McGraw-Hill Education
CONQUERING
ACT
Math and Science

McGraw-Hill Education
CONQUERING
ACT
Math and Science

FOURTH EDITION | Steven W. Dulan and Amy Dulan

New York   Chicago   San Francisco   Athens   London   Madrid   Mexico City
Milan   New Delhi   Singapore   Sydney   Toronto

1 2 3 4 5 6 7 8 9   LHS   25 24 23 22 21 20

ISBN 978-1-260-46259-3
MHID 1-260-46259-5

e-ISBN 978-1-260-46260-9
e-MHID 1-260-46260-9

ACT is a registered trademark of ACT, which was not involved in the production of, and does not endorse, this product.

McGraw-Hill Education products are available at special quantity discounts to use as premiums and sales promotions or for use in corporate training programs. To contact a representative, please visit the Contact Us pages at www.mhprofessional.com.

CONTENTS

ABOUT THE AUTHORS

Steven W. Dulan has been helping students prepare for success on the ACT and other standardized exams since 1989. He attended the Thomas M. Cooley Law School on a full honors scholarship after achieving a 99th percentile score on his Law School Admission Test (LSAT). In fact, Steve scored in the 99th percentile on every standardized test he has ever taken. While attending law school, Steve continued to teach standardized test prep classes (including ACT, SAT, PSAT, GRE, GMAT, and LSAT) an average of thirty hours each week, and tutored some of his fellow law students in a variety of subjects and in essay exam-writing techniques. Since 1997, Steve has served as president of Advantage Education®, a company dedicated to providing unparalleled test preparation. Thousands of students have benefited from his instruction, coaching, and admissions consulting and have gone on to their colleges of choice. Steve's students have gained admission to some of the most prestigious institutions in the world, and received many scholarships of their own. A few of them even beat his ACT score!

Amy Dulan put her analytical skills and nurturing personality to work as an ACT coach after receiving a psychology degree from Michigan State University in 1991. During forays into the corporate world over the next several years, Amy continued to tutor part time, eventually helping to found Advantage Education® in 1997. Since then, Amy has worked with thousands of high school students in both private and classroom settings, helping them to maximize their ACT scores. Her sense of humor and down-to-earth style allow Amy to connect with her students and make learning fun.

The techniques included in this book are the result of Steve's and Amy's experiences with students at all ability and motivation levels over many years.

"After working with Steve I was able to crack the ACT and got a 36 composite score! His help made all the difference in getting those last few points for a perfect score!"

C. S. (Student)

"Amy, thanks to you my daughter was able to get a 35 composite score on her ACT with a perfect 36 on the English test! Thank you for your time and commitment to her success."

J. Q. (Parent)

EXCITING ACT UPDATES!

There are three major changes to ACT that will be available beginning with the September 2020 test date.

ONLINE TESTING

First, the ACT will be available as an **online test** at select locations.

The sections, question types, timing, and scoring will remain the same. So, all the information and practice material in this book will still be relevant and helpful. The online test may be more comfortable for some students. For others, it might prove more stressful and distracting. Colleges will not know whether you take the online or paper test. This is strictly a matter of personal preference. The scores for online tests will be available as quickly as two days later. This is significantly faster than the paper test and may be helpful for students who are up against application deadlines.

The online test will be given at specified locations on ACT computers. It will not be available for home testing or on your own laptop, even at a testing center. Scratch paper will be available, and the testing software will include highlighting tools. You will be able to go back and change answers if there is time remaining in the section.

Some students prefer the comfortable environment of working on a computer screen. Others prefer to have the ability to mark on the page with their pencils as they work through the material. We advise you to try both environments before making your decision. *The Official Beginner's Guide for ACT* (a publication of ACT, Inc.) includes access to an online practice test so that you can see for yourself which option is best for you.

SUPERSCORING

Second, ACT will report a "**superscore**" for those who take more than one ACT. About one-third of all institutions currently allow superscoring. The change is that, now, ACT will automatically report the best score on each of your English, Math, Reading, and Science sections across all of the ACTs you take, and calculate your hypothetical composite score as though each of your best section scores were on the same full ACT. Colleges and universities will still each decide how to handle this information. Some will not consider the superscore in making admission decisions. Be sure to check with the schools and programs you are applying to for more information.

There is some research showing that superscores are better predictors of college GPA than single-day composite scores. The trend seems to be toward more institutions accepting superscores moving forward.

SECTION RETAKES

Third, if you have taken one complete, or "full-battery," ACT at any time since 2016, you may choose to **retake individual sections**. You may retake one, two, or three sections as an online test at select locations on any of the seven annual national test dates beginning with September 2020. You may NOT take individual sections as paper-and-pencil exams. In our opinion, this is the most exciting change. It means that, with proper planning, you could take your "full-panel" ACT on one day, and then do the writing section as a stand-alone test at a later date without the fatigue that is a major factor for many students. Some students will benefit from the reduced fatigue and stress when retaking only one, two, or three sections rather than an entire ACT exam.

One additional change is that ACT is removing the limit on retakes. In the past, a student could "only" take a lifetime maximum of 12 ACT exams. That limit is being rescinded starting in September 2020. However, with nearly 50 years combined ACT prep experience, the authors of this book have never met anyone who even came close to the 12-exam limit. We feel that this change is not significant for most test-takers.

See www.act.org/morechoices for more information.

McGraw-Hill Education
CONQUERING
ACT
Math and Science

INTRODUCTION

ABOUT THE ACT

The ACT is the fastest-growing and most widely accepted college entrance exam in the United States. It is designed to assess high school students' general educational development and their ability to complete college-level work. The authors of the ACT insist that the ACT is an achievement test, not a direct measure of abilities. It is not an IQ test, nor is it a measure of your worth as a human being. It is not even a perfect measure of how well you will do in college. Theoretically, each of us has a specific potential to learn and acquire skills. The ACT doesn't measure your natural, inborn ability. If it did, we wouldn't be as successful as we are at raising students' scores on ACT exams.

The ACT actually measures a certain knowledge base and skill set. It is "trainable," meaning that you can do better on your ACT if you work on learning the knowledge and gaining the skills that are tested.

STRUCTURE OF THE ACT

The ACT is made up of four multiple-choice tests—English, Mathematics, Reading, and Science—and one optional essay. There are 215 multiple-choice questions on the test. The multiple-choice tests are always given in the same order, followed by the essay. In fact, there is a lot of predictability when it comes to the ACT. The current exam still has a great deal in common with ACT exams from past years. This means that we basically know what is going to be on your ACT in terms of question types and content.

Following is a table giving a breakdown of the question types, number of each question type, and time allotted for each test section of the ACT:

ACT Structure		
Test	**Number of Questions and Time Allowed**	**Reporting Categories (Content and Skills Tested)**
English	75 Questions	*Conventions of Standard English*—Approximately 40 questions
	45 Minutes	*Production of Writing*—Approximately 25 questions
		Knowledge of Language—Approximately 10 questions
Math	60 Questions	*Preparing for Higher Math*—Approximately 35 questions
	60 Minutes	• Number and Quantity • Algebra • Functions • Geometry • Statistics and Probability *Integrating Essential Skills*—Approximately 25 questions
Reading	40 Questions	*Key Ideas and Details*—Approximately 20 questions
	35 Minutes	*Craft and Structure*—Approximately 15 questions
		Integration of Knowledge and Ideas—Approximately 5 questions
Science	40 Questions	*Interpretation of Data*—Approximately 20 questions
	35 Minutes	*Evaluation of Models, Inferences, and Results*—Approximately 10 questions
		Scientific Investigation—Approximately 10 questions
Writing		Optional 40-minute essay

Scoring the ACT

Each of the multiple-choice sections of the ACT (English Test, Mathematics Test, Reading Test, and Science Test) is given a score on a scale of 1 to 36. These four "scaled scores" are then averaged and rounded according to normal rounding rules to yield a Composite Score. It is this Composite Score that is most often meant when someone refers to your ACT score.

You don't have to be perfect to get a good score on the ACT. The truth is that you can miss a fair number of questions and still get a score that places you in the top 1 percent of all test takers. In fact, this test is so hard and the time limit is so unrealistic for most test takers that you can get a score that is at or above the national average (about a 21) even if you get almost half of the questions wrong.

The practice tests in this book are simulations created by experts to replicate the question types, difficulty level, and content areas that you will find on your real ACT Mathematics and Science Tests. The scoring worksheets provided are guides to computing approximate scores. Actual ACT exams are scored from tables that are unique to each test. The actual scaled scores depend on a number of factors: the number of students who take the test, the difficulty level of the items (questions and answer choices), and the performance of all of the students who take the test. Do not get too hung up on your test scores while you are practicing; the idea is to learn something from each practice experience and to get used to the "look and feel" of the ACT Mathematics and Science Tests.

Who Writes the ACT?

There is a company called ACT, Inc., that decides exactly what is going to be on your ACT exam. The experts at ACT, Inc., consult with classroom teachers at the high school and college levels. They look at high school and college curricula, and they employ educators and specialized psychologists called *psychometricians* (measurers of the mind), who know a lot about the human brain and how it operates under various conditions. Later in this book, we'll lay out the details of how you will be tested so that you can get yourself ready for the "contest" on test day.

Why Do ACT Exams Exist?

Colleges use the ACT for admissions decisions and sometimes for advanced placement decisions. The test is also used to make scholarship decisions. Because there are variations in grading standards and requirements among high schools around the country, the admissions departments at colleges use the ACT, in part, to help provide a standard for comparison. There are studies that reveal a fair amount of "grade inflation" at some schools; therefore, colleges cannot simply rely upon grade-point averages when evaluating academic performance.

How Do I Register for the ACT?

You should register for the ACT in advance. Do not just show up on test day with a Number 2 pencil and dive right in. The best source of information for all things ACT is, not surprisingly, the ACT website: www.act.org. There is also a very good chance that a guidance counselor and/or pre-college counselor at your school has an ACT Registration Book, which includes all the information that you'll need for your test registration.

◼◼ HOW TO USE THIS BOOK

This book contains general information about the ACT and chapters on the specific mathematics content areas tested, science skills tested, exercises, and in-format practice questions.

In a perfect situation, you will be reading this book at least several weeks before you take your actual ACT exam. If that is not the case, however, you can still benefit from this book. Look at the "General Test-Taking Information and Strategies" section in this chapter first, and then take the diagnostic tests in Chapter 2 and Chapter 11, which will help you to pinpoint areas of strength and weakness in your knowledge base and skill set. Even just a few hours of study and practice can have a beneficial impact on your ACT score.

If you are reading this only days before your ACT exam, it is important to mention that you should not preorder any ACT score reports. As of the writing of this book, ACT, Inc., allows you to pick and choose which scores you send out to colleges. So, you should send scores only after you have had a chance to review them yourself. If your score is not acceptable, you can always retake the ACT and send only the scores from your best testing day to your schools of choice. This is especially important if you are unsure of how you will score and if you are going in with only minimum preparation.

As you work with the practice questions in this book, be aware that most of them are simulated to match actual ACT items. If you work through all of the material provided, you can rest assured that there won't be any surprises on test day. Be aware, though, that ACT exams are sensitive to factors such as fatigue and stress; in addition, the time of day that you take the practice tests, your surroundings, and other things going on in your life can have an impact on your scores. Don't get worried if you see some variations because you are having an off day or because the practice test exposed a weakness in your knowledge base or skill set. Just use the information that you gather as a tool to help you improve.

In our experience, the students who see the largest increases in their scores are the ones who put in consistent effort over time. Try to keep your frustration to a minimum if you are struggling with the practice tests and aren't doing as well as you had hoped. Similarly, try to keep yourself from becoming overconfident when you have a great practice-testing day.

There is an explanation for each of the practice questions in this book. You will probably not need to read all of them. Sometimes you can tell right away why you answered a particular question incorrectly. We have seen countless students smack themselves on the forehead and say, "Stupid mistake." We try to refer to these errors as "concentration errors." Everyone makes them from time to time, and you should not worry when they occur. There is a good chance that your focus will be a little better on the real test as long as you train yourself properly with the aid of this book. You should distinguish between concentration errors and any holes in your knowledge base or understanding. If you have the time, it is worth reading the explanations for any of the questions that were at all challenging for you. Sometimes students get questions correct for the wrong reason, or because they guessed correctly. While you are practicing, you should mark any questions that you want to revisit and be sure to read the explanations for them.

> **Study Tip**
>
> Your score will improve with practice! Decide when you are going to take the ACT and allow sufficient practice time leading up to the test. We recommend six to eight weeks of preparation before the test.

GENERAL TEST-TAKING INFORMATION AND STRATEGIES

Now it's time to take a look at some general test-taking information and strategies that should help you approach the ACT with confidence. We'll start by discussing the importance of acquiring the skills necessary to maximize your ACT scores, and finish with some tips on how to handle stress before, during, and after the test. Additional chapters in this book include strategies and techniques specific to the ACT Mathematics and Science Tests.

KSA (Knowledge, Skills, Abilities)

Cognitive psychologists who study learning and thinking use the letters KSA to refer to the basic components of human performance in all human activities, from academics to athletics, playing music to playing games. The letters stand for Knowledge, Skills, and Abilities. As mentioned previously, the ACT measures a specific set of skills that can be improved through study and practice. You probably already understand this, since you are reading this book. In fact, many thousands of students over the years have successfully raised their ACT scores through study and practice.

Learning Facts vs. Acquiring Skills

The human brain stores and retrieves factual knowledge a little differently from the way it acquires and executes skills. Knowledge can generally be learned quickly and is fairly durable, even when you are under stress. You learn factual information by studying, and you acquire skills through practice. There is some overlap between these actions; you will learn while you practice, and vice versa. In fact, research shows that repetition is important for both information storage and skills acquisition.

As we just mentioned, repetition is necessary if you are to acquire and improve skills: knowing *about* a skill, or understanding how the skill should be executed, is not the same thing as actually having that skill. For instance, you might be told *about* a skill such as driving a car with a standard transmission, playing the piano, or typing on a computer keyboard. You might have a great teacher, have wonderful learning tools, and pay attention very carefully. You might *understand* everything perfectly. But the first few times that you actually attempt the skill, you will probably make some mistakes. In fact, you will probably experience some frustration because of the gap between your understanding of the skill and your actual ability to perform it. Perfecting skills takes practice. When skills have been repeated so many times that they can't be further improved, psychologists use the term *perfectly internalized skills*, which means that the skills are executed automatically, without any conscious thought. You need repetition to create the pathways in your brain that control your skills. Therefore, you shouldn't be satisfied with simply reading this book and then saying to yourself, "I get it." You will not reach your full ACT scoring potential unless you put in sufficient time practicing in addition to understanding and learning.

Practicing to Internalize Skills

We hope that you will internalize the skills you need for top performance on the ACT so that you don't have to spend time and energy figuring out what to do during the introduction to the exam. We are hoping that you will be well into each section while some of your less-prepared classmates are still reading the directions and trying to figure out exactly what they are supposed to be doing. We suggest that you practice sufficiently so that you develop your test-taking skills, and specifically good ACT-taking skills. While you practice, you should distinguish between practice that is meant to serve as a learning experience and practice that is meant to be a realistic simulation of what will happen on your actual ACT.

During practice that is meant for learning, it is okay to "cheat." You should feel free to disregard the time limits and just think about how the questions are put together; you can stop to look at the explanations included in this book. It is even okay to talk to others about what you are learning during your "learning practice." However, you also need to do some simulated testing practice, where you time yourself carefully and try to control as many variables in your environment as you can. Some research shows that you will have an easier time executing your skills and remembering information when the environment in which you are testing is similar to the environment in which you studied and practiced.

There is a psychological term, *cognitive endurance*, that refers to your ability to perform difficult mental tasks over an extended period of time. Just as with your physical endurance, you can build up your cognitive endurance through training. As you prepare yourself for the ACT, you should start off with shorter practice

---

Study Tip

Do not attempt any timed practice tests when you are mentally or physically exhausted. This will add unwanted stress to an already stressful situation. You must be realistic about how you spend your time and energy during the preparation process.

sessions and work up to the point where you can easily do a 35-minute Science Test and a 60-minute ACT Mathematics Test with no noticeable fatigue.

Now, let's explore the skills and strategies that are important to ensuring your success on the ACT.

Do the Easy Stuff First

First, you should get familiar with the format of each section of the ACT so that you can recognize questions that are likely to give you trouble. The format of the ACT is covered in Chapter 1.

All of the questions on an ACT test are weighted exactly equally. When you are taking the test, we suggest that you bypass pockets of resistance. Go around trouble spots and return to them later. It is a much better use of your time and energy to pick up all of the correct answers that you can early on, and then go back and work on the tougher questions. Learn to recognize the types of questions that are likely to give you trouble, and do not be goaded into a fight with them.

There will be some time-consuming questions that show up early in the ACT test sections; these are designed to lure you into wasting time that would be better spent answering some more reasonable questions later. Don't get caught up in these. Move on and come back to them later. By the time you take the test, you will have learned to recognize the types of questions that are likely to give you trouble. When you see them, don't be surprised. Just recognize them and work on the easier material first. If time permits, you can always come back and work on the challenging problems in the final minutes before the proctor calls, "Time!"

This book contains specific suggestions for which types of questions you should probably skip. You'll also develop likes and dislikes while practicing, meaning that you will know that certain question types are always going to be tough for you. By test day, you will have done enough timed practice that you will also develop a "feel" for how long you should be spending on each question. Be flexible. Even if a question is of a type that you can usually answer easily, do not spend more time than you should on it. There is usually time to come back if you leave a question too soon. However, once you waste a second of time, you cannot get it back.

Stay "On Point"

Most *incorrect* ACT answers are incorrect because they are irrelevant. This applies to all of the different question types in all of the various sections. For example, if you get very good at spotting and eliminating answer choices that are too big or too small on the ACT Mathematics and Science Tests, you'll go a long way toward improving your score. This can be more difficult than it sounds because some of the incorrect choices will contain numbers from the question, or will be the result of a small miscalculation.

Manage the Answer Sheet

Be certain to avoid the common mistake of marking the answer to each question on your answer document (bubble sheet) as you finish the question. In other words, you should NOT go to your answer sheet after each question. This is dangerous and wastes time. It is dangerous because you run an increased risk of marking your

> **Study Tip**
>
> Because what is easy for some people is not necessarily easy for others, do enough practice to be able to quickly recognize the types of questions that will be easy for *you*. Answer those questions first, then go back to work on the more difficult questions if time allows.

answer sheet incorrectly and perhaps not catching your error in time. It wastes time because you have to find your place on the answer sheet and then find your place back in the test booklet over and over again. The amount of time that is "wasted" as you mark each question is not large. But it adds up over the course of an entire test section and could cost you the amount of time you need to answer a few more questions correctly.

Instead, you should mark your answers in the test booklet and transfer your answers from the test booklet to the answer sheet in groups. On any of the sections, filling in circles (bubbles) on your answer sheet can be a good activity to keep you busy when you simply need a break to clear your head. Be sure to practice this technique until you are comfortable with it.

Use the Test Booklet

The ACT test booklets are meant to be used by one test taker only. You will not have any scratch paper for the multiple-choice tests on test day. You are expected to do all your note taking and figuring on the booklet itself. Generally, no one even bothers to look at the test booklet, since you cannot receive credit for anything that is written there. Your score comes only from the answers that you mark on the answer sheet. Therefore, you should feel comfortable marking up the questions, crossing off incorrect answer choices, making calculations, and so on, to help you to stay focused on relevant information.

Guess Wisely

Since there is no added scoring penalty for incorrect answers on the ACT, you should never leave a bubble on your answer sheet blank. We counted all of the correct answers on three recently released ACT exams and found that the distribution of answers by position on the answer sheet was almost exactly even. This means that there is no position that is more likely to be correct than any other. We use the term *position* when referring to the answer sheet because the letter assigned to each position changes depending on whether you are working on an odd-numbered or even-numbered question. On the Mathematics Test, the odd-numbered questions have answer choices that are labeled A, B, C, D, E and the even-numbered questions have answer choices that are labeled F, G, H, J, K. On the Science Test, the odd-numbered questions have answer choices that are labeled A, B, C, D and the even-numbered questions have answer choices that are labeled F, G, H, J. This system allows you to stay on track on your answer sheet.

Make educated guesses by eliminating answer choices. It's a good idea to add a symbol or two to the common repertoire to help you distinguish between the answer choices that you have eliminated and those that could be correct. For example, when you eliminate an answer choice, make a mark through the letter to indicate that you no longer consider it a viable choice:

> If a rectangle measures 18 meters by 24 meters, what is the length, in meters, of the diagonal of the rectangle?
>
> F. 18
> G. 24
> H. 30
> J. 42
> K. 900

Study Tip

The answers are distributed fairly evenly across the positions, so you should always guess the same position if you are guessing at random. Of course, if you can eliminate a choice or two, or if you have a hunch, then this advice doesn't apply.

The question just shown is fairly common. If you think that an answer choice *may* be correct, but you want to consider the remaining choices before you make your final decision, underline the answer choices you think are possible, as shown below. This might be a new step in your standard process:

If a rectangle measures 18 meters by 24 meters, what is the length, in meters, of the diagonal of the rectangle?

F. 18
G. 24
H. 30
J. 42
K. 900

Once you've decided on your final answer, circle it for later transfer to the answer sheet:

If a rectangle measures 18 meters by 24 meters, what is the length, in meters, of the diagonal of the rectangle?

F. 18
G. 24
(H) 30
J. 42
K. 900

If you have eliminated one or more of the answer choices and still don't feel comfortable guessing among those that remain, place a large **X** next to the question, leave the circle on your answer sheet empty, and come back to the question later if you have time. Try to budget your time so that you have at least a minute or two left at the end of each section to locate the questions you've marked with an **X** (because you will be making an educated guess), select one of the answer choices that you did not already eliminate, and fill in the corresponding circle on your answer sheet.

You also need to find out whether you are an answer changer. If you change an answer, are you more likely to change it *to* the correct answer or *from* the correct answer? You can learn this about yourself only by doing practice exams and paying attention to your tendencies. In general, we recommend sticking with your first choice.

Some students worry if they notice strings of the same answers on their answer sheets. This does not necessarily indicate a problem. When analyzing actual, released ACT exams, we counted strings of up to five questions long, all marked with the same answer position on the answer sheet, and all correct. You should not be too concerned even if you find a string of five answer choices that are all in the same position on the answer sheet.

Manage Stress

In college, stress arises from sources such as family expectations, fear of failure, heavy workload, competition, and difficult subjects. The ACT is designed to create similar stresses. The psychometricians we mentioned earlier, who contribute to the design of standardized tests, use artificial stressors to test how you will respond to the stress of college. In other words, they are actually trying to create a certain level of stress in you.

The main stressor is the time limit. The time limits are set on the ACT so that most students cannot finish all of the questions in the time allowed. Use the specific strategies mentioned in Chapter 3 and Chapter 12 to help you select as many correct answers as possible in the time allowed. Also, be sure to read Chapter 4 for a complete review of the concepts and subject matter tested on the ACT Mathematics Test.

Remember, if you practice enough, there should be no surprises on test day!

Relax to Succeed

Probably the worst thing that can happen to a test taker is to panic. When you panic, you can usually identify a specific set of easily recognizable symptoms: sweating, shortness of breath, muscle tension, increased pulse rate, tunnel vision, nausea, light-headedness, and, in rare cases, even loss of consciousness. These symptoms are the results of chemical changes in the brain brought on by some stimulus. The stimulus does not have to be external. Therefore, we can panic ourselves just by thinking about certain things. The stress chemical in your body called epinephrine, more commonly known as adrenaline, brings on these symptoms. Adrenaline changes the priorities in your brain activity. It moves blood and electrical energy away from some parts of the brain and to others. Specifically, it increases brain activity in the areas that control your body and decreases blood flow to the parts of your brain that are involved in complex thinking. Therefore, panic makes a person stronger and faster—and also less able to perform the type of critical thinking that is important on the ACT. It is not a bad thing to have a small amount of adrenaline in your bloodstream as a result of a healthy amount of excitement about your exam, but you should be careful not to panic before or during your test.

You can control your adrenaline levels by minimizing the unknown factors in the testing process. The biggest stress-inducing questions are: "What do the test writers expect?" "Am I ready?" and "How will I do on test day?"

If you spend your time and energy studying and practicing under realistic conditions before test day, you will have a much better chance of controlling your adrenaline levels and handling the exam with no panic.

The goals of your preparation should be to learn about the test, acquire the skills that are being measured by the test, and learn about yourself and how you respond to the different parts of the test. You need to be familiar with the material that is tested on each section of the test. Decide which questions you'll attempt to solve on test day and which ones you'll simply guess on. As you work through this book, make an assessment of the best use of your time and energy. Concentrate on the areas that will give you the highest score in the amount of time that you have until you take the ACT. This will give you a feeling of confidence on test day, even when you are facing very challenging questions.

Relaxation Techniques

The following are suggestions to help you feel as relaxed and confident as possible on test day.

Be Prepared

The more prepared you feel, the less likely it is that you'll be stressed on test day. Study and practice consistently during the time between now and your test day.

Be organized. Have your supplies and lucky testing clothes ready in advance. Make a practice trip to the test center before your test day.

Know Yourself

Get to know your strengths and weaknesses on the ACT and the things that help you to relax. Some test takers like to have a slightly anxious feeling to help them focus. Other folks do best when they are so relaxed that they are almost asleep. You will learn about yourself through practice.

Have a Plan of Attack

Know how you are going to work through each part of the exam. There is no time to create a plan of attack on test day. Practice enough that you internalize the skills that you will need if you are to do your best on each section, and you won't have to stop to think about what to do next.

Breathe

If you feel yourself tensing up, slow down and take deeper breaths. This will relax you and get more oxygen to your brain so that you can think more clearly.

Take Breaks

You cannot stay sharply focused on your ACT for the whole time in the testing center. You are certainly going to have distracting thoughts, or times when you just can't process all the information. When this happens, close your eyes, clear your mind, and then start back on your test. This process should take only a minute or so. You can pray, meditate, or just visualize a place or a person that helps you relax. Try thinking of something fun that you have planned to do after your test.

Be Aware of Time

Time yourself on test day. You should have timed yourself on some of your practice exams, so that you will have a sense of how long each section should take you. We suggest that you use an analog (dial face) watch. You can turn the hands on your watch back from noon to allow enough time for the section that you are working on. For example, set your watch to 11:00 for the 60-minute ACT Mathematics Test and to 11:25 for the 35-minute Science Test.

Clear Your Head

Remember, all that matters during the test is the test. All of life's other issues will have to be dealt with after your test is finished. You may find this attitude easier to achieve if you lose track of what time it is in the "outside world"—another benefit of resetting your watch.

Eat Right

Sugar is bad for stress and for brain function in general. Consuming refined sugar creates biological stress that has an impact on your brain chemistry. Keep it to a minimum for several days before your test. If you are actually addicted to caffeine (you can tell that you are if you get headaches when you skip a day), get your normal amount. Don't forget to eat regularly while you're preparing for the ACT. It's not a good idea to skip meals simply because you are experiencing some additional stress.

A Note on Music

Some types of music increase measured brain stress and interfere with clear thinking. Specifically, some rock, hip-hop, and dance rhythms, while great for certain occasions, can have detrimental effects on certain types of brain waves and interfere with learning and optimal test taking. Other music seems to help to organize brain waves and create a relaxed state that is conducive to learning and skills acquisition.

▰▰ WHAT TO DO ON TEST DAY

If you work through the material in this book and do some additional practice on released ACT items (visit act.org), you should be more than adequately prepared for the test. Use the following tips to help the entire testing process go smoothly.

Do a Dry Run

Make sure that you know how long it will take you to get to the testing center, where you will park, alternative routes, and so on. If you are taking the test in a place that is new to you, try to get into the building between now and test day so that you can absorb the sounds and smells, find out where the bathrooms and snack machines are, and so on.

Rest Up and Wake Up Early

You generally have to be at the testing center by 8:00 a.m. Set two alarms if you have to. Leave yourself plenty of time to get fully awake before you have to run out the door. Be sure to get enough rest the night before the test. The better rested you are, the better things seem. When you are fatigued, you are more likely to look on the dark side of things and worry more, which hurts your test scores.

Dress for Success

Wear loose, comfortable clothes in layers so that you can adjust to the temperature. Remember your watch. There might not be a clock in your testing room. (See page 10 for more information on timing!) Always check the ACT website for updates on what you can and cannot bring to the testing center.

Fuel Up

It is important that you eat something before you take the test. An empty stomach might be distracting and uncomfortable on test day. Low-sugar, high-protein foods are probably best. Get your normal dose of caffeine, if any. (Test day is not the time to "try coffee" for the first time!)

Bring Supplies

Bring your driver's license (or passport), your admission ticket, several sharpened Number 2 pencils, erasers, a timepiece, and your approved calculator. If you need them, bring your glasses or contact lenses. You won't be able to eat or drink while the test is in progress, but you can bring a snack for the break time.

Warm Up Your Brain

Read a newspaper or something similar, or review some practice material so that the ACT isn't the first thing you read on test day. If you review ACT material, make sure that it is something that you have worked through before, and focus on the part of the test that you tend to be best at. This is certainly the time to accentuate the positive!

Plan a Mini-Vacation

Most students find that it is easier for them to concentrate on their test preparation and on their ACT if they have a plan for some fun right after the test. Plan something that you can look forward to as a reward for all the hard work and energy that you're putting into preparing for and taking the test.

▄▄▄ WHAT'S NEXT?

The remaining chapters in this book include more detailed information about the format and scoring of the ACT Mathematics and Science Tests, a diagnostic test to evaluate your current readiness for each test, strategies specific to the ACT test, exercises to hone your skills, and practice questions in ACT format.

PART I

THE ACT MATHEMATICS TEST

CHAPTER 1
FORMAT AND SCORING

As mentioned in the Introduction, the ACT is made up of four multiple-choice tests (English, Mathematics, Reading, and Science) and an optional essay. This chapter will provide more information about the format of the ACT Mathematics Test and briefly discuss how this test is scored.

FORMAT

The ACT Mathematics Test includes 60 questions that are designed to measure your ability to reason mathematically, to understand basic math terminology, and to recall basic mathematical formulas and principles. You will have 60 minutes to answer these questions. You should be able to solve problems and apply relevant mathematics concepts in the following areas:

Preparing for Higher Math (Approximately 60% of the Questions)

This category has five subcategories.

- **Number & Quantity** (Approximately 10% of the Questions)
  Real and complex number systems
  Integer and rational exponents
  Vectors
  Matrices
- **Algebra** (Approximately 15% of the Questions)
  Linear expressions
  Polynomials
  Radicals
  Exponential relationships
- **Functions** (Approximately 15% of the Questions)
  Function definition, notation, representation, and application
  Linear, radical, piecewise, polynomial, and logarithmic functions
- **Geometry** (Approximately 15% of the Questions)
  Congruence, similarity relationships, surface area
  Volume measurements
  Triangles and circles
  Trigonometric ratios
  Equations of conic sections
- **Statistics & Probability** (Approximately 5% of the Questions)
  Center and spread of distributions
  Data collection methods

Bivariate data
Probabilities

Integrating Essential Skills (Approximately 40% of the Questions)

Rates and percentages
Proportional relationships
Area, surface area, and volume
Average and median

Each of these content areas will be further discussed in Chapter 4. In Chapter 5, you will have an opportunity to practice and build the skills necessary for success on the ACT Mathematics Test.

Anatomy of an ACT Mathematics Question

As mentioned in the introduction to this book, each multiple-choice mathematics question includes five answer choices (A, B, C, D, and E for odd-numbered questions, or F, G, H, J, and K for even-numbered questions). The answer choices correspond to the bubbles on your answer sheet. You may use an approved calculator to assist you in answering any of the multiple-choice questions, but none of the questions actually requires the use of a calculator to solve.

The basic structure of an ACT mathematics question is as follows:

1. If $5x - 6 = 14$, then what is the value of $8x$?　　**Question Stem**

    A.　$\dfrac{8}{5}$

    B.　4

    C.　$\dfrac{64}{5}$　　　**Answer Choices**

    D.　20

    E.　32

▮▮▮ SCORING

As noted earlier, each of the ACT multiple-choice tests is given a score on a scale of 1 to 36. In 2019, the average ACT Mathematics Test score in the United States was 21. Your score will be rounded to the nearest whole number before it is reported. Please refer to the ACT website, www.act.org, for more detailed information on your ACT scores.

Your ACT Mathematics Test score will be used along with the scores from the other ACT multiple-choice tests to calculate your composite score. Refer to the scoring worksheets provided with the answers to the practice tests in this book to calculate your approximate scaled score (1–36) for each test.

▮▮▮ WHAT'S NEXT?

Chapter 2 includes a diagnostic test, which you should use to determine your current readiness for the ACT Mathematics Test. Then, read Chapter 3, "Strategies and Techniques," to learn the best approach to answering the questions on the simulated tests included in this book, as well as on your actual ACT.

CHAPTER 2

ACT MATHEMATICS DIAGNOSTIC TEST

The following diagnostic test will assist you in evaluating your current readiness for the ACT Mathematics Test. Make an honest effort to answer each question, then review the explanations that follow. Don't worry if you are unable to answer many or most of the questions at this point. The rest of the book contains information and resources that will help you to maximize your ACT Mathematics Test scores. Once you have identified your areas of strength and weakness, you should review those particular sections in the book.

ACT MATHEMATICS DIAGNOSTIC TEST
Answer Sheet

MATHEMATICS

1 Ⓐ Ⓑ Ⓒ Ⓓ Ⓔ	16 Ⓕ Ⓖ Ⓗ Ⓙ Ⓚ	31 Ⓐ Ⓑ Ⓒ Ⓓ Ⓔ	46 Ⓕ Ⓖ Ⓗ Ⓙ Ⓚ
2 Ⓕ Ⓖ Ⓗ Ⓙ Ⓚ	17 Ⓐ Ⓑ Ⓒ Ⓓ Ⓔ	32 Ⓕ Ⓖ Ⓗ Ⓙ Ⓚ	47 Ⓐ Ⓑ Ⓒ Ⓓ Ⓔ
3 Ⓐ Ⓑ Ⓒ Ⓓ Ⓔ	18 Ⓕ Ⓖ Ⓗ Ⓙ Ⓚ	33 Ⓐ Ⓑ Ⓒ Ⓓ Ⓔ	48 Ⓕ Ⓖ Ⓗ Ⓙ Ⓚ
4 Ⓕ Ⓖ Ⓗ Ⓙ Ⓚ	19 Ⓐ Ⓑ Ⓒ Ⓓ Ⓔ	34 Ⓕ Ⓖ Ⓗ Ⓙ Ⓚ	49 Ⓐ Ⓑ Ⓒ Ⓓ Ⓔ
5 Ⓐ Ⓑ Ⓒ Ⓓ Ⓔ	20 Ⓕ Ⓖ Ⓗ Ⓙ Ⓚ	35 Ⓐ Ⓑ Ⓒ Ⓓ Ⓔ	50 Ⓕ Ⓖ Ⓗ Ⓙ Ⓚ
6 Ⓕ Ⓖ Ⓗ Ⓙ Ⓚ	21 Ⓐ Ⓑ Ⓒ Ⓓ Ⓔ	36 Ⓕ Ⓖ Ⓗ Ⓙ Ⓚ	51 Ⓐ Ⓑ Ⓒ Ⓓ Ⓔ
7 Ⓐ Ⓑ Ⓒ Ⓓ Ⓔ	22 Ⓕ Ⓖ Ⓗ Ⓙ Ⓚ	37 Ⓐ Ⓑ Ⓒ Ⓓ Ⓔ	52 Ⓕ Ⓖ Ⓗ Ⓙ Ⓚ
8 Ⓕ Ⓖ Ⓗ Ⓙ Ⓚ	23 Ⓐ Ⓑ Ⓒ Ⓓ Ⓔ	38 Ⓕ Ⓖ Ⓗ Ⓙ Ⓚ	53 Ⓐ Ⓑ Ⓒ Ⓓ Ⓔ
9 Ⓐ Ⓑ Ⓒ Ⓓ Ⓔ	24 Ⓕ Ⓖ Ⓗ Ⓙ Ⓚ	39 Ⓐ Ⓑ Ⓒ Ⓓ Ⓔ	54 Ⓕ Ⓖ Ⓗ Ⓙ Ⓚ
10 Ⓕ Ⓖ Ⓗ Ⓙ Ⓚ	25 Ⓐ Ⓑ Ⓒ Ⓓ Ⓔ	40 Ⓕ Ⓖ Ⓗ Ⓙ Ⓚ	55 Ⓐ Ⓑ Ⓒ Ⓓ Ⓔ
11 Ⓐ Ⓑ Ⓒ Ⓓ Ⓔ	26 Ⓕ Ⓖ Ⓗ Ⓙ Ⓚ	41 Ⓐ Ⓑ Ⓒ Ⓓ Ⓔ	56 Ⓕ Ⓖ Ⓗ Ⓙ Ⓚ
12 Ⓕ Ⓖ Ⓗ Ⓙ Ⓚ	27 Ⓐ Ⓑ Ⓒ Ⓓ Ⓔ	42 Ⓕ Ⓖ Ⓗ Ⓙ Ⓚ	57 Ⓐ Ⓑ Ⓒ Ⓓ Ⓔ
13 Ⓐ Ⓑ Ⓒ Ⓓ Ⓔ	28 Ⓕ Ⓖ Ⓗ Ⓙ Ⓚ	43 Ⓐ Ⓑ Ⓒ Ⓓ Ⓔ	58 Ⓕ Ⓖ Ⓗ Ⓙ Ⓚ
14 Ⓕ Ⓖ Ⓗ Ⓙ Ⓚ	29 Ⓐ Ⓑ Ⓒ Ⓓ Ⓔ	44 Ⓕ Ⓖ Ⓗ Ⓙ Ⓚ	59 Ⓐ Ⓑ Ⓒ Ⓓ Ⓔ
15 Ⓐ Ⓑ Ⓒ Ⓓ Ⓔ	30 Ⓕ Ⓖ Ⓗ Ⓙ Ⓚ	45 Ⓐ Ⓑ Ⓒ Ⓓ Ⓔ	60 Ⓕ Ⓖ Ⓗ Ⓙ Ⓚ

MATHEMATICS TEST

60 Minutes—60 Questions

DIRECTIONS: Solve each of the problems in the time allowed, then fill in the corresponding bubble on your answer sheet. Do not spend too much time on any one problem; skip the more difficult problems and go back to them later. You may use a calculator on this test. For this test, you should assume that figures are NOT necessarily drawn to scale, that all geometric figures lie in a plane, and that the word *line* is used to indicate a straight line.

1. For each of four months, the table below gives the number of games a basketball team played, the number of free throws the team attempted, and the number of free throws the team made.

Month	Games	Free Throws Attempted	Free Throws Made
September	4	78	69
October	6	107	93
November	8	120	102
December	5	83	76

To the nearest tenth, what is the average number of free throws that the team made per game in November?
A. 8.5
B. 10.2
C. 12.8
D. 15.0
E. 17.3

DO YOUR FIGURING HERE.

2. For the polygon below, the lengths of 2 sides are not given. Each angle between adjacent sides measures 90°. What is the polygon's perimeter, in centimeters?

F. 41
G. 47
H. 54
J. 62
K. 123

GO ON TO THE NEXT PAGE.

3. Which of the following inequalities represents the graph shown below on the real number line?

A. $-6 \leq x < 1$
B. $-5 \leq x \leq 0$
C. $-5 < x \leq -1$
D. $-5 < x \leq 0$
E. $-4 \leq x < -1$

DO YOUR FIGURING HERE.

4. What is the value of $3^{a-b} \times 4$ when $a = 1$ and $b = -2$?
F. -12
G. 24
H. 76
J. 94
K. 108

5. For integers y and z such that $yz = 24$, which of the following is NOT a possible value of z?
A. -12
B. -5
C. 6
D. 8
E. 24

6. The length of the base of a rectangular prism is 8 cm, and the width is 6 cm. If the height of the rectangular prism is 4 cm, what is its volume in cubic centimeters?
F. 192
G. 124
H. 86
J. 48
K. 24

7. A local radio station is selling airtime spots to advertisers for the upcoming week. The station charges $150 for one of the 85 30-second spots, and $270 for one of the 45 60-second spots. Which of the following expressions gives the total amount of money, in dollars, collected from selling all of the 60-second spots and S of the 30-second spots?
A. $150S + 12{,}150$
B. $150S + 270$
C. $85S + 12{,}150$
D. $45S + 10{,}000$
E. $S + 150$

GO ON TO THE NEXT PAGE.

8. In the figure below, W, X, and Y are collinear, the measure of angle WXZ is $4x°$, and the measure of angle YXZ is $8x°$. What is the measure of angle WXZ?

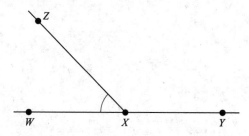

DO YOUR FIGURING HERE.

F. 15°
G. 60°
H. 80°
J. 95°
K. 120°

9. Haylee is living in a house with 11 other people, and each person will get her own room. There are 3 bedrooms on the first floor, 5 on the second, and 4 on the third. The housemates are deciding who gets what room by drawing numbers out of a hat. If Haylee draws first, what is the probability that she will get a room on the third floor?

A. $\dfrac{1}{12}$

B. $\dfrac{1}{6}$

C. $\dfrac{1}{4}$

D. $\dfrac{1}{3}$

E. $\dfrac{5}{12}$

10. Which of the following is a solution to the equation $x^2 - 49x = 0$?
F. 98
G. 49
H. 21
J. 7
K. −7

GO ON TO THE NEXT PAGE.

11. A group of high school students is planning to paint one side of the solid concrete wall around the elementary school playground as a way to give back to the community. The wall is 120 feet long and 8 feet tall. Assuming that 1 can of paint covers exactly 25 square feet, what is the minimum number of cans of paint the students will need in order to put 1 coat of paint on the wall?

A. 38
B. 39
C. 42
D. 47
E. 56

DO YOUR FIGURING HERE.

12. If the ratio of $3x$ to $7y$ is 1 to 7, what is the ratio of $6x$ to $7y$?

F. 3 to 7
G. 2 to 21
H. 2 to 7
J. 1 to 35
K. 1 to 14

13. A recent survey of college students on a big campus was conducted to find students' preferred method of getting to class. The results showed that 35% of students walk to class, 20% take the bus, 25% ride a bike, and 15% drive; the remaining students rollerblade to class. If each student preferred only 1 method of getting to class and 75 students preferred rollerblading, how many students were surveyed?

A. 900
B. 1,250
C. 1,500
D. 1,800
E. 2,225

14. The ratio of 40 to 32 is the same as the ratio of 30 to what number?

F. 15
G. 20
H. 24
J. 66
K. 70

15. $(3x^2 - 7x + 5) - (-2x + 8 - x^2)$ is equivalent to:

A. $2x^2 - 9x + 13$
B. $2x^2 - 5x + 3$
C. $4x^2 - 5x - 3$
D. $4x^2 + 5x + 13$
E. $6x^2 + 9x - 3$

16. A bleacher ticket for a high school baseball game costs \$8. Ryan decides to take his sister to the game as a birthday present. He gives her $\frac{1}{3}$ of the money he brought to buy two bleacher tickets and two hot dogs of equal cost. Later, Ryan decides to buy two bags of popcorn, which cost \$6 total. If Ryan has \$34 left, what was the price of one hot dog?

F. \$6.25
G. \$5.75
H. \$5.00
J. \$3.50
K. \$2.00

GO ON TO THE NEXT PAGE.

DO YOUR FIGURING HERE.

17. Mrs. Krantz gave her students a 15-question pop quiz on the week's algebra lesson. Which of the following percents is a possible score for the percent of questions that a student answered correctly if each question had equal weight? (Note: No partial credit was awarded.)

   A. 71%
   B. 73%
   C. 80%
   D. 86%
   E. 93%

18. The first 4 terms of a geometric sequence are $-\frac{1}{9}, \frac{1}{3}, -1,$ and 3. What is the 5th term?

   F. 9
   G. 3
   H. −6
   J. −9
   K. −12

19. $(5a - 2b)^2$ is equivalent to:

   A. $25a^2 - 20ab + 4b^2$
   B. $25a^2 - 10ab - 4b^2$
   C. $25a^2 - 4b^2$
   D. $25a^2 + 4b^2$
   E. $25a + 20ab + 4b^2$

20. Gary had a rectangular-shaped garden with sides of lengths 32 feet and 8 feet. He changed the garden into a square with the same area as the original rectangular-shaped garden. How many feet in length is each of the sides of the new square-shaped garden?

   F. 3
   G. $4\sqrt{2}$
   H. 12
   J. 16
   K. 24

21. What is the solution to the equation $4x - (-2x + 5) = -3$?

   A. $-\frac{1}{2}$
   B. $-\frac{1}{3}$
   C. $\frac{1}{4}$
   D. $\frac{1}{3}$
   E. 1

GO ON TO THE NEXT PAGE.

22. The area of △ABC below is 42 square inches. If $\overline{BD}$ is 7 inches long, how long is $\overline{AC}$, in inches?

DO YOUR FIGURING HERE.

    F. 9
    G. 10
    H. 12
    J. 15
    K. 21

23. Given $f(x) = 3x^2 + 6x + 11$, what is the value of $f(-5)$?
    A. −94
    B. −42
    C. 56
    D. 61
    E. 78

24. Which of the following data sets has the smallest standard deviation?
    F. 1, 17
    G. 1, 2, 3, 4
    H. 2, 2, 3, 6, 6, 8
    J. 15, 30, 40
    K. 80, 80, 80, 80, 80

25. The table below shows the age distribution of the varsity football team at Washington High School.

Age, in years	15	16	17	18
Percent of team	8	22	32	38

What percent of the team is at least 17 years old?
    A. 32%
    B. 38%
    C. 54%
    D. 65%
    E. 70%

26. What percent of $\frac{4}{8}$ is $\frac{1}{8}$?
    F. 20%
    G. 25%
    H. 30%
    J. 50%
    K. 60%

GO ON TO THE NEXT PAGE.

27. The sign below advertises a sale on car stereos. What is the sale price of a stereo with a regular price of $159.00?

DO YOUR FIGURING HERE.

HUGE SALE!
All Car Stereos
60% off the regular price!

- **A.** $58.75
- **B.** $63.60
- **C.** $79.50
- **D.** $95.40
- **E.** $103.10

28. The ratio of a side of square S to the base of triangle T is 2:6. The ratio of a side of square S to the height of triangle T is 2:4. What is the ratio of the area of square S to the area of triangle T?
- **F.** 1:3
- **G.** 3:2
- **H.** 4:1
- **J.** 4:10
- **K.** 4:24

29. In Algebra class, Mrs. Chan makes the statement "x varies inversely as the product of y^3 and z, and directly as w^2" and asks the students to translate it into an equation. Which of the following equations, with c as the constant of proportionality, is a correct translation of Mrs. Chan's statement?

- **A.** $x = \dfrac{cw^2}{y^3 z}$

- **B.** $x = \dfrac{cy^3 z}{w^2}$

- **C.** $x = \dfrac{w^2 y^3 z}{c}$

- **D.** $x = \dfrac{w^2}{cy^3 z}$

- **E.** $x = cw^2 y^3 z$

30. In a given isosceles triangle, the measure of each of the base angles is four times the measure of the vertex angle. What is the measure, in degrees, of the vertex angle?
- **F.** $20°$
- **G.** $30°$
- **H.** $45°$
- **J.** $70°$
- **K.** $80°$

31. Two friends have formed their own business performing magic shows. For a single month, in which x number of shows are performed, the friends' profit, P dollars, can be modeled by $P = x^2 - 30x - 1,000$. What is the least number of shows that the friends must perform in order for them not to lose money in any given month?
- **A.** 20
- **B.** 35
- **C.** 50
- **D.** 62
- **E.** 71

GO ON TO THE NEXT PAGE.

△ △ △ △ △ △ △ △ △ △

Use the following information to answer Questions 32–34.

DO YOUR FIGURING HERE.

A student is taking a course in speed reading. The results of different reading tests to determine reading speed (words per minute) over an 8-week period are plotted on the graph below, which also shows the line of best fit based on those results.

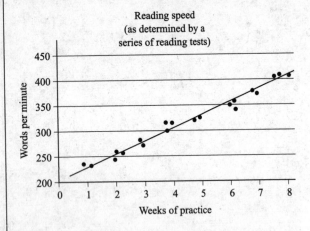

Reading speed
(as determined by a
series of reading tests)

Weeks of practice

32. According to the graph, how many total reading tests did the student take throughout the entire 8-week period?

F. 250
G. 56
H. 20
J. 16
K. 8

33. The slope of the line of best fit represents the increase in words per minute for each additional week of practice. Based on the slope of the line, by approximately how many words per minute can the student expect to increase his or her speed for each additional week of practice?

A. 100
B. 75
C. 50
D. 25
E. 10

34. The student continues the speed-reading course for another 8 weeks. Based on the graph, what is likely to be the student's reading speed (words per minute) at the end of 16 weeks?

F. 200
G. 600
H. 800
J. 1,600
K. Cannot be determined from the given information.

GO ON TO THE NEXT PAGE.

35. Which of the following is a *complete* factorization of the expression $4x^3y - 2x^2 + 6xy^2$?

A. $2xy(2x^2 - 1 + 3y)$
B. $x^2(2xy + 3y)$
C. $2x(2x^2y - x + 3y^2)$
D. $2xy - 1 + 3y^2$
E. $xy(4x^2 - 2 + 3y)$

DO YOUR FIGURING HERE.

36. Which of the following is an equation of the line that passes through the points $(-4, 5)$ and $(-8, -15)$ in the standard (x, y) coordinate plane?

F. $5x - y = -25$
G. $5x - 4y = 15$
H. $x + y = 5$
J. $\frac{5}{6}x = y + 5$
K. $-4x + 5y = -15$

37. What is the amplitude of the function $g(x) = \frac{1}{3}\cos(2x + \pi)$?

A. $\frac{1}{3}$
B. $\frac{1}{2}$
C. $\frac{3}{2}$
D. 2
E. -3

38. If the following system has a solution, what is the y coordinate of the solution?

$$2x - 5y = -17$$
$$4x + 3y = 31$$

F. 13
G. 9
H. 5
J. 1
K. The system has no solution.

39. If the equation $y = x^2 - 20$ were graphed in the standard (x, y) coordinate plane, the graph would be which of the following?

A. Parabola
B. Circle
C. Ellipse
D. Straight line
E. 2 rays forming an upside-down "V"

GO ON TO THE NEXT PAGE.

40. Reggie asked 120 students questions about reading. The results of the poll are shown in the table below.

Question	Yes	No
1. Have you read either a fiction or a non-fiction book in the last 6 months?	65	55
2. If you answered Yes to Question 1, have you read a fiction book in the last 6 months?	45	20
3. If you answered Yes to Question 1, have you read a nonfiction book in the last 6 months?	28	37

After completing the poll, Reggie wondered how many students had read both fiction *and* nonfiction in the last 6 months. How many of the students polled indicated that they had read both fiction and nonfiction in the last 6 months?

F. 73
G. 65
H. 47
J. 17
K. 8

41. Which set of numbers contains both solutions to the equation $x^2 - 2x - 8 = 0$?

A. $\{-4, -2, 0, 2, 6\}$
B. $\{-4, -3, 0, 3, 4\}$
C. $\{-4, -2, 1, 2, 4\}$
D. $\{-6, -4, 1, 4, 6\}$
E. $\{-8, -2, 0, 2, 8\}$

DO YOUR FIGURING HERE.

GO ON TO THE NEXT PAGE.

42. As shown in the figure below, a large slide is 60 feet long from start to finish and forms a 20° angle with the level ground.

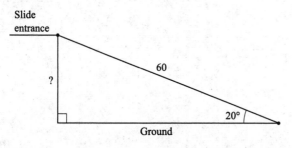

Slide entrance

?

60

20°

Ground

Given the trigonometric approximations in the table below, what is the height above the ground of the slide entrance, to the nearest 0.1 foot?

cos 20°	0.940
sin 20°	0.342
tan 20°	0.364

F. 18.8
G. 20.5
H. 21.8
J. 34.7
K. 56.3

43. If $a^2 - 3 \le 13$, what is the smallest real value a can have?
A. 0
B. −3
C. −4
D. −16
E. There is no smallest value for a.

44. A book has a sale price of $30.40, which is 20% off the original price. How much less than the original price is the sale price?
F. $10.40
G. $7.60
H. $6.08
J. $1.52
K. $0.38

45. What is the distance, in coordinate units, between the points $S(1, 1)$ and $T(3, 4)$ in the standard (x, y) coordinate plane?
A. 2
B. $\sqrt{13}$
C. 5
D. $2\sqrt{7}$
E. 9

DO YOUR FIGURING HERE.

GO ON TO THE NEXT PAGE.

46. Two friends, Erin and Pete, leave in separate cars at the same time from the same location to go on a ski trip. An hour into the drive, Erin stops to get gas, while Pete continues at a constant speed of 62 mph. By the time Erin gets back on the freeway, Pete is 8 miles ahead of her. Erin drives at 69 mph to catch up to Pete. Which of the following equations, when solved for t, gives the number of minutes it will take Erin to catch up to Pete?

F. $62t + 8 = 69t$
G. $1.03t + 8 = 1.15t$
H. $\dfrac{8 + 1.15t}{1.15t} = 1.03t$
J. $1.03t - 8 = 1.15t$
K. $1.15t = 10$

47. Which of the following defines the solution set for the system of inequalities shown below?

$$3x - 5 > 4$$
$$x + 2 \le 10$$

A. $x \le 8$
B. $x > 9$
C. $9 < x \le 10$
D. $-3 < x \le 8$
E. $3 < x \le 8$

48. At Northern College, 42 juniors are enrolled in a theater class and 29 juniors are enrolled in a computer graphics class. Of these juniors, 18 are enrolled in both classes. How many of the 104 juniors at Northern College are NOT enrolled in either a theater class or a computer graphics class?

F. 4
G. 25
H. 33
J. 46
K. 51

49. Given the function below, what is $f(6)$?

$$f(x) = \begin{cases} 3x + 1; \ x < 6 \\ -\dfrac{1}{3}x - 2; \ x \ge 6 \end{cases}$$

A. 0
B. $\dfrac{1}{2}$
C. 3
D. 6
E. 19

50. In the standard (x, y) coordinate plane, $(6, 10)$ is half-way between $(c, 2c - 5)$ and $(3c, c + 16)$. What is the value of c?

F. −2
G. 0
H. 3
J. 5
K. 9

DO YOUR FIGURING HERE.

GO ON TO THE NEXT PAGE.

51. $5^x + 5^x + 5^x + 5^x + 5^x = ?$

  A. 5^{x+1}

  B. 5^{x+2}

  C. 5^{x+5}

  D. 5^{5x}

  E. 5^{25x}

DO YOUR FIGURING HERE.

52. As shown in the (x, y, z) coordinate space below, the cube with vertices C through J has edges that are 3 coordinate units long. The coordinates of H are $(0, 0, 0)$, and I is on the y axis. What are the coordinates of F?

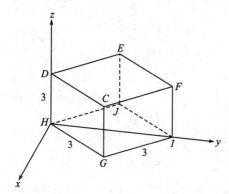

  F. $(0, 3, 3)$

  G. $(0, 3\sqrt{2}, 3)$

  H. $(0, 3\sqrt{2}, 0)$

  J. $(3, 3, 0)$

  K. $(3, \sqrt{2}, 0)$

53. Whenever a, b, and c are positive real numbers, which of the following expressions is equivalent to

$$5\log_4 a - \log_4 b + \frac{1}{3}\log_2 c \ ?$$

  A. $5\log_4(a^5 - b) + \log_2\left(\frac{1}{3}c\right)$

  B. $\log_4 \dfrac{a^5 b}{c}$

  C. $\log_4\left(\dfrac{b}{a^5}\right) + \log_2\left(\dfrac{c}{3}\right)$

  D. $5\log_4(a^5 - b) + \log_2(c^3)$

  E. $\log_4\left(\dfrac{a^5}{b}\right) + \log_2\left(\sqrt[3]{c}\right)$

54. If $-6 \le x \le -2$ and $4 \le y \le 7$, what is the maximum value of $|3x - y|$?

  F. 25

  G. 18

  H. 0

  J. 7

  K. 2

GO ON TO THE NEXT PAGE.

55. The measure of each interior angle of a regular n-sided polygon is $\dfrac{(n-2)180°}{n}$. A regular hexagon is shown below. What is the measure of the designated angle?

- **A.** 120°
- **B.** 162°
- **C.** 240°
- **D.** 256°
- **E.** 278°

56. Which of the following trigonometric functions has a period of π?
- **F.** $f(x) = 2 \cos \pi x$
- **G.** $f(x) = 2 \tan \pi x$
- **H.** $f(x) = \sin\left(\dfrac{1}{2}\pi x\right)$
- **J.** $f(x) = 2 \cos x$
- **K.** $f(x) = \sin 2x$

57. If $s^2 + t^2 = 145$, $st = 72$, and $t > s$, what is the value of $(s - 2t)^2$?
- **A.** −49
- **B.** −1
- **C.** 1
- **D.** 49
- **E.** 100

58. In the figure below, lines p and q are parallel and angle measures are as marked. If it can be determined, what is the value of a?

- **F.** 65°
- **G.** 45°
- **H.** 30°
- **J.** 20°
- **K.** Cannot be determined from the given information.

DO YOUR FIGURING HERE.

GO ON TO THE NEXT PAGE.

59. Given constants *p, q, r,* and *s* such that $x^2 + rx + p$ has factors of $(x + 2)$ and $(x + 4)$ and $x^2 + sx + q$ has factors of $(x + 3)$ and $(x + 7)$, what is *rs*?

A. 16
B. 18
C. 29
D. 60
E. 168

DO YOUR FIGURING HERE.

60. The determinant of any 2×2 matrix $\begin{bmatrix} a & b \\ c & d \end{bmatrix}$ is $ad - bc$.

The determinant of $\begin{bmatrix} (x-2) & 2 \\ 7 & (x+3) \end{bmatrix}$ is equal to 0. What are all possible values of *x*?

F. −1 and 9
G. −3 and 2
H. −4 and 5
J. −5 and 4
K. 0 only

END OF THE MATHEMATICS TEST.
STOP! IF YOU HAVE TIME LEFT OVER, CHECK YOUR WORK ON THIS SECTION ONLY.

ANSWER KEY

Mathematics Test

1. C	16. K	31. C	46. G
2. J	17. C	32. H	47. E
3. D	18. J	33. D	48. K
4. K	19. A	34. G	49. A
5. B	20. J	35. C	50. H
6. F	21. D	36. F	51. A
7. A	22. H	37. A	52. G
8. G	23. C	38. H	53. E
9. D	24. K	39. A	54. F
10. G	25. E	40. K	55. C
11. B	26. G	41. C	56. K
12. H	27. B	42. G	57. E
13. C	28. F	43. C	58. J
14. H	29. A	44. H	59. D
15. C	30. F	45. B	60. H

SCORING WORKSHEET

Scale Score	Raw Score Mathematics	Scale Score	Raw Score Mathematics
36	60	18	24–26
35	59	17	20–23
34	57–58	16	16–19
33	56	15	12–15
32	55	14	10–11
31	54	13	8–9
30	53	12	6–7
29	52	11	5
28	51–50	10	4
27	48–49	9	—
26	46–47	8	3
25	44–45	7	—
24	41–43	6	2
23	38–40	5	—
22	35–37	4	1
21	31–34	3	—
20	28–30	2	—
19	27	1	0

NOTE: Each actual ACT is scaled slightly differently based on a large amount of information gathered from the millions of tests ACT, Inc., scores each year. This scale will give you a fairly good idea of where you are in your preparation process. However, it should not be read as an absolute predictor of your actual ACT score. In fact, on practice tests, the scores are much less important than what you learn from analyzing your results.

ANSWERS AND EXPLANATIONS

1. **The correct answer is C.** This question asks you to calculate the average number of free throws that the team made per game in November. The number of free throws that the team attempted has no impact on the answer. Since the team played 8 games in November and made 102 free throws, the average number of free throws made per game is 102 ÷ 8, which is 12.75. Round to the nearest tenth to get 12.8.

2. **The correct answer is J.** The perimeter is the sum of the lengths of all sides of a polygon. There are 2 sides of the polygon that are not given, so you must first find the lengths of these 2 sides. To find the first unknown, subtract 6 from 11 to get 5 cm. The final unknown is $20 - 4 = 16$. Add up all of the sides to get the perimeter of the figure: $11 + 4 + 5 + 16 + 6 + 20 = 62$.

3. **The correct answer is D.** On this number line, the open circle at −5 and the line going to the right signify that the number is *strictly greater than* −5. Eliminate answer choices A, B, and E. The line connects with a closed circle at 0, which signifies that the number is *less than or equal to* 0. Therefore, the inequality can be expressed as $-5 < x \leq 0$.

4. **The correct answer is K.** To solve this problem follow these steps:

    Substitute the values given for a and b, then perform the subtraction of the exponents:
    $1 - (-2) = 3$
    Compute the exponent: $3^3 = 27$
    Multiply 27 by 4: $27 \times 4 = 108$

5. **The correct answer is B.** This problem deals with factors of 24. Because −5 is not a factor of 24, it is not a possible value of z.

6. **The correct answer is F.** The formula for the volume of a rectangular prism is Volume = Length × Width × Height. Substitute the given values into the formula: $8 \times 6 \times 4 = 192$.

7. **The correct answer is A.** If the radio station sold all 45 of the 60-second spots, it would collect 270×45, or $12,150. Eliminate answer choices B, D, and E. Since the 30-second spots each cost $150, the amount that station collects from selling S of them would be $150S$. Therefore, in total, the radio station would collect $150S + 12,150$.

8. **The correct answer is G.** In this problem, angle *WXZ* ($4x°$) and angle *YXZ* ($8x°$) must add up to 180° because they form a straight line. Therefore, you can set up an equation and solve for x:

    $4x + 8x = 180$
    $12x = 180$
    $x = 15$

    You are given that the measure of angle *WXZ* equals $4x°$, so angle *WXZ* must equal 4×15, or 60°.

9. **The correct answer is D.** If Mickey is the first to draw a number from the hat, he has a chance to get any of the 12 rooms that are available in the house. The probability that he will draw a room on the third floor can be expressed by $\frac{4}{12}$, since 4 out of the 12 rooms in the house are on the third floor. Simplifying this fraction gives a probability of $\frac{1}{3}$.

10. **The correct answer is G.** To solve this problem, first factor an x out of the given equation:

    $x^2 - 49x = 0$
    $x(x - 49) = 0$

    Now you can see that $x = 0$ and $x - 49 = 0$, so $x = 49$.

11. **The correct answer is B.** The first step in solving this problem is to determine the area of one side of the wall (Area = Length × Height): $120 \times 8 = 960$ square feet. Because one can of paint covers 25 square feet, the students would need 960 ÷ 25, or 38.4 cans of paint. The students need more than 38 cans, so they will have to purchase at least 39 cans of paint to have enough to paint the entire wall.

12. **The correct answer is H.** Remember that ratios can be expressed as fractions; $3x$ to $7y = \frac{3x}{7y}$, and $6x$ to $7y = \frac{6x}{7y}$. Therefore, you can set up an equation using fractions to compare the ratios given in the question:

    $$\text{If } \frac{3x}{7y} = \frac{1}{7}, \text{ then } \frac{6x}{7y} = ?$$

    Notice that the denominator is the same on the left side of both equations ($7y$). This means that the denominator will be the same on the right side of both equations as well. Now you know that the denominator will be 7, so you can eliminate answer choices G, J, and K. Notice that the numerator in the second fraction ($6x$) is two times the numerator in the first fraction ($3x$). If $3x = 1$, then $6x = 2$. The final ratio is $\frac{2}{7}$, or 2 to 7.

13. The correct answer is C. To solve this problem, you must first calculate the percentage of students who prefer to rollerblade to class. Do this by adding up the percentages from the other preferred methods (35 + 20 + 25 + 15 = 95), and subtracting the result from 100 (100 − 95 = 5). This shows that 5 percent of the students prefer to rollerblade. To solve for the total number of students surveyed, set up a proportion (75 students represent 5 percent of those surveyed, and x students represent 100 percent):

$$\frac{75}{5} = \frac{x}{100}$$
$$5x = 7,500$$
$$x = 1,500$$

14. The correct answer is H. To solve this problem, simply set up a proportion:

$$\frac{40}{32} = \frac{30}{x}$$

Now, cross-multiply and solve for x:

$$40x = 960$$
$$x = 24$$

15. The correct answer is C. To solve this problem, distribute the subtraction (negative sign) over the second quantity $(-2x + 8 - x^2)$ to get $2x - 8 + x^2$, then group like terms together:

$$3x^2 + x^2 - 7x + 2x + 5 - 8$$

Add like terms:

$$4x^2 - 5x - 3$$

16. The correct answer is K. To most easily solve this problem, start at the end and work your way back. Ryan is left with $34 after all of the purchases. The 2 bags of popcorn cost $6 total, which means that he had $40 before he bought them. The $40 represents $\frac{2}{3}$ of the money that Ryan started with, since he gave his sister $\frac{1}{3}$ of his total amount to buy tickets and hot dogs. To determine how much money he started with, set up an equation:

$$\frac{2}{3}x = 40$$

Multiply both sides by the inverse of the fraction to isolate x on the left side:

$$\frac{3}{2}\left(\frac{2}{3}x\right) = 40\left(\frac{3}{2}\right)$$
$$x = 60$$

This means that Ryan's sister spent $20 (60 − 40) on tickets and hot dogs. You are given that the bleacher seats cost $8 each, so she spent $16 (8 × 2) on them. That leaves $4 to be spent on the two hot dogs, so each hot dog must have cost $2.

17. The correct answer is C. This problem can be solved by testing each of the possible answers. The correct answer should indicate a whole number of questions answered correctly, as there is no way to answer a fraction of a question correctly on the quiz.

Answer choice A: 0.71 × 15 = 10.65
Answer choice B: 0.73 × 15 = 10.95
Answer choice C: 0.80 × 15 = 12
Answer choice D: 0.86 × 15 = 12.9
Answer choice E: 0.93 × 15 = 13.95

This shows that the only possible percentage of questions answered correctly is 80 percent, which is 12 out of 15 questions answered correctly.

18. The correct answer is J. A geometric sequence is a sequence such that each successive term is obtained from the previous term by multiplying that term by a fixed number called a *common ratio*. To get from $-\frac{1}{9}$ to $\frac{1}{3}$, you need to multiply $-\frac{1}{9}$ by −3. To make sure that this is the correct common ratio, try it for the remaining numbers $(\frac{1}{3} \times -3 = -1$, and $-1 \times -3 = 3$.) The 5th term will be 3 × −3, or −9.

19. The correct answer is A. In this problem, $(5a - 2b)^2$ can be expressed as $(5a - 2b)(5a - 2b)$. Use the FOIL method to solve:

$$25a^2 - 10ab - 10ab + 4b^2$$
$$25a^2 - 20ab + 4b^2$$

20. The correct answer is J. To calculate the area of the rectangular-shaped garden, multiply the length by the width: 32 × 8 = 256. You are given that the new square-shaped garden also has an area of 256. Since the area of a square with side x is x^2, the side of a square with area 256 can be found by taking the square root of 256; $\sqrt{256} = 16$.

21. The correct answer is D. To solve this problem, follow these steps, and remember the negative signs:

$$4x - (-2x + 5) = -3$$
$$4x + 2x - 5 = -3$$

Combine like terms and add 5 to both sides:

$$6x = 2$$

Divide both sides by 6:

$$x = \frac{1}{3}$$

22. The correct answer is H. The area of a triangle is given by the formula $A = \frac{1}{2}bh$, where b represents the base and h represents the height of the triangle. In this particular triangle, $\overline{AC}$ is the base, and $\overline{BD}$

(7 inches) is the height. Given this information, you can set up an equation to solve for $\overline{AC}$.

$$42 = \frac{1}{2}(b)(7)$$

Multiply by the inverse of $\frac{1}{2}$ on both sides.

$$(2)42 = (2)\frac{1}{2}(b)(7)$$
$$84 = 7b$$

Divide both sides by 7.

$$b = 12$$

The length of $\overline{AC}$ is 12 inches.

23. **The correct answer is C.** To determine the value of $f(-5)$, simply replace each instance of x in the equation with -5:

$$f(-5) = 3(-5)^2 + 6(-5) + 11$$
$$f(-5) = 3(25) - 30 + 11$$
$$f(-5) = 75 - 30 + 11$$
$$f(-5) = 56$$

24. **The correct answer is K.** Standard deviation is a measure of how spread out numbers are in a given data set, or how much the numbers in the data set deviate from the mean. Because the numbers in answer choice K do not deviate from the mean (they are all the same number), the data set has the smallest standard deviation.

25. **The correct answer is E.** This question asks what percent of the team is *at least* 17 years old, so the only ages that apply would be 17 and 18. Since 32 percent of the team is 17, and 38 percent is 18, the percent that is at least 17 is given by 32 + 38, or 70 percent of the team.

26. **The correct answer is G.** To answer this question, recognize that $\frac{1}{8}$ goes into $\frac{4}{8}$ four times, so $\frac{1}{8}$ is 25 percent of $\frac{4}{8}$. Alternatively, you could convert the fractions to their decimal equivalents and set up a proportion:

$$\frac{1}{8} = 0.125$$
$$\frac{4}{8} = 0.50$$

0.125 is to 0.50 as x is to 100

$$\frac{0.125}{0.5} = \frac{x}{100}$$
$$0.5x = 0.125 \times 100$$
$$0.5x = 12.5$$
$$x = 25$$

27. **The correct answer is B.** This problem can be solved in two different ways. First, you can calculate the amount that is being deducted from the original price during the sale and then subtract this amount from the original price. If the stereo is normally $159.00 and it is being sold at 60 percent off, that means that the price is reduced by 159×0.6, or $95.40. The stereo would then sell for $159 − $95.4, or $63.60. Alternatively, because the stereo is 60 percent off the original price, you could simply say that it is being sold for 40 percent of its regular price: $159 \times 0.4 = $63.60.

28. **The correct answer is F.** This problem deals with area and ratios. You are given that the ratio of one side of the square to the base of the triangle is 2:6, and that the ratio of another side of the square to the height of the triangle is 2:4. The area of the square is 2×2, or 4, because the area of a square is reached by multiplying two sides. The area of the triangle is $\frac{1}{2}(6)(4)$, or 12, since the area for a triangle is given by $A = \frac{1}{2}bh$. Therefore, the ratio of the area of the square to the area of the triangle would be 4:12, which can be reduced to 1:3.

29. **The correct answer is A.** In this problem, you are given an inverse variable expression and also a direct variable expression. The answer will be in the form of a fraction, with the direct expression as the numerator and the inverse expression as the denominator. To find the numerator, multiply by the constant of proportionality, which gives you cw^2. The denominator is "the product of y^3 and z," which is y^3z. Therefore, the answer is expressed as

$$x = \frac{cw^2}{y^3z}$$

30. **The correct answer is F.** In an isosceles triangle, 2 of the sides and 2 of the angles have the same measurement. This particular triangle has base angles that are 4 times greater than the vertex angle. Since the 3 angles must still add up to 180°, you can set up an equation:

$$4x + 4x + x = 180$$
$$9x = 180$$
$$x = 20$$

The vertex angle measures 20°.

31. **The correct answer is C.** To solve this problem, calculate the number of magic shows the friends must perform each month in order not to lose money on their business. Recognize that this means they will

"break even"; that is, their profit will be $0. The equation giving their profit ($P = x^2 - 30x - 1,000$) must equal 0. Try each answer choice to see which one yields a profit of $0:

Answer choice A: $20^2 - 30(20) - 1,000 = -1,200$; 20 shows gives a loss of $1,200.

Answer choice B: $35^2 - 30(35) - 1,000 = -825$; 35 shows gives a loss of $825.

Answer choice C: $50^2 - 30(50) - 1,000 = 0$; 50 shows gives no loss or profit.

There is no need to go any further because you have found the number of performances that yields zero loss and zero profit. Therefore, at this point, the friends are not losing money.

32. **The correct answer is H.** According to the information provided, the results of each test are plotted on the graph. There are 20 different points plotted on the graph, each corresponding to the results of a different reading test.

33. **The correct answer is D.** Looking at the values on the y axis of the graph, you can see that the student's reading speed increases by approximately 50 words per minute every 2 weeks (Week 1 = 225 wpm, Week 2 = 250 wpm, and so on). Thus, each week the student will increase his or her reading speed by approximately 25 words per minute.

34. **The correct answer is G.** According to the graph, the student's reading speed increases by 50 words per minute every 2 weeks. Therefore, after an additional 8 weeks, it is likely that the student's reading speed will have increased by 200 words per minute (50×4), meaning that the student should be able to read at $400 + 200$, or 600 words per minute.

35. **The correct answer is C.** To properly factor this expression, you must first find the greatest common factor (GCF). Determine the largest monomial that can be divided out of each of the terms. Looking strictly at the numbers (4, 2, 6), the GCF is 2. Looking at the variables (x^3y, x^2, xy^2), the GCF is x. So $2x$ is the GCF for the expression. Now perform the necessary multiplication to match the original expression:

First term: $4x^3y = 2x \times \mathbf{2x^2y}$

Second term: $-2x^2 = 2x \times \mathbf{-x}$

Third term: $6xy^2 = 2x \times \mathbf{3y^2}$

Therefore, the answer is $2x(2x^2y - x + 3y^2)$.

36. **The correct answer is F.** To find the equation of a line passing through two points, you must first determine the slope of the line, given by $\frac{(y_2 - y_1)}{(x_2 - x_1)}$:

$$\frac{(-15-5)}{(-8)-(-4)}$$
$$= \frac{(-15-5)}{(-8+4)}$$
$$= \frac{-20}{-4} = 5$$

Next, choose one of the points on the line and write an equation in slope-intercept form ($y = mx + b$, where m is the slope), to find the y-intercept (b). Using the point $(-4, 5)$ will yield an equation that looks like this:

$$y = 5x + b$$
$$5 = 5(-4) + b$$
$$5 = -20 + b$$
$$25 = b$$

This gives you an equation of $y = 5x + 25$ in slope-intercept form. Convert this to standard form ($Ax + By = C$):

$$y = 5x + 25$$
$$5x = y - 25$$
$$5x - y = -25$$

37. **The correct answer is A.** To solve this problem, remember that the amplitude of a function in the form $g(x) = A \cos (Bx + C)$ is $|A|$.

38. **The correct answer is H.** One way to solve this system of equations is to multiply one of them by a number that will allow you to eliminate one of the variables and isolate the other. In this system, multiply the top equation by -2:

$$-2(2x - 5y = -17)$$
$$-4x + 10y = 34$$

Now, when you add the two equations together, you can solve for y.

$$-4x + 10y = 34$$
$$\underline{+4x + 3y = 31}$$
$$0 + 13y = 65$$
$$13y = 65$$
$$y = 5$$

39. **The correct answer is A.** The formula for the classic parabola is $y = x^2$; therefore, the equation $y = x^2 - 20$ is the same parabola translated down by 20 units.

40. The correct answer is K. To solve this problem, first note that you must begin with the total number of students who answered Yes to Question 1 (65), *not* the total number of students (120). Next, find the number of students who answered Yes to both Question 2 and Question 3: 45 + 28 = 73. Since a total of 65 students answered Yes to Question 1, the number of students who read both fiction and nonfiction in the last six months is equal to 73 – 65, or 8.

41. The correct answer is C. To solve, find the values of x for which $x^2 - 2x - 8 = 0$ is true. There are several ways to solve quadratic equations such as this. In this case, factoring is probably the most efficient. To factor $x^2 - 2x - 8$, think of two numbers that can be multiplied to get –8 and added to get –2. Two such numbers are –4 and 2. The factored form is then $(x - 4)(x + 2)$. Now think about the values of x that make $(x - 4)(x + 2) = 0$ true: $(x - 4) = 0$ or $(x + 2) = 0$. Solving both of these equations yields $x = 4$ or $x = -2$. The only list that contains both the numbers 4 and –2 is {–4, –2, 1, 2, 4}, or answer choice C.

42. The correct answer is G. In this problem, you are given the length of the slide (60 ft) and the angle it forms with the level ground (20°). You are asked to solve for the height of the slide entrance. Since this side of the triangle is opposite to the 20° angle, you can use the sin function of this angle to find the height:

$\sin 20° = \dfrac{x}{60}$ (sin = opposite/hypotenuse)

$0.342 = \dfrac{x}{60}$ (you are given that sin 20° = 0.342)

$20.52 = x$ (multiply both sides by 60)

Rounding to the nearest 0.1 foot, the slide entrance is approximately 20.5 feet high.

43. The correct answer is C. If $a^2 - 3 \le 13$, then $a^2 \le 16$. The values of a for which $a^2 = 16$ are $a = 4$ and $a = -4$. Therefore $-4 \le a \le 4$. The smallest value that a can have is –4.

44. The correct answer is H. To solve this problem, first determine the original price. If the sale price is 20% off the original price, then the original price must be 120% of the sale price. $30.40(1.2) = $36.48. Therefore, the sale price is $36.48 – $30.40, which is $6.08 less than the original price.

45. The correct answer is B. The formula for the distance between two points on the x, y coordinate plane is given by $\sqrt{(x_2 - x_1) + (y_2 - y_1)}$. Substitute the numbers from the given points into this equation:

$\sqrt{(3 - 1)^2 + (4 - 1)^2}$

$\sqrt{(2)^2 + (3)^2}$

$\sqrt{4 + 9}$

$\sqrt{13}$

The distance between the two points is $\sqrt{13}$.

46. The correct answer is G. In order to determine how many minutes it will take Erin to catch up to Pete, you must first convert their respective driving speeds into minutes. (The answer choices should give you a clue.) If Pete is driving 62 miles per hour, he is driving $\dfrac{62}{60}$, or 1.03, miles per minute. Likewise, if Erin is driving 69 mph, she is driving at $\dfrac{69}{60}$, or 1.15, miles per minute. When Erin gets back on the freeway, Pete is 8 miles ahead of her, so the equation can be expressed as $1.03t + 8 = 1.15t$.

47. The correct answer is E. To find the solution set for this system of inequalities, simply solve each of the inequalities:

$$\left.\begin{array}{l} 3x - 5 > 4 \\ 3x > 9 \\ x > 3 \end{array}\right\} \text{First inequality}$$

$$\left.\begin{array}{l} x + 2 \le 10 \\ x \le 8 \end{array}\right\} \text{Second inequality}$$

After solving both inequalities, you are left with $3 < x \le 8$, which represents the solution set for both inequalities.

48. The correct answer is K. There are 42 juniors enrolled in a theater class, and 29 enrolled in a computer graphics class. This gives a total of 71 juniors enrolled in one or both of the classes. However, since 18 juniors are enrolled in *both* classes, there are really only 53 individual juniors total enrolled in these classes (subtract 18 from 71). Since there are 104 juniors at Northern College, 104 – 53, or 51, juniors are not enrolled in either class.

49. The correct answer is A. To solve this problem, first recognize that, because $x = 6$, you must solve the *second* inequality:

$f(x) = -\dfrac{1}{3}x - 2$

$f(6) = -\dfrac{1}{3}(6) - 2 = 2 - 2 = 0$

50. The correct answer is H. The formula for finding the midpoint of a line segment is given by $\left(\dfrac{x_1+x_2}{2}, \dfrac{y_1+y_2}{2}\right)$. In this problem, you are given the coordinates of the midpoint, and are asked to solve for c. To solve, set up an equation for either x or y (we've chosen x):

$$\dfrac{x_1+x_2}{2}=6 \quad \text{(6 is the } x \text{ coordinate of the given midpoint)}$$

$$\dfrac{c+3c}{2}=6 \quad \text{(} c \text{ and } 3c \text{ are the } x \text{ coordinates of the two given points on the line)}$$

$$\dfrac{4c}{2}=6$$
$$2c=6$$
$$c=3$$

51. The correct answer is A. To solve this problem, you must recall the rules governing exponents. First, simplify the equation, as shown below:

$$5^x + 5^x + 5^x + 5^x + 5^x = 5(5^x)$$

5 is equivalent to 5^1, and when you multiply like coefficients with exponents, you must add the exponents. Therefore, $5^1(5^x) = 5^{x+1}$.

52. The correct answer is G. Within the cube, HI bisects the side $HGIJ$ and forms two equal triangles. Since you are given that two of the sides of the triangle each measure 3, you can use the Pythagorean theorem to find the length of HI:

$$3^2 + 3^2 = x^2$$
$$9 + 9 = x^2$$
$$18 = x^2$$
$$\sqrt{x^2} = \sqrt{18}$$
$$x = \overline{9 \times 2}$$
$$x = 3\sqrt{2}$$

The length of HI is $3\sqrt{2}$. This means that I is located at $3\sqrt{2}$ on the y-axis. As for point F, it is located directly above point H, which is on the y axis, so its x-coordinate is 0. It is similar to I, as it is located at $3\sqrt{2}$ on the y axis, and is similar to D, as it is located at 3 on the z axis. Therefore, the coordinates for F are $(0, 3\sqrt{2}, 3)$.

53. The correct answer is E. To simplify $5 \log_4 a - \log_4 b + \dfrac{1}{3}\log_2 c$, first recall the properties of logarithms. The expression $5 \log_4 a$ can be written as $\log_4 a^5$. Likewise, $\dfrac{1}{3}\log_2 c$ can be written as $\log_2 c^{1/3}$, or $\log_2 (\sqrt[3]{c})$. Also, because $5 \log_4 a$ and $-\log_4 b$ are both logs of base 4, they can be combined to make $\log_4\left(\dfrac{a^5}{b}\right)$.

Therefore, the expression $5 \log_4 a - \log_4 b + \dfrac{1}{3}\log_2 c$ can be written as $\log_4\left(\dfrac{a^5}{b}\right) + \log_2(\sqrt[3]{c})$.

54. The correct answer is F. To find the maximum value in this problem, you simply need to get the highest number possible (within the limits set by the inequalities) within the absolute value signs. Because the absolute value will be positive, select a value for x that will result in the greatest value when multiplied by 3; $3 \times -6 = -18$. Likewise, select 7 for y because subtracting 7 from -18 will result in the largest possible number within the absolute value signs:

$$|3x - y|$$
$$|3(-6) - 7|$$
$$|-18 - 7|$$
$$|-25| = 25$$

55. The correct answer is C. Here you are given that the measure of each interior angle of an n-sided polygon is $\dfrac{(n-2)180°}{n}$. Since this figure is a hexagon (6 sides), substitute 6 for n to find the measure of each interior angle:

$$\dfrac{(6-2)180}{6} =$$
$$\dfrac{4 \times 180}{6} =$$
$$\dfrac{720}{6} = 120$$

The measure of each interior angle is 120°; however, the question is asking for the measure of the exterior angle. Since the two must add up to 360°, the exterior angle can be found with a simple equation:

$$120 + x = 360$$
$$x = 240$$

56. The correct answer is K. By definition, $f(x) = a \times \sin(bx + c)$. The period of this function is given by $\dfrac{2\pi}{b}$. For $f(x) = \sin 2x$, the period is $\dfrac{2\pi}{2}$, which is equal to π.

57. The correct answer is E. To solve, first determine all of the factors of 72: 1 and 72, 2 and 36, 3 and 24, 4 and 18, 6 and 12, and 8 and 9. Only 8 and 9 satisfy the second requirement that $s^2 + t^2 = 145$ ($8^2 = 64$ and $9^2 = 81$; $64 + 81 = 145$). Since $t > s$, then $t = 9$ and $s = 8$. Therefore, $(s - 2t)^2 = [8 - 2(9)]^2 = (8 - 18)^2 = (-10)^2 = 100$.

58. **The correct answer is J.** Suppose the line that creates the 45° angle was extended to intersect line p, as shown below.

A triangle that includes the angle with measure $a°$ is created. The triangle also has angles 45° (alternate interior angles) and $180° - 65° = 115°$ (supplementary angles). Since there are 180° within a triangle, $a = 180 - 115 - 45 = 20°$.

59. **The correct answer is D.** To solve this problem, apply the FOIL method to the given factors:

$(x + 2)(x + 4) = x^2 + 6x + 8$. You can see that $r = 6$ and $p = 8$.

$(x + 3)(x + 7) = x^2 + 10x + 21$. You can see that $s = 10$ and $q = 21$.

Therefore, $rs = (6)(10) = 60$.

60. **The correct answer is H.** To answer this question, substitute the given values into the definition of *determinant* and solve, as follows:

$$a = (x - 2)$$
$$b = 2$$
$$c = 7$$
$$d = (x + 3)$$

You are told that the determinant is equal to 0, so $ad - bc$ must equal 0:

$$(x - 2)(x + 3) - (2)(7) = 0$$
$$x^2 - x - 6 - 14 = 0$$
$$x^2 - x - 20 = 0$$

Factor the polynomial: $(x - 5)(x + 4) = 0$, so $x - 5 = 0$ and $x = 5$ AND $x + 4 = 0$, and $x = -4$.

CHAPTER 3

STRATEGIES AND TECHNIQUES

As mentioned in Chapter 1, the ACT Mathematics Test is designed to test your ability to reason mathematically, to understand basic math terminology, and to recall basic mathematics formulas and principles.

You will not receive credit for anything that you write in your test booklet, but you should use the available space to work through the problems so that you can check your work. Be sure to do enough practice to determine just how much space you need to solve various problems. You can use whatever space is available, but you cannot move to another test section in search of blank space that you can use to solve your math problems.

If you don't know the answer to a question, mark it in your test booklet and come back to it later if you have time. Cross off answer choices that you are able to eliminate. Make an educated guess if you are able to eliminate even one answer choice. The answer choices correspond to the bubbles on your answer sheet.

> You are not penalized for incorrect answers, so it is in your best interest to fill in every bubble on your answer sheet.

Study Tip
Please visit www.act.org for a list of approved calculators. As a general rule, calculators with memory and print functions are not allowed. The list of approved calculators is updated periodically, so check the website a couple of weeks before your test.

You can use an approved calculator to assist you in answering any of the multiple-choice questions, but none of the questions actually require the use of a calculator. If you do use your calculator, be sure that you are using it in the most efficient way possible. Do not just accept an answer from your calculator as correct. Always try to predict the answer, and if the result of your calculations is nowhere close to what you predicted, then consider trying the problem again.

The following strategies and techniques will help you to correctly answer as many of the questions on your ACT Mathematics Test as possible:

- Apply logic
- Draw pictures
- Answer the question that you are asked
- Don't quit early
- Let the answer choices guide you
- Substitute numbers for the variables
- Read the questions carefully

APPLY LOGIC

Even though you can use a calculator, most of the actual calculations you will need to do are fairly simple. In fact, the ACT test writers are just as likely to be testing your logical reasoning ability or your ability to follow directions as they are testing your ability to plug numbers into an equation. Consider the following example question:

If $b - c = 2$, and $a + c = 16$, then $a + b = ?$
A. 8
B. 14
C. 16
D. 18
E. 32

The correct answer is D. To solve this problem, first recognize that $(b - c) + (a + c) = a + b$. This is true because the c values cancel each other out, leaving you with $b + a$, which is equivalent to $a + b$. Therefore, $a + b$ must equal $2 + 16$, or 18.

▬ DRAW PICTURES

Many seemingly complex story problems will become considerably easier if you are able to visualize them. This strategy should not take a lot of time and can help you avoid making careless errors. Your sketch doesn't have to be beautiful; it just has to accurately depict the relationships in the problem. Sometimes you are given a figure or a table that you can work with (and write on); sometimes you just have to make your own. Consider the following example question:

The diagonal of a rectangular garden is 15 feet, and one side is 9 feet. What is the perimeter of the garden, in feet?

A. 135
B. 108
C. 68
D. 48
E. 42

The correct answer is E. To solve this problem, it is helpful to draw a picture, as shown below:

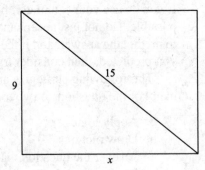

If a rectangular garden has a side of 9 feet and a diagonal of 15 feet, each half forms a right triangle with leg 9 and hypotenuse 15. Using the Pythagorean Theorem, the length of the other leg, x, can be determined using the following equation:

$$15^2 = 9^2 + x^2$$
$$x^2 = 225 - 81$$
$$x^2 = 144$$
$$x = 12$$

The perimeter of the rectangle is therefore $2(9) + 2(12)$, or 42, answer choice E.

ANSWER THE QUESTION THAT YOU ARE ASKED

If the problem requires three steps to reach a solution and you completed only two of the steps, it is likely that the answer you arrived at will be one of the choices. However, it will not be the correct choice! Consider the following example question:

> The rectangular garden shown in the figure below has a stone border 2 feet in width on all sides. What is the area, in square feet, of that portion of the garden that excludes the border?

6 ft

12 ft

> **A.** 4
> **B.** 16
> **C.** 40
> **D.** 56
> **E.** 72

The correct answer is B. This problem is asking for the area of the middle portion of the garden. To solve this problem, perform the following calculations, remembering that the border goes around the entire garden and therefore should be deducted from each dimension twice. First, subtract the border width from the length of the garden:

$$12 - 2(2) = 8$$

Next, subtract the border width from the width of the garden:

$$6 - 2(2) = 2$$

The area (Length × Width) of the portion of the garden that excludes the border is 8×2, or 16.

If you had accounted for the border on only one end of the length and width of the garden rather than both ends, you would have gotten answer choice C. Answer choice D is the area of the border around the garden. Answer choice E is the area of the entire garden, including the stone border.

DON'T QUIT EARLY

Some of the questions on the ACT Mathematics Test will appear quite difficult the first time you look at them. Often, though, you will be able to reason your way through the problem so that it makes sense. Keep in mind that these questions do not usually involve extensive calculations or complicated manipulations. Consider the following example question:

> If $0 < pr < 1$, then which of the following CANNOT be true?
> **A.** $p < 0$ and $r < 0$
> **B.** $p < -1$ and $r < 0$
> **C.** $p < -1$ and $r < -1$
> **D.** $p < 1$ and $r < 1$
> **E.** $p < 1$ and $r > 0$

The correct answer is C. At first glance, you might think that you don't have enough information to solve this problem. However, if you recognize that pr must be a positive fraction, since it lies between 0 and 1, you can work your way through the answer choices and eliminate those that could be true.

Answer choice A. If both p and r are less than 0, their product will be positive. It's possible for pr to be a positive fraction, since both p and r could be negative fractions, so eliminate answer choice A, because it could be true.

Answer choice B. If p is less than –1 and r is also a negative number, their product will be positive. It's possible for pr to be a positive fraction, since r could be a negative fraction, so eliminate answer choice B, because it could be true.

Answer choice C. If both p and r are less than –1, then pr will be greater than 1 (which violates the information given in the question), so this statement cannot be true, and answer choice C is correct.

Answer choice D. If both p and r are less than 1, their product can be positive. It's possible for pr to be a positive fraction, since both p and r could be either positive or negative fractions, so eliminate answer choice D, because it could be true.

Answer choice E. If p is less than 1, p can be a positive fraction. If r is greater than 0, it will be a positive number, and it's possible for pr to be a positive fraction; eliminate answer choice E, because it could be true.

Note: Once you have arrived at the correct answer, it's not necessary to work through any remaining answer choices. We did it here just to show you that D and E are, in fact, incorrect.

▇▇▇ LET THE ANSWER CHOICES GUIDE YOU

Sometimes, the quickest way to answer an ACT Mathematics question is to try the answer choices that the question gives you. The choices on the ACT Mathematics Test are often arranged in either ascending or descending order. For most of these problems, it makes sense to try the middle value (choice C or choice H) first. If this middle value is too small, for example, you can then eliminate the other two smaller choices.

Additionally, if the question asks you for the greatest or smallest possible value, start with the middle value to determine whether you are above or below the correct answer. Then work through the next smallest or largest remaining answer choice to verify that you have found the correct value. Remember that one of them is the correct choice. Consider the following example question:

If x is an integer and $y = 7x + 11$, what is the greatest value of x for which y is less than 50?

A. 7
B. 6
C. 5
D. 4
E. 3

The correct answer is C. Because the question asks for the greatest value of x, try answer choice C first, and substitute 5 for x:

Answer choice C: $y = 7(5) + 11 = 46$. This is less than 50, but you must be sure that it is the greatest possible value of x that works, so try the next largest answer.

Answer choice B: $y = 7(6) + 11 = 53$. This is not less than 50, so you can eliminate answer choice B and know that answer choice C is correct.

▬▬ SUBSTITUTE NUMBERS FOR THE VARIABLES

You can sometimes simplify your work on a given problem by using actual numbers as "stand-ins" for variables. This strategy works when you have variables in the question and the same variables in the answer choices. You can simplify the answer choices by substituting actual numbers for the variables. Pick numbers that are easy to work with and that meet the parameters of the information given in the question. If you use this strategy, remember that numbers on the ACT Mathematics Test can be either positive or negative and are sometimes whole numbers and sometimes fractions. You should also be careful not to use 1 or 0 as one of your stand-ins because they can create "identities," which can lead to more than one seemingly correct answer choice.

In addition, it is sometimes necessary to try more than one number to see whether the result always correctly responds to the question. If the numbers that you pick work for more than one answer choice, pick different numbers and try again.

Consider the following example questions:

Question 1:

If x and y are both positive even integers, which of the following must be even?

   I. x^y
   II. $(x + 1)^y$
   III. $x^{(y + 1)}$
A. I only
B. II only
C. I and II only
D. I and III only
E. II and III only

The correct answer is D. The question states that both x and y are positive even integers. Therefore, you can pick any positive even integer and substitute that value for x and y in each of the Roman numeral choices, as follows:

Roman numeral I (x^y): $2^2 = 4$, which is even; $4^2 = 16$, which is also even. Any positive even integer raised to another positive even integer will result in an even number; therefore, Roman numeral I correctly answers the question. At this point, you can safely eliminate any answer choices that do not contain Roman numeral I.

Roman numeral II [$(x + 1)^y$]: $(2 + 1)^2 = 3^2 = 9$, which is odd; $(4 + 1)^2 = 5^2 = 25$, which is also odd. When you add 1 to a positive even integer and raise the sum to a positive even integer, the result will be odd; therefore, Roman numeral II does not correctly answer the question. At this point, you can safely eliminate any remaining answer choices that contain Roman numeral II.

Roman numeral III ($x^{(y+1)}$): $2^{(2+1)} = 2^3 = 8$, which is even; $4^{(2+1)} = 4^3 = 64$, which is also even. Any positive even integer raised to an odd power will result in an even number; therefore, Roman numeral III correctly answers the question, and you can eliminate any remaining answer choices that do not contain Roman numeral III.

Question 2:

If a and b are positive consecutive odd integers, where $b > a$, which of the following is equal to $b^2 - a^2$?

F. $2a$
G. $4a$
H. $2a + 2$
J. $2a + 4$
K. $4a + 4$

The correct answer is K. You are given that a and b are positive consecutive odd integers, and that b is greater than a. Pick two numbers that fit the criteria: $a = 3$ and $b = 5$. Now, substitute these numbers into $b^2 - a^2$: $5^2 = 25$ and $3^2 = 9$; therefore, $b^2 - a^2 = 16$. Now, plug the value that you selected for a into the answer choices until one of them yields 16, as follows:

$2(3) = 6$; eliminate answer choice F.
$4(3) = 12$; eliminate answer choice G.
$2(3) + 2 = 8$; eliminate answer choice H.
$2(3) + 4 = 10$; eliminate answer choice J.
$4(3) + 4 = 16$; answer choice K is correct.

■ READ THE QUESTIONS CAREFULLY

Read all of the questions carefully, so that you know exactly what operations you are being asked to perform. When you are attempting ratio problems, for example, note whether the question is giving a part-to-part ratio or a part-to-whole ratio. The ratio of girls to boys in a class is a part-to-part ratio. The ratio of girls to students in a class is a part-to-whole ratio. Consider the following example question:

There are two types of candy in a bowl, chocolate and caramel. If the ratio of the number of pieces of chocolate candy to the number of pieces of caramel candy is 2:3, each of the following could be the total number of pieces of candy, EXCEPT:

A. 5
B. 12
C. 15
D. 20
E. 30

The correct answer is B. To solve this problem, you must realize that this is a part-to-part ratio of 2 pieces of chocolate candy to every 3 pieces of caramel candy, which means that for every 5 pieces of candy, 2 are chocolate and 3 are caramel. In order for the ratio to be exactly 2:3, the total number of pieces of candy in the bowl must be a multiple of 5. All of the possible answer choices are multiples of 5 except answer choice B.

Note: This is a special kind of ACT problem, in that you are actually looking for the answer choice that is *not* true. Be especially cautious when answering these questions; don't just select the first "right" answer that you see!

WHAT'S NEXT?

Chapter 4 reviews the content areas tested on the ACT Mathematics Test. If you need help with formulas and math terms, don't skip this chapter! Chapter 5 then gives you the opportunity to apply the strategies you just learned about and to continue building your math skills with dozens of practice questions and exercises.

PART II

ACT MATHEMATICS TEST CONTENT AREAS

CHAPTER 4

CONTENT AREAS TESTED

The ACT Mathematics Test questions are designed to measure both your basic mathematical skills and your ability to reason mathematically. You should be able to solve problems and apply relevant mathematics concepts in arithmetic, algebra, geometry, and data analysis.

The material covered on the Mathematics Test emphasizes the major content areas that are required for success in entry-level courses in college math. Nine scores are reported: a total test score based on all 60 questions and eight reporting category scores based on specific mathematical knowledge and skills.

This chapter provides a review of the mathematical concepts tested on the ACT Mathematics Test. Familiarize yourself with these mathematical concepts and be able to apply them to a variety of math problems included in the reporting categories listed here:

- Number & Quantity
- Algebra
- Functions
- Geometry
- Statistics & Probability
- Integrating Essential Skills

CONCEPTS

Following are the specific concepts addressed by the reporting categories. Additional information regarding the reporting categories can be found on the ACT website, www.act.org.

Operations Using Whole Numbers, Fractions, and Decimals

The ACT Mathematics Test requires you to add, subtract, multiply, and divide whole numbers, fractions, and decimals. When you are performing these operations, be sure to keep track of negative signs and line up decimal points in order to eliminate careless mistakes.

These questions might involve basic arithmetic operations, operations involving decimals, factoring, percents, ratios, proportions, sequences, number sets, number lines, absolute value, and prime numbers.

The Properties of Integers

The following are properties of integers that are commonly tested on the ACT Mathematics Test:

- Integers include both positive and negative whole numbers.
- Zero is considered an integer.
- Consecutive integers follow one another and differ by 1. For example, 6, 7, 8, and 9 are consecutive integers. Likewise, 0, −1, −2, and −3 are consecutive integers.
- The value of a number does not change when it is multiplied by 1. For example, $13 \times 1 = 13$.

Real Numbers

The following are properties of real numbers that are commonly tested on the ACT Mathematics Test:

- All real numbers correspond to points on the number line, as shown below:

- All real numbers except zero are either positive or negative. On a number line, such as that shown above, numbers that correspond to points to the right of zero are positive, and numbers that correspond to points to the left of zero are negative.
- For any two numbers on the number line, the number to the left is always less than the number to the right.
- Ordering is the process of arranging numbers from smallest to greatest or from greatest to smallest. The symbol > is used to represent "greater than," and the symbol < is used to represent "less than." To represent "greater than or equal to," use the symbol ≥; to represent "less than or equal to," use the symbol ≤.
- If any number n lies between 0 and any positive number x on the number line, then $0 < n < x$; in other words, n is greater than 0 but less than x. If n is any number on the number line between 0 and any positive number x, including 0 and x, then $0 \leq n \leq x$, which means that n is greater than or equal to 0 and less than or equal to x.
- If any number n lies between 0 and any negative number x on the number line, then $-x < n < 0$; in other words, n is greater than $-x$ but less than 0. If n is any number on the number line between 0 and any negative number x, including 0 and $-x$, then $-x \leq n \leq 0$, which means that n is greater than or equal to $-x$ and less than or equal to 0.

Order of Operations (PEMDAS)

The acronym PEMDAS stands for Parentheses, Exponents, Multiplication, Division, Addition, Subtraction. It should help you to remember to do the operations in the correct order, as follows:

P: First, do the operations within the *parentheses*, if any.
E: Next, do the *exponents*, if any.
M/D: Next, do the *multiplication and/or division*, in order from left to right.
A/S: Next, do the *addition and/or subtraction*, in order from left to right.

For example, $\dfrac{2(4+1)^2 \times 3}{5} - 7$ would be solved in the following order:

$$= \frac{2(5)^2 \times 3}{5} - 7$$

$$= \frac{2(25) \times 3}{5} - 7$$

$$= \frac{50 \times 3}{5} - 7$$

$$= \frac{150}{5} - 7$$

$$= 30 - 7 = 23$$

Decimals

The following are properties of decimals that are commonly tested on the ACT Mathematics Test:

- Place value refers to the value of a digit in a number relative to its position. Starting from the left of the decimal point, the values of the digits are ones, tens, hundreds, and so on. Starting to the right of the decimal point, the values of the digits are tenths, hundredths, thousandths, and so on.
- When adding and subtracting decimals, be sure to line up the decimal points. For example:

$$
\begin{array}{r}
236.78 \\
+113.21 \\
\hline
349.99
\end{array}
\qquad
\begin{array}{r}
78.90 \\
-23.42 \\
\hline
55.48
\end{array}
$$

- When multiplying decimals, it is not necessary to line up the decimal points. Simply multiply the numbers, then count the total number of places to the right of the decimal points in the decimals being multiplied to determine the placement of the decimal point in the product.

$$
\begin{array}{r}
17.330 \\
\times\ 0.35 \\
\hline
6.06550
\end{array}
$$

- When dividing decimals, first move the decimal point in the divisor to the right until the divisor becomes an integer. Then move the decimal point in the dividend the same number of places.

$$
\begin{array}{cc}
\text{dividend} & \text{divisor} \\
\downarrow & \downarrow
\end{array}
$$

For example: $58.345 \div 3.21 = 5834.5 \div 321$. (The decimal point was moved two places to the right.)

You can then perform the long division with the decimal point in the correct place in the quotient, as shown below:

$$
\begin{array}{r}
18.17 \\
321{\overline{\smash{)}\,5834.50}} \\
-321 \\
\hline
2624 \\
-2568 \\
\hline
565 \\
-321 \\
\hline
2440 \\
-2247 \\
\hline
193 \\
\text{and so on}
\end{array}
$$

Fractions

The following are properties of fractions and rational numbers that are commonly tested on the ACT Mathematics Test:

- The reciprocal of any number n is expressed as 1 over n, or $\frac{1}{n}$. The product of a number and its reciprocal is always 1. For example, the reciprocal of 3 is $\frac{1}{3}$, and $3 \times \frac{1}{3} = \frac{3}{3}$, which is equivalent to 1. By the same token, the reciprocal of $\frac{1}{3}$ is $\frac{3}{1}$, or 3.

- To change any fraction to a decimal, divide the numerator by the denominator. For example, $\frac{3}{4}$ is equivalent to $3 \div 4$, or 0.75.

- Multiplying and dividing both the numerator and the denominator of a fraction by the same nonzero number will result in an equivalent fraction. For example, $\frac{1}{4} \times \frac{3}{3} = \frac{3}{12}$, which can be reduced to $\frac{1}{4}$. This is true because whenever the numerator and the denominator are the same, the value of the fraction is 1; $\frac{3}{3} = 1$.

- When adding and subtracting like fractions, add or subtract the numerators and write the sum or difference over the denominator. So, $\frac{1}{8} + \frac{2}{8} = \frac{3}{8}$, and $\frac{4}{7} - \frac{2}{7} = \frac{2}{7}$.

- To simplify a fraction, find a common factor of both the numerator and the denominator. For example, $\frac{12}{15}$ can be simplified to $\frac{4}{5}$ by dividing both the numerator and the denominator by the common factor 3.

- To convert a mixed number to an improper fraction, multiply the whole number by the denominator of the fraction, add the result to the numerator, and place that value over the original denominator. For example, $3\frac{2}{5}$ is equivalent to $(3 \times 5) + 2$ over 5, or $\frac{17}{5}$.

- When multiplying fractions, multiply the numerators to get the numerator of the product, and multiply the denominators to get the denominator of the product. For example, $\frac{3}{5} \times \frac{7}{8} = \frac{21}{40}$.

- When dividing fractions, multiply the first fraction by the reciprocal of the second fraction. For example, $\frac{1}{3} \div \frac{1}{4} = \frac{1}{3} \times \frac{4}{1}$, which equals $\frac{4}{3}$, or $1\frac{1}{3}$.

Squares and Square Roots

The following are properties of squares and square roots that are commonly tested on the ACT Mathematics Test:

- Squaring a negative number yields a positive result. For example, $-2^2 = 4$.
- The square root of a number n is written as $\sqrt{n}$, or the nonnegative value a that fulfills the expression $a^2 = n$. For example, "the square root of 5" is expressed as $\sqrt{5}$, and $(\sqrt{5})^2 = 5$. A square root will always be a positive number.
- A number is considered a perfect square when the square root of that number is a whole number. The polynomial $a^2 \pm 2ab + b^2$ is also a perfect square because the solution set is $(a \pm b)^2$.

Exponents

The following are properties of exponents that are commonly tested on the ACT Mathematics Test:

- $a^m \times a^n = a^{(m+n)}$
  When multiplying the same base number raised to any power, add the exponents. For example: $3^2 \times 3^4 = 3^6$. Likewise, $3^6 = 3^2 \times 3^4$; $3^6 = 3^1 \times 3^5$; and $3^6 = 3^3 \times 3^3$.

- $(a^m)^n = a^{mn}$
  When raising an exponential expression to a power, multiply the exponent and the power. For example: $(3^2)^4 = 3^8$. Likewise, $3^8 = (3^2)^4$; $3^8 = (3^4)^2$; $3^8 = (3^1)^8$; and $3^8 = (3^8)^1$.

- $(ab)^m = a^m \times b^m$
  When multiplying two different base numbers and raising the product to a power, the product is equivalent to raising each number to the power, then multiplying the exponential expressions. For example: $(3 \times 2)^2 = 3^2 \times 2^2$, which equals 9×4, or 36. Likewise, $3^2 \times 2^2 = (3 \times 2)^2$, or 6^2, which equals 36.

- $\left(\dfrac{a}{b}\right)^m \times \dfrac{a^m}{b^m}$

  When dividing two different base numbers and raising the quotient to a power, the quotient is equivalent to raising each number to the power, then dividing the exponential expressions. For example: $\left(\dfrac{2}{3}\right)^2 = \dfrac{2^2}{3^2} = \dfrac{4}{9}$.

- $a^0 = 1$, when $a \neq 0$
  When you raise any number to the power of 0, the result is always 1.

- $a^{-m} = \dfrac{1}{a^m}$, when $a \neq 0$
  When you raise a number to a negative power, the result is equivalent to 1 over the number raised to the same positive power. For example: $3^{-2} = \dfrac{1}{3^2}$, or $\dfrac{1}{9}$.

Scientific Notation

When numbers are very large or very small, scientific notation is used to shorten them. Scientific notation is expressed by writing a positive number N that is equal to a number less than 10, times 10 raised to an integer. To form the scientific notation of a number, the decimal point is moved until it is placed after the first nonzero digit from the left in the number.

For example, 568,000,000 written in scientific notation would be 5.68×10^8, because the decimal point was moved 8 places to the left. Likewise, 0.0000000354 written in scientific notation would be 3.54×10^{-8}, because the decimal point was moved 8 places to the right.

Mean, Median, and Mode

The following are properties of the mean, median, and mode that are commonly tested on the ACT Mathematics Test:

- The arithmetic mean is equivalent to the average of a series of numbers. Calculate the average by dividing the sum of all of the numbers in the series by the total count of numbers in the series. For example: a student received scores of 80 percent, 85 percent, and 90 percent on 3 math tests. The average score received by the student on those tests is $80 + 85 + 90$ divided by 3, or $255 \div 3$, which is 85 percent.

- The median is the middle value of a series of numbers when those numbers are in either ascending or descending order. In the series (2, 4, 6, 8, 10) the median is 6. To find the median in a data set with an even number of items, find the average of the middle two numbers. In the series (3, 4, 5, 6) the median is 4.5.
- The mode is the number that appears most frequently in a series of numbers. In the series (2, 3, 4, 5, 6, 3, 7) the mode is 3, because 3 appears twice in the series and the other numbers each appear only once in the series.

Ratios, Proportions, and Percents

The following are properties of ratios, proportions, and percents that are commonly tested on the ACT Mathematics Test:

- A ratio expresses a mathematical comparison between two quantities. A ratio of 1 to 5, for example, is written as either $\frac{1}{5}$ or 1:5.
- When working with ratios, be sure to differentiate between part-to-part and part-to-whole ratios. In a part-to-part ratio, the elements being compared are parts of the whole. For example, if two components of a recipe are being compared to each other, it is a part-to-part ratio (2 cups of flour:1 cup of sugar). In a part-to-whole ratio, the elements being compared are one part of the whole to the whole itself. For example, if one group of students is being compared to the entire class, it is a part-to-whole ratio (13 girls:27 students).
- A proportion indicates that one ratio is equal to another ratio. For example, $\frac{1}{5} = \frac{x}{20}$ is a proportion, where $x = 4$.
- A percent is a fraction whose denominator is 100. The fraction $\frac{25}{100}$ is equal to 25 percent. To calculate the percent that one number is of another number, set up a ratio, as shown below:

What percent of 40 is 5?

5 is to 40 as x is to 100

$$\frac{5}{40} = \frac{x}{100}$$

Cross-multiply and solve for x:

$40x = 500$

$$x = \frac{500}{40} = 12.5$$

5 is 12.5% of 40

Note: If a price is discounted by p percent, then the discounted price is $(100 - p)$ percent of the original price. So, if a CD is on sale for 20 percent off the regular price, the sale price is equivalent to 80 percent of the original price.

Linear Equations with One Variable

The following are properties of linear equations with one variable that are commonly tested on the ACT Mathematics Test:

- In a linear equation with one variable, the variable cannot have an exponent or be in the denominator of a fraction. An example of a linear equation is $2x + 13 = 43$. The ACT Mathematics Test will most likely require you to solve for x in that equation. Do this by isolating x on the left side of the equation, as follows:

$$2x + 13 = 43$$
$$2x = 43 - 13$$
$$2x = 30$$
$$x = \frac{30}{2}, \text{ or } 15$$

- One common ACT example of a linear equation with one variable is in questions involving speed of travel. The basic formula to remember is Rate × Time = Distance. The question will generally give you two of these values, and you will have to solve for the remaining value.

Absolute Value

The absolute value of a number is indicated by placing that number inside two vertical lines. For example, the absolute value of 10 is written as follows: |10|. Absolute value can be defined as the numerical value of a real number without regard to its sign. This means that the absolute value of 10, |10|, is the same as the absolute value of −10, |−10|, in that they both equal 10. Think of it as the distance from −10 to 0 on the number line, and the distance from 0 to 10 on the number line . . . both distances equal 10 units.

Simple Probability

The following are properties of probability and outcomes that are commonly tested on the ACT Mathematics Test:

- Probability refers to the likelihood that an event will occur. For example, Jeff has 3 striped and 4 solid ties in his closet; therefore, he has a total of 7 ties in his closet. He has 3 chances to grab a striped tie out of the 7 total ties, because he has 3 striped ties. So, the likelihood of Jeff's grabbing a striped tie is 3 out of 7, which can also be expressed as 3:7 or $\frac{3}{7}$.

- Two specific events are considered independent if the outcome of one event has no effect on the outcome of the other event. For example, if you toss a coin, there is a 1 in 2, or $\frac{1}{2}$, chance that it will land on either heads or tails. If you toss the coin again, the outcome will be the same. To find the probability of two or more independent events occurring together, multiply the outcomes of the individual events. For example, the probability that both coin tosses will result in heads is or $\frac{1}{2} \times \frac{1}{2}$, or $\frac{1}{4}$.

The ACT Mathematics Test will assess your ability to calculate simple probabilities in everyday situations.

Functions

A function is a set of ordered pairs where no two of the ordered pairs have the same x value. In a function, each input (x value) has exactly one output (y value). An example of this relationship would be $y = x^2$. Here, y is a function of x because for any value of x, there is exactly one value of y. However, x is not a function of y because for certain values of y, there is more than one value of x. (If $y = 4$, x could be either 2 or −2.) The *domain* of a function refers to the x values, while the *range* of a function refers to the y values. If the values in the domain correspond to more than one value in the range, the relation is not a function.

Consider the following example:

For the function $f(x) = x^2 - 3x$, what is the value of $f(5)$?

Solve this problem by substituting 5 for x wherever x appears in the function:

$$f(x) = x^2 - 3x$$
$$f(5) = (5)^2 - (3)(5)$$
$$f(5) = 25 - 15$$
$$f(5) = 10$$

Polynomial Operations and Factoring Simple Quadratic Expressions

The following are properties of polynomial operations and factoring simple quadratic expressions that are commonly tested on the ACT Mathematics Test:

- A polynomial is the sum or difference of expressions like $2x^2$ and $14x$. The most common polynomial takes the form of a simple quadratic expression, such as $2x^2 + 14x + 8$, with the terms in decreasing order. The standard form of a simple quadratic expression is $ax^2 + bx + c$, where a, b, and c are whole numbers. When the terms include both a number and a variable, such as x, the number is called the *coefficient*. For example, in the expression $2x$, 2 is the coefficient of x.
- The ACT Mathematics Test will often require you to evaluate, or solve, a polynomial by substituting a given value for the variable, as follows:

For $x = -2$, $2x^2 + 14x + 8 = ?$

Substitute −2 for x and solve:

$$2(-2)^2 + 14(-2) + 8$$
$$= 2(4) + (-28) + 8$$
$$= 8 - 28 + 8 = -12$$

- You will also be required to add, subtract, multiply, and divide polynomials. To add or subtract polynomials, simply combine like terms, as in the following examples:

$$(2x^2 + 14x + 8) + (3x^2 + 5x + 32)$$
$$2x^2 + 3x^2 = 5x^2 \text{ and}$$
$$14x + 5x = 19x \text{ and}$$
$$8 + 32 = 40, \text{ so}$$
$$5x^2 + 19x + 40$$

$$(8x^2 + 11x + 23) - (7x^2 + 3x + 13)$$
$$8x^2 - 7x^2 = x^2, \text{ and}$$
$$11x - 3x = 8x, \text{ and}$$
$$23 - 13 = 10, \text{ so}$$
$$x^2 + 8x + 10$$

To multiply polynomials, use the distributive property to multiply each term of one polynomial by each term of the other polynomial. Following are some examples:

$$(3x)(x^2 + 4x - 2)$$

Multiply each term in the second polynomial by $3x$.

$$(3x^3 + 12x^2 - 6x)$$

___

$$(2x^2 + 5x)(x - 3)$$

Remember the *FOIL* method whenever you see this type of multiplication: multiply the *F*irst terms, then the *O*utside terms, then the *I*nside terms, then the *L*ast terms.

$$(2x^2 + 5x)(x - 3)$$
*F*irst terms: $(2x^2)(x) = 2x^3$
*O*utside terms: $(2x^2)(-3) = -6x^2$
*I*nside terms: $(5x)(x) = 5x^2$
*L*ast terms: $(5x)(-3) = -15x$

Now put the terms in decreasing order:

$$2x^3 + (-6x^2) + 5x^2 + (-15x)$$
$$= 2x^3 - 1x^2 - 15x$$

- You may also be asked to find the factors or solution sets of certain simple quadratic expressions. A factor or solution set takes the form ($x \pm$ some number). Simple quadratic expressions will usually have two of these factors or solution sets. Remember that the standard form of a simple quadratic expression is $ax^2 + bx + c$. To factor the equation, find two numbers that when multiplied together will give you c, and that when added together will give you b. The ACT Mathematics Test includes questions similar to the following:

  What are the solution sets for $x^2 + 9x + 20 = 0$?
  $$x^2 + 9x + 20 = 0$$
  $$(x + \underline{})(x + \underline{}) = 0$$

  5 and 4 are two numbers that when multiplied together give you 20, and that when added together give you 9.

  Therefore, $(x + 5)$ and $(x + 4)$ are the two solution sets for $x^2 + 9x + 20 = 0$.

Linear Inequalities with One Variable

The following are properties of linear inequalities with one variable that are commonly tested on the ACT Mathematics Test:

- Linear inequalities with one variable are solved in almost the same manner as linear equations with one variable: by isolating the variable on one side of the inequality (see previous examples).

- When an inequality is multiplied by a negative number, you must switch the sign.

For example, follow these steps to solve for x in the inequality $-2x + 2 < 6$:

$$-2x + 2 < 6$$
$$-2x < 4$$
$$-x < 2$$
$$x > -2$$

The Quadratic Formula

The quadratic formula is not tested specifically on the ACT. However, you may find it useful when you are attempting to answer questions that contain quadratic equations.

The quadratic formula is expressed as $x = \dfrac{-b \pm \sqrt{(b^2 - 4ac)}}{2a}$. This formula finds solutions to quadratic equations of the form $ax^2 + bx + c = 0$. It is the method that can be used in place of factoring for more complex polynomial expressions. The part of the formula $b^2 - 4ac$ is called the *discriminant* and can be used to quickly determine what kind of answer you should arrive at. If the discriminant is 0, then you will have only one solution. If the discriminant is positive, then you will have two real solutions. If the discriminant is negative, then you will have two complex solutions.

Radical and Rational Expressions

The following are properties of radical and rational expressions that are commonly tested on the ACT Mathematics Test:

- A radical is the root of a given quantity, indicated by the radical sign, $\sqrt{}$. For example, $\sqrt{9}$ is considered a radical, and 9 is the radicand. The following rules apply to radicals:

  ○ $\sqrt{a}$ means the "square root of a," $\sqrt[3]{a}$ means the "cube root of a," and so on

  ○ $\sqrt{a} \times \sqrt{b} = \sqrt{(ab)}$

  ○ $\sqrt[n]{a^n} = a$

  ○ $\sqrt[n]{\sqrt[m]{a}} = \sqrt[nm]{a}$

- A rational number is a number that can be expressed as a ratio of two integers. Fractions are rational numbers that represent a part of a whole number. To find the square root of a fraction, simply divide the square root of the numerator by the square root of the denominator. If the denominator is not a perfect square, rationalize the denominator by multiplying both the numerator and the denominator by a number that would make the denominator a perfect square. For example,

  $\dfrac{\sqrt{1}}{\sqrt{3}}$ can be rationalized in the following way:

  $$= \dfrac{\sqrt{(1 \times 12)}}{\sqrt{(3 \times 12)}}$$

$$= \frac{\sqrt{(12)}}{\sqrt{(36)}}$$

$$= \frac{\sqrt{(4)(3)}}{6}$$

$$= \frac{2\sqrt{3}}{6} = \frac{\sqrt{3}}{3}$$

Inequalities and Absolute Value Equations

An inequality with an absolute value will be in the form of $|ax + b| > c$, or $|ax + b| < c$. To solve $|ax + b| > c$, first drop the absolute value and create two separate inequalities with the word *or* between them. To solve $|ax + b| < c$, first drop the absolute value and create two separate inequalities with the word *and* between them. The first inequality will look just like the original inequality without the absolute value. For the second inequality, you must switch the inequality sign and change the sign of c.

For example, to solve $|x + 3| > 5$, first drop the absolute value sign and create two separate inequalities with the word *or* between them:

$$x + 3 > 5 \; or \; x + 3 < -5$$

Solve for x:

$$x > 2 \; or \; x < -8$$

To solve $|x + 3| < 5$, first drop the absolute value sign and create two separate inequalities with the word *and* between them:

$$x + 3 < 5 \; and \; x + 3 > -5$$

Solve for x:

$$x < 2 \; and \; x > -8$$

Sequences

The following are properties of sequences that are commonly tested on the ACT Mathematics Test:

- An arithmetic sequence is one in which the difference between one term and the next is the same. To find the nth term, use the formula $a_n = a_1 + (n - 1)d$, where d is the common difference.

- A geometric sequence is one in which the ratio between two terms is constant. For example, $\frac{1}{2}$, 1, 2, 4, 8, . . . is a geometric sequence in which 2 is the constant ratio. To find the nth term, use the formula $a_n = a_1(r)^{n-1}$, where r is the constant ratio.

Systems of Equations

The ACT Mathematics Test commonly includes questions that contain two equations and two unknowns. To solve a system of equations like this, follow the steps below:

$$4x + 5y = 21$$
$$5x + 10y = 30$$

If you multiply the top equation by -2, you will get

$$-8x - 10y = -42$$
$$5x + 10y = 30$$

Now you can add the two equations together:

$$-8x - 10y + 5x + 10y = -42 + 30$$
$$-3x = -12$$

Notice that the two y terms cancel each other out. Solving for x, you get $x = 4$. Now, choose one of the original two equations, substitute 4 for x, and solve for y:

$$4(4) + 5y = 21$$
$$16 + 5y = 21$$
$$5y = 5$$
$$y = 1$$

Logarithms

Logarithms are used to indicate exponents of certain numbers called *bases*, where $\log_a b = c$, if $a^c = b$. For example, $\log_2 16 = 4$ means that the log to the base 2 of 16 is 4, because $2^4 = 16$.

Consider the following example:

What value of x satisfies $\log_x 9 = 2$?

$\log_x 9 = 2$ means that the log to the base x of $9 = 2$.

So, x^2 must equal 9, and x must equal 3.

The ACT Mathematics Test might include one or two questions that require knowledge of the three most common logarithmic properties, shown next:

- $\log_b (xy) = \log_b x + \log_b y$

- $\log_b \left(\dfrac{x}{y} \right) = \log_b x - \log_b y$

- $\log_b (x^n) = n \log_b x$

Roots of Polynomials

When given a quadratic equation, $ax^2 + bx + c = 0$, you might be asked to find the roots of the equation. This means that you need to find what value(s) of x make the equation true. You may choose to either factor the quadratic equation or use the quadratic formula. For example, find the roots of $x^2 + 6x + 8 = 0$.

$$x^2 + 6x + 8 = 0$$
$$(x + 4)(x + 2) = 0; \text{ solve for } x$$
$$x + 4 = 0 \text{ and } x + 2 = 0, \text{ so } x = -4 \text{ and } x = -2.$$

The roots of $x^2 + 6x + 8 = 0$ are $x = -4$ and $x = -2$. Using the quadratic formula will yield the same solution.

Complex Numbers

Complex numbers are written in the form $a + bi$, where i is an imaginary number equal to the square root of -1. Thus, $i = \sqrt{(-1)}$. It also follows that $i^2 = (i)(i) = \left(\sqrt{(-1)}\right)\left(\sqrt{(-1)}\right) = -1$, $i^3 = (i^2)(i) = (-1)i = -i$, and $i^4 = (i^2)(i^2) = (-1)(-1) = 1$.

Complex numbers can be added, subtracted, multiplied, and divided as shown below:

Simply combine like terms when adding: $(5 + 3i) + (7 + 2i) = 12 + 5i$

Simply combine like terms when subtracting: $(3 + 6i) - (4 + 3i) = -1 + 3i$

Use the *FOIL* method when multiplying. $(2 + 3i)(4 - 2i)$

$= 8 - 4i + 12i - 6i^2$

$= 8 + 12i + 6 = 14 + 12i$ (Combine like terms, remembering that $i^2 = -1$.)

When dividing complex numbers, you must first eliminate all imaginary numbers from the denominator. Do this by multiplying the complex number in the denominator by its *conjugate*. The conjugate of $(a + bi)$ is simply $(a - bi)$:

$$\frac{(5 + 3i)}{(3 + 2i)}$$

First, multiply the numerator and denominator by $(3 - 2i)$; this will eliminate the imaginary number from the denominator.

$$= \frac{(5 + 3i)(3 - 2i)}{(3 + 2i)(3 - 2i)}$$

$$= \frac{15 - 10i + 9i - 6i^2}{9 - 6i + 6i - 4i^2}$$

$$= \frac{15 - i - 6(-1)}{9 - 4(-1)} = \frac{21 - i}{13}$$

Factorials

Factorials are represented by "!." The factorial of any positive number (n) is equal to the product of all positive numbers less than or equal to n. For example, $5! = 1 \times 2 \times 3 \times 4 \times 5 = 120$. You may also see the expression $n!$, which means $1 \times 2 \times 3 \times \ldots \times n$. Factorials are tested infrequently on the ACT Mathematics Test, so don't worry if you cannot remember these formulas.

When evaluating factorials, cancel out as many of the common terms as possible, as in the following example:

$$\frac{12!}{9!} = \frac{1 \times 2 \times 3 \ldots \times 9 \times 10 \times 11 \times 12}{1 \times 2 \times 3 \ldots \times 9}$$

The terms $1 \times 2 \times 3 \times \ldots \times 9$ in the numerator and the denominator cancel out, leaving you with an answer of $10 \times 11 \times 12 = 1,320$.

Additionally, it is valuable to remember that $0! = 1$, not 0.

Number Line Graphs

The most basic type of graphing is graphing on a number line. For the most part, you will be asked to graph inequalities like those shown below:

Equation of a Line

The standard form of an equation of a line is the form $Ax + By = C$. This can be transformed into the slope-intercept form of the equation of a line, $y = mx + b$, where m is the slope of the line and b is the y intercept (that is, the point at which the graph of the line crosses the y axis). The ACT Mathematics Test will often require you to put the equation of a line into the slope-intercept form to determine either the slope or the y intercept, as follows:

$$3x + 4y - 16 = 0$$

Put the equation in the slope-intercept form by isolating y on the left side:

$$4y = -3x + 16$$

$$y = -\frac{3}{4}x + 4$$

The slope of the line is $-\frac{3}{4}$, and the y intercept is 4.

Slope

The following are properties of slope that are commonly tested on the ACT Mathematics Test:

- The slope of a line is calculated by taking the change in y coordinates divided by the change in x coordinates from two given points on a line. The formula for slope is $m = \frac{(y_2 - y_1)}{(x_2 - x_1)}$, where (x_1, y_1) and (x_2, y_2) are the two given points. For example, the slope of a line that contains the points (6, 3) and (5, 2) is equivalent to $\frac{(6-5)}{(3-2)}$, or $\frac{1}{1}$, which equals 1.

- A positive slope means that the graph of the line goes upward and to the right. A negative slope means that the graph of the line goes downward and to the right. A horizontal line has a slope of 0, and a vertical line has an undefined slope because it never crosses the *y* axis. See the figure below for a visual representation of different slopes of a line.

Positive slope   Negative slope   0 slope   Undefined slope

Parallel and Perpendicular Lines

The following are properties of parallel and perpendicular lines that are commonly tested on the ACT Mathematics Test:

- Two lines are parallel if and only if they have the same slope. For example, the two lines with equations $2y = 6x + 7$ and $y = 3x - 14$ have the same slope (3).

- Two lines are perpendicular if and only if the slope of one of the lines is the negative reciprocal of the slope of the other line. In other words, if line *a* has a slope of 2 and line *b* has a slope of $-\frac{1}{2}$, the two lines are perpendicular.

Distance and Midpoint Formulas

The following are properties of distance and midpoint formulas that are commonly tested on the ACT Mathematics Test:

- To find the distance between two points in the (x, y) coordinate plane, use the distance formula $\sqrt{([x_2 - x_1]^2 + [y_2 - y_1]^2)}$, where (x_1, y_1) and (x_2, y_2) are the two given points. For example, if you are given the points (2, 3) and (4, 5), you would set up the following equation to determine the distance between the two points:

$$= \sqrt{(4-2)^2 + (5-3)^2}$$
$$= \sqrt{(2)^2 + (2)^2}$$
$$= \sqrt{4+4}$$
$$= \sqrt{8} = 2\sqrt{2}$$

- To find the midpoint of a line segment given two points on the line, use the midpoint formula $\left(\frac{[x_1 + x_2]}{2}, \frac{[y_1 + y_2]}{2} \right)$. For example, you would set up the following equation to determine the midpoint of the line segment between the two points (2, 3) and (4, 5):

$$\frac{(2+4)}{2} = \frac{6}{2} = 3; \text{ the } x\text{-value of the midpoint is 3.}$$
$$\frac{(3+5)}{2} = \frac{8}{2} = 4; \text{ the } y\text{-value of the midpoint is 4.}$$

Therefore, the midpoint of the line segment between the points (2, 3) and (4, 5) is (3, 4).

Translation and Reflection

The following are properties of translation and reflection that are commonly tested on the ACT Mathematics Test:

- A translation slides an object in the coordinate plane to the left or right or up or down. The object retains its shape and size and faces in the same direction as the original object. In the translation shown below, the triangle in the first graph has been translated x units down in the second graph.

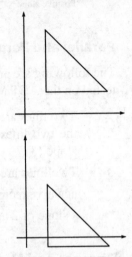

- A reflection flips an object in the coordinate plane over either the x axis or the y axis. When a reflection occurs across the x axis, the x coordinate remains the same, but the y coordinate is transformed into its opposite. When a reflection occurs across the y axis, the y coordinate remains the same, but the x coordinate is transformed into its opposite. The object retains its shape and size. The figure below shows a triangle that has been reflected across the y axis.

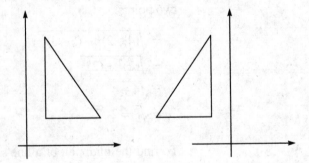

Properties and Relations of Plane Figures

The ACT Mathematics Test requires you to apply your knowledge of plane figures, such as triangles, quadrilaterals, other polygons, and circles. This section includes a description of many of the formulas that will help you to answer geometry questions more quickly.

Triangles

A triangle is a polygon with three sides and three angles. The following are properties of triangles that are commonly tested on the ACT Mathematics Test:

- In an equilateral triangle, all three sides have the same length, and each interior angle measures 60°, as shown below.

- In an isosceles triangle, two sides have the same length, and the angles opposite those sides are congruent, or equal, as shown below.

- In a right triangle, one of the angles measures 90°. The side opposite the right angle is the hypotenuse, and it is always the longest side, as shown below.

- The sum of the interior angles in any triangle is always 180°.
- The perimeter P of a triangle is the sum of the lengths of the sides.
- The area A of a triangle is equivalent to $\frac{1}{2}$ (base)(height). The height is equal to the perpendicular distance from an angle to a side, as shown below.

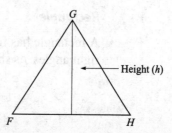

- In triangle *FGH* above, the height is the perpendicular line drawn from *G* to side *FH*. The height is *not* the distance from *F* to *G* or from *G* to *H*.
- The Pythagorean Theorem states that $a^2 + b^2 = c^2$, where *c* is the hypotenuse (the side opposite the right angle) of a right triangle and *a* and *b* are the two other sides of the triangle.
- In special right triangles, the side lengths have direct relationships, as shown below. You will not be tested directly on these relationships, but they will help you to answer some ACT Mathematics Test questions more quickly.

30°-60°-90° triangle

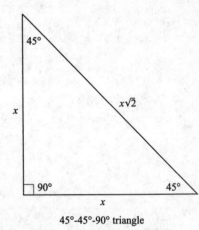

45°-45°-90° triangle

- The sides of a 3–4–5 special right triangle have the ratio 3:4:5.

Quadrilaterals

A quadrilateral is any four-sided object. The following are properties of quadrilaterals that are commonly tested on the ACT Mathematics Test:

Parallelogram

- In a parallelogram, the opposite sides are of equal length, and the opposite angles are equal, as shown below.

- The area *A* of a parallelogram is equivalent to (base)(height). The height is equal to the perpendicular distance from an angle to a side.
- The sum of the interior angles of a parallelogram is 360°.

Rectangle

- A rectangle has four sides (two sets of congruent, or equal, sides) and four right angles, as shown below. All rectangles are parallelograms.

- The sum of the angles in a rectangle is always 360° because a rectangle contains four 90° angles.
- The perimeter P of both a parallelogram and a rectangle is equivalent to $2l + 2w$, where l is the length and w is the width.
- The area A of a rectangle is equivalent to $(l)(w)$.
- The lengths of the diagonals of a rectangle are congruent, or equal in length. A diagonal is a straight line between opposite angles, as shown below.

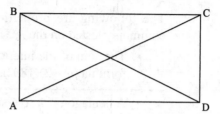

Square

- A square is a special rectangle in which all four sides are of equal length. All squares are rectangles.
- The length of each diagonal of a square is equivalent to the length of one side times $\sqrt{2}$. So, for example, a square with a side length of x would have diagonals equal to $x\sqrt{2}$, as shown below.

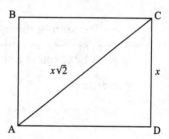

- The area A of a square is equivalent to one side squared (s^2).

Trapezoid

- A trapezoid is a polygon with four sides and four angles, as shown below.

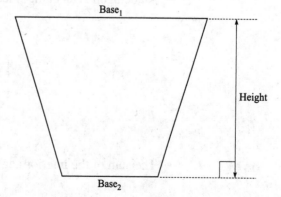

- The bases of a trapezoid (top and bottom) are never the same length.
- The sides of a trapezoid can be the same length (isosceles trapezoid), but they need not be.
- The perimeter P of a trapezoid is the sum of the lengths of the sides and the bases.

- The area A of a trapezoid is $A = \frac{1}{2}(\text{base}_1 + \text{base}_2)(\text{height})$. Height is the distance between the bases.
- The diagonals of a trapezoid have a unique feature. When the diagonals of a trapezoid intersect, the ratio of the top of the diagonals to the bottom of the diagonals is the same as the ratio of the top base to the bottom base.

Other Polygons

The following are properties of other polygons (multisided objects) that are commonly tested on the ACT Mathematics Test:

- The sum of the interior angles of any polygon can be calculated using the formula $(n - 2)(180°)$, where n is the number of sides.

- A pentagon is a five-sided figure, as shown below.

- The sum of the interior angles of a pentagon is $(5 - 2)(180°)$, or $540°$.

- A hexagon is a six-sided figure, as shown below.

- The sum of the interior angles of a hexagon is $(6 - 2)(180°)$, or $720°$.

- An octagon is an eight-sided figure, as shown below.

- The sum of the interior angles of an octagon is $(8 - 2)(180°)$, or $1,080°$.

Circles

The following are properties of circles that are commonly tested on the ACT Mathematics Test:

- The radius r of a circle is the distance from the center of the circle to any point on the circle.

- The diameter *d* of a circle is twice the radius, as shown below.

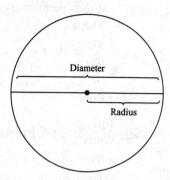

- The area *A* of a circle is equivalent to πr^2. So, the area of a circle with a radius of 3 is $3^2\pi$, or 9π.
- The circumference *C* of a circle is equivalent to $2\pi r$ or πd. So, the circumference of a circle with a radius of 3 is $2(3)\pi$, or 6π.
- The equation of a circle centered at the point (h, k) is $(x - h)^2 + (y - k)^2 = r^2$, where *r* is the radius of the circle.
- The complete arc of a circle has 360°.
- A tangent to a circle is a line that touches the circle at exactly one point.

Angles, Parallel Lines, and Perpendicular Lines

The following are properties of angles, parallel lines, and perpendicular lines that are commonly tested on the ACT Mathematics Test:

- A line is generally understood to mean a straight line.
- A line segment is the part of a line that lies between two points on the line.
- Two distinct lines are said to be parallel if they lie in the same plane and do not intersect.
- Two distinct lines are said to be perpendicular if their intersection creates right angles.
- When two parallel lines are cut by a transversal, each parallel line has four angles surrounding the intersection that are matched in measure and position with a counterpart at the other parallel line. The vertical (opposite) angles are congruent, and the adjacent angles are supplementary (they total 180°).

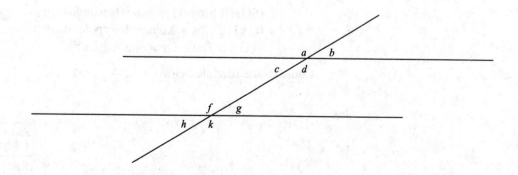

- ○ Vertical angles: $a = d = f = k$
- ○ Vertical angles: $b = c = g = h$
- ○ Supplementary angles: $a + b = 180°$

- ○ Supplementary angles: $c + d = 180°$
- ○ Supplementary angles: $f + g = 180°$
- ○ Supplementary angles: $h + k = 180°$

- An acute angle is any angle that is smaller than 90°.
- An obtuse angle is any angle that is greater than 90° and less than 180°.
- A right angle is an angle that measures exactly 90°.

Simple Three-Dimensional Geometry

The following are properties of three-dimensional figures that are commonly tested on the ACT Mathematics Test:

- The formula for the volume V of a rectangular solid is $V = lwh$, where l = length, w = width, and h = height.
- The surface area of a rectangular solid is the sum of the areas ($l \times w$) of the six faces of the solid. Think of each face as a square or a rectangle.
- The formula for the surface area of a rectangular solid is $A = 2(wl + lh + wh)$, where l = length, w = width, and h = height.

Basic Trigonometric Concepts

Trigonometry deals with the measures of the angles in a right triangle. The ACT Mathematics Test will generally ask you about only the sine, cosine, and tangent of those angles. Following are some basic trigonometric concepts that will help you to answer the four or five trigonometry questions that will appear on your actual ACT Mathematics Test correctly.

- The sine (sin) of each of the two smaller angles can be determined by the ratio of the length of the side opposite the given angle to the length of the hypotenuse: opposite/hypotenuse.
- The cosine (cos) can be determined by the ratio of the length of the side adjacent to the given angle to the length of the hypotenuse: adjacent/hypotenuse.
- The tangent (tan) can be determined by the ratio of the length of the side opposite to the given angle to the length of the side adjacent to the given angle: opposite/adjacent.
- The mnemonic device "SOHCAHTOA" can be used to help you remember these ratios.

> **(SOH): S**in = **O**pposite/**H**ypotenuse
> **(CAH): C**os = **A**djacent/**H**ypotenuse
> **(TOA): T**an = **O**pposite/**A**djacent

Consider the triangle below.

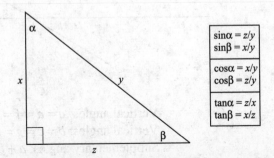

Advanced Trigonometric Concepts

You may find one or two questions on your ACT Mathematics Test that deal with more advanced trigonometric concepts, such as the secant, cosecant, and cotangent. The secant, cosecant, and cotangent can be found as follows:

- Sec (secant) = 1/cos
- Csc (cosecant) = 1/sin
- Cot (cotangent) = 1/tan

Radians

One or two of the many released ACT exams that we have evaluated contained a question about radians. We have included the following information to help you correctly answer any questions involving radians that might appear on your actual ACT Mathematics Test.

- To change from degrees to radians, multiply the angle measure by $\frac{\pi}{180}$. For example, for 120 degrees, $120\left(\frac{\pi}{180}\right) = \frac{120\pi}{180} = \frac{2\pi}{3}$ radians. Conversely, to change from radians to degrees, take the number of radians, multiply by 180, and drop the π.

Matrices

A matrix is used to organize data in columns and rows. The dimensions of a matrix refer to the number of rows and columns of a given matrix. For example, a 2×3 matrix, as shown below, has two rows and three columns:

$$\begin{bmatrix} 2 & 4 & 6 \\ 1 & 4 & 7 \end{bmatrix}$$

You can add and subtract matrices if each matrix has the same dimensions. Simply add or subtract the numbers that are in the same spot. For example:

$$\begin{bmatrix} 2 & 4 & 6 \\ 1 & 4 & 7 \end{bmatrix} + \begin{bmatrix} 3 & 1 & 2 \\ 8 & 5 & 1 \end{bmatrix} = \begin{bmatrix} 5 & 5 & 8 \\ 9 & 9 & 8 \end{bmatrix}$$

You can also multiply matrices. When you multiply a matrix by a number, you multiply every element in the matrix by the same number. For example:

$$a\begin{bmatrix} 5 & 5 & 8 \\ 9 & 9 & 8 \end{bmatrix} = \begin{bmatrix} 5a & 5a & 8a \\ 9a & 9a & 8a \end{bmatrix}$$

You might also be asked to calculate the determinant of a 2×2 matrix. The formula for calculating the determinant is:

$$\text{Matrix A:} \begin{bmatrix} a & b \\ c & d \end{bmatrix}$$

Determinant A: $ad - bc$

There may be one or two matrix questions on your ACT.

Vectors

By definition, a vector has both magnitude (size) and direction. A vector is depicted using an arrow. The length of the line shows its magnitude and the arrowhead points in the direction.

You can add two vectors by joining them head-to-tail:

You can also subtract vectors by first reversing the direction of the vector you want to subtract and then adding the vectors by joining them head-to-tail:

You could see one or two vector questions on your ACT.

■ WHAT'S NEXT?

Chapter 5, "Applying Strategies, Building Skills," includes practice questions in ACT format, divided by content area and difficulty level. Work through the questions, focusing on the areas that give you the most trouble. Then read the detailed explanations and refer back to Chapters 3 and 4 as needed.

CHAPTER 5

APPLYING STRATEGIES, BUILDING SKILLS

This chapter contains exercises designed to help you focus on the concepts that are generally tested on the ACT Mathematics Test in the areas of pre-algebra, elementary algebra, intermediate algebra, coordinate geometry, plane geometry, and trigonometry. The questions in this chapter, although they are in ACT format, are presented differently from those you will see on your ACT exam. They are separated first into broad content areas and then assigned one of three difficulty levels: easy, medium, or hard. We did this to give you an additional opportunity to practice working with and recognizing specific math concepts at varying levels of difficulty. Keep in mind that you are likely to see many different types of questions on your actual ACT, and that the questions given in this and subsequent chapters represent a sample of question types that have appeared on previous tests.

Chapters 6, 7, 8, and 9 each contain a simulated ACT Mathematics Test. These additional tests will allow you to become more familiar with the types of questions you will see on your actual ACT exam.

PRE-ALGEBRA

These questions will test your knowledge of operations using whole numbers, fractions, and decimals; square roots; scientific notation; linear equations with one variable; ratios, proportions, and percents; absolute value; simple probability; data interpretation; and very basic statistics.

Difficulty Level: Easy

1. The odometer on Jordan's car read 23,273 miles when he left on a trip and 23,650 miles when he returned. Jordan drove his car 6.5 hours on the trip. Based on the odometer readings, what was his average driving speed on the trip, in miles per hour?
   A. 53
   B. 58
   C. 60
   D. 65
   E. 67

2. For integers x and y such that $xy = 8$, which of the following is NOT a possible value of x?

F. -8
G. -6
H. -4
J. 1
K. 2

3. For the campers attending College Prep Camp this summer, the ratio of male campers to female campers is 3:5. Which of the following statements about the campers is (are) true?

   I.   For every 5 females, there are 3 males.
   II. There are more males than females.
   III. Males make up $\frac{3}{5}$ of the campers.

A. I only
B. II only
C. III only
D. II and III only
E. I, II, and III

4. Al needs $12\frac{1}{4}$ feet of lumber to complete a project. He has $8\frac{1}{2}$ feet of lumber. How many more feet of lumber does he need?

F. $3\frac{1}{2}$ feet

G. $3\frac{1}{3}$ feet

H. $3\frac{3}{4}$ feet

J. 4 feet

K. $4\frac{1}{3}$ feet

5. What is the solution to the equation $5b - (-b + 3) = 21$?

A. -4
B. 4
C. 6
D. 7
E. 13

6. What is the median of the data given below?

$$8, 13, 9, 8, 15, 14, 10$$

F. 8
G. 8.5
H. 10
J. 11
K. 15

7. What is the value of $|4 - x|$ if $x = 7$?
   A. −3
   B. 3
   C. 4
   D. 11
   E. 28

8. Mike had 2 more baseball cards than Jen. Then he bought 3 baseball cards from Jen. Now how many more baseball cards does Mike have than Jen?
   F. 12
   G. 8
   H. 6
   J. 2
   K. −4

Difficulty Level: Medium

9. The cost for a company to produce c computers in 1 year is $200c +$ $300,000. How many computers can the company produce in 1 year at a cost of $700,000?
   A. 2,000
   B. 2,667
   C. 3,500
   D. 5,000
   E. 5,333

10. $\left(\dfrac{1}{2}\right)^2 + \left(\dfrac{1}{3}\right)^2 + \left(\dfrac{1}{4}\right)^2 = ?$
    F. $\dfrac{1}{29}$

    G. $\dfrac{3}{29}$

    H. $\dfrac{61}{144}$

    J. $\dfrac{15}{32}$

    K. 9

11. If you add up 6 consecutive even integers that are each greater than 25, what is the smallest possible sum?
    A. 150
    B. 165
    C. 174
    D. 186
    E. 210

12. About what percent of $\dfrac{3}{5}$ is $\dfrac{1}{5}$?
    F. 20%
    G. 33%
    H. 50%
    J. 67%
    K. 300%

13. According to a recent survey of children about their favorite color, 20% of the children preferred red, 40% of the children preferred blue, 20% of the children preferred purple, and the remaining children preferred green. If each child preferred only 1 color and 30 children preferred green, how many children were surveyed?

A. 60
B. 90
C. 120
D. 150
E. 180

14. The ratio of a side of square X to the length of rectangle Y is 4:5. The ratio of a side of square X to the width of rectangle Y is 4:3. What is the ratio of the area of square X to the area of rectangle Y?

F. 12:15
G. 16:15
H. 18:15
J. 10:16
K. 12:16

Difficulty Level: Hard

15. For all nonzero a and b, $\dfrac{(a \times 0.01)(b \times 10^3)}{(a \times 10^{-2})(b \times 1,000)} = ?$

A. 1
B. 10
C. 10^5
D. $\dfrac{a}{b}$
E. $\dfrac{b^2}{a}$

16. Let $a \blacklozenge b = (a - b)^3$ for all integers a and b. Which of the following is the value of $3 \blacklozenge (-2)$?

F. 1
G. 19
H. 35
J. 125
K. 216

17. For any real number n, the equation $|x - n| = 8$ can be thought of as meaning "the distance on the real number line from x to n is 8 units." How far apart are the 2 solutions for n?

A. n
B. $2n$
C. $8 + n$
D. $\sqrt{8^2 + n^2}$
E. 16

18. What is the 211th digit after the decimal point in the repeating decimal $0.\overline{84382}$?

F. 9
G. 8
H. 4
J. 2
K. 0

▬ ELEMENTARY ALGEBRA

These questions will test your knowledge of operations involving functions, factoring simple quadratic equations, evaluating algebraic expressions using substitution, and properties of integer exponents.

Difficulty Level: Easy

1. For all a and b, $(2a - b)(a^2 + b) =$
  A. $2a^2 - b^2$
  B. $2a^3 - b^2$
  C. $2a^3 + ab - b^2$
  D. $2a^3 + 2ab - a^2b^2$
  E. $2a^3 - a^2b + 2ab - b^2$

2. The expression $x^2 - x - 42$ can be written as the product of two binomials with integer coefficients. One of the binomials is $(x - 7)$. Which of the following is the other binomial?
  F. $x^2 - 6$
  G. $x^2 + 6$
  H. $x - 6$
  J. $x + 6$
  K. $x + 7$

3. On a recent test, some questions were worth 3 points each, and the rest were worth 2 points each. Bailey answered correctly the same number of 3-point questions as 2-point questions and earned a score of 80. How many 2-point questions did she answer correctly?
  A. 10
  B. 13
  C. 15
  D. 16
  E. 18

4. Which of the following is equivalent to $10^{\frac{1}{2}}$?
  F. 5
  G. $\dfrac{1^2}{10}$
  H. $\sqrt{10}$
  J. $\sqrt[5]{10}$
  K. -1×10^2

5. What is the value of $4 \times 2^{a+b}$ when $a = -2$ and $b = 3$?
  A. -8
  B. 8
  C. 12
  D. 16
  E. 24

Difficulty Level: Medium

6. If x is a real number and $5^x = 625$, then $3 \times 3^x = ?$
  F. 5
  G. 9
  H. 45
  J. 125
  K. 243

7. Given $f(x) = 2x^2 - 3x + 6$, what is the value of $f(-4)$?
  A. 26
  B. 50
  C. 58
  D. 76
  E. 82

8. $(2a - 3b)^2$ is equivalent to:
  F. $4a^2 - 12ab + 9b^2$
  G. $4a^2 - 10ab + 9b^2$
  H. $4a^2 - 9b^2$
  J. $4a^2 + 9b^2$
  K. $4a - 6b$

Difficulty Level: Hard

9. If $h(x) = g(x) - f(x)$, where $g(x) = 5x^2 + 15x - 25$ and $f(x) = 5x^2 - 6x - 11$, then $h(x)$ is *always* divisible by which of the following?
  A. 17
  B. 9
  C. 7
  D. 5
  E. 3

10. Given $f(x) = \dfrac{x^3 + \frac{5}{8}}{x + \frac{1}{4}}$, what is $f\left(\frac{1}{2}\right)$?

  F. $\dfrac{7}{2}$

  G. $\dfrac{20}{8}$

  H. $\dfrac{36}{24}$

  J. 1

  K. $\dfrac{30}{20}$

■■■ INTERMEDIATE ALGEBRA

These questions will test your knowledge of operations involving the quadratic formula, radical and rational expressions, inequalities and absolute value equations, algebraic and geometric sequences, systems of equations, logarithms, roots of polynomials, and complex numbers.

Difficulty Level: Easy

1. The geometric mean of 2 positive numbers is the square root of the product of the 2 numbers. What is the geometric mean of 4 and 49?
   A. 9
   B. 14
   C. 26
   D. 98
   E. 196

2. If x is a real number such that $x^3 = 729$, then $x^2 + \sqrt{x} = ?$
   F. 9
   G. 27
   H. 30
   J. 84
   K. 90

3. What two numbers should be placed in the blanks below so that the difference between the consecutive numbers is the same?
   $$13, \_\_, \_\_, 34$$
   A. 19, 28
   B. 20, 27
   C. 21, 26
   D. 23, 24
   E. 24, 29

4. The first 5 terms of a geometric sequence are 0.75, −3, 12, −48, and 192. What is the 6th term?
   F. −768
   G. −144
   H. −75
   J. 132
   K. 255.75

Difficulty Level: Medium

5. What is the solution set of $|2a − 1| \geq 5$?
   A. $\{a: a \leq -4 \text{ or } a \geq 6\}$
   B. $\{a: a \leq -3 \text{ or } a \geq 3\}$
   C. $\{a: a \leq -2 \text{ or } a \geq 3\}$
   D. $\{a: a \geq 3\}$
   E. { } (the empty set)

6. If the following system of equations has a solution, what is the x coordinate of the solution?
   $$x + 6y = 24$$
   $$3x + 6y = 52$$
   F. 0
   G. 6
   H. 14
   J. 19
   K. The system has no solution.

7. For a single production run, when x items are made and sold, a company's profit, D dollars, can be modeled by $D = x^2 - 300x - 100,000$. What is the smallest number of items that must be made and sold in order for the company not to lose money on the production run?

A. 150
B. 200
C. 300
D. 350
E. 500

Difficulty Level: Hard

8. If $-4 \leq a \leq -3$ and $2 \leq b \leq 5$, what is the maximum value of $|a - 2b|$?

F. 7
G. 8
H. 13
J. 14
K. 20

9. For all positive integers n, which of the following is a correct ordering of the terms n^n, $(n!)^n$, and $(n!)^{n!}$?

A. $(n!)^{n!} \geq n^n \geq (n!)^n$
B. $(n!)^{n!} \geq (n!)^n \geq n^n$
C. $n^n \geq (n!)^n \geq (n!)^{n!}$
D. $(n!)^n \geq (n!)^{n!} \geq n^n$
E. $(n!)^n \geq n^n \geq (n!)^{n!}$

10. Whenever a, b, and c are positive real numbers, which of the following expressions is equivalent to $2\log_3 a + \frac{1}{2}\log_6 b - \log_3 c$?

F. $2\log_3 (a - c) + \log_6\left(\frac{b}{2}\right)$

G. $\log_3 (a - c) + \log_6 (\sqrt{b})$

H. $\log_3\left(\frac{c}{a^2}\right) + \log_6\left(\frac{b}{2}\right)$

J. $\log_3\left(\frac{a^2}{c}\right) + \log_6(\sqrt{b})$

K. $\log_3\left(\frac{a^2 b}{c}\right)$

◼◼ COORDINATE GEOMETRY

These questions will test your knowledge of operations involving number line graphs, the equation of a line, slope, and the distance and midpoint formulas.

Difficulty Level: Easy

1. Which of the following inequalities represents the graph shown below on the real number line?

A. $-4 \le x < 3$
B. $-4 \le x < 2$
C. $0 \le x < 3$
D. $4 \le x \le 4$
E. $3 < x \le -4$

2. As shown below, the diagonals of rectangle *RSTU* intersect at the point $(1, 4)$ in the standard (x, y) coordinate plane. Point *R* is at $(-3, 2)$. Which of the following are the coordinates of point *T*?

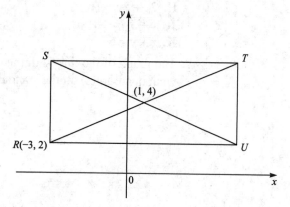

F. $(-3, 6)$
G. $(4, 5)$
H. $(5, 5)$
J. $(5, 6)$
K. $(7, 6)$

3. What is the slope of any line parallel to the line $2x - 3y = 7$?
A. -3
B. $-\dfrac{2}{3}$
C. $\dfrac{2}{3}$
D. 2
E. 3

4. If two lines in the standard (x, y) coordinate plane are perpendicular and the slope of one of the lines is -5, what is the slope of the other line?
F. -5
G. -1
H. $-\dfrac{1}{5}$
J. $\dfrac{1}{5}$
K. 5

Difficulty Level: Medium

5. What is the distance, in coordinate units, between the points (3, 5) and (−4, 1) in the standard (x, y) coordinate plane?
   A. $\sqrt{27}$
   B. $4\sqrt{2}$
   C. 8
   D. $8\sqrt{2}$
   E. $\sqrt{65}$

6. Which of the following is an equation of the line that passes through the points (−3, 11) and (1, 5) in the standard (x, y) coordinate plane?
   F. $3x + 2y = 13$
   G. $2x + 3y = 21$
   H. $2x + 2y = 16$
   J. $x + 3y = 16$
   K. $x + y = 6$

7. The graph of the line with the equation $-5y = 25$ does NOT have points in what quadrant(s) on the standard (x, y) coordinate plane below?

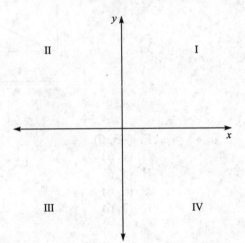

   A. Quadrant I only
   B. Quadrant II only
   C. Quadrant III only
   D. Quadrants I and II only
   E. Quadrants II and III only

Difficulty Level: Hard

8. An angle in the standard position in the standard (x, y) coordinate plane has its vertex at the origin and its initial side on the positive x axis. If the measure of the angle in the standard position is 2,585°, it has the same terminal side as an angle of each of the following measures EXCEPT:
   F. −1,375°
   G. −295°
   H. 65°
   J. 435°
   K. 785°

9. In the standard (x, y) coordinate plane, $\left(4, \dfrac{5}{3}\right)$ is halfway between $(a, a + 3)$ and $(2a, a - 5)$. What is the value of a?

A. $\dfrac{4}{3}$

B. $\dfrac{8}{3}$

C. 4

D. $\dfrac{9}{2}$

E. 6

10. What is the perimeter of quadrilateral $QRST$ if it has vertices with (x, y) coordinates $Q(0,0)$, $R(1,3)$, $S(4,4)$, and $T(3,1)$?

F. 100

G. 40

H. $6\sqrt{2} + 2\sqrt{10}$

J. $4\sqrt{10}$

K. $2\sqrt{10}$

▰ PLANE GEOMETRY

These questions will test your knowledge of operations involving plane figures such as circles, triangles, rectangles, parallelograms, and trapezoids; angles, parallel lines, and perpendicular lines; perimeter, area, and volume; and simple three-dimensional figures. Plane geometry questions make up a considerable portion of the more difficult math tested on the ACT Mathematics Test.

Difficulty Level: Easy

1. What is the volume, in cubic inches, of a cube whose edges each measure 3 inches in length?

A. 9

B. 12

C. 18

D. 27

E. 81

2. In the figure below, M, N, and O are collinear, the measure of angle MNP is $3x°$, and the measure of angle ONP is $6x°$. What is the measure of angle MNP?

F. 18°

G. 20°

H. 60°

J. 120°

K. 162°

3. For the polygon below, the lengths of 2 sides are not given. Each angle between adjacent sides measures 90°. What is the polygon's perimeter, in centimeters?

A. 45
B. 58
C. 87
D. 90
E. 180

4. The area of $\triangle ABC$ below is 40 square inches. If $\overline{AC}$ is 10 inches long, how long is the altitude $\overline{BD}$, in inches?

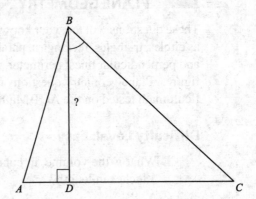

F. 4
G. 6
H. 8
J. 10
K. 12

5. What is the area, in square inches, of a trapezoid with a height of 6 inches and parallel bases of 9 inches and 7 inches, respectively?
A. 24
B. 32
C. 48
D. 96
E. 378

Difficulty Level: Medium

6. The area of a wheel is 78.5 inches. About how many revolutions does one of these wheels make when traveling 100 feet (1,200 inches) without slipping?

F. 12

G. 15

H. 38

J. 100

K. 942

7. In the figure below, if $a = 140$, what is the value of $b + c$?

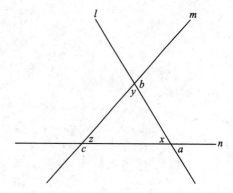

A. 320°

B. 220°

C. 180°

D. 140°

E. 50°

8. Triangles WXY and ZXY, shown below, are isosceles with base $\overline{XY}$. Segments $\overline{XZ}$ and $\overline{YZ}$ bisect $\angle WXY$ and $\angle WYX$, respectively. Which of the following angle congruences is necessarily true?

F. $\angle WXY \cong \angle WYZ$

G. $\angle WXZ \cong \angle WYX$

H. $\angle WXZ \cong \angle XYZ$

J. $\angle WYZ \cong \angle XWY$

K. $\angle XYZ \cong \angle XWY$

9. Mandy plans to carpet the entire floor of her bedroom. The floor is flat, and all adjacent sides meet at right angles, as shown below. Mandy can purchase 8-foot × 12-foot pieces of carpet on sale. What is the minimum number of pieces of carpet that she must purchase in order to carpet her bedroom floor?

A. 1
B. 2
C. 3
D. 4
E. 5

10. Triangle *ABC* is similar to triangle *XYZ*. $\overline{AB}$ is 5 inches long, $\overline{BC}$ is 8 inches long, and $\overline{AC}$ is 3 inches long. If the longest side of △*XYZ* is 20 inches long, what is the perimeter, in inches, of △*XYZ*?
F. 16
G. 28
H. 40
J. 64
K. 88

Difficulty Level: Hard

11. The noncommon rays of two adjacent angles form a straight angle. The measure of one angle is 3 times the measure of the other angle. What is the measure of the smaller angle?
A. 40°
B. 45°
C. 50°
D. 55°
E. 60°

12. A square has sides that are the same length as the radius of a circle. If the circle has a circumference of 64π units, how many units long is the perimeter of the square?
F. 8
G. 16
H. 32
J. 128
K. 256

13. In a certain rectangle *PQRS*, angle *QPS* and angle *PSR* are right angles. If the length of line $\overline{PR}$ is 34 units and the length of line $\overline{PS}$ is 30 units, what is the length of line $\overline{RS}$?

A. $\sqrt{30}$
B. 16
C. $\sqrt{34}$
D. $2\sqrt{514}$
E. 14

14. In the figure below, lines *a* and *b* are parallel and angle measures are as marked. If it can be determined, what is the value of *x*?

F. 30°
G. 40°
H. 55°
J. 70°
K. Cannot be determined from the given information.

15. Which of the following degree measures is equivalent to 3.75π radians?

A. 2,700°
B. 1,350°
C. 675°
D. 337.5°
E. 225°

16. The radius of a circle is $\dfrac{32}{\pi}$ centimeters. What is the area of the circle?

F. 64
G. 32π
H. $\dfrac{1024}{\pi}$
J. 1,024
K. $1,024\pi$

◼ TRIGONOMETRY

These questions will test your knowledge of operations involving trigonometry, including the relationships in right triangles, the definitions of trigonometric functions, graphing trigonometric functions, using trigonometric identities, and solving trigonometric equations. Since trigonometry is seen by the ACT as being "higher math," these practice questions are categorized as either medium or hard only; they make up a very small percentage of the ACT Mathematics Test, and will usually appear only in the latter half of the questions on your ACT Mathematics Test.

Difficulty Level: Medium

1. The sides of a right triangle measure 5 in., 12 in., and 13 in. What is the cosine of the acute angle adjacent to the side that measures 12 in.?

A. $\dfrac{5}{12}$

B. $\dfrac{5}{13}$

C. $\dfrac{12}{13}$

D. $\dfrac{13}{12}$

E. $\dfrac{12}{5}$

2. In the right triangle pictured below, r, s, and t are the lengths of its sides. What is the value of $\tan\alpha$?

F. $\dfrac{r}{t}$

G. $\dfrac{s}{t}$

H. $\dfrac{t}{r}$

J. $\dfrac{r}{s}$

K. $\dfrac{t}{s}$

3. If $\tan\beta = \dfrac{3}{4}$, then $\sin\beta = ?$

A. $\dfrac{3}{5}$

B. $\dfrac{3}{4}$

C. $\dfrac{4}{5}$

D. $\dfrac{4}{3}$

E. $\dfrac{5}{4}$

4. In the right triangle shown below, cos $\angle A$ = ?

F. $\dfrac{20}{21}$

G. $\dfrac{20}{29}$

H. $\dfrac{21}{29}$

J. $\dfrac{29}{21}$

K. $\dfrac{21}{20}$

Difficulty Level: Hard

5. For values of x where sin x, cos x, and tan x are all defined, $\dfrac{(\cos x)}{(\tan x)(\sin x)}$ = ?

A. $\dfrac{\cos^2 x}{\sin^2 x}$

B. $\tan^2 x$

C. 1

D. $\sin^2 x$

E. sec x

6. As shown in the figure below, a ramp leading from a loading dock is 35 feet long and forms a 15° angle with level ground.

Given the trigonometric approximations in the table below, what is the height above ground of the loading dock, to the nearest 0.1 foot?

cos 15°	0.966
tan 15°	0.268
sin 15°	0.259

F. 9.4

G. 9.1

H. 7.7

J. 7.4

K. 2.8

7. Whenever $\dfrac{\tan\alpha}{\sin\alpha}$ is defined, it is equivalent to:

A. $\cos\alpha$

B. $\dfrac{1}{\cos\alpha}$

C. $\dfrac{1}{\sin\alpha}$

D. $\dfrac{1}{\sin^2\alpha}$

E. $\dfrac{\cos\alpha}{\sin\alpha}$

ANSWERS AND EXPLANATIONS

PRE-ALGEBRA—DIFFICULTY LEVEL: EASY

1. **The correct answer is B.** Average speed is found by dividing the total distance traveled by the amount of time it took to travel that distance. Since Jordan's odometer began at 23,273 and read 23,650 at the end of the trip, the total distance can be found by subtracting 23,273 from 23,650. This distance, 377 miles, can then be divided by 6.5 hours (the total time) to find an average speed of 58 miles per hour.

2. **The correct answer is G.** Since integers are positive and negative whole numbers, any two integers that are multiplied together, as in the case of xy, to equal some other number must both be factors of that other number. In other words, both x and y must divide evenly into 8. Since the question is asking which of the following is NOT a possible value of x, you need to find the number that leaves a remainder when divided into 8; –6 leaves a remainder of one-third, while the other numbers all divide cleanly into 8.

3. **The correct answer is A.** The ratio in this question is a part-to-part ratio. This means that it is comparing one part of the group, males, to another part of the group, females. In part-to-part ratios, the top of the ratio has that many of the whole compared to the bottom of the ratio (3 males for every 5 females out of the total number of campers). A part-to-whole ratio is found by adding the two parts of the ratio together ($3 + 5 = 8$, so the ratio of male campers to total campers is 3:8). The only statement that is true, then, is Roman numeral I—that for every 5 females, there are 3 males. Roman numeral II is untrue, as there are clearly more females (5) than males (3), and Roman numeral III is untrue, since males make up $\frac{3}{8}$ of the campers, not $\frac{3}{5}$. Once you determined that Roman numeral I was a true statement, you could have eliminated answer choices B, C, and D, because they do not include Roman numeral I.

4. **The correct answer is H.** This problem requires you to subtract fractions, so the fractions must have the same denominator. The first step is to convert the mixed numbers to improper fractions. This can be accomplished by multiplying 12 by 4 (the denominator) and adding 1 (the numerator), to get $\frac{49}{4}$. Next, multiply 8 by 4 (twice the denominator) and add 2 (twice the numerator), to get $\frac{34}{4}$. Subtracting $\frac{34}{4}$ from $\frac{49}{4}$ leaves $\frac{15}{4}$, which reduces to $3\frac{3}{4}$ feet.

5. **The correct answer is B.** To solve this problem quickly, first multiply the quantity $(-b + 3)$ by -1, resulting in $5b + b - 3 = 21$. Simplifying this results in $6b = 24$. Dividing 24 by 6 leaves $b = 4$.

6. **The correct answer is H.** The median is the middle value in an ordered set of values. Therefore, the first step is to put the numbers in order, as follows:

   8, 8, 9, 10, 13, 14, 15

   As you can see, 10 is the middle value.

7. **The correct answer is B.** The absolute value of a number is indicated by placing that number inside two vertical lines. For example, the absolute value of 10 is written as follows: |10|. Absolute value can be defined as the numerical value of a real number without regard to its sign. This means that the absolute value of 10, |10|, is the same as the absolute value of –10, |–10|, in that they both equal 10. Think of it as the distance from –10 to 0 on the number line and the distance from 0 to 10 on the number line—both distances equal 10 units. In order to solve this problem, you must first substitute the number 7 for x to get |4 – 7|. Then, perform the operation within the vertical lines, so that you get |–3|. Since you must disregard the negative sign in order to determine absolute value, the absolute value of –3 is 3.

8. **The correct answer is G.** Mike originally had 2 more baseball cards than Jen. When he buys 3 baseball cards from Jen, he has at least 5 more baseball cards than Jen has. You can now eliminate answer choices J and K. The mathematical solution is as follows:

   $M = J + 2$ (original number of Mike's baseball cards)

   $M = J + 2 + 3$, or $J + 5$ (number of Mike's baseball cards after he buys 3 from Jen)

   $J = M - 3$ (number of Jen's baseball cards after she sold 3 to Mike)

   Since Jen now has 3 *fewer* baseball cards than she had before (because Mike bought them), Mike has $5 + 3$, or 8 more baseball cards than Jen now has.

PRE-ALGEBRA—DIFFICULTY LEVEL: MEDIUM

9. **The correct answer is A.** The easiest way to solve this problem is to create an equation in which cost is a function of the price per unit plus a fixed cost. Cost $= 200c + 300,000$. Substituting 700,000 for cost yields $700,000 = 200c + 300,000$. This can be simplified to $400,000 = 200c$, making c (the number of computers) $= 2,000$.

10. **The correct answer is H.** To solve this problem, first square each fraction: $\left(\frac{1}{2}\right)^2 + \left(\frac{1}{3}\right)^2 + \left(\frac{1}{4}\right)^2 = \frac{1}{4} + \frac{1}{9} + \frac{1}{16}$. Remember that to be added, fractions must have a common denominator. In this case, since 4 is a factor of 16, the lowest common denominator is $(9)(16) = 144$. To convert fractions into different denominators, you must multiply the top and bottom of a fraction by the *same* number. If $\frac{1}{4}$ is multiplied by $\frac{36}{36}$, the result is $\frac{36}{144}$. Likewise, multiplying $\frac{1}{9}$ by $\frac{16}{16}$ yields $\frac{16}{144}$, and multiplying $\frac{1}{16}$ by $\frac{9}{9}$ yields $\frac{9}{144}$. Therefore, $\frac{1}{4} + \frac{1}{9} + \frac{1}{16} = \frac{36}{144} + \frac{16}{144} + \frac{9}{144} = \frac{(36+16+9)}{144}$, or $\frac{61}{144}$.

11. **The correct answer is D.** Since you are asked for the smallest possible sum of six consecutive even integers greater than 25, add together the *next* six even numbers following 25. The smallest possible sum is then $26 + 28 + 30 + 32 + 34 + 36 = 186$.

12. **The correct answer is G.** In order to find what percentage one number is of another number, divide the part by the whole. In this case, divide $\frac{1}{5}$ by $\frac{3}{5}$ to get $\frac{1}{3}$. Another way to look at this problem would be to view $\frac{3}{5}$ as 60 and $\frac{1}{5}$ as 20 (translating the fractions into percentages themselves). This way, it is easy to tell that 20 is $\frac{1}{3}$ or 33 percent of 60.

13. **The correct answer is D.** Since the question gives you the number of students who preferred green, and it is asking for the total number of students surveyed, the first task is to determine what percentage of the total are the students who preferred green. The question states that 40 percent preferred one color, and 20 percent preferred each of two other colors; $40 + 20 + 20 = 80$. This leaves another 20 percent who prefer green. If the 30 students who prefer green make up 20 percent of the total, this can be turned into a ratio of 30:20 as x:100. Cross-multiply to get $20x = 3,000$, and $x = 150$.

14. **The correct answer is G.** To solve this problem, imagine a square with sides of length 4. The area of the square is $4 \times 4 = 16$. Next, imagine that the rectangle has length 5 and width 3. The area of the rectangle is $5 \times 3 = 15$. The ratio of the area of square X to the area of rectangle Y is 16:15.

PRE-ALGEBRA—DIFFICULTY LEVEL: HARD

15. **The correct answer is A.** To solve this problem, recall that $10^{-2} = 0.01 \left(10^{-2} = \frac{1}{10^2} = \frac{1}{100} = 0.01\right)$ and $10^3 = 1,000$. Substituting those numbers into the problem results in a fraction that has the same numerator and denominator, which has a value of 1, as shown below:

$$\frac{(a \times 0.01)(b \times 1.000)}{(a \times 0.01)(b \times 1.000)} = 1$$

16. **The correct answer is J.** Given that $a \blacklozenge b = (a - b)^3$ for all integers a and b, when $a = 3$ and $b = -2$, $a \blacklozenge b = [3 - (-2)]^3$.

    Subtracting a negative number is the same as adding: $[3 - (-2)]^3 = (3 + 2)^3$

    Complete the operations within the parentheses first: $(3 + 2)^3 = 5^3 = 125$

17. **The correct answer is E.** Because the equation $|x - n| = 8$ can be thought of as meaning "the distance on the real number line from x to n," there are two possible solutions for n: one that comes before x, and one that comes after x. If you know that the distance between x and n is 8, the distance between the two possible values of n on a number line must be twice that, or 16.

18. **The correct answer is G.** Notice that there are 5 digits in the repeating decimal (count only the digits after the decimal point). The fifth digit is the number 2, so every place that is a multiple of 5 will be the number 2. For example, 0.84392843928439284392 and so on. Since 210 is a multiple of 5, the 210th digit will be 2; likewise, since the number 8 always follows the number 2 in this repeating decimal, the 211th digit will be 8.

ELEMENTARY ALGEBRA—DIFFICULTY LEVEL: EASY

1. **The correct answer is E.** In this question, you are given the factored form and must find the equation. Use the *FOIL* method to find the equation. The *FOIL* method refers to the order in which you should multiply the elements of the factors. You must multiply the quantity $(2a - b)$ by the quantity $(a^2 + b)$ in the following order:

    First terms $\rightarrow 2a \times a^2 = 2a^3$
    Outside terms $\rightarrow 2a \times b = 2ab$
    Inside terms $\rightarrow -b \times a^2 = -ba^2$
    Last terms $\rightarrow -b \times b = -b^2$

    Then, add the results of these multiplications together:

    $2a^3 + ab + (-ba^2) + (-b^2)$, or $2a^3 + 2ab - ba^2 - b^2$

Finally, simplify and put the terms in descending order:

$$2a^3 - a^2b + 2ab - b^2.$$

2. **The correct answer is J.** This problem asks you to factor $x^2 - x - 42$. You are given one factor, $(x - 7)$; therefore, you must ask the question, "What multiplied by $(x - 7)$ yields $x^2 - x - 42$?" It makes sense that the other factor is either $(x - 6)$ or $(x + 6)$, because $7 \times 6 = 42$. Checking these two possibilities leaves $(x + 6)$ as the correct answer.

3. **The correct answer is D.** Since you don't know how many 2- or 3-point questions Bailey answered correctly, you can represent that number with a variable, q. The same variable can be used to represent the number of 2-point questions answered correctly and the number of 3-point questions answered correctly because Bailey answered the same number of questions of each type correctly. Bailey correctly answered the same number of 3-point questions as 2-point questions and earned a score of 80, which can be written mathematically as the equation $3q + 2q = 80$. Now, solve for q:

$$3q + 2q = 80$$
$$5q = 80$$
$$q = 16$$

4. **The correct answer is H.** To solve this problem, remember that any number taken to the $\frac{1}{2}$ power is the same as taking the square root of that number. Therefore, $10^{\frac{1}{2}} = \sqrt{10}$.

5. **The correct answer is B.** To solve this problem, substitute the given values for a and b, as follows:

$$4 \times 2^{a+b}, a = -2 \text{ and } b = 3$$
$$4 \times 2^{-2+3}$$
$$4 \times 2^1 = 4 \times 2 = 8; \text{ remember that an exponent of}$$
1 doesn't change the base.

ELEMENTARY ALGEBRA—DIFFICULTY LEVEL: MEDIUM

6. **The correct answer is K.** To solve this problem, first find the value of x in $5^x = 625$. One way to do this is to try exponents until you reach the correct value:

$$5^2 = 25$$
$$5^3 = 125$$
$$5^4 = 625$$

Therefore $x = 4$. To solve 3×3^x, simply substitute 4 for x:

$$3 \times 3^4$$
$$3 \times 81 = 243$$

7. **The correct answer is B.** To find the value of $f(-4)$ when $f(x) = 2x^2 - 3x + 6$, substitute -4 for x:

$$2x^2 - 3x + 6$$
$$= 2(-4)^2 - 3(-4) + 6$$
$$= 2(16) - (-12) + 6$$
$$= 32 + 12 + 6 = 50$$

8. **The correct answer is F.** To solve this problem, first expand $(2a - 3b)^2$, as follows:

$$(2a - 3b)^2 = (2a - 3b)(2a - 3b)$$

Next, perform the multiplication, and combine like terms:

FOIL: $4a^2 - 6ab - 6ab + 9b^2$
Combine like terms: $4a^2 - 12ab + 9b^2$

ELEMENTARY ALGEBRA—DIFFICULTY LEVEL: HARD

9. **The correct answer is C.** To solve this problem, simplify $h(x)$. Given that $h(x) = g(x) - f(x)$, where $g(x) = 5x^2 + 15x - 25$ and $f(x) = 5x^2 - 6x - 11$:

$$h(x) = (5x^2 + 15x - 25) - (5x^2 - 6x - 11)$$
$$= 5x^2 + 15x - 25 - 5x^2 + 6x + 11$$
Rearrange like terms: $h(x) = 5x^2 - 5x^2 + 15x + 6x - 25 + 11$
Simplify: $h(x) = 21x - 14$

Because 21 and 14 are both divisible by 7, $h(x)$ will always be divisible by 7.

10. **The correct answer is J.** To solve this problem, substitute $\frac{1}{2}$ for x in the equation and simplify, as shown next.

$$f(x) = \frac{x^3 = \frac{5}{8}}{x + \frac{1}{4}}, x = \frac{1}{2}$$

$$= \frac{\left(\frac{1}{2}\right)^3 + \frac{5}{8}}{\frac{1}{2} + \frac{1}{4}}$$

$$= \frac{\frac{1}{8} + \frac{5}{8}}{\frac{2}{4} + \frac{1}{4}}$$

$$= \frac{\frac{6}{8}}{\frac{3}{4}}$$

Recall that dividing by a fraction is the same as multiplying by the reciprocal:

$$= \frac{6}{8} \times \frac{4}{3} = \frac{24}{24} = 1$$

INTERMEDIATE ALGEBRA—DIFFICULTY LEVEL: EASY

1. **The correct answer is B.** Given that the geometric mean of 2 positive numbers is the square root of the product of the 2 numbers, the geometric mean of 4 and 49 is $\sqrt{(4 \times 49)} = \sqrt{196} = 14$.

2. **The correct answer is J.** To calculate the value of $x^2 + \sqrt{x}$, first solve $x^3 = 729$ for x. The solution is the cube root of 729, which is 9. Substitute 9 into the original expression; $9^2 + \sqrt{9}$. This expression simplifies to $81 + 3$, or 84.

3. **The correct answer is B.** To solve this problem, it is important to realize that the question is about an arithmetic sequence, a sequence in which each pair of successive terms differs by the same number. To find the difference, define d as that difference, 13 as the first term, and 34 as the fourth term. By definition, the second term is $13 + d$, and the third term is $13 + d + d$. The fourth term, 34, can also be written as $(13 + d + d) + d$. Using that expression, obtain the equation $34 = 13 + d + d + d$, or $34 = 13 + 3d$. After subtracting 13 from both sides, divide by 3, which results in $7 = d$. The difference is 7. Thus the second term is $13 + 7$, or 20, and the third term is $20 + 7$, or 27.

4. **The correct answer is F.** To find the 6th term in the sequence, first recognize the pattern that relates each term to the next. Recall that a geometric sequence is a sequence of numbers where each term after the first is found by multiplying the previous one by a *common ratio*. Given the first five terms 0.75, −3, 12, −48, and 192, the common ratio can be found by finding the ratio between any term and the one that precedes it. For instance:

$$\frac{192}{-48} = -4$$

$$-\frac{48}{12} = -4$$

$$\frac{12}{-3} = -4$$

It is apparent that the common ratio is −4. The 6th term can then be found by multiplying the 5th term, 192, by −4 to get $192(-4) = -768$.

INTERMEDIATE ALGEBRA—DIFFICULTY LEVEL: MEDIUM

5. **The correct answer is C.** To solve $|2a - 1| \geq 5$, recall that you must "split" this into two separate inequalities and then solve:

$2a - 1 \geq 5$	or	$2a - 1 \leq -5$
$2a \geq 6$	Add 1 to both sides	$2a \leq -4$
$a \geq 3$	Divide by 2	$a \leq -2$

We now have two inequalities that describe the solution set $\{a: a \leq -2 \text{ or } a \geq 3\}$.

6. **The correct answer is H.** This system is a prime target for the use of elimination as a solution strategy. Elimination involves subtracting one entire equation from another. This is possible because we can think of an equation as a balanced scale. Adding equal amounts to a balanced scale will not disturb the current balance.

$$x + 6y = 24$$
$$3x + 6y = 52$$

Subtract the bottom equation from the top equation:

$$x + 6y = 24$$
$$\underline{-(3x + 6y = 52)}$$
$$-2x + 0 = -28$$

Solve for x:

$$x = 14$$

7. **The correct answer is E.** Given that profit is modeled by $D = x^2 - 300x - 100,000$, the minimum number of items that must be produced for the company not to lose money will result in a profit of 0. To find the number of items, set the equation $D = x^2 - 300x - 100,000$ equal to 0 and solve for x by factoring (think of two numbers that multiply to get −100,000 and add to get −300):

$$0 = x^2 - 300x - 100,000$$
$$0 = (x - 500)(x + 200)$$

Therefore $x = 500$ or $x = -200$. Since it does not make sense to produce a negative quantity of items, the correct answer is 500. Also, note that −200 is not among the answer choices.

INTERMEDIATE ALGEBRA—DIFFICULTY LEVEL: HARD

8. **The correct answer is J.** To find the maximum values of $|a - 2b|$ given that $-4 \leq a \leq -3$ and $2 \leq b \leq 5$, start by using the extreme values for each variable. For a, we'll use −4 and −3. For b, we'll use 2 and 5. Now substitute different configurations of these extreme values into $|a - 2b|$ to find the maximum value:

$a = -4, b = 2$:	$\|-4 - 2(2)\| = \|-4 - 4\|$
	$= \|-8\| = 8$
$a = -4, b = 5$:	$\|-4 - 2(5)\| = \|-4 - 10\|$
	$= \|-14\| = 14$
$a = -3, b = 2$:	$\|-3 - 2(2)\| = \|-3 - 4\|$
	$= \|-7\| = 7$
$a = -3, b = 5$:	$\|-3 - 2(5)\| = \|-3 - 10\|$
	$= \|-13\| = 13$

The maximum value is 14.

9. **The correct answer is B.** Recall that $n!$ is the factorial of n. The factorial of a positive integer n is the product of that number n and all the positive integers less than n: $n(n-1)(n-2)$ ... and so on. This means that for all positive integers n, the following inequality holds: $n! \geq n$. Therefore $(n!)^n \geq n^n$ and $(n!)^{n!} \geq (n!)^n$. Note that you do not have to do any actual calculations to solve this problem; you just have to understand the relationships between various operations. The correct answer is $(n!)^{n!} \geq (n!)^n \geq n^n$.

10. **The correct answer is J.** To solve this problem, you must make use of several rules for simplifying logarithms. First, an exponent on everything inside of a log can be moved out front as a multiplier, and vice versa: $\log_b (m^n) = n \times \log_b (m)$. The expression $2\log_3 a + \frac{1}{2}\log_6 b - \log_3 c$ is equivalent to $\log_3 a^2 + \log_6 b^{\frac{1}{2}} - \log_3 c$. Next, as long as two logarithmic expressions have the same base, division inside the log can be turned into subtraction outside the log, and vice versa: $\log_b \left(\frac{m}{n}\right) = \log_b (m) - \log_b (n)$. Therefore, $\log_3 a^2 + \log_6 b^{\frac{1}{2}} - \log_3 c$ is equivalent to $\log_3 \left(\frac{a^2}{c}\right) + \log_6 \left(b^{\frac{1}{2}}\right)$. Finally, recall that taking a number to the $\frac{1}{2}$ power is the same as taking the square root. Therefore, the final answer is $\log_3 \left(\frac{a^2}{c}\right) + \log_6(\sqrt{b})$.

COORDINATE GEOMETRY—DIFFICULTY LEVEL: EASY

1. **The correct answer is A.** The number line graph shows a "closed circle" at –4 because x is "greater than or equal to" –4. Additionally, the number line graph shows an open circle at 3 because x is strictly "less than (but not equal to)" 3. The inequality $-4 \leq x < 3$ is correct because the first half of that combined inequality is merely $x \geq -4$ with the elements reversed.

2. **The correct answer is J.** Point (1, 4) serves as the midpoint of the segment RT. To find the coordinates of point T, find the difference between point $R(-3, 2)$ and the point at (1, 4).

$$x = [-1 - (-3)] = 4$$
$$y = (4 - 2) = 2$$

To find point T, simply add the distance from point R to the midpoint: $(1 + 4, 4 + 2) = (5, 6)$.

3. **The correct answer is C.** To solve this problem, recall that parallel lines always have the same slope. To find the slope of the line, convert the equation

$2x - 3y = 7$ into slope-intercept form ($y = mx + b$, where m is the slope):

$$2x - 3y = 7$$
$$-3y = -2x + 7$$
$$y = \frac{2}{3}x - \frac{7}{3}$$

Thus the slope of this line, and any line parallel to it, is $\frac{2}{3}$.

4. **The correct answer is J.** Perpendicular lines have slopes that are the "opposite reciprocal" of each other. That means that if one line has slope m, a line perpendicular to it must have slope $\frac{-1}{m}$. Given that the slope of the line is –5, the slope of a line perpendicular to it is $\frac{1}{5}$.

COORDINATE GEOMETRY—DIFFICULTY LEVEL: MEDIUM

5. **The correct answer is E.** The distance between the points (3, 5) and (–4, 1) can be found using the distance formula, which states that for two points (x_1, y_1) and (x_2, y_2), the distance between them is $d = \sqrt{[(x_1 - x_2)^2 + (y_1 - y_2)^2]}$. To solve, substitute the given points into the distance formula:

$$d = \sqrt{[(3 - (-4)]^2 + (5 - 1)^2}$$
$$d = \sqrt{[7^2 + 4^2]} = \sqrt{[49 + 16]} = \sqrt{65}.$$

6. **The correct answer is F.** To find the equation of a line, you need a point and a slope. To solve, first find the slope between the points (–3, 11) and (1, 5). The slope formula is $m = \frac{(y_2 - y_1)}{(x_2 - x_1)}$. For these points, $m = \frac{(5 - 11)}{[1 - (-3)]} = -\frac{6}{4} = -\frac{3}{2}$. Given the slope-intercept form of an equation, $y = mx + b$, where m is the slope and b is the y intercept, substitute a point (1, 5) and $m\left(-\frac{3}{2}\right)$ and then solve for b:

$$y = mx + b$$
$$5 = \left(-\frac{3}{2}\right)(1) + b$$

Convert 5 to $\frac{10}{2}$ and add $\frac{3}{2}$ to both sides.

$$\frac{13}{2} = b$$

Therefore, the equation is $y = \left(-\frac{3}{2}\right)x + \frac{13}{2}$. Convert to standard form: $\left(\frac{3}{2}\right)x + y = \frac{13}{2}$. Multiply the entire equation by 2 to get rid of the fraction: $3x + 2y = 13$.

7. **The correct answer is D.** To solve this problem, first simplify and graph the equation $-5y = 25$: $y = -5$. This line, shown below, has a slope of 0, and crosses two quadrants.

Since the question asks in which quadrants the line does NOT have points, the answer is only Quadrants I and II, answer choice D.

COORDINATE GEOMETRY—DIFFICULTY LEVEL: HARD

8. **The correct answer is J.** Angles that have the same terminal side are called *coterminal*. Coterminal angles are found by adding or subtracting whole-number multiples of 360°. To find coterminal angles of 2,585°, consider the expression $2,585° + n360°$, where n is an integer. You can generate a table of coterminal angles by varying the value of n:

$$2,585° + n360°$$

Value of n	−11	−10	−9	−8	−7	−6	−5	−4	−3	−2	−1	0
Angle°	−1,375	−1,015	−655	−295	65	425	785	1,145	1,505	1,865	2,225	2,585

From this table, you can determine that 435° cannot be the measure of the angle.

9. **The correct answer is B.** One way to find the value of a is to avoid the fractions and just look at the x coordinates. The x coordinate of the midpoint is found by averaging the values of the x coordinates. Therefore, the average of a and $2a$ is 4. Set up the following equation and solve for a:

$$\frac{a+2a}{2} = 4$$
$$a + 2a = 8$$
$$3a = 8$$
$$a = \frac{8}{3}$$

10. **The correct answer is J.** This question requires repeated use of the distance formula, which states that for two points (x_1, y_1) and (x_2, y_2), the distance

between them is $d = \sqrt{[(x_1 - x_2)^2 + (y_1 - y_2)^2]}$. Given that quadrilateral $QRST$ has vertices $Q(0,0)$, $R(1,3)$, $S(4,4)$, and $T(3,1)$, the perimeter can be found by taking the sum of $\overline{QR} + \overline{RS} + \overline{ST} + \overline{TQ}$.

$Q(0,0), R(1, 3): QR = \sqrt{[(0-1)^2 + (0-3)^2]} = \sqrt{(1+9)} = \sqrt{10}$

$R(1, 3), S(4, 4): RS = \sqrt{[(1-4)^2 + (3-4)^2]} = \sqrt{(9+1)} = \sqrt{10}$

$S(4, 4), T(3, 1): ST = \sqrt{[(4-3)^2 + (4-1)^2]} = \sqrt{(1+9)} = \sqrt{10}$

$T(3, 1), Q(0, 0): TQ = \sqrt{[(0-1)^2 + (0-3)^2]} = \sqrt{(1+9)} = \sqrt{10}$

The perimeter is therefore $\sqrt{10} + \sqrt{10} + \sqrt{10} + \sqrt{10} = 4\sqrt{10}$.

PLANE GEOMETRY—DIFFICULTY LEVEL: EASY

1. **The correct answer is D.** The volume of a rectangular prism is $l \times w \times h$. A cube is a special case in which the length, width, and height are all equal. The volume of a cube with edges of length 3 is $3 \times 3 \times 3 = 3^3 = 27$.

2. **The correct answer is H.** Because points M, N, and O are collinear, angle MNO has a measure of 180°. When it is split into two component angles, the sum of those component angles must equal 180°. Therefore, the measure of angle MNP plus the measure of angle ONP equals 180°. Since the measure of angle MNP is $3x°$ and the measure of angle ONP is $6x°$, it follows that $3x + 6x = 180$:

$$3x + 6x = 180$$
$$9x = 180$$
$$x = 20$$

The measure of angle MNP is $3x° = 3(20)° = 60°$.

3. **The correct answer is B.** Because all of the angles are known to be right angles, you can conclude that the length of all the right-facing sides must equal the length of all the left-facing sides. Since the length of the right-facing side is 9, the missing left-facing side will have length 5. Similarly, the length of all up-facing sides must equal the length of all down-facing sides, making the length of the missing up-facing side 8. The perimeter (beginning with the left-facing side and moving clockwise) is $5 + 8 + 4 + 12 + 9 + 20 = 58$ cm.

4. **The correct answer is H.** The area of a triangle is $\frac{1}{2}bh$ where b is the length of the base and h is the height of the triangle. In this case, $\overline{AC}$ is the base of the triangle and $\overline{BD}$ is the height. Substitute the given values into the formula and solve:

$$40 = \frac{1}{2}(10)h$$
$$40 = 5h$$
$$8 = h; \overline{BD} \text{ has length 8.}$$

5. **The correct answer is C.** To solve this problem, recall that the area of a trapezoid is found by multiplying the average of the parallel bases by the height. Since the parallel bases have length 9 and 7, the average is $\frac{(9+7)}{2} = \frac{16}{2} = 8$. The area is the average of the bases multiplied by the height, or $8 \times 6 = 48$ square inches.

PLANE GEOMETRY—DIFFICULTY LEVEL: MEDIUM

6. **The correct answer is H.** When a wheel makes one revolution, it goes completely around one time. The distance one time around a wheel is equal to the wheel's circumference. A wheel is a circle, so the formula for the circumference of a wheel is $C = 2\pi r$. You are given that the area of the wheel is 78.5 inches. The formula for the area of a circle $A = \pi r^2$, so $78.5 = \pi r^2$. Solve for r, the radius, as follows:

$$78.5 = \pi r^2$$
$$78.5 = 3.14(r^2)$$
$$25 = r^2$$
$$5 = r$$

Now calculate the circumference C of the wheel as follows:

$$C = 2\pi(5)$$
$$C = 2(3.14)(5) = 31.4$$

Because the circumference of the wheel is 31.4, one revolution of the wheel is equal to 31.4 inches. Divide the total number of inches traveled (1,200) by 31.4 to find the number of revolutions the wheel makes:

$$1,200 \div 31.4 = 38.2$$

The wheel makes about 38 revolutions.

7. **The correct answer is A.** To solve this problem, use the fact that supplementary angles add up to 180°. In the figure shown, x, y, and z form relationships with a, b, and c, respectively. Because a and x are vertical angles, they have the same measure. Angles b and y

are supplementary, so they add up to 180, making $y = 180 - b$. Likewise, $z = 180 - c$. Therefore, the sum of the angles within the triangle is $180 = x + y + z$, which is equivalent to $a + (180 - b) + (180 - c)$. You are given that $a = 140$, so substitute 140 for a, as follows:

$$180 = 140 + (180 - b) + (180 - c)$$
$$180 = 140 + 180 + 180 - b - c$$
$$180 = 500 - b - c$$
$$-320 = -b - c$$
$$320 = b + c$$

8. **The correct answer is H.** Because you are given that segments $\overline{XZ}$ and $\overline{YZ}$ bisect $\angle WXY$ and $\angle WYX$, respectively, you can conclude the following:

$$\angle WXZ \cong \angle YXZ$$
$$\angle WYZ \cong \angle XYZ$$

Furthermore, because you know that these two triangles are isosceles, you know that the base angles are congruent. Because of this congruence, you can conclude that the four angles written above are all congruent: $\angle WXZ \cong \angle YXZ \cong \angle WYZ \cong \angle XYZ$. Therefore, through transitivity, you can conclude that $\angle WXZ \cong \angle XYZ$.

9. **The correct answer is C.** Since Mandy's room is an L shape made up of a 14-foot × 7-foot rectangle and a 5-foot × 5-foot square, the area of her room is $(14 \times 12) + (5 \times 5) = 168 + 25$, or 193 square feet. An 8-foot × 12-foot piece of carpet covers 96 square feet $(8 \times 12 = 96)$, so the area of 193 square feet is slightly larger than what 2 pieces of carpet will cover. Therefore, Mandy will need at least 3 pieces of carpet.

10. **The correct answer is H.** When $\overline{AB}$ is 5 inches long, $\overline{BC}$ is 8 inches long, and $\overline{AC}$ is 3 inches long, $\triangle ABC$ has a perimeter of $5 + 8 + 3 = 16$. To find the perimeter of $\triangle XYZ$ when its longest side is 20, set up proportions to find the lengths of the sides. The sides of similar triangles are in proportion to each other. In this case, you can take the proportion of the longest sides, $20{:}8 \left(\frac{20}{8}\right)$, and apply it to the perimeter p as follows:

$$\frac{20}{8} = \frac{p}{16}$$
$$p = \frac{(20 \times 16)}{8} = 40$$

PLANE GEOMETRY—DIFFICULTY LEVEL: HARD

11. **The correct answer is B.** To solve this problem, remember that the noncommon rays of two adjacent angles are the sides of the angles that are *not*

shared. As shown in the figure below, these rays form a straight angle, or straight line, which you know contains 180°.

To find the measure of either angle, set up an equation: x (the measure of the smaller angle) + $3x$ (the measure of the larger angle) = 180°. Solve for x:

$$4x = 180°$$
$$x = 45°$$

12. **The correct answer is J.** The circumference of a circle is given by $2\pi r$, where r is the radius. If a circle has a circumference of 64π units, then $64\pi = 2\pi r$. Dividing both sides by 2π yields $r = 32$. Since the square has sides that are the same length as the radius of the circle, 32, the perimeter of that square is $4(32) = 128$.

13. **The correct answer is B.** You are given that angle QPS and angle PSR are right angles; you are also given the lengths of diagonal $\overline{PR}$ (34) and side $\overline{PS}$ (30). It may help to write the lengths of the various line segments on a diagram as shown below:

You should now see that you have the length of one side of the right triangle PRS (30) and the length of the hypotenuse (34). Use the Pythagorean Theorem to calculate the length of the remaining side:

$$a^2 + b^2 = c^2$$
$$30^2 + b^2 = 34^2$$
$$900 + b^2 = 1,156$$
$$b^2 = 256$$
$$b = 16$$

The length of $\overline{RS}$ is 16.

14. **The correct answer is G.** To solve this problem, it is helpful to extend the lines of the angle given in the diagram as shown below:

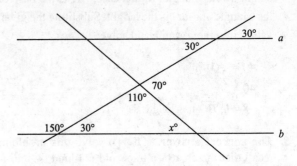

Make use of the properties of angles made by transversals that cross the parallel lines a and b. Also note the newly created triangle, which angle x is a part of. Given that opposite angles are congruent, one angle of that triangle is equal to 30°. Additionally, the supplement of the 70° angle is 110°. Knowing that two angles of a triangle are 110° and 30°, $x° + 140° = 180°$, and $x = 40°$.

15. **The correct answer is C.** To solve this problem, use the fact that π radians is equal to 180°. Given a radian measure, to convert to degrees, simply divide by π and multiply by 180:

$$\frac{3.75\pi}{\pi} = 3.75$$
$$3.75 \times 180 = 675°$$

16. **The correct answer is H.** The area of a circle is given by πr^2, where r is the radius. If the radius is $\frac{32}{\pi}$, then the area is $\pi\left(\frac{32}{\pi}\right)^2 = \frac{1,024\pi}{\pi^2} = \frac{1,024}{\pi}$.

TRIGONOMETRY—DIFFICULTY LEVEL: MEDIUM

1. **The correct answer is C.** The cosine of an angle in a right triangle is the ratio of the side adjacent to that angle to the hypotenuse of the triangle. Since the side adjacent measures 12 and the hypotenuse is 13 (always the longest side in a right triangle), the cosine of the angle is $\frac{12}{13}$.

2. **The correct answer is J.** The tangent is the ratio of the side opposite an angle in a right triangle to the side adjacent to that angle. According to the figure, the side opposite α is r and the side adjacent is s. Therefore $\tan \alpha = \frac{r}{s}$.

3. **The correct answer is A.** To solve this problem, recall that the tangent is the ratio of the side opposite an angle in a right triangle to the side adjacent to that angle. If $\tan \beta = \frac{3}{4}$, then you can think of this triangle as having legs of 3 and 4. The side opposite β is 3, and the side adjacent to β is 4. Now use the Pythagorean Theorem to find the length of the hypotenuse ($c^2 = a^2 + b^2$, where c is the hypotenuse and a and b are the legs in a right triangle). The hypotenuse in this case is 5. The sine of an angle in a right triangle is the ratio of the side opposite that angle to the hypotenuse of the triangle, making $\sin \beta = \frac{3}{5}$.

4. **The correct answer is H.** The cosine of any angle is calculated by dividing the length of the side adjacent to the acute angle by the hypotenuse $\left(\cos = \dfrac{\text{adj}}{\text{hyp}}\right)$, so $\cos \angle A = \dfrac{21}{x}$.

   To find the length of the hypotenuse, use the Pythagorean Theorem, $a^2 + b^2 = c^2$:

   $21^2 + 20^2 = c^2$

   $441 + 400 = 841 = c^2$

   $\sqrt{841} = \sqrt{c^2}$, so $c = 29$

   The cos of $\angle A = \dfrac{21}{29}$.

TRIGONOMETRY—DIFFICULTY LEVEL: HARD

5. **The correct answer is A.** By definition, the tangent of any angle is the sin/cos of that angle. Therefore, $\dfrac{(\cos x)}{(\tan x \sin x)}$ is equal to $\dfrac{\cos x}{\dfrac{(\sin x)}{(\cos x)}(\sin x)}$.

   Multiply both the numerator and denominator by $\cos x$ to get $\dfrac{\cos^2 x}{\sin^2 x}$.

6. **The correct answer is G.** The unknown side x is the side opposite the 15° angle. Recall that the sine of an angle in a right triangle is the ratio of the side opposite that angle to the hypotenuse of the triangle. $\sin 15° = \dfrac{x}{35}$.

   Substitute the approximated value for sin 15°:

   $0.259 = \dfrac{x}{35}$.

   $35(0.259) = x$

   $9.065 = x$, which is approximately 9.1

7. **The correct answer is B.** The ratio $\tan \alpha$ is defined as $\dfrac{\sin \alpha}{\cos \alpha}$. The ratio $\dfrac{\tan \alpha}{\sin \alpha}$ can be written as:

   $\dfrac{\sin \alpha}{\cos \alpha} \times \dfrac{1}{\sin \alpha}$

   This simplifies to $\dfrac{1}{\cos \alpha}$.

■■■■   WHAT'S NEXT?

Part III contains four simulated ACT Mathematics Practice Tests in ACT format. Apply the strategies and techniques that you learned in the previous chapters to answer as many of these questions as possible correctly. Review the explanations for the questions that you miss.

PART III

PRACTICE TESTS

PART III

PRACTICE
TESTS

CHAPTER 6

PRACTICE TEST 1 WITH EXPLANATIONS

ACT MATHEMATICS TEST 1

Answer Sheet

MATHEMATICS

1 Ⓐ Ⓑ Ⓒ Ⓓ Ⓔ	16 Ⓕ Ⓖ Ⓗ Ⓙ Ⓚ	31 Ⓐ Ⓑ Ⓒ Ⓓ Ⓔ	46 Ⓕ Ⓖ Ⓗ Ⓙ Ⓚ
2 Ⓕ Ⓖ Ⓗ Ⓙ Ⓚ	17 Ⓐ Ⓑ Ⓒ Ⓓ Ⓔ	32 Ⓕ Ⓖ Ⓗ Ⓙ Ⓚ	47 Ⓐ Ⓑ Ⓒ Ⓓ Ⓔ
3 Ⓐ Ⓑ Ⓒ Ⓓ Ⓔ	18 Ⓕ Ⓖ Ⓗ Ⓙ Ⓚ	33 Ⓐ Ⓑ Ⓒ Ⓓ Ⓔ	48 Ⓕ Ⓖ Ⓗ Ⓙ Ⓚ
4 Ⓕ Ⓖ Ⓗ Ⓙ Ⓚ	19 Ⓐ Ⓑ Ⓒ Ⓓ Ⓔ	34 Ⓕ Ⓖ Ⓗ Ⓙ Ⓚ	49 Ⓐ Ⓑ Ⓒ Ⓓ Ⓔ
5 Ⓐ Ⓑ Ⓒ Ⓓ Ⓔ	20 Ⓕ Ⓖ Ⓗ Ⓙ Ⓚ	35 Ⓐ Ⓑ Ⓒ Ⓓ Ⓔ	50 Ⓕ Ⓖ Ⓗ Ⓙ Ⓚ
6 Ⓕ Ⓖ Ⓗ Ⓙ Ⓚ	21 Ⓐ Ⓑ Ⓒ Ⓓ Ⓔ	36 Ⓕ Ⓖ Ⓗ Ⓙ Ⓚ	51 Ⓐ Ⓑ Ⓒ Ⓓ Ⓔ
7 Ⓐ Ⓑ Ⓒ Ⓓ Ⓔ	22 Ⓕ Ⓖ Ⓗ Ⓙ Ⓚ	37 Ⓐ Ⓑ Ⓒ Ⓓ Ⓔ	52 Ⓕ Ⓖ Ⓗ Ⓙ Ⓚ
8 Ⓕ Ⓖ Ⓗ Ⓙ Ⓚ	23 Ⓐ Ⓑ Ⓒ Ⓓ Ⓔ	38 Ⓕ Ⓖ Ⓗ Ⓙ Ⓚ	53 Ⓐ Ⓑ Ⓒ Ⓓ Ⓔ
9 Ⓐ Ⓑ Ⓒ Ⓓ Ⓔ	24 Ⓕ Ⓖ Ⓗ Ⓙ Ⓚ	39 Ⓐ Ⓑ Ⓒ Ⓓ Ⓔ	54 Ⓕ Ⓖ Ⓗ Ⓙ Ⓚ
10 Ⓕ Ⓖ Ⓗ Ⓙ Ⓚ	25 Ⓐ Ⓑ Ⓒ Ⓓ Ⓔ	40 Ⓕ Ⓖ Ⓗ Ⓙ Ⓚ	55 Ⓐ Ⓑ Ⓒ Ⓓ Ⓔ
11 Ⓐ Ⓑ Ⓒ Ⓓ Ⓔ	26 Ⓕ Ⓖ Ⓗ Ⓙ Ⓚ	41 Ⓐ Ⓑ Ⓒ Ⓓ Ⓔ	56 Ⓕ Ⓖ Ⓗ Ⓙ Ⓚ
12 Ⓕ Ⓖ Ⓗ Ⓙ Ⓚ	27 Ⓐ Ⓑ Ⓒ Ⓓ Ⓔ	42 Ⓕ Ⓖ Ⓗ Ⓙ Ⓚ	57 Ⓐ Ⓑ Ⓒ Ⓓ Ⓔ
13 Ⓐ Ⓑ Ⓒ Ⓓ Ⓔ	28 Ⓕ Ⓖ Ⓗ Ⓙ Ⓚ	43 Ⓐ Ⓑ Ⓒ Ⓓ Ⓔ	58 Ⓕ Ⓖ Ⓗ Ⓙ Ⓚ
14 Ⓕ Ⓖ Ⓗ Ⓙ Ⓚ	29 Ⓐ Ⓑ Ⓒ Ⓓ Ⓔ	44 Ⓕ Ⓖ Ⓗ Ⓙ Ⓚ	59 Ⓐ Ⓑ Ⓒ Ⓓ Ⓔ
15 Ⓐ Ⓑ Ⓒ Ⓓ Ⓔ	30 Ⓕ Ⓖ Ⓗ Ⓙ Ⓚ	45 Ⓐ Ⓑ Ⓒ Ⓓ Ⓔ	60 Ⓕ Ⓖ Ⓗ Ⓙ Ⓚ

MATHEMATICS TEST

60 Minutes—60 Questions

DIRECTIONS: Solve each of the problems in the time allowed, then fill in the corresponding bubble on your answer sheet (page 111). Do not spend too much time on any one problem; skip the more difficult problems and go back to them later. You may use a calculator on this test. For this test, you should assume that figures are NOT necessarily drawn to scale, that all geometric figures lie in a plane, and that the word *line* is used to indicate a straight line.

---

1. Which of the following expressions is equivalent to $6x + 12y - 15z$?
   A. $3(x + 12y - 15z)$
   B. $3(2x + 4y - 5z)$
   C. $3(3x + 4y) - 5z$
   D. $6(x + 2y - 3z)$
   E. $15(x + y - z)$

2. When written in symbols, "the product of a and b, raised to the third power" is represented as:
   F. $a^3 - b^3$
   G. $(a + b^3)$
   H. $(ab)^3$
   J. $\dfrac{a^3}{b^3}$
   K. ab^3

3. Tyler took a road trip on his motorcycle. When he left, the odometer read 22,687 miles, and when he returned, it read 23,002 miles. In total, Tyler rode for 5 hours. Based on the odometer readings, what was his average speed during the trip, to the nearest mile per hour?
   A. 79
   B. 76
   C. 64
   D. 63
   E. 58

4. The interior dimensions of a rectangular rabbit cage are 5 feet by 4 feet by 2 feet. What is the volume, in cubic feet, of the interior of the rabbit cage?
   F. 11
   G. 20
   H. 28
   J. 40
   K. 44

5. If z is a real number and $3^z = 81$, then $7 \times 2^z = ?$
   A. 14
   B. 28
   C. 56
   D. 84
   E. 112

DO YOUR FIGURING HERE.

GO ON TO THE NEXT PAGE.

6. For the students at Bayside College, the ratio of professors to students is 2:43. There are currently 9,030 students enrolled. Which of the following statements is (are) true?

    I. There are 420 professors.

    II. Each professor has 43 students in his or her course.

    III. Professors make up $\frac{2}{43}$ of the Bayside population.

  F. I only

  G. II only

  H. III only

  J. I and III only

  K. I, II, and III

7. If the probability that a specific event will occur is 0.09, what is the probability that the event will NOT occur?

  A. 0.00

  B. 0.11

  C. 0.70

  D. 0.91

  E. 1.00

8. As shown below, the diagonals of rectangle $ABCD$ intersect at the point $(-4, 2)$ in the standard (x, y) coordinate plane. Point D is at $(1, -1)$. Which of the following are the coordinates of point B?

  F. $(1, 5)$

  G. $(-6, 4)$

  H. $(-9, -1)$

  J. $(-9, 5)$

  K. $(-11, 6)$

9. $|5(-3) + 11| = ?$

  A. -4

  B. 3

  C. 4

  D. 13

  E. 26

10. The expression $5m(-3m + 6n) - 9mn$ is equivalent to:

  F. $30mn - 8m$

  G. $21mn - 15m^2$

  H. $15mn - 9m^2$

  J. $6mn$

  K. $-15m^2$

DO YOUR FIGURING HERE.

GO ON TO THE NEXT PAGE.

11. Jose recently took a history test on which certain questions were worth 3 points each, while the rest were worth 5 points each. He correctly answered the same number of 3-point questions as 5-point questions, and he earned a score of 72 points. How many 5-point questions did he answer correctly?

   A. 9
   B. 11
   C. 15
   D. 24
   E. 26

12. A rectangular poster measures 22 inches by 16 inches. Pietro estimates that the area is 264 square inches. His estimate is what percent *less* than the actual area?

   F. 75%
   G. 50%
   H. 45%
   J. 30%
   K. 25%

13. The *geometric mean* of 2 positive numbers is the square root of the product of the 2 numbers. What is the geometric mean of 16 and 64?

   A. 28
   B. 32
   C. 40
   D. 256
   E. 1,024

14. A model for the braking distance d feet required to stop a certain car when it is traveling x miles per hour is $d = \left(\dfrac{x^2}{20}\right) + x$. According to this model, what is the braking distance, in feet, required to stop this car when it is traveling at 30 miles per hour?

   F. 30
   G. 52
   H. 75
   J. 90
   K. 102

15. The expression $2x^2 + 10x - 28$ can be written as the product of 2 binomials with integer coefficients. One of the binomials is $(x + 7)$. Which of the following is the other binomial?

   A. $2x^2 - 4$
   B. $2x^2 + 4$
   C. $2x - 6$
   D. $2x - 4$
   E. $x + 4$

DO YOUR FIGURING HERE.

GO ON TO THE NEXT PAGE.

16. The table below shows the number of miles Mandy ran each day in the last week. What is the median of the data in the table?

Day	Number of Miles Run
Sun	15
Mon	17
Tue	12
Wed	23
Thu	13
Fri	15
Sat	24

DO YOUR FIGURING HERE.

F. 14.5
G. 15
H. 17
J. 23.5
K. 30

17. Given $f(x) = \dfrac{x^2 + \frac{3}{8}}{x + \frac{2}{5}}$, what is $f\left(\frac{1}{4}\right)$?

A. $\dfrac{35}{52}$

B. 1

C. $\dfrac{52}{30}$

D. $\dfrac{20}{9}$

E. $\dfrac{9}{2}$

18. Jim has $13 more than his friend Brian, who has x dollars. Jim spends $25 on Saturday, and then works on Sunday and earns $32. Which of the following is an expression for the amount of money, in dollars, that Jim has after working on Sunday?
F. 20
G. $x - 7$
H. $x - 20$
J. $2x + 7$
K. $x + 20$

19. Given that $\sqrt{2x} - 9 = 1$, $x = ?$
A. −32
B. 20
C. 25
D. 32
E. 50

GO ON TO THE NEXT PAGE.

20. Which of the following is a factored form of the expression $7x^2 + 10x - 8$?

    F. $(x - 1)(7x + 8)$
    G. $(x - 4)(7x + 2)$
    H. $(x - 8)(7x - 1)$
    J. $(x + 2)(7x - 4)$
    K. $(x + 4)(7x - 2)$

21. Which of the following is equivalent to $\sqrt[4]{8}$?

    A. $\dfrac{1}{8^4}$
    B. 1
    C. $\sqrt{2}$
    D. $8^{\frac{1}{4}}$
    E. 4^8

22. If x, y, and z are positive integers such that $x^y = a$ and $z^y = b$, then $ab =$?

    F. xz^y
    G. xz^{2y}
    H. $(xz)^y$
    J. $(xz)^{2y}$
    K. $(xz)^{\frac{y}{2}}$

23. The mean age of the 5 people in the room is 30 years. One of the 5 people, whose age is 50 years, leaves the room. What is the mean age of the 4 people remaining in the room?

    A. 14
    B. 20
    C. 25
    D. 30
    E. 35

24. When 5 consecutive odd integers that are each greater than 34 are added, what is the smallest possible sum?

    F. 195
    G. 185
    H. 152
    J. 147
    K. 144

DO YOUR FIGURING HERE.

GO ON TO THE NEXT PAGE.

25. The probability that Event X will occur is 0.3. The probability that Event Y will occur is 0.6. Given that Events X and Y are mutually exclusive, what is the probability that Event X *or* Event Y will occur?

A. 0.18
B. 0.2
C. 0.3
D. 0.4
E. 0.9

DO YOUR FIGURING HERE.

26. If $2x + 17 = |-35|$, then $x = $?

F. −26
G. −9
H. 5
J. 9
K. 26

27. Marianne went to the local market to purchase some fruit. Each box of oranges sold for $3, and each box of pears sold for $5. Marianne purchased a total of 18 boxes of fruit for $68. How many boxes of oranges did she purchase?

A. 5
B. 7
C. 9
D. 11
E. 16

28. In $\triangle ABD$ below, E lies on $\overline{AD}$, and w, x, y, and z are angle measures in degrees. The measure of angle D is 55°. What is $w + x + y + z$?

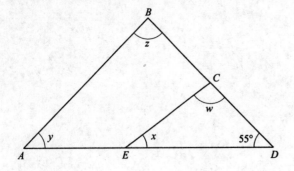

F. 85°
G. 125°
H. 250°
J. 260°
K. 305°

GO ON TO THE NEXT PAGE.

DO YOUR FIGURING HERE.

29. The diameter d of the rubber hoses manufactured by a certain company must satisfy the inequality $|d - 4| \leq 0.002$. What is the maximum diameter, in inches, that such a rubber hose may have?
   A. 0.008
   B. 2.000
   C. 3.998
   D. 4.000
   E. 4.002

30. If $x + 5 = y$ and $x + 6 = z$, what is the value of $z - y$?
   F. 11
   G. 1
   H. −1
   J. $2x + 11$
   K. $2x + 1$

31. In the standard (x, y) coordinate plane, point A has coordinates $(-2, 7)$ and point B has coordinates $(8, -3)$. If (r, s) is the midpoint of $\overline{AD}$, what is $r + s$?
   A. 0
   B. 2
   C. 4
   D. 5
   E. 10

Use the following information to answer Questions 32–34.

A local fitness club has a swimming pool—installed on level ground—that is a right cylinder with a diameter of 20 feet and a height of 5 feet. A diagram of the pool and its entry ladder is shown below.

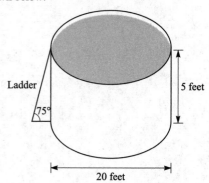

32. To the nearest cubic foot, what is the volume of water that will be in the pool when it is filled with water to a depth of 4 feet?
   (Note: The volume of a cylinder is given by $\pi r^2 h$, where r is the radius and h is the height.)
   F. 5,024
   G. 1,882
   H. 1,256
   J. 251
   K. 126

GO ON TO THE NEXT PAGE.

33. A solar cover is made for the pool. The cover will rest on the top of the pool and will include a wedge-shaped flap that forms a 30° angle at the center of the cover, as shown in the figure below. A zipper will be sewn along 1 side of the wedge-shaped flap and around the arc. Which of the following is closest to the length, in feet, of the zipper?

DO YOUR FIGURING HERE.

A. 41
B. 25
C. 20
D. 15
E. 10

34. A hose connected to a hydraulic pump was used to fill the pool. The pump had been on the medium setting for 10 hours and had filled the pool to the 3-foot mark when someone realized that the pump could be set to a higher setting that would increase the flow by 33%. The pool was then filled to the 4-foot mark at the greater flow rate. Which of the following graphs shows the relationship between the time spent filling the pool and the height of the water in the pool?

GO ON TO THE NEXT PAGE.

35. For all nonzero y and z, $\dfrac{(y \times 10^{-4})(z \times 1{,}000{,}000)}{(y \times 0.0001)(z \times 10^6)} = ?$

DO YOUR FIGURING HERE.

A. $\dfrac{1}{2}$

B. 1

C. 10

D. yz

E. $\dfrac{y^4}{z^5}$

36. For every pair of real numbers a and b such that $ab = 0$ and $\dfrac{a}{b} = 0$, which of the following statements is true?

F. $a = 0$ and $b = 0$

G. $a \neq 0$ and $b = 0$

H. $a = 0$ and $b \neq 0$

J. $a \neq 0$ and $b \neq 0$

K. None of the statements is true for every such pair of real numbers a and b.

37. Which of the following radian measures is equivalent to $810°$?

A. 2.5π

B. 3π

C. 4.5π

D. 5.2π

E. 6π

Use the following information to answer Questions 38–40.

Celina has a garden in her backyard that is shaped like a right triangle, as shown below.

144 ft

60 ft

38. If a bag of fertilizer costs $5.99 and covers approximately 360 square feet, which of the following is closest to the cost, in dollars, of fertilizing Celina's garden?

F. $37.00

G. $60.00

H. $72.00

J. $96.00

K. $144.00

GO ON TO THE NEXT PAGE.

39. Celina wants to put a fence around her garden to protect it from animals. Before she buys the fencing, she calculates the perimeter of the garden. What is its perimeter, in feet?

A. 204
B. 216
C. 300
D. 360
E. 408

40. The angle opposite the 60-foot side of the garden measures approximately 26.4°. Celina wants to change the shape of her garden. It will still be a right triangle with the 144-foot side as one leg, but she is going to extend the 60-foot side until the angle opposite that side is about 37°. By approximately how many feet would Celina need to extend the 60-foot side?
(Note: sin 37° = 0.60; cos 37° = 0.80; tan 37° = 0.75.)

F. 26
G. 48
H. 55
J. 60
K. 108

41. What is the point in the standard (x, y) coordinate plane that is the center of a circle with the equation $(x + 6)^2 + (y - 9)^2 = 25$?

A. $(-9, 6)$
B. $(-6, 9)$
C. $(0, 5)$
D. $(6, -9)$
E. $(9, -6)$

42. Brendan's average score after 4 math quizzes was 78. His score on the 5th quiz was 93. If all 5 of the quizzes are weighted equally, which of the following is closest to his average score after 5 quizzes?

F. 93
G. 90
H. 87
J. 81
K. 78

DO YOUR FIGURING HERE.

GO ON TO THE NEXT PAGE.

43. Ratings for a particular 2-hour television program reveal that the greatest number of viewers tuned in right at the start of the program and a majority of them remained tuned in for the 1st half-hour of the program. For the next hour, the number of viewers steadily declined, but it jumped back up for the last half-hour. Among the following graphs, which one best represents the relationship between the rating of the program, in thousands of viewers, and the time, in minutes, from the start to the finish of the program?

DO YOUR FIGURING HERE.

A.

B.

C.

D.

E.

GO ON TO THE NEXT PAGE.

DO YOUR FIGURING HERE.

44. Given that $a = 2$ and $b = 12$ for the proportion $\frac{a}{6} = \frac{k}{12}$, what is a when $b = 8$?

F. $\frac{3}{4}$

G. $\frac{4}{3}$

H. 3

J. 4

K. 12

45. In the figure below, a square is circumscribed about a circle with a diameter of 20 cm. Points Q, R, S, and T are the midpoints of the square's sides. What is the total area, in cm², of the shaded regions?

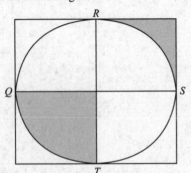

A. 20
B. 78.5
C. 100
D. 314
E. 400

46. Point $R(1, 5)$ is in the standard (x, y) coordinate plane. What must be the coordinates of point S so that the line $x = -3$ is the perpendicular bisector of $\overline{RS}$?

F. $(1, -11)$
G. $(-3, 5)$
H. $(-5, 1)$
J. $(-7, 5)$
K. $(-9, -3)$

47. A group has 20 members. The positions of president, vice president, and secretary will be assigned to 3 distinct members. Which of the following expressions gives the maximum number of distinct assignments that can be made?

A. 20^3
B. $20(3)$
C. $20(19)(18)$
D. $20(19)(18)(3)(2)(1)$
E. $\dfrac{20(19)(18)}{3(2)(1)}$

GO ON TO THE NEXT PAGE.

48. Which of the following is the solution to the statement for the inequality shown below?

$$-4 < 1 - 5x < 11$$

F. $-2 < x < 1$

G. $-1 < 5x < 6$

H. $2 > x > -1$

J. $4 > x > -5$

K. $-2 > x > -4$

49. What is the distance, in units, between the points in the standard (x, y) coordinate plane $(-1, 3)$ and $(-6, -9)$?

A. 17

B. 13

C. 12

D. 9

E. 5

50. What is the perimeter of parallelogram *ABCD* that has vertices with (x, y) coordinates $A(-3, -2)$, $B(-1, 5)$, $C(4, 6)$, and $D(2, -1)$?

F. 15

G. $2\sqrt{10} + 2\sqrt{29}$

H. $2\sqrt{53} + 2\sqrt{26}$

J. $2\sqrt{79}$

K. 158

51. The graph of the line with equation $-2x - 3y = -15$ does NOT have points in what quadrant(s) of the standard (x, y) coordinate plane below?

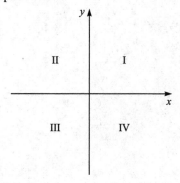

A. Quadrant I only

B. Quadrant II only

C. Quadrant III only

D. Quadrant IV only

E. Quadrants II and IV only

52. Lines *a* and *b* intersect at point $(2, 5)$ in the standard (x, y) coordinate plane. Lines *a* and *c* intersect at point $(1, 4)$. Which of the following is an equation for line *a*?

F. $y = 3x$

G. $y = 4x$

H. $y = x + 3$

J. $y = 3x - 1$

K. Cannot be determined from the given information

DO YOUR FIGURING HERE.

GO ON TO THE NEXT PAGE.

DO YOUR FIGURING HERE.

53. $3^0 + 3^2 + 3^{-2} = ?$

   A. 0

   B. $\dfrac{1}{9}$

   C. 9

   D. $10\dfrac{1}{9}$

   E. 19

54. Let p be a negative odd integer. The expression pq^3 is a positive even integer whenever q is any member of which of the following sets?

   F. Negative even integers

   G. Negative odd integers

   H. Positive even integers

   J. Positive odd integers

   K. All integers

55. In the (x, y) coordinate plane, what is the radius of the circle with a diameter having endpoints $(-2, 8)$ and $(1, 4)$?

   A. 2.5

   B. 5

   C. 9

   D. 16.5

   E. 25

56. The graph of the function $f(x) = \dfrac{x^3 - 4}{x^2 + 3x - 10}$ is shown in the standard (x, y) coordinate plane below. Which of the following, if any, is a list of each of the *vertical* asymptotes of $f(x)$?

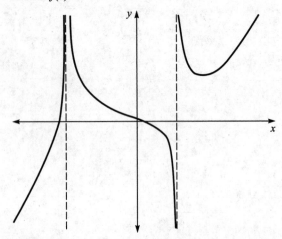

   F. $x = 0$

   G. $x = -5$ and $x = 2$

   H. $x = -1$ and $x = 7$

   J. $y = 3x - 10$

   K. This function has no vertical asymptotes.

57. The roots of a polynomial are $-\frac{3}{5}$ and $\frac{1}{3}$. Which one of the following could be the polynomial?

   A. $y = 4(3x + 5)(3x - 1)$

   B. $y = 4(5x + 3)(3x - 1)$

   C. $y = (5x - 3)(3x + 1)$

   D. $y = \left(x + \frac{5}{3}\right)(3x + 1)$

   E. $y = (x + 3)(x - 1)$

58. What is the real value of a in the equation $\log_2 2 + \log_2 32 = \log_4 a$?

   F. 4,096

   G. 2,048

   H. 128

   J. 64

   K. 6

59. If $h(x) = f(x) + g(x)$, where $f(x) = 3x^2 - 5x - 11$ and $g(x) = -3x^2 + 23x - 16$, then $h(x)$ is *always* divisible by which of the following?

   A. 2

   B. 6

   C. 9

   D. 12

   E. 18

60. What is the maximum value of $2a$ for a and b satisfying the system of inequalities below?

$$a \geq 0$$
$$b \geq 0$$
$$a + b \leq 8$$

   F. 1

   G. 2

   H. 8

   J. 16

   K. Cannot be determined from the given information

DO YOUR FIGURING HERE.

END OF THE MATHEMATICS TEST.
STOP! IF YOU HAVE TIME LEFT OVER, CHECK YOUR WORK ON THIS SECTION ONLY.

ANSWER KEY

Mathematics Test

1. B	16. G	31. D	46. J
2. H	17. A	32. H	47. C
3. D	18. K	33. D	48. F
4. J	19. E	34. F	49. B
5. E	20. J	35. B	50. H
6. F	21. D	36. H	51. C
7. D	22. H	37. C	52. H
8. J	23. C	38. H	53. D
9. C	24. F	39. D	54. F
10. G	25. E	40. G	55. A
11. A	26. J	41. B	56. G
12. K	27. D	42. J	57. B
13. B	28. H	43. A	58. F
14. H	29. E	44. H	59. C
15. D	30. F	45. C	60. J

SCORING WORKSHEET

Scale Score	Raw Score Mathematics	Scale Score	Raw Score Mathematics
36	60	18	24–26
35	59	17	20–23
34	57–58	16	16–19
33	56	15	12–15
32	55	14	10–11
31	54	13	8–9
30	53	12	6–7
29	52	11	5
28	51–50	10	4
27	48–49	9	—
26	46–47	8	3
25	44–45	7	—
24	41–43	6	2
23	38–40	5	—
22	35–37	4	1
21	31–34	3	—
20	28–30	2	—
19	27	1	0

NOTE: Each actual ACT is scaled slightly differently based on a large amount of information gathered from the millions of tests ACT, Inc., scores each year. This scale will give you a fairly good idea of where you are in your preparation process. However, it should not be read as an absolute predictor of your actual ACT score. In fact, on practice tests, the scores are much less important than what you learn from analyzing your results.

ANSWERS AND EXPLANATIONS

1. **The correct answer is B.** To solve this problem, factor out 3, as it is the greatest common factor of the three monomials ($3 \times 2 = 6$, $3 \times 4 = 12$, $3 \times -5 = -15$). Use these values to simplify the expression:

$$6x + 12y - 15z$$
$$= 3(2x + 4y - 5z)$$

Once you determined that 3 was the greatest common factor, you could eliminate answer choices D and E.

2. **The correct answer is H.** The product of two numbers is found by multiplying them ($a \times b$ in this case). Raising the product of a and b to the third power is represented by $(ab)^3$, since you are raising the entire product to the third power, not just one of the variables (as shown in answer choice K).

3. **The correct answer is D.** Before you can calculate Tyler's average speed, you must find out how far he traveled. If his odometer read 22,687 when he left and 23,002 when he returned, he traveled 315 miles ($23,002 - 22,687$). You are given that he drove for 5 hours, so you can use the formula Distance = Rate × Time to find his average speed:

$$315 = R(5)$$
$$R = 63$$

His average speed was 63 miles per hour.

4. **The correct answer is J.** The volume of a rectangle is given by Length × Height × Width. For the rabbit cage, the volume would be ($5 \times 4 \times 2$) = 40 cubic feet.

5. **The correct answer is E.** The first step in solving this problem is to determine the value of z. You are given that 3 raised to the power of z equals 81. Therefore, z must equal 4 ($3^4 = 81$). Use this value to solve 7×2^z:

$$7 \times 2^4 = 7 \times 16 = 112$$

6. **The correct answer is F.** You are given the ratio of professors to students (2:43) and the number of students (9,030). You can use this information to set up a proportion to determine the number of professors:

$$\frac{2}{43} = \frac{x}{9,030}$$

$$18,060 = 43x$$
$$x = 420$$

There are 420 professors at Bayside, so Roman numeral I is true. Eliminate answer choices G and H because they do not include Roman numeral I. Roman numeral II is not supported by any of the given information (you don't know the total number of courses); therefore it is not true. There is not enough information given for Roman numeral III (i.e., other employees of the school), so it also is not true. Since only Roman numeral I is true, answer choice F is correct.

7. **The correct answer is D.** In simple probability, the probability that an event will occur plus the probability that that event will not occur must equal 1. Therefore, if the probability that a specific event will occur is 0.09, then the probability that it will not occur is $1.00 - 0.09 = 0.91$, answer choice D.

8. **The correct answer is J.** To find the value of B, you can use the midpoint formula. Since the diagonals of the rectangle intersect at point (-4, 2), this is the midpoint of segments $\overline{BD}$ and $\overline{AC}$. The formula for determining the midpoint of a segment with endpoints (x_1, y_1) and (x_2, y_2) is $\left(\dfrac{x_1 + x_2}{2}, \dfrac{y_1 + y_2}{2}\right)$.

You already have the coordinates of the midpoint and point D, so you can use these to determine the coordinates of point B:

x coordinate:
$$-4 = \frac{1 + x_2}{2}$$
$$-8 = 1 + x_2$$
$$-9 = x_2$$

y coordinate:
$$2 = \frac{-1 + y_2}{2}$$
$$4 = -1 + y_2$$
$$5 = y_2$$

The coordinates of point B are (-9, 5).

9. **The correct answer is C.** To answer this question, perform the math within the absolute value signs:

$$5(-3) + 11 = -15 + 11 = -4$$

Because absolute value must be positive, the correct answer is 4.

10. **The correct answer is G.** To solve this problem, distribute $5m$ as shown next:

$$5m(-3m + 6n) - 9mn$$
$$= -15m^2 + 30mn - 9mn$$
$$= -15m^2 + 21mn$$
$$= 21mn - 15m^2$$

11. **The correct answer is A.** Since Jose answered the same number of 3-point questions correctly as he did 5-point questions, you can set up an equation:

$5x + 3x = 72$ (5 points times the number of 5-point questions answered correctly, plus 3 points times the number of 3-point questions answered correctly, equals 72)

$8x = 72$
$x = 9$

Jose answered nine 5-point questions and nine 3-point questions correctly.

12. **The correct answer is K.** First, you need to find the actual area of the poster, which is $22 \times 16 = 352$ square inches. Next, find the percentage of the actual area that is represented by Pietro's estimate $\left(\dfrac{264}{352} = 0.75\right)$. Pietro's estimate of the area is 75 percent of the actual area; therefore, his estimate is 25 percent less than the actual area.

13. **The correct answer is B.** You are told that the geometric mean is the square root of the product of two numbers. To find the geometric mean of 16 and 64, first find the product of the two numbers $(16 \times 64 = 1{,}024)$. Now, take the square root of this number $(\sqrt{1{,}024} = 32)$. The geometric mean of 16 and 64 is 32.

14. **The correct answer is H.** To solve this problem, insert 30 into the equation wherever there is an instance of x:

$d = (30^2 \div 20) + 30$
$d = (900 \div 20) + 30$
$d = 45 + 30$
$d = 75$

When traveling 30 miles per hour, the braking distance for this car would be 75 feet.

15. **The correct answer is D.** To solve this problem, you can test the answer choices to see which one, when multiplied by the given binomial, $(x + 7)$, equals $2x^2 + 10x - 28$ (remember to use the *FOIL* method):

Answer choice A: $(2x^2 - 4)(x + 7) = 2x^3 + 14x^2 - 4x - 28$. Eliminate answer choice A.

Answer choice B: $(2x^2 + 4)(x + 7) = 2x^3 + 14x^2 + 4x + 28$. Eliminate answer choice B.

Answer choice C: $(2x - 6)(x + 7) = 2x^2 + 14x - 6x - 42 = 2x^2 + 8x - 42$. Eliminate answer choice C.

Answer choice D: $(2x - 4)(x + 7) = 2x^2 + 14x - 4x - 28 = 2x^2 + 10x - 28$.
Answer choice D is correct, so there is no need to test answer choice E.

16. **The correct answer is G.** The median of any ordered set of data is the value that lies in the middle. The first step is to put each of the values in the "Number of Miles Run" column in order, as follows: 12, 13, 15, 15, 17, 23, 24. Since the value 15 is in the middle, it is the median.

17. **The correct answer is A.** To solve this problem, substitute $\dfrac{1}{4}$ for every instance of x in the equation:

$$f(x) = \dfrac{\left(\dfrac{1}{4}\right)^2 + \dfrac{3}{8}}{\dfrac{1}{4} + \dfrac{2}{5}}$$

$$f(x) = \dfrac{\dfrac{1}{16} + \dfrac{3}{8}}{\dfrac{1}{4} + \dfrac{2}{5}}$$

Find the least common denominators, and add the fractions in the numerator and the denominator:

$$f(x) = \dfrac{\dfrac{1}{16} + \dfrac{6}{16}}{\dfrac{5}{20} + \dfrac{8}{20}}$$

$$f(x) = \dfrac{\dfrac{7}{16}}{\dfrac{13}{20}}$$

Dividing by a fraction is equivalent to multiplying by the reciprocal of the fraction:

$$f(x) = \dfrac{7}{16} \times \dfrac{20}{13} = \dfrac{140}{208}, \text{ which reduces to } \dfrac{35}{52}.$$

18. **The correct answer is K.** Jim started with $13 more than Brian, who has x dollars, so the amount of money that Jim started with can be expressed as $x + 13$. If Jim spends $25, then his total can be expressed as $x + 13 - 25$, which equals $x - 12$. The next day, Jim earns $32, so the amount of money that he now has can be expressed as $x - 12 + 32 = x + 20$.

19. **The correct answer is E.** To solve this problem, first add 9 to both sides of the equation to get $\sqrt{2x} = 10$. Next, square both sides to get $2x = 100$, and $x = 50$.

20. **The correct answer is J.** To solve this problem, test each of the answer choices until you find the correct factored form (use the FOIL method):

Answer choice F: $(x-1)(7x+8) = 7x^2 + 8x - 7x - 8 = 7x^2 + x - 8$. Eliminate answer choice F.

Answer choice G: $(x-4)(7x+2) = 7x^2 + 2x - 28x - 8 = 7x^2 - 26x - 8$. Eliminate answer choice G.

Answer choice H: $(x-8)(7x-1) = 7x^2 - x - 56x + 8 = 7x^2 - 57x + 8$. Eliminate answer choice H.

Answer choice J: $(x+2)(7x-4) = 7x^2 - 4x + 14x - 8 = 7x^2 + 10x - 8$.

Answer choice J is the correct factored form of the expression, so there is no need to test answer choice K.

21. **The correct answer is D.** This problem tests your knowledge of roots and exponents. The expression $\sqrt[4]{8}$ means the fourth root of 8, and represents the number that when raised to the fourth power equals 8. This can also be written as $8^{\frac{1}{4}}$, answer choice D.

22. **The correct answer is H.** Even though the question includes variables, you should treat them as if they were numbers. Therefore, the rules of exponents apply. First note that $ab = (x^y)(z^y)$. Since you are raising both x and z to the same power, $ab = (x^y)(z^y) = (xz)^y$.

23. **The correct answer is C.** To solve this problem, first recognize that if the mean age of the 5 people in the room is 30 years, the total number of "years in the room" is $30 \times 5 = 150$. When the 50-year-old person leaves the room, the total number of "years in the room" is 100. Therefore, the mean age of the 4 people remaining in the room must be $100 \div 4$, or 25.

24. **The correct answer is F.** To find the smallest possible sum, take the 5 consecutive odd integers that are the closest to 34 (remember, they all must be greater than 34). These numbers would be 35, 37, 39, 41, and 43. Add them together: $35 + 37 + 39 + 41 + 43 = 195$.

25. **The correct answer is E.** This question is asking you to determine whether one event OR the other will occur. Since the events are mutually exclusive (the occurrence of one is not dependent on the occurrence of the other), you simply add the probabilities.

26. **The correct answer is J.** The absolute value of a number is its numerical value without regard to its sign. Start by finding the absolute value in the equation ($|-35| = 35$). Now solve for x:

$2x + 17 = 35$
$2x = 18$
$x = 9$

27. **The correct answer is D.** To solve this problem, set up two different equations:

$x + y = 18$

x is the number of boxes of oranges, and y is the number of boxes of pears; a total of 18 boxes was purchased.

$3x + 5y = 68$

3 times the number of boxes of oranges plus 5 times the number of boxes of pears equals 68 total dollars spent.

Now, solve the first equation for y in terms of x:

$y = 18 - x$

Take this value for y and substitute it into the second equation to solve for x:

$3x + 5(18 - x) = 68$
$3x + 90 - 5x = 68$
$-2x + 90 = 68$
$-2x = -22$
$x = 11$

Marianne purchased 11 boxes of oranges.

28. **The correct answer is H.** The three angles of a triangle must always add up to $180°$. As you can see in the figure, there is a smaller triangle within triangle $\triangle ABD$ ($\triangle DCE$). Since you are given that the measure of angle D is $55°$, the measures of angles x and w must add up to $125°$ ($125 + 55 = 180$). This goes for angles y and z as well. If $x + w = 125$, and $y + z = 125$, then $w + x + y + z = 250$.

29. **The correct answer is E.** The first step in solving this problem is clearing the absolute value according to the pattern:

$|d - 4| \le 0.002$
$-0.002 \le d - 4 \le 0.002$

This is the pattern for "less than." Now, solve for d:

$3.998 \le d \le 4.002$

Since d is less than or equal to 4.002, the maximum value of the diameter is 4.002 inches. Watch out for answer choice C, which is the smallest possible diameter.

30. **The correct answer is F.** To answer this question, recognize that $z - y = x + 6 - x + 5$. Now add the like terms:

$z - y = x + 6 - x + 5$
$z - y = x - x + 6 + 5$
$z - y = 11$

31. **The correct answer is D.** To solve this problem, find the midpoint of the segment between points (−2, 7) and (8, −3) by taking the average of the x coordinates and the average of the y coordinates. The midpoint is $\left[\dfrac{(-2+8)}{2}, \dfrac{(7+-3)}{2}\right] = (3,2)$. Therefore the quantity $x + y$ is $3 + 2 = 5$.

32. **The correct answer is H.** The volume of a cylinder is given by $\pi r^2 h$, where r is the radius and h is the height. In this case, the radius is 10 because it is half the diameter, which is 20. The height h is 4, since the pool was filled to that depth. Therefore the volume of water in the pool is $\pi(10)^2(4) = 3.14(100)(4) = 1{,}256 \text{ ft}^3$.

33. **The correct answer is D.** The length of the zipper includes the radius, 10, and the length of the arc formed by the 30° angle. Eliminate answer choice E, because you know the length must be greater than 10. Calculate this measurement by finding the circumference of the circle, which is given by πd, where d is the diameter, and then multiplying by the ratio $\dfrac{30}{360}$, since the arc occupies only 30 of the 360 degrees in an entire circle. The circumference is $\pi(20) = 62.8$. The arc length is $62.8 \times \left(\dfrac{30}{360}\right)$, which is equivalent to $62.8 \div 12$, or approximately 5. The total length of the zipper, then, is approximately $10 + 5 = 15$ feet.

34. **The correct answer is F.** Since the pool is filling at a constant rate for the first 10 hours, the graph should show a straight line that increases (rises) from left to right. At some point, the slope of that line should increase (become steeper) because the flow increases. Only the graph in answer choice F reflects this description of the rate of flow.

35. **The correct answer is B.** To solve this problem, write out the numbers that are given in scientific notation:

$$(y \times 10^{-4}) = y \times 0.0001$$

Remember, $10^{-4} = \dfrac{1}{10^4} = \dfrac{1}{10{,}000} = 0.0001$

$$(z \times 10^6) = z \times 1{,}000{,}000$$

Now, rewrite the expression with these numbers:

$$\frac{(y \times 0.0001)(z \times 1{,}000{,}000)}{(y \times 0.0001)(z \times 1{,}000{,}000)}$$

As you can see, the numerator is the same as the denominator; therefore, when dividing the two, the answer will be 1.

36. **The correct answer is H.** To answer this question, first notice that b cannot be 0 because $\dfrac{a}{0}$ does not equal 0. Eliminate answer choices F and G. Next,

because b cannot equal 0, a MUST equal 0 because $ab = 0$.

37. **The correct answer is C.** To find the measure of an angle in radians, take the angle measure and divide it by 180π:

$$\frac{810}{180}\pi = 04.5\pi$$

38. **The correct answer is H.** To solve this problem, you must first find the area of Celina's garden. Since the garden is in the shape of a triangle, use the formula for the area of a triangle $\left(A = \dfrac{1}{2}hb\right)$:

$$A = \frac{1}{2}(144)(60)$$
$$A = 4{,}320 \text{ square feet}$$

If one bag of fertilizer covers 360 square feet, then Celina will need 12 bags of fertilizer $\left(\dfrac{4{,}320}{360}\right)$. You are given that one bag costs \$5.99, so the total cost of fertilizing the garden would be $5.99 \times 12 = 71.88$ (round up to \$72.00).

39. **The correct answer is D.** To find the perimeter of the garden, you must first find the length of the missing side. Use the Pythagorean Theorem to solve:

$$a^2 + b^2 = c^2$$
$$60^2 + 144^2 = c^2$$
$$3{,}600 + 20{,}736 = c^2$$
$$24{,}336 = c^2$$
$$c = 156$$

The perimeter of the garden is $60 + 144 + 156 = 360$ feet.

40. **The correct answer is G.** To solve this problem, it is a good idea to draw a picture of the new shape of the garden, as shown below:

The only information that you have now is the length of the side adjacent to the 37° angle (144), and you need to find the value of the length opposite to the 37° angle. The trigonometric function that uses the adjacent side and the opposite side is the tangent (tan = opp/adj). For the missing side, this can be expressed as:

$$\tan 37° = \frac{x}{144}$$
$$144\tan 37° = x$$
$$144(0.75) = x$$
$$x = 108$$

If the side opposite the 37° angle is going to be 108 feet, this means that it will need to be extended by 48 feet (108 − 60).

41. **The correct answer is B.** The equation of a circle is given by $(x - h)^2 + (y - k)^2 = r^2$, where (h, k) are the coordinates of the center of the circle, and r is the radius. For this circle, h is −6 and k is 9, so the center of the circle is (−6, 9).

42. **The correct answer is J.** If Brendan's average score after 4 quizzes was 78, then his total score on all 4 quizzes is $4 \times 78 = 312$. He scored 93 on the 5th quiz, so he now has a total of 405 (312 + 93). His average after taking the 5th quiz will be 81 $\left(\frac{405}{5}\right)$.

43. **The correct answer is A.** The correct representation of the program's ratings on a graph would show the highest number at the start, with a slight decline during the first 30 minutes. For the next 60 minutes (from 30 to 90 on the graph), there should be a steady downward slope. During the last 30 minutes (from 90 to 120), the graph should go back up. The only graph that correctly displays this information is answer choice A.

44. **The correct answer is H.** To answer this question, first solve for k in the given equation:

$$\frac{a}{6} = \frac{k}{12}$$
$$6k = 12a$$
$$k = \frac{12a}{6}$$
$$k = 2a$$

You are given that $a = 2$, so k must equal 4. You are also given that, when $a = 2$, $b = 12$, so $\frac{a}{6} = \frac{4}{b}$, and $ab = 24$. Therefore, when $b = 8$, a must equal 3, since $3 \times 8 = 24$.

45. **The correct answer is C.** Since the square is circumscribed about a circle with diameter 20 cm, the length of each of the sides of the square is also 20 cm. Therefore, the area of the entire square is $(20)^2 = 400$ cm². However, the question asks for the area, in square centimeters, of the shaded regions. Based on the figure, it is apparent that the shaded regions occupy a total of one-quarter of

the entire square. Therefore, the area of the shaded regions is $\frac{400}{4} = 100$ cm².

46. **The correct answer is J.** The line $x = -3$ is a vertical line that intersects the x axis at −3. Since it is the perpendicular bisector of $\overline{RS}$, the segment $\overline{RS}$ must be horizontal. Every point on a horizontal segment has the same y coordinate. Therefore, the y coordinate of S must be the same as the y coordinate of R, which is 5. Eliminate answer choices F, H, and K. Furthermore, since the segment is bisected by the vertical line, it must be bisected at (−3, 5). The points R and S are equidistant from the point of bisection. Therefore, the only possible answer is the point (−7, 5), as it and (1, 5) are equidistant from (−3, 5). Watch out for answer choice G, which is a partial answer.

47. **The correct answer is C.** Because this question asks for *distinct* assignments, remember that there are 20 members to choose from for president, but once the president has been chosen, only 19 members remain for the position of vice president. Once the vice president has been chosen, only 18 members remain for the position of secretary. Therefore, the maximum number of distinct assignments is $20 \times 19 \times 18$, answer choice C.

48. **The correct answer is F.** The best way to solve this problem is to treat the given inequality as two separate inequalities.

$$-4 < 1 - 5x \quad and \quad 1 - 5x < 11$$

Solve each inequality:

$$-4 < 1 - 5x \qquad 1 - 5x < 11$$
$$-5 < -5x \qquad -5x < 10$$
$$1 > x \qquad x > -2$$

Remember that you must switch the direction of the sign when you divide by a negative number. Therefore, x is between 1 and −2.

49. **The correct answer is B.** To solve this problem, use the distance formula $(d = \sqrt{(x_2 - x_1)^2 + (y_2 - y_1)^2})$ to find the distance between the points (−1, 3) and (−6, −9).

$$d = \sqrt{((-1) - (-6))^2 + (3 - (-9))^2}$$
$$d = \sqrt{(-1 + 6)^2 + (3 + 9)^2}$$
$$d = \sqrt{(5)^2 + (12)^2}$$
$$d = \sqrt{25 + 144}$$
$$d = \sqrt{169} = 13$$

50. **The correct answer is H.** The perimeter of parallelogram ABCD is equal to the sum of the sides. The measure of each side is the distance between corresponding points. To solve this problem, use

the distance formula $\left(d = \sqrt{(x_2 - x_1)^2 + (y_2 - y_1)^2}\right)$ to find the distance between A and B:

$$d = \sqrt{(-1) - (-3))^2 + (5 - (-2))^2}$$
$$d = \sqrt{(-1 + 3)^2 + (5 + 2)^2}$$
$$d = \sqrt{(2)^2 + (7)^2}$$
$$d = \sqrt{4 + 49}$$
$$d = \sqrt{53}$$

Now, use the same formula to find the distance between A and D:

$$d = \sqrt{(2 - (-3))^2 + (-1 - (-2))^2}$$
$$d = \sqrt{(2 + 3)^2 + (-1 + 2)^2}$$
$$d = \sqrt{(5)^2 + (1)^2)}$$
$$d = \sqrt{25 + 1}$$
$$d = \sqrt{26}$$

Since this is a parallelogram, the distance between D and C is the same as the distance between A and B; likewise, the distance from B to C is the same as the distance from A to D. Therefore, the perimeter of the parallelogram is $2\sqrt{53} + 2\sqrt{26}$.

51. The correct answer is C. First convert the given equation to slope-intercept form, as follows:

$$-2x - 3y = -15$$
$$-3y = 2x - 15$$
$$y = \frac{-2}{3}x + 5$$

The slope of the line is $\frac{-2}{3}$, and the y intercept is 5. Now, you can draw the line in the (x, y) coordinate plane. After plotting a few points on the graph, it is clear that the line passes through every quadrant except for the third, as shown in the figure below.

Also, note that the line crosses the y axis at 5 and has a negative slope. This should help you to eliminate some answer choices quickly.

52. The correct answer is H. Since two points determine a line, it is possible to find an equation for line a because you are given that it passes through the points $(2, 5)$ and $(1, 4)$. To find an equation, first calculate the slope using the slope formula $\frac{(y_2 - y_1)}{(x_2 - x_1)}$.

$$\frac{(5 - 4)}{(2 - 1)}$$
$$= \frac{1}{1} = 1$$

Now that you know that the slope is 1, use the point-slope formula for a line, $(y - y_1) = m(x - x_1)$, for slope m and point (x_1, y_1). You can use either point in this calculation:

$$y - 4 = 1(x - 1)$$
$$y - 4 = x - 1$$
$$y = x + 3$$

53. The correct answer is D. To solve, simplify the expression $3^0 + 3^2 + 3^{-2}$. Apply a couple of exponent rules. First, any nonzero number to the zero power is 1. Also, negative exponents indicate reciprocals, meaning $3^{-2} = \frac{1}{3^2} = \frac{1}{9}$. Therefore $3^0 + 3^2 + 3^{-2} = 1 + 9 + \frac{1}{9} = 10\frac{1}{9}$.

54. The correct answer is F. One way to solve this problem is to look for the relationship among the variables. Because you're given that pq^3 is a positive even integer, and p is a negative odd integer, q^3 has to be a negative integer. Eliminate answer choices H, J, and K. Now, since pq^3 is a positive *even* integer and p is a negative *odd* integer, q must be a negative even integer. Try picking some numbers to test this reasoning:

Let $p = -3$ and $q = -2$

$pq^3 = -3(-2^3) = -3(-8) = 24$, which is a positive even integer.

55. The correct answer is A. You are given the endpoints of the diameter of the circle, so you can use the distance formula to determine the value of the diameter:

$$d = \sqrt{(1 - (-2))^2 + (4 - 8)^2}$$
$$d = \sqrt{(1 + 2)^2 + (-4)^2}$$
$$d = \sqrt{(3)^2 + (-4)^2}$$

$$d = \sqrt{9+16}$$
$$d = \sqrt{25}$$
$$d = 5$$

The radius is half of the diameter, so for this circle it is $2.5 \left(\frac{5}{2}\right)$.

56. The correct answer is G. You can find the vertical asymptotes of a function by finding the values that would set the denominator equal to zero (the values that are disallowed in the domain). To find these values, set the denominator equal to zero and solve:

$$x^2 + 3x - 10 = 0$$

Find two values that when multiplied equal −10, and when added together equal 3 (the only possible values are 5 and −2).

$$(x+5)(x-2) = 0$$
$$x + 5 = 0 \text{ or } x - 2 = 0$$

Set both binomials equal to 0.

$$x = -5 \text{ or } x = 2$$

This tells you that you cannot have either −5 or 2 in the domain, and therefore these are the two vertical asymptotes of the function (where the graph can't go).

57. The correct answer is B. You are given that the polynomial has roots $\frac{-3}{5}$ and $\frac{1}{3}$, which means that the values of $\frac{-3}{5}$ and $\frac{1}{3}$ for x result in the value of the entire polynomial being zero. To solve, you could substitute the given values into the polynomials in the answer choices. You could also generate your own polynomial using factors that correspond to each root. For instance, the root $\frac{-3}{5}$ corresponds to the factor $(5x + 3)$. Similarly the root $\frac{1}{3}$ corresponds to the factor $(3x - 1)$.

58. The correct answer is F. To find the value of a in the equation $\log_2 2 + \log_2 32 = \log_4 a$, first simplify the expression $\log_2 2 + \log_2 32$. According to the rules of logarithms, $\log_2 2 + \log_2 32 = \log_2 (2 \cdot 32) = \log_2 (64)$. By the definition of a logarithm, $\log_2 (64) = x$ means $64 = 2^x$. Therefore, $x = 6$. Since $\log_4 a = 6$, $a = 4^6 = 4{,}096$.

59. The correct answer is C. You are given that $h(x) = f(x) + g(x)$, and also the values for $f(x)$ and $g(x)$. Use these values to solve for $h(x)$:

$$h(x) = (3x^2 - 5x - 11) + (-3x^2 + 23x - 16)$$
$$h(x) = 3x^2 - 3x^2 - 5x + 23x - 11 - 16$$
$$h(x) = 18x - 27$$
$$h(x) = 9(2x - 3)$$

After solving, it is clear that $h(x)$ will always be divisible by 9.

60. The correct answer is J. Given that the sum of a and b has a maximum value (8), a will be greatest when b takes its lowest possible value. Since $b \geq 0$, a could be as great as 8 and still satisfy $a + b \leq 8$. Therefore, $2a$ can be as great as $2(8) = 16$.

CHAPTER 7

PRACTICE TEST 2 WITH EXPLANATIONS

■ **ANSWER SHEET**

ACT MATHEMATICS TEST 2
Answer Sheet

MATHEMATICS

1 Ⓐ Ⓑ Ⓒ Ⓓ Ⓔ	16 Ⓕ Ⓖ Ⓗ Ⓙ Ⓚ	31 Ⓐ Ⓑ Ⓒ Ⓓ Ⓔ	46 Ⓕ Ⓖ Ⓗ Ⓙ Ⓚ
2 Ⓕ Ⓖ Ⓗ Ⓙ Ⓚ	17 Ⓐ Ⓑ Ⓒ Ⓓ Ⓔ	32 Ⓕ Ⓖ Ⓗ Ⓙ Ⓚ	47 Ⓐ Ⓑ Ⓒ Ⓓ Ⓔ
3 Ⓐ Ⓑ Ⓒ Ⓓ Ⓔ	18 Ⓕ Ⓖ Ⓗ Ⓙ Ⓚ	33 Ⓐ Ⓑ Ⓒ Ⓓ Ⓔ	48 Ⓕ Ⓖ Ⓗ Ⓙ Ⓚ
4 Ⓕ Ⓖ Ⓗ Ⓙ Ⓚ	19 Ⓐ Ⓑ Ⓒ Ⓓ Ⓔ	34 Ⓕ Ⓖ Ⓗ Ⓙ Ⓚ	49 Ⓐ Ⓑ Ⓒ Ⓓ Ⓔ
5 Ⓐ Ⓑ Ⓒ Ⓓ Ⓔ	20 Ⓕ Ⓖ Ⓗ Ⓙ Ⓚ	35 Ⓐ Ⓑ Ⓒ Ⓓ Ⓔ	50 Ⓕ Ⓖ Ⓗ Ⓙ Ⓚ
6 Ⓕ Ⓖ Ⓗ Ⓙ Ⓚ	21 Ⓐ Ⓑ Ⓒ Ⓓ Ⓔ	36 Ⓕ Ⓖ Ⓗ Ⓙ Ⓚ	51 Ⓐ Ⓑ Ⓒ Ⓓ Ⓔ
7 Ⓐ Ⓑ Ⓒ Ⓓ Ⓔ	22 Ⓕ Ⓖ Ⓗ Ⓙ Ⓚ	37 Ⓐ Ⓑ Ⓒ Ⓓ Ⓔ	52 Ⓕ Ⓖ Ⓗ Ⓙ Ⓚ
8 Ⓕ Ⓖ Ⓗ Ⓙ Ⓚ	23 Ⓐ Ⓑ Ⓒ Ⓓ Ⓔ	38 Ⓕ Ⓖ Ⓗ Ⓙ Ⓚ	53 Ⓐ Ⓑ Ⓒ Ⓓ Ⓔ
9 Ⓐ Ⓑ Ⓒ Ⓓ Ⓔ	24 Ⓕ Ⓖ Ⓗ Ⓙ Ⓚ	39 Ⓐ Ⓑ Ⓒ Ⓓ Ⓔ	54 Ⓕ Ⓖ Ⓗ Ⓙ Ⓚ
10 Ⓕ Ⓖ Ⓗ Ⓙ Ⓚ	25 Ⓐ Ⓑ Ⓒ Ⓓ Ⓔ	40 Ⓕ Ⓖ Ⓗ Ⓙ Ⓚ	55 Ⓐ Ⓑ Ⓒ Ⓓ Ⓔ
11 Ⓐ Ⓑ Ⓒ Ⓓ Ⓔ	26 Ⓕ Ⓖ Ⓗ Ⓙ Ⓚ	41 Ⓐ Ⓑ Ⓒ Ⓓ Ⓔ	56 Ⓕ Ⓖ Ⓗ Ⓙ Ⓚ
12 Ⓕ Ⓖ Ⓗ Ⓙ Ⓚ	27 Ⓐ Ⓑ Ⓒ Ⓓ Ⓔ	42 Ⓕ Ⓖ Ⓗ Ⓙ Ⓚ	57 Ⓐ Ⓑ Ⓒ Ⓓ Ⓔ
13 Ⓐ Ⓑ Ⓒ Ⓓ Ⓔ	28 Ⓕ Ⓖ Ⓗ Ⓙ Ⓚ	43 Ⓐ Ⓑ Ⓒ Ⓓ Ⓔ	58 Ⓕ Ⓖ Ⓗ Ⓙ Ⓚ
14 Ⓕ Ⓖ Ⓗ Ⓙ Ⓚ	29 Ⓐ Ⓑ Ⓒ Ⓓ Ⓔ	44 Ⓕ Ⓖ Ⓗ Ⓙ Ⓚ	59 Ⓐ Ⓑ Ⓒ Ⓓ Ⓔ
15 Ⓐ Ⓑ Ⓒ Ⓓ Ⓔ	30 Ⓕ Ⓖ Ⓗ Ⓙ Ⓚ	45 Ⓐ Ⓑ Ⓒ Ⓓ Ⓔ	60 Ⓕ Ⓖ Ⓗ Ⓙ Ⓚ

MATHEMATICS TEST

60 Minutes—60 Questions

DIRECTIONS: Solve each of the problems in the time allowed, then fill in the corresponding bubble on your answer sheet (page 139). Do not spend too much time on any one problem; skip the more difficult problems and go back to them later. You may use a calculator on this test. For this test, you should assume that figures are NOT necessarily drawn to scale, that all geometric figures lie in a plane, and that the word *line* is used to indicate a straight line.

1. In triangle *ABC* below, the measure of angle *B* is 70 degrees, and the measure of angle *A* is half the measure of angle *B*. What is the measure of angle *C*?

DO YOUR FIGURING HERE.

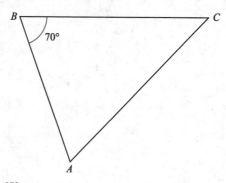

    A. 65°
    B. 70°
    C. 75°
    D. 80°
    E. 85°

2. Twenty-one students agreed to contribute an equal amount of money to buy a gift for their teacher. If a total of $70.40 had been collected after 16 students paid their shares, what was the total price of the gift?
    F. $54.40
    G. $92.40
    H. $188.00
    J. $1,126.40
    K. $1,478.40

3. The minimum fine for driving in excess of the speed limit is $25. An additional $6 is added to the minimum fine for each mile per hour (mph) in excess of the speed limit. Omar was issued a $103 fine for speeding in a 55-mph speed limit zone. For driving at what speed, in mph, was Omar fined?
    A. 13
    B. 52
    C. 62
    D. 68
    E. 72

GO ON TO THE NEXT PAGE.

DO YOUR FIGURING HERE.

4. In a circuit, $E = IR$, where E = number of volts, I = number of amperes, and R = number of ohms. How much resistance, in ohms, does a circuit possess if the number of volts is 24 and the current is 8 amperes?
   F. 2
   G. 3
   H. 4
   J. 24
   K. 32

5. In the figure below, line s is parallel to line t, and line p is a transversal crossing both lines s and t. Which of the following lists 3 angles that are equal in measure?

   A. angle a, angle b, angle c
   B. angle a, angle c, angle d
   C. angle a, angle c, angle f
   D. angle a, angle d, angle e
   E. angle b, angle d, angle e

6. What value of a makes $\frac{2}{3}a + 5 = 11$ true?
   F. 4
   G. $5\frac{1}{3}$
   H. 9
   J. $10\frac{2}{3}$
   K. 24

7. $\frac{35.65}{0.05} = ?$
   A. 0.713
   B. 7.13
   C. 71.30
   D. 713.0
   E. 7,130.0

8. What is the slope of the line that is perpendicular to the line given by the equation $3y + 6x = -5$?
   F. -2
   G. $\frac{-5}{3}$
   H. $\frac{-1}{2}$
   J. $\frac{1}{2}$
   K. 3

9. If $x = -4$, then $24 + 3 - x^2 = ?$
   A. 11
   B. 25
   C. 29
   D. 31
   E. 43

GO ON TO THE NEXT PAGE.

10. A pair of shoes that originally costs $75.00 is on sale at 40% off. If the sales tax on the shoes is 7% of the purchase price, how much would it cost to buy the pair of shoes at the sale price?

F. $33.15
G. $40.00
H. $42.90
J. $45.00
K. $48.15

DO YOUR FIGURING HERE.

11. Which of the following graphs represents $x > 7$?

A.

B.
5 6 7 8 9 10 11 12

C.
5 6 7 8 9 10 11 12

D.
5 6 7 8 9 10 11 12

E.
5 6 7 8 9 10 11 12

12. If the ratio of $2p$ to $11r$ is 1 to 6, what is the ratio of $6p$ to $11r$?

F. 1 to 18
G. 3 to 6
H. 3 to 33
J. 1 to 6
K. 3 to 22

13. Which of the following equations could be used to determine the value of x?

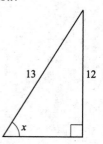

A. $13 \sin x = 5$
B. $12 \tan x = 5$
C. $12 \cos x = 13$
D. $5 \tan x = 12$
E. $\frac{\cos x}{5} = 12$

14. A rectangular soccer field has an area of 4,500 square meters. The length of the field is 10 meters more than twice the width. Which of the following equations could be used to find the width w, in feet, of the soccer field?

F. $w^2 = 4{,}500 - 10w$
G. $2(w + 10) + w = 4{,}500$
H. $w + 10(2w) = 4{,}500$
J. $w(2w + 10) = 4{,}500$
K. $w(w^2 + 10) = 4{,}500$

GO ON TO THE NEXT PAGE.

DO YOUR FIGURING HERE.

15. While riding his bike at a rate of 14 miles per hour (mph), Alan takes 1.20 hours to ride the entire length of a trail. How many hours would it take him to complete the same ride if he rode at 8 mph?

  A. 1.40
  B. 1.75
  C. 2.10
  D. 2.55
  E. 9.60

16. Last year on his vegetable farm, Phil planted carrots in a square-shaped plot, with sides measuring 18 feet. This year, he changed this plot into a rectangular design with the same area as the original square section. If the new width of this section is 12 feet, what is its length, in feet?

  F. 18
  G. 21
  H. 27
  J. 30
  K. 36

17. An apartment complex has 30 apartments that each rent for $320 per month. If 70% of the apartments are rented for 6 months, how much rent will be charged in total for those apartments for the 6 months?

  A. $6,720
  B. $9,600
  C. $22,450
  D. $40,320
  E. $57,600

18. In the figure below, W, X, and Z are collinear. If the measure of angle Y is 87° and the measure of angle YXW is 128°, what is the measure of angle Z?

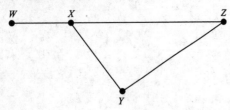

  F. 35°
  G. 41°
  H. 52°
  J. 78°
  K. 139°

19. What is the value of x in the solution for the system of equations below?

$$-2x + 3y = 30$$

$$4x - \frac{1}{4}y = -14$$

  A. −27
  B. −16
  C. −9
  D. −4
  E. −3

DO YOUR FIGURING HERE.

20. What is the product of the complex numbers $(-2i + 5)$ and $(2i + 5)$?

   F. 3
   G. 21
   H. 29
   J. $20i - 21$
   K. $20i + 21$

21. For all x, $-5x(x - 2) - (4x - 7x^2) + (-3x) = ?$

   A. $-12x^2 - 11x$
   B. $-12x^2 + 9x$
   C. $2x^2 + 3x$
   D. $2x^2 + 9x$
   E. $12x^2 + 11x$

22. 4^{-3} is equivalent to:

   F. 64
   G. 12
   H. $\dfrac{1}{64}$
   J. -4
   K. -64

23. If $x = \dfrac{5}{2}$ is one solution of the equation $2x^2 + kx - 20 = 0$, what is the value of k?

   A. -5
   B. -3
   C. 2
   D. 3
   E. 8

24. In triangle QRS shown below, $\overline{RT}$ bisects angle QRS. The measure of angle QRS is 118°, and angle Q measures 44°. What is the measure of angle RTS?

   F. 77°
   G. 90°
   H. 103°
   J. 109°
   K. 118°

GO ON TO THE NEXT PAGE.

25. Emily wants to enclose an area of her backyard for her dogs. She has 52 feet of fencing. The width of the enclosed area can be between 9 and 12 feet. If she wants to use all of the fencing, what are the possible dimensions for the length of the enclosed area, in feet?

A. Between 13 and 15
B. Between 14 and 17
C. Between 28 and 34
D. Between 40 and 43
E. All of the fencing cannot be used.

26. Let x and y represent real numbers with the property $|x - y - 1| > 0$. Which of the following statements about x and y CANNOT be true?

F. $x - y < 1$
G. $x - y = 1$
H. $x < 1$ and $y > 0$
J. $x < 1$ and $y = 1$
K. $x < 0$ and $y > 0$

27. In the figure below, angle K is a right angle, $\overline{JL}$ is 17 inches long, and $\overline{KL}$ is 8 inches long. If the measure of angle J is s, then $\tan s = ?$

A. $\dfrac{17}{8}$

B. $\dfrac{17}{15}$

C. $\dfrac{15}{17}$

D. $\dfrac{8}{15}$

E. $\dfrac{8}{17}$

28. For what value of r does the quadratic equation $x^2 - 2x + r = 0$ have solutions of $x = 4$ and $x = -2$?

F. -8
G. -2
H. 2
J. 6
K. 8

29. Given that the function f defined as $f(x) = 3 - 5x$ has domain $\{-2, 0, 1\}$, what is the range of f?

A. $\{1, 3, 5\}$
B. $\{1, 2, 10\}$
C. $\{1, 5, 8\}$
D. $\{-2, 5, 7\}$
E. $\{-2, 3, 13\}$

DO YOUR FIGURING HERE.

GO ON TO THE NEXT PAGE.

30. In the figure below, $\overline{KO}$ is parallel to $\overline{LN}$, points J, K, L, and M are collinear; and $\overline{KN}$ is the same length as $\overline{LN}$. If the measure of angle LNK is 40°, what is the measure of angle JKO?

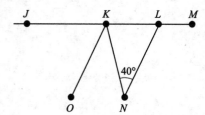

DO YOUR FIGURING HERE.

   F. 100°
   G. 70°
   H. 55°
   J. 40°
   K. 25°

31. If $2a^2 - 5 \le 67$, what is the smallest real value a can have?
   A. 36
   B. 12
   C. −6
   D. −12
   E. There is no smallest value for a.

32. The length of one side of a square is 11 units. What is the length, in units, of the diagonal of the square?
   F. $22\sqrt{2}$
   G. $\sqrt{22}$
   H. $11\sqrt{3}$
   J. $11\sqrt{2}$
   K. 11

33. What is the radius of a circle in the standard (x, y) coordinate plane with an equation of $(x + 9)^2 + (y + 7)^2 = 64$?
   A. 64
   B. 32
   C. 16
   D. 12
   E. 8

34. Duke's Dog Grooming asked each of 20 customers to give a rating of its service. The table below summarizes the 20 customer ratings.

Rating	Number of Customers
3	6
2	8
1	2
0	4

Which of the following values is closest to the mean of the 20 customer ratings?
   F. 3.3
   G. 2.7
   H. 2.3
   J. 2.0
   K. 1.8

GO ON TO THE NEXT PAGE.

35. In a local basketball league, teams must have at least six players, but no more than ten. There are 25 teams in the league, and the number of persons on each team varies as shown in the chart below. What is the average number of persons per team, to the nearest whole number, for these 25 teams?

Number of players on the team	6	7	6	9	10
Number of teams	3	6	4	9	3

A. 5
B. 6
C. 7
D. 8
E. 9

DO YOUR FIGURING HERE.

36. In the figure below, the circle centered at K is contained within the square $ABCD$. The length of $\overline{KL}$ is 7 inches. If the circle is cut out of the square, how much of the area, in square inches, of the square, will remain?

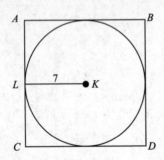

F. $196 - 49\pi$
G. $196 - 14\pi$
H. 14π
J. 49π
K. $196 + 14\pi$

37. What is the equation of the line that has the same slope as the line $2x - 8y = 13$ but the same y intercept as the line $y + 5 = -3x$?

A. $y = -3x - \dfrac{13}{8}$

B. $y = -\dfrac{1}{4}x + 5$

C. $y = \dfrac{1}{4}x - 5$

D. $y = 2x + \dfrac{13}{8}$

E. $y = 3x - 5$

GO ON TO THE NEXT PAGE.

38. Which of the following represents the solution set of the inequality $4x + 2 \geq 7x + 11$?

DO YOUR FIGURING HERE.

F. ⟵─┼─┼─●─┼─┼─┼─┼─┼─┼─┼─┼─┼─┼─┼─┼─┼⟶
   −8 −7 −6 −5 −4 −3 −2 −1 0 1 2 3 4 5 6 7 8

G. ⟵─┼─┼─┼─┼─┼─┼─┼─┼─┼─┼─┼─┼─┼─●─┼─┼⟶
   −8 −7 −6 −5 −4 −3 −2 −1 0 1 2 3 4 5 6 7 8

H. ⟵─┼─┼─┼─┼─●─┼─┼─┼─┼─┼─┼─┼─┼─┼─┼─┼⟶
   −8 −7 −6 −5 −4 −3 −2 −1 0 1 2 3 4 5 6 7 8

J. ⟵─┼─┼─┼─┼─┼─┼─┼─┼─┼─┼─●─┼─┼─┼─┼─┼⟶
   −8 −7 −6 −5 −4 −3 −2 −1 0 1 2 3 4 5 6 7 8

K. ⟵─┼─┼─┼─┼─●─┼─┼─┼─┼─┼─┼─┼─┼─┼─┼─┼⟶
   −8 −7 −6 −5 −4 −3 −2 −1 0 1 2 3 4 5 6 7 8

39. What is the value of s if the line in the standard (x, y) coordinate plane that passes through the points $(3s, 16)$ and $(2s, 6)$ has slope $-\frac{5}{2}$?
A. −11
B. −4
C. 0
D. 4
E. 11

40. The formula for calculating simple interest is $I = Prt$, where I is the number of dollars of interest paid, P is the initial amount borrowed (principal), r is the fixed annual interest rate, and t is the time, in years, of the loan. To buy a computer, Trey took out a loan that was repaid over two years at an annual interest rate of 11%. If Trey paid $308 total in interest, how much did he originally borrow?
F. $3,388
G. $2,250
H. $1,400
J. $1,025
K. $616

41. Three vertices of a rectangle in the standard (x, y) coordinate plane have coordinates $(−5, 2)$, $(6, 2)$, and $(6, −1)$. What are the coordinates of the fourth vertex?
A. $(−6, −1)$
B. $(−2, −6)$
C. $(−5, −1)$
D. $(2, −1)$
E. $(2, 0)$

42. If $\sqrt{4x} − 2 = 6$, then $x = ?$
F. 4
G. 8
H. 16
J. 24
K. 32

GO ON TO THE NEXT PAGE.

DO YOUR FIGURING HERE.

43. Eugenia used a calculator to find her monthly expenses. When trying to multiply a number Z by 4, she accidentally multiplied it by 7, and her result was 39 more than the correct value. Which of the following equations would correctly determine Z?

A. $7Z - 39 = 4Z$

B. $7Z + 4Z = 39$

C. $7Z = 4Z - 39$

D. $\dfrac{7 - 39}{Z} = \dfrac{4}{Z}$

E. $\dfrac{7}{Z} + 39 = \dfrac{4}{Z}$

44. What is the sum of all the values of x that satisfy the equation $3x^2 - 15x - 42 = 0$?

F. 9

G. 5

H. 2

J. –5

K. –9

45. If the first term in an arithmetic series is 5, the last term is 159, and the sum is 1,230, what are the 2nd, 3rd, and 4th terms?

A. 10, 15, 20

B. 16, 27, 38

C. 20, 35, 50

D. $43\dfrac{1}{2}$, 82, 159

E. 126, 137, 148

46. Student tickets for a volleyball game cost $3 each, and nonstudent tickets cost $5 each. A total of $360 worth of tickets were sold. If S represents the number of student tickets sold, which of the following is a general formula for the total number of dollars collected from the sale of nonstudent tickets?

F. $3S + 360$

G. $5S + 360$

H. $8S - 360$

J. $15S$

K. $360 - 3S$

47. Which of the following represents the values of x that are solutions for the inequality $(x + 7)(8 - 2x) \geq 0$?

A. $x \leq -7$ or $x \geq 4$

B. $x \leq -4$ or $x \geq 7$

C. $\dfrac{1}{7} \leq x \leq \dfrac{1}{4}$

D. $-4 \leq x \leq 7$

E. $-7 \leq x \leq 4$

GO ON TO THE NEXT PAGE.

48. In the figure below, angle Y is a right angle, and the measure of angle X is 45°. What is the ratio of the length of $\overline{YZ}$ to the length of $\overline{XZ}$?

 DO YOUR FIGURING HERE.

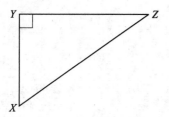

F. $\dfrac{1}{\sqrt{3}}$

G. $\dfrac{1}{\sqrt{2}}$

H. $\dfrac{\sqrt{2}}{\sqrt{3}}$

J. $\dfrac{\sqrt{2}}{1}$

K. $\dfrac{\sqrt{3}}{1}$

49. If $\tan\theta = \dfrac{6}{-8}$ and $0° \le \theta \le 180°$, then $\cos\theta = ?$

A. $\dfrac{10}{8}$

B. $\dfrac{6}{10}$

C. $\dfrac{-8}{10}$

D. $\dfrac{-10}{8}$

E. $\dfrac{-10}{6}$

50. At George Washington High School, 65% of this year's senior class members have taken at least 6 science courses. Of the remaining class members, 40% have taken 4 or 5 science courses. Assuming no seniors took more than 6 science courses, what percent of the senior class members have taken fewer than 4 science courses?

F. 0%

G. 8%

H. 14%

J. 21%

K. 35%

GO ON TO THE NEXT PAGE.

51. In the figure below, rectangle *WXYZ* has sides with length of 12 units and width of 4 units. Also, *F* and *G* are the midpoints of $\overline{WX}$ and $\overline{YZ}$, respectively. What is the perimeter, in units, of quadrilateral *WFYG*?

A. $8 + 6\sqrt{15}$
B. $12 + 4\sqrt{13}$
C. $12 + 4\sqrt{15}$
D. $16\sqrt{13}$
E. 40

52. A line in the standard (*x*, *y*) coordinate plane has slope $\frac{3}{2}$ and goes through the point (−3, −2). If the point with coordinates (*a*, 7) is on the line, then *a* = ?
F. −9
G. −3
H. 3
J. 5
K. 9

53. The list of numbers 42, 37, 30, *A*, *B*, and 15 has a median of 25. The mode of the list of numbers is 15. To the nearest whole number, what is the mean of the list?
A. 15
B. 20
C. 27
D. 28
E. 30

54. Which of the following inequalities characterizes the values of *a* for which the inequality $5a - 13 \geq -3a + 19$ is true?
F. $a \leq 4$
G. $a \leq 16$
H. $a \geq -4$
J. $a \geq 4$
K. $a \geq 16$

DO YOUR FIGURING HERE.

DO YOUR FIGURING HERE.

55. In the figure below, the lengths of $\overline{KL}$, $\overline{JL}$, and $\overline{LM}$ are given, in inches. What is the area, in square inches, of triangle *JML*?

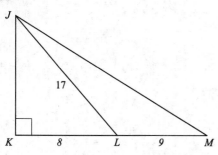

A. 28.6
B. 35
C. 67.5
D. 127.5
E. 135

56. Which of the following intervals contains the solution to the equation $-x + 7 = \dfrac{2x - 19}{3}$?

F. $6 < x \le 7$
G. $7 < x \le 8$
H. $11 < x \le 12$
J. $16 < x \le 17$
K. $20 < x \le 21$

57. In the figure below, *Q* and *R* lie on the circle centered at *O*, $\overline{OQ}$ is 12 units long, and the measure of angle *QOR* is 120°. How many units long is minor arc *QR*?

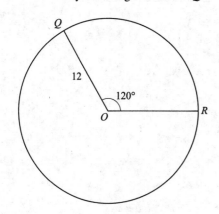

A. 2π
B. 4π
C. 8π
D. 16π
E. 24π

GO ON TO THE NEXT PAGE.

58. Given the graph in the standard (x, y) coordinate plane below, which of the following statements is true about the slopes m_1 and m_2 of line 1 and line 2, respectively?

DO YOUR FIGURING HERE.

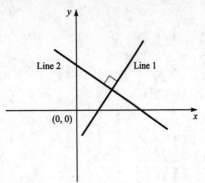

F. $m_1 = \dfrac{-1}{m_2}$

G. $m_1 = -m_2$

H. $m_1 = \dfrac{1}{2m_2}$

J. $m_1 = m_2$

K. $m_1 = 2m_2$

59. The ratio of x to y is 6 to 1, and the ratio of y to z is 12 to 1. What is the value of $\dfrac{2x+3y}{4y+3z}$?

A. $\dfrac{5}{17}$

B. $\dfrac{60}{17}$

C. 4

D. $\dfrac{48}{7}$

E. 24

60. Point $M(3, -7)$ is in the standard (x, y) coordinate plane. What must be the coordinates of point N so that the line $y = -3$ is the perpendicular bisector of $\overline{MN}$?

F. $(1, -7)$

G. $(3, -9)$

H. $(3, -5)$

J. $(3, -3)$

K. $(3, 1)$

END OF THE MATHEMATICS TEST.
STOP! IF YOU HAVE TIME LEFT OVER, CHECK YOUR WORK ON THIS SECTION ONLY.

ANSWER KEY

Mathematics Test

1. C	16. H	31. C	46. K
2. G	17. D	32. J	47. E
3. D	18. G	33. E	48. G
4. G	19. E	34. K	49. C
5. D	20. H	35. D	50. J
6. H	21. C	36. F	51. B
7. D	22. H	37. C	52. H
8. J	23. D	38. K	53. C
9. A	24. H	39. B	54. J
10. K	25. B	40. H	55. C
11. A	26. G	41. C	56. G
12. G	27. D	42. H	57. C
13. D	28. F	43. A	58. F
14. J	29. E	44. G	59. B
15. C	30. G	45. B	60. K

SCORING WORKSHEET

Scale Score	Raw Score Mathematics	Scale Score	Raw Score Mathematics
36	60	18	24–26
35	59	17	20–23
34	57–58	16	16–19
33	56	15	12–15
32	55	14	10–11
31	54	13	8–9
30	53	12	6–7
29	52	11	5
28	51–50	10	4
27	48–49	9	—
26	46–47	8	3
25	44–45	7	—
24	41–43	6	2
23	38–40	5	—
22	35–37	4	1
21	31–34	3	—
20	28–30	2	—
19	27	1	0

NOTE: Each actual ACT is scaled slightly differently based on a large amount of information gathered from the millions of tests ACT, Inc., scores each year. This scale will give you a fairly good idea of where you are in your preparation process. However, it should not be read as an absolute predictor of your actual ACT score. In fact, on practice tests, the scores are much less important than what you learn from analyzing your results.

ANSWERS AND EXPLANATIONS

1. **The correct answer is C.** You are given that angle B measures $70°$ and that the measure of angle A is half that of angle B. Therefore, angle A must measure $35° \left(\frac{70}{2} \right)$. Since the three angles of a triangle add up to $180°$, angle C must equal $180° - 70° - 35°$, or $75°$.

2. **The correct answer is G.** The problem states that the students *agreed to contribute an equal amount of money* for the gift. If $70.40 was collected from 16 students, then each of them contributed $4.40 $\left(\frac{\$70.40}{16} = \$4.40 \right)$.

   Since 21 students are involved, the total bill for the gift is $4.40 × 21 = $92.40. You could have safely eliminated answer choices J and K because they are too large; you know that about $\frac{2}{3}$ of the students have paid their share, and the total collection is only $70.40. Also, answer choice F cannot be correct because it is less than $70.40.

3. **The correct answer is D.** Omar paid a total of $103 for his speeding ticket. You are given that the basic fine for speeding is $25, so he was charged an additional $78 ($103 − $25). If the charge for each mile per hour over the speed limit is $6, then Omar was driving 13 mph $\left(\frac{\$78}{\$6} = 13 \right)$ over the 55-mph speed limit, or 68 mph.

4. **The correct answer is G.** To solve this problem, substitute the given values into the equation. You are given that the number of volts is 24 and that the current is 8 amperes. Substitute these values into the equation, as follows:

   $$E = IR$$
   $$24 = 8R$$
   $$R = 3$$

   Therefore, the circuit possesses a resistance of 3 ohms.

5. **The correct answer is D.** When parallel lines are cut by a transversal, the angles created have special relationships. For instance, opposite angles are congruent (have the same measure), which means that angles a and d are equal, and angles e and h are also equal. Also, same-side interior angles are equal, which means that angles a and e are equal. Only answer choice D includes angles that have the same measure.

6. **The correct answer is H.** To answer this question, simply solve for a:

   $$\frac{2}{3}a + 5 = 11$$

$$\frac{2}{3}a = 6$$
$$a = 6 \left(\frac{3}{2} \right)$$
$$a = \frac{18}{2} = 9$$

7. **The correct answer is D.** To solve this problem, you can use simple division; carefully enter the numbers in your calculator:

   $$35.65 \div 0.05 = 713.0$$

   You could also use long division to solve this problem.

8. **The correct answer is J.** To solve this problem, first convert the given equation to slope-intercept form ($y = mx + b$, where m is the slope of the line):

   $$3y + 6x = -5$$
   $$3y = -6x - 5$$
   $$y = -2x - \frac{5}{3}$$

   The slope of this line is -2. Since perpendicular slopes are negative reciprocals, the correct answer is $\frac{1}{2}$.

9. **The correct answer is A.** The problem states that $x = -4$, so to solve, substitute -4 wherever there is an instance of x (carefully track the negative signs!):

   $$24 + 3 - x^2$$
   $$= 24 + 3 - (-4)^2$$
   $$= 24 + 3 - (16) = 11$$

10. **The correct answer is K.** As stated in the problem, the shoes are 40% off. Therefore, they are selling for 60% of their original cost ($75.00 × 0.6 = $45.00). The sales tax is 7%, so the total sales tax is $3.15 ($45 × 0.07). In all, the pair of shoes will cost $45.00 + $3.15 = $48.15.

11. **The correct answer is A.** The graph of $x > 7$ is represented by an open point at 7 and a line going to the right of 7. The only choice that correctly shows this is A.

12. **The correct answer is G.** You are given that the ratio of $2p$ to $11r$ is 1 to 6, and you know that $6p$ is equivalent to $3 × 2p$. Therefore, the ratio of $6p$ to $11r$ is 3 to 6.

13. **The correct answer is D.** To solve this problem, first find the missing value of the leg of the triangle that is adjacent to x. Use the Pythagorean Theorem:

    $$a^2 + 12^2 = 13^2$$
    $$a^2 + 144 = 169$$
    $$a^2 = 25$$

$a = \sqrt{25}$
$a = 5$

For x, $\sin = \frac{12}{13}$, $\cos = \frac{5}{13}$, and $\tan = \frac{12}{5}$. Test the answer choices to see which one correctly represents its respective trigonometric function:

Answer choice A: $13 \sin x = 5$; $\sin x = \frac{5}{13}$. Eliminate answer choice A.

Answer choice B: $12 \tan x = 5$; $\tan x = \frac{5}{12}$. Eliminate answer choice B.

Answer choice C: $12 \cos x = 13$; $\cos x = \frac{13}{12}$. Eliminate answer choice C.

Answer choice D: $5 \tan x = 12$; $\tan x = \frac{12}{5}$. This is the correct answer.

Answer choice D is the only answer that correctly represents one of the trigonometric functions for x.

14. **The correct answer is J.** The area of a rectangle is given by length × width. You are given that the area is 4,500 square meters and that the length is 10 meters more than twice the width. The length can be expressed as $2w + 10$. To solve for w, use the area formula:

$l \times w = A$
$(2w + 10) \times w = 4,500$

Find the common factors:

$w(2w + 10) = 4,500$

15. **The correct answer is C.** To solve this problem, use the distance formula (Distance = Rate × Time) to first determine the length of the trail. If Alan traveled at 14 mph for 1.2 hours, then the trail must be $14 \times 1.2 = 16.8$ miles long. Use the same formula to find out how long it would take Alan to complete the same ride at 8 mph:

$16.8 = 8t$
$t = 2.1$

It would take Alan 2.1 hours to complete the trail at a speed of 8 mph.

16. **The correct answer is H.** To solve this problem, you first need to calculate the area of the original plot. If it was a square shape with sides lengths measuring 18 feet, then the area is $18 \times 18 = 324$ square feet. The plot is changed to a rectangular shape, but it still has the same area. You can solve the problem by using the formula for the area of a rectangle (Area = Length × Width), since you already know the area and the width:

$324 = l \times 12$
$l = 27$

17. **The correct answer is D.** To solve this problem, first determine how many apartments are being rented. If 70% of the 30 apartments are being rented, then there are 21 (30×0.7) apartments being rented. If the rent is $320 a month and each apartment is rented for 6 months, then the total amount of rent charged will be $21 \times 320 \times 6 = \$40,320$. Watch out for answer choice A, which is a partial answer, representing the amount of rent collected for the apartments in 1 month.

18. **The correct answer is G.** In this problem, you are given that the measure of angle YXW is 128°. Since this angle forms a line with angle X, the two must add up to 180°. Therefore, angle X must equal $180 - 128 = 52°$. Likewise, the three angles of a triangle must add up to 180°. You know that angle Y is 87° and angle X is 52°, so angle Z must equal $180 - 87 - 52 = 41°$.

19. **The correct answer is E.** To solve this problem, you first need to eliminate one of the variables. In this problem, it makes the most sense to eliminate x. This can be done by multiplying the first equation by 2:

$2(-2x + 3y) = 2(30)$
$= -4x + 6y = 60$

Now add the two equations:

$$-4x + 6y = 60$$
$$+4x - \frac{1}{4}y = -14$$
$$\overline{5\frac{3}{4}y = 46}$$

Finally, solve for y ($5\frac{3}{4}$ is equivalent to 5.75):

$5.75y = 46$
$y = 8$

Now that you know the value of y, you can solve one of the equations to find x (solve the most simple equation):

$-2x + 3(8) = 30$
$-2x + 24 = 30$
$-2x = 6$
$x = -3$

20. **The correct answer is H.** To answer this question, multiply the two quantities using the FOIL method (remember that i^2 is equal to -1):

$(-2i + 5)(2i + 5) =$
$-4i^2 - 10i + 10i + 25 =$
$-4i^2 + 25 =$
$-4(-1) + 25 = 4 + 25 = 29$

21. **The correct answer is C.** To solve this problem, first perform the multiplication in the first part of the problem (carefully track the negative signs):

$$-5x(x-2) = -5x^2 + 10x$$

Now, write out the entire equation and perform the addition and subtraction (again, track the negative signs):

$$-5x^2 + 10x - 4x + 7x^2 - 3x$$

Group like terms together:

$$= (-5x^2 + 7x^2) + (10x - 4x - 3x)$$
$$= 2x^2 + 3x$$

22. **The correct answer is H.** A general rule of exponents says that $x^{-n} = \dfrac{1}{x^n}$. Following this rule, 4^{-3} would be $\dfrac{1}{4^3} = \dfrac{1}{64}$.

23. **The correct answer is D.** You are given that $x = \dfrac{5}{2}$ is one of the solutions to the equation, so backtrack to find the factor:

$$x = \frac{5}{2}$$
$$2x = 5$$
$$2x - 5 = 0$$

This solution must be multiplied by $x + 4$, as that is the only term that would result in the equation $2x^2 + kx - 20 = 0$. To solve for k, simply use the *FOIL* method for the two binomials:

$$(2x - 5)(x + 4) = 0$$
$$2x^2 + 8x - 5x - 20 = 0$$
$$2x^2 + 3x - 20 = 0$$

Therefore, k is equal to 3.

24. **The correct answer is H.** The three angles of a triangle always add up to $180°$. Since you are given the measures of angles Q ($44°$) and R ($118°$), the measure of angle S must be $180 - 44 - 118 = 18°$. You are given that $\overline{RT}$ bisects angle QRS, so in each of the two smaller triangles, angle R equals $59°$. You now have two of the angles in triangle RTS, so the measure of angle RTS must be $180 - 18 - 59 = 103°$.

25. **The correct answer is B.** You are given that Emily has and wants to use all 52 feet of fencing and that the width of the enclosure is going to be between 9 and 12 feet. You can use the formula for perimeter to find the possible dimensions for the length:

$$2W + 2L = \text{Perimeter}$$
$$2(9) + 2L = 52, \text{ or } 2(12) + 2L = 52$$
$$18 + 2L = 52, \text{ or } 24 + 2L = 52$$

$$2L = 34, \text{ or } 2L = 28$$
$$L = 17, \text{ or } L = 14$$

The length of the dog enclosure must be between 14 and 17 feet.

26. **The correct answer is G.** One way to solve this problem is to apply some logic based on the information in the question. You're given that $|x - y - 1| > 0$, so the quantity $x - y$ must be any value other than 1. If the quantity $x - y = 1$, then the given statement cannot be true: $|1 - 1|$ is NOT greater than 0.

27. **The correct answer is D.** To solve this problem, find the missing side length by using the Pythagorean Theorem:

$$a^2 + b^2 = c^2$$
$$8^2 + b^2 = 17^2$$
$$64 + b^2 = 289$$
$$b^2 = 225$$
$$b = \sqrt{225}$$
$$b = 15$$

The tangent of an angle is the ratio of the side opposite the angle to the adjacent side (opposite/adjacent). Therefore, $\tan s = \dfrac{8}{15}$.

28. **The correct answer is F.** If the quadratic equation has solutions of 4 and -2, then its factors must be $(x - 4)(x + 2)$. Apply the FOIL method to get $x^2 - 2x - 8$, which means that $r = -8$.

29. **The correct answer is E.** Remember that domain refers to the x-values and range refers to the $f(x)$ values. Simply plug the given x-values into the function and solve:

$$f(x) = 3 - 5x$$
$$f(-2) = 3 - 5(-2) = 3 + 10 = 13$$

Now, check the answer choices. Because only answer choice E includes 13, it must be the correct answer.

30. **The correct answer is G.** Since $\overline{KO}$ is parallel to $\overline{LN}$ angle JKO is equal to angle KLN. Also, because $\overline{KN}$ is the same length as $\overline{LN}$ triangle KNL is isosceles. The two missing angles must be the same and must add up to $140°$ ($180° - 40°$). Therefore, the angles must each equal $70°$ ($70° + 70° + 40° = 180°$). Because angle KLN measures $70°$, angle JKO must have the same measurement.

31. **The correct answer is C.** To solve this problem, first reduce the inequality:

$$2a^2 - 5 \leq 67$$

$$2a^2 \leq 72$$
$$a^2 \leq 36$$
$$a \leq 6$$

Eliminate answer choices A and B because you know that a must be either equal to or less than 6. Now, work through the remaining answer choices, substituting the values for a in the inequality. Answer choice C:

$$2(-6)^2 - 5 \leq 67$$
$$2(36) - 5 \leq 67$$
$$72 - 5 \leq 67$$
$$67 \leq 67$$

Any number less than −6 will yield an answer greater than 67, which would make the inequality untrue.

32. **The correct answer is J.** To solve this problem, it is helpful to draw a picture of the square to give yourself a visual representation of what you are trying to find.

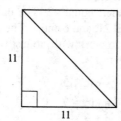

Since all of the angles in a square measure 90°, the diagonal splits the square into two triangles with angles measuring 45°, 45°, and 90°, as seen in the picture. For a 45°–45°–90° triangle, the sides measure 1, 1, and $\sqrt{2}$, respectively. You already know that the length of each of the sides of the square is 11, so the length of the diagonal must be $11\sqrt{2}$.

33. **The correct answer is E.** The standard equation for a circle with center (h, k) and radius r is $(x - h)^2 + (y - k)^2 = r^2$. In the equation given in this problem, $r^2 = 64$, so the radius must be $\sqrt{64} = 8$.

34. **The correct answer is K.** To answer this question, remember that the mean is the average. Calculate the average rating by finding the total value of the ratings and divide it by the total number of customers:

$$6 \times 3 = 18$$
$$8 \times 2 = 16$$
$$2 \times 1 = 2$$
$$4 \times 0 = 0$$

The total value of the ratings is $18 + 16 + 2 + 0 = 36$, and $36 \div 20 = 1.8$, answer choice K.

35. **The correct answer is D.** To solve this problem, you first need to determine how many players there are in the league. Multiply each of the "number of players on the team" by its respective "number of teams":

$$6 \times 3 = 18$$
$$7 \times 6 = 42$$
$$6 \times 4 = 24$$
$$9 \times 9 = 81$$
$$10 \times 3 = 30$$

Now, add all of these numbers together:

$$18 + 42 + 24 + 81 + 30 = 195$$

There are 195 players in the league. Since you are given that there are 25 teams in the league, the average number of players per team is $195 \div 25 = 7.8$. The question asks you to round to the nearest whole number, so the correct answer is 8.

36. **The correct answer is F.** The circle is centered at K, so line segment KL is the radius of the circle. The area of a circle is given by the formula $A = \pi r^2$. For this circle, the area would be $\pi(7^2) = 49\pi$. Since the radius of the circle is 7, the diameter is 14, which is also the measure of the sides of the square. The area of the square is $14 \times 14 = 196$. Therefore, if the circle was cut out of the square, the remaining area would be $196 - 49\pi$.

37. **The correct answer is C.** To solve this problem, first find the slope of the first line by changing the equation to slope-intercept form ($y = mx + b$):

$$2x - 8y = 13$$
$$-8y = -2x + 13$$
$$y = \frac{1}{4}x - \frac{13}{8}$$

The slope of this line is $\frac{1}{4}$. Eliminate answer choices A, B, D, and E. The correct answer must be C. If you have time, you can confirm this by finding the y intercept of the second line:

$$y + 5 = -3x$$
$$y = -3x - 5$$

The y intercept of this equation is −5.
A line with the same slope as the first line and the same y intercept as the second line would have the equation $y = \frac{1}{4}x - 5$.

38. **The correct answer is K.** To solve this problem, first solve the inequality for x:

$$4x + 2 \geq 7x + 11$$
$$-9 \geq 3x$$
$$-3 \geq x$$

The inequality means "x is less than or equal to -3." This is represented by a closed point at -3 and a line going to the left. The only answer choice that shows this is K.

39. The correct answer is B. In this problem, you are given two points on a line and the slope of the line. To solve for s, use the equation $(y_2 - y_1) = m(x_2 - x_1)$, where m is the slope of the line, and (x_1, y_1) and (x_2, y_2) are the given points on the line:

$$6 - 16 = -\frac{5}{2}(2s - 3s)$$
$$-10 = -\frac{5}{2}(-s)$$
$$-10 = \frac{5}{2}s$$
$$-20 = 5s$$
$$-4 = s$$

40. The correct answer is H. In this problem, you are given the time over which the loan is to be paid back (t), the interest rate (r), and the total amount of interest paid (I). You are asked to find the amount borrowed (P). To solve, substitute the given values into the formula for calculating interest:

$$I = Prt$$
$$308 = P(0.11)(2)$$
$$308 = 0.22P$$
$$P = 1,400$$

Trey took out a $1,400 loan.

41. The correct answer is C. To solve this problem, draw the (x, y) coordinate plane and plot the three given points, as shown below:

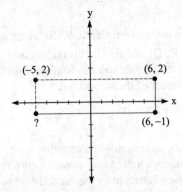

You can see that the missing point must be in Quadrant III (both x and y coordinates are negative) in order to form a rectangle. This eliminates answer choices D and E. Because the figure is a rectangle, opposite sides are parallel, which means the x coordinate of the missing point must be -5, and the y coordinate must be -1.

42. The correct answer is H. To solve this problem, first isolate the variable in the equation:

$$\sqrt{4x} - 2 = 6$$
$$\sqrt{4x} = 8$$

Next, square both sides to get rid of the square root and then solve for x:

$$(\sqrt{4x})^2 = 8^2$$
$$4x = 64$$
$$x = 16$$

43. The correct answer is A. By pressing the "7" button instead of the "4," Eugenia's result was 39 more than the correct answer. Since the correct answer would be $4Z$, her mistake yields $4Z + 39$, which is equal to $7Z$. Therefore, the equation to determine Z can be expressed $7Z - 39 = 4Z$.

44. The correct answer is G. The first step is to determine the binomials to which the given polynomial can be reduced. Find two numbers that, when multiplied together, equal 42. The only options are 1 and 42, 2 and 21, and 6 and 7. The most logical pair (and easiest to work with) to test would be 6 and 7, as shown next:

$$(3x + 6)(x - 7) = 0$$
$$3x + 6 = 0 \text{ and } x - 7 = 0$$
$$3x = -6 \text{ and } x = 7$$
$$x = -2 \text{ and } x = 7$$

The sum of the solutions is $-2 + 7 = 5$.

45. The correct answer is B. In this problem, you are given the sum of the series (1,230) and the values of the first (5) and last (159) terms. The equation for finding the sum of the first n terms of a series is $S_n = \frac{n(a_1 + a_n)}{2}$. Here, a_1 is the first term in the series. Use this formula to determine the number of values that are in the series (159 is the nth number in the series):

$$1,230 = \frac{n(5 + 159)}{2}$$
$$2,460 = n(164)$$
$$15 = n$$

Now you know that 159 is the 15th term in the series. Since it is also the last term, there must be a total of 15 terms in the series. To find the 2nd, 3rd, and 4th terms of the series, you must first find the common difference (d). This can be found by using the formula for finding the nth term of an arithmetic series, which is $a_n = a_1 + (n - 1)d$. Use the values that you have for the first and last terms of the series to solve for d:

$$159 = 5 + (15 - 1)d$$
$$159 = 5 + 14d$$
$$154 = 14d$$
$$d = 11$$

The common difference is 11. This is the number that is added to each term to get the next term in the series. Since the first number in the series is 5, the 2nd must be 16 $(5 + 11)$, the 3rd is 27 $(16 + 11)$, and the 4th is 38 $(27 + 11)$.

46. **The correct answer is K.** You are given that a total of $360 worth of tickets was sold and that student tickets cost $3. To determine the number of dollars collected from nonstudent tickets, subtract $3S$ from the total number of dollars collected. This is expressed mathematically as $360 - 3S$.

47. **The correct answer is E.** To solve this problem, set up two different inequalities:

$$x + 7 \geq 0 \text{ and } 8 - 2x \geq 0$$
$$= x \geq -7 \text{ and } 8 \geq 2x$$
$$= x \geq -7 \text{ and } x \leq 4$$
$$= -7 \leq x \leq 4$$

48. **The correct answer is G.** You are given that angle Y is 90° and that angle X is 45°, so angle Z must be 45° as well $(90 + 45 + 45 = 180)$. For a 45°–45°–90° triangle, the sides measure 1, 1, and $\sqrt{2}$, respectively. Therefore, the ratio of $\overline{YZ}$ to $\overline{XZ}$ would be $\frac{1}{\sqrt{2}}$.

49. **The correct answer is C.** To solve this problem, begin by drawing a diagram using the (x, y) coordinate plane, as shown below:

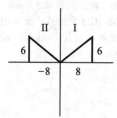

Since $0° \leq \theta° \leq 180°$, θ must be in either Quadrant I or Quadrant II. You are given that $\tan \theta = \frac{6}{-8}$, so you know that θ is in Quadrant II, because the adjacent side is negative. Using the Pythagorean Theorem, you can find the missing side of the triangle:

$$6^2 + (-8)^2 = c^2$$
$$36 + 64 = c^2$$
$$100 = c^2$$
$$c = 10$$

The cosine of an angle is given by adjacent/hypotenuse, so for θ it is $\frac{-8}{10}$.

50. **The correct answer is J.** If 65% of the senior class members have taken at least 6 science courses, then 35% have taken fewer than 6 science courses. Of these remaining students, 40% have taken 4 or 5 science courses. To find the percentage of the entire class that this represents, multiply 0.35 by 0.40, which equals 0.14. This tells you that 14% of the senior class members took 4 or 5 science courses. Therefore, the percentage of the senior class that took fewer than 4 science courses would be 21% $(35 - 14)$.

51. **The correct answer is B.** Since F and G are midpoints, they split $\overline{WX}$ and $\overline{ZY}$ each into two sections of 6 units. They also form two equal triangles (WZG and FXY). Looking at triangle WZG, you already know that $\overline{WZ}$ is 4 units (the width of the rectangle), and that $\overline{ZG}$ is 6 units. Use the Pythagorean Theorem to find the value of $\overline{WG}$:

$$4^2 + 6^2 = c^2$$
$$16 + 36 = c^2$$
$$52 = c^2$$
$$c = \sqrt{52}$$
$$c = \sqrt{4} \times \sqrt{13}$$
$$c = 2\sqrt{13}$$

Now you can find the perimeter of quadrilateral $WFYG$. $\overline{WF}$ and $\overline{GY}$ both equal 6, and $\overline{WG}$ and $\overline{FY}$ both equal $2\sqrt{13}$, so the perimeter is

$$2L + 2W$$
$$2(6) + 2(2\sqrt{13})$$
$$12 + 4\sqrt{13}$$

52. **The correct answer is H.** To solve this problem, set up an equation in the form $(y_2 - y_1) = m(x_2 - x_1)$:

$$(7 - (-2)) = \frac{3}{2}(a - (-3))$$
$$(7 + 2) = \frac{3}{2}(a + 3)$$
$$9 = \frac{3}{2}a + 4\frac{1}{2}$$
$$4\frac{1}{2} = \frac{3}{2}a$$
$$a = 3$$

53. **The correct answer is C.** To solve this problem, first put the list in numerical order:

15, 30, 37, 42

You are given that 15 is the mode, which means that 15 appears most often in the list. Therefore, at least one of the unknown values must be 15:

15, 15, 30, 37, 42

You are also given that the median, or middle value, is 25, so the other unknown value must be 20 because 25 is exactly halfway between 20 and 30:

15, 15, 20, 30, 37, 42

Now you can calculate the mean: $15 + 15 + 20 + 30 + 37 + 42 = 159$ and $159 \div 6 = 26.5$, which rounds up to 27.

54. **The correct answer is J.** Don't let the wording of this problem trip you up. It is simply asking you to solve the inequality for a:

$$5a - 13 \geq -3a + 19$$
$$8a \geq 32$$
$$a \geq 4$$

55. **The correct answer is C.** The area for a triangle is given by the formula $A = \frac{1}{2}bh$ (base × height). You are given the length of the base ($\overline{LM} = 9$), and you need to find the height. Notice that two right triangles are formed (JKL and JKM). For triangle JKL, you already have the values of two sides, so you can use the Pythagorean Theorem to find the third:

$$a^2 + b^2 = c^2$$
$$a^2 + 8^2 = 17^2$$
$$a^2 + 64 = 289$$
$$a^2 = 225$$
$$a = 15$$

Therefore, the length of $\overline{JK}$ is 15 inches. You can use this value to solve for the area of triangle JML, as it represents the height of the triangle:

$$A = \frac{1}{2}(9)(15)$$
$$A = \frac{1}{2}(135)$$
$$A = 67.5$$

56. **The correct answer is G.** This question asks you to solve the given equation. To do so, use cross-multiplication:

$$-x + 7 = \frac{2x - 19}{3}$$
$$3(-x + 7) = 2x - 19$$
$$-3x + 21 = 2x - 19$$
$$40 = 5x$$
$$8 = x$$

The only interval that includes $x = 8$ is the one given in answer choice G.

57. **The correct answer is C.** The formula for the length of an arc of a circle is given by $s = r\theta$, where s = arc length, r = radius of the circle, and θ = measure of the central angle, in radians. Also, the minor arc of a circle is the shorter of two arcs between two points on a circle. For this problem, you know that the radius is 12 units long, and the central angle is 120° $\left(\frac{2\pi}{3} \text{ in radians}\right)$. You can now set up an equation to solve:

$$s = rv$$
$$s = 12\left(\frac{2\pi}{3}\right)$$
$$s = \frac{24\pi}{3}$$
$$s = 8\pi$$

The measure of the minor arc is 8π.

58. **The correct answer is F.** The two lines depicted in the picture are perpendicular. By definition, perpendicular lines have negative reciprocal slopes. Therefore, when the slope of one line is x, the slope of a line perpendicular to that line will be $-\left(\frac{1}{x}\right)$. This relationship is represented in answer choice F.

59. **The correct answer is B.** One way to solve this problem is to recognize that ratios can be written as fractions:

x to y = 6 to 1 is the same as $\frac{x}{y} = \frac{6}{1}$, and $x = 6y$

y to z = 12 to 1 is the same as $\frac{y}{z} = \frac{12}{1}$, and $z = \frac{y}{12}$

Now you can substitute the x and z values into the given fraction (the y variable will eventually cancel out because it is in both the numerator and the denominator):

$$\frac{2x + 3y}{4y + 3z} = \frac{2(6y) + 3y}{4y + \frac{3y}{12}}$$
$$\frac{12y + 3y}{\frac{48y}{12} + \frac{3y}{12}} =$$
$$\frac{15y}{\frac{51y}{12}} =$$
$$15y\left(\frac{12}{51y}\right) = \frac{180}{51}$$

Now, check the answer choices against your answer. You will see that $\frac{180}{51}$ reduces to $\frac{60}{17}$.

60. The correct answer is K. To solve this problem, draw a picture of the (x, y) coordinate plane to give you a visual representation.

First, draw the line $y = -3$, and then plot all of the points that are given as possible answers, as shown below:

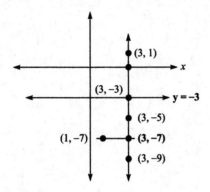

The correct answer must form a line with the point $(3, -7)$ that is perpendicular to $y = -3$. You can eliminate answer choice F, as this forms a line parallel to $y = -3$. Also, the correct answer must be as far away from $y = -3$ as $(3, -7)$ is (same point on the x axis; 4 away on the y axis). The only choice that correctly matches both criteria is the point $(3, 1)$, answer choice K.

CHAPTER 8

PRACTICE TEST 3 WITH EXPLANATIONS

ACT MATHEMATICS TEST 3
Answer Sheet

MATHEMATICS

1 Ⓐ Ⓑ Ⓒ Ⓓ Ⓔ	16 Ⓕ Ⓖ Ⓗ Ⓙ Ⓚ	31 Ⓐ Ⓑ Ⓒ Ⓓ Ⓔ	46 Ⓕ Ⓖ Ⓗ Ⓙ Ⓚ
2 Ⓕ Ⓖ Ⓗ Ⓙ Ⓚ	17 Ⓐ Ⓑ Ⓒ Ⓓ Ⓔ	32 Ⓕ Ⓖ Ⓗ Ⓙ Ⓚ	47 Ⓐ Ⓑ Ⓒ Ⓓ Ⓔ
3 Ⓐ Ⓑ Ⓒ Ⓓ Ⓔ	18 Ⓕ Ⓖ Ⓗ Ⓙ Ⓚ	33 Ⓐ Ⓑ Ⓒ Ⓓ Ⓔ	48 Ⓕ Ⓖ Ⓗ Ⓙ Ⓚ
4 Ⓕ Ⓖ Ⓗ Ⓙ Ⓚ	19 Ⓐ Ⓑ Ⓒ Ⓓ Ⓔ	34 Ⓕ Ⓖ Ⓗ Ⓙ Ⓚ	49 Ⓐ Ⓑ Ⓒ Ⓓ Ⓔ
5 Ⓐ Ⓑ Ⓒ Ⓓ Ⓔ	20 Ⓕ Ⓖ Ⓗ Ⓙ Ⓚ	35 Ⓐ Ⓑ Ⓒ Ⓓ Ⓔ	50 Ⓕ Ⓖ Ⓗ Ⓙ Ⓚ
6 Ⓕ Ⓖ Ⓗ Ⓙ Ⓚ	21 Ⓐ Ⓑ Ⓒ Ⓓ Ⓔ	36 Ⓕ Ⓖ Ⓗ Ⓙ Ⓚ	51 Ⓐ Ⓑ Ⓒ Ⓓ Ⓔ
7 Ⓐ Ⓑ Ⓒ Ⓓ Ⓔ	22 Ⓕ Ⓖ Ⓗ Ⓙ Ⓚ	37 Ⓐ Ⓑ Ⓒ Ⓓ Ⓔ	52 Ⓕ Ⓖ Ⓗ Ⓙ Ⓚ
8 Ⓕ Ⓖ Ⓗ Ⓙ Ⓚ	23 Ⓐ Ⓑ Ⓒ Ⓓ Ⓔ	38 Ⓕ Ⓖ Ⓗ Ⓙ Ⓚ	53 Ⓐ Ⓑ Ⓒ Ⓓ Ⓔ
9 Ⓐ Ⓑ Ⓒ Ⓓ Ⓔ	24 Ⓕ Ⓖ Ⓗ Ⓙ Ⓚ	39 Ⓐ Ⓑ Ⓒ Ⓓ Ⓔ	54 Ⓕ Ⓖ Ⓗ Ⓙ Ⓚ
10 Ⓕ Ⓖ Ⓗ Ⓙ Ⓚ	25 Ⓐ Ⓑ Ⓒ Ⓓ Ⓔ	40 Ⓕ Ⓖ Ⓗ Ⓙ Ⓚ	55 Ⓐ Ⓑ Ⓒ Ⓓ Ⓔ
11 Ⓐ Ⓑ Ⓒ Ⓓ Ⓔ	26 Ⓕ Ⓖ Ⓗ Ⓙ Ⓚ	41 Ⓐ Ⓑ Ⓒ Ⓓ Ⓔ	56 Ⓕ Ⓖ Ⓗ Ⓙ Ⓚ
12 Ⓕ Ⓖ Ⓗ Ⓙ Ⓚ	27 Ⓐ Ⓑ Ⓒ Ⓓ Ⓔ	42 Ⓕ Ⓖ Ⓗ Ⓙ Ⓚ	57 Ⓐ Ⓑ Ⓒ Ⓓ Ⓔ
13 Ⓐ Ⓑ Ⓒ Ⓓ Ⓔ	28 Ⓕ Ⓖ Ⓗ Ⓙ Ⓚ	43 Ⓐ Ⓑ Ⓒ Ⓓ Ⓔ	58 Ⓕ Ⓖ Ⓗ Ⓙ Ⓚ
14 Ⓕ Ⓖ Ⓗ Ⓙ Ⓚ	29 Ⓐ Ⓑ Ⓒ Ⓓ Ⓔ	44 Ⓕ Ⓖ Ⓗ Ⓙ Ⓚ	59 Ⓐ Ⓑ Ⓒ Ⓓ Ⓔ
15 Ⓐ Ⓑ Ⓒ Ⓓ Ⓔ	30 Ⓕ Ⓖ Ⓗ Ⓙ Ⓚ	45 Ⓐ Ⓑ Ⓒ Ⓓ Ⓔ	60 Ⓕ Ⓖ Ⓗ Ⓙ Ⓚ

MATHEMATICS TEST

60 Minutes—60 Questions

DIRECTIONS: Solve each of the problems in the time allowed, then fill in the corresponding bubble on your answer sheet (page 167). Do not spend too much time on any one problem; skip the more difficult problems and go back to them later. You may use a calculator on this test. For this test, you should assume that figures are NOT necessarily drawn to scale, that all geometric figures lie in a plane, and that the word *line* is used to indicate a straight line.

1. $(4x - 5)(3x + 1)$ is equivalent to:
   A. $7x - 4$
   B. $12x^2 - 5$
   C. $7x^2 + 11x - 4$
   D. $12x^2 - 11x - 5$
   E. $16x + 20$

2. The square root of a certain number is approximately 3.316. The certain number is between what 2 integers?
   F. 3 and 4
   G. 5 and 6
   H. 9 and 12
   J. 25 and 30
   K. 33 and 39

3. Adam attempted 33 field goals throughout the football season and made 26 of them. Approximately what percentage of his field goals did he make during the season?
   A. 27%
   B. 33%
   C. 66%
   D. 72%
   E. 79%

4. What (x, y) pair is the solution to the system of equations below?

   $$-2x + 4y = -18$$
   $$4x - 5y = 30$$

   F. $(5, -2)$
   G. $(3, 3)$
   H. $(0, 0)$
   J. $(-3, -3)$
   K. $(-5, 2)$

5. If the measure of each interior angle in a regular polygon is 90, how many sides does the polygon have?
   A. 8
   B. 6
   C. 5
   D. 4
   E. 3

DO YOUR FIGURING HERE.

GO ON TO THE NEXT PAGE.

DO YOUR FIGURING HERE.

6. For all positive integers x, what is the greatest common factor of the numbers $256x$ and $144x$?
   F. 12
   G. 16
   H. x
   J. $16x$
   K. $24x$

7. Kathleen and Natalie are putting new carpet in their apartment. Kathleen used $22\frac{3}{4}$ square yards of carpet in the living room, and Natalie used $12\frac{1}{2}$ square yards of carpet in the dining room. If 50 square yards of carpet was purchased, how many square yards were left after laying down new carpet in both rooms?
   A. $12\frac{3}{4}$
   B. $14\frac{1}{4}$
   C. $14\frac{1}{2}$
   D. $14\frac{3}{4}$
   E. $16\frac{1}{4}$

8. In the figure below, parallel lines q and r are intersected by line s. What is the value of x?

   F. 9
   G. 16
   H. 20
   J. 40
   K. 55

9. The equation of a circle is $x^2 + y^2 = 81$. If this circle is graphed in the standard (x, y) coordinate plane, what will be the y intercepts?
   A. $(0, 3)$ and $(0, -3)$
   B. $(0, 9)$ and $(0, -9)$
   C. $(0, 12)$ and $(0, -12)$
   D. $(0, 18)$ and $(0, -18)$
   E. $(0, 27)$ and $(0, -27)$

GO ON TO THE NEXT PAGE.

10. A new rectangular soccer field is being constructed at John Adams High School. The length of the field must be $(4x - 3)$ yards, and the width must be $5x$ yards. Which of the following expressions in terms of x gives the number of square yards of grass needed to cover the field?

F. $x - 3$

G. $9x - 3$

H. $20x - 15x^2$

J. $15x^2 + 9x$

K. $20x^2 - 15x$

11. In the geometric sequence

$$4, 10, 25, 62\frac{1}{2}, N, \ldots$$

what is the 5th term, N?

A. $144\frac{3}{4}$

B. $148\frac{1}{2}$

C. $156\frac{1}{4}$

D. $156\frac{1}{2}$

E. $162\frac{1}{4}$

12. What are the values for x that satisfy the equation $(x + y)(x + z) = 0$?

F. y and z

G. y and $-z$

H. $-yz$

J. $-y$ and z

K. $-y$ and $-z$

13. What fraction lies exactly halfway between $\frac{1}{3}$ and $\frac{3}{5}$?

A. $\frac{7}{15}$

B. $\frac{2}{5}$

C. $\frac{1}{2}$

D. $\frac{2}{3}$

E. $\frac{14}{15}$

DO YOUR FIGURING HERE.

GO ON TO THE NEXT PAGE.

△ △ △ △ △ △ △ △ △ △

14. Each night at closing time over a full workweek, Cory counted the number of customers who shopped at his store that day and recorded it in the table shown below. For that workweek, what was the average number of customers per day at Cory's store?

Day	Number of Customers
Monday	20
Tuesday	26
Wednesday	21
Thursday	17
Friday	31

F. 26
G. 23
H. 21
J. 20
K. 18

15. Sasha is going to Italy over his spring break. When he arrives, he has to exchange his U.S. dollars for euros. If the exchange rate between the number of U.S. dollars (u) and euros (e) is expressed in the equation $0.77u = e$, approximately how many euros will Sasha receive in exchange for his 675 U.S. dollars?

A. 877
B. 730
C. 520
D. 493
E. 465

16. When doing a problem, Barb meant to divide a number by 2, but instead she accidentally multiplied the number by 2. Which of the following calculations could Barb then do to the result to obtain the result she originally wanted?

F. Divide by 4
G. Divide by 2
H. Multiply by 4
J. Multiply by 2
K. Subtract the original number

17. There is a bowl with 48 different marbles in it. In the bowl, there are 14 red marbles, 12 blue, 9 green, 8 yellow, and 5 white. If Corbin reaches into the bowl without looking, what is the probability that he will draw a marble that is either blue or white?

A. $\frac{21}{48}$
B. $\frac{17}{48}$
C. $\frac{12}{48}$
D. $\frac{9}{48}$
E. $\frac{5}{48}$

DO YOUR FIGURING HERE.

GO ON TO THE NEXT PAGE.

18. If $n = 2$, what is the value of $n(-6)^n - 9n$?
  F. 126
  G. 81
  H. 54
  J. 18
  K. -90

19. Which of the following is a factor of $(2z^2 - z - 15)$?
  A. $2z - 5$
  B. $2z - 15$
  C. $z^2 - 3$
  D. $z + 15$
  E. $z - 3$

20. If the point with coordinates $(-2, y_1)$ lies on the graph of $y = -4x + 5$, what is the value of y_1?
  F. 13
  G. 8
  H. 3
  J. 1
  K. -3

21. If $8y = 6x + 14$, then $x = ?$
  A. $y - 14$
  B. $\dfrac{8y}{6} + 14$
  C. $\dfrac{4y + 7}{3}$
  D. $\dfrac{4y - 7}{3}$
  E. $\dfrac{8y + 14}{6}$

22. A packet of fruit snacks is filled by weight in the factory. If each fruit snack weighs about 0.04 ounce, about how many are needed to fill a packet with 1.2 ounces of fruit snacks?
  F. 12
  G. 30
  H. 36
  J. 48
  K. 75

23. What is the difference between the mean and the median of the set $\{5, 7, 8, 12\}$?
  A. 0
  B. 0.5
  C. 4
  D. 7.5
  E. 8

24. The area of a circle is 121π square units. What is the diameter, in units, of the circle?
  F. π
  G. 11
  H. 22
  J. 11π
  K. 121

DO YOUR FIGURING HERE.

GO ON TO THE NEXT PAGE.

DO YOUR FIGURING HERE.

25. For all x, $\dfrac{-5(-2x)^3}{10x}$ is equivalent to:

    A. $100x^2$
    B. $4x^2$
    C. x^3
    D. $-4x^2$
    E. $-100x^2$

26. A set of numbers consists of all the odd integers that are greater than 1 and less than 25. What is the probability that a number picked at random from the set will be divisible by 3?

    F. $\dfrac{3}{25}$

    G. $\dfrac{1}{8}$

    H. $\dfrac{1}{3}$

    J. $\dfrac{4}{11}$

    K. $\dfrac{7}{13}$

27. Two numbers are *reciprocals* if their product is 1. If m and n are reciprocals and $0 < m < 1$, then n must be:
    A. less than -1
    B. between 0 and -1
    C. equal to 0
    D. between 0 and 1
    E. greater than 1

28. Which of the following is equivalent to

    $(5x - 2x^2) - (3x - 11) + (x^2 - 6)$?

    F. $x^4 - 2x^2 - 17$
    G. $-x^4 + 2x^2 + 5$
    H. $-x^4 + 2x^2 - 17$
    J. $-x^2 + 2x + 5$
    K. $-x^2 + 2x - 17$

29. The edges of a cube are 4 inches long. What is the surface area, in square inches, of this cube?
    A. 144
    B. 96
    C. 64
    D. 24
    E. 16

GO ON TO THE NEXT PAGE.

30. A ladder is set up at a 50° angle to the second-story window of a house, which is 28 feet above the ground. Which of the following equations gives the height x, in feet, of the ladder?

DO YOUR FIGURING HERE.

   F. $\cos 50° = \dfrac{28}{x}$

   G. $\sec 50° = \dfrac{28}{x}$

   H. $\tan 50° = \dfrac{28}{x}$

   J. $\csc 50° = \dfrac{28}{x}$

   K. $\text{sine} 50° = \dfrac{28}{x}$

31. Ian's points-per-game average was exactly 26 after the first 6 games of the basketball season. He scored 18, 30, 21, 24, and 36 points, respectively, in the first 5 games. How many points did he score in the 6th game?

   A. 18
   B. 23
   C. 26
   D. 27
   E. 32

32. In the standard (x, y) coordinate plane, what is the slope of the line $3x - 9y = 12$?

   F. -3

   G. $-\dfrac{1}{3}$

   H. $\dfrac{1}{3}$

   J. $\dfrac{4}{3}$

   K. 3

33. What is the mode of the following set of scores?

      47, 89, 75, 77, 56, 89, 46, 89, 72

   A. 47
   B. 56
   C. 71
   D. 75
   E. 89

GO ON TO THE NEXT PAGE.

34. In the isosceles trapezoid *WXYZ* shown below, $\overline{GF}$ is an altitude, and all lengths are given in inches. What is the perimeter of trapezoid *WXYZ*, in inches?

   F. 71
   G. 76
   H. 78
   J. 90
   K. 98

35. For what positive values of *x* is it true that
$x^2 > 5x > x + 24$?
   A. No positive values
   B. Only positive values less than 3
   C. Only values between 3 and 6
   D. Only values greater than 6
   E. All positive values

36. What is the smallest positive whole number that is divisible by both 14 and 16 with zero remainder?
   F. 2
   G. 32
   H. 84
   J. 112
   K. 224

37. If all the angles in the figure shown below are right angles and each dimension given is in centimeters, then what is the area of the figure, in square centimeters?

   A. 62
   B. 106
   C. 132
   D. 156
   E. 166

DO YOUR FIGURING HERE.

GO ON TO THE NEXT PAGE.

38. What is the distance, in units, between the points (5, 2) and (−3, 6) in the standard (x, y) coordinate plane?

DO YOUR FIGURING HERE.

F. $4\sqrt{5}$

G. 8

H. $4\sqrt{3}$

J. 2

K. $-\dfrac{1}{2}$

39. Consider all products ab such that a is divisible by 8 and b is divisible by 14. Which of the following whole numbers is NOT a factor of each product ab?

A. 4

B. 8

C. 12

D. 56

E. 112

40. On the local television station, commercial airtime sells for p dollars per minute. Which of the following expressions gives the cost, in dollars, of x minutes and y seconds of commercial airtime?

F. $p\left(\dfrac{x}{60}+y\right)$

G. $p(x+60y)$

H. $p\left(x+\dfrac{y}{60}\right)$

J. $\dfrac{p(x+y)}{60}$

K. $p(60x+y)$

41. For all positive values of j, k, and s, which of the following is equivalent to $\dfrac{j^5(j^2)(k^3)^4}{s^{-7}}$?

A. $j^{10}k^7s^7$

B. $j^7k^7s^7$

C. $j^7k^{12}s^7$

D. $\dfrac{j^{10}k^7}{s^7}$

E. $\dfrac{j^7k^{12}}{s^7}$

GO ON TO THE NEXT PAGE.

DO YOUR FIGURING HERE.

42. If *a* is a negative number, for which of the following values of *b* is $|a - b|$ greatest?

   F. −10
   G. −4
   H. 0
   J. 4
   K. 10

43. On February 1, Mr. Well's electric meter read 5,468 kilowatt-hours (kwh). On March 1, the meter read 7,678 kwh, but the utility company did not send an agent to take the reading. Instead, it estimated that Mr. Well had used 2,150 kwh of electricity that month and billed him for that estimated amount. If each kwh costs $0.12, what, if any, amount of money will Mr. Well owe the utility company beyond what he was actually billed?

   A. $3.87
   B. $4.08
   C. $5.25
   D. $7.20
   E. He does not owe them any money

44. If 2 interior angles of a triangle measure 40° and 85°, respectively, which of the following describes the location of the shortest side of the triangle?

   F. Always opposite the 40° angle
   G. Always between the 40° and the 85° angle
   H. Always opposite the 85° angle
   J. Opposite either the 85° angle or the unknown angle
   K. Cannot be determined from the information given

45. On the number line below, what is the coordinate of the point between *Y* and *Z* that is three times as far from point *Z* as from point *Y*?

   A. −9
   B. −7
   C. −3
   D. −1
   E. 1

GO ON TO THE NEXT PAGE.

46. If $x + y = 2$, $y + z = 5$, and $x + y + z = 10$, then $y = ?$
- **F.** −3
- **G.** 0
- **H.** 1
- **J.** 3
- **K.** $\dfrac{17}{3}$

DO YOUR FIGURING HERE.

47. What is the total when the product of 57 and 0.22 is added to 7% of 57?
- **A.** 16.99
- **B.** 16.53
- **C.** 12.54
- **D.** 8.55
- **E.** 3.99

48. Which of the following expressions, if any, are equivalent for all real numbers n?

   I. $-|n|$
   II. $|-n|$
   III. $\sqrt{(-n)^2}$

- **F.** I and II only
- **G.** I and III only
- **H.** II and III only
- **J.** I, II, and III
- **K.** None of the expressions are equivalent.

49. Coach McLeod will use a circle graph to show how the members of his team spend their time during a 3-hour practice. The size of the sector representing each drill is proportional to the amount of time spent in that drill. During practice, the team members spend 36 minutes on the punt return drill. How many degrees should the central angle measure in the sector representing the punt return drill?
- **A.** 30.5°
- **B.** 36°
- **C.** 49.75°
- **D.** 72°
- **E.** 144°

50. If $r \neq 0$, s is a real number, $r^3 = 2s$, and $r^5 = 18s$, then what is one possible value of r?
- **F.** 3
- **G.** 5
- **H.** 9
- **J.** s^2
- **K.** Cannot be determined from the information given

GO ON TO THE NEXT PAGE.

DO YOUR FIGURING HERE.

51. The volume of a sphere is given by the formula $V = \frac{4}{3}\pi r^3$, and its surface area by the formula $S = 4\pi r^2$, where r is the radius of the sphere. What is the surface area of a sphere, in square inches, if its volume is $\frac{2,048\pi}{3}$?

A. 32π
B. 144π
C. 256π
D. 324π
E. 512π

52. Jim and Steve both work as lifeguards at the local beach. Their lookout towers are located about 22 yards apart, at the same elevation. A victim is spotted waving for help in the water at angles of 39° and 54° from the line of sight between the lookout towers, as indicated in the diagram below. Which of the following expressions, if any, gives the approximate distance, in yards, between the victim and Steve's tower?
(Note: The *law of sines* states that the ratio of the sine of an angle to the length of the side opposite an angle is the same for all interior angles in the same triangle.)

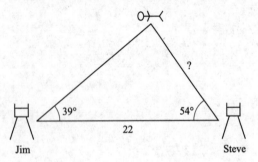

Jim

22

Steve

F. $\sqrt{39^2 + 54^2}$

G. $\dfrac{22\tan 54°}{\tan 87°}$

H. $22\sin 54°$

J. $\dfrac{22\sin 39°}{\sin 87°}$

K. The distance cannot be approximated without more information.

DO YOUR FIGURING HERE.

53. For a population that grows at a constant rate of $r\%$ per year, the formula $P(t) = p_o\left(1 + \dfrac{r}{100}\right)^t$ models the population t years after an initial population of p_o is counted. The population of the city of Midtown was 557,000 in 2005. Assume the population grows at a constant rate of 2% per year. According to this formula, which of the following is an expression for the population of Midtown in the year 2010?

A. $(557{,}000 \times 1.02)^5$
B. $(557{,}000 \times 1.2)^5$
C. $557{,}000(1.02)^5$
D. $557{,}000(1.2)^5$
E. $557{,}000(3)^5$

54. In the standard (x, y) coordinate plane, line k_1 has an equation of $2x + 6y = 11$. If line k_2 is perpendicular to line k_1, what is the slope of line k_2?

F. 3
G. $\dfrac{11}{6}$
H. 1
J. $-\dfrac{1}{3}$
K. -3

55. A parabola with an equation of the form $y = ax^2 + bx + c$ has the point $(-4, 2)$ as its vertex. If $(0, -5)$ also lies on this parabola, which of the following is another point on the parabola?

A. $(-8, -5)$
B. $(-5, 8)$
C. $(-2, 3)$
D. $(0, 5)$
E. $(3, -2)$

56. Which of the following is a graph of the solution set for the inequality $|2y + 3| \le 11$?

F.

G.

H.

J.

K.

GO ON TO THE NEXT PAGE.

57. A function *G* is defined as follows:

$$\text{For } x > 0, G(x) = x^3 + 3x^2 - 3x + 1$$
$$\text{For } x < 0, G(x) = x^3 + 3x^2 + 3x + 1$$

What is the value of $G(-1)$?

A. 6
B. 3
C. 0
D. −3
E. −6

58. A number is increased by 40%, and the resulting number is then decreased by 25%. The final number is what percent of the original number?

F. 115%
G. 105%
H. 85%
J. 15%
K. Cannot be determined with the given information

59. If $a > 0$ and $b < 0$, which of the following *must* be true for the value of $b - a$?

A. $b - a > a$
B. $b - a > 0$
C. $b - a > b$
D. $b - a > ab$
E. $b - a < b$

60. The length of one side of a square is decreased by 40%. By approximately what percent would the length of an adjacent side have to be *increased* so that the area of the new figure (a rectangle) is the same as the area of the original square?

F. 33%
G. 40%
H. 55%
J. 67%
K. 75%

DO YOUR FIGURING HERE.

END OF THE MATHEMATICS TEST.
STOP! IF YOU HAVE TIME LEFT OVER, CHECK YOUR WORK ON THIS SECTION ONLY.

ANSWER KEY

Mathematics Test

1. D	16. F	31. D	46. J
2. H	17. B	32. H	47. B
3. E	18. H	33. E	48. H
4. F	19. E	34. G	49. D
5. D	20. F	35. D	50. F
6. J	21. D	36. J	51. C
7. D	22. G	37. C	52. J
8. H	23. B	38. F	53. C
9. B	24. H	39. C	54. F
10. K	25. B	40. H	55. A
11. C	26. J	41. C	56. H
12. K	27. E	42. K	57. C
13. A	28. J	43. D	58. G
14. G	29. B	44. F	59. E
15. C	30. K	45. B	60. J

SCORING WORKSHEET

Scale Score	Raw Score Mathematics	Scale Score	Raw Score Mathematics
36	60	18	24–26
35	59	17	20–23
34	57–58	16	16–19
33	56	15	12–15
32	55	14	10–11
31	54	13	8–9
30	53	12	6–7
29	52	11	5
28	51–50	10	4
27	48–49	9	—
26	46–47	8	3
25	44–45	7	—
24	41–43	6	2
23	38–40	5	—
22	35–37	4	1
21	31–34	3	—
20	28–30	2	—
19	27	1	0

NOTE: Each actual ACT is scaled slightly differently based on a large amount of information gathered from the millions of tests ACT, Inc., scores each year. This scale will give you a fairly good idea of where you are in your preparation process. However, it should not be read as an absolute predictor of your actual ACT score. In fact, on practice tests, the scores are much less important than what you learn from analyzing your results.

ANSWERS AND EXPLANATIONS

1. **The correct answer is D.** To solve this problem, use the distributive property to expand $(4x - 5)(3x + 1)$. You might know this as the *FOIL* method because you multiply the *f*irst terms together, then the *o*utside terms, then the *i*nside terms, and finally the *l*ast terms. In this case, $(4x - 5)(3x + 1) = (4x)(3x) + (4x)(1) - (5)(3x) - (5)(1) = 12x^2 + 4x - 15x - 5$. Combine like terms to get $12x^2 - 11x - 5$.

2. **The correct answer is H.** To solve this problem, you could use your calculator to square 3.316, but another way to solve this problem is to recognize that $3^2 = 9$, so 3.316^2 must be slightly greater than 9.

3. **The correct answer is E.** To solve this problem, divide the number of field goals made by the number attempted, then multiply by 100 to get the percent. Since Adam attempted 33 field goals and made 26, the percentage made is $\frac{26}{33} \times 100 = 78.\overline{78}\%$, which rounds up to 79%.

4. **The correct answer is F.** One way to solve this problem is to solve one of the equations for x or y and use substitution. It does not matter which equation you solve first:

$$-2x + 4y = -18$$
$$-2x = -4y - 18$$
$$x = \frac{-4}{-2}y - \frac{18}{-2} = 2y + 9$$

Now substitute $2y + 9$ for x into the equation $4x - 5y = 30$:

$$4(2y + 9) - 5y = 30$$
$$8y + 36 - 5y = 30$$
$$3y + 36 = 30$$
$$3y = -6$$
$$y = -2$$

At this point, it is not necessary to find the x coordinate because only one answer choice has a y coordinate of -2. The correct answer could also have been found by substituting each answer choice into both of the equations. The correct answer choice works in both equations.

5. **The correct answer is D.** A polygon whose interior angles each measure 90 is a rectangle (or a square, which is a special rectangle). You could also have applied the formula $S = 180(n - 2)$, where S is the sum of the measures of the interior angles of a regular polygon. A regular polygon has n congruent angles, so $S = 90n$:

$$90n = 180(n - 2)$$
$$90n = 180n - 360$$
$$90n = 360$$
$$n = 4$$

6. **The correct answer is J.** It is clear that x is a factor of both $256x$ and $144x$. Eliminate answer choices F and G. Now find the greatest common factor of 256 and 144.

   Factors of 256: 1, 2, 4, 8, **16**, 32, 64, 128, 256

   Factors of 144: 1, 2, 3, 4, 6, 8, 9, 12, **16**, 18, 24, 36, 48, 72, 144

   The greatest common factor is $16x$.

7. **The correct answer is D.** To solve this problem, find the total quantity of carpet used and subtract that sum from 50. To add $22\frac{3}{4}$ and $12\frac{1}{2}$, first find common denominators: the least common multiple of 2 and 4, which is 4. Now convert $12\frac{1}{2}$ to $12\frac{2}{4}$. Add the numbers to get $22 + 12 + \frac{3}{4} + \frac{2}{4} = 22 + 12 + \frac{5}{4} = 22 + 12 + 1 + \frac{1}{4} = 35\frac{1}{4}$. Subtracting $35\frac{1}{4}$ from 50 yields $14\frac{3}{4}$.

8. **The correct answer is H.** By definition, the angles with measure $2x°$ and $7x°$ are interior angles. Interior angles that are formed by cutting two parallel lines by a transversal are supplementary, meaning that their sum is $180°$. Therefore, $2x + 7x = 180$. Solve for x:

$$2x + 7x = 180$$
$$9x = 180$$
$$x = 20$$

9. **The correct answer is B.** Circles have an equation of the form $(x - h)^2 + (y - k)^2 = r^2$, where the circle has center (h, k) and radius r. A circle with equation $x^2 + y^2 = 81$ has its center at $(0, 0)$ because $(x - 0)^2 = x^2$ and $(y - 0)^2 = y^2$, and a radius of $\sqrt{81} = 9$. Therefore, the circle will intersect the y axis 9 units above and 9 units below the origin at points $(0, 9)$ and $(0, -9)$.

10. **The correct answer is K.** The area of a rectangle is found by multiplying length by width. Since the width of the field is $(4x - 3)$ yards and the length is $5x$ yards, the area is given by $5x(4x - 3)$. To simplify, use the distributive property to get $(5x)(4x) - (5x)(3) = 20x^2 - 15x$.

11. **The correct answer is C.** To solve this problem, recall that a geometric sequence is formed by multiplying each successive term by a constant number to get the next term. Call this constant number k, so that $4k = 10$, $10k = 25$, $25k = 62\frac{1}{2}$, and so on. In all of these cases, $k = 2.5$. Therefore, the 5th term can be found by multiplying the 4th term, $62\frac{1}{2}$, by the quantity 2.5. The result is 156.25, or $156\frac{1}{4}$.

12. **The correct answer is K.** To answer this question, set each quantity equal to 0 and solve for x:

$$x + y = 0$$
$$x = -y$$
$$x + z = 0$$
$$x = -z$$

13. **The correct answer is A.** The first step in solving this problem is to find the Lowest Common Denominator (LCD). Because both 3 and 5 divide evenly into 15, 15 is the LCD. $\frac{1}{3} = \frac{5}{15}$ and $\frac{3}{5} = \frac{9}{15}$. The fraction that is exactly halfway between $\frac{5}{15}$ and $\frac{9}{15}$ is $\frac{7}{15}$.

14. **The correct answer is G.** In this case, average refers to the mean. To find the mean, add the values, then divide that sum by the total number of values. Since there are 5 values (Monday through Friday), divide the sum by 5: $\frac{(20 + 26 + 21 + 17 + 31)}{5} = \frac{115}{5} = 23$.

15. **The correct answer is C.** In this problem, $u = 675$. Since $0.77u = e$, $0.77(675) = e = 519.75$, or about 520 euros. Because the exchange rate is less than 1, you could have eliminated answer choices A and B.

16. **The correct answer is F.** One way to solve this problem is to pick a number for Barb. Suppose that her number was 4. What Barb did: $4 \times 2 = 8$. What Barb meant to do: $4 \div 2 = 2$. So in order to obtain the result she originally wanted, she must divide the accidental result by 4.

17. **The correct answer is B.** Since there are 12 blue and 5 white marbles, there are 17 marbles that Corbin could draw out of a total of 48 marbles. Therefore, the probability that Corbin draws a marble that is either blue or white is $\frac{17}{48}$.

18. **The correct answer is H.** To solve $n(-6)^n - 9n$ for $n = 2$, substitute 2 for n in the expression as follows:

$$2(-6)^2 - 9(2)$$
$$= 2(36) - 18$$
$$= 72 - 18 = 54$$

19. **The correct answer is E.** To solve this problem, factor the quadratic equation $2z^2 - z - 15$ as follows:

$$(2z + 5)(z - 3)$$

You are asked to find one factor, and only $(z - 3)$ is among the choices, so answer choice E must be correct.

20. **The correct answer is F.** To find the y coordinate of a particular x value on the line $y = -4x + 5$, simply plug in the x value: $y_1 = -4(-2) + 5 = 8 + 5 = 13$.

21. **The correct answer is D.** To answer this question, solve $8y = 6x + 14$ for x:

$$8y = 6x + 14$$
$$8y - 14 = 6x$$
$$\frac{8y - 14}{6} = x; \text{ simplify by dividing by 2}$$
$$\frac{4y - 7}{3} = x$$

22. **The correct answer is G.** To solve this problem, divide the total weight of a packet (1.2 ounces) by the weight of an individual snack (0.04 ounces). The result is $\frac{1.2}{0.04} = 30$. There are 30 fruit snacks in a packet.

23. **The correct answer is B.** The mean is the average of all 4 numbers: $5 + 7 + 8 + 12 = 32$; $32 \div 4 = 8$; therefore, the mean is 8. The median is the middle number of the ordered set. Since there are four numbers in the set, the median is halfway between the two middle numbers, 7 and 8. Therefore, the median is 7.5, and the difference between the mean and the median is $8 - 7.5 = 0.5$.

24. **The correct answer is H.** The area of a circle is given by πr^2, where r is the radius. Since the area is given as 121π, $r = \sqrt{121} = 11$. The diameter of a circle is equal to twice the length of the radius, or $2(11) = 22$.

25. **The correct answer is B.** To simplify, follow the proper order of operations:

$$\frac{-5(-2x)^3}{10x}$$

Compute exponents first:

$$= \frac{-5(-8x^3)}{10x}$$

Perform the multiplication in the numerator next:

$$= \frac{40x^3}{10x}$$

Simplify and cancel terms:

$$= 4x^2$$

26. The correct answer is J. To solve this problem, first list the odd integers greater than 1 but less than 25: 3, 5, 7, 9, 11, 13, 15, 17, 19, 21, 23. There are eleven such integers. Now, select the integers from that set that are divisible by 3: 3, 9, 15, and 21. The probability that a number picked at random from the set will be divisible by 3 is $\frac{4}{11}$.

27. The correct answer is E. This is a good time to use a "stand-in" to calculate the correct answer. Since $0 < m < 1$, pick a number for m that satisfies the requirements, such as $\frac{1}{2}$. The reciprocal of $\frac{1}{2}$ is 2 because $2\left(\frac{1}{2}\right) = 1$. Therefore, if $m = \frac{1}{2}$, then $n = 2$. The only choice that works is that n must be greater than 1. You can try other values for m and n with the same results.

28. The correct answer is J. To solve this problem, distribute subtraction to each term within the parentheses, then combine like terms, as shown below:

$$(5x - 2x^2) - (3x - 11) + (x^2 - 6)$$
$$= 5x - 2x^2 - 3x + 11 + x^2 - 6$$
$$= -2x^2 + x^2 + 5x - 3x + 11 - 6$$
$$= -x^2 + 2x + 5$$

29. The correct answer is B. To solve this problem, recall that a cube has 6 square-shaped faces. Therefore, the surface area is equal to 6 times the area of one of the square faces. Since an edge of the cube has length 4, one face has area $4^2 = 16$. The total surface area is $6(16) = 96$ square inches.

30. The correct answer is K. To solve this problem, recall that the sine of an angle in a right triangle is the ratio of the opposite side to the hypotenuse. In this case, the side opposite the 50° angle has length 28 and the hypotenuse has length x; $\sin 50° = \frac{28}{x}$.

31. The correct answer is D. In this question, average refers to mean. The mean score of the first 6 games is 26. If the number of points Ian scored in the 6th game is given by x, then $\frac{(18+30+21+24+36+x)}{6} = 26$. Solve for x:

$$\frac{(18+30+21+24+36+x)}{6} = 26$$
$$(129+x) = 6(26) = 156$$
$$x = 156 - 129 = 27$$

32. The correct answer is H. To find the slope of the line $3x - 9y = 12$, convert the equation to slope-intercept form ($y = mx + b$, where m is the slope and b is the y intercept):

$$3x - 9y = 12$$
$$-9y = -3x + 12$$
$$y = \frac{-3}{-9}x + \frac{12}{-9}$$
$$m(\text{slope}) = \frac{-3}{-9} = \frac{1}{3}$$

33. The correct answer is E. To solve this problem, recall that the mode is the value that appears most often in the list. First, rearrange the list in order of value to get 46, 47, 56, 72, 75, 77, 89, 89, 89. You can see that 89 appears 3 times in the list.

34. The correct answer is G. To solve this problem, think of the bottom side as having the length of the top side plus two additional lengths (the small legs of the right triangles formed below):

Since the height and hypotenuse are given, use the Pythagorean Theorem to find the length of the missing leg:

$$12^2 + a^2 = 13^2$$
$$144 + a^2 = 169$$
$$a^2 = 25$$
$$a = 5$$

The length of each leg is 5, making the total length of the bottom side $20 + 2(5) = 30$. The perimeter is then $20 + 13 + 13 + 30 = 76$.

35. The correct answer is D. To solve this problem, use sample values to evaluate the validity of the statement $x^2 > 5x > x + 24$. Since the answer choices use the values 3 and 6, it is logical to start with those values, then try others.

$x = 3$:	$3^2 > 5(3) > 3 + 24$	False
$x = 6$:	$6^2 > 5(6) > 6 + 24$	False
$x = 7$:	$7^2 > 5(7) > 7 + 24$	True

Therefore, the statement must be valid only for values of x greater than 6.

36. The correct answer is J. To solve this problem, find the least common multiple of 14 and 16. Multiples of 14 include 14, 28, 42, 56, 70, 84, 98, 112 . . . . Multiples of 16 include 16, 32, 48, 64, 80, 96, 112 . . . . It is easy to see that 112 is the smallest positive whole number that is divisible by both 14 and 16 with zero remainder. You could find a common multiple by finding the product of 14 and 16, but in this case it is not the *least* common multiple. Watch out for answer choice F, which is the smallest common factor (other than 1) of both 14 and 16.

37. The correct answer is C. To solve this problem, break the figure into three rectangles as shown below:

The dimensions of the large rectangle can be determined by subtracting the length of the small rectangle at the top (2) from 10 to get 8. The large rectangle has length 14 and width 8, making its area (14)(8) = 112. The area of the whole figure must be greater than 112, so eliminate answer choices A and B. The smallest rectangle has length 1 and width 2, making its area (1)(2) = 2. Finally, the dimensions of the third rectangle can be found by determining the length of the "gap" on its upper left side. The gap is 8 − 6 = 2, making the total length of that side 2 + 4 = 6. Its area is (6)(3) = 18. The total area is 112 + 18 + 2 = 132.

38. The correct answer is F. To find the distance between the points (5, 2) and (−3, 6), use the distance formula (the distance between the points (x_1, y_1) and (x_2, y_2) is $d = \sqrt{(x_2 - x_1)^2 + (y_2 - y_1)^2}$:

$$\sqrt{(-3-5)^2 + (6-2)^2}$$
$$= \sqrt{(-8)^2 + (4)^2}$$
$$= \sqrt{64 + 16} = \sqrt{80}$$
$$= \sqrt{16} \times \sqrt{5} = 4\sqrt{5}$$

39. The correct answer is C. The quickest way to solve this problem is to recognize that if *a* is divisible by 8 and *b* is divisible by 14, then *ab* must be divisible by 8 × 14, which is 112. The only answer choice that does not divide evenly into 112 is 12.

40. The correct answer is H. Since *x* represents minutes of airtime and *y* represents seconds of airtime, find the total number of minutes of commercial airtime. To do so, convert the number of seconds into minutes by dividing by 60 (60 seconds in a minute): $\frac{y}{60}$. The total minutes is therefore $x + \frac{y}{60}$. Since commercial airtime sells for *p* dollars per minute, the total cost is $p\left(x + \frac{y}{60}\right)$.

41. The correct answer is C. This problem requires the use of three different exponent rules. First, to simplify $j^5(j^2)$, simply add the exponents to get j^7. Eliminate answer choices A and D. Second, $(k^3)^4$ can be simplified by multiplying the exponents to get k^{12}. Eliminate answer choice B. Finally, $\frac{1}{s^{-7}} = s^7$. Therefore, the correct answer is $j^7k^{12}s^7$.

42. The correct answer is K. One way to solve this problem is to pick a value for *a*, then try the answer choices for *b*. Let's say that *a* = −2.

F. $|-2 - (-10)| = |-2 + 10| = |-8| = 8$
G. $|-2 - (-4)| = |-2 + 4| = |-2| = 2$
H. $|-2 - 0| = |-2| = 2$
J. $|-2 - 4| = |-6| = 6$
K. $|-2 - 10| = |-12| = 12$

43. The correct answer is D. The first step is to calculate the amount of electricity that Mr. Well actually used by finding the difference between the two meter readings: 7,678 − 5,468 = 2,210 kwh. Although he was estimated to have used 2,150 kwh, he actually used 2,210 − 2,150 = 60 kwh more. Therefore, Mr. Well owes the utility company for 60 kwh beyond what he was actually billed for. The amount owed is 60(0.12) = $7.20.

44. The correct answer is F. The length of a side of a triangle is proportional to the measure of the angle opposite it. Two angles of this triangle are 40° and 85°, and since the sum of the angles in a triangle is always 180°, the third angle measure is 180 − (40 + 85) = 55°. Therefore, the shortest side of this triangle is opposite the smallest angle, 40°.

45. The correct answer is B. Since point *Y* is located at −11 and point *Z* is located at 5, the distance between them is 16. Think of the 16 units between the two points as being in four equal sections of 4 units each. A point that is three times as far from point *Z* as from point *Y* will be located at the end of the first section of 4 units to the right of *Y*. Since point *Y* is located at −11, this point is located at −11 + 4, or −7.

46. The correct answer is J. To solve this problem, solve the first two equations, substitute the results into the third equation, then solve for y:

$$x + y = 2; x = 2 - y$$
$$y + z = 5; z = 5 - y$$

$$2 - y + y + 5 - y = 10$$
$$2 + 5 - y = 10$$
$$7 - y = 10$$
$$-y = -3$$
$$y = 3$$

47. The correct answer is B. To solve this problem, first compute the two values, then take the sum. The product of 57 and 0.22 is $0.22(57) = 12.54$, and 7% of 57 is $0.07(57) = 3.99$. The sum of 12.54 and 3.99 is $12.54 + 3.99 = 16.53$.

48. The correct answer is H. To solve this problem, pick a value for n and test the Roman numerals. Let $n = 2$:

  I. $-|n| = -|2| = -2$
  II. $|-n| = |-2| = 2$
  III. $\sqrt{(-n)^2} = \sqrt{(-2)^2} = \sqrt{4} = 2$

You can see that only II and III are equivalent because Roman numeral I will always be negative.

49. The correct answer is D. A three-hour practice consists of 180 minutes ($3 \times 60 = 180$). Each minute of practice represents $2°$ on a circle graph, as there are 360 degrees in a circle. A 36-minute drill will occupy $2(36) = 72°$ on a circle (pie) graph.

50. The correct answer is F. To solve this problem, use substitution. You are given that $r^3 = 2s$ and $r^5 = 18s$. Since $r^5 = 18s$, then $r^5 = 9(2s)$. You are given that $r^3 = 2s$, so $r^5 = 9(r^3)$. Solve for r as follows:

$$r^5 = 9r^3$$
$$r^2 = 9$$
$$r = 3$$

51. The correct answer is C. To solve this problem, first find the radius of the sphere. Since the volume is $\dfrac{2{,}048\pi}{3}$ and the formula is $V = \dfrac{4}{3}\pi r^3$, set these quantities equal and solve for r:

$$\frac{2{,}048\pi}{3} = \frac{4}{3}\pi r^3$$
$$512 = r^3$$
$$r = 8$$

Now that you know the radius is 8, find the surface area as follows:

$$S = 4\pi r^2$$
$$S = 4\pi(8)^2$$
$$S = 4\pi(64)$$
$$S = 256\pi$$

52. The correct answer is J. The first step in solving this problem is to find the unknown angle. Since the sum of the angles in a triangle must be $180°$, the unknown angle is $180 - (39 + 54) = 87°$. The *law of sines* states that the ratio of the sine of an angle to the length of the side opposite that angle is the same for all interior angles in the same triangle. Set the unknown side equal to x, and solve:

$$\frac{22}{\sin 87°} = \frac{x}{\sin 39°}$$
$$\frac{22 \sin 39°}{\sin 87°} = x$$

53. The correct answer is C. Given that $P(t) = p_o\left(1 + \dfrac{r}{100}\right)^t$, substitute the values $p_o = 557{,}000$, $r = 2$, and $t = 5$ to get $P(t) = 557{,}000\left(1 + \dfrac{2}{100}\right)$. Next, simplify the expression to get $P(t) = 557{,}000\,(1 + 0.02)^5 = 557{,}000(1.02)^5$.

54. The correct answer is F. To solve, first find the slope of line k_1, which has an equation of $2x + 6y = 11$. To do so, convert it to slope-intercept form ($y = mx + b$, where m is the slope and b is the y intercept).

$$2x + 6y = 11$$
$$6y = -2x + 11$$
$$y = -\frac{2}{6}x + \frac{11}{6}$$

The slope is $-\dfrac{2}{6}$, which reduces to $-\dfrac{1}{3}$.

Since k_2 is perpendicular to k_1, the slopes are negative reciprocals, and the slope of line k_2 is 3.

55. The correct answer is A. Parabolas have a line of symmetry that runs through the vertex. Since the point $(0, -5)$ has an x coordinate that is 4 units to the right of the vertex, there will be a corresponding point with the same y coordinate four units to the left of the vertex. Since the vertex is $(-4, 2)$, a point 4 units to the left will have an x coordinate of $-4 - 4 = -8$. Therefore, the point is $(-8, -5)$.

56. The correct answer is H. To solve this problem, break up $|2y + 3| \leq 11$ into two inequalities (because of the absolute value) and solve for y, as shown below:

First inequality	Second inequality
$2y + 3 \leq 11$	$2y + 3 \geq -11$
$2y \leq 8$	$2y \geq -14$
$y \leq 4$	$y \geq -7$

Now look for the graph that shows the intersection of these two inequalities ($4 \geq y \geq -7$). Because the inequalities are inclusive ("less than or equal to" and "greater than or equal to"), the correct graph will have closed circles. Only answer choice H satisfies these conditions.

57. The correct answer is C. To solve this problem, substitute -1 for x in the appropriate equation. Since $-1 < 0$, use $G(x) = x^3 + 3x^2 + 3x + 1$ as follows:

$$G(-1) = (-1)^3 + 3(-1)^2 + 3(-1) + 1$$
$$G(-1) = -1 + 3 - 3 + 1 = 0$$

58. The correct answer is G. To solve this problem, select a number as a stand-in. A good number to select is 100, since you are using percents. Increasing 100 by 40% yields 140. To decrease 140 by 25%, multiply 140 by 0.75 (which is 100% minus 25%), which gives you 105. Therefore, the resulting number is 105% of the original number.

59. The correct answer is E. Given that a is positive and b is negative, the difference $(b - a)$ is negative. Try some numbers: $a = 1$ and $b = -1$; $-1 - 1 = -2$. Since a is positive and nonzero, $b - a$ must be less than b; therefore, $b - a < b$ is the correct answer.

60. The correct answer is J. This problem might be simplified by using a number as a stand-in. Use 10 as the original length of the side of the square because it is an easy number to work with. The original area of the square is $10^2 = 100$. If the length of one side is reduced by 40%, leaving 60% of the length intact, the new length is 6, creating a rectangle with a length of 6, a width of 10, and an area of 60. The area of the original square was 100, which means that you must increase the area of the newly created rectangle by $100 - 60$, or 40. Set up a proportion as follows, where x is the percent of increase:

40 is to 60 as x is to 100

$$\frac{40}{60} = \frac{x}{100}$$

Cross-multiply and solve for x:

$$60x = 4,000$$
$$x = 66.6$$

The adjacent side will need to be increased by about 67%.

CHAPTER 9

PRACTICE TEST 4 WITH EXPLANATIONS

ACT MATHEMATICS TEST 4
Answer Sheet

MATHEMATICS

1 Ⓐ Ⓑ Ⓒ Ⓓ Ⓔ	16 Ⓕ Ⓖ Ⓗ Ⓙ Ⓚ	31 Ⓐ Ⓑ Ⓒ Ⓓ Ⓔ	46 Ⓕ Ⓖ Ⓗ Ⓙ Ⓚ
2 Ⓕ Ⓖ Ⓗ Ⓙ Ⓚ	17 Ⓐ Ⓑ Ⓒ Ⓓ Ⓔ	32 Ⓕ Ⓖ Ⓗ Ⓙ Ⓚ	47 Ⓐ Ⓑ Ⓒ Ⓓ Ⓔ
3 Ⓐ Ⓑ Ⓒ Ⓓ Ⓔ	18 Ⓕ Ⓖ Ⓗ Ⓙ Ⓚ	33 Ⓐ Ⓑ Ⓒ Ⓓ Ⓔ	48 Ⓕ Ⓖ Ⓗ Ⓙ Ⓚ
4 Ⓕ Ⓖ Ⓗ Ⓙ Ⓚ	19 Ⓐ Ⓑ Ⓒ Ⓓ Ⓔ	34 Ⓕ Ⓖ Ⓗ Ⓙ Ⓚ	49 Ⓐ Ⓑ Ⓒ Ⓓ Ⓔ
5 Ⓐ Ⓑ Ⓒ Ⓓ Ⓔ	20 Ⓕ Ⓖ Ⓗ Ⓙ Ⓚ	35 Ⓐ Ⓑ Ⓒ Ⓓ Ⓔ	50 Ⓕ Ⓖ Ⓗ Ⓙ Ⓚ
6 Ⓕ Ⓖ Ⓗ Ⓙ Ⓚ	21 Ⓐ Ⓑ Ⓒ Ⓓ Ⓔ	36 Ⓕ Ⓖ Ⓗ Ⓙ Ⓚ	51 Ⓐ Ⓑ Ⓒ Ⓓ Ⓔ
7 Ⓐ Ⓑ Ⓒ Ⓓ Ⓔ	22 Ⓕ Ⓖ Ⓗ Ⓙ Ⓚ	37 Ⓐ Ⓑ Ⓒ Ⓓ Ⓔ	52 Ⓕ Ⓖ Ⓗ Ⓙ Ⓚ
8 Ⓕ Ⓖ Ⓗ Ⓙ Ⓚ	23 Ⓐ Ⓑ Ⓒ Ⓓ Ⓔ	38 Ⓕ Ⓖ Ⓗ Ⓙ Ⓚ	53 Ⓐ Ⓑ Ⓒ Ⓓ Ⓔ
9 Ⓐ Ⓑ Ⓒ Ⓓ Ⓔ	24 Ⓕ Ⓖ Ⓗ Ⓙ Ⓚ	39 Ⓐ Ⓑ Ⓒ Ⓓ Ⓔ	54 Ⓕ Ⓖ Ⓗ Ⓙ Ⓚ
10 Ⓕ Ⓖ Ⓗ Ⓙ Ⓚ	25 Ⓐ Ⓑ Ⓒ Ⓓ Ⓔ	40 Ⓕ Ⓖ Ⓗ Ⓙ Ⓚ	55 Ⓐ Ⓑ Ⓒ Ⓓ Ⓔ
11 Ⓐ Ⓑ Ⓒ Ⓓ Ⓔ	26 Ⓕ Ⓖ Ⓗ Ⓙ Ⓚ	41 Ⓐ Ⓑ Ⓒ Ⓓ Ⓔ	56 Ⓕ Ⓖ Ⓗ Ⓙ Ⓚ
12 Ⓕ Ⓖ Ⓗ Ⓙ Ⓚ	27 Ⓐ Ⓑ Ⓒ Ⓓ Ⓔ	42 Ⓕ Ⓖ Ⓗ Ⓙ Ⓚ	57 Ⓐ Ⓑ Ⓒ Ⓓ Ⓔ
13 Ⓐ Ⓑ Ⓒ Ⓓ Ⓔ	28 Ⓕ Ⓖ Ⓗ Ⓙ Ⓚ	43 Ⓐ Ⓑ Ⓒ Ⓓ Ⓔ	58 Ⓕ Ⓖ Ⓗ Ⓙ Ⓚ
14 Ⓕ Ⓖ Ⓗ Ⓙ Ⓚ	29 Ⓐ Ⓑ Ⓒ Ⓓ Ⓔ	44 Ⓕ Ⓖ Ⓗ Ⓙ Ⓚ	59 Ⓐ Ⓑ Ⓒ Ⓓ Ⓔ
15 Ⓐ Ⓑ Ⓒ Ⓓ Ⓔ	30 Ⓕ Ⓖ Ⓗ Ⓙ Ⓚ	45 Ⓐ Ⓑ Ⓒ Ⓓ Ⓔ	60 Ⓕ Ⓖ Ⓗ Ⓙ Ⓚ

MATHEMATICS TEST

60 Minutes—60 Question

DIRECTIONS. Solve each of the problems in the time allowed, then fill in the corresponding bubble on your answer sheet (page 193). Do not spend too much time on any one problem; skip the more difficult problems and go back to them later.

You may use a calculator on this test. For this test, you should assume that figures are NOT necessarily drawn to scale, that all geometric figures lie in a plane, and that the word *line* is used to indicate a straight line.

DO YOUR FIGURING HERE.

1. Katie plans to purchase a motorcycle that costs $4,600. In addition, she has to pay $450 for insurance and $320 for taxes. If Katie has $3,200 saved, what amount must she borrow to be able to buy the motorcycle and pay the expenses?
   A. $630
   B. $1,400
   C. $1,850
   D. $2,170
   E. $7,800

2. What is the greatest common factor of the monomials $18x^2$, $27x^4$, and $30x^3$?
   F. $3x^2$
   G. $3x^4$
   H. $9x^2$
   J. $18x^2$
   K. $30x^3$

3. $6a^7 \times 9a^3$ is equivalent to:
   A. $54a^{21}$
   B. $54a^{10}$
   C. $54a^4$
   D. $15a^{21}$
   E. $15a^{10}$

4. In parallelogram *WXYZ* shown below, $\overline{WY}$ is perpendicular to $\overline{YZ}$, and the measure of angle *WZY* is 72°. What is the measure of angle *XYW*?

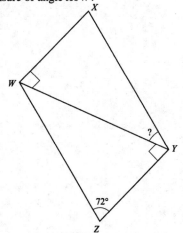

   F. 12°
   G. 18°
   H. 36°
   J. 58°
   K. 72°

GO ON TO THE NEXT PAGE.

DO YOUR FIGURING HERE.

5. What is the value of the expression $\dfrac{20,000}{Y^2 - 12Y + 100} + 5Y$
   when $Y = 50$?
   A. 130
   B. 155
   C. 200
   D. 260
   E. 310

6. For the variables y and z, $a = 3y^4 - z^2$ and $b = -5y^3$. Which of the following expressions represents the product ab?
   F. $-15y^{12} + 5yz^6$
   G. $-15y^7 + 5y^3z^2$
   H. $-8y^7 + z^2$
   J. $-2y^3 - z^2$
   K. $-2y - z^2$

7. What is the slope of the line $12y + 4x = 17$?
   A. 17
   B. 12
   C. 4
   D. $\dfrac{17}{12}$
   E. $-\dfrac{1}{3}$

8. Mars has much less gravity than Earth, so objects on Mars weigh about 38% of what they would weigh on Earth. If Jason weighs 175 pounds on Earth, about how many pounds would he weigh on Mars?
   F. 66.5
   G. 89
   H. 108.5
   J. 241
   K. 460.5

9. Brad's volleyball team won 25 of its 45 games, and had 2 ties. What fraction of the 45 games did the team lose?
   A. $\dfrac{3}{5}$
   B. $\dfrac{5}{9}$
   C. $\dfrac{2}{5}$
   D. $\dfrac{1}{3}$
   E. $\dfrac{2}{9}$

GO ON TO THE NEXT PAGE.

10. In the figure below, $\overline{ML}$ is perpendicular to $\overline{LK}$, and points L, K, and J are collinear. If the measure of angle LMK is 62°, what is the measure of angle MKJ?

DO YOUR FIGURING HERE.

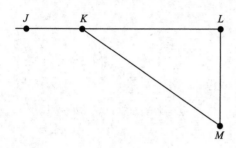

  F. 28°
  G. 76°
  H. 118°
  J. 134°
  K. 152°

11. In Boardman City, the daily low temperatures, in degrees Fahrenheit (°F), during the first week in January were −13, −8, 10, 2, 23, 31, and 30. To the nearest 1°F, what was the mean daily low temperature for that week?
  A. −3
  B. 10
  C. 11
  D. 18
  E. 25

12. In the (x, y) coordinate plane, what is the radius of the circle $(x − 1)^2 + (y + 2)^2 = 8$?
  F. 1
  G. $\sqrt{2}$
  H. 2
  J. $\sqrt{8}$
  K. 8

13. What value of x makes the proportion below true?

$$\frac{10}{10+x} = \frac{36}{45}$$

  A. 2.5
  B. 9
  C. 12
  D. 18
  E. 27.5

GO ON TO THE NEXT PAGE.

14. $|-5| + 2|-4| - |7| = ?$
- F. 10
- G. 6
- H. 3
- J. −4
- K. −20

DO YOUR FIGURING HERE.

15. If $18x$ is 40% of 180, then $x = ?$
- A. 4
- B. 10
- C. 24
- D. 38
- E. 72

16. The expression $(6s - 2)(4s - 7)$ is equivalent to:
- F. $24s^2 - 50s + 14$
- G. $24s^2 - 34s - 14$
- H. $24s^2 + 14$
- J. $10s^2 - 50s + 14$
- K. $10s^2 - 14$

17. If $f(x) = 5x^2 - 3x - 27$, then $f(-4) = ?$
- A. 385
- B. 172
- C. 65
- D. 41
- E. −95

18. If $n < 0$, which of the following best describes a general relationship between n^2 and n^3?
- F. $n^2 < n^3$
- G. $n^2 > n^3$
- H. $n^2 = n^3$
- J. $-n^2 = n^3$
- K. $\dfrac{1}{n^2} < n^3$

19. The endpoints of line $\overline{QR}$ on the real number line are −5 and 11. What is the coordinate of the midpoint of $\overline{QR}$?
- A. −2
- B. 0
- C. 3
- D. 6
- E. 8

GO ON TO THE NEXT PAGE.

20. If the sine of an angle is −0.5 and its cosine is 0.7, what is its secant?

DO YOUR FIGURING HERE.

  F. $\dfrac{-1}{0.5}$

  G. $\dfrac{-0.7}{0.5}$

  H. $\dfrac{-0.5}{0.7}$

  J. $\dfrac{-0.5}{1}$

  K. $\dfrac{1}{0.7}$

21. What is the point in the standard (x, y) coordinate plane that is the center of a circle with the equation $(x + 3)^2 + (y - 7)^2 = 16$?

  A. $(7, 3)$
  B. $(4, 4)$
  C. $(3, -7)$
  D. $(-3, 4)$
  E. $(-3, 7)$

22. Through the 3rd game of the football season, Reggie had scored 2 more touchdowns than Tom. In the 4th game, Tom scored 3 touchdowns while Reggie had none. After being injured, Tom missed the next 3 games, during which Reggie scored 5 touchdowns. Over the 8th and 9th games, Tom scored 4 touchdowns and Reggie scored 2 touchdowns total. In the 10th game, Reggie scored 3 touchdowns while Tom scored 1. At the end of the 10th game, who between Tom and Reggie had more touchdowns, and by how many?

  F. Tom by 4
  G. Tom by 2
  H. Neither
  J. Reggie by 2
  K. Reggie by 4

23. If $7x - 3(x - 6) = 2(x - 7) + 10$, then $x = $?

  A. 6
  B. $\dfrac{9}{2}$
  C. 2
  D. −11
  E. $\dfrac{-37}{3}$

GO ON TO THE NEXT PAGE.

24. For all x, which of the following is a factor of $10x^2 + 14x - 12$?

   F. $(x + 3)$
   G. $(2x - 4)$
   H. $(5x - 3)$
   J. $(5x + 3)$
   K. $(5x + 4)$

DO YOUR FIGURING HERE.

25. A group of college students started a landscaping business. The students charge $24 per hour for a job that requires more than 5 hours. For any job that requires 5 hours or less, they charge a flat rate of $125. If h represents the number of hours that the job requires, which of the following expressions gives the charge, in dollars, for a job requiring more than 5 hours to complete?

   A. $125h$
   B. $-24h + 125$
   C. $24h - 125$
   D. $24h$
   E. $24h + 125$

26. The ratio of Kevin's age to his nephew's age is 9:2. The sum of their ages is 44. How old is Kevin?

   F. 40
   G. 36
   H. 35
   J. 33
   K. 22

27. What is the distance, in units, between the points with standard (x, y) coordinates $(-2, 3)$ and $(-6, 10)$?

   A. $\sqrt{65}$
   B. $\sqrt{91}$
   C. 11
   D. $\sqrt{113}$
   E. $\sqrt{185}$

28. What is the value of $7b - (2a^3 + 4b^2)$ if $a = -5$ and $b = -3$?

   F. 265
   G. 235
   H. 193
   J. -174
   K. -235

29. When $\dfrac{2x^2 - x - 15}{2x + 5}$ is defined, it is equivalent to which of the following expressions?

A. -3

B. $-x^2 + 3$

C. $\dfrac{1}{x - 3}$

D. $x - 15$

E. $x - 3$

30. Two transversals intersect at X, a point between 2 parallel lines s and t. The measures of angles are as marked on the figure below. What is the measure of angle WYX?

F. $42°$

G. $57°$

H. $63°$

J. $75°$

K. $105°$

31. Which of the following is NOT a solution of $(x + 5)(x - 2)(x - 9)(x + 2) = 0$?

A. -9

B. -5

C. -2

D. 2

E. 9

32. A convenience store is having a sale that offers a 50-cent discount on any size bottle of cola. For any given bottle, P is the price in cents, and S is the size of the bottle, in ounces. Which of the following formulas determines the price per ounce of the cola, in cents, after the discount?

F. $\dfrac{S}{50P}$

G. $\dfrac{P - 50}{S}$

H. $\dfrac{P}{S - 50}$

J. $\dfrac{P + 50}{S}$

K. $\dfrac{50P}{S}$

DO YOUR FIGURING HERE.

GO ON TO THE NEXT PAGE.

33. Aaron drove to visit a friend. He drove 410 miles in 6 hours and 15 minutes. What was his average speed, to the nearest tenth of a mile per hour?

A. 62.4
B. 63.2
C. 65.6
D. 66.7
E. 68.3

34. For the right triangle below, cos θ = ?

F. 0.28
G. 0.29
H. 0.96
J. 1.04
K. 3.57

35. Jill told Jordan that if she spends up to $400 from her savings account, her savings account would have at least $\frac{2}{3}$ as much in it as it has now. From Jill's statement, Jordan can deduce that the least amount of money Jill could have in her savings account now is:

A. $400
B. $600
C. $900
D. $1200
E. $1400

36. Molly is planning her birthday party at a local skating rink. For renting the rink, she was given the following prices:

Number of guests	Price
10	$130
15	$180
20	$230
25	$280
30	$330

Which of the following equations, where G represents the number of guests and P represents the price in dollars, best fits the information in the price list?

F. $P = 50G + 100$
G. $P = 50G$
H. $P = 10G + 30$
J. $P = 5G + 80$
K. $P = G + 120$

GO ON TO THE NEXT PAGE.

37. In a circle with diameter 10 inches, shown below, how many inches in length is an arc that has a central angle of 120°?

DO YOUR FIGURING HERE.

A. $\dfrac{3\pi}{12}$

B. $\dfrac{5\pi}{12}$

C. $\dfrac{10\pi}{3}$

D. $\dfrac{16\pi}{3}$

E. $\dfrac{20\pi}{3}$

38. What is the sum of the first 8 terms of the geometric sequence 2, 6, 18, 54, . . . ?
F. 4,374
G. 6,560
H. 7,243
J. 13,121
K. 14,260

39. The circle below has a diameter of 8 inches. Which of the following is closest to the area, in square inches, of the square inscribed in the circle?

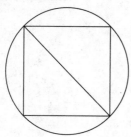

A. 16
B. 24
C. 32
D. 64
E. 120

40. The length of a rectangle is 3 times its width. The area of the rectangle is 48 square feet. What is the width, in feet, of the rectangle?
F. 4
G. 8
H. 12
J. 16
K. 22

GO ON TO THE NEXT PAGE.

DO YOUR FIGURING HERE.

represents $\frac{1}{8}$ of 6?

C. 0.75
D. 0.075
E. 0.0075

42. If $a^2 - 4 = 4 - a^2$, what are all possible values of a?

    F. 0 only
    G. 2 only
    H. 4 only
    J. −2 and 2 only
    K. −2, 0, and 2

43. Which of the following graphs in the standard (x, y) coordinate plane represents the equation $2y - 6 = 3x$?

A.

B.

C.

D.

E.

GO ON TO THE NEXT PAGE.

44. In the figure below, all distances are in inches and all angles are right angles. A straight line drawn from point Q to point T would be how many inches long?

DO YOUR FIGURING HERE.

   F. 9
   G. 11
   H. 14
   J. 15
   K. 17

45. What is the sixth term of the geometric sequence whose second term is −2 and whose fifth term is 16?
   A. −64
   B. −32
   C. 38
   D. 64
   E. 128

46. The diagonal of a rectangle is 17 units long, and one side is 15 units long. How many units squared is the area of the rectangle?
   F. 46
   G. 120
   H. 136
   J. 208
   K. 255

47. The area of a circle is 25π square units. What is the circumference of the circle?
   A. 5
   B. 10
   C. 5π
   D. 25
   E. 10π

48. The expression $\dfrac{a-b}{a+b}$ has the value 0 if and only if:

   F. $a - b \neq 0$ and $a + b \neq 0$
   G. $a - b \neq 0$ and $a + b = 0$
   H. $a - b = 0$ and $a + b \neq 0$
   J. $a \neq 0$ and $b \neq 0$
   K. $a = 0$ and $b = 0$

GO ON TO THE NEXT PAGE.

49. When 4 times the number x is added to 12, the result is 8. What number results when 2 times x is added to 11?

   A. −1
   B. 5
   C. 8
   D. 9
   E. 13

DO YOUR FIGURING HERE.

50. Which of the following inequalities is represented by the shaded region shown below?

   F. $y + \dfrac{2}{3}x \geq 4$

   G. $y \geq \dfrac{2}{3}x + 4$

   H. $y + 4 \leq \dfrac{2}{3}x$

   J. $y + \dfrac{2}{3}x \leq 4$

   K. $y \leq \dfrac{2}{3}x + 4$

51. An emergency exit ramp goes from the door of a plane to the ground. If the ramp is 29 feet long and the end of the ramp is 21 feet away from the plane, how many feet above the ground is the start of the ramp?

   A. 1,282
   B. 400
   C. 53
   D. $\sqrt{1,282}$
   E. 20

52. What is the slope of the line that is perpendicular to the line determined by the equation $2x + 6y = 11$?

   F. 11
   G. 3
   H. $-\dfrac{1}{3}$

   J. $-\dfrac{11}{2}$

   K. −6

GO ON TO THE NEXT PAGE.

DO YOUR FIGURING HERE.

53. Which of the following expresses all and only the values of x that satisfy $|3x - 5| > 13$?

   A. $-6 < x < \dfrac{8}{3}$

   B. $-\dfrac{8}{3} < x < 6$

   C. $x < -6$ or $x > \dfrac{8}{3}$

   D. $x < -\dfrac{8}{3}$ or $x > 6$

   E. $x < \dfrac{8}{3}$ or $x > -6$

54. Given the sets A = {1, 3, 5, 7} and B = {0, 1, 2, 3}, which of the following defines a function f from B onto A?
   F. $f(x) = x + 1$
   G. $f(x) = 2x + 1$
   H. $f(x) = 3x + 1$
   J. $f(x) = 2x - 1$
   K. $f(x) = 3x - 1$

55. If $b = 19 - (5 + a)^3$, for which of the following values of a will b have its maximum value?
   A. 19
   B. 5
   C. 1
   D. −5
   E. −19

56. Chuck drinks 9 bottles of water in 2 days. At this rate, how many bottles of water will Chuck drink in $2 + d$ days?

   F. $9 + \dfrac{9d}{2}$

   G. $2 + \dfrac{d}{2}$

   H. $\dfrac{9}{2} + \dfrac{9}{2d}$

   J. $\dfrac{9}{2} + \dfrac{d}{2}$

   K. $\dfrac{9}{2} + d$

57. In the (x, y) coordinate plane, a line passes through the point $(-4, 6)$ and has a slope of $-\dfrac{1}{3}$. What is the x coordinate of a point on the line having a y coordinate of 3?
   A. −13
   B. −8
   C. 3
   D. 5
   E. 9

GO ON TO THE NEXT PAGE.

58. A rectangle has a perimeter of 36 units, and its length is twice its width. A right triangle has sides with lengths of 5, 12, and 13 units. What is the difference in the areas of these figures, in square units?

F. 7
G. 26
H. 42
J. 50
K. 84

59. How many zeros are there in the integer representation of the product of 3 thousand and 7 billion?

A. 11
B. 12
C. 13
D. 14
E. 15

60. If $\cos x = -\dfrac{\sqrt{2}}{2}$ and $\dfrac{\pi}{2} < x < \pi$, what is the value of $\tan x$?

F. $-\sqrt{2}$
G. -1
H. $1\sqrt{2}$
J. 1
K. $\sqrt{3}$

DO YOUR FIGURING HERE.

END OF THE MATHEMATICS TEST.
STOP! IF YOU HAVE TIME LEFT OVER, CHECK YOUR WORK ON THIS SECTION ONLY.

ANSWER KEY

Mathematics Test

1. D	16. F	31. A	46. G
2. F	17. C	32. G	47. E
3. B	18. G	33. C	48. H
4. G	19. C	34. F	49. D
5. D	20. K	35. D	50. K
6. G	21. E	36. H	51. E
7. E	22. K	37. C	52. G
8. F	23. D	38. G	53. D
9. C	24. H	39. C	54. G
10. K	25. D	40. F	55. E
11. C	26. G	41. C	56. F
12. J	27. A	42. J	57. D
13. A	28. H	43. E	58. H
14. G	29. E	44. K	59. B
15. A	30. H	45. B	60. G

SCORING WORKSHEET

Scale Score	Raw Score Mathematics	Scale Score	Raw Score Mathematics
36	60	18	24–26
35	59	17	20–23
34	57–58	16	16–19
33	56	15	12–15
32	55	14	10–11
31	54	13	8–9
30	53	12	6–7
29	52	11	5
28	51–50	10	4
27	48–49	9	—
26	46–47	8	3
25	44–45	7	—
24	41–43	6	2
23	38–40	5	—
22	35–37	4	1
21	31–34	3	—
20	28–30	2	—
19	27	1	0

NOTE: Each actual ACT is scaled slightly differently based on a large amount of information gathered from the millions of tests ACT, Inc., scores each year. This scale will give you a fairly good idea of where you are in your preparation process. However, it should not be read as an absolute predictor of your actual ACT score. In fact, on practice tests, the scores are much less important than what you learn from analyzing your results.

ANSWERS AND EXPLANATIONS

1. **The correct answer is D.** To solve this problem, first calculate the total amount that Katie will have to pay for the motorcycle:

$4,600 (cost)
+$450 (insurance)
+$320 (taxes)
= $5,370 (total)

Eliminate answer choice E, because she won't have to borrow more than the total cost.

If she has $3,200 saved, then the amount that she must borrow in order to buy the motorcycle and pay the expenses is $5,370 − $3,200, or $2,170.

2. **The correct answer is F.** The greatest common factor, or GCF, is the greatest factor that divides two or more numbers. Looking at the numbers alone (18, 27, and 30), the greatest number that divides all three of them is 3. Eliminate answer choices H, J, and K. In terms of the variables (x^2, x^4, and x^3), the greatest number that divides all three is x^2. Therefore, the greatest common factor of these monomials is $3x^2$.

3. **The correct answer is B.** To solve this problem, you need to multiply like terms. Remember, when multiplying any two powers of the same base, simply add the powers together:

$$6a^7 \times 9a^3$$
$$= (6 \times 9)(a^7 \times a^3)$$
$$= 54a^{10}$$

If you started by simply multiplying 6×9, you could have quickly eliminated answer choices D and E.

4. **The correct answer is G.** Within parallelogram *WXYZ*, there are two equal triangles (*WYZ* and *YWX*). The measure of angle *YZW* is 72°; this is also the measure of angle *WXY*. The three angles of a triangle must add up to 180°, so the measure of angle *XYW* must equal 180° − 90° − 72°, or 18°.

5. **The correct answer is D.** To solve this problem, substitute 50 for all instances of *Y* in the equation and solve:

$$\frac{20,000}{Y^2 - 12Y + 100} + 5Y$$
$$= \frac{20,000}{(50)^2 - 12(50) + 100} + 5(50)$$
$$= \frac{20,000}{2,500 - 600 + 100} + 250$$
$$= \frac{20,000}{2,000} + 250$$
$$= 10 + 250 = 260$$

6. **The correct answer is G.** This problem asks you to multiply *a* and *b*. Remember, when multiplying two powers of the same base, add the powers together. For two powers with different bases, simply keep the powers the same:

$$(3y^4 - z^2)(-5y^3)$$
$$= -15y^7 + 5y^3z^2$$

If you started by simply multiplying 3×-5, you could have quickly eliminated answer choices H, J, and K.

7. **The correct answer is E.** To find the slope of this line, you first must convert the equation to slope-intercept form ($y = mx + b$):

$$12y + 4x = 17$$
$$12y = -4x + 17$$
$$y = \frac{-4}{12x} + \frac{17}{12}$$
$$y = \frac{-1}{3x} + \frac{17}{12}$$

The slope of the line is $-\frac{1}{3}$.

8. **The correct answer is F.** You are given that objects on Mars weigh about 38% of what they would weigh on Earth. Therefore, if Jason weighs 175 pounds on Earth, he would weigh about 175 × 0.38, or 66.5 pounds, on Mars.

9. **The correct answer is C.** Brad's team won 25 of its 45 games and had 2 ties, so it must have lost 18 games (45 − 25 − 2). Set up a fraction to show the relationship between games lost and games played:

$$\frac{18}{45} = \frac{9 \times 2}{9 \times 5} = \frac{2}{5}$$

10. **The correct answer is K.** You are given that $\overline{ML}$ is perpendicular to $\overline{LK}$, so angle *MLK* measures 90°. Also given is the value of angle *LMK* (62°). The three angles of a triangle must add up to 180°, so angle *MKL* must equal 28° (180°−90°−62°). Angle *MKL* and angle *MKJ* form a line, so they must also add up to 180°. Therefore, angle *MKJ* measures 152°(180° − 28°).

11. **The correct answer is C.** To calculate the mean, or average, temperature, first find the total number of degrees for the week: −13 + −8 + 10 + 2 + 23 + 31 + 30 = 75. Now, divide 75 by the number of days in the week: 75 ÷ 7 = 10.7, which rounds to 11.

12. **The correct answer is J.** The standard form for the equation of a circle is $(x - h)^2 + (y - k)^2 = r^2$, where (h, k) is the circle's center and r is its radius. In this case, $r^2 = 8$, so $r = \sqrt{8}$.

13. **The correct answer is A.** To answer this question, cross-multiply and solve for x:

$$\frac{10}{10 + x} = \frac{36}{45}$$

$$10(45) = 36(10 + x)$$
$$450 = 360 + 36x$$
$$90 = 36x$$
$$2.5 = x$$

14. **The correct answer is G.** This problem deals with absolute values. The absolute value of a number is its numerical value without regard to its sign. Simplify the equation by finding the necessary absolute values ($|-5| = 5, |-4| = 4, |7| = 7$):

$$5 + 2(4) - 7$$
$$= 5 + 8 - 7$$
$$= 6$$

15. **The correct answer is A.** To solve this problem, first find 40% of 180:

$$(0.40 \times 180 = 72)$$

You can now set up an equation to solve for x:

$$18x = 72$$
$$x = 4$$

16. **The correct answer is F.** When multiplying binomials, use the *FOIL* (first, outside, inside, last) method:

$$(6s - 2)(4s - 7) =$$
First: $6s \times 4s = 24s^2$
Outside: $6s \times -7 = -42s$
Inside: $-2 \times 4s = -8s$
Last: $-2 \times -7 = 14$

Now, combine like terms:

$$24s^2 - 42s - 8s + 14$$
$$= 24s^2 - 50s + 14$$

Once you determined that the first value was $24s^2$, you could safely eliminate answer choices J and K.

17. **The correct answer is C.** To solve this problem, substitute -4 for any instance of x in the function:

$$5x^2 - 3x - 27$$
$$= 5(-4^2) - 3(-4) - 27$$
$$= 5(16) + 12 - 27$$
$$= 80 + 12 - 27 = 65$$

18. **The correct answer is G.** You are given that $n < 0$, which means that n is negative. Pick a negative number for n, and try the answer choices. Make $n = -2$:

F. $n^2 < n^3$; $-2^2 = 4$, and $-2^3 = -8$, so this inequality is false.

G. $n^2 > n^3$; $-2^2 = 4$, and $-2^3 = -8$, so this inequality is true, which means this must be the correct answer.

19. **The correct answer is C.** To solve this problem, first determine how far it is from each point to 0 (-5 is 5 spaces away from 0; 11 is 11 spaces away from 0). Therefore, the two points are 16 spaces away from each other ($5 + 11 = 16$). The midpoint of the line would be 8 spaces away from each of the endpoints ($-5 + 8 = 3$, $11 - 8 = 3$). Therefore, the midpoint of the line is 3.

20. **The correct answer is K.** The definition of secant is $\frac{1}{\text{cosine}}$, so for this angle, the secant would be $\frac{1}{0.7}$.

21. **The correct answer is E.** The equation of a circle is given by $(x - h)^2 + (y - k)^2 = r^2$, where (h, k) is the center of the circle and r is the radius. In the given circle, h is -3 and k is 7, so the center of the circle is $(-3, 7)$.

22. **The correct answer is K.** One way to solve this problem is to create a chart to track the touchdowns made by each player (for simplicity, assume that Tom did not score any touchdowns in Games 1–3):

Game number	Tom's touchdowns	Reggie's touchdowns
1–3	0	2
4	3	0
5–7	0	5
8 & 9	4	2
10	1	3
Total number of touchdowns	8	12

At the end of 10 games, Reggie is ahead of Tom by 4 touchdowns.

23. **The correct answer is D.** To solve this problem, simplify each side of the equation by performing the necessary multiplication:

$$7x - 3(x - 6) = 2(x - 7) + 10$$
$$7x - 3x + 18 = 2x - 14 + 10$$
$$4x + 18 = 2x - 4$$
$$2x = -22$$
$$x = -11$$

24. **The correct answer is H.** To solve this problem, first simplify the polynomial:

$$10x^2 + 14x - 12$$
$$= 2(5x^2 + 7x - 6)$$

Now factor $5x^2 + 7x - 6$, as follows:

$$5x^2 + 7x - 6$$
$$= (5x - 3)(x + 2)$$

The only answer choice that includes one of the factors of $10x^2 + 14x - 12$ is answer choice H.

25. **The correct answer is D.** You are given that the students charge $24 per hour for a job that requires more than 5 hours. The question asks you for the expression that shows how much they charge for a job requiring more than 5 hours, which is $24 times the number of hours it takes. This can be expressed mathematically as $24h$.

26. **The correct answer is G.** You are given that the ratio of Kevin's age to his nephew's age is 9:2. Therefore, Kevin's age must be a multiple of 9, making answer choice G the only possible option.

27. **The correct answer is A.** The formula for the distance between two points in the (x, y) coordinate plane is $\sqrt{(x_2 - x_1)^2 + (y_2 - y_1)^2}$, where (x_1, y_1) and (x_2, y_2) are the coordinates of the two points. Use the formula with the two points that are given:

$$= \sqrt{[-6 - (-2)]^2 + (10 - 3)^2}$$
$$= \sqrt{(-4)^2 + (7)^2}$$
$$= \sqrt{16 + 49}$$
$$= \sqrt{65}$$

This cannot be simplified further, so the distance between the points is $\sqrt{65}$.

28. **The correct answer is H.** To solve this problem, substitute the given values for a and b into the equation as follows:

$$7b - (2a^3 + 4b^2)$$
$$= 7(-3) - [2(-5)^3 + 4(-3)^2]$$
$$= -21 - [2(-125) + 4(9)]$$
$$= -21 - (-250 + 36)$$
$$= -21 - (-214)$$
$$= -21 + 214 = 193$$

29. **The correct answer is E.** To solve this problem, first simplify by factoring the numerator:

$$2x^2 - x - 15 = (2x + 5)(x - 3)$$

You now have $\dfrac{(2x + 5)(x - 3)}{2x + 5}$ so you can cancel out $2x + 5$, leaving you with $x - 3$.

30. **The correct answer is H.** Before you can find the measure of angle WYX, you must find a few missing angles. Notice that the points W, Y, and X form a small triangle. Therefore, the three angles within the triangle must add up to 180°. Angle YXW has the same measurement as the 42° angle that is given in the picture, as they are vertical angles. Angle VWX is an alternate interior angle of the given 105° angle, so they have the same measurement. Because this angle forms a line with angle YWX, the two must add up to 180°, so angle YWX equals 75° (180 − 105). You now have two of the three angles in the triangle (42° and 75°). The missing measurement is that of angle WYX, and it must equal 63° (180 − 42 − 75 = 63).

31. **The correct answer is A.** To find the solutions to the equation, set each of the four binomials equal to 0:

- $(x + 5) = 0$ $x = -5$
- $(x - 2) = 0$ $x = 2$
- $(x - 9) = 0$ $x = 9$
- $(x + 2) = 0$ $x = -2$

The solutions to the equation are −5, −2, 2, and 9. The only answer choice that is not a possible solution is −9.

32. **The correct answer is G.** If the price of any bottle of cola is P, then the price after the 50-cent discount will be $P - 50$. To determine the price per ounce of the cola, you need to divide the discounted price by the number of ounces in the bottle (S). Therefore, the formula is expressed as $\dfrac{P - 50}{S}$.

33. **The correct answer is C.** If Aaron drove for 6 hours and 15 minutes, he drove for 6.25 hours $\left(\dfrac{15 \text{ min}}{60 \text{ min}} = 0.25 \text{ hour}\right)$. His average speed can be calculated by dividing the distance he traveled (410 miles) by the time he spent driving (6.25 hours), which equals 65.6 miles per hour.

34. **The correct answer is F.** To solve this problem, first find the missing length of the leg of the triangle using the Pythagorean Theorem:

$$a^2 + b^2 = c^2$$
$$a^2 + 24^2 = 25^2$$
$$a^2 + 576 = 625$$
$$a^2 = 49$$
$$a = \sqrt{49}$$
$$a = 7$$

The cosine of an angle is given by $\dfrac{\text{adjacent}}{\text{hypotenuse}}$. For angle θ, the cosine is $\dfrac{7}{25}$, which equals 0.28.

35. **The correct answer is D.** If Jill spent \$400 and still had $\dfrac{2}{3}$ of her savings account available, then \$400 must be equal to $\dfrac{1}{3}$ of Jill's savings account. Therefore, Jill has \$1200 in her savings account.

36. **The correct answer is H.** According to the information given, the price (P) is always 30 more than 10 times the number of guests (G). For example, $10 \times 10 = 100$ and $130 = 100 + 30$. This can be expressed by the equation $P = 10G + 30$.

37. **The correct answer is C.** The formula for the arc of a circle is given by $s = r\theta$, where s is the arc length, r is the radius of the circle, and θ is the measure of the central angle, in radians. You are given that the diameter of the circle is 10 inches, so the radius is $\dfrac{10}{2}$, or 5. To convert a degree measure of an angle to radians, multiply by $\dfrac{\pi}{180}$. For 120°:

$$120 \times \frac{\pi}{180}$$
$$= \frac{120\pi}{180}$$
$$= \frac{2\pi}{3}$$

Now, use the values you found for the radius and the degree measure in radians to solve for the arc length:

$$s = 5\left(\frac{2\pi}{3}\right)$$
$$s = \frac{10\pi}{3}$$

38. **The correct answer is G.** To find the sum of terms in a geometric sequence, use the formula $S_n = \dfrac{a_1(1-r^n)}{(1-r)}$ where S_n is the sum of the first n terms in a sequence, a_1 is the first term in the sequence, r is the common ratio in the sequence, and n is the number of terms you are adding up. For this sequence, the common ratio is 3 ($2 \times 3 = 6$, $6 \times 3 = 18$, etc.).

To solve, substitute the values that you have into the formula:

$$S_8 = \frac{2(1-3^8)}{(1-3)}$$
$$S_8 = \frac{2(1-6{,}561)}{-2}$$
$$S_8 = \frac{2(-6{,}560)}{-2}$$
$$S_8 = \frac{-13{,}120}{-2}$$
$$S_8 = 6{,}560$$

39. **The correct answer is C.** To solve this problem, recognize that the diameter of the circle is also the diagonal of the square. Since the diagonal divides the square into two 45-45-90 right triangles, use the Pythagorean Theorem ($a^2 + b^2 = c^2$) to calculate the length of the sides. The sides are the same length, so set each side equal to x: $2x^2 = 8^2$, $2x^2 = 64$, and $x^2 = 32$.

40. **The correct answer is F.** The area of a rectangle is defined as $A = L \times W$. For this rectangle, you are given that the length is 3 times the width and that the area is 48 square feet. Knowing this, you can set up an equation (since the length is 3 times the width, the length can be expressed as $3W$):

$$48 = 3W \times W$$
$$48 = 3W^2$$
$$16 = W^2$$
$$W = \sqrt{16}$$
$$W = 4$$

41. **The correct answer is C.** To solve this problem, multiply $\dfrac{1}{8}$ by 6, which equals $\dfrac{3}{4}$, or 0.75 in decimal form. You could also divide 6 by 8 to get the answer. You could also make an educated guess because you know that $\dfrac{1}{2}$ of 6 is 3, so $\dfrac{1}{8}$ of 6 must be less than 3.

42. **The correct answer is J.** To answer this question, solve the given equation for a:

$$a^2 - 4 = 4 - a^2$$
$$2a^2 = 8$$
$$a^2 = 4$$

Therefore, $a = 2$ and $a = -2$.

43. **The correct answer is E.** To solve this problem, first change the equation so that it is in slope-intercept form ($y = mx + b$):

$$2y - 6 = 3x$$
$$2y = 3x + 6$$
$$y = \frac{3x + 6}{2}$$

The line represented by this equation has a slope of $\frac{3}{2}$ and a y intercept of 3. Eliminate answer choices B and C. Next, determine the slope of the remaining choices:

Answer choice A: $\frac{(6-3)}{(5-0)} = \frac{3}{5}$

Answer choice D: $\frac{(9-3)}{(2-0)} = \frac{6}{2} = 3$

Answer choice E: $\frac{(6-3)}{(2-0)} = \frac{3}{2}$

44. **The correct answer is K.** This problem looks a bit more complicated than it actually is. To solve, first draw a line from Q to T. You can see that by adding a few more lines, you can form a right triangle. Creating a new point, X, you can see that $\overline{RX}$ is the same length as $\overline{ST}$ (4), and that $\overline{XT}$ is the same as $\overline{RS}$ (8).

You now have the length of two of the legs of triangle QXT (15 and 8), and $\overline{QT}$ represents the hypotenuse. Use the Pythagorean Theorem to find the length of $\overline{QT}$:

$$a^2 + b^2 = c^2$$
$$8^2 + 15^2 = c^2$$
$$64 + 225 = c^2$$
$$289 = c^2$$
$$c = \sqrt{289}$$
$$c = 17$$

The length of $\overline{QT}$ is 17 inches.

45. **The correct answer is B.** A geometric sequence is a sequence of numbers where each term after the first is found by multiplying the previous one by a fixed, nonzero number called the common ratio. Your first step in answering this question is to find the common ratio and then fill in the missing terms in the sequence. Since the second term is −2, −2 is a good logical choice for the common ratio. That would make the six terms of the sequence 1, −2, 4, −8, 16, and −32.

46. **The correct answer is G.** To solve this problem, draw a picture to give yourself a visual representation of what you need to find. You are given that the length of the diagonal is 17 units, and the length of one side is 15 units.

As you can see, the diagonal splits the rectangle into two equal right triangles. Use the Pythagorean Theorem to solve for the missing side:

$$a^2 + b^2 = c^2$$
$$a^2 + 15^2 = 17^2$$
$$a^2 + 225 = 289$$
$$a^2 = 64$$
$$a = \sqrt{64}$$
$$a = 8$$

To find the area of the rectangle, take the length times the width (15×8), which equals 120 square units.

47. **The correct answer is E.** The circumference of a circle is given by $C = \pi \times d$, where d is the diameter of the circle. For this problem, you are given only the area of the circle (25π). The area of a circle is given by $A = \pi r^2$. You can use this equation to find the radius of the circle:

$$25\pi = \pi r^2$$
$$25 = r^2$$
$$r = \sqrt{25}$$
$$r = 5$$

Since you know that the radius of the circle is 5, the diameter is twice that, which equals 10. Now you can solve for the circumference: $C = 10\pi$.

48. **The correct answer is H.** A fraction will have the value 0 if and only if the numerator is 0. If the denominator is 0, the fraction will be undefined. These statements are represented mathematically in answer choice H.

49. The correct answer is D. The first step in answering this question is to set up an equation and solve for x. You are given that when 4 times the number x is added to 12, the result is 8. This translates into the equation $4x + 12 = 8$. Therefore, $4x = -4$ and $x = -1$. Now, create a second equation based on the given information, and substitute -1 for x: $2x + 11 = 2(-1) + 11 = -2 + 11 = 9$.

50. The correct answer is K. The graph shows a solid line with the area below the line shaded. This tells you that y is less than (because the shaded region is below the line) or equal to (because the line is solid) the inequality, so you would use the $\leq$ symbol. Eliminate answer choices F and G. Now you need to determine the slope and the y intercept of the line. Since the line crosses the y axis at $(0, 4)$, the y intercept (b) is 4. The two points of the line that you are given are $(0, 4)$ and $(-6, 0)$. You can use these to determine the slope (m) of the line:

$$m = \frac{0-4}{-6-0}$$

$$m = \frac{-4}{-6}$$

$$m = \frac{2}{3}$$

Finally, use the information you have found to write the inequality in slope-intercept form ($y = mx + b$):

$$y \leq \frac{2}{3}x + 4$$

51. The correct answer is E. Using the given values in this problem, draw a picture and form a right triangle:

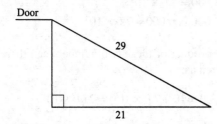

Since you are given two values of side lengths of the triangle, use the Pythagorean Theorem to find the missing value, which is the height of the start of the ramp:

$$a^2 + b^2 = c^2$$
$$a^2 + 21^2 = 29^2$$
$$a^2 + 441 = 841$$
$$a^2 = 400$$
$$a = \sqrt{400}$$
$$a = 20$$

The start of the ramp is 20 feet above the ground.

52. The correct answer is G. To solve the problem, first find the slope of the line that you are given by converting the equation to slope-intercept form:

$$2x + 6y = 11$$
$$6y = -2x + 11$$
$$y = -\frac{1}{3}x + \frac{11}{6}$$

The slope of this line is $-\frac{1}{3}$. To find the slope of a line perpendicular to this line, take the negative reciprocal of the first line's slope. The negative reciprocal of $-\frac{1}{3}$ is $-\frac{1}{3}$ divided by -1, which equals 3.

53. The correct answer is D. When dealing with an inequality that has an absolute value, you need to set up two separate inequalities, as shown next:

$$|3x - 5| > 13$$
$$3x - 5 > 13 \text{ or } 3x - 5 < -13$$
$$3x > 18 \text{ or } 3x < -8$$
$$x > 6 \text{ or } x < -\frac{8}{3}$$

54. The correct answer is G. To answer this question, test the answer choices with the values given in the sets. Because the question asks for a function f from B onto A, the values in set B will be x, and the corresponding values in set A will be $f(x)$.

F. $f(x) = x + 1$: $f(0) = 0 + 1 = 1$
   $f(1) = 1 + 1 \neq 3$, so eliminate answer choice F.

G. $f(x) = 2x + 1$: $f(0) = 2(0) + 1 = 1$
   $f(1) = 2(1) + 1 = 3$
   $f(2) = 2(2) + 1 = 5$
   $f(3) = 2(3) + 1 = 7$

All of the values work, so G is the correct answer.

55. The correct answer is E. The best way to solve this problem is to use the given equation and test the answer choices to see which yields the greatest value. Replace a with each of the values in the answer choices, and solve the equations:

Answer choice A: $b = 19 - (5 + 19)^3$
$$b = 19 - (24)^3$$
$$b = 19 - 13,824$$
$$b = -13,805$$

Answer choice B: $b = 19 - (5 + 5)^3$
$b = 19 - (10)^3$
$b = 19 - 1,000$
$b = -981$

Answer choice C: $b = 19 - (5 + 1)^3$
$b = 19 - (6)^3$
$b = 19 - 216$
$b = -197$

Answer choice D: $b = 19 - [5 + (-5)]^3$
$b = 19 - (0)^3$
$b = 19 - 0$
$b = 19$

Answer choice E: $b = 19 - [5 + (-19)]^3$
$b = 19 - (-14)^3$
$b = 19 - (-2,744)$
$b = 2,763$

Answer choice E yields the greatest value.

56. **The correct answer is F.** If Chuck drinks 9 bottles of water in 2 days and continues drinking at this constant rate, the number of bottles he drinks in d days can be expressed by $\frac{9d}{2}$. The problem asks you how many bottles he will drink in $2 + d$ days. Since you already know that he drinks 9 bottles in 2 days, and he will drink $\frac{9d}{2}$ bottles in d days, he will drink $9 + \frac{9d}{2}$ bottles in $2 + d$ days.

57. **The correct answer is D.** To solve this problem, use the equation $y_2 - y_1 = m(x_2 - x_1)$, using the points $(-4, 6)$ and $(x, 3)$ and the given slope, $-\frac{1}{3}$:

$$(3 - 6) = -\frac{1}{3}[x - (-4)]$$
$$-3 = -\frac{1}{3}(x + 4)$$
$$-3 = -\frac{1}{3}x - \frac{4}{3}$$
$$9 = x + 4$$
$$5 = x$$

58. **The correct answer is H.** You are asked to find the difference in the areas of the two given figures, so you must first find the area of each figure. For the rectangle, you are given that the perimeter is 36 units and that its length is twice its width (this can be expressed

as $L = 2W$). Use the formula for perimeter ($P = 2L + 2W$) to find the values of the length and the width:

$$36 = 2(2W) + 2W$$
$$36 = 4W + 2W$$
$$36 = 6W$$
$$6 = W$$

The length of the rectangle is $2W$, or 2×6, which equals 12. The formula for the area of a rectangle is $A = L \times W$. For this rectangle, the area would be 6×12, or 72 square units.

Draw a picture of the triangle to help you visualize the problem:

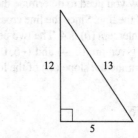

The area of a triangle is given by $A = \frac{1}{2}bh$, where $b = $ base and $h = $ height. In this triangle, the base is 5 and the height is 12, so the area is $\frac{1}{2}(5)(12)$, or 30 square units. The difference in the areas of the two figures is $72 - 30$, or 42 square units.

59. **The correct answer is B.** To solve this problem, write the numbers out in scientific notation, as follows:

$$3,000 = 3.0 \times 10^3$$
$$7,000,000,000 = 7.0 \times 10^9$$

The product of these two numbers can therefore be written as:

$$(3.0 \times 10^3)(7.0 \times 10^9) = 21.0 \times 10^{12}$$

Remember, when multiplying exponents with the same base, simply add the two numbers together.

Therefore, there are 12 zeros in the product of 3 thousand and 7 billion.

60. **The correct answer is G.** Recall that when $\frac{\pi}{2} < x < \pi$ on the unit circle, the point is in Quadrant II, which has negative values for the cosine and positive values for the sine. The value $\frac{\sqrt{2}}{2}$ corresponds with the angles

45°, 135°, 225°, and 315°, or $\dfrac{\pi}{4}, \dfrac{3\pi}{2}, \dfrac{5\pi}{2}$, and $\dfrac{7\pi}{2}$, respectively. These angles have sine and cosine values with the same magnitude, so you are left to determine the correct sign. As stated earlier, in Quadrant II, cosine values are negative and sine values are positive. Therefore, if the cosine is $-\dfrac{\sqrt{2}}{2}$ the sine is $\dfrac{\sqrt{2}}{2}$. Tangent is defined as $\dfrac{\text{sine}}{\text{cosine}}$; therefore, $\tan \dfrac{\left(\dfrac{\sqrt{2}}{2}\right)}{\left(-\dfrac{\sqrt{2}}{2}\right)} = -1.$

PART IV

THE ACT SCIENCE TEST

CHAPTER 10

FORMAT AND SCORING

The ACT Science Test measures the interpretation, analysis, evaluation, reasoning, and problem-solving skills that apply to the study of the natural sciences. The questions require you to recognize and understand the basic concepts related to the information contained within the passages, critically examine the hypotheses developed, and generalize from the given information to draw conclusions or make predictions.

> You may have to do some math on the ACT Science Test. You are not, however, allowed to use a calculator. Only basic arithmetic computation will be necessary to answer these questions. You can do math scratch work right on your test booklet. In most cases, it is useful to round values before you perform any computations.

■■■ FORMAT

The ACT Science Test usually includes 7 passages, each followed by 4 to 7 multiple-choice questions, for a total of 40 questions. The content areas found in the passages are biology, chemistry, physics, and earth sciences. You do not need to have advanced knowledge of these content areas; you only need to be able to interpret the information as it is presented, and to understand the scientific method and experimental design. All of the information required to answer the questions is contained within the passages. If you have completed two years of science coursework in high school, you will usually have all of the background knowledge necessary to understand the passages and answer the questions correctly.

The ACT Science Test passages come in three basic formats:

1. **Data Representation.** These passages mostly involve charts and graphs. The questions ask you to read information from them, or to spot trends within the data presented. There will be three Data Representation passages on your test, each followed by four to six questions.
2. **Research Summaries.** These passages explain the setup of an experiment or a series of experiments and the results that were obtained. There will be three Research Summaries passages on your test, each followed by four to six questions.
3. **Conflicting Viewpoints.** These passages are a lot like Reading Comprehension passages. Generally, there will be two scientists or two students who disagree on a specific scientific point, and each will present an argument

defending his or her position and/or attacking the other, conflicting position. There will be one Conflicting Viewpoints passage on your test, followed by seven questions.

Anatomy of an ACT Science Question

On the ACT Science Test, each multiple-choice question includes four answer choices (A, B, C, and D for odd-numbered questions, or F, G, H, and J for even-numbered questions). The answer choices correspond to the bubbles on your answer sheet.

The basic structure of an ACT Science question is as follows:

Passage I

Several scientists considered the different environmental factors and their influence on the growth of certain bacteria. The following experiments used *E. coli* bacteria and a controlled temperature to measure the effect of pH levels, nutrients, and growth factors in biosynthesis on the number of bacteria produced within a given time period.

Experiment 1

An *E. coli* bacterium was placed in each of 3 petri dishes with the same nutrient concentration. The pH level of each of the petri dishes was recorded, and the dishes were left alone. After 6 hours, the percent growth of *E. coli* bacteria was recorded (Table 1).

Dish	pH level	Percent growth
1	6	34
2	7	84
3	8	26

1. According to Table 1, what might best contribute to the growth of *E. coli* bacteria? ⎫ **Question Stem**

A. a pH level above 8 ⎫
B. a pH level below 6 ⎬ **Answer Choices**
C. a pH level near 7 ⎪
D. a pH level above 7 ⎭

▮▮▮ SCORING

As noted earlier, each of the ACT multiple-choice tests is given a score on a scale of 1 to 36. In 2019, the average ACT Science Test score in the United States was 20.7. Your score will be rounded to the nearest whole number before it is reported.

Your ACT Science Test score will be used along with the scores for the other ACT multiple-choice tests to calculate your composite score. Refer to the scoring worksheets provided with the answers to the practice tests in this book to calculate your approximate scaled score (1–36) for each test.

■■■ WHAT'S NEXT?

Chapter 11 includes a diagnostic test, which you should use to determine your current readiness for the ACT Science Test. Then, read Chapter 12, "Strategies and Techniques," to learn the best approach to answering the questions on the simulated tests included in this book, as well as on your actual ACT.

CHAPTER 11

ACT SCIENCE DIAGNOSTIC TEST

This chapter will assist you in evaluating your current readiness for the ACT Science Test. Make an honest effort to answer each question, then review the explanations that follow. Don't worry if you are unable to answer many or most of the questions at this point. The rest of the book contains information and resources that will help you to maximize your ACT Science Test scores. Once you have identified your areas of strength and weakness, you should review those particular sections in the book.

SCIENCE TEST
Answer Sheet

SCIENCE

1 Ⓐ Ⓑ Ⓒ Ⓓ	16 Ⓕ Ⓖ Ⓗ Ⓙ	31 Ⓐ Ⓑ Ⓒ Ⓓ
2 Ⓕ Ⓖ Ⓗ Ⓙ	17 Ⓐ Ⓑ Ⓒ Ⓓ	32 Ⓕ Ⓖ Ⓗ Ⓙ
3 Ⓐ Ⓑ Ⓒ Ⓓ	18 Ⓕ Ⓖ Ⓗ Ⓙ	33 Ⓐ Ⓑ Ⓒ Ⓓ
4 Ⓕ Ⓖ Ⓗ Ⓙ	19 Ⓐ Ⓑ Ⓒ Ⓓ	34 Ⓕ Ⓖ Ⓗ Ⓙ
5 Ⓐ Ⓑ Ⓒ Ⓓ	20 Ⓕ Ⓖ Ⓗ Ⓙ	35 Ⓐ Ⓑ Ⓒ Ⓓ
6 Ⓕ Ⓖ Ⓗ Ⓙ	21 Ⓐ Ⓑ Ⓒ Ⓓ	36 Ⓕ Ⓖ Ⓗ Ⓙ
7 Ⓐ Ⓑ Ⓒ Ⓓ	22 Ⓕ Ⓖ Ⓗ Ⓙ	37 Ⓐ Ⓑ Ⓒ Ⓓ
8 Ⓕ Ⓖ Ⓗ Ⓙ	23 Ⓐ Ⓑ Ⓒ Ⓓ	38 Ⓕ Ⓖ Ⓗ Ⓙ
9 Ⓐ Ⓑ Ⓒ Ⓓ	24 Ⓕ Ⓖ Ⓗ Ⓙ	39 Ⓐ Ⓑ Ⓒ Ⓓ
10 Ⓕ Ⓖ Ⓗ Ⓙ	25 Ⓐ Ⓑ Ⓒ Ⓓ	40 Ⓕ Ⓖ Ⓗ Ⓙ
11 Ⓐ Ⓑ Ⓒ Ⓓ	26 Ⓕ Ⓖ Ⓗ Ⓙ	
12 Ⓕ Ⓖ Ⓗ Ⓙ	27 Ⓐ Ⓑ Ⓒ Ⓓ	
13 Ⓐ Ⓑ Ⓒ Ⓓ	28 Ⓕ Ⓖ Ⓗ Ⓙ	
14 Ⓕ Ⓖ Ⓗ Ⓙ	29 Ⓐ Ⓑ Ⓒ Ⓓ	
15 Ⓐ Ⓑ Ⓒ Ⓓ	30 Ⓕ Ⓖ Ⓗ Ⓙ	

SCIENCE TEST

35 Minutes—40 Questions

DIRECTIONS: This test includes seven passages, each followed by several questions. Read each passage and choose the best answer to each question. After you have selected your answer, fill in the corresponding bubble on your answer sheet. You should refer to the passages as often as necessary when answering the questions. You may NOT use a calculator on this test.

PASSAGE I

The cells of multicellular organisms are constantly communicating: sending, receiving, and interpreting signals from other cells and from the environment in order to compose the appropriate responses. One normal component of cell health and development is *apoptosis*, which is an example of this communication between cells. Apoptosis is a normal and healthy process that regulates the death of a cell that is unnecessary, unwanted, or damaged. The cell responds to a variety of signals that instruct it to kill itself.

Apoptosis can be induced by either an internal signal or an external signal. Internal signals are produced when the cell experiences cellular stress, such as exposure to radiation and chemicals, or a viral infection. External signals are received by cell surface receptors and are transmitted to the cytoplasm, the fluid on the inside of the cell, which begins to self-destruct. External signals occur when other cells recognize virus-infected cells nearby and send a message to try to stop the spread of a disease such as cancer. One of the methods by which cytoxic T lymphocytes (CTLs) kill nearby virus-infected cells is by inducing apoptosis.

Once a signal has been transmitted to a cell, the cytoplasm begins to shrink, followed by the breakdown of proteins within the cell, which causes the cell to take on a horseshoe-like shape. The cell will continue to shrink, forming tiny blisters (indicated by an arrow in Figure 1) that make it easier for *phagocytic* cells to do their job and remove the fragmented cell from the tissues of an organism. This process is illustrated in Figure 1.

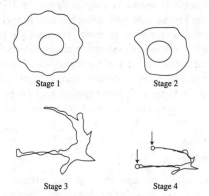

Figure 1

1. Information in the passage best supports the hypothesis that the number of virus-infected cells decreases as which of the following increases?
   A. phagocytic cells
   B. CTL-induced apoptosis
   C. cell surface receptors
   D. external signals

2. Based on information in the passage, all of the following are true about apoptosis EXCEPT:
   F. apoptosis of a cell may be stimulated by both internal and external signals.
   G. it is abnormal for a cell to induce its own death through apoptosis.
   H. a signal is transmitted to a cell before disintegration occurs.
   J. apoptosis may occur during the natural development of an organism.

3. According to Figure 1 and information in the passage, a cell that is prepared for removal by a *phagocytic* cell looks most like which of the following?

   A.

   B.

   C.

   D.

GO ON TO THE NEXT PAGE.

4. According to Figure 1, during which stage of apoptosis do small blisters appear on the cell?

F. Stage 1
G. Stage 2
H. Stage 3
J. Stage 4

5. Is the claim "CTLs act in response to internal signals" consistent with the information provided?

A. No, because CTLs are unique cells found within the nucleus.
B. No, because CTLs respond to external signals from nearby virus-infected cells.
C. Yes, because CTLs kill virus-infected cells, and a viral infection is an internal signal.
D. Yes, because CTLs send signals to each other to start the process of apoptosis.

PASSAGE II

In nature, different types of organisms often form *symbiotic* (mutually beneficial) relationships with each other. One such example of this is between certain types of fungi and plants; this relationship is known as a *mycorrhiza*. The association provides the fungus with food through access to sugars from photosynthesis in the plant. In return, the plant gains the use of the fungi's surface area to absorb mineral nutrients from the soil. It is believed that without the assistance of fungi, these plants would not be able to absorb crucial nutrients, including phosphates, from the soil. Two experiments were performed to study the effect that the plant-fungi relationship has on plant growth.

Experiment 1

For six weeks, several specimens of four different types of plants were grown in a climate-controlled greenhouse. The average growth of each type of plant was recorded every two weeks. The soil used for the plants was treated to remove any trace of fungi to establish expected growth without the plant-fungi association. The results are shown in Table 1.

Table 1			
Plant Type	**Average Plant Growth (in.)**		
	Week 2	**Week 4**	**Week 6**
1	1.2	2.8	3.7
2	0.9	2.1	3.6
3	1.3	2.7	3.3
4	1.1	2.6	3.2

Experiment 2

In this experiment, several specimens of four different types of plants were grown in a climate-controlled greenhouse for six weeks, and the average growth of each type of plant was recorded every two weeks. This time, however, untreated soil that contained fungi was used. The results are shown in Table 2.

Table 2			
Plant Type	**Average Plant Growth (in.)**		
	Week 2	**Week 4**	**Week 6**
1	2.6	3.8	5.1
2	2.9	4.1	5.9
3	1.9	3.9	5.4
4	1.7	2.6	3.4

Information on the plant types used is given in Table 3.

Table 3			
Plant Type	**Root Structure**	**Native Climate Type**	**Leaf Type**
1	Diffuse	Prairie	Grass-like
2	Taproot	Northern Forest	Evergreen Needle
3	Taproot	Prairie	Broad
4	Diffuse	Tropical Forest	Broad

6. In Experiment 2, which plant type most likely did NOT have a symbiotic relationship with the fungi?

F. Plant Type 1
G. Plant Type 2
H. Plant Type 3
J. Plant Type 4

7. A botanist claims that a symbiotic relationship exists between each of the plant types studied and the fungi that occur naturally in the soil. The claim is *inconsistent* with the results of Experiment 2 for which plant type?

A. Plant Type 1
B. Plant Type 2
C. Plant Type 3
D. Plant Type 4

GO ON TO THE NEXT PAGE.

8. Suppose a set of trials had been done in Experiment 1 in which fungi were introduced to the soil after Week 4. Plant growth during Week 6 would most likely have been:
 F. greater for Plant Types 2 and 3 only.
 G. less for Plant Types 1 and 4 only.
 H. greater for Plant Types 1, 2, and 3.
 J. less for all plant types.

9. Studies show that, in nature, specimens of Plant Type 2 reach an average height of 6.1 inches after 6 weeks of growth. Which of the following statements is most accurate based on the data presented?
 A. Plant Type 2 grows naturally in northern forests with fungi present in the soil.
 B. Plant Type 2 grows naturally in northern forests without fungi present in the soil.
 C. Plant Type 2 uses its diffuse root system to absorb nutrients from the soil.
 D. Plant Type 2 uses its broad evergreen needles to absorb nutrients from the soil.

10. During which time period did Plant Type 3 show the least amount of growth?
 F. Experiment 1, Week 2 to Week 4
 G. Experiment 1, Week 4 to Week 6
 H. Experiment 2, Week 2 to Week 4
 J. Experiment 2, Week 4 to Week 6

11. Suppose a fifth plant type was grown in Experiment 2 and the following average growth was reported:

Plant Type	Average Plant Growth (in.)		
	Week 2	Week 4	Week 6
5	1.6	2.7	3.4

This plant most likely:
 A. has a diffuse root system, broad leaves, and grows naturally in the prairie.
 B. has a taproot system, evergreen needles, and grows naturally in northern forests.
 C. has a diffuse root system, broad leaves, and grows naturally in tropical forests.
 D. has a taproot system, grasslike leaves, and grows naturally in the prairie.

PASSAGE III

The Great Lakes are a group of five large lakes located in the United States and Canada. They are the largest group of freshwater lakes in the world, and the Great Lakes–St. Lawrence River system is the largest freshwater system in the world. Recently, near-historic low water levels have plagued the water system. Two scientists discuss the causes of low water levels in the Great Lakes.

Scientist 1

Water levels are part of the ebb and flow of nature. The determining factor in whether the water level will rise, fall, or remain stable is the difference between the amount of water coming into a lake and the amount of water going out. When several months of above-average precipitation occur with cooler, cloudy conditions that cause less evaporation, the lake levels gradually rise. Likewise, the lowering of water levels will result from prolonged periods of lower-than-average precipitation and warmer temperatures.

The recent decline of water levels in the Great Lakes, now at lows not seen since the mid–1960s, is due to a number of causes. Higher levels of evaporation caused by warmer-than-usual temperatures in recent years, a series of mild winters, and a below-average snowpack in the Lake Superior basin have all contributed to the phenomenon. Since precipitation, evaporation, and runoff are the major factors affecting the water supply to the lakes, levels cannot be controlled or accurately predicted

for more than a few weeks into the future. Furthermore, the influence of human regulation of lake levels is very ineffective. Because water is added through snow and rain, and taken away through evaporation, nature has most of the control.

Scientist 2

Several human activities have affected the levels and flow of the water in the Great Lakes. For example, structures have been built to regulate the outflows of both Lake Superior and Lake Ontario. Lake Superior has been regulated since 1921 as a result of hydroelectric and navigation developments in the St. Mary's River, such as the Soo Locks. Lake Ontario has been regulated since 1960 after completion of the St. Lawrence Seaway and Power Project. Diversions bring water into, and take water out of, the Great Lakes. Many such diversions were constructed for hydropower generation and logging. For example, the Lake Michigan diversion at Chicago moves water out of Lake Michigan and into the Mississippi River for domestic, navigation, hydroelectric, and sanitation purposes.

In addition, the St. Clair and Detroit Rivers have been dredged and modified. This has caused some drop in the levels of Lakes Michigan and Huron. Channel and shoreline modifications in connecting the channels of the Great Lakes have affected lake levels and flows as well, because the infilling of shoreline areas can reduce the flow-carrying capacity of the river. Furthermore, the extensive use of groundwater deposited in massive aquifers (underground layers of water-bearing permeable rock) in the Midwest has affected the lake levels.

GO ON TO THE NEXT PAGE.

Vast quantities of water deposited in aquifers surrounding the Great Lakes are taken to population centers outside of the Great Lakes' watershed (region of land whose water drains into a specified body of water). Thus, the water is not replenished.

12. Which of the following generalizations about water levels is most consistent with Scientist 1's viewpoint?
   F. Human intervention has the greatest impact on water levels.
   G. Natural forces have the greatest impact on water levels.
   H. Humans and nature have an identical impact on water levels.
   J. Neither humans nor nature can have an impact on water levels.

13. With which of the following statements would both scientists be likely to agree?
   A. It is critical that the water in the Great Lakes be replenished somehow.
   B. The Great Lakes are most stable when humans intervene.
   C. Water levels in the Great Lakes cannot be affected by natural phenomena.
   D. The Great Lakes have changed over time solely as a result of the ebb and flow of nature.

14. According to Scientist 2, which of the following would be most likely to have the greatest impact on water levels in the Great Lakes?
   F. Higher temperatures during the summer months
   G. Longer periods of frigid cold during the winter months
   H. A heavier-than-normal snowfall in Canada
   J. Construction of a dam on the Detroit River

15. Based on Scientist 2's viewpoint, the Mississippi River contains water diverted from:
   A. the St. Lawrence Seaway.
   B. Lake Michigan.
   C. the Lake Superior Basin.
   D. Canada.

16. Scientist 1's viewpoint would most likely be *weakened* by which of the following statements?
   F. Lake level fluctuation has severe consequences for coastal communities.
   G. Studies have shown that precipitation and evaporation levels have been stable for the last 50 years.
   H. Studies detailing aquifer use announce a dramatic increase in volume in the last 5 years.
   J. Recreational boating releases thousands of gallons of petroleum-based chemicals into the water system each year.

17. Given the information regarding the location of the Great Lakes, which of the following would most likely NOT be true of the Great Lakes?
   A. The Great Lakes contain only freshwater.
   B. The Great Lakes empty directly into the Atlantic Ocean.
   C. The Great Lakes supply freshwater to several midwestern states.
   D. The Great Lakes are at least partially frozen in the winter.

18. Suppose a study of water levels in Lake Superior revealed that water levels have remained stable since the construction of the Soo Locks. How would this discovery most likely affect the scientists' viewpoints, if at all?
   F. It would strengthen Scientist 1's viewpoint only.
   G. It would weaken Scientist 2's viewpoint only.
   H. It would strengthen both scientists' viewpoints.
   J. It would have no effect on either scientist's viewpoint.

PASSAGE IV

Horses are susceptible to hoof infections that can seriously impair the horses' ability to walk. Horse breeders routinely administer dietary supplements in addition to the horses' regular feed in order to prevent these infections. A side effect of one of these supplements, supplement X, is increased urination, which can sometimes lead to dehydration in the animal.

Twenty (20) adult horses, each weighing approximately 1,000 pounds, were randomly selected and assigned to two groups of 10 horses each. Group R received dietary supplement X, while Group S received a placebo. Each horse in both groups received the same amount of feed and water each day. The horses were placed in individual stalls for 7 days, during which time their urine output was measured. The results are shown in Figure 1.

Figure 1

GO ON TO THE NEXT PAGE.

19. Which of the following generalizations best fits the results of the study?
- **A.** The effects of dietary supplement X on urinary output cannot be immediately detected.
- **B.** Dietary supplements should be administered over time in order to be effective.
- **C.** Dietary supplement X has no effect on urinary output in horses.
- **D.** The horses in Group R urinated less frequently than did the horses in Group S.

20. In order to best determine the effects of dietary supplement X in this experiment, one should examine:
- **F.** the type of feed that each horse was given.
- **G.** the amount of feed that each horse was given.
- **H.** the urinary output of each horse over time.
- **J.** the average urinary output of a third group.

21. Based on the information in Figure 1, on which day did the control group have the highest urinary output?
- **A.** Day 7
- **B.** Day 4
- **C.** Day 3
- **D.** Day 1

22. During the study, several of the horses in Group R began showing signs of dehydration. According to the passage, what is the most likely cause of this?
- **F.** The low urinary output of the horses in Group R.
- **G.** The amount of water that the horses in Group R were given.
- **H.** The high urinary output of the horses in Group R.
- **J.** The lack of supplements in the diet of the horses in Group R.

23. Which of the following statements is supported by the data presented in Figure 1?
- **A.** Urinary output increased over time for Group S only.
- **B.** Urinary output increased over time for Group R only.
- **C.** Urinary output increased over time for neither Group R nor Group S.
- **D.** Urinary output increased over time for both Group R and Group S.

24. Do the results of the study show that dietary supplement X could cause dehydration in horses?
- **F.** Yes, because the urinary output increased over time in the group that received the supplement.
- **G.** Yes, because the control group maintained a relatively constant urinary output.
- **H.** No, because the urinary output stayed the same over time in the group that received the supplement.
- **J.** No, because the urinary output of the control group was not adequately measured.

PASSAGE V

Carbon-14 dating is a process that uses radioactivity to determine the age of an organic material. It is typically used to establish the age of archaeological artifacts, such as bones, insect remains, plant fibers, or any material that was once living or was derived from something that was living.

Each radioactive substance has a *half-life*, which is the amount of time that it takes for the initial amount of the substance to be reduced by 50% (also called radioactive decay). The half-life of carbon-14 is approximately 5,730 years. Figure 1 shows the half-life decay of carbon-14, with each increment on the *x* axis representing one half-life.

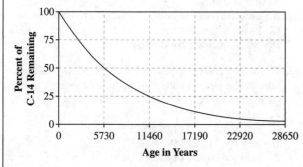

Figure 1

Carbon-14 is a naturally occurring radioactive isotope that is continually generated in the upper atmosphere. It is absorbed by all living things and is ingested by humans and animals. The ratio of normal carbon (carbon-12) to carbon-14 in the air and in all living things is nearly constant. As soon as something that was living dies, it stops taking in new carbon. Carbon-12 will remain constant, and carbon-14 will continue to decay. To determine the object's age, the ratio of carbon-12 to carbon-14 must be observed and compared to the ratio of carbon-12 to carbon-14 in all living things. With this information, scientists can determine the age of something that is no longer living.

Figure 2 shows the ages of different organic materials and each material's *carbon ratio*. The carbon ratio is a comparison of the present amount of carbon-14 (A) to the original amount of carbon-14 (A_0) in an object. The original amount of carbon-14 is the amount that the organic material contained while it was still living.

GO ON TO THE NEXT PAGE.

Figure 2

25. What is the approximate age in years of an organic material with 12.5% carbon-14 remaining?
    A. 1,430
    B. 5,730
    C. 17,190
    D. 28,650

26. Inorganic (nonliving) rocks cannot be dated using the carbon-14 method. Which of the following best explains why?
    F. Only animals and humans contain carbon-12 and carbon-14.
    G. The carbon ratio of inorganic materials is too high.
    H. Only materials that were once living can be dated using the carbon-14 method.
    J. The carbon ratio of inorganic materials is too low.

27. Which of the following best explains the relationship between the carbon ratio and the age of an object?
    A. As the carbon ratio decreases, the age increases.
    B. As the carbon ratio decreases, the age decreases.
    C. A ratio close to 1 signifies an older object.
    D. A ratio close to 0 signifies an age of less than 1,000 years.

28. According to information in the passage, which of the following is NOT true? Carbon-14:
    F. remains constant as carbon-12 decays after an organism dies.
    G. has a half-life of 5,730 years.
    H. decays while carbon-12 remains constant after an organism dies.
    J. is used to determine the age of organic materials.

PASSAGE VI

The molar heat of fusion is the amount of heat necessary to melt (or freeze) 1.00 mole of a substance at its melting point at a constant pressure. The molar heat of fusion for water is 6.02 kilojoules per mole (kJ/mol).

The equation for the molar heat of fusion is:

$$q = \Delta H_{fus} \text{ (mass/molar mass)}$$

In this equation, q is the total amount of heat involved, ΔH_{fus} represents the molar heat of fusion (this value is a constant for a given substance), and (mass/molar mass) represents the number of moles of a given substance.

Table 1 lists the molar heats of fusion, boiling points, and melting points for several elements.

Table 1

Element	Melting Point (°C)	Boiling Point (°C)	ΔH_{fus} (kJ/mol)
Calcium	839.00	1,484.00	8.54
Silver	961.92	2,212.00	11.30
Iron	1,535.00	2,750.00	13.80
Nickel	1,453.00	2,732.00	17.46

Note: Measured at a pressure of 1 atmosphere (atm).

29. According to the passage, ΔH_{fus} of water:
    A. is less than ΔH_{fus} of calcium.
    B. is greater than ΔH_{fus} of calcium.
    C. is greater than ΔH_{fus} of nickel.
    D. cannot be determined.

30. The energy required to melt 1.00 mole of iron at 1,535°C and constant pressure of 1 atm is:
    F. 6.02 kJ.
    G. 8.54 kJ.
    H. 13.80 kJ.
    J. 2,750.00 kJ.

31. According to the table, as the energy required to melt 1 mole of the given elements increases, the melting points:
    A. increase only.
    B. decrease only.
    C. increase, then decrease.
    D. neither increase nor decrease.

32. The boiling point of potassium is 759.90°C. If potassium follows the general pattern of the other elements in the table, its molar heat of fusion would be:
    F. below 8 kJ/mol.
    G. between 8 and 11 kJ/mol.
    H. between 11 and 14 kJ/mol.
    J. between 14 and 18 kJ/mol.

33. The molar heat of fusion is directly related to the strength of the forces that hold molecules together; strong forces make it difficult for molecules to break away into the liquid or gaseous phase. Data in the table support the conclusion that those forces are stronger in:

A. calcium than in silver.
B. silver than in nickel.
C. iron than in calcium.
D. iron than in nickel.

34. It was hypothesized that the molar heat of fusion will increase as the boiling point increases. Based on the data in the table, which of the following pairs of elements support(s) this hypothesis?

  I. Nickel and iron
  II. Water and calcium
  III. Silver and iron

F. I only
G. III only
H. II and III only
J. I, II, and III

PASSAGE VII

Compost is the name given to a mixture of decaying leaves and other organic material. This mixture is often used as fertilizer. Several students designed experiments to test the effect of various types of soil and various combinations of soil and compost on plant growth.

Experiment 1

The students dug a soil sample from an empty field next to the school. They put soil into 4 different clay pots, and mixed in various amounts of compost so that the volume of soil mixture was the same in each pot. They then planted the same number of basil seeds (4) in each pot. The soil/compost mixtures for each pot are shown in Table 1.

Table 1

Soil/Compost Mixture (Pot #)	% Soil/% Compost
1	25%/75%
2	50%/50%
3	75%/25%
4	100% soil

The clay pots were placed next to each other on a windowsill and watered at the same time each day. The students took care to ensure that the pots each received the same amount of sunlight and water each day. After 2 weeks, the students began recording the growth of the basil plants. They continued recording these data for two more weeks. The results are shown in Table 2.

Table 2

Soil/Compost Mixture (Pot #)	Average Plant Height (cm)			Average Number of Leaves		
	14 days	21 days	28 days	14 days	21 days	28 days
1	4.2	5.3	6.2	3	5.5	8
2	3.8	4.8	5.1	3	4.5	6.5
3	3.3	4.4	4.8	2	4	5.5
4	3.2	4.1	4.4	2	3.5	4.5

Experiment 2

The students repeated Experiment 1, with the following changes: each pot contained a different soil type, and no compost was used. This experiment was begun at the same time as Experiment 1. The results of Experiment 2 are shown in Table 3.

Table 3

Soil Type	Average Plant Height (cm)			Average Number of Leaves		
	14 days	21 days	28 days	14 days	21 days	28 days
Sand (1)	2.4	2.9	3.4	1	2.5	3.5
Potting soil (2)	3.9	4.7	5.3	3	4	6
Soil from a field near the school (3)	3.2	4.2	4.3	2	3.5	4.5
Mixture of sand and potting soil (4)	3.1	3.3	4.2	2	4	5.5

35. According to the results of Experiment 1, what percentage of compost yielded the highest average number of leaves?

A. 100%
B. 75%
C. 50%
D. 25%

36. Based on the results of Experiment 2, which soil type yielded the most overall growth after 28 days?

F. sand
G. potting soil
H. soil from the field near the school
J. a mixture of sand and potting soil

37. Based on the results of Experiment 1, which soil/compost mixture yielded the greatest average plant height after the first 2 weeks?

A. 4
B. 3
C. 2
D. 1

GO ON TO THE NEXT PAGE.

38. Experiment 2 was different from Experiment 1 in that none of the clay pots:

F. was watered during the first 2 weeks.

G. contained any compost.

H. contained any soil.

J. was placed on the windowsill.

39. The results of Soil Type 3 in Experiment 2 and Pot 4 in Experiment 1 were almost identical. This is most likely because:

A. the same amount of compost was used.

B. the plants were allowed to grow for 2 more weeks.

C. the pots were the same size.

D. the same type of soil was used.

40. In Experiment 2, how many seeds were planted in each clay pot?

F. 4

G. 14

H. 21

J. Cannot be determined from the information given.

END OF THE SCIENCE TEST.
STOP! IF YOU HAVE TIME LEFT OVER, CHECK YOUR WORK ON THIS SECTION ONLY.

ANSWER KEY

Science Test

1. B	11. C	21. D	31. C
2. G	12. G	22. H	32. F
3. B	13. A	23. B	33. C
4. J	14. J	24. F	34. H
5. B	15. B	25. C	35. B
6. J	16. G	26. H	36. G
7. D	17. B	27. A	37. D
8. H	18. G	28. F	38. G
9. A	19. A	29. A	39. D
10. G	20. H	30. H	40. F

SCORING WORKSHEET

Scale Score	Raw Score Science	Scale Score	Raw Score Science
36	39–40	18	15–16
35	38	17	14
34	37	16	12–13
33	36	15	11
32	—	14	10
31	35	13	9
30	34	12	8
29	33	11	7
28	32	10	6
27	31	9	5
26	29–30	8	4
25	27–28	7	3
24	25–26	6	—
23	23–24	5	2
22	21–22	4	—
21	20	3	1
20	18–19	2	—
19	17	1	0

NOTE: Each actual ACT is scaled slightly differently based on a large amount of information gathered from the millions of tests ACT, Inc., scores each year. This scale will give you a fairly good idea of where you are in your preparation process. However, it should not be read as an absolute predictor of your actual ACT score. In fact, on practice tests, the scores are much less important than what you learn from analyzing your results.

ANSWERS AND EXPLANATIONS

Passage I

1. **The correct answer is B.** According to the passage, "One of the methods by which cytoxic T lymphocytes (CTLs) kill nearby virus-infected cells is by inducing apoptosis."

2. **The correct answer is G.** According to the passage, "One normal component of cell health and development is *apoptosis*, which is an example of this communication between cells. Apoptosis is a normal and healthy process that regulates the death of a cell that is unnecessary, unwanted, or damaged."

3. **The correct answer is B.** The passage states, "Once a signal has been transmitted to a cell, the cytoplasm begins to shrink, followed by the breakdown of proteins within the cell, which causes the cell to take on a horseshoe-like shape. The cell will continue to shrink, forming tiny blisters (indicated by an arrow in Figure 1) that make it easier for *phagocytic* cells to do their job and remove the fragmented cell from the tissues of an organism." This is shown by the cell in answer choice B.

4. **The correct answer is J.** The passage states, "Once a signal has been transmitted to a cell, the cytoplasm begins to shrink, followed by the breakdown of proteins within the cell, which causes the cell to take on a horseshoe-like shape. The cell will continue to shrink, forming tiny blisters (indicated by an arrow in Figure 1) that make it easier for *phagocytic* cells to do their job and remove the fragmented cell from the tissues of an organism." Figure 1 shows the blisters appearing in Stage 4.

5. **The correct answer is B.** According to the passage, "External signals are received by cell surface receptors and are transmitted to the cytoplasm, the fluid on the inside of the cell, which begins to self-destruct. External signals occur when other cells recognize virus-infected cells nearby and send a message to try to stop the spread of a disease such as cancer. One of the methods by which cytoxic T lymphocytes (CTLs) kill nearby virus-infected cells is by inducing apoptosis."

Passage II

6. **The correct answer is J.** According to the passage, "The plant gains the use of the fungi's surface area to absorb mineral nutrients from the soil. It is believed that without the assistance of fungi, these plants would not be able to absorb crucial nutrients, including phosphates, from the soil." This indicates that the plants will

probably grow more efficiently in the presence of fungi. The results of Experiment 2 are shown in Table 2. The data for Plant Type 4 show less growth than those for any of the other plant types, suggesting that Plant Type 4 does not have a symbiotic relationship with the fungi.

7. **The correct answer is D.** According to the passage, "The plant gains the use of the fungi's surface area to absorb mineral nutrients from the soil. It is believed that without the assistance of fungi, these plants would not be able to absorb crucial nutrients, including phosphates, from the soil." This indicates that the plants will probably grow more efficiently in the presence of fungi. The results of Experiment 2 are shown in Table 2. The data for Plant Type 4 show less growth than those for any of the other plant types, suggesting that Plant Type 4 does not have a symbiotic relationship with the fungi.

8. **The correct answer is H.** According to the passage, "The plant gains the use of the fungi's surface area to absorb mineral nutrients from the soil. It is believed that without the assistance of fungi, these plants would not be able to absorb crucial nutrients, including phosphates, from the soil." This indicates that the plants will probably grow more efficiently in the presence of fungi. No fungi were present in Experiment 1; fungi were present in Experiment 2. When comparing the data from each experiment for Plant Type 4, you see very little change, suggesting that Plant Type 4 does not have a symbiotic relationship with the fungi. Therefore, the presence of fungi would be beneficial only to Plant Types 1, 2, and 3.

9. **The correct answer is A.** According to Table 3, Plant Type 2 is native to northern forests, and has a taproot system and evergreen needles. Eliminate answer choice C. You can also use common sense to eliminate answer choice D; it is unlikely that a plant's leaves or needles would absorb nutrients from the soil. Table 2 shows that after 6 weeks, Plant Type 2 had very nearly reached its average height of 6.1 inches, suggesting that Plant Type 2 has a symbiotic relationship with fungi found naturally in the soil.

10. **The correct answer is G.** According to Table 1, Plant Type 3 grew only 0.6 inch from Week 4 to Week 6, which is the least amount of growth for any of the time periods shown in the answer choices.

11. **The correct answer is C.** Based on the new information and the information in Tables 1 and 2, Plant Type 5 is most like Plant Type 4. According to Table 3, Plant

Type 4 has a diffuse root system and broad leaves, and grows naturally in tropical forests.

Passage III

12. The correct answer is G. According to Scientist 1, "Water levels are part of the ebb and flow of nature." This is most consistent with answer choice G.

13. The correct answer is A. Because both scientists are studying water levels in the Great Lakes, and because both appear to be concerned about declining water levels, it makes sense that both scientists would agree that it is critical that the water in the Great Lakes be replenished somehow.

14. The correct answer is J. According to Scientist 2, "Several human activities have affected the levels and flow of the water in the Great Lakes." Scientist 2 also points out that "the St. Clair and Detroit Rivers have been dredged and modified. This has caused some drop in the levels of Lakes Michigan and Huron." Therefore, you can assume that construction of a dam on the Detroit River would affect water levels in the Great Lakes.

15. The correct answer is B. According to Scientist 2, "The Lake Michigan diversion at Chicago moves water out of Lake Michigan and into the Mississippi River for domestic, navigation, hydroelectric, and sanitation purposes."

16. The correct answer is G. If studies have shown that precipitation and evaporation levels have been stable for the last 50 years, Scientist 1's viewpoint would be weakened. This is because Scientist 1 says that a recent increase in evaporation has contributed to lower lake levels: "The recent decline of water levels in the Great Lakes, now at lows not seen since the mid-1960s, is due to a number of causes. Higher levels of evaporation caused by warmer-than-usual temperatures in recent years. . . ." Because this statement would be disproved, the scientist's viewpoint would be weakened.

17. The correct answer is B. The passage indicates that the Great Lakes are located in the Midwest, specifically near Michigan, Wisconsin, Illinois, Indiana, and Ohio. In addition, Canada contains a portion of the Great Lakes. Therefore, it would not be true that the Great Lakes empty directly into the Atlantic Ocean.

18. The correct answer is G. According to Scientist 2, "Several human activities have affected the levels

and flow of the water in the Great Lakes." If it were true that the Soo Locks did not affect water levels in the Great Lakes, Scientist 2's viewpoint would be weakened.

Passage IV

19. The correct answer is A. According to the results of the experiment, the increase in urine output caused by dietary supplement X could not be immediately detected. On Days 1 and 2, the horses that received a placebo had a greater average urine output than Group R. It does not become apparent until Day 3 that the dietary supplement is steadily increasing the urine output of the Group R horses.

20. The correct answer is H. In order to best determine the effects of dietary supplement X in this experiment, one should examine the urinary output of each horse over time. This would provide more information on the effects of dietary supplement X on each horse.

21. The correct answer is D. Figure 1 shows the control group (Group S) having the highest average urine output per horse on Day 1 (2.1 gallons).

22. The correct answer is H. The passage states: "A side effect of one of these supplements, supplement X, is increased urination, which can sometimes lead to dehydration in the animal." This suggests that the reason that several horses began showing signs of dehydration is because of their high urinary output.

23. The correct answer is B. Figure 1 shows that over the course of the seven days, the urinary output for each horse in Group R increased, but the urinary output for the horses in Group S remained about the same (with some minor fluctuations), which best supports answer choice B.

24. The correct answer is F. Over time, the urinary output for the group that received the supplement increased. According to the passage, increased urination can sometimes lead to dehydration, which supports the statement that dietary supplement X could cause dehydration in horses. Answer choice H can be eliminated because the table suggests that this answer choice is false.

Passage V

25. The correct answer is C. To answer this question, look at Figure 1 and draw a horizontal line from the point on the y axis representing 12.5% (halfway between 0 and 25%) until it intersects the curved line. This intersection occurs at 17,190 years.

26. The correct answer is H. According to the passage, "Carbon-14 is a naturally occurring radioactive isotope that is continually generated in the upper atmosphere. It is absorbed by all living things and is ingested by humans and animals." Therefore, a nonliving rock cannot be carbon dated.

27. The correct answer is A. According to Figure 2, younger objects have higher carbon ratios. As an object ages, its carbon ratio decreases.

28. The correct answer is F. According to the passage, "Carbon-12 will remain constant, and carbon-14 will continue to decay."

Passage VI

29. The correct answer is A. The passage states that the molar heat of fusion (ΔH_{fus}) of water is 6.02. This value is less than the molar heat of fusion of calcium.

30. The correct answer is H. According to the passage, the molar heat of fusion (ΔH_{fus}) is "the amount of heat necessary to melt (or freeze) 1.00 mole of a substance at its melting point at a constant pressure." The table indicates that the molar heat of fusion for iron is 13.8 kJ/mol.

31. The correct answer is C. According to the passage, the molar heat of fusion (ΔH_{fus}) is "the amount of heat necessary to melt (or freeze) 1.00 mole of a substance at its melting point at a constant pressure." The table shows that the molar heat of fusion and the melting point both increase for calcium, silver, and iron, but the melting point decreases as the molar heat of fusion continues to increase for nickel. This best supports answer choice C.

32. The correct answer is F. The table shows that, in general, higher boiling points result in a higher molar heat of fusion. Therefore, because the boiling point for potassium is lower than the boiling point for calcium, it is likely that the molar heat of fusion for potassium will be lower than the molar heat of fusion for calcium.

33. The correct answer is C. You are given that the molar heat of fusion is directly related to the strength of the forces that hold molecules together; therefore, higher molar heats of fusion will indicate stronger bonds between molecules. Iron has a higher molar heat of fusion than calcium, so the forces holding molecules together will be stronger in iron than in calcium.

34. The correct answer is H. To answer this question, compare the boiling points and molar heats of fusion for each of the pairs of elements:

I. Nickel and iron. The boiling point of iron is higher than the boiling point of nickel, but the molar heat of fusion is lower for iron than it is for nickel. Roman numeral I does *not* support the hypothesis, so eliminate answer choices F and J.

II. Water and calcium. The boiling point of water is lower than the boiling point of calcium, and the molar heat of fusion is lower for water than it is for calcium. Roman numeral II supports the hypothesis, so eliminate answer choice G.

The process of elimination leaves you with answer choice H, but if you evaluate Roman numeral III, you will see that it also supports the hypothesis.

Passage VII

35. The correct answer is B. Based on the data in Table 2, Pot 1 yielded the highest average number of leaves. Table 1 indicates that this pot contained 75 percent compost and 25 percent soil.

36. The correct answer is G. According to Table 3, the average height of the plants grown in potting soil was 5.3 centimeters, and the average number of leaves on the plants grown in potting soil was 6. This best supports answer choice G.

37. The correct answer is D. According to Table 2, after 14 days, the soil/compost mixture that yielded the greatest average plant height was mixture 1, with an average plant height of 4.2 centimeters.

38. The correct answer is G. The passage states that in Experiment 2, "Each pot contained a different soil type, and no compost was used." The other answer choices are not supported by the passage.

39. The correct answer is D. Based on the data in Tables 2 and 3, soil from near the school was used in Pot 4 in Experiment 1 and in Pot 3 in Experiment 2. This would most likely account for the nearly identical results recorded. The other answer choices are not supported by the data.

40. The correct answer is F. The passage indicates that 4 basil seeds were placed in each pot in Experiment 1. The only differences between Experiment 1 and Experiment 2 were the soil types used and the fact that no compost was used. Therefore, the same number of seeds (4) was planted in each pot in Experiment 2.

CHAPTER 12

STRATEGIES AND TECHNIQUES

As mentioned in Chapter 10, the ACT Science Test is designed to measure the interpretation, analysis, evaluation, reasoning, and problem-solving skills that apply to the study of the natural sciences. You will be required to recognize and understand the basic concepts related to the information contained within the passages, critically examine the hypotheses developed, and generalize from given information to draw conclusions or make predictions.

You will not receive credit for anything that you write in your test booklet, but you should use any available space in the Science Test section to organize data, make notes, or do simple math calculations. This work can help you to stay focused and can lead you more easily to the correct answer.

If you don't know the answer to a question, mark the question in your test booklet and come back to it later if you have time. Cross off answer choices that you are able to eliminate. Make an educated guess if you are able to eliminate even one answer choice. Remember that every correct answer counts on the ACT, so it is in your best interest to fill in every bubble on your answer sheet.

The following strategies will help you to answer as many of the questions on your ACT Science Test as possible correctly:

- Prioritize
- Apply logic and common sense
- Be "trendy"
- Ignore "sciency" language
- Read the questions carefully
- Predict answers

PRIORITIZE

For some students, the task of completing all seven Science passages in the time allowed can be daunting. Prioritizing the passages can help you to work efficiently—remember, the goal is to answer as many questions as possible correctly. Sometimes it makes sense to slow down a bit and focus on five or six of the passages, then simply guess on the remaining questions. Practice sufficiently to determine which types of passages consistently give you trouble, and save those passages for last.

There are a few factors to consider when deciding which passage(s) you will sacrifice. For example, you should certainly look at the subject matter. Most students have distinct preferences for the passages that deal with experiments and the results of studies because the data are presented in a fairly straightforward manner. If you decide to focus on five or six passages on test day, let your practice help guide you when you are deciding which passages to sacrifice. Choose the format that fits you best. If you are having a hard time making sense of the passage that you start with, move on to some less confusing material. The best way to know which passages to do first on test day is to practice ahead of time so that you can recognize the passages that are likely to give you the most points for the time that you put in.

APPLY LOGIC AND COMMON SENSE

Once you have chosen your first passage to attack, take a moment or two to understand the main idea or ideas presented before you dig into the questions. Then, focus on the questions, as they will almost always tell you exactly where in the passage you can find the answer. Common sense will help to keep you from being fooled by some of the distracters that are "way out." For instance, if the passage is describing an experiment done with living animals in a laboratory, and the question asks about temperatures that are likely to result in a certain behavior, you could certainly rule out an answer choice that says, "400 degrees Fahrenheit."

Because the questions typically tell you exactly where to look for the answer ("Based on the results of Experiment 1, … "), don't take the time to read the passage first. After a quick evaluation to determine whether you will attempt the passage, go right to the questions. Stay focused on the data, and remember that logic and common sense will always prevail.

BE "TRENDY"

Many of the Science questions reward test takers who can spot trends in the data presented. When charts or graphs are given, take a moment to figure out which variables are being charted and note any apparent relationships between them. A *direct relationship* is when one variable increases as the other increases. An *inverse relationship* is when one variable *decreases* as another increases. Sometimes the data reveal a lack of relationship. As you have learned in your science classes, this is often the result of experimentation and observation.

IGNORE "SCIENCY" LANGUAGE

There will certainly be language on the Science Test that is new to you. Don't get worried when you see words that you have never seen before. The ACT usually defines terms that are absolutely essential to your understanding. You can answer questions about some terms without even knowing exactly what they mean as long as you focus on the data and the overall idea of the passage.

Never spend time trying to figure out how to pronounce any of the unfamiliar terms that you run across. That is simply a waste of time and energy. Remember, this is not a test of your scientific knowledge! It is a test of your ability to apply strategic thinking, logic, and common sense when answering questions that relate to scientific data.

READ THE QUESTIONS CAREFULLY

Start at the beginning of each group of questions. Read the question and make sure that you understand it. Paraphrase it if you need to. This means to put the question into your own words. If you paraphrase, keep your language simple. Pretend you are "translating" the question to an average eighth grader. If you are sure that the eighth grader you are imagining can understand the question, then you are ready to answer it.

Isolate key words and phrases in the question by circling or underlining them. Pay attention to whether the question asks you to focus on the results of a specific study or experiment. You can sometimes quickly eliminate answer choices that respond to a data set that is NOT being asked about in the question.

■■■ PREDICT ANSWERS

> **Study Tip**
>
> Simplify the question and predict an answer based on the data. Trust the data, and don't over-analyze either the questions or your answers!

Once you have found the information among the data that will provide the answer that you are looking for, try to answer the question in your mind. Do this before you look at the answer choices. Remember, three out of every four answer choices are incorrect. Not only are they incorrect, but they were written by experts to confuse you. They are less likely to confuse you if you have a clear idea of what the answer should be before you read the answer choices. If you can predict an answer for the question, then skim the choices presented and look for the answer that you predicted. You may have to be a little flexible to recognize it. If you can recognize a paraphrase of your predicted answer, mark it. The odds that you will have managed to predict one of the "distracter" (incorrect) answer choices are slim. Mark the question if you are unsure. You can always come back to it later if there is time.

The rest of this chapter will provide an overview of the scientific method, a brief review of basic scientific concepts, an introduction to the types of questions you will see on the ACT Science Test, and sample questions with explanations.

■■■ THE SCIENTIFIC METHOD

The scientific method is the process by which scientists attempt to construct an accurate representation of the world. This process is fundamental to scientific investigation and the acquisition of new knowledge based upon actual physical evidence and careful observation. The scientific method is a means of building a supportable, documented understanding of our world.

The scientific method includes four essential elements:

1. Observation
2. Hypothesis
3. Prediction
4. Experiment

During the *observation* phase, the experimenter will directly observe and measure the phenomenon that is being studied. Careful notes should be taken, and all pertinent data should be recorded so that the phenomenon (thing being observed) can be accurately described.

The experimenter will then generate a *hypothesis* to explain the phenomenon. He or she will speculate as to the reason for the phenomenon, based on the observations made and recorded.

Next, the experimenter will make *predictions* to test the hypothesis. These predictions are tested with scientific experiments, designed to either prove or disprove the hypothesis. The scientific method requires that any hypothesis be either ruled out or modified if the predictions are clearly and consistently incompatible with the experimental results.

If the experiments bear out the hypothesis, it may come to be regarded as a *theory* or *law of nature*. However, it is possible that new information and discoveries could contradict any hypothesis, at any stage of experimentation.

The passages included on the ACT Science Test have been written with the scientific method in mind. You can often use common sense along with a basic understanding of this process to answer many of the questions.

Experimental Design

When scientists design experiments to test their hypotheses, they have to be careful to avoid "confounding of variables." This means that they have to isolate, as much as possible, one variable at a time so that they can reveal the relationships between the variables, if any. An *independent variable* (one that is manipulated by the experimenter) is under the control of the scientist. As the scientist changes the independent variable, it is hoped that the *dependent variable* (observed by the experimenter) will change as a result, and that a relationship can be established.

A *control* is an element of the experiment that is not subjected to the same changes in the independent variable as the *experimental* elements. For instance, if we want to find out how the consumption of sugar affects the fatigue level of ACT takers, we would have to be sure to have at least a few ACT takers who do not consume any sugar so that we can measure the "baseline" or "natural" fatigue level of ACT takers for comparison to the group that consumes sugar. If there were no control group, we wouldn't be able to say for sure that sugar has any impact on the fatigue level of ACT takers. If all of the test takers consumed sugar, and all of them were sleepy, we would face a "confounding of variables" situation because the sleepiness could be caused by any other factor that the group had in common, like the ACT itself!

Some of the ACT Science passages refer to "studies" rather than experiments. An experiment is an artificial situation that is created by the researcher. A study is simply a careful, documented observation. Studies can include some of the elements of experiments, such as control groups.

■ PRACTICE QUESTIONS

As mentioned previously, the ACT Science Test includes three basic passage types: Data Representation, Research Summaries, and Conflicting Viewpoints. In this section, we will further describe those passage types and provide examples of each.

Data Representation

Data Representation passages present scientific information in tables, charts, graphs, and figures similar to those that you might find in a scientific journal or other scientific publication. The questions associated with Data Representation passages will ask you to interpret and analyze the data shown in the tables, charts, graphs, and figures. Following is a Data Representation passage and several questions. The answers and explanations are given at the end of this chapter.

A virus is a tiny particle that needs a multi cellular host, like a plant or an animal, in which to live and replicate. Unlike bacteria, viruses cannot live and reproduce without a host. Viruses wait in the environment and enter a host through the nose, the mouth, or a cut in the skin. Once it is successfully inside an organism, the virus finds a host cell to invade, causing infection and disease.

The average time that elapses between exposure to a virus and the appearance of symptoms is called the *incubation period*. The period of time during which a person with a viral infection is capable of passing the virus on to others is called the *contagious period*.

Table 1 shows the incubation period and the contagious period for several skin infections caused by viruses. All of the viruses in Table 1 attack host cells that line the skin.

Table 1			
Infection	**Incubation period**	**Contagious period begins**	**Contagious period ends**
Chicken pox	11–23 days	4 days after symptoms appear	When all sores have scabbed over
Roseola	8–10 days	Onset of fever	When rash is gone
Measles	9–13 days	5 days before rash appears	7 days after rash is gone
Erythema infectiosum	5–14 days	7 days before rash appears	When rash appears
Hand, foot, and mouth disease	2–6 days	Onset of sores in mouth	When fever is gone

Table 2 shows the incubation period and the contagious period for several respiratory infections caused by viruses. All of the viruses in Table 2 attack host cells that line the respiratory tract.

Table 2			
Infection	**Incubation period**	**Contagious period begins**	**Contagious period ends**
Bronchiolitis	3–7 days	Onset of cough	7 days after onset of cough
Common cold	1–3 days	Onset of symptoms	1 day after fever is gone
Influenza	1–2 days	Onset of symptoms	1 day after fever is gone
Viral sore throat	3–6 days	Onset of symptoms	When fever is gone
Croup	1–5 days	Onset of cough	When fever is gone

1. Roseola is an infant skin disease that is characterized by a high fever for 3 to 5 days and a red rash (appearing once the fever has subsided) that lasts for approximately 48 hours. According to Table 1, the virus that causes roseola is contagious for:
   A. 1–3 days.
   B. 2–5 days.
   C. 5–7 days.
   D. 8–10 days.

2. Based on Table 1, which of the following is the most common symptom of skin disease?
   F. Scabs
   G. Mouth sores
   H. Fever
   J. Rash

3. According to Table 1 and Table 2, the viral infection that takes the least amount of time to produce any symptoms is:
   A. chicken pox.
   B. croup.
   C. influenza.
   D. viral sore throat.

4. Which of the following would most likely reduce the contagious period of the virus that causes chicken pox?
   F. A cream that dries out the sores
   G. Pain relievers that quickly reduce high fevers
   H. Medicine that encourages scratching
   J. An ointment that moistens the sores

5. The HIV virus causes a progressive infection that damages the immune system. Which of the following is most likely true of the HIV virus?
   A. The HIV virus has one of the shortest contagious periods of any known virus.
   B. The HIV virus attacks the cells of the immune system.
   C. The incubation period of the HIV virus is similar to those of respiratory viruses.
   D. The incubation period of the HIV virus is shorter than most.

Research Summary

Research Summary passages provide descriptions of one or more related experiments or studies. The passages usually include a discussion of the design, methods, and results of the experiments or studies. The corresponding questions will ask you to comprehend, evaluate, and interpret the procedures and results. Following is a Research Summary passage and several questions. The answers and explanations are given at the end of this chapter.

Several scientists considered some different environmental factors and their influence on the growth of certain bacteria. The following experiments used *Salmonella* bacteria to measure the effect of pH levels, nutrients, and temperature on the number of bacteria produced within a given time period.

Experiment 1

A known quantity of *Salmonella* bacteria was placed in each of 3 petri dishes with the same nutrient concentration at the same temperature. The pH level of the nutrient concentration in each dish was varied according to Table 1. On the pH scale, 7 represents neutral, values less than 7 indicate an acid, and values greater than 7 indicate a base. The lids of the petri dishes were replaced, and the dishes were left alone. After 6 hours, the percent growth of *Salmonella* bacteria was recorded (Table 1).

Table 1		
Dish	**pH level**	**Percent growth**
1	5	27
2	7	81
3	9	38

Experiment 2

A known quantity of *Salmonella* bacteria was placed in each of 3 petri dishes with different nutrient concentrations in the form of organic compounds. The temperature and pH level (neutral 7) were held constant in each sample. The lids of the petri dishes were replaced, and the dishes were left alone. After 6 hours, the percent growth of *Salmonella* bacteria was recorded (Table 2).

Table 2			
Dish	Organic compound	Percent of dry weight	Percent growth
1	Carbon	50	37
	Oxygen	20	
	Nitrogen	15	
2	Carbon	25	16
	Oxygen	10	
	Nitrogen	7	
3	Carbon	12.5	8
	Oxygen	5	
	Nitrogen	20	

Experiment 3

A known quantity of *Salmonella* bacteria was placed in each of 3 petri dishes at different temperatures. The pH level and nutrient concentrations were held constant. The lids of the petri dishes were replaced, and the dishes were left alone. After 6 hours, the percent growth of *Salmonella* bacteria was recorded (Table 3).

Table 3		
Dish	Temperature (°C)	Percent growth
1	10	13
2	40	83
3	90	24

1. According to Table 1, what might best contribute to the growth of *Salmonella* bacteria?
   A. A pH level above 9
   B. A pH level below 5
   C. A pH level near 7
   D. A pH level near 5

2. According to the results of the three experiments, which combination of the three factors studied would be expected to produce the highest percent growth?
   F. pH level of 5, Organic Compounds in Dish 2, Temperature of 40°C
   G. pH level of 7, Organic Compounds in Dish 2, Temperature of 10°C
   H. pH level of 7, Organic Compounds in Dish 1, Temperature of 40°C
   J. pH level of 9, Organic Compounds in Dish 1, Temperature of 90°C

3. Which of the following conclusions is strengthened by the results of Experiment 1?
  A. *Salmonella* bacteria reproduce most efficiently in an acidic environment.
  B. *Salmonella* bacteria reproduce most efficiently in a neutral environment.
  C. *Salmonella* bacteria cannot reproduce in a basic environment.
  D. *Salmonella* bacteria cannot reproduce in an acidic environment.

4. Bacteria will often reproduce until all of the available nutrients have been depleted. How could the experiment be altered to maximize the length of time that bacteria will reproduce?
  F. Change the observation time from 6 hours to 12 hours.
  G. Regularly resupply each group of bacteria with unlimited nutrients.
  H. Increase the rate of growth by decreasing the pH levels.
  J. Do not test the effect of different nutrient combinations on growth.

5. The nutritional requirements of a bacterium are determined by the makeup of the elements within its cells. According to the experiments, which of the following elements are present in the cells of a *Salmonella* bacterium?
  A. Nitrogen and hydrogen
  B. Bases and vitamins
  C. Nitrogen and acids
  D. Carbon and oxygen

6. The experiments recorded the percent growth that occurred after a 6-hour period. Bacteria often reproduce at a rate that varies drastically from one stage to the next. The best way to study the different stages of growth would be to record the percent growth:
  F. after 2 hours only.
  G. after 4 hours, then again after 6 hours.
  H. after 8 hours only.
  J. every 15 minutes for 3 hours.

Conflicting Viewpoints

The Conflicting Viewpoints passage provides information on more than one alternative hypothesis or theory related to an observable event or phenomenon. The viewpoints presented are usually inconsistent with one another. Questions associated with the Conflicting Viewpoints passage ask you to comprehend, evaluate, and compare differing hypothesis and theories. Following is a Conflicting Viewpoints passage and several questions. The answers and explanations are given at the end of this chapter.

Remote sensing of the environment is defined as any technique for obtaining information about certain objects through the analysis of data collected by special instruments. These instruments are not in direct physical contact with the objects that are being investigated, and can include photographic cameras, mechanical scanners, and radar systems. Two scientists present their views on different types of remote sensing techniques.

Scientist 1

Remote sensing is best achieved through the use of aerial photographs. These photographs supply researchers with a vast amount of data, which can often be used for additional studies. Large areas can be covered rapidly and at a much lower cost. In fact, it is often possible to share the charges for aerial photography with scientists conducting different research in the same area. Large-scale phenomena can be more easily identified in aerial photographs. In addition, wetlands, rugged terrain, and prohibited areas can be accessed via the air. It is often not necessary to get permission to fly over restricted or hard-to-reach locations.

Scientist 2

The best way to remotely sense the environment is to conduct a ground survey. Measurements are very precise, and field operators become familiar with the physical and cultural features of the landscape. This familiarity allows researchers to gain a deeper understanding of the environment. Minute details can be closely observed and documented. Weather factors that may impede or inhibit aerial photography are generally not a problem during ground surveys. Remote sensors can be strategically placed throughout an area to record data that can be collected at a later date.

1. Is the claim that previously uncharted jungle terrain can best be researched on foot consistent with Scientist 2's viewpoint?
   A. No, because aerial photography is best conducted remotely.
   B. No, because precise measurements are required in ground surveys.
   C. Yes, because ground surveys yield the most precise data.
   D. Yes, because wetlands are easily accessible via the air.

2. Scientist 1's viewpoint contains the basic assumption that:
   F. remote sensing is the only means to gather important data.
   G. aerial photographs can be effectively and accurately interpreted.
   H. ground surveys are the primary remote sensing techniques used today.
   J. aerial photographs cannot provide adequate information.

3. Scientist 1 would most likely state that which of the following is an important consideration in deciding upon a remote sensing technique?
   A. Cost
   B. Culture
   C. Climate
   D. Education

4. According to information in Scientist 2's viewpoint, accurate measurements are possible because:
   F. large areas can be easily accessed.
   G. field operators are not familiar with the landscape.
   H. a vast amount of data can be gathered.
   J. details can be more easily observed.

5. Both scientists would most likely agree that:
   A. it is necessary to get permission to remotely sense restricted areas.
   B. remote sensing of the environment can yield useful data.
   C. remote sensing is best achieved using photographic instruments.
   D. it is impossible to identify large-scale phenomena.

6. Scientist 1 would most likely support which of the following statements about remote sensing instruments?
   F. Strategic placement of remote sensors is critical in gathering useful data.
   G. Remote sensing instruments cannot tolerate high altitudes.
   H. Photographic instruments can be modified to capture an entire ground area instantaneously.
   J. Rugged terrain cannot be remotely sensed with any of the instruments currently in use.

7. Scientist 2 states that:
   A. aerial photographs often supply researchers with an excess of data.
   B. physical and cultural features of the landscape can often be overlooked during a ground survey.
   C. large-scale phenomena can easily be seen from the air.
   D. ground surveys can yield highly accurate data, despite potentially bad weather conditions.

ANSWERS AND EXPLANATIONS

Data Representation

1. **The correct answer is C.** According to Table 1, roseola is contagious from the "onset of fever" until the "rash is gone." The question states that the fever lasts for 3 to 5 days, and, after that, a rash appears that lasts for 48 hours, or 2 more days. Determine the contagious period by adding the 2 days that the rash lasts to both 3 and 5. So, the contagious period for roseola can be anywhere from $3 + 2 = 5$ days to $5 + 2 = 7$ days, or 5–7 days.

2. **The correct answer is J.** The symptoms listed in Table 1 include sores, fever, and rash, and rash appears most often. Therefore, answer choice J is correct.

3. **The correct answer is C.** The passage defines the *incubation period* as the "average time that elapses between exposure to a virus and the appearance of symptoms." Therefore, the question is asking you to look at incubation periods. According to Table 2, influenza has an incubation period of 1–2 days, the shortest time period listed in the incubation period column, so answer choice C is correct.

4. **The correct answer is F.** According to Table 1, the contagious period for chicken pox ends when "all sores have scabbed over." Therefore, the contagious period for chicken pox is most likely to be reduced if the sores dry up and scab over more quickly. Answer choice A best accomplishes this.

5. **The correct answer is B.** The passage states that all of the skin infections in Table 1 are caused by viruses that attack the cells that line the skin. The passage goes on to say that all of the respiratory viruses in Table 2 are caused by viruses that attack cells that line the respiratory tract. In other words, a virus attacks the cells that correspond to the part of the body that will be damaged by the disease. Therefore, if HIV damages the immune system, then you can assume that the virus attacks the cells of the immune system, answer choice B. The other answer choices are not supported by the passage.

Research Summary

1. **The correct answer is C.** According to Table 1, *Salmonella* bacteria had the largest percent growth at a pH level of 7. This information suggests that a pH level near 7 might best contribute to the growth of the bacteria.

2. **The correct answer is H.** To answer this question, you must look at the results in all of the tables and choose the conditions that create the highest percent growth of bacteria. In Table 1, a pH level of 7 created the highest percent growth (81%) of the bacteria. In Table 2, the organic compound in Dish 1 created the highest percent growth (37%) of the bacteria. In Table 3, a temperature of 40°C created the highest percent growth (83%) of the bacteria. Combining these three conditions would be expected to produce the highest percent growth.

3. **The correct answer is B.** Table 1 shows that the *Salmonella* bacteria reproduced most efficiently at a pH of 7 (neutral). A conclusion stating that *Salmonella* bacteria reproduce most efficiently in a neutral environment would reaffirm the results of Experiment 1.

4. **The correct answer is G.** To maximize the length of time that bacteria will reproduce, the bacteria must not run out of nutrients. In order to make sure that the nutrients are not depleted, the bacteria groups must be regularly resupplied with unlimited nutrients. Answer choice J can be eliminated because it is irrelevant to the purpose of the question.

5. **The correct answer is D.** According to Table 2, the bacteria grew more efficiently in environments with more carbon and oxygen and less nitrogen. This information suggests that nitrogen is not present in the cells of a *Salmonella* bacterium. Answer choice B can be eliminated because this information was not tested in any of the experiments.

6. **The correct answer is J.** Because bacteria reproduce at a rate that varies from one stage to the next, testing at 15-minute intervals allows study of the different stages of growth most effectively.

Conflicting Viewpoints

1. **The correct answer is C.** Scientist 2 believes that the "best way to remotely sense the environment is to conduct a ground survey." Ground surveys (conducted at least partially on foot) yield the most precise measurements and allow surveyors to become more intimate with the environment.

2. **The correct answer is G.** Scientist 1 believes that aerial photographs are the best means by which to remotely sense the environment. Therefore, Scientist 1 must believe that aerial photographs can be interpreted effectively and accurately. The other answer choices are not supported by Scientist 1's viewpoint.

3. **The correct answer is A.** Scientist 1 states that aerial photography can be cost-effective, and that it might be "possible to share the charges for aerial photography with scientists conducting different research in the same area." This suggests that Scientist 1 is somewhat concerned about the cost of aerial photography. The other answer choices are not supported by the passage.

4. **The correct answer is J.** Scientist 2 states that in a ground survey, "details can be closely observed and documented." The other answer choices are not supported by information in Scientist 2's viewpoint.

5. **The correct answer is B.** While the scientists disagree on which is the best type of remote sensing, they would most likely both agree that remote sensing can be very useful.

6. **The correct answer is H.** Scientist 1 indicates that aerial photographs are the best method for remotely sensing the environment. Scientist 1 goes on to say that "large areas can be covered rapidly." This suggests that Scientist 1 would support the idea that photographic instruments can be modified to capture large-scale images.

7. **The correct answer is D.** Scientist 2 argues that ground surveys are the best means by which to remotely sense the environment, and that weather factors are "generally not a problem during ground surveys." This best supports answer choice D.

WHAT'S NEXT?

Part V contains two simulated ACT Science practice tests in format. Apply the strategies and techniques that you have learned to answer as many of these questions as possible correctly. Review the explanations for the questions that you miss.

PART V

PRACTICE TESTS

CHAPTER 13

PRACTICE TEST 1
WITH EXPLANATIONS

SCIENCE TEST
Answer Sheet

SCIENCE

1 Ⓐ Ⓑ Ⓒ Ⓓ	16 Ⓕ Ⓖ Ⓗ Ⓙ	31 Ⓐ Ⓑ Ⓒ Ⓓ
2 Ⓕ Ⓖ Ⓗ Ⓙ	17 Ⓐ Ⓑ Ⓒ Ⓓ	32 Ⓕ Ⓖ Ⓗ Ⓙ
3 Ⓐ Ⓑ Ⓒ Ⓓ	18 Ⓕ Ⓖ Ⓗ Ⓙ	33 Ⓐ Ⓑ Ⓒ Ⓓ
4 Ⓕ Ⓖ Ⓗ Ⓙ	19 Ⓐ Ⓑ Ⓒ Ⓓ	34 Ⓕ Ⓖ Ⓗ Ⓙ
5 Ⓐ Ⓑ Ⓒ Ⓓ	20 Ⓕ Ⓖ Ⓗ Ⓙ	35 Ⓐ Ⓑ Ⓒ Ⓓ
6 Ⓕ Ⓖ Ⓗ Ⓙ	21 Ⓐ Ⓑ Ⓒ Ⓓ	36 Ⓕ Ⓖ Ⓗ Ⓙ
7 Ⓐ Ⓑ Ⓒ Ⓓ	22 Ⓕ Ⓖ Ⓗ Ⓙ	37 Ⓐ Ⓑ Ⓒ Ⓓ
8 Ⓕ Ⓖ Ⓗ Ⓙ	23 Ⓐ Ⓑ Ⓒ Ⓓ	38 Ⓕ Ⓖ Ⓗ Ⓙ
9 Ⓐ Ⓑ Ⓒ Ⓓ	24 Ⓕ Ⓖ Ⓗ Ⓙ	39 Ⓐ Ⓑ Ⓒ Ⓓ
10 Ⓕ Ⓖ Ⓗ Ⓙ	25 Ⓐ Ⓑ Ⓒ Ⓓ	40 Ⓕ Ⓖ Ⓗ Ⓙ
11 Ⓐ Ⓑ Ⓒ Ⓓ	26 Ⓕ Ⓖ Ⓗ Ⓙ	
12 Ⓕ Ⓖ Ⓗ Ⓙ	27 Ⓐ Ⓑ Ⓒ Ⓓ	
13 Ⓐ Ⓑ Ⓒ Ⓓ	28 Ⓕ Ⓖ Ⓗ Ⓙ	
14 Ⓕ Ⓖ Ⓗ Ⓙ	29 Ⓐ Ⓑ Ⓒ Ⓓ	
15 Ⓐ Ⓑ Ⓒ Ⓓ	30 Ⓕ Ⓖ Ⓗ Ⓙ	

SCIENCE TEST

35 Minutes—40 Questions

DIRECTIONS: This test includes several passages, each followed by several questions. Read the passage and choose the best answer to each question. After you have selected your answer, fill in the corresponding bubble on your answer sheet. You should refer to the passages as often as necessary when answering the questions. You may NOT use a calculator on this test.

PASSAGE I

Some science students are debating four hypotheses regarding the origin of the asteroid belt located between Mars and Jupiter, based on the following observations:

Observations

Observation 1. If all of the asteroids were gathered together, the diameter of the object formed would be less than half the diameter of Earth's Moon.

Observation 2. The total mass of the asteroid belt is only 4% that of the Moon. One asteroid alone, Ceres, contains $\frac{1}{3}$ of the total mass of the asteroid belt.

Observation 3. Asteroids are largely composed of silicate, with some deposits of iron and nickel, a composition proportionately similar to that of the terrestrial planets. Some asteroids also contain carbon and other elements.

Observation 4. There is a strong orbital resonance (overlapping gravity) with Jupiter in the region of the asteroid belt, which keeps the asteroids in an orbit around the sun.

Observation 5. In reality, the asteroids within the belt are very far apart, not clustered together.

Observation 6. Within the early solar system, the velocity of collisions within the region of the asteroid belt was much higher than it is currently.

Hypothesis 1

The material that composes the asteroids is similar to that of the terrestrial planets. The belt probably formed during the same period when the planets were forming, and because of the strong orbital resonance with the gas giant Jupiter and high-velocity collisions, chunks of the material were pulled away from various planets and trapped in orbit. This also explains the varying composition of the asteroids throughout the belt.

Hypothesis 2

All of the material that makes up the asteroids in the asteroid belt is similar to the material that makes up the terrestrial planets. The velocity of collisions in the early solar system was at one time high enough to break planets apart as they formed. Since one asteroid has $\frac{1}{3}$ the total mass of the belt, the asteroids are most likely the result of a partially formed planet that broke apart and became trapped in an orbit between Mars and Jupiter.

Hypothesis 3

The asteroids most likely came from somewhere outside the solar system. As they passed through space at varying intervals, they were trapped by the large orbital resonance of Jupiter and formed a "belt." The vast distances between most of the asteroids in the belt are evidence that they did not come from a single source, but arrived at different points in the belt's development.

Hypothesis 4

The asteroids could not once have been a planet, because there is not enough material within the entire belt to form a planet-sized object. The lack of material, shown by the total diameter and mass of the objects within the belt, is proof that the asteroids are no more than large particles left over from the formation of the terrestrial planets from a single cloud of material.

GO ON TO THE NEXT PAGE.

1. According to Hypothesis 1, most of the matter composing the asteroids in the belt came from:
   A. Earth's moon.
   B. a partially formed planet between Mars and Jupiter.
   C. the same material that composes the planets that are most similar to Earth.
   D. a planet outside of Earth's solar system.

2. Hypothesis 4 includes the assertion that the asteroids are made up of particles left over from a single cloud of material. This assertion explains which of the following observations?
   F. Observations 1 and 2
   G. Observation 4 only
   H. Observations 5 and 6
   J. Observation 3 only

3. Recent discoveries indicate that the gravity from Jupiter is so strong that, even given enough raw material, planets could not form around Jupiter. Which of the hypotheses is supported by this information?
   A. Hypothesis 1 only
   B. Hypothesis 1 and Hypothesis 3 only
   C. Hypothesis 1 and Hypothesis 4 only
   D. Hypothesis 1, Hypothesis 2, and Hypothesis 4

4. Supporters of Hypothesis 2 would most likely agree that, at the time the asteroid belt formed, the planets were:
   F. still in the process of forming.
   G. completely formed as they are seen today.
   H. no more than a cloud of material in space.
   J. all the size of asteroids.

5. Which of the following assumptions regarding the asteroid belt's origins is implicit in Hypothesis 2?
   A. The asteroids' composition is identical to that of the Moon.
   B. The asteroids have several different sources of origin.
   C. The asteroid belt is older than Jupiter.
   D. The asteroid belt is younger than Jupiter.

6. With which of the following statements would supporters of all four hypotheses agree?
   F. There is not enough scientific data to prove the existence of asteroids.
   G. Asteroids are made up of the same material as that which makes up Mars.
   H. The asteroid belt lies entirely outside of the solar system.
   J. The objects that are currently in an orbit between Mars and Jupiter are asteroids.

7. Consider the crust of a terrestrial planet to have a proportion of silicate to iron to nickel of 10,000:100:10. Based on the information in the passage, the ratio of these substances in the composition of an average asteroid is likely to be:
   A. 500:10:1
   B. 1,000:50:5
   C. 10,000:100:10
   D. 10,000:500:50

PASSAGE II

Amino acids are the building blocks of proteins. They are formed together based on DNA and its interaction with RNA. The process first starts with *transcription*, where the base sequence DNA is copied to form messenger RNA (mRNA). It then travels to a ribosome, where transfer RNA (tRNA) finds and delivers amino acids that match the base sequence of the mRNA, a process called *translation*. The amino acids then bond together to form peptide strands. These strands fold and bond together to form proteins. This process is depicted in Figure 1.

Figure 1

Each 3-base unit on the mRNA forms a *codon*, which corresponds to a specific amino acid. Table 1 displays the 64 codons that scientists have identified.

GO ON TO THE NEXT PAGE.

AAU	Asparagine	CAU	Histidine	GAU	Aspartic acid	UAU		Tyrosine
AAC		CAC		GAC		UAC		
AAA	Lysine	CAA	Glutamine	GAA	Glutamic acid	UAA		Stop**
AAG		CAG		GAG		UAG		
ACU	Threonine	CCU	Proline	GCU	Alanine	UCU		Serine
ACC		CCC		GCC		UCC		
ACA		CCA		GCA		UCA		
ACG		CCG		GCG		UCG		
AGU	Serine	CGU	Arginine	GGU	Glycine	UGU		Cysteine
AGC		CGC		GGC		UGC		
AGA	Arginine	CGA		GGA		UGA		Stop**
AGG		CGG		GGG		UGG		Tryptophan
AUU	Isoleucine	CUU	Leucine	GUU	Valine	UUU		Phenylalanine
AUC		CUC		GUC		UUC		
AUA		CUA		GUA		UUA		Leucine
AUG	Methionine	CUG		GUG		UUG		

Table 1

**Stop codons specify the end of the polypeptide chain.

8. According to Table 1, the mRNA strand shown below, when read from left to right, encodes for which amino acids?

C U G A G A U G G

F. Arginine, glutamic acid, methionine
G. Leucine, arginine, tryptophan
H. Leucine, serine, cysteine
J. Lysine, isoleucine, tyrosine

9. Based on the information in Table 1, all of the following codons encode for the same amino acid EXCEPT:
A. AGA
B. AGG
C. AGU
D. CGU

10. If the codon labeled A, shown below in a mRNA strand, was changed to CCA, what would be the effect on the translation of this mRNA strand?

A

U U G A C C G G A

F. The amino acid specified by codon A would be the only variation.
G. The amino acid specified by codon A and the amino acids specified by the following codons would be altered.
H. The original polypeptide strand would be identical to the new polypeptide strand.
J. Translation would stop because CCA is a stop codon.

GO ON TO THE NEXT PAGE.

11. According to the passage, the correct ordering of substances used in the synthesis of proteins is which of the following?

A. DNA → RNA → protein → amino acids → polypeptides

B. DNA → tRNA → mRNA + amino acids

C. RNA → DNA → tRNA + amino acids

D. DNA → mRNA → tRNA + amino acids

12. A strand of mRNA must have a minimum of how many base units in order to produce a polypeptide chain 7 amino acids long, if there is no stop codon?

F. 7

G. 14

H. 21

J. 28

13. How many amino acids are encoded by more than four different codons?

A. None

B. 1

C. 2

D. 3

PASSAGE III

Benzene gas is carcinogenic; it has been linked to causing cancers such as leukemia and lymphoma. Cars are a major source of atmospheric benzene gas in urban areas. A group of researchers hypothesize that cars emit more benzene gas at colder temperatures, compared to warmer temperatures, during the first 15 minutes. The following experiments were designed to test this hypothesis.

Experiment 1

To collect car exhaust, the researchers attached a hose from the tailpipe of a car to a plastic bag. The engine was started, and researchers used a syringe to extract 1-mL samples of exhaust at 2-minute intervals. The samples were injected into a gas chromatograph, an instrument used to separate a mixture of gases into its individual components. Researchers determined the percent by volume of benzene in the exhaust by comparing the exhaust with mixtures of known benzene concentrations. Samples of exhaust were taken from 4 cars tested at an external temperature of $-10\,°C$. The results were recorded in Table 1.

Table 1				
Time after starting (min)	Percent of benzene in the exhaust at –10°C:			
	1976 Model X	1976 Model Y	1995 Model X	1995 Model Y
1	1.7	1.6	0.6	0.1
3	2.0	1.9	0.5	0.6
5	4.3	3.8	0.7	1.2
7	1.8	5.0	0.5	1.5
9	1.6	4.5	0.3	1.3
11	1.5	4.0	0.3	1.0
13	1.4	3.5	0.3	1.0

Experiment 2

The procedure from Experiment 1 was repeated at an external temperature of 20°C. The results were recorded in Table 2.

Table 2				
Time after starting (min)	Percent of benzene in the exhaust at 20°C:			
	1976 Model X	1976 Model Y	1995 Model X	1995 Model Y
1	1.0	0.4	0.1	0.1
3	1.4	1.0	0.2	0.5
5	1.7	3.0	0.3	0.7
7	0.8	3.5	0.1	0.4
9	0.7	3.5	0.1	0.3
11	0.5	3.2	0.1	0.2
13	0.5	2.5	0.1	0.1
15	0.4	2.4	0.1	0.1

14. In Experiment 2, which of the following factors varied?

F. The temperature at which the engine was started

G. The year in which the cars were made

H. The volume of exhaust that was collected

J. The method of collecting samples

GO ON TO THE NEXT PAGE.

15. Do the results of Experiment 1 support the hypothesis that, at a given time and temperature, the exhaust of newer cars contains less benzene gas than the exhaust of older cars?

   A. Yes; the highest percent of benzene was in the exhaust of the 1995 Model Y
   B. Yes; both 1995 models had percents of benzene that were lower than those of either 1976 model.
   C. No; the highest percent of benzene was in the exhaust of the 1976 Model Y.
   D. No; both 1976 models had percents of benzene that were lower than those of either 1995 model.

16. Based on the results of the experiments and the information in the table below, cars in which of the following cities would most likely contribute the greatest amount of benzene to the atmosphere in January? (Assume that the types, numbers, and ages of cars used in each city are approximately equal.)

City	Average temperature (°F) in January
Green Bay	22.2
Chicago	28.9
Denver	39.8
Sacramento	67.5

   F. Green Bay
   G. Chicago
   H. Denver
   J. Sacramento

17. Assume that the 1976 Model X car was left running for another 2 minutes at 20°C. What would the percent benzene in the exhaust most likely be?

   A. Greater than 0.4
   B. Between 0.4 and 0.3
   C. Between 2.4 and 2.5
   D. Greater than 2.5

18. Many states require annual testing of cars to determine the levels of benzene and other gases in their exhaust emissions. Based on the experiments, in order to determine the maximum percent of benzene found in a car's exhaust, during which of the following times after starting a car would it be best to sample the exhaust?

   F. 1–3 min
   G. 5–7 min
   H. 11–13 min
   J. 13 min or longer

19. Experiment 1 and Experiment 2 differ in that in Experiment 1:

   A. older cars were used.
   B. the temperature was lower.
   C. the starting times were adjusted.
   D. more exhaust was collected.

PASSAGE IV

In the United States, 1 in 4 people suffer from some type of allergy. An allergy is an overreaction of the body's immune system to a foreign substance, which is called an *allergen*. An allergen can be ingested (eaten), injected, inhaled into the lungs, or absorbed by the skin. Once an allergen has been introduced to the body, the body can react by producing a variety of symptoms, including the following: coughing and sneezing; itchy, watery eyes; a runny nose; and a scratchy throat. In extreme cases, a person may experience a rash, hives, low blood pressure, difficulty in breathing, an asthma attack, or even death. Although allergies and their symptoms can be managed, there is no known cure.

Allergies are characterized by the specific allergens that trigger symptoms, as well as the method by which the allergy can be introduced. The most common types of allergies, their method of introduction, and their common triggers are listed in Table 1.

Table 1		
Allergy type	**Method**	**Common triggers**
Indoor	Inhalation	Pet dander, dust mites, mold spores
Outdoor	Inhalation	Tree, grass, and weed pollen; mold spores
Food and drug	Ingestion	Peanuts, shellfish, wheat, dairy
	Injection	Penicillin
Skin	Absorption	Latex, poison ivy/oak/sumac
Insect	Injection	Hornets/wasps/bees, fire ants

GO ON TO THE NEXT PAGE.

Many people suffer from "seasonal allergies," which occur at specific times of the year. The most common seasonal allergies result from outdoor allergens such as tree, grass, and weed pollen. The pollen and spores from these allergens all vary in concentration throughout the year, thus making reactions greater at certain times of the year than at others.

Pollen can be counted at research stations and measured in terms of the number of pollen grains per cubic meter of air. Table 2 shows the scale for determining the intensity of allergen counts.

Table 2			
	Allergen in terms of number of pollen grains or spores per cubic meter of air		
Intensity	**Grass**	**Tree**	**Weed**
Not present	0	0	0
Low	1–5	1–16	1–9
Moderate	6–20	17–90	10–50
High	21–200	91–1,500	51–500
Very high	>201	>1,500	> 500

A study was conducted to measure the allergen counts for grass pollen, tree pollen, and weed pollen in an area over the course of one year. The results are shown in Figure 1.

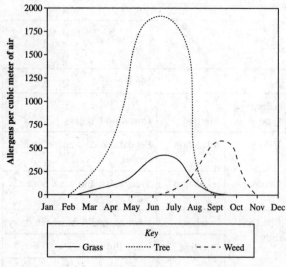

Figure 1

20. According to the study, which factor most affects the presence of grass, weed, and tree pollen?
   F. the method of introduction
   G. the symptoms produced
   H. the allergic reactions of people in the area
   J. the time of year

21. According to the study, grass and tree pollen are similar to each other in that:
   A. neither allergen is present from February to May.
   B. all people experience the same symptoms from both allergens.
   C. both experience elevated allergen counts from May to August.
   D. tree and grass pollen produces identical symptoms in all sufferers.

22. Based on the results of the study, one could generalize that, compared to allergic reactions to grass pollen, allergic reactions to weed pollen:
   F. are greatest from mid-August to October.
   G. are greatest during the summer months.
   H. remain constant throughout the year.
   J. are more difficult to measure.

23. Seasonal allergies most likely result from allergens that are:
   A. inhaled into the lungs.
   B. ingested.
   C. injected.
   D. absorbed by the skin.

24. According to Table 2, a tree pollen count of 1,000 would be considered:
   F. low.
   G. moderate.
   H. high.
   J. very high.

GO ON TO THE NEXT PAGE.

PASSAGE V

A high school cooking class made frozen yogurt using the apparatus shown in Figure 1. The frozen yogurt mixture (Y1) was stirred at a constant rate.

electric motor

steel container

frozen yogurt mixture

salt/ice mixture

stirring paddle

Figure 1

During the mixing time, the temperature of the frozen yogurt mixture (Y1), as well as that of the salt/ice mixture, fluctuated. Figure 2 illustrates the change in temperature related to the mixing time.

The resistance to flow, or *viscosity*, of any frozen yogurt mixture is directly proportional to the current drawn by the motor required to turn the stirring paddles. The cooking students monitored the current, as it changed with the mixing times, for three yogurt mixtures (Y1, Y2, and Y3). The results were plotted in Figure 3.

mixing time (min)

| frozen yogurt mixture (Y1) |
| ----- salt/ice mixture |

Figure 2

viscosity

Figure 3

GO ON TO THE NEXT PAGE.

25. According to Figure 2, the salt/ice mixture and the frozen yogurt mixture were at the same temperature after approximately how much time had elapsed?

A. 2 minutes
B. 6 minutes
C. 9 minutes
D. 12 minutes

26. According to Figures 2 and 3, as the temperature of the salt/ice mixture increased, the viscosity of Y1:

F. decreased only.
G. increased only.
H. decreased, then increased.
J. increased, then decreased.

27. Students observed the viscosity of a fourth frozen yogurt mixture (Y4). If the current at 0 min was 1.2 amperes, how did the initial viscosity of Y4 compare with that of Y1, Y2, and Y3?

A. The viscosity of Y4 was less than that of Y1, Y2, and Y3.
B. The viscosity of Y4 was less than that of Y1 and Y2, but equal to that of Y3.
C. The viscosity of Y4 was greater than that of Y1 and Y2, but less than that of Y3.
D. The viscosity of Y4 was greater than that of Y1, Y2, and Y3.

28. Based on the results shown in Figure 3, when the yogurt has been mixed for 10 minutes, the current drawn by the motor to stir Y2 is closest to:

F. 1.4 amperes.
G. 1.5 amperes.
H. 1.6 amperes.
J. 1.7 amperes.

29. Once frozen yogurt has a viscosity that requires a current of 2.2 amperes to turn the stirring paddles, it is considered finished. According to the information in Figure 3, which frozen yogurt mixture has the shortest completion time?

A. Y1
B. Y2
C. Y3
D. All three frozen yogurt mixtures have the same completion time.

30. Students were required to explain the conduction of heat within the frozen yogurt mixer as stirring time increased. Using the information from Figures 1 and 2, which of the following is the best explanation?

F. Heat was conducted by the stirring paddles from the motor to the frozen yogurt mixture.
G. Heat was conducted by the stirring paddles from the frozen yogurt mixture to the motor.
H. Heat was conducted by the steel container from the frozen yogurt mixture to the salt/ice mixture.
J. Heat was conducted by the steel container from the salt/ice mixture to the frozen yogurt mixture.

PASSAGE VI

Nuts vary in the amount of fats, proteins, and carbohydrates that they contain. *Energy content* is the number of calories found in a nut, and it is based on the nut's composition. There are approximately 4 Calories per gram (Cal/g) of carbohydrates and protein, and approximately 9 Cal/g of fats.

A nutrition class designed the following experiments to discover the composition and energy content of shelled pecans, peanuts, walnuts, and almonds.

Experiment 1

A 10-g sample of pecans was crushed, mixed with 40 g of ethanol, and placed in a machine that stirred it for 24 hours. The ethanol will dissolve only fat. The remaining solids were filtered off and saved for future experiments. The ethanol was then allowed to evaporate, leaving the fat content of the pecan. The mass was then determined. This procedure was repeated for the remaining nuts.

Experiment 2

The remaining solids from Experiment 1 were used to determine the protein content. The procedure from Experiment 1 was followed, except that a mild acid was used to dissolve only the protein.

Experiment 3

The remaining solids from Experiment 2 were used to determine the carbohydrate content. The procedure from Experiment 1 was followed, except that a strong acid was used to dissolve the carbohydrates.

Experiment 4

A *bomb calorimeter* measures the heat given off when a substance is burned in pure oxygen. 10-g samples of each nut were placed in the bomb calorimeter to determine the energy content of each nut.

The results from all 4 experiments were recorded in a single table (Table 1).

Table 1			
Nut sample	Fats (g)	Proteins (g)	Carbohydrates (g)	Energy content (Cal)
Pecans	7.2	0.9	1.4	71.4
Peanuts	4.9	2.6	1.6	60.3
Walnuts	4.7	2.3	1.1	54.8
Almonds	4.1	1.9	1.3	51.2

GO ON TO THE NEXT PAGE.

31. According to the students' results, the sample of nuts with the lowest energy content is the sample with the fewest:
    A. carbohydrates.
    B. proteins.
    C. fats.
    D. proteins and carbohydrates.

32. Based on the results of the experiments, as fat content increases, energy content:
    F. increases only for all nuts.
    G. decreases only for all nuts.
    H. increases for some nuts, and decreases for other nuts.
    J. remains stable for all nuts.

33. In Experiment 3, the nut with the highest overall carbohydrate level was the:
    A. pecan.
    B. peanut.
    C. walnut.
    D. almond.

34. According to the results of Experiment 4, the number of calories in 10 g of walnuts is closest to:
    F. 5.
    G. 9.
    H. 42.
    J. 55.

35. Data from the passage indicate that a nut containing 4.5 grams of fat would most likely have an energy content:
    A. lower than 51.2 Cal.
    B. between 51.2 Cal and 54.8 Cal.
    C. between 60.3 Cal and 71.4 Cal.
    D. higher than 71.4 Cal.

PASSAGE VII

In 2008, NASA's *Messenger* spacecraft completed a flyby of the planet Mercury, and its cameras captured more than 1,200 high-resolution and color images of the planet, revealing another 30 percent of Mercury's surface that had never before been seen by any spacecraft. Throughout its mission, *Messenger*'s instruments will explore Mercury's polar deposits, crust and mantle, crustal composition, and geologic evolution. Understanding the forces that shaped the planet is fundamental to understanding the formation of the other terrestrial planets, particularly Earth.

Table 1 lists some of Earth's parameters. Table 2 lists some of Mercury's parameters, as well as the parameter ratios of Mercury and Earth.

Table 1	
Mass (10^{24} kg)	5.9736
Volume (10^{10} km^3)	108.321
Equatorial radius (km)	6,378.1
Mean density (kg/m^3)	5,515.0
Surface gravity (m/s^2)	9.798
Solar irradiance (W/m^2)	1,367.6
Average temperature (°C)	15.0

Table 2		
	Mercury parameters	Mercury/ Earth ratios
Mass (10^{24} kg)	0.03302	0.0553
Volume (10^{10} km^3)	6.083	0.0562
Equatorial radius (km)	2,439.7	0.383
Mean density (kg/m^3)	5,427.0	0.984
Surface gravity (m/s^2)	3.70	0.378
Solar irradiance (W/m^2)	9,126.6	6.673
Average temperature (°C)	167.0	11.133

36. Based on the data presented, Mercury is *most* like Earth with regard to:
    F. mass.
    G. equatorial radius.
    H. mean density.
    J. average temperature.

37. For any given parameter, the data indicate that compared to Earth, Mercury's parameters are:
    A. always lower.
    B. always higher.
    C. sometimes higher, sometimes lower.
    D. difficult to measure.

GO ON TO THE NEXT PAGE.

38. Based on the data presented, the gravitational pull on Earth is:

   F. less than the gravitational pull on Mercury.

   G. greater than the gravitational pull on Mercury.

   H. equal to the gravitational pull on Mercury.

   J. directly proportional to the gravitational pull on Mercury.

39. According to Table 2, the Mercury/Earth ratio of planetary volume is:

   A. 108.321×10^{10} km^3.

   B. 6.083×10^{10} km^3.

   C. 5.9736×10^{10} km^3.

   D. 0.0562×10^{10} km^3.

40. According to the passage, the *Messenger* mission is significant because:

   F. it has already revealed precisely how Mercury was formed.

   G. it will provide insight into the underlying geologic forces responsible for the formation of Earth.

   H. it is NASA's first mission to Mercury.

   J. it has provided information necessary for the recalculation of many of Earth's bulk parameters.

END OF THE SCIENCE TEST.

STOP! IF YOU HAVE TIME LEFT OVER, CHECK YOUR WORK ON THIS SECTION ONLY.

ANSWER KEY

Science Test

1. C	11. D	21. C	31. C
2. J	12. H	22. F	32. F
3. A	13. D	23. A	33. B
4. F	14. G	24. H	34. J
5. D	15. B	25. D	35. B
6. J	16. F	26. G	36. H
7. C	17. B	27. B	37. C
8. G	18. G	28. J	38. G
9. C	19. B	29. B	39. D
10. G	20. J	30. H	40. G

SCORING WORKSHEET

Scale Score	Raw Score Science	Scale Score	Raw Score Science
36	39–40	18	15–16
35	38	17	14
34	37	16	12–13
33	36	15	11
32	—	14	10
31	35	13	9
30	34	12	8
29	33	11	7
28	32	10	6
27	31	9	5
26	29–30	8	4
25	27–28	7	3
24	25–26	6	—
23	23–24	5	2
22	21–22	4	—
21	20	3	1
20	18–19	2	—
19	17	1	0

NOTE: Each actual ACT is scaled slightly differently based on a large amount of information gathered from the millions of tests ACT, Inc., scores each year. This scale will give you a fairly good idea of where you are in your preparation process. However, it should not be read as an absolute predictor of your actual ACT score. In fact, on practice tests, the scores are much less important than what you learn from analyzing your results.

■ **ANSWERS AND EXPLANATIONS**

Passage I

1. **The correct answer is C.** Hypothesis 1 states, "The material that composes the asteroids is similar to that of the terrestrial planets." Because Earth is a terrestrial planet, answer choice C is correct.

2. **The correct answer is J.** According to Observation 3, "Asteroids are largely composed of silicate, with some deposits of iron and nickel, a composition proportionately similar to that of the terrestrial planets. Some asteroids also contain carbon and other elements." This is the only observation that discusses the composition of the asteroids.

3. **The correct answer is A.** Only Hypothesis 1 suggests that the material in the asteroid belt shares a similar composition with that in the terrestrial planets, and also mentions Jupiter's "strong orbital resonance." The new data would support this hypothesis.

4. **The correct answer is F.** According to Hypothesis 2, "All of the material that makes up the asteroids in the asteroid belt is similar to the material that makes up the terrestrial planets. The velocity of collisions in the early solar system was at one time high enough to break planets apart *as they formed*."

5. **The correct answer is D.** Because Hypothesis 2 states that the asteroids became trapped in an orbit between Mars and Jupiter as the asteroids were being formed, Jupiter must already have been in existence.

6. **The correct answer is J.** Each of the hypotheses states that the objects are asteroids. The hypotheses differ in their theories concerning the origin and composition of the asteroids.

7. **The correct answer is C.** Most of the information in the passage indicates that the asteroids are similar in composition to the terrestrial planets. Therefore, you can assume that the ratios would be the same.

Passage II

8. **The correct answer is G.** Based on the information in Table 1, CUG codes for leucine, AGA codes for arginine, and UGG codes for tryptophan. Remember that each codon corresponds to a specific amino acid and is formed from a 3-base unit.

9. **The correct answer is C.** According to Table 1, AGA, AGG, and CGU all encode for arginine, whereas AGU encodes for serine.

10. **The correct answer is F.** Only the labeled codon is changed; the following codons remain the same.

11. **The correct answer is D.** Both Figure 1 and the information in the introductory paragraph indicate that the synthesis of proteins begins with DNA, followed by the formation of messenger RNA (mRNA). The mRNA travels to the ribosome, where translation occurs, which involves transfer RNA (tRNA) and amino acids.

12. **The correct answer is H.** According to the passage, "Each 3-base unit on the mRNA forms a *codon*, which corresponds to a specific amino acid." The passage also states that a stop codon indicates the end of a polypeptide chain. Therefore, it will take 3×7 or 21 base units.

13. **The correct answer is D.** According to Table 1, arginine, serine, and leucine are encoded by more than four different codons.

Passage III

14. **The correct answer is G.** In Experiment 2, the only factor that varied was the year in which the cars were made. The temperature was constant, the same volume of gas was collected from each car, and the method of collecting samples was the same for each car.

15. **The correct answer is B.** The results of Experiment 1 are shown in Table 1. According to Table 1, the percent of benzene was lower for cars built in 1995.

16. **The correct answer is F.** According to the passage, "A group of researchers hypothesize that cars emit more benzene gas at colder temperatures, compared to warmer temperatures, during the first 15 minutes." The results of the experiments support this hypothesis; therefore, cars in the city with the coldest average temperature will emit more benzene.

17. **The correct answer is B.** According to Table 2, after 15 minutes, the 1976 Model X car emitted 0.4 percent benzene. The table also shows a general downward trend in the amount of benzene emitted after the first 5 minutes; in fact, the percent emitted appears to decrease by 0.1 every two minutes. Therefore, you can conclude that after another 2 minutes, the percent of benzene emitted would be somewhere between 0.4 and 0.3.

18. **The correct answer is G.** Because both Table 1 and Table 2 show a significant drop in the percent of benzene emitted between 5 minutes and 7 minutes, it

would make sense to sample the exhaust during this time interval.

19. **The correct answer is B.** According to the passage, Experiment 1 was conducted at an external temperature of −10°C, while Experiment 2 was conducted at an external temperature of 20°C.

Passage IV

20. **The correct answer is J.** Figure 1 shows the pollen count for grass, tree, and weed pollen. According to Figure 1, the presence of pollen fluctuates depending on the time of year. Also, the passage states, "The most common seasonal allergies result from outdoor allergens such as tree, grass, and weed pollen. The pollen and spores from these allergens all vary in concentration throughout the year, thus making reactions greater at certain times of the year than at others."

21. **The correct answer is C.** Figure 1 shows a peak in pollen counts for both grass and tree pollen starting in May and ending in August.

22. **The correct answer is F.** According to Figure 1, weed pollen counts increase from mid-August through September; they begin to decrease in October.

23. **The correct answer is A.** According to the passage, "Many people suffer from 'seasonal allergies,' which occur at specific times of the year. The most common seasonal allergies result from outdoor allergens such as tree, grass, and weed pollen. The pollen and spores from these allergens all vary in concentration throughout the year, thus making reactions greater at certain times of the year than at others." This information best supports answer choice A.

24. **The correct answer is H.** Table 2 indicates that an allergen count of tree pollen between 91 and 1,500 is considered high.

Passage V

25. **The correct answer is D.** Figure 2 shows the lines representing temperature merging after about 12 minutes. This means that the temperatures were the same at that point.

26. **The correct answer is G.** Figure 2 shows that, over time, the temperature of the ice increased. Likewise, Figure 3 shows that, over time, the viscosity of Y1 increased.

27. **The correct answer is B.** According to Figure 3, a current of 1.2 amperes was used for Y3 at the onset of

mixing. Therefore, the initial viscosity of Y4 should be identical to that of Y3. Only answer choice B makes that connection.

28. **The correct answer is J.** In Figure 3, Y2 is represented by a square. At 10 minutes, the square representing Y2 is just under 1.8 amperes, which means that the current is closest to 1.7 amperes.

29. **The correct answer is B.** To answer this question, find the yogurt that reached 2.2 amperes in the shortest amount of time. Figure 3 shows that it took about 12 minutes for Y2 to reach a current of 2.2 amperes, whereas Y1 and Y3 took slightly longer.

30. **The correct answer is H.** Data in the passage show that the temperature of the ice increased while the temperature of the frozen yogurt mixture decreased. Therefore, heat was being conducted from the yogurt mixture to the ice/salt mixture through the container that enclosed the yogurt mixture.

Passage VI

31. **The correct answer is C.** Table 1 shows that the nuts with the highest levels of fat had higher energy content. There is a direct relationship between the number of fat grams and the number of Calories (energy content).

32. **The correct answer is F.** Table 1 shows that the nuts with the highest levels of fat had higher energy content. There is a direct relationship between the number of fat grams and the number of Calories (energy content).

33. **The correct answer is B.** The results of Experiment 3 are shown in Table 1. According to Table 1, the peanut sample contained 1.6 grams of carbohydrates, more than any of the other samples.

34. **The correct answer is J.** According to the passage, "10-g samples of each nut were placed in the bomb calorimeter to determine the energy content of each nut" in Experiment 4. Table 1 shows that the energy content (Calories) of the walnut sample was 54.8, or about 55.

35. **The correct answer is B.** According to Table 1, a nut with a fat content of 4.5 would most likely have an energy content somewhere between that of almonds (fat content of 4.1) and that of walnuts (fat content of 4.7). Therefore, the energy content of the untested nut would be somewhere between 51.2 and 54.8 Calories.

Passage VII

36. The correct answer is H. According to Table 2, the Mercury/Earth ratio of mean density is very close to 1.0, indicating very similar densities.

37. The correct answer is C. Table 2 shows a variation among the ratios; mass, volume, equatorial radius, and surface gravity are all quite low, whereas mean density is nearly identical, and solar irradiance and average temperatures have significantly higher ratios.

38. The correct answer is G. Table 1 shows that Earth's surface gravity is 9.798 m/s^2, and Table 2 shows that Mercury's surface gravity is 3.70 m/s^2.

39. The correct answer is D. To answer this question, simply locate volume on Table 2 and follow the row across to the Mercury/Earth ratio column.

40. The correct answer is G. The passage states, *"Messenger*'s instruments will explore Mercury's polar deposits, crust and mantle, crustal composition, and geologic evolution. Understanding the forces that shaped the planet is fundamental to understanding the formation of the other terrestrial planets, particularly Earth." This best supports answer choice G.

CHAPTER 14

PRACTICE TEST 2 WITH EXPLANATIONS

SCIENCE TEST
Answer Sheet

SCIENCE

1 Ⓐ Ⓑ Ⓒ Ⓓ	16 Ⓕ Ⓖ Ⓗ Ⓙ	31 Ⓐ Ⓑ Ⓒ Ⓓ
2 Ⓕ Ⓖ Ⓗ Ⓙ	17 Ⓐ Ⓑ Ⓒ Ⓓ	32 Ⓕ Ⓖ Ⓗ Ⓙ
3 Ⓐ Ⓑ Ⓒ Ⓓ	18 Ⓕ Ⓖ Ⓗ Ⓙ	33 Ⓐ Ⓑ Ⓒ Ⓓ
4 Ⓕ Ⓖ Ⓗ Ⓙ	19 Ⓐ Ⓑ Ⓒ Ⓓ	34 Ⓕ Ⓖ Ⓗ Ⓙ
5 Ⓐ Ⓑ Ⓒ Ⓓ	20 Ⓕ Ⓖ Ⓗ Ⓙ	35 Ⓐ Ⓑ Ⓒ Ⓓ
6 Ⓕ Ⓖ Ⓗ Ⓙ	21 Ⓐ Ⓑ Ⓒ Ⓓ	36 Ⓕ Ⓖ Ⓗ Ⓙ
7 Ⓐ Ⓑ Ⓒ Ⓓ	22 Ⓕ Ⓖ Ⓗ Ⓙ	37 Ⓐ Ⓑ Ⓒ Ⓓ
8 Ⓕ Ⓖ Ⓗ Ⓙ	23 Ⓐ Ⓑ Ⓒ Ⓓ	38 Ⓕ Ⓖ Ⓗ Ⓙ
9 Ⓐ Ⓑ Ⓒ Ⓓ	24 Ⓕ Ⓖ Ⓗ Ⓙ	39 Ⓐ Ⓑ Ⓒ Ⓓ
10 Ⓕ Ⓖ Ⓗ Ⓙ	25 Ⓐ Ⓑ Ⓒ Ⓓ	40 Ⓕ Ⓖ Ⓗ Ⓙ
11 Ⓐ Ⓑ Ⓒ Ⓓ	26 Ⓕ Ⓖ Ⓗ Ⓙ	
12 Ⓕ Ⓖ Ⓗ Ⓙ	27 Ⓐ Ⓑ Ⓒ Ⓓ	
13 Ⓐ Ⓑ Ⓒ Ⓓ	28 Ⓕ Ⓖ Ⓗ Ⓙ	
14 Ⓕ Ⓖ Ⓗ Ⓙ	29 Ⓐ Ⓑ Ⓒ Ⓓ	
15 Ⓐ Ⓑ Ⓒ Ⓓ	30 Ⓕ Ⓖ Ⓗ Ⓙ	

SCIENCE TEST

35 Minutes—40 Questions

DIRECTIONS: This test includes several passages, each followed by several questions. Read the passage and choose the best answer to each question. After you have selected your answer, fill in the corresponding bubble on your answer sheet. You should refer to the passages as often as necessary when answering the questions. You may NOT use a calculator on this test.

PASSAGE I

Predation is an interaction between individuals of two species in which one is harmed (the prey) and the other is helped (the predator). Predation can occur both *among* plants and animals and *between* plants and animals. Some biologists contend that *herbivores*, or plant eaters, are predators. Table 1 indicates some characteristics and examples of certain predators.

Table 1

Predator	Characteristics	Examples
Herbivore	Eats plants only. Can be very selective in the plants eaten.	Rabbits, deer, some birds, some insects.
Carnivore	Eats herbivores and other carnivores.	Lions, wolves, some birds, some insects.
Parasite	Feeds on another organism's parts, generally without killing the organism.	Bacteria, some worms, some plants.

Predation is very important in maintaining a natural balance in any given ecosystem. For example, without predators, prey populations tend to grow exponentially. Without prey, predator populations tend to decline exponentially. Predators consume individual members of the prey population, thereby controlling the overall numbers in the ecosystem. The number of prey consumed depends on both the number of prey present and the number of predators present.

The rate of change in the number of prey is a function of the birth of new prey minus the death of other prey, due either to predation or to other causes. The death rate is assumed to depend on the number of available prey and the number of predators. The rate of change in the number of predators is a function of the birth of new predators (which depends on the number of prey) minus the death of some predators.

Over long periods of time, predator and prey tend to balance each other out. This is called the *predator-prey cycle*. Prey numbers will increase when predator numbers decrease. When the number of prey reaches a certain point, predators will start to increase until they eat enough prey to cause a decline in prey numbers. When this happens, the number of predators will begin to decrease because they can't find enough prey to eat, and the cycle will begin again. Figure 1 represents an example of a *predator-prey cycle*.

Figure 1

1. Based on information in the passage and in Table 1, a herbivore is:
   A. a predator only.
   B. both a parasite and a predator.
   C. prey only.
   D. both a predator and prey.

2. According to information in the passage, the number of prey consumed in an ecosystem is dependent on:
   F. the rate of change in the number of prey.
   G. the total number of predators that die as a result of predation.
   H. the type of parasites available in the ecosystem.
   J. the number of predators present and the number of prey present.

3. Based on Figure 1, during the first year, predator numbers were mostly:
   A. higher than prey numbers.
   B. lower than prey numbers.
   C. equal to prey numbers.
   D. unable to be determined.

GO ON TO THE NEXT PAGE.

4. Studies have shown that a certain species of deer will eat only a specific type of plant found in the deer's natural habitat, and nothing else. Is this finding supported by the information in the passage?

F. No, because a deer is a herbivore, which means that it eats all plants.

G. No, because a deer is a carnivore and does not eat plants.

H. Yes, because a deer is a herbivore, and herbivores can be selective eaters.

J. Yes, because a deer is a prey animal, so it must use caution when eating.

5. Based on Figure 1, during which year was the greatest number of prey animals available?

A. 1
B. 2
C. 3
D. 4

PASSAGE II

When connection to a municipal water system is not feasible, wells are drilled to access groundwater. Engineers employed by a company that was interested in developing a remote plot of land conducted studies to compare the water quality of two possible well locations on the land. Water quality is determined by a number of factors, including the levels of nitrates, lead, microbes, pH, hardness (calcium carbonate), and alkalinity. The water samples were kept at a constant temperature of 72°F throughout the entire study. The results include the ideal level or concentration of each chemical and the readings of each test for the two different 100-mL samples of water (Table 1).

Table 1			
Factor	**Ideal**	**Sample 1**	**Sample 2**
Nitrates	< 10 mg/L	8 mg/L	7 mg/L
Lead	< 0.015 mg/L	0.01 mg/L	0.008 mg/L
Iron	< 0.3 mg/L	0.45 mg/L	0.40 mg/L
pH	6.5–8.5	6.0	7.5
Hardness	80–100 mg/L	40 mg/L	200 mg/L
Alkalinity	200–500 mg/L	120 mg/L	350 mg/L
Total dissolved solids	< 1,500 mg/L	1,050 mg/L	900 mg/L

The pH scale measures how acidic or basic a substance is on a scale of 0 to 14. Lower numbers indicate increasing acidity, and higher numbers indicate increasing basicity. The normal pH level of groundwater systems is between 6 and 8.5. Water with a low pH (< 6.5) could be acidic, soft, and corrosive and could contain elevated levels of toxic metals that might cause premature damage to metal piping. A pH > 8.5 indicates that the water is hard. Hard water does not pose a health risk, but it can cause mineral deposits on fixtures and dishes and can have a bad taste and odor.

Alkalinity is the water's capacity to resist changes in pH that would make the water more acidic. This resistance is achieved through a process called *buffering* (a buffered solution resists changes in pH until the buffer is used up). The alkalinity of natural water is determined by the soil and bedrock through which it passes. The main sources of natural alkalinity are rocks that contain carbonate, bicarbonate, and hydroxide compounds. These compounds, however, also cause hardness, which is less desirable in a drinking source. To illustrate the effect of alkalinity on pH stability, acid was added to two 100-mL sample solutions that initially had a pH of 6.5. One of the solutions had 200 mg/L alkalinity, while the other tested at zero alkalinity. The pH of the two solutions was recorded after every addition of acid and is shown in the figures below.

0 Alkalinity Solution

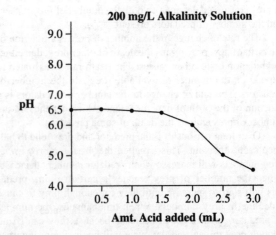

200 mg/L Alkalinity Solution

GO ON TO THE NEXT PAGE.

6. Which of the following statements best describes the concentration of lead in Sample 1?

F. The concentration of lead in Sample 1 is above the ideal level.

G. The concentration of lead in Sample 1 may be corrosive to surfaces.

H. The concentration of lead in Sample 1 is at or below the ideal level.

J. The concentration of lead in Sample 1 is too low to be measured.

7. An ideal alkalinity prevents pH levels from becoming too acidic. Which statement is best supported by this fact?

A. An alkalinity test is not necessary when testing drinking water.

B. Alkalinity above 500 mg/L is ideal in drinking water.

C. Ideal water samples will have a very low alkalinity (below 200 mg/L).

D. A properly buffered water source will have reduced corrosive effects.

8. The test results of Sample 1 indicate that:

F. the water from Sample 1 is probably balanced and safe.

G. the water from Sample 1 is too acidic and corrosive.

H. alkalinity levels are high enough to prevent the water from Sample 1 from becoming overly acidic.

J. the water tested in Sample 1 is hard water.

9. Based on the test results, Sample 2 is acceptable as a water source as long as the developers:

A. are willing to accept high iron levels and hard water.

B. are willing to accept high lead levels and soft water.

C. are willing to accept high alkalinity levels and soft water.

D. treat the water to reduce its corrosive nature.

10. Suppose a chemical could be added to treat the high iron levels in either sample. The chemical additive would be safe to use with Sample 2 but NOT Sample 1 if:

F. the chemical additive reduced pH levels by 1.

G. the chemical additive caused an increase in hardness levels.

H. the chemical additive increased alkalinity by 100 mg/L.

J. the chemical additive increased the amount of dissolved solids by 200 mg/L.

PASSAGE III

Precession is defined as a top's revolution around an imaginary line that is perpendicular to the surface at the point of contact. Figure 1 illustrates precession. Students designed two experiments to study precession.

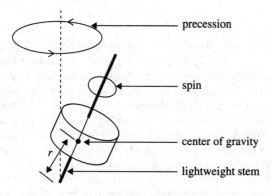

Figure 1

Experiment 1

To achieve a specified spin rate (revolutions per minute, or rpm), students attached an electric motor to the top. Once the top reached the specified spin rate, the motor was removed. Students then counted the number of precessions per minute. The procedure was repeated for different spin rates, and the results were recorded in Table 1.

Table 1	
Spin rate (rpm)	**Precession rate (rpm)**
450	15
550	10
750	7
1,150	4

Experiment 2

Students used the same top as in Experiment 1, but used different lengths of lightweight stems. The new stems varied the distance from the top's center of gravity to the surface (*r*). The electric motor was used to achieve the same spin rate for each trial. The number of precessions for each trial was counted and recorded in Table 2.

Table 2	
r (inches)	**Precession rate (rpm)**
1	3.5
2	7
3	11
4	16

GO ON TO THE NEXT PAGE.

11. How would one best investigate the effect of a top's mass on the precession rate if the spin rate is constant?
    A. Use tops with motors permanently attached.
    B. Use tops that are the same size and have the same shape, but are made from different metals.
    C. Try different tops and test them in a vacuum.
    D. Try tops with equal mass, but with stems of different lengths.

12. Based on the results of Experiment 2, one can conclude that the precession rate of a top increases as the stem:
    F. decreases in length.
    G. increases in length.
    H. remains the same length.
    J. reaches a specified spin rate.

13. Which of the following graphs best represents the change in the precession rate with increasing spin rate as shown in Experiment 1?

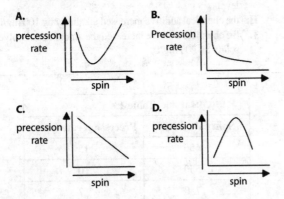

A.
B.
C.
D.

14. Based on Table 1, if a spin rate of 900 had been recorded, the precession rate would most likely have been closest to:
    F. 0 rpm.
    G. 3 rpm.
    H. 5.5 rpm.
    J. 12.5 rpm.

15. If the spin rate used in Experiment 2 was 500 rpm, what is most likely the value of r in Experiment 1?
    A. 3 inches
    B. 5 inches
    C. 7 inches
    D. 10 inches

16. If the techniques of Experiment 1 had not been perfected first, how would this have affected Experiment 2?
    F. The mass of the top would have been a factor.
    G. The spin rate might not have been the same in each trial.
    H. The top's mass might have redistributed itself.
    J. The top's stem would have been removed.

PASSAGE IV

The U.S. Environmental Protection Agency (EPA) monitors the sea level (the average height of the sea) and reports that it has risen approximately 20 centimeters in the last 100 years. Scientists have also determined that the sea level has risen a total of 120 meters since the last ice age, which ended approximately 10,000 years ago. Two scientists discuss whether the increasing temperature of the ocean waters or the melting of the polar icecaps is responsible for the rise in sea level.

Scientist 1

The rise in sea level occurs when pieces of the polar icecap called icebergs melt. Icebergs are sections of frozen glaciers that break away from landmasses and float into the ocean. Global warming and the resulting climate change lead to the formation of icebergs. The warmer temperatures weaken the glaciers, allowing more cracks to form and making ice more likely to break away. As soon as the ice floats into the ocean, the sea level rises. Even though the rise is relatively small, the cumulative effect of many icebergs breaking off and entering the sea could be devastating. Major ice-covered landmasses include Antarctica, the North Pole, and Greenland, all of which contain a large portion of ice above the permafrost zone. Global warming directly affects the melting of these polar icecaps, particularly in Greenland, which is closer to the equator and more likely to be affected by rising temperatures. It is hypothesized that the sea level would increase 7 meters (20 feet) if the ice covering Greenland were to melt. Although it is highly unlikely, if the ice covering all of Antarctica, which includes 90% of the world's ice, were to melt, the sea level would rise more than 61 meters (200 feet).

Scientist 2

The major cause of the rise in sea level is thermal expansion. Thermal expansion is the increase in the volume of matter when it is heated. Water is most dense at approximately 39.2°F. At any temperature above this temperature, water will expand and, therefore, occupy more space. In other words, the density of the water decreases as the water temperature increases.

GO ON TO THE NEXT PAGE.

The ocean absorbs heat from the atmosphere. As the atmosphere becomes warmer, so will the ocean waters. Warmer temperatures caused by global warming contribute to the rising temperatures of the ocean, which cause the water to naturally expand, thus elevating sea levels. According to reports, thermal expansion may be responsible for up to 7 cm of sea level increase during this century. Although this may seem like a small amount, this rise in sea level could be very detrimental, particularly to coastal cities. Coastal erosion, increased storm-surge flooding, and changes in the water quality and characteristics are just a few of the effects threatening these areas.

17. Which of the following best describes the major point of difference between the scientists' viewpoints?
   A. the major contributing factor of global warming
   B. the effects of global warming on the environment
   C. the effects of rising sea levels
   D. the major cause of rising sea levels

18. With which of the following statements would both scientists likely agree?
   F. The probability of the icecaps melting is very small.
   G. Global warming contributes to rising sea levels.
   H. Global warming affects sea level more than it affects any other aspect of the environment.
   J. The increasing sea level is not a major concern.

19. Which of the following statements best describes how Scientist 1 would explain why the icecaps of Antarctica are in no danger of melting, as opposed to the icecaps of Greenland?
   A. Antarctica and Greenland are both close to the equator.
   B. The average temperature in Antarctica is –37°F, far below the temperatures in Greenland.
   C. Antarctica and Greenland are too far away from the equator.
   D. The average amount of ice that has melted is greater in Antarctica than it is in Greenland.

20. According to Scientist 2, global warming increases the temperature of the atmosphere, thus:
   F. decreasing the density of the water in the ocean.
   G. reducing the amount of water in the ocean.
   H. increasing the amount of water in the ocean.
   J. changing the composition of icecaps.

21. Scientist 1's viewpoint would most likely be *weakened* by which of the following statements?
   A. It is nearly impossible for ice above the permafrost zone to melt.
   B. The effect of thermal expansion on sea level is minimal.
   C. Thermal expansion has no effect on the melting of icecaps.
   D. Icebergs form rapidly in Greenland, which is covered by large ice masses.

22. Scientist 2 claims that all of the following are issues facing coastal cities EXCEPT:
   F. coastal erosion.
   G. increased flooding.
   H. a greater number of storms.
   J. changes in water quality.

23. Based on Scientist 2's viewpoint, even a small increase in sea level could result in:
   A. thermal expansion.
   B. the formation of icebergs.
   C. increased air temperatures.
   D. alteration of the world's coastlines.

PASSAGE V

Aphids are small plant-eating insects known to feed on rosebushes. In the cultivation of roses, certain pesticides are often applied when the presence of aphids is detected. However, the flowers that are treated with the pesticides sometimes are not as vibrant or as fragrant as those that did not receive the pesticide treatment. Two experiments were done to study the effect of certain pesticides on rosebushes.

Experiment 1

A gardener filled 125 pots with Soil Type 1. No pesticide was added to the soil in 25 pots. The other pots were divided into four groups of 25, and the soils in each group were treated with 5, 15, 25, or 35 ppm of either Pesticide A or Pesticide B. All other factors were held constant. Fully grown rosebushes with

buds but no flowers were planted after the pesticide was placed in the soil. After 30 days, the rosebushes were uprooted and sun-dried, and the number of petals was counted. The results are shown in Table 1.

Table 1		
Pesticide dose (ppm)	**Number of petals**	
	Pesticide A	**Pesticide B**
5	12	15
15	2	7
25	9	14
35	5	7
None	14	14

GO ON TO THE NEXT PAGE.

Experiment 2

Experiment 1 was repeated with 100 pots of Soil Type 1 and 100 pots of Soil Type 2. The same pesticide doses and type and number of rosebushes were used. All other factors were held constant. After 30 days, the rosebushes were uprooted and weighed. The results are shown in Table 2.

Table 2				
	Average weight of rosebush (oz)			
Pesticide dose (ppm)	Soil Type 1		Soil Type 2	
	Pesticide A	Pesticide B	Pesticide A	Pesticide B
5	47.5	51.4	52.7	61.2
15	37.1	42.3	40.3	51.7
25	27.5	32.9	31.1	40.3
35	19.7	22.1	23.6	29.7

Note: Average plant weight with untreated Soil Type 1 was 42.1 oz; average plant weight with untreated Soil Type 2 was 24.7 oz.

Information on the composition of the two soil types used is given in Table 3.

Table 3				
Soil type	pH level	Organic matter (%)	Clay (%)	Sand (%)
1	4.1	3.0	12.5	84.5
2	3.9	8.5	11.0	80.5

24. Which of the following sets of rosebushes served as the control in Experiment 1?
   F. Rosebushes grown in soil with no pesticide added
   G. Rosebushes grown in soil treated with 15 ppm of Pesticide A
   H. Rosebushes grown in soil treated with 15 ppm of Pesticide B
   J. Rosebushes grown in soil treated with 35 ppm of Pesticide A

25. Which of the following, if true, best explains why the pesticides were applied to the soil as opposed to being placed directly on the rosebushes?
   A. Pesticide is always placed in the soil when dealing with aphids and all other pests.
   B. Rosebushes are not affected when pesticide is applied to the soil.
   C. The experiments were testing how water levels affect growth patterns.
   D. The aphids lay their eggs in the soil, and early treatment is most effective.

26. Assume that there is a direct correlation between plant weight and the number of petals on the flowers. If a rosebush was grown in Soil Type 2, one would predict that the number of petals would be *lowest* under which of the following conditions?
   F. Pesticide B at 35 ppm
   G. Pesticide A at 35 ppm
   H. Pesticide B at 25 ppm
   J. Pesticide A at 15 ppm

27. Assume that a rosebush was grown in soil treated with varying doses of a third pesticide (Pesticide C). Based on the results of the experiments, what prediction, if any, about the effect of Pesticide C on the growth of this rosebush can be made?
   A. Pesticide C would have no impact on the growth of the rosebush.
   B. Pesticide C would interfere with the growth of this rosebush by making it smaller.
   C. Pesticide C would interfere with the growth of this rosebush by making it less fragrant.
   D. No prediction can be made on the basis of the results.

28. The results of Experiment 2 indicate that, at every pesticide dose, average plant weight was *lowest* under which of the following conditions?
   F. Pesticide B and Soil Type 1
   G. Pesticide A and Soil Type 1
   H. Pesticide B and Soil Type 2
   J. Pesticide A and Soil Type 2

29. According to information in the passage, which of the following most likely contributed to the higher average weight of rosebushes grown in Soil Type 2?
   A. Higher pH levels in the soil
   B. Lower pesticide doses applied to the soil
   C. Higher percentage of organic matter in the soil
   D. Lower initial number of petals on the rosebushes

GO ON TO THE NEXT PAGE.

PASSAGE VI

A group of students designed the following experiments to study the viscosity of different types of liquids. *Viscosity* is defined as a fluid's resistance to flow. Therefore, higher viscosity will mean higher resistance to flow and longer flow times.

Experiment 1

At a temperature of 20°C, the density of water (H_2O) was determined using the following equation:

$$Density = \frac{mass\ (g)}{volume\ (mL)}$$

A 10.0-mL sample of H_2O was placed in a *viscometer*. The viscometer was positioned to allow the H_2O to flow through the capillary tubing, as shown in Figure 1. The time it took for all of the liquid to flow through the capillary tubing was measured. Students tested a total of four types of liquids. The results are displayed in Table 1.

Figure 1

Table 1		
Liquid	**Density (g/mL)**	**Flow time (sec)**
Water	1.01	30
Methanol	0.79	80
Pentane	0.63	20
Sunflower oil	0.92	2,190

Experiment 2

Students took a plastic eyedropper and labeled it with two marks that were 3 cm apart (see Figure 2). The students then filled the dropper with Liquid A at 20°C until it was at the level of the top line. The students measured the time

it took for the liquid to reach the end point when the liquid was allowed to flow freely out of the dropper. The students repeated the procedure for a total of four different liquids at three different temperatures. The results were recorded in Table 2.

Figure 2

Table 2			
Liquid	**Flow time (sec) at 5°C**	**Flow time (sec) at 20°C**	**Flow time (sec) at 40°C**
A	46.8	21.9	10.8
B	30.3	15.6	8.1
C	65.4	31.5	14.7
D	111.8	47.6	17.7

30. If Experiment 2 were repeated at a temperature of 30°C, the flow time for Liquid A in the eyedropper would most likely be closest to:
- **F.** 10 sec.
- **G.** 15 sec.
- **H.** 20 sec.
- **J.** 30 sec.

31. One of the students tested an additional substance in Experiment 1. She found that 10.0 mL of the liquid had a mass of 20.0 g. What is the density of this liquid?
- **A.** 0.5 g/mL
- **B.** 2.0 g/mL
- **C.** 10.0 g/mL
- **D.** 20.0 g/mL

GO ON TO THE NEXT PAGE.

32. According to Table 2, as temperature increases, flow time:

F. increases for all liquids only.

G. decreases for all liquids only.

H. remains constant for all liquids.

J. increases for some liquids and decreases for others.

33. In which of the following ways are the designs of Experiments 1 and 2 different? In Experiment 1:

A. only oils were tested, while in Experiment 2 other substances were tested.

B. the effect of density on viscosity was investigated, while in Experiment 2 the effect of temperature on viscosity was investigated.

C. more samples were tested than were tested in Experiment 2.

D. a different instrument was used to measure the viscosity than was used in Experiment 2.

34. Which of the following lists the four liquids measured in Experiment 1 in order of increasing viscosity?

F. Water, pentane, methanol, sunflower oil

G. Sunflower oil, methanol, water, pentane

H. Pentane, water, methanol, sunflower oil

J. Water, methanol, pentane, sunflower oil

35. How would the flow times measured in Experiment 1 differ, if at all, if the capillary tubing in the viscometer had an inside diameter of 1.7 mm? The measured flow times would:

A. be shorter.

B. be longer.

C. remain the same.

D. be shorter or longer, depending on the liquid.

PASSAGE VII

Turf grasses are often planted to create lawns. Kentucky bluegrass is the most common type of turf grass used in the northern part of the United States. To keep up their lawns, homeowners are encouraged to apply fertilizer up to five times a year. Inorganic fertilizers contain three common elements (nitrogen, phosphorus, and potassium) for the development of plant color, strength, and health. Turf grass does not take up all of these nutrients, leading to the development of nutrient-rich soil. One problem with high-nutrient soil occurs with the onset of rain and irrigation. When water enters the soil, it picks up a portion of the excess nitrogen from the soil. This water, now termed *leachate*, flows into waterways. The leaching of nitrogen into natural waterways can throw off the environmental equilibrium of the aquatic ecosystem, resulting in an increase in plant growth, which leads to higher fish fatality. Leaching into waterways used for drinking water can lead to health problems in humans.

A study was performed to examine the degree of nitrogen (N) leaching in Kentucky bluegrass turf; two plots were compared. Plot A, with a low N rate application, received 98 kg N/ha annually from 2000 to 2005. Plot B, with a high N rate application, received 245 kg N/ha annually from 2000 to 2002. From 2003 to 2005, the annual amount of nitrogen applied was decreased to 196 kg N/ha. Table 1 shows the flow-weighted means of NO_3-N concentration in the leachate. Figure 1 shows the percent concentration of NO_3-N in the leachate.

Table 1		
	Mean flow rate (mg/L)	
Year	**Plot A**	**Plot B**
2000	2.1	14.7
2001	3.7	18.9
2002	4.8	25.3
2003	6.3	29.7
2004	2.6	8.8
2005	3.6	11.6

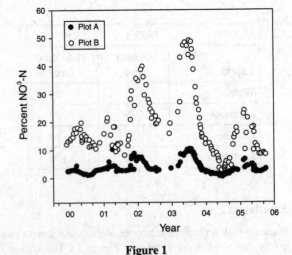

Figure 1

GO ON TO THE NEXT PAGE.

36. According to the passage, which of the following statements is (are) true?

    I. Excess nitrogen in lakes can cause a decrease in the population of fish.

    II. Kentucky bluegrass is the most common turf grass used in the Pacific Southwest.

    III. Rainwater absorbs nitrogen from nutrient-dense soil and carries it to rivers.

    F. I only
    G. I and II
    H. I and III
    J. I, II, and III

37. Compared to the mean flow rate of Plot A, the mean flow rate of Plot B is:

    A. always slower.
    B. always faster.
    C. sometimes slower, sometimes faster, depending on the year.
    D. more difficult to measure.

38. During which year did the highest percent of NO_3-N concentration in Plot A and Plot B occur?

    F. 2000
    G. 2002
    H. 2003
    J. 2005

39. According to the EPA, the mean flow rate of NO_3-N must be less than 10 mg/L. Following this standard, which fertilizing regimen is the safest?

    A. 245 kg N/ha/yr
    B. 196 kg N/ha/yr
    C. 98 kg N/ha/yr
    D. None of the tested regimens are safe.

40. The data from the study support which of the following conclusions?

    F. During the time span studied, the amount of nitrogen leaching into the soil followed an oscillating pattern.

    G. During the time span studied, the NO_3-N concentration in the leachate increased linearly.

    H. During the time span studied, the NO_3-N concentration in the leachate decreased linearly.

    J. Nitrogen leaching did not follow a recognizable pattern.

END OF THE SCIENCE TEST.
STOP! IF YOU HAVE TIME LEFT OVER, CHECK YOUR WORK ON THIS SECTION ONLY.

■■ **ANSWER KEY**

Science Test

1. D	11. B	21. A	31. B
2. J	12. G	22. H	32. G
3. A	13. C	23. D	33. B
4. H	14. H	24. F	34. H
5. B	15. A	25. D	35. A
6. H	16. G	26. G	36. H
7. D	17. D	27. D	37. B
8. G	18. G	28. G	38. H
9. A	19. B	29. C	39. C
10. F	20. F	30. G	40. F

■■ **SCORING WORKSHEET**

Scale Score	Raw Score Science	Scale Score	Raw Score Science
36	39–40	18	15–16
35	38	17	14
34	37	16	12–13
33	36	15	11
32	—	14	10
31	35	13	9
30	34	12	8
29	33	11	7
28	32	10	6
27	31	9	5
26	29–30	8	4
25	27–28	7	3
24	25–26	6	—
23	23–24	5	2
22	21–22	4	—
21	20	3	1
20	18–19	2	—
19	17	1	0

NOTE: Each actual ACT is scaled slightly differently based on a large amount of information gathered from the millions of tests ACT, Inc., scores each year. This scale will give you a fairly good idea of where you are in your preparation process. However, it should not be read as an absolute predictor of your actual ACT score. In fact, on practice tests, the scores are much less important than what you learn from analyzing your results.

ANSWERS AND EXPLANATIONS

Passage I

1. **The correct answer is D.** Table 1 lists characteristics of certain predators. Since "herbivore" is listed in the table, a herbivore is a predator. The passage also indicates that some scientists contend that herbivores are predators. According to Table 1, carnivores eat herbivores, which means that a herbivore is also a prey animal.

2. **The correct answer is J.** The passage states, "The number of prey consumed depends on both the number of prey present and the number of predators present." The other answer choices are not supported by the passage.

3. **The correct answer is A.** In Figure 1, predators are indicated by a dashed line. During the first year, the number of predators was generally higher than was the number of prey.

4. **The correct answer is H.** According to Table 1, a deer is a herbivore, so eliminate answer choice G. Table 1 also indicates that herbivores can be selective eaters, which means that they may choose to eat a certain type of plant over other types of plants.

5. **The correct answer is B.** To answer this question, find the location on Figure 1 where the line representing prey reaches its highest point. This occurs during the second year.

Passage II

6. **The correct answer is H.** According to Table 1, the ideal level of lead is less than 0.015 mg/L. Because the lead level in Sample 1 is 0.01 mg/L, it is below the ideal level.

7. **The correct answer is D.** The passage states, "Alkalinity is the water's capacity to resist changes in pH that would make the water more acidic. This resistance is achieved through a process called *buffering* (a buffered solution resists changes in pH until the buffer is used up)." Because increased acidity can lead to corrosion, answer choice D makes the most sense.

8. **The correct answer is G.** The test results of Sample 1 are shown in Table 1. According to Table 1, Sample 1 has a lower than ideal pH, which means that the sample is acidic.

9. **The correct answer is A.** The test results of Sample 2 are shown in Table 1. According to Table 1, Sample 2 has higher than ideal iron and hardness levels.

10. **The correct answer is F.** Because Sample 1 is already at a lower than ideal pH level (meaning that the water is acidic), reducing the pH level will serve to increase both the acidity and the level of certain toxic metals in the water.

Passage III

11. **The correct answer is B.** Different metals will most likely have different masses. Therefore, if the size, shape, and spin rate remain constant, varying the masses of the tops will give you a good test of the effect of mass on precession rate.

12. **The correct answer is G.** The results of Experiment 2 are shown in Table 2. According to Table 2, as r increases, precession rate also increases.

13. **The correct answer is C.** The results of Experiment 1 are shown in Table 1. According to Table 1, as spin rate increases, precession rate decreases. This is an inverse relationship, best represented by the graph shown in answer choice C.

14. **The correct answer is H.** A spin rate of 900 would most likely result in a precession rate somewhere between 7 and 4. Only answer choice H falls within this range.

15. **The correct answer is A.** The r value (stem length) is not shown for Experiment 1, but it can be extrapolated based on the information given in the question and the data in Tables 1 and 2. Based on Table 1, a spin rate of 500 would be likely to result in a precession rate somewhere between 10 and 15. According to Table 2, a precession rate between 10 and 15 would mean that the stem was probably 3 inches long.

16. **The correct answer is G.** Experiment 1 tested spin rates of the tops. Therefore, any further testing of spin rate would probably have been affected if the techniques used in Experiment 1 had not been perfected.

Passage IV

17. **The correct answer is D.** According to the passage, Scientist 1 believes that the rise in sea levels is caused by melting of the polar icecaps, whereas Scientist 2 believes that the rise in sea levels is caused by thermal expansion.

18. **The correct answer is G.** Because both scientists are studying various effects of global warming on increased levels of ocean waters, it makes sense that the scientists would both agree that global warming contributes to rising sea levels.

19. **The correct answer is B.** According to Scientist 1, "Global warming directly affects the melting of these polar icecaps, particularly in Greenland, which is closer to the equator and more likely to be affected by rising temperatures." Therefore, because Antarctica has lower average temperatures than does Greenland, it makes sense that Scientist 1 would suggest that Antarctica's icecaps are safe.

20. **The correct answer is F.** Scientist 2 states, "The density of the water decreases as the water temperature increases. The ocean absorbs heat from the atmosphere. As the atmosphere becomes warmer, so will the ocean waters." This best supports answer choice F.

21. **The correct answer is A.** Scientist 1 states, "Major ice-covered landmasses include Antarctica, the North Pole, and Greenland, all of which contain a large portion of ice above the permafrost zone. Global warming directly affects the melting of these polar icecaps." Therefore, if it were true that ice above the permafrost zone did not melt, Scientist 1's viewpoint would be weakened.

22. **The correct answer is H.** According to Scientist 2, "Coastal erosion, increased storm-surge flooding, and changes in the water quality and characteristics are just a few of the effects threatening these areas." A greater number of storms is not mentioned.

23. **The correct answer is D.** According to Scientist 2, "Although this may seem like a small amount, this rise in sea level could be very detrimental, particularly to coastal cities. Coastal erosion, increased storm-surge flooding, and changes in the water quality and characteristics are just a few of the effects threatening these areas."

Passage V

24. **The correct answer is F.** In Experiment 1, the control group (the group that the results are compared to) was the group of rosebushes that were grown in soil with no pesticide added.

25. **The correct answer is D.** The best way to answer this question is by the process of elimination. Answer

choices A and B are incorrect because they do not explain why the pesticides were applied to the soil as opposed to being placed directly on the rosebushes. Answer choice C is incorrect because this explanation is irrelevant to the topic of the passage. Answer choice D is the correct answer, because if early treatment of aphids was most effective, it would make sense to apply to the pesticides to the soil in order to kill the eggs.

26. **The correct answer is G.** If there is a direct correlation between plant weight and the number of petals on the flowers, the lower the average weight of the rosebush, the lower the number of petals. A rosebush grown in Soil Type 2 with Pesticide A at 35 ppm (23.6 oz) would have the lowest number of petals.

27. **The correct answer is D.** If Pesticide C was used to treat a rosebush, no prediction could be made on the basis of the previous results because no information about Pesticide C was given. Answer choice C can be eliminated because the fragrance of the flowers was not tested in this experiment, and therefore no information about this is provided.

28. **The correct answer is G.** The results of Experiment 2 are shown in Table 2. According to the table, in every row, the average weight of the rosebushes was lowest for Soil Type 1 and Pesticide A.

29. **The correct answer is C.** According to Table 3, the percentage of organic material in Soil Type 2 was significantly higher than the percentage of organic material in Soil Type 1. The other factors are either very similar for each soil or part of the experiment, so answer choice C makes the most sense.

Passage VI

30. **The correct answer is G.** The results of Experiment 2 are shown in Table 2. According to Table 2, the flow time of Liquid A at 20° was 21.9 seconds and the flow time at 40° was 10.8 seconds. It makes sense that the flow time at 30° would fall about halfway between these two rates.

31. **The correct answer is B.** The formula in the passage indicates that density is equal to mass divided by volume. Therefore, the density of the additional substance would be equal to 20 divided by 10, which is 2.

32. **The correct answer is G.** Table 2 shows that as the temperature increases from 5° to 20° to 40°, all of the flow times decrease.

33. The correct answer is B. According to the passage, "A group of students designed the following experiments to study the viscosity of different types of liquids. *Viscosity* is defined as a fluid's resistance to flow. Therefore, higher viscosity will mean higher resistance to flow and longer flow times." Experiment 1 was designed to test flow time based on density at a constant temperature, while Experiment 2 was designed to test flow time at various temperatures.

34. The correct answer is H. According to the passage, "*Viscosity* is defined as a fluid's resistance to flow. Therefore, higher viscosity will mean higher resistance to flow and longer flow times." To answer this question, first find the liquid in Table 1 with the shortest flow time. Pentane has the shortest flow time (20 seconds), so only answer choice H will work.

35. The correct answer is A. Increasing the diameter of the capillary tubing should allow the fluids to flow more quickly. Therefore, the flow times should be shorter for all of the liquids.

Passage VII

36. The correct answer is H. The passage does not support the statement in Roman numeral II; in fact, the passage states, "Kentucky bluegrass is the most common type of turf grass used in the northern part of the United States."

37. The correct answer is B. Table 1 shows that during each year tested, the mean flow rate was always slower for Plot A than for Plot B.

38. The correct answer is H. To answer this question, look at Figure 1. The highest percent of NO_3-N for both plots occurred during 2003, although the concentrations at Plot B were much higher.

39. The correct answer is C. According to the passage, "Plot A, with a low N rate application, received 98 kg N/ha annually from 2000 to 2005. Plot B, with a high N rate application, received 245 kg N/ha annually from 2000 to 2002. From 2003 to 2005, the annual amount of nitrogen applied was decreased to 196 kg N/ha." Table 1 shows that the mean flow rate at Plot A was consistently below 10 mg/L, so an application of 98 kg/ha would be the safest.

40. The correct answer is F. Based on Figure 1, the NO_3-N concentrations fluctuated from year to year (more so at Plot B than at Plot A), which means that the amount of nitrogen leaching into the soil followed an oscillating pattern.

CHAPTER 15

PRACTICE TEST 3 WITH EXPLANATIONS

SCIENCE TEST
Answer Sheet

SCIENCE

1 (A)(B)(C)(D)
2 (F)(G)(H)(J)
3 (A)(B)(C)(D)
4 (F)(G)(H)(J)
5 (A)(B)(C)(D)
6 (F)(G)(H)(J)
7 (A)(B)(C)(D)
8 (F)(G)(H)(J)
9 (A)(B)(C)(D)
10 (F)(G)(H)(J)
11 (A)(B)(C)(D)
12 (F)(G)(H)(J)
13 (A)(B)(C)(D)
14 (F)(G)(H)(J)
15 (A)(B)(C)(D)

16 (F)(G)(H)(J)
17 (A)(B)(C)(D)
18 (F)(G)(H)(J)
19 (A)(B)(C)(D)
20 (F)(G)(H)(J)
21 (A)(B)(C)(D)
22 (F)(G)(H)(J)
23 (A)(B)(C)(D)
24 (F)(G)(H)(J)
25 (A)(B)(C)(D)
26 (F)(G)(H)(J)
27 (A)(B)(C)(D)
28 (F)(G)(H)(J)
29 (A)(B)(C)(D)
30 (F)(G)(H)(J)

31 (A)(B)(C)(D)
32 (F)(G)(H)(J)
33 (A)(B)(C)(D)
34 (F)(G)(H)(J)
35 (A)(B)(C)(D)
36 (F)(G)(H)(J)
37 (A)(B)(C)(D)
38 (F)(G)(H)(J)
39 (A)(B)(C)(D)
40 (F)(G)(H)(J)

SCIENCE TEST

35 Minutes—40 Questions

DIRECTIONS: This test includes several passages, each followed by several questions. Read the passage and choose the best answer to each question. After you have selected your answer, fill in the corresponding bubble on your answer sheet. You should refer to the passages as often as necessary when answering the questions. You may NOT use a calculator on this test.

PASSAGE I

Many different units of measurement are used in chemistry. A *mole* is a unit of measure that is approximately equivalent to 6×10^{23} molecules or units of a compound. So, the number of glucose molecules in 1 mole of glucose equals the number of KI (potassium iodide) units in 1 mole of KI. *Molality* (m) is a unit of concentration defined as follows:

$$m = \frac{\text{moles of solute}}{\text{kg of solvent}}$$

When any substance is dissolved in a solvent, the boiling and freezing points of the solution will differ from the boiling and freezing points of the original pure solvent, depending on the concentration of the solute particles. Figure 1 shows how the boiling point of H_2O at 1 atm of pressure varies with concentration for 3 solutes. Figure 2 shows how the freezing point of H_2O at 1 atm of pressure varies with concentration for 3 solutes.

Figure 1

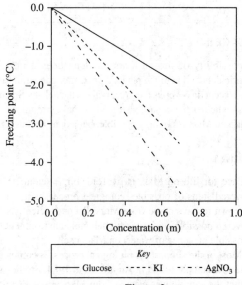

Figure 2

1. Based on the trends in Figure 1, which of the following aqueous solutions would have the lowest boiling point?
   A. 1.8 m Glucose
   B. 1.6 m KI
   C. 1.4 m KI
   D. 1.2 m AgNO$_3$

2. Consider an aqueous solution with a boiling point of 101.6°C. According to the passage, which of the following is likely true about the aqueous solution?
   F. The aqueous solution has a molality less than 0.0.
   G. The aqueous solution has a molality between 0.0 and 0.4.
   H. The aqueous solution has a molality between 0.8 and 1.0.
   J. The aqueous solution has a molality greater than 1.0.

3. Based on Figure 2, the freezing point of a solution composed of 0.95 moles of KI dissolved in 1 kg of H_2O would be closest to which of the following?
   A. −5.6°C
   B. −4.8°C
   C. −3.6°C
   D. −2.9°C

GO ON TO THE NEXT PAGE.

4. Based on Figure 2, as the mass of glucose dissolved in a given amount of solvent increases, the freezing point of the solution will:
   F. increase linearly.
   G. increase, but not linearly.
   H. decrease linearly.
   J. decrease, but not linearly.

5. A student claimed that, per formula unit, adding $AgNO_3$ changes the boiling point of H_2O more than adding KI. Does Figure 1 support this claim?
   A. No, because at a given concentration, $AgNO_3$ caused a smaller increase in the boiling point.
   B. No, because at a given concentration, $AgNO_3$ caused a smaller decrease in the boiling point.
   C. Yes, because at a given concentration, $AgNO_3$ caused a greater decrease in the boiling point.
   D. Yes, because at a given concentration, $AgNO_3$ caused a greater increase in the boiling point.

PASSAGE II

The possibility of life on Mars has long been a matter of scientific debate due to the planet's proximity and similarity to Earth. Recent discoveries have reenergized the debate. Scientists discuss whether the conditions on Mars make life impossible, or if life on Mars is not only possible, but a demonstrated fact.

Scientist 1

Evidence for life on Mars is twofold. First, scientists have discovered signs of possible biological processes in meteorites known to have come from Mars. Second, scientists have discovered possible evidence of a habitable environment (i.e., the possible presence of water) on Mars itself.

Most of the support for biological processes comes from a meteorite sample found in Antarctica in 1984. Studies indicate that the sample was ejected from Mars about 17 million years ago and has spent 11,000 years on Earth. Composition analysis has revealed a kind of mineral that, on Earth, is only found in association with certain microorganisms. Moreover, electron-scanning microscopes detected possible fossil remains of *nanobacteria*, a bacteria-like life-form only nanometers in length.

In 2000, evidence for water under the surface of Mars was discovered in the form of flood-like gullies. Deep subsurface water deposits near the planet's liquid core might form a present-day habitat for life. In this environment, Martian life would most likely be found in soil sediments formed in water. Further data is needed to confirm this hypothesis.

Scientist 2

There is no definite proof of life on Mars. The possible microfossils discovered on the Antarctica meteorite are inconclusive at best. The scientific community is not convinced that *nanobacteria* exist at all, due to the fact that they are too small to contain RNA genetic code. Other meteorites have been hailed as signs of life because they contain evidence of carbon deposits. While carbon is the basis of life, it is also the fourth most common element in the universe. Its presence may suggest life, but it does not prove it.

It is true that scientists have found suggestions of water in the form of flood-like gullies. However, astronomers have also found similar gullies on the Moon, which is believed never to have had liquid water on its surface. I believe that, as on the Moon, the Mars gullies are the result of micrometeorite impacts.

6. Which of the following criticisms might Scientist 1 logically make about Scientist 2's conclusion that the microfossils are NOT evidence of life on Mars?
   F. Scientist 2 ignores the mineral data that reinforces the identification of *nanobacteria*.
   G. Scientist 2 does not understand the means by which RNA operates within *nanobacteria*.
   H. Scientist 2 has misidentified the origin of the meteorites.
   J. Scientist 2 does not understand the importance of Antarctica in the development of the hypothesis supporting the existence of life on Mars.

7. Scientist 2's hypothesis would be most strongly supported by the finding that sediment rocks on Mars:
   A. are 17 million years old.
   B. contain evidence of *nanobacteria*.
   C. contain carbon deposits.
   D. contain salinity at a level that is toxic to life.

8. About which of the following points do the scientists agree?
   F. Evidence of water has been found on Mars.
   G. Electro-scanning microscopes have detected *nanobacteria* fossils in Martian soil.
   H. A Martian meteorite has been discovered on Earth.
   J. Flood-like gullies on Mars are caused by micrometeorite impacts.

GO ON TO THE NEXT PAGE.

9. Which of the following is an assumption likely made by Scientist 1?
   A. Mars is a planet unlike any others in the solar system.
   B. Martian life requires the presence of water.
   C. *Nanobacteria* are precursors to more advanced life-forms.
   D. All Martian soil must be formed by water.

10. Which of the following observations would more strongly support Scientist 1 than Scientist 2?
    F. Evidence of carbon molecules on Mars
    G. Evidence proving that gullies on Mars were created by micrometeorites
    H. Evidence of sediment in meteorites from Mars found on Earth
    J. Evidence showing bacterial remains in Martian soil samples

11. Which of the following observations would provide evidence to support Scientist 2's theory but NOT Scientist 1's theory?
    A. The discovery that the Moon once had surface water
    B. The scientific community's decision to reclassify life-forms to include silicon-based organisms in addition to carbon-based organisms
    C. Scientific data proving that *nanobacteria* cannot reproduce, and are, therefore not organic life-forms
    D. The discovery of *nanobacteria* in soil sediments on Mars

12. Suppose further study of the Antarctic meteorite revealed that it might not have originated on Mars. How would this discovery most likely affect the scientist's viewpoints, if at all?
    F. It would weaken Scientist 1's viewpoint only.
    G. It would weaken Scientist 2's viewpoint only.
    H. It would strengthen both scientists' viewpoints.
    J. It would have no effect on either scientist's viewpoint.

PASSAGE III

The factors that affect the growth of microorganisms include water availability (A_w), pH, and temperature. Table 1 lists some microorganisms and their respective pH range for growth. Figure 1 shows a pH scale. Table 2 lists some microorganisms and their optimum temperature range for growth. Table 3 lists the minimum A_w necessary for the growth of some microorganisms.

Figure 1

Table 1

Microorganism	Minimum pH	Optimum pH	Maximum pH
Sulfolobus acidocaldarius	1.0	2.0–3.0	5.0
Bacillus acidocaldarius	2.0	4.0	6.0
Lactobacillus acidophilus	4.0–4.6	5.8–6.6	6.8
Staphylococcus aureus	4.2	7.0–7.5	8.3
Escherichia coli	4.4	6.0–7.0	9.0
Pseudomonas aeruginosa	5.6	6.6–7.0	8.0
Thiobacillus novellus	5.7	7.0	9.0
Streptococcus pneumoniae	6.5	7.8	9.3

Table 2

Microorganism	Optimum Temperature (°C)
Vibrio marinus	15
Thiobacillus novellus	25–30
Staphylococcus aureus	30–37
Escherichia coli	37
Streptococcus pneumoniae	37
Pseudomonas aeruginosa	37
Sulfolobus acidocaldarius	75–85

Table 3

Microorganism	Minimum A_w
Caulobacter	1.00
Spirillum	1.00
Pseudomonas	0.91
Salmonella/Escherichia coli	0.91
Lactobacillus	0.90
Bacillus	0.90
Staphylococcus	0.85
Halococcus	0.75

Note: Pure water has an A_w of 1.00.

GO ON TO THE NEXT PAGE.

13. Which of the following ranks the microorganisms from those requiring a more acidic growth medium to those requiring a less acidic growth medium?

A. *Sulfolobus acidocaldarius, Streptococcus pneumoniae, Staphylococcus aureus*

B. *Sulfolobus acidocaldarius, Staphylococcus aureus, Streptococcus pneumoniae*

C. *Staphylococcus aureus, Streptococcus pneumoniae, Sulfolobus acidocaldarius*

D. *Streptococcus pneumoniae, Sulfolobus acidocaldarius, Staphylococcus aureus*

14. According to Table 1, *Escherichia coli* will experience optimum growth at which of the following pH levels?

F. 4.4
G. 6.5
H. 7.8
J. 12.3

15. Table 2 indicates that, compared to *Streptococcus pneumoniae*, *Escherichia coli* has an optimum growth temperature that is:

A. lower.
B. higher.
C. the same.
D. not measurable.

16. Which set of data best supports the claim that *Bacillus acidocaldarius* is more acidic than *Pseudomonas aeruginosa*?

F. Figure 1
G. Table 1
H. Table 2
J. Table 3

17. Based on the passage, which of the following microorganisms requires the *least* amount of water to grow?

F. *Spirillum*
G. *Pseudomonas*
H. *Staphylococcus*
J. *Halococcus*

PASSAGE IV

A major source of air pollutants is exhaust from motor vehicles. CO and SO_2 are two pollutants found in car exhaust. Environmentalists performed two experiments to ascertain the levels and behavior of these two pollutants near busy roadways.

Experiment 1

Environmentalists studied the correlation between CO levels and vehicle use. They measured CO levels hourly for 24 hours, $\frac{1}{2}$ mile (mi) downwind from six different roadways. The combination of speed limit and *vehicle usage* (number of vehicles per day) differed between each roadway. An average CO value for each roadway was calculated in parts per billion (ppb), with the results displayed in Table 1.

Table 1		
Roadway Speed Limit (mi/hr)	Vehicle Usage (vehicles/day)	Average CO Level (ppb)
45	15,000	107
	20,000	112
	25,000	117
70	15,000	110
	20,000	117
	25,000	125

Experiment 2

Environmentalists measured the levels of CO and SO_2 at 0, 1, and 2 miles downwind from the 70 mi/hr roadway, which averaged 20,000 vehicles per day. The level of CO decreased from 134 ppb at 0 mi to 100 ppb at 2 mi. The level of SO_2 decreased from 52 ppb at 0 mi to 12 ppb at 2 mi.

(Note: The levels of CO and SO_2 found far from pollution sources are 50 ppb and 5 ppb, respectively.)

18. In Experiment 2, which of the following factors was varied?

F. Number of roadways
G. Number of vehicles per day traveling on the roadway
H. Distance from the roadway
J. Speed limit on the roadway

19. According to the results, which of the following would the environmentalists suggest to decrease levels of CO in an area?

A. Reduce speed limits on the roadways
B. Reduce the number of cars traveling on the roadways
C. Increase speed limits on the roadways
D. Change the way CO emissions are measured

GO ON TO THE NEXT PAGE.

20. Based on the experimental results, if one compared SO_2 levels near a major roadway to those in a remote forest, SO_2 levels:
    F. near the roadway would be higher than in the forest.
    G. near the roadway would be lower than in the forest.
    H. near the roadway would be the same as those in the forest.
    J. would be detectable only in the forest.

21. Motor vehicle exhaust also introduces formaldehyde into the air. If formaldehyde behaves similarly to CO and SO_2 in the experiments, the environmentalists would hypothesize that formaldehyde levels:
    A. would decrease over time.
    B. would stay the same over time.
    C. are higher when closer to roadways compared to farther away.
    D. are lower when closer to roadways compared to farther away.

22. According to the results obtained by the environmentalists, as the distance from the roadway increases:
    F. CO and SO_2 levels both increase.
    G. CO and SO_2 levels both decrease.
    H. CO levels decrease and SO_2 levels increase.
    J. CO levels increase and SO_2 levels decrease.

23. A seventh road was added to the experiment. It has a speed limit of 45 mi/hr and a vehicle usage of 50,000 vehicles per day. One would hypothesize that $\frac{1}{2}$ mi downwind from this roadway CO levels are:
    A. less than 107 ppb.
    B. between 107 and 112 ppb.
    C. between 112 and 117 ppb.
    D. above 117 ppb.

PASSAGE V

Some students wanted to study the effects of concentration and temperature on *chemical kinetics*, which describes the reaction rates of chemical processes. The students prepared five 400 mL beakers containing different concentrations of potassium iodate (KIO_3), as shown in Table 1. All beakers were kept at room temperature (25°C), except for Beaker 4 (45°C) and Beaker 5 (10°C).

Table 1					
	Beaker 1	Beaker 2	Beaker 3	Beaker 4	Beaker 5
KIO_3	0.04 M	0.07 M	0.02 M	0.04 M	0.04 M
Distilled Water	150 mL	100 mL	175 mL	150 mL	150 mL

The students next prepared five identical 250 mL beakers (6–10), each containing 10 mL of 0.20 M sodium metabisulfite solution, 30 mL of 2% starch solution, and 40 mL of distilled water. These beakers were kept at room temperature (25°C).

Experiment 1

To test the effect of concentration on reaction rate, the students first poured the contents of Beaker 6 into Beaker 1 and recorded the rate at which the initial mixing of the two solutions caused the solution to turn blue. This was the control reaction. The students then poured the contents of Beaker 7 into Beaker 2 and poured the contents of Beaker 8 into Beaker 3. They recorded the rate at which the solutions turned blue. The results are shown in Table 2.

Experiment 2

To test the effect of temperature on reaction rate, the students poured the contents of Beaker 9 into Beaker 4, and poured the contents of Beaker 10 into Beaker 5. The rate at which each solution turned blue was also recorded in Table 2.

Table 2					
	6 → 1	7 → 2	8 → 3	9 → 4	10 → 5
KIO_3	0.04 M	0.07 M	0.02 M	0.04 M	0.04 M
Temperature	Room (25°C)	Room (25°C)	Room (25°C)	Warm (45°C)	Cool (10°C)
Reaction Rate (s)	6	3	12	4	8

24. Based on the information presented, what is the relationship between KIO_3 and reaction rate?
    F. As KIO_3 concentration increases, reaction rate increases only.
    G. As KIO_3 concentration increases, reaction rate decreases only.
    H. As KIO_3 concentration increases, reaction rate increases, then decreases.
    J. No relationship can be determined based on the data.

25. The students added sodium metabisulfite to the second set of beakers most likely because:
    A. it would not fit in the first set of beakers.
    B. it is the same temperature as distilled water.
    C. it is the easiest chemical to measure.
    D. it reacts with KIO_3 to turn the solution blue.

GO ON TO THE NEXT PAGE.

26. The students theorized that, at a constant KIO_3 concentration, as temperature increases, reaction rate increases. Does the data support this theory?
    F. Yes, because, at a constant KIO_3 concentration, the reaction rate was faster at 10°C than it was at 25°C.
    G. Yes, because, at a constant KIO_3 concentration, the reaction rate was faster at 45°C than it was at 25°C.
    H. No, because, at a constant KIO_3 concentration, the reaction rate was slower at 45°C than it was at 25°C.
    J. No, because, at a constant KIO_3 concentration, the reaction rate was slower at 25°C than it was at 10°C.

27. Based on the results of Experiments 1 and 2, the fastest reaction rate occurred when:
    A. Beaker 9 was mixed with Beaker 4.
    B. Beaker 8 was mixed with Beaker 3.
    C. Beaker 7 was mixed with Beaker 2.
    D. Beaker 6 was mixed with Beaker 1.

28. In which of the following ways was Experiment 2 different from Experiment 1? In Experiment 2:
    F. the students used different quantities of sodium metabisulfite.
    G. KIO_3 concentrations were varied.
    H. reaction rate was not measured.
    J. the students did not generate a control reaction.

29. A catalyst acts to increase *chemical kinetics*. It has been determined that sulfuric acid acts as a catalyst for the reaction studied in these experiments. Suppose 10 mL of sulfuric acid had been added to a beaker containing 150 mL of distilled water and 0.04 M of KIO_3, and the contents of the beaker had been mixed with a beaker containing 0.02 M of sodium metabisulfite and 40 mL of distilled water at room temperature. The reaction rate would most likely be:
    A. <6 seconds.
    B. equal to 6 seconds.
    C. >6 seconds, but <8 seconds.
    D. >8 seconds.

PASSAGE VI

Minerals can be identified by different characteristics such as hardness, color, specific gravity (density), and luster. Minerals with a specific gravity less than 2.0 are considered light weight, those with a specific gravity between 2.0 and 4.5 are considered average in weight, and those with a specific gravity greater than 4.5 are considered heavy.

Table 1 lists minerals according to the Mohs Hardness Scale, in order of hardness from soft (1) to hard (10). Luster describes how a mineral reflects light; minerals with a high reflectance are considered shiny, or metallic, while those with a low reflectance are considered dull. Table 2 describes different levels of luster for some minerals. Table 3 lists some common minerals and their identifying characteristics.

Table 1	
Mohs Hardness Scale	**Mineral**
1	Talc
2	Gypsum
3	Calcite
4	Fluorite
5	Apatite
6	Feldspar
7	Quartz
8	Topaz
9	Corundum
10	Diamond

Table 2	
Luster	**Description**
Metallic (splendent)	Opaque and reflective like metal
Submetallic	Opaque to nearly opaque and reflects well; thin splinters are translucent
Vitreous (glassy)	Reflective like glass
Adamantine (brilliant)	Transparent to translucent; extraordinarily brilliant and shiny
Resinous	Appears honey-like but not necessarily the same color
Silky	Fine fibrous structure, similar to silk cloth
Pearly	Like a shirt button or inside of mollusk shell; usually iridescent (rainbow-like)
Greasy (oily)	Appears coated with grease or oil
Pitchy	Tar-like; usually radioactive
Waxy	Appears coated with wax
Dull (earthly)	Poor reflective qualities; porous or rough

GO ON TO THE NEXT PAGE.

Table 3				
Mineral	**Color**	**Luster**	**Hardness**	**Specific Gravity**
Gypsum	Colorless, white, gray, brown, beige, orange, pink, yellow, light red, green	Vitreous to pearly	1.5–2	2.3–2.4
Halite	Colorless, white, red, yellow, orange, pink, green, blue, violet, gray	Vitreous	2–2.5	2.6
Calcite	All colors; may be multicolored	Vitreous	3	2.7
Anhydrite	Colorless, white, light yellow, gray, blue, orange-red, red, pink, lilac	Vitreous to pearly	3–3.5	2.9–3.0
Chalcopyrite	Brass yellow to golden yellow	Metallic	3.5–4	4.1–4.3
Pyrite	Yellowish gray to gray	Metallic	6–6.5	4.9–5.2

30. A mineral has been located that is blue, reflective like glass, and registers between 2 and 3 on the Mohs Scale. This mineral is most likely:

F. apatite.
G. pyrite.
H. gypsum.
J. calcite.

31. According to the passage, pyrite is most likely:
A. dull.
B. highly reflective.
C. porous.
D. coated with wax.

32. According to the passage, which of the following pairs of minerals is most similar?
F. Calcite and topaz
G. Halite and anhydrite
H. Talc and diamond
J. Feldspar and gypsum

33. According to Table 3, as a mineral's hardness increases, its specific gravity:
A. increases only.
B. decreases only.
C. doubles.
D. remains constant.

34. According to the passage, which of the following minerals listed in Table 1 most likely has the lowest specific gravity?
F. Quartz
G. Diamond
H. Talc
J. Topaz

PASSAGE VII

Resource supply in nature can be highly dynamic. Fluctuations in certain resources may change community composition and species diversity. For example, seasonal changes in weather have major effects on phytoplankton communities. It has been found that in temperate lakes, there is a growing season during the spring and early summer months, while during the late summer growth rate becomes stable, and organisms die off or enter resting stages in the winter. This environmental variation leads to a regular succession of species over the growing season, called *seasonal succession*.

Seasonal succession has long fascinated plankton ecologists. They theorize that growth and composition of phytoplankton depends strongly on light availability. Scientists examined how fluctuating light affects phytoplankton growth in a temperate lake.

Study 1

Light fluctuations can alter growth rates of phytoplankton. Some species are depressed and some are stimulated by light fluctuations, whereas growth rates typically remain constant in unchanging light. Growth of 2 separate species of phytoplankton—*Nitzschia* and *Sphaerocystis*—was observed over time. Figure 1 shows the minimum light requirements for growth of the 2 species, as a function of the proportion of light available during each period (p) studied. Figure 2 illustrates the application of a mathematical model to growth rate of the 2 species of phytoplankton.

GO ON TO THE NEXT PAGE.

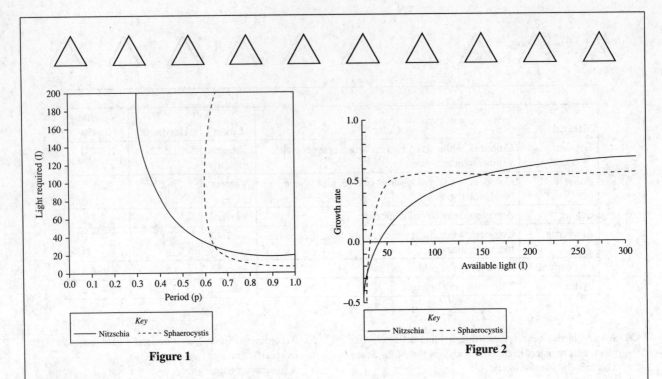

Figure 1

Figure 2

Study 2

The growth of the same 2 species observed in Study 1 was measured during the spring, summer, and fall, in order to determine whether the seasonally changing day length contributed to changes in population densities. The results are shown in Figure 3.

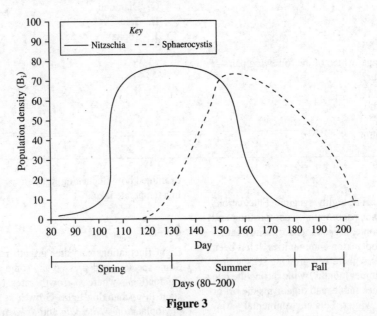

Days (80–200)

Figure 3

35. In Study 1, as available light increased, growth rate of both phytoplankton species:
    A. decreased only.
    B. increased only.
    C. first decreased, then leveled off.
    D. first increased, then leveled off.

GO ON TO THE NEXT PAGE.

36. According to the results of Study 2, how did seasonal changes affect the population density of both phytoplankton species?

   F. Seasonal changes increased the population of *Nitzschia* but decreased the population of *Sphaerocystis*.

   G. Seasonal changes decreased the population of *Nitzschia* but increased the population of *Sphaerocystis*.

   H. Seasonal changes resulted in population density fluctuations in both species.

   J. Seasonal changes had no effect on the population of either species.

37. Based on the results of Study 1, if growth rate of *Nitzschia* had been measured when I was 400, the expected growth rate would have been closest to which of the following values?

   A. −0.5
   B. 0.2
   C. 0.4
   D. 0.7

38. Suppose that, during the early spring, the overall light available to a temperate lake was consistently between 10 and 50 I. Based on the information presented, population density of *Nitzschia* at the rate was most likely:

   F. less than 10 B_i.
   G. between 10 B_i and 80 B_i.
   H. between 80 B_i and 100 B_i.
   J. greater than 100 B_i.

39. According to Figure 3, at 190 days, the population densities of the phytoplankton were closest to which of the following?

	Nitzschia	Sphaerocystis
A.	5 B_i	80 B_i
B.	5 B_i	45 B_i
C.	20 B_i	5 B_i
D.	45 B_i	5 B_i

40. According to Figure 1, the minimum light required for growth was the same for both phytoplankton species during:

   F. Period 0.3.
   G. Period 0.4.
   H. Period 0.5.
   J. Period 0.6.

END OF THE SCIENCE TEST.
STOP! IF YOU HAVE TIME LEFT OVER, CHECK YOUR WORK ON THIS SECTION ONLY.

■ **ANSWER KEY**

Science Test

1. A	11. C	21. C	31. B
2. H	12. F	22. G	32. G
3. B	13. B	23. D	33. A
4. H	14. G	24. J	34. H
5. D	15. C	25. D	35. D
6. F	16. G	26. G	36. H
7. D	17. J	27. C	37. D
8. H	18. H	28. J	38. F
9. B	19. A	29. A	39. B
10. J	20. F	30. J	40. J

■ **SCORING WORKSHEET**

Scale Score	Raw Score Science	Scale Score	Raw Score Science
36	39–40	18	15–16
35	38	17	14
34	37	16	12–13
33	36	15	11
32	—	14	10
31	35	13	9
30	34	12	8
29	33	11	7
28	32	10	6
27	31	9	5
26	29–30	8	4
25	27–28	7	3
24	25–26	6	—
23	23–24	5	2
22	21–22	4	—
21	20	3	1
20	18–19	2	—
19	17	1	0

NOTE: Each actual ACT is scaled slightly differently based on a large amount of information gathered from the millions of tests ACT, Inc., scores each year. This scale will give you a fairly good idea of where you are in your preparation process. However, it should not be read as an absolute predictor of your actual ACT score. In fact, on practice tests, the scores are much less important than what you learn from analyzing your results.

ANSWERS AND EXPLANATIONS

Passage I

1. **The correct answer is A.** Figure 1 shows that as concentration increases, boiling point increases. Also, based on the figure, of the three solutions, glucose has the lowest boiling point.

2. **The correct answer is H.** To answer this question, look at Figure 1 and find 101.6 along the y-axis (Boiling point). Then, look at the x-axis (Concentration) to see that a boiling point of 101.6 matches up to a concentration between 0.8 and 1.0.

3. **The correct answer is B.** To answer this question, look at Figure 2 and find 0.95 along the x-axis (Concentration). Then, look at the y-axis (Freezing point) to see that a concentration of 0.95 matches up with a freezing point slightly above –5°C.

4. **The correct answer is H.** To answer this question, first note that Figure 2 shows a linear relationship between freezing point and concentration. Therefore, you can eliminate answer choices G and J. Now, remember that –5°C is *less than* –1°C, so as concentration (m) increases, the freezing point decreases.

5. **The correct answer is D.** According to Figure 1, the slope of the line representing $AgNO_3$ is steeper than the slope of the line representing KI. Therefore, the student's claim is supported by the data.

Passage II

6. **The correct answer is F.** According to Scientist 1, ". . . electron-scanning microscopes detected possible fossil remains of *nanobacteria*, a bacteria-like life-form only nanometers in length." Scientist 2, on the other hand, claims that the ". . . scientific community is not convinced that *nanobacteria* exist at all . . ." and fails to mention the mineral data to which Scientist 1 refers.

7. **The correct answer is D.** Scientist 2 believes that the evidence for life on Mars is inconclusive at best. Therefore, if it were discovered that sediment rocks on Mars contain salinity at a level that is toxic to life, Scientist 2's assertion about possible life on Mars would be supported.

8. **The correct answer is H.** The only conclusion that can be supported by the evidence presented in both viewpoints is that a Martian meteorite has been discovered on Earth. The other answer choices are either not supported by evidence, or are points of contention between the scientists.

9. **The correct answer is B.** According to Scientist 1, ". . . scientists have discovered possible evidence of a habitable environment (i.e., the possible presence of water) on Mars itself." Likewise, Scientist 1 claims that ". . . Martian life would most likely be found in soil sediments formed in water." It seems reasonable to conclude that Scientist 1 assumes that Martian life requires the presence of water.

10. **The correct answer is J.** Scientist 1 states that "Composition analysis has revealed a kind of mineral that, on Earth, is only found in association with certain microorganisms. Moreover, electron-scanning microscopes detected possible fossil remains of *nanobacteria*, a bacteria-like life-form only nanometers in length." If bacterial remains were observed in Martian soil samples, Scientist 1's position would be supported.

11. **The correct answer is C.** Because Scientist 1 claims that *nanobacteria* are life-forms possibly found on Mars, any claim that *nanobacteria* are NOT life-forms would refute that claim.

12. **The correct answer is F.** Scientist 1's claim regarding possible life on Mars is supported by evidence from the Martian meteorite. If further study of the meteorite indicated that it did not originate on Mars, Scientist 1's viewpoint would be weakened.

Passage III

13. **The correct answer is B.** According to Figure 1, lower pH levels indicate higher acidity. Look at Table 1 to place the microorganisms mentioned in the answer choices in order of lowest pH to highest pH.

14. **The correct answer is G.** According to Table 1, *Escherichia coli* has an optimum pH level of 6.0–7.0, making answer choice G the most logical.

15. **The correct answer is C.** According to Table 2, both microorganisms have an optimum growth temperature of 37°.

16. **The correct answer is G.** Although Figure 1 shows the pH scale, Table 1 provides the information about pH levels necessary to compare the microorganisms mentioned in the question.

17. The correct answer is J. According to the passage, A_W indicates water availability. *Halococcus* has the lowest minimum A_W, so it requires the least amount of water to grow.

Passage IV

18. The correct answer is H. In Experiment 2, environmentalists "measured the levels of CO and SO_2 at 0, 1, and 2 miles downwind from the 70 mi/hr roadway, which averaged 20,000 vehicles per day."

19. The correct answer is A. Based on the data, average CO levels were lower when the speed limit was 45 than when the speed limit was 70. Therefore, it would make sense that reducing speed limits would lead to a decrease in CO levels.

20. The correct answer is F. According to the data, the level of SO_2 decreases as you move farther away from the roadways. Therefore, SO_2 levels near the roadways would likely be higher than SO_2 levels in a remote forest.

21. The correct answer is C. The question indicates that formaldehyde behaves similarly to CO and SO_2, so we can assume that formaldehyde levels would be similar to CO and SO_2 levels. According to the data, CO and SO_2 levels are higher when closer to roadways compared to farther away.

22. The correct answer is G. According to the data, CO and SO_2 levels are higher when closer to roadways compared to farther away. Therefore, you can assume that as distance from the roadway increases, CO and SO_2 levels would both decrease.

23. The correct answer is D. According to Table 1, a road with a speed limit of 45 and a vehicle usage of 25,000 vehicles per day has an average CO level of 117 ppb. The table also indicates that as vehicle usage increases, average CO levels increase. You can conclude that a road with a speed limit of 45 and a vehicle usage of 50,000 vehicles per day would have average CO levels greater than 117 ppb.

Passage V

24. The correct answer is J. According to Table 2, at a KIO_3 level of 0.04, a reaction rate of 4, 6, and 8 was observed. Therefore, you cannot determine a relationship between KIO_3 and reaction rate based on the data.

25. The correct answer is D. According to the passage, the students recorded the time it took for the solutions to turn blue. It makes sense they added sodium metabisulfate because it reacts with KIO_3 to turn the solution blue.

26. The correct answer is G. According to Table 2, when the KIO_3 concentration was 0.04, the reaction rate at 45°C was 4 seconds and the reaction rate at 25°C was 6 seconds.

27. The correct answer is C. Table 2 shows that the fastest reaction rate was 3 seconds when Beaker 7 was mixed with Beaker 2.

28. The correct answer is J. In Experiment 1, ". . . the students first poured the contents of Beaker 6 into Beaker 1 and recorded the rate at which the initial mixing of the two solutions caused the solution to turn blue. This was the control reaction." No such control reaction was recorded in Experiment 2.

29. The correct answer is A. The question describes the experimental procedure involving Beakers 1, 4, and 5 (0.04 M of KIO_3) at room temperature (25°C). Based on Table 2, the reaction rate of 0.04 M of KIO_3 at 25°C was 6 seconds. Therefore, the addition of a catalyst would likely cause the reaction time to be less than 6 seconds.

Passage VI

30. The correct answer is J. To answer this question, first look at Table 1. The question says that the mineral is between 2 and 3 on the Mohs Hardness Scale, so it is likely either gypsum or calcite. Next, find gypsum and calcite on Table 3. Because the mineral in the question is blue, and calcite can be any color, the mineral is most likely calcite.

31. The correct answer is B. To answer this question, find pyrite on Table 3. Table 3 indicates that pyrite is metallic, so it is most likely highly reflective.

32. The correct answer is G. One way to answer this question is to analyze each of the mineral pairs in the answer choices based on where they appear in the tables. Based on Table 3, halite and anhydrite are very similar in color, luster, hardness, and specific gravity.

33. The correct answer is A. Based on Table 3, as hardness increases, specific gravity also increases.

34. The correct answer is H. To answer this question, note that, according to Table 3, as hardness increases, specific gravity also increases. Therefore, the mineral with the lowest number on the Mohs Hardness Scale will have the lowest specific gravity.

Passage VII

35. **The correct answer is D.** The results of Study 1 are shown in Figure 1 and Figure 2. The question asks specifically about available light, which is shown in Figure 2. According to Figure 2, the growth rate for both species increased until the available light reached approximately 50–100 I, at which point the growth rate began to level off.

36. **The correct answer is H.** The results of Study 2 are shown in Figure 3. Based on Figure 3, the population density for both species fluctuated throughout the year.

37. **The correct answer is D.** According to Figure 2, the growth rate of *Nitzschia* leveled off at about 0.7 when I was approximately 50. You can reasonably conclude based on the data that the growth rate would remain stable at 0.7.

38. **The correct answer is F.** To answer this question, first look at Figure 2. When the available light (I) was between 10 and 50, the growth rate was approximately 0.0 to 0.5 for *Nitzschia*. Likewise, Figure 3 shows that, in early spring, population density (B_i) was approximately 0 to 10.

39. **The correct answer is B.** To answer this question efficiently, start with *Nitzschia*. According to Figure 3, at 190 days, the population density of *Nitzschia* was approximately 5 B_i. Therefore, the correct answer must be either A or B. Next, find that, at 190 days, the population density of *Sphaerocystis* was between 40 and 50, so answer choice B must be correct.

40. **The correct answer is J.** The minimum light required for growth will be the same at the point at which the lines cross. According to Figure 1, the lines cross during Period 0.6.

CHAPTER 16

PRACTICE TEST 4 WITH EXPLANATIONS

SCIENCE TEST
Answer Sheet

SCIENCE

1 Ⓐ Ⓑ Ⓒ Ⓓ	16 Ⓕ Ⓖ Ⓗ Ⓙ	31 Ⓐ Ⓑ Ⓒ Ⓓ
2 Ⓕ Ⓖ Ⓗ Ⓙ	17 Ⓐ Ⓑ Ⓒ Ⓓ	32 Ⓕ Ⓖ Ⓗ Ⓙ
3 Ⓐ Ⓑ Ⓒ Ⓓ	18 Ⓕ Ⓖ Ⓗ Ⓙ	33 Ⓐ Ⓑ Ⓒ Ⓓ
4 Ⓕ Ⓖ Ⓗ Ⓙ	19 Ⓐ Ⓑ Ⓒ Ⓓ	34 Ⓕ Ⓖ Ⓗ Ⓙ
5 Ⓐ Ⓑ Ⓒ Ⓓ	20 Ⓕ Ⓖ Ⓗ Ⓙ	35 Ⓐ Ⓑ Ⓒ Ⓓ
6 Ⓕ Ⓖ Ⓗ Ⓙ	21 Ⓐ Ⓑ Ⓒ Ⓓ	36 Ⓕ Ⓖ Ⓗ Ⓙ
7 Ⓐ Ⓑ Ⓒ Ⓓ	22 Ⓕ Ⓖ Ⓗ Ⓙ	37 Ⓐ Ⓑ Ⓒ Ⓓ
8 Ⓕ Ⓖ Ⓗ Ⓙ	23 Ⓐ Ⓑ Ⓒ Ⓓ	38 Ⓕ Ⓖ Ⓗ Ⓙ
9 Ⓐ Ⓑ Ⓒ Ⓓ	24 Ⓕ Ⓖ Ⓗ Ⓙ	39 Ⓐ Ⓑ Ⓒ Ⓓ
10 Ⓕ Ⓖ Ⓗ Ⓙ	25 Ⓐ Ⓑ Ⓒ Ⓓ	40 Ⓕ Ⓖ Ⓗ Ⓙ
11 Ⓐ Ⓑ Ⓒ Ⓓ	26 Ⓕ Ⓖ Ⓗ Ⓙ	
12 Ⓕ Ⓖ Ⓗ Ⓙ	27 Ⓐ Ⓑ Ⓒ Ⓓ	
13 Ⓐ Ⓑ Ⓒ Ⓓ	28 Ⓕ Ⓖ Ⓗ Ⓙ	
14 Ⓕ Ⓖ Ⓗ Ⓙ	29 Ⓐ Ⓑ Ⓒ Ⓓ	
15 Ⓐ Ⓑ Ⓒ Ⓓ	30 Ⓕ Ⓖ Ⓗ Ⓙ	

SCIENCE TEST

35 Minutes—40 Questions

DIRECTIONS: This test includes several passages, each followed by several questions. Read the passage and choose the best answer to each question. After you have selected your answer, fill in the corresponding bubble on your answer sheet. You should refer to the passages as often as necessary when answering the questions. You may NOT use a calculator on this test.

PASSAGE I

Cats and humans have coexisted for thousands of years. Because of the close relationship that can develop between cats and humans, humans can sometimes acquire cat scratch disease (CSD). It is a bacterial disease caused by the spread of *Bartonella henselae* from a cat to a human via a scratch or bite (traumatic cat contact). About 40% of cats carry *B. henselae* at some point in their lives. These cats do not show any signs of illness, which makes it impossible to determine which cats can spread CSD. While CSD rarely proves fatal, it can result in several painful and potentially dangerous symptoms. Table 1 shows some symptoms and their onset and typical duration.

Table 1

Symptom	Onset	Typical Duration
Infection at the site of scratch or bite	3–30 days after contact	1–4 weeks
Prolonged fever	5–30 days after contact	1–2 weeks
Swollen lymph nodes	7–30 days after contact	4–8 weeks
Fatigue	7–30 days after contact	3–4 weeks

Clinical diagnosis of CSD can sometimes be difficult. Table 2 lists 4 criteria, 3 of which must be met in order for a patient to be diagnosed with CSD. Most people recover in 2–5 months, but it can take up to one year for the swelling in the lymph nodes to disappear completely.

Table 2

1	History of traumatic cat contact
2	Positive skin-test response to CSD skin-test antigens
3	Characteristic lymph node lesions
4	Negative laboratory investigation for unexplained lymphadenopathy (nodes that are abnormal in either size, consistency, or number)

1. On the basis of the data in Table 1, if a person were infected with *B. henselae* after traumatic cat contact, one would predict that symptoms would begin appearing:
   A. in 3–4 weeks.
   B. after 30 days.
   C. after 3 days.
   D. immediately.

2. According to the passage, the symptom that develops most quickly is:
   F. fatigue.
   G. lymph node swelling.
   H. prolonged fever.
   J. infection.

3. Suppose that a patient presents with a history of traumatic cat contact and lymph node lesions. The patient has been previously diagnosed with abnormally large lymph nodes. Should this patient be diagnosed with CSD?
   A. Yes, because the patient meets 3 of the 4 criteria listed in Table 2.
   B. Yes, because the patient exhibits at least 1 of the 4 symptoms listed in Table 1.
   C. No, because the patient only meets 2 of the 4 criteria listed in Table 2.
   D. No, because the patient must exhibit all of the symptoms listed in Table 1.

4. According to the passage, which symptom requires the longest recovery time?
   F. Infection
   G. Prolonged fever
   H. Swollen lymph nodes
   J. Fatigue

GO ON TO THE NEXT PAGE.

5. Which of the following statements about CSD is supported by the information presented in the passage?
    A. CSD, though rarely fatal, can cause pain and discomfort in humans that can last up to one year.
    B. CSD symptoms generally disappear completely within 2 months of the onset of the disease.
    C. CSD, a bacterial disease, is typically spread to humans by cats showing signs of illness.
    D. CSD proves fatal in approximately 40% of cats.

PASSAGE II

To publish a brochure on bicycle safety, college officials needed to calculate *D*, a bicycle's total stopping distance. The distance is measured from the time a bicyclist first reacts to an emergency until the bicycle comes to a complete stop. Officials use 2 methods to calculate the total stopping distance.

In Method 1, *R* is the distance a bicycle travels during a bicyclist's estimated reaction time of 0.67 seconds, and *B* is the average distance traveled once the brakes are applied. Method 2 uses the equation *D* = (initial speed in ft/sec) × 1.5 seconds. Table 1 shows the results from both methods used to determine *D* at various initial speeds.

Table 1				
Initial Speed (ft/sec)	Method 1			Method 2
	R (ft)	B (ft)	D (ft)	D (ft)
9	6	5	11	13.5
13	9	10	19	19.5
18	12	13	25	27
22	15	16	31	33

6. In Method 1, *D* equals:
    F. *R* + *B*.
    G. *R* − *B*.
    H. *R* × *B*.
    J. *R* ÷ *B*.

7. According to Table 1, the value of *D* is most similar for Method 1 and Method 2 when the initial speed is closest to:
    A. 9 ft/sec.
    B. 13 ft/sec.
    C. 18 ft/sec.
    D. 22 ft/sec.

8. A bicyclist was traveling 9 ft/sec when she spotted a squirrel in the road and immediately applied her brakes. It took her 1.5 sec from the time she spotted the squirrel until she brought her bicycle to a complete stop. According to Method 2, how far did her bicycle travel during the 1.5 sec interval?
    F. 11 ft
    G. 13.5 ft
    H. 22 ft
    J. 27 ft

9. Based on Table 1, if the initial speed of a bicycle is 25 ft/sec, *D*, according to Method 2, will be:
    A. less than 20 ft.
    B. between 20 ft and 33 ft.
    C. between 33 ft and 40 ft.
    D. greater than 40 ft.

10. Compared to *R* at an initial speed of 9 ft/sec, *R* at an initial speed of 18 ft/sec is:
    F. ¼ as great.
    G. ½ as great.
    H. 2 times as great.
    J. 4 times as great.

GO ON TO THE NEXT PAGE.

PASSAGE III

Astronomers have observed that many neutron stars accrete (gradually add) different gases from a companion star. Hydrogen (H) that is accreted onto the neutron star is continually fused into helium (He). When there is enough helium present on the surface of the star, the helium quickly fuses into carbon (C), and a nuclear reaction ignites and triggers an explosion known as an *x-ray burst*. These bursts generally last about 10 seconds (s) at a temperature of approximately 10^9 K. As accretion continues, additional x-ray bursts can be seen. Thermally unstable H/He burning occurs when the accretion rate is less than 2×10^{-10} M/yr. Figure 1 illustrates the H/He ignition temperature required to initiate the first x-ray burst at low accretion rates. Figure 2 shows the intensity of the same x-ray burst over time.

Astronomers predicted that the sedimentation (accumulation) of isotopes such as carbon and oxygen (O) will affect the "fuel" required for the x-ray bursts. Over time, the heavier nuclei—carbon and oxygen—in the accumulated fuel layer settle downward and the lightest nuclei—hydrogen—float upward. Occasionally, a "superburst" is seen that lasts for approximately one hour and is likely caused by unstable C burning in the deepest accretion layers.

Figure 1

Figure 2

11. According to the passage, in the 30 seconds following the first x-ray burst at low accretion rates, temperature:
    A. decreases only.
    B. increases only.
    C. increases, then decreases.
    D. decreases, then increases.

12. According to Figures 1 and 2, at approximately what intensity did the x-ray burst reach a temperature of 10^9 K?
    F. 500 cts/s
    G. 1,500 cts/s
    H. 2,000 cts/s
    J. 3,500 cts/s

13. Which of the following statements is best supported by the information in the passage?
    A. When the accretion rate exceeds 2×10^{-10} M/yr, no x-ray bursts will be observed.
    B. As H converts to He over time, the accretion rate decreases.
    C. When the accretion layer temperature increases, C and O isotope levels in the accretion layer decrease.
    D. As H floats upward in the accretion layer, C and O isotope levels on the surface of the neutron star increase.

14. According to Figure 2, approximately 60 seconds after the x-ray burst its intensity was closest to:
    F. 4,500 cts/s.
    G. 3,000 cts/s.
    H. 1,000 cts/s.
    J. 250 cts/s.

15. Based on information in the passage, an x-ray burst will occur during which of the following combinations of temperature and intensity?

	Temperature	Intensity
A.	10^8	3,500 cts/s
B.	10^9	3,500 cts/s
C.	10^8	250 cts/s
D.	10^9	250 cts/s

GO ON TO THE NEXT PAGE.

PASSAGE IV

The geologic time scale follows the evolution of life on Earth. It began with the Precambrian Era and continues through the current Cenozoic Era. Each era is divided into one or more periods. The periods are often described by the life-forms that evolved during each period. Table 1 lists the eras, periods, some representative life-forms, and the duration of each period.

Table 1			
Era	Period	Representative Life-Forms	Duration (million years ago)
Cenozoic	Quaternary	wooly mammoth, horses, humans	1.8 mya to present
Cenozoic	Tertiary	mastadon, whales, early primates	65–1.8 mya
Mesozoic	Cretaceous	angiosperms, sea urchins	144–65 mya
Mesozoic	Jurassic	birds, frogs, toads	206–44 mya
Mesozoic	Triassic	ferns, primitive amphibians	248–206 mya
Paleozoic	Permian	dragonflies, beetles, conifers	290–248 mya
Paleozoic	Carboniferous	cockroaches, first reptiles	354–290 mya
Paleozoic	Devonian	spiders, mites, psilophyta plants	417–54 mya
Paleozoic	Silurian	sharks, nautiloids	443–417 mya
Paleozoic	Ordovician	corals, clams, primitive fish	490–443 mya
Paleozoic	Cambrian	sponges, trilobites	540–490 mya
Precambrian	Proterozoic	algae, protozoa	4,500–540 mya

The creation of fossils allows us to determine which animals lived during each period. The process of fossil creation begins when an organism dies. After an organism dies, its body decays over time and only the hard parts—such as teeth and bones—are left. Sediment settles over the organism's skeleton. As time goes by, more and more layers of sediment are deposited on the remains. This causes great pressure on the underlying layers and compresses them. When the compacted sediment is changed into sedimentary rock, a fossil is formed.

Scientists typically use two techniques to determine the age of a fossil. The first method is called *relative dating*, which considers the positions of the different rocks in sequence (in relation to each other) and the different types of fossils that are found in the rocks. The second method is called *absolute dating*, which analyzes the amount of radioactive decay in the minerals of the rocks. The *principle of lateral continuity* is applied to dating fossils when fossils of the same species have previously been found and it is possible to establish accurately the age of those fossils. Likewise, a fossil will always be younger than any fossils found in the rock beds beneath it; this is called the *principle of superposition*.

16. Using relative dating, a scientist has determined that a fossil is approximately 150 million years old. According to the passage, the fossil could be the remains of a:
    F. primate.
    G. mammoth.
    H. frog.
    J. whale.

17. According to the passage, the process by which fossils are created begins when:
    A. the sediment is compressed.
    B. the organism dies.
    C. the principle of lateral continuity is applied.
    D. the skeleton decays.

18. Periods can be further divided into epochs. The Pleistocene Epoch is known as "The Great Ice Age," and lasted from about 1.6 mya to about 10,000 years ago. Based on the information presented, during which era was the Pleistocene Epoch?
    F. Precambrian
    G. Paleozoic
    H. Mesozoic
    J. Cenozoic

19. According to the passage, which of the following places the organisms in order from earliest evolution to most recent evolution?
    A. Humans, sea urchins, sharks, algae
    B. Sea urchins, sharks, algae, humans
    C. Algae, sharks, sea urchins, humans
    D. Algae, sea urchins, sharks, humans

GO ON TO THE NEXT PAGE.

20. A student claimed that, during the Devonian Period, the ozone layer formed and the first air-breathing arthropods evolved on land. Is this claim supported by the data presented in Table 1?

F. Yes, because the representative life of the Devonian Period includes spiders and mites, which are air-breathing arthropods.

G. Yes, because, prior to the Devonian Period, spiders and mites did not breathe air.

H. No, because the representative life of the Devonian Period does not include any air-breathing organisms.

J. No, because air-breathing arthropods did not evolve until 417–354 mya.

21. Suppose that a fossil is found in a layer of rock *below* another layer of rock that is 200 million years old. According to the passage, the fossil:

A. will be less than 200 million years old.

B. will be exactly 200 million years old.

C. will be more than 200 million years old.

D. will be too old to accurately date using the principle of superposition.

PASSAGE V

Rumination is the process of regurgitating food after a meal and then chewing, swallowing, and digesting the food. Some students evaluated the effects of saturated and unsaturated fatty acid supplements (FS) on feed intake and rumination in cows. Eight cows were studied over a period of 7 days.

Experiment 1

Each of 4 cows was given 15 kg of food, which included 35% forage (hay), 24% oats, and 41% corn, at 8:00 a.m. each day. The cows were given free access to fresh water, and their behaviors were monitored. Different amounts of FS were given to each cow at mealtime. The effects of the supplement on the amount of food consumed (meal size), number of rumination bouts (NRB), and duration of rumination bouts (DRB) was measured. The results are recorded in Tables 1–3.

Table 1								
	% FS Given	Day 1 Meal Size	Day 2 Meal Size	Day 3 Meal Size	Day 4 Meal Size	Day 5 Meal Size	Day 6 Meal Size	Day 7 Meal Size
Cow 1	0.0 %	13.8 kg	13.7 kg	13.8 kg	13.4 kg	13.9 kg	13.5 kg	13.8 kg
Cow 2	2.5 %	13.5 kg	13.4 kg	13.0 kg	13.0 kg	12.9 kg	12.8 kg	12.8 kg
Cow 3	5.0 %	13.5 kg	12.8 kg	12.4 kg	12.2 kg	12.0 kg	12.1 kg	11.8 kg
Cow 4	7.5 %	13.4 kg	12.4 kg	12.2 kg	11.8 kg	11.5 kg	10.8 kg	10.5 kg

Table 2								
	% FS Given	Day 1 NRB	Day 2 NRB	Day 3 NRB	Day 4 NRB	Day 5 NRB	Day 6 NRB	Day 7 NRB
Cow 1	0.0 %	6	5	5	6	5	5	5
Cow 2	2.5 %	5	6	4	5	4	4	5
Cow 3	5.0 %	5	5	4	5	5	6	5
Cow 4	7.5 %	6	4	6	5	5	5	5

Table 3								
	% FS Given	Day 1 DRB	Day 2 DRB	Day 3 DRB	Day 4 DRB	Day 5 DRB	Day 6 DRB	Day 7 DRB
Cow 1	0.0 %	25.2 min.	25.1 min.	24.9 min.	24.8 min.	25.1 min.	25.2 min.	25.2 min.
Cow 2	2.5 %	24.6 min.	24.3 min.	23.9 min.	23.6 min.	23.4 min.	23.1 min.	23.0 min.
Cow 3	5.0 %	24.2 min.	23.9 min.	23.7 min.	23.5 min.	22.9 min.	22.9 min.	22.8 min.
Cow 4	7.5 %	23.9 min.	23.5 min.	23.2 min.	22.4 min.	21.9 min.	20.3 min.	19.5 min.

Note: DRB is the average length of time in minutes, rounded to the nearest tenth, of all recorded rumination bouts per cow.

GO ON TO THE NEXT PAGE.

Experiment 2

Each of the 4 remaining cows was given 2.5% FS at 3 different meals each day. The meals were given at the same times each day. The total percentage of the food makeup was the same as in Experiment 1, but each cow was given 5 kg of food at each meal. The cows were given free access to fresh water, and their behaviors were monitored. Meal sizes, number of rumination bouts (NRB), and duration of rumination bouts (DRB) were measured. The results are recorded in Tables 4–6.

		Day 1 Meal Size	Day 2 Meal Size	Day 3 Meal Size	Day 4 Meal Size	Day 5 Meal Size	Day 6 Meal Size	Day 7 Meal Size
Cow 5	1st meal	4.5 kg	4.4 kg	4.3 kg	4.3 kg	4.1 kg	4.1 kg	4.0 kg
	2nd meal	4.8 kg	4.6 kg	4.5 kg	4.4 kg	4.3 kg	4.2 kg	4.1 kg
	3rd meal	4.6 kg	4.4 kg	4.4 kg	4.3 kg	4.2 kg	4.1 kg	4.0 kg
Cow 6	1st meal	4.6 kg	4.5 kg	4.3 kg	4.4 kg	4.1 kg	4.0 kg	4.0 kg
	2nd meal	4.3 kg	4.4 kg	4.5 kg	4.3 kg	4.2 kg	4.1 kg	3.9 kg
	3rd meal	4.9 kg	4.6 kg	4.4 kg	4.3 kg	4.1 kg	4.2 kg	4.2 kg
Cow 7	1st meal	4.8 kg	4.5 kg	4.3 kg	4.3 kg	4.2 kg	4.1 kg	3.9 kg
	2nd meal	4.3 kg	4.3 kg	4.3 kg	4.3 kg	4.1 kg	4.1 kg	3.8 kg
	3rd meal	4.5 kg	4.4 kg	4.3 kg	4.3 kg	4.2 kg	4.1 kg	4.1 kg
Cow 8	1st meal	4.5 kg	4.3 kg	4.2 kg	4.1 kg	4.1 kg	4.1 kg	4.0 kg
	2nd meal	4.7 kg	4.6 kg	4.4 kg	4.3 kg	4.2 kg	4.1 kg	4.0 kg
	3rd meal	4.6 kg	4.5 kg	4.3 kg	4.3 kg	4.1 kg	4.1 kg	3.9 kg

Table 4

	Day 1 NRB	Day 2 NRB	Day 3 NRB	Day 4 NRB	Day 5 NRB	Day 6 NRB	Day 7 NRB
Cow 5	5	6	4	6	4	4	5
Cow 6	5	6	5	5	4	5	5
Cow 7	5	5	4	5	5	4	6
Cow 8	5	6	4	5	4	5	5

Table 5

	Day 1 DRB	Day 2 DRB	Day 3 DRB	Day 4 DRB	Day 5 DRB	Day 6 DRB	Day 7 DRB
Cow 5	24.9 min.	24.5 min.	24.3 min.	23.9 min.	23.5 min.	23.3 min.	23.1 min.
Cow 6	24.6 min.	24.2 min.	23.9 min.	23.6 min.	23.4 min.	23.2 min.	23.0 min.
Cow 7	24.7 min.	24.7 min.	24.0 min.	23.5 min.	23.4 min.	22.9 min.	22.9 min.
Cow 8	24.9 min.	24.5 min.	24.2 min.	23.8 min.	23.5 min.	23.3 min.	23.1 min.

Table 6

Note: DRB is the average length of time in minutes, rounded to the nearest tenth, of all recorded rumination bouts per cow.

GO ON TO THE NEXT PAGE.

22. Based on the information presented, the cows in Experiment 2 behaved most like which cow in Experiment 1?
   F. Cow 1
   G. Cow 2
   H. Cow 3
   J. Cow 4

23. The main purpose of Experiment 2 was to determine how varying the:
   A. type of food given to each cow affected the number and duration of rumination bouts.
   B. quantity of FS given to each cow affected water intake, food intake, and number of rumination bouts.
   C. duration of rumination bouts affected food and water intake.
   D. number of meals affected food intake, duration of rumination bouts, and number of rumination bouts.

24. According to the results of the experiments, as the % FS given to each cow was increased, the number of rumination bouts:
   F. increased only for all cows.
   G. decreased only for all cows.
   H. increased and then decreased for all cows.
   J. remained relatively stable for all cows.

25. A student claimed that, overall, meal size decreased over time for the cows in Experiment 2. Do the data support this claim?
   A. Yes, because for Cows 5–8, the meal size on Day 1 was larger than the meal size on Day 7.
   B. Yes, because for Cows 1–4, the meal size on Day 1 was larger than the meal size on Day 7.
   C. No, because for Cows 5–8, the meal size on Day 7 was larger than the meal size on Day 1.
   D. No, because for Cows 1–4, the meal size on Day 7 was larger than the meal size on Day 1.

26. According to the results of Experiment 1, as saturated and unsaturated fatty acid supplement intake increases:
   F. meal size increases.
   G. meal size decreases.
   H. meal size increases, then decreases.
   J. meal size is not affected.

27. Which of the following statements is *least* consistent with the results of the experiments?
   A. The amount of food consumed by the cows in Experiment 1 was affected by saturated and unsaturated fatty acid supplement intake.
   B. The number and duration of rumination bouts in cows in both experiments were not affected overall by saturated and unsaturated fatty acid supplement intake.
   C. The level of saturated and unsaturated fatty acid supplement intake affected meal size in the cows in Experiment 1.
   D. Increased FS levels greatly affected the number of rumination bouts in the cows in Experiment 2.

PASSAGE VI

Spider mites are small plant-eating insects known to feed on hibiscus plants. In the cultivation of hibiscus, certain pesticides are often applied when the presence of spider mites is detected. Spider mites cause the leaves of hibiscus plants to become yellow and mottled. Two experiments were done to study the effect of certain pesticides on spider mites.

Experiment 1

A gardener filled 125 pots with Soil Type A. No pesticide was added to the soil in 25 pots. The other pots were divided into four groups of 25 and the soils in each group were treated with 5, 15, 25, or 35 ppm of either Pesticide 1 or Pesticide 2. All other factors were held constant. Fully-grown hibiscus were planted after the pesticide was placed in the soil. After 30 days

the hibiscus were uprooted, and the number of mottled yellow leaves was counted. The results are shown in Table 1.

Table 1		
	Number of Mottled Yellow Leaves	
Pesticide Dose (ppm)	**Pesticide 1**	**Pesticide 2**
5	12	15
15	2	7
25	9	14
35	5	7
None	14	14

GO ON TO THE NEXT PAGE.

Experiment 2

Experiment 1 was repeated with 100 pots of Soil Type 1 and 100 pots of Soil Type 2. The same pesticide doses and type and number of hibiscus were used. All other factors were held constant. After 30 days the hibiscus were uprooted and weighed. The results are shown in Table 2.

Table 2				
	Average Weight of Hibiscus (oz)			
Pesticide Dose (ppm)	Soil Type A		Soil Type B	
	Pesticide 1	Pesticide 2	Pesticide 1	Pesticide 2
5	47.5	51.4	52.7	61.2
15	37.1	42.3	40.3	51.7
25	27.5	32.9	31.1	40.3
35	19.7	22.1	23.6	29.7

Note: Average plant weight with untreated Soil Type A was 42.1 oz; average plant weight with untreated Soil Type B was 24.7 oz.

Information on the composition of the two soil types used is given in Table 3.

Table 3			
Soil Type	pH Level	Organic Matter (%)	Clay (%)
A	4.1	3.0	12.5
B	3.9	6.5	6.3

28. What was the total weight of the hibiscus plants grown in Soil Type A treated with Pesticide 1?
F. 42.1 oz
G. 66.8 oz
H. 131.8 oz
J. Cannot be determined from the given information

29. Which of the following sets of hibiscus served as the control in Experiment 1?
A. Hibiscus grown in soil with no pesticide added
B. Hibiscus grown in soil treated with 15 ppm of Pesticide 1
C. Hibiscus grown in soil treated with 15 ppm of Pesticide 2
D. Hibiscus grown in soil treated with 35 ppm of Pesticide 1

30. Which of the following, if true, best explains why the pesticides were applied to the soil as opposed to being placed directly on the hibiscus leaves?
F. Pesticide is always placed in the soil when dealing with spider mites or other pests.
G. The pesticides were comprised of very small, dry spheres.
H. The experiments were testing how water levels affect growth patterns.
J. Hibiscus generally do not have leaves.

31. Assume that there is an indirect correlation between plant weight and the number of mottled yellow leaves. If the hibiscus was grown in Soil Type B, one would predict that the number of mottled yellow leaves would be *lowest* under which of the following conditions?
A. Pesticide 1 at 5 ppm
B. Pesticide 1 at 35 ppm
C. Pesticide 2 at 5 ppm
D. Pesticide 2 at 35 ppm

32. Assume that a hibiscus was grown in soil treated with varying doses of a third pesticide (Pesticide 3). Based on the results of the experiments, what prediction, if any, about the effect of Pesticide 3 on the growth of this hibiscus can be made?
F. Pesticide 3 would have no impact on the growth of the hibiscus.
G. Pesticide 3would interfere with the growth of the hibiscus by making them smaller.
H. Pesticide 3 would interfere with the growth of the hibiscus by turning the leaves yellow.
J. No prediction can be made on the basis of the results.

33. The results of Experiment 2 indicate that, at every pesticide dose, average plant weight was *lowest* under which of the following conditions?
A. Pesticide 2 and Soil Type A
B. Pesticide 1 and Soil Type A
C. Pesticide 2 and Soil Type B
D. Pesticide 1 and Soil Type B

PASSAGE VI

The K-T (Cretaceous-Tertiary) boundary is a geological marker dated to approximately 65.5 ± 0.3 mya (million years ago). The boundary is associated with the Cretaceous–Tertiary mass extinction event that resulted in significant species loss, including that of all nonavian dinosaurs. Two scientists discuss their theories about the cause of this mass extinction.

Scientist 1

The K-T boundary extinction is best explained by the Alvarez hypothesis. This theory, propounded by Luiz and Walter Alvarez, suggests that an extremely large extraterrestrial body (i.e., meteor) crashed into Earth, causing tsunamis and dust clouds that killed off most photosynthesizing life-forms within a very short time period.

Primary support for the meteor impact theory lies in measurements of REE (Rare Earth Elements) taken at the K-T boundary layer. Specifically, the Alvarez team found an abundance of Iridium (Ir) hundreds of times higher than would be expected on the surface of Earth. This elevated level of Ir has been found at K-T boundary sites across the planet. Not only is Ir relatively abundant in meteorites, these particular Ir samples have an isotopic composition typical of extraterrestrial bodies, not of Earth's crust. Further support for the Alvarez hypothesis is found in the meteor impact site at Chicxulub in the Yucatan Peninsula. The Chicxulub crater is the correct age, as it has been dated to 65 mya. It is large enough to account for the worldwide layer of Ir and the mass extinctions.

Scientist 2

A meteorite the size of the one that caused the Chicxulub Crater would have been a major stressor on contemporary life-forms. However, it is not the only possible cause of the K-T boundary extinctions. The Deccan Traps hypothesis suggests that volcanic activity in the Deccan Plateau of west-central India may have caused atmospheric conditions similar to those implicated in the Alvarez hypothesis. The massive volcanic activity, which lasted more than 800,000 years, would have caused greenhouse/global-warming conditions sufficient to result in cataclysmic species loss. Moreover, research indicates that the eruptions occurred during the K-T boundary, but prior to the Chicxulub meteorite. Even Walter Alvarez acknowledges that other factors, like the Deccan Traps, may have irrevocably weakened Earth species before the Chicxulub event.

34. Which of the following figures representing the distribution of Ir in clay soil samples taken at an archeological dig site would best support the Alvarez hypothesis?

F.

G.

H.

J.

GO ON TO THE NEXT PAGE.

35. Supporters of both hypotheses would agree with which of the following conclusions about meteoric impacts?
- **A.** The Ir measurements at the K-T boundary are too low to indicate a sufficiently large meteoric impact.
- **B.** The Chicxulub meteorite was the only prehistoric event large enough to have caused mass extinctions.
- **C.** A meteoric impact the size of Chicxulub could have resulted in massive species deaths.
- **D.** Volcanic activity was the primary cause of the K-T boundary mass extinctions.

36. Which of the following statements would most likely *contradict* the view that Ir found in the K-T boundary layer originated from the Chicxulub meteorite?
- **F.** Ir has been detected in the K-T boundary layer on the Yucatan peninsula.
- **G.** The amount of Ir in Earth's surface is similar to the amount of Ir at Earth's core.
- **H.** The Ir isotope in the K-T boundary layer is the most commonly found Ir isotope in meteorites.
- **J.** The Chicxulub impact occurred 5 million years before the K-T boundary.

37. Scientists estimate that the K-T mass extinctions occurred between 65.2 and 65.8 million years ago. Based on this information, which of the following new observations would most seriously challenge the Alvarez hypothesis?
- **A.** Some smaller species were found to have survived the mass extinctions.
- **B.** Recent core samples from Chicxulub prove the impact occurred about 500,000 years before the mass extinction.
- **C.** The Deccan Traps volcanic activity was much stronger than initially believed.
- **D.** Other meteorite craters have been found that are contemporaneous to the Chicxulub crater.

38. According to the Alvarez hypothesis, which of the following hypothetical observations would best support the theory that a meteorite caused the K-T mass extinctions?
- **F.** Physical evidence of a meteorite causing large tsunamis and dust clouds
- **G.** Physical evidence of periodic extinctions in several different paleontological eras
- **H.** Fossil evidence of large predators surviving the Chicxulub impact
- **J.** Fossil evidence of omnivores surviving the K-T extinctions

39. Which of the following discoveries would *weaken* Scientist 2's argument?
- **A.** Finding that massive volcanic eruptions can have a long-term environmental impact
- **B.** Finding that there is no evidence of volcanic activity prior to the time of the Chicxulub meteorite
- **C.** Finding that the mass extinctions resulted from some other cataclysmic event
- **D.** Finding that most dinosaur species had already been weakened by global warming at the time of the Chicxulub meteorite

40. Based on Scientist 2's viewpoint, volcanic activity in the Deccan Plateau caused all of the following EXCEPT:
- **F.** dust clouds that led to mass extinctions.
- **G.** increased levels of greenhouse gases.
- **H.** a geologic marker.
- **J.** a crater in the Yucatan Peninsula.

END OF THE SCIENCE TEST.
STOP! IF YOU HAVE TIME LEFT OVER, CHECK YOUR WORK ON THIS SECTION ONLY.

ANSWER KEY

Science Test

1. C	11. C	21. C	31. C
2. J	12. J	22. G	32. J
3. C	13. A	23. D	33. B
4. H	14. J	24. J	34. H
5. A	15. B	25. A	35. C
6. F	16. H	26. G	36. J
7. B	17. B	27. D	37. B
8. G	18. J	28. H	38. F
9. C	19. C	29. A	39. B
10. H	20. F	30. G	40. J

SCORING WORKSHEET

Scale Score	Raw Score Science	Scale Score	Raw Score Science
36	39–40	18	15–16
35	38	17	14
34	37	16	12–13
33	36	15	11
32	—	14	10
31	35	13	9
30	34	12	8
29	33	11	7
28	32	10	6
27	31	9	5
26	29–30	8	4
25	27–28	7	3
24	25–26	6	—
23	23–24	5	2
22	21–22	4	—
21	20	3	1
20	18–19	2	—
19	17	1	0

NOTE: Each actual ACT is scaled slightly differently based on a large amount of information gathered from the millions of tests ACT, Inc., scores each year. This scale will give you a fairly good idea of where you are in your preparation process. However, it should not be read as an absolute predictor of your actual ACT score. In fact, on practice tests, the scores are much less important than what you learn from analyzing your results.

ANSWERS AND EXPLANATIONS

Passage I

1. **The correct answer is C.** According to Table 1, the first onset of a symptom occurs 3 days after contact.

2. **The correct answer is J.** According to Table 1, infection at the site of a scratch or bite occurs as soon as 3 days after contact.

3. **The correct answer is C.** The passage states that 3 of the 4 criteria "must be met in order for a patient to be diagnosed with CSD." Therefore a patient with a history of cat contact and lymph node lesions would not qualify for diagnosis.

4. **The correct answer is H.** Based on Table 1, swollen lymph nodes have a typical duration of 4–8 weeks. The passage also states that "it can take up to one year for the swelling in the lymph nodes to disappear completely."

5. **The correct answer is A.** According to the passage, "While CSD rarely proves fatal, it can result in several painful and potentially dangerous symptoms." The passage also states that "it can take up to one year for the swelling in the lymph nodes to disappear completely."

Passage II

6. **The correct answer is F.** To answer this question, look at Table 1. The value of D is equivalent to R + B for each speed listed.

7. **The correct answer is B.** According to Table 1, when the initial speed is 13 ft/sec, the value of D for Method 1 is 19 and the value of D for Method 2 is 19.5.

8. **The correct answer is G.** According to Table 1, at an initial speed of 9 ft/sec, D is 13.5.

9. **The correct answer is C.** Table 1 shows that as initial speed increases, D increases. The greatest initial speed listed in the table is 22 ft/sec, which corresponds to a D value of 33 for Method 2. The rate of increase for D is approximately 6 feet for every 3 second increase in initial speed, so answer choice C makes the most logical sense.

10. **The correct answer is H.** According to Table 1, at an initial speed of 9 ft/sec, R = 6 for Method 1 and R = 13.5 for Method 2. At an initial speed of 18 ft/sec, R = 12 for Method 1 and R = 27 for Method 2.

Passage III

11. **The correct answer is C.** Figure 1 shows the relationship between temperature and time. According to the graph, over time, the temperature initially increased, then begins to decrease once it reaches 10^9 K.

12. **The correct answer is J.** According to Figure 1, a temperature of 10^9 K was reached at approximately 10 seconds. According to Figure 2, at approximately 10 seconds, the intensity was closest to 3,500 cts/s.

13. **The correct answer is A.** According to the passage, "Thermally unstable H/He burning occurs when the accretion rate is less than 2×10^{-10} M/yr." Therefore, it is likely that at a higher accretion rate, no x-ray bursts will be observed.

14. **The correct answer is J.** Figure 2 shows that intensity levels off at about 250 cts/s after about 15 seconds, and remains at 250 cts/s until at least 67.5 seconds.

15. **The correct answer is B.** To answer this question, start with temperature. According to the passage, x-ray "bursts generally last about 10 seconds (s) at a temperature of approximately 10^9 K." Eliminate answer choices A and C. Next, look at Figure 2, which shows that, at approximately 10 seconds, the intensity is 3,500 cts/s.

Passage IV

16. **The correct answer is H.** According to Table 1, during the Jurassic Period, which lasted from 201–144 million years ago, representative life-forms included birds, frogs, and toads.

17. **The correct answer is B.** The passage states that, "The process of fossil creation begins when an organism dies."

18. **The correct answer is J.** According to the table, the Cenozoic Era started approximately 1.8 million years ago and continues to the present day. The Pleistocene Epoch falls within this time range.

19. The correct answer is C. To answer this question, first find the *oldest* organism. According to the table, algae evolved during the Precambrian Period; therefore, algae must be in the first position on this list. Eliminate answer choices A and B. Next, move up the table to see that sharks evolved before sea urchins, so answer choice C is correct.

20. The correct answer is F. According to the table, representative life-forms of the Devonian Period included spiders and mites, both of which are air breathing arthropods.

21. The correct answer is C. The passage states that, ". . . a fossil will always be younger than any fossils found in the rock beds beneath it; this is called the *principle of superposition.*" Therefore, a fossil found *below* a 200-million-year-old layer of rock will be older than the rock above it.

Passage V

22. The correct answer is G. To answer this question, start with an analysis of the easiest data to read, which is in the tables showing the NRB results. When you compare Table 2 with Table 5, you can see that Cow 2 has NRB values that are very similar to the NRB values of each cow on Table 5. Likewise, a comparison of DRB values in Table 3 and Table 6 show that all of the cows in Experiment 2 have DRB values very similar to the DRB values of Cow 2.

23. The correct answer is D. According to the passage, the cows in Experiment 1 received one meal per day, whereas the cows in Experiment 2 received the same type and amount of food, but the meals were given three times per day.

24. The correct answer is J. According to Table 2, the NRB values either varied slightly or stayed the same at each %FS given over the seven days the experiment was conducted.

25. The correct answer is A. According to Table 4, for each cow, the meal size on Day 1 was larger than the meal size on Day 7.

26. The correct answer is G. The passage states that, ". . . students evaluated the effects of saturated and unsaturated fatty acid supplements (FS) on feed intake and rumination in cows." Table 1 shows that, as %FS increases, meal size decreases.

27. The correct answer is D. In Experiment 2, 2.5%FS was given to each cow, which is a relatively low amount of FS. Also, when you look at Experiment 1, you see that an increase in FS has very little impact on the NRB values, so you can extrapolate those results to reach a logical conclusion regarding the relationship between FS and NRB values.

Passage VI

28. The correct answer is H. To answer this question, simply add the weights listed under Soil Type A, Pesticide 1 on Table 2.

29. The correct answer is A. A control is an element of the experiment that is not manipulated and which serves as a baseline. Because the experiments were conducted to study the effect of certain pesticides on spider mites, the control would be the hibiscus grown in soil with no pesticide added.

30. The correct answer is G. If the pesticides were comprised of very small, dry spheres, it is likely that those spheres would simply roll off the leaves. However, if the spherical pesticides were placed in the soil, they would more likely be dissolved into any water applied to the soil and then absorbed into the plant's root system.

31. The correct answer is C. Because there is an *indirect* correlation between plant weight and number of mottled yellow leaves, the plant with the highest weight would likely have the fewest mottled yellow leaves.

32. The correct answer is J. You are not given any information about Pesticide 3, so you cannot make a prediction about the effectiveness of Pesticide 3.

33. The correct answer is B. The lowest weight listed on Table 2 is 19.7 oz, which resulted in Soil Type A with Pesticide 1.

Passage VII

34. The correct answer is H. According to the passage, "The K-T (Cretaceous-Tertiary) boundary is a geological marker dated to approximately 65.5 ± 0.3 mya (million years ago)." The Alvarez hypothesis "suggests that an extremely large extraterrestrial body (i.e., meteor) crashed into Earth, causing tsunamis and dust clouds that killed off most photosynthesizing life-forms within a very short time period. Primary support for the meteor impact theory lies in measurements of REE (Rare Earth Elements) taken at the K-T boundary layer. Specifically, the Alvarez team found an abundance of Iridium (Ir) hundreds of times higher than would be expected on the surface of Earth. This elevated level of Ir has been found at K-T boundary sites across the planet." The graph in answer choice H shows high Ir concentrations at approximately 65 mya.

35. **The correct answer is C.** Both scientists conclude that a large meteoric impact could have resulted in massive species deaths. Scientist 1's argument is based on the impact theory, while Scientist 2 states a meteorite could have caused the extinctions, but it is not the only explanation.

36. **The correct answer is J.** If the Chicxulub impact occurred significantly earlier than the K-T boundary was formed, then the Ir found in the K-T boundary layer likely did not come from the Chicxulub impact.

37. **The correct answer is B.** According to Scientist 1, "The K-T boundary extinction is best explained by the Alvarez hypothesis. This theory, propounded by Luiz and Walter Alvarez, suggests that an extremely large extraterrestrial body (i.e., meteor) crashed into Earth. . . ." If the Chicxulub impact occurred significantly earlier than the K-T mass extinctions, then the Alvarez hypothesis would be weakened.

38. **The correct answer is F.** According to the Alvarez hypothesis, ". . . an extremely large extraterrestrial body (i.e., meteor) crashed into Earth, causing tsunamis and dust clouds that killed off most photosynthesizing life-forms within a very short time period."

39. **The correct answer is B.** According to Scientist 2, "The Deccan Traps hypothesis suggests that volcanic activity in the Deccan Plateau of west-central India may have caused atmospheric conditions similar to those implicated in the Alvarez hypothesis. The massive volcanic activity, which lasted more than 800,000 years, would have caused greenhouse/global-warming conditions sufficient to result in cataclysmic species loss. Moreover, research indicates that the eruptions occurred during the K-T boundary, but prior to the Chicxulub meteorite."

40. **The correct answer is J.** According to the passage, the Chicxulub Crater was formed by a meteor impact, not volcanic eruptions.

PART VI

APPENDICES

APPENDIX A

GLOSSARY OF MATHEMATICS TERMS AND FORMULAS

A

Absolute value.

The absolute value of a number is its distance from 0 on the number line, without regard to its direction from 0. Therefore, absolute value will always be positive. Think of it as the distance from −10 to 0 on the number line, and also the distance from 0 to 10 on the number line. Both distances equal 10 units.

The absolute value is indicated by enclosing a number within two vertical lines:

$|-3| = 3$ and $|3| = 3$

Absolute value inequalities.

To solve an absolute value inequality, you must set up two solutions. The way that you set these up depends on whether the inequality uses a less-than symbol (either < or ≤) or a greater-than symbol (either > or ≥). For an inequality with a less-than symbol, you set up two parts to the solution with the connecting word *and*. For an inequality with a greater-than symbol, you set up two parts to the solution with the connecting word *or*.

- If the symbol is < or ≤ and $a > 0$, then the solutions to $|x| < a$ are:

$$x < a \text{ and } x > -a$$

- If the symbol is < or ≤ and $a < 0$, then the solution to $|x| < a$ is all real numbers (because absolute value must be a positive number or 0, it is always greater than a negative number).

- If the symbol is > or ≥ and $a > 0$, then the solutions to $|x| > a$ are:

$$x > a \text{ or } x < -a$$

- If the symbol is > or ≥ and $a < 0$, then there is no solution (because absolute value must be a positive number or 0, it cannot be less than a negative number).

Acute angle. An angle with a measurement of less than 90 degrees.

Adjacent angle. Either of two angles having a common side and a common vertex. For example, in the following figure, angles a and b are adjacent:

Arc. A portion of the circumference of a circle. A circle has a major arc, which is the larger of the two arcs between two points on a circle, and a minor arc, which is the smaller of the two arcs:

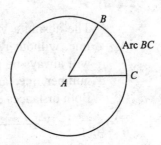

The complete arc of a circle has 360 degrees.

The equation used to find the arc of a circle is $s = r\theta$, where s is the arc length, r is the radius of the circle, and θ is the measure of the central angle in radians (angle A would be the central angle in the figure shown).

Area. The number of square units that covers a given shape or figure. The following are formulas for the areas of some common figures:

- Square: side (s) squared (s^2).
- Rectangle: length (l) times width (w) ($l \times w$).
- Circle: π times the radius (r) squared (πr^2).
- Triangle: one-half the base (b) times the height (h) $\left(\frac{1}{2} b \times h\right)$
- Parallelogram: base times height ($b \times h$).

Arithmetic mean (see average). The arithmetic mean is equivalent to the average of a series of numbers. Calculate the arithmetic mean by dividing the sum of all of the numbers in the series by the total count of numbers in the series. For example, a student received scores of 80%, 85%, and 90% on 3 math tests. The average, or mean, score received by the student on those tests is $80 + 85 + 90$ divided by 3, or $\frac{255}{3}$, which is 85%.

Associative property. According to this property, changing the grouping of numbers does not change the sum or the product. The associative property of multiplication can be expressed as $(a \times b) \times c = a \times (b \times c)$. Likewise, the associative property of addition can be expressed as $(a + b) + c = a + (b + c)$.

Average (see arithmetic mean).

The arithmetic mean of a group of values. Calculate the average by dividing the sum of all of the numbers in the series by the total count of numbers in the series. For example, a student received scores of 80%, 85%, and 90% on 3 math tests. The average score received by the student on those tests is 80 + 85 + 90 divided by 3, or 255/3, which is 85%.

■■ **B**

Base.

In geometry, the base is the bottom of a plane figure. For example, in the right triangle shown below, AC is the base:

In algebra, the base is the number that is raised to various powers. For example, 4^2 indicates a base of 4 raised to the power of 2.

■■ **C**

Circle.

The set of all points in a plane at a fixed distance, called the *radius*, from a given point, the center.

The following are properties of circles that are commonly tested on the ACT:

- The radius r of a circle is the distance from the center of the circle to any point on the circle.
- The diameter d of a circle is twice the radius.
- The area A of a circle is equivalent to πr^2. For example, the area of a circle with a radius of 3 is $3^2\pi$, or 9π.
- The circumference C of a circle is equivalent to $2\pi r$ or πd. For example, the circumference of a circle with a radius of 3 is $2(3)\pi$, or 6π.
- The equation of a circle centered at the point (h, k) is $(x - h)^2 + (y - k)^2 = r^2$, where r is the radius of the circle.
- The complete arc of a circle has 360°.

Circumference.

The distance around a circle. The circumference of a circle is equal to π times the diameter of the circle (πd). This can also be expressed as $2\pi r$, because the diameter, d, is twice the radius, r.

Collinear.

Refers to points that pass through or lie on the same straight line.

Commutative property.

According to this property, changing the order of numbers that you are either adding or multiplying does not change either the sum or the product. The commutative property of addition is expressed as $a + b = b + a$. Likewise, the commutative property of multiplication is expressed as $a \times b = b \times a$, or $ab = ba$.

Complementary angles.

Two angles that, when added together, equal 90°.

Congruent.

Any shapes or figures, including line segments and angles, with the same size or measure. For example, in the triangle below, sides AB and BC are congruent, and angles A and C are congruent.

Coordinate plane.

A plane, typically defined with the coordinates x and y, where the two axes are at right angles to each other. The horizontal axis is the x axis and the vertical axis is the y axis, as shown in the following figure:

You can locate any point on the coordinate plane by an ordered pair of numbers. The ordered pair (0, 0), where the x and y axes meet, is the origin.

The coordinate plane is divided into four quadrants, as shown in the following figure:

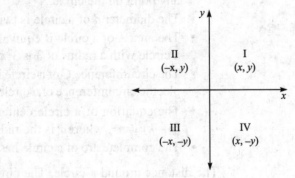

Cosecant (see trigonometric functions).

For an angle in a right triangle, the cosecant (csc) of an angle is defined as $\frac{1}{\sin}$.

Cosine (see trigonetric functions).

For an angle in a right triangle, the cosine (cos) is defined as the ratio of the side adjacent to the angle to the hypotenuse. $\text{Cos} = \frac{\text{adj}}{\text{hyp}}$.

Cotangent (see trigonometric functions).

For an angle in a right triangle, the cotangent (cot) is defined as $\frac{\cos}{\sin}$, or $\frac{1}{\tan}$.

D

Decimal.

The point that separates values less than 1 from those greater than 1. In our number system, digits can be placed to the left and right of a decimal point. *Place value* refers to the value of a digit in a number relative to its position. Starting from the left of the decimal point, the values of the digits are ones, tens, hundreds, and so on. Starting to the right of the decimal point, the values of the digits are tenths, hundredths, thousandths, and so on.

When adding and subtracting decimals, be sure to line up the decimal points, as shown here:

$$
\begin{array}{r}
236.78 \\
+113.21 \\
\hline
349.99
\end{array}
\qquad
\begin{array}{r}
78.90 \\
-23.42 \\
\hline
55.48
\end{array}
$$

When multiplying decimals, it is not necessary to line up the decimal points. Just as you would do when multiplying whole numbers, start on the right, and multiply each digit in the top number by each digit in the bottom number, and then add the products. Finally, place the decimal point in the answer by starting at the right and moving left a number of places equal to the sum of the decimal places in both numbers that were multiplied. Refer to the following example:

$$
\begin{array}{r}
2.357 \quad \text{(3 decimal places)} \\
\times\, 0.78 \quad \text{(2 decimal places)} \\
\hline
18856 \\
+164990 \quad \text{(5 decimal places)} \\
\hline
1.83846
\end{array}
$$

When dividing decimals, first move the decimal point in the divisor to the right until the divisor becomes an integer. Then move the decimal point in the dividend the same number of places:

$58.345 \div 3.21 = 5834.5 \div 321$. (The decimal point was moved two places to the right)

You can then perform long division with the decimal point in the correct place in the quotient, as shown below:

$$
\begin{array}{r}
18.17 \\
321\overline{)\ 5834.50} \\
-321 \\
\hline
2634 \\
-2568 \\
\hline
568 \\
-321 \\
\hline
2440 \\
-2247 \\
\hline
193
\end{array}
$$

Denominator.

The bottom part of a fraction. For example, in the fraction $\frac{2}{5}$, 5 is the denominator.

Diagonal.

A line segment that connects two nonadjacent vertices in any polygon. In the following rectangle, AC and BD are diagonals:

The lengths of the diagonals of a rectangle are congruent, or equal in length, so $AC = BD$.

Diameter.

A line segment that joins two points on a circle and passes through the center of the circle, as shown in the following figure, where AB is the diameter:

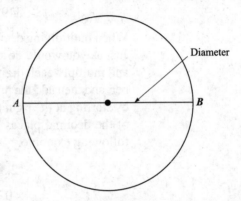

The diameter (d) of a circle is twice the radius (r).

Distance formula.

To find the distance between two points in the (x, y) coordinate plane, use the Distance Formula $\sqrt{[(x_2 - x_1)^2 + (y_2 - y_1)^2]}$ where (x_1, y_1) and (x_2, y_2) are the two given points. For example, if you are given the points (2, 3) and (4, 5), you would set up the following equation determine the distance between the two points:

$$\sqrt{(4-2)^2 + (5-3)^2} = \sqrt{(4-2)^2 + (5-3)^2}$$
$$= \sqrt{2^2 + 2^2}$$
$$= \sqrt{8}$$
$$= 2\sqrt{2}$$

Distributive property.

This property is used when an expression involves both addition and multiplication. The distributive property of multiplication is expressed as $a(b + c) = ab + ac$, where the variable a is distributed to the variables b and c. For example, $x(x + 3) = x^2 + 3x$.

Divisible.

Capable of being divided, usually with no remainder. For example, 6 is divisible by 2, and the result is 3 with no remainder.

Domain.

Refers to the x, or independent variable, values of a function. For example, take the function $y = 2x$. All of the various numbers that could be used for x make up the domain of the function. The domain of this function would be all real numbers, since x could accept any real number.

■■■ **E**

Equilateral triangle.

A triangle in which all of the sides are congruent and each of the angles equals 60 degrees.

Exponent.

A number that indicates the operation of repeated multiplication. A number with an exponent is said to be "raised to the power" of that exponent. For example, 2^3 indicates 2 raised to the power of 3, which equals $2 \times 2 \times 2$. In this example, 3 is the exponent.

The following are properties of exponents that are commonly tested on the ACT:

1. $a^m \times a^n = a^{(m+n)}$
   When multiplying the same base number raised to any power, add the exponents. For example, $3^2 \times 3^4 = 3^6$. Likewise, $3^6 = 3^2 \times 3^4$; $3^6 = 3^1 \times 3^5$; and $3^6 = 3^3 \times 3^3$.

2. $(a^m)^n = a^{mn}$
   When raising an exponential expression to a power, multiply the exponent and the power. For example, $(3^2)^4 = 3^8$. Likewise, $3^8 = (3^2)^4$; $3^8 = (3^4)^2$; $3^8 = (3^1)^8$; and $3^8 = (3^8)^1$.

3. $(ab)^m = a^m \times b^m$
   When multiplying two different base numbers and raising the product to a power, the product is equivalent to raising each number to the power and multiplying the exponential expressions. For example, $(3 \times 2)^2 = 3^2 \times 2^2$, which equals 9×4, or 36. Likewise, $3^2 \times 2^2 = (3 \times 2)^2$, or 6^2, which equals 36.

4. $\left(\dfrac{a}{b}\right)^m = \dfrac{a^m}{b^m}$

   When dividing two different base numbers and raising the quotient to a power, the quotient is equivalent to raising each number to the power and dividing the exponential expressions. For example,
   $$\left(\frac{2}{3}\right)^2 = \frac{2^2}{3^2}, \text{ or } \frac{4}{9}$$

5. $a^0 = 1$, when $a \neq 0$
   When you raise any number to the power of 0, the result is always 1.

6. $a^{-m} = \dfrac{1}{a^m}$, when $a \neq 0$

   When you raise a number to a negative power, the result is equivalent to 1 over the number raised to the same positive power.
   For example, $3^{-2} = \dfrac{1}{3^2}$, or $\dfrac{1}{9}$

■■■ **F**

Factor.

One of two or more expressions that are multiplied together to get a product. For example, in the equation $2 \times 3 = 6$, 2 and 3 are factors of 6. Likewise, in the equation $x^2 + 5x + 6$, $(x + 2)$ and $(x + 3)$ are factors. Common factors include all of the factors that two or more numbers share. For example, 1, 2, 4, and 8 are all factors of 8, and 1, 2, 3, and 6 are all factors of 6. Therefore, 8 and 6 have common factors of 1 and 2.

You may be required to find the factors or solution sets of certain simple quadratic expressions. A factor or solution set takes the form $(x \pm \text{some number})$. Simple quadratic expressions will usually have 2 of these factors or solution sets. For example, the solution sets of $x^2 - 4$ are $(x + 2)$ and $(x - 2)$.

To find common factors, simply look for the elements that two expressions have in common. For example, in the expression $x^2 + 3x$, the common factor is x: $x(x + 3)$ is the factored form of the original expression.

FOIL method.

A method of multiplying two binomials, such as $(x + 2)$ and $(x + 3)$, according to the following steps:

_F_irst. Multiply the first terms together: $(x)(x) = x^2$.
_O_utside. Multiply the outside terms together: $(x)(3) = 3x$.
_I_nside. Multiply the inside terms together: $(2)(x) = 2x$.
_L_ast. Multiply the last terms together: $(2)(3) = 6$.

Now, combine like terms to get $x^2 + 5x + 6$.

Fraction.

An expression that indicates the quotient of two quantities. For example, $\frac{2}{3}$ is a fraction, where 2 is the numerator and 3 is the denominator. The following are properties of fractions and rational numbers that are commonly tested on the ACT:

- To change any fraction to a decimal, divide the numerator by the denominator. For example, $\frac{3}{4}$ is equivalent to $3 \div 4$, or 0.75.
- Equivalent fractions are fractions that name the same amount. For example, $\frac{1}{3} = \frac{2}{6} = \frac{3}{9} = \frac{4}{12}$ and so on.
- Multiplying and dividing both the numerator and the denominator of a fraction by the same nonzero number will result in an equivalent fraction. For example, $\frac{1}{4} \times \frac{3}{3} = \frac{3}{12}$ which can be reduced to $\frac{1}{4}$. This is true because whenever the numerator and the denominator are the same, the value of the fraction is 1; $\frac{3}{3} = 1$.
- When adding and subtracting like fractions (fractions with the same denominator), add or subtract the numerators and write the sum or difference over the denominator. So, $\frac{1}{8} + \frac{2}{8} = \frac{3}{8}$ and $\frac{4}{7} - \frac{2}{7} = \frac{2}{7}$
- To simplify a fraction, find a common factor of both the numerator and the denominator. For example, $\frac{12}{15}$ can be simplified to $\frac{4}{5}$ by dividing both the numerator and the denominator by the common factor 3.
- To convert a mixed number to an improper fraction, multiply the whole number by the denominator of the fraction, add the result to the numerator of the fraction, and place that value over the original denominator. For example, $3\frac{2}{5}$ is equivalent to $(3 \times 5) + 2$ over 5, or $\frac{17}{5}$.
- When multiplying fractions, multiply the numerators to get the numerator of the product, and multiply the denominators to get the denominator of the product. For example, $\frac{3}{5} \times \frac{7}{8} = \frac{21}{40}$.
- When dividing fractions, multiply the first fraction by the reciprocal of the second fraction. For example, $\frac{1}{3} \div \frac{1}{4} = \frac{1}{3} \times \frac{4}{1}$, which equals $\frac{4}{3}$ or $1\frac{1}{3}$

Frequency distribution.

A frequency distribution is often a more convenient way to express a set of measurements. A frequency distribution table or graph shows the frequency of occurrence of each value in the set. Following is an example of a frequency distribution table:

Rank	Degree of agreement	Number of students
1	Strongly agree	23
2	Somewhat agree	31
3	Somewhat disagree	12
4	Strongly disagree	7

Function.

A set of ordered pairs where no two of the ordered pairs have the same x value. In a function, each input (x value) has exactly one output (y value). An example of this relationship would be $y = x^2$. Here, y is a function of x because for any value of x, there is exactly one value of y. However, x is not a function of y because for certain values of y, there is more than one value of x. The *domain* of a function refers to the x values, while the *range* of a function refers to the y values. For example, $f(x) = 2x + 3$. If $x = 3$, then $f(x) = 9$. For every x, only one $f(x)$, or y, exists. If any of the values in the domain correspond to more than one value in the range, the relation is not a function.

G

Greatest common factor (GCF).

The largest number that will divide evenly into any 2 or more numbers. For example: 1, 2, 4, and 8 are all factors of 8, and 1, 2, 3, and 6 are all factors of 6. Therefore, the greatest common factor of 8 and 6 is 2.

H

Hexagon.

A six-sided figure, as shown below:

The sum of the interior angles of a hexagon is $(6 - 2)(180°)$, or $720°$.

Hypotenuse.

The leg of a right triangle that is opposite the right angle. For example, in the right triangle shown in the following figure, BC is the hypotenuse:

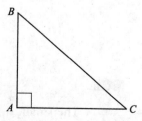

The hypotenuse is always the longest leg of a right triangle.

━━ I

Inequality.

A mathematical expression that shows that two quantities are not equal. For example, $2x < 8$ is an inequality that means that $2x$ is less than 8. Likewise, $3a > 17$ is an inequality that means that $3a$ is greater than 17.

The following are properties of inequalities that are commonly tested on the ACT:

- Inequalities can usually be worked with in the same way that equations are worked with. For example, to solve for x in the inequality $2x > 8$, simply divide both sides by 2 to get $x > 4$.
- When an inequality is multiplied by a negative number, you must switch the sign.
    For example, follow these steps to solve for x in the inequality $-2x + 2 < 6$:
$$-2x + 2 < 6$$
$$-2x < 4$$
$$-x < 2$$
$$x > -2$$

Integer.

The following are properties of integers that are commonly tested on the ACT:

- Integers include both positive and negative whole numbers.
- Zero is considered an integer.
- Consecutive integers follow one another and differ by 1. For example, 6, 7, 8, and 9 are consecutive integers.
- The value of a number does not change when it is multiplied by 1. For example, $13 \times 1 = 13$.

Interior angle.

An angle inside two adjacent sides of a polygon. The sum of the interior angles of a triangle is always 180 degrees. The sum of the interior angles of a parallelogram is always 360 degrees.

Irrational number.

A number that cannot be exactly expressed as the ratio of two integers. In other words, if a number cannot be written as a fraction, it is an irrational number. Numbers such as $\sqrt{2}$ and π(pi) are irrational numbers.

Isosceles triangle.

A triangle in which two sides have the same length, as shown below:

━━ L

Least common denominator (LCD).

The smallest multiple of the denominators of two or more fractions. For example, the LCD of $\frac{3}{4}$ and $\frac{2}{5}$ is 20.

Least common multiple (LCM).

The smallest number that any two or more numbers will divide evenly into. For example, the common multiples of 3 and 4 are 12, 24, 36, and so on; 12 is the smallest common multiple and is, therefore, the LCM of 3 and 4.

Like terms.

Terms that contain the same variables raised to the same power. For example, $3x^2$ and $10x^2$ are like terms that can be added to get $13x^2$; $-x$ and $4x$ are like terms that can be added to get $3x$; and $\frac{1}{11}$ and $\frac{5}{11}$ are like terms that can be added to get $\frac{6}{11}$.

Line.

A straight set of points that extends into infinity in both directions, as shown in the following figure:

Line segment.

Two points on a line and all the points in between, as shown in the following figure:

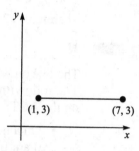

Logarithm.

A logarithm of a number x in a base b is a number n such that $x = b^n$, where b must not be 0 or a root of 1. This is most often written as a logarithmic equation, which looks like $\log_b (x) = n$.

The following are properties of logarithms that are commonly tested on the ACT:

- Logarithms are the inverse of exponentials. The logarithmic equation $\log_b (x) = n$ is equivalent to the exponential equation $b^n = x$. For example: $\log_x 81 = 4$ is equivalent to $x^4 = 81$.
- In any base, the logarithm of 1 is 0 ($\log_b 1 = 0$).
- In any base, the logarithm of the base itself is 1 ($\log_b b = 1$).

M

Median.

The middle value of a series of numbers when those numbers are in either ascending or descending order. In the series (2, 4, 6, 8, 10), the median is 6. To find the median in an even set of data, find the average of the middle two numbers. In the series (3, 4, 5, 6), the median is 4.5.

Midpoint.

The center point of a line segment. To find the midpoint of a line given two points on the line, use the formula $\left[\frac{(x_1 + x_2)}{2}, \frac{(y_1 + y_2)}{2} \right]$. For example, you would set up the following equation to determine the midpoint of the line between the two points (2, 3) and (4, 5):

- $\frac{(2+4)}{2} = \frac{6}{2} = 3$; the x value of the midpoint is 3.

- $\dfrac{(3+5)}{2} = \dfrac{8}{2} = 4$; the y value of the midpoint is 4.

- Therefore, the midpoint of the line between the points (2, 3) and (4, 5) is (3, 4).

Mode. The number that appears most frequently in a series of numbers. In the series (2, 3, 4, 5, 6, 3, 7) the mode is 3, because 3 appears twice in the series and the other numbers each appear only once in the series.

Multiple. A number is a multiple of another number if it can be expressed as the product of that number and a second number. For example, $2 \times 3 = 6$, so 6 is a multiple of both 2 and 3.

Common multiples include all of the multiples that two or more numbers share. For example:

Multiples of 3 include $3 \times 4 = 12$; $3 \times 8 = 24$; and $3 \times 12 = 36$.
Multiples of 4 include $4 \times 3 = 12$; $4 \times 6 = 24$; and $4 \times 9 = 36$.

Therefore, 12, 24, and 36 are all common multiples of both 3 and 4.

N

Number line. The line on which every point represents a real number.
The following are properties of a number line that are commonly tested on the ACT:

- On a number line, numbers that correspond to points to the right of 0 are positive, and numbers that correspond to points to the left of 0 are negative.
- For any two numbers on the number line, the number to the left is less than the number to the right.
- If any number n lies between 0 and any positive number x on the number line, then $0 < n < x$; in other words, n is greater than 0 but less than x. If n is any number on the number line between 0 and any positive number x, including 0 and x, then $0 \le n \le x$, which means that n is greater than or equal to 0 and less than or equal to x.
- If any number n lies between 0 and any negative number x on the number line, then $-x < n < 0$; in other words, n is greater than $-x$ but less than 0. If n is any number on the number line between 0 and any negative number x, including 0 and $-x$, then $-x \le n \le 0$, which means that n is greater than or equal to $-x$ and less than or equal to 0.

Numerator. The top part of a fraction. For example, in the fraction $\dfrac{2}{5}$, 2 is the numerator.

O

Obtuse angle. An angle that is greater than 90 degrees and less than 180 degrees.

Octagon. An eight-sided figure, as shown below:

The sum of the interior angles of an octagon is $(8 - 2)(180°)$, or $1,080°$.

Ordering (see inequality).

The process of arranging numbers from smallest to greatest or from greatest to smallest. The symbol > is used to represent "greater than," and the symbol < is used to represent "less than." To represent "greater than or equal to," use the symbol ≥; to represent "less than or equal to," use the symbol ≤.

P

Parallel.

When two distinct lines lie in the same plane and do not intersect, they are parallel. Two lines are parallel if and only if they have the same slope. For example, the two lines with equations $2y = 6x + 7$ and $y = 3x - 14$ have the same slope (3), and are therefore parallel.

Parallelogram.

A quadrilateral in which the opposite sides are of equal length and the opposite angles are equal, as shown in the following figure:

$$GH = FJ$$
$$GF = HJ$$
$$\angle F = \angle H$$
$$\angle G = \angle J$$

The sum of the angles in a parallelogram is always 360 degrees.

The area A of a parallelogram is equivalent to (base)(height). The height is equal to the perpendicular distance from an angle to a side. In the parallelogram shown above, the height is the distance from G to the bottom side, or base, or the distance from J to the top side, or base. The height is **not** the distance from G to F or the distance from H to J.

PEMDAS.

An acronym that describes the correct order in which to perform mathematical operations. The acronym PEMDAS stands for Parentheses, Exponents, Multiplication, Division, Addition, Subtraction. It should help you to remember to do the operations in the correct order, as follows:

1. **P:** First, do the operations within the *parentheses*, if any.
2. **E:** Next, do the *exponents*, if any.
3. **M/D:** Next, do the *multiplication and/or division*, in order from left to right.
4. **A/S:** Next, do the *addition and/or subtraction*, in order from left to right.

For example, $\dfrac{2(4+1)^2 \times 3}{5} - 7$ would be solved in the following order

$$\dfrac{2(5)^2 \times 3}{5} - 7$$

$$= \dfrac{2(25) \times 3}{5} - 7$$

$$= \dfrac{50 \times 3}{5} - 7$$

$$= \dfrac{150}{5} - 7$$

$$= 30 - 7 = 23$$

Pentagon.   A five-sided figure, as shown below:

The sum of the interior angles of a pentagon is $(5-2)(180°)$, or $540°$.

Percent.   Refers to one part in one hundred. A percent is a fraction whose denominator is 100. The fraction 25/100 is equal to 25%. To calculate the percent that one number is of another number, set up a ratio, as shown below:

What percent of 40 is 5?
5 is to 40 as x is to 100

$$\dfrac{5}{40} = \dfrac{x}{100}$$

Cross-multiply and solve for x:

$$40x = 500$$

$$x = \dfrac{500}{40} = 12.5$$

5 is 12.5% of 40

If a price is discounted by p percent, then the discounted price is $(100 - p)$ percent of the original price.

Perimeter.   The distance around any shape or object. Following are the formulas for the perimeter of some common figures:

- The perimeter P of both a parallelogram and a rectangle is equivalent to $2l + 2w$, where l is the length and w is the width.
- The perimeter P of other polygons is the sum of the lengths of the sides.
- The perimeter P of a triangle is the sum of the lengths of the sides.

Perpendicular.   Two distinct lines are perpendicular if their intersection creates a right angle. Two lines are perpendicular if and only if the slope of one of the lines is the negative reciprocal of the slope of the other line. In other words, if line *a* has a slope of 2 and line *b* has a slope of $-\frac{1}{2}$, the two lines are perpendicular. The figure below shows two perpendicular lines:

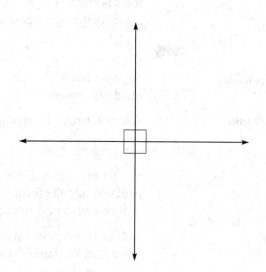

Point.	A location in a plane or in space that has no dimensions.
Point-slope form (see slope-intercept form).	The equation of a line in the form $y = mx + b$, where *m* is the slope and *b* is the *y* intercept (that is, the point at which the graph of the line crosses the *y* axis).
Polygon.	A closed plane figure made up of at least three line segments that are joined. For example, a triangle, a rectangle, and an octagon are all polygons.
Polynomial.	A mathematic expression consisting of more than two terms. $2x^2 + 4x + 4$ is a simple quadratic equation, and is also a polynomial.
Prime number.	Any number that can be divided only by itself and by 1; 1 and the number itself are the only factors of a prime number. For example, 2, 3, 5, 7, and 11 are prime numbers.
Probability.	The likelihood that an event will occur. For example, Jeff has 3 striped and 4 solid ties in his closet; therefore, he has a total of 7 ties in his closet. He has 3 chances to grab a striped tie out of the 7 total ties, because he has 3 striped ties. So, the likelihood of Jeff's grabbing a striped tie is 3 out of 7, which can also be expressed as 3:7 or $\frac{3}{7}$.

Two specific events are considered independent if the outcome of one event has no effect on the outcome of the other event. For example, if you toss a coin, there is a 1 in 2, or $\frac{1}{2}$, chance that it will land on either heads or tails. If you toss the coin again, the probability of its landing on heads or tails will be the same as in the first toss. To find the probability of two or more independent events occurring together, multiply the outcomes of the individual events. For example, the probability that both coin tosses will result in heads is $\frac{1}{2} \times \frac{1}{2}$, or $\frac{1}{4}$.

Product.	The result of multiplication. For example, 32 is the product of 8 and 4.

Proportion.

Indicates that one ratio is equal to another ratio. For example, $\frac{1}{5} = \frac{x}{20}$ is a proportion.

Pythagorean Theorem.

This theorem applies only to finding the length of the sides in right triangles; it states that $a^2 + b^2 = c^2$, where c is the hypotenuse (the side opposite the right angle) of the right triangle, and a and b are the two other sides of the triangle.

Q

Quadratic equation.

An equation of the form $ax^2 + bx + c$, where $a \neq 0$. $2x^2 + 4x + 4$ is a simple quadratic equation.

Quadratic formula.

Given a quadratic equation of the form $ax^2 + bx + c$, the quadratic formula can be used to solve the equation. It is written as $x = \frac{-b \pm \sqrt{b^2 - 4ac}}{2a}$.

To solve, substitute the given values for a, b, and c in the quadratic equation into the formula. Keep in mind that the $\pm$ sign indicates that there will be both a negative and a positive solution to the equation.

Quadrilateral.

A four-sided polygon with four angles. A parallelogram, a rectangle, a square, and a trapezoid are all examples of quadrilaterals.

Quotient.

The result of division. For example, 3 is the quotient of 18 and 6.

R

Radian.

A unit of angular measure. A circle has 2π radians, so $1° = \frac{\pi}{180}$. To convert a degree measurement to radians, multiply by $\frac{\pi}{180}$. For example, 90° in radians is equal to $90\left(\frac{\pi}{180}\right)$, or $\frac{\pi}{2}$.

Radius.

The distance from the center of a circle to any point on the circle, as shown in the following circle with center C:

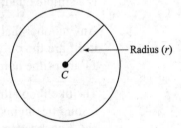

Range.

The y values of a function.

Ratio.

A mathematical comparison between two quantities. A ratio of 1 to 5, for example, is written as either $\frac{1}{5}$ or 1:5.

When working with ratios, be sure to differentiate between part-to-part ratios and part-to-whole ratios. For example, if two components of a recipe are being compared to each other, it is a part-to-part ratio (2 cups of flour:1 cup of sugar). On the other hand, if one group of students is being compared to the entire class, it is a part-to-whole ratio (13 girls:27 students).

Rational number.

A fraction whose numerator and denominator are both integers and whose denominator does not equal zero.

Real number.

Any rational or irrational number used to express quantities, lengths, amounts, and so on. All real numbers except zero are either positive or negative. All real numbers correspond to points on the number line, as shown below:

On a number line, such as that shown above, numbers that correspond to points to the right of zero are positive, and numbers that correspond to points to the left of zero are negative.

Reciprocal.

Given a number n, the reciprocal is expressed as 1 over n, or $\frac{1}{n}$. The product of a number and its reciprocal is always 1. In other words $\frac{1}{3} \times \frac{3}{1} = \frac{3}{3}$, which is equivalent to 1.

Rectangle.

A polygon with four sides (two sets of congruent, or equal, sides) and four right angles. All rectangles are parallelograms. Shown below is an example of a rectangle:

Width (w)

Length (l)

- The sum of the angles in a rectangle is always 360 degrees, because a rectangle contains four 90-degree angles.
- The perimeter P of a rectangle is equivalent to $2l + 2w$, where l is the length and w is the width.
- The area A of a rectangle is equivalent to $(l)(w)$.
- The lengths of the diagonals of a rectangle are congruent, or equal in length.
- A square is a special rectangle in which all four sides are of equal length. All squares are rectangles.
- The length of each diagonal of a square is equivalent to the length of one side times $\sqrt{2}$. So, for example, a square with a side length of x would have diagonals equal to $x\sqrt{2}$.

Reflection.

A reflection flips an object in the coordinate plane over either the x axis or the y axis. When a reflection occurs across the x axis, the x coordinate remains the same, but the y coordinate is transformed into its opposite. When a reflection occurs across the y axis, the y coordinate remains the same, but the x coordinate is transformed into its opposite. The object retains its shape and size. The figures below show a triangle that has been reflected across the y axis:

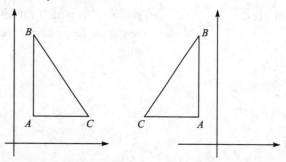

Right angle.

An angle that measures 90 degrees.

S

Scientific notation.

When numbers are very large or very small, they are often expressed using scientific notation. Scientific notation is indicated by setting a positive number N equal to a number greater than or equal to 1 and less than 10, then multiplying that number by 10 raised to an integer. The integer depends on the number of places to the left or right that the decimal was moved. For example, 667,000,000 written in scientific notation would be 6.67×10^8 because the decimal was moved 8 places to the left, and 0.0000000298 written in scientific notation would be 2.98×10^{-8} because the decimal was moved 8 places to the right.

Secant (see trigonometric functions).

For an angle in a right triangle, the secant is $\dfrac{1}{\cos}$.

Sequence.

The following are properties of arithmetic and geometric sequences that are commonly tested on the ACT:

- An *arithmetic* sequence is one in which the difference between one term and the next is the same. For example, the following sequence is an arithmetic sequence because the difference between the terms is 2: 1, 3, 5, 7, 9. To find the nth term, use the formula $a_n = a_1 + (n - 1)d$, where d is the common difference.

- A *geometric* sequence is one in which the ratio between two consecutive terms is constant. For example, $\frac{1}{2}$, 1, 2, 4, 8, …, is a geometric sequence where 2 is the constant ratio. To find the nth term, use the formula $a_n = a_1(r)^{n-1}$, where r is the constant ratio.

Set.

The following are properties of number sets that are commonly tested on the ACT:

- A set is a collection of numbers. The numbers are elements or members of the set. For example, {2, 4, 6, 8} is the set of positive, even integers less than 10.

- The union of two sets includes all of the elements in each set. For example, if Set A = {2, 4, 6, 8} and Set B = {1, 3, 5, 7, 9}, then {1, 2, 3, 4, 5, 6, 7, 8, 9} is the union of Set A and Set B.

- The intersection of two sets identifies the common elements of the two sets. For example, if Set A = {1, 2, 3, 4} and Set B = {2, 4, 6, 8} then {2, 4} is the intersection of Set A and Set B.

Similar triangles.

Triangles in which the measures of the corresponding angles are equal and the corresponding sides are in proportion, as shown in the following figure:

Sine (see trigonometric functions).

For an angle in a right triangle, the sine (sin) is the ratio of the side opposite the angle to the hypotenuse. $\text{Sin} = \dfrac{\text{opp}}{\text{hyp}}$.

Slope.

The change in y coordinates divided by the change in x coordinates from two given points on a line. The formula for slope is $m = \dfrac{(y_2 - y_1)}{(x_2 - x_1)}$, where (x_1, y_1) and (x_2, y_2) are the two given points. For example, the slope of a line that contains the points (3, 6) and (2, 5) is equivalent to $\dfrac{(6-5)}{(3-2)}$, or $\dfrac{1}{1}$, which equals 1.

A positive slope means that the graph of the line will go up and to the right. A negative slope means that the graph of the line will go down and to the right. A horizontal line has slope 0, while a vertical line has an undefined slope, because it never crosses the y axis. See the figures below.

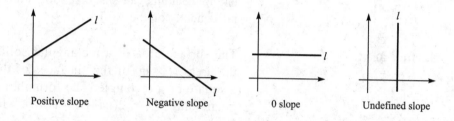

Positive slope   Negative slope   0 slope   Undefined slope

Slope-intercept form (see point-slope form).

The slope-intercept (standard) form of the equation of a line is $y = mx + b$, where m is the slope of the line and b is the y intercept (that is, the point at which the graph of the line crosses the y axis).

SOHCAHTOA (see trigonometric functions).

An acronym that can assist you in remembering the basic trigonometric functions:

(SOH) SIN = OPPOSITE/HYPOTENUSE
(CAH) COS = ADJACENT/HYPOTENUSE
(TOA) TAN = OPPOSITE/ADJACENT

Special triangles.

Triangles whose sides have special ratios. The following are angle measures and side lengths for special right triangles:

30°-60°-90° triangle   45°-45°-90° triangle

The sides of a 3-4-5 special right triangle have the ratio 3:4:5.

Square.

A number multiplied by itself. The following are properties of squares that are commonly tested on the ACT:

- Squaring a negative number yields a positive result. For example, $(-2)^2 = 4$.
- A number is considered a perfect square when the square root of that number is a whole number. The polynomial $a^2 \pm 2ab + b^2$ is also a perfect square because the solution set is $(a \pm b)^2$.

Square root.

The square root of a number n is written as $\sqrt{n}$, or the nonnegative value a that fulfills the expression $a^2 = n$. For example, "the square root of 5" is expressed as $\sqrt{5}$, and $(\sqrt{5})^2 = 5$. A square root will always be a positive number.

Standard deviation.

Calculated by finding the arithmetic mean of the data set, finding the difference between the mean and each of the n values of the data set, squaring each of the differences, finding the average of the squared differences, and taking the nonnegative square root of this average. This calculation is used infrequently on the ACT.

Surface area.

The surface area of a rectangular solid (shown below) is the sum of the areas ($l \times w$) of the six faces of the solid. Think of each face as a square or a rectangle. The formula for the surface area of a rectangular solid is $A = 2(wl + lh + wh)$, where l = length, w = width, and h = height.

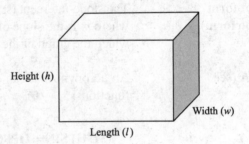

The equation for the surface area of a sphere with radius $r = 4\pi r^2$.

System of equations.

A collection of two or more equations with the same set of unknowns. In solving a system of equations, find values for each of the unknowns that satisfy every equation in the system.

T

Tangent.

A line perpendicular to the radius of a circle that touches the circle at one point.

In trigonometry, the tangent (tan) of an angle in a right triangle is the ratio of the side opposite the angle to the side adjacent to the angle (see definition for **trigonometric functions**). $\text{Tan} = \dfrac{\text{opp}}{\text{adj}}$.

Translation.

A translation slides an object in the coordinate plane to the left or right, or up or down. The object retains its shape and size, and faces in the same direction. In the figure below, the triangle in the first graph is translated 4 units down in the second graph:

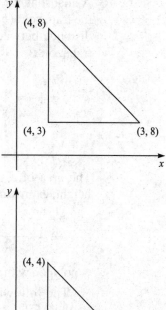

Transversal.

A line that intersects two other lines. In the following figure, line n is the transversal:

When two parallel lines are cut by a transversal, each parallel line has four angles surrounding the intersection, each of which is matched in measure and position with a counterpart at the other parallel line. The vertical (opposite) angles are congruent, and the adjacent angles are supplementary (they total 180°). See the figure below.

- Vertical angles: $a = d = f = k$
- Vertical angles: $b = c = g = h$
- Supplementary angles: $a + b = 180°$
- Supplementary angles: $c + d = 180°$

- Supplementary angles: $f + g = 180°$
- Supplementary angles: $h + k = 180°$

Trapezoid.

A quadrilateral with exactly one pair of parallel sides, called the bases of the trapezoid (b_1 and b_2). The height of the trapezoid is the perpendicular distance between the two bases (h). Shown below is an example of a trapezoid:

The area of a trapezoid is equal to the average of the bases times the height, expressed as:

$$A = \frac{(b_1 + b_2)h}{2}$$

Triangle.

A polygon with three vertices and three sides that are straight line segments.

The following are properties of triangles that are commonly tested on the ACT:

- In an equilateral triangle, all three sides have the same length, and each interior angle measures 60 degrees.
- In an isosceles triangle, two sides have the same length, and the angles opposite those sides are congruent.
- In a right triangle, one of the angles measures 90 degrees. The side opposite the right angle is the hypotenuse, and it is always the longest side.
- The sum of the interior angles in any triangle is always 180 degrees.
- The perimeter P of a triangle is the sum of the lengths of the sides.
- The area A of a triangle is equivalent to $\frac{1}{2}$(base)(height). The height is equal to the perpendicular distance from an angle to a side. Following are examples of the height of a given triangle:

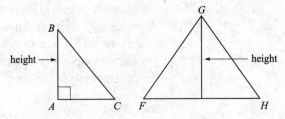

Trigonometric functions.

Functions of an angle that are commonly defined as ratios of two sides of a right triangle containing the angle.

The following are properties of trigonometric functions that are commonly tested on the ACT (use the triangle below as a reference to the definitions):

- In a right triangle, the *sine* (sin) of an angle is defined as the ratio of the leg opposite the angle to the hypotenuse (opposite/hypotenuse). In the triangle shown above, $\sin x = \frac{4}{5}$.
- In a right triangle, the *cosine* (cos) of an angle is defined as the ratio of the leg adjacent to the angle to the hypotenuse (adjacent/hypotenuse). In the triangle shown above, $\cos x = \frac{3}{5}$.
- In a right triangle, the *tangent* (tan) of an angle is defined as the ratio of the leg opposite the angle to the adjacent leg (opposite/adjacent). In the triangle shown above, $\tan x = \frac{4}{3}$.
- In a right triangle, the *cosecant* (csc) of an angle is defined as $\frac{1}{\sin}$. In the triangle shown above, $\csc x = \frac{5}{4}$.
- In a right triangle, the *secant* (sec) of an angle is defined as $\frac{1}{\cos}$. In the triangle shown above, $\sec x = \frac{5}{3}$.
- In a right triangle, the *cotangent* (cot) of an angle is defined as $\frac{\cos}{\sin}$, or $\frac{1}{\tan}$. In the triangle shown above, $\cot x = \frac{3}{4}$.

See SOHCAHTOA.

V–Y

Vertical angle.

One of two opposite angles that are formed by intersecting lines. Vertical angles are congruent. In the following figure, angles a and b are vertical angles:

Volume.

A measure of space or capacity of a three-dimensional object. The following are properties of volume that are commonly tested on the ACT:

- The formula for the volume of a rectangular solid is $V = lwh$, where l = length, w = width, and h = height.
- The formula for the volume of a cube is the length of a side (s) cubed (s^3).
- The formula for the volume of a sphere is $\left(\frac{3}{4}\right)\pi r^3$, where r is the radius of the sphere.

Word problem.

A type of question on the ACT that uses words as well as, or sometimes instead of, mathematical symbols. When solving word problems, translate the verbal statements into algebraic expressions. For example:

- "Greater than," "more than," and "sum of" mean addition (+).
- "Less than," "fewer than," and "difference" mean subtraction (−).
- "Of," "by," and "product" mean multiplication (×).
- "Per" means division (÷).

Y intercept.

The point at which a line crosses the y axis in the x, y coordinate plane. In the figure below, the y intercept is 2:

GLOSSARY OF SCIENTIFIC TERMS

The following list includes some scientific terms that have appeared on previously released ACTs. While the ACT Science Test is not a test of scientific knowledge, a basic understanding of some of these terms might help you to better understand the passages and increase your confidence on test day.

A

Acceleration.	The rate of change of velocity
Aerobic respiration.	The breakdown of glucose in the body of an animal to supply muscles with oxygen
Aerosol.	Solid or liquid particles suspended in a gas
Alkalinity.	Having a pH greater than 7 (contrast with *basic*, which means having a pH less than 7)
Altitude.	Elevation above a level of reference, usually given in feet above sea level
Amino acids.	Organic compounds that link together to form proteins
Anatomical.	Related to the structure of an organism
Antigen.	A substance such as a toxin or enzyme that is capable of eliciting an immune response
Antitoxin.	An antibody created for and capable of neutralizing a toxin
Asteroids.	Small celestial bodies that revolve around the sun, with diameters between a few and several hundred kilometers
Asthenosphere.	The lower layer of the Earth's crust

B

Bacteria.	Single-celled microorganisms
Basalt.	Solidified lava; a dense, dark gray, fine-grained igneous rock
Basic.	Having a pH less than 7 (contrast with *alkalinity*, which means having a pH greater than 7)
Biomass.	Total mass of all the living matter within a given area
Biosynthesis.	The production of a chemical compound within the body
Boiling point.	The temperature at which a liquid changes state from a liquid to a gas

■■■ C

Capillary. A very slim tube; one of a network of extremely small blood vessels

Carbohydrate. Sugars and starches that serve as a major energy source for animals

Celsius. A temperature scale in which the freezing point of water is 0° and the boiling point is 100° under normal atmospheric conditions

Cerebral edema. Brain swelling

Chlorophyll. The green coloring of plants is essential to the production of carbohydrates by photosynthesis

Cholesterol. A soft, waxy compound found in the body and in the food we eat

Colloid. A gelatinous material

Compressibility. The ease with which pressure can alter the volume of matter

Condense. To become more compact; to change from a vapor to a liquid

■■■ D

Diffusion time. The time that it takes for a material to spread from one area to another

Dilute. To weaken the strength of a solution

Disperse. To scatter or spread out

Dissolution. The process of dissolving or disintegrating

Drag force. The force that resists or slows down motion through a medium such as air

■■■ E

Ecology. The field of science that concentrates on relationships between organisms and their environments

Emulsion. A state in which one liquid is suspended in another because the liquids will not dissolve in one another

Equilibrium. A state of balance

Experimental variables. Elements of an experiment that are changed (distinguished from constants, which are held the same in order to produce significant results)

■■■ F

Fahrenheit. A temperature scale in which the boiling point of water is 212° and the freezing point is 32°

Fermentation. The chemical process of breaking down an organic substance into simpler substances, such as the fermentation of sugar to alcohol

Foliation. The alternating layers of different mineral compositions within solid rocks

Friction. The force resistant to motion

G

Galvanism.	A direct electric current produced by chemical reactions
Gas.	A substance (such as air) that possesses the quality of indefinite expansion
Gas chromatograph.	A device used to detect the composition of an unknown material
Gastric emptying.	The movement of food from the stomach to the small intestine, and finally into the colon
Gravity.	The force of attraction between two bodies of mass

H

Herbivore.	A plant-eating organism
Humidity.	A measure of how damp the air is
Hydrogen bonding.	The chemical bonding of a hydrogen atom with another electronegative atom

I

Igneous rocks.	Rocks that are formed by the cooling and solidification of molten magma
Ignition temperature.	The temperature that a fuel must reach before combustion can begin
Indigenous.	Native to or naturally existing in a certain area
Interstitial.	Fluid outside of cells; in the small spaces between other things
Intracellular.	Fluid in cells
Isotopes.	Two or more atoms with an identical atomic number and differing electric charges

K

Kelvin.	A temperature scale in which 0 K is absolute zero, the freezing point of water is 273 K, and the boiling point of water is 373 K

L

Lipid.	An oily or waxy organic compound that cannot be dissolved in water
Liquid.	A material that is neither solid nor gas; flowing freely
Lithosphere.	The outer part of the Earth that includes the crust and upper mantle

M

Macrophages.	Protective cells
Manometer.	A device that measures the pressure of liquids and gases
Melting point.	The temperature at which a solid softens into a liquid
Mesosphere.	A layer of the atmosphere 50 to 80 kilometers above the Earth's surface

Metamorphism.   The process of altering solid rocks by changing their temperature, pressure, and chemistry

Meteorite.   A meteor that reaches the surface of the Earth before it is entirely vaporized

Microorganism.   An organism of microscopic or very small size

Mole.   A unit of measurement for the molecular weight of a substance

Molecular weight.   The weight of all the atoms in a molecule

▄▄▄ N

Nanometer.   One billionth of a meter

Newton.   The amount of force needed to accelerate a 1-kilogram mass at a rate of 1 meter per second, per second

▄▄▄ O

Organic matter.   Matter that is derived from living or formerly living organisms

Organism.   A living thing, either plant or animal

▄▄▄ P

pH.   A scale that measures how acidic or basic a substance is on a scale of 0 to 14. Lower numbers indicate increasing acidity, and higher numbers indicate increasing basicity

Photophores.   Organs that produce light

Photosynthesis.   The process by which plants turn carbon dioxide and water into energy with the aid of sunlight

Pigmentation.   Coloration

Protein.   A compound that consists of amino acids and plays various structural, mechanical, and nutritional roles within organisms

▄▄▄ R

Radioactive decay.   A natural process by which an atom of a radioactive isotope spontaneously decays into another element

▄▄▄ S

Saturation.   A state of being completely full or soaked

Scientific inquiry.   A method of investigation based on experiment and observation and the application of the scientific method

Solid.   Neither gas nor liquid; of the same or coherent texture

Solute.   A dissolved substance

Solution.   A homogenous mixture of two or more substances

Specific gravity.   The ratio of the density of one substance to the density of another substance

Stratosphere.   A layer of the atmosphere between the troposphere and the mesosphere

Supercooled.   Below freezing but remaining liquid

Suspension.   The state of a substance when its particles are combined together but have not been dissolved in a fluid or solid

Synthetic polymer.   A man-made, repeating chain of atoms

▬ T

Territorial.   The protective behavior that is displayed when an animal is defending its area

Thermal degradation.   A process of combustion in which materials in a fuel are broken down into several by-products

Thermosphere.   The outermost layer of the atmosphere

Troposphere.   The lowest part of the Earth's atmosphere

▬ V

Vapor pressure.   The pressure exerted by a vapor

Vaporize.   To change into a gas

Velocity.   Speed of motion

Vertical migrators.   Marine species that travel toward the surface of the ocean to feed

Viscosity.   A fluid's resistance to flow

▬ W

Wavelength.   The distance between repeating peaks or crests of waves

APPENDIX C

QUICK REVIEW SHEET

This review contains useful information about preparing for the ACT Mathematics and Science Tests. Be sure that you read the book and take the practice tests before referring to this sheet. Review the information included on this sheet prior to entering the testing center, paying close attention to the areas in which you feel you need the most review. This sheet should not be used as a substitute for actual preparation; it is simply a review of important information presented in detail elsewhere in this book.

GENERAL TEST-TAKING STRATEGIES

1. Relax.

   - Don't panic if you are having a hard time answering the questions! You do not have to answer all the questions correctly to get a good score.
   - Take a few moments to relax if you get stressed during the test. Put your pencil down, close your eyes, take some deep breaths, and stop testing. When you get back to the test, you will feel better.

2. Do the easy stuff first.

   - You don't have to do the questions in each section in order. Skip the hard ones and come back to them later.
   - Keep moving so that you don't waste valuable time. If you get stuck on a question, move on!

3. Manage your answer sheet.

   - Do not go to your answer sheet after each question. Mark your answers in the book, and then transfer them every one to two pages. Pay attention to question numbers, especially if you skip a question. Your score depends on what is filled in on your answer sheet.

4. Use the test booklet.

   - Do the math! Draw pictures to help you figure out problems, and use the space available to write down your calculations.
   - Circle your answer choices, cross out answers that you have eliminated, and mark questions that you need to come back to later. If you cannot eliminate an answer choice and you think that it might work, underline it.

5. Be aware of time.

   - Pace yourself. You learned in practice which questions you should focus on and which questions you should skip and come back to later if you have the time.
   - Time yourself with a watch. Do not rely on the proctor's official time announcements.
   - You have only a limited amount of time. Read and work actively through the test.
   - Stay focused. Ignore the things going on around you that you cannot control.
   - Check over your answers if you have time remaining.

6. Guess effectively.

   - *Never* leave a question blank; make educated guesses when you can, and fill in your random guessing choices on the remaining questions.

- Eliminate answer choices that you know are wrong. The more you can eliminate, the better your chance of getting the question right.

7. Don't change your mind.

- Do not second-guess yourself. Your first answer choice is more likely to be correct. If you're not completely comfortable with your first choice, place a question mark next to your answer and come back to it later if you have time.
- Change your answer only when you are sure that it's wrong.

▰ MATH CONCEPTS AND STRATEGIES

Following are general math concepts and strategies, as well as specific strategies for the multiple-choice questions.

General Math Concepts

1. The area of a circle is $A = \pi r^2$, where r is the radius of the circle.
2. The circumference of a circle is $C = 2\pi r$, where r is the radius of the circle. The circumference can also be expressed as πd because the diameter is always twice the radius.
3. The area of a rectangle is $A = lw$, where l is the length of the rectangle and w is the width of the rectangle.
4. The area of a triangle is $A = \frac{1}{2} bh$, where b is the base of the triangle and h is the height of the triangle.
5. The volume of a rectangular prism is $V = lwh$, where l is the length of the rectangular prism, w is the width of the rectangular prism, and h is the height of the rectangular prism.
6. The volume of a cylinder is $V = \pi r^2 h$, where r is the radius of one of the bases of the cylinder and h is the height of the cylinder.
7. The perimeter is the distance around any object.
8. The Pythagorean Theorem states that $c^2 = a^2 + b^2$ (or $a^2 + b^2 = c^2$), where c is the hypotenuse of a right triangle and a and b are two sides of the triangle.
9. The following are angle measures and side

lengths for special right triangles:

30°-60°-90° triangle   45°-45°-90° triangle

10. In an equilateral triangle, all three sides have the same length.
11. In an isosceles triangle, two sides have the same length.
12. The complete arc of a circle has 360°.
13. A straight line has 180°.
14. A prime number is any number that can be divided only by itself and by 1.
15. Squaring a negative number yields a positive number.
16. To change any fraction to a decimal, divide the numerator by the denominator.
17. If two numbers have one or more divisors in common, those are the common factors of the numbers.
18. To calculate the mean, or average, of a list of values, divide the sum of the values by the number of values in the list.
19. The median is the middle value of a list, where the values are in either ascending or descending order.
20. The mode is the value that appears most often in a list.
21. A ratio expresses a mathematical comparison between two quantities ($\frac{1}{4}$ or 1:4).
22. A proportion is an equation involving two ratios ($\frac{1}{4} = \frac{x}{8}$ or 1:4 = x:8).
23. When multiplying exponential expressions with the same base, add the exponents.
24. When dividing exponential expressions with the same base, subtract the exponents.
25. When raising one power to another power, multiply the exponents.

General Math Strategies

1. Draw pictures or create tables as necessary to help you figure out problems.
2. Look for a way to reason through the problem. Don't just go for your calculator.
3. When reading word problems, translate them into mathematical equations. (Jenny has 5 more CDs than Amy is equivalent to $J = A + 5$.)
4. Paraphrase questions to make sure that you are answering what is asked. Cross out any irrelevant information given in the question.
5. Remember to estimate or predict answers when you can. It is often possible to eliminate all but the correct answer choice without doing any actual math.
6. Once you've eliminated an answer choice, cross it out.

Multiple-Choice Question Strategies

1. Look at the format of the answer choices before you attempt to work through the problem. Remember that the answer choices will be in either ascending or descending order where appropriate.
2. Even if the format of the question is unfamiliar to you, read through it and consider the answer choices carefully. You might know how to solve the problem.

SCIENCE CONCEPTS AND STRATEGIES

The following are general concepts and strategies for the Science Test.

General Science Concepts

1. The ACT Science Test is not a test of your scientific knowledge.
2. On a graph, a line with a positive slope indicates a direct relationship.
3. On a graph, a line with a negative slope indicates an inverse relationship.

General Science Strategies

1. Focus on the data. Most of the questions will ask you about trends in or relationships between the data.
2. Paraphrase the questions—simplify the language as much as possible.
3. Predict answers when you can, and eliminate answer choices that are not supported by the data.

APPENDIX D

ADDITIONAL RESOURCES

The purpose of this book is to help you prepare for the ACT Mathematics and Science Tests. While this book provides you with helpful information about the tests and realistic practice materials to get you ready for the real thing, the following additional resources might be useful in your preparation:

ACT, INC.

The ACT website at http://www.act.org offers a wealth of up-to-date information about the ACT.

The Real ACT Prep Guide, published by ACT, is a great source of practice material. This book is usually available at all the major bookstores and online.

TEXTBOOKS AND HUMAN RESOURCES

Middle school and high school textbooks are extremely valuable resources. The content areas tested on the ACT are the same content areas that you've been studying in school. Hence, textbooks cover many of the relevant skills and subjects you will need for success on the ACT. If you do not have your textbooks, your school library should have copies that you can use.

Don't forget to talk to your teachers and to older students who have some experience with the ACT. They might be able to shed some additional light on getting ready for the test. It is in your best interest to be as well prepared as possible on test day.

Student Solutions Manual

Cindy Trimble & Associates

Intermediate Algebra

FIFTH EDITION

Elayn Martin-Gay

PEARSON

Prentice
Hall

Upper Saddle River, NJ 07458

Editorial Director, Mathematics: Christine Hoag
Editor-in-Chief: Paul Murphy
Sponsoring Editor: Mary Beckwith
Assistant Editor: Georgina Brown
Senior Managing Editor: Linda Mihatov Behrens
Project Manager: Kristy S. Mosch
Art Director: Heather Scott
Supplement Cover Manager: Paul Gourhan
Supplement Cover Designer: Victoria Colotta
Operations Specialist: Ilene Kahn
Senior Operations Supervisor: Diane Peirano

© 2009 Pearson Education, Inc.
Pearson Prentice Hall
Pearson Education, Inc.
Upper Saddle River, NJ 07458

Printed in the United States of America

10 9 8 7 6 5 4 3 2 1

ISBN-13: 978-0-13-603052-2   Standalone

ISBN-10:   0-13-603052-1   Standalone

ISBN-13: 978-0-13-603053-9   Value Pack

ISBN-10:   0-13-603053-X   Value Pack

Pearson Education Ltd., London
Pearson Education Singapore, Pte. Ltd.
Pearson Education Canada, Inc.
Pearson Education—Japan
Pearson Education Australia PTY, Limited
Pearson Education North Asia, Ltd., Hong Kong
Pearson Educación de Mexico, S.A. de C.V.
Pearson Education Malaysia, Pte. Ltd.
Pearson Education Upper Saddle River, New Jersey

Contents

Chapter 1

Practice Exercises

1. Let $b = 3.5$ and $h = 8$.

$$A = \frac{1}{2}bh$$

$$A = \frac{1}{2}(3.5)(8) = 14$$

The area is 14 square centimeters.

2. Let $p = 17$ and $q = 3$.
$$2p - q = 2(17) - 3 = 34 - 3 = 31$$

3. **a.** $\{6, 7, 8, 9\}$

   b. $\{41, 42, 43, ...\}$

4. **a.** True, since 7 is a natural number and therefore an element of the set.

   b. True, since 6 is not an element of the set $\{1, 3, 5, 7\}$.

5. **a.** True; every integer is a real number.

   b. False; $\sqrt{8}$ is an irrational number.

   c. True; every whole number is a rational number.

   d. False; since the element 2 in the first set is not an element of the second set.

6. **a.** $|4| = 4$ since 4 is located 4 units from 0 on the number line.

   b. $\left|-\frac{1}{2}\right| = \frac{1}{2}$ since $-\frac{1}{2}$ is $\frac{1}{2}$ unit from 0 on the number line.

   c. $|1| = 1$ since 1 is 1 unit from 0 on the number line.

   d. $-|6.8| = -6.8$
   The negative sign outside the absolute value bars means to take the opposite of the absolute value of 6.8.

   e. $-|-4| = -4$
   Since $|-4| = 4$, $-|-4| = -4$.

7. **a.** The opposite of 5.4 is -5.4.

   b. The opposite of $-\frac{3}{5}$ is $\frac{3}{5}$.

   c. The opposite of 18 is -18.

8. **a.** $3 \cdot x$ or $3x$

   b. $2x - 5$

   c. $3\frac{5}{8} + x$

   d. $\frac{x}{2}$

   e. $x - 14$

   f. $5(x + 10)$

Vocabulary and Readiness Check

1. Letters that represent numbers are called <u>variables</u>.

2. Finding the <u>value</u> of an expression means evaluating the expression.

3. The <u>absolute value</u> of a number is that number's distance from 0 on the number line.

4. An <u>expression</u> is formed by numbers and variables connected by operations such as addition, subtraction, multiplication, division, raising to powers, and/or taking roots.

5. The <u>natural numbers</u> are $\{1, 2, 3, ...\}$.

6. The <u>whole numbers</u> are $\{0, 1, 2, 3, ...\}$.

7. The <u>integers</u> are $\{..., -3, -2, -1, 0, 1, 2, 3, ...\}$.

8. The number $\sqrt{5}$ is an <u>irrational number</u>.

9. The number $\frac{5}{7}$ is a <u>rational number</u>.

10. The opposite of a is <u>$-a$</u>.

Exercise Set 1.2

1. $5x = 5(7) = 35$

3. $9.8z = 9.8(3.1) = 30.38$

5. $ab = \left(\dfrac{1}{2}\right)\left(\dfrac{3}{4}\right) = \dfrac{3}{8}$

7. $3x + y = 3(6) + (4) = 18 + 4 = 22$

9. $400t = 400(5) = 2000$ miles

11. $lw = (5.1)(4) = 20.4$
The display needs 20.4 sq ft of floor space.

13. $2948t = 2948(3.6) = \$10{,}612.80$

15. $\{1, 2, 3, 4, 5\}$

17. $\{11, 12, 13, 14, 15, 16\}$

19. $\{0\}$

21. $\{0, 2, 4, 6, 8\}$

23.

25.

27.

29. Answers may vary

31. $\left\{3, 0, \sqrt{36}\right\}$

33. $\left\{3, \sqrt{36}\right\}$

35. $\left\{\sqrt{7}\right\}$

37. $-11 \in \{x | x \text{ is an integer}\}$

39. $-6 \notin \{2, 4, 6, \ldots\}$

41. $12 \subseteq \{1, 3, 5, \ldots\}$

43. $\dfrac{1}{2} \notin \{x | x \text{ is an irrational number}\}$

45. True; every integer is a real number.

47. True; -1 is an integer.

49. False; 0 is not a natural number.

51. False; $\sqrt{5}$ is an irrational number.

53. True; every natural number is an integer.

55. False; the number $\sqrt{7}$, for example, is a real number, but it is not a rational number.

57. Answers may vary

59. $-|2| = -2$ (the opposite of $|2|$)

61. $|-4| = 4$ since -4 is located 4 units from 0 on the number line.

63. $|0| = 0$ since 0 is located 0 units from 0 on the number line.

65. $-|-3| = -3$ (the opposite of $|-3|$)

67. Answers may vary

69. The opposite of -6.2 is $-(-6.2) = 6.2$.

71. The opposite of $\dfrac{4}{7}$ is $-\dfrac{4}{7}$.

73. The opposite of $-\dfrac{2}{3}$ is $\dfrac{2}{3}$.

75. The opposite of 0 is 0.

77. $2x$

79. $2x + 5$

81. $x - 10$

83. $x + 2$

85. $\dfrac{x}{11}$

87. $12 - 3x$

89. $x + 2.3$ or $x + 2\dfrac{3}{10}$

91. $1\dfrac{1}{3} - x$

93. $\dfrac{5}{4 - x}$

95. $2(x + 3)$

97. The height of the bar representing China is about 137. Therefore, 137 million tourists are predicted for China.

99. The height of the bar representing Spain is about 69. Therefore, 69 million tourists are predicted for Spain.

101. Answers may vary

Section 1.3

Practice Exercises

1. a. $-6 + (-2) = -(6 + 2) = -8$

  b. $5 + (-8) = -3$

  c. $-4 + 9 = 5$

  d. $(-3.2) + (-4.9) = -8.1$

  e. $-\dfrac{3}{5} + \dfrac{2}{3} = -\dfrac{9}{15} + \dfrac{10}{15} = \dfrac{1}{15}$

2. a. $3 - 11 = 3 + (-11) = -8$

  b. $-6 - (-3) = -6 + (3) = -3$

  c. $-7 - 5 = -7 + (-5) = -12$

  d. $4.2 - (-3.5) = 4.2 + 3.5 = 7.7$

  e. $\dfrac{5}{7} - \dfrac{1}{3} = \dfrac{5 \cdot 3}{7 \cdot 3} - \dfrac{1 \cdot 7}{3 \cdot 7} = \dfrac{15}{21} + \left(-\dfrac{7}{21}\right) = \dfrac{8}{21}$

  f. $3 - 1.2 = 3 + (-1.2) = 1.8$

  g. $2 - 9 = 2 + (-9) = -7$

3. a. $13 + 5 - 6 = 18 - 6 = 12$

  b. $-6 - 2 + 4 = -8 + 4 = -4$

4. a. Since the signs of the two numbers are different or unlike, the product is negative.
$(-5)(3) = -15$

  b. Since the signs of the two numbers are the same, the product is positive.
$(-7)\left(-\dfrac{1}{14}\right) = \dfrac{7}{14} = \dfrac{1}{2}$

  c. $5.1(-2) = -10.2$

d. $14(0) = 0$

  e. $\left(-\dfrac{1}{4}\right)\left(\dfrac{8}{13}\right) = -\dfrac{8}{52} = -\dfrac{2}{13}$

  f. $6(-1)(-2)(3) = -6(-2)(3) = 12(3) = 36$

  g. $5(-2.3) = -11.5$

5. a. Since the signs are different or unlike, the quotient is negative.
$\dfrac{-16}{8} = -2$

  b. Since the signs are the same, the quotient is positive.
$\dfrac{-15}{-3} = 5$

  c. $-\dfrac{2}{3} \div 4 = -\dfrac{2}{3} \cdot \dfrac{1}{4} = -\dfrac{1}{6}$

  d. $\dfrac{54}{-9} = -6$

  e. $-\dfrac{1}{12} \div \left(-\dfrac{3}{4}\right) = -\dfrac{1}{12} \cdot -\dfrac{4}{3} = \dfrac{1}{9}$

  f. $\dfrac{0}{-7} = 0$

6. a. $2^3 = 2 \cdot 2 \cdot 2 = 8$

  b. $\left(\dfrac{1}{3}\right)^2 = \left(\dfrac{1}{3}\right)\left(\dfrac{1}{3}\right) = \dfrac{1}{9}$

  c. $-6^2 = -(6 \cdot 6) = -36$

  d. $(-6)^2 = (-6)(-6) = 36$

  e. $-4^3 = -(4 \cdot 4 \cdot 4) = -64$

  f. $(-4)^3 = (-4)(-4)(-4) = -64$

7. a. $\sqrt{49} = 7$ since 7 is positive and $7^2 = 49$.

  b. $\sqrt{\dfrac{1}{16}} = \dfrac{1}{4}$ since $\left(\dfrac{1}{4}\right)^2 = \dfrac{1}{16}$.

c. $-\sqrt{64} = -8$

d. $\sqrt{-64}$ is not a real number.

e. $\sqrt{100} = 10$ since $10^2 = 100.$

8. a. $\sqrt[3]{64} = 4$ since $4^3 = 64.$

b. $\sqrt[5]{-1} = -1$ since $(-1)^5 = -1.$

c. $\sqrt[4]{10,000} = 10$ since $10^4 = 10,000.$

9. a. $14 - 3 \cdot 4 = 14 - 12 = 2$

b. $3(5-8)^2 = 3(-3)^2 = 3(9) = 27$

c. $\dfrac{|-5|^2 + 4}{\sqrt{4} - 3} = \dfrac{5^2 + 4}{2 - 3} = \dfrac{25 + 4}{-1} = \dfrac{29}{-1} = -29$

10. $5 - [(3-5) + 6(2-4)] = 5 - [-2 + 6(-2)]$
$$= 5 - [-2 + (-12)]$$
$$= 5 - [-14]$$
$$= 5 + 14$$
$$= 19$$

11. $\dfrac{-2\sqrt{12+4} - (-3)^2}{6^2 + |1-9|} = \dfrac{-2\sqrt{16} - (-3)^2}{6^2 + |-8|}$
$$= \dfrac{-2(4) - 9}{36 + 8}$$
$$= \dfrac{-8 - 9}{44}$$
$$= -\dfrac{17}{44}$$

12. For each expression, replace x with 16 and y with -5.

a. $2x - 7y = 2(16) - 7(-5) = 32 + 35 = 67$

b. $-4y^2 = -4(-5)^2 = -4(25) = -100$

c. $\dfrac{\sqrt{x}}{y} - \dfrac{y}{x} = \dfrac{\sqrt{16}}{-5} - \dfrac{-5}{16}$
$$= -\dfrac{4}{5} + \dfrac{5}{16}$$
$$= -\dfrac{4}{5} \cdot \dfrac{16}{16} + \dfrac{5}{16} \cdot \dfrac{5}{5}$$
$$= -\dfrac{64}{80} + \dfrac{25}{80}$$
$$= -\dfrac{39}{80}$$

13. When $x = -5,$
$$\dfrac{9}{5}x + 32 = \dfrac{9}{5}(-5) + 32 = -9 + 32 = 23.$$
When $x = 10,$
$$\dfrac{9}{5}x + 32 = \dfrac{9}{5}(10) + 32 = 18 + 32 = 50.$$
When $x = 25,$
$$\dfrac{9}{5}x + 32 = \dfrac{9}{5}(25) + 32 = 45 + 32 = 77.$$
The completed table is

Degrees Celsius	x	-5	10	25
Degrees Fahrenheit	$\dfrac{9}{5}x + 32$	23	50	77

Vocabulary and Readiness Check

1. $-\dfrac{1}{7} = \dfrac{-1}{7} = \dfrac{1}{-7};$ b, c

2. $\dfrac{-x}{y} = \dfrac{x}{-y} = -\dfrac{x}{y};$ a, b

3. $\dfrac{5}{-(x+y)} = \dfrac{-5}{(x+y)} = -\dfrac{5}{(x+y)};$ b, d

4. $-\dfrac{(y+z)}{3y} = \dfrac{-(y+z)}{3y} = \dfrac{(y+z)}{-3y};$ a, d

5. $\dfrac{-9x}{-2y} = \dfrac{9x}{2y};$ b

6. $\dfrac{-a}{-b} = \dfrac{a}{b};$ a

7. $0 \cdot a = \underline{0}$

8. $\dfrac{0}{4}$ simplifies to $\underline{0}$ while $\dfrac{4}{0}$ is <u>undefined</u>.

9. The <u>reciprocal</u> of the nonzero number b is $\dfrac{1}{b}$.

10. The fraction $-\dfrac{a}{b} = \dfrac{-a}{\underline{b}} = \dfrac{a}{\underline{-b}}$.

11. An <u>exponent</u> is a shorthand notation for repeated multiplication of the same number.

12. In $(-5)^2$, the 2 is the <u>exponent</u> and the -5 is the <u>base</u>.

13. The opposite of squaring a number is taking the <u>square root</u> of a number.

14. Using order of operations, $9 \div 3 \cdot 3 = \underline{9}$.

Exercise Set 1.3

1. $-3 + 8 = 5$

3. $-14 + (-10) = -24$

5. $-4.3 - 6.7 = -11$

7. $13 - 17 = -4$

9. $\dfrac{11}{15} - \left(-\dfrac{3}{5}\right) = \dfrac{11}{15} + \dfrac{9}{15} = \dfrac{20}{15} = \dfrac{4}{3}$

11. $19 - 10 - 11 = 9 - 11 = -2$

13. $-\dfrac{4}{5} - \left(-\dfrac{3}{10}\right) = -\dfrac{4}{5} + \dfrac{3}{10} = -\dfrac{8}{10} + \dfrac{3}{10} = -\dfrac{5}{10} = -\dfrac{1}{2}$

15. $8 - 14 = -6$

17. $-5 \cdot 12 = -60$

19. $-7 \cdot 0 = 0$

21. $\dfrac{0}{-2} = 0$

23. $\dfrac{-9}{3} = -3$

25. $\dfrac{-12}{-4} = 3$

27. $3\left(-\dfrac{1}{18}\right) = -\dfrac{3}{18} = -\dfrac{1}{6}$

29. $(-0.7)(-0.8) = 0.56$

31. $9.1 \div -1.3 = \dfrac{9.1}{1} \cdot \dfrac{1}{-1.3} = -7$

33. Multiplying from left to right gives $(-4)(-2)(-1) = 8(-1) = -8$.

35. $-7^2 = -(7 \cdot 7) = -49$

37. $(-6)^2 = (-6)(-6) = 36$

39. $(-2)^3 = (-2)(-2)(-2) = 4(-2) = -8$

41. $\left(-\dfrac{1}{3}\right)^3 = \left(-\dfrac{1}{3}\right)\left(-\dfrac{1}{3}\right)\left(-\dfrac{1}{3}\right) = -\dfrac{1}{27}$

43. $\sqrt{49} = 7$ since 7 is positive and $7^2 = 49$.

45. $-\sqrt{\dfrac{4}{9}} = -\dfrac{2}{3}$ since $\left(\dfrac{2}{3}\right)^2 = \dfrac{4}{9}$.

47. $\sqrt[3]{64} = 4$ since $4^3 = 64$.

49. $\sqrt[4]{81} = 3$ since $3^4 = 81$.

51. $\sqrt{-100}$ is not a real number.

53. $3(5-7)^4 = 3(-2)^4 = 3(16) = 48$

55. $-3^2 + 2^3 = -9 + 8 = -1$

57. $\dfrac{3.1 - (-1.4)}{-0.5} = \dfrac{3.1 + 1.4}{-0.5} = \dfrac{4.5}{-0.5} = -9$

59. $(-3)^2 + 2^3 = 9 + 8 = 17$

61. $-8 \div 4 \cdot 2 = -2 \cdot 2 = -4$

63. $-8\left(-\dfrac{3}{4}\right) - 8 = 6 - 8 = -2$

65. $2 - [(7-6) + (9-19)] = 2 - [1 + (-10)]$
$= 2 - (-9)$
$= 11$

67. $\dfrac{(-9+6)(-1^2)}{-2-2} = \dfrac{(-3)(-1)}{-4} = \dfrac{3}{-4} = -\dfrac{3}{4}$

69. $\left(\sqrt[3]{8}\right)(-4) - \left(\sqrt{9}\right)(-5) = (2)(-4) - (3)(-5)$
$$= -8 - (-15)$$
$$= -8 + 15$$
$$= 7$$

71. $25 - [(3-5) + (14-18)]^2 = 25 - [(-2) + (-4)]^2$
$$= 25 - (-6)^2$$
$$= 25 - 36$$
$$= -11$$

73. $\dfrac{\left(3-\sqrt{9}\right) - (-5-1.3)}{-3} = \dfrac{(3-3) - (-6.3)}{-3}$
$$= \dfrac{0 + 6.3}{-3}$$
$$= \dfrac{6.3}{-3}$$
$$= -2.1$$

75. $\dfrac{|3-9| - |-5|}{-3} = \dfrac{6-5}{-3} = \dfrac{1}{-3} = -\dfrac{1}{3}$

77. $\dfrac{3(-2+1)}{5} - \dfrac{-7(2-4)}{1-(-2)} = \dfrac{3(-1)}{5} - \dfrac{-7(-2)}{1+2}$
$$= \dfrac{-3}{5} - \dfrac{14}{3}$$
$$= -\dfrac{9}{15} - \dfrac{70}{15}$$
$$= -\dfrac{79}{15}$$

79. $\dfrac{\frac{1}{3}\cdot 9 - 7}{3 + \frac{1}{2}\cdot 4} = \dfrac{3-7}{3+2} = \dfrac{-4}{5} = -\dfrac{4}{5}$

81. $3\{-2 + 5[1 - 2(-2+5)]\} = 3\{-2 + 5[1 - 2(3)]\}$
$$= 3\{-2 + 5[1 - 6]\}$$
$$= 3\{-2 + 5[-5]\}$$
$$= 3\{-2 + [-25]\}$$
$$= 3\{-27\}$$
$$= -81$$

83. $\dfrac{-4\sqrt{80+1} + (-4)^2}{3^3 + |-2(3)|} = \dfrac{-4\sqrt{81} + (-4)^2}{3^3 + |-6|}$
$$= \dfrac{-4(9) + 16}{27 + 6}$$
$$= \dfrac{-36 + 16}{27 + 6}$$
$$= \dfrac{-20}{33}$$
$$= -\dfrac{20}{33}$$

85. Let $x = 9$, $y = -2$.
$9x - 6y = 9(9) - 6(-2) = 81 + 12 = 93$

87. Let $y = -2$.
$-3y^2 = -3(-2)^2 = -3(4) = -12$

89. Let $x = 9$, $y = -2$.
$\dfrac{\sqrt{x}}{y} - \dfrac{y}{x} = \dfrac{\sqrt{9}}{-2} - \dfrac{-2}{9}$
$$= \dfrac{3}{-2} + \dfrac{2}{9}$$
$$= -\dfrac{27}{18} + \dfrac{4}{18}$$
$$= -\dfrac{23}{18}$$

91. Let $x = 9$, $y = -2$.
$\dfrac{3 + 2|x-y|}{x+2y} = \dfrac{3 + 2|9 - (-2)|}{9 + 2(-2)}$
$$= \dfrac{3 + 2|9+2|}{9 + 2(-2)}$$
$$= \dfrac{3 + 2|11|}{9 + (-4)}$$
$$= \dfrac{3 + 22}{5}$$
$$= \dfrac{25}{5}$$
$$= 5$$

93. Let $x = 9$, $y = -2$.

$$\frac{y^3 + \sqrt{x-5}}{|4x - y|} = \frac{(-2)^3 + \sqrt{9-5}}{|4 \cdot 9 - (-2)|}$$

$$= \frac{-8 + \sqrt{4}}{|36 + 2|}$$

$$= \frac{-8 + 2}{|38|}$$

$$= \frac{-6}{38}$$

$$= -\frac{3}{19}$$

95. a. $y = 5$: $8 + 2y = 8 + 2(5) = 8 + 10 = 18$
$y = 7$: $8 + 2y = 8 + 2(7) = 8 + 14 = 22$
$y = 10$: $8 + 2y = 8 + 2(10) = 8 + 20 = 28$
$y = 100$: $8 + 2y = 8 + 2(100) = 8 + 200 = 208$
The completed table is:

Length	y	5	7	10	100
Perimeter	$8 + 2y$	18	22	28	208

    b. The perimeter increases as length increases; answers may vary.

97. a. $x = 10$: $\dfrac{100x + 5000}{x} = \dfrac{100(10) + 5000}{10}$

$$= \frac{1000 + 5000}{10}$$

$$= \frac{6000}{10}$$

$$= 600$$

$x = 100$: $\dfrac{100x + 5000}{x} = \dfrac{100(100) + 5000}{100}$

$$= \frac{10,000 + 5000}{100}$$

$$= \frac{15,000}{100}$$

$$= 150$$

$x = 1000$: $\dfrac{100x + 5000}{x} = \dfrac{100(1000) + 5000}{1000}$

$$= \frac{100,000 + 5000}{1000}$$

$$= \frac{105,000}{1000}$$

$$= 105$$

The completed table is:

Number of Bookshelves	x	10	100	1000
Cost per Bookshelf	$\dfrac{100x+5000}{x}$	600	150	105

    b. The cost per bookshelf decreases as the number of bookshelves increases; answers may vary.

99. Let $x_1 = 2$, $x_2 = 4$, $y_1 = -3$, $y_2 = 2$.
$$\frac{y_2 - y_1}{x_2 - x_1} = \frac{2-(-3)}{4-2} = \frac{2+3}{4-2} = \frac{5}{2}$$

101. $1 - \dfrac{1}{5} - \dfrac{3}{7} = \dfrac{35}{35} - \dfrac{7}{35} - \dfrac{15}{35} = \dfrac{13}{35}$

103. $10{,}203 - 5998 = 4205$ meters

105. $(2 + 7) \cdot (1 + 3) = 9 \cdot 4 = 36$

107. Answers may vary

109. $\sqrt{10} \approx 3.1623$

111. $\sqrt{7.9} \approx 2.8107$

113. $\dfrac{-1.682 - 17.895}{(-7.102)(-4.691)} \approx -0.5876$

115. Look for the bar representing 15 years. Choose the positive number, 15.6%.

117. Look for the bar representing 15 years. Find the difference.
$15.6 - (-2.1) = 15.6 + 2.1 = 17.7\%$

119. This type of investment is recommended for long term investments. Short term investing appears to be very volatile.

Integrated Review

  1. Let $z = -4$.
$z^2 = (-4)^2 = (-4)(-4) = 16$

  2. Let $z = -4$.
$-z^2 = -(-4)^2 = -(-4)(-4) = -16$

  3. Let $x = -1$, $y = 3$, $z = -4$.
$$\frac{4x - z}{2y} = \frac{4(-1) - (-4)}{2(3)} = \frac{-4+4}{6} = \frac{0}{6} = 0$$

  4. Let $x = -1$, $y = 3$, $z = -4$.
$$\begin{aligned} x(y - 2z) &= -1[3 - 2(-4)] \\ &= -1[3 + 8] \\ &= -1[11] \\ &= -11 \end{aligned}$$

  5. $-7 - (-2) = -7 + 2 = -5$

  6. $\dfrac{9}{10} - \dfrac{11}{12} = \dfrac{9}{10} \cdot \dfrac{6}{6} - \dfrac{11}{12} \cdot \dfrac{5}{5} = \dfrac{54}{60} - \dfrac{55}{60} = -\dfrac{1}{60}$

  7. $\dfrac{-13}{2-2} = \dfrac{-13}{0}$ is undefined.

  8. $(1.2)^2 - (2.1)^2 = 1.44 - 4.41 = -2.97$

  9. $\sqrt{64} - \sqrt[3]{64} = 8 - 4 = 4$

  10. $-5^2 - (-5)^2 = -25 - 25 = -50$

  11. $\begin{aligned} 9 + 2[(8-10)^2 + (-3)^2] &= 9 + 2[(-2)^2 + (-3)^2] \\ &= 9 + 2(4 + 9) \\ &= 9 + 2(13) \\ &= 9 + 26 \\ &= 35 \end{aligned}$

  12. $\begin{aligned} 8 - 6\left[\sqrt[3]{8}(-2) + \sqrt{4}(-5)\right] &= 8 - 6[2(-2) + 2(-5)] \\ &= 8 - 6[(-4) + (-10)] \\ &= 8 - 6(-14) \\ &= 8 + 84 \\ &= 92 \end{aligned}$

  13. $-15 - 2x$

  14. $3x + 5$

  15. 0 is a whole number that is not a natural number.

  16. True

Section 1.4

Practice Exercises

  1. $\underbrace{\text{The product of} -4 \text{ and } x}_{\displaystyle -4x} \ \underset{\displaystyle =}{\overset{\downarrow}{\text{is}}} \ \underset{\displaystyle 20}{\overset{\downarrow}{20}}$

2. $\underbrace{\text{Three times}}_{3}$ $\underbrace{\text{the difference of } z \text{ and } 3}_{(z-3)}$ $\underbrace{\text{equals}}_{=}$ $\underbrace{9.}_{9}$

3. $\underbrace{\text{The sum of } x \text{ and } 5}_{x+5}$ $\underbrace{\text{is the same as}}_{=}$ $\underbrace{3 \text{ less than twice } x.}_{2x-3}$

4. $\underbrace{\text{The sum of } y \text{ and } 2}_{y+2}$ $\underbrace{\text{is}}_{=}$ $\underbrace{4 \text{ more than the quotient of } z \text{ and } 8.}_{4+\dfrac{z}{8}}$

5. a. $-6 < -5$ since -6 lies to the left of -5 on the number line.

$$-10\,-9\,-8\,-7\,-6\,-5\,-4\,-3\,-2\,-1\ \ 0\ \ 1$$

    b. $\dfrac{24}{3} = 8$

    c. $0 > -7$ since 0 lies to the right of -7 on the number line.

$$-9\,-8\,-7\,-6\,-5\,-4\,-3\,-2\,-1\ \ 0\ \ 1\ \ 2$$

    d. $2.76 > 2.67$ since 2.76 lies to the right of 2.67 on the number line.

$$\begin{array}{c} 2.67\quad 2.76 \\ \hline 1\qquad 2\qquad 3 \end{array}$$

6. a. $x - 3 \le 5$

    b. $y \ne -4$

    c. $2 < 4 + \dfrac{1}{2}z$

7. a. The opposite of -7 is $-(-7) = 7$.

    b. The opposite of 4.7 is -4.7.

    c. The opposite of $-\dfrac{3}{8}$ is $-\left(-\dfrac{3}{8}\right) = \dfrac{3}{8}$.

8. a. The reciprocal of $-\dfrac{5}{3}$ is $-\dfrac{3}{5}$ because $-\dfrac{5}{3}\left(-\dfrac{3}{5}\right) = 1$.

    b. The reciprocal of 14 is $\dfrac{1}{14}$.

    c. The reciprocal of -2 is $-\dfrac{1}{2}$.

9. $8 + 13x = 13x + 8$

10. $3 \cdot (11b) = (3 \cdot 11)b = 33b$

11. a. $4(x + 5y) = 4 \cdot x + 4 \cdot 5y = 4x + 20y$

b. $\begin{aligned}-(3 - 2z) &= -1(3 - 2z) \\ &= -1 \cdot 3 + (-1)(-2z) \\ &= -3 + 2z\end{aligned}$

c. $\begin{aligned}0.3x(y - 3) &= 0.3x \cdot y - 0.3x \cdot 3 \\ &= 0.3xy - 0.9x\end{aligned}$

12. a. In words: Value of a dime   ·   number of dimes

$\qquad\qquad\qquad\qquad\downarrow\qquad\qquad\qquad\qquad\downarrow$

Translate: 0.10 x , or $0.10x$

b. In words: number of grams of   ·   number of
              carbohydrates in one   cookies
                      cookie

$\qquad\qquad\qquad\qquad\downarrow\qquad\qquad\qquad\qquad\downarrow$

Translate: 26 y , or $26y$

c. In words: cost of one   ·   number of cards
              birthday card

$\qquad\qquad\qquad\qquad\downarrow\qquad\qquad\qquad\qquad\downarrow$

Translate: 1.75 z , or $1.75z$

d. In words: Discount   ·   purchase price

$\qquad\qquad\qquad\qquad\downarrow\qquad\qquad\qquad\qquad\downarrow$

Translate: 0.15 t , or $0.15t$

13. a. If two numbers have a sum of 16 and one number is x, the other number is the rest of 16.

In words: Sixteen   minus x

$\qquad\qquad\quad\downarrow\qquad\quad\downarrow\qquad\quad\downarrow$

Translate: 16   – x

b. In words: One hundred   minus   one angle, x
              eighty

$\qquad\qquad\qquad\downarrow\qquad\qquad\downarrow\qquad\qquad\downarrow$

Translate: 180   – x

c. The next consecutive even integer is always two more than the previous even integer.

In words:	first integer	plus	two
	↓	↓	↓
Translate:	x	$+$	2

d.

In words:	younger brother's age	plus	nine
	↓	↓	↓
Translate:	x	$+$	9

14. a. $6ab - ab = 6ab - 1ab = (6-1)ab = 5ab$

b. $4x - 5 + 6x = 4x + 6x - 5$
$= (4+6)x - 5$
$= 10x - 5$

c. $17p - 9$ cannot be simplified further since $17p$ and -9 are not like terms.

15. a. $5pq - 2pq - 11 - 4pq + 18$
$= 5pq - 2pq - 4pq - 11 + 18$
$= (5 - 2 - 4)pq + (-11 + 18)$
$= -1pq + (7)$
$= -pq + 7$

b. $3x^2 + 7 - 2(x^2 - 6) = 3x^2 + 7 - 2x^2 + 12$
$= 3x^2 - 2x^2 + 7 + 12$
$= x^2 + 19$

c. $(3.7x + 2.5) - (-2.1x - 1.3)$
$= 3.7x + 2.5 + 2.1x + 1.3$
$= 3.7x + 2.1x + 2.5 + 1.3$
$= 5.8x + 3.8$

d. $\dfrac{1}{5}(15c - 25d) - \dfrac{1}{2}(8c + 6d + 1) + \dfrac{3}{4}$
$= 3c - 5d - 4c - 3d - \dfrac{1}{2} + \dfrac{3}{4}$
$= -c - 8d + \dfrac{1}{4}$

Vocabulary and Readiness Check

	Symbol	Meaning
1.	$<$	is less than
2.	$>$	is greater than
3.	$\neq$	is not equal to
4.	$=$	is equal to
5.	$\geq$	is greater than or equal to
6.	$\leq$	is less than or equal to

7. The opposite of nonzero number a is $\underline{-a}$.

8. The reciprocal of nonzero number a is $\underline{\dfrac{1}{a}}$.

9. The <u>commutative</u> property has to do with "order."

10. The <u>associative</u> property has to do with "grouping."

11. $a(b + c) = ab + ac$ illustrates the <u>distributive</u> property.

12. Terms with the same variable(s) raised to the same powers are called <u>like</u> terms.

13. The <u>terms</u> of an expression are the addends of the expression.

14. The process of adding or subtracting like terms is called <u>combining</u> like terms.

Exercise Set 1.4

1. The sum of 10 and x is -12.
        ↓   ↓
     $10 + x$ $= -12$
or $10 + x = -12$

3. Twice x plus 5   is the same as -14.
                           ↓
     $2x + 5$ $=$ -14
or $2x + 5 = -14$

5.　The quotient of n and 5　is　4 times n.

$$\frac{n}{5} \quad\quad = \quad\quad 4n$$

　or $\dfrac{n}{5} = 4n$

7.　The difference of z and one-half　is the same as　the product of z and one-half.

$$z - \frac{1}{2} \quad\quad = \quad\quad \frac{1}{2}z$$

　or $z - \dfrac{1}{2} = \dfrac{1}{2}z$

9.　The product of 7 and x　is less than or equal to -21.

$$7x \quad\quad \leq \quad\quad -21$$

　or $7x \leq -21$

11.　Twice the difference of x and 6　is greater than　the reciprocal of 11.

$$2(x - 6) \quad\quad > \quad\quad \frac{1}{11}$$

　or $2(x - 6) > \dfrac{1}{11}$

13.　Twice the difference of x and 6　is　-27.

$$2(x - 6) \quad\quad = -27$$

　or $2(x - 6) = -27$

15.　$-16 > -17$ since -16 is to the right of -17 on the number line.

17.　$7.4 = 7.40$

19.　$\dfrac{7}{11} < \dfrac{9}{11}$ since $7 < 9$.

21.　$\dfrac{1}{2} < \dfrac{5}{8}$ since $\dfrac{1}{2}$ is to the left of $\dfrac{5}{8}$ on the number line.

23.　$-7.9 < -7.09$ since -7.9 is to the left of -7.09 on the number line.

	Number	Opposite	Reciprocal
25.	5	–5	$\frac{1}{5}$
27.	–8	8	$-\frac{1}{8}$
29.	$-\frac{1}{7}$	$\frac{1}{7}$	–7
31.	0	0	Undefined
33.	$\frac{7}{8}$	$-\frac{7}{8}$	$\frac{8}{7}$

35. Zero; for every real number x, $0 \cdot x \neq 1$, so 0 has no reciprocal. It is the only real number that has no reciprocal because if $x \neq 0$, then $x \cdot \dfrac{1}{x} = 1$ by definition.

37. $7x + y = y + 7x$

39. $z \cdot w = w \cdot z$

41. $\dfrac{1}{3} \cdot \dfrac{x}{5} = \dfrac{x}{5} \cdot \dfrac{1}{3}$

43. No, subtraction is not commutative. Answers may vary (for example, $8 - 5 \neq 5 - 8$).

45. $5 \cdot (7x) = (5 \cdot 7)x$

47. $(x + 1.2) + y = x + (1.2 + y)$

49. $(14z) \cdot y = 14(z \cdot y)$

51. $12 - (5 - 3) = 10$; $(12 - 5) - 3 = 4$; subtraction is not associative.

53. $3(x + 5) = 3 \cdot x + 3 \cdot 5 = 3x + 15$

55. $-(2a + b) = -1(2a + b)$
$= -1 \cdot 2a + (-1) \cdot b$
$= -2a - b$

57. $2(6x + 5y + 2z) = 2 \cdot 6x + 2 \cdot 5y + 2 \cdot 2z$
$= 12x + 10y + 4z$

59. $-4(x - 2y + 7) = -4 \cdot x + (-4)(-2y) + (-4)(7)$
$= -4x + 8y - 28$

61. $0.5x(6y - 3) = 0.5x \cdot 6y - 0.5x \cdot 3 = 3xy - 1.5x$

63. $3x + 6 = 6 + 3x$

65. $\dfrac{2}{3} + \left(-\dfrac{2}{3}\right) = 0$

67. $7 \cdot 1 = 7$

69. $10(2y) = (10 \cdot 2)y$

71. $a(b + c) = ab + ac$

73. In words: $\boxed{\text{Value of a dime}} \cdot \boxed{\text{Number of dimes}}$
Translate: $0.1 \cdot d$ or $0.1d$

75. If two numbers have a sum of 112 and one number is x, then the other number is the "rest of 112." So, in other words, we have
$\boxed{\text{One hundred twelve}} - \boxed{x}$
Translate: $112 - x$

77. In words: $\boxed{\text{Ninety}} - \boxed{5x}$
Translate: $90 - 5x$

79. In words: $\boxed{\text{Cost of a book}} \cdot \boxed{\text{Number of books}}$
Translate: $\$35.61y$

81. The next even integer would be 2 more than the given even integer. In words:
$\boxed{\text{Even integer}} + \boxed{\text{Two}}$
Translate: $2x + 2$

83. $5y - 14 + 7y - 20y = 5y + 7y - 20y - 14$
$= (5 + 7 - 20)y - 14$
$= -8y - 14$

85. $-11c - (4 - 2c) = -11c - 4 + 2c$
$= -11c + 2c - 4$
$= (-11 + 2)c - 4$
$= -9c - 4$

87. $(8 - 5y) - (4 + 3y) = 8 - 5y - 4 - 3y$
$= -5y - 3y + 8 - 4$
$= (-5 - 3)y + 4$
$= -8y + 4$ or $4 - 8y$

89. $-4(yz + 3) - 7yz + 1 + y^2$
$= -4yz - 12 - 7yz + 1 + y^2$
$= y^2 - 4yz - 7yz - 11$
$= y^2 + (-4 - 7)yz - 11$
$= y^2 - 11yz - 11$

91. $-(8-t)+(2t-6) = -8+t+2t-6$
$$= t+2t-8-6$$
$$= (1+2)t-14$$
$$= 3t-14$$

93. $5(2z^3-6)+10(3-z^3) = 10z^3-30+30-10z^3$
$$= 10z^3-10z^3-30+30$$
$$= (10-10)z^3+0$$
$$= 0$$

95. $7n+3(2n-6)-2 = 7n+6n-18-2$
$$= (7+6)n-20$$
$$= 13n-20$$

97. $6.3y-9.7+2.2y-11.1 = 6.3y+2.2y-9.7-11.1$
$$= (6.3+2.2)y-20.8$$
$$= 8.5y-20.8$$

99. $\dfrac{7}{8}a-\dfrac{11}{12}-\dfrac{1}{2}a+\dfrac{5}{6} = \dfrac{7}{8}a-\dfrac{1}{2}a-\dfrac{11}{12}+\dfrac{5}{6}$
$$= \left(\dfrac{7}{8}-\dfrac{1}{2}\right)a-\dfrac{11}{12}+\dfrac{10}{12}$$
$$= \left(\dfrac{7}{8}-\dfrac{4}{8}\right)a-\dfrac{1}{12}$$
$$= \dfrac{3}{8}a-\dfrac{1}{12}$$

101. $4(5y+12) = 20y+48$

103. $\dfrac{1}{2}(10x-2)-\dfrac{1}{6}(60x-5y) = 5x-1-10x+\dfrac{5}{6}y$
$$= 5x-10x+\dfrac{5}{6}y-1$$
$$= -5x+\dfrac{5}{6}y-1$$

105. $\dfrac{1}{3}(6x-33y)-\dfrac{1}{8}(24x-40y+1)-\dfrac{1}{3}$
$$= 2x-11y-3x+5y-\dfrac{1}{8}-\dfrac{1}{3}$$
$$= 2x-3x-11y+5y-\dfrac{3}{24}-\dfrac{8}{24}$$
$$= (2-3)x+(-11+5)y-\dfrac{11}{24}$$
$$= -x-6y-\dfrac{11}{24}$$

107. $5(7y) = (5\cdot 7)y$

109. $6.5y-4.4(1.8x-3.3)+10.95$
$$= 6.5y-7.92x+14.52+10.95$$
$$= 6.5y-7.92x+25.47$$

111. It is not the case that two rectangles with the same perimeter will necessarily have the same area. Take a rectangle that is 5 in. by 5 in. and another that is 8 in. by 2 in. Both have the same perimeter, but the areas are 25 square inches and 16 square inches, respectively.

113. Locate 2050 on the 'Year' axis. Travel up vertically until you hit the line. Travel left horizontally until you hit the 'Population'-axis. Read the value. The predicted population over 65 in 2050 is 80 million.

115. Locate 2000 on the 'Year'-axis. Travel up vertically until you hit the line. Travel left horizontally until you hit the 'Population'-axis. Read the value. The population over 65 in 2000 was 35 million.

117. $(2.5)(8.1\%) = 20.25\%$

Chapter 1 Vocabulary Check

1. An <u>algebraic expression</u> is formed by numbers and variables connected by the operations of addition, subtraction, multiplication, division, raising to powers, and/or taking roots.

2. The <u>opposite</u> of a number a is $-a$.

3. $3(x-6) = 3x-18$ by the <u>distributive</u> property.

4. The <u>absolute value</u> of a number is the distance between the number and 0 on the number line.

5. An <u>exponent</u> is a shorthand notation for repeated multiplication of the same factor.

6. A letter that represents a number is called a <u>variable</u>.

7. The symbols < and > are called <u>inequality</u> symbols.

8. If a is not 0, then a and $\dfrac{1}{a}$ are called <u>reciprocals</u>.

9. $A+B = B+A$ by the <u>commutative</u> property.

10. $(A+B)+C = A+(B+C)$ by the <u>associative</u> property.

11. The numbers 0, 1, 2, 3, ... are called <u>whole</u> numbers.

12. If a number corresponds to a point on the number line, we know that number is a <u>real</u> number.

Chapter 1 Review

1. $7x = 7(3) = 21$

2. $st = (1.6)(5) = 8$

3. One hour is $60(60) = 3600$ seconds.
$90t = 90(3600) = 324,000$
324,000 wing beats per hour.

4. $\{x|x$ is an odd integer between -2 and $4\}$
$= \{-1, 1, 3\}$

5. $\{x|x$ is an even integer between -3 and $7\}$
$= \{-2, 0, 2, 4, 6\}$

6. There are no whole numbers that are negative.
$\varnothing$

7. All natural numbers are rational numbers.
$\varnothing$

8. $\{x|x$ is a whole number greater than $5\}$
$= \{6, 7, 8, ...\}$

9. $\{x|x$ is an integer less than $3\} = \{..., -1, 0, 1, 2\}$

10. Since $D = \{2, 4, 6, 8, 10, ..., 16\}$, $10 \in D$ is true.

11. Since $B = \{5, 9, 11\}$, $B \in 9$ is false.

12. $\sqrt{169} = 13$, which is a rational number. So $\sqrt{169} \notin G$ is true.

13. Since $F = \{ \ \}$ and 0 is not an element of the empty set, then $0 \notin F$ is true.

14. Since $E = \{x|x$ is a rational number$\}$ and π is irrational, then $\pi \in E$ is false.

15. Since $H = \{x|x$ is a real number$\}$ and π is a real number, then $\pi \in H$ is true.

16. Since $\sqrt{4} = 2$ and $G = \{x|x$ is an irrational number$\}$, and 2 is a rational number, then $\sqrt{4} \in G$ is false.

17. Since $E = \{x|x$ is a rational number$\}$ and -9 is a rational number, then $-9 \in E$ is true.

18. Since $A = \{6, 10, 12\}$ and $D = \{2, 4, 6, 8, 10, 12, 14, 16\}$, then $A \subseteq D$ is true.

19. Since $C = \{..., -3, -2, -1, 0, 1, 2, 3, ...\}$ and $B = \{5, 9, 11\}$, then $C \nsubseteq B$ is true.

20. Since $C = \{..., -3, -2, -1, 0, 1, 2, 3, ...\}$ and $E = \{x|x$ is a rational number$\}$, and all integers are rational numbers, then $C \nsubseteq E$ is false.

21. Since $F = \{ \ \}$ and $H = \{x|x$ is a real number$\}$, and the empty set is a subset of all sets, then $F \subseteq H$ is true.

22. A set is always a subset of itself, so $B \subseteq B$ is true.

23. $D = \{2, 4, 6, ..., 16\}$ and $C = \{..., -3, -2, -1, 0, 1, 2, 3, ...\}$
Every element of D is also an element of C, so $D \subseteq C$ is true.

24. $C = \{..., -3, -2, -1, 0, 1, 2, 3, ...\}$ and $H = \{x|x$ is a real number$\}$.
Every integer is a real number, so $C \subseteq H$ is true.

25. $G = \{x|x$ is an irrational number$\}$ and $H = \{x|x$ is a real number$\}$
Every irrational number is also a real number, so $G \subseteq H$ is true.

26. Since $B = \{5, 9, 11\}$, and B does not contain the set $\{5\}$, then $\{5\} \in B$ is false.

27. Since $B = \{5, 9, 11\}$, and $\{5\}$ is a subset of B, then $\{5\} \subseteq B$ is true.

28. Whole numbers: $\left\{5, \dfrac{8}{2}, \sqrt{9}\right\}$

29. Natural numbers: $\left\{5, \dfrac{8}{2}, \sqrt{9}\right\}$

30. Rational numbers: $\left\{5, -\dfrac{2}{3}, \dfrac{8}{2}, \sqrt{9}, 0.3, 1\dfrac{5}{8}, -1\right\}$

31. Irrational numbers: $\left\{\sqrt{7}, \pi\right\}$

32. Real numbers:
$$\left\{5, -\frac{2}{3}, \frac{8}{2}, \sqrt{9}, 0.3, \sqrt{7}, 1\frac{5}{8}, -1, \pi\right\}$$

33. Integers: $\left\{5, \frac{8}{2}, \sqrt{9}, -1\right\}$

34. The opposite of $-\frac{3}{4}$ is $-\left(-\frac{3}{4}\right) = \frac{3}{4}$.

35. The opposite of 0.6 is –0.6.

36. The opposite of 0 is $-0 = 0$.

37. The opposite of 1 is –1.

38. The reciprocal of $-\frac{3}{4}$ is $\frac{1}{\left(-\frac{3}{4}\right)} = -\frac{4}{3}$.

39. The reciprocal of 0.6 is $\frac{1}{0.6}$.

40. The reciprocal of 0 is $\frac{1}{0}$ which is undefined.

41. The reciprocal of 1 is $\frac{1}{1} = 1$.

42. $-7 + 3 = -4$

43. $-10 + (-25) = -35$

44. $5(-0.4) = -2$

45. $(-3.1)(-0.1) = 0.31$

46. $-7 - (-15) = -7 + 15 = 8$

47. $9 - (-4.3) = 9 + 4.3 = 13.3$

48. $(-6)(-4)(0)(-3) = 0$

49. $(-12)(0)(-1)(-5) = 0$

50. $(-24) \div 0$ is undefined.

51. $0 \div (-45) = 0$

52. $(-36) \div (-9) = 4$

53. $60 \div (-12) = -5$

54. $\left(-\frac{4}{5}\right) - \left(-\frac{2}{3}\right) = -\frac{4}{5} + \frac{2}{3} = -\frac{12}{15} + \frac{10}{15} = -\frac{2}{15}$

55. $\left(\frac{5}{4}\right) - \left(-2\frac{3}{4}\right) = \frac{5}{4} + \frac{11}{4} = \frac{16}{4} = 4$

56. $1 - \frac{1}{4} - \frac{1}{3} = \frac{12}{12} - \frac{3}{12} - \frac{4}{12} = \frac{5}{12}$

57. $-5 + 7 - 3 - (-10) = 2 - 3 + 10 = -1 + 10 = 9$

58. $8 - (-3) + (-4) + 6 = 8 + 3 - 4 + 6$
$$= 11 - 4 + 6$$
$$= 7 + 6$$
$$= 13$$

59. $3(4-5)^4 = 3(-1)^4 = 3(1) = 3$

60. $6(7-10)^2 = 6(-3)^2 = 6(9) = 54$

61. $\left(-\frac{8}{15}\right) \cdot \left(-\frac{2}{3}\right)^2 = -\frac{8}{15} \cdot \frac{4}{9} = -\frac{32}{135}$

62. $\left(-\frac{3}{4}\right)^2 \cdot \left(-\frac{10}{21}\right) = \left(\frac{9}{16}\right)\left(-\frac{10}{21}\right) = -\frac{15}{56}$

63. $\dfrac{-\frac{6}{15}}{\frac{8}{25}} = -\frac{6}{15} \div \frac{8}{25} = -\frac{6}{15} \cdot \frac{25}{8} = -\frac{150}{120} = -\frac{5}{4}$

64. $\dfrac{\frac{4}{9}}{-\frac{8}{45}} = \frac{4}{9} \div \left(-\frac{8}{45}\right) = \frac{4}{9} \cdot \left(-\frac{45}{8}\right) = -\frac{180}{72} = -\frac{5}{2}$

65. $-\frac{3}{8} + 3(2) \div 6 = -\frac{3}{8} + 6 \div 6 = -\frac{3}{8} + 1 = -\frac{3}{8} + \frac{8}{8} = \frac{5}{8}$

66. $5(-2) - (-3) - \frac{1}{6} + \frac{2}{3} = -10 + 3 - \frac{1}{6} + \frac{2}{3}$
$$= -7 - \frac{1}{6} + \frac{2}{3}$$
$$= -\frac{42}{6} - \frac{1}{6} + \frac{4}{6}$$
$$= -\frac{39}{6}$$
$$= -6\frac{1}{2}$$

67. $\left| 2^3 - 3^2 \right| - \left| 5 - 7 \right| = \left| 8 - 9 \right| - \left| -2 \right|$
$$= \left| -1 \right| - 2$$
$$= 1 - 2$$
$$= -1$$

68. $\left| 5^2 - 2^2 \right| + \left| 9 \div (-3) \right| = \left| 25 - 4 \right| + \left| -3 \right|$
$$= \left| 21 \right| + 3$$
$$= 21 + 3$$
$$= 24$$

69. $(2^3 - 3^2) - (5 - 7) = (8 - 9) - (-2) = -1 + 2 = 1$

70. $(5^2 - 2^4) + [9 \div (-3)] = (25 - 16) + (-3)$
$$= 9 + (-3)$$
$$= 6$$

71. $\dfrac{(8-10)^3 - (-4)^2}{2 + 8(2) \div 4} = \dfrac{(-2)^3 - 16}{2 + 16 \div 4}$
$$= \dfrac{-8 - 16}{2 + 4}$$
$$= \dfrac{-24}{6}$$
$$= -4$$

72. $\dfrac{(2+4)^2 + (-1)^5}{12 \div 2 \cdot 3 - 3} = \dfrac{(6)^2 + (-1)}{6 \cdot 3 - 3}$
$$= \dfrac{36 - 1}{18 - 3}$$
$$= \dfrac{35}{15}$$
$$= \dfrac{7}{3}$$

73. $\dfrac{(4-9) + 4 - 9}{10 - 12 \div 4 \cdot 8} = \dfrac{(-5) + 4 - 9}{10 - 3 \cdot 8}$
$$= \dfrac{-1 - 9}{10 - 24}$$
$$= \dfrac{-10}{-14}$$
$$= \dfrac{5}{7}$$

74. $\dfrac{3 - 7 - (7 - 3)}{15 + 30 \div 6 \cdot 2} = \dfrac{-4 - (4)}{15 + 5 \cdot 2} = \dfrac{-8}{15 + 10} = \dfrac{-8}{25} = -\dfrac{8}{25}$

75. $\dfrac{\sqrt{25}}{4 + 3 \cdot 7} = \dfrac{5}{4 + 21} = \dfrac{5}{25} = \dfrac{1}{5}$

76. $\dfrac{\sqrt{64}}{24 - 8 \cdot 2} = \dfrac{8}{24 - 16} = \dfrac{8}{8} = 1$

77. Let $x = 0$, $y = 3$, $z = -2$.
$$x^2 - y^2 + z^2 = (0)^2 - (3)^2 + (-2)^2$$
$$= 0 - 9 + 4$$
$$= -5$$

78. Let $x = 0$, $y = 3$, $z = -2$.
$$\dfrac{5x + z}{2y} = \dfrac{5(0) + (-2)}{2(3)} = \dfrac{0 - 2}{6} = \dfrac{-2}{6} = -\dfrac{1}{3}$$

79. Let $y = 3$, $z = -2$.
$$\dfrac{-7y - 3z}{-3} = \dfrac{-7(3) - 3(-2)}{-3} = \dfrac{-21 + 6}{-3} = \dfrac{-15}{-3} = 5$$

80. Let $x = 0$, $y = 3$, $z = -2$.
$$(x - y + z)^2 = (0 - 3 + (-2))^2$$
$$= (-3 - 2)^2$$
$$= (-5)^2$$
$$= 25$$

81. a. When $r = 1$, $2\pi r = 2\pi(1) = 2(3.14) = 6.28$.
When $r = 10$,
$2\pi r = 2\pi(10) = 20(3.14) = 62.8$.
When $r = 100$,
$2\pi r = 2\pi(100) = 200(3.14) = 628$.

r	1	10	100
$2\pi r$	6.28	62.8	628

    b. As the radius increases, the circumference increases.

82. $5xy - 7xy + 3 - 2 + xy = 5xy - 7xy + xy + 3 - 2$
$$= (5 - 7 + 1)xy + (3 - 2)$$
$$= (-1)xy + 1$$
$$= -xy + 1$$

83. $4x + 10x - 19x + 10 - 19$
$$= (4 + 10 - 19)x + (10 - 19)$$
$$= -5x + (-9)$$
$$= -5x - 9$$

84.
$$6x^2 + 2 - 4(x^2 + 1) = 6x^2 + 2 - 4x^2 - 4$$
$$= 6x^2 - 4x^2 + 2 - 4$$
$$= (6-4)x^2 + (2-4)$$
$$= 2x^2 + (-2)$$
$$= 2x^2 - 2$$

85.
$$-7(2x^2 - 1) - x^2 - 1 = -14x^2 + 7 - x^2 - 1$$
$$= -14x^2 - x^2 + 7 - 1$$
$$= (-14-1)x^2 + (7-1)$$
$$= -15x^2 + 6$$

86.
$$(3.2x - 1.5) - (4.3x - 1.2) = 3.2x - 1.5 - 4.3x + 1.2$$
$$= 3.2x - 4.3x - 1.5 + 1.2$$
$$= (3.2 - 4.3)x - 0.3$$
$$= -1.1x - 0.3$$

87.
$$(7.6x + 4.7) - (1.9x + 3.6) = 7.6x + 4.7 - 1.9x - 3.6$$
$$= 7.6x - 1.9x + 4.7 - 3.6$$
$$= (7.6 - 1.9)x + 4.7 - 3.6$$
$$= 5.7x + 1.1$$

88. $\underbrace{\text{Twelve}}\underset{\downarrow}{\text{is}} \underbrace{\text{the product of } x \text{ and negative } 4}.$

$\quad\quad 12 \quad = \quad\quad\quad -4x$

or $12 = -4x$

89. $\underbrace{\text{The sum of } n \text{ and twice } n} \underset{\downarrow}{\text{ is }} \underbrace{\text{negative fifteen}}.$

$\quad\quad n + 2n \quad\quad = \quad\quad -15$

90. $\underbrace{\text{Four}}\underbrace{\text{times}} \underbrace{\text{the sum of } y \text{ and three}}\underset{\downarrow}{\text{ is }}\underset{\downarrow}{-1}.$

$\quad\quad 4 \quad\cdot\quad\quad (y+3) \quad\quad = -1$

or $4(y + 3) = -1$

91. $\underbrace{\text{The difference of } t \text{ and } 5}, \underbrace{\text{multiplied by}} \underset{\downarrow}{\text{six}} \underset{\downarrow}{\text{is}} \underset{\downarrow}{\text{four}}.$

$\quad\quad\quad (t-5) \quad\quad\quad\quad \cdot \quad\quad 6 = 4$

or $6(t - 5) = 4$

92. $\underbrace{\text{Seven subtracted from } z} \underset{\downarrow}{\text{ is }} \underset{\downarrow}{\text{six}}.$

$\quad\quad\quad z - 7 \quad\quad\quad = 6$

or $z - 7 = 6$

93. $\underbrace{\text{Ten less than the product of } x \text{ and nine}} \underset{\downarrow}{\text{ is }} \underset{\downarrow}{\text{five}}.$

$\quad\quad\quad\quad 9x - 10 \quad\quad\quad = 5$

or $9x - 10 = 5$

94. $\underbrace{\text{The difference of } x \text{ and } 5}\ \underbrace{\text{is at least}}\ \underset{\downarrow}{12}$.

$ x - 5 \geq 12$

or $x - 5 \geq 12$

95. $\underbrace{\text{The opposite of four}}\ \underbrace{\text{is less than}}\ \underbrace{\text{the product of } y \text{ and seven}}$.

$ -4 < 7y$

or $-4 < 7y$

96. $\underbrace{\text{Two-thirds}}\ \underbrace{\text{is not equal to}}\ \underbrace{\text{twice}}\ \underbrace{\text{the sum of } n \text{ and one-fourth}}$.

$ \dfrac{2}{3} \neq 2\cdot \left(n+\dfrac{1}{4}\right)$

or $\dfrac{2}{3} \neq 2\left(n+\dfrac{1}{4}\right)$

97. $\underbrace{\text{The sum of } t \text{ and six}}\ \underbrace{\text{is not more than}}\ \underbrace{\text{negative twelve}}$.

$ t + 6 \leq -12$

or $t + 6 \leq -12$

98. $(M + 5) + P = M + (5 + P)$: Associative Property of Addition

99. $5(3x - 4) = 15x - 20$: Distributive Property

100. $(-4) + 4 = 0$: Additive Inverse Property

101. $(3 + x) + 7 = 7 + (3 + x)$: Commutative Property of Addition

102. Associative and Commutative Properties of Multiplication
To see this: $(XY)Z = X(YZ) = (YZ)X$

103. $\left(-\dfrac{3}{5}\right)\cdot\left(-\dfrac{5}{3}\right) = 1$: Multiplicative Inverse Property

104. $T \cdot 0 = 0$: Multiplication Property of Zero

105. $(ab)c = a(bc)$: Associative Property of Multiplication

106. $A + 0 = A$: Additive Identity Property

107. $8 \cdot 1 = 8$: Multiplicative Identity Property

108. $5x - 15z = 5(x - 3z)$

109. $(7 + y) + (3 + x) = (3 + x) + (7 + y)$

110. $0 = 2 + (-2)$, for example

111. $1 = 2 \cdot \dfrac{1}{2}$, for example

112. $[(3.4)(0.7)]5 = (3.4)[(0.7)(5)]$

113. $7 = 7 + 0$

114. $-9 > -12$, since -9 is to the right of -12 on the number line.

115. $0 > -6$, since 0 is to the right of -6 on the number line.

116. $-3 < -1$, since -3 is to the left of -1 on the number line.

117. $7 = |-7|$

118. $-5 < -(-5)$, since $-(-5) = 5$.

119. $-(-2) > -2$, since $-(-2) = 2$.

120. The opposite of $-\dfrac{3}{4}$ is $\dfrac{3}{4}$.

The reciprocal of $-\dfrac{3}{4}$ is $-\dfrac{4}{3}$.

121. If the opposite of the number is -5, then the number is $-(-5) = 5$. The reciprocal of 5 is $\dfrac{1}{5}$.

122. $-2\left(5x + \dfrac{1}{2}\right) + 7.1 = -2 \cdot 5x + (-2) \cdot \dfrac{1}{2} + 7.1$

$= -10x - 1 + 7.1$

$= -10x + 6.1$

123. $\sqrt{36} \div 2 \cdot 3 = 6 \div 2 \cdot 3 = 3 \cdot 3 = 9$

124. $-\dfrac{7}{11} - \left(-\dfrac{1}{11}\right) = -\dfrac{7}{11} + \dfrac{1}{11} = -\dfrac{6}{11}$

125. $10 - (-1) + (-2) + 6 = 10 + 1 + (-2) + 6$

$= 11 + (-2) + 6$

$= 9 + 6$

$= 15$

126. $\left(-\dfrac{2}{3}\right)^3 \div \dfrac{10}{9} = -\dfrac{8}{27} \div \dfrac{10}{9}$

$= -\dfrac{8}{27} \cdot \dfrac{9}{10}$

$= -\dfrac{2 \cdot 4 \cdot 9}{3 \cdot 9 \cdot 2 \cdot 5}$

$= -\dfrac{4}{15}$

127. $\dfrac{(3-5)^2 + (-1)^3}{1 + 2(3 - (-1))^2} = \dfrac{(-2)^2 + (-1)^3}{1 + 2(3+1)^2}$

$= \dfrac{4 + (-1)}{1 + 2(4)^2}$

$= \dfrac{3}{1 + 2(16)}$

$= \dfrac{3}{1 + 32}$

$= \dfrac{3}{33}$

$= \dfrac{1}{11}$

128. $\dfrac{1}{3}(9x - 3y) - (4x - 1) + 4y$

$= \dfrac{1}{3} \cdot 9x - \dfrac{1}{3} \cdot 3y - 4x + 1 + 4y$

$= 3x - y - 4x + 1 + 4y$

$= 3x - 4x - y + 4y + 1$

$= -x + 3y + 1$

129. 1976: $76.8 - 75 = 1.8$
1981: $77.8 - 76.8 = 1.0$
1986: $78.2 - 77.8 = 0.4$
1991: $78.9 - 78.2 = 0.7$
1996: $79.1 - 78.9 = 0.2$
2001: $79.8 - 79.1 = 0.7$
2006: $80.8 - 79.8 = 1.0$

Year	Increase in Life Expectancy (in Years) from 5 Years Earlier
1976	1.8
1981	1.0
1986	0.4
1991	0.7
1996	0.2
2001	0.7
2006	1.0

Chapter 1 Test

1. True; -2.3 lies to the right of -2.33 on the number line.

2. False; $-6^2 = -36$, while $(-6)^2 = 36$.

3. False; $-5 - 8 = -13$, while $-(5 - 8) = -(-3) = 3$.

4. False; $(-2)(-3)(0) = 0$, while $\dfrac{(-4)}{0}$ is undefined.

5. True

6. False; for example, $\dfrac{1}{2}$ is a rational number that is not an integer.

7. $5 - 12 \div 3(2) = 5 - 4(2) = 5 - 8 = -3$

8. $5^2 - 3^4 = 25 - 81 = -56$

9. $(4-9)^3 - |{-4} - 6|^2 = (-5)^3 - |{-10}|^2$
$$\begin{aligned}
&= -125 - 10^2 \\
&= -125 - 100 \\
&= -225
\end{aligned}$$

10. $12 + \{6 - [5 - 2(-5)]\} = 12 + \{6 - [5 + 10]\}$
$$\begin{aligned}
&= 12 + (6 - 15) \\
&= 12 + (-9) \\
&= 12 - 9 \\
&= 3
\end{aligned}$$

11. $\dfrac{6(7-9)^3 + (-2)}{(-2)(-5)(-5)} = \dfrac{6(-2)^3 - 2}{10(-5)}$
$$\begin{aligned}
&= \dfrac{6(-8) - 2}{-50} \\
&= \dfrac{-48 - 2}{-50} \\
&= \dfrac{-50}{-50} \\
&= 1
\end{aligned}$$

12. $\dfrac{\left(4 - \sqrt{16}\right) - (-7 - 20)}{-2(1-4)^2} = \dfrac{(4-4) - (-27)}{-2(-3)^2}$
$$\begin{aligned}
&= \dfrac{0 + 27}{-2(9)} \\
&= \dfrac{27}{-18} \\
&= -\dfrac{3}{2}
\end{aligned}$$

13. Let $q = 4$ and $r = -2$.
$q^2 - r^2 = (4)^2 - (-2)^2 = 16 - 4 = 12$

14. Let $q = 4$, $r = -2$, and $t = 1$.
$\dfrac{5t - 3q}{3r - 1} = \dfrac{5(1) - 3(4)}{3(-2) - 1} = \dfrac{5 - 12}{-6 - 1} = \dfrac{-7}{-7} = 1$

15. a. When $x = 1$, $5.75x = 5.75(1) = 5.75$.
     When $x = 3$, $5.75x = 5.75(3) = 17.25$.
     When $x = 10$, $5.75x = 5.75(10) = 57.50$.
     When $x = 20$, $5.75x = 5.75(20) = 115.00$.

x	1	3	10	20
$5.75x$	5.75	17.25	57.50	115.00

  b. As the number of adults increases the total cost increases.

16. $\underbrace{\text{Twice}}\ \underbrace{\text{the sum of } x \text{ and five}}\ \underbrace{\text{is}}\ \underbrace{30}.$

$\quad 2\cdot \qquad\qquad (x+5) \qquad\quad = 30$

or $2(x+5) = 30$

17. $\underbrace{\text{The square of the difference of six and } y}\ \underbrace{\text{divided by}}\ \underbrace{\text{seven}}\ \underbrace{\text{is not equal to}}\ \underbrace{10}.$

$\qquad\qquad (6-y)^2 \qquad\qquad\qquad \div \qquad 7 \qquad \neq \qquad 10$

or $\dfrac{(6-y)^2}{7} \neq 10$

18. $\underbrace{\text{The product of nine and } z}, \ \underbrace{\text{divided by}}\ \underbrace{\text{the absolute value of } -12}\ \underbrace{\text{is not equal to}}\ \underbrace{10}.$

$\qquad\quad 9z \qquad\qquad \div \qquad\qquad |-12| \qquad\qquad \neq \qquad 10$

or $\dfrac{9z}{|-12|} \neq 10$

19. $\underbrace{\text{Three}}\ \underbrace{\text{times}}\ \underbrace{\text{the quotient of } n \text{ and five}}\ \underbrace{\text{is}}\ \underbrace{\text{the opposite of } n}.$

$\quad 3 \qquad \cdot \qquad\qquad \dfrac{n}{5} \qquad\qquad = \qquad -n$

or $3\left(\dfrac{n}{5}\right) = -n$

20. $\underbrace{\text{Twenty}}\ \underbrace{\text{is equal to}}\ \underbrace{6 \text{ subtracted from twice } x}.$

$\quad 20 \qquad = \qquad\qquad 2x-6$

or $20 = 2x - 6$

21. $\underbrace{\text{Negative two}}\ \underbrace{\text{is equal to}}\ \underbrace{x}\ \underbrace{\text{divided by}}\ \underbrace{\text{the sum of } x \text{ and five}}.$

$\quad -2 \qquad = \qquad x \qquad \div \qquad\qquad (x+5)$

or $-2 = \dfrac{x}{x+5}$

22. $6(x-4) = 6x - 24$: Distributive Property

23. $(4+x)+z = 4+(x+z)$: Associative Property of Addition

24. $(-7)+7 = 0$: Additive Inverse Property

25. $(-18)(0) = 0$: Multiplication Property of Zero

26. Let 0.05 be the value of each nickel and 0.1 be the value of each dime. If there are n nickels, and d dimes, then the total amount of money is $0.05n + 0.1d$.

27. $-2(3x + 7) = -6x - 14$

28.
$$\frac{1}{3}a - \frac{3}{8} + \frac{1}{6}a - \frac{3}{4} = \frac{1}{3}a + \frac{1}{6}a - \frac{3}{8} - \frac{3}{4}$$
$$= \left(\frac{1}{3} + \frac{1}{6}\right)a - \frac{3}{8} - \frac{3}{4}$$
$$= \left(\frac{2}{6} + \frac{1}{6}\right)a - \frac{3}{8} - \frac{6}{8}$$
$$= \left(\frac{3}{6}\right)a - \frac{9}{8}$$
$$= \frac{1}{2}a - \frac{9}{8}$$

29.
$$4y + 10 - 2(y + 10) = 4y + 10 - 2y - 20$$
$$= 4y - 2y + 10 - 20$$
$$= (4 - 2)y - 10$$
$$= 2y - 10$$

30.
$$(8.3x - 2.9) - (9.6x - 4.8)$$
$$= 8.3x - 2.9 - 9.6x + 4.8$$
$$= 8.3x - 9.6x - 2.9 + 4.8$$
$$= (8.3 - 9.6)x + 1.9$$
$$= -1.3x + 1.9$$

Chapter 2

Section 2.1

Practice Exercises

1.
$$3x + 7 = 22$$
$$3x + 7 - 7 = 22 - 7$$
$$3x = 15$$
$$\frac{3x}{3} = \frac{15}{3}$$
$$x = 5$$

2.
$$2.5 = 3 - 2.5t$$
$$2.5 - 3 = 3 - 2.5t - 3$$
$$-0.5 = -2.5t$$
$$\frac{-0.5}{-2.5} = \frac{-2.5t}{-2.5}$$
$$0.2 = t$$

3.
$$-8x - 4 + 6x = 5x + 11 - 4x$$
$$-2x - 4 = x + 11$$
$$-2x - 4 - x = x + 11 - x$$
$$-3x - 4 = 11$$
$$-3x - 4 + 4 = 11 + 4$$
$$-3x = 15$$
$$\frac{-3x}{-3} = \frac{15}{-3}$$
$$x = -5$$

4.
$$3(x - 5) = 6x - 3$$
$$3x - 15 = 6x - 3$$
$$3x - 15 - 6x = 6x - 3 - 6x$$
$$-3x - 15 = -3$$
$$-3x - 15 + 15 = -3 + 15$$
$$-3x = 12$$
$$\frac{-3x}{-3} = \frac{12}{-3}$$
$$x = -4$$

5.
$$\frac{y}{2} - \frac{y}{5} = \frac{1}{4}$$
$$20\left(\frac{y}{2} - \frac{y}{5}\right) = 20\left(\frac{1}{4}\right)$$
$$20\left(\frac{y}{2}\right) - 20\left(\frac{y}{5}\right) = 5$$
$$10y - 4y = 5$$
$$6y = 5$$
$$\frac{6y}{6} = \frac{5}{6}$$
$$y = \frac{5}{6}$$

6.
$$x - \frac{x - 2}{12} = \frac{x + 3}{4} + \frac{1}{4}$$
$$12\left(x - \frac{x - 2}{12}\right) = 12\left(\frac{x + 3}{4} + \frac{1}{4}\right)$$
$$12 \cdot x - 12\left(\frac{x - 2}{12}\right) = 12\left(\frac{x + 3}{4}\right) + 12 \cdot \frac{1}{4}$$
$$12x - (x - 2) = 3(x + 3) + 3$$
$$12x - x + 2 = 3x + 9 + 3$$
$$11x + 2 = 3x + 12$$
$$11x + 2 - 3x = 3x + 12 - 3x$$
$$8x + 2 = 12$$
$$8x + 2 - 2 = 12 - 2$$
$$8x = 10$$
$$\frac{8x}{8} = \frac{10}{8}$$
$$x = \frac{5}{4}$$

7.
$$0.15x - 0.03 = 0.2x + 0.12$$
$$100(0.15x - 0.03) = 100(0.2x + 0.12)$$
$$100(0.15x) - 100(0.03) = 100(0.2x) + 100(0.12)$$
$$15x - 3 = 20x + 12$$
$$15x - 20x = 12 + 3$$
$$-5x = 15$$
$$\frac{-5x}{-5} = \frac{15}{-5}$$
$$x = -3$$

8.
$$4x - 3 = 4(x + 5)$$
$$4x - 3 = 4x + 20$$
$$4x - 3 - 4x = 4x + 20 - 4x$$
$$-3 = 20$$

This equation is false no matter what value the variable x might have. Thus, there is no solution. The solution set is { } or $\varnothing$.

9.
$$5x - 2 = 3 + 5(x - 1)$$
$$5x - 2 = 3 + 5x - 5$$
$$5x - 2 = -2 + 5x$$
$$5x - 2 + 2 = -2 + 5x + 2$$
$$5x = 5x$$
$$5x - 5x = 5x - 5x$$
$$0 = 0$$

Since $0 = 0$ is a true statement for every value of x, all real numbers are solutions. The solution set is $\{x | x$ is a real number$\}$.

Vocabulary and Readiness Check

1. Equations with the same solution set are called equivalent equations.

2. A value for the variable in an equation that makes the equation a true statement is called a solution of the equation.

3. By the addition property of equality, $y = -3$ and $y - 7 = -3 - 7$ are equivalent equations.

4. By the multiplication property of equality,
$2y = -3$ and $\dfrac{2y}{2} = \dfrac{-3}{2}$ are equivalent equations.

5. $\dfrac{1}{3}x - 5$ expression

6. $2(x - 3) = 7$ equation

7. $\dfrac{5}{9}x + \dfrac{1}{3} = \dfrac{2}{9} - x$ equation

8. $\dfrac{5}{9}x + \dfrac{1}{3} - \dfrac{2}{9} - x$ expression

9. $2x + 3 = 2x + 3$
Since the two sides of the equation are identical, the equation is true for any value of x. All real numbers are solutions.

10. $2x + 1 = 2x + 3$
Adding 1 to a number and adding 3 to the same number will not result in equal numbers for any value of x. There is no solution.

11. $5x - 2 = 5x - 7$
Subtracting 2 from a number and subtracting 7 from the same number will not result in equal numbers for any value of x. There is no solution.

12. $5x - 3 = 5x - 3$
Since the two sides of the equation are identical, the equation is true for any value of x. All real numbers are solutions.

Exercise Set 2.1

1. $-5x = -30$
$$\frac{-5x}{-5} = \frac{-30}{-5}$$
$$x = 6$$
Check: $-5x = -30$
$$-5(6) \stackrel{?}{=} -30$$
$$-30 = -30 \quad \text{True}$$
The solution is 6.

3. $-10 = x + 12$
$$-10 - 12 = x + 12 - 12$$
$$-22 = x$$
Check: $-10 = x + 12$
$$-10 \stackrel{?}{=} -22 + 12$$
$$-10 = -10 \quad \text{True}$$
The solution is -22.

5. $x - 2.8 = 1.9$
$$x - 2.8 + 2.8 = 1.9 + 2.8$$
$$x = 4.7$$
Check: $x - 2.8 = 1.9$
$$4.7 - 2.8 \stackrel{?}{=} 1.9$$
$$1.9 = 1.9 \quad \text{True}$$
The solution is 4.7.

7. $5x - 4 = 26 + 2x$
$$5x - 2x = 26 + 4$$
$$3x = 30$$
$$\frac{3x}{3} = \frac{30}{3}$$
$$x = 10$$
Check: $5x - 4 = 26 + 2x$
$$5(10) - 4 \stackrel{?}{=} 26 + 2(10)$$
$$50 - 4 \stackrel{?}{=} 26 + 20$$
$$46 = 46 \quad \text{True}$$
The solution is 10.

9.
$$-4.1 - 7z = 3.6$$
$$-4.1 - 7z + 4.1 = 3.6 + 4.1$$
$$-7z = 7.7$$
$$\frac{-7z}{-7} = \frac{7.7}{-7}$$
$$z = -1.1$$

Check:
$$-4.1 - 7z = 3.6$$
$$-4.1 - 7(-1.1) \stackrel{?}{=} 3.6$$
$$-4.1 + 7.7 \stackrel{?}{=} 3.6$$
$$3.6 = 3.6 \quad \text{True}$$

The solution is -1.1.

11.
$$5y + 12 = 2y - 3$$
$$5y + 12 - 2y = 2y - 3 - 2y$$
$$3y + 12 = -3$$
$$3y + 12 - 12 = -3 - 12$$
$$3y = -15$$
$$\frac{3y}{3} = \frac{-15}{3}$$
$$y = -5$$

Check:
$$5y + 12 = 2y - 3$$
$$5(-5) + 12 \stackrel{?}{=} 2(-5) - 3$$
$$-25 + 12 \stackrel{?}{=} -10 - 3$$
$$-13 = -13 \quad \text{True}$$

The solution is -5.

13.
$$3x - 4 - 5x = x + 4 + x$$
$$-4 - 2x = 2x + 4$$
$$-2x - 2x = 4 + 4$$
$$-4x = 8$$
$$x = -2$$

Check:
$$3x - 4 - 5x = x + 4 + x$$
$$3(-2) - 4 - 5(-2) \stackrel{?}{=} -2 + 4 - 2$$
$$-6 - 4 + 10 \stackrel{?}{=} 0$$
$$0 = 0 \quad \text{True}$$

The solution is -2.

15.
$$8x - 5x + 3 = x - 7 + 10$$
$$3x + 3 = x + 3$$
$$2x = 0$$
$$x = 0$$

Check:
$$8x - 5x + 3 = x - 7 + 10$$
$$8(0) - 5(0) + 3 \stackrel{?}{=} (0) - 7 + 10$$
$$0 + 3 \stackrel{?}{=} 3$$
$$3 = 3 \quad \text{True}$$

The solution is 0.

17.
$$5x + 12 = 2(2x + 7)$$
$$5x + 12 = 4x + 14$$
$$x + 12 = 14$$
$$x = 2$$

Check:
$$5x + 12 = 2(2x + 7)$$
$$5(2) + 12 \stackrel{?}{=} 2(2(2) + 7)$$
$$10 + 12 \stackrel{?}{=} 2(4 + 7)$$
$$22 \stackrel{?}{=} 2(11)$$
$$22 = 22 \quad \text{True}$$

The solution is 2.

19.
$$3(x - 6) = 5x$$
$$3x - 18 = 5x$$
$$-18 = 2x$$
$$-9 = x$$

Check:
$$3(x - 6) = 5x$$
$$3((-9) - 6) \stackrel{?}{=} 5(-9)$$
$$3(-15) \stackrel{?}{=} -45$$
$$-45 = -45 \quad \text{True}$$

The solution is -9.

21.
$$-2(5y - 1) - y = -4(y - 3)$$
$$-10y + 2 - y = -4y + 12$$
$$-7y + 2 = 12$$
$$-7y = 10$$
$$y = -\frac{10}{7}$$

Check:
$$-2(5y - 1) - y = -4(y - 3)$$
$$-2\left(5\left(-\frac{10}{7}\right) - 1\right) - \left(-\frac{10}{7}\right) \stackrel{?}{=} -4\left(\left(-\frac{10}{7}\right) - 3\right)$$
$$-2\left(-\frac{50}{7} - 1\right) + \frac{10}{7} \stackrel{?}{=} -4\left(-\frac{31}{7}\right)$$
$$-2\left(-\frac{57}{7}\right) + \frac{10}{7} \stackrel{?}{=} \frac{124}{7}$$
$$\frac{114}{7} + \frac{10}{7} \stackrel{?}{=} \frac{124}{7}$$
$$\frac{124}{7} = \frac{124}{7} \quad \text{True}$$

The solution is $-\dfrac{10}{7}$.

23. $\dfrac{x}{2} + \dfrac{x}{3} = \dfrac{3}{4}$

$12\left(\dfrac{x}{2} + \dfrac{x}{3}\right) = 12\left(\dfrac{3}{4}\right)$

$6x + 4x = 9$

$10x = 9$

$x = \dfrac{9}{10}$

Check: $\dfrac{x}{2} + \dfrac{x}{3} = \dfrac{3}{4}$

$\dfrac{9}{10}\cdot\dfrac{1}{2} + \dfrac{9}{10}\cdot\dfrac{1}{3} \overset{?}{=} \dfrac{3}{4}$

$\dfrac{9}{20} + \dfrac{3}{10} \overset{?}{=} \dfrac{3}{4}$

$\dfrac{3}{4} = \dfrac{3}{4}$ True

The solution is $\dfrac{9}{10}$.

25. $\dfrac{3t}{4} - \dfrac{t}{2} = 1$

$4\left(\dfrac{3t}{4} - \dfrac{t}{2}\right) = 4(1)$

$3t - 2t = 4$

$t = 4$

Check: $\dfrac{3t}{4} - \dfrac{t}{2} = 1$

$\dfrac{3(4)}{4} - \dfrac{(4)}{2} \overset{?}{=} 1$

$3 - 2 \overset{?}{=} 1$

$1 = 1$ True

The solution is 4.

27. $\dfrac{n-3}{4} + \dfrac{n+5}{7} = \dfrac{5}{14}$

$28\left(\dfrac{n-3}{4}\right) + 28\left(\dfrac{n+5}{7}\right) = 28\left(\dfrac{5}{14}\right)$

$7(n-3) + 4(n+5) = 2(5)$

$7n - 21 + 4n + 20 = 10$

$11n - 1 = 10$

$11n = 11$

$n = 1$

Check: $\dfrac{n-3}{4} + \dfrac{n+5}{7} = \dfrac{5}{14}$

$\dfrac{(1)-3}{4} + \dfrac{(1)+5}{7} \overset{?}{=} \dfrac{5}{14}$

$\dfrac{-2}{4} + \dfrac{6}{7} \overset{?}{=} \dfrac{5}{14}$

$\dfrac{-1}{2} + \dfrac{6}{7} \overset{?}{=} \dfrac{5}{14}$

$-\dfrac{7}{14} + \dfrac{12}{14} \overset{?}{=} \dfrac{5}{14}$

$\dfrac{5}{14} = \dfrac{5}{14}$ True

The solution is 1.

29. $0.6x - 10 = 1.4x - 14$

$-0.8x - 10 = -14$

$-0.8x = -4$

$x = 5$

Check: $0.6x - 10 = 1.4x - 14$

$0.6(5) - 10 \overset{?}{=} 1.4(5) - 14$

$3 - 10 \overset{?}{=} 7 - 14$

$-7 = -7$ True

The solution is 5.

31. $\dfrac{3x-1}{9} + x = \dfrac{3x+1}{3} + 4$

$9\left(\dfrac{3x-1}{9} + x\right) = 9\left(\dfrac{3x+1}{3} + 4\right)$

$(3x-1) + 9x = 3(3x+1) + 36$

$3x - 1 + 9x = 9x + 3 + 36$

$12x = 9x + 40$

$3x = 40$

$x = \dfrac{40}{3}$

Check: $\dfrac{3x-1}{9} + x = \dfrac{3x+1}{3} + 4$

$\dfrac{3\left(\frac{40}{3}\right)-1}{9} + \dfrac{40}{3} \overset{?}{=} \dfrac{3\left(\frac{40}{3}\right)+1}{3} + 4$

$\dfrac{39}{9} + \dfrac{120}{9} \overset{?}{=} \dfrac{41}{3} + \dfrac{12}{3}$

$\dfrac{53}{3} = \dfrac{53}{3}$ True

The solution is $\dfrac{40}{3}$.

33.
$$1.5(4-x) = 1.3(2-x)$$
$$10[1.5(4-x)] = 10[1.3(2-x)]$$
$$15(4-x) = 13(2-x)$$
$$60-15x = 26-13x$$
$$-2x = -34$$
$$x = 17$$
Check: $1.5(4-x) = 1.3(2-x)$
$$1.5(4-17) \overset{?}{=} 1.3(2-17)$$
$$1.5(-13) \overset{?}{=} 1.3(-15)$$
$$-19.5 = -19.5 \quad \text{True}$$
The solution is 17.

35.
$$4(n+3) = 2(6+2n)$$
$$4n+12 = 12+4n$$
$$0 = 0$$
This is true for all x. Therefore, all real numbers are solutions.

37.
$$3(x+1)+5 = 3x+2$$
$$3x+3+5 = 3x+2$$
$$3x+8 = 3x+2$$
$$8 = 2$$
This is false for any x. Therefore, no solution exists, $\varnothing$.

39.
$$2(x-8)+x = 3(x-6)+2$$
$$2x-16+x = 3x-18+2$$
$$3x-16 = 3x-16$$
$$0 = 0$$
This is true for all x. Therefore, all real numbers are solutions.

41.
$$4(x+5) = 3(x-4)+x$$
$$4x+20 = 3x-12+x$$
$$4x+20 = 4x-12$$
$$20 = -12$$
This is false for any x. Therefore, no solution exists, $\varnothing$.

43.
$$\frac{3}{8}+\frac{b}{3} = \frac{5}{12}$$
$$24\left(\frac{3}{8}\right)+24\left(\frac{b}{3}\right) = 24\left(\frac{5}{12}\right)$$
$$9+8b = 10$$
$$8b = 1$$
$$b = \frac{1}{8}$$

45.
$$x-10 = -6x-10$$
$$x+6x = -10+10$$
$$7x = 0$$
$$x = 0$$

47.
$$5(x-2)+2x = 7(x+4)-38$$
$$5x-10+2x = 7x+28-38$$
$$7x-10 = 7x-10$$
$$0 = 0$$
This is true for all x. Therefore, all real numbers are solutions.

49.
$$y+0.2 = 0.6(y+3)$$
$$y+0.2 = 0.6y+1.8$$
$$0.4y = 1.6$$
$$y = 4$$

51.
$$\frac{1}{4}(a+2) = \frac{1}{6}(5-a)$$
$$\frac{1}{4}a+\frac{1}{2} = \frac{5}{6}-\frac{1}{6}a$$
$$\frac{1}{4}a+\frac{1}{6}a = \frac{5}{6}-\frac{1}{2}$$
$$\frac{3}{12}a+\frac{2}{12}a = \frac{5}{6}-\frac{3}{6}$$
$$\frac{5}{12}a = \frac{2}{6}$$
$$a = \frac{2}{6}\cdot\frac{12}{5}$$
$$a = \frac{4}{5}$$

53.
$$2y+5(y-4) = 4y-2(y-10)$$
$$2y+5y-20 = 4y-2y+20$$
$$7y-20 = 2y+20$$
$$7y-2y = 20+20$$
$$5y = 40$$
$$y = 8$$

55.
$$6x-2(x-3) = 4(x+1)+4$$
$$6x-2x+6 = 4x+4+4$$
$$4x+6 = 4x+8$$
$$4x-4x = 8-6$$
$$0 = 2$$
This is false for any x. Therefore, the solution set is $\varnothing$.

57.
$$\frac{m-4}{3}-\frac{3m-1}{5} = 1$$
$$15\left(\frac{m-4}{3}\right)-15\left(\frac{3m-1}{5}\right) = 15(1)$$
$$5(m-4)-3(3m-1) = 15$$
$$5m-20-9m+3 = 15$$
$$-4m-17 = 15$$
$$-4m = 32$$
$$m = -8$$

59. $8x - 12 - 3x = 9x - 7$
$5x - 12 = 9x - 7$
$5x - 9x = -7 + 12$
$-4x = 5$
$x = -\dfrac{5}{4}$

61. $-(3x - 5) - (2x - 6) + 1 = -5(x - 1) - (3x + 2) + 3$
$-3x + 5 - 2x + 6 + 1 = -5x + 5 - 3x - 2 + 3$
$-5x + 12 = -8x + 6$
$3x = -6$
$x = -2$

63. $\dfrac{1}{3}(y + 4) + 6 = \dfrac{1}{4}(3y - 1) - 2$
$12\left[\dfrac{1}{3}(y + 4) + 6\right] = 12\left[\dfrac{1}{4}(3y - 1) - 2\right]$
$4(y + 4) + 12 \cdot 6 = 3(3y - 1) - 12 \cdot 2$
$4y + 16 + 72 = 9y - 3 - 24$
$4y + 88 = 9y - 27$
$-5y = -115$
$y = 23$

65. $2[7 - 5(1 - n)] + 8n = -16 + 3[6(n + 1) - 3n]$
$2[7 - 5 + 5n] + 8n = -16 + 3[6n + 6 - 3n]$
$2(2 + 5n) + 8n = -16 + 3(3n + 6)$
$4 + 10n + 8n = -16 + 9n + 18$
$4 + 18n = 2 + 9n$
$9n = -2$
$n = -\dfrac{2}{9}$

67. Quotient means to divide. The quotient of 8 and a number: $\dfrac{8}{x}$

69. Product means to multiply. The product of 8 and a number: $8x$

71. Five subtracted from twice a number: $2x - 5$

73. Subtract 19 instead of adding;
$3x + 19 = 13$
$2x = -6$
$\dfrac{2x}{2} = \dfrac{-6}{2}$
$x = -3$

75. $0.4 - 1.6 = -1.2$, not 1.2;
$9x + 1.6 = 4x + 0.4$
$5x = -1.2$
$\dfrac{5x}{5} = \dfrac{-1.2}{5}$
$x = -0.24$

77. a. $4(x + 1) + 1 = 4x + 4 + 1 = 4x + 5$

   b. $4(x + 1) + 1 = -7$
$4x + 4 + 1 = -7$
$4x + 5 = -7$
$4x = -12$
$x = -3$
The solution is -3.

   c. Answers may vary

79. Answers may vary

81. $3.2x + 4 = 5.4x - 7$
$3.2x + 4 - 4 = 5.4x - 7 - 4$
$3.2x = 5.4x - 11$
From this we see that $K = -11$.

83. $\dfrac{7}{11}x + 9 = \dfrac{3}{11}x - 14$
$\dfrac{7}{11}x + 9 - 9 = \dfrac{3}{11}x - 14 - 9$
$\dfrac{7}{11}x = \dfrac{3}{11}x - 23$
From this we see that $K = -23$.

85. Answers may vary

87. $x(x - 6) + 7 = x(x + 1)$
$x^2 - 6x + 7 = x^2 + x$
$-6x + 7 = x$
$7 = 7x$
$1 = x$

89. $3x(x + 5) - 12 = 3x^2 + 10x + 3$
$3x^2 + 15x - 12 = 3x^2 + 10x + 3$
$15x - 12 = 10x + 3$
$5x = 15$
$x = 3$

91. $2.569x = -12.48534$

$$\frac{2.569x}{2.569} = \frac{-12.48534}{2.569}$$

$$x = -4.86$$

Check: $2.569x = -12.48534$

$2.569(-4.86) \stackrel{?}{=} -12.48534$

$-12.48534 = -12.48534$ True

The solution is -4.86.

93. $2.86z - 8.1258 = -3.75$

$$2.86z = 4.3758$$

$$\frac{2.86z}{2.86} = \frac{4.3758}{2.86}$$

$$z = 1.53$$

Check: $2.86z - 8.1258 = -3.75$

$2.86(1.53) - 8.1258 \stackrel{?}{=} -3.75$

$-3.75 = -3.75$ True

The solution is 1.53.

Section 2.2

Practice Exercises

1. a.   In words:

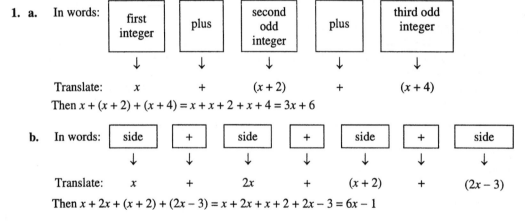

Translate: x $+$ $(x+2)$ $+$ $(x+4)$

Then $x + (x+2) + (x+4) = x + x + 2 + x + 4 = 3x + 6$

   b.   In words:

Translate: x $+$ $2x$ $+$ $(x+2)$ $+$ $(2x-3)$

Then $x + 2x + (x+2) + (2x-3) = x + 2x + x + 2 + 2x - 3 = 6x - 1$

2. If x = number of arrivals and departures at Frankfurt airport,
then $x + 15.7$ = number at London, and $x + 1.6$ = number at Paris.

Translate: x $+$ $(x+15.7)$ $+$ $(x+1.6)$

Then $x + (x+15.7) + (x+1.6) = x + x + 15.7 + x + 1.6 = 3x + 17.3$

3. Let x = the first number, then $3x - 8$ = the second number, and $5x$ = the third number.
The sum of the three numbers is 118.
$$x + (3x - 8) + 5x = 118$$
$$x + 3x + 5x - 8 = 118$$
$$9x - 8 = 118$$
$$9x = 126$$
$$x = 14$$
The numbers are 14, $3x - 8 = 3(14) - 8 = 34$, and $5x = 5(14) = 70$.

4. Let x = the original price. Then $0.4x$ = the discount. The original price, minus the discount, is equal to $270.
$$x - 0.4x = 270$$
$$0.6x = 270$$
$$x = \frac{270}{0.6} = 450$$
The original price was $450.

5. Let x = width, then $2x - 16$ = length.
The perimeter is 160 inches.
$$2(x) + 2(2x - 16) = 160$$
$$2x + 4x - 32 = 160$$
$$6x - 32 = 160$$
$$6x = 192$$
$$x = 32$$
$$2x - 16 = 2(32) - 16 = 48$$
The width is 32 inches and the length is 48 inches.

6. Let x = first odd integer, then $x + 2$ = second odd integer, and $x + 4$ = third odd integer.
The sum of the integers is 81.
$$x + (x + 2) + (x + 4) = 81$$
$$3x + 6 = 81$$
$$3x = 75$$
$$x = 25$$
$$x + 2 = 27$$
$$x + 4 = 29$$
The integers are 25, 27, and 29.

Vocabulary and Readiness Check

1. 130% of a number _>_ the number.

2. 70% of a number _<_ the number.

3. 100% of a number _=_ the number.

4. 200% of a number _>_ the number.

		First Integer	All Described Integers
5.	Four consecutive integers	31	31, 32, 33, 34
6.	Three consecutive odd integers	31	31, 33, 35
7.	Three consecutive even integers	18	18, 20, 22
8.	Four consecutive even integers	92	92, 94, 96, 98
9.	Three consecutive integers	y	$y, y + 1, y + 2$
10.	Three consecutive even integers	$z (z$ is even$)$	$z, z + 2, z + 4$
11.	Four consecutive integers	p	$p, p + 1, p + 2, p + 3$
12.	Three consecutive odd integers	s (s is odd)	$s, s + 2, s + 4$

Exercise Set 2.2

1. The perimeter is the sum of the lengths of the four sides.
    $y + y + y + y = 4y$

3. Let z = first integer, then $z + 1$ = second integer, and $z + 2$ = third integer.
    $z + (z + 1) + (z + 2) = z + z + z + 1 + 2 = 3z + 3$

5. Find the sum of x nickels worth 5¢ each, and $(x + 3)$ dimes worth 10¢ each, and $2x$ quarters worth 25¢ each.
    $$5x + 10(x + 3) + 25(2x) = 5x + 10x + 30 + 50x$$
    $$= 65x + 30$$
    The total amount is $(65x + 30)$ cents.

7. $4x + 3(2x + 1) = 4x + 6x + 3 = 10x + 3$

9. The length of the side denoted by ? is $10 - 2 = 8$. Similarly, the length of the unmarked side is
    $(x - 3) - (x - 10) = x - 3 - x + 10 = 7$.
    Thus the perimeter of the floor plan is given by $(x - 10) + 2 + 7 + 8 + (x - 3) + 10 = 2x + 14$.

11. Let x = the number.
    $$4(x - 2) = 2 + 4x + 2x$$
    $$4x - 8 = 2 + 6x$$
    $$-2x = 10$$
    $$x = -5$$
    The number is -5.

13. Let x = the first number, then
$5x$ = the second number, and
$x + 100$ = the third number.
$$x + 5x + (x + 100) = 415$$
$$7x + 100 = 415$$
$$7x = 315$$
$$x = 45$$
$5x = 225$
$x + 100 = 145$
The numbers are 45, 225, and 145.

15. 29% of $2271 = 0.29 \cdot 2271 = 658.59$;
$2271 - 658.59 = 1612.41$.
Approximately 1612.41 million acres are not federally owned.

17. 85.3% of $2748 = 0.853 \cdot 2748 \approx 2344$
Approximately 2344 minor earthquakes occurred in 2006.

19. 15% of $1500 = 0.15 \cdot 1500 = 225$
$1500 - 225 = 1275$
1275 are willing to do business with any size retailer.

21. $100\% - (55\% + 7\% + 9\% + 7\%) = 100\% - 78\%$
$$= 22\%$$

23. 7% of $5957 = 0.07 \cdot 5957 = 416.99$
About 417 employees spend more than 3 hours per day using e-mail.

25. Let x = population in 2001.
$$x + 0.054x = 31.6$$
$$1.054x = 31.6$$
$$x \approx 29.98$$
The population of Canada in 2001 was about 29.98 million.

27. $$x + 4x + (x + 6) = 180$$
$$6x + 6 = 180$$
$$6x = 174$$
$$x = 29$$
$4x = 4(29) = 116$
$x + 6 = 29 + 6 = 35$
The angles measure 29°, 35°, and 116°.

29. $$(4x) + (5x + 1) + (5x + 3) = 102$$
$$14x + 4 = 102$$
$$14x = 98$$
$$x = 7$$
$4x = 4(7) = 28$
$5x + 1 = 5(7) + 1 = 36$
$5x + 3 = 5(7) + 3 = 38$
The sides measure 28 meters, 36 meters, and 38 meters.

31. $$x + (2.5x - 9) + x + 1.5x = 99$$
$$6x - 9 = 99$$
$$6x = 108$$
$$x = 18$$
$1.5x = 1.5(18) = 27$
$2.5x - 9 = 2.5(18) - 9 = 36$
The sides measure 18 inches, 18 inches, 27 inches, and 36 inches.

33. Let x = first integer; then
$x + 1$ = next integer and
$x + 2$ = third integer.
$$x + (x + 1) + (x + 2) = 228$$
$$3x + 3 = 228$$
$$3x = 225$$
$$x = 75$$
$x + 1 = 75 + 1 = 76$
$x + 2 = 75 + 2 = 77$
The integers are 75, 76, and 77.

35. Let x = first even integer, then
$x + 2$ = second even integer, and
$x + 4$ = third even integer.
$$2x + (x + 4) = 268{,}222$$
$$3x + 4 = 268{,}222$$
$$3x = 268{,}218$$
$$x = 89{,}406$$
$x + 2 = 89{,}408$
$x + 4 = 89{,}410$
Fallon's zip code is 89406, Fernley's zip code is 89408, and Gardnerville Ranchos's zip code is 89410.

37. $$(2x - 51) + \left(\frac{3}{2}x + 3\right) + x = 780$$
$$\frac{9}{2}x - 48 = 780$$
$$\frac{9}{2}x = 828$$
$$x = 828 \cdot \frac{2}{9}$$
$$x = 184$$
$2x - 51 = 2(184) - 51 = 317$
$\frac{3}{2}x + 3 = \frac{3}{2}(184) + 3 = 279$

Occupation	Increase in Number of Jobs (in thousands) from 2000 to 2012
Security guards	317 thousand
Home health aides	279 thousand
Computer system analysts	184 thousand
Total	780 thousand

39. Let x = number of medical assistant jobs (in thousands), then $2x + 173$ = number of postsecondary teacher jobs (in thousands), and $3x - 22$ = number of registered nurse jobs (in thousands).
$$x + (2x + 173) + (3x - 22) = 1441$$
$$6x + 151 = 1441$$
$$6x = 1290$$
$$x = 215$$
$2x + 173 = 2(215) + 173 = 603$
$3x - 22 = 3(215) - 22 = 623$
The predicted job growth:
medical assistant: 215 thousand;
postsecondary teacher jobs: 603 thousand;
registered nurses: 623 thousand

41. Let x = no. of seats in the 737-200;
then $x + 21$ = no. in the 737-300 and $2x - 36$ = no. in the 757-200.
$$x + (x + 21) + (2x - 36) = 437$$
$$4x - 15 = 437$$
$$4x = 452$$
$$x = 113$$
$x + 21 = 113 + 21 = 134$
$2x - 33 = 2(113) - 36 = 190$
The 737-200 has 113 seats. The 737-300 has 134 seats. The 757-200 has 190 seats.

43. Let x = price before taxes.
$$x + 0.08x = 464.40$$
$$1.08x = 464.40$$
$$x = 430$$
The price was \$430 before taxes.

45. Let x = expected population.
$$x = 44.2 - 0.056(44.2)$$
$$x = 44.2 - 2.4752$$
$$x \approx 41.7$$
The expected population of South Africa in 2050 is 41.7 million.

47. Let x = measure of the angle; then $180 - x$ = measure of its supplement.
$$x = 3(180 - x) + 20$$
$$x = 540 - 3x + 20$$
$$4x = 560$$
$$x = 140$$
$180 - x = 180 - 140 = 40$
The angles measure 140° and 40°.

49. Let x = measure of second angle; then $2x$ = measure of first angle and $3x - 12$ = measure of third angle.
$$x + 2x + (3x - 12) = 180$$
$$6x - 12 = 180$$
$$6x = 192$$
$$x = 32$$
$2x = 2(32) = 64$
$3x - 12 = 3(32) - 12 = 84$
The angles measure 64°, 32°, and 84°.

51. Let x = the length of a side of the square. Then $x + 6$ = the length of a side of the triangle.
$$4x = 3(x + 6)$$
$$4x = 3x + 18$$
$$x = 18$$
The sides of the square are 18 cm and the sides of the triangle are 24 cm.

53. Let x = first even integer, then $x + 2$ = second even integer, and $x + 4$ = third even integer.
$$x + (x + 4) = 156$$
$$2x + 4 = 156$$
$$2x = 152$$
$$x = 76$$
$x + 2 = 78$
$x + 4 = 80$
The integers are 76, 78, and 80.

55. $$x + 5x + (6x - 3) = 483$$
$$12x - 3 = 483$$
$$12x = 486$$
$$x = 40.5$$
$5x = 5(40.5) = 202.5$
$6x - 3 = 6(40.5) - 3 = 240$
The sides measure 40.5 feet, 202.5 feet, and 240 feet.

57. $$3x + 14.6 = 197.6$$
$$3x = 183.0$$
$$x = 61.0$$
The arrivals and departures are as follows:
Los Angeles: $x = 61.0$ million
Atlanta: $x + 13.3 = 61.0 + 13.3 = 74.3$ million
Chicago: $x + 1.3 = 61.0 + 1.3 = 62.3$ million

59. Let x = hours for halogen; then
$25x$ = hours for fluorescent and
$x - 2500$ = hours for incandescent.
$$x + 25x + (x - 2500) = 105,500$$
$$27x - 2500 = 105,500$$
$$27x = 108,000$$
$$x = 4000$$
$25x = 100,000; x - 2500 = 1500$
The halogen has 4000 bulb hours.
The fluorescent has 100,000 bulb hours.
The incandescent has 1500 bulb hours.

61. Let x = height, then $2x + 12$ = length.
$$2(x) + 2(2x + 12) = 312$$
$$2x + 4x + 24 = 312$$
$$6x + 24 = 312$$
$$6x = 288$$
$$x = 48$$
$2x + 12 = 2(48) + 12 = 108$
The height is 48 inches and the length is
108 inches.

63. a. $4.7 + 0.05 \cdot 4.7 = 4.7 + 0.235 \approx 4.9$
The total sales in 2006 were \$4.9 billion.

b. $0.25 \cdot 4.9 \approx 1.23$
The amount spent on running shoes in 2006
was \$1.23 billion.

65. Let x = subscribers in Russia, then
$4x - 3.1$ = subscribers in China, and
$x + 4.3$ = subscribers in United States.
$$x + (4x - 3.1) + (x + 4.3) = 34.8$$
$$6x + 1.2 = 34.8$$
$$6x = 33.6$$
$$x = 5.6$$
$4x - 3.1 = 4(5.6) - 3.1 = 19.3$
$x + 4.3 = 5.6 + 4.3 = 9.9$
The percents of world subscribers are as follows:
Russia: 5.6%, China: 19.3%; U.S.: 9.9%.

67. Let x = pages in first book.
$x + 1.54x$ = pages in final book
$$x + 1.54x = 784$$
$$2.54x = 784$$
$$x \approx 309$$
There are 309 pages in *Harry Potter and the*
Sorcerer's Stone.

69. Let x = first odd integer (Canada), then
$x + 2$ = second odd integer (U.S.), and
$x + 4$ = third odd integer (Germany).
$$x + 2(x + 2) + 4(x + 4) = 69$$
$$x + 2x + 4 + 4x + 16 = 69$$
$$7x + 20 = 69$$
$$7x = 49$$
$$x = 7$$
$x + 2 = 9$
$x + 4 = 11$
The number of gold medals won are as follows:
Germany: 11; U.S.: 9; Canada: 7

71. $ab + 6bc = 0(-1) + 6(-1)(9) = 0 - 6(9) = -54$

73. $2n^2 + 3m^2 = 2(-2)^2 + 3(7)^2$
$$= 2(4) + 3(49)$$
$$= 8 + 147$$
$$= 155$$

75. $\dfrac{1}{3}lwh = \dfrac{1}{3}(37.8)(5.6)(7.9) = 557.424$

77. Answers may vary

79. $180 - x = 2(90 - x) + 50$
$$180 - x = 180 - 2x + 50$$
$$180 - x = 230 - 2x$$
$$x = 50$$
The angle is 50°.

81. a. $\qquad y = -49.4x + 1756.8$
$$0 = -49.4x + 1756.8$$
$$-1756.8 = -49.4x$$
$$35 \approx x$$
$1997 + 35 = 2032$
The average annual number of cigarettes
smoked will be 0 during the year 2032.

b. $y = -49.4x + 1756.8$
$y = -49.4(15) + 1756.8$
$y = 1015.8$
The predicted average annual number of
cigarettes smoked by an American adult in
2012 is 1015.8.

c. $1015.8 \div 365 \approx 3$
An American adult will smoke an average
of 3 cigarettes a day in 2012.
No; answers may vary; possible answer:
This is the daily number of cigarettes for all
American adults—smokers and non-
smokers.

83. $R = C$
$60x = 50x + 5000$
$10x = 5000$
$x = 500$
$R = 60x = 60(500) = 30,000$
$C = 50x + 5000 = 50(500) + 5000 = 30,000$
To break even, 500 boards must be sold. You need $30,000 to produce the 500 boards.

85. The company makes a profit.

Section 2.3

Practice Exercises

1. $I = Prt$
$\dfrac{I}{Pr} = \dfrac{Prt}{Pr}$
$\dfrac{I}{Pr} = t$ or $t = \dfrac{I}{Pr}$

2. $7x - 2y = 5$
$7x - 2y - 7x = 5 - 7x$
$-2y = 5 - 7x$
$\dfrac{-2y}{-2} = \dfrac{5 - 7x}{-2}$
$y = \dfrac{7}{2}x - \dfrac{5}{2}$

3. $A = P + Prt$
$A - P = P + Prt - P$
$A - P = Prt$
$\dfrac{A - P}{Pt} = \dfrac{Prt}{Pt}$
$\dfrac{A - P}{Pt} = r$ or $r = \dfrac{A - P}{Pt}$

4. Let $P = 8000$, $r = 6\% = 0.06$, $t = 4$, $n = 2$.
$A = P\left(1 + \dfrac{r}{n}\right)^{nt}$
$A = 8000\left(1 + \dfrac{0.06}{2}\right)^{2 \cdot 4}$
$A = 8000(1.03)^8$
$A \approx 8000(1.266770081)$
$A \approx 10,134.16$
Russ will have $10,134.16 in his account.

5. Let $d = 192$ and $r = 7.5$.
$d = rt$
$192 = 7.5t$
$\dfrac{192}{7.5} = \dfrac{7.5t}{7.5}$
$25.6t = t$
They spent 25.6 hours cycling, or 25 hours 36 minutes.

Exercise Set 2.3

1. $D = rt$
$\dfrac{D}{r} = \dfrac{rt}{r}$
$\dfrac{D}{r} = t$
$t = \dfrac{D}{r}$

3. $I = PRT$
$\dfrac{I}{PT} = \dfrac{PRT}{PT}$
$\dfrac{I}{PT} = R$
$R = \dfrac{I}{PT}$

5. $9x - 4y = 16$
$9x - 4y - 9x = 16 - 9x$
$-4y = 16 - 9x$
$\dfrac{-4y}{-4} = \dfrac{16 - 9x}{-4}$
$y = \dfrac{9x - 16}{4}$

7. $P = 2L + 2W$
$P - 2L = 2W$
$\dfrac{P - 2L}{2} = \dfrac{2W}{2}$
$\dfrac{P - 2L}{2} = W$
$W = \dfrac{P - 2L}{2}$

9.
$$J = AC - 3$$
$$J + 3 = AC$$
$$\frac{J+3}{C} = \frac{AC}{C}$$
$$\frac{J+3}{C} = A$$
$$A = \frac{J+3}{C}$$

11.
$$W = gh - 3gt^2$$
$$W = g(h - 3t^2)$$
$$\frac{W}{h - 3t^2} = \frac{g(h - 3t^2)}{h - 3t^2}$$
$$\frac{W}{h - 3t^2} = g$$
$$g = \frac{W}{h - 3t^2}$$

13.
$$T = C(2 + AB)$$
$$T = 2C + ABC$$
$$T - 2C = 2C + ABC - 2C$$
$$T - 2C = ABC$$
$$\frac{T - 2C}{AC} = \frac{ABC}{AC}$$
$$\frac{T - 2C}{AC} = B$$
$$B = \frac{T - 2C}{AC}$$

15.
$$C = 2\pi r$$
$$\frac{C}{2\pi} = \frac{2\pi r}{2\pi}$$
$$\frac{C}{2\pi} = r$$
$$r = \frac{C}{2\pi}$$

17.
$$E = I(r + R)$$
$$E = Ir + IR$$
$$E - IR = Ir + IR - IR$$
$$E - IR = Ir$$
$$\frac{E - IR}{I} = \frac{Ir}{I}$$
$$\frac{E - IR}{I} = r$$
$$r = \frac{E - IR}{I}$$

19.
$$s = \frac{n}{2}(a + L)$$
$$2s = 2 \cdot \frac{n}{2}(a + L)$$
$$2s = n(a + L)$$
$$2s = na + nL$$
$$2s - na = na + nL - na$$
$$2s - na = nL$$
$$\frac{2s - na}{n} = \frac{nL}{n}$$
$$\frac{2s - na}{n} = L$$
$$L = \frac{2s - na}{n}$$

21.
$$N = 3st^4 - 5sv$$
$$N - 3st^4 = 3st^4 - 5sv - 3st^4$$
$$N - 3st^4 = -5sv$$
$$\frac{N - 3st^4}{-5s} = \frac{-5sv}{-5s}$$
$$\frac{3st^4 - N}{5s} = v$$
$$v = \frac{3st^4 - N}{5s}$$

23.
$$S = 2LW + 2LH + 2WH$$
$$S - 2LW = 2LW + 2LH + 2WH - 2LW$$
$$S - 2LW = 2LH + 2WH$$
$$S - 2LW = H(2L + 2W)$$
$$\frac{S - 2LW}{2L + 2W} = \frac{H(2L + 2W)}{2L + 2W}$$
$$\frac{S - 2LW}{2L + 2W} = H$$
$$H = \frac{S - 2LW}{2L + 2W}$$

25. $A = P\left(1 + \dfrac{r}{n}\right)^{nt} = 3500\left(1 + \dfrac{0.03}{n}\right)^{10n}$

n	1	2	4
A	\$4703.71	\$4713.99	\$4719.22

n	12	365
A	\$4722.74	\$4724.45

27. $A = P\left(1+\dfrac{r}{n}\right)^{nt} = 6000\left(1+\dfrac{0.04}{n}\right)^{5n}$

a. $n = 2$

$A = 6000\left(1+\dfrac{0.04}{2}\right)^{5\cdot2} \approx 7313.97$

$7313.97

b. $n = 4$

$A = 6000\left(1+\dfrac{0.04}{4}\right)^{5\cdot4} \approx 7321.14$

$7321.14

c. $n = 12$

$A = 6000\left(1+\dfrac{0.04}{12}\right)^{5\cdot12} \approx 7325.98$

$7325.98

29. $C = \dfrac{5}{9}(F-32)$

$C = \dfrac{5}{9}(104-32)$

$C = \dfrac{5}{9}(72)$

$C = 40°$

The day's high temperature was 40°C.

31. $d = rt$

$2(90) = 50t$

$180 = 50t$

$\dfrac{180}{50} = t$

$t = 3.6$

She takes 3.6 hours or 3 hours, 36 minutes to make the round trip.

33. $A = s^2 = (64)^2 = 4096 \text{ ft}^2;\ \dfrac{4096}{24} \approx 171$

There should be 171 packages of tiles bought.

35. $A = \dfrac{1}{2}bh$

$18 = \dfrac{1}{2}(4)h$

$18 = 2h$

$9 = h$

The height is 9 feet.

37. The area of one pair of walls is $2\cdot14\cdot8 = 224 \text{ ft}^2$ and the area of the other walls is $2\cdot16\cdot8 = 256 \text{ ft}^2$ for a total of 480 ft^2. Multiplying by 2, the number of coats, yields 960 ft^2. Dividing this by 500 yields 1.92. Thus, 2 gallons should be purchased.

39. a. $V = \pi r^2 h$

$V = \pi(4.2)^2(2.12)$

$V \approx 1174.86$

The volume of the cylinder is 1174.86 cubic meters.

b. $V = \dfrac{4}{3}\pi r^3$

$V = \dfrac{4}{3}\pi(4.2)^3$

$V \approx 310.34$

The volume of the sphere is 310.34 cubic meters.

c. $V = 1174.86 + 310.34 = 1485.20$

The volume of the tank is 1485.20 cubic meters.

41. 19 hours 5 minutes $= 19\dfrac{5}{60}$ hours

$d = rt$

$2447.8 = r\left(19\dfrac{5}{60}\right)$

$128.3 \approx r$

Her average speed was 128.3 miles per hour.

43. $V = \pi r^2 h$

1 mile = 5280 feet

1.3 miles = 6864 feet

$3800 = \pi r^2(6864)$

$0.42 \approx r$

The radius of the hole is 0.42 feet.

45. $C = \pi d = \pi(41.125) = 41.125\pi \text{ ft} \approx 129.1325 \text{ ft}$

The circumference of Eartha is $41.125\pi \approx 129.1325$ feet.

47. $A = P\left(1 + \dfrac{r}{n}\right)^{nt}$

$= 10,000\left(1 + \dfrac{0.085}{4}\right)^{4 \cdot 2}$

$= 10,000(1 + 0.02125)^8$

$\approx \$11,831.96$

$\$11,831.96 - \$10,000 = \$1831.96$

49. $C = 4h + 9f + 4p$

$C - 4h - 4p = 9f$

$\dfrac{C - 4h - 4p}{9} = f$

$f = \dfrac{C - 4h - 4p}{9}$

51. $C = 4h + 9f + 4p$

$C = 4(7) + 9(14) + 4(6)$

$C = 178$

There are 178 calories in this serving.

53. $C = 4h + 9f + 4p$

$130 = 4(31) + 9(0) + 4p$

$130 = 124 + 4p$

$6 = 4p$

$\dfrac{6}{4} = p$

$p = 1.5$

There are 1.5 g of protein provided by this serving of raisins.

55. $-3, -2, -1$ satisfy $x < 0$.

57. $-3, -2, -1, 0, 1$ satisfy $x + 5 \le 6$ or $x \le 1$.

59. Answers may vary

61. $AU = \dfrac{\text{miles}}{92,900,000}$ or $\dfrac{\text{million miles}}{92.9}$

Planet	AU from Sun
Mercury	0.388
Venus	0.723
Earth	1.00
Mars	1.523
Jupiter	5.202
Saturn	9.538
Uranus	19.193
Neptune	30.065
Pluto	39.505

63. Answers may vary

$\dfrac{1,700,000,000}{250,000,000} = 6.8$

It cost \$6.80 per person to build the *Endeavor*.

65. 4 times a year; answers may vary

67. $\dfrac{168 \text{ mi}}{1 \text{ hr}} \cdot \dfrac{5280 \text{ ft}}{1 \text{ mi}} \cdot \dfrac{1 \text{ hr}}{60 \text{ min}} \cdot \dfrac{1 \text{ min}}{60 \text{ sec}} = 246.4 \text{ ft/sec}$

$d = rt$

$60.5 \text{ ft} = 246.6 \text{ ft/sec} \cdot t$

$0.25 \text{ sec} \approx t$

The ball would reach the plate in approximately 0.25 second.

69. $P(\text{yellow}) = \dfrac{2}{8} = \dfrac{1}{4}$

71. $P(\text{blue}) = \dfrac{3}{8}$

73. $P(\text{black or yellow}) = P(\text{black}) + P(\text{yellow})$

$= \dfrac{1}{8} + \dfrac{2}{8}$

$= \dfrac{3}{8}$

75. $P(\text{yellow, blue, or black})$

$= P(\text{yellow}) + P(\text{blue}) + P(\text{black})$

$= \dfrac{2}{8} + \dfrac{3}{8} + \dfrac{1}{8}$

$= \dfrac{6}{8}$

$= \dfrac{3}{4}$

77. $P(\text{red, yellow, green, blue, or black})$

$= P(\text{red}) + P(\text{yellow}) + P(\text{green}) + P(\text{blue})$

$\qquad\qquad + P(\text{black})$

$= \dfrac{1}{8} + \dfrac{2}{8} + \dfrac{1}{8} + \dfrac{3}{8} + \dfrac{1}{8}$

$= 1$

79. 1

Section 2.4

Practice Problems

1. a. $\{x|x < 3.5\}$ $(-\infty, 3.5)$

         3.5

   b. $\{x|x \geq -3\}$ $[-3, \infty)$

         −3

   c. $\{x|-1 \leq x < 4\}$ $[-1, 4)$

         −1   4

2. $x + 5 > 9$

     $x + 5 - 5 > 9 - 5$

        $x > 4$

    $(4, \infty)$

         4

3. $8x + 21 \leq 2x - 3$

    $8x + 21 - 2x \leq 2x - 3 - 2x$

      $6x + 21 \leq -3$

    $6x + 21 - 21 \leq -3 - 21$

         $6x \leq -24$

        $\dfrac{6x}{6} \leq \dfrac{-24}{6}$

          $x \leq -4$

   $(-\infty, -4]$

         −4

4. a. $\dfrac{2}{5}x \geq \dfrac{4}{15}$

     $\dfrac{5}{2} \cdot \dfrac{2}{5}x \geq \dfrac{5}{2} \cdot \dfrac{4}{15}$

         $x \geq \dfrac{2}{3}$

   $\left[\dfrac{2}{3}, \infty\right)$

         $\dfrac{2}{3}$

   b. $-2.4x < 9.6$

      $\dfrac{-2.4x}{-2.4} > \dfrac{9.6}{-2.4}$

        $x > -4$

    $(-4, \infty)$

         −4

5. $-(4x + 6) \leq 2(5x + 9) + 2x$

     $-4x - 6 \leq 10x + 18 + 2x$

      $-4x - 6 \leq 12x + 18$

   $-4x - 6 + 4x \leq 12x + 18 + 4x$

        $-6 \leq 16x + 18$

     $-6 - 18 \leq 16x + 18 - 18$

        $-24 \leq 16x$

       $\dfrac{-24}{16} \leq \dfrac{16x}{16}$

        $-\dfrac{3}{2} \leq x$

   $\left[-\dfrac{3}{2}, \infty\right)$

         $-\dfrac{3}{2}$

6. $\dfrac{3}{5}(x - 3) \geq x - 7$

    $5\left[\dfrac{3}{5}(x - 3)\right] \geq 5(x - 7)$

       $3(x - 3) \geq 5(x - 7)$

        $3x - 9 \geq 5x - 35$

    $3x - 9 - 5x \geq 5x - 35 - 5x$

       $-2x - 9 \geq -35$

    $-2x - 9 + 9 \geq -35 + 9$

        $-2x \geq -26$

       $\dfrac{-2x}{-2} \leq \dfrac{-26}{-2}$

         $x \leq 13$

   $(-\infty, 13]$

         13

7. $4(x - 2) < 4x + 5$

       $4x - 8 < 4x + 5$

    $4x - 8 - 4x < 4x + 5 - 4x$

         $-8 < 5$

This is a true statement for all values of x. The solution set is $\{x|x$ is a real number$\}$ or $(-\infty, \infty)$.

         0

8. In words:

900	+	commission (15% of sales)	$\geq$	2400

$$\downarrow \quad \downarrow \quad\quad \downarrow \quad\quad \downarrow \quad \downarrow$$

Translate: 900   +   0.15x $\geq$ 2400

$$900 + 0.15x \geq 2400$$
$$900 + 0.15x - 900 \geq 2400 - 900$$
$$0.15x \geq 1500$$
$$x \geq 10{,}000$$

Sales must be greater than or equal to $10,000 per month.

9. $-9.2t + 527.33 < 250$
$$-9.2t < -277.33$$
$$t > 30.14$$

The annual consumption of cigarettes will be less than 250 billion more than 30.14 years after 1990, or in approximately $31 + 1990 = 2021$ and after.

Vocabulary and Readiness Check

1. d. $(-\infty, -5)$

2. c. $[-11, \infty)$

3. b. $\left(-2.5, \dfrac{7}{4}\right]$

4. a. $\left[-\dfrac{10}{3}, 0.2\right)$

5. The set $\{x \mid x \geq -0.4\}$ written in interval notation is $\underline{[-0.4, \infty)}$.

6. The set $\{x \mid x < -0.4\}$ written in interval notation is $\underline{(-\infty, -0.4)}$.

7. The set $\{x \mid x \leq -0.4\}$ written in interval notation is $\underline{(-\infty, -0.4]}$.

8. The set $\{x \mid x > -0.4\}$ written in interval notation is $\underline{(-0.4, \infty)}$.

9. $3x > -14$ no

10. $-3x \leq 14$ yes

11. $-3x < -14$ yes

12. $-x \geq 23$ yes

Exercise Set 2.4

1. $\{x \mid x < -3\}$
$(-\infty, -3)$

3. $\{x | x \geq 0.3\}$
$[0.3, \infty)$

0.3

5. $\{x | -7 \leq x\}$
$[-7, \infty)$

−7

7. $\{x | -2 < x < 5\}$
$(-2, 5)$

−2   5

9. $\{x | 5 \geq x > -1\}$
$(-1, 5]$

−1   5

11. $x - 7 \geq -9$
$x \geq -2$
$[-2, \infty)$

−2

13. $7x < 6x + 1$
$x < 1$
$(-\infty, 1)$

1

15. $8x - 7 \leq 7x - 5$
$x - 7 \leq -5$
$x \leq 2$
$(-\infty, 2]$

2

17. $\dfrac{3}{4} x \geq 6$

$\dfrac{4}{3} \cdot \dfrac{3}{4} x \geq \dfrac{4}{3} \cdot 6$

$x \geq 8$
$[8, \infty)$

8

19. $5x < -23.5$
$x < -4.7$
$(-\infty, -4.7)$

−4.7

21. $-3x \geq 9$
$x \leq -3$
$(-\infty, -3]$

−3

23. $-2x + 7 \geq 9$
$-2x \geq 2$
$x \leq -1$
$(-\infty, -1]$

25. $15 + 2x \geq 4x - 7$
$15 \geq 2x - 7$
$22 \geq 2x$
$11 \geq x$ or $x \leq 11$
$(-\infty, 11]$

27. $4(2x + 1) > 4$
$8x + 4 > 4$
$8x > 0$
$x > 0$
$(0, \infty)$

29. $3(x - 5) < 2(2x - 1)$
$3x - 15 < 4x - 2$
$-15 < x - 2$
$-13 < x$
$x > -13$
$(-13, \infty)$

31. $\dfrac{5x + 1}{7} - \dfrac{2x - 6}{4} \geq -4$

$28\left(\dfrac{5x + 1}{7} - \dfrac{2x - 6}{4}\right) \geq 28(-4)$

$4(5x + 1) - 7(2x - 6) \geq -112$
$20x + 4 - 14x + 42 \geq -112$
$6x + 46 \geq -112$
$6x \geq -158$
$x \geq -\dfrac{79}{3}$

$\left[-\dfrac{79}{3}, \infty\right)$

33. $-3(2x-1) < -4[2+3(x+2)]$
$-6x+3 < -4(2+3x+6)$
$-6x+3 < -4(8+3x)$
$-6x+3 < -32-12x$
$6x+3 < -32$
$6x < -35$
$x < -\dfrac{35}{6}$
$\left(-\infty, -\dfrac{35}{6}\right)$

35. $x+9 < 3$
$x+9-9 < 3-9$
$x < -6$
$(-\infty, -6)$

37. $-x < -4$
$\dfrac{-x}{-1} > \dfrac{-4}{-1}$
$x > 4$
$(4, \infty)$

39. $-7x \le 3.5$
$\dfrac{-7x}{-7} \ge \dfrac{3.5}{-7}$
$x \ge -0.5$
$[-0.5, \infty)$

41. $\dfrac{1}{2}+\dfrac{2}{3} \ge \dfrac{x}{6}$
$6\left(\dfrac{1}{2}+\dfrac{2}{3}\right) \ge 6\left(\dfrac{x}{6}\right)$
$3+4 \ge x$
$7 \ge x$
$x \le 7$
$(-\infty, 7]$

43. $-5x+4 \le -4(x-1)$
$-5x+4 \le -4x+4$
$-x \le 0$
$x \ge 0$
$[0, \infty)$

45. $\dfrac{3}{4}(x-7) \ge x+2$
$4\left[\dfrac{3}{4}(x-7)\right] \ge 4(x+2)$
$3(x-7) \ge 4(x+2)$
$3x-21 \ge 4x+8$
$-x-21 \ge 8$
$-x \ge 29$
$x \le -29$
$(-\infty, -29]$

47. $0.8x+0.6x \ge 4.2$
$1.4x \ge 4.2$
$x \ge 3$
$[3, \infty)$

49. $4(x-6)+2x-4 \ge 3(x-7)+10x$
$4x-24+2x-4 \ge 3x-21+10x$
$6x-28 \ge 13x-21$
$-28 \ge 7x-21$
$-7 \ge 7x$
$-1 \ge x$
$x \le -1$
$(-\infty, -1]$

51. $14-(5x-6) \ge -6(x+1)-5$
$14-5x+6 \ge -6x-6-5$
$-5x+20 \ge -6x-11$
$x+20 \ge -11$
$x \ge -31$
$[-31, \infty)$

53. $\dfrac{1}{2}(3x-4) \le \dfrac{3}{4}(x-6)+1$
$4\left[\dfrac{1}{2}(3x-4)\right] \le 4\left[\dfrac{3}{4}(x-6)+1\right]$
$2(3x-4) \le 3(x-6)+4$
$6x-8 \le 3x-18+4$
$6x-8 \le 3x-14$
$3x-8 \le -14$
$3x \le -6$
$x \le -2$
$(-\infty, -2]$

55. $\dfrac{-x+2}{2}-\dfrac{1-5x}{8}<-1$

$8\left(\dfrac{-x+2}{2}-\dfrac{1-5x}{8}\right)<8(-1)$

$4(-x+2)-(1-5x)<-8$

$-4x+8-1+5x<-8$

$x+7<-8$

$x<-15$

$(-\infty,-15)$

57. $\dfrac{x+5}{5}-\dfrac{3+x}{8}\ge-\dfrac{3}{10}$

$40\left(\dfrac{x+5}{5}-\dfrac{3+x}{8}\right)\ge40\left(-\dfrac{3}{10}\right)$

$8(x+5)-5(3+x)\ge-12$

$8x+40-15-5x\ge-12$

$3x+25\ge-12$

$3x\ge-37$

$x\ge-\dfrac{37}{3}$

$\left[-\dfrac{37}{3},\infty\right)$

59. $\dfrac{x+3}{12}+\dfrac{x-5}{15}<\dfrac{2}{3}$

$60\left(\dfrac{x+3}{12}+\dfrac{x-5}{15}\right)<60\left(\dfrac{2}{3}\right)$

$5(x+3)+4(x-5)<20(2)$

$5x+15+4x-20<40$

$9x-5<40$

$9x<45$

$x<5$

$(-\infty,5)$

61. $0.4(4x-3)<1.2(x+2)$

$10[0.4(4x-3)]<10[1.2(x+2)]$

$4(4x-3)<12(x+2)$

$16x-12<12x+24$

$4x-12<24$

$4x<36$

$x<9$

$(-\infty,9)$

63. $\dfrac{2}{5}x-\dfrac{1}{4}\le\dfrac{3}{10}x-\dfrac{4}{5}$

$20\left[\dfrac{2}{5}x-\dfrac{1}{4}\right]\le20\left[\dfrac{3}{10}x-\dfrac{4}{5}\right]$

$4\cdot2x-5\le2\cdot3x-4\cdot4$

$8x-5\le6x-16$

$2x-5\le-16$

$2x\le-11$

$x\le-\dfrac{11}{2}$

$\left(-\infty,-\dfrac{11}{2}\right]$

65. $4(x-1)\ge4x-8$

$4x-4\ge4x-8$

$-4\ge-8$ (True for all x)

All real numbers

$(-\infty,\infty)$

67. $7x<7(x-2)$

$7x<7x-14$

$0<-14$ (False)

No solution; $\varnothing$

69. Let x = her score on the final.

a. Then $\dfrac{72+67+82+79+2x}{6}\ge77$

$300+2x\ge462$

$2x\ge162$

$x\ge81$

$\{x|x\ge81\}$

b. A final exam grade of 81 or higher will result in an average of 77 or higher.

71. a. Let x = weight of the luggage and cargo.
Then $6(160)+x\le2000$

$960+x\le2000$

$x\le1040$

$\{x|x\le1040\}$

b. The plane can carry a maximum of 1040 pounds of luggage and cargo.

73. a. Let x be the number of boxes.

$147+66x\le1500$

$66x\le1353$

$x\le\dfrac{1353}{66}$

$x\le20.5$

$\{x|x\le20\}$

b. The number of boxes that can be moved at one time is at most 20.

75. Let n = number of calls made in a given month.

   a. Then
$$25 < 13 + 0.06n$$
$$12 < 0.06n$$
$$200 < n \text{ or } n > 200$$
$$\{n|n > 200\}$$

   b. Plan 1 is more economical than Plan 2 when 200 or more calls are made.

77. $F \geq \dfrac{9}{5}C + 32$

$F \geq \dfrac{9}{5}(500) + 32$

$F \geq 932°$

$\{F|F \geq 932°\}$

Glass is a liquid at temperatures of 932°F or higher.

79. a. $651.2t + 28,472 > 42,000$
$$651.2t > 13,528$$
$$t > 20.8$$
t is more than 20.8, so $t \geq 21$.
$1990 + 21 = 2011$
Salaries will be greater than \$42,000 in 2011.

   b. Answers may vary

81. The consumption of whole milk is decreasing. The graph of the line is going down over time.

83. $t = 2010 - 2000 = 10$
$y = -0.19t + 7.6$
$y = -0.19(10) + 7.6$
$y = -1.9 + 7.6$
$y = 5.7$
The consumption of whole milk in 2010 will be 5.7 gallons per person per year.

85. $-0.19t + 7.6 < 6$
$$-0.19t < -1.6$$
$$t > 8.4$$
$2000 + 8 = 2008$
Consumption of whole milk will be less than 6 gallons per person per year during 2008.

87. Answers may vary

89. $x < 5$ and $x > 1$
The integers are 2, 3, and 4.

91. $x \geq -2$ and $x \geq 2$
The integers are 2, 3, 4, ...

93.
$$2x - 6 = 4$$
$$2x - 6 + 6 = 4 + 6$$
$$2x = 10$$
$$\frac{2x}{2} = \frac{10}{2}$$
$$x = 5$$

95.
$$-x + 7 = 5x - 6$$
$$-x - 5x = -6 - 7$$
$$-6x = -13$$
$$\frac{-6x}{-6} = \frac{-13}{-6}$$
$$x = \frac{13}{6}$$

97. $\{x|x \geq 2\}, [2, \infty)$

99.

$(-\infty, 0)$

101. $\{x|-2 < x \leq 1.5\}$

103.
$$2x - 3 = 5$$
$$2x - 3 + 3 = 5 + 3$$
$$2x = 8$$
$$\frac{2x}{2} = \frac{8}{2}$$
$$x = 4$$
$\{4\}$

105.
$$2x - 3 > 5$$
$$2x - 3 + 3 > 5 + 3$$
$$2x > 8$$
$$\frac{2x}{2} > \frac{8}{2}$$
$$x > 4$$
$(4, \infty)$

107. Answers may vary

109. Answers may vary

111. Answers may vary

The Bigger Picture

1.
$$3x - 4 = 3(2x - 1) + 7$$
$$3x - 4 = 6x - 3 + 7$$
$$3x - 4 = 6x + 4$$
$$3x - 4 - 6x = 6x + 4 - 6x$$
$$-3x - 4 = 4$$
$$-3x - 4 + 4 = 4 + 4$$
$$-3x = 8$$
$$\frac{-3x}{-3} = \frac{8}{-3}$$
$$x = -\frac{8}{3}$$

2.
$$5 + 2x = 5(x + 1)$$
$$5 + 2x = 5x + 5$$
$$5 + 2x - 5x = 5x + 5 - 5x$$
$$5 - 3x = 5$$
$$5 - 3x - 5 = 5 - 5$$
$$-3x = 0$$
$$\frac{-3x}{-3} = \frac{0}{-3}$$
$$x = 0$$

3.
$$\frac{x + 3}{2} > 1$$
$$2\left(\frac{x + 3}{2}\right) > 2(1)$$
$$x + 3 > 2$$
$$x + 3 - 3 > 2 - 3$$
$$x > -1$$
$$(-1, \infty)$$

4.
$$\frac{x - 2}{2} - \frac{x - 4}{3} = \frac{5}{6}$$
$$6\left(\frac{x - 2}{2} - \frac{x - 4}{3}\right) = 6\left(\frac{5}{6}\right)$$
$$3(x - 2) - 2(x - 4) = 5$$
$$3x - 6 - 2x + 8 = 5$$
$$x + 2 = 5$$
$$x + 2 - 2 = 5 - 2$$
$$x = 3$$

5.
$$\frac{7}{5} + \frac{y}{10} = 2$$
$$10\left(\frac{7}{5} + \frac{y}{10}\right) = 10(2)$$
$$2(7) + y = 20$$
$$14 + y = 20$$
$$14 + y - 14 = 20 - 14$$
$$y = 6$$

6.
$$5 + 2x = 2(x + 1)$$
$$5 + 2x = 2x + 2$$
$$5 + 2x - 2x = 2x + 2 - 2x$$
$$5 = 2 \quad \text{False}$$
This false statement indicates that there is no solution. The solution set is $\varnothing$.

7.
$$4(x - 2) + 3x \geq 9(x - 1) - 2$$
$$4x - 8 + 3x \geq 9x - 9 - 2$$
$$7x - 8 \geq 9x - 11$$
$$7x - 8 - 9x \geq 9x - 11 - 9x$$
$$-2x - 8 \geq -11$$
$$-2x - 8 + 8 \geq -11 + 8$$
$$-2x \geq -3$$
$$\frac{-2x}{-2} \leq \frac{-3}{-2}$$
$$x \leq \frac{3}{2}$$
$$\left(-\infty, \frac{3}{2}\right]$$

8.
$$6(x + 1) - 2 = 6x + 4$$
$$6x + 6 - 2 = 6x + 4$$
$$6x + 4 = 6x + 4$$
$$6x + 4 - 6x = 6x + 4 - 6x$$
$$4 = 4 \quad \text{True}$$
This true statement indicates that all real numbers are solutions of the equation. The solution set is $(-\infty, \infty)$.

Integrated Review

1.
$$-4x = 20$$
$$\frac{-4x}{-4} = \frac{20}{-4}$$
$$x = -5$$

2.
$$-4x < 20$$
$$\frac{-4x}{-4} > \frac{20}{-4}$$
$$x > -5$$
$$(-5, \infty)$$

3. $\dfrac{3x}{4} \geq 2$

$4\left(\dfrac{3x}{4}\right) \geq 4(2)$

$3x \geq 8$

$x \geq \dfrac{8}{3}$

$\left[\dfrac{8}{3}, \infty\right)$

4. $5x + 3 \geq 2 + 4x$

$x + 3 \geq 2$

$x \geq -1$

$[-1, \infty)$

5. $6(y - 4) = 3(y - 8)$

$6y - 24 = 3y - 24$

$3y = 0$

$y = 0$

6. $-4x \leq \dfrac{2}{5}$

$-20x \leq 2$

$x \geq -\dfrac{1}{10}$

$\left[-\dfrac{1}{10}, \infty\right)$

7. $-3x \geq \dfrac{1}{2}$

$2(-3x) \geq 2\left(\dfrac{1}{2}\right)$

$-6x \geq 1$

$x \leq -\dfrac{1}{6}$

$\left(-\infty, -\dfrac{1}{6}\right]$

8. $5(y + 4) = 4(y + 5)$

$5y + 20 = 4y + 20$

$y = 0$

9. $7x < 7(x - 2)$

$7x < 7x - 14$

$0 < -14$ (False)

No Solution; $\varnothing$

10. $\dfrac{-5x + 11}{2} \leq 7$

$2\left(\dfrac{-5x + 11}{2}\right) \leq 2(7)$

$-5x + 11 \leq 14$

$-5x \leq 3$

$x \geq -\dfrac{3}{5}$

$\left[-\dfrac{3}{5}, \infty\right)$

11. $-5x + 1.5 = -19.5$

$-5x + 1.5 - 1.5 = -19.5 - 1.5$

$-5x = -21$

$\dfrac{-5x}{-5} = \dfrac{-21}{-5}$

$x = 4.2$

12. $-5x + 4 = -26$

$-5x = -30$

$x = 6$

13. $5 + 2x - x = -x + 3 - 14$

$5 + x = -x - 11$

$5 + 2x = -11$

$2x = -16$

$x = -8$

14. $12x + 14 < 11x - 2$

$x + 14 < -2$

$x < -16$

$(-\infty, -16)$

15. $\dfrac{x}{5} - \dfrac{x}{4} = \dfrac{x - 2}{2}$

$20\left(\dfrac{x}{5} - \dfrac{x}{4}\right) = 20\left(\dfrac{x - 2}{2}\right)$

$4x - 5x = 10(x - 2)$

$-x = 10x - 20$

$-11x = -20$

$x = \dfrac{20}{11}$

16. $12x - 12 = 8(x - 1)$

$12x - 12 = 8x - 8$

$4x - 12 = -8$

$4x = 4$

$x = 1$

17. $2(x-3) > 70$
$$2x - 6 > 70$$
$$2x > 76$$
$$x > 38$$
$$(38, \infty)$$

18. $-3x - 4.7 = 11.8$
$$-3x - 4.7 + 4.7 = 11.8 + 4.7$$
$$-3x = 16.5$$
$$\frac{-3x}{-3} = \frac{16.5}{-3}$$
$$x = -5.5$$

19. $-2(b-4) - (3b-1) = 5b + 3$
$$-2b + 8 - 3b + 1 = 5b + 3$$
$$-5b + 9 = 5b + 3$$
$$-10b = -6$$
$$b = \frac{-6}{-10} = \frac{3}{5}$$

20. $8(x+3) < 7(x+5) + x$
$$8x + 24 < 7x + 35 + x$$
$$8x + 24 < 8x + 35$$
$$24 < 35 \quad \text{(True for all } x\text{)}$$
All real numbers; $(-\infty, \infty)$

21. $\dfrac{3t+1}{8} = \dfrac{5+2t}{7} + 2$
$$56\left(\frac{3t+1}{8}\right) = 56\left(\frac{5+2t}{7}\right) + 56(2)$$
$$7(3t+1) = 8(5+2t) + 112$$
$$21t + 7 = 40 + 16t + 112$$
$$21t + 7 = 16t + 152$$
$$5t = 145$$
$$t = 29$$

22. $4(x-6) - x = 8(x-3) - 5x$
$$4x - 24 - x = 8x - 24 - 5x$$
$$3x - 24 = 3x - 24$$
$$-24 = -24 \quad \text{(True for all } x\text{)}$$
The solution is all real numbers.

23. $\dfrac{x}{6} + \dfrac{3x-2}{2} < \dfrac{2}{3}$
$$6\left(\frac{x}{6} + \frac{3x-2}{2}\right) < 6\left(\frac{2}{3}\right)$$
$$x + 3(3x-2) < 4$$
$$x + 9x - 6 < 4$$
$$10x - 6 < 4$$
$$10x < 10$$
$$x < 1$$
$$(-\infty, 1)$$

24. $\dfrac{y}{3} + \dfrac{y}{5} = \dfrac{y+3}{10}$
$$30\left(\frac{y}{3}\right) + 30\left(\frac{y}{5}\right) = 30\left(\frac{y+3}{10}\right)$$
$$10y + 6y = 3(y+3)$$
$$16y = 3y + 9$$
$$13y = 9$$
$$y = \frac{9}{13}$$

25. $5(x-6) + 2x > 3(2x-1) - 4$
$$5x - 30 + 2x > 6x - 3 - 4$$
$$7x - 30 > 6x - 7$$
$$x > 23$$
$$(23, \infty)$$

26. $14(x-1) - 7x \le 2(3x-6) + 4$
$$14x - 14 - 7x \le 6x - 12 + 4$$
$$7x - 14 \le 6x - 8$$
$$x \le 6$$
$$(-\infty, 6]$$

27. $\dfrac{1}{4}(3x+2) - x \ge \dfrac{3}{8}(x-5) + 2$
$$8\left[\frac{1}{4}(3x+2) - x\right] \ge 8\left[\frac{3}{8}(x-5) + 2\right]$$
$$2(3x+2) - 8x \ge 3(x-5) + 16$$
$$6x + 4 - 8x \ge 3x - 15 + 16$$
$$-2x + 4 \ge 3x + 1$$
$$3 \ge 5x$$
$$\frac{3}{5} \ge x \quad \text{or} \quad x \le \frac{3}{5}$$
$$\left(-\infty, \frac{3}{5}\right]$$

28. $\dfrac{1}{3}(x-10)-4x > \dfrac{5}{6}(2x+1)-1$

$$6\left[\dfrac{1}{3}(x-10)-4x\right] > 6\left[\dfrac{5}{6}(2x+1)-1\right]$$
$$2(x-10)-24x > 5(2x+1)-6$$
$$2x-20-24x > 10x+5-6$$
$$-22x-20 > 10x-1$$
$$-19 > 32x$$
$$-\dfrac{19}{32} > x \quad \text{or} \quad x < -\dfrac{19}{32}$$

$$\left(-\infty, -\dfrac{19}{32}\right)$$

Section 2.5

Practice Exercises

1. $A = \{1, 3, 5, 7, 9\}$ and $B = \{1, 2, 3, 4\}$
The numbers 1 and 3 are in sets A and B.
The intersection is $\{1, 3\}$. $A \cap B = \{1, 3\}$.

2. $x+3 < 8$ and $2x-1 < 3$
     $x < 5$ and $2x < 4$
     $x < 5$ and $x < 2$

$\{x | x < 5\}, (-\infty, 5)$

5

$\{x | x < 2\}, (-\infty, 2)$

2

$\{x | x < 5 \text{ and } x < 2\} = \{x | x < 2\}$

2

The solution set is $(-\infty, 2)$.

3. $4x \le 0$ and $3x+2 > 8$
     $x \le 0$ and $3x > 6$
     $x \le 0$ and $x > 2$

$\{x | x \le 0\}, (-\infty, 0]$

0

$\{x | x > 2\}, (2, \infty)$

2

$\{x | 4x \le 0 \text{ and } 3x + 2 > 8\} = \{\ \} \text{ or } \varnothing$

4. $3 < 5 - x < 9$
    $3 - 5 < 5 - x - 5 < 9 - 5$
        $-2 < -x < 4$
     $\dfrac{-2}{-1} > \dfrac{-x}{-1} > \dfrac{4}{-1}$
        $2 > x > -4$
   or $-4 < x < 2$
The solution set is $(-4, 2)$.

5. $-4 \le \dfrac{x}{2} - 1 \le 3$

$$2(-4) \le 2\left(\dfrac{x}{2} - 1\right) \le 2(3)$$
$$-8 \le x - 2 \le 6$$
$$-8 + 2 \le x - 2 + 2 \le 6 + 2$$
$$-6 \le x \le 8$$

The solution set is $[-6, 8]$.

6. $A = \{1, 3, 5, 7, 9\}$ and $B = \{2, 3, 4, 5, 6\}$.
The numbers that are in either set or both sets are
$\{1, 2, 3, 4, 5, 6, 7, 9\}$. This set is the union,
$A \cup B$.

7. $8x + 5 \le 8$ or $x - 1 \ge 2$
      $8x \le 3$ or $x \ge 3$
       $x \le \dfrac{3}{8}$ or $x \ge 3$

$\left\{x \Big| x \le \dfrac{3}{8}\right\}, \left(-\infty, \dfrac{3}{8}\right]$

$\dfrac{3}{8}$

$\{x | x \ge 3\}, [3, \infty)$

3

$\left\{x \Big| x \le \dfrac{3}{8} \text{ or } x \ge 3\right\} = \left(-\infty, \dfrac{3}{8}\right] \cup [3, \infty)$

$\dfrac{3}{8}$ 3

The solution set is $\left(-\infty, \dfrac{3}{8}\right] \cup [3, \infty)$.

8. $-3x - 2 > -8$ or $5x > 0$
     $-3x > -6$ or $x > 0$
       $x < 2$ or $x > 0$

$\{x | x < 2\}, (-\infty, 2)$

2

$\{x | x > 0\}, (0, \infty)$

0

$\{x | x < 2 \text{ or } x > 0\}, (-\infty, \infty)$

The solution set is $(-\infty, \infty)$.

Vocabulary and Readiness Check

1. Two inequalities joined by the words "and" or
"or" are called <u>compound</u> inequalities.

2. The word <u>and</u> means intersection.

3. The word <u>or</u> means union.

4. The symbol $\cap$ means intersection.

5. The symbol $\cup$ represents union.

6. The symbol $\varnothing$ is the empty set.

7. The inequality $-2 \le x < 1$ means $-2 \le x$ <u>and</u> $x < 1$.

8. $\{x | x < 0 \text{ and } x > 0\} = \underline{\varnothing}$.

Exercise Set 2.5

1. $C \cup D = \{2, 3, 4, 5, 6, 7\}$

3. $A \cap D = \{4, 6\}$

5. $A \cup B = \{..., -2, -1, 0, 1, ...\}$

7. $B \cap D = \{5, 7\}$

9. $B \cup C = \{x | x \text{ is an odd integer or } x = 2 \text{ or } x = 4\}$

11. $A \cap C = \{2, 4\}$

13. $x < 1$ and $x > -3$
$-3 < x < 1$
$(-3, 1)$

15. $x \le -3$ and $x \ge -2$
$\varnothing$

17. $x < -1$ and $x < 1$
$x < -1$
$(-\infty, -1)$

19. $x + 1 \ge 7$ and $3x - 1 \ge 5$
$x \ge 6$ and $3x \ge 6$
$x \ge 2$

$x \ge 6$
$[6, \infty)$

21. $4x + 2 \le -10$ and $2x \le 0$
$4x \le -12$ and $x \le 0$
$x \le -3$

$x \le -3$
$(-\infty, -3]$

23. $-2x < -8$ and $x - 5 < 5$
$x > 4$ and $x < 10$
$(4, 10)$

25. $5 < x - 6 < 11$
$11 < x < 17$
$(11, 17)$

27. $-2 \le 3x - 5 \le 7$
$3 \le 3x \le 12$
$1 \le x \le 4$
$[1, 4]$

29. $1 \le \dfrac{2}{3}x + 3 \le 4$

$-2 \le \dfrac{2}{3}x \le 1$

$-3 \le x \le \dfrac{3}{2}$

$\left[-3, \dfrac{3}{2}\right]$

31. $-5 \le \dfrac{-3x + 1}{4} \le 2$

$4(-5) \le 4\left(\dfrac{-3x + 1}{4}\right) \le 4(2)$

$-20 \le -3x + 1 \le 8$

$-21 \le -3x \le 7$

$7 \ge x \ge -\dfrac{7}{3}$

$-\dfrac{7}{3} \le x \le 7$

$\left[-\dfrac{7}{3}, 7\right]$

33. $x < 4$ or $x < 5$
$(-\infty, 5)$

35. $x \le -4$ or $x \ge 1$
$(-\infty, -4] \cup [1, \infty)$

37. $x > 0$ or $x < 3$
$(-\infty, \infty)$

39. $-2x \le -4$ or $5x - 20 \ge 5$
         $x \ge 2$ or $5x \ge 25$
                              $x \ge 5$

   $x \ge 2$
   $[2, \infty)$

41. $x + 4 < 0$ or $6x > -12$
         $x < -4$ or $x > -2$
   $(-\infty, -4) \cup (-2, \infty)$

43. $3(x-1) < 12$ or $x + 7 > 10$
         $x - 1 < 4$ or $x > 3$
            $x < 5$
   $(-\infty, \infty)$

45. $x < \dfrac{2}{3}$ and $x > -\dfrac{1}{2}$

   $-\dfrac{1}{2} < x < \dfrac{2}{3}$

   $\left(-\dfrac{1}{2}, \dfrac{2}{3}\right)$

47. $x < \dfrac{2}{3}$ or $x > -\dfrac{1}{2}$

   $(-\infty, \infty)$

49. $0 \le 2x - 3 \le 9$
   $3 \le 2x \le 12$

   $\dfrac{3}{2} \le x \le 6$

   $\left[\dfrac{3}{2}, 6\right]$

51. $\dfrac{1}{2} < x - \dfrac{3}{4} < 2$

   $4\left(\dfrac{1}{2}\right) < 4\left(x - \dfrac{3}{4}\right) < 4(2)$

      $2 < 4x - 3 < 8$
      $5 < 4x < 11$

   $\dfrac{5}{4} < x < \dfrac{11}{4}$

   $\left(\dfrac{5}{4}, \dfrac{11}{4}\right)$

53. $x + 3 \ge 3$ and $x + 3 \le 2$
         $x \ge 0$ and $x \le -1$
   No solution exists.
   $\varnothing$

55. $3x \ge 5$ or $-\dfrac{5}{8}x - 6 > 1$

   $x \ge \dfrac{5}{3}$ or $-\dfrac{5}{8}x > 7$

                          $x < -\dfrac{56}{5}$

   $\left(-\infty, -\dfrac{56}{5}\right) \cup \left[\dfrac{5}{3}, \infty\right)$

57. $0 < \dfrac{5 - 2x}{3} < 5$

      $0 < 5 - 2x < 15$

   $\dfrac{-5}{-2} > \dfrac{-2x}{-2} > \dfrac{10}{-2}$

      $\dfrac{5}{2} > x > -5$

      $-5 < x < \dfrac{5}{2}$

   $\left(-5, \dfrac{5}{2}\right)$

59. $-6 < 3(x - 2) \le 8$
   $-6 < 3x - 6 \le 8$
    $0 < 3x \le 14$

   $0 < x < \dfrac{14}{3}$

   $\left(0, \dfrac{14}{3}\right]$

61. $-x + 5 > 6$ and $1 + 2x \le -5$
         $-x > 1$ and $2x \le -6$
          $x < -1$ and $x \le -3$

   $x \le -3$
   $(-\infty, -3]$

63. $3x + 2 \le 5$ or $7x > 29$

         $3x \le 3$ or $x > \dfrac{29}{7}$

         $x \le 1$ or $x > \dfrac{29}{7}$

   $(-\infty, 1] \cup \left(\dfrac{29}{7}, \infty\right)$

65. $5 - x > 7$ and $2x + 3 \ge 13$
         $-x > 2$ and $2x \ge 10$
          $x < -2$ and $x \ge 5$
   No solution exists.
   $\varnothing$

67.
$$-\frac{1}{2} \le \frac{4x-1}{6} < \frac{5}{6}$$
$$6\left(-\frac{1}{2}\right) \le 6\left(\frac{4x-1}{6}\right) < 6\left(\frac{5}{6}\right)$$
$$-3 \le 4x-1 < 5$$
$$-2 \le 4x < 6$$
$$-\frac{1}{2} \le x < \frac{3}{2}$$
$$\left[-\frac{1}{2}, \frac{3}{2}\right)$$

69.
$$\frac{1}{15} < \frac{8-3x}{15} < \frac{4}{5}$$
$$15\left(\frac{1}{15}\right) < 15\left(\frac{8-3x}{15}\right) < 15\left(\frac{4}{5}\right)$$
$$1 < 8-3x < 12$$
$$-7 < -3x < 4$$
$$-\frac{4}{3} < x < \frac{7}{3}$$
$$\left(-\frac{4}{3}, \frac{7}{3}\right)$$

71.
$$0.3 < 0.2x - 0.9 < 1.5$$
$$1.2 < 0.2x < 2.4$$
$$6 < x < 12$$
$$(6, 12)$$

73. $|-7| - |19| = 7 - 19 = -12$

75. $-(-6) - |-10| = 6 - 10 = -4$

77. $|x| = 7$
$$x = -7, 7$$

79. $|x| = 0$
$$x = 0$$

81. The years that the consumption of bottled water was greater than 20 gallons per person were 2003, 2004, and 2005. The years that consumption of diet soda was greater than 14 gallons per person were 2003, 2004, and 2005. The years in common are 2003, 2004, and 2005.

83.
$$-29 \le C \le 35$$
$$-29 \le \frac{5}{9}(F-32) \le 35$$
$$-52.5 \le F - 32 \le 63$$
$$-20.2 \le F \le 95$$
$$-20.2° \le F \le 95°$$

85.
$$70 \le \frac{68+65+75+78+2x}{6} \le 79$$
$$420 \le 286 + 2x \le 474$$
$$134 \le 2x \le 188$$
$$67 \le x \le 94$$
If Christian scores between 67 and 94 inclusive on his final exam, he will receive a C in the course.

87. $2x - 3 < 3x + 1 < 4x - 5$
$$2x-3 < 3x+1 \quad \text{and} \quad 3x+1 < 4x-5$$
$$-x < 4 \qquad\quad \text{and} \qquad -x < -6$$
$$x > -4 \qquad\quad \text{and} \qquad x > 6$$
$$x > 6$$
$$(6, \infty)$$

89. $-3(x-2) \le 3 - 2x \le 10 - 3x$
$$-3x+6 \le 3-2x \quad \text{and} \quad 3-2x \le 10-3x$$
$$-x \le -3 \qquad\quad \text{and} \qquad x \le 7$$
$$x \ge 3$$
$$3 \le x \le 7$$
$$[3, 7]$$

91. $5x - 8 < 2(2 + x) < -2(1 + 2x)$
$$5x-8 < 4+2x \quad \text{and} \quad 4+2x < -2-4x$$
$$3x < 12 \qquad\quad \text{and} \qquad 6x < -6$$
$$x < 4 \qquad\quad \text{and} \qquad x < -1$$
$$x < -1$$
$$(-\infty, -1)$$

The Bigger Picture

1. $x - 2 \le 1 \quad \text{and} \quad 3x - 1 \ge -4$
$$x \le 3 \quad \text{and} \qquad 3x \ge -3$$
$$\qquad\qquad\qquad\qquad x \ge -1$$
$$-1 \le x \le 3$$
$$[-1, 3]$$

2. $-2 < x - 1 < 5$
$$-2+1 < x-1+1 < 5+1$$
$$-1 < x < 6$$
$$(-1, 6)$$

3. $-2x + 2.5 = -7.7$
$$-2x = -10.2$$
$$x = 5.1$$

4. $-5x > 20$

$$\frac{-5x}{-5} < \frac{20}{-5}$$

$$x < -4$$

$$(-\infty, -4)$$

5. $x \le -3$ or $x \le -5$

$$x \le -3$$

$$(-\infty, -3]$$

6. $5x < -10$ or $3x - 4 > 2$

$x < -2$ or $3x > 6$

$\phantom{5x < -2 \text{ or } 3x}x > 2$

$$(-\infty, -2) \cup (2, \infty)$$

7. $\dfrac{5t}{2} - \dfrac{3t}{4} = 7$

$$4\left(\frac{5t}{2} - \frac{3t}{4}\right) = 4(7)$$

$$2(5t) - 3t = 28$$

$$10t - 3t = 28$$

$$7t = 28$$

$$t = 4$$

8. $5(x - 3) + x + 2 \ge 3(x + 2) + 2x$

$$5x - 15 + x + 2 \ge 3x + 6 + 2x$$

$$6x - 13 \ge 5x + 6$$

$$6x - 5x \ge 13 + 6$$

$$x \ge 19$$

$$[19, \infty)$$

Section 2.6

Practice Exercises

1. $|q| = 7$

$q = 7$ or $q = -7$

The solution set is $\{-7, 7\}$.

2. $|2x - 3| = 5$

$2x - 3 = 5$ or $2x - 3 = -5$

$2x = 8$ or $2x = -2$

$x = 4$ or $x = -1$

The solution set is $\{-1, 4\}$.

3. $\left|\dfrac{x}{5} + 1\right| = 15$

$\dfrac{x}{5} + 1 = 15$ or $\dfrac{x}{5} + 1 = -15$

$\dfrac{x}{5} = 14$ or $\dfrac{x}{5} = -16$

$\phantom{\dfrac{x}{5}}x = 70$ or $\phantom{\dfrac{x}{5}}x = -80$

The solutions are -80 and 70.

4. $|3x| + 8 = 14$

$$|3x| = 6$$

$3x = 6$ or $3x = -6$

$x = 2$ or $x = -2$

The solutions are -2 and 2.

5. $|z| = 0$

The solution is 0.

6. $3|z| + 9 = 7$

$$3|z| = -2$$

$$|z| = -\frac{2}{3}$$

The absolute value of a number is never negative, so there is no solution. The solution set is $\{\ \}$ or $\varnothing$.

7. $\left|\dfrac{5x + 3}{4}\right| = -8$

The absolute value of a number is never negative, so there is no solution. The solution set is $\{\ \}$ or $\varnothing$.

8. $|2x + 4| = |3x - 1|$

$2x + 4 = 3x - 1$ or $2x + 4 = -(3x - 1)$

$-x + 4 = -1$ $2x + 4 = -3x + 1$

$ -x = -5$ $5x + 4 = 1$

$ x = 5$ $5x = -3$

$$x = -\frac{3}{5}$$

The solutions are $-\dfrac{3}{5}$ and 5.

9. $|x - 2| = |8 - x|$

$x - 2 = 8 - x$ or $x - 2 = -(8 - x)$

$2x - 2 = 8$ $x - 2 = -8 + x$

$ 2x = 10$ $-2 = -8$ False

$ x = 5$

The solution is 5.

Vocabulary and Readiness Check

1. $|x - 2| = 5$
   C. $x - 2 = 5$ or $x - 2 = -5$

2. $|x - 2| = 0$
   A. $x - 2 = 0$

3. $|x - 2| = |x + 3|$
   B. $x - 2 = x + 3$ or $x - 2 = -(x + 3)$

4. $|x + 3| = 5$
   E. $x + 3 = 5$ or $x + 3 = -5$

5. $|x + 3| = -5$
   D. $\varnothing$

Exercise Set 2.6

1. $|x| = 7$
   $x = 7$ or $x = -7$

3. $|3x| = 12.6$
   $3x = 12.6$ or $3x = -12.6$
   $x = 4.2$ or $x = -4.2$

5. $|2x - 5| = 9$
   $2x - 5 = 9$ or $2x - 5 = -9$
   $2x = 14$ or $2x = -4$
   $x = 7$ or $x = -2$

7. $\left| \dfrac{x}{2} - 3 \right| = 1$

   $\dfrac{x}{2} - 3 = 1$ or $\dfrac{x}{2} - 3 = -1$

   $2\left(\dfrac{x}{2} - 3\right) = 2(1)$ or $2\left(\dfrac{x}{2} - 3\right) = 2(-1)$

   $x - 6 = 2$ or $x - 6 = -2$
   $x = 8$ or $x = 4$

9. $|z| + 4 = 9$
   $|z| = 5$
   $z = -5$ or $z = -5$

11. $|3x| + 5 = 14$
    $|3x| = 9$
    $3x = 9$ or $3x = -9$
    $x = 3$ or $x = -3$

13. $|2x| = 0$
    $2x = 0$
    $x = 0$

15. $|4n + 1| + 10 = 4$
    $|4n + 1| = -6$ which is impossible.
    The solution set is $\varnothing$.

17. $|5x - 1| = 0$
    $5x - 1 = 0$
    $5x = 1$
    $x = \dfrac{1}{5}$

19. $|x| = 5$

21. $|5x - 7| = |3x + 11|$
    $5x - 7 = 3x + 11$ or $5x - 7 = -(3x + 11)$
    $2x = 18$ or $5x - 7 = -3x - 11$
    $x = 9$ or $8x = -4$
    $x = -\dfrac{1}{2}$

23. $|z + 8| = |z - 3|$
    $z + 8 = z - 3$ or $z + 8 = -(z - 3)$
    $8 = -3$ or $z + 8 = -z + 3$
    $2z = -5$
    $z = -\dfrac{5}{2}$

    The only solution is $-\dfrac{5}{2}$.

25. Answers may vary

27. $|x| = 4$
    $x = 4$ or $x = -4$

29. $|y| = 0;\ y = 0$

31. $|z| = -2$ is impossible. The solution set is $\varnothing$.

33. $|7 - 3x| = 7$
    $7 - 3x = 7$ or $7 - 3x = -7$
    $-3x = 0$ or $-3x = -14$
    $x = 0$ or $x = \dfrac{14}{3}$

35. $|6x| - 1 = 11$
$$|6x| = 12$$
$$6x = 12 \quad \text{or} \quad 6x = -12$$
$$x = 2 \quad \text{or} \quad x = -2$$

37. $|4p| = -8$ is impossible. The solution set is $\varnothing$.

39. $|x - 3| + 3 = 7$
$$|x - 3| = 4$$
$$x - 3 = 4 \quad \text{or} \quad x - 3 = -4$$
$$x = 7 \quad \text{or} \quad x = -1$$

41. $\left|\dfrac{z}{4} + 5\right| = -7$ is impossible. The solution set is $\varnothing$.

43. $|9v - 3| = -8$ is impossible. The solution set is $\varnothing$.

45. $|8n + 1| = 0$
$$8n + 1 = 0$$
$$8n = -1$$
$$n = -\frac{1}{8}$$

47. $|1 - 6c| - 7 = -3$
$$|1 - 6c| = 4$$
$$1 - 6c = 4 \quad \text{or} \quad 1 - 6c = -4$$
$$6c = 3 \quad \text{or} \quad 6c = -5$$
$$c = \frac{1}{2} \quad \text{or} \quad c = -\frac{5}{6}$$

49. $|5x + 1| = 11$
$$5x + 1 = 11 \quad \text{or} \quad 5x + 1 = -11$$
$$5x = 10 \quad \text{or} \quad 5x = -12$$
$$x = 2 \quad \text{or} \quad x = -\frac{12}{5}$$

51. $|4x - 2| = |-10|$
$$|4x - 2| = 10$$
$$4x - 2 = 10 \quad \text{or} \quad 4x - 2 = -10$$
$$4x = 12 \quad \text{or} \quad 4x = -8$$
$$x = 3 \quad \text{or} \quad x = -2$$

53. $|5x + 1| = |4x - 7|$
$$5x + 1 = 4x - 7 \quad \text{or} \quad 5x + 1 = -(4x - 7)$$
$$x = -8 \quad \text{or} \quad 5x + 1 = -4x + 7$$
$$9x = 6$$
$$x = \frac{2}{3}$$

55. $|6 + 2x| = -|-7|$
$|6 + 2x| = -7$ which is impossible. The solution set is $\varnothing$.

57. $|2x - 6| = |10 - 2x|$
$$2x - 6 = 10 - 2x \quad \text{or} \quad 2x - 6 = -(10 - 2x)$$
$$4x = 16 \quad \text{or} \quad 2x - 6 = -10 + 2x$$
$$x = 4 \quad \text{or} \quad -6 = -10$$
$-6 = -10$ is impossible. The only solution is 4.

59. $\left|\dfrac{2x - 5}{3}\right| = 7$
$$\frac{2x - 5}{3} = 7 \quad \text{or} \quad \frac{2x - 5}{3} = -7$$
$$2x - 5 = 21 \quad \text{or} \quad 2x - 5 = -21$$
$$2x = 26 \quad \text{or} \quad 2x = -16$$
$$x = 13 \quad \text{or} \quad x = -8$$

61. $2 + |5n| = 17$
$$|5n| = 15$$
$$5n = 15 \quad \text{or} \quad 5n = -15$$
$$n = 3 \quad \text{or} \quad n = -3$$

63. $\left|\dfrac{2x - 1}{3}\right| = |-5|$
$$\left|\frac{2x - 1}{3}\right| = 5$$
$$\frac{2x - 1}{3} = 5 \quad \text{or} \quad \frac{2x - 1}{3} = -5$$
$$2x - 1 = 15 \quad \text{or} \quad 2x - 1 = -15$$
$$2x = 16 \quad \text{or} \quad 2x = -14$$
$$x = 8 \quad \text{or} \quad x = -7$$

65. $|2y - 3| = |9 - 4y|$
$$2y - 3 = 9 - 4y \quad \text{or} \quad 2y - 3 = -(9 - 4y)$$
$$6y = 12 \quad \text{or} \quad 2y - 3 = -9 + 4y$$
$$y = 2 \quad \text{or} \quad -2y = -6$$
$$y = 3$$

67. $\left|\dfrac{3n+2}{8}\right| = |-1|$

$\left|\dfrac{3n+2}{8}\right| = 1$

$\dfrac{3n+2}{8} = 1$ or $\dfrac{3n+2}{8} = -1$

$3n+2 = 8$ or $3n+2 = -8$

$3n = 6$ or $3n = -10$

$n = 2$ or $n = -\dfrac{10}{3}$

69. $|x+4| = |7-x|$

$x+4 = 7-x$ or $x+4 = -(7-x)$

$2x = 3$ or $x+4 = -7+x$

$x = \dfrac{3}{2}$ or $4 = -7$

$4 = -7$ is impossible. The only solution is $\dfrac{3}{2}$.

71. $\left|\dfrac{8c-7}{3}\right| = -|-5|$

$\left|\dfrac{8c-7}{3}\right| = -5$ which is impossible.

The solution set is $\varnothing$.

73. Answers may vary

75. 34% of cheese consumption came from cheddar cheese.

77. $33\% \cdot (120 \text{ pounds}) = 0.33(120 \text{ pounds})$
$= 39.6 \text{ pounds}$

We might expect they consumed 39.6 pounds.

79. $|x| \geq -2$
Answers may vary; 0, 1, 2, 3, 4, for example

81. $|y| < 0$
No solution

83. $|x-7| = 2$

85. $|2x-1| = 4$

87. $|ax+b| = c$

a. one solution if $c = 0$

b. no solutions if c is a negative number

c. two solutions if c is a positive number

Section 2.7

Practice Exercises

1. $|x| < 2$
The solution set of this inequality contains all numbers whose distance from 0 is less than 2. The solution set is $(-2, 2)$.

2. $|b+1| < 3$
$-3 < b+1 < 3$
$-3-1 < b+1-1 < 3-1$
$-4 < b < 2$
$(-4, 2)$

3. $|3x-2| + 5 \leq 9$
$|3x-2| \leq 9-5$
$|3x-2| \leq 4$
$-4 \leq 3x-2 \leq 4$
$-4+2 \leq 3x-2+2 \leq 4+2$
$-2 \leq 3x \leq 6$
$-\dfrac{2}{3} \leq x \leq 2$
$\left[-\dfrac{2}{3}, 2\right]$

4. $\left|3x + \dfrac{5}{8}\right| < -4$

The absolute value of a number is always nonnegative and can never be less than -4. The solution set is $\{\ \}$ or $\varnothing$.

5. $|y+4| \geq 6$
$y+4 \leq -6$ or $y+4 \geq 6$
$y+4-4 \leq -6-4$ or $y+4-4 \geq 6-4$
$y \leq -10$ or $y \geq 2$
$(-\infty, -10] \cup [2, \infty)$

6. $|4x+3| + 5 > 3$
$|4x+3| + 5 - 5 > 3 - 5$
$|4x+3| > -2$

The absolute value of any number is always nonnegative and thus is always greater than -2.
$(-\infty, \infty)$

7. $\left|\dfrac{x}{2}-3\right|-5>-2$

$\left|\dfrac{x}{2}-3\right|-5+5>-2+5$

$\left|\dfrac{x}{2}-3\right|>3$

$\dfrac{x}{2}-3<-3$ or $\dfrac{x}{2}-3>3$

$2\left(\dfrac{x}{2}-3\right)<2(-3)$ or $2\left(\dfrac{x}{2}-3\right)>2(3)$

$x-6<-6$ or $x-6>6$

$x<0$ or $x>12$

$(-\infty,0)\cup(12,\infty)$

8. $\left|\dfrac{3(x-2)}{5}\right|\le 0$

$\dfrac{3(x-2)}{5}=0$

$5\left[\dfrac{3(x-2)}{5}\right]=5(0)$

$3(x-2)=0$

$3x-6=0$

$3x=6$

$x=2$

The solution set is $\{2\}$.

Vocabulary and Readiness Check

1. D

2. E

3. C

4. B

5. A

Exercise Set 2.7

1. $|x|\le 4$

$-4\le x\le 4$

$[-4,4]$

3. $|x-3|<2$

$-2<x-3<2$

$1<x<5$

$(1,5)$

5. $|x+3|<2$

$-2<x+3<2$

$-5<x<-1$

$(-5,-1)$

7. $|2x+7|\le 3$

$-13\le 2x+7\le 13$

$-20\le 2x\le 6$

$-10\le x\le 3$

$[-10,3]$

9. $|x|+7\le 12$

$|x|\le 5$

$-5\le x\le 5$

$[-5,5]$

11. $|3x-1|<-5$

No real solutions; $\varnothing$

13. $|x-6|-7\le -1$

$|x-6|\le 6$

$-6\le x-6\le 6$

$0\le x\le 12$

$[0,12]$

15. $|x|>3$

$x<-3$ or $x>3$

$(-\infty,-3)\cup(3,\infty)$

17. $|x+10|\ge 14$

$x+10\le -14$ or $x+10\ge 14$

$x\le -24$ or $x\ge 4$

$(-\infty,-24]\cup[4,\infty)$

19. $|x|+2>6$

$|x|>4$

$x<-4$ or $x>4$

$(-\infty,-4)\cup(4,\infty)$

21. $|5x| > -4$

All real numbers

$(-\infty, \infty)$

23. $|6x-8|+3 > 7$

$|6x-8| > 4$

$6x-8 < -4$ or $6x-8 > 4$

$6x < 4$ or $6x > 12$

$x < \dfrac{2}{3}$ or $x > 2$

$\left(-\infty, \dfrac{2}{3}\right) \cup (2, \infty)$

25. $|x| \le 0$

$|x| = 0$

$x = 0$

27. $|8x + 3| > 0$ only excludes $|8x + 3| = 0$

$8x+3 = 0$

$8x = -3$

$x = -\dfrac{3}{8}$

All real numbers except $-\dfrac{3}{8}$.

$\left(-\infty, -\dfrac{3}{8}\right) \cup \left(-\dfrac{3}{8}, \infty\right)$

29. $|x| \le 2$

$-2 \le x \le 2$

$[-2, 2]$

31. $|y| > 1$

$y < -1$ or $y > 1$

$(-\infty, -1) \cup (1, \infty)$

33. $|x - 3| < 8$

$-8 < x-3 < 8$

$-5 < x < 11$

$(-5, 11)$

35. $|0.6x - 3| > 0.6$

$0.6x-3 < -0.6$ or $0.6x - 3 > 0.6$

$0.6x < 2.4$ or $0.6x > 3.6$

$x < 4$ or $x > 6$

$(-\infty, 4) \cup (6, \infty)$

37. $5+|x| \le 2$

$|x| \le -3$

No real solution

$\varnothing$

39. $|x| > -4$

All real numbers

$(-\infty, \infty)$

41. $|2x - 7| \le 11$

$-11 \le 2x-7 \le 11$

$-4 \le 2x \le 18$

$-2 \le x \le 9$

$[-2, 9]$

43. $|x + 5|+2 \ge 8$

$|x+5| \ge 6$

$x+5 \le -6$ or $x + 5 \ge 6$

$x \le -11$ or $x \ge 1$

$(-\infty, -11] \cup [1, \infty)$

45. $|x| > 0$ only excludes $|x| = 0$, or $x = 0$.

All real numbers except $x = 0$

$(-\infty, 0) \cup (0, \infty)$

47. $9+|x| > 7$

$|x| > -2$

All real numbers

$(-\infty, \infty)$

49. $6 + |4x - 1| \le 9$

$\qquad |4x - 1| \le 3$

$-3 \le 4x - 1 \le 3$

$-2 \le 4x \le 4$

$-\dfrac{1}{2} \le x \le 1$

$\left[-\dfrac{1}{2}, 1 \right]$

51. $\left| \dfrac{2}{3}x + 1 \right| > 1$

$\dfrac{2}{3}x + 1 < -1 \quad$ or $\quad \dfrac{2}{3}x + 1 > 1$

$\quad \dfrac{2}{3}x < -2 \quad$ or $\quad \dfrac{2}{3}x > 0$

$\qquad x < -3 \quad$ or $\qquad x > 0$

$(-\infty, -3) \cup (0, \infty)$

53. $|5x + 3| < -6$

No real solution

$\varnothing$

55. $\left| \dfrac{8x - 3}{4} \right| \le 0$

$\dfrac{8x - 3}{4} = 0$

$8x - 3 = 0$

$8x = 3$

$x = \dfrac{3}{8}$

$\left\{ \dfrac{3}{8} \right\}$

57. $|1 + 3x| + 4 < 5$

$\qquad |1 + 3x| < 1$

$-1 < 1 + 3x < 1$

$-2 < 3x < 0$

$-\dfrac{2}{3} < x < 0$

$\left(-\dfrac{2}{3}, 0 \right)$

59. $\left| \dfrac{x + 6}{3} \right| > 2$

$\dfrac{x + 6}{3} < -2 \quad$ or $\quad \dfrac{x + 6}{3} > 2$

$x + 6 < -6 \quad$ or $\quad x + 6 > 6$

$\quad x < -12 \quad$ or $\qquad x > 0$

$(-\infty, -12) \cup (0, \infty)$

61. $-15 + |2x - 7| \le -6$

$\qquad |2x - 7| \le 9$

$-9 \le 2x - 7 \le 9$

$-2 \le 2x \le 16$

$-1 \le x \le 8$

$[-1, 8]$

63. $\left| 2x + \dfrac{3}{4} \right| - 7 \le -2$

$\left| 2x + \dfrac{3}{4} \right| \le 5$

$-5 \le 2x + \dfrac{3}{4} \le 5$

$-20 \le 8x + 3 \le 20$

$-23 \le 8x \le 17$

$-\dfrac{23}{8} \le x \le \dfrac{17}{8}$

$\left[-\dfrac{23}{8}, \dfrac{17}{8} \right]$

65. $|2x-3| < 7$
$-7 < 2x-3 < 7$
$-4 < 2x < 10$
$-2 < x < 5$
$(-2, 5)$

67. $|2x-3| = 7$
$2x-3 = 7$ or $2x-3 = -7$
$2x = 10$ or $2x = -4$
$x = 5$ or $x = -2$

69. $|x-5| \geq 12$
$x-5 \leq -12$ or $x-5 \geq 12$
$x \leq -7$ or $x \geq 17$
$(-\infty, -7] \cup [17, \infty)$

71. $|9+4x| = 0$
$9+4x = 0$
$4x = -9$
$x = -\dfrac{9}{4}$

73. $|2x+1|+4 < 7$
$|2x+1| < 3$
$-3 < 2x+1 < 3$
$-4 < 2x < 2$
$-2 < x < 1$
$(-2, 1)$

75. $|3x-5|+4 = 5$
$|3x-5| = 1$
$3x-5 = 1$ or $3x-5 = -1$
$3x = 6$ or $3x = 4$
$x = 2$ or $x = \dfrac{4}{3}$

77. $|x+11| = -1$ is impossible. The solution set is $\varnothing$.

79. $\left|\dfrac{2x-1}{3}\right| = 6$
$\dfrac{2x-1}{3} = 6$ or $\dfrac{2x-1}{3} = -6$
$2x-1 = 18$ or $2x-1 = -18$
$2x = 19$ or $2x = -17$
$x = \dfrac{19}{2}$ or $x = -\dfrac{17}{2}$

81. $\left|\dfrac{3x-5}{6}\right| > 5$
$\dfrac{3x-5}{6} < -5$ or $\dfrac{3x-5}{6} > 5$
$3x-5 < -30$ or $3x-5 > 30$
$3x < -25$ or $3x > 35$
$x < -\dfrac{25}{3}$ or $x > \dfrac{35}{3}$
$\left(-\infty, -\dfrac{25}{3}\right) \cup \left(\dfrac{35}{3}, \infty\right)$

83. $P(\text{rolling a 2}) = \dfrac{1}{6}$

85. $P(\text{rolling a 7}) = 0$

87. $P(\text{rolling a 1 or 3}) = \dfrac{1}{3}$

89. $3x-4y = 12$
$3(2)-4y = 12$
$6-4y = 12$
$-4y = 6$
$y = -\dfrac{3}{2} = -1.5$

91. $3x-4y = 12$
$3x-4(-3) = 12$
$3x+12 = 12$
$3x = 0$
$x = 0$

93. $|x| < 7$

95. $|x| \leq 5$

97. Answers may vary

99. $|3.5-x| < 0.05$
$-0.05 < 3.5-x < 0.05$
$-3.55 < -x < -3.45$
$3.55 > x > 3.45$
$3.45 < x < 3.55$

The Bigger Picture

1. $9x-14 = 11x+2$
$9x-11x = 14+2$
$-2x = 16$
$x = -8$

2. $|x - 4| = 17$

$x - 4 = -17$ or $x - 4 = 17$

$x = -13$ or $x = 21$

3. $x - 1 \le 5$ or $3x - 2 \le 10$

$x \le 6$ or $3x \le 12$

$x \le 6$ or $x \le 4$

$(-\infty, 6]$

4. $-x < 7$ and $4x \le 20$

$x > -7$ and $x \le 5$

$(-7, 5]$

5. $|x - 2| = |x + 15|$

$x - 2 = x + 15$ or $x - 2 = -(x + 15)$

$-2 = 15$ False $x - 2 = -x - 15$

$2x - 2 = -15$

$2x = -13$

$x = -\dfrac{13}{2}$

The only solution is $-\dfrac{13}{2}$.

6. $9y - 6y + 1 = 4y + 10 - y + 3$

$3y + 1 = 3y + 13$

$1 = 13$

$\varnothing$

7. $\quad 1.5x - 3 = 1.2x - 18$

$1.5x - 1.2x = 3 - 18$

$0.3x = -15$

$x = -50$

8. $\quad \dfrac{7x + 1}{8} - 3 = x + \dfrac{2x + 1}{4}$

$8\left(\dfrac{7x + 1}{8} - 3\right) = 8\left(x + \dfrac{2x + 1}{4}\right)$

$7x + 1 - 8 \cdot 3 = 8x + 2(2x + 1)$

$7x + 1 - 24 = 8x + 4x + 2$

$7x - 23 = 12x + 2$

$7x - 12x = 2 + 23$

$-5x = 25$

$x = -5$

9. $|5x+2|-10 \le -3$

$\quad\;\; |5x+2| \le 7$

$\quad -7 \le 5x+2 \le 7$

$\quad -9 \le 5x \le 5$

$\quad -\dfrac{9}{5} \le x \le 1$

$\left[-\dfrac{9}{5}, 1\right]$

10. $|x+11| > 2$

$\quad x+11 > 2 \quad$ or $\quad x+11 < -2$

$\qquad x > -9 \quad$ or $\qquad x < -13$

$(-\infty, -13) \cup (-9, \infty)$

11. $|9x+2|-1=24$

$\quad\; |9x+2| = 25$

$9x+2 = -25 \quad$ or $\quad 9x+2 = 25$

$\quad 9x = -27 \quad$ or $\qquad 9x = 23$

$\qquad x = -3 \quad$ or $\qquad x = \dfrac{23}{9}$

12. $\left|\dfrac{3x-1}{2}\right| = |2x+5|$

$\dfrac{3x-1}{2} = -(2x+5) \qquad$ or $\qquad \dfrac{3x-1}{2} = 2x+5$

$2\left(\dfrac{3x-1}{2}\right) = 2[-(2x+5)] \quad$ or $\quad 2\left[\dfrac{3x-1}{2}\right] = 2(2x+5)$

$\quad 3x-1 = -4x-10 \qquad$ or $\qquad 3x-1 = 4x+10$

$\quad 3x+4x = -10+1 \qquad$ or $\qquad 3x-4x = 10+1$

$\qquad\quad 7x = -9 \qquad$ or $\qquad\quad -x = 11$

$\qquad\quad x = -\dfrac{9}{7} \qquad$ or $\qquad\quad x = -11$

Chapter 2 Vocabulary Check

1. The statement "$x < 5$ or $x > 7$" is called a <u>compound inequality</u>.

2. An equation in one variable that has no solution is called a <u>contradiction</u>.

3. The <u>intersection</u> of two sets is the set of all elements common to both sets.

4. The <u>union</u> of two sets is the set of all elements that belong to either of the sets.

5. An equation in one variable that has every number (for which the equation is defined) as a solution is called an <u>identity</u>.

6. The equation $d = rt$ is also called a <u>formula</u>.

7. A number's distance from 0 is called its <u>absolute value</u>.

8. When a variable in an equation is replaced by a number and the resulting equation is true, then that number is called a <u>solution</u> of the equation.

9. The integers 17, 18, 19 are examples of <u>consecutive integers</u>.

10. The statement $5x - 0.2 < 7$ is an example of a <u>linear inequality in one variable</u>.

11. The statement $5x - 0.2 = 7$ is an example of a <u>linear equation in one variable</u>.

Chapter 2 Review

1. $4(x-5) = 2x - 14$
$$4x - 20 = 2x - 14$$
$$2x = 6$$
$$x = 3$$

2. $x + 7 = -2(x+8)$
$$x + 7 = -2x - 16$$
$$3x = -23$$
$$x = -\frac{23}{3}$$

3. $3(2y-1) = -8(6+y)$
$$6y - 3 = -48 - 8y$$
$$14y = -45$$
$$y = -\frac{45}{14}$$

4. $-(z+12) = 5(2z-1)$
$$-z - 12 = 10z - 5$$
$$-11z = 7$$
$$z = -\frac{7}{11}$$

5. $n - (8+4n) = 2(3n-4)$
$$n - 8 - 4n = 6n - 8$$
$$-3n = 6n$$
$$-9n = 0$$
$$n = 0$$

6. $4(9v+2) = 6(1+6v) - 10$
$$36v + 8 = 6 + 36v - 10$$
$$36v + 8 = 36v - 4$$
$$8 = -4$$
No solution, or $\varnothing$

7. $0.3(x-2) = 1.2$
$$10[0.3(x-2) = 10(1.2)$$
$$3(x-2) = 12$$
$$3x - 6 = 12$$
$$3x = 18$$
$$x = 6$$

8. $1.5 = 0.2(c - 0.3)$
$$1.5 = 0.2c - 0.06$$
$$100(1.5) = 100(0.2c - 0.06)$$
$$150 = 20c - 6$$
$$156 = 20c$$
$$7.8 = c$$

9. $-4(2-3x) = 2(3x-4) + 6x$
$$-8 + 12x = 6x - 8 + 6x$$
$$-8 + 12x = 12x - 8$$
$$-8 = -8$$
All real numbers

10. $6(m-1) + 3(2-m) = 0$
$$6m - 6 + 6 - 3m = 0$$
$$3m = 0$$
$$m = 0$$

11. $6 - 3(2g+4) - 4g = 5(1-2g)$
$$6 - 6g - 12 - 4g = 5 - 10g$$
$$-6 - 10g = 5 - 10g$$
$$-6 = 5$$
No solution, $\varnothing$

12. $20 - 5(p+1) + 3p = -(2p-15)$
$$20 - 5p - 5 + 3p = -2p + 15$$
$$15 - 2p = -2p + 15$$
$$15 = 15$$
All real numbers

13. $\dfrac{x}{3} - 4 = x - 2$
$$3\left(\dfrac{x}{3} - 4\right) = 3(x-2)$$
$$x - 12 = 3x - 6$$
$$-2x = 6$$
$$x = -3$$

14.
$$\frac{9}{4}y = \frac{2}{3}y$$
$$12\left(\frac{9}{4}y\right) = 12\left(\frac{2}{3}y\right)$$
$$27y = 8y$$
$$19y = 0$$
$$y = 0$$

15.
$$\frac{3n}{8} - 1 = 3 + \frac{n}{6}$$
$$24\left(\frac{3n}{8} - 1\right) = 24\left(3 + \frac{n}{6}\right)$$
$$9n - 24 = 72 + 4n$$
$$5n = 96$$
$$n = \frac{96}{5}$$

16.
$$\frac{z}{6} + 1 = \frac{z}{2} + 2$$
$$6\left(\frac{z}{6} + 1\right) = 6\left(\frac{z}{2} + 2\right)$$
$$z + 6 = 3z + 12$$
$$-2z = 6$$
$$z = -3$$

17.
$$\frac{y}{4} - \frac{y}{2} = -8$$
$$4\left(\frac{y}{4} - \frac{y}{2}\right) = 4(-8)$$
$$y - 2y = -32$$
$$-y = -32$$
$$y = 32$$

18.
$$\frac{2x}{3} - \frac{8}{3} = x$$
$$2x - 8 = 3x$$
$$-8 = x$$

19.
$$\frac{b-2}{3} = \frac{b+2}{5}$$
$$5(b-2) = 3(b+2)$$
$$5b - 10 = 3b + 6$$
$$2b = 16$$
$$b = 8$$

20.
$$\frac{2t-1}{3} = \frac{3t+2}{15}$$
$$15\left(\frac{2t-1}{3}\right) = 15\left(\frac{3t+2}{15}\right)$$
$$5(2t-1) = 3t+2$$
$$10t - 5 = 3t + 2$$
$$7t = 7$$
$$t = 1$$

21.
$$\frac{2(t+1)}{3} = \frac{2(t-1)}{3}$$
$$3\left[\frac{2(t+1)}{3}\right] = 3\left[\frac{2(t-1)}{3}\right]$$
$$2(t+1) = 2(t-1)$$
$$2t + 2 = 2t - 2$$
$$2 = -2$$
No solution, $\varnothing$

22.
$$\frac{3a-3}{6} = \frac{4a+1}{15} + 2$$
$$30\left(\frac{3a-3}{6}\right) = 30\left(\frac{4a+1}{15} + 2\right)$$
$$5(3a-3) = 2(4a+1) + 30(2)$$
$$15a - 15 = 8a + 2 + 60$$
$$15a - 15 = 8a + 62$$
$$7a = 77$$
$$a = 11$$

23. Let x = the number.
$$2(x-3) = 3x+1$$
$$2x - 6 = 3x + 1$$
$$-7 = x$$
The number is -7.

24. Let x = smaller number, then
$x + 5$ = larger number.
$$x + x + 5 = 285$$
$$2x = 280$$
$$x = 140$$
$$x + 5 = 145$$
The numbers are 140 and 145.

25. $40\% \cdot 130 = 0.40 \cdot 130 = 52$

26. $1.5\% \cdot 8 = 0.015 \cdot 8 = 0.12$

27. Let x = number of CDs sold in 2000.
$$x - 0.25x = 705.4$$
$$0.75x = 705.4$$
$$x \approx 940.5$$
There were 940.5 million music CDs sold by
U.S. manufacturers in 2000.

28. Let n = the first integer, then
$n + 1$ = the second integer,
$n + 2$ = the third integer, and
$n + 3$ = the fourth integer.
$$(n+1)+(n+2)+(n+3)-2n = 16$$
$$n + 6 = 16$$
$$n = 10$$
Therefore, the integers are 10, 11, 12, and 13.

29. Let x = smaller odd integer, then
$x + 2$ = larger odd integer.
$$5x = 3(x+2)+54$$
$$5x = 3x+6+54$$
$$2x = 60$$
$$x = 30$$
Since this is not odd, no such consecutive odd integers exist.

30. Let x = width of the playing field, then
$2x - 5$ = length of the playing field.
$$2x + 2(2x-5) = 230$$
$$2x + 4x - 10 = 230$$
$$6x = 240$$
$$x = 40$$
Then $2x - 5 = 2(40) - 5 = 75$. The field is
75 meters long and 40 meters wide.

31. Let m = number of miles of driven.
$$2(19.95)+0.12(m-200) = 46.86$$
$$39.90+0.12m-24 = 46.86$$
$$0.12m+15.90 = 46.86$$
$$0.12m = 30.96$$
$$m = 258$$

32. Solve $R = C$.
$$16.50x = 4.50x+3000$$
$$12x = 3000$$
$$x = 250$$
Thus, 250 calculators must be produced and sold
in order to break even.

33. $V = LWH$
$$W = \frac{V}{LH}$$

34. $C = 2\pi r$
$$\frac{C}{2\pi} = r$$

35. $5x - 4y = -12$
$$5x + 12 = 4y$$
$$y = \frac{5x+12}{4}$$

36. $5x - 4y = -12$
$$5x = 4y - 12$$
$$x = \frac{4y-12}{5}$$

37. $y - y_1 = m(x - x_1)$
$$m = \frac{y-y_1}{x-x_1}$$

38.
$$y - y_1 = m(x-x_1)$$
$$y - y_1 = mx - mx_1$$
$$y - y_1 + mx_1 = mx$$
$$\frac{y-y_1+mx_1}{m} = x$$

39.
$$E = I(R+r)$$
$$E = IR+Ir$$
$$I - IR = Ir$$
$$\frac{E-IR}{I} = r$$

40.
$$S = vt + gt^2$$
$$S - vt = gt^2$$
$$\frac{S-vt}{t^2} = g$$

41. $T = gr + gvt$
$$T = g(r+vt)$$
$$g = \frac{T}{r+vt}$$

42.
$$I = Prt + P$$
$$I = P(rt+1)$$
$$\frac{I}{rt+1} = P$$

43. $A = P\left(1+\dfrac{r}{n}\right)^{nt} = 3000\left(1+\dfrac{0.03}{n}\right)^{7n}$

a. $A = 3000\left(1+\dfrac{0.03}{2}\right)^{14} \approx \$3695.27$

b. $A = 3000\left(1+\dfrac{0.03}{52}\right)^{364} \approx \$3700.81$

44. $C = \frac{5}{9}(F - 32)$

$C = \frac{5}{9}(90 - 32)$

$C = \frac{5}{9}(58)$

$C = \frac{290}{9} \approx 32.2$

$90°F$ is $\left(\frac{290}{9}\right)°C \approx 32.2°C.$

45. Let x = original width, then
$x + 2$ = original length.
$(x+4)(x+2+4) = x(x+2) + 88$
$(x+4)(x+6) = x^2 + 2x + 88$
$x^2 + 10x + 24 = x^2 + 2x + 88$
$8x = 64$
$x = 8$
$x + 2 = 10$
The original width is 8 in. and the original length
is 10 in.

46. Area $= 18 \times 21 = 378 \text{ ft}^2$
Packages $= \frac{378}{24} = 15.75$
There are 16 packages needed.

47. $3(x - 5) > -(x + 3)$
$3x - 15 > -x - 3$
$4x > 12$
$x > 3$
$(3, \infty)$

48. $-2(x + 7) \geq 3(x + 2)$
$-2x - 14 \geq 3x + 6$
$-5x \geq 20$
$x \leq -4$
$(-\infty, -4]$

49. $4x - (5 + 2x) < 3x - 1$
$4x - 5 - 2x < 3x - 1$
$2x - 5 < 3x - 1$
$-x < 4$
$x > -4$
$(-4, \infty)$

50. $3(x - 8) < 7x + 2(5 - x)$
$3x - 24 < 7x + 10 - 2x$
$3x - 24 < 5x + 10$
$-2x < 34$
$x > -17$
$(-17, \infty)$

51. $24 \geq 6x - 2(3x - 5) + 2x$
$24 \geq 6x - 6x + 10 + 2x$
$24 \geq 10 + 2x$
$14 \geq 2x$
$7 \geq x$
$(-\infty, 7]$

52. $\frac{x}{3} + \frac{1}{2} > \frac{2}{3}$
$6\left(\frac{x}{3} + \frac{1}{2}\right) > 6\left(\frac{2}{3}\right)$
$2x + 3 > 4$
$2x > 1$
$x > \frac{1}{2}$
$\left(\frac{1}{2}, \infty\right)$

53. $x + \frac{3}{4} < -\frac{x}{2} + \frac{9}{4}$
$4\left(x + \frac{3}{4}\right) < 4\left(-\frac{x}{2} + \frac{9}{4}\right)$
$4x + 3 < -2x + 9$
$6x < 6$
$x < 1$
$(-\infty, 1)$

54. $\frac{x - 5}{2} \leq \frac{3}{8}(2x + 6)$
$8\left(\frac{x - 5}{2}\right) \leq 8\left[\frac{3}{8}(2x + 6)\right]$
$4(x - 5) \leq 3(2x + 6)$
$4x - 20 \leq 6x + 18$
$-2x \leq 38$
$x \geq -19$
$[-19, \infty)$

55. Let n = number of pounds of laundry.
$15 < 0.5(10) + 0.4(n - 10)$
$15 < 5 + 0.4n - 4$
$15 < 1 + 0.4n$
$14 < 0.4n$
$35 < n$
It is more economical to use the housekeeper for
more than 35 pounds of laundry per week.

56. $500 \le F \le 1000$

$500 \le \dfrac{9}{5}C + 32 \le 1000$

$468 \le \dfrac{9}{5}C \le 968$

$260 \le C \le 538$

Rounded to the nearest degree, firing temperatures range from 260°C to 538°C.

57. Let x = the score from the last judge.

$\dfrac{9.5 + 9.7 + 9.9 + 9.7 + 9.7 + 9.6 + 9.5 + x}{8} \ge 9.65$

$67.6 + x \ge 77.2$

$x \ge 9.6$

The last judge must give Nana at least a 9.6 for her to win the silver medal.

58. Let x = the amount saved each summer.

$4000 \le 2x + 500 \le 8000$

$3500 \le 2x \le 7500$

$1750 \le x \le 3750$

She must save between \$1750 and \$3750 each summer.

59. $1 \le 4x - 7 \le 3$

$8 \le 4x \le 10$

$2 \le x \le \dfrac{5}{2}$

$\left[2, \dfrac{5}{2}\right]$

60. $-2 \le 8 + 5x < -1$

$-10 \le 5x \le -9$

$-2 \le x \le -\dfrac{9}{5}$

$\left[-2, \dfrac{9}{5}\right)$

61. $-3 < 4(2x - 1) < 12$

$-3 < 8x - 4 < 12$

$1 < 8x < 16$

$\dfrac{1}{8} < x < 2$

$\left(\dfrac{1}{8}, 2\right)$

62. $-6 < x - (3 - 4x) < -3$

$-6 < x - 3 + 4x < -3$

$-6 < 5x - 3 < -3$

$-3 < 5x < 0$

$-\dfrac{3}{5} < x < 0$

$\left(-\dfrac{3}{5}, 0\right)$

63. $\dfrac{1}{6} < \dfrac{4x - 3}{3} \le \dfrac{4}{5}$

$30\left(\dfrac{1}{6}\right) < 30\left(\dfrac{4x - 3}{3}\right) \le 30\left(\dfrac{4}{5}\right)$

$5 < 10(4x - 3) \le 24$

$5 < 40x - 30 \le 24$

$35 < 40x \le 54$

$\dfrac{7}{8} < x \le \dfrac{27}{20}$

$\left(\dfrac{7}{8}, \dfrac{27}{20}\right]$

64. $x \le 2$ and $x > -5$

$-5 < x \le 2$

$(-5, 2]$

65. $3x - 5 > 6$ or $-x < -5$

     $3x > 11$ or $x > 5$

        $x > \dfrac{11}{3}$ or $x > 5$

$x > \dfrac{11}{3}$

$\left(\dfrac{11}{3}, \infty\right)$

66. $|x - 7| = 9$

$x - 7 = 9$ or $x - 7 = -9$

    $x = 16$ or $x = -2$

67. $|8 - x| = 3$

$8 - x = 3$ or $8 - x = -3$

   $-x = -5$ or $-x = -11$

     $x = 5$ or $x = 11$

68. $|2x + 9| = 9$

$2x + 9 = 9$ or $2x + 9 = -9$

     $2x = 0$ or $2x = -18$

       $x = 0$ or $x = -9$

69. $|-3x+4|=7$

$$-3x+4=7 \quad \text{or} \quad -3x+4=-7$$
$$-3x=3 \quad \text{or} \quad -3x=-11$$
$$x=-1 \quad \text{or} \quad x=\frac{11}{3}$$

70. $|3x-2|+6=10$

$$|3x-2|=4$$
$$3x-2=4 \quad \text{or} \quad 3x-2=-4$$
$$3x=6 \quad \text{or} \quad 3x=-2$$
$$x=2 \quad \text{or} \quad x=-\frac{2}{3}$$

71. $5+|6x+1|=5$

$$|6x+1|=0$$
$$6x+1=0$$
$$6x=-1$$
$$x=-\frac{1}{6}$$

72. $-5=|4x-3|$

The solution set is $\varnothing$.

73. $|5-6x|+8=3$

$$|5-6x|=-5$$

The solution set is $\varnothing$.

74. $-8=|x-3|-10$

$$2=|x-3|$$
$$x-3=2 \quad \text{or} \quad x-3=-2$$
$$x=5 \quad \text{or} \quad x=1$$

75. $\left|\dfrac{3x-7}{4}\right|=2$

$$\frac{3x-7}{4}=2 \quad \text{or} \quad \frac{3x-7}{4}=-2$$
$$3x-7=8 \quad \text{or} \quad 3x-7=-8$$
$$3x=15 \quad \text{or} \quad 3x=-1$$
$$x=5 \quad \text{or} \quad x=-\frac{1}{3}$$

76. $|6x+1|=|15+4x|$

$$6x+1=15+4x \quad \text{or} \quad 6x+1=-(15+4x)$$
$$2x=14 \quad\quad\;\; \text{or} \quad 6x+1=-15-4x$$
$$x=7 \quad\quad\;\; \text{or} \quad 10x=-16$$
$$x=-\frac{8}{5}$$

77. $|5x-1|<9$

$$-9<5x-1<9$$
$$-8<5x<10$$
$$-\frac{8}{5}<x<2$$
$$\left(-\frac{8}{5},2\right)$$

78. $|6+4x|\geq 10$

$$6+4x\leq-10 \quad \text{or} \quad 6+4x\geq 10$$
$$4x\leq-16 \quad \text{or} \quad 4x\geq 4$$
$$x\leq-4 \quad \text{or} \quad x\geq 1$$
$$(-\infty,-4]\cup[1,\infty)$$

79. $|3x|-8>1$

$$|3x|>9$$
$$3x<-9 \quad \text{or} \quad 3x>9$$
$$x<-3 \quad \text{or} \quad x>3$$
$$(-\infty,-3)\cup(3,\infty)$$

80. $9+|5x|<24$

$$|5x|<15$$
$$-15<5x<15$$
$$-3<x<3$$
$$(-3,3)$$

81. $|6x-5|\leq-1$

The solution set is $\varnothing$.

82. $\left| 3x + \dfrac{2}{5} \right| \geq 4$

$$3x + \frac{2}{5} \leq -4 \quad \text{or} \quad 3x + \frac{2}{5} \geq 4$$

$$5\left(3x + \frac{2}{5}\right) \leq 5(-4) \quad \text{or} \quad 5\left(3x + \frac{2}{5}\right) \geq 5(4)$$

$$15x + 2 \leq -20 \quad \text{or} \quad 15x + 2 \geq 20$$

$$15x \leq -22 \quad \text{or} \quad 15x \geq 18$$

$$x \leq -\frac{22}{15} \quad \text{or} \quad x \geq \frac{6}{5}$$

$$\left(-\infty, -\frac{22}{15}\right] \cup \left[\frac{6}{5}, \infty\right)$$

83. $\left| \dfrac{x}{3} + 6 \right| - 8 > -5$

$$\left| \frac{x}{3} + 6 \right| > 3$$

$$\frac{x}{3} + 6 < -3 \quad \text{or} \quad \frac{x}{3} + 6 > 3$$

$$\frac{x}{3} < -9 \quad \text{or} \quad \frac{x}{3} > -3$$

$$x < -27 \quad \text{or} \quad x > -9$$

$$(-\infty, -27) \cup (-9, \infty)$$

84. $\left| \dfrac{4(x-1)}{7} \right| + 10 < 2$

$$\left| \frac{4(x-1)}{7} \right| < -8$$

The solution set is $\varnothing$.

85. $\dfrac{x-2}{5} + \dfrac{x+2}{2} = \dfrac{x+4}{3}$

$$30\left(\frac{x-2}{5} + \frac{x+2}{2}\right) = 30\left(\frac{x+4}{3}\right)$$

$$6(x-2) + 15(x+2) = 10(x+4)$$

$$6x - 12 + 15x + 30 = 10x + 40$$

$$21x + 18 = 10x + 40$$

$$11x = 22$$

$$x = 2$$

86. $\dfrac{2z-3}{4} - \dfrac{4-z}{2} = \dfrac{z+1}{3}$

$$12\left(\frac{2z-3}{4} - \frac{4-z}{2}\right) = 12\left(\frac{z+1}{3}\right)$$

$$3(2z-3) - 6(4-z) = 4(z+1)$$

$$6z - 9 - 24 + 6z = 4z + 4$$

$$12z - 33 = 4z + 4$$

$$8z = 37$$

$$z = \frac{37}{8}$$

87. Let x = number of tourists for France, then
$x + 9$ = number of tourists for United States, and
$x + 44$ = number of tourists for China.

$$x + (x+9) + (x+44) = 332$$

$$3x + 53 = 332$$

$$3x = 279$$

$$x = 93$$

$x + 9 = 102$
$x + 44 = 137$
China is predicted to have 137 million tourists,
whereas the United States is predicted to have
102 million and France, 93 million.

88. $\qquad A = \dfrac{h}{2}(B + b)$

$$2A = hB + hb$$

$$2A - hb = hB$$

$$\frac{2A - hb}{h} = B$$

89. $\qquad V = \dfrac{1}{3}\pi r^2 h$

$$3V = \pi r^2 h$$

$$\frac{3V}{\pi r^2} = h$$

90. $V_{\text{box}} = lwh = 8 \cdot 5 \cdot 3 = 120 \text{ in}^3$, while

$V_{\text{cyl}} = \pi r^2 h = \pi \cdot 3^2 \cdot 6 = 54\pi \approx 170 \text{ in}^3$

Therefore, the cylinder holds more ice cream.

91. $d = rt$ or $r = \dfrac{d}{t}$

11:00 A.M. to 1:15 P.M. is 2.25 hours.

$r = \dfrac{130}{2.25} \approx 58$

His average speed was 58 mph.

92. $48 + x \geq 5(2x + 4) - 2x$

$48 + x \geq 10x + 20 - 2x$

$48 + x \geq 8x + 20$

$28 \geq 7x$

$4 \geq x$

$(-\infty, 4]$

93. $\dfrac{3(x-2)}{5} > \dfrac{-5(x-2)}{3}$

$15\left[\dfrac{3(x-2)}{5}\right] > 15\left[\dfrac{-5(x-2)}{3}\right]$

$9(x-2) > -25(x-2)$

$9x - 18 > -25x + 50$

$34x > 68$

$x > 2$

$(2, \infty)$

94. $0 \leq \dfrac{2(3x+4)}{5} \leq 3$

$5(0) \leq 5\left[\dfrac{2(3x+4)}{5}\right] \leq 5(3)$

$0 \leq 2(3x+4) \leq 15$

$0 \leq 6x + 8 \leq 15$

$-8 \leq 6x \leq 7$

$-\dfrac{4}{3} \leq x \leq \dfrac{7}{6}$

$\left[-\dfrac{4}{3}, \dfrac{7}{6}\right]$

95. $x \leq 2$ or $x > -5$

$(-\infty, \infty)$

96. $-2x \leq 6$ and $-2x + 3 < -7$

$x \geq -3$ and $-2x < -10$

$x \geq -3$ and $x > 5$

$x > 5$

$(5, \infty)$

97. $|7x| - 26 = -5$

$|7x| = 21$

$7x = 21$ or $7x = -21$

$x = 3$ or $x = -3$

98. $\left|\dfrac{9-2x}{5}\right| = -3$

The solution set is $\varnothing$.

99. $|x - 3| = |7 + 2x|$

$x - 3 = 7 + 2x$ or $x - 3 = -(7 + 2x)$

$-10 = x$ or $x - 3 = -7 - 2x$

$3x = -4$

$x = -\dfrac{4}{3}$

100. $|6x - 5| \geq -1$

Since $|6x - 5|$ is nonnegative for all numbers x, the solution set is $(-\infty, \infty)$.

101. $\left|\dfrac{4x-3}{5}\right| < 1$

$-1 < \dfrac{4x-3}{5} < 1$

$-5 < 4x - 3 < 5$

$-2 < 4x < 8$

$-\dfrac{1}{2} < x < 2$

$\left(-\dfrac{1}{2}, 2\right)$

Chapter 2 Test

1. $8x + 14 = 5x + 44$

$3x = 30$

$x = 10$

2. $9(x + 2) = 5[11 - 2(2 - x) + 3]$

$9x + 18 = 5[11 - 4 + 2x + 3]$

$9x + 18 = 5[10 + 2x]$

$9x + 18 = 50 + 10x$

$-x = 32$

$x = -32$

3. $3(y - 4) + y = 2(6 + 2y)$

$3y - 12 + y = 12 + 4y$

$4y - 12 = 12 + 4y$

$-12 = 12$

No solution, $\varnothing$

4. $7n - 6 + n = 2(4n - 3)$

$8n - 6 = 8n - 6$

$-6 = -6$

All real numbers

5.
$$\frac{7w}{4} + 5 = \frac{3w}{10} + 1$$
$$20\left(\frac{7w}{4} + 5\right) = 20\left(\frac{3w}{10} + 1\right)$$
$$35w + 100 = 6w + 20$$
$$29w = -80$$
$$w = -\frac{80}{29}$$

6.
$$\frac{z+7}{9} + 1 = \frac{2z+1}{6}$$
$$18\left(\frac{z+7}{9} + 1\right) = 18\left(\frac{2z+1}{6}\right)$$
$$2(z+7) + 18 = 3(2z+1)$$
$$2z + 14 + 18 = 6z + 3$$
$$2z + 32 = 6z + 3$$
$$2z - 6z = 3 - 32$$
$$-4z = -29$$
$$z = \frac{29}{4}$$

7. $|6x - 5| - 3 = -2$
$$|6x - 5| = 1$$
$$6x - 5 = 1 \quad \text{or} \quad 6x - 5 = -1$$
$$6x = 6 \quad \text{or} \quad 6x = 4$$
$$x = 1 \quad \text{or} \quad x = \frac{2}{3}$$

8. $|8 - 2t| = -6$
No solution, $\varnothing$

9. $|2x - 3| = |4x + 5|$
$$2x - 3 = 4x + 5 \quad \text{or} \quad 2x - 3 = -(4x + 5)$$
$$2x - 4x = 5 + 3 \quad \text{or} \quad 2x - 3 = -4x - 5$$
$$-2x = 8 \quad \text{or} \quad 2x + 4x = -5 + 3$$
$$x = -4 \quad \text{or} \quad 6x = -2$$
$$x = -4 \quad \text{or} \quad x = -\frac{1}{3}$$

10. $|x - 5| = |x + 2|$
$$x - 5 = x + 2 \quad \text{or} \quad x - 5 = -(x + 2)$$
$$-5 = 2 \text{ False} \quad \text{or} \quad x - 5 = -x - 2$$
$$2x = 3$$
$$x = \frac{3}{2}$$

Since $-5 = 2$ is not possible, the only solution is $\frac{3}{2}$.

11. $3x - 4y = 8$
$$3x - 8 = 4y$$
$$y = \frac{3x - 8}{4}$$

12. $S = gt^2 + gvt$
$$S = g(t^2 + vt)$$
$$g = \frac{S}{t^2 + vt}$$

13. $F = \frac{9}{5}C + 32$
$$F - 32 = \frac{9}{5}C$$
$$C = \frac{5}{9}(F - 32)$$

14. $3(2x - 7) - 4x > -(x + 6)$
$$6x - 21 - 4x > -x - 6$$
$$2x - 21 > -x - 6$$
$$3x > 15$$
$$x > 5$$
$(5, \infty)$

15.
$$\frac{3x - 2}{3} - \frac{5x + 1}{4} \geq 0$$
$$12\left[\frac{3x - 2}{3} - \frac{5x + 1}{4}\right] \geq 12(0)$$
$$4(3x - 2) - 3(5x + 1) \geq 0$$
$$12x - 8 - 15x - 3 \geq 0$$
$$-3x - 11 \geq 0$$
$$-3x \geq 11$$
$$x \leq -\frac{11}{3}$$
$$\left(-\infty, -\frac{11}{3}\right]$$

16. $-3 < 2(x - 3) \leq 4$
$$-3 < 2x - 6 \leq 4$$
$$3 < 2x \leq 10$$
$$\frac{3}{2} < x \leq 5$$
$$\left(\frac{3}{2}, 5\right]$$

17. $|3x+1| > 5$

$3x+1 < -5$ or $3x+1 > 5$

$3x < -6$ or $3x > 4$

$x < -2$ or $x > \dfrac{4}{3}$

$(-\infty, -2) \cup \left(\dfrac{4}{3}, \infty\right)$

18. $|x-5| - 4 < -2$

$|x-5| < 2$

$-2 < x-5 < 2$

$3 < x < 7$

$(3, 7)$

19. $x \geq 5$ and $x \geq 4$

$[5, \infty)$

20. $x \geq 5$ or $x \geq 4$

$[4, \infty)$

21. $-1 \leq \dfrac{2x-5}{3} < 2$

$3(-1) \leq 3\left(\dfrac{2x-5}{3}\right) < 3(2)$

$-3 \leq 2x-5 < 6$

$-3+5 \leq 2x-5+5 < 6+5$

$2 \leq 2x < 11$

$\dfrac{2}{2} \leq \dfrac{2x}{2} < \dfrac{11}{2}$

$1 \leq x < \dfrac{11}{2}$

$\left[1, \dfrac{11}{2}\right)$

22. $6x+1 > 5x+4$ or $1-x > -4$

$x > 3$ or $5 > x$

$(-\infty, \infty)$

23. $12\% \cdot 80 = 0.12 \cdot 80 = 9.6$

24. Let x = number employed in 2004.

$x + 0.55x = 357,000$

$1.55x = 357,000$

$x \approx 230,323$

There were 230,323 employees in 2004.

25. Recall that $C = 2\pi r$. Here $C = 78.5$.

$78.5 = 2\pi r$

$r = \dfrac{78.5}{2\pi} = \dfrac{39.25}{\pi}$

Also, recall that $A = \pi r^2$.

$A = \pi\left(\dfrac{39.25}{\pi}\right)^2 \approx \dfrac{39.25^2}{3.14} \approx 490.63$

Dividing this by 60 yields approximately 8.18. Therefore, about 8 hunting dogs could safely be kept in the pen.

26. Solve $R > C$.

$7.4x > 3910 + 2.8x$

$4.6x > 3910$

$x > 850$

Therefore, more than 850 sunglasses must be produced and sold in order for them to yield a profit.

27. $A = P\left(1 + \dfrac{r}{n}\right)^{nt}$

$= 2500\left(1 + \dfrac{0.035}{4}\right)^{4 \cdot 10}$

$= \$3542.27$

28. Let x = population of New York, then
$x + 1.3$ = population of Seoul, Korea, and
$2x - 10.2$ = population of Tokyo.

$x + (x+1.3) + (2x-10.2) = 78.3$

$4x - 8.9 = 78.3$

$4x = 87.2$

$x = 21.8$

$x + 1.3 = 23.1$

$2x - 10.2 = 33.4$

The populations are as follows:
New York: 21.8 million,
Seoul: 23.1 million,
Tokyo: 33.4 million.

Chapter 2 Cumulative Review

1. a. $\{101, 102, 103, ...\}$

b. $\{2, 3, 4, 5\}$

2. a. $\{-2, -1, 0, 1, 2, 3, 4\}$

b. $\{4\}$

3. a. $|3| = 3$

b. $\left|-\dfrac{1}{7}\right| = \dfrac{1}{7}$

c. $-|2.7| = -2.7$

d. $-|-8| = -8$

e. $|0| = 0$

4. a. The opposite of $\dfrac{2}{3}$ is $-\dfrac{2}{3}$.

b. The opposite of -9 is 9.

c. The opposite of 1.5 is -1.5.

5. a. $-3 + (-11) = -14$

b. $3 + (-7) = -4$

c. $-10 + 15 = 5$

d. $-8.3 + (-1.9) = -10.2$

e. $-\dfrac{2}{3} + \dfrac{3}{7} = -\dfrac{14}{21} + \dfrac{9}{21} = -\dfrac{5}{21}$

6. a. $-2 - (-10) = -2 + 10 = 8$

b. $1.7 - 8.9 = -7.2$

c. $-\dfrac{1}{2} - \dfrac{1}{4} = -\dfrac{2}{4} - \dfrac{1}{4} = -\dfrac{3}{4}$

7. a. $\sqrt{9} = 3$ since $3^2 = 9$.

b. $\sqrt{25} = 5$ since $5^2 = 25$.

c. $\sqrt{\dfrac{1}{4}} = \dfrac{1}{2}$ since $\left(\dfrac{1}{2}\right)^2 = \dfrac{1}{4}$.

d. $-\sqrt{36} = -6$ since $6^2 = 36$.

e. $\sqrt{-36}$ is not a real number.

8. a. $-3(-2) = 6$

b. $-\dfrac{3}{4}\left(-\dfrac{4}{7}\right) = \dfrac{3}{7}$

c. $\dfrac{0}{-2} = 0$

d. $\dfrac{-20}{-2} = 10$

9. Let $x = 4$, $y = -3$.

a. $3x - 7y = 3(4) - 7(-3) = 12 + 21 = 33$

b. $-2y^2 = -2(-3)^2 = -2(9) = -18$

c. $\dfrac{\sqrt{x}}{y} - \dfrac{y}{x} = \dfrac{\sqrt{4}}{-3} - \dfrac{-3}{4}$

$= -\dfrac{2}{3} + \dfrac{3}{4}$

$= -\dfrac{8}{12} + \dfrac{9}{12}$

$= \dfrac{1}{12}$

10. a. $\sqrt[4]{1} = 1$ since $1^4 = 1$.

b. $\sqrt[3]{8} = 2$ since $2^3 = 8$.

c. $\sqrt[4]{81} = 3$ since $3^4 = 81$.

11. a. $x + 5 = 20$

b. $2(3 + y) = 4$

c. $x - 8 = 2x$

d. $\dfrac{z}{9} = 9 + z$

12. a. $-3 > -5$ since -3 is to the right of -5 on the number line.

b. $\dfrac{-12}{-4} = 3$

c. $0 > -2$ since 0 is to the right of -2 on the number line.

13. $7x + 5 = 5 + 7x$

14. $5 \cdot (7x) = (5 \cdot 7)x = 35x$

15. $2x + 5 = 9$
$2x = 4$
$x = 2$

16. $11.2 = 1.2 - 5x$
$10 = -5x$
$-2 = x$

17. $6x - 4 = 2 + 6(x - 1)$
$6x - 4 = 2 + 6x - 6$
$6x - 4 = 6x - 4$
$-4 = -4,$ which is always true.
All real numbers

18. $2x + 1.5 = -0.2 + 1.6x$
$0.4x = -1.7$
$x = -4.25$

19. a. Let $x =$ the first integer. Then
$x + 1 =$ the second integer and
$x + 2 =$ the third integer.
$x + (x + 1) + (x + 2) = 3x + 3$

    b. $x + (5x) + (6x - 3) = 12x - 3$

20. a. Let $x =$ the first integer. Then
$x + 1 =$ the second integer and
$x + 2 =$ the third integer.
$x + (x + 1) + (x + 2) = 3x + 3$

    b. $4(3x + 1) = 12x + 4$

21. Let $x =$ first number, then
$2x + 3 =$ second number and
$4x =$ third number.
$x + (2x + 3) + 4x = 164$
$7x + 3 = 164$
$7x = 161$
$x = 23$
$2x + 3 = 2(23) + 3 = 49$
$4x = 4(23) = 92$
The three numbers are 23, 49 and 92.

22. Let $x =$ first number, then
$3x + 2 =$ second number.
$(3x + 2) - x = 24$
$2x + 2 = 24$
$2x = 22$
$x = 11$
$3x + 2 = 3(11) + 2 = 35$
The two numbers are 11 and 35.

23. $3y - 2x = 7$
$3y = 2x + 7$
$y = \dfrac{2x + 7}{3},$ or $y = \dfrac{2x}{3} + \dfrac{7}{3}$

24. $7x - 4y = 10$
$7x = 4y + 10$
$x = \dfrac{4y + 10}{7},$ or $x = \dfrac{4y}{7} + \dfrac{10}{7}$

25. $A = \dfrac{1}{2}(B + b)h$
$2A = (B + b)h$
$2A = Bh + bh$
$2A - Bh = bh$
$\dfrac{2A - Bh}{h} = b$

26. $P = 2l + 2w$
$P - 2w = 2l$
$\dfrac{P - 2w}{2} = l$

27. a. $\{x | x \geq 2\}$

$[2, \infty)$

    b. $\{x | x < -1\}$

$(-\infty, -1)$

    c. $\{x | 0.5 < x \leq 3\}$

$(0.5, 3]$

28. a. $\{x | x \leq -3\}$

$(-\infty, -3]$

    b. $\{x | -2 \leq x < 0.1\}$

$[-2, 0.1)$

29. $-(x - 3) + 2 \leq 3(2x - 5) + x$
$-x + 3 + 2 \leq 6x - 15 + x$
$-x + 5 \leq 7x - 15$
$20 \leq 8x$
$\dfrac{5}{2} \leq x$

$\left[\dfrac{5}{2}, \infty\right)$

30. $2(7x - 1) - 5x > -(-7x) + 4$
$14x - 2 - 5x > 7x + 4$
$9x - 2 > 7x + 4$
$2x > 6$
$x > 3$
$(3, \infty)$

31. $2(x+3) > 2x+1$
$2x+6 > 2x+1$
$6 > 1$; True for all real numbers x.
$(-\infty, \infty)$

32. $4(x+1)-3 < 4x+1$
$4x+4-3 < 4x+1$
$4x+1 < 4x+1$
$1 < 1$ Never true
$\varnothing$

33. $A = \{2, 4, 6, 8\}$, $B = \{3, 4, 5, 6\}$; the numbers 4 and 6 are in both sets so the intersection of A and B is $\{4, 6\}$.

34. The elements in either set or both sets are -2, -1, $0, 1, 2, 3, 4$, and 5, so the union is $\{-2, -1, 0, 1, 2, 3, 4, 5\}$.

35. $x-7 < 2$ and $2x+1 < 9$
$x < 9$ and $2x < 8$
$\phantom{x-7 < 9 \text{ and } 2x+1}x < 4$
$x < 4$
$(-\infty, 4)$

36. $x+3 \le 1$ or $3x-1 < 8$
$x \le -2$ or $3x < 9$
$\phantom{x+3 \le -2 \text{ or } 3x-1}x < 3$
$x < 3$
$(-\infty, 3)$

37. $A = \{2, 4, 6, 8\}$ and $B = \{3, 4, 5, 6\}$, so the union of A and B is $\{2, 3, 4, 5, 6, 8\}$.

38. $\varnothing$; there are no elements in common.

39. $-2x-5 < -3$ or $6x < 0$
$-2x < 2$ or $x < 0$
$\phantom{-2x-5 < }x > -1$
All real numbers
$(-\infty, \infty)$

40. $-2x-5 < -3$ and $6x < 0$
$-2x < 2$ and $x < 0$
$\phantom{-2x-5 < }x > -1$
$-1 < x < 0$
$(-1, 0)$

41. $|p| = 2$
$p = 2$ or $p = -2$

42. $|x| = 5$
$x = 5$ or $x = -5$

43. $\left|\dfrac{x}{2} - 1\right| = 11$

$\dfrac{x}{2} - 1 = 11$ or $\dfrac{x}{2} - 1 = -11$

$\dfrac{x}{2} = 12$ or $\dfrac{x}{2} = -10$

$x = 24$ or $x = -20$

44. $\left|\dfrac{y}{3} + 2\right| = 10$

$\dfrac{y}{3} + 2 = 10$ or $\dfrac{y}{3} + 2 = -10$

$\dfrac{y}{3} = 8$ or $\dfrac{y}{3} = -12$

$y = 24$ or $y = -36$

45. $|x-3| = |5-x|$
$x-3 = 5-x$ or $x-3 = -(5-x)$
$2x = 8$ or $x-3 = -5+x$
$x = 4$ or $-3 = -5$
Since $-3 = -5$ is not possible, the only solution is 4.

46. $|x+3| = |7-x|$
$x+3 = 7-x$ or $x+3 = -(7-x)$
$2x = 4$ or $x-3 = -7+x$
$x = 2$ or $-3 = -7$
Since $-3 = -7$ is not possible, the only solution is 2.

47. $|x| \le 3$
$-3 \le x \le 3$
$[-3, 3]$

48. $|x| > 1$
$x < -1$ or $x > 1$
$(-\infty, -1) \cup (1, \infty)$

49. $|2x+9| + 5 > 3$
$|2x+9| > -2$
Since $|2x + 9|$ is nonnegative for all numbers x, the solution set is $(-\infty, \infty)$.

50. $|3x+1| + 9 < 1$
$|3x+1| < -8$
The solution set is $\varnothing$.

Chapter 3

Practice Exercises

1. The six points are graphed as shown.

   a. $(3, -4)$ lies in quadrant IV.

   b. $(0, -2)$ is on the y-axis.

   c. $(-2, 4)$ lies in quadrant II.

   d. $(4, 0)$ is on the x-axis.

   e. $\left(-1\frac{1}{2}, -2\right)$ is in quadrant III.

   f. $(2.5, 3.5)$ is in quadrant I.

2. Let $x = 1$ and $y = 4$.
$$4x + y = 8$$
$$4(1) + 4 \overset{?}{=} 8$$
$$4 + 4 \overset{?}{=} 8$$
$$8 = 8 \quad \text{True}$$
Let $x = 0$ and $y = 6$.
$$4x + y = 8$$
$$4(0) + 6 \overset{?}{=} 8$$
$$0 + 6 \overset{?}{=} 8$$
$$6 = 8 \quad \text{False}$$
Let $x = 3$ and $y = -4$.
$$4x + y = 8$$
$$4(3) + (-4) \overset{?}{=} 8$$
$$12 - 4 \overset{?}{=} 8$$
$$8 = 8 \quad \text{True}$$
Thus, $(0, 6)$ is not a solution, but both $(1, 4)$ and $(3, -4)$ are solutions.

3. **a.** Since x is products sold, find 6000 along the x-axis and move vertically up until you reach a point on the line. From this point on the line, move horizontally to the left until you reach the y-axis. Its value on the y-axis is 4200, which means if $6000 worth of products is sold, the salary for the month is $4200.

   b. Since y is monthly salary, find 4800 along the y-axis and move horizontally to the right until you reach a point on the line. Move vertically downward until you reach the x-axis. The corresponding x-value is 9000. This means that $9000 worth of products sold gives a salary of $4800 for the month. For the salary to be greater than $4800, products sold must be greater than $9000.

4. $y = -3x - 2$

   This is a linear equation. (In standard form, it is $3x + y = -2$.) Since the equation is solved for y, we choose three x-values.
   Let $x = 0$.
   $$y = -3x - 2$$
   $$y = -3 \cdot 0 - 2$$
   $$y = -2$$
   Let $x = -1$.
   $$y = -3x - 2$$
   $$y = -3(-1) - 2$$
   $$y = 1$$
   Let $x = -2$.
   $$y = -3x - 2$$
   $$y = -3(-2) - 2$$
   $$y = 4$$
   The three ordered pairs $(0, -2)$, $(-1, 1)$, and $(-2, 4)$ are listed in the table.

x	y
0	-2
-1	1
-2	4

$y = -3x - 2$

5. $y = -\dfrac{1}{2}x$

To avoid fractions, we choose x-values that are multiples of 2. To find the y-intercept, we let $x = 0$.

If $x = 0$, then $y = -\dfrac{1}{2}(0)$, or 0.

If $x = 2$, then $y = -\dfrac{1}{2}(2)$, or -1.

If $x = -2$, then $y = -\dfrac{1}{2}(-2)$, or 1.

x	y
0	0
2	-1
-2	1

$y = -\dfrac{1}{2}x$

6. $y = 2x^2$

This equation is not linear because of the x^2 term. Its graph is not a line.

If $x = -3$, then $y = 2(-3)^2$, or 18.

If $x = -2$, then $y = 2(-2)^2$, or 8.

If $x = -1$, then $y = 2(-1)^2$, or 2.

If $x = 0$, then $y = 2(0)^2$, or 0.

If $x = 1$, then $y = 2(1)^2$, or 2.

If $x = 2$, then $y = 2(2)^2$, or 8.

If $x = 3$, then $y = 2(3)^2$, or 18.

x	y
-3	18
-2	8
-1	2
0	0
1	2
2	8
3	18

7. $y = -|x|$

This equation is not linear because it cannot be written in the form $Ax + By = C$. Its graph is not a line.

If $x = -3$, then $y = -|-3|$, or -3.

If $x = -2$, then $y = -|-2|$, or -2.

If $x = -1$, then $y = -|-1|$, or -1.

If $x = 0$, then $y = -|0|$, or 0.

If $x = 1$, then $y = -|1|$, or -1.

If $x = 2$, then $y = -|2|$, or -2.

If $x = 3$, then $y = -|3|$, or -3.

x	y
−3	−3
−2	−2
−1	−1
0	0
1	−1
2	−2
3	−3

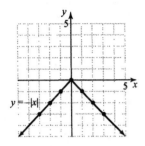

$y = -|x|$

Graphing Calculator Explorations

1.

2.

3.

4.

5.

6.

7.

8.

Vocabulary and Readiness Check

1. Point *A* is (5, 2).

2. Point *B* is (2, 5).

3. Point *C* is (3, 0).

4. Point *D* is (−1, 3).

5. Point *E* is (−5, −2).

6. Point *F* is (−3, 5).

7. Point *G* is (−1, 0).

8. Point *H* is (0, −3).

9. (2, 3); QI

10. (0, 5); *y*-axis

11. (−2, 7); QII

12. (−3, 0); *x*-axis

13. (−1, −4); QIII

14. (4, −2); QIV

15. $(0, -100)$; *y*-axis

16. $(10, 30)$; QI

17. $(-10, -30)$; QIII

18. $(0, 0)$; *x*- and *y*-axis

19. $(-87, 0)$; *x*-axis

20. $(-42, 17)$; QII

Exercise Set 3.1

1. $(3, 2)$ is in quadrant I

3. $(-5, 3)$ is in quadrant II.

5. $\left(5\dfrac{1}{2}, -4\right)$ is in quadrant IV.

7. $(0, 3.5)$ is on the *y*-axis.

9. $(-2, -4)$ is in quadrant III.

11. $(x, -y)$ lies in quadrant IV.

13. $(x, 0)$ lies on the *x*-axis.

15. $(-x, -y)$ lies in quadrant III.

17. Let $x = 0$, $y = 5$.
$$y = 3x - 5$$
$$5 = 3 \cdot 0 - 5$$
$$5 = -5$$
False; no

Let $x = -1$, $y = -8$.
$$y = 3x - 5$$
$$-8 = 3 \cdot (-1) - 5$$
$$-8 = -8$$
True; yes

19. Let $x = 1$, $y = 0$.
$$-6x + 5y = -6$$
$$-6(1) + 5(0) = -6$$
$$-6 = -6$$
True; yes

Let $x = 2$, $y = \dfrac{6}{5}$.
$$-6x + 5y = -6$$
$$-6(2) + 5\left(\dfrac{6}{5}\right) = -6$$
$$-6 = -6$$
True; yes

21. Let $x = 1$, $y = 2$.

$y = 2x^2$

$2 = 2(1)^2$

$2 = 2$

True; yes

Let $x = 3$, $y = 18$.

$y = 2x^2$

$18 = 2(3)^2$

$18 = 18$

True; yes

23. Let $x = 2$, $y = 8$.

$y = x^3$

$8 = (2)^3$

$8 = 8$

True; yes

Let $x = 3$, $y = 9$,

$y = x^3$

$9 = (3)^3$

$9 = 27$

False; no

25. Let $x = 1$, $y = 3$.

$y = \sqrt{x} + 2$

$3 = \sqrt{1} + 2$

$3 = 3$

True; yes

Let $x = 4$, $y = 4$.

$y = \sqrt{x} + 2$

$4 = \sqrt{4} + 2$

$4 = 4$

True; yes

27. $x + y = 3$

Linear

x	y
0	3
3	0
1	2

29. $y = 4x$

Linear

x	y
-1	-4
0	0
1	4

31. $y = 4x - 2$

Linear

x	y
0	-2
$\frac{1}{2}$	0
1	2

33. $y = |x| + 3$
Not linear

x	y
−2	5
−1	4
0	3
1	4
2	5

35. $2x − y = 5$
Linear

x	y
$2\frac{1}{2}$	0
0	−5
1	−3

37. $y = 2x^2$
Not linear

x	y
−2	8
−1	2
0	0
1	2
2	8

39. $y = x^2 − 3$
Not linear

x	y
−2	1
−1	−2
0	−3
1	−2
2	1

41. $y = −2x$
Linear

x	y
−1	2
0	0
1	−2

43. $y = -2x + 3$
Linear

x	y
−1	5
0	3
1	1

45. $y = |x + 2|$
Not linear

x	y
−4	2
−3	1
−2	0
−1	1
0	2

47. $y = x^3$
Not linear

x	y
−3	−27
−2	−8
−1	−1
0	0
1	1
2	8

49. $y = -|x|$
Not linear

x	y
−2	−2
−2	−1
0	0
1	−1
2	−2

51. $y = \dfrac{1}{3}x - 1$

Linear

x	y
-3	-2
0	-1
3	0

53. $x = -\dfrac{3}{2}x + 1$

Linear

x	y
-2	4
0	1
2	-2

55. $3(x-2) + 5x = 6x - 16$

$3x - 6 + 5x = 6x - 16$

$8x - 6 = 6x - 16$

$2x = -10$

$x = -5$

The solution is -5.

57. $3x + \dfrac{2}{5} = \dfrac{1}{10}$

$30x + 4 = 1$

$30x = -3$

$x = -\dfrac{1}{10}$

The solution is $-\dfrac{1}{10}$.

59. $3x \le -15$

$x \le -5$

$(-\infty, -5]$

61. $2x - 5 > 4x + 3$

$-2x > 8$

$x < -4$

$(-\infty, -4)$

63. The first coordinate, -1, indicates that the point is 1 unit to the left of the y-axis. The second coordinate, 5.3, indicates that the point is 5.3 units above the x-axis. The answer is b.

65. Look for the graph where the only nonzero y-values are 40 and 60. The answer is b.

67. Look for the graph where all the y-values are between 10 and 30. The answer is c.

69. The first segment in the graph with y-coordinate greater than 0.25 begins in February 1991. Thus, 1991 is the first year that the price of a first-class stamp rose above \$0.25.

71. Answers may vary

73. $y = x^2 - 4x + 7$

x	y
0	7
1	4
2	3
3	4
4	7

75. a. $y = 2x + 6$

x	y
0	6
1	8
2	10

b. When x is 4, y is 14. Thus, when the length is 4 inches, the perimeter is 14 inches.

77. When $x = 0$, $y = 7$. Thus, the purchase price was $7000.

79. $7000 - 6500 = \$500$

81. Depreciation is the same from year to year.

83. They are parallel.

85. Answers may vary

87. "The y-value is -3 decreased by twice the x-value" is written as $y = -3 - 2x$.

89. "The y-value is 5 decreased by the square of the x-value" is written as $y = 5 - x^2$.

91.

93.

Section 3.2

Practice Exercises

1. a. The domain is the set of all first coordinates, $\{4, 5\}$. The range is the set of all second coordinates, $\{1, -3, -2, 6\}$.

b. Ordered pairs are not listed here but are given in graph form. The relation is $\{(3, -4), (3, -3), (3, -2), (3, -1), (3, 0), (3, 1), (3, 2), (3, 3), (3, 4)\}$. The domain is $\{3\}$. The range is $\{-4, -3, -2, -1, 0, 1, 2, 3, 4\}$.

c.   The domain is the set of inputs, {Administrative Secretary, Game Developer, Engineer, Restaurant Manager, Marketing}. The range is comprised of the numbers in the set of outputs that correspond to elements in the set of inputs, {27, 73, 50, 35}.

2. a.   Although the ordered pairs (3, 1) and (9, 1) have the same *y*-value, each *x*-value is assigned to only one *y*-value, so this set of ordered pairs is a function.

    b.   The *x*-value −2 is assigned to two *y*-values, −3 and 4, in this graph, so this relation does not define a function.

    c.   This relation is a function because although two different people may have the same birth date, each person has only one birth date. This means that each element in the first set is assigned to only one element in the second set.

3.   The relation $y = -3x + 5$ is a function if each *x*-value corresponds to just one *y*-value. For each *x*-value substituted into the equation $y = -3x + 5$, the multiplication and addition performed on each gives a single result, so only one *y*-value will be associated with each *x*-value. Thus, $y = -3x + 5$ is a function.

4.   The relation $y = -x^2$ is a function if each *x*-value corresponds to just one *y*-value. For each *x*-value substituted into the equation $y = -x^2$, squaring each gives a single result, so only one *y*-value will be associated with each *x*-value. Thus, $y = -x^2$ is a function.

5. a.   Yes, this is the graph of a function since no vertical line will intersect this graph more than once.

    b.   Yes, this is the graph of a function since no vertical line will intersect this graph more than once.

    c.   No, this is not the graph of a function. Note that vertical lines can be drawn that intersect the graph in two points.

d.   Yes, this is the graph of a function since no vertical line will intersect this graph more than once.

e.   No, this is not the graph of a function. A vertical line can be drawn that intersects this line at every point.

6. a.   By the vertical line test, the graph is the graph of a function. The *x*-values are graphed from −1 to 2, so the domain is [−1, 2]. The *y*-values are graphed from −2 to 9, so the range is [−2, 9].

    b.   By the vertical line test, the graph is not the graph of a function. The *x*-values are graphed from −1 to 1, so the domain is [−1, 1]. The *y*-values are graphed from −4 to 4, so the range is [−4, 4].

    c.   By the vertical line test, the graph is the graph of a function. The arrows indicate that the graph continues forever. All *x*-values are graphed, so the domain is (−∞, ∞). The *y*-values for 4 and numbers less than 4 are graphed, so the range is (−∞, 4].

    d.   By the vertical line test, the graph is the graph of a function. The arrows indicate that the graph continues forever. All *x*-values and all *y*-values are graphed, so the domain is (−∞, ∞) and the range is (−∞, ∞).

7. a.   Substitute 1 for *x* in *f*(*x*).
$$f(x) = 3x - 2$$
$$f(1) = 3(1) - 2 = 3 - 2 = 1$$

    b.   Substitute 1 for *x* in *g*(*x*).
$$g(x) = 5x^2 + 2x - 1$$
$$g(1) = 5(1)^2 + 2(1) - 1$$
$$= 5 + 2 - 1 = 6$$

c. Substitute 0 for x in $f(x)$.

$f(x) = 3x - 2$

$f(0) = 3(0) - 2 = 0 - 2 = -2$

d. Substitute -2 for x in $g(x)$.

$g(x) = 5x^2 + 2x - 1$

$g(-2) = 5(-2)^2 + 2(-2) - 1$

$= 5(4) - 4 - 1$

$= 20 - 4 - 1 = 15$

8. a. To find $f(1)$, find the y-value when $x = 1$. We see from the graph that when $x = 1$, y or $f(x) = -3$. Thus, $f(1) = -3$.

b. $f(0) = -2$ from the ordered pair $(0, -2)$.

c. $g(-2) = 3$ from the ordered pair $(-2, 3)$.

d. $g(0) = 1$ from the ordered pair $(0, 1)$.

e. To find x-values such that $f(x) = 1$, we are looking for any ordered pairs on the graph of f whose $f(x)$ or y-value is 1. They are $(-1, 1)$ and $(3, 1)$. Thus, $f(-1) = 1$ and $f(3) = 1$. The x-values are -1 and 3.

f. Find ordered pairs on the graph of g whose $g(x)$ or y-value is -2. There is one such ordered pair, $(-3, -2)$. Thus, $g(-3) = -2$. The only x-value is -3.

9. Find the year 2003 and move upward until you reach the graph. From the point on the graph, move horizontally to the left until the other axis is reached. In 2003, approximately \$35 billion was spent.

10. Find $f(2012)$.

$f(x) = 2.602x - 5178$

$f(2012) = 2.602(2012) - 5178$

$= 57.224$

We predict that \$57.224 billion will be spent in 2012.

Graphing Calculator Explorations

1.

2.

3.

4.

5.

6.

Vocabulary and Readiness Check

1. The intersection of the x-axis and y-axis is a point, called the <u>origin</u>.

2. To find an x-intercept, let <u>y</u> = 0 and solve for <u>x</u>.

3. To find a y-intercept, let <u>x</u> = 0 and solve for <u>y</u>.

4. The graph of $Ax + By = C$, where A and B are not both 0 is a <u>line</u>.

5. The graph of $y = |x|$ looks <u>V-shaped</u>.

6. The graph of $y = x^2$ is a <u>parabola</u>.

7. A <u>relation</u> is a set of ordered pairs.

8. The <u>range</u> of a relation is the set of all second components of the ordered pairs.

9. The <u>domain</u> of a relation is the set of all first components of the ordered pairs.

10. A <u>function</u> is a relation in which each first component in the ordered pairs corresponds to *exactly* one second component.

11. By the vertical line test, all linear equations are functions except those whose graphs are <u>vertical</u> lines.

12. If $f(-2) = 1.7$, the corresponding ordered pair is <u>(−2, 1.7)</u>.

Exercise Set 3.2

1. The domain is the set of all first coordinates and the range is the set of all second coordinates.
Domain = {−1, 0, −2, 5}
Range = {7, 6, 2}
Function since each x-value corresponds to exactly one y-value.

3. The domain is the set of all first coordinates and the range is the set of all second coordinates.
Domain = {−2, 6, −7}
Range = {4, −3, −8}
The relation is not a function since −2 is paired with both 4 and −3.

5. The domain is the set of all first coordinates and the range is the set of all second coordinates.
Domain = {1}
Range = {1, 2, 3, 4}
The relation is not a function since 1 is paired with both 1 and 2 for example.

7. The domain is the set of all first coordinates and the range is the set of all second coordinates.
Domain = $\left\{\dfrac{3}{2}, 0\right\}$

Range = $\left\{\dfrac{1}{2}, -7, \dfrac{4}{5}\right\}$

The relation is not a function since $\dfrac{3}{2}$ is paired

with both $\dfrac{1}{2}$ and −7.

9. The domain is the set of all first coordinates and the range is the set of all second coordinates.
Domain = {−3, 0, 3}
Range = {−3, 0, 3}
Function since each x-value corresponds to exactly one y-value.

11. Points on graph: (−1, 2), (1, 1), (2, 1), (3, 1)
Domain = {−1, 1, 2, 3}
Range = {2, 1}
Function since each x-value corresponds to exactly one y-value.

13. Domain = {Iowa, Alaska, Delaware, Illinois, Connecticut, New York}
Range = {5, 1, 19, 29}
Function since each input corresponds to exactly one output.

15. Domain = {32°, 104°, 212°, 50°}
Range = {0°, 40°, 10°, 100°}
Function since each input corresponds to exactly one output.

17. Domain = {0}
Range = {2, −1, 5, 100}
Not a function since the input 0 corresponds to more than one output.

19. This relation is a function because although two different students may have the same final grade average, each student has only one final grade average. This means that each element in the first set is assigned to only one element in the second set.

21. This relation is not a function because more than one person in Cincinnati has blue eyes. This means that one element in the first set is assigned to more than one element in the second set.

23. Yes, this is the graph of a function since no vertical line will intersect this graph more than once.

25. No, this is not the graph of a function. Note that vertical lines can be drawn that intersect the graph in two points. The y-axis is such a vertical line.

27. Yes, this is the graph of a function since no vertical line will intersect this graph more than once.

29. The x-values are graphed from 0 to +∞; domain = $[0, \infty)$
The arrows indicate the y-values continue forever; range = $(-\infty, \infty)$
The relation is not a function since it fails the vertical line test (try $x = 1$).

31. The x-values are graphed from -1 to 1; domain $= [-1, 1]$

The arrows indicate the y-values continue forever; range $= (-\infty, \infty)$

The relation is not a function since it fails the vertical line test (try $x = 0$).

33. The arrows indicate the x-values continue forever; domain $= (-\infty, \infty)$

The y-values do not include $(-3, 3)$; range $= (-\infty, -3] \cup [3, \infty)$

The relation is not a function since it fails the vertical line test (try $x = 2$).

35. The x-values are graphed from 2 to 7; domain $= [2, 7]$

The y-values are graphed from 1 to 6; range $= [1, 6]$

The relation is not a function since it fails the vertical line test (try $x = 4$).

37. The only x-value is 2; domain $= \{-2\}$
The y-values continue forever; range $= (-\infty, \infty)$
The relation is not a function since it fails the vertical line test (try $x = -2$).

39. The x-values continue forever; domain $= (-\infty, \infty)$

The y-values are 3 and less; range $= (-\infty, 3]$
Function since it passes the vertical line test.

41. Answers may vary

43. $y = x + 1$
For each x-value substituted into the equation $y = x + 1$, the addition performed gives a single result, so only one y-value will be associated with each x-value. Thus, $y = x + 1$ is a function.

45. $x = 2y^2$
The x-value 8 is associated with two y-values, -2 and 2. Thus, $x = 2y^2$ is not a function.

47. $y - x = 7$
For each x-value substituted into the equation $y - x = 7$, the process of solving for y gives a single result, so only one y-value will be associated with each x-value. Thus, $y - x = 7$ is a function.

49. $y = \dfrac{1}{x}$

For each x-value substituted into the equation $y = \dfrac{1}{x}$, the division performed gives a single result, so only one y-value will be associated with each x-value. Thus, $y = \dfrac{1}{x}$ is a function.

51. $y = 5x - 12$

For each x-value substituted into the equation $y = 5x - 12$, the multiplication and addition performed on each gives a single result, so only one y-value will be associated with each x-value. Thus, $y = 5x - 12$ is a function.

53. $x = y^2$

The x-value 4 is associated with two y-values, -2 and 2. Thus, $x = y^2$ is not a function.

55. $f(x) = 3x + 3$
$f(4) = 3(4) + 3 = 12 + 3 = 15$

57. $h(x) = 5x^2 - 7$
$$\begin{aligned} h(-3) &= 5(-3)^2 - 7 \\ &= 5(9) - 7 \\ &= 45 - 7 \\ &= 38 \end{aligned}$$

59. $g(x) = 4x^2 - 6x + 3$
$$\begin{aligned} g(2) &= 4(2)^2 - 6(2) + 3 \\ &= 4(4) - 12 + 3 \\ &= 16 - 12 + 3 \\ &= 7 \end{aligned}$$

61. $g(x) = 4x^2 - 6x + 3$
$$\begin{aligned} g(0) &= 4(0)^2 - 6(0) + 3 \\ &= 4(0) - 0 + 3 \\ &= 0 - 0 + 3 \\ &= 3 \end{aligned}$$

63. $f(x) = \dfrac{1}{2}x$

a. $f(0) = \dfrac{1}{2}(0) = 0$

b. $f(2) = \dfrac{1}{2}(2) = 1$

c. $f(-2) = \dfrac{1}{2}(-2) = -1$

65. $g(x) = 2x^2 + 4$

a. $g(-11) = 2(-11)^2 + 4$
$= 2(121) + 4$
$= 242 + 4$
$= 246$

b. $g(-1) = 2(-1)^2 + 4$
$= 2(1) + 4$
$= 2 + 4$
$= 6$

c. $g\left(\dfrac{1}{2}\right) = 2\left(\dfrac{1}{2}\right)^2 + 4$
$= 2\left(\dfrac{1}{4}\right) + 4$
$= \dfrac{1}{2} + \dfrac{8}{2}$
$= \dfrac{9}{2}$

67. $f(x) = -5$

a. $f(2) = -5$

b. $f(0) = -5$

c. $f(606) = -5$

69. $f(x) = 1.3x^2 - 2.6x + 5.1$

a. $f(2) = 1.3(2)^2 - 2.6(2) + 5.1$
$= 1.3(4) - 5.2 + 5.1$
$= 5.2 - 5.2 + 5.1$
$= 5.1$

b. $f(-2) = 1.3(-2)^2 - 2.6(-2) + 5.1$
$= 1.3(4) + 5.2 + 5.1$
$= 5.2 + 5.2 + 5.1$
$= 15.5$

c. $f(3.1) = 1.3(3.1)^2 - 2.6(3.1) + 5.1$
$= 1.3(9.61) - 8.06 + 5.1$
$= 12.493 - 8.06 + 5.1$
$= 9.533$

71. If $f(1) = -10$, then $y = -10$ when $x = 1$. The ordered pair is $(1, -10)$.

73. If $g(4) = 56$, then $y = 56$ when $x = 4$. The ordered pair is $(4, 56)$.

75. The ordered pair $(-1, -2)$ is on the graph of f. Thus, $f(-1) = -2$.

77. The ordered pair $(2, 0)$ is on the graph of g. Thus, $g(2) = 0$.

79. There are two ordered pairs on the graph of f with a y-value of -5, $(-4, -5)$ and $(0, -5)$. The x-values are -4 and 0.

81. To the right of the y-axis, there is one ordered pair on the graph of g with a y-value of 4, $(3, 4)$. The x-value is 3.

83. Infinite number
The reason is that a graph is a function as long as it passes the vertical line test. So it does not matter if the equation of the graph takes on the value 0 many times.

85. a. Find the year 1996 and move upward until you reach the graph. From the point on the graph, move horizontally to the left until the other axis is reached. In 1996, approximately \$17 billion was spent.

b. Find $f(1996)$.
$f(x) = 2.602x - 5178$
$f(1996) = 2.602(1996) - 5178$
$= 15.592$
Approximately \$15.592 billion was spent in 1996.

87. Since 2012 is 12 years after 2000, find $f(12)$.
$f(x) = 0.42x + 10.5$
$f(12) = 0.42(12) + 10.5$
$= 15.54$
We predict that diamond production will be \$15.54 billion in 2012.

89. $f(x) = x + 7$

91. $A(r) = \pi r^2$

$A(5) = \pi(5)^2 = 25\pi$ square centimeters

93. $V(x) = x^3$

$V(14) = (14)^3 = 2744$ cubic inches

95. $H(f) = 2.59f + 47.24$

$H(46) = 2.59(46) + 47.24$

$= 166.38$ centimeters

97. $D(x) = \dfrac{136}{25}x$

$D(30) = \dfrac{136}{25}(30) = 163.2$ milligrams

99. $C(x) = 2.28x + 94.86$

a. $C(5) = 2.28(5) + 94.86 = 106.24$

The per capita consumption of poultry was about 106.26 lb in 2006.

b. 2007 gives $x = 6$.

$C(6) = 2.28(6) + 94.86 = 108.54$ pounds

101. $x - y = -5$

x	0	–5	1
y	5	0	6

103. $7x + 4y = 8$

x	0	$\dfrac{8}{7}$	$\dfrac{12}{7}$
y	2	0	–1

105. $y = 6x$

x	0	0	–1
y	0	0	–6

107. Yes, it is possible to find the perimeter. The sum of the lengths of the two sides parallel to the side measuring 45 meters is also 45 meters. The sum of the lengths of the two sides parallel to the side measuring 40 meters is also 40 meters. The perimeter is $45 + 45 + 40 + 40 = 170$ meters.

109. $f(7) = 50$ means that $y = 50$ when $x = 7$. We conclude that the given statement is false, since it does not follow from $f(7) = 50$.

111. Since $f(7) = 50$ when $f(x) = 10x - 20$, the statement is true.

113. $g(x) = -3x + 12$

a. $g(s) = -3s + 12$

b. $g(r) = -3r + 12$

115. $f(x) = x^2 - 12$

a. $f(12) = (12)^2 - 12 = 144 - 12 = 132$

b. $f(a) = a^2 - 12$

117. Answers may vary

Section 3.3

Practice Exercises

1. $f(x) = 4x$, $g(x) = 4x - 3$

x	$f(x)$	$g(x)$
0	0	–3
–1	–4	–7
1	4	1

2. $f(x) = -2x$, $g(x) = -2x + 5$

x	$f(x)$	$g(x)$
0	0	5
–1	2	7
1	–2	3
2	–4	1

3. a. The y-intercept of $f(x) = \dfrac{3}{4}x - \dfrac{2}{5}$ is
$$\left(0, -\frac{2}{5}\right).$$

   b. The y-intercept of $y = 2.6x + 4.1$ is
$(0, 4.1)$.

4. $4x - 5y = -20$

Let $x = 0$.
$$4x - 5y = -20$$
$$4 \cdot 0 - 5y = -20$$
$$-5y = -20$$
$$y = 4$$

Let $y = 0$.
$$4x - 5y = -20$$
$$4x - 5 \cdot 0 = -20$$
$$4x = -20$$
$$x = -5$$

Let $x = -2$.
$$4x - 5y = -20$$
$$4(-2) - 5y = -20$$
$$-8 - 5y = -20$$
$$-5y = -12$$
$$y = \frac{12}{5} = 2\frac{2}{5}$$

The ordered pairs are in the table.

x	y
0	4
–5	0
–2	$2\frac{2}{5}$

5. $y = -3x$

If $x = 0$, then $y = -3(0) = 0$.
If $x = 1$, then $y = -3(1) = -3$.
If $x = -1$, then $y = -3(-1) = 3$.

The ordered pairs are in the table.

x	y
0	0
1	–3
–1	3

6. $x = -4$

The equation can be written as $x + 0y = -4$. For any y-value chosen, notice that x is -4.

x	y
-4	-3
-4	0
-4	3

7. $y = 4$

The equation can be written as $0x + y = 4$. For any x-value chosen, notice that y is 4.

x	y
-3	4
0	4
3	4

Graphing Calculator Explorations

1. $x = 3.5y$

$$y = \frac{x}{3.5}$$

2. $-2.7y = x$

$$y = \frac{x}{-2.7} = -\frac{x}{2.7}$$

3. $5.78x + 2.31y = 10.98$

$2.31y = -5.78x + 10.98$

$$y = -\frac{5.78}{2.31}x + \frac{10.98}{2.31}$$

4. $-7.22x + 3.89y = 12.57$

$3.89y = 7.22x + 12.57$

$$y = \frac{7.22}{3.89}x + \frac{12.57}{3.89}$$

5. $y - |x| = 3.78$

$$y = |x| + 3.78$$

6. $3y - 5x^2 = 6x - 4$

$$3y = 5x^2 + 6x - 4$$

$$y = \frac{5}{3}x^2 + 2x - \frac{4}{3}$$

7. $y - 5.6x^2 = 7.7x + 1.5$

$$y = 5.6x^2 + 7.7x + 1.5$$

8. $y + 2.6|x| = -3.2$

$$y = -2.6|x| - 3.2$$

Vocabulary and Readiness Check

1. A <u>linear</u> function can be written in the form $f(x) = mx + b$.

2. In the form $f(x) = mx + b$, the y-intercept is <u>(0, b)</u>.

3. The graph of $x = c$ is a <u>vertical</u> line with x-intercept <u>(c, 0)</u>.

4. The graph of $y = c$ is a <u>horizontal</u> line with y-intercept <u>(0, c)</u>.

5. To find an x-intercept, let <u>y</u> = 0 or <u>f(x)</u> = 0 and solve for <u>x</u>.

6. To find a y-intercept, let <u>x</u> = 0 and solve for <u>y</u>.

Exercise Set 3.3

1. $f(x) = -2x$

x	0	-1	1
y	0	2	-2

Plot the points to obtain the graph.

3. $f(x) = -2x + 3$

x	0	1	-1
y	3	1	5

Plot the points to obtain the graph.

5. $f(x) = \frac{1}{2}x$

x	0	2	-2
y	0	1	-1

Plot the points to obtain the graph.

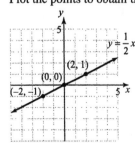

7. $f(x) = \frac{1}{2}x - 4$

x	0	2	4
y	-4	-3	-2

Plot the points to obtain the graph.

$$y = \frac{1}{2}x - 4$$

9. The graph of $f(x) = 5x - 3$ is the graph of $f(x) = 5x$ shifted down 3 units. The correct graph is C.

11. The graph of $f(x) = 5x + 1$ is the graph of $f(x) = 5x$ shifted up 1 unit. The correct graph is D.

13. $x - y = 3$

Let $x = 0$.   Let $y = 0$.   Let $x = 2$.
$0 - y = 3$ $x - 0 = 3$ $2 - y = 3$
$y = -3$ $x = 3$ $y = -1$

x	0	3	2
y	−3	0	−1

$$f(x) = x - 3$$

15. $x = 5y$

Let $x = 0$.   Let $x = 5$.   Let $x = -5$.
$0 = 5y$ $5 = 5y$ $-5 = 5y$
$y = 0$ $y = 1$ $y = -1$

x	0	5	−5
y	0	1	−1

$$f(x) = \frac{x}{5}$$

17. $-x + 2y = 6$

Let $x = 0$.   Let $y = 0$.   Let $x = 2$.
$-0 + 2y = 6$ $-x + 2(0) = 6$ $-2 + 2y = 6$
$y = 3$ $x = -6$ $y = 4$

x	0	−6	2
y	3	0	4

$$f(x) = \frac{1}{2}x + 3$$

19. $2x - 4y = 8$

Let $x = 0$.   Let $y = 0$.
$2(0) - 4y = 8$ $2x - 4(0) = 8$
$y = -2$ $x = 4$
Let $x = 2$.
$2(2) - 4y = 8$
$y = -1$

x	0	4	2
y	−2	0	−1

$$f(x) = \frac{1}{2}x - 2$$

21. Answers may vary

23. $x = -1$

Vertical line with x-intercept at -1

25. $y = 0$

Horizontal line with y-intercept at 0

27. $y + 7 = 0$

$y = -7$

Horizontal line with y-intercept at -7

29. The graph of $y = 2$ is a horizontal line with y-intercept $(0, 2)$. The correct graph is C.

31. The graph of $x - 2 = 0$ or $x = 2$ is a vertical line with x-intercept $(2, 0)$. The correct graph is A.

33. The vertical line $x = 0$ has y-intercepts.

35. $x + 2y = 8$

37. $3x + 5y = 7$

39. $x + 8y = 8$

41. $5 = 6x - y$

43. $-x + 10y = 11$

45. $y = \dfrac{3}{2}$

47. $2x + 3y = 6$

49. $x + 3 = 0$, or $x = -3$

51. $f(x) = \dfrac{3}{4}x + 2$

53. $f(x) = x$

55. $f(x) = \dfrac{1}{2}x$

57. $f(x) = 4x - \dfrac{1}{3}$

59. $x = -3$

61. $|x - 3| = 6$

$x - 3 = 6$ or $x - 3 = -6$

$x = 9$ or $\quad x = -3$

The solution set is $\{-3, 9\}$.

63. $|2x + 5| > 3$

$2x + 5 < -3$ or $2x + 5 > 3$

$2x < -8$ or $\quad 2x > -2$

$x < -4$ or $\quad x > -1$

$(-\infty, -4) \cup (-1, \infty)$

65. $|3x - 4| \le 2$

$-2 \le 3x - 4 \le 2$

$2 \le 3x \le 6$

$\dfrac{2}{3} \le x \le 2$

$\left[\dfrac{2}{3}, 2\right]$

67. $\dfrac{-6 - 3}{2 - 8} = \dfrac{-9}{-6} = \dfrac{3}{2}$

69. $\dfrac{-8 - (-2)}{-3 - (-2)} = \dfrac{-8 + 2}{-3 + 2} = \dfrac{-6}{-1} = 6$

71. $\dfrac{0 - 6}{5 - 0} = \dfrac{-6}{5} = -\dfrac{6}{5}$

73. $2x + 3y = 1500$

    a. $2(0) + 3y = 1500$

            $3y = 1500$

              $y = 500$

       (0, 500); If no tables are produced, 500 chairs can be produced.

    b. $2x + 3(0) = 1500$

              $2x = 1500$

               $x = 750$

       (750, 0); If no chairs are produced, 750 tables can be produced.

    c. $2(50) + 3y = 1500$

            $100 + 3y = 1500$

                $3y = 1400$

                  $y = 466.7$

       466 chairs

75. $C(x) = 0.2x + 24$

    a. $C(200) = 0.2(200) + 24$

                  $= 40 + 24$

                  $= 64$

       \$64

    b.

    c.   The line moves upward from left to right.

77. $f(x) = 107.3x + 1245.62$

    a.   Since 2015 is 15 years after 2000, find $f(15)$.

           $f(15) = 107.3(15) + 1245.62$

                 $= 1609.5 + 1245.62$

                 $= 2855.12$

       In 2015, the yearly cost of attending a two-year college will be approximately \$2855.12.

    b.   Let $f(x) = 2500$.

           $2500 = 107.3x + 1245.62$

         $1254.38 = 107.3x$

         $\dfrac{1254.38}{107.3} = x$

           $11.69 \approx x$

       Round up to 12. The yearly cost of attending a two-year college will first exceed \$2500 in 2012, 12 years after 2000.

c.   Answers may vary.

79.

81.

83. **a.** $y = -4x + 2$ is a line parallel to $y = -4x$ but with y-intercept $(0, 2)$.

   b. $y = -4x - 5$ is a line parallel to $y = -4x$ but with y-intercept $(0, -5)$.

85.   The graph shows the graph of $y = |x|$ shifted up 1 unit. Its equation is $y = |x| + 1$. The correct answer is b.

87.   The graph shows the graph of $y = |x|$ shifted down 1 unit. Its equation is $y = |x| - 1$. The correct answer is a.

Section 3.4

Practice Exercises

1.   Let $(x_1, y_1) = (4, 0)$ and $(x_2, y_2) = (-2, 3)$.
$$m = \frac{y_2 - y_1}{x_2 - x_1}$$
$$= \frac{3 - 0}{-2 - 4}$$
$$= \frac{3}{-6}$$
$$= -\frac{1}{2}$$

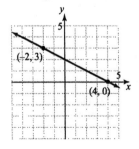

2.   Let $(x_1, y_1) = (-5, -4)$ and $(x_2, y_2) = (5, 2)$.
$$m = \frac{y_2 - y_1}{x_2 - x_1}$$
$$= \frac{2 - (-4)}{5 - (-5)}$$
$$= \frac{6}{10}$$
$$= \frac{3}{5}$$

3. $f(x) = -4x + 6$ or $y = -4x + 6$
We need two points. We find the intercepts.
Let $x = 0$.
$y = -4 \cdot 0 + 6 = 6$
Let $y = 0$.
$0 = -4x + 6$
$4x = 6$
$$x = \frac{6}{4} = \frac{3}{2}$$

The intercepts are $(0, 6)$ and $\left(\frac{3}{2}, 0\right)$. Let
$(x_1, y_1) = (0, 6)$ and $(x_2, y_2) = \left(\frac{3}{2}, 0\right)$.
$$m = \frac{y_2 - y_1}{x_2 - x_1}$$
$$= \frac{0 - 6}{\frac{3}{2} - 0}$$
$$= \frac{-6}{\frac{3}{2}}$$
$$= -\frac{6}{1} \cdot \frac{2}{3}$$
$$= -\frac{12}{3}$$
$$= -4$$

4. $2x - 3y = 9$

Write the equation in slope-intercept form by solving for y.

$$2x - 3y = 9$$
$$-3y = -2x + 9$$
$$\frac{-3y}{-3} = \frac{-2x}{-3} + \frac{9}{-3}$$
$$y = \frac{2}{3}x - 3$$

The coefficient of x, $\frac{2}{3}$, is the slope, and the y-intercept is $(0, -3)$.

5. $f(x) = 2.7x + 38.64$

The year 2012 corresponds to $x = 16$.

$$f(16) = 2.7(16) + 38.64$$
$$= 43.2 + 38.64$$
$$= 81.84$$

We predict that in 2012 the price of an adult one-day pass will be about \$81.84.

6. $x = 4$

The graph of $x = 4$ is a vertical line. We choose two points on the line, $(4, 0)$ and $(4, 3)$. Let $(x_1, y_1) = (4, 0)$ and $(x_2, y_2) = (4, 3)$.

$$m = \frac{y_2 - y_1}{x_2 - x_1}$$
$$= \frac{3 - 0}{4 - 4}$$
$$= \frac{3}{0}$$

Since $\frac{3}{0}$ is undefined, the slope of the vertical line $x = 4$ is undefined.

7. $y = -3$

The graph of $y = -3$ is a horizontal line. We choose two points on the line, $(0, -3)$ and $(4, -3)$. Let $(x_1, y_1) = (0, -3)$ and $(x_2, y_2) = (4, -3)$.

$$m = \frac{y_2 - y_1}{x_2 - x_1}$$
$$= \frac{-3 - (-3)}{4 - 0}$$
$$= \frac{0}{4}$$
$$= 0$$

The slope of the horizontal line $y = -3$ is 0.

8. a. Find the slope of each line.

$$x - 2y = 3$$
$$-2y = -x + 3$$
$$\frac{-2y}{-2} = \frac{-x}{-2} + \frac{3}{-2}$$
$$y = \frac{1}{2}x - \frac{3}{2}$$

The slope is $\frac{1}{2}$.

$$2x + y = 3$$
$$y = -2x + 3$$

The slope is -2. The product of the slopes is $-1 \left[\frac{1}{2}(-2) = -1 \right]$. The lines are perpendicular.

b. Find the slope of each line.

$$4x - 3y = 2$$
$$-3y = -4x + 2$$
$$\frac{-3y}{-3} = \frac{-4x}{-3} + \frac{2}{-3}$$
$$y = \frac{4}{3}x - \frac{2}{3}$$

The slope is $\frac{4}{3}$. The y-intercept is $\left(0, -\frac{2}{3} \right)$.

$$-8x + 6y = -6$$
$$6y = 8x - 6$$
$$\frac{6y}{6} = \frac{8x}{6} - \frac{6}{6}$$
$$y = \frac{4}{3}x - 1$$

The slope is $\frac{4}{3}$. The y-intercept is $(0, -1)$.

The slopes of both lines are $\frac{4}{3}$. The y-intercepts are different, so the lines are not the same. Therefore, the lines are parallel.

Graphing Calculator Explorations

1.

$y = 18.4$

2.

$y = 11.5$

3.

$x = -1.5$

4.

$x = 10.5$

5.

$y = 14.0$

$x = 4.2$

$x = -9.4$

6.

$x = 23.1$

$x = -1.5$

$x = 2.7$

Vocabulary and Readiness Check

1. The measure of the steepness or tilt of a line is called <u>slope</u>.

2. The slope of a line through two points is measured by the ratio of <u>vertical</u> change to <u>horizontal</u> change.

3. If a linear equation is in the form $y = mx + b$, or $f(x) = mx + b$, the slope of the line is <u>m</u> and the y-intercept is <u>$(0, b)$</u>.

4. The form $y = mx + b$ or $f(x) = mx + b$ is the <u>slope-intercept</u> form.

5. The slope of a <u>horizontal</u> line is 0.

6. The slope of a <u>vertical</u> line is undefined.

7. Two perpendicular lines have slopes whose product is <u>−1</u>.

8. Two non-vertical lines are parallel if they have <u>the same</u> slope and different <u>y-intercepts</u>.

9. $m = \dfrac{7}{6}$ slants upward.

10. $m = -3$ slants downward.

11. Since $m = 0$, the line is horizontal.

12. Since the slope is undefined, the line is vertical.

Exercise Set 3.4

1. $m = \dfrac{11 - 2}{8 - 3} = \dfrac{9}{5}$

3. $m = \dfrac{8-1}{1-3} = \dfrac{7}{-2} = -\dfrac{7}{2}$

5. $m = \dfrac{3-8}{4-(-2)} = \dfrac{-5}{6} = -\dfrac{5}{6}$

7. $m = \dfrac{-4-(-6)}{4-(-2)} = \dfrac{-4+6}{4+2} = \dfrac{2}{6} = \dfrac{1}{3}$

9. $m = \dfrac{11-(-1)}{-12-(-3)} = \dfrac{12}{-9} = -\dfrac{4}{3}$

11. $m = \dfrac{5-5}{3-(-2)} = \dfrac{0}{5} = 0$

13. $m = \dfrac{-5-1}{-1-(-1)} = \dfrac{-6}{0}$

undefined slope

15. $m = \dfrac{0-6}{-3-0} = \dfrac{-6}{-3} = 2$

17. $m = \dfrac{4-2}{-3-(-1)} = \dfrac{2}{-2} = -1$

19. The slope of l_1 is negative, and the slope of l_2 is positive. Since a positive number is greater than any negative number, l_2 has the greater slope.

21. The slope of l_1 is negative, and the slope of l_2 is 0. Since 0 is greater than any negative number, l_2 has the greater slope.

23. Both lines have positive slope. Since l_2 is steeper, it has the greater slope.

25. $f(x) = 5x - 2$
$m = 5$, $b = -2$ so y-intercept is $(0, -2)$.

27. $2x + y = 7$
$\qquad y = -2x + 7$
$m = -2$, $b = 7$ so y-intercept is $(0, 7)$.

29. $2x - 3y = 10$
$\qquad -3y = -2x + 10$
$\qquad y = \dfrac{2}{3}x - \dfrac{10}{3}$
$m = \dfrac{2}{3}$, $b = -\dfrac{10}{3}$ so y-intercept is $\left(0, -\dfrac{10}{3}\right)$.

31. $f(x) = \dfrac{1}{2}x$
$m = \dfrac{1}{2}$, $b = 0$ so y-intercept is $(0, 0)$.

33. $f(x) = 2x + 3$
The slope is 2, and the y-intercept is $(0, 3)$. The correct graph is A.

35. $f(x) = -2x + 3$
The slope is -2, and the y-intercept is $(0, 3)$. The correct graph is B.

37. $x = 1$ is a vertical line.
m is undefined.

39. $y = -3$ is a horizontal line.
$m = 0$

41. $x + 2 = 0$
$\qquad x = -2$
This is a vertical line. m is undefined.

43. Answers may vary

45. $f(x) = -x + 5$ or $y = -1x + 5$
$m = -1$, $b = 5$ so y-intercept is $(0, 5)$.

47. $-6x + 5y = 30$
$\qquad 5y = 6x + 30$
$\qquad y = \dfrac{6}{5}x + 6$
$m = \dfrac{6}{5}$, $b = 6$ so y-intercept is $(0, 6)$.

49. $3x + 9 = y$
$\qquad y = 3x + 9$
$m = 3$, $b = 9$ so y-intercept is $(0, 9)$.

51. $y = 4$
$m = 0$, $b = 4$ so y-intercept is $(0, 4)$.

53. $f(x) = 7x$
$m = 7$, $b = 0$ so y-intercept is $(0, 0)$.

55. $6 + y = 0$
$\qquad y = -6$
$m = 0$, $b = -6$ so y-intercept is $(0, -6)$.

57. $2 - x = 3$
$\qquad x = -1$
m is undefined. There is no y-intercept.

59. $f(x) = -3x + 6$ $g(x) = 3x + 5$
    $m = -3$ $m = 3$
Neither, since their slopes are not equal nor does their product equal -1.

61. $-4x + 2y = 5$ $2x - y = 7$
            $y = 2x + \dfrac{5}{2}$ $y = 2x - 7$
                        $m = 2$
    $m = 2$
Parallel, since they have the same slope.

63. $-2x + 3y = 1$ $3x + 2y = 12$
        $y = \dfrac{2}{3}x + \dfrac{1}{3}$ $y = -\dfrac{3}{2}x + 6$
    $m = \dfrac{2}{3}$ $m = -\dfrac{3}{2}$
Perpendicular, since the product of their slopes is -1.

65. Answers may vary

67. Two points on the line: $(0, 0)$, $(2, 3)$
    $m = \dfrac{3 - 0}{2 - 0} = \dfrac{3}{2}$

69. Two points on the line: $(4, 0)$, $(0, 2)$
    $m = \dfrac{2 - 0}{0 - 4} = \dfrac{2}{-4} = -\dfrac{1}{2}$

71. $m = \dfrac{8}{12} = \dfrac{2}{3}$

73. $m = \dfrac{-1600 \text{ ft.}}{2.5 \text{ mi}}$
    $= \dfrac{-1600 \text{ ft.}}{2.5(5280 \text{ ft.})}$
    $= \dfrac{-1600}{13,200} \approx -0.12$

75. $y = 694.9x + 43,884.9$

    a. The year 2009 corresponds to $x = 9$.
    $y = 694.9(9) + 43,884.9$
    $\quad = 6254.1 + 43,884.9$
    $\quad = 50,139$
    We predict that in 2009 an American man with an associate's degree will earn $50,139.

    b. The slope is 694.9. The annual income increases $694.90 every year.

    c. The y-intercept is $(0, 43,884.9)$. When $x = 0$, or in 2000, the average annual income was $43,884.90.

77. $-66x + 2y = 84$

    a. Solve for y.
    $-66x + 2y = 84$
    $\quad\quad 2y = 66x + 84$
    $\quad\quad \dfrac{2y}{2} = \dfrac{66x}{2} + \dfrac{84}{2}$
    $\quad\quad y = 33x + 42$
    The slope is 33, and the y-intercept is $(0, 42)$.

    b. The number of WiFi hotspots increases 33 thousand for every 1 year.

    c. There were 42,000 WiFi hotspots in 2003.

79. $f(x) = 291.5x + 2944.05$

    a. The slope is 291.5. The yearly cost of tuition increases $291.50 every 1 year.

    b. The y-intercept is $(0, 2944.05)$. The yearly cost of tuition when $x = 0$, or in 2000, was $2944.05.

81. $y - 2 = 5(x + 6)$
    $y - 2 = 5x + 30$
    $\quad\; y = 5x + 32$

83. $y - (-1) = 2(x - 0)$
    $\quad y + 1 = 2x$
    $\quad\quad y = 2x - 1$

85. The denominator in the first fraction should be $7 - (-2)$.
    $m = \dfrac{-14 - 6}{7 - (-2)} = \dfrac{-20}{9} = -\dfrac{20}{9}$

87. The numerator in the first fraction should be $-10 - (-5)$. The denominator in the first fraction should be $-8 - (-11)$.
    $m = \dfrac{-10 - (-5)}{-8 - (-11)} = \dfrac{-5}{3} = -\dfrac{5}{3}$

89. $f(x) = -\dfrac{7}{2}x - 6$ or $y = -\dfrac{7}{2}x - 6$

$m = -\dfrac{7}{2}$

The slope of a parallel line is $-\dfrac{7}{2}$.

91. $f(x) = -\dfrac{7}{2}x - 6$ or $y = -\dfrac{7}{2}x - 6$

$m = -\dfrac{7}{2}$

The slope of a perpendicular line is $\dfrac{2}{7}$.

93. $5x - 2y = 6 \Rightarrow y = \dfrac{5}{2}x - 3$

$m = \dfrac{5}{2}$

The slope of a parallel line is $\dfrac{5}{2}$.

95. $5x - 2y = 6 \Rightarrow y = \dfrac{5}{2}x - 3$

$m = \dfrac{5}{2}$

The slope of a perpendicular line is $-\dfrac{2}{5}$.

97. a. $(6, 20)$

   b. $(10, 13)$

   c. $m = \dfrac{13 - 20}{10 - 6} = \dfrac{-7}{4} = -\dfrac{7}{4} = -1.75$

     The rate of change is -1.75 yd per sec.

   d. $F(22, 2)$, $G(26, 8)$

     $m = \dfrac{8 - 2}{26 - 22} = \dfrac{6}{4} = \dfrac{3}{2} = 1.5$

     The rate of change is 1.5 yd per sec.

99. $-4x + 2y = 5$ or $y = 2x + \dfrac{5}{2}$

      $2x - y = 7$ or $y = 2x - 7$

101. a. $y = \dfrac{1}{2}x + 1$

     $y = x + 1$

     $y = 2x + 1$

   b. $y = -\dfrac{1}{2}x + 1$

     $y = -x + 1$

     $y = -2x + 1$

   c. True

Section 3.5

Practice Exercises

1. We are given the slope, $-\dfrac{3}{4}$, and the

   y-intercept, $(0, 4)$.

   Let $m = -\dfrac{3}{4}$ and $b = 4$.

   $y = mx + b$

   $y = -\dfrac{3}{4}x + 4$

2. $y = \dfrac{3}{4}x + 2$

The slope is $\dfrac{3}{4}$, and the y-intercept is $(0, 2)$. Plot $(0, 2)$. Then plot a second point by starting at $(0, 2)$, rising 3 units up, and running 4 units to the right. The second point is $(4, 5)$.

3. $x + 2y = 6$

Solve for y.

$$x + 2y = 6$$
$$2y = -x + 6$$
$$y = -\frac{1}{2}x + 3$$

The slope is $-\frac{1}{2}$, and the y-intercept is (0, 3).

Plot (0, 3). Then plot a second point by starting at (0, 3), moving 1 unit down, and moving 2 units to the right. The second point is (2, 2).

4. Use the point-slope form with $m = -4$ and $(x_1, y_1) = (-2, 5)$.

$$y - y_1 = m(x - x_1)$$
$$y - 5 = -4[x - (-2)]$$
$$y - 5 = -4(x + 2)$$
$$y - 5 = -4x - 8$$
$$y = -4x - 3$$

5. First find the slope.

$$m = \frac{0 - 2}{2 - (-1)} = \frac{-2}{3} = -\frac{2}{3}$$

Use the slope and one of the points in the point-slope form. We use (2, 0).

$$y - y_1 = m(x - x_1)$$
$$y - 0 = -\frac{2}{3}(x - 2)$$
$$y = -\frac{2}{3}x + \frac{4}{3}$$
$$f(x) = -\frac{2}{3}x + \frac{4}{3}$$

6. The points on the graph have coordinates (-2, 3) and (1, 1). Find the slope.

$$m = \frac{1 - 3}{1 - (-2)} = \frac{-2}{3} = -\frac{2}{3}$$

Use the slope and one of the points in the point-slope form. We use (1, 1).

$$y - y_1 = m(x - x_1)$$
$$y - 1 = -\frac{2}{3}(x - 1)$$
$$3(y - 1) = -2(x - 1)$$
$$3y - 3 = -2x + 2$$
$$2x + 3y = 5$$

7. Let x = the number of years after 2000 and y = the number of houses sold in the year corresponding to x. We have two ordered pairs, (2, 7513) and (6, 9198). Find the slope.

$$m = \frac{9198 - 7513}{6 - 2}$$
$$= \frac{1685}{4}$$
$$= 421.25$$

Use the slope and one of the points in the point-slope form. We use (2, 7513).

$$y - y_1 = m(x - x_1)$$
$$y - 7513 = 421.25(x - 2)$$
$$y - 7513 = 421.25x - 842.5$$
$$y = 421.25x + 6670.5$$

The year 2014 corresponds to $x = 14$.

$$y = 421.25(14) + 6670.5$$
$$= 5897.5 + 6670.5$$
$$= 12,568$$

We predict that there will 12,568 house sales in 2014.

8. A horizontal line has an equation of the form $y = b$. Since the line contains the point (6, -2), the equation is $y = -2$.

9. Since the line has undefined slope, the line must be vertical. A vertical line has an equation of the form $x = c$. Since the line contains the point (6, -2), the equation is $x = 6$.

10. Solve the given equation for y.

$$3x + 4y = 1$$
$$4y = -3x + 1$$
$$y = -\frac{3}{4}x + \frac{1}{4}$$

The slope of this line is $-\frac{3}{4}$, so the slope of any line parallel to it is also $-\frac{3}{4}$. Use this slope and the point (8, -3) in the point-slope form.

$$y - y_1 = m(x - x_1)$$
$$y - (-3) = -\frac{3}{4}(x - 8)$$
$$4(y + 3) = -3(x - 8)$$
$$4y + 12 = -3x + 24$$
$$3x + 4y = 12$$

11. Solve the given equation for y.
$$3x + 4y = 1$$
$$4y = -3x + 1$$
$$y = -\frac{3}{4}x + \frac{1}{4}$$

The slope of this line is $-\frac{3}{4}$, so the slope of any line perpendicular to it is the negative reciprocal of $-\frac{3}{4}$, or $\frac{4}{3}$. Use this slope and the point $(8, -3)$ in the point-slope form.

$$y - y_1 = m(x - x_1)$$
$$y - (-3) = \frac{4}{3}(x - 8)$$
$$3(y + 3) = 4(x - 8)$$
$$3y + 9 = 4x - 32$$
$$3y = 4x - 41$$
$$y = \frac{4}{3}x - \frac{41}{3}$$
$$f(x) = \frac{4}{3}x - \frac{41}{3}$$

Vocabulary and Readiness Check

1. $m = -4$, $b = 12$ so y-intercept is $(0, 12)$.

2. $m = \frac{2}{3}$, $b = -\frac{7}{2}$ so y-intercept is $\left(0, -\frac{7}{2}\right)$.

3. $m = 5$, $b = 0$ so y-intercept is $(0, 0)$.

4. $m = -1$, $b = 0$ so y-intercept is $(0, 0)$.

5. $m = \frac{1}{2}$, $b = 6$ so y-intercept is $(0, 6)$.

6. $m = -\frac{2}{3}$, $b = 5$ so y-intercept is $(0, 5)$.

7. The lines both have slope 12 and they have different y-intercepts, $(0, 6)$ and $(0, -2)$, so they are parallel.

8. The lines both have slope -5 and they have different y-intercepts, $(0, 8)$ and $(0, -8)$, so they are parallel.

9. The line have slopes -9 and $\frac{3}{2}$. The slopes are not equal and their product is not -1, so the lines are neither parallel nor perpendicular.

10. The line have slopes 2 and $\frac{1}{2}$. The slopes are not equal and their product is not -1, so the lines are neither parallel nor perpendicular.

Exercise Set 3.5

1. $m = -1$, $b = 1$
$$y = mx + b$$
$$y = -1x + 1$$
$$y = -x + 1$$

3. $m = 2$, $b = \frac{3}{4}$
$$y = mx + b$$
$$y = 2x + \frac{3}{4}$$

5. $m = \frac{2}{7}$, $b = 0$
$$y = mx + b$$
$$y = \frac{2}{7}x + 0$$
$$y = \frac{2}{7}x$$

7. $y = 5x - 2$
possible points: $(0, -2)$, $(1, 3)$

9. $4x + y = 7$
$$y = -4x + 7$$
possible points: $(0, 7), (1, 3)$

11. $-3x + 2y = 3$
$$2y = 3x + 3$$
$$y = \frac{3}{2}x + \frac{3}{2}$$
possible points: $\left(0, \frac{3}{2}\right), \left(2, \frac{9}{2}\right)$

13. $y - y_1 = m(x - x_1)$
$$y - 2 = 3(x - 1)$$
$$y - 2 = 3x - 3$$
$$y = 3x - 1$$

15. $y - y_1 = m(x - x_1)$
$$y - (-3) = -2(x - 1)$$
$$y + 3 = -2x + 2$$
$$y = -2x - 1$$

17. $y - y_1 = m(x - x_1)$
$$y - 2 = \frac{1}{2}[x - (-6)]$$
$$y - 2 = \frac{1}{2}(x + 6)$$
$$y - 2 = \frac{1}{2}x + 3$$
$$y = \frac{1}{2}x + 5$$

19. $y - y_1 = m(x - x_1)$
$$y - 0 = -\frac{9}{10}[x - (-3)]$$
$$y = -\frac{9}{10}(x + 3)$$
$$y = -\frac{9}{10}x - \frac{27}{10}$$

21. $m = \dfrac{6 - 0}{4 - 2} = \dfrac{6}{2} = 3$
$$y - 0 = 3(x - 2)$$
$$y = 3x - 6$$
$$f(x) = 3x - 6$$

23. $m = \dfrac{13 - 5}{-6 - (-2)} = \dfrac{8}{-4} = -2$
$$y - 5 = -2[x - (-2)]$$
$$y - 5 = -2(x + 2)$$
$$y - 5 = -2x - 4$$
$$y = -2x + 1$$
$$f(x) = -2x + 1$$

25. $m = \dfrac{-3 - (-4)}{-4 - (-2)} = \dfrac{1}{-2} = -\dfrac{1}{2}$
$$y - (-4) = -\frac{1}{2}[x - (-2)]$$
$$y + 4 = -\frac{1}{2}(x + 2)$$
$$2y + 8 = -(x + 2)$$
$$2y + 8 = -x - 2$$
$$2y = -x - 10$$
$$y = -\frac{1}{2}x - 5$$
$$f(x) = -\frac{1}{2}x - 5$$

27. $m = \dfrac{-9 - (-8)}{-6 - (-3)} = \dfrac{-1}{-3} = \dfrac{1}{3}$
$$y - (-8) = \frac{1}{3}[x - (-3)]$$
$$y + 8 = \frac{1}{3}(x + 3)$$
$$3y + 24 = x + 3$$
$$3y = x - 21$$
$$y = \frac{1}{3}x - 7$$
$$f(x) = \frac{1}{3}x - 7$$

29. $m = \dfrac{\frac{7}{10} - \frac{4}{10}}{-\frac{1}{5} - \frac{3}{5}} = \dfrac{\frac{3}{10}}{-\frac{4}{5}} = \dfrac{3}{10}\left(-\dfrac{5}{4}\right) = -\dfrac{3}{8}$

$y - \dfrac{4}{10} = -\dfrac{3}{8}\left(x - \dfrac{3}{5}\right)$

$y - \dfrac{4}{10} = -\dfrac{3}{8}x + \dfrac{9}{40}$

$y = -\dfrac{3}{8}x + \dfrac{5}{8}$

$f(x) = -\dfrac{3}{8}x + \dfrac{5}{8}$

31. $(0, 3), (1, 1)$

$m = \dfrac{1-3}{1-0} = \dfrac{-2}{1} = -2$

$b = 3$

$y = -2x + 3$

$2x + y = 3$

33. $(-2, 1), (4, 5)$

$m = \dfrac{5-1}{4-(-2)} = \dfrac{4}{6} = \dfrac{2}{3}$

$y - 1 = \dfrac{2}{3}(x + 2)$

$3y - 3 = 2(x + 2)$

$3y - 3 = 2x + 4$

$2x - 3y = -7$

35. $f(0) = -2$

37. $f(2) = 2$

39. $f(x) = -6$

$f(-2) = -6$

$x = -2$

41. $y = mx + b$

$-4 = 0(-2) + b$

$-4 = b$

$y = -4$

43. Every vertical line is in the form $x = c$. Since the line passes through the point $(4, 7)$, its equation is $x = 4$.

45. Every horizontal line is in the form $y = c$. Since the line passes through the point $(0, 5)$, its equation is $y = 5$.

47. $y = 4x - 2$ so $m = 4$

$y - 8 = 4(x - 3)$

$y - 8 = 4x - 12$

$y = 4x - 4$

$f(x) = 4x - 4$

49. $3y = x - 6$ or $y = \dfrac{1}{3}x - 2$ so

$m = \dfrac{1}{3}$ and $m_\perp = -3$

$y - (-5) = -3(x - 2)$

$y + 5 = -3x + 6$

$y = -3x + 1$

$f(x) = -3x + 1$

51. $3x + 2y = 5$

$2y = -3x + 5$

$y = -\dfrac{3}{2}x + \dfrac{5}{2}$ so $m = -\dfrac{3}{2}$

$y - (-3) = -\dfrac{3}{2}[x - (-2)]$

$2(y + 3) = -3(x + 2)$

$2y + 6 = -3(x + 2)$

$2y + 6 = -3x - 6$

$y = -\dfrac{3}{2}x - 6$

$f(x) = -\dfrac{3}{2}x - 6$

53. $y - 3 = 2[x - (-2)]$

$y - 3 = 2(x + 2)$

$y - 3 = 2x + 4$

$2x - y = -7$

55. $m = \dfrac{2-6}{5-1} = \dfrac{-4}{4} = -1$

$y - 6 = -1(x - 1)$

$y - 6 = -x + 1$

$y = -x + 7$

$f(x) = -x + 7$

57. $y = -\dfrac{1}{2}x + 11$

$2y = -x + 22$

$x + 2y = 22$

59. $m = \dfrac{-6-(-4)}{0-(-7)} = \dfrac{-2}{7} = -\dfrac{2}{7}$

$$y = -\dfrac{2}{7}x - 6$$
$$7y = -2x - 42$$
$$2x + 7y = -42$$

61. $y - 0 = -\dfrac{4}{3}[x - (-5)]$

$$3y = -4(x + 5)$$
$$3y = -4x - 20$$
$$4x + 3y = -20$$

63. Every vertical line is in the form $x = c$. Since the line passes through the point $(-2, -10)$, its equation is $x = -2$.

65. $2x + 4y = 8$

$$4y = -2x + 8$$
$$y = -\dfrac{1}{2}x + 2 \text{ so } m = -\dfrac{1}{2}$$
$$y - (-2) = -\dfrac{1}{2}(x - 6)$$
$$2(y + 2) = -(x - 6)$$
$$2y + 4 = -x + 6$$
$$x + 2y = 2$$

67. Lines with slopes of 0 are horizontal. Every horizontal line is in the form $y = c$. Since the line passes through $(-9, 12)$, its equation is $y = 12$.

69. $8x - y = 9$

$$y = 8x - 9 \text{ so } m = 8$$
$$y - 1 = 8(x - 6)$$
$$y - 1 = 8x - 48$$
$$8x - y = 47$$

71. A line perpendicular to $y = 9$ will have the form $x = c$. Since the line passes through the point $(5, -6)$, its equation is $x = 5$.

73. $m = \dfrac{-5-(-8)}{-6-2} = \dfrac{3}{-8} = -\dfrac{3}{8}$

$$y - (-8) = -\dfrac{3}{8}(x - 2)$$
$$8(y + 8) = -3(x - 2)$$
$$8y + 64 = -3x + 6$$
$$y = -\dfrac{3}{8}x - \dfrac{29}{4}$$
$$f(x) = -\dfrac{3}{8}x - \dfrac{29}{4}$$

75. a. $(1, 30{,}000)$, $(4, 66{,}000)$

$$m = \dfrac{66{,}000 - 30{,}000}{4 - 1} = 12{,}000$$
$$y - 30{,}000 = 12{,}000(x - 1)$$
$$y = 12{,}000x + 18{,}000$$
$$P(x) = 12{,}000x + 18{,}000$$

b. $P(7) = 12{,}000(7) + 18{,}000$
$$= \$102{,}000$$

c. $126{,}000 = 12{,}000x + 18{,}000$
$$x = \dfrac{126{,}000 - 18{,}000}{12{,}000}$$
$$x = 9 \text{ years}$$

77. a. $(3, 10{,}000)$, $(5, 8000)$

$$m = \dfrac{8000 - 10{,}000}{5 - 3} = -1000$$
$$y - 10{,}000 = -1000(x - 3)$$
$$y - 10{,}000 = -1000x + 3{,}000$$
$$y = -1000x + 13{,}000$$

b. $y = -1000(3.5) + 13{,}000$
$$y = 9500$$
9500 Fun Noodles

79. a. We have two ordered pairs, $(0, 150{,}900)$ and $(5, 222{,}000)$. Find the slope.

$$m = \dfrac{222{,}000 - 150{,}900}{5 - 0}$$
$$= \dfrac{71{,}100}{5}$$
$$= 14{,}220$$

Use the slope and the y-intercept, $(0, 150{,}900)$ to write the equation.
$$y = mx + b$$
$$y = 14{,}220x + 150{,}900$$

b. The year 2010 corresponds to $x = 9$.
$$y = 14{,}220(9) + 150{,}900$$
$$= 127{,}980 + 150{,}900$$
$$= 278{,}880$$
We predict that the median existing home price will be $278,880 in 2010.

c. The slope is 14,220. Every year the median price of a home increases by $14,220.

81. a. $(0, 387)$, $(10, 589)$
$$m = \frac{589 - 387}{10 - 0} = \frac{202}{10} = 20.2$$
$$y - 387 = 20.2(x - 0)$$
$$y = 20.2x + 387$$

b. $x = 2013 - 2004 = 9$
$$y = 20.2(9) + 387$$
$$= 568.8 \text{ thousand people}$$

83. $2x - 7 \le 21$
$$2x \le 28$$
$$x \le 14$$
$$(-\infty, 14]$$

85. $5(x - 2) \ge 3(x - 1)$
$$5x - 10 \ge 3x - 3$$
$$2x \ge 7$$
$$x \ge \frac{7}{2}$$
$$\left[\frac{7}{2}, \infty\right)$$

87. $\dfrac{x}{2} + \dfrac{1}{4} < \dfrac{1}{8}$
$$8\left(\frac{x}{2} + \frac{1}{4}\right) < 8\left(\frac{1}{8}\right)$$
$$4x + 2 < 1$$
$$4x < -1$$
$$x < -\frac{1}{4}$$
$$\left(-\infty, -\frac{1}{4}\right)$$

89. Since any vertical line intersects any horizontal line in a right angle, the statement is true.

91. $m = \dfrac{1 - (-1)}{-5 - 3} = \dfrac{2}{-8} = -\dfrac{1}{4}$ so $m_\perp = 4$
$$M((3, -1), (5, 1)) = \left(\frac{3 - 5}{2}, \frac{-1 + 1}{2}\right) = (1, 0)$$
$$y - 0 = 4[x - (-1)]$$
$$y = 4(x + 1)$$
$$y = 4x + 4$$
$$-4x + y = 4$$

93. $m = \dfrac{-4 - 6}{-22 - (-2)} = \dfrac{-10}{-20} = \dfrac{1}{2}$ so $m_\perp = -2$
$$M((-2, 6), (-22, -4)) = \left(\frac{-2 - 22}{2}, \frac{6 - 4}{2}\right)$$
$$= (-12, 1)$$
$$y - 1 = -2[x - (-12)]$$
$$y - 1 = -2(x + 12)$$
$$y - 1 = -2x - 24$$
$$2x + y = -23$$

95. $m = \dfrac{7 - 3}{-4 - 2} = \dfrac{4}{-6} = -\dfrac{2}{3}$ so $m_\perp = \dfrac{3}{2}$
$$M((2, 3), (-4, 7)) = \left(\frac{2 - 4}{2}, \frac{3 + 7}{2}\right)$$
$$= (-1, 5)$$
$$y - 5 = \frac{3}{2}[x - (-1)]$$
$$2(y - 5) = 3(x + 1)$$
$$2y - 10 = 3x + 3$$
$$3x - 2y = -13$$

97. Answers may vary

99. $f(x) = -x + 7$

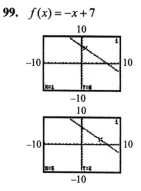

101. $4x + 3y = -20$

103. $y = 4x - 2$
$y = 4x - 4$

Integrated Review

1. $y = -2x$

x	-1	0	1
y	2	0	-2

2. $3x - 2y = 6$

x	0	2	4
y	-3	0	3

3. $x = -3$
The graph of $x = -3$ is a vertical line.

4. $y = 1.5$

5. $m = \dfrac{-5 - (-5)}{3 - (-2)} = \dfrac{0}{5} = 0$

6. $m = \dfrac{5 - 2}{0 - 5} = \dfrac{3}{-5} = -\dfrac{3}{5}$

7. $y = 3x - 5$
$m = 3; \; (0, -5)$

8. $5x - 2y = 7$
$\qquad -2y = -5x + 7$
$\qquad \quad y = \dfrac{5}{2}x - \dfrac{7}{2}$
$\qquad m = \dfrac{5}{2}; \; \left(0, -\dfrac{7}{2}\right)$

9. $y = 8x - 6 \quad y = 8x + 6$
$m = 8 \qquad m = 8$
Parallel, since their slopes are equal.

10. $y = \dfrac{2}{3}x + 1$ $\qquad\qquad 2y + 3x = 1$
$\quad m = \dfrac{2}{3}$ $\qquad\qquad\quad 2y = -3x + 1$
$\qquad\qquad\qquad\qquad\qquad y = -\dfrac{3}{2}x + \dfrac{1}{2}$
$\qquad\qquad\qquad\qquad\quad m = -\dfrac{3}{2}$

Perpendicular, since the product of their slopes is -1.

11. $m = \dfrac{2-6}{5-1} = \dfrac{-4}{4} = -1$

$y - 6 = -1(x - 1)$

$y - 6 = -x + 1$

$\qquad y = -x + 7$

12. Every vertical line is in the form $x = c$. Since the line passes through the point $(-2, -10)$, its equation is $x = -2$.

13. Every horizontal line is in the form $y = c$. Since the line passes through the point $(1, 0)$, its equation is $y = 0$.

14. $m = \dfrac{-5 - (-9)}{-6 - 2} = \dfrac{4}{-8} = -\dfrac{1}{2}$

$y - (-9) = -\dfrac{1}{2}(x - 2)$

$2(y + 9) = -1(x - 2)$

$2y + 18 = -x + 2$

$2y = -x - 16$

$\quad y = -\dfrac{1}{2}x - 8$

$f(x) = -\dfrac{1}{2}x - 8$

15. $y - 4 = -5[x - (-2)]$

$y - 4 = -5(x + 2)$

$y - 4 = -5x - 10$

$\quad y = -5x - 6$

$f(x) = -5x - 6$

16. $\quad y = -4x + \dfrac{1}{3}$

$f(x) = -4x + \dfrac{1}{3}$

17. $\quad y = \dfrac{1}{2}x - 1$

$f(x) = \dfrac{1}{2}x - 1$

18. $y - 0 = 3\left(x - \dfrac{1}{2}\right)$

$\quad y = 3x - \dfrac{3}{2}$

19. $3x - y = 5$

$\quad y = 3x - 5$

$m = 3$

$y - (-5) = 3[x - (-1)]$

$\quad y + 5 = 3(x + 1)$

$\quad y + 5 = 3x + 3$

$\qquad y = 3x - 2$

20. $4x - 5y = 10$

$-5y = -4x + 10$

$y = \dfrac{4}{5}x - 2; \quad m = \dfrac{4}{5} \quad$ so $\quad m_\perp = -\dfrac{5}{4}$

Therefore, $y = -\dfrac{5}{4}x + 4$.

21. $4x + y = \dfrac{2}{3}$

$y = -4x + \dfrac{2}{3}; \quad m = -4 \quad$ so $\quad m_\perp = \dfrac{1}{4}$

$y - (-3) = \dfrac{1}{4}(x - 2)$

$4(y + 3) = x - 2$

$4y + 12 = x - 2$

$\quad 4y = x - 14$

$\quad y = \dfrac{1}{4}x - \dfrac{7}{2}$

22. $5x + 2y = 2$

$2y = -5x + 2$

$y = -\dfrac{5}{2}x + 1$

$m = -\dfrac{5}{2}$

$y - 0 = -\dfrac{5}{2}[x - (-1)]$

$\quad y = -\dfrac{5}{2}(x + 1)$

$2y = -5(x + 1)$

$2y = -5x - 5$

$\quad y = -\dfrac{5}{2}x - \dfrac{5}{2}$

23. A line having undefined slope is vertical. Therefore, the equation is $x = -1$.

24. $y - 3 = 0[x - (-1)]$

$y - 3 = 0$

$\quad y = 3$

Section 3.6

Practice Exercises

1. $f(x) = \begin{cases} -4x - 2 & \text{if } x \le 0 \\ x + 1 & \text{if } x > 0 \end{cases}$

Since $4 > 0$, $f(4) = 4 + 1 = 5$.

Since $-2 \le 0$, $f(-2) = -4(-2) - 2 = 8 - 2 = 6$.

Since $0 \le 0$, $f(0) = -4(0) - 2 = 0 - 2 = -2$.

2. $f(x) = \begin{cases} -4x - 2 & \text{if } x \le 0 \\ x + 1 & \text{if } x > 0 \end{cases}$

For $x \le 0$:

x	$f(x)$
–2	6
–1	2
0	–2

For $x > 0$:

x	$f(x)$
1	2
2	3
3	4

Graph a closed circle at (0, –2). Graph an open circle at (0, 1), which is found by substituting 0 for x in $f(x) = x + 1$.

3. $f(x) = x^2$ and $g(x) = x^2 - 3$

The graph of $g(x) = x^2 - 3$ is the graph of $f(x) = x^2$ moved downward 3 units.

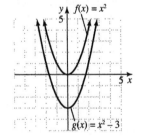

4. $f(x) = \sqrt{x}$ and $g(x) = \sqrt{x} + 1$

The graph of $g(x) = \sqrt{x} + 1$ is the graph of $f(x) = \sqrt{x}$ moved upward 1 unit.

5. $f(x) = |x|$ and $g(x) = |x - 3|$

x	$f(x)$	$g(x)$
–2	2	5
–1	1	4
0	0	3
1	1	2
2	2	1
3	3	0
4	4	1
5	5	2

6. $f(x) = |x|$ and $g(x) = |x - 2| + 3$

The graph of $g(x)$ is the same as the graph of $f(x)$ shifted 2 units to the right and 3 units up.

7. $h(x) = -(x+2)^2 - 1$

The graph of $h(x) = -(x+2)^2 - 1$ is the same as the graph of $f(x) = x^2$ reflected about the x-axis, then moved 2 units to the left and 1 unit downward.

$h(x) = -(x+2)^2 - 1$

Vocabulary and Readiness Check

1. The graph that corresponds to $y = \sqrt{x}$ is C.

2. The graph that corresponds to $y = x^2$ is B.

3. The graph that corresponds to $y = x$ is D.

4. The graph that corresponds to $y = |x|$ is A.

Exercise Set 3.6

1. $f(x) = \begin{cases} 2x & \text{if } x < 0 \\ x+1 & \text{if } x \ge 0 \end{cases}$

For $x < 0$:   For $x \ge 0$:

x	$f(x)$
-3	-6
-2	-4
-1	-2

x	$f(x)$
0	1
1	2
2	3

Graph a closed circle at $(0, 1)$. Graph an open circle at $(0, 0)$, which is found by substituting 0 for x in $f(x) = 2x$.

3. $f(x) = \begin{cases} 4x+5 & \text{if } x \le 0 \\ \frac{1}{4}x+2 & \text{if } x > 0 \end{cases}$

For $x \le 0$:   For $x > 0$:

x	$f(x)$
-2	-3
-1	1
0	5

x	$f(x)$
1	$2\frac{1}{4}$
2	$2\frac{1}{2}$
4	3

Graph a closed circle at $(0, 5)$. Graph an open circle at $(0, 2)$, which is found by substituting 0 for x in $f(x) = \frac{1}{4}x+2$.

5. $g(x) = \begin{cases} -x & \text{if } x \le 1 \\ 2x+1 & \text{if } x > 1 \end{cases}$

For $x \le 1$:   For $x > 1$:

x	$g(x)$
-1	1
0	0
1	-1

x	$g(x)$
2	5
3	7
4	9

Graph a closed circle at $(1, -1)$. Graph an open circle at $(1, 3)$, which is found by substituting 1 for x in $g(x) = 2x+1$.

7. $f(x) = \begin{cases} 5 & \text{if } x < -2 \\ 3 & \text{if } x \geq -2 \end{cases}$

For $x < -2$:   For $x \geq -2$:

x	$f(x)$
-5	5
-4	5
-3	5

x	$f(x)$
-2	3
-1	3
0	3

Graph a closed circle at $(-2, 3)$. Graph an open circle at $(-2, 5)$, which is found by substituting -2 for x in $f(x) = 5$.

9. $f(x) = \begin{cases} -2x & \text{if } x \leq 0 \\ 2x+1 & \text{if } x > 0 \end{cases}$

For $x \leq 0$:   For $x > 0$:

x	$f(x)$
-1	2
0	0

x	$f(x)$
1	3
2	5

Graph a closed circle at $(0, 0)$. Graph an open circle at $(0, 1)$, which is found by substituting 0 for x in $f(x) = 2x+1$.

The function is defined for all real numbers, so the domain is $(-\infty, \infty)$. The function takes on all y-values greater than or equal to 0, so the range is $[0, \infty)$.

11. $h(x) = \begin{cases} 5x-5 & \text{if } x < 2 \\ -x+3 & \text{if } x \geq 2 \end{cases}$

For $x < 2$:   For $x \geq 2$:

x	$h(x)$
0	-5
1	0

x	$h(x)$
2	1
3	0

Graph a closed circle at $(2, 1)$. Graph an open circle at $(2, 5)$, which is found by substituting 2 for x in $h(x) = 5x-5$.

The function is defined for all real numbers, so the domain is $(-\infty, \infty)$. The function takes on all y-values less than 5, so the range is $(-\infty, 5)$.

13. $f(x) = \begin{cases} x+3 & \text{if } x < -1 \\ -2x+4 & \text{if } x \geq -1 \end{cases}$

For $x < -1$:   For $x \geq -1$:

x	$f(x)$
-4	-1
-3	0
-2	1

x	$f(x)$
-1	6
0	4
1	2

Graph a closed circle at $(-1, 6)$. Graph an open circle at $(-1, 2)$, which is found by substituting -1 for x in $f(x) = x+3$.

The function is defined for all real numbers, so the domain is $(-\infty, \infty)$. The function takes on all y-values less than or equal to 6, so the range is $(-\infty, 6]$.

15. $g(x) = \begin{cases} -2 & \text{if } x \leq 0 \\ -4 & \text{if } x \geq 1 \end{cases}$

For $x \leq 0$:   For $x \geq 1$:

x	$g(x)$
-2	-2
-1	-2
0	-2

x	$g(x)$
1	-4
2	-4
3	-4

Graph closed circles at $(0, -2)$ and $(1, -4)$.

The function is defined for $x \leq 0$ or $x \geq 1$, so the domain is $(-\infty, 0] \cup [1, \infty)$. The function takes on two y-values, -2 and -4, so the range is $\{-2, -4\}$.

17. $f(x) = |x| + 3$

The graph of $f(x) = |x| + 3$ is the same as the graph of $y = |x|$ shifted up 3 units.

19. $f(x) = \sqrt{x} - 2$

The graph of $f(x) = \sqrt{x} - 2$ is the same as the graph of $y = \sqrt{x}$ shifted down 2 units.

21. $f(x) = |x - 4|$

The graph of $f(x) = |x - 4|$ is the same as the graph of $y = |x|$ shifted right 4 units.

23. $f(x) = \sqrt{x + 2}$

The graph of $f(x) = \sqrt{x + 2}$ is the same as the graph of $y = \sqrt{x}$ shifted left 2 units.

25. $y = (x - 4)^2$

The graph of $y = (x - 4)^2$ is the same as the graph of $y = x^2$ shifted right 4 units.

27. $f(x) = x^2 + 4$

The graph of $f(x) = x^2 + 4$ is the same as the graph of $y = x^2$ shifted up 4 units.

29. $f(x) = \sqrt{x-2} + 3$

The graph of $f(x) = \sqrt{x-2} + 3$ is the same as the graph of $y = \sqrt{x}$ shifted right 2 units and up 3 units.

31. $f(x) = |x-1| + 5$

The graph of $f(x) = |x-1| + 5$ is the same as the graph of $y = |x|$ shifted right 1 unit and up 5 units.

33. $f(x) = \sqrt{x+1} + 1$

The graph of $f(x) = \sqrt{x+1} + 1$ is the same as the graph of $y = \sqrt{x}$ shifted left 1 unit and up 1 unit.

35. $f(x) = |x+3| - 1$

The graph of $f(x) = |x+3| - 1$ is the same as the graph of $y = |x|$ shifted left 3 units and down 1 unit.

37. $g(x) = (x-1)^2 - 1$

The graph of $g(x) = (x-1)^2 - 1$ is the same as the graph of $y = x^2$ shifted right 1 unit and down 1 unit.

39. $f(x) = (x+3)^2 - 2$

The graph of $f(x) = (x+3)^2 - 2$ is the same as the graph of $y = x^2$ shifted left 3 units and down 2 units.

41. $f(x) = -(x-1)^2$

The graph of $f(x) = -(x-1)^2$ is the same as the graph of $y = x^2$ reflected about the x-axis and then shifted right 1 unit.

43. $h(x) = -\sqrt{x} + 3$

The graph of $h(x) = -\sqrt{x} + 3$ is the same as the graph of $y = \sqrt{x}$ reflected about the x-axis and then shifted up 3 units.

45. $h(x) = -|x+2| + 3$

The graph of $h(x) = -|x+2| + 3$ is the same as the graph of $y = |x|$ reflected about the x-axis and then shifted left 2 units and up 3 units.

47. $f(x) = (x-3) + 2$

Since the function can be simplified to $f(x) = x - 1$, we see that its graph is a line with slope $m = 1$ and y-intercept $(0, -1)$.

49. The graph of $y = -1$ is a horizontal line with y-intercept $(0, -1)$. The correct graph is A.

51. The graph of $x = 3$ is a vertical line with x-intercept $(3, 0)$. The correct graph is D.

53. Answers may vary

55. $f(x) = \begin{cases} -\frac{1}{2}x & \text{if } x \le 0 \\ x+1 & \text{if } 0 < x \le 2 \\ 2x-1 & \text{if } x > 2 \end{cases}$

Some points for $x \le 0$: $(-4, 2), (-2, 1), (0, 0)$
Closed dot at $(0, 0)$
Some points for $0 < x \le 2$: $(1, 2), (2, 3)$
Open dot at $(0, 1)$, closed dot at $(2, 3)$
Some points for $x > 2$: $(3, 5), (4, 7)$
There would be an open dot at $(2, 3)$ except that it gets filled by the middle piece of the graph.

57. $f(x) = \sqrt{x-2} + 3$

The function is defined when $x - 2 \geq 0$, or $x \geq 2$, so the domain is $[2, \infty)$. The function takes on all y-values greater than or equal to 3, so the range is $[3, \infty)$.

59. $h(x) = -|x+2| + 3$

The function is defined for all real numbers, so the domain is $(-\infty, \infty)$. The function takes on all y-values less than or equal to 3, so the range is $(-\infty, 3]$.

61. $f(x) = 5\sqrt{x-20} + 1$

The function is defined when $x - 20 \geq 0$, or $x \geq 20$, so the domain is $[20, \infty)$.

63. $h(x) = 5|x-20| + 1$

The function is defined for all real numbers, so the domain is $(-\infty, \infty)$.

65. $g(x) = 9 - \sqrt{x+103}$

The function is defined when $x + 103 \geq 0$, or $x \geq -103$, so the domain is $[-103, \infty)$.

67. $f(x) = \begin{cases} |x| & \text{if } x \leq 0 \\ x^2 & \text{if } x > 0 \end{cases}$

For $x \leq 0$:   For $x > 0$:

x	$f(x)$
−2	2
−1	1
0	0

x	$f(x)$
1	1
2	4
3	9

Graph a closed circle at (0, 0). The graph of $f(x) = x^2$ for $x > 0$ also approaches the point (0, 0).

The function is defined for all real numbers, so the domain is $(-\infty, \infty)$. The function takes on all

y-values greater than or equal to 0, so the range is $[0, \infty)$.

69. $g(x) = \begin{cases} |x-2| & \text{if } x < 0 \\ -x^2 & \text{if } x \geq 0 \end{cases}$

For $x < 0$:   For $x \geq 0$:

x	$g(x)$
−3	5
−2	4
−1	3

x	$g(x)$
0	0
1	−1
2	−4

Graph an open circle at (0, 2). Graph a closed circle at (0, 0).

The function is defined for all real numbers, so the domain is $(-\infty, \infty)$. The function takes on all y-values such $y > 2$ or $y \leq 0$, so the range is $(-\infty, 0] \cup (2, \infty)$.

Section 3.7

Practice Exercises

1. $3x + y < 8$

The boundary line is $3x + y = 8$. Graph a dashed boundary line because the inequality symbol is $<$. The point (0, 0) is not on the boundary line, so we use it as a test point. Replace x with 0 and y with 0 in the original inequality.

$3x + y < 8$
$3(0) + 0 < 8$
$\quad 0 < 8 \quad$ True

Since (0, 0) satisfies the inequality, shade the half-plane that contains (0, 0). Every point in the shaded half-plane satisfies the original inequality.

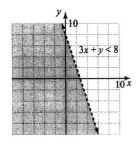

2. $x \ge 3y$

First graph the boundary line $x = 3y$. Graph a solid boundary line because the inequality symbol is $\ge$. We choose (0, 1) as a test point.

$x \ge 3y$

$0 \ge 3(1)$

$0 \ge 3$ False

Since this point does not satisfy the inequality, shade the half-plane on the opposite side of the boundary line from (0, 1). The graph of $x \ge 3y$ is the boundary line together with the shaded region.

3. The intersection of $x \le 3$ and $y \le x - 2$

Graph each inequality. The intersection of the two graphs is all points common to both regions, as shown by the darker shading in the graph.

$x \le 3$
$y \le x - 2$

4. The union of $2x - 3y \le -2$ or $y \ge 1$

Graph each inequality. The union of the two inequalities is both shaded regions, including the boundary lines, as shown in the graph.

Exercise Set 3.7

1. $x < 2$

Graph $x = 2$ as a dashed line. Shade to the left of the line.

3. $x - y \ge 7$

Graph $x - y = 7$ as a solid line.
Test: (0, 0)

$0 - 0 \ge 7$

   $0 \ge 7$ False

Shade the half-plane that does not contain (0, 0).

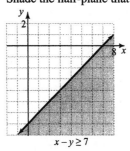

$x - y \ge 7$

5. $3x + y > 6$

Graph $3x + y = 6$ as a dashed line.
Test: (0, 0)

$3(0) + 0 > 6$

   $0 > 6$ False

Shade the half-plane that does not contain (0, 0).

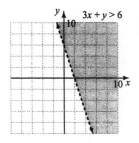

7. $y \le -2x$

Graph $y = -2x$ as a solid line.
Test: $(1, 1)$
$1 \le -2(1)$
$1 \le -2$ False
Shade the half-plane that does not contain $(1, 1)$.

9. $2x + 4y \ge 8$

Graph $2x + 4y = 8$ as a solid line.
Test: $(0, 0)$
$2(0) + 4(0) \ge 8$
        $0 \ge 8$ False
Shade the half-plane that does not contain $(0, 0)$.

11. $5x + 3y > -15$

Graph $5x + 3y = -15$ as a dashed line.
Test: $(0, 0)$
$5(0) + 3(0) > -15$
        $0 > -15$ True
Shade the half-plane that contains $(0, 0)$.

13. Answers may vary. A dashed boundary line should be used when the inequality contains a < or >.

15. $x \ge 3$ and $y \le -2$

The intersection is shown by the darker shading in the graph.

17. $x \le -2$ or $y \ge 4$

The union is both shaded regions, including the boundary line.

19. $x - y < 3$ and $x > 4$

The intersection is shown by the darker shading in the graph.

21. $x + y \leq 3$ or $x - y \geq 5$

The union is both shaded regions, including the boundary lines.

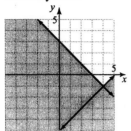

23. $y \geq -2$

Graph $y = -2$ as a solid line.
Test: (0, 0)
$0 \geq -2$ True
Shade the half-plane that contains (0, 0).

25. $x - 6y < 12$
$\quad -6y < 12 - x$
$\quad\quad y > \dfrac{1}{6}x - 2$

Graph the boundary line as a dashed line.
Test: (0, 0)
$0 > \dfrac{1}{6}(0) - 2$ True

Shade the half-plane that contains (0, 0).

27. $x > 5$

Graph $x = 5$ as a dashed line.
Test: (0, 0)
$0 > 5$ False
Shade the half-plane that does not contain (0, 0).

29. $-2x + y \leq 4$
$\quad\quad y \leq 2x + 4$

Graph the boundary line as a solid line.
Test: (0, 0)
$0 \leq 2(0) + 4$ True
Shade the half-plane that contains (0, 0).

31. $x - 3y < 0$
$\quad -3y < -x$
$\quad\quad y > \dfrac{x}{3}$

Graph the boundary line as a dashed line.
Test: (0, 1)
$1 > \dfrac{0}{3}$ True

Shade the half-plane that contains (0, 1).

33. $3x - 2y \leq 12$
$\quad -2y \leq -3x + 12$
$\quad\quad y \geq \dfrac{3}{2}x - 6$

Graph the boundary line as a solid line.
Test: (0, 0)
$3(0) - 2(0) \leq 12$ True
Shade the half-plane that contains (0, 0).

35. $x - y > 2$ or $y < 5$
     $y < x - 2$ or $y < 5$

Graph each inequality. The union of the two inequalities is both shaded regions, as shown by the shading in the graph below.

41. $x \geq -2$ and $x \leq 1$
     $-2 \leq x \leq 1$

Graph each inequality. The intersection of the two inequalities is all points common to both regions, as shown by the shading in the graph below.

37. $x + y \leq 1$ and $y \leq -1$
     $y \leq -x + 1$ and $y \leq -1$

Graph each inequality. The intersection of the two inequalities is all points common to both regions, as shown by the shading in the graph below.

43. $x + y \leq 0$ or $3x - 6y \geq 12$
     $y \leq -x$ or $-6y \geq -3x + 12$

     $y \leq -x$ or $y \leq \dfrac{1}{2}x - 2$

Graph each inequality. The union of the two inequalities is both shaded regions, as shown by the shading in the graph below.

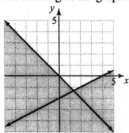

39. $2x + y > 4$ or $x \geq 1$
     $y > -2x + 4$ or $x \geq 1$

Graph each inequality. The union of the two inequalities is both shaded regions, as shown by the shading in the graph below.

45. $2x - y > 3$ and $x > 0$
     $y < 2x - 3$ and $x > 0$

Graph each inequality. The intersection of the two inequalities is all points common to both regions, as shown by the shading in the graph below.

47. $y \leq 2x + 3$

The boundary line should be solid, and the half-plane below the boundary line should be shaded. The correct graph is D.

49. $y > 2x + 3$

The boundary line should be dashed, and the half-plane above the boundary line should be shaded. The correct graph is A.

51. The boundary line, $x = 2$, is solid, and the half-plane with x-values greater than 2 is shaded. The inequality is $x \geq 2$.

53. The boundary line, $y = -3$, is solid, and the half-plane with y-values less than -3 is shaded. The inequality is $y \leq -3$.

55. The boundary line, $y = 4$, is dashed, and the half-plane with y-values greater than 4 is shaded. The inequality is $y > 4$.

57. The boundary line, $x = 1$, is dashed, and the half-plane with x-values less than 1 is shaded. The inequality is $x < 1$.

59. $2^3 = 2 \cdot 2 \cdot 2 = 8$

61. $-5^2 = -(5 \cdot 5) = -25$

63. $(-2)^4 = (-2)(-2)(-2)(-2) = 16$

65. $\left(\dfrac{3}{5}\right)^3 = \dfrac{3^3}{5^3} = \dfrac{27}{125}$

67. Domain: [1, 5]
Range: [1, 3]
Since it fails the vertical line test it is not a function.

69. $x \leq 20$ and $y \geq 10$

71. $\begin{cases} x \geq 0 \\ y \geq 0 \\ 2x + 4y \leq 40 \end{cases}$

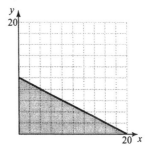

Chapter 3 Vocabulary Check

1. A <u>relation</u> is a set of ordered pairs.

2. The graph of every linear equation in two variables is a <u>line</u>.

3. The statement $-x + 2y > 0$ is called a <u>linear inequality</u> in two variables.

4. <u>Standard</u> form of linear equation in two variables is $Ax + By = C$.

5. The <u>range</u> of a relation is the set of all second components of the ordered pairs of the relation.

6. <u>Parallel</u> lines have the same slope and different y-intercepts.

7. <u>Slope-intercept</u> form of a linear equation in two variables is $y = mx + b$.

8. A <u>function</u> is a relation in which each first component in the ordered pairs corresponds to exactly one second component.

9. In the equation $y = 4x - 2$, the coefficient of x is the <u>slope</u> of its corresponding graph.

10. Two lines are <u>perpendicular</u> if the product of their slopes is −1.

11. To find the x-intercept of a linear equation, let <u>y</u> = 0 and solve for the other variable.

12. The <u>domain</u> of a relation is the set of all first components of the ordered pairs of the relation.

13. A <u>linear function</u> is a function that can be written in the form $f(x) = mx + b$.

14. To find the y-intercept of a linear equation, let <u>x</u> = 0 and solve for the other variable.

15. The equation $y − 8 = −5(x + 1)$ is written in <u>point-slope</u> form.

Chapter 3 Review

1. $A(2, −1)$, quadrant IV
   $B(−2, 1)$, quadrant II
   $C(0, 3)$, y-axis
   $D(−3, −5)$, quadrant III

2. $A(−3, 4)$, quadrant II
   $B(4, −3)$, quadrant IV
   $C(−2, 0)$, x-axis
   $D(−4, 1)$, quadrant II

3. $7x − 8y = 56$

   $(0, 56)$; No
   $7(0) − 8(56) \stackrel{?}{=} 56$
   $\quad −448 = 56$, False

   $(8, 0)$; Yes
   $7(8) − 8(0) \stackrel{?}{=} 56$
   $\quad 56 = 56$, True

4. $−2x + 5y = 10$

   $(−5, 0)$; Yes
   $−2(−5) + 5(0) \stackrel{?}{=} 10$
   $\qquad 10 = 10$, True

   $(1, 1)$, No
   $−2(1) + 5(1) \stackrel{?}{=} 10$
   $\qquad 3 = 10$, False

5. $x = 13$

   $(13, 5)$; Yes
   $13 = 13$, True
   $(13, 13)$; Yes
   $13 = 13$, True

6. $y = 2$

   $(7, 2)$; Yes
   $2 = 2$, True
   $(2, 7)$; No
   $7 = 2$, False

7. $y = 3x$; Linear

x	−1	0	1
y	−3	0	3

8. $y = 5x$; Linear

x	−1	0	1
y	−5	0	5

9. $3x - y = 4$; Linear

Find three ordered pair solutions, or find x- and y-intercepts, or find m and b.

10. $x - 3y = 2$; Linear

Find three ordered pair solutions, or find x- and y-intercepts, or find m and b.

11. $y = |x| + 4$; Nonlinear

x	–3	–2	–1	0	1	2	3
y	7	6	5	4	5	6	7

12. $y = x^2 + 4$; Nonlinear

x	–3	–2	–1	0	1	2	3
y	13	8	5	4	5	8	13

13. $y = -\dfrac{1}{2}x + 2$; Linear

Find three ordered pair solutions, or find x- and y-intercepts, or find m and b.

14. $y = -x + 5$; Linear

Find three ordered pair solutions, or find x- and y-intercepts, or find m and b.

15. $y = 2x - 1$; Linear

Find three ordered pair solutions, or find x- and y-intercepts, or find m and b.

16. $y = \frac{1}{3}x + 1$; Linear

    Find three ordered pair solutions, or find x- and y-intercepts, or find m and b.

17. $y = -1.36x$; Linear

    Find three ordered pair solutions, or find x- and y-intercepts, or find m and b.

18. $y = 2.1x + 5.9$

    Find three ordered pair solutions, or find x- and y-intercepts, or find m and b.

19. The domain is the set of all first coordinates (or inputs) and the range is the set of all second coordinates (or outputs).

    Domain: $\left\{ -\frac{1}{2}, 6, 0, 25 \right\}$

    Range: $\left\{ \frac{3}{4}, -12, 25 \right\}$

    Function since each x-value corresponds to exactly one y-value.

20. The domain is the set of all first coordinates (or inputs) and the range is the set of all second coordinates (or outputs).

    Domain: $\left\{ \frac{3}{4}, -12, 25 \right\}$

    Range: $\left\{ -\frac{1}{2}, 6, 0, 25 \right\}$

    Not a function since $\frac{3}{4}$ (or 0.75) is paired with

    both $-\frac{1}{2}$ and 6.

21. The domain is the set of all first coordinates (or inputs) and the range is the set of all second coordinates (or outputs).
    Domain: {2, 4, 6, 8}
    Range: {2, 4, 5, 6}
    Not a function since 2 is paired with both 2 and 4.

22. The domain is the set of all first coordinates (or inputs) and the range is the set of all second coordinates (or outputs).
    Domain:
    {Triangle, Square, Rectangle, Parallelogram}
    Range: {3, 4}
    Function since each input is paired with exactly one output.

23. Domain: $(-\infty, \infty)$

    Range: $(-\infty, -1] \cup [1, \infty)$

    Not a function since it fails the vertical line test.

24. Domain: $\{-3\}$
    Range: $(-\infty, \infty)$
    Not a function since it fails the vertical line test.

25. Domain: $(-\infty, \infty)$
    Range: {4}
    Function since it passes the vertical line test.

26. Domain: $[-1, 1]$
    Range: $[-1, 1]$
    Not a function since it fails the vertical line test.

27. $f(x) = x - 5$
    $f(2) = (2) - 5 = -3$

28. $g(x) = -3x$
    $g(0) = -3(0) = 0$

29. $g(x) = -3x$

$g(-6) = -3(-6) = 18$

30. $h(x) = 2x^2 - 6x + 1$

$h(-1) = 2(-1)^2 - 6(-1) + 1$
$= 2(1) + 6 + 1$
$= 9$

31. $h(x) = 2x^2 - 6x + 1$

$h(1) = 2(1)^2 - 6(1) + 1 = 2 - 6 + 1 = -3$

32. $f(x) = x - 5$

$f(5) = (5) - 5 = 0$

33. $J(x) = 2.54x$

$J(150) = 2.54(150) = 381$ pounds

34. $J(x) = 2.54x$

$J(2000) = 2.54(2000) = 5080$ pounds

35. The point $(-1, 0)$ is on the graph, so $f(-1) = 0$.

36. The point $(1, -2)$ is on the graph, so $f(1) = -2$.

37. $f(x) = 1$

$f(-2) = f(4) = 1$
$x = -2, 4$

38. $f(x) = -1$

$f(0) = f(2) = -1$
$x = 0, 2$

39. $f(x) = x$ or $y = x$

$m = 1, \ b = 0$

40. $f(x) = -\dfrac{1}{3}x$ or $y = -\dfrac{1}{3}x$

$m = -\dfrac{1}{3}, \ b = 0$

41. $g(x) = 4x - 1$ or $y = 4x - 1$

$m = 4, \ b = -1$

42. $f(x) = 3x + 1$

The y-intercept should be $(0, 1)$. The correct graph is C.

43. $f(x) = 3x - 2$

The y-intercept should be $(0, -2)$. The correct graph is A.

44. $f(x) = 3x + 2$

The y-intercept should be $(0, 2)$. The correct graph is B.

45. $f(x) = 3x - 5$

The y-intercept should be $(0, -5)$. The correct graph is D.

46. $4x + 5y = 20$

Let $x = 0$ Let $y = 0$

$4(0) + 5y = 20$ $4x + 5(0) = 20$

$\qquad y = 4$ $\qquad x = 5$

$(0, 4)$ $(5, 0)$

47. $3x - 2y = -9$

Let $x = 0$ Let $y = 0$

$3(0) - 2y = -9$ $3x - 2(0) = -9$

$\qquad y = \dfrac{9}{2}$ $\qquad x = -3$

$\qquad\qquad$ $(-3, 0)$

$\left(0, \dfrac{9}{2}\right)$

48. $4x - y = 3$

Let $x = 0$ Let $y = 0$

$4(0) - y = 3$ $4x - (0) = 3$

$\qquad y = -3$ $\qquad x = \dfrac{3}{4}$

$(0, -3)$

$\qquad\qquad\qquad$ $\left(\dfrac{3}{4}, 0\right)$

49. $2x + 6y = 9$

Let $x = 0$ Let $y = 0$

$2(0) + 6y = 9$ $2x + 6(0) = 9$

$\qquad y = \dfrac{3}{2}$ $\qquad x = \dfrac{9}{2}$

$\left(0, \dfrac{3}{2}\right)$ $\left(\dfrac{9}{2}, 0\right)$

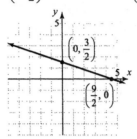

50. $y = 5$

Horizontal line with y-intercept 5.

51. $x = -2$

Vertical line with x-intercept –2.

52. $x - 2 = 0$

$\qquad x = 2$

53. $y + 3 = 0$
$$y = -3$$

54. $C(x) = 0.3x + 42$

   a. $C(150) = 0.3(150) + 42$
$$= 45 + 42$$
$$= 87$$

     $87

   b. $m = 0.3, \ b = 42$

55. $m = \dfrac{-4 - 8}{6 - 2} = \dfrac{-12}{4} = -3$

56. $m = \dfrac{13 - 9}{5 - (-3)} = \dfrac{4}{8} = \dfrac{1}{2}$

57. $m = \dfrac{6 - (-4)}{-3 - (-7)} = \dfrac{10}{4} = \dfrac{5}{2}$

58. $m = \dfrac{7 - (-2)}{-5 - 7} = \dfrac{9}{-12} = -\dfrac{3}{4}$

59. $6x - 15y = 20$
$$-15y = -6x + 20$$
$$y = \dfrac{2}{5}x - \dfrac{4}{3}$$
$$m = \dfrac{2}{5}, \ b = -\dfrac{4}{3}, \ \text{y-intercept} \left(0, -\dfrac{4}{3}\right)$$

60. $4x + 14y = 21$
$$14y = -4x + 21$$
$$y = -\dfrac{2}{7}x + \dfrac{3}{2}$$
$$m = -\dfrac{2}{7}, \ b = \dfrac{3}{2}, \ \text{y-intercept} \left(0, \dfrac{3}{2}\right)$$

61. $y - 3 = 0$
$$y = 3; \ \text{Slope} = 0$$

62. $x = -5$; Vertical line
Slope is undefined.

63. The slope of l_1 is negative, and the slope of l_2 is positive. Since a positive number is greater than any negative number, l_2 has the greater slope.

64. The slope of l_1 is 0, and the slope of l_2 is positive. Since a positive number is greater than 0, l_2 has the greater slope.

65. The slope of l_1 and the slope of l_2 are both positive. Since l_2 is steeper, it has the greater slope.

66. The slope of l_1 is 0, and the slope of l_2 is negative. Since a negative number is less than 0, l_1 has the greater slope.

67. $y = 0.3x + 42$

   a. $m = 0.3$; the cost increases by $0.30 for each additional mile driven.

   b. $b = 42$; the cost for 0 miles driven is $42.

68. $f(x) = -2x + 6$ $g(x) = 2x - 1$
$m = -2$ $m = 2$
Neither; The slopes are not the same and their product is not -1.

69. $-x + 3y = 2$ $6x - 18y = 3$
$$y = \dfrac{1}{3}x + \dfrac{2}{3} \qquad\qquad y = \dfrac{1}{3}x - \dfrac{1}{6}$$
$$m = \dfrac{1}{3} \qquad\qquad\qquad m = \dfrac{1}{3}$$
Parallel, since their slopes are equal.

70. $y = -x + 1$
$m = -1, \ b = 1$

71. $y = 4x - 3$
$m = 4, \ b = -3$

72. $3x - y = 6$
$y = 3x - 6$
$m = 3, \ b = -6$

73. $y = -5x$
$m = -5, \ b = 0$

74. Every horizontal line is in the form $y = c$. Since the line passes through the point $(3, -1)$, its equation is $y = -1$.

75. Every vertical line has the form $x = c$. Since the line passes through the point $(-2, -4)$, its equation is $x = -2$.

76. A line parallel to $x = 6$ has the form $x = c$. Since the line passes through $(-4, -3)$, its equation is $x = -4$.

77. Lines with slope 0 are horizontal, and have the form $y = c$. Since it passes through $(2, 5)$, its equation is $y = 5$.

78. $y - y_1 = m(x - x_1)$
$y - 5 = 3[x - (-3)]$
$y - 5 = 3(x + 3)$
$y - 5 = 3x + 9$
$3x - y = -14$

79. $y - y_1 = m(x - x_1)$
$y - (-2) = 2(x - 5)$
$y + 2 = 2x - 10$
$2x - y = 12$

80. $m = \dfrac{-2 - (-1)}{-4 - (-6)} = \dfrac{-1}{2} = -\dfrac{1}{2}$
$y - y_1 = m(x - x_1)$
$y - (-1) = -\dfrac{1}{2}[x - (-6)]$
$2(y + 1) = -(x + 6)$
$2y + 2 = -x - 6$
$x + 2y = -8$

81. $m = \dfrac{-8 - 3}{-4 - (-5)} = \dfrac{-11}{1} = -11$
$y - y_1 = m(x - x_1)$
$y - 3 = -11[x - (-5)]$
$y - 3 = -11(x + 5)$
$y - 3 = -11x - 55$
$11x + y = -52$

82. $x = 4$ has undefined slope.
A line perpendicular to $x = 4$ has slope = 0 and is therefore horizontal.
$y = 3$

83. $y = 8$ has slope = 0.
A line parallel to $y = 8$ has slope = 0.
$y = -5$

84. $y = mx + b$

$$y = -\frac{2}{3}x + 4$$

$$f(x) = -\frac{2}{3}x + 4$$

85. $y = mx + b$

$$y = -x - 2$$

$$f(x) = -x - 2$$

86. $6x + 3y = 5$

$$3y = -6x + 5$$

$$y = -2x + \frac{5}{3} \text{ so } m = -2$$

$$y - y_1 = m(x - x_1)$$

$$y - (-6) = -2(x - 2)$$

$$y + 6 = -2x + 4$$

$$y = -2x - 2$$

$$f(x) = -2x - 2$$

87. $3x + 2y = 8$

$$2y = -3x + 8$$

$$y = -\frac{3}{2}x + 4 \text{ so } m = -\frac{3}{2}$$

$$y - y_1 = m(x - x_1)$$

$$y - (-2) = -\frac{3}{2}[x - (-4)]$$

$$2(y + 2) = -3(x + 4)$$

$$2y + 4 = -3x - 12$$

$$2y = -3x - 16$$

$$y = -\frac{3}{2}x - 8$$

$$f(x) = -\frac{3}{2}x - 8$$

88. $4x + 3y = 5$

$$3y = -4x + 5$$

$$y = -\frac{4}{3}x + \frac{5}{3}$$

$$\text{so } m = -\frac{4}{3} \text{ and } m_\perp = \frac{3}{4}$$

$$y - y_1 = m(x - x_1)$$

$$y - (-1) = \frac{3}{4}[x - (-6)]$$

$$4(y + 1) = 3(x + 6)$$

$$4y + 4 = 3x + 18$$

$$4y = 3x + 14$$

$$y = \frac{3}{4}x + \frac{7}{2}$$

$$f(x) = \frac{3}{4}x + \frac{7}{2}$$

89. $2x - 3y = 6$

$$-3y = -2x + 6$$

$$y = \frac{2}{3}x - 2$$

$$\text{so } m = \frac{2}{3} \text{ and } m_\perp = -\frac{3}{2}$$

$$y - y_1 = m(x - x_1)$$

$$y - 5 = -\frac{3}{2}[x - (-4)]$$

$$2(y - 5) = -3(x + 4)$$

$$2y - 10 = -3x - 12$$

$$2y = -3x - 2$$

$$y = -\frac{3}{2}x - 1$$

$$f(x) = -\frac{3}{2}x - 1$$

90. a. Use ordered pairs (0, 71) and (5, 82)

$$m = \frac{82 - 71}{5 - 0} = \frac{11}{5} = 2.2 \text{ and } b = 71$$

$$y = 2.2x + 71$$

b. $x = 2009 - 2000 = 9$

$y = 2.2(9) + 71 = 90.8$

About 91% of US drivers will be wearing seat belts.

91. a. Use ordered pairs (0, 43) and (22, 60)

$$m = \frac{60 - 43}{22 - 0} = \frac{17}{22} \text{ and } b = 43$$

$$y = \frac{17}{22}x + 43$$

b. $x = 2010 - 1998 = 12$

$y = \dfrac{17}{22}(12) + 43 \approx 52.3$

There will be about 52 million people reporting arthritis.

92. $f(x) = \begin{cases} -3x & \text{if } x < 0 \\ x - 3 & \text{if } x \geq 0 \end{cases}$

For $x < 0$:   For $x \geq 0$:

x	$f(x)$
−3	9
−2	6
−1	3

x	$f(x)$
0	−3
1	−2
2	−1

Graph a closed circle at (0, −3). Graph an open circle at (0, 0), which is found by substituting 0 for x in $f(x) = -3x$.

93. $g(x) = \begin{cases} -\dfrac{1}{5}x & \text{if } x \leq -1 \\ -4x + 2 & \text{if } x > -1 \end{cases}$

For $x \leq -1$:   For $x > -1$:

x	$g(x)$
−5	1
−3	$\frac{3}{5}$
−1	$\frac{1}{5}$

x	$g(x)$
0	2
1	−2
2	−6

Graph a closed circle at $\left(-1, \dfrac{1}{5}\right)$. Graph an open circle at (−1, 6), which is found by substituting −1 for x in $g(x) = -4x + 2$.

94. $y = \sqrt{x} - 4$

The graph of $f(x) = \sqrt{x} - 4$ is the same as the graph of $y = \sqrt{x}$ shifted down 4 units.

95. $f(x) = \sqrt{x - 4}$

The graph of $f(x) = \sqrt{x - 4}$ is the same as the graph of $y = \sqrt{x}$ shifted right 4 units.

96. $g(x) = |x - 2| - 2$

The graph of $g(x) = |x - 2| - 2$ is the same as the graph of $y = |x|$ shifted right 2 units and down 2 units.

97. $h(x) = -(x+3)^2 - 1$

The graph of $h(x) = -(x+3)^2 - 1$ is the same as

the graph of $y = x^2$ reflected about the

x-axis and then shifted left 3 units and down
1 unit.

98. $3x + y > 4$

$\qquad y > -3x + 4$

Graph the boundary line as dashed.
Test: (0, 0)
$3(0) + 0 > 4$ False
Shade the half-plane that does not include (0, 0).

99. $\dfrac{1}{2}x - y < 2$

$\qquad y > \dfrac{1}{2}x - 2$

Graph the boundary line as dashed.
Test: (0, 0)

$\dfrac{1}{2}(0) - 0 < 2$ True

Shade the half-plane that contains (0, 0).

100. $5x - 2y \le 9$

$\qquad -2y \le -5x + 9$

$\qquad y \ge \dfrac{5}{2}x - \dfrac{9}{2}$

Graph the boundary line as solid.
Test: (0, 0)
$5(0) - 2(0) \le 9$ True
Shade the half-plane that contains (0, 0).

101. $3y \ge x$

$\qquad y \ge \dfrac{x}{3}$

Graph the boundary line as solid.
Test: (0, 1)
$3(1) \ge 0$ True
Shade the half-plane that contains (0, 1).

102. $y < 1$

Graph the boundary line as dashed. Shade the
half-plane below $y = 1$.

103. $x > -2$

Graph the boundary line as dashed. Shade the half-plane to the right of $x = -2$.

104. $y > 2x + 3$ or $x \le -3$

Graph each inequality. The union of the two inequalities is both shaded regions, as shown by the graph below.

105. $2x < 3y + 8$ and $y \ge -2$

Graph each inequality. The intersection of the two inequalities is all points common to both regions, as shown by the shading in the graph below.

106. $3x - 2y = -9$

Let $x = 0$. 　　　　　　　Let $y = 0$.

$3x - 2y = -9$ 　　　　　
$3(0) - 2y = -9$ 　　　　$3x - 2y = -9$
$-2y = -9$ 　　　　　　$3x - 2(0) = -9$
　　　　　　　　　　　$3x = -9$
$y = \dfrac{9}{2}$ 　　　　　　$x = -3$

The intercepts are $\left(0, \dfrac{9}{2}\right)$ and $(-3, 0)$.

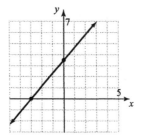

107. $x = -4y$ or $y = -\dfrac{1}{4}x$

The slope is $-\dfrac{1}{4}$, and the y-intercept is $(0, 0)$.

108. $3y \ge x$

Graph the boundary line $3y = x$ or $y = \dfrac{1}{3}x$ as a solid line.

Test $(0, 1)$.

$3y \ge x$
$3(1) \ge 0$
$3 \ge 0$ 　True

Shade the half-plane that contains $(0, 1)$.

109. Vertical; through $\left(-7, -\dfrac{1}{2}\right)$

A vertical line has an equation of the form $x = a$, where a is the x-coordinate of any point on the line. The equation is $x = -7$.

110. Slope 0; through $\left(-4, \dfrac{9}{2}\right)$

    A line with slope 0 is horizontal, and a horizontal line has an equation of the form $y = b$, where b is the y-coordinate of any point on the line. The equation is $y = \dfrac{9}{2}$.

111. Slope $\dfrac{3}{4}$; through $(-8, -4)$

$$y - y_1 = m(x - x_1)$$
$$y - (-4) = \frac{3}{4}(x - (-8))$$
$$y + 4 = \frac{3}{4}(x + 8)$$
$$4(y + 4) = 3(x + 8)$$
$$4y + 16 = 3x + 24$$
$$4y = 3x + 8$$
$$y = \frac{3}{4}x + 2$$

112. Through $(-3, 8)$ and $(-2, 3)$
Find the slope.
$$m = \frac{3 - 8}{-2 - (-3)} = \frac{-5}{1} = -5$$

Use the slope and one of the points in the point-slope form. We use $(-2, 3)$.
$$y - y_1 = m(x - x_1)$$
$$y - 3 = -5(x - (-2))$$
$$y - 3 = -5(x + 2)$$
$$y - 3 = -5x - 10$$
$$y = -5x - 7$$

113. Through $(-6, 1)$; parallel to $y = -\dfrac{3}{2}x + 11$

The slope of a line parallel to $y = -\dfrac{3}{2}x + 11$ will

have the same slope, $-\dfrac{3}{2}$.
$$y - y_1 = m(x - x_1)$$
$$y - 1 = -\frac{3}{2}(x - (-6))$$
$$y - 1 = -\frac{3}{2}(x + 6)$$
$$2(y - 1) = -3(x + 6)$$
$$2y - 2 = -3x - 18$$
$$2y = -3x - 16$$
$$y = -\frac{3}{2}x - 8$$

114. Through $(-5, 7)$; perpendicular to $5x - 4y = 10$
Find the slope of $5x - 4y = 10$.
$$5x - 4y = 10$$
$$-4y = -5x + 10$$
$$y = \frac{5}{4}x - \frac{5}{2}$$

The slope is $\dfrac{5}{4}$. The slope of any line

perpendicular to this line is the negative

reciprocal of $\dfrac{5}{4}$, or $-\dfrac{4}{5}$.
$$y - y_1 = m(x - x_1)$$
$$y - 7 = -\frac{4}{5}(x - (-5))$$
$$y - 7 = -\frac{4}{5}(x + 5)$$
$$5(y - 7) = -4(x + 5)$$
$$5y - 35 = -4x - 20$$
$$5y = -4x + 15$$
$$y = -\frac{4}{5}x + 3$$

115. $f(x) = \begin{cases} x - 2 & \text{if } x \le 0 \\ -\dfrac{x}{3} & \text{if } x \ge 3 \end{cases}$

For $x \le 0$:   For $x \ge 3$:

x	$f(x)$
-2	-4
-1	-3
0	-2

x	$f(x)$
3	-1
4	$-\dfrac{4}{3}$
6	-2

Graph closed circles at $(0, -2)$ and $(3, -1)$.

116. $g(x) = \begin{cases} 4x - 3 & \text{if } x \leq 1 \\ 2x & \text{if } x > 1 \end{cases}$

For $x \leq 1$:   For $x > 1$:

x	$g(x)$
-1	-7
0	-3
1	1

x	$g(x)$
2	4
3	6
4	8

Graph a closed circle at (1, 1). Graph an open circle at (1, 2), which is found by substituting 1 for x in $g(x) = 2x$.

117. $f(x) = \sqrt{x - 2}$

The graph of $f(x) = \sqrt{x - 2}$ is the same as the graph of $y = \sqrt{x}$ shifted right 2 units.

118. $f(x) = |x + 1| - 3$

The graph of $f(x) = |x + 1| - 3$ is the same as the graph of $y = |x|$ shifted left 1 unit and down 3 units.

Chapter 3 Test

1.

A is in quadrant IV.
B is on the x-axis, no quadrant.
C is in quadrant II.

2. $2x - 3y = -6$
$-3y = -2x - 6$
$y = \dfrac{2}{3}x + 2$
$m = \dfrac{2}{3}, \ b = 2$

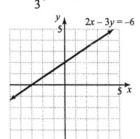

3. $4x + 6y = 7$
$6y = -4x + 7$
$y = -\dfrac{2}{3}x + \dfrac{7}{6}$
$m = -\dfrac{2}{3}, \ b = \dfrac{7}{6}$

4. $f(x) = \frac{2}{3}x$ or $y = \frac{2}{3}x$

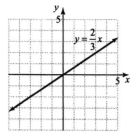

5. $y = -3$

Horizontal line with y-intercept at -3.

6. $m = \frac{10 - (-8)}{-7 - 5} = \frac{18}{-12} = -\frac{3}{2}$

7. $3x + 12y = 8$

$12y = -3x + 8$

$y = -\frac{1}{4}x + \frac{2}{3}$

$m = -\frac{1}{4}$, $b = \frac{2}{3}$, so y-intercept is $\left(0, \frac{2}{3}\right)$.

8. $f(x) = (x-1)^2$

x	-2	-1	0	1	2	3	4
y	9	4	1	0	1	4	9

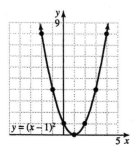

9. $f(x) = |x| + 2$

x	-3	-2	-1	0	1	2	3
y	5	4	3	2	3	4	5

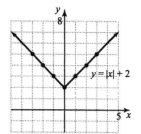

10. Horizontal; through $(2, -8)$

A horizontal line has an equation of the form $y = b$, where b is the y-coordinate of any point on the line. The equation is $y = -8$.

11. Vertical; through $(-4, -3)$

A vertical line has an equation of the form $x = a$, where a is the x-coordinate of any point on the line. The equation is $x = -4$.

12. Perpendicular to $x = 5$; through $(3, -2)$

The line $x = 5$ is vertical, so any line perpendicular to it is horizontal. A horizontal line has an equation of the form $y = b$, where b is the y-coordinate of any point on the line. The equation is $y = -2$.

13. $y - y_1 = m(x - x_1)$

$y - (-1) = -3(x - 4)$

$y + 1 = -3x + 12$

$3x + y = 11$

14. $y - y_1 = m(x - x_1)$

$y - (-2) = 5(x - 0)$

$y + 2 = 5x$

$5x - y = 2$

15. $m = \dfrac{-3-(-2)}{6-4} = \dfrac{-1}{2} = -\dfrac{1}{2}$

$y - y_1 = m(x - x_1)$

$y - (-2) = -\dfrac{1}{2}(x - 4)$

$2(y + 2) = -(x - 4)$

$2y + 4 = -x + 4$

$2y = -x$

$y = -\dfrac{1}{2}x$

$f(x) = -\dfrac{1}{2}x$

16. $3x - y = 4$

$y = 3x - 4$

$m = 3$ so $m_\perp = -\dfrac{1}{3}$

$y - y_1 = m(x - x_1)$

$y - 2 = -\dfrac{1}{3}[x - (-1)]$

$3(y - 2) = -(x + 1)$

$3y - 6 = -x - 1$

$3y = -x + 5$

$y = -\dfrac{1}{3}x + \dfrac{5}{3}$

$f(x) = -\dfrac{1}{3}x + \dfrac{5}{3}$

17. $2y + x = 3$

$2y = -x + 3$

$y = -\dfrac{1}{2}x + 3$ so $m = -\dfrac{1}{2}$

$y - y_1 = m(x - x_1)$

$y - (-2) = -\dfrac{1}{2}(x - 3)$

$2(y + 2) = -(x - 3)$

$2y + 4 = -x + 3$

$2y = -x - 1$

$y = -\dfrac{1}{2}x - \dfrac{1}{2}$

$f(x) = -\dfrac{1}{2}x - \dfrac{1}{2}$

18. $2x - 5y = 8$

$-5y = -2x + 8$

$y = \dfrac{2}{5}x - \dfrac{8}{5}$ so $m_1 = \dfrac{2}{5}$

$m_2 = \dfrac{-1-4}{-1-1} = \dfrac{-5}{-2} = \dfrac{5}{2}$

Therefore, lines L_1 and L_2 are neither parallel nor perpendicular since their slopes are not equal and the product of their slopes is not -1.

19. $x \le -4$

Graph a solid boundary line and shade the half-plane to the left of $x = -4$.

20. $2x - y > 5$

$y < 2x - 5$

Graph the boundary line as a dashed line.
Test: $(0, 0)$
$2(0) - 0 > 5$ False
Shade the half-plane that does not contain the point $(0, 0)$.

21. $2x + 4y < 6$ and $y \le 4$

$4y < -2x + 6$ and $y \le 4$

$y < -\dfrac{1}{2}x + \dfrac{3}{2}$ and $y \le 4$

Graph each inequality. The intersection of the two inequalities is all points common to both regions, as shown by the shading in the graph below.

22. Domain: $(-\infty, \infty)$
Range: $\{5\}$
Function since it passes the vertical line test.

23. Domain: $\{-2\}$
Range: $(-\infty, \infty)$
Not a function since it fails the vertical line test.

24. Domain: $(-\infty, \infty)$
Range: $[0, \infty)$
Function since it passes the vertical line test.

25. Domain: $(-\infty, \infty)$
Range: $(-\infty, \infty)$
Function since it passes the vertical line test.

26. $f(x) = 1031x + 25{,}193$

   a. $x = 0$
      $f(0) = 1031(0) + 25{,}193 = 25{,}193$
      The average earnings in 2000 were $25,193.

   b. $x = 2007 - 2000 = 7$
      $f(7) = 1031(7) + 25{,}193 = 32{,}410$
      The average earnings in 2007 were $32,410.

   c. $40{,}000 \le 1031x + 25{,}193$
      $14{,}807 \le 1031x$
        $14.4 \le x$
      $2000 + 15 = 2015$
      The average earnings will be greater than
      $40,000 in 2015.

   d. slope $= 1031$; the yearly earnings for high
      school graduates increases $1031 per year.

   e. $(0, 25{,}193)$; the yearly earnings for a high
      school graduate in 2000 were $25,193.

27. $f(x) = \begin{cases} -\frac{1}{2}x & \text{if } x \le 0 \\ 2x - 3 & \text{if } x > 0 \end{cases}$

For $x \le 0$:   For $x > 0$:

x	$f(x)$
-4	2
-2	1
0	0

x	$f(x)$
1	-1
2	1
3	3

Graph a closed circle at $(0, 0)$. Graph an open
circle at $(0, -3)$, which is found by substituting 0
for x in $f(x) = 2x - 3$.

28. $f(x) = (x - 4)^2$

The graph of $f(x) = (x - 4)^2$ is the same as the
graph of $y = x^2$ shifted right 4 units.

29. $g(x) = -|x + 2| - 1$

The graph of $g(x) = -|x + 2| - 1$ is the same as
the graph of $y = |x|$ reflected about the
x-axis and then shifted left 2 units and down
1 unit.

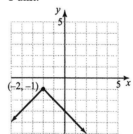

30. $h(x) = \sqrt{x} - 1$

The graph of $h(x) = \sqrt{x} - 1$ is the same as the
graph of $y = \sqrt{x}$ shifted down 1 unit.

Chapter 3 Cumulative Review

1. $3x - y = 3(15) - (4) = 45 - 4 = 41$

2. a. $-4 + (-3) = -7$

     b. $\dfrac{1}{2} - \left(-\dfrac{1}{3}\right) = \dfrac{3}{6} + \dfrac{2}{6} = \dfrac{5}{6}$

     c. $7 - 20 = -13$

3. a. True, 3 is a real number

     b. False, $\dfrac{1}{5}$ is not an irrational number.

     c. False, every rational number is not an integer, for example, $\dfrac{2}{3}$.

     d. False, since 1 is not in the second set.

4. a. The opposite of -7 is 7.

     b. The opposite of 0 is 0.

     c. The opposite of $\dfrac{1}{4}$ is $-\dfrac{1}{4}$.

5. a. $2 - 8 = -6$

     b. $-8 - (-1) = -8 + 1 = -7$

     c. $-11 - 5 = -16$

     d. $10.7 - (-9.8) = 10.7 + 9.8 = 20.5$

     e. $\dfrac{2}{3} - \dfrac{1}{2} = \dfrac{4}{6} - \dfrac{3}{6} = \dfrac{1}{6}$

     f. $1 - 0.06 = 0.94$

     g. $4 - 7 = -3$

6. a. $\dfrac{-42}{-6} = 7$

     b. $\dfrac{0}{14} = 0$

     c. $-1(-5)(-2) = 5(-2) = -10$

7. a. $3^2 = 3 \cdot 3 = 9$

     b. $\left(\dfrac{1}{2}\right)^4 = \dfrac{1}{2^4} = \dfrac{1}{16}$

     c. $-5^2 = -(5 \cdot 5) = -25$

     d. $(-5)^2 = (-5)(-5) = 25$

     e. $-5^3 = -(5 \cdot 5 \cdot 5) = -125$

     f. $(-5)^3 = (-5)(-5)(-5) = -125$

8. a. Distributive Property

     b. Commutative Property of Addition

9. a. $-1 > -2$ since -1 is to the right of -2 on the number line.

     b. $\dfrac{12}{4} = 3$

     c. $-5 < 0$ since -5 is to the left of 0 on the number line.

     d. $-3.5 \le -3.05$ since -3.5 is to the left of -3.05 on the number line.

10. $2x^2$

     a. $2(7)^2 = 2(49) = 98$

     b. $2(-7)^2 = 2(49) = 98$

11. a. The reciprocal of 11 is $\dfrac{1}{11}$.

     b. The reciprocal of -9 is $-\dfrac{1}{9}$.

     c. The reciprocal of $\dfrac{7}{4}$ is $\dfrac{4}{7}$.

12. $\begin{aligned}[t] -2 + 3[5 - (7 - 10)] &= -2 + 3[5 - (-3)] \\ &= -2 + 3(8) \\ &= -2 + 24 \\ &= 22 \end{aligned}$

13.
$$0.6 = 2 - 3.5c$$
$$-1.4 = -3.5c$$
$$\frac{-1.4}{-3.5} = \frac{-3.5c}{-3.5}$$
$$0.4 = c$$

14.
$$2(x-3) = -40$$
$$2x - 6 = -40$$
$$2x = -34$$
$$x = -17$$

15.
$$3x + 5 = 3(x+2)$$
$$3x + 5 = 3x + 6$$
$$5 = 6 \text{ False}$$
The solution is $\varnothing$.

16.
$$5(x-7) = 4x - 35 + x$$
$$5x - 35 = 5x - 35$$
$$-35 = -35 \text{ True for any number}$$
The solution is all real numbers.

17. a. If x is the first integer, then the next two consecutive integers are $x + 1$ and $x + 2$. The sum is $x + (x+1) + (x+2) = 3x + 3$.

    b. The perimeter is found by adding the lengths of the sides.
$$x + 5x + (6x - 3) = 12x - 3$$

18. 25% of $16 = 0.25(16) = 4$

19. Let x = the lowest of the scores. Then the other two scores are $x + 2$ and $x + 4$.
$$x + (x+2) + (x+4) = 264$$
$$3x + 6 = 264$$
$$3x = 258$$
$$x = 86$$
$$x + 2 = 86 + 2 = 88$$
$$x + 4 = 86 + 4 = 90$$
The scores are 86, 88, and 90.

20. Let x = first odd integer, then $x + 2$ = next odd integer and $x + 4$ = third odd integer.
$$x + (x+2) + (x+4) = 213$$
$$3x + 6 = 213$$
$$3x = 207$$
$$x = 69$$
$$x + 2 = 69 + 2 = 71$$
$$x + 4 = 69 + 4 = 73$$
The integers are 69, 71, and 73.

21.
$$V = lwh$$
$$\frac{V}{lw} = \frac{lwh}{lw}$$
$$\frac{V}{lw} = h$$

22.
$$7x + 3y = 21$$
$$3y = -7x + 21$$
$$y = -\frac{7}{3}x + 7$$

23.
$$x - 2 < 5$$
$$x < 7$$
$$(-\infty, 7) \text{ or } \{x | x < 7\}$$

24.
$$-x - 17 \geq 9$$
$$-x \geq 26$$
$$x \leq -26$$
$$(-\infty, -26]$$

25.
$$\frac{2}{5}(x-6) \geq x - 1$$
$$5\left[\frac{2}{5}(x-6)\right] \geq 5[x-1]$$
$$2(x-6) \geq 5x - 5$$
$$2x - 12 \geq 5x - 5$$
$$-3x \geq 7$$
$$x \leq -\frac{7}{3}$$
$$\left(-\infty, -\frac{7}{3}\right]$$

26.
$$3x + 10 > \frac{5}{2}(x-1)$$
$$2(3x+10) > 2\left[\frac{5}{2}(x-1)\right]$$
$$6x + 20 > 5(x-1)$$
$$6x + 20 > 5x - 5$$
$$x > -25$$
$$(-25, \infty)$$

27.
$$2x \geq 0 \text{ and } 4x - 1 \leq -9$$
$$x \geq 0 \text{ and } \quad\quad 4x \leq -8$$
$$x \geq 0 \text{ and } \quad\quad x \leq -2$$
The solution set is $\varnothing$.

28. $x - 2 < 6$ and $3x + 1 > 1$
$x < 8$ and $3x > 0$
$x < 8$ and $x > 0$
$0 < x < 8$
$(0, 8)$

29. $5x - 3 \le 10$ or $x + 1 \ge 5$
$5x \le 13$ or $x \ge 4$
$x \le \dfrac{13}{5}$ or $x \ge 4$
$\left(-\infty, \dfrac{13}{5} \right] \cup [4, \infty)$

30. $x - 2 < 6$ or $3x + 1 > 1$
$x < 8$ or $3x > 0$
$x < 8$ or $x > 0$
$(-\infty, \infty)$

31. $|5w + 3| = 7$
$5w + 3 = 7$ or $5w + 3 = -7$
$5w = 4$ or $5w = -10$
$w = \dfrac{4}{5}$ or $w = -2$
The solution set is $\left\{ -2, \dfrac{4}{5} \right\}$.

32. $|5x - 2| = 3$
$5x - 2 = 3$ or $5x - 2 = -3$
$5x = 5$ or $5x = -1$
$x = 1$ or $x = -\dfrac{1}{5}$
The solution set is $\left\{ -\dfrac{1}{5}, 1 \right\}$.

33. $|3x + 2| = |5x - 8|$
$3x + 2 = 5x - 8$ or $3x + 2 = -(5x - 8)$
$-2x = -10$ or $3x + 2 = -5x + 8$
$x = 5$ or $8x = 6$
$x = \dfrac{3}{4}$
The solution set is $\left\{ \dfrac{3}{4}, 5 \right\}$.

34. $|7x - 2| = |7x + 4|$
$7x - 2 = 7x + 4$ or $7x - 2 = -(7x + 4)$
$-2 = 4$ or $7x - 2 = -7x - 4$
False or $14x = -2$
$x = -\dfrac{1}{7}$
The solution set is $\left\{ -\dfrac{1}{7} \right\}$.

35. $|5x + 1| + 1 \le 10$
$|5x + 1| \le 9$
$-9 \le 5x + 1 \le 9$
$-10 \le 5x \le 8$
$-2 \le x \le \dfrac{8}{5}$
$\left[-2, \dfrac{8}{5} \right]$

36. $|-x + 8| - 2 \le 8$
$|-x + 8| \le 10$
$-10 \le -x + 8 \le 10$
$-18 \le -x \le 2$
$18 \ge x \ge -2$
$-2 \le x \le 18$
$[-2, 18]$

37. $|y - 3| > 7$
$y - 3 < -7$ or $y - 3 > 7$
$y < -4$ or $y > 10$
$(-\infty, -4) \cup (10, \infty)$

38. $|x + 3| > 1$
$x + 3 < -1$ or $x + 3 > 1$
$x < -4$ or $x > -2$
$(-\infty, -4) \cup (-2, \infty)$

39. $3x - y = 12$
$3(0) - (-12) \stackrel{?}{=} 12$
$12 = 12$ True
$(0, -12)$ is a solution.
$3(1) - 9 \stackrel{?}{=} 12$
$-6 = 12$ False
$(1, 9)$ is not a solution.
$3(2) - (-6) \stackrel{?}{=} 12$
$6 + 6 \stackrel{?}{=} 12$
$12 = 12$ True
$(2, -6)$ is a solution.

40. $7x + 2y = 10$

$$2y = -7x + 10$$

$$y = -\frac{7}{2}x + 5$$

$$m = -\frac{7}{2}, \ y\text{-intercept} = (0, 5)$$

41. Yes, $y = 2x + 1$ is a function (graph the function and use the vertical line test).

42. No, it is not a function (by the vertical line test).

43. a. $f(x) = \frac{1}{2}x + \frac{3}{7}$

$$y = mx + b$$

$$b = \frac{3}{7}$$

$$y\text{-intercept} = \left(0, \frac{3}{7}\right)$$

b. $y = -2.5x - 3.2$

$$y = mx + b$$

$$b = -3.2$$

$$y\text{-intercept} = (0, -3.2)$$

44. $m = \dfrac{y_2 - y_1}{x_2 - x_1} = \dfrac{9 - 6}{0 - (-1)} = \dfrac{3}{1} = 3$

45. $f(x) = \dfrac{2}{3}x + 4$

$y = mx + b$

The slope of the line is m, the coefficient of x,

$\dfrac{2}{3}$.

46. Vertical; through $\left(-2, \ -\dfrac{3}{4}\right)$

A vertical line has an equation of the form $x = a$, where a is the x-coordinate of any point on the line. The equation is $x = -2$.

47. y-intercept $= (0, -3)$ means that $b = -3$. Using the equation $y = mx + b$, we have $y = \dfrac{1}{4}x - 3$.

48. Horizontal; through $\left(-2, \ -\dfrac{3}{4}\right)$

A horizontal line has an equation of the form $y = b$, where b is the y-coordinate of any point on the line. The equation is $y = -\dfrac{3}{4}$.

49. $2x - y < 6$

Graph the boundary line as a dashed line.
Test: $(0, 0)$
$2(0) - 0 < 6$ True
Shade the half-plane that contains the point $(0, 0)$.

50. $m = \dfrac{7 - 5}{-4 - (-2)} = \dfrac{2}{-4 + 2} = \dfrac{2}{-2} = -1$

$$y - y_1 = m(x - x_1)$$

$$y - 5 = -1[x - (-2)]$$

$$y - 5 = -(x + 2)$$

$$y - 5 = -x - 2$$

$$x + y = 3$$

Chapter 4

Section 4.1

Practice Exercises

1. a. $\begin{cases} -x-4y=1 \\ 2x+y=5 \end{cases}$

Replace x with 3 and y with -1 in each equation.
$$-x-4y=1$$
$$-3-4(-1) \overset{?}{=} 1$$
$$-3+4 \overset{?}{=} 1$$
$$1=1 \quad \text{True}$$

$$2x+y=5$$
$$2(3)+(-1) \overset{?}{=} 5$$
$$6-1 \overset{?}{=} 5$$
$$5=5 \quad \text{True}$$

Since $(3, -1)$ makes both equations true, it is a solution.

b. $\begin{cases} 4x+y=-4 \\ -x+3y=8 \end{cases}$

Replace x with -2 and y with 4 in each equation.
$$4x+y=-4$$
$$4(-2)+4 \overset{?}{=} -4$$
$$-8+4 \overset{?}{=} -4$$
$$-4=-4 \quad \text{True}$$

$$-x+3y=8$$
$$-(-2)+3(4) \overset{?}{=} 8$$
$$2+12 \overset{?}{=} 8$$
$$14=8 \quad \text{False}$$

Since $(-2, 4)$ does not make both equations true, it is not a solution.

2. a. $\begin{cases} 3x-2y=4 \\ -9x+6y=-12 \end{cases}$

The graphs appear to be the same line. Notice that if both sides of the first equation

are multiplied by -3, the result is the second equation. Any solution of one equation satisfies the other equation as well. There are an infinite number of solutions in the form $\{(x, y) | 3x - 2y = 4\}$ or $\{(x, y) | -9x + 6y = -12\}$.

b. $\begin{cases} y = 5x \\ 2x+y=7 \end{cases}$

These lines intersect at one point as shown in the graph. The coordinates of the point appear to be $(1, 5)$. Check by replacing x with 1 and y with 5 in both equations.

$$y=5x \qquad\qquad 2x+y=7$$
$$5 \overset{?}{=} 5(1) \qquad\qquad 2(1)+5 \overset{?}{=} 7$$
$$5=5 \quad \text{True} \qquad\qquad 2+5 \overset{?}{=} 7$$
$$\qquad\qquad\qquad\qquad\quad 7=7 \quad \text{True}$$

Since $(1, 5)$ satisfies both equations, we conclude that $(1, 5)$ is the solution of the system.

c. $\begin{cases} y = \dfrac{3}{4}x+1 \\ 3x-4y=12 \end{cases}$

The lines appear to be parallel. The first equation is in point-slope. Write the second equation in point-slope form.

$$3x - 4y = 12$$
$$-4y = -3x + 12$$
$$y = \frac{3}{4}x - 3$$

The graphs have the same slope, $\frac{3}{4}$, but different y-intercepts, so the lines are parallel. The system has no solution.

3. $\begin{cases} y = 4x + 7 \\ 2x + y = 4 \end{cases}$

In the first equation, we are told that y is equal to $4x + 7$, so we substitute $4x + 7$ for y in the second equation and solve for x.
$$2x + y = 4$$
$$2x + (4x + 7) = 4$$
$$6x + 7 = 4$$
$$6x = -3$$
$$x = \frac{-3}{6} = -\frac{1}{2}$$

To find the y-coordinate, we replace x with $-\frac{1}{2}$ in the first equation.
$$y = 4x + 7$$
$$y = 4\left(-\frac{1}{2}\right) + 7$$
$$y = -2 + 7 = 5$$

The solution is $\left(-\frac{1}{2}, 5\right)$.

4. $\begin{cases} -\dfrac{x}{3} + \dfrac{y}{4} = \dfrac{1}{2} \\ \dfrac{x}{4} - \dfrac{y}{2} = -\dfrac{1}{4} \end{cases}$

Multiply each equation by its LCD to clear fractions.
$$\begin{cases} 12\left(-\dfrac{x}{3} + \dfrac{y}{4}\right) = 12\left(\dfrac{1}{2}\right) \\ 4\left(\dfrac{x}{4} - \dfrac{y}{2}\right) = 4\left(-\dfrac{1}{4}\right) \end{cases}$$
$$\begin{cases} -4x + 3y = 6 \\ x - 2y = -1 \end{cases}$$

Solve the second equation for x.
$$x - 2y = -1$$
$$x = 2y - 1$$

Replace x with $2y - 1$ in the first equation.

$$-4x + 3y = 6$$
$$-4(2y - 1) + 3y = 6$$
$$-8y + 4 + 3y = 6$$
$$-5y + 4 = 6$$
$$-5y = 2$$
$$y = -\frac{2}{5}$$

To find the x-coordinate, replace y with $-\frac{2}{5}$ in $x = 2y - 1$.
$$x = 2\left(-\frac{2}{5}\right) - 1 = -\frac{4}{5} - 1 = -\frac{4}{5} - \frac{5}{5} = -\frac{9}{5}$$

The solution is $\left(-\frac{9}{5}, -\frac{2}{5}\right)$.

5. $\begin{cases} 3x - y = 5 \\ 5x + y = 11 \end{cases}$

We add the equations.
$$3x - y = 5$$
$$\underline{5x + y = 11}$$
$$8x \qquad = 16$$
$$x = 2$$

Replace x with 2 in the second equation to find y.
$$5x + y = 11$$
$$5(2) + y = 11$$
$$10 + y = 11$$
$$y = 1$$

The solution is $(2, 1)$.

6. $\begin{cases} 3x - 2y = -6 \\ 4x + 5y = -8 \end{cases}$

We can eliminate y if we multiply both sides of the first equation by 5 and both sides of the second equation by 2.
$$\begin{cases} 5(3x - 2y) = 5(-6) \\ 2(4x + 5y) = 2(-8) \end{cases}$$
$$\begin{cases} 15x - 10y = -30 \\ \underline{8x + 10y = -16} \end{cases}$$
$$23x \qquad\quad = -46$$
$$x = -2$$

To find y, replace x with -2 in either equation.
$$4x + 5y = -8$$
$$4(-2) + 5y = -8$$
$$-8 + 5y = -8$$
$$5y = 0$$
$$y = 0$$

The solution is $(-2, 0)$.

7. $\begin{cases} 8x + y = 6 \\ 2x + \dfrac{y}{4} = -2 \end{cases}$

If we multiply the second equation by -4, the coefficients of x will be opposites.

$\begin{cases} 8x + y = 6 \\ -4\left(2x + \dfrac{y}{4}\right) = -4(-2) \end{cases}$

$\begin{cases} 8x + y = 6 \\ -8x - y = 8 \end{cases}$

$\overline{\qquad 0 = 14 \quad \text{False}}$

The system has no solution. The solution set is $\{\ \}$ or $\varnothing$.

8. $\begin{cases} -3x + 2y = -1 \\ 9x - 6y = 3 \end{cases}$

To eliminate x, we multiply both sides of the first equation by 3.

$\begin{cases} 3(-3x + 2y) = 3(-1) \\ 9x - 6y = 3 \end{cases}$

$\begin{cases} -9x + 6y = -3 \\ 9x - 6y = 3 \end{cases}$

$\overline{\qquad 0 = 0 \quad \text{True}}$

There are an infinite number of solutions. The solution set is $\{(x, y)|{-3x + 2y = -1}\}$ or $\{(x, y)|9x - 6y = 3\}$.

Graphing Calculator Explorations

1.

$(2.11, 0.17)$

2.

$(-1.12, -5.02)$

3.

$(0.57, -1.97)$

4.

$(-1.38, 1.35)$

Vocabulary and Readiness Check

1. A system with no solution has lines that are parallel. The correct graph is B.

2. A system with an infinite number of solutions has lines that are the same. The correct graph is C.

3. A system with solution $(1, -2)$ has lines that intersect at $(1, -2)$. The correct graph is A.

4. A system with solution $(-3, 0)$ has lines that intersect at $(-3, 0)$. The correct graph is D.

Exercise Set 4.1

1. $\begin{cases} x - y = 3 \\ 2x - 4y = 8 \end{cases}$

$\quad x - y = 3$

$2 - (-1) \overset{?}{=} 3$

$\qquad 3 = 3 \quad \text{True}$

$\quad 2x - 4y = 8$

$2(2) - 4(-1) \overset{?}{=} 8$

$\quad 4 + 4 \overset{?}{=} 8$

$\qquad 8 = 8 \quad \text{True}$

Yes, $(2, -1)$ is a solution.

3. $\begin{cases} 2x - 3y = -9 \\ 4x + 2y = -2 \end{cases}$

$\quad 2x - 3y = -9$

$2(3) - 3(5) \overset{?}{=} -9$

$\quad 6 - 15 \overset{?}{=} -9$

$\qquad -9 = -9 \quad \text{True}$

$\quad 4x + 2y = -2$

$4(3) + 2(5) \overset{?}{=} -2$

$\quad 12 + 10 \overset{?}{=} -2$

$\qquad 22 = -2 \quad \text{False}$

No, $(3, 5)$ is not a solution.

5. $\begin{cases} 3x + 7y = -19 \\ -6x = 5y + 8 \end{cases}$

$3x + 7y = -19$

$3\left(\dfrac{2}{3}\right) + 7(-3) \stackrel{?}{=} -19$

$2 + (-21) \stackrel{?}{=} -19$

$-19 = -19$ True

$-6x = 5y + 8$

$-6\left(\dfrac{2}{3}\right) \stackrel{?}{=} 5(-3) + 8$

$-4 \stackrel{?}{=} -15 + 8$

$-4 = -7$ False

No, $\left(\dfrac{2}{3}, -3\right)$ is not a solution.

7. $\begin{cases} x + y = 1 \\ x - 2y = 4 \end{cases}$

$(2, -1)$

The solution is $(2, -1)$.

9. $\begin{cases} 2y - 4x = 0 \\ x + 2y = 5 \end{cases}$

$(1, 2)$

The solution is $(1, 2)$.

11. $\begin{cases} 3x - y = 4 \\ 6x - 2y = 4 \end{cases}$

The solution set is $\varnothing$.

13. No; answers may vary

15. $\begin{cases} x + y = 10 \\ y = 4x \end{cases}$

Replace y with $4x$ in E1.

$x + (4x) = 10$

$5x = 10$

$x = 2$

Replace x with 2 in E2.

$y = 4(2)$

$y = 8$

The solution is $(2, 8)$.

17. $\begin{cases} 4x - y = 9 \\ 2x + 3y = -27 \end{cases}$

Solve E1 for y.

$4x - y = 9$

$y = 4x - 9$

Replace y with $4x - 9$ in E2.

$2x + 3(4x - 9) = -27$

$2x + 12x - 27 = -27$

$14x = 0$

$x = 0$

Replace x with 0 in E1.

$4(0) - y = 9$

$y = -9$

The solution is $(0, -9)$.

19. $\begin{cases} \dfrac{1}{2}x + \dfrac{3}{4}y = -\dfrac{1}{4} \\ \dfrac{3}{4}x - \dfrac{1}{4}y = 1 \end{cases}$

Clear fractions by multiplying each equation by 4.

$\begin{cases} 2x + 3y = -1 \\ 3x - y = 4 \end{cases}$

Now solve E2 for y.

$3x - y = 4$

$y = 3x - 4$

Replace y with $3x - 4$ in E1.

$2x + 3(3x - 4) = -1$

$2x + 9x - 12 = -1$

$11x = 11$

$x = 1$

Replace x with 1 in equation $y = 3x - 4$.

$y = 3(1) - 4$

$y = -1$

The solution is $(1, -1)$.

21. $\begin{cases} \dfrac{x}{3} + y = \dfrac{4}{3} \\ -x + 2y = 11 \end{cases}$

Clear fractions by multiplying the first equation by 3.

$\begin{cases} x + 3y = 4 \\ -x + 2y = 11 \end{cases}$

Solve E2 for x.

$2y - 11 = x$

$x = 2y - 11$

Replace x with $2y - 11$ in E1.

$(2y - 11) + 3y = 4$

$5y = 15$

$y = 3$

Replace y with 3 in equation $x = 2y - 11$.

$x = 2(3) - 11$

$x = -5$

The solution is $(-5, 3)$.

23. $\begin{cases} -x + 2y = 0 \\ x + 2y = 5 \end{cases}$

E1 + E2: $\begin{array}{r} -x + 2y = 0 \\ x + 2y = 5 \\ \hline 4y = 5 \end{array}$

$y = \dfrac{5}{4}$

Replace y with $\dfrac{5}{4}$ in E1.

$-x + 2\left(\dfrac{5}{4}\right) = 0$

$-x + \dfrac{5}{2} = 0$

$\dfrac{5}{2} = x$

The solution is $\left(\dfrac{5}{2}, \dfrac{5}{4}\right)$.

25. $\begin{cases} 5x + 2y = 1 \\ x - 3y = 7 \end{cases}$

Multiply E2 by –5.

$\begin{cases} 5x + 2y = 1 \\ -5x + 15y = -35 \end{cases}$

E1 + E2: $\begin{array}{r} 5x + 2y = 1 \\ -5x + 15y = -35 \\ \hline 17y = -34 \end{array}$

$y = -2$

Replace y with –2 in E2.

$x - 3(-2) = 7$

$x + 6 = 7$

$x = 1$

The solution is $(1, -2)$.

27. $\begin{cases} \dfrac{3}{4}x + \dfrac{5}{2}y = 11 \\ \dfrac{1}{16}x - \dfrac{3}{4}y = -1 \end{cases}$

Clear fractions by multiplying E1 by 4 and E2 by 16.

$\begin{cases} 3x + 10y = 44 \\ x - 12y = -16 \end{cases}$

Multiply E2 by –3.

$\begin{cases} 3x + 10y = 44 \\ -3x + 36y = 48 \end{cases}$

E1 + E2: $\begin{array}{r} 3x + 10y = 44 \\ -3x + 36y = 48 \\ \hline 46y = 92 \end{array}$

$y = 2$

Replace y with 2 in the equation $x - 12y = -16$.

$x - 12(2) = -16$

$x - 24 = -16$

$x = 8$

The solution is $(8, 2)$.

29. $\begin{cases} 3x - 5y = 11 \\ 2x - 6y = 2 \end{cases}$

Multiply E1 by 2 and E2 by –3.

$\begin{cases} 6x - 10y = 22 \\ -6x + 18y = -6 \end{cases}$

E1 + E2: $\begin{array}{r} 6x - 10y = 22 \\ -6x + 18y = -6 \\ \hline 8y = 16 \end{array}$

$y = 2$

Replace y with 2 in E2.

$$2x - 6(2) = 2$$
$$2x - 12 = 2$$
$$2x = 14$$
$$x = 7$$

The solution is (7, 2).

31. $\begin{cases} x - 2y = 4 \\ 2x - 4y = 4 \end{cases}$

Multiply E1 by –2.

$\begin{cases} -2x + 4y = -8 \\ 2x - 4y = 4 \end{cases}$

E1 + E2: $\begin{aligned} -2x + 4y &= -8 \\ \underline{2x - 4y} &= \underline{4} \\ 0 &= -4 \quad \text{False} \end{aligned}$

Inconsistent system; the solution set is $\varnothing$.

33. $\begin{cases} 3x + y = 1 \\ 2y = 2 - 6x \end{cases}$

$\begin{cases} 3x + y = 1 \\ 6x + 2y = 2 \end{cases}$

Multiply E1 by –2.

$\begin{cases} -6x - 2y = -2 \\ 6x + 2y = 2 \end{cases}$

E1 + E2: $\begin{aligned} -6x - 2y &= -2 \\ \underline{6x + 2y} &= \underline{2} \\ 0 &= 0 \quad \text{True} \end{aligned}$

Dependent system; the solution set is
$\{(x, y) | 3x + y = 1\}$.

35. $\begin{cases} 2x + 5y = 8 \\ 6x + y = 10 \end{cases}$

Multiply E1 by –3.

$\begin{cases} -6x - 15y = -24 \\ 6x + y = 10 \end{cases}$

E1 + E2: $\begin{aligned} -6x - 15y &= -24 \\ \underline{6x + y} &= \underline{10} \\ -14y &= -14 \\ y &= 1 \end{aligned}$

Replace y with 1 in E2.
$$6x + 1 = 10$$
$$6x = 9$$
$$x = \frac{9}{6} = \frac{3}{2}$$

The solution is $\left(\frac{3}{2}, 1\right)$.

37. $\begin{cases} x + y = 1 \\ x - 2y = 4 \end{cases}$

Multiply E1 by –1.

$\begin{cases} -x - y = -1 \\ x - 2y = 4 \end{cases}$

E1 + E2: $\begin{aligned} -x - y &= -1 \\ \underline{x - 2y} &= \underline{4} \\ -3y &= 3 \\ y &= -1 \end{aligned}$

Replace y with –1 in E1.
$$x + (-1) = 1$$
$$x - 1 = 1$$
$$x = 2$$

The solution is (2, –1).

39. $\begin{cases} \dfrac{1}{3}x + y = \dfrac{4}{3} \\ -\dfrac{1}{4}x - \dfrac{1}{2}y = -\dfrac{1}{4} \end{cases}$

Clear fractions by multiplying E1 by 3 and E2 by 4.

$\begin{cases} x + 3y = 4 \\ -x - 2y = -1 \end{cases}$

E1 + E2: $\begin{aligned} x + 3y &= 4 \\ \underline{-x - 2y} &= \underline{-1} \\ y &= 3 \end{aligned}$

Replace y with 3 in the equation $x + 3y = 4$.
$$x + 3(3) = 4$$
$$x + 9 = 4$$
$$x = -5$$

The solution is (–5, 3).

41. $\begin{cases} 2x + 6y = 8 \\ 3x + 9y = 12 \end{cases}$

Multiply E1 by –3 and E2 by 2.

$\begin{cases} -6x - 18y = -24 \\ 6x + 18y = 24 \end{cases}$

E1 + E2: $\begin{aligned} -6x - 18y &= -24 \\ \underline{6x + 18y} &= \underline{24} \\ 0 &= 0 \quad \text{True} \end{aligned}$

Dependent system; the solution is
$\{(x, y) | 3x + 9y = 12\}$.

43. $\begin{cases} 4x + 2y = 5 \\ 2x + y = -1 \end{cases}$

Multiply E2 by –2.

$\begin{cases} 4x + 2y = 5 \\ -4x - 2y = 2 \end{cases}$

E1 + E2: $4x + 2y = 5$
$\underline{-4x - 2y = 2}$
$0 = 7$ False

Inconsistent system; the solution set is $\varnothing$.

45. $\begin{cases} 10y - 2x = 1 \\ 5y = 4 - 6x \end{cases}$

$\begin{cases} 10y - 2x = 1 \\ 5y + 6x = 4 \end{cases}$

Multiply E2 by –2.

$\begin{cases} 10y - 2x = 1 \\ -10y - 12x = -8 \end{cases}$

E1 + E2: $10y - 2x = 1$
$\underline{-10y - 12x = -8}$
$-14x = -7$
$x = \dfrac{1}{2}$

Replace x with $\dfrac{1}{2}$ in the equation $5y = 4 - 6x$.

$5y = 4 - 6\left(\dfrac{1}{2}\right)$

$5y = 4 - 3$
$5y = 1$
$y = \dfrac{1}{5}$

The solution is $\left(\dfrac{1}{2}, \dfrac{1}{5}\right)$.

47. $\begin{cases} 5x - 2y = 27 \\ -3x + 5y = 18 \end{cases}$

Multiply E1 by 3 and E2 by 5.

$\begin{cases} 15x - 6y = 81 \\ -15x + 25y = 90 \end{cases}$

E1 + E2: $15x - 6y = 81$
$\underline{-15x + 25y = 90}$
$19y = 171$
$y = 9$

Replace y with 9 in E1.
$5x - 2(9) = 27$
$5x - 18 = 27$
$5x = 45$
$x = 9$
The solution is (9, 9).

49. $\begin{cases} x = 3y + 2 \\ 5x - 15y = 10 \end{cases}$

Replace x with $3y + 2$ in E2.

$5(3y + 2) - 15y = 10$
$15y + 10 - 15y = 10$
$10 = 10$ True
The system is dependent. The solution is
$\{(x, y)\,|\,x = 3y + 2\}$.

51. $\begin{cases} 2x - y = -1 \\ y = -2x \end{cases}$

Replace y with $-2x$ in E1.
$2x - (-2x) = -1$
$4x = -1$
$x = -\dfrac{1}{4}$

Replace x with $-\dfrac{1}{4}$ in E2.

$y = -2\left(-\dfrac{1}{4}\right)$

$y = \dfrac{1}{2}$

The solution is $\left(-\dfrac{1}{4}, \dfrac{1}{2}\right)$.

53. $\begin{cases} 2x = 6 \\ y = 5 - x \end{cases}$

E1 yields $x = 3$.
Replace x with 3 in E2.
$y = 5 - 3$
$y = 2$
The solution is (3, 2).

55. $\begin{cases} \dfrac{x+5}{2} = \dfrac{6-4y}{3} \\ \dfrac{3x}{5} = \dfrac{21-7y}{10} \end{cases}$

Multiply E1 by 6 and E2 by 10.

$\begin{cases} 3x + 15 = 12 - 8y \\ 6x = 21 - 7y \end{cases}$

$\begin{cases} 3x + 8y = -3 \\ 6x + 7y = 21 \end{cases}$

Multiply E1 by –2.

$\begin{cases} -6x - 16y = 6 \\ 6x + 7y = 21 \end{cases}$

E1 + E2: $-6x - 16y = 6$
$\underline{6x + 7y = 21}$
$-9y = 27$
$y = -3$

Replace y with –3 in the equation $3x + 8y = -3$.

$$3x + 8(-3) = -3$$
$$3x - 24 = -3$$
$$3x = 21$$
$$x = 7$$

The solution is $(7, -3)$.

57. $\begin{cases} 4x - 7y = 7 \\ 12x - 21y = 24 \end{cases}$

Multiply E1 by –3.

$\begin{cases} -12x + 21y = -21 \\ 12x - 21y = 24 \end{cases}$
$$\overline{\ 0 = 3 \quad \text{False}}$$

Inconsistent system; the solution set is $\varnothing$.

59. $\begin{cases} \dfrac{2}{3}x - \dfrac{3}{4}y = -1 \\ -\dfrac{1}{6}x + \dfrac{3}{8}y = 1 \end{cases}$

Multiply E1 by 12 and E2 by 24.

$\begin{cases} 8x - 9y = -12 \\ -4x + 9y = 24 \end{cases}$

E1 + E2: $\quad 8x - 9y = -12$
$$\underline{-4x + 9y = 24}$$
$$4x = 12$$
$$x = 3$$

Replace x with 3 in the equation $-4x + 9y = 24$.
$$-4(3) + 9y = 24$$
$$-12 + 9y = 24$$
$$9y = 36$$
$$y = 4$$

The solution is $(3, 4)$.

61. $\begin{cases} 0.7x - 0.2y = -1.6 \\ 0.2x - y = -1.4 \end{cases}$

Multiply both equations by 10.

$\begin{cases} 7x - 2y = -16 \\ 2x - 10y = -14 \end{cases}$

Multiply E1 by –5.

$\begin{cases} -35x + 10y = 80 \\ 2x - 10y = -14 \end{cases}$

E1 + E2: $-35x + 10y = 80$
$$\underline{2x - 10y = -14}$$
$$-33x = 66$$
$$x = -2$$

Replace x with –2 in the equation $7x - 2y = -16$.

$$7(-2) - 2y = -16$$
$$-14 - 2y = -16$$
$$-2y = -2$$
$$y = 1$$

The solution is $(-2, 1)$.

63. $\begin{cases} 4x - 1.5y = 10.2 \\ 2x + 7.8y = -25.68 \end{cases}$

Multiply E2 by –2.

$\begin{cases} 4x - 1.5y = 10.2 \\ -4x - 15.6y = 51.36 \end{cases}$

E1 + E2: $\quad 4x - 1.5y = 10.2$
$$\underline{-4x - 15.6y = 51.36}$$
$$-17.1y = 61.56$$
$$y = -3.6$$

Replace y with –3.6 in E1.
$$4x - 1.5(-3.6) = 10.2$$
$$4x + 5.4 = 10.2$$
$$4x = 4.8$$
$$x = 1.2$$

The solution is $(1.2, -3.6)$.

65. $\quad 3x - 4y + 2z = 5$
$$3(1) - 4(2) + 2(5) \overset{?}{=} 5$$
$$3 - 8 + 10 \overset{?}{=} 5$$
$$5 = 5$$

True

67. $\quad -x - 5y + 3z = 15$
$$-(0) - 5(-1) + 3(5) \overset{?}{=} 15$$
$$0 + 5 + 15 \overset{?}{=} 15$$
$$20 = 15$$

False

69. $\quad 3x + 2y - 5z = 10$
$$\underline{-3x + 4y + z = 15}$$
$$6y - 4z = 25$$

71. $\quad 10x + 5y + 6z = 14$
$$\underline{-9x + 5y - 6z = -12}$$
$$x + 10y = 2$$

73. Find the coordinates of the equilibrium point, (5000, 21). This represents 5000 DVDs at $21 per DVD.

75. Supply is greater than demand because the line representing supply is above that for demand.

77. $\begin{cases} y = 2.5x \\ y = 0.9x + 3000 \end{cases}$

Substitute.
$2.5x = 0.9x + 3000$
$1.6x = 3000$
$\quad x = 1875$
$\quad y = 2.5(1875) = 4687.5$
The point of intersection is $(1875, 4687.5)$.

79. Makes money because revenue is greater than cost at $x = 2000$.

81. For values of $x > 1875$ because the x-value at the intersection is 1875.

83. Answers may vary; one possibility:
$\begin{cases} -2x + y = 1 \\ x - 2y = -8 \end{cases}$

85. Red meat: $y = -0.3x + 113$
Poultry: $y = x + 68$

   a. $m_{\text{red meat}} = -0.3$ and $m_{\text{poultry}} = 1$.

     Consumption of red meat is decreasing while consumption of poultry is increasing.

   b. $\begin{cases} y = -0.3x + 113 \\ y = x + 68 \end{cases}$

     Substitute.
     $-0.3x + 113 = x + 68$
              $45 = 1.3x$
              $35 = x$
     $y = 35 + 68 = 103$
     The solution is $(35, 103)$.

   c. $x = 35 \Rightarrow 2000 + 35 = 2035$
     In the year 2035, red meat and poultry consumption will each be about 103 pounds per person.

87. $\begin{cases} \dfrac{1}{x} + y = 12 \\ \dfrac{3}{x} - y = 4 \end{cases}$

Replacing $\dfrac{1}{x}$ with a, we have
$\begin{cases} a + y = 12 \\ 3a - y = 4 \end{cases}$

Adding the two new equations we get
$4a = 16$
$\quad a = 4$

Replace a with 4 in the equation $a + y = 12$.
$4 + y = 12$
$\quad y = 8$

Since $a = 4$, $x = \dfrac{1}{4}$.

The solution is $\left(\dfrac{1}{4}, 8 \right)$.

89. $\begin{cases} \dfrac{1}{x} + \dfrac{1}{y} = 5 \\ \dfrac{1}{x} - \dfrac{1}{y} = 1 \end{cases}$

Replace $\dfrac{1}{x}$ with a and $\dfrac{1}{y}$ with b.

$\begin{cases} a + b = 5 \\ a - b = 1 \end{cases}$

Adding the two new equations we get
$2a = 6$
$\quad a = 3$

Replace a with 3 in the equation $a + b = 5$.
$3 + b = 5$
$\quad b = 2$

Since $a = 3$, $x = \dfrac{1}{3}$. Similarly, $y = \dfrac{1}{2}$.

The solution is $\left(\dfrac{1}{3}, \dfrac{1}{2} \right)$.

91. $\begin{cases} \dfrac{2}{x} + \dfrac{3}{y} = -1 \\ \dfrac{3}{x} - \dfrac{2}{y} = 18 \end{cases}$

Replace $\dfrac{1}{x}$ with a and $\dfrac{1}{y}$ with b.

$\begin{cases} 2a + 3b = -1 \\ 3a - 2b = 18 \end{cases}$

Multiply E1 by 2 and E2 by 3 to obtain
$\begin{cases} 4a + 6b = -2 \\ 9a - 6b = 54 \end{cases}$

Adding these last two equations we have
$13a = 52$
$\quad a = 4$

Replace a with 4 in the equation $2a + 3b = -1$.
$2(4) + 3b = -1$
$\quad\quad\quad 3b = -9$
$\quad\quad\quad\; b = -3$

Since $a = 4$, $x = \dfrac{1}{4}$. Similarly, $y = -\dfrac{1}{3}$.

The solution is $\left(\dfrac{1}{4}, -\dfrac{1}{3} \right)$.

93. $\begin{cases} \dfrac{2}{x} - \dfrac{4}{y} = 5 \\ \dfrac{1}{x} - \dfrac{2}{y} = \dfrac{3}{2} \end{cases}$

Replace $\dfrac{1}{x}$ with a and $\dfrac{1}{y}$ with b.

$\begin{cases} 2a - 4b = 5 \\ a - 2b = \dfrac{3}{2} \end{cases}$

Multiply E2 by 2.

$\begin{cases} 2a - 4b = 5 \\ 2a - 4b = 3 \end{cases}$

This system is inconsistent. The solution set is $\varnothing$.

Section 4.2

Practice Exercises

1. $\begin{cases} 3x + 2y - z = 0 & (1) \\ x - y + 5z = 2 & (2) \\ 2x + 3y + 3z = 7 & (3) \end{cases}$

Multiply equation (2) by 2 and add to equation (1) to eliminate y.

$\begin{cases} 3x + 2y - z = 0 \\ 2(x - y + 5z) = 2(2) \end{cases}$

$\begin{array}{r} 3x - 2y \ \ - z = 0 \\ \underline{2x - 2y + 10z = 4} \\ 5x \quad\quad + 9z = 4 \quad (4) \end{array}$

Multiply equation (2) by 3 and add to equation (3) to eliminate y again.

$\begin{cases} 3(x - y + 5z) = 3(2) \\ 2x + 3y + 3z = 7 \end{cases}$

$\begin{array}{r} 3x - 3y + 15z = 6 \\ \underline{2x + 3y \ \ + 3z = 7} \\ 5x + \quad\quad 18z = 13 \quad (5) \end{array}$

Multiply equation (4) by -1 and add to equation (5) to eliminate x.

$\begin{cases} -1(5x + 9z) = -1(4) \\ 5x + 18z = 13 \end{cases}$

$\begin{array}{r} -5x \ \ - 9z = -4 \\ \underline{5x + 18z = 13} \\ 9z = 9 \\ z = 1 \end{array}$

Replace z with 1 in equation (4) or (5).

$\begin{aligned} 5x + 9z &= 4 \\ 5x + 9(1) &= 4 \\ 5x &= -5 \\ x &= -1 \end{aligned}$

Replace x with -1 and z with 1 in equation (1), (2), or (3).

$\begin{aligned} x - y + 5z &= 2 \\ -1 - y + 5(1) &= 2 \\ -y + 4 &= 2 \\ -y &= -2 \\ y &= 2 \end{aligned}$

The solution is $(-1, 2, 1)$. To check, let $x = -1$, $y = 2$, and $z = 1$ in all three original equations of the system.

2. $\begin{cases} 6x - 3y + 12z = 4 & (1) \\ -6x + 4y - 2z = 7 & (2) \\ -2x + y - 4z = 3 & (3) \end{cases}$

Multiply equation (3) by 3 and add to equation (1) to eliminate x.

$\begin{cases} 6x - 3y + 12z = 4 \\ 3(-2x + y - 4z) = 3(3) \end{cases}$

$\begin{array}{r} 6x - 3y + 12z = 4 \\ \underline{-6x + 3y - 12z = 9} \\ 0 = 13 \quad \text{False} \end{array}$

Since the statement is false, this system is inconsistent and has no solution. The solution set is $\{ \ \}$ or $\varnothing$.

3. $\begin{cases} 3x + 4y \quad\quad = 0 & (1) \\ 9x \quad\quad - 4z = 6 & (2) \\ -2y + 7z = 1 & (3) \end{cases}$

Equation (2) has no term containing the variable y. Eliminate y using equations (1) and (3). Multiply equation (3) by 2 and add to equation (1).

$\begin{cases} 3x + 4y = 0 \\ 2(-2y + 7z) = 2(1) \end{cases}$

$\begin{array}{r} 3x + 4y \quad\quad = 0 \\ \underline{-4y + 14z = 2} \\ 3x \quad\quad + 14z = 2 \quad (4) \end{array}$

Multiply equation (4) by -3 and add to equation (2) to eliminate x.

$$\begin{cases} 9x - 4z = 6 \\ -3(3x + 14z) = -3(2) \end{cases}$$

$$\begin{cases} 9x \quad -4z = 6 \\ \underline{-9x - 52z = -6} \end{cases}$$
$$\qquad -56z = 0$$
$$\qquad z = 0$$

Replace z with 0 in equation (2) and solve for x.
$$9x - 4z = 6$$
$$9x - 4(0) = 6$$
$$9x = 6$$
$$x = \frac{6}{9} = \frac{2}{3}$$

Replace z with 0 in equation (3) and solve for y.
$$-2y + 7z = 1$$
$$-2y + 7(0) = 1$$
$$-2y = 1$$
$$y = -\frac{1}{2}$$

The solution is $\left(\frac{2}{3}, -\frac{1}{2}, 0\right)$.

4. $\begin{cases} 2x + y - 3z = 6 & (1) \\ x + \dfrac{1}{2}y - \dfrac{3}{2}z = 3 & (2) \\ -4x - 2y + 6z = -12 & (3) \end{cases}$

Multiply both sides of equation (2) by 2 to eliminate fractions, and multiply both sides of equation (3) by $-\dfrac{1}{2}$ since all coefficients in equation (3) are divisible by 2 and the coefficient of x is negative. The resulting system is

$$\begin{cases} 2x + y - 3z = 6 \\ 2x + y - 3z = 6 \\ 2x + y - 3z = 6 \end{cases}$$

Since the three equations are identical, there are infinitely many solutions of the system. The equations are dependent. The solution set can be written as $\{(x, y, z) | 2x + y - 3z = 6\}$.

5. $\begin{cases} x + 2y + 4z = 16 & (1) \\ x \quad\quad + 2z = -4 & (2) \\ \quad\quad y - 3z = 30 & (3) \end{cases}$

Solve equation (2) for x and equation (3) for y.
$$x + 2z = -4 \qquad\qquad y - 3z = 30$$
$$x = -2z - 4 \qquad\qquad y = 3z + 30$$

Substitute $-2z - 4$ for x and $3z + 30$ for y in equation (1) and solve for z.

$$x + 2y + 4z = 16$$
$$(-2z - 4) + 2(3z + 30) + 4z = 16$$
$$-2z - 4 + 6z + 60 + 4z = 16$$
$$8z + 56 = 16$$
$$8z = -40$$
$$z = -5$$

Use $x = -2z - 4$ to find x:
$x = -2(-5) - 4 = 10 - 4 = 6$.
Use $y = 3z + 30$ to find y:
$y = 3(-5) + 30 = -15 + 30 = 15$.
The solution is (6, 15, −5).

Exercise Set 4.2

1. $\quad x + y + z = 3 \qquad\qquad -x + y + z = 5$
$\quad\quad (-1) + 3 + 1 \overset{?}{=} 3 \qquad -(-1) + 3 + 1 \overset{?}{=} 5$
$\qquad\qquad\quad 3 = 3 \qquad\qquad\qquad\quad 5 = 5$
a is true. $\qquad\qquad$ b is true.
$\quad -x + y + 2z = 0 \qquad\quad x + 2y - 3z = 2$
$\quad -(-1) + 3 + 2(1) \overset{?}{=} 0 \quad (-1) + 2(3) - 3(1) \overset{?}{=} 2$
$\qquad\qquad\qquad 6 = 0 \qquad\qquad\qquad\qquad 2 = 2$
c is false. $\qquad\qquad$ d is true.
Therefore, equations a, b, and d.

3. Yes; answers may vary

5. $\begin{cases} x - y + z = -4 & (1) \\ 3x + 2y - z = 5 & (2) \\ -2x + 3y - z = 15 & (3) \end{cases}$

Add E1 and E2.
$$4x + y = 1$$

Add E1 and E3.
$$-x + 2y = 11$$

Solve the new system:
$$\begin{cases} 4x + y = 1 \\ -x + 2y = 11 \end{cases}$$

Multiply the second equation by 4.
$$\begin{cases} 4x + y = 1 \\ -4x + 8y = 44 \end{cases}$$

Add the equations.
$$4x + y = 1$$
$$\underline{-4x + 8y = 44}$$
$$\qquad 9y = 45$$
$$\qquad y = 5$$

Replace y with 5 in the equation $4x + y = 1$.
$$4x + 5 = 1$$
$$4x = -4$$
$$x = -1$$

Replace x with −1 and y with 5 in E1.

$(-1)-(5)+z=-4$
$-6+z=-4$
$z=2$
The solution is $(-1, 5, 2)$.

7. $\begin{cases} x+y \quad\;\; =3 \quad (1) \\ \quad\;\; 2y \quad =10 \;\; (2) \\ 3x+2y-3z=1 \quad (3) \end{cases}$

Solve E2 for y: $y=5$
Replace y with 5 in E1.
$x+5=3$
$x=-2$
Replace x with -2 and y with 5 in E3.
$3(-2)+2(5)-3z=1$
$-6+10-3z=1$
$4-3z=1$
$-3z=-3$
$z=1$
The solution is $(-2, 5, 1)$.

9. $\begin{cases} 2x+2y+z=1 \quad (1) \\ -x+y+2z=3 \quad (2) \\ x+2y+4z=0 \quad (3) \end{cases}$

Add E2 and E3.
$3y+6z=3$ or $y+2z=1$
Multiply E2 by 2 and add to E1.
$-2x+2y+4z=6$
$\underline{2x+2y+z=1}$
$4y+5z=7$

Solve the new system:
$\begin{cases} y+2z=1 \\ 4y+5z=7 \end{cases}$

Multiply the first equation by -4.
$\begin{cases} -4y-8z=-4 \\ 4y+5z=7 \end{cases}$

Add the equations.
$-4y-8z=-4$
$\underline{4y+5z=7}$
$-3z=3$
$z=-1$
Replace z with -1 in the equation $y+2z=1$.
$y+2(-1)=1$
$y-2=1$
$y=3$
Replace y with 3 and z with -1 in E3.
$x+2(3)+4(-1)=0$
$x+6-4=0$
$x+2=0$
$x=-2$
The solution is $(-2, 3, -1)$.

11. $\begin{cases} x-2y+z=-5 \quad (1) \\ -3x+6y-3z=15 \quad (2) \\ 2x-4y+2z=-10 \quad (3) \end{cases}$

Multiply E2 by $-\dfrac{1}{3}$ and E3 by $\dfrac{1}{2}$.

$\begin{cases} x-2y+z=-5 \\ x-2y+z=-5 \\ x-2y+z=-5 \end{cases}$

All three equations are identical. There are infinitely many solutions. The solution set is $\{(x, y, z) | x-2y+z=-5\}$.

13. $\begin{cases} 4x-y+2z=5 \quad (1) \\ 2y+z=4 \quad (2) \\ 4x+y+3z=10 \quad (3) \end{cases}$

Multiply E1 by -1 and add to E3.
$-4x+y-2z=-5$
$\underline{4x+y+3z=10}$
$2y+z=5$ (4)
Multiply E4 by -1 and add to E2.
$-2y-z=-5$
$\underline{2y+z=4}$
$0=-1$ False
Inconsistent system; the solution set is $\varnothing$.

15. $\begin{cases} x+ \quad\;\; 5z=0 \quad (1) \\ 5x+y \quad\;\; =0 \quad (2) \\ \quad\;\; y-3z=0 \quad (3) \end{cases}$

Multiply E3 by -1 and add to E2.
$-y+3z=0$
$\underline{5x+y \quad\;\; =0}$
$5x+ \quad 3z=0$ (4)
Multiply E1 by -5 and add to E4.
$-5x-25z=0$
$\underline{5x+ \quad 3z=0}$
$-22z=0$
$z=0$
Replace z with 0 in E4.
$5x+3(0)=0$
$5x=0$
$x=0$
Replace x with 0 in E2.
$5(0)+y=0$
$y=0$
The solution is $(0, 0, 0)$.

17. $\begin{cases} 6x - 5z = 17 \quad (1) \\ 5x - y + 3z = -1 \quad (2) \\ 2x + y = -41 \quad (3) \end{cases}$

Add E2 and E3.

$7x + 3z = -42 \quad (4)$

Multiply E4 by 5, multiply E1 by 3, and add.

$35x + 15z = -210$

$\underline{18x - 15z = 51}$

$53x = -159$

$ x = -3$

Replace x with -3 in E1.

$6(-3) - 5z = 17$

$-18 - 5z = 17$

$-5z = 35$

$z = -7$

Replace x with -3 in E3.

$2(-3) + y = -41$

$-6 + y = -41$

$y = -35$

The solution is $(-3, -35, -7)$.

19. $\begin{cases} x + y + z = 8 \quad (1) \\ 2x - y - z = 10 \quad (2) \\ x - 2y - 3z = 22 \quad (3) \end{cases}$

Add E1 and E2.

$3x = 18 \text{ or } x = 6$

Add twice E1 to E3.

$2x + 2y + 2z = 16$

$\underline{x - 2y - 3z = 22}$

$3x - z = 38$

Replace x with 6 in this equation.

$3(6) - z = 38$

$18 - z = 38$

$-z = 20$

$z = -20$

Replace x with 6 and z with -20 in E1.

$6 + y + (-20) = 8$

$y - 14 = 8$

$y = 22$

The solution is $(6, 22, -20)$.

21. $\begin{cases} x + 2y - z = 5 \quad (1) \\ 6x + y + z = 7 \quad (2) \\ 2x + 4y - 2z = 5 \quad (3) \end{cases}$

Add E1 and E2.

$7x + 3y = 12 \quad (4)$

Add twice E2 to E3.

$12x + 2y + 2z = 14$

$\underline{2x + 4y - 2z = 5}$

$14x + 6y = 19 \quad (5)$

Multiply E4 by -2 and add to E5.

$-14x - 6y = -24$

$\underline{14x + 6y = 19}$

$0 = -5 \quad \text{False}$

Inconsistent system; the solution set is $\varnothing$.

23. $\begin{cases} 2x - 3y + z = 2 \quad (1) \\ x - 5y + 5z = 3 \quad (2) \\ 3x + y - 3z = 5 \quad (3) \end{cases}$

Add -2 times E2 to E1.

$2x - 3y + z = 2$

$\underline{-2x + 10y - 10z = -6}$

$7y - 9z = -4 \quad (4)$

Add -3 times E2 to E3.

$-3x + 15y - 15z = -9$

$\underline{3x + y - 3z = 5}$

$16y - 18z = -4$

Solve the new system:

$\begin{cases} 7y - 9z = -4 \quad (4) \\ 16y - 18z = -4 \quad (5) \end{cases}$

Multiply E4 by -2 and add to E5.

$-14y + 18z = 8$

$\underline{16y - 18z = -4}$

$2y = 4$

$y = 2$

Replace y with 2 in E4.

$7(2) - 9z = -4$

$-9z = -18$

$z = 2$

Replace y with 2 and z with 2 in E1.

$2x - 3(2) + 2 = 2$

$2x = 6$

$x = 3$

The solution is $(3, 2, 2)$.

25. $\begin{cases} -2x - 4y + 6z = -8 \quad (1) \\ x + 2y - 3z = 4 \quad (2) \\ 4x + 8y - 12z = 16 \quad (3) \end{cases}$

Add 2 times E2 to E1.

$2x + 4y - 6z = 8$

$\underline{-2x - 4y + 6z = -8}$

$0 = 0$

Add -4 times E2 to E3.

$$-4x - 8y + 12z = -16$$
$$\underline{4x + 8y - 12z = 16}$$
$$0 = 0$$

The system is dependent.
The solution set is $\{(x, y, z)|x + 2y - 3z = 4\}$.

27. $\begin{cases} 2x + 2y - 3z = 1 & (1) \\ y + 2z = -14 & (2) \\ 3x - 2y = -1 & (3) \end{cases}$

Add E1 to E3.
$5x - 3z = 0$ (4)
Add twice E2 to E3.
$$2y + 4z = -28$$
$$\underline{3x - 2y = -1}$$
$$3x + 4z = -29 \quad (5)$$

Multiply E4 by 4, multiply E5 by 3, and add.
$$20x - 12z = 0$$
$$\underline{9x + 12z = -87}$$
$$29x = -87$$
$$x = -3$$

Replace x with –3 in E4.
$$5(-3) - 3z = 0$$
$$3z = -15$$
$$z = -5$$

Replace z with –5 in E2.
$$y + 2(-5) = -14$$
$$y - 10 = -14$$
$$y = -4$$

The solution is (–3, –4, –5).

29. $\begin{cases} x + 2y - z = 5 & (1) \\ -3x - 2y - 3z = 11 & (2) \\ 4x + 4y + 5z = -18 & (3) \end{cases}$

Add E1 and E2.
$-2x - 4z = 16$ or $x + 2z = -8$ (4)
Add twice E2 to E3.
$$-6x - 4y - 6z = 22$$
$$\underline{4x + 4y + 5z = -18}$$
$$-2x - z = 4 \quad (5)$$

Solve the new system:
$\begin{cases} x + 2z = -8 & (4) \\ -2x - z = 4 & (5) \end{cases}$
Add twice E4 to E5.
$$2x + 4z = -16$$
$$\underline{-2x - z = 4}$$
$$3z = -12$$
$$z = -4$$

Replace z with –4 in E4.

$$x + 2(-4) = -8$$
$$x - 8 = -8$$
$$x = 0$$

Replace x with 0 and z with –4 in E1.
$$0 + 2y - (-4) = 5$$
$$2y = 1$$
$$y = \frac{1}{2}$$

The solution is $\left(0, \frac{1}{2}, -4\right)$.

31. $\begin{cases} \dfrac{3}{4}x - \dfrac{1}{3}y + \dfrac{1}{2}z = 9 & (1) \\ \dfrac{1}{6}x + \dfrac{1}{3}y - \dfrac{1}{2}z = 2 & (2) \\ \dfrac{1}{2}x - y + \dfrac{1}{2}z = 2 & (3) \end{cases}$

Multiply E1 by 12, multiply E2 by 6, and multiply E3 by 2.
$\begin{cases} 9x - 4y + 6z = 108 & (4) \\ x + 2y - 3z = 12 & (5) \\ x - 2y + z = 4 & (6) \end{cases}$

Add twice E5 to E4.
$$2x + 4y - 6z = 24$$
$$\underline{9x - 4y + 6z = 108}$$
$$11x = 132$$
$$x = 12$$

Add E5 and E6.
$2x - 2z = 16$ or $x - z = 8$
Replace x with 12 in this equation.
$$12 - z = 8$$
$$z = 4$$

Replace x with 12 and z with 4 in E6.
$$12 - 2y + 4 = 4$$
$$12 - 2y = 0$$
$$-2y = -12$$
$$y = 6$$

The solution is (12, 6, 4).

33. Let $x =$ the first number, then
$2x =$ the second number.
$$x + 2x = 45$$
$$3x = 45$$
$$x = 15$$
$$2x = 2(15) = 30$$

The numbers are 15 and 30.

35. $2(x-1)-3x = x-12$
$2x-2-3x = x-12$
$-x-2 = x-12$
$-2x = -10$
$x = 5$

37. $-y-5(y+5) = 3y-10$
$-y-5y-25 = 3y-10$
$-6y-25 = 3y-10$
$-9y = 15$
$y = -\dfrac{15}{9} = -\dfrac{5}{3}$

39. Answers may vary

41. Answers may vary

43. $\begin{cases} x+\ y+\ z = 1 & (1) \\ 2x-\ y+\ z = 0 & (2) \\ -x+2y+2z = -1 & (3) \end{cases}$

Add E1 and E3.
$3y+3z = 0$ or $y+z = 0$ (4)
Add –2 times E1 to E2.
$-2x-2y-2z = -2$
$\underline{2x-\ y+\ z = 0}$
$\quad -3y-\ z = -2$ (5)
Add E4 and E5.
$-2y = -2$
$y = 1$
Replace y with 1 in E4.
$1+z = 0$
$z = -1$
Replace y with 1 and z with –1 in E1.
$x+1+(-1) = 1$
$x = 1$
The solution is (1, 1, –1), and
$\dfrac{x}{8}+\dfrac{y}{4}+\dfrac{z}{3} = \dfrac{1}{8}+\dfrac{1}{4}-\dfrac{1}{3}$
$\qquad = \dfrac{3}{24}+\dfrac{6}{24}-\dfrac{8}{24}$
$\qquad = \dfrac{1}{24}.$

45. $\begin{cases} x+y\quad -w = 0 & (1) \\ \quad y+2z+w = 3 & (2) \\ x\quad -z\quad = 1 & (3) \\ 2x-y\quad -w = -1 & (4) \end{cases}$

Add E1 and E2.
$x+2y+2z = 3$ (5)
Add E2 and E4.

$2x+2z = 2$ or $x+z = 1$ (6)
Add E3 and E6.
$x-z = 1$
$\underline{x+z = 1}$
$2x\quad = 2$
Replace x with 1 in E3.
$1-z = 1$
$z = 0$
Replace x with 1 and z with 0 in E5.
$1+2y+2(0) = 3$
$1+2y = 3$
$2y = 2$
$y = 1$
Replace y with 1, and z with 0 in E2.
$1+2(0)+w = 3$
$1+w = 3$
$w = 2$
The solution is (1, 1, 0, 2).

47. $\begin{cases} x+y+z+w = 5 & (1) \\ 2x+y+z+w = 6 & (2) \\ x+y+z\quad = 2 & (3) \\ x+y\quad = 0 & (4) \end{cases}$

Add –1 times E4 to E3.
$-x-y\quad = 0$
$\underline{x+y+z = 2}$
$z = 2$
Replace z with 2 in E1 and E2.
$\begin{cases} x+y+w = 3 & (5) \\ 2x+y+w = 4 & (6) \end{cases}$
Add –1 times E5 to E6.
$-x-y-w = -3$
$\underline{2x+y+w = 4}$
$x\quad = 1$
Replace x with 1 in E4.
$1+y = 0$
$y = -1$
Replace x with 1, y with –1, and z with 2 in E1.
$1+(-1)+2+w = 5$
$2+w = 5$
$w = 3$
The solution is (1, –1, 2, 3).

49. Answers may vary

Section 4.3

Practice Exercises

1. a. We are given a system of equations.
$$\begin{cases} y = -0.16x + 113.9 \\ y = 1.06x + 62.3 \end{cases}$$
We want to know the year x in which the pounds y are the same. Since both equations are solved for y, we use the substitution method. Substitute $-0.16x + 113.9$ for y in the second equation.
$$-0.16x + 113.9 = 1.06x + 62.3$$
$$-1.22x = -51.6$$
$$x = \frac{-51.6}{-1.22} \approx 42.30$$
Since we are only asked to give the year, we need only solve for x. The consumption of red meat and poultry will be the same about 42.30 years after 1995, or in about 2037.

b. Yes; answers may vary.

2. Let x = first number
y = second number
"A first number is five more than a second number" is translated as $x = y + 5$. "Twice the first number is 2 less than 3 times the second number" is translated as $2x = 3y - 2$.
We solve the following system.
$$\begin{cases} x = y + 5 \\ 2x = 3y - 2 \end{cases}$$
Since the first equation is solved for x, we use substitution. Substitute $y + 5$ for x in the second equation.
$$2(y + 5) = 3y - 2$$
$$2y + 10 = 3y - 2$$
$$12 = y$$
Replace y with 12 in the equation $x = y + 5$ and solve for x.
$$x = 12 + 5 = 17$$
The numbers are 12 and 17.

3. Let x = speed of the V150
y = speed of the Atlantique
We summarize the information in a chart. Both trains have traveled two hours.

	Rate	•	Time	=	Distance
V150	x		2		$2x$
Atlantique	y		2		$2y$

The trains are 2150 kilometers apart, so the sum of the distances is 2150: $2x + 2y = 2150$.
The V150 is 75 kph faster than the Atlantique: $x = y + 75$.
We solve the following system.
$$\begin{cases} 2x + 2y = 2150 \\ x = y + 75 \end{cases}$$
Since the second equation is solved for x, we use substitution. Substitute $y + 75$ for x in the first equation.
$$2(y + 75) + 2y = 2150$$
$$2y + 150 + 2y = 2150$$
$$4y + 150 = 2150$$
$$4y = 2000$$
$$y = 500$$
To find x, we replace y with 500 in the second equation.
$$x = 500 + 75 = 575$$
The speed of the V150 is 575 kph, and the speed of the Atlantique is 500 kph.

4. Let x = amount of 99% acid
y = amount of water (0%)
Both x and y are measured in liters. We use a table to organize the given data.

	Amount	Acid Strength	Amount of Pure Acid
99% acid	x	99%	$0.99x$
Water	y	0%	$0y$

The amount of 99% acid and water combined must equal 1 liter, so $x + y = 1$.
The amount of pure acid in the mixture must equal the sum of the amounts of pure acid in the 99% acid and in the water, so
$0.99x + 0y = 0.05(1)$, which simplifies to $0.99x = 0.05$.
We solve the following system.
$$\begin{cases} x + y = 1 \\ 0.99x = 0.05 \end{cases}$$
Since the second equation does not contain y, we solve it for x.
$$0.99x = 0.05$$
$$x = \frac{0.05}{0.99} \approx 0.05$$
To find y, we replace x with 0.05 in the first equation.

$x + y = 1$
$0.05 + y = 1$
$y = 0.95$

The teacher should use 0.05 liter of the 99% HCL solution and 0.95 liter of water.

5. Let x = the number of packages.
The firm charges the customer $4.50 for each package, so the revenue equation is $R(x) = 4.5x$.
Each package costs $2.50 to produce and the equipment costs $3000, so the cost equation is $C(x) = 2.5x + 3000$.
Since the break-even point is when $R(x) = C(x)$, we solve the equation $4.5x = 2.5x + 3000$.
$$4.5x = 2.5x + 3000$$
$$2x = 3000$$
$$x = 1500$$
The company must sell 1500 packages to break even.

6. Let x = measure of smallest angle
y = measure of largest angle
z = measure of third angle
The sum of the measures is 180°:
$x + y + z = 180$.

The measure of the largest angle is 40° more than the measure of the smallest angle:
$y = x + 40$.

The measure of the remaining angle is 20° more than the measure of the smallest angle:
$y = x + 20$.

We solve the following system.
$$\begin{cases} x + y + z = 1180 \\ y = x + 40 \\ z = x + 20 \end{cases}$$
We substitute $x + 40$ for y and $x + 20$ for z in the first equation.
$$x + (x + 40) + (x + 20) = 180$$
$$3x + 60 = 180$$
$$3x = 120$$
$$x = 40$$
Then $y = x + 40 = 40 + 40 = 80$ and $z = x + 20 = 40 + 20 = 60$.
The angle measures are 40°, 60°, and 80°.

Exercise Set 4.3

1. Let x = the first number, and
y = the second number.
$$\begin{cases} x = y + 2 & (1) \\ 2x = 3y - 4 & (2) \end{cases}$$
Substitute $x = y + 2$ in E2.

$2(y + 2) = 3y - 4$
$2y + 4 = 3y - 4$
$y = 8$
Replace y with 8 in E1.
$x = 8 + 2 = 10$
The numbers are 10 and 8.

3. a. Let x = length of Enterprise, and
y = length of Nimitz.
$$\begin{cases} x + y = 2193 & (1) \\ x - y = 9 & (2) \end{cases}$$
Add E1 and E2.
$2x = 2202$
$x = 1101$
Replace x with 1101 in E1.
$1101 + y = 2193$
$y = 1092$

The Enterprise is 1101 feet long and the Nimitz is 1092 feet long.

b. Since 100 yards is equivalent to 300 feet, we divide the length of the Enterprise by 300 feet.
$$\frac{1101}{300} = 3.67 \text{ football fields}$$

5. Let p = the speed of the plane in still air, and
w = the speed of the wind.
$$\begin{cases} p + w = 560 & (1) \\ p - w = 480 & (2) \end{cases}$$
Add E1 and E2.
$2p = 1040$
$p = 520$
Replace p with 520 in E1.
$520 + w = 560$
$w = 40$
The speed of the plane in still air is 520 mph and the speed of the wind is 40 mph.

7. Let x = number of quarts of 4% butterfat milk, and y = number of quarts of 1% butterfat milk.
$$\begin{cases} x + y = 60 & (1) \\ 0.04x + 0.01y = 0.02(60) & (2) \end{cases}$$
Multiply E2 by −100 and add to E1.
$$x + y = 60$$
$$\underline{-4x - y = -120}$$
$$-3x = -60$$
$$x = 20$$

Replace x with 20 in E1.

$20 + y = 60$

$y = 40$

There should be 20 quarts of 4% butterfat used and 40 quarts of 1% butterfat used.

9. Let x = number of students studied abroad in the United Kingdom and
y = number of students studied abroad in Italy.

$$\begin{cases} x + \quad y = 56,929 \quad (1) \\ \quad\quad x = y + 7213 \quad (2) \end{cases}$$

Substitute $y + 7213$ for x in E1.

$(y + 7213) + y = 56,929$

$2y + 7213 = 56,929$

$2y = 49,716$

$y = 24,858$

Replace y with 24,858 in E2.

$x = 24,858 + 7213 = 32,071$

The United Kingdom had 32,071 students and Italy had 24,858 students.

11. Let l = the number of large frames, and
s = the number of small frames.

$$\begin{cases} \quad l + s = 22 \quad (1) \\ 15l + 8s = 239 \quad (2) \end{cases}$$

Multiply E1 by −8 and add to E2.

$-8l - 8s = -176$

$\underline{15l + 8s = 239}$

$7l \quad\quad = 63$

$l = 9$

Replace l with 9 in E1.

$9 + s = 22$

$s = 13$

She bought 9 large frames and 13 small frames.

13. Let x = the first number, and
y = the second number.

$$\begin{cases} \quad x = y - 2 \quad (1) \\ 2x = 3y + 4 \quad (2) \end{cases}$$

Substitute $x = y - 2$ in E2.

$2(y - 2) = 3y + 4$

$2y - 4 = 3y + 4$

$y = -8$

Replace y with −8 in E1.

$x = -8 - 2 = -10$

The numbers are −10 and −8.

15. $$\begin{cases} y = 5.3x + 39.5 \quad (1) \\ y = 4.5x + 45.5 \quad (2) \end{cases}$$

Substitute $5.3x + 39.5$ for y in E2.

$5.3x + 39.5 = 4.5x + 45.5$

$0.8x = 6$

$x = 7.5$

$2000 + 7 = 2007$

The year was 2007.

17. Let x = price of each tablet, and
y = the price of each pen.

$$\begin{cases} 7x + \quad 4y = 6.40 \quad (1) \\ 2x + 19y = 5.40 \quad (2) \end{cases}$$

Multiply E1 by 2 and E2 by −7 and add.

$14x + \quad 8y = 12.8$

$\underline{-14x - 133y = -37.80}$

$-125y = -25$

$y = 0.20$

Replace y with 0.20 in E1.

$7x + 4(0.20) = 6.40$

$7x + 0.80 = 6.40$

$7x = 5.60$

$x = 0.80$

Tablets cost $0.80 each and pens cost $0.20 each.

19. Let p = the speed of the plane in still air, and
w = the speed of the wind.
First note:

$\dfrac{2160 \text{ mi}}{3 \text{ hr}} = 720$ mph and $\dfrac{2160 \text{ mi}}{4 \text{ hr}} = 540$ mph

Now,

$$\begin{cases} p + w = 720 \\ p - w = 540 \end{cases}$$

Add E1 and E2.

$2p = 1260$

$p = 630$

Replace p with 630 in E1.

$630 + w = 720$

$w = 90$

The speed of the plane in still air is 630 mph and the speed of the wind is 90 mph.

21. a. Answers may vary, but depend on the slope of each function.

b. $$\begin{cases} y = -1379.4x + 150,604 \quad (1) \\ y = 478.4x + 157,838 \quad\quad (2) \end{cases}$$

Substitute $478.4x + 157,838$ for y in E1.

$$478.4x + 157,838 = -1379.4x + 150,604$$
$$1857.8x = -7234$$
$$x = \frac{-7234}{1857.8} \approx -3.89$$
$$1995 + (-3.89) = 1991.11$$
They were the same in 1991.

23. Let x = length of shortest two sides, and y = length of the longest side.
$$\begin{cases} 2x + y = 93 & (1) \\ y = x + 9 & (2) \end{cases}$$
Replace y with $x+9$ in E1.
$$2x + (x+9) = 93$$
$$3x + 9 = 93$$
$$3x = 84$$
$$x = 28$$
Replace x with 28 in E2.
$$y = 28 + 9 = 37$$
The three sides are 28 cm, 28 cm, and 37 cm.

25. Cost for Hertz: $H(x) = 25 + 0.10x$

Cost for Budget: $B(x) = 20 + 0.25x$

We want to find when $B(x) = 2 \cdot H(x)$
$$20 + 0.25x = 2(25 + 0.10x)$$
$$20 + 0.25x = 50 + 0.20x$$
$$0.05x = 30$$
$$x = 600$$
The Budget charge will be twice that of the Hertz charge at 600 miles.

27. $\begin{cases} x + y = 180 \\ x = y - 30 \end{cases}$

Replace x with $y - 30$ in E1.
$$(y - 30) + y = 180$$
$$2y - 30 = 180$$
$$2y = 210$$
$$y = 105$$
Replace y with 105 in E2.
$$x = 105 - 30 = 75$$
The value of x is 75° and the value of y is 105°.

29. $C(x) = 30x + 10,000$
$$R(x) = 46x$$
$$46x = 30x + 10,000$$
$$16x = 10,000$$
$$x = 625$$
625 units

31. $C(x) = 1.2x + 1500$
$$R(x) = 1.7x$$
$$1.7x = 1.2x + 1500$$
$$0.5x = 1500$$
$$x = 3000$$
3000 units

33. $C(x) = 75x + 160,000$
$$R(x) = 200x$$
$$200x = 75x + 160,000$$
$$125x = 160,000$$
$$x = 1280$$
1280 units

35. **a.** $R(x) = 450x$

b. $C(x) = 200x + 6000$

c. $R(x) = C(x)$
$$450x = 200x + 6000$$
$$250x = 6000$$
$$x = 24 \text{ desks}$$

37. Let x = units of Mix A, y = units of Mix B, and z = units of Mix C.
$$\begin{cases} 4x + 6y + 4z = 30 & (1) \\ 6x + y + z = 16 & (2) \\ 3x + 2y + 12z = 24 & (3) \end{cases}$$
Multiply E2 by –6 and add to E1.
$$\begin{array}{r} -36x - 6y - 6z = -96 \\ 4x + 6y + 4z = 30 \\ \hline -32x \quad\quad - 2z = -66 \end{array}$$ or $16x + z = 33$ (4)

Multiply E2 by –2 and add to E3.
$$\begin{array}{r} -12x - 2y - 2z = -32 \\ 3x + 2y + 12z = 24 \\ \hline -9x + \quad 10z = -8 \end{array}$$ (5)

Multiply E4 by –10 and add to E5.
$$\begin{array}{r} -160x - 10z = -330 \\ -9x + 10z = -8 \\ \hline -169x \quad\quad = -338 \end{array}$$
$$x = 2$$
Replace x with 2 in E4.
$$16(2) + z = 33$$
$$32 + z = 33$$
$$z = 1$$
Replace x with 2 and z with 1 in E2.
$$6(2) + y + 1 = 16$$
$$y = 3$$
You need 2 units of Mix A, 3 units of Mix B, and 1 unit of Mix C.

39. Let x = length of shortest side,
y = length of longest side, and
z = length of the other two sides

$$\begin{cases} x+y+2z=29 & (1) \\ \quad\quad y=2x & (2) \\ \quad\quad z=x+2 & (3) \end{cases}$$

Substitute $y=2x$ and $z=x+2$ in E1.

$x+(2x)+2(x+2)=29$
$x+2x+2x+4=29$
$5x=25$
$x=5$

Replace x with 5 in E2 and E3.

$y=2(5)\quad\quad z=5+2$
$y=10\quad\quad z=7$

The sides are 5 in., 7 in., 7 in., and 10 in.

41. Let x = the first number
y = the second number, and
z = the third number.

$$\begin{cases} x+y+z=40 \\ \quad x=y+5 \\ \quad x=2z \end{cases}$$

$$\begin{cases} x+y+z=40 & (1) \\ x-y\quad\;=5 & (2) \\ x-\;\;2z=0 & (3) \end{cases}$$

Add E1 and E2.

$2x+z=45\quad(4)$

Multiply E3 by -2 and add to E4.

$-2x+4z=0$
$\underline{2x\;+z=45}$
$5z=45$
$z=9$

Replace z with 9 in E3.

$x-2(9)=0$
$x=18$

Replace x with 18 in E2.

$18-y=5$
$y=13$

The numbers are 18, 13, and 9.

43. Let x = number of free throws,
y = number of two-point field goals, and
z = number of three-point field goals

$$\begin{cases} x+2y+3z=860 \\ \quad\quad y=2z-65 \\ \quad\quad x=y-34 \end{cases}$$

$$\begin{cases} x+2y+3z=860 & (1) \\ \quad\; y-2z=-65 & (2) \\ x-y\quad\quad=-34 & (3) \end{cases}$$

Multiply E3 by -1 and add to E1.

$-x+\quad y\quad\quad=34$
$\underline{x+2y+3z=860}$
$3y+3z=894\;$ or $\;y+z=298\;\;(4)$

Multiply E4 by -1 and add to E2.

$-y-z=-298$
$\underline{y-2z=-65}$
$-3z=-363$
$z=121$

Replace z with 121 in E2.

$y-2(121)=-65$
$y-242=-65$
$y=177$

Replace y with 177 in E3.

$x-177=-34$
$x=143$

She made 143 free throws, 177 two-point field goals, and 121 three-point field goals.

45. $$\begin{cases} x+y+z=180 \\ y+2x+5=180 \\ z+2x-5=180 \end{cases}$$

$$\begin{cases} x+y+z=180 & (1) \\ 2x+y\quad\;=175 & (2) \\ 2x+\;\;z=185 & (3) \end{cases}$$

Multiply E1 by -1 and add to E2.

$-x-y-z=-180$
$\underline{2x+y\quad\;=175}$
$x\quad\;-z=-5\;\;(4)$

Add E3 and E4.

$3x=180$
$x=60$

Replace x with 60 in E4.

$60-z=-5$
$z=65$

Replace x with 60 in E2.

$2(60)+y=175$
$120+y=175$
$y=55$

$x=60$, $y=55$, and $z=65$

47. $$\begin{cases} 3x-\;y+\;z=2 & (1) \\ -x+2y+3z=6 & (2) \end{cases}$$

Multiply E1 by 2 and add to E2.

$6x-2y+2z=4$
$\underline{-x+2y+3z=6}$
$5x\quad\quad+5z=10$
$5x+5z=10$

49. $\begin{cases} x + 2y - z = 0 & (1) \\ 3x + y - z = 2 & (2) \end{cases}$

Multiply E1 by –3 and add to E2.

$-3x - 6y + 3z = 0$

$\underline{3x + y - z = 2}$

$-5y + 2z = 2$

$-5y + 2z = 2$

51. Let x = number filed in 1996

y = number filed in 2006

$\begin{cases} y = x + 25,765 \\ x + y = 2,144,653 \end{cases}$

Substitute $x + 25,765$ for y in E2.

$x + (x + 25,765) = 2,144,653$

$2x + 25,765 = 2,144,653$

$2x = 2,118,888$

$x = 1,059,444$

Replace x with 1,059,444 in E1.

$y = 1,059,444 + 25,765 = 1,085,209$

There were 1,059,444 bankruptcy petitions filed in 1996 and 1,085,209 filed in 2006.

53. a. Replace $f(x)$ with y in each equation.

$\begin{cases} y = 0.85x + 41.75 & (1) \\ y = 1.13x + 10.49 & (2) \end{cases}$

Substitute $0.85x + 41.75$ for y in E2.

$0.85x + 41.75 = 1.13x + 10.49$

$31.26 = 0.28x$

$\dfrac{31.26}{0.28} = x$

$112 \approx x$

Replace x with 112 in E1.

$y = 0.85(112) + 41.75 \approx 137$

The solution is (112, 137).

b. 112 months is 9 years, 4 months.

Since the first month is February 2007, the 112th month is 9 years and 4 months later, or June 2016.

55. $y = ax^2 + bx + c$

$(1, 2)$: $2 = a + b + c$ (1)

$(2, 3)$: $3 = 4a + 2b + c$ (2)

$(-1, 6)$: $6 = a - b + c$ (3)

Add E1 and E3 to obtain

$2a + 2c = 8$, or $a + c = 4$ (4)

Multiply E3 by 2 and add to E2 to get

$15 = 6a + 3c$, or $2a + c = 5$ (5)

Multiply E4 by –1 and add to E5 to get $a = 1$.

Replace a with 1 in E4.

$1 + c = 4$ so $c = 3$

Replace a with 1 and c with 3 in E1.

$2 = 1 + b + 3$

$-2 = b$

Therefore, $a = 1$, $b = -2$, and $c = 3$.

57. $y = ax^2 + bx + c$

$(4, 2.47)$: $2.47 = 16a + 4b + c$ (1)

$(7, 0.6)$: $0.6 = 49a + 7b + c$ (2)

$(8, 1.1)$: $1.1 = 64a + 8b + c$ (3)

Multiply E1 by –1 and add to E2.

$-16a - 4b - c = -2.47$

$\underline{49a + 7b + c = 0.6}$

$33a + 3b \quad = -1.87$ (4)

Multiply E1 by –1 and add to E3.

$-16a - 4b - c = -2.47$

$\underline{64a + 8b + c = 1.1}$

$48a + 4b \quad = -1.37$ (5)

Multiply E4 by –4, E5 by 3, and add.

$-132a - 12b = 7.48$

$\underline{144a + 12b = -4.11}$

$12a \quad\quad = 3.37$

$a = \dfrac{3.37}{12} \approx 0.2808$

Use this value in E4.

$33(0.2808) + 3b = -1.87$

$3b = -11.1364$

$b = -3.7121$

From E1 we now have

$16(0.2808) + 4(-3.7121) + c = 2.47$

$-10.3556 + c = 2.47$

$c = 12.8256$

So, $a = 0.28$, $b = -3.71$, and $c = 12.83$.

September is represented by $x = 9$:

$y = 0.28x^2 - 3.71x + 12.83$

$= 0.28(9)^2 - 3.71(9) + 12.83$

$= 2.12$ inches

Integrated Review

1. A system with solution (1, 2) has lines that intersect at (1, 2). The correct graph is C.

2. A system with solution (–2, 3) has lines that intersect at (–2, 3). The correct graph is D.

3. A system with no solution has lines that are parallel. The correct graph is A.

4. A system with an infinite number of solutions has lines that are the same. The correct graph is B.

5. $\begin{cases} x + y = 4 & (1) \\ \quad y = 3x & (2) \end{cases}$

Substitute $y = 3x$ in E1.

$x + (3x) = 4$
$\qquad 4x = 4$
$\qquad\ x = 1$

Replace x with 1 in E2.

$y = 3x = 3(1) = 3$

The solution is $(1, 3)$.

6. $\begin{cases} x - y = -4 & (1) \\ \quad y = 4x & (2) \end{cases}$

Substitute $y = 4x$ in E1.

$x - (4x) = -4$
$\quad -3x = -4$
$\qquad\ x = \dfrac{4}{3}$

Replace x with $\dfrac{4}{3}$ in E2.

$y = 4x = 4\left(\dfrac{4}{3}\right) = \dfrac{16}{3}$

The solution is $\left(\dfrac{4}{3}, \dfrac{16}{3}\right)$.

7. $\begin{cases} \ x + y = 1 & (1) \\ x - 2y = 4 & (2) \end{cases}$

Multiply E1 by -1 and add to E2.

$\begin{array}{r} -x - y = -1 \\ x - 2y = 4 \\ \hline -3y = 3 \\ y = -1 \end{array}$

Replace y with -1 in E1.

$x + (-1) = 1$
$\quad x - 1 = 1$
$\qquad\ x = 2$

The solution is $(2, -1)$.

8. $\begin{cases} 2x - y = 8 & (1) \\ x + 3y = 11 & (2) \end{cases}$

Multiply E1 by 3 and add to E2.

$\begin{array}{r} 6x - 3y = 24 \\ x + 3y = 11 \\ \hline 7x \quad\ = 35 \\ x = 5 \end{array}$

Replace x with 5 in E1.

$2(5) - y = 8$
$\quad 10 - y = 8$
$\qquad\quad\ y = 2$

The solution is $(5, 2)$.

9. $\begin{cases} 2x + 5y = 8 & (1) \\ 6x + \ y = 10 & (2) \end{cases}$

Multiply E2 by -5 and add to E1.

$\begin{array}{r} 2x + 5y = 8 \\ -30x - 5y = -50 \\ \hline -28x \qquad = -42 \\ x = \dfrac{3}{2} \end{array}$

Replace x with $\dfrac{3}{2}$ in E2.

$6\left(\dfrac{3}{2}\right) + y = 10$
$\qquad 9 + y = 8$
$\qquad\qquad y = 1$

The solution is $\left(\dfrac{3}{2}, 1\right)$.

10. $\begin{cases} \dfrac{1}{8}x - \dfrac{1}{2}y = -\dfrac{5}{8} & (1) \\ -3x - 8y = 0 & (2) \end{cases}$

Multiply E1 by -16 and add to E2.

$\begin{array}{r} -2x + 8y = 10 \\ -3x - 8y = 0 \\ \hline -5x \qquad = 10 \\ x = -2 \end{array}$

Replace x with -2 in E2.

$-3(-2) - 8y = 0$
$\qquad 6 - 8y = 0$
$\qquad\quad -8y = -6$
$\qquad\qquad\ y = \dfrac{-6}{-8} = \dfrac{3}{4}$

The solution is $\left(-2, \dfrac{3}{4}\right)$.

11. $\begin{cases} \ 4x - 7y = 7 & (1) \\ 12x - 21y = 24 & (2) \end{cases}$

Multiply E1 by -3 and add to E2.

$\begin{array}{r} -12x + 21y = -21 \\ 12x - 21y = 24 \\ \hline 0 = 3 \ \ \text{False} \end{array}$

The system is inconsistent. The solution set is $\varnothing$.

12. $\begin{cases} 2x - 5y = 3 & (1) \\ -4x + 10y = -6 & (2) \end{cases}$

Multiply E1 by 2 and add to E2.

$\begin{array}{r} 4x - 10y = 6 \\ -4x + 10y = -6 \\ \hline 0 = 0 \quad \text{True} \end{array}$

The system is dependent. The solution set is $\{(x, y) | 2x - 5y = 3\}$.

13. $\begin{cases} y = \dfrac{1}{3}x \\ 5x - 3y = 4 \end{cases}$

Substitute $\dfrac{1}{3}x$ for y in E2.

$5x - 3\left(\dfrac{1}{3}x\right) = 4$

$\qquad 5x - x = 4$

$\qquad\quad 4x = 4$

$\qquad\quad\ x = 1$

Replace x with 1 in E1.

$y = \dfrac{1}{3}(1) = \dfrac{1}{3}$

The solution is $\left(1,\ \dfrac{1}{3}\right)$.

14. $\begin{cases} y = \dfrac{1}{4}x \\ 2x - 4y = 3 \end{cases}$

Substitute $\dfrac{1}{4}x$ for y in E2.

$2x - 4\left(\dfrac{1}{4}x\right) = 3$

$\qquad 2x - x = 3$

$\qquad\quad\ x = 3$

Replace x with 3 in E1.

$y = \dfrac{1}{4}(3) = \dfrac{3}{4}$

The solution is $\left(3,\ \dfrac{3}{4}\right)$.

15. $\begin{cases} x + y \quad = 2 & (1) \\ -3y + z = -7 & (2) \\ 2x + y - z = -1 & (3) \end{cases}$

Add E2 and E3.

$2x - 2y = -8 \text{ or } x - y = -4 \quad (4)$

Add E1 and E4.

$2x = -2$

$\ x = -1$

Replace x with -1 in E1.

$-1 + y = 2$

$\quad\ y = 3$

Replace y with 3 in E2.

$-3(3) + z = -7$

$\quad -9 + z = -7$

$\qquad\qquad z = 2$

The solution is $(-1, 3, 2)$.

16. $\begin{cases} y + 2z = -3 & (1) \\ x - 2y \quad = 7 & (2) \\ 2x - y + z = 5 & (3) \end{cases}$

Multiply E2 by -2 and add to E3.

$\begin{array}{r} -2x + 4y \quad\ = -14 \\ 2x - y + z = 5 \\ \hline 3y + z = -9 \quad (4) \end{array}$

Multiply E4 by -2 and add to E1.

$\begin{array}{r} -6y - 2z = 18 \\ y + 2z = -3 \\ \hline -5y \qquad = 15 \\ y = -3 \end{array}$

Replace y with -3 in E4.

$3(-3) + z = -9$

$\qquad\qquad z = 0$

Replace y with -3 in E2.

$x - 2(-3) = 7$

$\quad\ x + 6 = 7$

$\qquad\quad x = 1$

The solution is $(1, -3, 0)$.

17. $\begin{cases} 2x + 4y - 6z = 3 & (1) \\ -x + y - z = 6 & (2) \\ x + 2y - 3z = 1 & (3) \end{cases}$

Multiply E3 by -2 and add to E1.

$\begin{array}{r} -2x - 4y + 6z = -2 \\ 2x + 4y - 6z = 3 \\ \hline 0 = 1 \quad \text{False} \end{array}$

The system is inconsistent. The solution set is $\varnothing$.

18. $\begin{cases} x - y + 3z = 2 & (1) \\ -2x + 2y - 6z = -4 & (2) \\ 3x - 3y + 9z = 6 & (3) \end{cases}$

Multiply E1 by 2 and add to E2.

$\begin{array}{r} 2x - 2y + 6z = 4 \\ -2x + 2y - 6z = -4 \\ \hline 0 = 0 \quad \text{True} \end{array}$

The system is dependent. The solution set is $\{(x, y) | x - y + 3z = 2\}$.

19. $\begin{cases} x+y-4z=5 & (1) \\ x-y+2z=-2 & (2) \\ 3x+2y+4z=18 & (3) \end{cases}$

Add E1 and E2.

$2x-2z=3$ (4)

Multiply E2 by 2 and add to E3.

$2x-2y+4z=-4$
$\underline{3x+2y+4z=18}$
$5x\quad\quad+8z=14$ (5)

Multiply E4 by 4 and add to E5.

$8x-8z=12$
$\underline{5x+8z=14}$
$13x\quad\quad=26$
$x=2$

Replace x with 2 in E4.

$2(2)-2z=3$
$-2z=-1$
$z=\dfrac{1}{2}$

Replace x with 2 and z with $\dfrac{1}{2}$ in E1.

$2+y-4\left(\dfrac{1}{2}\right)=5$

$2+y-2=5$

$y=5$

The solution is $\left(2,5,\dfrac{1}{2}\right)$.

20. $\begin{cases} 2x-y+3z=2 & (1) \\ x+y-6z=0 & (2) \\ 3x+4y-3z=6 & (3) \end{cases}$

Add E1 and E3.

$5x+3y=8$ (4)

Multiply E1 by 2 and add to E2.

$4x-2y+6z=4$
$\underline{x+\ y-6z=0}$
$5x-y\quad\quad=4$ (5)

Multiply E5 by 3 and add to E4.

$15x-3y=12$
$\underline{5x+3y=8}$
$20x\quad\quad=20$
$x=1$

Replace x with 1 in E5.

$5(1)-y=4$
$-y=-1$
$y=1$

Replace both x and y with 1 in E1.

$2(1)-1+3z=2$
$1+3z=2$
$3z=1$
$z=\dfrac{1}{3}$

The solution is $\left(1,1,\dfrac{1}{3}\right)$.

21. Let x = the first number and
y = the second number.

$\begin{cases} x=y-8 & (1) \\ 2x=y+11 & (2) \end{cases}$

Substitute $x=y-8$ in E2.

$2(y-8)=y+11$
$2y-16=y+11$
$y=27$

Replace y with 27 in E1.

$x=27-8=19$

The numbers are 19 and 27.

22. Let x = measure of the two smallest angles,
y = measure of the third angle, and
z = measure of the fourth angle.

$\begin{cases} 2x+y+z=360 \\ y=x+30 \\ z=x+50 \end{cases}$

Substitute $y=x+30$ and $z=x+50$ in the first equation.

$2x+(x+30)+(x+50)=360$
$4x+80=360$
$4x=280$
$x=70$

so $y=70+30=100$ and $z=70+50=120$

The two smallest angles are 70°, the third angle is 100°, and the fourth angle is 120°.

Section 4.4

Practice Exercises

1. $\begin{cases} x+4y=-2 \\ 3x-y=7 \end{cases}$

The corresponding matrix is $\begin{bmatrix} 1 & 4 & | & -2 \\ 3 & -1 & | & 7 \end{bmatrix}$. The element in the first row, first column is already 1. Multiply row 1 by -3 and add to row 2 to get a 0 below the 1.

$\begin{bmatrix} 1 & 4 & | & -2 \\ -3(1)+3 & -3(4)+(-1) & | & -3(-2)+7 \end{bmatrix}$

$$\begin{bmatrix} 1 & 4 & | & -2 \\ 0 & -13 & | & 13 \end{bmatrix}$$

We change -13 to a 1 by dividing row 2 by -13.

$$\begin{bmatrix} 1 & 4 & | & -2 \\ 0 & \frac{-13}{-13} & | & \frac{13}{-13} \end{bmatrix}$$

$$\begin{bmatrix} 1 & 4 & | & -2 \\ 0 & 1 & | & -1 \end{bmatrix}$$

The last matrix corresponds to $\begin{cases} x+4y=-2 \\ \quad\;\; y=-1 \end{cases}$

To find x, we let $y=-1$ in the first equation.
$$x+4y=-2$$
$$x+4(-1)=-2$$
$$x-4=-2$$
$$x=2$$
The solution is $(2, -1)$.

2. $\begin{cases} x-3y=3 \\ -2x+6y=4 \end{cases}$

The corresponding matrix is $\begin{bmatrix} 1 & -3 & | & 3 \\ -2 & 6 & | & 4 \end{bmatrix}$. The

element in the first row, first column is already 1. Multiply row 1 by 2 and add to row 2 to get a 0 below the 1.

$$\begin{bmatrix} 1 & -3 & | & 3 \\ 2(1)+(-2) & 2(-3)+6 & | & 2(3)+4 \end{bmatrix}$$

$$\begin{bmatrix} 1 & -3 & | & 3 \\ 0 & 0 & | & 10 \end{bmatrix}$$

The corresponding system is $\begin{cases} x-3y=3 \\ \quad\;\; 0=10 \end{cases}$

The equation $0 = 10$ is false. Hence, the system is inconsistent and has no solution. The solution set is $\varnothing$.

3. $\begin{cases} x+3y-z=0 \\ 2x+y+3z=5 \\ -x-2y+4z=7 \end{cases}$

The corresponding matrix is $\begin{bmatrix} 1 & 3 & -1 & | & 0 \\ 2 & 1 & 3 & | & 5 \\ -1 & -2 & 4 & | & 7 \end{bmatrix}$.

The element in the first row, first column is already 1. Multiply row 1 by -2 and add to row 2 to get a 0 below the 1 in row 2. Add row 1 to row 3 to get a 0 below the 1 in row 3.

$$\begin{bmatrix} 1 & 3 & -1 & | & 0 \\ -2(1)+2 & -2(3)+1 & -2(-1)+3 & | & -2(0)+5 \\ 1+(-1) & 3+(-2) & -1+4 & | & 0+7 \end{bmatrix}$$

$$\begin{bmatrix} 1 & 3 & -1 & | & 0 \\ 0 & -5 & 5 & | & 5 \\ 0 & 1 & 3 & | & 7 \end{bmatrix}$$

Now we want a 1 where the -5 is now. Interchange rows 2 and 3.

$$\begin{bmatrix} 1 & 3 & -1 & | & 0 \\ 0 & 1 & 3 & | & 7 \\ 0 & -5 & 5 & | & 5 \end{bmatrix}$$

Now we want a 0 below the 1. Multiply row 2 by 5 and add to row 3.

$$\begin{bmatrix} 1 & 3 & -1 & | & 0 \\ 0 & 1 & 3 & | & 7 \\ 5(0)+0 & 5(1)+(-5) & 5(3)+5 & | & 5(7)+5 \end{bmatrix}$$

$$\begin{bmatrix} 1 & 3 & -1 & | & 0 \\ 0 & 1 & 3 & | & 7 \\ 0 & 0 & 20 & | & 40 \end{bmatrix}$$

Finally, divide row 3 by 20.

$$\begin{bmatrix} 1 & 3 & -1 & | & 0 \\ 0 & 1 & 3 & | & 7 \\ 0 & 0 & \frac{20}{20} & | & \frac{40}{20} \end{bmatrix}$$

$$\begin{bmatrix} 1 & 3 & -1 & | & 0 \\ 0 & 1 & 3 & | & 7 \\ 0 & 0 & 1 & | & 2 \end{bmatrix}$$

This matrix corresponds to the system
$$\begin{cases} x+3y-z=0 \\ \quad\;\; y+3z=7 \\ \qquad\quad z=2 \end{cases}$$

The z-coordinate is 2. Replace z with 2 in the second equation and solve for y.
$$y+3z=7$$
$$y+3(2)=7$$
$$y+6=7$$
$$y=1$$
To find x, we let $z=2$ and $y=1$ in the first equation.
$$x+3y-z=0$$
$$x+3(1)-2=0$$
$$x+1=0$$
$$x=-1$$
The solution is $(-1, 1, 2)$.

Vocabulary and Readiness Check

1. A <u>matrix</u> is a rectangular array of numbers.

2. Each of the numbers in a matrix is called an <u>element</u>.

3. The numbers aligned horizontally in a matrix are in the same <u>row</u>.

4. The numbers aligned vertically in a matrix are in the same <u>column</u>.

5. Any two columns may be interchanged. <u>false</u>

6. Any two rows may be interchanged. <u>true</u>

7. The elements in a row may be added to their corresponding elements in another row. <u>true</u>

8. The elements of a column may be multiplied by any nonzero number. <u>false</u>

Exercise Set 4.4

1. $\begin{cases} x + y = 1 \\ x - 2y = 4 \end{cases}$

$\begin{bmatrix} 1 & 1 & | & 1 \\ 1 & -2 & | & 4 \end{bmatrix}$

Multiply R1 by –1 and add to R2.

$\begin{bmatrix} 1 & 1 & | & 1 \\ 0 & -3 & | & 3 \end{bmatrix}$

Divide R2 by –3.

$\begin{bmatrix} 1 & 1 & | & 1 \\ 0 & 1 & | & -1 \end{bmatrix}$

This corresponds to $\begin{cases} x + y = 1 \\ y = -1 \end{cases}$.

$x + (-1) = 1$
$x - 1 = 1$
$x = 2$
The solution is $(2, -1)$.

3. $\begin{cases} x + 3y = 2 \\ x + 2y = 0 \end{cases}$

$\begin{bmatrix} 1 & 3 & | & 2 \\ 1 & 2 & | & 0 \end{bmatrix}$

Multiply R1 by –1 and add to R2.

$\begin{bmatrix} 1 & 3 & | & 2 \\ 0 & -1 & | & -2 \end{bmatrix}$

Multiply R2 by –1.

$\begin{bmatrix} 1 & 3 & | & 2 \\ 0 & 1 & | & 2 \end{bmatrix}$

This corresponds to $\begin{cases} x + 3y = 2 \\ y = 2 \end{cases}$.

$x + 3(2) = 2$
$x + 6 = 2$
$x = -4$
The solution is $(-4, 2)$.

5. $\begin{cases} x - 2y = 4 \\ 2x - 4y = 4 \end{cases}$

$\begin{bmatrix} 1 & -2 & | & 4 \\ 2 & -4 & | & 4 \end{bmatrix}$

Multiply R1 by –2 and add to R2.

$\begin{bmatrix} 1 & -2 & | & 4 \\ 0 & 0 & | & -4 \end{bmatrix}$

This corresponds to $\begin{cases} x - 2y = 4 \\ 0 = -4 \end{cases}$.

This is an inconsistent system. The solution is $\varnothing$.

7. $\begin{cases} 3x - 3y = 9 \\ 2x - 2y = 6 \end{cases}$

$\begin{bmatrix} 3 & -3 & | & 9 \\ 2 & -2 & | & 6 \end{bmatrix}$

Divide R1 by 3.

$\begin{bmatrix} 1 & -1 & | & 3 \\ 2 & -2 & | & 6 \end{bmatrix}$

Multiply R1 by –2 and add to R2.

$\begin{bmatrix} 1 & -1 & | & 3 \\ 0 & 0 & | & 0 \end{bmatrix}$

This corresponds to $\begin{cases} x - y = 3 \\ 0 = 0 \end{cases}$.

This is a dependent system. The solution is $\{(x, y) | x - y = 3\}$.

9. $\begin{cases} x + y \phantom{{}-4z}= 3 \\ \phantom{x+{}} 2y \phantom{{}-4z}= 10 \\ 3x + 2y - 4z = 12 \end{cases}$

$\begin{bmatrix} 1 & 1 & 0 & | & 3 \\ 0 & 2 & 0 & | & 10 \\ 3 & 2 & -4 & | & 12 \end{bmatrix}$

Multiply R1 by –3 and add to R3.

$\begin{bmatrix} 1 & 1 & 0 & | & 3 \\ 0 & 2 & 0 & | & 10 \\ 0 & -1 & -4 & | & 3 \end{bmatrix}$

Divide R2 by 2.

$\begin{bmatrix} 1 & 1 & 0 & | & 3 \\ 0 & 1 & 0 & | & 5 \\ 0 & -1 & -4 & | & 3 \end{bmatrix}$

Add R2 to R3.

$\begin{bmatrix} 1 & 1 & 0 & | & 3 \\ 0 & 1 & 0 & | & 5 \\ 0 & 0 & -4 & | & 8 \end{bmatrix}$

Divide R3 by –4.

$$\begin{bmatrix} 1 & 1 & 0 & 3 \\ 0 & 1 & 0 & 5 \\ 0 & 0 & 1 & -2 \end{bmatrix}$$

This corresponds to $\begin{cases} x+y=3 \\ \quad y=5 \\ \quad z=-2 \end{cases}$.

$x+5=3$
$\quad x=-2$
The solution is $(-2, 5, -2)$.

11. $\begin{cases} 2y-\ z=-7 \\ x+4y+\ z=-4 \\ 5x-y+2z=13 \end{cases}$

$$\begin{bmatrix} 0 & 2 & -1 & -7 \\ 1 & 4 & 1 & -4 \\ 5 & -1 & 2 & 13 \end{bmatrix}$$

Interchange R1 and R2.

$$\begin{bmatrix} 1 & 4 & 1 & -4 \\ 0 & 2 & -1 & -7 \\ 5 & -1 & 2 & 13 \end{bmatrix}$$

Multiply R1 by -5 and add to R3.

$$\begin{bmatrix} 1 & 4 & 1 & -4 \\ 0 & 2 & -1 & -7 \\ 0 & -21 & -3 & 33 \end{bmatrix}$$

Divide R2 by 2.

$$\begin{bmatrix} 1 & 4 & 1 & -4 \\ 0 & 1 & -\frac{1}{2} & -\frac{7}{2} \\ 0 & -21 & -3 & 33 \end{bmatrix}$$

Multiply R2 by 21 and add to R3.

$$\begin{bmatrix} 1 & 4 & 1 & -4 \\ 0 & 1 & -\frac{1}{2} & -\frac{7}{2} \\ 0 & 0 & -\frac{27}{2} & -\frac{81}{2} \end{bmatrix}$$

Multiply R2 by $-\dfrac{2}{27}$.

$$\begin{bmatrix} 1 & 4 & 1 & -4 \\ 0 & 1 & -\frac{1}{2} & -\frac{7}{2} \\ 0 & 0 & 1 & 3 \end{bmatrix}$$

This corresponds to $\begin{cases} x+4y+z=-4 \\ \quad y-\frac{1}{2}z=-\frac{7}{2} \\ \qquad z=3 \end{cases}$.

$y-\dfrac{1}{2}(3)=-\dfrac{7}{2}$
$y-\dfrac{3}{2}=-\dfrac{7}{2}$
$\quad y=-2$
$x+4(-2)+3=-4$
$\quad x-8+3=-4$
$\qquad x=1$
The solution is $(1, -2, 3)$.

13. $\begin{cases} x-4=0 \\ x+y=1 \end{cases}$ or $\begin{cases} x\quad=4 \\ x+y=1 \end{cases}$

$$\begin{bmatrix} 1 & 0 & 4 \\ 1 & 1 & 1 \end{bmatrix}$$

Multiply R1 by -1 and add to R2.

$$\begin{bmatrix} 1 & 0 & 4 \\ 0 & 1 & -3 \end{bmatrix}$$

This corresponds to $\begin{cases} x=4 \\ y=-3 \end{cases}$.

The solution is $(4, -3)$.

15. $\begin{cases} x+y+z=2 \\ 2x\quad-z=5 \\ \quad 3y+z=2 \end{cases}$

$$\begin{bmatrix} 1 & 1 & 1 & 2 \\ 2 & 0 & -1 & 5 \\ 0 & 3 & 1 & 2 \end{bmatrix}$$

Multiply R1 by -2 and add to R2.

$$\begin{bmatrix} 1 & 1 & 1 & 2 \\ 0 & -2 & -3 & 1 \\ 0 & 3 & 1 & 2 \end{bmatrix}$$

Divide R2 by -2.

$$\begin{bmatrix} 1 & 1 & 1 & 2 \\ 0 & 1 & \frac{3}{2} & -\frac{1}{2} \\ 0 & 3 & 1 & 2 \end{bmatrix}$$

Multiply R2 by -3 and add to R3.

$$\begin{bmatrix} 1 & 1 & 1 & 2 \\ 0 & 1 & \frac{3}{2} & -\frac{1}{2} \\ 0 & 0 & -\frac{7}{2} & \frac{7}{2} \end{bmatrix}$$

Multiply R3 by $-\dfrac{2}{7}$.

$$\begin{bmatrix} 1 & 1 & 1 & 2 \\ 0 & 1 & \frac{3}{2} & -\frac{1}{2} \\ 0 & 0 & 1 & -1 \end{bmatrix}$$

This corresponds to $\begin{cases} x+y+z = 2 \\ y+\dfrac{3}{2}z = -\dfrac{1}{2} \\ z = -1 \end{cases}$.

$$y+\frac{3}{2}(-1) = -\frac{1}{2}$$
$$y-\frac{3}{2} = -\frac{1}{2}$$
$$y = 1$$
$$x+1+(-1) = 2$$
$$x = 2$$

The solution is $(2, 1, -1)$.

17. $\begin{cases} 5x-2y = 27 \\ -3x+5y = 18 \end{cases}$

$\begin{bmatrix} 5 & -2 & | & 27 \\ -3 & 5 & | & 18 \end{bmatrix}$

Divide R1 by 5.

$\begin{bmatrix} 1 & -\frac{2}{5} & | & \frac{27}{5} \\ -3 & 5 & | & 18 \end{bmatrix}$

Multiply R1 by 3 and add to R2.

$\begin{bmatrix} 1 & -\frac{2}{5} & | & \frac{27}{5} \\ 0 & \frac{19}{5} & | & \frac{171}{5} \end{bmatrix}$

Multiply R2 by $\dfrac{5}{19}$.

$\begin{bmatrix} 1 & -\frac{2}{5} & | & \frac{27}{5} \\ 0 & 1 & | & 9 \end{bmatrix}$

This corresponds to $\begin{cases} x-\dfrac{2}{5}y = \dfrac{27}{5} \\ y = 9 \end{cases}$.

$$x-\frac{2}{5}(9) = \frac{27}{5}$$
$$x-\frac{18}{5} = \frac{27}{5}$$
$$x = 9$$

The solution is $(9, 9)$.

19. $\begin{cases} 4x-7y = 7 \\ 12x-21y = 24 \end{cases}$

$\begin{bmatrix} 4 & -7 & | & 7 \\ 12 & -21 & | & 24 \end{bmatrix}$

Divide R1 by 4.

$\begin{bmatrix} 1 & -\frac{7}{4} & | & \frac{7}{4} \\ 12 & -21 & | & 24 \end{bmatrix}$

Multiply R1 by -12 and add to R2.

$\begin{bmatrix} 1 & -\frac{7}{4} & | & \frac{7}{4} \\ 0 & 0 & | & 3 \end{bmatrix}$

This corresponds to $\begin{cases} x-\dfrac{7}{4}y = \dfrac{7}{4} \\ 0 = 3 \end{cases}$.

This is an inconsistent system. The solution set is $\varnothing$.

21. $\begin{cases} 4x-y+2z = 5 \\ 2y+z = 4 \\ 4x+y+3z = 10 \end{cases}$

$\begin{bmatrix} 4 & -1 & 2 & | & 5 \\ 0 & 2 & 1 & | & 4 \\ 4 & 1 & 3 & | & 10 \end{bmatrix}$

Divide R1 by 4.

$\begin{bmatrix} 1 & -\frac{1}{4} & \frac{1}{2} & | & \frac{5}{4} \\ 0 & 2 & 1 & | & 4 \\ 4 & 1 & 3 & | & 10 \end{bmatrix}$

Multiply R1 by -4 and add to R3.

$\begin{bmatrix} 1 & -\frac{1}{4} & \frac{1}{2} & | & \frac{5}{4} \\ 0 & 2 & 1 & | & 4 \\ 0 & 2 & 1 & | & 5 \end{bmatrix}$

Divide R2 by 2.

$\begin{bmatrix} 1 & -\frac{1}{4} & \frac{1}{2} & | & \frac{5}{4} \\ 0 & 1 & \frac{1}{2} & | & 2 \\ 0 & 2 & 1 & | & 5 \end{bmatrix}$

Multiply R2 by -2 and add to R3.

$\begin{bmatrix} 1 & -\frac{1}{4} & \frac{1}{2} & | & \frac{5}{4} \\ 0 & 1 & \frac{1}{2} & | & 2 \\ 0 & 0 & 0 & | & 1 \end{bmatrix}$

This corresponds to $\begin{cases} x-\dfrac{1}{4}y+\dfrac{1}{2}z = \dfrac{5}{4} \\ y+\dfrac{1}{2}z = 2 \\ 0 = 1 \end{cases}$.

This is an inconsistent system. The solution set is $\varnothing$.

23. $\begin{cases} 4x+y+\ z=3 \\ -x+y-2z=-11 \\ x+2y+2z=-1 \end{cases}$

$$\begin{bmatrix} 4 & 1 & 1 & | & 3 \\ -1 & 1 & -2 & | & -11 \\ 1 & 2 & 2 & | & -1 \end{bmatrix}$$

Interchange R1 and R3.

$$\begin{bmatrix} 1 & 2 & 2 & | & -1 \\ -1 & 1 & -2 & | & -11 \\ 4 & 1 & 1 & | & 3 \end{bmatrix}$$

Add R1 to R2. Multiply R1 by –4 and add to R3.

$$\begin{bmatrix} 1 & 2 & 2 & | & -1 \\ 0 & 3 & 0 & | & -12 \\ 0 & -7 & -7 & | & 7 \end{bmatrix}$$

Divide R2 by 3.

$$\begin{bmatrix} 1 & 2 & 2 & | & -1 \\ 0 & 1 & 0 & | & -4 \\ 0 & -7 & -7 & | & 7 \end{bmatrix}$$

Multiply R2 by 7 and add to R3.

$$\begin{bmatrix} 1 & 2 & 2 & | & -1 \\ 0 & 1 & 0 & | & -4 \\ 0 & 0 & -7 & | & -21 \end{bmatrix}$$

Divide R3 by –7.

$$\begin{bmatrix} 1 & 2 & 2 & | & -1 \\ 0 & 1 & 0 & | & -4 \\ 0 & 0 & 1 & | & 3 \end{bmatrix}$$

This corresponds to $\begin{cases} x+2y+2z=-1 \\ \quad y \quad\quad =-4. \\ \quad\quad\quad z=3 \end{cases}$

$$x+2(-4)+2(3)=-1$$
$$x-8+6=-1$$
$$x=1$$

The solution is (1, –4, 3).

25. No vertical line intersects the graph more than once. It is the graph of a function.

27. The *y*-axis is a vertical line that intersects the graph more than once. It is not the graph of a function.

29. $(-1)(-5)-(6)(3)=5-18=-13$

31. $(4)(-10)-(2)(-2)=-40+4=-36$

33. $(-3)(-3)-(-1)(-9)=9-9=0$

35. The matrix should have four columns, so (a) is not the correct matrix. The matrix should have a 0 in the first column, second row since the coefficient of *x* in the second equation is 0, so (b) is not the correct matrix. The correct matrix is (c).

37. a. Solve the system $\begin{cases} 2.3x+y=52 \\ -5.4x+y=14 \end{cases}$.

$$\begin{bmatrix} 2.3 & 1 & | & 52 \\ -5.4 & 1 & | & 14 \end{bmatrix}$$

Since getting 1 in the first column would lead to repeating decimals, we multiply R1 by –1 and add to R2.

$$\begin{bmatrix} 2.3 & 1 & | & 52 \\ -7.7 & 0 & | & -38 \end{bmatrix}$$

This corresponds to $\begin{cases} 2.3x+y=52 \\ -7.7x \quad\quad =-38 \end{cases}$.

From the second equation,

$$x=\frac{-3.8}{-7.7}\approx 4.935.$$

Thus, the percent of U.S. households owning black-and-white television sets was the same as the percent of U.S. households owning a microwave oven in the end of 1984 (about 4.9 years after 1980).

b. Solve the television equation for *y*: $y=-2.3x+52$. Thus, for 1980,

$y=-2.3(0)+52=52$, and for 1993,

$y=-2.3(13)+52=22.1$.

Solve the microwave equation for *y*:
$y=5.4x+14$. Thus, for 1980
$y=5.4(0)+14=14$, and for 1993,
$y=5.4(13)+14=84.2$.

In 1980, a greater percent of (and hence more) U.S. households owned black-and-white television sets. In 1993, more households owned a microwave oven. The percent owning black-and-white television sets is decreasing and the percent owning a microwave oven is increasing.
Answers may vary.

c. Let $y = 0$ in the television equation.

$$2.3x + y = 52$$
$$2.3x + 0 = 52$$
$$x = \frac{52}{2.3} \approx 22.6$$

According to this model, the percent of U.S. households owning a black-and-white television set will be 0% about 22.6 years after 1980, or sometime in 2002.

39. Answers may vary

Section 4.5

Practice Exercises

1. $\begin{cases} 4x \geq y \\ x + 3y \geq 6 \end{cases}$

Graph both inequalities on the same set of axes. The solution is the intersection of the solution regions.

For $4x \geq y$, the boundary line is the graph of $4x = y$. The boundary line is solid since the inequality means $4x > y$ or $4x = y$. The test point $(1, 0)$ satisfies the inequality, so we shade the half-plane that includes $(1, 0)$.

For $x + 3y \geq 6$, sketch the solid boundary line $x + 3y = 6$. The test point $(0, 0)$ does not satisfy the inequality, so shade the half-plane that does not include $(0, 0)$.

The solution of the system is the darker shaded region. This solution includes parts of both boundary lines.

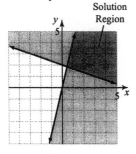

2. $\begin{cases} x - y < 1 \\ y < 4 \\ 3x + y > -3 \end{cases}$

Graph all three inequalities on the same set of axes. All boundary lines are dashed since the inequality symbols are < and >. The solution set of the system is the shaded region. The boundary

lines are not a part of the solution.

3. $\begin{cases} -2x + 5y \leq 10 \\ x \leq 4 \\ x \geq 0 \\ y \geq 0 \end{cases}$

Graph the inequalities on the same set of axes. The intersection of the inequalities is the solution region. It is the only shaded region in this graph and includes the portion of all four boundary lines that border the shaded region.

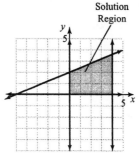

Vocabulary and Readiness Check

1. Two or more linear inequalities form a <u>system</u> of linear inequalities.

2. An ordered pair that satisfies each inequality in a system is a <u>solution</u> of the system.

3. The point where two boundary lines intersect is a <u>corner</u> point.

4. The solution region of a system of inequalities consists of the <u>intersection</u> of the solution regions of the inequalities in the system.

Exercise Set 4.5

1. $\begin{cases} y \geq x + 1 \\ y \geq 3 - x \end{cases}$

Graph both inequalities on the same set of axes. The solution is the intersection of the solution regions. The solution of the system is the darker shaded region. This solution includes parts of both boundary lines.

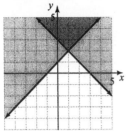

3. $\begin{cases} y < 3x - 4 \\ y \le x + 2 \end{cases}$

Graph both inequalities on the same set of axes. The solution is the intersection of the solution regions. The solution of the system is the darker shaded region. This solution includes the part of the solid boundary line that borders the region but not the dashed boundary line or the point where the boundary lines intersect.

5. $\begin{cases} y < -2x - 2 \\ y > x + 4 \end{cases}$

Graph both inequalities on the same set of axes. The solution is the intersection of the solution regions. The solution of the system is the darker shaded region. The boundary lines are not a part of the solution.

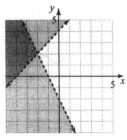

7. $\begin{cases} y \ge -x + 2 \\ y \le 2x + 5 \end{cases}$

Graph both inequalities on the same set of axes. The solution is the intersection of the solution regions. The solution of the system is the darker shaded region. This solution includes parts of

both boundary lines.

9. $\begin{cases} x \ge 3y \\ x + 3y \le 6 \end{cases}$

Graph both inequalities on the same set of axes. The solution is the intersection of the solution regions. The solution of the system is the darker shaded region. This solution includes parts of both boundary lines.

11. $\begin{cases} x \le 2 \\ y \ge -3 \end{cases}$

Graph both inequalities on the same set of axes. The solution is the intersection of the solution regions. The solution of the system is the darker shaded region. This solution includes parts of both boundary lines.

13. $\begin{cases} y \ge 1 \\ x < -3 \end{cases}$

Graph both inequalities on the same set of axes. The solution is the intersection of the solution regions. The solution of the system is the darker shaded region. This solution includes the part of the solid boundary line that borders the region but not the dashed boundary line or the point where the boundary lines intersect.

15. $\begin{cases} y+2x \geq 0 \\ 5x-3y \leq 12 \\ y \leq 2 \end{cases}$

Graph all three inequalities on the same set of axes. The solution set of the system is the shaded region. The parts of the boundary lines that border the shaded region are part of the solution.

17. $\begin{cases} 3x-4y \geq -6 \\ 2x+y \leq 7 \\ y \geq -3 \end{cases}$

Graph all three inequalities on the same set of axes. The solution set of the system is the shaded region. The parts of the boundary lines that border the shaded region are part of the solution.

19. $\begin{cases} 2x+y \leq 5 \\ x \leq 3 \\ x \geq 0 \\ y \geq 0 \end{cases}$

Graph the inequalities on the same set of axes. The intersection of the inequalities is the solution region. It is the only shaded region in this graph and includes the portion of all four boundary lines that border the shaded region.

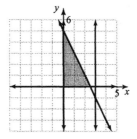

21. $\begin{cases} y < 5 \\ x > 3 \end{cases}$

Both boundary lines should be dashed. The region including (5, 0) should be shaded since (5, 0) satisfies both inequalities. The correct graph is C.

23. $\begin{cases} y \leq 5 \\ x < 3 \end{cases}$

The boundary line $y = 5$ should be solid. The correct graph is D.

25. $(-3)^2 = (-3)(-3) = 9$

27. $\left(\dfrac{2}{3}\right)^2 = \dfrac{2}{3} \cdot \dfrac{2}{3} = \dfrac{2 \cdot 2}{3 \cdot 3} = \dfrac{4}{9}$

29. $(-2)^2 - (-3) + 2(-1) = 4 - (-3) + 2(-1)$
$= 4 - (-3) + (-2)$
$= 4 + 3 - 2$
$= 7 - 2$
$= 5$

31. $8^2 + (-13) - 4(-2) = 64 + (-13) - 4(-2)$
$= 64 + (-13) - (-8)$
$= 64 - 13 + 8$
$= 51 + 8$
$= 59$

33. $\begin{cases} y \leq 3 \\ y \geq 3 \end{cases}$

The only y-values that satisfy both inequalities are those that equal 3. The solution of the system is the line $y = 3$.

35. Answers may vary.

Chapter 4 Vocabulary Check

1. Two or more linear equations in two variables form a <u>system of equations</u>.

2. A <u>solution</u> of a system of two equations in two variables is an ordered pair that makes both equations true.

3. A <u>consistent</u> system of equations has at least one solution.

4. If a matrix has the same number of rows and columns, it is called a <u>square</u> matrix.

5. An <u>inconsistent</u> system of equations has no solution.

6. A <u>matrix</u> is a rectangular array of numbers.

Chapter 4 Review

1. $\begin{cases} 3x + 10y = 1 & (1) \\ x + 2y = -1 & (2) \end{cases}$

(1)

(2) From E2: $x = -2y - 1$
Replace x with $-2y - 1$ in E1.
$$3(-2y - 1) + 10y = 1$$
$$-6y - 3 + 10y = 1$$
$$4y = 4$$
$$y = 1$$
Replace y with 1 in the equation $x = -2y - 1$.
$$x = -2(1) - 1 = -3$$
The solution is $(-3, 1)$.

(3) Multiply E2 by -3 and add to E1.
$$3x + 10y = 1$$
$$-3x - 6y = 3$$
$$\overline{4y = 4}$$
$$y = 1$$
Replace y with 1 in E2.
$$x + 2(1) = -1$$
$$x + 2 = -1$$
$$x = -3$$
The solution is $(-3, 1)$.

2. $\begin{cases} y = \dfrac{1}{2}x + \dfrac{2}{3} & (1) \\ 4x + 6y = 4 & (2) \end{cases}$

(1)

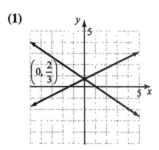

(2) Replace y with $\dfrac{1}{2}x + \dfrac{2}{3}$ in E2.
$$4x + 6\left(\frac{1}{2}x + \frac{2}{3}\right) = 4$$
$$4x + 3x + 4 = 4$$
$$x = 0$$
Replace x with 0 in E1.
$$y = \frac{1}{2}(0) + \frac{2}{3} = \frac{2}{3}$$
The solution is $\left(0, \dfrac{2}{3}\right)$.

(3) Rewrite the system: $\begin{cases} -\dfrac{1}{2}x + y = \dfrac{2}{3} \\ 4x + 6y = 4 \end{cases}$.

Multiply the first equation by -6.
$$\begin{cases} 3x - 6y = -4 \\ 4x + 6y = 4 \end{cases}$$
Add these equations.
$$7x = 0$$
$$x = 0$$
Replace x with 0 in second equation.
$$4(0) + 6y = 4$$
$$6y = 4$$
$$y = \frac{4}{6} = \frac{2}{3}$$
The solution is $\left(0, \dfrac{2}{3}\right)$.

3. $\begin{cases} 2x - 4y = 22 & (1) \\ 5x - 10y = 15 & (2) \end{cases}$

(1)

(2) Solve E1 for x.

$2x - 4y = 22$

$2x = 4y + 22$

$x = 2y + 11$

Replace x with $2y + 11$ in E2.

$5(2y + 11) - 10y = 15$

$10y + 55 - 10y = 15$

$55 = 15$ False

This is an inconsistent system. The solution is $\varnothing$.

(3) Multiply E1 by 5 and E2 by –2.

$\begin{cases} 10x - 20y = 110 \\ -10x + 20y = -30 \end{cases}$

Add these equations.

$10x - 20y = 110$

$\underline{-10x + 20y = -30}$

$0 = 80$ False

This is an inconsistent system. The solution is $\varnothing$.

4. $\begin{cases} 3x - 6y = 12 & (1) \\ 2y = x - 4 & (2) \end{cases}$

(1)

(2) Solve E2 for x.

$x = 2y + 4$

Replace x with $2y + 4$ in E1.

$3(2y + 4) - 6y = 12$

$6y + 12 - 6y = 12$

$12 = 12$ True

This is a dependent system. The solution is $\{(x, y)|3x - 6y = 12\}$.

(3) $\begin{cases} 3x - 6y = 12 & (1) \\ -x + 2y = -4 & (2) \end{cases}$

Multiply E2 by 3.

$\begin{cases} 3x - 6y = 12 \\ -3x + 6y = -12 \end{cases}$

Add these equations.

$3x - 6y = 12$

$\underline{-3x + 6y = -12}$

$0 = 0$ True

This is a dependent system. The solution is $\{(x, y)|3x - 6y = 12\}$.

5. $\begin{cases} \dfrac{1}{2}x - \dfrac{3}{4}y = -\dfrac{1}{2} & (1) \\ \dfrac{1}{8}x + \dfrac{3}{4}y = \dfrac{19}{8} & (2) \end{cases}$

(1)

(2) Clear fractions by multiplying E1 by 4 and E2 by 8.

$\begin{cases} 2x - 3y = -2 & (1) \\ x + 6y = 19 & (2) \end{cases}$

Solve the new E2 for x.

$x = -6y + 19$

Replace x with $-6y + 19$ in new E1.

$2(-6y + 19) - 3y = -2$

$-12y + 38 - 3y = -2$

$-15y = -40$

$y = \dfrac{-40}{-15} = \dfrac{8}{3}$

Replace y with $\dfrac{8}{3}$ in the equation

$x = -6y + 19$.

$$x = -6\left(\frac{8}{3}\right) + 19$$
$$x = -16 + 19$$
$$x = 3$$

The solution is $\left(3, \dfrac{8}{3}\right)$.

(3) Add the equations.

$$\frac{1}{2}x - \frac{3}{4}y = -\frac{1}{2}$$
$$\frac{1}{8}x + \frac{3}{4}y = \frac{19}{8}$$
$$\overline{\quad\frac{5}{8}x \qquad = \frac{15}{8}\quad}$$
$$5x = 15$$
$$x = 3$$

Replace x with 3 in E1.

$$\frac{1}{2}(3) - \frac{3}{4}y = -\frac{1}{2}$$
$$-\frac{3}{4}y = -2$$
$$-3y = -8$$
$$y = \frac{8}{3}$$

The solution is $\left(3, \dfrac{8}{3}\right)$.

6. $\begin{cases} y = 32x & (1) \\ y = 15x + 25{,}500 & (2) \end{cases}$

Multiply E1 by –1 and add to E2.

$$-y = -32$$
$$\underline{\quad y = 15x + 25{,}500\quad}$$
$$0 = -17x + 25{,}500$$
$$17x = 25{,}500$$
$$x = 1500$$

Replace x with 1500 in E1.
$$y = 32(1500) = 48{,}000$$

The number of backpacks that the company must sell is 1500.

7. $\begin{cases} x + \quad z = 4 & (1) \\ 2x - y \quad = 4 & (2) \\ x + y - z = 0 & (3) \end{cases}$

Adding E2 and E3 gives $3x - z = 4$ (4)
Adding E1 and E4 gives $4x = 8$ or $x = 2$
Replace x with 2 in E1.
$$2 + z = 4$$
$$z = 2$$
Replace x with 2 and z with 2 in E3.

$$2 + y - 2 = 0$$
$$y = 0$$
The solution is (2, 0, 2).

8. $\begin{cases} 2x + 5y \quad = 4 & (1) \\ x - 5y + z = -1 & (2) \\ 4x \quad - z = 11 & (3) \end{cases}$

Add E2 and E3.
$$5x - 5y = 10 \quad (4)$$
Add E1 and E4.
$$7x = 14$$
$$x = 2$$
Replace x with 2 in E1.
$$2(2) + 5y = 4$$
$$4 + 5y = 4$$
$$5y = 0$$
$$y = 0$$
Replace x with 2 in E3.
$$4(2) - z = 11$$
$$8 - z = 11$$
$$z = -3$$
The solution is (2, 0, –3).

9. $\begin{cases} 4y + 2z = 5 & (1) \\ 2x + 8y \quad = 5 & (2) \\ 6x \quad + 4z = 1 & (3) \end{cases}$

Multiply E1 by –2 and add to E2.
$$-8y - 4z = -10$$
$$\underline{2x + 8y \qquad = 5\quad}$$
$$2x \qquad - 4z = -5 \quad (4)$$
Add E3 and E4.
$$8x = -4$$
$$x = -\frac{1}{2}$$

Replace x with $-\dfrac{1}{2}$ in E2.

$$2\left(-\frac{1}{2}\right) + 8y = 5$$
$$-1 + 8y = 5$$
$$8y = 6$$
$$y = \frac{3}{4}$$

Replace x with $-\dfrac{1}{2}$ in E3.

$$6\left(-\frac{1}{2}\right)+4z=1$$
$$-3+4z=1$$
$$4z=4$$
$$z=1$$

The solution is $\left(-\frac{1}{2},\frac{3}{4},1\right)$.

10. $\begin{cases} 5x+7y=9 & (1) \\ 14y-z=28 & (2) \\ 4x+2z=-4 & (3) \end{cases}$

Dividing E3 by 2 gives $2x+z=-2$.
Add this equation to E2.
$$2x+z=-2$$
$$\underline{14y-z=28}$$
$$2x+14y=26 \text{ or } x+7y=13 \quad (4)$$
Multiply E4 by -1 and add to E1.
$$-x-7y=-13$$
$$\underline{5x+7y=9}$$
$$4x=-4$$
$$x=-1$$
Replace x with -1 in E4.
$$-1+7y=13$$
$$7y=14$$
$$y=2$$
Replace x with -1 in E3.
$$4(-1)+2z=-4$$
$$-4+2z=-4$$
$$2z=0$$
$$z=0$$
The solution is $(-1, 2, 0)$.

11. $\begin{cases} 3x-2y+2z=5 & (1) \\ -x+6y+z=4 & (2) \\ 3x+14y+7z=20 & (3) \end{cases}$

Multiply E2 by 3 and add to E1.
$$3x-2y+2z=5$$
$$\underline{-3x+18y+3z=12}$$
$$16y+5z=17 \quad (4)$$
Multiply E3 by -1 and add to E1.
$$3x-2y+2z=5$$
$$\underline{-3x-14y-7z=-20}$$
$$-16y-5z=-15 \quad (5)$$
Add E4 and E5.
$$16y+5z=17$$
$$\underline{-16y-5z=-15}$$
$$0=2 \quad \text{False}$$
The system is inconsistent. The solution is $\varnothing$.

12. $\begin{cases} x+2y+3z=11 & (1) \\ y+2z=3 & (2) \\ 2x+2z=10 & (3) \end{cases}$

Multiply E2 by -2 and add to E1.
$$x+2y+3z=11$$
$$\underline{-2y-4z=-6}$$
$$x-z=5 \quad (4)$$
Multiply E4 by 2 and add to E3.
$$2x+2z=10$$
$$\underline{2x-2z=10}$$
$$4x=20$$
$$x=5$$
Replace x with 5 in E3.
$$2(5)+2z=10$$
$$10+2z=10$$
$$2z=0$$
$$z=0$$
Replace z with 0 in E2.
$$y+2(0)=3$$
$$y+0=3$$
$$y=3$$
The solution is $(5, 3, 0)$.

13. $\begin{cases} 7x-3y+2z=0 & (1) \\ 4x-4y-z=2 & (2) \\ 5x+2y+3z=1 & (3) \end{cases}$

Multiply E2 by 2 and add to E1.
$$7x-3y+2z=0$$
$$\underline{8x-8y-2z=4}$$
$$15x-11y=4 \quad (4)$$
Multiply E2 by 3 and add to E3.
$$12x-12y-3z=6$$
$$\underline{5x+2y+3z=1}$$
$$17x-10y=7 \quad (5)$$
Solve the new system.
$$\begin{cases} 15x-11y=4 & (4) \\ 17x-10y=7 & (5) \end{cases}$$
Multiply E4 by -10, multiply E5 by 11, and add.
$$-150x+110y=-40$$
$$\underline{187x-110y=77}$$
$$37x=37$$
$$x=1$$
Replace x with 1 in E4.
$$15(1)-11y=4$$
$$15-11y=4$$
$$-11y=-11$$
$$y=1$$
Replace x with 1 and y with 1 in E1.

$7(1) - 3(1) + 2z = 0$

$4 + 2z = 0$

$2z = -4$

$z = -2$

The solution is (1, 1, –2).

14. $\begin{cases} x - 3y - 5z = -5 & (1) \\ 4x - 2y + 3z = 13 & (2) \\ 5x + 3y + 4z = 22 & (3) \end{cases}$

Multiply E1 by –4 and add to E2.

$-4x + 12y + 20z = 20$

$\underline{4x - 2y + 3z = 13}$

$10y + 23z = 33$ (4)

Multiply E1 by –5 and add to E3.

$-5x + 15y + 25z = 25$

$\underline{5x + 3y + 4z = 22}$

$18y + 29z = 47$ (5)

Solve the new system.

$\begin{cases} 10y + 23z = 33 & (4) \\ 18y + 29z = 47 & (5) \end{cases}$

Multiply E4 by 9, multiply E5 by –5 and add.

$90y + 207z = 297$

$\underline{-90y - 145z = -235}$

$62z = 62$

$z = 1$

Replace z with 1 in E4.

$10y + 23(1) = 33$

$10y = 10$

$y = 1$

Replace y with 1 and z with 1 in E1.

$x - 3(1) - 5(1) = -5$

$x - 8 = -5$

$x = 3$

The solution is (3, 1, 1).

15. Let x = the first number, y = the second number, and z = the third number.

$\begin{cases} x + y + z = 98 & (1) \\ x + y = z + 2 & (2) \\ y = 4x & (3) \end{cases}$

Replace y with $4x$ in E1 and E2.

$x + 4x + z = 98$

$5x + z = 98$ (4)

$x + 4x = z + 2$

$5x - z = 2$ (5)

Add E4 and E5.

$5x + z = 98$

$\underline{5x - z = 2}$

$10x = 100$

$x = 10$

Replace x with 10 in E3.

$y = 4(10) = 40$

Replace x with 10 and y with 40 in E2.

$10 + 40 = z + 2$

$50 = z + 2$

$48 = z$

The numbers are 10, 40, and 48.

16. Let x = the first number and y = the second number.

$\begin{cases} x = 3y & (1) \\ 2(x + y) = 168 & (2) \end{cases}$

Replace x with $3y$ in E2.

$2(3y + y) = 168$

$8y = 168$

$y = 21$

Replace y with 21 in E1.

$x = 3(21) = 63$

The numbers are 63 and 21.

17. Let x = speed of first car and y = speed of the second car.

$\begin{cases} 4x + 4y = 492 & (1) \\ y = x + 7 & (2) \end{cases}$

Replace y with $x + 7$ in E1.

$4x + 4(x + 7) = 492$

$8x + 28 = 492$

$8x = 464$

$x = 58$

Replace x with 58 in E2.

$y = 58 + 7 = 65$

The cars are going 58 and 65 miles per hour.

18. Let w = the width of the foundation and l = the length of the foundation.

$\begin{cases} l = 3w & (1) \\ 2w + 2l = 296 & (2) \end{cases}$

Replace l with $3w$ in E2.

$2w + 2(3w) = 296$

$2w + 6w = 296$

$8w = 296$

$w = 37$

Replace w with 37 in E1.

$l = 3(37) = 111$

The foundation is 37 feet wide and 111 feet long.

19. Let x = liters of 10% solution and
y = liters of 60% solution.

$$\begin{cases} x + y = 50 & (1) \\ 0.10x + 0.60y = 0.40(50) & (2) \end{cases}$$

Solve E1 for y.
$y = 50 - x$

Replace y with $50 - x$ in E2.

$$0.10x + 0.60(50 - x) = 0.40(50)$$
$$10[0.10x + 0.60(50 - x)] = 10[0.40(50)]$$
$$x + 6(50 - x) = 4(50)$$
$$x + 300 - 6x = 200$$
$$-5x = -100$$
$$x = 20$$

Replace x with 20 in the equation $y = 50 - x$.
$y = 50 - 20 = 30$

He should use 20 liters of 10% solution and 30 liters of 60% solution.

20. Let c = pounds of chocolate used,
n = pounds of nuts used, and
r = pounds of raisins used.

$$\begin{cases} r = 2n & (1) \\ c + n + r = 45 & (2) \\ 3.00c + 2.70n + 2.25r = 2.80(45) & (3) \end{cases}$$

Replace r with $2n$ in E2.

$$c + n + 2n = 45$$
$$c + 3n = 45$$
$$c = -3n + 45$$

Replace r with $2n$ and c with $-3n + 45$ in E3.

$$3.00(-3n + 45) + 2.70n + 2.25(2n) = 126$$
$$-9n + 135 + 2.7n + 4.5n = 126$$
$$-1.8n + 135 = 126$$
$$-1.8n = -9$$
$$n = 5$$

Replace n with 5 in E1.
$r = 2(5) = 10$

Replace n with 5 and r with 10 in E2.

$$c + 5 + 10 = 45$$
$$c + 15 = 45$$
$$c = 30$$

She should use 30 pounds of creme-filled chocolates, 5 pounds of chocolate-covered nuts, and 10 pounds of chocolate-covered raisins.

21. Let x = the number of pennies,
y = the number of nickels, and
z = the number dimes.

$$\begin{cases} x + y + z = 53 & (1) \\ 0.01x + 0.05y + 0.10z = 2.77 & (2) \\ y = z + 4 & (3) \end{cases}$$

Clear the decimals from E2 by multiplying by 100.
$x + 5y + 10z = 277$ (4)

Replace y with $z + 4$ in E1.
$x + z + 4 + z = 53$
$\quad x + 2z = 49$ (5)

Replace y with $z + 4$ in E4.
$x + 5(z + 4) + 10z = 277$
$\quad x + 15z = 257$ (6)

Solve the new system.

$$\begin{cases} x + 2z = 49 & (5) \\ x + 15z = 257 & (6) \end{cases}$$

Multiply E5 by -1 and add to E6.

$$\begin{array}{r} -x - 2z = -49 \\ x + 15z = 257 \\ \hline 13z = 208 \\ z = 16 \end{array}$$

Replace z with 16 in E3.
$x + 2(16) = 49$
$\quad x + 32 = 49$
$\quad\quad x = 17$

Replace z with 16 in E3.
$y = 16 + 4 = 20$

He has 17 pennies, 20 nickels, and 16 dimes in his jar.

22. Let l = rate of interest on the larger investment and s = the rate of interest on the smaller investment, both expressed as decimals.

$$\begin{cases} 10,000l + 4000s = 1250 & (1) \\ l = s + 0.02 & (2) \end{cases}$$

Replace l with $s + 0.02$ in E1.

$$10,000(s + 0.02) + 4000s = 1250$$
$$10,000s + 200 + 4000s = 1250$$
$$14,000s = 1050$$
$$s = \frac{1050}{14,000} = 0.075$$

and $l = 0.075 + 0.02 = 0.095$.
The interest rate on the larger investment is 9.5% and the rate on the smaller investment is 7.5%.

23. Let x = length of the equal side and
y = length of the third side.

$$\begin{cases} 2x + y = 73 & (1) \\ y = x + 7 & (2) \end{cases}$$

Replace y with $x + 7$ in E1.
$2x + x + 7 = 73$
$\quad\quad 3x = 66$
$\quad\quad\; x = 22$
Replace x with 22 in E2.

$y = 22 + 7 = 29$

Two sides of the triangle have length 22 cm and the third side has length 29 cm.

24. Let f = the first number, s = the second number, and t = the third number.

$$\begin{cases} f + s + t = 295 & (1) \\ f = s + 5 & (2) \\ f = 2t & (3) \end{cases}$$

Solve E2 for s and E3 for t.

$s = f - 5$

$t = \dfrac{f}{2}$

Replace s with $f - 5$ and t with $\dfrac{f}{2}$ in E1.

$$f + f - 5 + \frac{f}{2} = 295$$

$$\frac{5}{2}f = 300$$

$$f = 120$$

Replace f with 300 in the equation $s = f - 5$.

$s = 120 - 5 = 115$

Replace f with 120 the equation $\dfrac{f}{2}$.

$$t = \frac{120}{2} = 60$$

The first number is 120, the second number is 115, and the third number is 60.

25. $\begin{cases} 3x + 10y = 1 \\ x + 2y = -1 \end{cases}$

$$\begin{bmatrix} 3 & 10 & | & 1 \\ 1 & 2 & | & -1 \end{bmatrix}$$

Interchange R1 and R2.

$$\begin{bmatrix} 1 & 2 & | & -1 \\ 3 & 10 & | & 1 \end{bmatrix}$$

Multiply R1 by –3 and add to R2.

$$\begin{bmatrix} 1 & 2 & | & -1 \\ 0 & 4 & | & 4 \end{bmatrix}$$

Divide R2 by 4.

$$\begin{bmatrix} 1 & 2 & | & -1 \\ 0 & 1 & | & 1 \end{bmatrix}$$

This corresponds to $\begin{cases} x + 2y = -1 \\ y = 1 \end{cases}$.

$x + 2(1) = -1$

$x = -3$

The solution is $(-3, 1)$.

26. $\begin{cases} 3x - 6y = 12 \\ 2y = x - 4 \end{cases}$, or $\begin{cases} 3x - 6y = 12 \\ -x + 2y = -4 \end{cases}$

$$\begin{bmatrix} 3 & -6 & | & 12 \\ -1 & 2 & | & -4 \end{bmatrix}$$

Divide R1 by 3.

$$\begin{bmatrix} 1 & -2 & | & 4 \\ -1 & 2 & | & -4 \end{bmatrix}$$

Add R1 to R2.

$$\begin{bmatrix} 1 & -2 & | & 4 \\ 0 & 0 & | & 0 \end{bmatrix}$$

This corresponds to $\begin{cases} x - 2y = 4 \\ 0 = 0 \end{cases}$.

This is a dependent system. The solution is $\{(x, y) | x - 2y = 4\}$.

27. $\begin{cases} 3x - 2y = -8 \\ 6x + 5y = 11 \end{cases}$

$$\begin{bmatrix} 3 & -2 & | & -8 \\ 6 & 5 & | & 11 \end{bmatrix}$$

Divide R1 by 3.

$$\begin{bmatrix} 1 & -\frac{2}{3} & | & -\frac{8}{3} \\ 6 & 5 & | & 11 \end{bmatrix}$$

Multiply R1 by –6 and add to R2.

$$\begin{bmatrix} 1 & -\frac{2}{3} & | & -\frac{8}{3} \\ 0 & 9 & | & 27 \end{bmatrix}$$

Divide R2 by 9.

$$\begin{bmatrix} 1 & -\frac{2}{3} & | & -\frac{8}{3} \\ 0 & 1 & | & 3 \end{bmatrix}$$

This corresponds to $\begin{cases} x - \frac{2}{3}y = -\frac{8}{3} \\ y = 3 \end{cases}$.

$$x - \frac{2}{3}(3) = -\frac{8}{3}$$

$$x - 2 = -\frac{8}{3}$$

$$x = -\frac{2}{3}$$

The solution is $\left(-\dfrac{2}{3}, 3\right)$.

28. $\begin{cases} 6x - 6y = -5 \\ 10x - 2y = 1 \end{cases}$

$$\begin{bmatrix} 6 & -6 & | & -5 \\ 10 & -2 & | & 1 \end{bmatrix}$$

Divide R1 by 6.

$$\begin{bmatrix} 1 & -1 & \Big| & -\frac{5}{6} \\ 10 & -2 & \Big| & 1 \end{bmatrix}$$

Multiply R1 by –10 and add to R2.

$$\begin{bmatrix} 1 & -1 & \Big| & -\frac{5}{6} \\ 0 & 8 & \Big| & \frac{28}{3} \end{bmatrix}$$

Divide R2 by 8.

$$\begin{bmatrix} 1 & -1 & \Big| & -\frac{5}{6} \\ 0 & 1 & \Big| & \frac{7}{6} \end{bmatrix}$$

Add R2 to R1.

$$\begin{bmatrix} 1 & 0 & \Big| & \frac{1}{3} \\ 0 & 1 & \Big| & \frac{7}{6} \end{bmatrix}$$

This corresponds to $\begin{cases} x = \dfrac{1}{3} \\ y = \dfrac{7}{6} \end{cases}$. The solution is

$\left(\dfrac{1}{3}, \dfrac{7}{6} \right)$.

29. $\begin{cases} 3x - 6y = 0 \\ 2x + 4y = 5 \end{cases}$

$$\begin{bmatrix} 3 & -6 & \Big| & 0 \\ 2 & 4 & \Big| & 5 \end{bmatrix}$$

Divide R1 by 3.

$$\begin{bmatrix} 1 & -2 & \Big| & 0 \\ 2 & 4 & \Big| & 5 \end{bmatrix}$$

Multiply R1 by –2 and add to R2.

$$\begin{bmatrix} 1 & -2 & \Big| & 0 \\ 0 & 8 & \Big| & 5 \end{bmatrix}$$

Divide R2 by 8.

$$\begin{bmatrix} 1 & -2 & \Big| & 0 \\ 0 & 1 & \Big| & \frac{5}{8} \end{bmatrix}$$

This corresponds to $\begin{cases} x - 2y = 0 \\ y = \dfrac{5}{8} \end{cases}$.

$$x - 2\left(\frac{5}{8} \right) = 0$$
$$x - \frac{5}{4} = 0$$
$$x = \frac{5}{4}$$

The solution is $\left(\dfrac{5}{4}, \dfrac{5}{8} \right)$.

30. $\begin{cases} 5x - 3y = 10 \\ -2x + y = -1 \end{cases}$

$$\begin{bmatrix} 5 & -3 & \Big| & 10 \\ -2 & 1 & \Big| & -1 \end{bmatrix}$$

Divide R1 by 5.

$$\begin{bmatrix} 1 & -\frac{3}{5} & \Big| & 2 \\ -2 & 1 & \Big| & -1 \end{bmatrix}$$

Multiply R1 by 2 and add to R2.

$$\begin{bmatrix} 1 & -\frac{3}{5} & \Big| & 2 \\ 0 & -\frac{1}{5} & \Big| & 3 \end{bmatrix}$$

Multiply R2 by –5.

$$\begin{bmatrix} 1 & -\frac{3}{5} & \Big| & 2 \\ 0 & 1 & \Big| & -15 \end{bmatrix}$$

This corresponds to $\begin{cases} x - \dfrac{3}{5} y = 2 \\ y = -15 \end{cases}$.

$$x - \frac{3}{5}(-15) = 2$$
$$x + 9 = 2$$
$$x = -7$$

The solution is (–7, –15).

31. $\begin{cases} 0.2x - 0.3y = -0.7 \\ 0.5x + 0.3y = 1.4 \end{cases}$

$$\begin{bmatrix} 0.2 & -0.3 & \Big| & -0.7 \\ 0.5 & 0.3 & \Big| & 1.4 \end{bmatrix}$$

Multiply both rows by 10 to clear decimals.

$$\begin{bmatrix} 2 & -3 & \Big| & -7 \\ 5 & 3 & \Big| & 14 \end{bmatrix}$$

Divide R1 by 2.

$$\begin{bmatrix} 1 & -\frac{3}{2} & \Big| & -\frac{7}{2} \\ 5 & 3 & \Big| & 14 \end{bmatrix}$$

Multiply R1 by –5 and add to R2.

$$\begin{bmatrix} 1 & -\frac{3}{2} & \Big| & -\frac{7}{2} \\ 0 & \frac{21}{2} & \Big| & \frac{63}{2} \end{bmatrix}$$

Multiply R2 by $\dfrac{2}{21}$.

$$\begin{bmatrix} 1 & -\frac{3}{2} & \Big| & -\frac{7}{2} \\ 0 & 1 & \Big| & 3 \end{bmatrix}$$

This corresponds to $\begin{cases} x - \dfrac{3}{2} y = -\dfrac{7}{2} \\ y = 3 \end{cases}$.

$$x - \frac{3}{2}(3) = -\frac{7}{2}$$
$$x - \frac{9}{2} = -\frac{7}{2}$$
$$x = 1$$

The solution is $(1, 3)$.

32. $\begin{cases} 3x + 2y = 8 \\ 3x - y = 5 \end{cases}$

$\begin{bmatrix} 3 & 2 & | & 8 \\ 3 & -1 & | & 5 \end{bmatrix}$

Divide R1 by 3.

$\begin{bmatrix} 1 & \frac{2}{3} & | & \frac{8}{3} \\ 3 & -1 & | & 5 \end{bmatrix}$

Multiply R1 by –3 and add to R2.

$\begin{bmatrix} 1 & \frac{2}{3} & | & \frac{8}{3} \\ 0 & -3 & | & -3 \end{bmatrix}$

Divide R2 by –3.

$\begin{bmatrix} 1 & \frac{2}{3} & | & \frac{8}{3} \\ 0 & 1 & | & 1 \end{bmatrix}$

This corresponds to $\begin{cases} x + \dfrac{2}{3}y = \dfrac{8}{3} \\ y = 1 \end{cases}$.

$$x + \frac{2}{3}(1) = \frac{8}{3}$$
$$x = 2$$

The solution is $(2, 1)$.

33. $\begin{cases} x \quad + z = 4 \\ 2x - y \quad = 0 \\ x + y - z = 0 \end{cases}$

$\begin{bmatrix} 1 & 0 & 1 & | & 4 \\ 2 & -1 & 0 & | & 0 \\ 1 & 1 & -1 & | & 0 \end{bmatrix}$

Multiply R1 by –2 and add to R2. Multiply R1 by –1 and add to R3.

$\begin{bmatrix} 1 & 0 & 1 & | & 4 \\ 0 & -1 & -2 & | & -8 \\ 0 & 1 & -2 & | & -4 \end{bmatrix}$

Multiply R2 by –1.

$\begin{bmatrix} 1 & 0 & 1 & | & 4 \\ 0 & 1 & 2 & | & 8 \\ 0 & 1 & -2 & | & -4 \end{bmatrix}$

Multiply R2 by –1 and add to R3.

$\begin{bmatrix} 1 & 0 & 1 & | & 4 \\ 0 & 1 & 2 & | & 8 \\ 0 & 0 & -4 & | & -12 \end{bmatrix}$

Divide R3 by –4.

$\begin{bmatrix} 1 & 0 & 1 & | & 4 \\ 0 & 1 & 2 & | & 8 \\ 0 & 0 & 1 & | & 3 \end{bmatrix}$

This corresponds to $\begin{cases} x + z = 4 \\ y + 2z = 8 \\ z = 3 \end{cases}$.

$$y + 2(3) = 8$$
$$y + 6 = 8$$
$$y = 2$$
$$x + 3 = 4$$
$$x = 1$$

The solution is $(1, 2, 3)$.

34. $\begin{cases} 2x + 5y \quad = 4 \\ x - 5y + z = -1 \\ 4x \quad - z = 11 \end{cases}$

$\begin{bmatrix} 2 & 5 & 0 & | & 4 \\ 1 & -5 & 1 & | & -1 \\ 4 & 0 & -1 & | & 11 \end{bmatrix}$

Interchange R1 and R2.

$\begin{bmatrix} 1 & -5 & 1 & | & -1 \\ 2 & 5 & 0 & | & 4 \\ 4 & 0 & -1 & | & 11 \end{bmatrix}$

Multiply R1 by –2 and add to R2. Multiply R1 by –4 and add to R3.

$\begin{bmatrix} 1 & -5 & 1 & | & -1 \\ 0 & 15 & -2 & | & 6 \\ 0 & 20 & -5 & | & 15 \end{bmatrix}$

Divide R2 by 15.

$\begin{bmatrix} 1 & -5 & 1 & | & -1 \\ 0 & 1 & -\frac{2}{15} & | & \frac{2}{5} \\ 0 & 20 & -5 & | & 15 \end{bmatrix}$

Multiply R2 by –20 and add to R3.

$\begin{bmatrix} 1 & -5 & 1 & | & -1 \\ 0 & 1 & -\frac{2}{15} & | & \frac{2}{5} \\ 0 & 0 & -\frac{7}{3} & | & 7 \end{bmatrix}$

Multiply R3 by $-\dfrac{3}{7}$.

$\begin{bmatrix} 1 & -5 & 1 & | & -1 \\ 0 & 1 & -\frac{2}{15} & | & \frac{2}{5} \\ 0 & 0 & 1 & | & -3 \end{bmatrix}$

This corresponds to $\begin{cases} x - 5y + z = -1 \\ y - \dfrac{2}{15}z = \dfrac{2}{5} \\ z = -3 \end{cases}$.

$$y - \frac{2}{15}(-3) = \frac{2}{5}$$
$$y + \frac{2}{5} = \frac{2}{5}$$
$$y = 0$$
$$x - 5(0) + (-3) = -1$$
$$x - 3 = -1$$
$$x = 2$$

The solution is (2, 0, –3).

35. $\begin{cases} 3x - y = 11 \\ x + 2z = 13 \\ y - z = -7 \end{cases}$

$$\begin{bmatrix} 3 & -1 & 0 & | & 11 \\ 1 & 0 & 2 & | & 13 \\ 0 & 1 & -1 & | & -7 \end{bmatrix}$$

Interchange R1 and R2.

$$\begin{bmatrix} 1 & 0 & 2 & | & 13 \\ 3 & -1 & 0 & | & 11 \\ 0 & 1 & -1 & | & -7 \end{bmatrix}$$

Interchange R2 and R3.

$$\begin{bmatrix} 1 & 0 & 2 & | & 13 \\ 0 & 1 & -1 & | & -7 \\ 3 & -1 & 0 & | & 11 \end{bmatrix}$$

Multiply R1 by –3 and add to R3.

$$\begin{bmatrix} 1 & 0 & 2 & | & 13 \\ 0 & 1 & -1 & | & -7 \\ 0 & -1 & -6 & | & -28 \end{bmatrix}$$

Add R2 to R3.

$$\begin{bmatrix} 1 & 0 & 2 & | & 13 \\ 0 & 1 & -1 & | & -7 \\ 0 & 0 & -7 & | & -35 \end{bmatrix}$$

Divide R3 by –7.

$$\begin{bmatrix} 1 & 0 & 2 & | & 13 \\ 0 & 1 & -1 & | & -7 \\ 0 & 0 & 1 & | & 5 \end{bmatrix}$$

This corresponds to $\begin{cases} x + 2z = 13 \\ y - z = -7 \\ z = 5 \end{cases}$.

$$y - 5 = -7$$
$$y = -2$$
$$x + 2(5) = 13$$
$$x = 3$$

The solution is (3, –2, 5).

36. $\begin{cases} 5x + 7y + 3z = 9 \\ 14y - z = 28 \\ 4x + 2z = -4 \end{cases}$

$$\begin{bmatrix} 5 & 7 & 3 & | & 9 \\ 0 & 14 & -1 & | & 28 \\ 4 & 0 & 2 & | & -4 \end{bmatrix}$$

Divide R1 by 5.

$$\begin{bmatrix} 1 & \frac{7}{5} & \frac{3}{5} & | & \frac{9}{5} \\ 0 & 14 & -1 & | & 28 \\ 4 & 0 & 2 & | & -4 \end{bmatrix}$$

Multiply R1 by –4 and add to R3.

$$\begin{bmatrix} 1 & \frac{7}{5} & \frac{3}{5} & | & \frac{9}{5} \\ 0 & 14 & -1 & | & 28 \\ 0 & -\frac{28}{5} & -\frac{2}{5} & | & -\frac{56}{5} \end{bmatrix}$$

Divide R2 by 14.

$$\begin{bmatrix} 1 & \frac{7}{5} & \frac{3}{5} & | & \frac{9}{5} \\ 0 & 1 & -\frac{1}{14} & | & 2 \\ 0 & -\frac{28}{5} & -\frac{2}{5} & | & -\frac{56}{5} \end{bmatrix}$$

Multiply R2 by $\frac{28}{5}$ and add to R3.

$$\begin{bmatrix} 1 & \frac{7}{5} & \frac{3}{5} & | & \frac{9}{5} \\ 0 & 1 & -\frac{1}{14} & | & 2 \\ 0 & 0 & -\frac{4}{5} & | & 0 \end{bmatrix}$$

Multiply R3 by $-\frac{5}{4}$.

$$\begin{bmatrix} 1 & \frac{7}{5} & \frac{3}{5} & | & \frac{9}{5} \\ 0 & 1 & -\frac{1}{14} & | & 2 \\ 0 & 0 & 1 & | & 0 \end{bmatrix}$$

This corresponds to $\begin{cases} x + \frac{7}{5}y + \frac{3}{5}z = \frac{9}{5} \\ y - \frac{1}{14}z = 2 \\ z = 0 \end{cases}$.

$$y - \frac{1}{14}(0) = 2$$
$$y = 2$$
$$x + \frac{7}{5}(2) + \frac{3}{5}(0) = \frac{9}{5}$$
$$x + \frac{14}{5} = \frac{9}{5}$$
$$x = -1$$

The solution is (–1, 2, 0).

37. $\begin{cases} 7x - 3y + 2z = 0 \\ 4x - 4y - z = 2 \\ 5x + 2y + 3z = 1 \end{cases}$

$$\begin{bmatrix} 7 & -3 & 2 & | & 0 \\ 4 & -4 & -1 & | & 2 \\ 5 & 2 & 3 & | & 1 \end{bmatrix}$$

Interchange R1 and R2.

$$\begin{bmatrix} 4 & -4 & -1 & | & 2 \\ 7 & -3 & 2 & | & 0 \\ 5 & 2 & 3 & | & 1 \end{bmatrix}$$

Divide R1 by 4.

$$\begin{bmatrix} 1 & -1 & -\frac{1}{4} & | & \frac{1}{2} \\ 7 & -3 & 2 & | & 0 \\ 5 & 2 & 3 & | & 1 \end{bmatrix}$$

Multiply R1 by –7 and add to R2. Multiply R1 by –5 and add to R3.

$$\begin{bmatrix} 1 & -1 & -\frac{1}{4} & | & \frac{1}{2} \\ 0 & 4 & \frac{15}{4} & | & -\frac{7}{2} \\ 0 & 7 & \frac{17}{4} & | & -\frac{3}{2} \end{bmatrix}$$

Divide R2 by 4.

$$\begin{bmatrix} 1 & -1 & -\frac{1}{4} & | & \frac{1}{2} \\ 0 & 1 & \frac{15}{16} & | & -\frac{7}{8} \\ 0 & 7 & \frac{17}{4} & | & -\frac{3}{2} \end{bmatrix}$$

Multiply R2 by –7 and add to R3.

$$\begin{bmatrix} 1 & -1 & -\frac{1}{4} & | & \frac{1}{2} \\ 0 & 1 & \frac{15}{16} & | & -\frac{7}{8} \\ 0 & 0 & -\frac{37}{16} & | & -\frac{37}{8} \end{bmatrix}$$

Multiply R3 by $-\dfrac{16}{37}$.

$$\begin{bmatrix} 1 & -1 & -\frac{1}{4} & | & \frac{1}{2} \\ 0 & 1 & \frac{15}{16} & | & -\frac{7}{8} \\ 0 & 0 & 1 & | & -2 \end{bmatrix}$$

This corresponds to $\begin{cases} x - y - \dfrac{1}{4}z = \dfrac{1}{2} \\ y + \dfrac{15}{16}z = -\dfrac{7}{8} \\ z = -2 \end{cases}$.

$$y + \frac{15}{16}(-2) = -\frac{7}{8}$$
$$y - \frac{15}{8} = -\frac{7}{8}$$
$$y = 1$$

$$x - 1 - \frac{1}{4}(-2) = \frac{1}{2}$$
$$x - 1 + \frac{1}{2} = \frac{1}{2}$$
$$x = 1$$

The solution is $(1, 1, -2)$.

38. $\begin{cases} x + 2y + 3z = 14 \\ y + 2z = 3 \\ 2x \quad - 2z = 10 \end{cases}$

$$\begin{bmatrix} 1 & 2 & 3 & | & 14 \\ 0 & 1 & 2 & | & 3 \\ 2 & 0 & -2 & | & 10 \end{bmatrix}$$

Multiply R1 by –2 and add to R3.

$$\begin{bmatrix} 1 & 2 & 3 & | & 14 \\ 0 & 1 & 2 & | & 3 \\ 0 & -4 & -8 & | & -18 \end{bmatrix}$$

Multiply R2 by 4 and add to R3.

$$\begin{bmatrix} 1 & 2 & 3 & | & 14 \\ 0 & 1 & 2 & | & 3 \\ 0 & 0 & 0 & | & -6 \end{bmatrix}$$

This corresponds to $\begin{cases} x + 2y + 3z = 14 \\ y + 2z = 3 \\ 0 = -6 \end{cases}$.

This system is inconsistent. The solution is $\varnothing$.

39. $\begin{cases} y \geq 2x - 3 \\ y \leq -2x + 1 \end{cases}$

Graph both inequalities on the same set of axes. The solution is the intersection of the solution regions. The solution of the system is the darker shaded region. This solution includes parts of both boundary lines.

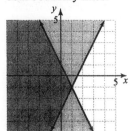

40. $\begin{cases} y \le -3x - 3 \\ y \le 2x + 7 \end{cases}$

Graph both inequalities on the same set of axes. The solution is the intersection of the solution regions. The solution of the system is the darker shaded region. This solution includes parts of both boundary lines.

41. $\begin{cases} x + 2y > 0 \\ x - y \le 6 \end{cases}$

Graph both inequalities on the same set of axes. The solution is the intersection of the solution regions. The solution of the system is the darker shaded region. This solution includes the part of the solid boundary line that borders the region but not the dashed boundary line or the point where the boundary lines intersect.

42. $\begin{cases} x - 2y \ge 7 \\ x + y \le -5 \end{cases}$

Graph both inequalities on the same set of axes. The solution is the intersection of the solution regions. The solution of the system is the darker shaded region. This solution includes parts of both boundary lines.

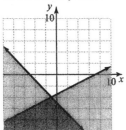

43. $\begin{cases} 3x - 2y \le 4 \\ 2x + y \ge 5 \\ y \le 4 \end{cases}$

Graph all three inequalities on the same set of axes. The solution set of the system is the shaded region. The parts of the boundary lines that border the shaded region are part of the solution.

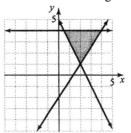

44. $\begin{cases} 4x - y \le 0 \\ 3x - 2y \ge -5 \\ y \ge -4 \end{cases}$

Graph all three inequalities on the same set of axes. The solution set of the system is the shaded region. The parts of the boundary lines that border the shaded region are part of the solution.

45. $\begin{cases} x + 2y \le 5 \\ x \le 2 \\ x \ge 0 \\ y \ge 0 \end{cases}$

Graph the inequalities on the same set of axes. The intersection of the inequalities is the solution region. It is the only shaded region in this graph and includes the portion of all four boundary lines that border the shaded region.

46. $\begin{cases} x+3y \le 7 \\ y \le 5 \\ x \ge 0 \\ y \ge 0 \end{cases}$

Graph the inequalities on the same set of axes. The intersection of the inequalities is the solution region. It is the only shaded region in this graph and includes the portion of all four boundary lines that border the shaded region.

47. $\begin{cases} y = x-5 \\ y = -2x+2 \end{cases}$

We substitute $x - 5$ for y in the second equation.
$$x-5 = -2x+2$$
$$3x = 7$$
$$x = \frac{7}{3}$$

Replace x with $\frac{7}{3}$ in the first equation.

$$y = \frac{7}{3} - 5 = \frac{7}{3} - \frac{15}{3} = -\frac{8}{3}$$

The solution is $\left(\frac{7}{3}, -\frac{8}{3} \right)$.

48. $\begin{cases} \frac{2}{5}x + \frac{3}{4}y = 1 \\ x + 3y = -2 \end{cases}$

Multiply both sides of the first equation by 20 to eliminate fractions.

$\begin{cases} 20\left(\frac{2}{5}x + \frac{3}{4}y \right) = 20(1) \\ x+3y = -2 \end{cases}$

$\begin{cases} 8x+15y = 20 \\ x+3y = -2 \end{cases}$

Multiply both sides of the second equation by -5 and add to the first equation to eliminate y.

$\begin{array}{r} 8x+15y = 20 \\ -5x-15y = 10 \\ \hline 3x = 30 \\ x = 10 \end{array}$

To find y, replace x with 10 in the second equation.
$$10+3y = -2$$
$$3y = -12$$
$$y = -4$$
The solution is (10, –4).

49. $\begin{cases} 5x-2y = 10 \\ x = \frac{2}{5}y+2 \end{cases}$

Multiply both sides of the second equation by 5.

$\begin{cases} 5x-2y = 10 \\ 5x = 5\left(\frac{2}{5}y+2 \right) \end{cases}$

$\begin{cases} 5x-2y = 10 \\ 5x = 2y+10 \end{cases}$

Subtract $2y$ from both sides of the second equation.

$\begin{cases} 5x-2y = 10 \\ 5x-2y = 10 \end{cases}$

The equations are the same. The system has an infinite number of solutions. The solution set can be written as $\{(x, y)| 5x - 2y = 10\}$.

50. $\begin{cases} x-4y = 4 \\ \frac{1}{8}x - \frac{1}{2}y = 3 \end{cases}$

Multiply the second by -8 and add to the first equation to eliminate x.

$\begin{cases} x-4y = 4 \\ -x+4y = -24 \end{cases}$

The equation $0 = -20$ is false. The system has no solution. The solution set is { } or $\varnothing$.

51. $\begin{cases} x-3y+2z = 0 \\ 9y- z = 22 \\ 5x +3z = 10 \end{cases}$

The corresponding matrix is $\begin{bmatrix} 1 & -3 & 2 & | & 0 \\ 0 & 9 & -1 & | & 22 \\ 5 & 0 & 3 & | & 10 \end{bmatrix}$

Multiply row 1 by -5 and add to row 3.
$$\begin{bmatrix} 1 & -3 & 2 & | & 0 \\ 0 & 9 & -1 & | & 22 \\ 0 & 15 & -7 & | & 10 \end{bmatrix}$$

Divide row 2 by 9.
$$\begin{bmatrix} 1 & -3 & 2 & | & 0 \\ 0 & 1 & -\frac{1}{9} & | & \frac{22}{9} \\ 0 & 15 & -7 & | & 10 \end{bmatrix}$$

Multiply row 2 by −15 and add to row 3.

$$\begin{bmatrix} 1 & -3 & 2 & | & 0 \\ 0 & 1 & -\frac{1}{9} & | & \frac{22}{9} \\ 0 & 0 & -\frac{48}{9} & | & -\frac{240}{9} \end{bmatrix}$$

Multiply row 3 by $-\frac{9}{48}$.

$$\begin{bmatrix} 1 & -3 & 2 & | & 0 \\ 0 & 1 & -\frac{1}{9} & | & \frac{22}{9} \\ 0 & 0 & 1 & | & 5 \end{bmatrix}$$

This matrix represents the system

$$\begin{cases} x - 3y + 2z = 0 \\ y - \frac{1}{9}z = \frac{22}{9} \\ z = 5 \end{cases}$$

Replace z with 5 in the second equation to find y.

$$y - \frac{1}{9}(5) = \frac{22}{9}$$

$$y = \frac{22}{9} + \frac{5}{9} = \frac{27}{9} = 3$$

Replace y with 3 and z with 5 in the first equation to find x.

$$x - 3(3) + 2(5) = 0$$
$$x - 9 + 10 = 0$$
$$x + 1 = 0$$
$$x = -1$$

The solution is (−1, 3, 5).

52. Let x = the first number
y = the second number
We solve the system

$$\begin{cases} x = 3y - 5 \\ x + y = 127 \end{cases}$$

We substitute $3y - 5$ for x in the second equation.

$$(3y - 5) + y = 127$$
$$4y - 5 = 127$$
$$4y = 132$$
$$y = 33$$

We replace y with 33 in the first equation to find x.

$$x = 3(33) - 5 = 99 - 5 = 94$$

The numbers are 33 and 94.

53. Let x = length of the shortest side
y = length of the second side
z = length of the third side
We solve the system

$$\begin{cases} x + y + z = 126 \\ y = 2x \\ z = x + 14 \end{cases}$$

We substitute $2x$ for y and $x + 14$ for z in the first equation.

$$x + 2x + (x + 14) = 126$$
$$4x + 14 = 126$$
$$4x = 112$$
$$x = 28$$

Now we find y and z.

$$y = 2x = 2(28) = 56$$
$$z = x + 14 = 28 + 14 = 42$$

The lengths are 28 units, 42 units, and 56 units.

54. $$\begin{cases} y \le 3x - \frac{1}{2} \\ 3x + 4y \ge 6 \end{cases}$$

Graph both inequalities on the same set of axes. The solution is the intersection of the solution regions. The solution of the system is the darker shaded region. This solution includes parts of both boundary lines.

55. We solve the system

$$\begin{cases} y = -443x + 2584 \\ y = 500x + 551 \end{cases}$$

We substitute $-443x + 2584$ for y in the second equation.

$$-443x + 2584 = 500x + 551$$
$$-994x = -2033$$
$$x = \frac{-2033}{-994} \approx 2.05$$

The amount spent on VCR decks and DVD players was the same about 2 years after 1998, or in 2000.

Chapter 4 Test

1. $\begin{cases} 2x - y = -1 & (1) \\ 5x + 4y = 17 & (2) \end{cases}$

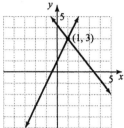

By elimination:
Multiply E1 by 4 and add it to E2.

$$8x - 4y = -4$$
$$\underline{5x + 4y = 17}$$
$$13x \quad = 13$$
$$x = 1$$

Replace x with 1 in E2.
$$5(1) + 4y = 17$$
$$4y = 12$$
$$y = 3$$
The solution is $(1, 3)$.

2. $\begin{cases} 7x - 14y = 5 & (1) \\ \quad x = 2y & (2) \end{cases}$

By substitution:
Replace x with $2y$ in E1.
$$7(2y) - 14y = 5$$
$$14y - 14y = 5$$
$$0 = 5 \text{ False}$$

The system is inconsistent. The solution set is $\varnothing$.

3. $\begin{cases} 4x - 7y = 29 \\ 2x + 5y = -11 \end{cases}$

Multiply E2 by −2 and add to E1.

$$-4x - 10y = 22$$
$$\underline{4x - 7y = 29}$$
$$-17y = 51$$
$$y = -3$$

Replace y with −3 in E1.

$$4x - 7(-3) = 29$$
$$4x + 21 = 29$$
$$4x = 8$$
$$x = 2$$
The solution is $(2, -3)$.

4. $\begin{cases} 15x + 6y = 15 \\ 10x + 4y = 10 \end{cases}$

Divide E1 by 3 and E2 by 2.

$\begin{cases} 5x + 2y = 5 \\ 5x + 2y = 5 \end{cases}$

The system is dependent. The solution is
$\{(x, y) | 10x + 4y = 10\}$.

5. $\begin{cases} 2x - 3y \quad = 4 & (1) \\ \quad 3y + 2z = 2 & (2) \\ x \quad - z = -5 & (3) \end{cases}$

Add E1 and E2.
$$2x + 2z = 6 \text{ or } x + z = 3 \quad (4)$$
Add E3 and E4.
$$x + z = 3$$
$$\underline{x - z = -5}$$
$$2x \quad = -2$$
$$x = -1$$
Replace x with −1 in E3.
$$-1 - z = -5$$
$$-z = -4 \text{ so } z = 4$$
Replace x with −1 in E1.
$$2(-1) - 3y = 4$$
$$-2 - 3y = 4$$
$$-3y = 6$$
$$y = -2$$
The solution is $(-1, -2, 4)$.

6. $\begin{cases} 3x - 2y - z = -1 & (1) \\ 2x - 2y \quad = 4 & (2) \\ 2x \quad - 2z = -12 & (3) \end{cases}$

Multiply E2 by −1 and add to E1.
$$3x - 2y - z = -1$$
$$\underline{-2x + 2y \quad = -4}$$
$$x \quad - z = -5 \quad (4)$$
Multiply E4 by −2 and add to E3.
$$2x - 2z = -12$$
$$\underline{-2x + 2z = 10}$$
$$0 = -2 \text{ False}$$

The system is inconsistent. The solution set is $\varnothing$.

7. $\begin{cases} \dfrac{x}{2} + \dfrac{y}{4} = -\dfrac{3}{4} \\ x + \dfrac{3}{4}y = -4 \end{cases}$

Clear fractions by multiplying both equations by 4.

$\begin{cases} 2x + y = -3 \quad (1) \\ 4x + 3y = -16 \quad (2) \end{cases}$

Multiply E1 by –2 and add to E2.

$-4x - 2y = 6$

$\underline{4x + 3y = -16}$

$y = -10$

Replace y with –10 in E1.

$2x + (-10) = -3$

$2x = 7 \quad$ so $\quad x = \dfrac{7}{2}$

The solution is $\left(\dfrac{7}{2}, -10 \right)$.

8. $\begin{cases} x - y = -2 \\ 3x - 3y = -6 \end{cases}$

$\begin{bmatrix} 1 & -1 & | & -2 \\ 3 & -3 & | & -6 \end{bmatrix}$

Multiply R1 by –3 and add to R2.

$\begin{bmatrix} 1 & -1 & | & -2 \\ 0 & 0 & | & 0 \end{bmatrix}$

This corresponds to $\begin{cases} x - y = -2 \\ 0 = 0 \end{cases}$.

This is a dependent system. The solution is $\{(x, y) | x - y = -2\}$.

9. $\begin{cases} x + 2y = -1 \\ 2x + 5y = -5 \end{cases}$

$\begin{bmatrix} 1 & 2 & | & -1 \\ 2 & 5 & | & -5 \end{bmatrix}$

Multiply R1 by –2 and add to R2.

$\begin{bmatrix} 1 & 2 & | & -1 \\ 0 & 1 & | & -3 \end{bmatrix}$

This corresponds to $\begin{cases} x + 2y = -1 \\ y = -3 \end{cases}$.

$x + 2(-3) = -1$

$x - 6 = -1$

$x = 5$

The solution is (5, –3).

10. $\begin{cases} x - y - z = 0 \\ 3x - y - 5z = -2 \\ 2x + 3y = -5 \end{cases}$

$\begin{bmatrix} 1 & -1 & -1 & | & 0 \\ 3 & -1 & -5 & | & -2 \\ 2 & 3 & 0 & | & -5 \end{bmatrix}$

Multiply R1 by –3 and add to R2. Multiply R1 by –2 and add to R3.

$\begin{bmatrix} 1 & -1 & -1 & | & 0 \\ 0 & 2 & -2 & | & -2 \\ 0 & 5 & 2 & | & -5 \end{bmatrix}$

Divide R2 by 2.

$\begin{bmatrix} 1 & -1 & -1 & | & 0 \\ 0 & 1 & -1 & | & -1 \\ 0 & 5 & 2 & | & -5 \end{bmatrix}$

Multiply R2 by –5 and add to R3.

$\begin{bmatrix} 1 & -1 & -1 & | & 0 \\ 0 & 1 & -1 & | & -1 \\ 0 & 0 & 7 & | & 0 \end{bmatrix}$

Divide R3 by 7.

$\begin{bmatrix} 1 & -1 & -1 & | & 0 \\ 0 & 1 & -1 & | & -1 \\ 0 & 0 & 1 & | & 0 \end{bmatrix}$

This corresponds to $\begin{cases} x - y - z = 0 \\ y - z = -1 \\ z = 0 \end{cases}$.

$y - 0 = -1$

$y = -1$

$x - (-1) - 0 = 0$

$x + 1 = 0$

$x = -1$

The solution is (–1, –1, 0).

11. Let x = double occupancy rooms and y = single occupancy rooms.

$\begin{cases} x + y = 80 \quad (1) \\ 90x + 80y = 6930 \quad (2) \end{cases}$

Multiply E1 by –80 and add to E2.

$-80x - 80y = -6400$

$\underline{90x + 80y = 6930}$

$10x = 530$

$x = 53$

Replace x with 53 in E1.

$53 + y = 80$

$y = 27$

53 double-occupancy and 27 single-occupancy rooms are occupied.

12. Let x = gallons of 10% solution and
y = gallons of 20% solution.

$$\begin{cases} x + y = 20 & (1) \\ 0.10x + 0.20y = 0.175(20) & (2) \end{cases}$$

Multiply E1 by –0.10 add to E2.

$$\begin{array}{r} -0.10x - 0.10y = -2.0 \\ 0.10x + 0.20y = 3.5 \\ \hline 0.10y = 1.5 \\ y = 15 \end{array}$$

Replace y with 15 in E1.

$$x + 15 = 20$$
$$x = 5$$

They should use 5 gallons of 10% fructose solution and 15 gallons of the 20% solution.

13. $R(x) = 4x$ and $C(x) = 1.5x + 2000$

Break even occurs when $R(x) = C(x)$.

$$4x = 1.5x + 2000$$
$$2.5x = 2000$$
$$x = 800$$

The company must sell 800 packages to break even.

14. Let x = measure of the smallest angle. Then the largest angle has a measure of $5x - 3$, and the remaining angle has a measure of $2x - 1$. The sum of the three angles must add to 180°:

$$a + b + c = 180$$
$$x + (5x - 3) + (2x - 1) = 180$$
$$x + 5x - 3 + 2x - 1 = 180$$
$$8x - 4 = 180$$
$$8x = 184$$
$$x = 23$$
$$5x - 3 = 5(23) - 3 = 115 - 3 = 112$$
$$2x - 1 = 2(23) - 1 = 46 - 1 = 45$$

The angle measures are 23°, 45°, and 112°.

15. $\begin{cases} 2y - x \geq 1 \\ x + y \geq -4 \\ y \leq 2 \end{cases}$

Graph all three inequalities on the same set of axes. The solution set of the system is the shaded region. The parts of the boundary lines that border the shaded region are part of the solution.

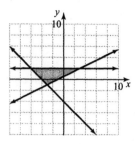

Chapter 4 Cumulative Review

1. a. Since 3 is a natural number, the statement is true.

b. Since 7 is not one of the three numbers listed in the set, the statement is true.

2. a. Since 7 is not an element of the second set, the first set is not a subset of the second set. The statement is false.

b. Since all three numbers in the first set are also elements of the second set, the first set is a subset of the second set. The statement is true.

3. a. $11 + 2 - 7 = 13 - 7 = 6$

b. $-5 - 4 + 2 = -9 + 2 = -7$

4. a. $-7 - (-2) = -7 + 2 = -5$

b. $14 - 38 = -24$

5. a. The opposite of 4 is –4.

b. The opposite of $\frac{3}{7}$ is $-\frac{3}{7}$.

c. The opposite of –11.2 is 11.2.

6. a. The reciprocal of 5 is $\frac{1}{5}$.

b. The reciprocal of $-\frac{2}{3}$ is $-\frac{3}{2}$.

7. a. $3(2x + y) = 6x + 3y$

b. $-(3x - 1) = -3x + 1$

c. $0.7a(b - 2) = 0.7ab - 1.4a$

8. a. $7(3x - 2y + 4) = 21x - 14y + 28$

b. $-(-2s - 3t) = 2s + 3t$

9. a. $3x - 5x + 4 = (3 - 5)x + 4 = -2x + 4$

b. $7yz + yz = (7 + 1)yz = 8yz$

c. $4z + 6.1 = 4z + 6.1$

10. a. $5y^2 - 1 + 2(y^2 + 2) = 5y^2 - 1 + 2y^2 + 4$
$$= 7y^2 + 3$$

b. $(7.8x - 1.2) - (5.6x - 2.4)$
$= 7.8x - 1.2 - 5.6x + 2.4$
$= 2.2x + 1.2$

11. $-4x - 1 + 5x = 9x + 3 - 7x$
$$x - 1 = 2x + 3$$
$$-x = 4$$
$$x = -4$$

12. $8y - 14 = 6y - 14$
$$2y = 0$$
$$y = 0$$

13. $0.3x + 0.1 = 0.27x - 0.02$
$$0.03x = -0.12$$
$$x = -4$$

14. $2(m - 6) - m = 4(m - 3) - 3m$
$$2m - 12 - m = 4m - 12 - 3m$$
$$m - 12 = m - 12$$
$$0 = 0 \quad \text{Always True}$$
The solution is all real numbers.

15. Let x = length of the third side, then
$2x + 12$ = length of the two equal sides.
$$x + (2x + 12) + (2x + 12) = 149$$
$$5x + 24 = 149$$
$$5x = 125$$
$$x = 25$$
$$2(25) + 12 = 50 + 12 = 62$$
The sides are 25 cm, 62 cm, and 62 cm.

16. Let x = measure of the equal angles,
$x + 10$ = measure of the third angle, and
$\dfrac{1}{2}x$ = measure of the fourth angle.

$$x + x + (x + 10) + \frac{1}{2}x = 360$$
$$\frac{7}{2}x + 10 = 360$$
$$\frac{7}{2}x = 350$$
$$7x = 700$$
$$x = 100$$
$$x + 10 = 100 + 10 = 110$$
$$\frac{1}{2}x = \frac{1}{2}(100) = 50$$

The measure of the angles are 100°, 100°, 110°, and 50°.

17. $3x + 4 \geq 2x - 6$
$$x \geq -10$$

18. $5(2x - 1) > -5$
$$10x - 5 > -5$$
$$10x > 0$$
$$x > 0$$
$$(0, \infty)$$

19. $2 < 4 - x < 7$
$$-2 < -x < 3$$
$$2 > x > -3$$
$$-3 < x < 2$$
$$(-3, 2)$$

20. $-1 < \dfrac{-2x - 1}{3} < 1$
$$3(-1) < 3\left[\frac{-2x - 1}{3}\right] < 3(1)$$
$$-3 < -2x - 1 < 3$$
$$-2 < -2x < 4$$
$$1 > x > -2$$
$$-2 < x < 1$$
$$(-2, 1)$$

21. $|2x| + 5 = 7$
$$|2x| = 2$$
$$2x = 2 \quad \text{or} \quad 2x = -2$$
$$x = 1 \quad \text{or} \quad x = -1$$
The solution set is $\{-1, 1\}$.

22. $|x-5|=4$
　　$x-5=4$ or $x-5=-4$
　　　$x=9$ or 　$x=1$
　　The solution set is $\{1, 9\}$.

23. $|m-6|<2$
　　$-2<m-6<2$
　　　$4<m<8$
　　$(4, 8)$

24. $|2x+1|>5$
　　$2x+1<-5$ or $2x+1>5$
　　　$2x<-6$ or 　$2x>4$
　　　$x<-3$ or 　　$x>2$
　　$(-\infty, -3)\cup(2, \infty)$

25.

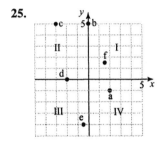

　　a. $(2, -1)$ is in Quadrant IV.

　　b. $(0, 5)$ is on the *y*-axis.

　　c. $(-3, 5)$ is in Quadrant II.

　　d. $(-2, 0)$ is on the *x*-axis.

　　e. $\left(-\dfrac{1}{2}, -4\right)$ is in Quadrant III.

　　f. $(1.5, 1.5)$ is in Quadrant I.

26. a. $(-1, -5)$ is in Quadrant III.

　　b. $(4, -2)$ is in Quadrant IV.

　　c. $(0, 2)$ is on the *y*-axis.

27. No; for the input $x = 4$, there are two outputs, $y = \pm2$.

28. $-2x+\dfrac{1}{2}y=-2,$ or $y=4x-4$

29. $f(x)=7x^2-3x+1,\ g(x)=3x-2$

　　a. $f(1)=7(1)^2-3(1)+1=7-3+1=5$

　　b. $g(1)=3(1)-2=3-2=1$

　　c. $f(-2)=7(-2)^2-3(-2)+1$
　　　　　$=7(4)+6+1$
　　　　　$=28+6+1$
　　　　　$=35$

　　d. $g(0)=3(0)-2=0-2=-2$

30. $f(x)=3x^2$

　　a. $f(5)=3(5)^2=3(25)=75$

　　b. $f(-2)=3(-2)^2=3(4)=12$

31. $g(x)=2x+1$ and $f(x)=2x$

The graph of g is the graph of f shifted 1 unit up.

32. $m=\dfrac{9-6}{0-(-2)}=\dfrac{3}{2}$

33. $3x - 4y = 4$
$$-4y = -3x + 4$$
$$y = \frac{3}{4}x - 1$$
$$m = \frac{3}{4}, \ \text{y-intercept} = (0, -1)$$

34. $y = 2$
$$m = 0, \ \text{y-intercept} = (0, 2)$$

35. a. $3x + 7y = 4$
$$7y = -3x + 4$$
$$y = -\frac{3}{7}x + \frac{4}{7}$$
$$m = -\frac{3}{7}$$
$$6x + 14y = 7$$
$$14y = -6x + 7$$
$$y = -\frac{3}{7}x + \frac{1}{2}$$
$$m = -\frac{3}{7}$$
Parallel, since the slopes are equal.

b. $-x + 3y = 2$
$$3y = x + 2$$
$$y = \frac{1}{3}x + \frac{2}{3}$$
$$m = \frac{1}{3}$$
$$2x + 6y = 5$$
$$6y = -2x + 5$$
$$y = -\frac{1}{3}x + \frac{5}{6}$$
$$m = -\frac{1}{3}$$
Neither, since the slopes are not equal and their product is not -1.

36. $y - (-9) = \frac{1}{5}(x - 0)$
$$y + 9 = \frac{1}{5}x$$
$$y = \frac{1}{5}x - 9$$

37. $m = \dfrac{-5 - 0}{-4 - 4} = \dfrac{-5}{-8} = \dfrac{5}{8}$
$$y - 0 = \frac{5}{8}(x - 4)$$
$$y = \frac{5}{8}x - \frac{5}{2}$$
$$f(x) = \frac{5}{8}x - \frac{5}{2}$$

38. $f(x) = \dfrac{1}{2}x - \dfrac{1}{3}$ or $y = \dfrac{1}{2}x - \dfrac{1}{3}$
$$m = \frac{1}{2} \ \text{ so } \ m_{\perp} = -2$$
$$y - 6 = -2[x - (-2)]$$
$$y - 6 = -2(x + 2)$$
$$y - 6 = -2x - 4$$
$$y = -2x + 2$$

39. $3x \geq y$, or $y \leq 3x$
Graph the boundary line $y = 3x$ with a solid line because the inequality symbol is $\leq$.
Test: $(0, 1)$
$$3x \geq y$$
$$3(0) \geq 1$$
$$0 \geq 1 \ \text{ False}$$
Shade the half-plane that does not contain $(0, 1)$.

40. $x \geq 1$
Graph the boundary line $x = 1$ with a solid line because the inequality symbol is $\geq$.
Shade the half-plane that does not contain $(0, 0)$.

41. a. $\begin{cases} -x+y=2 \\ 2x-y=-3 \end{cases}$

$-(-1)+1=2$
$1+1=2$
$2=2$ True

$2(-1)-(1)=-3$
$-2-1=-3$
$-3=-3$ True
Yes, $(-1, 1)$ is a solution.

b. $\begin{cases} 5x+3y=-1 \\ x-y=1 \end{cases}$

$5(-2)+3(3)=-1$
$-10+9=-1$
$-1=-1$ True

$-2-3=-1$
$-5=-1$ False
No, $(-2, 3)$ is not a solution.

42. $\begin{cases} 5x+\ y=-2 \quad (1) \\ 4x-2y=-10 \quad (2) \end{cases}$

Multiply E1 by 2 and add to E2.
$10x+2y=-4$
$\underline{4x-2y=-10}$
$14x\qquad=-14$
$\quad x=-1$
Replace x with -1 in E1.
$5(-1)+y=-2$
$-5+y=-2$
$y=3$
The solution is $(-1, 3)$.

43. $\begin{cases} 3x-y+z=-15 \quad (1) \\ x+2y-z=1 \quad (2) \\ 2x+3y-2z=0 \quad (3) \end{cases}$

Add E1 and E2.
$4x+y=-14$ (4)
Multiply E1 by 2 and add to E3.
$6x-2y+2z=-30$
$\underline{2x+3y-2z=0}$
$8x+y\qquad=-30$ (5)
Solve the new system:
$\begin{cases} 4x+y=-14 \quad (4) \\ 8x+y=-30 \quad (5) \end{cases}$
Multiply E4 by -1 and add to E5.
$-4x-y=14$
$\underline{8x+y=-30}$
$4x\qquad=-16$
$\quad x=-4$

Replace x with -4 in E4.
$4(-4)+y=-14$
$-16+y=-14$
$y=2$
Replace x with -4 and y with 2 in E1.
$3(-4)-(2)+z=-15$
$-12-2+z=-15$
$-14+z=-15$
$z=-1$
The solution is $(-4, 2, -1)$.

44. $\begin{cases} x-2y+\ z=0 \quad (1) \\ 3x-y-2z=-15 \quad (2) \\ 2x-3y+3z=7 \quad (3) \end{cases}$

Multiply E1 by 2 and add to E2.
$2x-4y+2z=0$
$\underline{3x-y-2z=-15}$
$5x-5y\qquad=-15$ or $x-y=-3$ (4)
Multiply E1 by -3 and add to E3.
$-3x+6y-3z=0$
$\underline{2x-3y+3z=7}$
$-x+3y\qquad=7$ (5)
Add E4 and E5.
$2y=4$
$y=2$
Replace y with 2 in E4.
$x-2=-3$
$x=-1$
Replace x with -1 and y with 2 in E1.
$-1-2(2)+z=0$
$-5+z=0$
$z=5$
The solution is $(-1, 2, 5)$.

45. $\begin{cases} x+3y=5 \\ 2x-y=-4 \end{cases}$

$\begin{bmatrix} 1 & 3 & | & 5 \\ 2 & -1 & | & -4 \end{bmatrix}$

Multiply R1 by -2 and add to R2.
$\begin{bmatrix} 1 & 3 & | & 5 \\ 0 & -7 & | & -14 \end{bmatrix}$

Divide R2 by -7.
$\begin{bmatrix} 1 & 3 & | & 5 \\ 0 & 1 & | & 2 \end{bmatrix}$

This corresponds to $\begin{cases} x+3y=5 \\ y=2 \end{cases}$.

$$x + 3(2) = 5$$
$$x + 6 = 5$$
$$x = -1$$
The solution is $(-1, 2)$.

46. $\begin{cases} -6x + 8y = 0 & (1) \\ 9x - 12y = 2 & (2) \end{cases}$

Divide E1 by -2 and E2 by 3.

$\begin{cases} 3x - 4y = 0 \\ 3x - 4y = \dfrac{2}{3} \end{cases}$

This system is inconsistent. The solution set is $\varnothing$.

Chapter 5

Practice Exercises

1. a. $3^4 \cdot 3^2 = 3^{4+2} = 3^6$

   b. $x^5 \cdot x^2 = x^{5+2} = x^7$

   c. $y \cdot y^3 \cdot y^5 = (y^1 \cdot y^3) \cdot y^5 = y^4 \cdot y^5 = y^9$

2. a. $(5z^3)(7z) = 5(7)z^3 z^1 = 35z^4$

   b. $(-4.1t^5 q^3)(5tq^5) = -4.1(5)t^5 t^1 q^3 q^5$
   $$= -20.5t^6 q^8$$

3. a. $5^0 = 1$

   b. $-5^0 = -(5^0) = -(1) = -1$

   c. $(3x - 8)^0 = 1$

   d. $3x^0 = 3(1) = 3$

4. a. $\dfrac{z^8}{z^3} = z^{8-3} = z^5$

   b. $\dfrac{3^9}{3^3} = 3^{9-3} = 3^6$

   c. $\dfrac{45x^7}{5x^3} = 9x^{7-3} = 9x^4$

   d. $\dfrac{24a^{14}b^6}{18a^7 b^6} = \dfrac{4}{3}a^{14-7}b^{6-6}$
   $$= \dfrac{4}{3}a^7 b^0$$
   $$= \dfrac{4}{3}a^7 \text{ or } \dfrac{4a^7}{3}$$

5. a. $6^{-2} = \dfrac{1}{6^2} = \dfrac{1}{36}$

   b. $(-2)^{-6} = \dfrac{1}{(-2)^6} = \dfrac{1}{64}$

   c. $3x^{-5} = 3 \cdot \dfrac{1}{x^5} = \dfrac{3}{x^5}$

   d. $(5y)^{-1} = \dfrac{1}{(5y)^1} = \dfrac{1}{5y}$

   e. $\dfrac{k^4}{k^{11}} = k^{4-11} = k^{-7} = \dfrac{1}{k^7}$

   f. $\dfrac{5^3}{5^5} = 5^{3-5} = 5^{-2} = \dfrac{1}{5^2} = \dfrac{1}{25}$

   g. $5^{-1} + 2^{-2} = \dfrac{1}{5^1} + \dfrac{1}{2^2} = \dfrac{1}{5} + \dfrac{1}{4} = \dfrac{4}{20} + \dfrac{5}{20} = \dfrac{9}{20}$

   h. $\dfrac{1}{z^{-8}} = \dfrac{1}{\frac{1}{z^8}} = 1 \div \dfrac{1}{z^8} = 1 \cdot \dfrac{z^8}{1} = z^8$

6. a. $\dfrac{z^{-8}}{z^3} = z^{-8-3} = z^{-11} = \dfrac{1}{z^{11}}$

   b. $\dfrac{7t^3}{t^{-5}} = 7 \cdot t^{3-(-5)} = 7t^8$

   c. $\dfrac{3^{-2}}{3^{-4}} = 3^{-2-(-4)} = 3^{-2+4} = 3^2 = 9$

   d. $\dfrac{5a^{-5}b^3}{15a^2 b^{-4}} = \dfrac{a^{-5-2}b^{3-(-4)}}{3} = \dfrac{a^{-7}b^7}{3} = \dfrac{b^7}{3a^7}$

   e. $\dfrac{(2x^{-5})(x^6)}{x^5} = \dfrac{2x^{-5+6}}{x^5}$
   $$= \dfrac{2x^1}{x^5}$$
   $$= 2x^{1-5}$$
   $$= 2x^{-4}$$
   $$= \dfrac{2}{x^4}$$

7. a. $x^{3a} \cdot x^4 = x^{3a+4}$

   b. $\dfrac{x^{3t-2}}{x^{t-3}} = x^{(3t-2)-(t-3)} = x^{3t-2-t+3} = x^{2t+1}$

8. a. Move the decimal point until the number is between 1 and 10. The decimal point is moved 4 places and the original number is 10 or greater, so the count is positive 4.

$$65,000 = 6.5 \times 10^4$$

b. Move the decimal point until the number is between 1 and 10. The decimal point is moved 5 places and the original number is less than 1, so the count is -5.

$$0.000038 = 3.8 \times 10^{-5}$$

9. a. Since the exponent is positive, move the decimal point 5 places to the right.

$$6.2 \times 10^5 = 620,000$$

b. Since the exponent is negative, more the decimal point 2 places to the left.

$$3.109 \times 10^{-2} = 0.03109$$

Graphing Calculator Explorations

1. $(3 \times 10^{11})(2 \times 10^{32}) = 6 \times 10^{43}$

2. $(6 \times 10^{14}) \div (3 \times 10^9) = 2 \times 10^5$

3. $(5.2 \times 10^{23})(7.3 \times 10^4) = 3.796 \times 10^{28}$

4. $(4.38 \times 10^{41}) \div (3 \times 10^{17}) = 1.46 \times 10^{24}$

Vocabulary and Readiness Check

1. $9x^5$; base x

2. yz^5; base z

3. -3^5; base 3

4. $(-3)^5$; base -3

5. $(y^7)^5$; base y^7

6. $9 \cdot 2^5$; base 2

7. $5x^{-1}y^{-2} = \dfrac{5}{xy^2}$

8. $7xy^{-4} = \dfrac{7x}{y^4}$

9. $a^2 b^{-1} c^{-5} = \dfrac{a^2}{bc^5}$

10. $a^{-4} b^2 c^{-6} = \dfrac{b^2}{a^4 c^6}$

11. $\dfrac{y^{-2}}{x^{-4}} = \dfrac{x^4}{y^2}$

12. $\dfrac{x^{-7}}{z^{-3}} = \dfrac{z^3}{x^7}$

Exercise Set 5.1

1. $4^2 \cdot 4^3 = 4^{2+3} = 4^5$

3. $x^5 \cdot x^3 = x^{5+3} = x^8$

5. $m \cdot m^7 \cdot m^6 = m^{1+7+6} = m^{14}$

7. $(4xy)(-5x) = -20x^{1+1}y = -20x^2 y$

9. $(-4x^3 p^2)(4y^3 x^3) = -16x^{3+3}y^3 p^2$
$$= -16x^6 y^3 p^2$$

11. $-8^0 = -(8^0) = -1$

13. $(4x+5)^0 = 1$

15. $-x^0 = -(x^0) = -(1) = -1$

17. $4x^0 + 5 = 4(1) + 5 = 4 + 5 = 9$

19. $\dfrac{a^5}{a^2} = a^{5-2} = a^3$

21. $-\dfrac{26z^{11}}{2z^7} = -13z^{11-7} = -13z^4$

23. $\dfrac{x^9 y^6}{x^8 y^6} = x^{9-8} y^{6-6} = x^1 y^0 = x$

25. $\dfrac{12x^4 y^7}{9xy^5} = \dfrac{4x^{4-1}y^{7-5}}{3} = \dfrac{4}{3}x^3 y^2$

27. $\dfrac{-36a^5 b^7 c^{10}}{6ab^3 c^4} = -6a^{5-1}b^{7-3}c^{10-4} = -6a^4 b^4 c^6$

29. $4^{-2} = \dfrac{1}{4^2} = \dfrac{1}{16}$

31. $(-3)^{-3} = \dfrac{1}{(-3)^3} = \dfrac{1}{-27} = -\dfrac{1}{27}$

33. $\dfrac{x^7}{x^{15}} = x^{7-15} = x^{-8} = \dfrac{1}{x^8}$

35. $5a^{-4} = \dfrac{5}{a^4}$

37. $\dfrac{x^{-7}}{y^{-2}} = \dfrac{y^2}{x^7}$

39. $\dfrac{x^{-2}}{x^5} = x^{-2-5} = x^{-7} = \dfrac{1}{x^7}$

41. $\dfrac{8r^4}{2r^{-4}} = 4r^{4-(-4)} = 4r^8$

43. $\dfrac{x^{-9}x^4}{x^{-5}} = \dfrac{x^{-9+4}}{x^{-5}} = \dfrac{x^{-5}}{x^{-5}} = x^{-5-(-5)} = x^0 = 1$

45. $\dfrac{2a^{-6}b^2}{18ab^{-5}} = \dfrac{a^{-6-1}b^{2-(-5)}}{9} = \dfrac{a^{-7}b^7}{9} = \dfrac{b^7}{9a^7}$

47. $\dfrac{(24x^8)(x)}{20x^{-7}} = \dfrac{6x^{8+1}}{5x^{-7}} = \dfrac{6x^{9-(-7)}}{5} = \dfrac{6x^{16}}{5}$

49. $-7x^3 \cdot 20x^9 = -7 \cdot 20x^{3+9} = -140x^{12}$

51. $x^7 \cdot x^8 \cdot x = x^{7+8+1} = x^{16}$

53. $2x^3 \cdot 5x^7 = 2 \cdot 5x^{3+7} = 10x^{10}$

55. $(5x)^0 + 5x^0 = 1 + 5 \cdot 1 = 1 + 5 = 6$

57. $\dfrac{z^{12}}{z^{15}} = z^{12-15} = z^{-3} = \dfrac{1}{z^3}$

59. $3^0 - 3t^0 = 1 - 3 \cdot 1 = 1 - 3 = -2$

61. $\dfrac{y^{-3}}{y^{-7}} = y^{-3-(-7)} = y^4$

63. $4^{-1} + 3^{-2} = \dfrac{1}{4^1} + \dfrac{1}{3^2}$
$= \dfrac{1}{4} + \dfrac{1}{9}$
$= \dfrac{9}{36} + \dfrac{4}{36}$
$= \dfrac{13}{36}$

65. $3x^{-1} = \dfrac{3}{x^1} = \dfrac{3}{x}$

67. $\dfrac{r^4}{r^{-4}} = r^{4-(-4)} = r^8$

69. $\dfrac{x^{-7}y^{-2}}{x^2 y^2} = x^{-7-2}y^{-2-2} = x^{-9}y^{-4} = \dfrac{1}{x^9 y^4}$

71. $(-4x^2 y)(3x^4)(-2xy^5)$
$= -4(3)(-2)x^2 \cdot x^4 \cdot x \cdot y \cdot y^5$
$= 24x^{2+4+1} \cdot y^{1+5}$
$= 24x^7 y^6$

73. $2^{-4} \cdot x = \dfrac{x}{2^4} = \dfrac{x}{16}$

75. $\dfrac{5^{17}}{5^{13}} = 5^{17-13} = 5^4 = 625$

77. $\dfrac{8^{-7}}{8^{-6}} = 8^{-7-(-6)} = 8^{-7+6} = 8^{-1} = \dfrac{1}{8}$

79. $\dfrac{9^{-5}a^4}{9^{-3}a^{-1}} = 9^{-5-(-3)}a^{4-(-1)}$
$= 9^{-5+3}a^{4+1}$
$= 9^{-2}a^5$
$= \dfrac{a^5}{9^2}$
$= \dfrac{a^5}{81}$

81. $\dfrac{14x^{-2}yz^{-4}}{2xyz} = \dfrac{14}{2} \cdot x^{-2-1}y^{1-1}z^{-4-1}$

$\qquad\qquad = 7x^{-3}y^{0}z^{-5}$

$\qquad\qquad = \dfrac{7}{x^{3}z^{5}}$

83. $x^{5} \cdot x^{7a} = x^{5+7a}$ or x^{7a+5}

85. $\dfrac{x^{3t-1}}{x^{t}} = x^{3t-1-t} = x^{2t-1}$

87. $x^{4a} \cdot x^{7} = x^{4a+7}$

89. $\dfrac{z^{6x}}{z^{7}} = z^{6x-7}$

91. $\dfrac{x^{3t} \cdot x^{4t-1}}{x^{t}} = \dfrac{x^{3t+(4t-1)}}{x^{t}} = x^{7t-1-t} = x^{6t-1}$

93. $31,250,000 = 3.125 \times 10^{7}$

95. $0.016 = 1.6 \times 10^{-2}$

97. $67,413 = 6.7413 \times 10^{4}$

99. $0.0125 = 1.25 \times 10^{-2}$

101. $0.000053 = 5.3 \times 10^{-5}$

103. $344,992,000,000 = 3.44992 \times 10^{11}$

105. $3,500,00 = 3.5 \times 10^{6}$

107. $124,000,000,000 = 1.24 \times 10^{11}$

109. $0.001 = 1.0 \times 10^{-3}$

111. $3.6 \times 10^{-9} = 0.0000000036$

113. $9.3 \times 10^{7} = 93,000,000$

115. $1.278 \times 10^{6} = 1,278,000$

117. $7.35 \times 10^{12} = 7,350,000,000,000$

119. $4.03 \times 10^{-7} = 0.000000403$

121. $3.0 \times 10^{8} = 300,000,000$

123. $1.53 \times 10^{11} = \$153,000,000,000$

125. $(5 \cdot 2)^{2} = (10)^{2} = 100$

127. $\left(\dfrac{3}{4}\right)^{3} = \left(\dfrac{3}{4}\right)\left(\dfrac{3}{4}\right)\left(\dfrac{3}{4}\right) = \dfrac{3 \cdot 3 \cdot 3}{4 \cdot 4 \cdot 4} = \dfrac{27}{64}$

129. $(2^{3})^{2} = 8^{2} = 64$

131. Answers may vary

133. Answers may vary

135. a. $x^{a} \cdot x^{a} = x^{a+a} = x^{2a}$

    b. $x^{a} + x^{a} = 2x^{a}$

    c. $\dfrac{x^{a}}{x^{b}} = x^{a-b}$

    d. $x^{a} \cdot x^{b} = x^{a+b}$

    e. $x^{a} + x^{b} = x^{a} + x^{b}$

137. 7^{13}

139. 7^{-11}

Section 5.2

Practice Exercises

1. a. $(z^{3})^{5} = z^{3 \cdot 5} = z^{15}$

    b. $(5^{2})^{2} = 5^{2 \cdot 2} = 5^{4} = 625$

    c. $(3^{-1})^{3} = 3^{-1 \cdot 3} = 3^{-3} = \dfrac{1}{3^{3}} = \dfrac{1}{27}$

    d. $(x^{-4})^{-6} = x^{-4(-6)} = x^{24}$

2. a. $(2x^{3})^{5} = 2^{5} \cdot (x^{3})^{5} = 2^{5} \cdot x^{3 \cdot 5} = 32x^{15}$

    b. $\left(\dfrac{3}{5}\right)^{2} = \dfrac{3^{2}}{5^{2}} = \dfrac{9}{25}$

c. $\left(\dfrac{2a^5}{b^7}\right)^4 = \dfrac{(2a^5)^4}{(b^7)^4} = \dfrac{2^4 \cdot (a^5)^4}{(b^7)^4} = \dfrac{16a^{20}}{b^{28}}$

d. $\left(\dfrac{3^{-2}}{x}\right)^{-1} = \dfrac{(3^{-2})^{-1}}{x^{-1}} = \dfrac{3^2}{x^{-1}} = 9x$

e. $(a^{-2}b^{-5}c^4)^{-2} = (a^{-2})^{-2} \cdot (b^{-5})^{-2} \cdot (c^4)^{-2}$
$\qquad = a^4 b^{10} c^{-8}$
$\qquad = \dfrac{a^4 b^{10}}{c^8}$

3. a. $(3ab^{-5})^{-3} = 3^{-3} a^{-3} (b^{-5})^{-3}$
$\qquad = 3^{-3} a^{-3} b^{15}$
$\qquad = \dfrac{b^{15}}{3^3 a^3}$
$\qquad = \dfrac{b^{15}}{27a^3}$

b. $\left(\dfrac{y^{-7}}{y^{-4}}\right)^{-5} = \dfrac{(y^{-7})^{-5}}{(y^{-4})^{-5}}$
$\qquad = \dfrac{y^{35}}{y^{20}}$
$\qquad = y^{35-20}$
$\qquad = y^{15}$

c. $\left(\dfrac{3}{8}\right)^{-2} = \dfrac{3^{-2}}{8^{-2}} = \dfrac{8^2}{3^2} = \dfrac{64}{9}$

d. $\dfrac{9^{-2} a^{-4} b^3}{a^2 b^{-5}} = 9^{-2}\left(\dfrac{a^{-4}}{a^2}\right)\left(\dfrac{b^3}{b^{-5}}\right)$
$\qquad = 9^{-2} a^{-4-2} b^{3-(-5)}$
$\qquad = 9^{-2} a^{-6} b^8$
$\qquad = \dfrac{b^8}{9^2 a^6}$
$\qquad = \dfrac{b^8}{81a^6}$

4. a. $\left(\dfrac{5a^4 b}{a^{-8} c}\right)^{-3} = \left(\dfrac{5a^{12} b}{c}\right)^{-3}$
$\qquad = \dfrac{5^{-3} a^{-36} b^{-3}}{c^{-3}}$
$\qquad = \dfrac{c^3}{5^3 a^{36} b^3}$
$\qquad = \dfrac{c^3}{125 a^{36} b^3}$

b. $\left(\dfrac{2x^4}{5y^{-2}}\right)^3 \left(\dfrac{x^{-4}}{10y^{-2}}\right)^{-1} = \dfrac{8x^{12}}{125y^{-6}} \cdot \dfrac{x^4}{10^{-1} y^2}$
$\qquad = \dfrac{8 \cdot 10 \cdot x^{12} x^4 y^6}{125 y^2}$
$\qquad = \dfrac{16 x^{16} y^4}{25}$

5. a. $x^{-2a} (3x^a)^3 = x^{-2a} \cdot 3^3 \cdot x^{a \cdot 3}$
$\qquad = 27 x^{-2a+3a}$
$\qquad = 27 x^a$

b. $\dfrac{(y^{3b})^3}{y^{4b-3}} = \dfrac{y^{9b}}{y^{4b-3}}$
$\qquad = y^{9b-(4b-3)}$
$\qquad = y^{9b-4b+3}$
$\qquad = y^{5b+3}$

6. a. $(3.4 \times 10^4)(5 \times 10^{-7})$
$\qquad = 3.4 \times 5 \times 10^4 \times 10^{-7}$
$\qquad = 17.0 \times 10^{-3}$
$\qquad = (1.7 \times 10^1) \times 10^{-3}$
$\qquad = 1.7 \times 10^{-2}$

b. $\dfrac{5.6 \times 10^8}{4 \times 10^{-2}} = \left(\dfrac{5.6}{4}\right)\left(\dfrac{10^8}{10^{-2}}\right)$
$\qquad = 1.4 \times 10^{8-(-2)}$
$\qquad = 1.4 \times 10^{10}$

7.
$$\frac{2400 \times 0.0000014}{800}$$
$$= \frac{(2.4 \times 10^3)(1.4 \times 10^{-6})}{8 \times 10^2}$$
$$= \frac{2.4(1.4)}{8} \cdot \frac{10^3 \cdot 10^{-6}}{10^2}$$
$$= 0.42 \times 10^{-5}$$
$$= (4.2 \times 10^{-1}) \times 10^{-5}$$
$$= 4.2 \times 10^{-6}$$

Vocabulary and Readiness Check

1. $(x^4)^5 = x^{4(5)} = x^{20}$

2. $(5^6)^2 = 5^{6(2)} = 5^{12}$

3. $x^4 \cdot x^5 = x^{4+5} = x^9$

4. $x^7 \cdot x^8 = x^{7+8} = x^{15}$

5. $(y^6)^7 = y^{6(7)} = y^{42}$

6. $(x^3)^4 = x^{3(4)} = x^{12}$

7. $(z^4)^9 = z^{4(9)} = z^{36}$

8. $(z^3)^7 = z^{3(7)} = z^{21}$

9. $(z^{-6})^{-3} = z^{-6(-3)} = z^{18}$

10. $(y^{-4})^{-2} = y^{-4(-2)} = y^8$

Exercise Set 5.2

1. $(3^{-1})^2 = 3^{-1(2)} = 3^{-2} = \frac{1}{3^2} = \frac{1}{9}$

3. $(x^4)^{-9} = x^{4(-9)} = x^{-36} = \frac{1}{x^{36}}$

5. $(y)^{-5} = y^{-5} = \frac{1}{y^5}$

7. $(3x^2y^3)^2 = 3^2(x^2)^2(y^3)^2$
$$= 9x^{2(2)}y^{3(2)}$$
$$= 9x^4y^6$$

9. $\left(\frac{2x^5}{y^{-3}}\right)^4 = \frac{2^4(x^5)^4}{(y^{-3})^4}$
$$= \frac{16x^{5(4)}}{y^{-3(4)}}$$
$$= \frac{16x^{20}}{y^{-12}}$$
$$= 16x^{20}y^{12}$$

11. $(a^2bc^{-3})^{-6} = (a^2)^{-6}b^{-6}(c^{-3})^{-6}$
$$= a^{2(-6)}b^{-6}c^{-3(-6)}$$
$$= a^{-12}b^{-6}c^{18}$$
$$= \frac{c^{18}}{a^{12}b^6}$$

13. $\left(\frac{x^7y^{-3}}{z^{-4}}\right)^{-5} = \frac{(x^7)^{-5}(y^{-3})^{-5}}{(z^{-4})^{-5}}$
$$= \frac{x^{-35}y^{15}}{z^{20}}$$
$$= \frac{y^{15}}{x^{35}z^{20}}$$

15. $(5^{-1})^3 = 5^{-1(3)} = 5^{-3} = \frac{1}{5^3} = \frac{1}{125}$

17. $\left(\frac{x^{-9}}{x^{-4}}\right)^{-3} = \frac{(x^{-9})^{-3}}{(x^{-4})^{-3}} = \frac{x^{27}}{x^{12}} = x^{27-12} = x^{15}$

19. $\left(\frac{5x^7y^4}{10x^3y^{-2}}\right)^{-3} = \left(\frac{x^4y^6}{2}\right)^{-3}$
$$= \frac{(x^4)^{-3}(y^6)^{-3}}{(2)^{-3}}$$
$$= (2)^3x^{-12}y^{-18}$$
$$= \frac{8}{x^{12}y^{18}}$$

21. $\frac{8^{-2}x^{-3}y^{11}}{x^2y^{-5}} = \frac{x^{-3-2}y^{11-(-5)}}{8^2} = \frac{x^{-5}y^{16}}{64} = \frac{y^{16}}{64x^5}$

23. $\left(\frac{4p^6}{p^9}\right)^3 = \left(\frac{4}{p^3}\right)^3 = \frac{4^3}{(p^3)^3} = \frac{64}{p^9}$

25. $(-xy^0x^2a^3)^{-3} = (-x^3a^3)^{-3}$
$$= (-1)^3(x^3)^{-3}(a^3)^{-3}$$
$$= -1x^{-9}a^{-9}$$
$$= -\frac{1}{x^9a^9}$$

27. $\left(\dfrac{x^{-1}y^{-2}}{5^{-3}}\right)^{-5} = \dfrac{(x^{-1})^{-5}(y^{-2})^{-5}}{(5^{-3})^{-5}} = \dfrac{x^5y^{10}}{5^{15}}$

29. $(x^7)^{-9} = x^{7(-9)} = x^{-63} = \dfrac{1}{x^{63}}$

31. $\left(\dfrac{7}{8}\right)^3 = \dfrac{7^3}{8^3} = \dfrac{343}{512}$

33. $(4x^2)^2 = 4^2(x^2)^2 = 16x^4$

35. $(-2^{-2}y)^3 = (-2^{-2})^3y^3$
$$= -2^{-6}y^3$$
$$= -\frac{y^3}{2^6}$$
$$= -\frac{y^3}{64}$$

37. $\left(\dfrac{4^{-4}}{y^3x}\right)^{-2} = \dfrac{(4^{-4})^{-2}}{(y^3)^{-2}x^{-2}} = \dfrac{4^8}{y^{-6}x^{-2}} = 4^8x^2y^6$

39. $\left(\dfrac{1}{4}\right)^{-3} = \dfrac{1^{-3}}{4^{-3}} = \dfrac{4^3}{1^3} = \dfrac{64}{1} = 64$

41. $\left(\dfrac{3x^5}{6x^4}\right)^4 = \left(\dfrac{x^{5-4}}{2}\right)^4 = \left(\dfrac{x}{2}\right)^4 = \dfrac{x^4}{2^4} = \dfrac{x^4}{16}$

43. $\dfrac{(y^3)^{-4}}{y^3} = \dfrac{y^{-12}}{y^3} = y^{-12-3} = y^{-15} = \dfrac{1}{y^{15}}$

45. $\left(\dfrac{2x^{-3}}{y^{-1}}\right)^{-3} = \dfrac{2^{-3}(x^{-3})^{-3}}{(y^{-1})^{-3}} = \dfrac{x^9}{2^3y^3} = \dfrac{x^9}{8y^3}$

47. $\dfrac{3^{-2}a^{-5}b^6}{4^{-2}a^{-7}b^{-3}} = \dfrac{4^2a^{-5-(-7)}b^{6-(-3)}}{3^2} = \dfrac{16a^2b^9}{9}$

49. $(4x^6y^5)^{-2}(6x^4y^3) = 4^{-2}(x^6)^{-2}(y^5)^{-2}\cdot 6x^4y^3$
$$= \frac{1}{4^2}x^{-12}y^{-10}\cdot 6x^4y^3$$
$$= \frac{6}{16}x^{-12+4}y^{-10+3}$$
$$= \frac{3x^{-8}y^{-7}}{8}$$
$$= \frac{3}{8x^8y^7}$$

51. $x^6(x^6bc)^{-6} = x^6(x^6)^{-6}b^{-6}c^{-6}$
$$= \frac{x^6x^{-36}}{b^6c^6}$$
$$= \frac{x^{-30}}{b^6c^6}$$
$$= \frac{1}{x^{30}b^6c^6}$$

53. $\dfrac{2^{-3}x^2y^{-5}}{5^{-2}x^7y^{-1}} = \dfrac{5^2x^{2-7}y^{-5-(-1)}}{2^3}$
$$= \frac{25x^{-5}y^{-4}}{8}$$
$$= \frac{25}{8x^5y^4}$$

55. $\left(\dfrac{2x^2}{y^4}\right)^3\left(\dfrac{2x^5}{y}\right)^{-2} = \dfrac{2^3x^{2(3)}2^{-2}x^{5(-2)}}{y^{4(3)}y^{-2}}$
$$= \frac{8x^6x^{-10}}{2^2y^{12}y^{-2}}$$
$$= \frac{2x^{-4}}{y^{10}}$$
$$= \frac{2}{x^4y^{10}}$$

57. $(x^{3a+6})^3 = x^{(3a+6)\cdot 3} = x^{9a+18}$

59. $\dfrac{x^{4a}(x^{4a})^3}{x^{4a-2}} = \dfrac{x^{4a}\cdot x^{12a}}{x^{4a-2}}$
$$= \frac{x^{4a+12a}}{x^{4a-2}}$$
$$= x^{16a-(4a-2)}$$
$$= x^{12a+2}$$

61. $(b^{5x-2})^{2x} = b^{(5x-2)\cdot 2x} = b^{10x^2-4x}$

63. $\dfrac{(y^{2a})^8}{y^{a-3}} = \dfrac{y^{16a}}{y^{a-3}} = y^{16a-(a-3)} = y^{15a+3}$

65. $\left(\dfrac{2x^{3t}}{x^{2t-1}}\right)^4 = \dfrac{2^4 x^{3t(4)}}{x^{(2t-1)\cdot 4}}$

$= \dfrac{16x^{12t}}{x^{8t-4}}$

$= 16x^{12t-(8t-4)}$

$= 16x^{4t+4}$

67. $\dfrac{25x^{2a+1}y^{a-1}}{5x^{3a+1}y^{2a-3}} = \left(\dfrac{25}{5}\right)\left(\dfrac{x^{2a+1}}{x^{3a+1}}\right)\left(\dfrac{y^{a-1}}{y^{2a-3}}\right)$

$= 5x^{2a+1-(3a+1)}y^{a-1-(2a-3)}$

$= 5x^{2a+1-3a-1}y^{a-1-2a+3}$

$= 5x^{-a}y^{-a+2}$

69. $(5\times 10^{11})(2.9\times 10^{-3}) = 5\times 2.9\times 10^{11+(-3)}$

$= 14.5\times 10^8$

$= 1.45\times 10^1 \times 10^8$

$= 1.45\times 10^9$

71. $(2\times 10^5)^3 = 2^3 \times 10^{5(3)} = 8\times 10^{15}$

73. $\dfrac{3.6\times 10^{-4}}{9\times 10^2} = \dfrac{3.6}{9}\times 10^{-4-2}$

$= 0.4\times 10^{-6}$

$= 4\times 10^{-1}\times 10^{-6}$

$= 4\times 10^{-7}$

75. $\dfrac{0.0069}{0.023} = \dfrac{6.9\times 10^{-3}}{2.3\times 10^{-2}}$

$= \dfrac{6.9}{2.3}\times 10^{-3-(-2)}$

$= 3\times 10^{-1}$

77. $\dfrac{18,200\times 100}{91,000} = \dfrac{1.82\times 10^4 \times 1\times 10^2}{9.1\times 10^4}$

$= \dfrac{1.82\times 10^6}{9.1\times 10^4}$

$= 0.2\times 10^{6-4}$

$= 2\times 10^{-1}\times 10^2$

$= 2\times 10^{-1+2}$

$= 2\times 10^1$

79. $\dfrac{6000\times 0.006}{0.009\times 400} = \dfrac{6\times 10^3 \times 6\times 10^{-3}}{9\times 10^{-3}\times 4\times 10^2}$

$= \dfrac{36\times 10^0}{36\times 10^{-1}}$

$= 1\times 10^{0-(-1)}$

$= 1\times 10^1$

81. $\dfrac{0.00064\times 2000}{16,000} = \dfrac{6.4\times 10^{-4}\times 2\times 10^3}{1.6\times 10^4}$

$= \dfrac{12.8\times 10^{-1}}{1.6\times 10^4}$

$= 8\times 10^{-1-4}$

$= 8\times 10^{-5}$

83. $\dfrac{66,000\times 0.001}{0.002\times 0.003} = \dfrac{6.6\times 10^4 \times 1\times 10^{-3}}{2\times 10^{-3}\times 3\times 10^{-3}}$

$= \dfrac{6.6\times 10^1}{6\times 10^{-6}}$

$= 1.1\times 10^{1-(-6)}$

$= 1.1\times 10^7$

85. $\dfrac{9.24\times 10^{15}}{(2.2\times 10^{-2})(1.2\times 10^{-5})}$

$= \dfrac{9.24}{(2.2)(1.2)}\cdot 10^{15-(-2)-(-5)}$

$= 3.5\times 10^{22}$

87. $200,000\times 10^{-8} = (2\times 10^5)\times 10^{-8}$

$= 2\times 10^{-3}$ second

89. $(3.8\times 10^{-6})(1.64\times 10^{-5}) = 6.232\times 10^{-11}$

The volume is 6.232×10^{-11} cubic meter.

91. $12m - 14 - 15m - 1 = -3m - 15$

93. $-9y - (5 - 6y) = -9y - 5 + 6y = -3y - 5$

95. $5(x - 3) - 4(2x - 5) = 5x - 15 - 8x + 20$
$$= -3x + 5$$

97. $\left(\dfrac{3x^{-1}}{y^{-3}}\right)\left(5x^{-7}\right) = \dfrac{3 \cdot 5x^{-1+(-7)}}{y^{-3}}$

$$= \dfrac{15x^{-8}}{y^{-3}}$$

$$= \dfrac{15y^3}{x^8}$$

The area is $\dfrac{15y^3}{x^8}$ square feet.

99.
$$D = \dfrac{M}{V}$$

$$3.12 \times 10^{-2} = \dfrac{M}{4.269 \times 10^{14}}$$

$$(3.12 \times 10^{-2})(4.269 \times 10^{14}) = M$$

$$3.12 \times 4.269 \times 10^{-2+14} = M$$

$$13.31928 \times 10^{12} = M$$

$$1.331928 \times 10^1 \times 10^{12} = M$$

$$1.331928 \times 10^{13} = M$$

The mass is 1.331928×10^{13} tons.

101. $a^{-2} = \dfrac{1}{a^2}$

Since 1 and a^2 are both positive, their quotient cannot be negative. Therefore, no, there is no such a.

103. $\dfrac{3.016 \times 10^8}{3.536 \times 10^6} = \dfrac{3.016}{3.536} \times 10^{8-6}$

$$= 0.85 \times 10^2$$

$$= 85$$

The population density for the United States in 2007 was 85 people per square mile.

105. $\dfrac{2.82 \times 10^9}{4.44 \times 10^8} = \dfrac{2.82}{4.44} \times 10^{9-8}$

$$= 0.64 \times 10^1$$

$$= 6.4$$

The Tokyo subway's volume is 6.4 times greater than that of Toronto's subway.

107. $\dfrac{4.87 \times 10^6}{15.38 \times 10^6} = \dfrac{4.87}{15.38} \times 10^{6-6}$

$$= 0.317 \times 10^0$$

$$= 31.7\%$$

Therefore, 31.7% of the residents of Beijing could speak a foreign language.

Section 5.3

Practice Exercises

1. a. $4x^5$: The exponent on x is 5, so the degree of the term is 5.

b. $-4^3 y^3$: The exponent on y is 3, so the degree of the term is 3.

c. The degree of z, or z^1, is 1.

d. $65a^3 b^7 c$: The degree is the sum of the exponents on the variables, or $3 + 7 + 1 = 11$.

e. The degree of 36, which can be written as $36x^0$, is 0.

Polynomial	Degree	Classification
2. a. $3x^4 + 2x^2 - 3$	4	trinomial
b. $9abc^3$	5	monomial
c. $8x^5 + 5x^3$	5	binomial

3.

Term	Degree
$2x^3 y$	4
$-3x^3 y^2$	5
$-9y^5$	5
9.6	0

The largest degree of any term is 5, so the degree of this polynomial is 5.

4. a. Substitute -1 for x and simplify.

$$P(x) = -5x^2 + 2x - 8$$
$$P(-1) = -5(-1)^2 + 2(-1) - 8$$
$$= -5 - 2 - 8$$
$$= -15$$

b. Substitute 3 for x and simplify.

$$P(x) = -5x^2 + 2x - 8$$
$$P(3) = -5(3)^2 + 2(3) - 8$$
$$= -45 + 6 - 8$$
$$= -47$$

5. $P(t) = -16t^2 + 290$

Let $t = 0$: $P(0) = -16(0)^2 + 290 = 290$

Let $t = 2$: $P(2) = -16(2)^2 + 290 = 226$

The height of the object at $t = 0$ second is 290 feet and the height at $t = 2$ seconds is 226 feet.

6. a. $8x^4 - 5x^4 - 5x = (8-5)x^4 - 5x$
$$= 3x^4 - 5x$$

b. $4ab - 5b + 3ab + 2b$
$$= 4ab + 3ab - 5b + 2b$$
$$= (4+3)ab + (-5+2)b$$
$$= 7ab - 3b$$

7. a. $(3a^4b - 5ab^2 + 7) + (9ab^2 - 12)$
$$= 3a^4b - 5ab^2 + 7 + 9ab^2 - 12$$
$$= 3a^4b - 5ab^2 + 9ab^2 + 7 - 12$$
$$= 3a^4b + 4ab^2 - 5$$

b. $(2x^5 - 3y + x - 6) + (4y - 2x - 3)$
$$= 2x^5 - 3y + x - 6 + 4y - 2x - 3$$
$$= 2x^5 - 3y + 4y + x - 2x - 6 - 3$$
$$= 2x^5 + y - x - 9$$

8. $(5x^3 - 3x^2 - 9x - 8) + (x^3 + 9x^2 + 2x)$
$$= 5x^3 + x^3 - 3x^2 + 9x^2 - 9x + 2x - 8$$
$$= 6x^3 + 6x^2 - 7x - 8$$

9. $(13a^4 - 7a^3 - 9) - (-2a^4 + 8a^3 - 12)$
$$= 13a^4 - 7a^3 - 9 + 2a^4 - 8a^3 + 12$$
$$= 13a^4 + 2a^4 - 7a^3 - 8a^3 - 9 + 12$$
$$= 15a^4 - 15a^3 + 3$$

10. $(11x^2y^2 - 7xy^2) - (5x^2y^2 - 3xy^2 + 5y^3)$
$$= 11x^2y^2 - 7xy^2 - 5x^2y^2 + 3xy^2 - 5y^3$$
$$= 6x^2y^2 - 4xy^2 - 5y^3$$

11. The degree of $f(x)$ is 3, which means that its graph has the shape of **C**.

Graphing Calculator Explorations

1. $(2x^2 + 7x + 6) + (x^3 - 6x^2 - 14)$
$$= x^3 - 4x^2 + 7x - 8$$

2. $(-14x^3 - x + 2) + (-x^3 + 3x^2 + 4x)$
$$= -15x^3 + 3x^2 + 3x + 2$$

3. $(1.8x^2 - 6.8x - 1.7) - (3.9x^2 - 3.6x)$
$$= -2.1x^2 - 3.2x - 1.7$$

4. $(-4.8x^2 + 12.5x - 7.8) - (3.1x^2 - 7.8x)$
$$= -7.9x^2 + 20.3x - 7.8$$

5. $(1.29x - 5.68) + (7.69x^2 - 2.55x + 10.98)$
$$= 7.69x^2 - 1.26x + 5.3$$

6. $(-0.98x^2 - 1.56x + 5.57) + (4.36x - 3.71)$
$= -0.98x^2 + 2.8x + 1.86$

Vocabulary and Readiness Check

1. The numerical factor of a term is the <u>coefficient</u>.

2. A <u>polynomial</u> is a finite sum of terms in which all variables are raised to nonnegative integer powers and no variables appear in any denominator.

3. A <u>binomial</u> is a polynomial with 2 terms.

4. A <u>monomial</u> is a polynomial with 1 term.

5. A <u>trinomial</u> is a polynomial with 3 terms.

6. The degree of a term is the sum of the exponents on the <u>variables</u> in the term.

7. The <u>degree</u> of a polynomial is the largest degree of all its terms.

8. <u>Like</u> terms contain the same variables raised to the same powers.

9. $5x + x = 6x$

10. $5x - x = 4x$

11. $y + y = 2y$

12. $z^2 + z^2 = 2z^2$

13. $7xy^2 - y^2 = 7xy^2 - y^2$

14. $x^3 - 9x^3 = -8x^3$

Exercise Set 5.3

1. 4 has degree 0.

3. $5x^2$ has degree 2.

5. $-3xy^2$ has degree $1 + 2 = 3$.

7. $-8^7 y^3$ has degree 3 (note: the degree on the *variable* is 3).

9. $3.78ab^3c^5$ has degree $1 + 3 + 5 = 9$.

11. $6x + 0.3$ has degree 1 and is a binomial.

13. $3x^2 - 2x + 5$ has degree 2 and is a trinomial.

15. $-3^4 xy^2$ has degree $1 + 2 = 3$ and is a monomial.

17.

Term	Degree
$x^2 y$	3
$-4xy^2$	3
$5x$	1
y^4	4

19. $P(x) = x^2 + x + 1$
$P(7) = 7^2 + 7 + 1 = 49 + 7 + 1 = 57$

21. $Q(x) = 5x^2 - 1$
$Q(-10) = 5(-10)^2 - 1$
$\qquad = 5(100) - 1$
$\qquad = 500 - 1$
$\qquad = 499$

23. $Q(x) = 5x^2 - 1$
$Q\left(\dfrac{1}{4}\right) = 5\left(\dfrac{1}{4}\right)^2 - 1$
$\qquad = 5\left(\dfrac{1}{16}\right) - 1$
$\qquad = \dfrac{5}{16} - \dfrac{16}{16}$
$\qquad = -\dfrac{11}{16}$

25. $P(t) = -16t^2 + 1125$
$P(2) = -16(2)^2 + 1125 = 1061$ feet

27. $P(t) = -16t^2 + 1125$
$P(6) = -16(6)^2 + 1125 = 549$ feet

29. $5y + y = 6y$

31. $4x + 7x - 3 = 11x - 3$

33. $4xy + 2x - 3xy - 1 = xy + 2x - 1$

35. $7x^2 - 2xy + 5y^2 - x^2 + xy + 11y^2$
$= 6x^2 - xy + 16y^2$

37. $(9y^2 - 8) + (9y^2 - 9) = 18y^2 - 17$

39. $\quad x^2 + xy - y^2$
$\quad \underline{2x^2 - 4xy + 7y^2}$
$\quad 3x^2 - 3xy + 6y^2$

41. $\quad x^2 - 6x + 3$
$\quad \underline{+ (2x + 5)}$
$\quad x^2 - 4x + 8$

43. $(9y^2 - 7y + 5) - (8y^2 - 7y + 2)$
$= 9y^2 - 7y + 5 - 8y^2 + 7y - 2$
$= y^2 + 3$

45. $(4x^2 + 2x) - (6x^2 - 3x)$
$= 4x^2 + 2x - 6x^2 + 3x$
$= -2x^2 + 5x$

47. $\quad 3x^2 - 4x + 8$
$\quad \underline{-5x^2 + 7}$
$\quad -2x^2 - 4x + 15$

49. $(5x - 11) + (-x - 2) = 5x - 11 - x - 2$
$ = 4x - 13$

51. $(7x^2 + x + 1) - (6x^2 + x - 1)$
$= 7x^2 + x + 1 - 6x^2 - x + 1$
$= x^2 + 2$

53. $(7x^3 - 4x + 8) + (5x^3 + 4x + 8x)$
$= 7x^3 - 4x + 8 + 5x^3 + 4x + 8x$
$= 12x^3 + 8x + 8$

55. $\quad 9x^3 - 2x^2 + 4x - 7$
$\quad \underline{-2x^3 + 6x^2 + 4x - 3}$
$\quad 7x^3 + 4x^2 + 8x - 10$

57. $(y^2 + 4yx + 7) + (-19y^2 + 7yx + 7)$
$= y^2 + 4yx + 7 - 19y^2 + 7yx + 7$
$= -18y^2 + 11yx + 14$

59. $(3x^3 - b + 2a - 6) + (-4x^3 + b + 6a - 6)$
$= 3x^3 - b + 2a - 6 - 4x^3 + b + 6a - 6$
$= -x^3 + 8a - 12$

61. $(4x^2 - 6x + 2) - (-x^2 + 3x + 5)$
$= 4x^2 - 6x + 2 + x^2 - 3x - 5$
$= 5x^2 - 9x - 3$

63. $(-3x + 8) + (-3x^2 + 3x - 5)$
$= -3x + 8 - 3x^2 + 3x - 5$
$= -3x^2 + 3$

65. $(-3 + 4x^2 + 7xy^2) + (2x^3 - x^2 + xy^2)$
$= -3 + 4x^2 + 7xy^2 + 2x^3 - x^2 + xy^2$
$= 2x^3 + 3x^2 + 8xy^2 - 3$

67. $\quad 6y^2 - 6y + 4$
$\quad \underline{y^2 + 6y - 7}$
$\quad 7y^2 - 3$

69. $\quad 3x^2 + 15x + 8$
$\quad \underline{2x^2 + 7x + 8}$
$\quad 5x^2 + 22x + 16$

71. $\quad \dfrac{1}{2}x^2 - \dfrac{1}{3}x^2y \phantom{- \dfrac{8}{3}x^2y^2} + 2y^3$
$\quad \underline{\dfrac{1}{4}x^2 \phantom{- \dfrac{1}{3}x^2y} - \dfrac{8}{3}x^2y^2 - \dfrac{1}{2}y^3}$
$\quad \dfrac{3}{4}x^2 - \dfrac{1}{3}x^2y - \dfrac{8}{3}x^2y^2 + \dfrac{3}{2}y^3$

73. $(5q^4 - 2q^2 - 3q) + (-6q^4 + 3q^2 + 5)$
$= 5q^4 - 2q^2 - 3q - 6q^4 + 3q^2 + 5$
$= -q^4 + q^2 - 3q + 5$

75.
$$7x^2 + 4x + 9$$
$$+\ 8x^2 + 7x - 8$$
$$\overline{15x^2 + 11x + 1}$$
$$-\qquad\ 3x + 7$$
$$\overline{15x^2 + 8x - 6}$$

77. $(4x^4 - 7x^2 + 3) + (2 - 3x^4)$
$$= 4x^4 - 7x^2 + 3 + 2 - 3x^4$$
$$= x^4 - 7x^2 + 5$$

79. $\left(\dfrac{2}{3}x^2 - \dfrac{1}{6}x + \dfrac{5}{6}\right) - \left(\dfrac{1}{3}x^2 + \dfrac{5}{6}x - \dfrac{1}{6}\right)$
$$= \dfrac{2}{3}x^2 - \dfrac{1}{6}x + \dfrac{5}{6} - \dfrac{1}{3}x^2 - \dfrac{5}{6}x + \dfrac{1}{6}$$
$$= \dfrac{1}{3}x^2 - x + 1$$

81. If $L = 5$, $W = 4$, and $H = 9$, then
$$2HL + 2LW + 2HW$$
$$= 2(9)(5) + 2(5)(4) + 2(9)(4)$$
$$= 90 + 40 + 72$$
$$= 202$$
The surface area is 202 square inches.

83. $P(t) = -16t^2 + 300t$

    a. $P(1) = -16(1)^2 + 300(1) = 284$ feet

    b. $P(2) = -16(2)^2 + 300(2) = 536$ feet

    c. $P(3) = -16(3)^2 + 300(3) = 756$ feet

    d. $P(4) = -16(4)^2 + 300(4) = 944$ feet

    e. Answers may vary

    f.
$$0 = -16t^2 + 300t$$
$$0 = -4t(4t - 75)$$
$$4t - 75 = 0$$
$$4t = 75$$
$$t = \dfrac{75}{4} = 18.75$$
       19 sec

85. $P(x) = 45x - 100,000$
$$P(4000) = 45(4000) - 100,000$$
$$= 80,000$$
The profit is $80,000.

87. $R(x) = 2x$
$$R(20,000) = 2(20,000)$$
$$= 40,000$$
The revenue is $40,000.

89. A: The degree of $f(x)$ is 2, so the graph has the shape of A or C. The coefficient of x^2 is a positive number, so the graph has the shape of A.

91. D: The degree of $g(x)$ is 3, so the graph has the shape of B or D. The coefficient of x^3 is a negative number, so the graph has the shape of D.

93. $5(3x - 2) = 15x - 10$

95. $-2(x^2 - 5x + 6) = -2x^2 + 10x - 12$

97. The opposite of $8x - 6$ is $-(8x - 6)$ or $-8x + 6$; a and c.

99. $(12x - 1.7) - (15x + 6.2)$
$$= 12x - 1.7 - 15x - 6.2$$
$$= -3x - 7.9$$

101. Answers may vary

103. Answers may vary

105. $(4x^{2a} - 3x^a + 0.5) - (x^{2a} - 5x^a - 0.2)$
$$= 4x^{2a} - 3x^a + 0.5 - x^{2a} + 5x^a + 0.2$$
$$= 3x^{2a} + 2x^a + 0.7$$

107. $(8x^{2y} - 7x^y + 3) + (-4x^{2y} + 9x^y - 14)$
$$= 8x^{2y} - 7x^y + 3 - 4x^{2y} + 9x^y - 14$$
$$= 4x^{2y} + 2x^y - 11$$

109. $P = 2l + 2w$
$$= 2(3x^2 - x + 2y) + 2(x + 5y)$$
$$= 6x^2 - 2x + 4y + 2x + 10y$$
$$= 6x^2 + 14y$$
The perimeter is $P = (6x^2 + 14y)$ units.

111. $P(x) + Q(x) = (3x + 3) + (4x^2 - 6x + 3)$
$$= 3x + 3 + 4x^2 - 6x + 3$$
$$= 4x^2 - 3x + 6$$

113. $Q(x) - R(x) = (4x^2 - 6x + 3) - (5x^2 - 7)$
$$= 4x^2 - 6x + 3 - 5x^2 + 7$$
$$= -x^2 - 6x + 10$$

115. $2[Q(x)] - R(x)$
$$= 2(4x^2 - 6x + 3) - (5x^2 - 7)$$
$$= 8x^2 - 12x + 6 - 5x^2 + 7$$
$$= 3x^2 - 12x + 13$$

117. $3[R(x)] + 4[P(x)] = 3(5x^2 - 7) + 4(3x + 3)$
$$= 15x^2 - 21 + 12x + 12$$
$$= 15x^2 + 12x - 9$$

119. $P(x) = 2x - 3$

    a. $P(a) = 2a - 3$

    b. $P(-x) = 2(-x) - 3 = -2x - 3$

    c. $P(x + h) = 2(x + h) - 3 = 2x + 2h - 3$

121. $P(x) = 4x$

    a. $P(a) = 4a$

    b. $P(-x) = 4(-x) = -4x$

    c. $P(x + h) = 4(x + h) = 4x + 4h$

123. $P(x) = 4x - 1$

    a. $P(a) = 4a - 1$

    b. $P(-x) = 4(-x) - 1 = -4x - 1$

    c. $P(x + h) = 4(x + h) - 1 = 4x + 4h - 1$

125. $f(x) = 0.07x^2 - 0.8x + 3.6$

    a. Jan 2004 means that $x = 1$.
$$f(1) = 0.07(1)^2 - 0.8(1) + 3.6$$
$$= 2.9 \text{ million}$$

    b. Oct 2006 means that $x = 34$.
$$f(34) = 0.07(34)^2 - 0.8(34) + 3.6$$
$$= 57.3 \text{ million}$$

    c. May 2009 means that $x = 65$.
$$f(65) = 0.07(65)^2 - 0.8(65) + 3.6$$
$$= 247.4 \text{ million}$$

    d. Answers may vary

127. $f(x) = -0.39x^2 + 2.49x + 38.7$

    a. 2003 means that $x = 4$.
$$f(4) = -0.39(4)^2 + 2.49(4) + 38.7$$
$$= 42.4 \text{ million}$$

    b. 2008 means that $x = 9$.
$$f(9) = -0.39(9)^2 + 2.49(9) + 38.7$$
$$= 29.5 \text{ million}$$

129. $f(x) = -0.005x^2 + 0.377x + 1.71$

    a. 2003 means that $x = 8$.
$$f(8) = -0.005(8)^2 + 0.377(8) + 1.71$$
$$= 4.4 \text{ million}$$

    b. 2010 means that $x = 15$.
$$f(15)$$
$$= -0.005(15)^2 + 0.377(15) + 1.71$$
$$= 6.2 \text{ million}$$

Section 5.4

Practice Exercises

1. a. $(3x^4)(2x^2) = 3(2)(x^4)(x^2) = 6x^6$

    b. $(-5m^4np^3)(-8mnp^5)$
$$= -5(-8)(m^4m)(n \cdot n)(p^3p^5)$$
$$= 40m^5n^2p^8$$

2. a. $3x(7x - 1) = 3x(7x) + 3x(-1)$
$$= 21x^2 - 3x$$

    b. $-5a^2(3a^2 - 6a + 5)$
$$= -5a^2(3a^2) + (-5a^2)(-6a)$$
$$+ (-5a^2)(5)$$
$$= -15a^4 + 30a^3 - 25a^2$$

c. $-mn^3(5m^2n^2 + 2mn - 5m)$

$= -mn^3(5m^2n^2) + (-mn^3)(2mn)$

$\quad + (-mn^3)(-5m)$

$= -5m^3n^5 - 2m^2n^4 + 5m^2n^3$

3. a. $(x+5)(2x+3) = x(2x+3) + 5(2x+3)$

$= 2x^2 + 3x + 10x + 15$

$= 2x^2 + 13x + 15$

b. $(3x-1)(x^2 - 6x + 2)$

$= 3x(x^2 - 6x + 2) + (-1)(x^2 - 6x + 2)$

$= 3x^3 - 18x^2 + 6x - x^2 + 6x - 2$

$= 3x^3 - 19x^2 + 12x - 2$

4.

$$\begin{array}{r} x^2 - 4x - 5 \\ 3x^2 + 2 \\ \hline 2x^2 - 8x - 10 \\ 3x^4 - 12x^3 - 15x^2 \\ \hline 3x^4 - 12x^3 - 13x^2 - 8x - 10 \end{array}$$

5. $(x-5)(x+3)$

$= x \cdot x + 3 \cdot x + (-5)x + (-5)(3)$

$= x^2 + 3x - 5x - 15$

$= x^2 - 2x - 15$

6. a. $(3x-5)(2x-7)$

$= 3x(2x) + 3x(-7) + (-5)(2x)$

$\quad + (-5)(-7)$

$= 6x^2 - 21x - 10x + 35$

$= 6x^2 - 31x + 35$

b. $(2x^2 - 3y)(4x^2 + y)$

$= 8x^4 + 2x^2y - 12x^2y - 3y^2$

$= 8x^4 - 10x^2y - 3y^2$

7. a. $(x+6)^2 = x^2 + 2 \cdot x \cdot 6 + 6^2$

$= x^2 + 12x + 36$

b. $(x-2)^2 = x^2 - 2 \cdot x \cdot 2 + 2^2$

$= x^2 - 4x + 4$

c. $(3x+5y)^2$

$= (3x)^2 + 2(3x)(5y) + (5y)^2$

$= 9x^2 + 30xy + 25y^2$

d. $(3x^2 - 8b)^2$

$= (3x^2)^2 - 2(3x^2)(8b) + (8b)^2$

$= 9x^4 - 48x^2b + 64b^2$

8. a. $(x-7)(x+7) = x^2 - 7^2 = x^2 - 49$

b. $(2a+5)(2a-5) = (2a)^2 - 5^2$

$= 4a^2 - 25$

c. $\left(5x^2 + \dfrac{1}{4}\right)\left(5x^2 - \dfrac{1}{4}\right) = (5x^2)^2 - \left(\dfrac{1}{4}\right)^2$

$= 25x^4 - \dfrac{1}{16}$

d. $(a^3 - 4b^2)(a^3 + 4b^2) = (a^3)^2 - (4b^2)^2$

$= a^6 - 16b^4$

9. $[2 + (3x - y)]^2$

$= 2^2 + 2(2)(3x - y) + (3x - y)^2$

$= 4 + 4(3x - y) + (3x)^2 - 2(3x) \cdot y + y^2$

$= 4 + 12x - 4y + 9x^2 - 6xy + y^2$

10. $[(3x - y) - 5][(3x - y) + 5]$

$= (3x - y)^2 - 5^2$

$= (3x)^2 - 2(3x)(y) + y^2 - 25$

$= 9x^2 - 6xy + y^2 - 25$

11. $(x+4)(x-4)(x^2 - 16)$

$= (x^2 - 16)(x^2 - 16)$

$= (x^2 - 16)^2$

$= x^4 - 32x^2 + 256$

12. $f(x) = x^2 - 3x + 5$

$f(h+1) = (h+1)^2 - 3(h+1) + 5$

$= h^2 + 2h + 1 - 3h - 3 + 5$

$= h^2 - h + 3$

Graphing Calculator Explorations

1. $(x+4)(x-4) = x^2 - 16$

2. $(x+3)(x+3) = x^2 + 6x + 9$

3. $(3x-7)^2 = 9x^2 - 42x + 49$

4. $(5x-2)^2 = 25x^2 - 20x + 4$

5. $(5x+1)(x^2 - 3x - 2) = 5x^3 - 14x^2 - 13x - 2$

6. $(7x+4)(2x^2 + 3x - 5) = 14x^3 + 29x^2 - 23x - 20$

Vocabulary and Readiness Check

1. $(6x^3)\left(\dfrac{1}{2}x^3\right) = \underline{3x^6}$

2. $(x+7)^2 = \underline{x^2 + 14x + 49}$

3. $(x+7)(x-7) = \underline{x^2 - 49}$

4. The product of $(3x-1)(4x^2 - 2x + 1)$ is a polynomial of degree 3.

5. If $f(x) = x^2 + 1$ then $f(a+1) = \underline{(a+1)^2 + 1}$.

6. $[x + (2y+1)]^2$
   $= \underline{[x + (2y+1)][x + (2y+1)]}$

Exercise Set 5.4

1. $(-4x^3)(3x^2) = -4(3)x^5 = -12x^5$

3. $3x(4x+7) = 3x(4x) + 3x(7)$
           $= 12x^2 + 21x$

5. $-6xy(4x + y) = -6xy(4x) - 6xy(y)$
                 $= -24x^2y - 6xy^2$

7. $-4ab(xa^2 + ya^2 - 3)$
    $= -4ab(xa^2) - 4ab(ya^2) - 4ab(-3)$
    $= -4a^3bx - 4a^3by + 12ab$

9.
$$
\begin{array}{r}
2x + 4 \\
\times \quad x - 3 \\
\hline
-6x - 12 \\
2x^2 + 4x \\
\hline
2x^2 - 2x - 12
\end{array}
$$

11. $(2x+3)(x^3 - x + 2)$
    $= 2x(x^3 - x + 2) + 3(x^3 - x + 2)$
    $= 2x^4 - 2x^2 + 4x + 3x^3 - 3x + 6$
    $= 2x^4 + 3x^3 - 2x^2 + x + 6$

13.
$$
\begin{array}{r}
3x - 2 \\
\times \quad 5x + 1 \\
\hline
3x - 2 \\
15x^2 - 10x \\
\hline
15x^2 - 7x - 2
\end{array}
$$

15.
$$
\begin{array}{r}
3m^2 + 2m - 1 \\
\times \quad 5m + 2 \\
\hline
6m^2 + 4m - 2 \\
15m^3 + 10m^2 - 5m \\
\hline
15m^3 + 16m^2 - m - 2
\end{array}
$$

17. $(x-3)(x+4) = x \cdot x + x(4) - 3 \cdot x - 3(4)$
              $= x^2 + 4x - 3x - 12$
              $= x^2 + x - 12$

19. $(5x+8y)(2x-y)$
$$= 5x \cdot 2x + 5x(-y) + 8y(2x) + 8y(-y)$$
$$= 10x^2 - 5xy + 16xy - 8y^2$$
$$= 10x^2 + 11xy - 8y^2$$

21. $(3x-1)(x+3) = 3x \cdot x + 3x \cdot 3 - 1 \cdot x - 1 \cdot 3$
$$= 3x^2 + 9x - x - 3$$
$$= 3x^2 + 8x - 3$$

23. $\left(3x + \dfrac{1}{2}\right)\left(3x - \dfrac{1}{2}\right)$
$$= 3x(3x) + 3x\left(-\dfrac{1}{2}\right) + \dfrac{1}{2}(3x) + \dfrac{1}{2}\left(-\dfrac{1}{2}\right)$$
$$= 9x^2 - \dfrac{3}{2}x + \dfrac{3}{2}x - \dfrac{1}{4}$$
$$= 9x^2 - \dfrac{1}{4}$$

25. $(5x^2 - 2y^2)(x^2 - 3y^2)$
$$= 5x^4 - 15x^2y^2 - 2x^2y^2 + 6y^4$$
$$= 5x^4 - 17x^2y^2 + 6y^4$$

27. $(x+4)^2 = x^2 + 2(x)(4) + 4^2$
$$= x^2 + 8x + 16$$

29. $(6y-1)(6y+1) = (6y)^2 - 1^2 = 36y^2 - 1$

31. $(3x-y)^2 = (3x)^2 - 2(3x)(y) + y^2$
$$= 9x^2 - 6xy + y^2$$

33. $(5b-6y)(5b+6y) = (5b)^2 - (6y)^2$
$$= 25b^2 - 36y^2$$

35. $[3+(4b+1)]^2$
$$= 3^2 + 2(3)(4b+1) + (4b+1)^2$$
$$= 9 + 6(4b+1) + (4b)^2 + 2(4b)(1) + 1^2$$
$$= 9 + 24b + 6 + 16b^2 + 8b + 1$$
$$= 16b^2 + 32b + 16$$

37. $[(2s-3)-1][(2s-3)+1]$
$$= (2s-3)^2 - 1^2$$
$$= (2s)^2 - 2(2s)(3) + 3^2 - 1$$
$$= 4s^2 - 12s + 9 - 1$$
$$= 4s^2 - 12s + 8$$

39. $[(xy+4)-6]^2$
$$= (xy+4)^2 - 2(xy+4)(6) + 6^2$$
$$= (xy)^2 + 2(xy)(4) + 4^2 - 12(xy+4) + 36$$
$$= x^2y^2 + 8xy + 16 - 12xy - 48 + 36$$
$$= x^2y^2 - 4xy + 4$$

41. Answers may vary

43. $(x+y)(x-y)(x^2-y^2) = (x^2-y^2)(x^2-y^2)$
$$= (x^2)^2 - 2x^2y^2 + (y^2)^2$$
$$= x^4 - 2x^2y^2 + y^4$$

45. $(x-2)^4 = (x-2)^2(x-2)^2$
$$= (x^2 - 4x + 4)(x^2 - 4x + 4)$$

$$
\begin{array}{r}
x^2 - 4x + 4 \\
\times \quad x^2 - 4x + 4 \\
\hline
4x^2 - 16x + 16 \\
-4x^3 + 16x^2 - 16x \\
x^4 - 4x^3 + 4x^2 \\
\hline
x^4 - 8x^3 + 24x^2 - 32x + 16
\end{array}
$$

47. $(x-5)(x+5)(x^2+25) = (x^2-25)(x^2+25)$
$$= (x^2)^2 - 25^2$$
$$= x^4 - 625$$

49. $(3x+1)(3x+5)$
$$= (3x)^2 + 3x(5) + 1(3x) + 1(5)$$
$$= 9x^2 + 15x + 3x + 5$$
$$= 9x^2 + 18x + 5$$

51. $(2x^3+5)(5x^2+4x+1)$
$$= 2x^3(5x^2+4x+1) + 5(5x^2+4x+1)$$
$$= 10x^5 + 8x^4 + 2x^3 + 25x^2 + 20x + 5$$

53. $(7x-3)(7x+3) = (7x)^2 - 3^2 = 49x^2 - 9$

55.
$$
\begin{array}{r}
3x^2 + 4x - 4 \\
\times \quad 3x + 6 \\
\hline
18x^2 + 24x - 24 \\
9x^3 + 12x^2 - 12x \\
\hline
9x^3 + 30x^2 + 12x - 24
\end{array}
$$

57. $\left(4x+\dfrac{1}{3}\right)\left(4x-\dfrac{1}{2}\right)$

$= (4x)^2 + 4x\left(-\dfrac{1}{2}\right) + \dfrac{1}{3}(4x) + \dfrac{1}{3}\left(-\dfrac{1}{2}\right)$

$= 16x^2 - 2x + \dfrac{4}{3}x - \dfrac{1}{6}$

$= 16x^2 - \dfrac{2}{3}x - \dfrac{1}{6}$

59. $(6x+1)^2 = (6x)^2 + 2(6x)(1) + 1^2$

$= 36x^2 + 12x + 1$

61. $(x^2 + 2y)(x^2 - 2y) = (x^2)^2 - (2y)^2$

$= x^4 - 4y^2$

63.
$$
\begin{array}{r}
5a^2b^2 - 6a - 6b \\
\times \qquad -6a^2b^2 \\
\hline
-30a^4b^4 + 36a^3b^2 + 36a^2b^3
\end{array}
$$

65. $(a-4)(2a-4) = 2a^2 - 4a - 8a + 16$

$= 2a^2 - 12a + 16$

67. $(7ab + 3c)(7ab - 3c) = (7ab)^2 - (3c)^2$

$= 49a^2b^2 - 9c^2$

69. $(m-4)^2 = m^2 - 2(m)(4) + 4^2$

$= m^2 - 8m + 16$

71. $(3x+1)^2 = (3x)^2 + 2(3x)(1) + 1^2$

$= 9x^2 + 6x + 1$

73. $(y-4)(y-3) = y^2 - 3y - 4y + 12$

$= y^2 - 7y + 12$

75. $(x+y)(2x-1)(x+1)$

$= (x+y)(2x^2 + 2x - x - 1)$

$= (x+y)(2x^2 + x - 1)$

$= x(2x^2 + x - 1) + y(2x^2 + x - 1)$

$= 2x^3 + x^2 - x + 2x^2y + xy - y$

$= 2x^3 + 2x^2y + x^2 + xy - x - y$

77.
$$
\begin{array}{r}
3x^2 + 2x - 1 \\
\times \qquad 3x^2 + 2x - 1 \\
\hline
-3x^2 - 2x + 1 \\
6x^3 + 4x^2 - 2x \\
9x^4 + 6x^3 - 3x^2 \\
\hline
9x^4 + 12x^3 - 2x^2 - 4x + 1
\end{array}
$$

79.
$$
\begin{array}{r}
4x^2 - 2x + 5 \\
\times \qquad 3x + 1 \\
\hline
4x^2 - 2x + 5 \\
12x^3 - 6x^2 + 15x \\
\hline
12x^3 - 2x^2 + 13x + 5
\end{array}
$$

81. $f(x) = x^2 - 3x$

$f(a) = a^2 - 3a$

83. $f(x) = x^2 - 3x$

$f(a+h) = (a+h)^2 - 3(a+h)$

$= a^2 + 2ah + h^2 - 3a - 3h$

85. $f(x) = x^2 - 3x$

$f(b-2) = (b-2)^2 - 3(b-2)$

$= b^2 - 4b + 4 - 3b + 6$

$= b^2 - 7b + 10$

87. $y = -2x + 7$

$m = -2$

89. $3x - 5y = 14$

$-5y = -3x + 14$

$y = \dfrac{3}{5}x - \dfrac{14}{5}$

$m = \dfrac{3}{5}$

91. Since any vertical line crosses the graph at most once, it is a function.

93. $7y(3z - 2) + 1 = 21yz - 14y + 1$

95. Answers may vary

97. $F(x) = x^2 + 3x + 2$

   a. $F(a+h) = (a+h)^2 + 3(a+h) + 2$
$$= a^2 + 2ah + h^2 + 3a + 3h + 2$$

   b. $F(a) = a^2 + 3a + 2$

   c. $F(a+h) - F(a)$
$$= a^2 + 2ah + h^2 + 3a + 3h + 2 - (a^2 + 3a + 2)$$
$$= 2ah + h^2 + 3h$$

99. $5x^2 y^n (6y^{n+1} - 2)$
$$= 5x^2 y^n (6y^{n+1}) + 5x^2 y^n (-2)$$
$$= 30x^2 y^{2n+1} - 10x^2 y^n$$

101. $(x^a + 5)(x^{2a} - 3)$
$$= x^a \cdot x^{2a} + x^a(-3) + 5(x^{2a}) + 5(-3)$$
$$= x^{3a} - 3x^a + 5x^{2a} - 15$$

103. Area $= \pi r^2$
$$= \pi(5x - 2)^2$$
$$= \pi(25x^2 - 20x + 4) \text{ square km}$$

105. Area $= (3x - 2)^2 - x^2$
$$= (9x^2 - 12x + 4) - x^2$$
$$= (8x^2 - 12x + 4) \text{ square inches}$$

107. One operation is addition, the other is multiplication.

   a. $(3x+5) + (3x+7) = 6x + 12$

   b. $(3x+5)(3x+7)$
$$= 9x^2 + 21x + 15x + 35$$
$$= 9x^2 + 36x + 35$$

109. $P(x) \cdot R(x) = (5x)(x+5)$
$$= 5x \cdot x + 5x \cdot 5$$
$$= 5x^2 + 25x$$

111. $[Q(x)]^2 = (x^2 - 2)^2$
$$= (x^2)^2 - 2(x^2)(2) + 2^2$$
$$= x^4 - 4x^2 + 4$$

113. $R(x) \cdot Q(x) = (x+5)(x^2 - 2)$
$$= x^3 - 2x + 5x^2 - 10$$
$$= x^3 + 5x^2 - 2x - 10$$

Section 5.5

Practice Exercises

1. $32x^4 y^2 = 2 \cdot 2 \cdot 2 \cdot 2 \cdot 2 \cdot x^4 \cdot y \cdot y$
$48x^3 y = 2 \cdot 2 \cdot 2 \cdot 2 \cdot 3 \cdot x^3 \cdot y$
$24y^2 = 2 \cdot 2 \cdot 2 \cdot 3 \cdot y \cdot y$
$\text{GCF} = 2 \cdot 2 \cdot 2 \cdot y = 8y$

2. **a.** The GCF of $6x^2$, 9, and $15x$ is 3.
$$6x^2 + 9 + 15x = 3(2x^2) + 3(3) + 3(5x)$$
$$= 3(2x^2 + 3 + 5x)$$

   b. There is no common factor of the terms $3x$ and $-8y^3$ other than 1 (or -1).
$$3x - 8y^3$$

   c. The GCF of $8a^4$ and $-2a^3$ is $2a^3$.
$$8a^4 - 2a^3 = 2a^3 \cdot 4a - 2a^3 \cdot 1$$
$$= 2a^3(4a - 1)$$

3. Factor out the GCF of the two terms, $8x^3 y^2$.
$$64x^5 y^2 - 8x^3 y^2 = 8x^3 y^2 \cdot 8x^2 - 8x^3 y^2 \cdot 1$$
$$= 8x^3 y^2 (8x^2 - 1)$$

4. Factor out the GCF of the three terms, $-xy^2$.
$$-9x^4 y^2 + 5x^2 y^2 + 7xy^2$$
$$= -xy^2 \cdot 9x^3 - xy^2(-5x) - xy^2(-7)$$
$$= -xy^2(9x^3 - 5x - 7)$$

5. The GCF is $(x + 4)$.
$$3(x+4) + 5b(x+4) = (x+4)(3 + 5b)$$

6. $8b(a^3 + 2y) - (a^3 + 2y)$
$$= 8b(a^3 + 2y) - 1(a^3 + 2y)$$
$$= (a^3 + 2y)(8b - 1)$$

7. $xy + 2y - 10 - 5x = (xy + 2y) + (-10 - 5x)$
$$= y(x+2) - 5(2+x)$$
$$= y(x+2) - 5(x+2)$$
$$= (x+2)(y-5)$$

8. $a^3 + 2a^2 + 5a + 10 = (a^3 + 2a^2) + (5a + 10)$
$$= a^2(a+2) + 5(a+2)$$
$$= (a+2)(a^2 + 5)$$

9. $x^2y^2 + 3y^2 - 5x^2 - 15$
$= (x^2y^2 + 3y^2) + (-5x^2 - 15)$
$= y^2(x^2 + 3) - 5(x^2 + 3)$
$= (x^2 + 3)(y^2 - 5)$

10. $pq + 3p - q - 3 = (pq + 3p) + (-q - 3)$
$= p(q + 3) - 1(q + 3)$
$= (q + 3)(p - 1)$

Vocabulary and Readiness Check

1. The reverse of multiplying is <u>factoring</u>.

2. The greatest common factor (GCF) of x^7, x^3, x^5 is <u>x^3</u>.

3. In general, the GCF of a list of common variables raised to powers is the <u>least</u> exponent in the list.

4. Factoring means writing as a <u>product</u>.

5. True or false: A factored form of $2xy^3 + 10xy$ is $2xy \cdot y^2 + 2xy \cdot 5$. <u>false</u>

6. True or false: A factored form of $x^3 - 6x^2 + x$ is $x(x^2 - 6x)$. <u>false</u>

7. True or false: A factored form of $5x - 5y + x^3 - x^2y$ is $5(x - y) + x^2(x - y)$. <u>false</u>

8. True or false: A factored form of $5x - 5y + x^3 - x^2y$ is $(x - y)(5 + x^2)$. <u>true</u>

9. $6 = 2 \cdot 3$
$12 = 2 \cdot 2 \cdot 3$
$GCF = 2 \cdot 3 = 6$

10. $9 = 3 \cdot 3$
$27 = 3 \cdot 3 \cdot 3$
$GCF = 3 \cdot 3 = 9$

11. $15x = 3 \cdot 5 \cdot x$
$10 = 2 \cdot 5$
$GCF = 5$

12. $9x = 3 \cdot 3 \cdot x$
$12 = 2 \cdot 2 \cdot 3$
$GCF = 3$

13. $13x = 13 \cdot x$
$2x = 2 \cdot x$
$GCF = x$

14. $4y = 4 \cdot y$
$5y = 5 \cdot y$
$GCF = y$

15. $7x = 7 \cdot x$
$14x = 2 \cdot 7 \cdot x$
$GCF = 7x$

16. $8z = 2 \cdot 2 \cdot 2 \cdot z$
$4z = 2 \cdot 2 \cdot z$
$GCF = 2 \cdot 2 \cdot z = 4z$

Exercise Set 5.5

1. a^8, a^5, and a^3; $GCF = a^3$

3. $x^2y^3z^3$, y^2z^3, and xy^2z^2; $GCF = y^2z^2$

5. $6x^3y$, $9x^2y^2$, and $12x^2y$; $GCF = 3x^2y$

7. $10x^3yz^3$, $20x^2z^5$, $45xz^3$; $GCF = 5xz^3$

9. $18x - 12 = 6 \cdot 3x - 6 \cdot 2 = 6(3x - 2)$

11. $4y^2 - 16xy^3 = 4y^2 \cdot 1 - 4y^2 \cdot 4xy$
$= 4y^2(1 - 4xy)$

13. $6x^5 - 8x^4 + 2x^3 = 2x^3(3x^2) - 2x^3(4x) + 2x^3(1)$
$= 2x^3(3x^2 - 4x + 1)$

15. $8a^3b^3 - 4a^2b^2 + 4ab + 16ab^2$
$= 4ab(2a^2b^2) - 4ab(ab) + 4ab(1) + 4ab(4b)$
$= 4ab(2a^2b^2 - ab + 1 + 4b)$

17. $6(x + 3) + 5a(x + 3) = (x + 3)(6 + 5a)$

19. $2x(z + 7) + (z + 7) = (z + 7)(2x + 1)$

21. $3x(x^2 + 5) - 2(x^2 + 5) = (x^2 + 5)(3x - 2)$

23. Answers may vary

25. $ab + 3a + 2b + 6 = a(b + 3) + 2(b + 3)$
$= (a + 2)(b + 3)$

27. $ac + 4a - 2c - 8 = a(c+4) - 2(c+4)$
$$= (a-2)(c+4)$$

29. $2xy - 3x - 4y + 6 = x(2y-3) - 2(2y-3)$
$$= (x-2)(2y-3)$$

31. $12xy - 8x - 3y + 2 = 4x(3y-2) - (3y-2)$
$$= (4x-1)(3y-2)$$

33. $6x^3 + 9 = 3(2x^3) + 3(3) = 3(2x^3 + 3)$

35. $x^3 + 3x^2 = x^2(x) + x^2(3) = x^2(x+3)$

37. $8a^3 - 4a = 4a(2a^2) - 4a(1) = 4a(2a^2 - 1)$

39. $-20x^2 y + 16xy^3 = -4xy(5x) - 4xy(4y^2)$
$$= -4xy(5x - 4y^2)$$

41. $10a^2 b^3 + 5ab^2 - 15ab^3$
$$= 5ab^2(2ab) + 5ab^2(1) - 5ab^2(3b)$$
$$= 5ab^2(2ab + 1 - 3b)$$

43. $9abc^2 + 6a^2 bc - 6ab + 3bc$
$$= 3b(3ac^2) + 3b(2a^2 c) + 3b(-2a) + 3b(c)$$
$$= 3b(3ac^2 + 2a^2 c - 2a + c)$$

45. $4x(y-2) - 3(y-2) = (y-2)(4x-3)$

47. $6xy + 10x + 9y + 15$
$$= 2x(3y+5) + 3(3y+5)$$
$$= (2x+3)(3y+5)$$

49. $xy + 3y - 5x - 15 = y(x+3) - 5(x+3)$
$$= (x+3)(y-5)$$

51. $6ab - 2a - 9b + 3 = 2a(3b-1) - 3(3b-1)$
$$= (3b-1)(2a-3)$$

53. $12xy + 18x + 2y + 3$
$$= 6x(2y+3) + 1(2y+3)$$
$$= (6x+1)(2y+3)$$

55. $2m(n-8) - (n-8) = (2m-1)(n-8)$

57. $15x^3 y^2 - 18x^2 y^2 = 3x^2 y^2 \cdot 5x - 3x^2 y^2 \cdot 6$
$$= 3x^2 y^2(5x-6)$$

59. $2x^2 + 3xy + 4x + 6y$
$$= x(2x+3y) + 2(2x+3y)$$
$$= (2x+3y)(x+2)$$

61. $5x^2 + 5xy - 3x - 3y = 5x(x+y) - 3(x+y)$
$$= (x+y)(5x-3)$$

63. $x^3 + 3x^2 + 4x + 12 = x^2(x+3) + 4(x+3)$
$$= (x+3)(x^2+4)$$

65. $x^3 - x^2 - 2x + 2 = x^2(x-1) - 2(x-1)$
$$= (x-1)(x^2-2)$$

67. $(5x^2)(11x^5) = 5(11)x^2 x^5 = 55x^7$

69. $(5x^2)^3 = 5^3(x^2)^3 = 125x^6$

71. $(x+2)(x-5) = x^2 - 5x + 2x - 10$
$$= x^2 - 3x - 10$$

73. $(x+3)(x+2) = x^2 + 3x + 2x + 6$
$$= x^2 + 5x + 6$$

75. $(y-3)(y-1) = y^2 - 1y - 3y + 3$
$$= y^2 - 4y + 3$$

77. d

    a. $2(5x^2 - x + 1) = 10x^2 - 2x + 2$

    b. $2(5x^2 - x) = 10x^2 - 2x$

    c. $2(5x^2 - x - 2) = 10x^2 - 2x - 4$

    d. $2(5x^2 - x - 1) = 10x^2 - 2x - 2$

79. $2\pi r^2 + 2\pi rh = 2\pi r(r+h)$

81. $A = 5600 + 5600rt$
$A = 5600(1) + 5600(rt)$
$A = 5600(1 + rt)$

83. Answers may vary

85. None

  a. $(2-x)(3-y) = 6 - 2y - 3x + xy$
                       $= xy - 3x - 2y + 6$

  b. $(-2+x)(-3+y) = 6 - 2y - 3x + xy$
                           $= xy - 3x - 2y + 6$

  c. $(x-2)(y-3) = xy - 3x - 2y + 6$

  d. $(-x+2)(-y+3) = xy - 3x - 2y + 6$

87. a is correct

  a. $3(4x^2 + 3x + 1) = 12x^2 + 9x + 3$

  b. $3(4x^2 + 3x - 1) = 12x^2 + 9x - 3$

  c. $3(4x^2 + 3x - 3) = 12x^2 + 9x - 9$

  d. $3(4x^2 + 3x) = 12x^2 + 9x$

89. $A = P + PRT$
    $A = P(1 + RT)$

91. $3y^n + 3y^{2n} + 5y^{8n} = y^n \cdot 3 + y^n \cdot 3y^n + y^n \cdot 5y^{7n}$
                            $= y^n(3 + 3y^n + 5y^{7n})$

93. $3x^{5a} - 6x^{3a} + 9x^{2a}$
    $= 3x^{2a} \cdot x^{3a} - 3x^{2a} \cdot 2x^a + 3x^{2a} \cdot 3$
    $= 3x^{2a}(x^{3a} - 2x^a + 3)$

95. $h(t) = -16t^2 + 224$

  a. $h(t) = -16(t^2 - 14)$

  b. $h(2) = -16(2)^2 + 224$
             $= -16(4) + 224$
             $= -64 + 224$
             $= 160$ feet
      $h(2) = -16(2^2 - 14)$
             $= -16(4 - 14)$
             $= -16(-10)$
             $= 160$ feet

  c. Answers may vary

Section 5.6

Practice Exercises

1. Find two integers whose product is 6 and whose sum is 5. Since our integers must have a positive product and a positive sum, look for positive factors.

Positive Factors of 6	Sum of Factors
1, 6	$1 + 6 = 7$
3, 2	$3 + 2 = 5$ (correct)

$x^2 + 5x + 6 = (x+3)(x+2)$

2. Find two integers whose product is 24 and whose sum is -11. Since our integers must have a positive product and a negative sum, look for negative factors.

Negative Factors of 24	Sum of Factors
$-1, -24$	$-1 + (-24) = -25$
$-2, -12$	$-2 + (-12) = -14$
$-3, -8$	$-3 + (-8) = -11$ (correct)
$-4, -6$	$-4 + (-6) = -10$

$x^2 - 11x + 24 = (x-3)(x-8)$

3. $3x^3 - 9x^2 - 30x = 3x(x^2 - 3x - 10)$
Find two integers whose product is -10 and whose sum is -3. The numbers are -5 and 2.
$3x^3 - 9x^2 - 30x = 3x(x^2 - 3x - 10)$
                          $= 3x(x-5)(x+2)$

4. $2b^2 - 18b - 22 = 2(b^2 - 9b - 11)$
Find two integers whose product is -11 and whose sum is -9.

Factors	Sum
$-1, 11$	10
$1, -11$	-10

Neither of the pairs has a sum of -9, so no further factoring is possible.
$2b^2 - 18b - 22 = 2(b^2 - 9b - 11)$

5. Factors of $2x^2$: $2x \cdot x$
Factors of 6: $1 \cdot 6$ and $2 \cdot 3$
$(2x + 6)(x + 1) \Rightarrow 2x + 6x = 8x$ (incorrect middle term)
$(2x + 1)(x + 6) \Rightarrow 12x + x = 13x$ (correct middle term)
$(2x + 2)(x + 3) \Rightarrow 6x + 2x = 8x$ (incorrect middle term)
$(2x + 3)(x + 2) \Rightarrow 4x + 3x = 7x$ (incorrect middle term)
$2x^2 + 13x + 6 = (2x + 1)(x + 6)$

6. Factors of $4x^2$: $4x \cdot x$ and $2x \cdot 2x$
Factors of -6: $-6 \cdot 1, 6 \cdot -1, 2 \cdot -3, -2 \cdot 3$
$(4x - 6)(x + 1) \Rightarrow 4x - 6x = -2x$ (incorrect)
$(4x + 6)(x - 1) \Rightarrow -4x + 6x = 2x$ (incorrect)
$(4x + 2)(x - 3) \Rightarrow -12x + 2x = -10x$ (incorrect)
$(4x - 3)(x + 2) \Rightarrow 8x - 3x = 5x$ (correct)
$4x^2 + 5x - 6 = (4x - 3)(x + 2)$

7. $18b^4 - 57b^3 + 30b^2 = 3b^2(6b^2 - 19b + 10)$

Factors of $6b^2$: $2b \cdot 3b, 6b \cdot b$
Negative factors of 10: $-1 \cdot -10, -5 \cdot -2$
$(2b - 1)(3b - 10) \Rightarrow -20b - 3b = -23b$ (incorrect)
$(2b - 10)(3b - 1) \Rightarrow -2b - 30b = -32b$ (incorrect)
$(2b - 5)(3b - 2) \Rightarrow -4b - 15b = -19b$ (correct)
$18b^4 - 57b^3 + 30b^2 = 3b^2(6b^2 - 19b + 10)$
$\qquad = 3b^2(2b - 5)(3b - 2)$

8. No greatest common factor can be factored out.
Factors of $25x^2$: $25x \cdot x, 5x \cdot 5x$
Factors of $4y^2$: $4y \cdot y, 2y \cdot 2y$
Try possible combinations.
$25x^2 + 20xy + 4y^2 = (5x + 2y)(5x + 2y)$
$\qquad\qquad\qquad = (5x + 2y)^2$

9. $20x^2 + 23x + 6$
$a = 20, b = 23, c = 6$
Find two numbers whose product is
$a \cdot c = 20 \cdot 6 = 120$, and whose sum is b, 23. The two numbers are 8 and 15.
$20x^2 + 23x + 6 = 20x^2 + 8x + 15x + 6$
$\qquad = 4x(5x + 2) + 3(5x + 2)$
$\qquad = (5x + 2)(4x + 3)$

10. $15x^2 + 4x - 3$
$a = 15, b = 4, c = -3$
Find two numbers whose product is
$a \cdot c = 15(-3) = -45$ and whose sum is b, 4. The two numbers are 9 and -5.
$15x^2 + 4x - 3 = 15x^2 + 9x - 5x - 3$
$\qquad = 3x(5x + 3) - 1(5x + 3)$
$\qquad = (5x + 3)(3x - 1)$

11. Let $y = x + 1$.
$3(x + 1)^2 - 7(x + 1) - 20 = 3y^2 - 7y - 20$
$\qquad\qquad\qquad\qquad = (3y + 5)(y - 4)$
Replace y with $x + 1$.
$(3y + 5)(y - 4) = [3(x + 1) + 5][(x + 1) - 4)]$
$\qquad\qquad = (3x + 3 + 5)(x + 1 - 4)$
$\qquad\qquad = (3x + 8)(x - 3)$
Thus, $3(x + 1)^2 - 7(x + 1) - 20 = (3x + 8)(x - 3)$.

12. Let $y = x^2$.
$6x^4 - 11x^2 - 10 = 6y^2 - 11y - 10$
$\qquad\qquad\qquad = (3y + 2)(2y - 5)$
Replace y with x^2.
$(3y + 2)(2y - 5) = (3x^2 + 2)(2x^2 - 5)$

Vocabulary and Readiness Check

1. $10 = 2 \cdot 5$
$7 = 2 + 5$
2 and 5

2. $12 = 2 \cdot 2 \cdot 3 = 2 \cdot 6$
$8 = 2 + 6$
2 and 6

3. $24 = 2 \cdot 2 \cdot 2 \cdot 3 = 8 \cdot 3$
$11 = 8 + 3$
8 and 3

4. $30 = 2 \cdot 3 \cdot 5 = 10 \cdot 3$
$13 = 10 + 3$
10 and 3

Exercise Set 5.6

1. $x^2 + 9x + 18 = (x + 6)(x + 3)$

3. $x^2 - 12x + 32 = (x - 4)(x - 8)$

5. $x^2 + 10x - 24 = (x + 12)(x - 2)$

7. $x^2 - 2x - 24 = (x-6)(x+4)$

9. Note that the GCF is 3.
$$3x^2 - 18x + 24 = 3(x^2 - 6x + 8)$$
$$= 3(x-2)(x-4)$$

11. Note that the GCF is $4z$.
$$4x^2 z + 28xz + 40z = 4z(x^2 + 7x + 10)$$
$$= 4z(x+2)(x+5)$$

13. Note that the GCF is 2.
$$2x^2 - 24x - 64 = 2(x^2 - 12x - 32)$$

15. $5x^2 + 16x + 3 = (5x+1)(x+3)$

17. $2x^2 - 11x + 12 = (2x-3)(x-4)$

19. $2x^2 + 25x - 20$ is prime.

21. $4x^2 - 12x + 9 = (2x-3)(2x-3)$
$$= (2x-3)^2$$

23. Note that the GCF is 2.
$$12x^2 + 10x - 50 = 2(6x^2 + 5x - 25)$$
$$= 2(3x-5)(2x+5)$$

25. Note that the GCF is y^2.
$$3y^4 - y^3 - 10y^2 = y^2(3y^2 - y - 10)$$
$$= y^2(3y+5)(y-2)$$

27. Note that the GCF is $2x$.
$$6x^3 + 8x^2 + 24x = 2x(3x^2 + 4x + 12)$$

29. $2x^2 - 5xy - 3y^2 = (2x+y)(x-3y)$

31. Note that the GCF is 2, so that
$$28y^2 + 22y + 4 = 2(14y^2 + 11y + 2).$$
$ac = 28$; the two numbers are 4 and 7.
$$14y^2 + 11y + 2 = 14y^2 + 7y + 4y + 2$$
$$= 7y(2y+1) + 2(2y+1)$$
$$= (7y+2)(2y+1)$$
So, $28y^2 + 22y + 4 = 2(7y+2)(2y+1)$.

33. $2x^2 + 15x - 27$; $ac = -54$ so the two numbers are 18 and –3.
$$2x^2 + 15x - 27 = 2x^2 + 18x - 3x - 27$$
$$= 2x(x+9) - 3(x+9)$$
$$= (2x-3)(x+9)$$

35. Let $y = x^2$. Then we have
$$x^4 + x^2 - 6 = y^2 + y - 6 = (y+3)(y-2).$$
This yields $(x^2 + 3)(x^2 - 2)$.

37. Let $y = 5x + 1$. Then we have
$$(5x+1)^2 + 8(5x+1) + 7 = y^2 + 8y + 7$$
$$= (y+1)(y+7).$$
This yields
$$[(5x+1) + 1][(5x+1) + 7] = (5x+2)(5x+8).$$

39. Let $y = x^3$. Then we have
$$x^6 - 7x^3 + 12 = y^2 - 7y + 12$$
$$= (y-4)(y-3).$$
This yields $(x^3 - 4)(x^3 - 3)$.

41. Let $y = a + 5$. Then we have
$$(a+5)^2 - 5(a+5) - 24 = y^2 - 5y - 24$$
$$= (y-8)(y+3).$$
This yields
$$[(a+5) - 8][(a+5) + 3] = (a-3)(a+8).$$

43. $x^2 - 24x - 81 = (x-27)(x+3)$

45. $x^2 - 15x - 54 = (x-18)(x+3)$

47. $3x^2 - 6x + 3 = 3(x^2 - 2x + 1)$
$$= 3(x-1)(x-1)$$
$$= 3(x-1)^2$$

49. $3x^2 - 5x - 2 = (3x+1)(x-2)$

51. $8x^2 - 26x + 15 = (4x-3)(2x-5)$

53. $18x^4 + 21x^3 + 6x^2 = 3x^2(6x^2 + 7x + 2)$
$$= 3x^2(3x+2)(2x+1)$$

55. $x^2 + 8xz + 7z^2 = (x+z)(x+7z)$

57. $x^2 - x - 12$; $ac = -12$ so the two numbers are -4 and 3.

$$x^2 - x - 12 = x^2 - 4x + 3x - 12$$
$$= x(x-4) + 3(x-4)$$
$$= (x+3)(x-4)$$

59. $3a^2 + 12ab + 12b^2 = 3(a^2 + 4ab + 4b^2)$
$$= 3(a+2b)(a+2b)$$
$$= 3(a+2b)^2$$

61. $x^2 + 4x + 5$ is prime.

63. Let $y = x + 4$. Then

$$2(x+4)^2 + 3(x+4) - 5$$
$$= 2y^2 + 3y - 5$$
$$= (2y+5)(y-1)$$
$$= [2(x+4)+5][(x+4)-1]$$
$$= (2x+8+5)(x+3)$$
$$= (2x+13)(x+3)$$

65. $6x^2 - 49x + 30 = (3x-2)(2x-15)$

67. Let $y = x^2$. Then

$$x^4 - 5x^2 - 6 = y^2 - 5y - 6$$
$$= (y-6)(y+1)$$
$$= (x^2 - 6)(x^2 + 1)$$

69. $6x^3 - x^2 - x = x(6x^2 - x - 1)$
$$= x(3x+1)(2x-1)$$

71. $12a^2 - 29ab + 15b^2 = (4a-3b)(3a-5b)$

73. $9x^2 + 30x + 25 = (3x+5)(3x+5)$
$$= (3x+5)^2$$

75. $3x^2 y - 11xy + 8y = y(3x^2 - 11x + 8)$
$$= y(3x-8)(x-1)$$

77. $2x^2 + 2x - 12 = 2(x^2 + x - 6)$
$$= 2(x+3)(x-2)$$

79. Let $y = x - 4$. Then

$$(x-4)^2 + 3(x-4) - 18$$
$$= y^2 + 3y - 18$$
$$= (y+6)(y-3)$$
$$= [(x-4)+6][(x-4)-3]$$
$$= (x+2)(x-7)$$

81. Let $y = x^3$. Then

$$2x^6 + 3x^3 - 9 = 2y^2 + 3y - 9$$
$$= (2y-3)(y+3)$$
$$= (2x^3 - 3)(x^3 + 3)$$

83. $72xy^4 - 24xy^2 z + 2xz^2 = 2x(36y^4 - 12y^2 z + z^2)$
$$= 2x(6y^2 - z)(6y^2 - z)$$
$$= 2x(6y^2 - z)^2$$

85. $2x^3 y + 2x^2 y - 12xy = 2xy(x^2 + x - 6)$
$$= 2xy(x+3)(x-2)$$

87. $x^2 + 6xy + 5y^2 = (x+5y)(x+y)$

89. $(x-3)(x+3) = x^2 - 3^3 = x^2 - 9$

91. $(2x+1)^2 = (2x)^2 + 2(2x)(1) + 1^2$
$$= 4x^2 + 4x + 1$$

93.
$$\begin{array}{r} x^2 + 2x + 4 \\ x - 2 \\ \hline -2x^2 - 4x - 8 \\ x^3 + 2x^2 + 4x \\ \hline x^3 \qquad\qquad -8 \end{array}$$

95. $x^2 + bx + 6$
$6 = 2 \cdot 3$ or $6 = (-2)(-3)$
$6 = 1 \cdot 6$ or $6 = (-1)(-6)$
$(x+2)(x+3) = x^2 + 5x + 6$
$(x-2)(x-3) = x^2 - 5x + 6$
$(x+1)(x+6) = x^2 + 7x + 6$
$(x-1)(x-6) = x^2 - 7x + 6$
$b = \pm 5$ and $b = \pm 7$

97. $V(x) = x^3 + 2x^2 - 8x$
$$= x(x^2 + 2x - 8)$$
$$= x(x+4)(x-2)$$

99. $h(t) = -16t^2 + 80t + 576$

  a. $h(0) = -16(0)^2 + 80(0) + 576 = 576$ ft

$$h(2) = -16(2)^2 + 80(2) + 576$$
$$= -16(4) + 160 + 576$$
$$= -64 + 160 + 576$$
$$= 672 \text{ ft}$$
$$h(4) = -16(4)^2 + 80(4) + 576$$
$$= -16(16) + 320 + 576$$
$$= -256 + 320 + 576$$
$$= 640 \text{ ft}$$
$$h(6) = -16(6)^2 + 80(6) + 576$$
$$= -16(36) + 480 + 576$$
$$= -576 + 480 + 576$$
$$= 480 \text{ ft}$$

  b. Answers may vary

  c. $h(t) = -16t^2 + 80t + 576$
$$= -16(t^2 - 5t - 36)$$
$$= -16(t - 9)(t + 4)$$

101. $x^{2n} + 10x^n + 16 = (x^n + 2)(x^n + 8)$

103. $x^{2n} - 3x^n - 18 = (x^n - 6)(x^n + 3)$

105. $2x^{2n} + 11x^n + 5 = (2x^n + 1)(x^n + 5)$

107. $4x^{2n} - 12x^n + 9 = (2x^n - 3)(2x^n - 3)$
$$= (2x^n - 3)^2$$

109. $x^4 + 6x^3 + 5x^2 = x^2(x^2 + 6x + 5)$
$$= x^2(x + 5)(x + 1)$$

111. $30x^3 + 9x^2 - 3x = 3x(10x^2 + 3x - 1)$
$$= 3x(5x - 1)(2x + 1)$$

Section 5.7

Practice Exercises

1. $b^2 + 16b + 64 = b^2 + 2(b)(8) + 8^2 = (b + 8)^2$

2. $45x^2 b - 30xb + 5b = 5b(9x^2 - 6x + 1)$
$$= 5b[(3x)^2 - 2(3x)(1) + 1^2]$$
$$= 5b(3x - 1)^2$$

3. a. $x^2 - 16 = x^2 - 4^2 = (x + 4)(x - 4)$

  b. $25b^2 - 49 = (5b)^2 - 7^2 = (5b - 7)(5b + 7)$

  c. $45 - 20x^2 = 5(9 - 4x^2)$
$$= 5[3^2 - (2x)^2]$$
$$= 5(3 - 2x)(3 + 2x)$$

  d. $y^2 - \dfrac{1}{81} = y^2 - \left(\dfrac{1}{9}\right)^2 = \left(y - \dfrac{1}{9}\right)\left(y + \dfrac{1}{9}\right)$

4. a. $x^4 - 10,000 = (x^2)^2 - 100^2$
$$= (x^2 + 100)(x^2 - 100)$$
$$= (x^2 + 100)(x + 10)(x - 10)$$

  b. $(x + 2)^2 - 49 = (x + 2)^2 - 7^2$
$$= [(x + 2) + 7][(x + 2) - 7]$$
$$= (x + 2 + 7)(x + 2 - 7)$$
$$= (x + 9)(x - 5)$$

5. $m^2 + 6m + 9 - n^2 = (m^2 + 6m + 9) - n^2$
$$= (m + 3)^2 - n^2$$
$$= [(m + 3) + n][(m + 3) - n]$$
$$= (m + 3 + n)(m + 3 - n)$$

6. $x^3 + 64 = x^3 + 4^3$
$$= (x + 4)(x^2 - x \cdot 4 + 4^2)$$
$$= (x + 4)(x^2 - 4x + 16)$$

7. $a^3 + 8b^3 = a^3 + (2b)^3$
$$= (a + 2b)[a^2 - a(2b) + (2b)^2]$$
$$= (a + 2b)(a^2 - 2ab + 4b^2)$$

8. $27 - y^3 = 3^3 - y^3$
$$= (3 - y)(3^2 + 3 \cdot y + y^2)$$
$$= (3 - y)(9 + 3y + y^2)$$

9. $b^3 x^2 - 8x^2 = x^2(b^3 - 8)$
$$= x^2(b^3 - 2^3)$$
$$= x^2(b - 2)(b^2 + b \cdot 2 + 2^2)$$
$$= x^2(b - 2)(b^2 + 2b + 4)$$

Vocabulary and Readiness Check

1. $81y^2 = (9y)^2$

2. $4z^2 = (2z)^2$

3. $64x^6 = (8x^3)^2$

4. $49y^6 = (7y^3)^2$

5. $125 = 5^3$

6. $216 = 6^3$

7. $8x^3 = (2x)^3$

8. $27y^3 = (3y)^3$

9. $64y^6 = (4x^2)^3$

10. $x^3 y^6 = (xy^2)^3$

Exercise Set 5.7

1. $x^2 + 6x + 9 = x^2 + 2 \cdot x \cdot 3 + 3^2 = (x + 3)^2$

3. $4x^2 - 12x + 9 = (2x)^2 - 2 \cdot 2x \cdot 3 + 3^2$
$$= (2x - 3)^2$$

5. $3x^2 - 24x + 48 = 3(x^2 - 8x + 16)$
$$= 3(x - 4)^2$$

7. $9y^2 x^2 + 12yx^2 + 4x^2 = x^2(9y^2 + 12y + 4)$
$$= x^2(3y + 2)^2$$

9. $x^2 - 25 = x^2 - 5^2 = (x + 5)(x - 5)$

11. $9 - 4z^2 = 3^2 - (2z)^2 = (3 + 2z)(3 - 2z)$

13. $(y + 2)^2 - 49 = (y + 2)^2 - 7^2$
$$= [(y + 2) + 7][(y + 2) - 7]$$
$$= (y + 9)(y - 5)$$

15. $64x^2 - 100 = 4(16x^2 - 25)$
$$= 4[(4x)^2 - 5^2]$$
$$= 4(4x + 5)(4x - 5)$$

17. $x^2 + 27 = x^3 + 3^3 = (x + 3)(x^2 - 3x + 9)$

19. $z^3 - 1 = z^3 - 1^3 = (z - 1)(z^2 + z + 1)$

21. $m^3 + n^3 = (m + n)(m^2 - mn + n^2)$

23. $x^3 y^2 - 27y^2 = y^2(x^3 - 27)$
$$= y^2(x^3 - 3^3)$$
$$= y^2(x - 3)(x^2 + 3x + 9)$$

25. $a^3 b + 8b^4 = b(a^3 + 8b^3)$
$$= b[a^3 + (2b)^3]$$
$$= b(a + 2b)(a^2 - 2ab + 4b^2)$$

27. $125y^3 - 8x^3 = (5y)^3 - (2x)^3$
$$= (5y - 2x)(25y^2 + 10xy + 4x^2)$$

29. $(x^2 + 6x + 9) - y^2 = (x + 3)^2 - y^2$
$$= (x + 3 + y)(x + 3 - y)$$

31. $(x^2 - 10x + 25) - y^2 = (x - 5)^2 - y^2$
$$= (x - 5 + y)(x - 5 - y)$$

33. $(4x^2 + 4x + 1) - z^2 = (2x + 1)^2 - z^2$
$$= (2x + 1 + z)(2x + 1 - z)$$

35. $9x^2 - 49 = (3x)^2 - 7^2 = (3x + 7)(3x - 7)$

37. $x^2 - 12x + 36 = x^2 - 2 \cdot x \cdot 6 + 6^2 = (x - 6)^2$

39. $x^4 - 81 = (x^2 + 9)(x^2 - 9)$
$$= (x^2 + 9)(x + 3)(x - 3)$$

41. $(x^2 + 8x + 16) - 4y^2 = (x+4)^2 - (2y)^2$
$$= (x+4+2y)(x+4-2y)$$

43. $(x+2y)^2 - 9 = (x+2y)^2 - 3^2$
$$= (x+2y+3)(x+2y-3)$$

45. $x^3 - 216 = x^3 - 6^3 = (x-6)(x^2 + 6x + 36)$

47. $x^3 + 125 = x^3 + 5^3 = (x+5)(x^2 - 5x + 25)$

49. $4x^2 + 25$ is prime.

51. $4a^2 + 12a + 9 = (2a)^2 + 2 \cdot 2a \cdot 3 + 3^2 = (2a+3)^2$

53. $18x^2 y - 2y = 2y(9x^2 - 1)$
$$= 2y(3x+1)(3x-1)$$

55. $8x^3 + y^3 = (2x)^3 + y^3$
$$= (2x+y)(4x^2 - 2xy + y^2)$$

57. $x^6 - y^3 = (x^2)^3 - y^3$
$$= (x^2 - y)(x^4 + x^2 y + y^2)$$

59. $(x^2 + 16x + 64) - x^4 = (x+8)^2 - (x^2)^2$
$$= (x+8+x^2)(x+8-x^2)$$

61. $3x^6 y^2 + 81y^2 = 3y^2(x^6 + 27)$
$$= 3y^2[(x^2)^3 + 3^3]$$
$$= 3y^2(x^2 + 3)(x^4 - 3x^2 + 9)$$

63. $(x+y)^3 + 125$
$$= (x+y)^3 + 5^3$$
$$= [(x+y) + 5][(x+y)^2 - 5(x+y) + 25]$$
$$= (x+y+5)(x^2 + 2xy + y^2 - 5x - 5y + 25)$$

65. $(2x+3)^3 - 64$
$$= (2x+3)^3 - 4^3$$
$$= [(2x+3) - 4][(2x+3)^2 + 4(2x+3) + 16]$$
$$= (2x-1)(4x^2 + 12x + 9 + 8x + 12 + 16)$$
$$= (2x-1)(4x^2 + 20x + 37)$$

67. $x - 5 = 0$
$$x = 5$$

69. $3x + 1 = 0$
$$3x = -1$$
$$x = -\frac{1}{3}$$

71. $-2x = 0$
$$x = 0$$

73. $-5x + 25 = 0$
$$-5x = -25$$
$$x = 5$$

75. No; $x^2 - 4$ can be factored further.
$$5x(x^2 - 4) = 5x(x^2 - 2^2) = 5x(x+2)(x-2)$$

77. Yes; $7y(a^2 + a + 1)$ is factored completely.

79. Area $= \pi R^2 - \pi r^2$
$$= \pi(R^2 - r^2)$$
$$= \pi(R+r)(R-r) \text{ sq units}$$

81. Volume $= x^3 - y^2 x$
$$= x(x^2 - y^2)$$
$$= x(x+y)(x-y) \text{ cubic units}$$

83. $\frac{1}{2} \cdot b = \frac{1}{2} \cdot 6 = 3$ so $c = 3^2 = 9$

85. $\frac{1}{2} \cdot b = \frac{1}{2}(-14) = -7$ so $c = (-7)^2 = 49$

87. $\frac{1}{2} \cdot c = \frac{c}{2}$ so $\left(\frac{c}{2}\right)^2 = 16$
$$\frac{c^2}{4} = 16$$
$$c^2 = 64$$
$$c = \pm 8$$

89. $x^6 - 1$

    a. $(x^3)^2 - 1^2$
$$= (x^3 + 1)(x^3 - 1)$$
$$= (x+1)(x^2 - x + 1)(x-1)(x^2 + x + 1)$$

    b. $(x^2)^3 - 1^3 = (x^2 - 1)(x^4 + x^2 + 1)$
$$= (x+1)(x-1)(x^4 + x^2 + 1)$$

c.   No; answers may vary

91. $x^{2n} - 36 = (x^n)^2 - 6^2 = (x^n + 6)(x^n - 6)$

93. $25x^{2n} - 81 = (5x^n)^2 - 9^2$
$$= (5x^n + 9)(5x^n - 9)$$

95. $x^{4n} - 625 = (x^{2n})^2 - 25^2$
$$= (x^{2n} + 25)(x^{2n} - 25)$$
$$= (x^{2n} + 25)[(x^n)^2 - 5^2]$$
$$= (x^{2n} + 25)(x^n + 5)(x^n - 5)$$

Integrated Review

Practice Exercises

1. a. $12x^2y - 3xy = 3xy(4x) + 3xy(-1)$
$$= 3xy(4x - 1)$$

b. $49x^2 - 4 = (7x)^2 - 2^2 = (7x + 2)(7x - 2)$

c. $5x^2 + 2x - 3 = (5x - 3)(x + 1)$

d. $3x^2 + 6 + x^3 + 2x = 3(x^2 + 2) + x(x^2 + 2)$
$$= (x^2 + 2)(3 + x)$$

e. $4x^2 + 20x + 25 = (2x)^2 + 2 \cdot 2x \cdot 5 + 5^2$
$$= (2x + 5)^2$$

f. $b^2 + 100$ cannot be factored.

2. a. $64x^3 + y^3 = (4x)^3 + y^3$
$$= (4x + y)[(4x)^2 - 4x \cdot y + y^2]$$
$$= (4x + y)(16x^2 - 4xy + y^2)$$

b. $7x^2y^2 - 63y^4 = 7y^2(x^2 - 9y^2)$
$$= 7y^2[x^2 - (3y)^2]$$
$$= 7y^2(x - 3y)(x + 3y)$$

c. $3x^2 + 12x + 12 - 3b^2$
$$= 3(x^2 + 4x + 4 - b^2)$$
$$= 3[(x + 2)^2 - b^2]$$
$$= 3(x + 2 + b)(x + 2 - b)$$

d. $x^5y^4 + 27x^2y$
$$= x^2y(x^3y^3 + 27)$$
$$= x^2y[(xy)^3 + 3^3]$$
$$= x^2y(xy + 3)(x^2y^2 - 3xy + 9)$$

e. $(x + 7)^2 - 81y^2 = (x + 7)^2 - (9y)^2$
$$= (x + 7 + 9y)(x + 7 - 9y)$$

Integrated Review Exercise Set

1. $(-y^2 + 6y - 1) + (3y^2 - 4y - 10)$
$$= -y^2 + 6y - 1 + 3y^2 - 4y - 10$$
$$= 2y^2 + 2y - 11$$

2. $(5z^4 - 6z^2 + z + 1) - (7z^4 - 2z + 1)$
$$= 5z^4 - 6z^2 + z + 1 - 7z^4 + 2z - 1$$
$$= -2z^4 - 6z^2 + 3z$$

3. $(x^2 - 6x + 2) - (x - 5) = x^2 - 6x + 2 - x + 5$
$$= x^2 - 7x + 7$$

4. $(2x^2 + 6x - 5) + (5x^2 - 10x) = 7x^2 - 4x - 5$

5. $(5x - 3)^2 = (5x)^2 - 2(5x)(3) + 3^2$
$$= 25x^2 - 30x + 9$$

6. $\dfrac{5x^2 - 14x - 3}{5x + 1} = \dfrac{(x - 3)(5x + 1)}{5x + 1} = x - 3$

7.

$$
\begin{array}{r}
2x^3 - 4x^2 + 5x - 3 \\
x + 2 \overline{)\, 2x^4 + 0x^3 - 3x^2 + 5x - 2} \\
\underline{2x^4 + 4x^3} \\
-4x^3 - 3x^2 \\
\underline{-4x^3 - 8x^2} \\
5x^2 + 5x \\
\underline{5x^2 + 10x} \\
-5x - 2 \\
\underline{-5x - 10} \\
8
\end{array}
$$

$92x^4 - 3x^2 + 5x - 2) \div (x + 2)$
$$= 2x^3 - 4x^2 + 5x - 5 + \dfrac{8}{x + 2}$$

8.

$$
\begin{array}{r}
x^2 - 3x - 2 \\
\times \qquad 4x - 1 \\
\hline
-x^2 + 3x + 2 \\
4x^3 - 12x^2 - 8x \\
\hline
4x^3 - 13x^2 - 5x + 2
\end{array}
$$

9. $x^2 - 8x + 16 - y^2 = (x-4)^2 - y^2$
$$= (x - 4 + y)(x - 4 - y)$$

10. $12x^2 - 22x - 20 = 2(6x^2 - 11x - 10)$
$$= 2(3x + 2)(2x - 5)$$

11. $x^4 - x = x(x^3 - 1) = x(x-1)(x^2 + x + 1)$

12. Let $y = 2x + 1$. Then

$(2x+1)^2 - 3(2x+1) + 2$
$= y^2 - 3y + 2$
$= (y - 2)(y - 1)$
$= [(2x+1) - 2][(2x+1) - 1]$
$= (2x - 1)(2x)$
$= 2x(2x - 1)$

13. $14x^2 y - 2xy = 2xy(7x - 1)$

14. $24ab^2 - 6ab = 6ab(4b - 1)$

15. $4x^2 - 16 = 4(x^2 - 4) = 4(x + 2)(x - 2)$

16. $9x^2 - 81 = 9(x^2 - 9) = 9(x + 3)(x - 3)$

17. $3x^2 - 8x - 11 = (3x - 11)(x + 1)$

18. $5x^2 - 2x - 3 = (5x + 3)(x - 1)$

19. $4x^2 + 8x - 12 = 4(x^2 + 2x - 3)$
$$= 4(x + 3)(x - 1)$$

20. $6x^2 - 6x - 12 = 6(x^2 - x - 2)$
$$= 6(x - 2)(x + 1)$$

21. $4x^2 + 36x + 81 = (2x)^2 + 2 \cdot 2x \cdot 9 + 9^2$
$$= (2x + 9)^2$$

22. $25x^2 + 40x + 16 = (5x)^2 + 2 \cdot 5x \cdot 4 + 4^2$
$$= (5x + 4)^2$$

23. $8x^3 + 125y^3 = (2x)^3 + (5y)^3$
$$= (2x + 5y)(4x^2 - 10xy + 25y^2)$$

24. $27x^3 - 64y^3 = (3x)^3 - (4y)^3$
$$= (3x - 4y)(9x^2 + 12xy + 16y^2)$$

25. $64x^2 y^3 - 8x^2 = 8x^2(8y^3 - 1)$
$$= 8x^2[(2y)^3 - 1^3]$$
$$= 8x^2(2y - 1)(4y^2 + 2y + 1)$$

26. $27x^5 y^4 - 216x^2 y$
$= 27x^2 y(x^3 y^3 - 8)$
$= 27x^2 y[(xy)^3 - 2^3]$
$= 27x^2 y(xy - 2)(x^2 y^2 + 2xy + 4)$

27. $(x + 5)^3 + y^3$
$= [(x + 5) + y][(x + 5)^2 - (x + 5)y + y^2]$
$= (x + y + 5)(x^2 + 10x + 25 - xy - 5y + y^2)$
$= (x + y + 5)(x^2 + 10x - xy - 5y + y^2 + 25)$

28. $(y - 1)^3 + 27x^3$
$= (y - 1)^3 + (3x)^3$
$= [(y - 1) + 3x][(y - 1)^2 - (y - 1)(3x) + (3x)^2]$
$= (y - 1 + 3x)(y^2 - 2y + 1 - 3xy + 3x + 9x^2)$

29. Let $y = 5a - 3$. Then
$(5a - 3)^2 - 6(5a - 3) + 9 = y^2 - 6y + 9$
$= (y - 3)(y - 3)$
$= (y - 3)^2$
$= [(5a - 3) - 3]^2$
$= (5a - 6)^2$

30. Let $y = 4r + 1$. Then
$(4r + 1)^2 + 8(4r + 1) + 16 = y^2 + 8y + 16$
$= (y + 4)(y + 4)$
$= (y + 4)^2$
$= [(4r + 1) + 4]^2$
$= (4r + 5)^2$

31. $7x^2 - 63x = 7x(x - 9)$

32. $20x^2 + 23x + 6 = (4x + 3)(5x + 2)$

33. $ab - 6a + 7b - 42 = a(b - 6) + 7(b - 6)$
$\qquad\qquad\qquad = (a + 7)(b - 6)$

34. $20x^2 - 220x + 600 = 20(x^2 - 11x + 30)$
$\qquad\qquad\qquad\quad = 20(x - 6)(x - 5)$

35. $x^4 - 1 = (x^2)^2 - 1^2$
$\qquad\quad = (x^2 + 1)(x^2 - 1)$
$\qquad\quad = (x^2 + 1)(x + 1)(x - 1)$

36. $15x^2 - 20x = 5x(3x - 4)$

37. $10x^2 - 7x - 33 = (5x - 11)(2x + 3)$

38. $45m^3n^3 - 27m^2n^2 = 9m^2n^2(5mn - 3)$

39. $5a^3b^3 - 50a^3b = 5a^3b(b^2 - 10)$

40. $x^4 + x = x(x^3 + 1)$
$\qquad\quad = x(x^3 + 1^3)$
$\qquad\quad = x(x + 1)(x^2 - x + 1)$

41. $16x^2 + 25$ is a prime polynomial.

42. $20x^3 + 20y^3 = 20(x^3 + y^3)$
$\qquad\qquad\quad = 20(x + y)(x^2 - xy + y^2)$

43. $10x^3 - 210x^2 + 1100x = 10x(x^2 - 21x + 110)$
$\qquad\qquad\qquad\qquad\quad = 10x(x - 11)(x - 10)$

44. $9y^2 - 42y + 49 = (3y)^2 - 2 \cdot 3y \cdot 7 + 7^2$
$\qquad\qquad\qquad = (3y - 7)^2$

45. $64a^3b^4 - 27a^3b$
$\quad = a^3b(64b^3 - 27)$
$\quad = a^3b[(4b)^3 - 3^3]$
$\quad = a^3b(4b - 3)(16b^2 + 12b + 9)$

46. $y^4 - 16 = (y^2)^2 - 4^2$
$\qquad\quad = (y^2 + 4)(y^2 - 4)$
$\qquad\quad = (y^2 + 4)(y + 2)(y - 2)$

47. $2x^3 - 54 = 2(x^3 - 27)$
$\qquad\quad = 2(x^3 - 3^3)$
$\qquad\quad = 2(x - 3)(x^2 + 3x + 9)$

48. $2sr + 10s - r - 5 = 2s(r + 5) - 1(r + 5)$
$\qquad\qquad\qquad = (2s - 1)(r + 5)$

49. $3y^5 - 5y^4 + 6y - 10 = y^4(3y - 5) + 2(3y - 5)$
$\qquad\qquad\qquad\qquad = (y^4 + 2)(3y - 5)$

50. $64a^2 + b^2$ is a prime polynomial.

51. $100z^3 + 100 = 100(z^3 + 1)$
$\qquad\qquad\quad = 100(z + 1)(z^2 - z + 1)$

52. $250x^4 - 16x = 2x(125x^3 - 8)$
$\qquad\qquad\quad = 2x[(5x)^3 - 2^3]$
$\qquad\qquad\quad = 2x(5x - 2)(25x^2 + 10x + 4)$

53. $4b^2 - 36b + 81 = (2b)^2 - 2 \cdot 2b \cdot 9 + 9^2$
$\qquad\qquad\qquad = (2b - 9)^2$

54. $2a^5 - a^4 + 6a - 3 = a^4(2a - 1) + 3(2a - 1)$
$\qquad\qquad\qquad\quad = (a^4 + 3)(2a - 1)$

55. Let $x = y - 6$. Then
$\quad (y - 6)^2 + 3(y - 6) + 2 = x^2 + 3x + 2$
$\qquad\qquad\qquad\qquad\qquad = (x + 2)(x + 1)$
$\qquad\qquad\qquad\qquad\qquad = [(y - 6) + 2][(y - 6) + 1]$
$\qquad\qquad\qquad\qquad\qquad = (y - 4)(y - 5)$

56. Let $x = c + 2$. Then
$\quad (c + 2)^2 - 6(c + 2) + 5 = x^2 - 6x + 5$
$\qquad\qquad\qquad\qquad\qquad = (x - 5)(x - 1)$
$\qquad\qquad\qquad\qquad\qquad = [(c + 2) - 5][(c + 2) - 1]$
$\qquad\qquad\qquad\qquad\qquad = (c - 3)(c + 1)$

57. Area $= 3^2 - 4x^2 = 3^2 - (2x)^2 = (3 + 2x)(3 - 2x)$

Section 5.8

Practice Exercises

1. $(x + 8)(x - 5) = 0$
$\quad x + 8 = 0 \quad$ or $\quad x - 5 = 0$
$\qquad x = -8 \quad$ or $\qquad x = 5$

Both solutions check. The solution set is $\{-8, 5\}$.

2. $3x^2 + 10x - 8 = 0$

$(3x - 2)(x + 4) = 0$

$3x - 2 = 0$ or $x + 4 = 0$

$3x = 2$

$x = \dfrac{2}{3}$ or $x = -4$

Both solutions check. The solution set is
$\left\{ -4, \dfrac{2}{3} \right\}$.

3. $x(3x + 14) = -8$

$3x^2 + 14x = -8$

$3x^2 + 14x + 8 = 0$

$(3x + 2)(x + 4) = 0$

$3x + 2 = 0$ or $x + 4 = 0$

$3x = -2$

$x = -\dfrac{2}{3}$ or $x = -4$

The solutions are $-\dfrac{2}{3}$ and -4.

4. $8(x^2 + 3) + 4 = -8x(x + 3) + 19$

$8x^2 + 24 + 4 = -8x^2 - 24x + 19$

$16x^2 + 24x + 9 = 0$

$(4x + 3)(4x + 3) = 0$

$4x + 3 = 0$ or $4x + 3 = 0$

$4x = -3$ or $4x = -3$

$x = -\dfrac{3}{4}$ or $x = -\dfrac{3}{4}$

The solution is $-\dfrac{3}{4}$.

5. $4x^2 = \dfrac{15}{2}x + 1$

$2(4x^2) = 2\left(\dfrac{15}{2}x + 1 \right)$

$8x^2 = 15x + 2$

$8x^2 - 15x - 2 = 0$

$(8x + 1)(x - 2) = 0$

$8x + 1 = 0$ or $x - 2 = 0$

$8x = -1$

$x = -\dfrac{1}{8}$ or $x = 2$

The solutions are $-\dfrac{1}{8}$ and 2.

6. $x^3 = 2x^2 + 3x$

$x^3 - 2x^2 - 3x = 0$

$x(x^2 - 2x - 3) = 0$

$x(x - 3)(x + 1) = 0$

$x = 0$ or $x - 3 = 0$ or $x + 1 = 0$

$x = 3$ or $x = -1$

The solutions are 0, 3, and -1.

7. $x^3 - 9x = 18 - 2x^2$

$x^3 + 2x^2 - 9x - 18 = 0$

$x^2(x + 2) - 9(x + 2) = 0$

$(x + 2)(x^2 - 9) = 0$

$(x + 2)(x + 3)(x - 3) = 0$

$x + 2 = 0$ or $x + 3 = 0$ or $x - 3 = 0$

$x = -2$ or $x = -3$ or $x = 3$

The solutions are 3, -3, and -2.

8. Let $h = 0$.

$-16t^2 + 96t = 0$

$-16t(t - 6) = 0$

$-16t = 0$ or $t - 6 = 0$

$t = 0$ or $t = 6$

The rocket will return to the ground in 6 seconds.

9. Let $x =$ first even integer, then $x + 2 =$ next even integer, and $x + 4 =$ third even integer.

$x^2 + (x + 2)^2 = (x + 4)^2$

$x^2 + x^2 + 4x + 4 = x^2 + 8x + 16$

$x^2 - 4x - 12 = 0$

$(x - 6)(x + 2) = 0$

$x - 6 = 0$ or $x + 2 = 0$

$x = 6$ or $x = -2$

Discard $x = -2$ since length cannot be negative. The legs are $x = 6$ units, $x + 2 = 8$ units, and $x + 4 = 10$ units.

10. The graph of $f(x) = (x - 1)(x + 3)$ has two x-intercepts, (1, 0) and (-3, 0), so the graph is C.
The graph of $g(x) = x(x + 3)(x - 2)$ has three x-intercepts, (0, 0), (-3, 0), and (2, 0), so the graph is A.
The graph of $h(x) = (x - 3)(x + 2)(x - 2)$ has three x-intercepts, (3, 0), (-2, 0), and (2, 0), so the graph is B.

Graphing Calculator Explorations

1. $y = x^2 + 3x - 2$

The intercepts are -3.562, 0.562.

2. $y = 5x^2 - 7x + 1$

The intercepts are 0.161, 1.239.

3. $y = 2.3x^2 - 4.4x - 5.6$

The intercepts are -0.874, 2.787.

4. $y = 0.2x^2 + 6.2x + 2.1$

The intercepts are -30.658, -0.342.

5. $y = 0.09x^2 - 0.13x - 0.08$

The intercepts are -0.465, 1.910.

6. $y = x^2 + 0.08x - 0.01$

The intercepts are -0.148, 0.068.

Vocabulary and Readiness Check

1. $(x-3)(x+5) = 0$
$x - 3 = 0$ or $x + 5 = 0$
$x = 3$ or $\quad x = -5$
The solutions are -5, 3.

2. $(y+5)(y+3) = 0$
$y + 5 = 0$ or $y + 3 = 0$
$y = -5$ or $\quad y = -3$
The solutions are -5, -3.

3. $(z-3)(z+7) = 0$
$z - 3 = 0$ or $z + 7 = 0$
$z = 3$ or $\quad z = -7$
The solutions are -7, 3.

4. $(c-2)(c-4)=0$

$c-2=0$ or $c-4=0$

$c=2$ or $\quad c=4$

The solutions are 2, 4.

5. $x(x-9)=0$

$x=0$ or $x-9=0$

$\qquad\qquad x=9$

The solutions are 0, 9.

6. $w(w+7)=0$

$w=0$ or $w+7=0$

$\qquad\qquad w=-7$

The solutions are -7, 0.

Exercise Set 5.8

1. $(x+3)(3x-4)=0$

$x+3=0$ or $3x-4=0$

$x=-3$ or $\quad 3x=4$

$\qquad\qquad\qquad x=\dfrac{4}{3}$

The solutions are $-3, \dfrac{4}{3}$.

3. $3(2x-5)(4x+3)=0$

$2x-5=0$ or $4x+3=0$

$2x=5$ or $\quad 4x=-3$

$x=\dfrac{5}{2}$ or $\quad x=-\dfrac{3}{4}$

The solutions are $-\dfrac{3}{4},\dfrac{5}{2}$.

5. $x^2+11x+24=0$

$(x+8)(x+3)=0$

$x+8=0$ or $x+3=0$

$x=-8$ or $\quad x=-3$

The solutions are $-8, -3$.

7. $12x^2+5x-2=0$

$(4x-1)(3x+2)=0$

$4x-1=0$ or $3x+2=0$

$4x=1$ or $\quad 3x=-2$

$x=\dfrac{1}{4}$ or $\quad x=-\dfrac{2}{3}$

The solutions are $-\dfrac{2}{3},\dfrac{1}{4}$.

9. $\qquad z^2+9=10z$

$z^2-10z+9=0$

$(z-9)(z-1)=0$

$z-9=0$ or $z-1=0$

$z=9$ or $\quad z=1$

The solutions are 1, 9.

11. $\qquad x(5x+2)=3$

$5x^2+2x-3=0$

$(5x-3)(x+1)=0$

$5x-3=0$ or $x+1=0$

$5x=3$ or $\quad x=-1$

$x=\dfrac{3}{5}$

The solutions are $-1, \dfrac{3}{5}$.

13. $x^2-6x=x(8+x)$

$x^2-6x=8x+x^2$

$-14x=0$

$x=0$

The solution is 0.

15. $\dfrac{z^2}{6}-\dfrac{z}{2}-3=0$

$z^2-3z-18=0$

$(z-6)(z+3)=0$

$z-6=0$ or $z+3=0$

$z=6$ or $\quad z=-3$

The solutions are -3, 6.

17. $\dfrac{x^2}{2}+\dfrac{x}{20}=\dfrac{1}{10}$

$10x^2+x=2$

$10x^2+x-2=0$

$(5x-2)(2x+1)=0$

$5x-2=0$ or $2x+1=0$

$5x=2$ or $\quad 2x=-1$

$x=\dfrac{2}{5}$ or $\quad x=-\dfrac{1}{2}$

The solutions are $-\dfrac{1}{2},\dfrac{2}{5}$.

19.
$$\frac{4t^2}{5} = \frac{t}{5} + \frac{3}{10}$$
$$8t^2 = 2t + 3$$
$$8t^2 - 2t - 3 = 0$$
$$(4t - 3)(2t + 1) = 0$$
$$4t - 3 = 0 \text{ or } 2t + 1 = 0$$
$$4t = 3 \text{ or } 2t = -1$$
$$t = \frac{3}{4} \text{ or } t = -\frac{1}{2}$$
The solutions are $-\frac{1}{2}, \frac{3}{4}$.

21. $(x + 2)(x - 7)(3x - 8) = 0$
$$x + 2 = 0 \text{ or } x - 7 = 0 \text{ or } 3x - 8 = 0$$
$$x = -2 \text{ or } x = 7 \text{ or } 3x = 8$$
$$x = \frac{8}{3}$$
The solutions are $-2, 7, \frac{8}{3}$.

23.
$$y^3 = 9y$$
$$y^3 - 9y = 0$$
$$y(y^2 - 9) = 0$$
$$y(y + 3)(y - 3) = 0$$
$$y = 0 \text{ or } y + 3 = 0 \text{ or } y - 3 = 0$$
$$y = -3 \text{ or } y = 3$$
The solutions are $-3, 0, 3$.

25.
$$x^3 - x = 2x^2 - 2$$
$$x^3 - 2x^2 - x + 2 = 0$$
$$x^2(x - 2) - 1(x - 2) = 0$$
$$(x^2 - 1)(x - 2) = 0$$
$$(x + 1)(x - 1)(x - 2) = 0$$
$$x + 1 = 0 \text{ or } x - 1 = 0 \text{ or } x - 2 = 0$$
$$x = -1 \text{ or } x = 1 \text{ or } x = 2$$
The solutions are $-1, 1, 2$.

27. Answers may vary

29. $(2x + 7)(x - 10) = 0$
$$2x + 7 = 0 \text{ or } x - 10 = 0$$
$$2x = -7 \text{ or } x = 10$$
$$x = -\frac{7}{2}$$
The solutions are $-\frac{7}{2}, 10$.

31. $3x(x - 5) = 0$
$$3x = 0 \text{ or } x - 5 = 0$$
$$x = 0 \text{ or } x = 5$$
The solutions are $0, 5$.

33. $x^2 - 2x - 15 = 0$
$$(x - 5)(x + 3) = 0$$
$$x - 5 = 0 \text{ or } x + 3 = 0$$
$$x = 5 \text{ or } x = -3$$
The solutions are $-3, 5$.

35.
$$12x^2 + 2x - 2 = 0$$
$$2(6x^2 + x - 1) = 0$$
$$2(3x - 1)(2x + 1) = 0$$
$$3x - 1 = 0 \text{ or } 2x + 1 = 0$$
$$3x = 1 \text{ or } 2x = -1$$
$$x = \frac{1}{3} \text{ or } x = -\frac{1}{2}$$
The solutions are $-\frac{1}{2}, \frac{1}{3}$.

37.
$$w^2 - 5w = 36$$
$$w^2 - 5w - 36 = 0$$
$$(w - 9)(w + 4) = 0$$
$$w - 9 = 0 \text{ or } w + 4 = 0$$
$$w = 9 \text{ or } w = -4$$
The solutions are $-4, 9$.

39. $25x^2 - 40x + 16 = 0$
$$(5x - 4)^2 = 0$$
$$5x - 4 = 0$$
$$5x = 4$$
$$x = \frac{4}{5}$$
The solution is $\frac{4}{5}$.

41.
$$2r^3 + 6r^2 = 20r$$
$$2r^3 + 6r^2 - 20r = 0$$
$$2r(r^2 + 3r - 10) = 0$$
$$2r(r + 5)(r - 2) = 0$$
$$2r = 0 \text{ or } r + 5 = 0 \text{ or } r - 2 = 0$$
$$r = 0 \text{ or } r = -5 \text{ or } r = 2$$
The solutions are $-5, 0, 2$.

43. $z(5z-4)(z+3)=0$

$z=0$ or $5z-4=0$ or $z+3=0$

$\qquad\qquad\qquad 5z=4$ or $\qquad z=-3$

$\qquad\qquad\qquad z=\dfrac{4}{5}$

The solutions are -3, 0, $\dfrac{4}{5}$.

45. $2z(z+6)=2z^2+12z-8$

$2z^2+12z=2z^2+12z-8$

$\qquad\qquad 0=-8$ False

No solutions exist; $\varnothing$.

47. $(x-1)(x+4)=24$

$x^2+3x-4=24$

$x^2+3x-28=0$

$(x+7)(x-4)=0$

$x+7=0$ or $x-4=0$

$\qquad x=-7$ or $\qquad x=4$

The solutions are -7, 4.

49. $\dfrac{x^2}{4}-\dfrac{5}{2}x+6=0$

$x^2-10x+24=0$

$(x-6)(x-4)=0$

$x-6=0$ or $x-4=0$

$\qquad x=6$ or $\qquad x=4$

The solutions are 4, 6.

51. $y^2+\dfrac{1}{4}=-y$

$\qquad 4y^2+1=-4y$

$\quad 4y^2+4y+1=0$

$\qquad (2y+1)^2=0$

$\qquad\quad 2y+1=0$

$\qquad\qquad 2y=-1$

$\qquad\qquad\; y=-\dfrac{1}{2}$

The solution is $-\dfrac{1}{2}$.

53. $\qquad y^3+4y^2=9y+36$

$y^3+4y^2-9y-36=0$

$y^2(y+4)-9(y+4)=0$

$\qquad (y^2-9)(y+4)=0$

$(y+3)(y-3)(y+4)=0$

$y+3=0$ or $y-3=0$ or $y+4=0$

$\quad y=-3$ or $\qquad y=3$ or $\qquad y=-4$

The solutions are -4, -3, 3.

55. $\qquad 2x^3=50x$

$\quad 2x^3-50x=0$

$2x(x^2-25)=0$

$2x(x+5)(x-5)=0$

$2x=0$ or $x+5=0$ or $x-5=0$

$x=0$ or $\qquad x=-5$ or $\qquad x=5$

The solutions are -5, 0, 5.

57. $x^2+(x+1)^2=61$

$x^2+x^2+2x+1=61$

$\qquad 2x^2+2x-60=0$

$\qquad 2(x^2+x-30)=0$

$\qquad 2(x+6)(x-5)=0$

$x+6=0$ or $x-5=0$

$\quad x=-6$ or $\qquad x=5$

The solutions are -6, 5.

59. $\qquad m^2(3m-2)=m$

$\qquad 3m^3-2m^2=m$

$\quad 3m^3-2m^2-m=0$

$\quad m(3m^2-2m-1)=0$

$\quad m(3m+1)(m-1)=0$

$m=0$ or $3m+1=0$ or $m-1=0$

$\qquad\qquad 3m=-1$ or $\qquad m=1$

$\qquad\qquad\; m=-\dfrac{1}{3}$

The solutions are $-\dfrac{1}{3}$, 0, 1.

61.
$$3x^2 = -x$$
$$3x^2 + x = 0$$
$$x(3x+1) = 0$$
$$x = 0 \quad \text{or} \quad 3x + 1 = 0$$
$$3x = -1$$
$$x = -\frac{1}{3}$$

The solutions are $-\frac{1}{3}$, 0.

63.
$$x(x-3) = x^2 + 5x + 7$$
$$x^2 - 3x = x^2 + 5x + 7$$
$$-8x = 7$$
$$x = -\frac{7}{8}$$

The solution is $-\frac{7}{8}$.

65.
$$3(t-8) + 2t = 7 + t$$
$$3t - 24 + 2t = 7 + t$$
$$5t - 24 = 7 + t$$
$$4t = 31$$
$$t = \frac{31}{4}$$

The solution is $\frac{31}{4}$.

67.
$$-3(x-4) + x = 5(3-x)$$
$$-3x + 12 + x = 15 - 5x$$
$$-2x + 12 = 15 - 5x$$
$$3x = 3$$
$$x = 1$$

The solution is 1.

69. **a** and **d** are incorrect because the right side of the equation is not zero.

71. Let n = the one number and
$n + 5$ = the other number.
$$n(n+5) = 66$$
$$n^2 + 5n - 66 = 0$$
$$(n+11)(n-6) = 0$$
$$n + 11 = 0 \quad \text{or} \quad n - 6 = 0$$
$$n = -11 \quad \text{or} \quad n = 6$$

The two solutions are –11 and –6 and 6 and 11.

73. Let d = amount of cable needed. Then from the Pythagorean theorem, $d^2 = 45^2 + 60^2 = 5625$ so $d = \sqrt{5625} = 75$ ft.

75.
$$C(x) = x^2 - 15x + 50$$
$$9500 = x^2 - 15x + 50$$
$$0 = x^2 - 15x - 9450$$
$$0 = (x-105)(x+90)$$
$$x - 105 = 0 \quad \text{or} \quad x + 90 = 0$$
$$x = 105 \quad \text{or} \quad x = -90$$

Disregard the negative; 105 units.

77. Let x = one leg of a right triangle and
$x - 3$ = the other leg of the right triangle.
$$15^2 = x^2 + (x-3)^2$$
$$225 = x^2 + x^2 - 6x + 9$$
$$225 = 2x^2 - 6x + 9$$
$$0 = 2x^2 - 6x - 216$$
$$0 = 2(x^2 - 3x - 108)$$
$$0 = 2(x-12)(x+9)$$
$$x - 12 = 0 \quad \text{or} \quad x + 9 = 0$$
$$x = 12 \quad \text{or} \quad x = -9$$

Disregarding the negative solution, we find that one leg of the right triangle is 12 cm and the other leg is 9 cm.

79. Note that the outer rectangle has lengths of $2x + 12$ and $2x + 16$. Thus, the area of the border is $(2x + 12)(2x + 16) - 12 \cdot 16$. Set this equal to 128 and solve for x.
$$(2x+12)(2x+16) - 12 \cdot 16 = 128$$
$$4x^2 + 56x + 192 - 192 = 128$$
$$4x^2 + 56x = 128$$
$$4x^2 + 56x - 128 = 0$$
$$x^2 + 14x - 32 = 0$$
$$(x+16)(x-2) = 0$$
$$x + 16 = 0 \quad \text{or} \quad x - 2 = 0$$
$$x = -16 \quad \text{or} \quad x = 2$$

Since x must be positive, we see that $x = 2$ inches.

81. The sunglasses will hit the ground when
$h(t)$ equals 0.

$$-16t^2 + 1600 = 0$$
$$-16(t^2 - 100) = 0$$
$$-16(t - 10)(t + 10) = 0$$
$$t - 10 = 0 \quad \text{or} \quad t + 10 = 0$$
$$t = 10 \quad \text{or} \qquad t = -10$$

The sunglasses will hit the ground 10 seconds after being dropped.

83. Let the width of the floor $= w$. Then the length is
$2w - 3$ and so the area is

$$(2w - 3)w = 90$$
$$2w^2 - 3w - 90 = 0$$
$$(2w - 15)(w + 6) = 0$$
$$2w - 15 = 0 \qquad \text{or} \quad w + 6 = 0$$
$$2w = 15 \qquad \text{or} \qquad w = -6$$
$$w = \frac{15}{2} = 7.5$$

Disregard -6.
$$2w - 3 = 2(7.5) - 3 = 15 - 3 = 12$$
The width is 7.5 ft and the length is 12 ft.

85.
$$0.5x^2 = 50$$
$$0.5x^2 - 50 = 0$$
$$5x^2 - 500 = 0$$
$$x^2 - 100 = 0$$
$$(x + 10)(x - 10) = 0$$
$$x + 10 = 0 \quad \text{or} \quad x - 10 = 0$$
$$x = -10 \quad \text{or} \qquad x = 10$$

Disregard the negative solution. A 10-inch square tier is needed, provided each person has one serving.

87. The object will hit the ground when $h(t)$ equals
0.

$$-16t^2 + 80t + 576 = 0$$
$$-16(t^2 - 5t - 36) = 0$$
$$-16(t - 9)(t + 4) = 0$$
$$t - 9 = 0 \quad \text{or} \quad t + 4 = 0$$
$$t = 9 \quad \text{or} \qquad t = -4$$

The object will hit the ground 9 seconds after being dropped.

89. E; x-intercepts $(2, 0)$, $(-5, 0)$

91. F; x-intercepts $(0, 0)$, $(-3, 0)$, $(3, 0)$

93. B; x-intercepts $\left(-\dfrac{1}{2}, 0\right)$, $(-4, 0)$

95. $(-3, 0)$, $(0, 2)$; function, because any vertical line will cross only once.

97. $(-4, 0)$, $(0, 2)$, $(4, 0)$, $(0, -2)$; not a function, because a vertical line can be drawn that crosses twice.

99. Answers may vary

101. $(x - 5)(x + 2) = 0$
$$x - 5 = 0 \quad \text{or} \quad x + 2 = 0$$
$$x = 5 \quad \text{or} \qquad x = -2$$

103.
$$y(y - 5) = -6$$
$$y^2 - 5y + 6 = 0$$
$$(y - 2)(y - 3) = 0$$
$$y - 2 = 0 \quad \text{or} \quad y - 3 = 0$$
$$y = 2 \quad \text{or} \qquad y = 3$$

105. $(x^2 + x - 6)(3x^2 - 14x - 5) = 0$
$$x^2 + x - 6 = 0 \quad \text{or} \quad 3x^2 - 14x - 5 = 0$$
$$(x + 3)(x - 2) = 0 \quad \text{or} \quad (3x + 1)(x - 5) = 0$$
$$x + 3 = 0 \quad \text{or} \quad x - 2 = 0 \quad \text{or} \quad 3x + 1 = 0$$
$$x = -3 \qquad x = 2 \qquad 3x = -1$$
$$x = -\frac{1}{3}$$
or $x - 5 = 0$
$$x = 5$$
The solutions are -3, $-\dfrac{1}{3}$, 2, 5.

107. No; answers may vary

109. Answers may vary
Ex.: $(x - 6)(x - 7) = x^2 - 13x + 42 = 0$

111. Answers may vary
Ex.: $(x - 4)(x + 3) = x^2 - x - 12 = 0$

The Bigger Picture

1. $|7x - 3| = |5x - 9|$
$$7x - 3 = 5x + 9 \quad \text{or} \quad 7x - 3 = -(5x + 9)$$
$$2x = 12 \qquad\qquad 7x - 3 = -5x - 9$$
$$x = 6 \qquad\qquad 12x = -6$$
$$x = -\frac{1}{2}$$

2. $\left|\dfrac{x+2}{5}\right| < 1$

$-1 < \dfrac{x+2}{5} < 1$

$-5 < x+2 < 5$

$-7 < x < 3$

$(-7, 3)$

3. $3(x-6)+2 = 9+5(3x-1)$

$3x-18+2 = 9+15x-5$

$3x-16 = 15x+4$

$-12x = 20$

$x = -\dfrac{5}{3}$

4. $(x-6)(2x+3) = 0$

$x-6 = 0$ or $2x+3 = 0$

$x = 6$ or $x = -\dfrac{3}{2}$

5. $|-3x+10| \ge -2$

The absolute value of any expression is always ≥ 0. Therefore, the solution is $(-\infty, \infty)$.

6. $|-2x-5| = 11$

$-2x-5 = -11$ or $-2x-5 = 11$

$-2x = -6$ or $-2x = 16$

$x = 3$ or $x = -8$

7. $x(x-7) = 30$

$x^2 - 7x = 30$

$x^2 - 7x - 30 = 0$

$(x+3)(x-10) = 0$

$x+3 = 0$ or $x-10 = 0$

$x = -3$ or $x = 10$

8. $8x-4 \ge 15x-4$

$-7x \ge 0$

$x \le 0$

The solution set is $(-\infty, 0]$.

Chapter 5 Vocabulary Check

1. A <u>polynomial</u> is a finite sum of terms in which all variables are raised to nonnegative integer powers and no variables appear in any denominator.

2. <u>Factoring</u> is the process of writing a polynomial as a product.

3. <u>Exponents</u> are used to write repeated factors in a more compact form.

4. The <u>degree of a term</u> is the sum of the exponents on the variables contained in the term.

5. A <u>monomial</u> is a polynomial with three terms.

6. If a is not 0, $a^0 = \underline{1}$.

7. A <u>trinomial</u> is a polynomial with three terms.

8. A polynomial equation of degree 2 is also called a <u>quadratic equation</u>.

9. A positive number is written in <u>scientific notation</u> if it is written as the product of a number a, such that $1 \le a < 10$ and a power of 10.

10. The <u>degree of a polynomial</u> is the largest degree of all of its terms.

11. A <u>binomial</u> is a polynomial with two terms.

12. If a and b are real numbers and $a \cdot b = \underline{0}$, then $a = 0$ and $b = 0$.

Chapter 5 Review

1. $(-2)^2 = (-2)(-2) = 4$

2. $(-3)^4 = (-3)(-3)(-3)(-3) = 81$

3. $-2^2 = -(2 \cdot 2) = -4$

4. $-3^4 = -(3 \cdot 3 \cdot 3 \cdot 3) = -81$

5. $8^0 = 1$

6. $-9^0 = -1$

7. $-4^{-2} = -\dfrac{1}{4^2} = -\dfrac{1}{16}$

8. $(-4)^2 = \dfrac{1}{(-4)^2} = \dfrac{1}{16}$

9. $-xy^2 \cdot y^3 \cdot xy^2 z = -x^{1+1} y^{2+3+2} z = -x^2 y^7 z$

10. $(-4xy)(-3xy^2b) = (-4)(-3)x^{1+1}y^{1+2}b$
$$= 12x^2y^3b$$

11. $a^{-14}a^5 = a^{-14+5} = a^{-9} = \dfrac{1}{a^9}$

12. $\dfrac{a^{16}}{a^{17}} = a^{16-17} = a^{-1} = \dfrac{1}{a}$

13. $\dfrac{x^{-7}}{x^4} = x^{-7-4} = x^{-11} = \dfrac{1}{x^{11}}$

14. $\dfrac{9a(a^{-3})}{18a^{15}} = \dfrac{a^{1-3-15}}{2} = \dfrac{a^{-17}}{2} = \dfrac{1}{2a^{17}}$

15. $\dfrac{y^{6p-3}}{y^{6p+2}} = y^{(6p-3)-(6p+2)}$
$$= y^{6p-3-6p-2}$$
$$= y^{-5}$$
$$= \dfrac{1}{y^5}$$

16. $36{,}890{,}000 = 3.689 \times 10^7$

17. $-0.000362 = -3.62 \times 10^{-4}$

18. $1.678 \times 10^{-6} = 0.000001678$

19. $4.1 \times 10^5 = 410{,}000$

20. $(8^5)^3 = 8^{5 \cdot 3} = 8^{15}$

21. $\left(\dfrac{a}{4}\right)^2 = \dfrac{a^2}{4^2} = \dfrac{a^2}{16}$

22. $(3x)^3 = 3^3 x^3 = 27x^3$

23. $(-4x)^{-2} = \dfrac{1}{(-4x)^2} = \dfrac{1}{(-4)^2 x^2} = \dfrac{1}{16x^2}$

24. $\left(\dfrac{6x}{5}\right)^2 = \dfrac{(6x)^2}{5^2} = \dfrac{36x^2}{25}$

25. $(8^6)^{-3} = 8^{6(-3)} = 8^{-18} = \dfrac{1}{8^{18}}$

26. $\left(\dfrac{4}{3}\right)^{-2} = \dfrac{4^{-2}}{3^{-2}} = \dfrac{3^2}{4^2} = \dfrac{9}{16}$

27. $(-2x^3)^{-3} = \dfrac{1}{(-2x^3)^3}$
$$= \dfrac{1}{(-2)^3(x^3)^3}$$
$$= \dfrac{1}{-8x^9}$$
$$= -\dfrac{1}{8x^9}$$

28. $\left(\dfrac{8p^6}{4p^4}\right)^{-2} = (2p^2)^{-2} = 2^{-2}p^{-4} = \dfrac{1}{4p^4}$

29. $(-3x^{-2}y^2)^3 = (-3)^3(x^{-2})^3(y^2)^3$
$$= -27x^{-6}y^6$$
$$= -\dfrac{27y^6}{x^6}$$

30. $\left(\dfrac{x^{-5}y^{-3}}{z^3}\right)^{-5} = \dfrac{x^{25}y^{15}}{z^{-15}} = x^{25}y^{15}z^{15}$

31. $\dfrac{4^{-1}x^3yz}{x^{-2}yx^4} = \dfrac{x^{3-(-2)-4}z}{4} = \dfrac{x^{3+2-4}z}{4} = \dfrac{xz}{4}$

32. $(5xyz)^{-4}(x^{-2})^{-3} = \dfrac{1}{(5xyz)^4}x^6$
$$= \dfrac{x^6}{5^4 x^4 y^4 z^4}$$
$$= \dfrac{x^2}{625y^4z^4}$$

33. $\dfrac{2(3yz)^{-3}}{y^{-3}} = \dfrac{2(3)^{-3}y^{-3}z^{-3}}{y^{-3}} = \dfrac{2}{3^3 z^3} = \dfrac{2}{27z^3}$

34. $x^{4a}(3x^{5a})^3 = x^{4a}(3^3 x^{15a})$
$$= 27x^{4a+15a}$$
$$= 27x^{19a}$$

35. $\dfrac{4y^{3x-3}}{2y^{2x+4}} = 2y^{(3x-3)-(2x+4)}$

$\qquad = 2y^{3x-3-2x-4}$

$\qquad = 2y^{x-7}$

36. $\dfrac{(0.00012)(144,000)}{0.0003} = \dfrac{(1.2\times10^{-4})(1.44\times10^5)}{3\times10^{-4}}$

$\qquad\qquad = 0.576\times10^5$

$\qquad\qquad = 5.76\times10^4$

37. $\dfrac{(-0.00017)(0.00039)}{3000}$

$= \dfrac{(-1.7\times10^{-4})(3.9\times10^{-4})}{3\times10^3}$

$= -2.21\times10^{-4-4-3}$

$= -2.21\times10^{-11}$

38. $\dfrac{27x^{-5}y^5}{18x^{-6}y^2}\cdot\dfrac{x^4y^{-2}}{x^{-2}y^3} = \dfrac{3x^{-5+4}y^{5-2}}{2x^{-6-2}y^{2+3}}$

$\qquad = \dfrac{3x^{-1}y^3}{2x^{-8}y^5}$

$\qquad = \dfrac{3}{2}x^{-1-(-8)}y^{3-5}$

$\qquad = \dfrac{3}{2}x^7y^{-2}$

$\qquad = \dfrac{3x^7}{2y^2}$

39. $\dfrac{3x^5}{y^{-4}}\cdot\dfrac{(3xy^{-3})^{-2}}{(z^{-3})^{-4}} = \dfrac{3x^5\cdot3^{-2}x^{-2}y^6}{y^{-4}z^{12}}$

$\qquad = \dfrac{3^{1-2}x^{5-2}y^{6-(-4)}}{z^{12}}$

$\qquad = \dfrac{3^{-1}x^3y^{10}}{z^{12}}$

$\qquad = \dfrac{x^3y^{10}}{3z^{12}}$

40. $\dfrac{(x^w)^2}{(x^{w-4})^{-2}} = \dfrac{x^{2w}}{x^{-2(w-4)}}$

$\qquad = \dfrac{x^{2w}}{x^{-2w+8}}$

$\qquad = x^{2w-(-2w+8)}$

$\qquad = x^{4w-8}$

41. The degree of the polynomial
$x^2y-3xy^3z+5x+7y$ is the degree of the term
$-3xy^3z$ which is 5.

42. $3x+2$ has degree 1.

43. $4x+8x-6x^2-6x^2y = (4+8)x-6x^2-6x^2y$

$\qquad = 12x-6x^2-6x^2y$

44. $-8xy^3+4xy^3-3x^3y = (-8+4)xy^3-3x^3y$

$\qquad\qquad = -4xy^3-3x^3y$

45. $(3x+7y)+(4x^2-3x+7)+(y-1)$

$= 3x+7y+4x^2-3x+7+y-1$

$= 4x^2+(3-3)x+(7+1)y+(7-1)$

$= 4x^2+8y+6$

46. $(4x^2-6xy+9y^2)-(8x^2-6xy-y^2)$

$= 4x^2-6xy+9y^2-8x^2+6xy+y^2$

$= (4-8)x^2+(9+1)y^2$

$= -4x^2+10y^2$

47. $(3x^2-4b+28)+(9x^2-30)-(4x^2-6b+20)$

$= 3x^2-4b+28+9x^2-30-4x^2+6b-20$

$= (3+9-4)x^2+(-4+6)b+(28-30-20)$

$= 8x^2+2b-22$

48. $(9xy+4x^2+18)+(7xy-4x^3-9x)$

$= 9xy+4x^2+18+7xy-4x^3-9x$

$= -4x^3+4x^2+(9+7)xy-9x+18$

$= -4x^3+4x^2+16xy-9x+18$

49. $(3x^2y-7xy-4)+(9x^2y+x)-(x-7)$

$= 3x^2y-7xy-4+9x^2y+x-x+7$

$= (3+9)x^2y-7xy+(-4+7)$

$= 12x^2y-7xy+3$

50. $\begin{array}{r} x^2-5x+7 \\ -\quad(x+4) \\ \hline x^2-6x+3 \end{array}$

51.
$$\begin{array}{l} x^3 \quad\ +2xy^2-y \\ \underline{+\ \ (x-4xy^2\quad -7)} \\ x^3+x-2xy^2-y-7 \end{array}$$

52. $P(6) = 9(6)^2 - 7(6) + 8 = 290$

53. $P(-2) = 9(-2)^2 - 7(-2) + 8 = 58$

54. $P(-3) = 9(-3)^2 - 7(-3) + 8 = 110$

55. $\begin{aligned} P(x) + Q(x) &= (2x-1) + (x^2 + 2x - 5) \\ &= 2x - 1 + x^2 + 2x - 5 \\ &= x^2 + 4x - 6 \end{aligned}$

56. $\begin{aligned} 2[P(x)] - Q(x) &= 2(2x-1) - (x^2 + 2x - 5) \\ &= 4x - 2 - x^2 - 2x + 5 \\ &= -x^2 + 2x + 3 \end{aligned}$

57. $\begin{aligned} & 2(2x^2y - 6x + 1) + 2(x^2y + 5) \\ &= 4x^2y - 12x + 2 + 2x^2y + 10 \\ &= (6x^2y - 12x + 12) \text{ cm} \end{aligned}$

58. $-6x(4x^2 - 6x + 1) = -24x^3 + 36x^2 - 6x$

59. $\begin{aligned} & -4ab^2(3ab^3 + 7ab + 1) \\ &= -4ab^2(3ab^3) - 4ab^2(7ab) - 4ab^2(1) \\ &= -12a^2b^5 - 28a^2b^3 - 4ab^2 \end{aligned}$

60. $\begin{aligned} (x-4)(2x+9) &= 2x^2 + 9x - 8x - 36 \\ &= 2x^2 + x - 36 \end{aligned}$

61. $\begin{aligned} (-3xa + 4b)^2 &= (-3xa)^2 + 2(-3xa)(4b) + (4b)^2 \\ &= 9x^2a^2 - 24xab + 16b^2 \end{aligned}$

62.
$$\begin{array}{l} \quad\quad 9x^2 + 4x + 1 \\ \underline{\quad\quad\quad\quad\quad 4x - 3} \\ \ -27x^2 - 12x - 3 \\ \underline{36x^3 + 16x^2\ + 4x} \\ 36x^3 - 11x^2\ - 8x - 3 \end{array}$$

63. $\begin{aligned} (5x-9y)(3x+9y) &= 15x^2 + 45xy - 27xy + 81y^2 \\ &= 15x^2 + 18xy - 81y^2 \end{aligned}$

64. $\begin{aligned} \left(x - \frac{1}{3}\right)\left(x + \frac{2}{3}\right) &= x^2 + \frac{2}{3}x - \frac{1}{3}x - \frac{1}{3}\left(\frac{2}{3}\right) \\ &= x^2 + \frac{1}{3}x - \frac{2}{9} \end{aligned}$

65. $\begin{aligned} & (x^2 + 9x + 1)^2 \\ &= (x^2 + 9x + 1)(x^2 + 9x + 1) \\ &= x^2(x^2 + 9x + 1) + 9x(x^2 + 9x + 1) + 1(x^2 + 9x + 1) \\ &= x^4 + 9x^3 + x^2 + 9x^3 + 81x^2 + 9x + x^2 + 9x + 1 \\ &= x^4 + 18x^3 + 83x^2 + 18x + 1 \end{aligned}$

66. $\begin{aligned} (3x - y)^2 &= (3x)^2 - 2(3x)y + y^2 \\ &= 9x^2 - 6xy + y^2 \end{aligned}$

67. $\begin{aligned} (4x + 9)^2 &= (4x)^2 + 2(4x)(9) + 9^2 \\ &= 16x^2 + 72x + 81 \end{aligned}$

68. $(x + 3y)(x - 3y) = x^2 - (3y)^2 = x^2 - 9y^2$

69. $\begin{aligned} & [4 + (3a - b)][4 - (3a - b)] \\ &= 4^2 - (3a - b)^2 \\ &= 16 - [(3a)^2 - 2(3a)b + b^2] \\ &= 16 - (9a^2 - 6ab + b^2) \\ &= 16 - 9a^2 + 6ab - b^2 \end{aligned}$

70. $\begin{aligned} & P(x) \cdot Q(x) \\ &= (2x - 1)(x^2 + 2x - 5) \\ &= 2x(x^2 + 2x - 5) - 1(x^2 + 2x - 5) \\ &= 2x^3 + 4x^2 - 10x - x^2 - 2x + 5 \\ &= 2x^3 + 3x^2 - 12x + 5 \end{aligned}$

71. $\begin{aligned} \text{Area} &= lw \\ &= (3y + 7z)(3y - 7z) \\ &= (3y)^2 - (7z)^2 \\ &= (9y^2 - 49z^2) \text{ square units} \end{aligned}$

72. $\begin{aligned} 4a^b(3a^{b+2} - 7) &= 4a^b(3a^{b+2}) + 4a^b(-7) \\ &= 12a^{b+b+2} - 28a^b \\ &= 12a^{2b+2} - 28a^b \end{aligned}$

73. $\begin{aligned} (4xy^z - b)^2 &= (4xy^z)^2 - 2(4xy^z)b + b^2 \\ &= 4^2x^2(y^z)^2 - 8xy^zb + b^2 \\ &= 16x^2y^{2z} - 8xy^zb + b^2 \end{aligned}$

74. $(3x^a - 4)(3x^a + 4) = (3x^a)^2 - 4^2$
$$= 3^2(x^a)^2 - 16$$
$$= 9x^{2a} - 16$$

75. $16x^3 - 24x^2 = 8x^2(2x - 3)$

76. $36y - 24y^2 = 12y(3 - 2y)$

77. $6ab^2 + 8ab - 4a^2b^2 = 2ab(3b + 4 - 2ab)$

78. $14a^2b^2 - 21ab^2 + 7ab = 7ab(2ab - 3b + 1)$

79. $6a(a + 3b) - 5(a + 3b) = (6a - 5)(a + 3b)$

80. $4x(x - 2y) - 5(x - 2y) = (4x - 5)(x - 2y)$

81. $xy - 6y + 3x - 18 = y(x - 6) + 3(x - 6)$
$$= (y + 3)(x - 6)$$

82. $ab - 8b + 4a - 32 = b(a - 8) + 4(a - 8)$
$$= (b + 4)(a - 8)$$

83. $pq - 3p - 5q + 15 = p(q - 3) - 5(q - 3)$
$$= (p - 5)(q - 3)$$

84. $x^3 - x^2 - 2x + 2 = x^2(x - 1) - 2(x - 1)$
$$= (x^2 - 2)(x - 1)$$

85. Area $= 2xy - x^2 = x(2y - x)$ sq units

86. $x^2 - 14x - 72 = (x - 18)(x + 4)$

87. $x^2 + 16x - 80 = (x - 4)(x + 20)$

88. $2x^2 - 18x + 28 = 2(x^2 - 9x + 14)$
$$= 2(x - 7)(x - 2)$$

89. $3x^2 + 33x + 54 = 3(x^2 + 11x + 18)$
$$= 3(x + 9)(x + 2)$$

90. $2x^3 - 7x^2 - 9x = x(2x^2 - 7x - 9)$
$$= x(2x - 9)(x + 1)$$

91. $3x^2 + 2x - 16 = (3x + 8)(x - 2)$

92. $6x^2 + 17x + 10 = (6x + 5)(x + 2)$

93. $15x^2 - 91x + 6 = (15x - 1)(x - 6)$

94. $4x^2 + 2x - 12 = 2(2x^2 + x - 6)$
$$= 2(2x - 3)(x + 2)$$

95. $9x^2 - 12x - 12 = 3(3x^2 - 4x - 4)$
$$= 3(3x + 2)(x - 2)$$

96. $y^2(x + 6)^2 - 2y(x + 6)^2 - 3(x + 6)^2$
$$= (x + 6)^2(y^2 - 2y - 3)$$
$$= (x + 6)^2(y - 3)(y + 1)$$

97. Let $y = x + 5$. Then
$$(x + 5)^2 + 6(x + 5) + 8 = y^2 + 6y + 8$$
$$= (y + 4)(y + 2)$$
$$= [(x + 5) + 4][(x + 5) + 2]$$
$$= (x + 9)(x + 7)$$

98. $x^4 - 6x^2 - 16 = (x^2 - 8)(x^2 + 2)$

99. $x^4 + 8x^2 - 20 = (x^2 + 10)(x^2 - 2)$

100. $x^2 - 100 = x^2 - 10^2 = (x + 10)(x - 10)$

101. $x^2 - 81 = x^2 - 9^2 = (x + 9)(x - 9)$

102. $2x^2 - 32 = 2(x^2 - 16)$
$$= 2(x^2 - 4^2)$$
$$= 2(x + 4)(x - 4)$$

103. $6x^2 - 54 = 6(x^2 - 9)$
$$= 6(x^2 - 3^2)$$
$$= 6(x + 3)(x - 3)$$

104. $81 - x^4 = 9^2 - (x^2)^2$
$$= (9 + x^2)(9 - x^2)$$
$$= (9 + x^2)(3 + x)(3 - x)$$

105. $16 - y^4 = 4^2 - (y^2)^2$
$$= (4 + y^2)(4 - y^2)$$
$$= (4 + y^2)(2 + y)(2 - y)$$

106. $(y + 2)^2 - 25 = (y + 2)^2 - 5^2$
$$= [(y + 2) + 5][(y + 2) - 5]$$
$$= (y + 7)(y - 3)$$

107. $(x-3)^2 - 16 = (x-3)^2 - 4^2$
$$= [(x-3)+4][(x-3)-4]$$
$$= (x+1)(x-7)$$

108. $x^3 + 216 = x^3 + 6^3$
$$= (x+6)(x^2 - 6 \cdot x + 6^2)$$
$$= (x+6)(x^2 - 6x + 36)$$

109. $y^3 + 512 = y^3 + 8^3$
$$= (y+8)(y^2 - 8 \cdot y + 8^2)$$
$$= (y+8)(y^2 - 8y + 64)$$

110. $8 - 27y^3 = 2^3 - (3y)^3$
$$= (2-3y)(4 + 2 \cdot 3y + (3y)^2)$$
$$= (2-3y)(4 + 6y + 9y^2)$$

111. $1 - 64y^3 = 1^3 - (4y)^3$
$$= (1-4y)(1^2 + 1 \cdot 4y + (4y)^2)$$
$$= (1-4y)(1 + 4y + 16y^2)$$

112. $6x^4 y + 48xy = 6xy(x^3 + 8)$
$$= 6xy(x^3 + 2^3)$$
$$= 6xy(x+2)(x^2 - 2x + 2^2)$$
$$= 6xy(x+2)(x^2 - 2x + 4)$$

113. $2x^5 + 16x^2 y^3 = 2x^2(x^3 + 8y^3)$
$$= 2x^2(x^3 + (2y)^3)$$
$$= 2x^2(x+2y)(x^2 - x \cdot 2y + (2y)^2)$$
$$= 2x^2(x+2y)(x^2 - 2xy + 4y^2)$$

114. $x^2 - 2x + 1 - y^2 = (x^2 - 2x + 1) - y^2$
$$= (x-1)^2 - y^2$$
$$= [(x-1)+y][(x-1)-y]$$
$$= (x-1+y)(x-1-y)$$

115. $x^2 - 6x + 9 - 4y^2 = (x^2 - 6x + 9) - 4y^2$
$$= (x-3)^2 - (2y)^2$$
$$= [(x-3)+2y][(x-3)-2y]$$
$$= (x-3+2y)(x-3-2y)$$

116. $4x^2 + 12x + 9 = (2x+3)(2x+3)$
$$= (2x+3)^2$$

117. $16a^2 - 40ab + 25b^2 = (4a-5b)(4a-5b)$
$$= (4a-5b)^2$$

118. Volume $= \pi R^2 h - \pi r^2 h$
$$= \pi h(R^2 - r^2)$$
$$= \pi h(R+r)(R-r) \text{ cubic units}$$

119. $(3x-1)(x+7) = 0$
$3x - 1 = 0$ or $x + 7 = 0$
$x = \dfrac{1}{3}$ or $\quad x = -7$

The solutions are $-7, \dfrac{1}{3}$.

120. $3(x+5)(8x-3) = 0$
$x + 5 = 0$ or $8x - 3 = 0$
$x = -5$ or $\quad x = \dfrac{3}{8}$

The solutions are $-5, \dfrac{3}{8}$.

121. $5x(x-4)(2x-9) = 0$
$5x = 0$ or $x - 4 = 0$ or $2x - 9 = 0$
$x = 0$ or $\quad x = 4$ or $\quad x = \dfrac{9}{2}$

The solutions are $0, 4, \dfrac{9}{2}$.

122. $6(x+3)(x-4)(5x+1) = 0$
$x + 3 = 0$ or $x - 4 = 0$ or $5x + 1 = 0$
$x = -3$ or $\quad x = 4$ or $\quad 5x = -1$
$$x = -\dfrac{1}{5}$$

The solutions are $-\dfrac{1}{5}, -3, 4$.

123.
$$2x^2 = 12x$$
$$2x^2 - 12x = 0$$
$$2x(x-6) = 0$$
$2x = 0$ or $x - 6 = 0$
$x = 0$ or $\quad x = 6$
The solutions are $0, 6$.

124.
$$4x^3 - 36x = 0$$
$$4x(x^2 - 9) = 0$$
$$4x(x+3)(x-3) = 0$$
$$4x = 0 \text{ or } x+3 = 0 \text{ or } x-3 = 0$$
$$x = 0 \text{ or } \quad x = -3 \text{ or } \quad x = 3$$
The solutions are $-3, 0, 3$.

125.
$$(1-x)(3x+2) = -4x$$
$$3x + 2 - 3x^2 - 2x = -4x$$
$$-3x^2 + x + 2 = -4x$$
$$-3x^2 + 5x + 2 = 0$$
$$3x^2 - 5x - 2 = 0$$
$$(3x+1)(x-2) = 0$$
$$3x + 1 = 0 \text{ or } x - 2 = 0$$
$$3x = -1 \text{ or } \quad x = 2$$
$$x = -\frac{1}{3}$$
The solutions are $-\frac{1}{3}, 2$.

126.
$$2x(x-12) = -40$$
$$2x^2 - 24x = -40$$
$$2x^2 - 24x + 40 = 0$$
$$2(x^2 - 12x + 20) = 0$$
$$2(x-10)(x-2) = 0$$
$$x - 10 = 0 \text{ or } x - 2 = 0$$
$$x = 10 \text{ or } \quad x = 2$$
The solutions are $2, 10$.

127.
$$3x^2 + 2x = 12 - 7x$$
$$3x^2 + 9x - 12 = 0$$
$$3(x^2 + 3x - 4) = 0$$
$$3(x+4)(x-1) = 0$$
$$x + 4 = 0 \text{ or } x - 1 = 0$$
$$x = -4 \text{ or } \quad x = 1$$
The solutions are $-4, 1$.

128.
$$2x^2 + 3x = 35$$
$$2x^2 + 3x - 35 = 0$$
$$(2x-7)(x+5) = 0$$
$$2x - 7 = 0 \text{ or } x + 5 = 0$$
$$2x = 7 \text{ or } \quad x = -5$$
$$x = \frac{7}{2}$$
The solutions are $-5, \frac{7}{2}$.

129.
$$x^3 - 18x = 3x^2$$
$$x^3 - 3x^2 - 18x = 0$$
$$x(x^2 - 3x - 18) = 0$$
$$x(x-6)(x+3) = 0$$
$$x = 0 \text{ or } x - 6 = 0 \text{ or } x + 3 = 0$$
$$x = 6 \text{ or } \quad x = -3$$
The solutions are $-3, 0, 6$.

130.
$$19x^2 - 42x = -x^3$$
$$x^3 + 19x^2 - 42x = 0$$
$$x(x^2 + 19x - 42) = 0$$
$$x(x+21)(x-2) = 0$$
$$x = 0 \text{ or } x + 21 = 0 \text{ or } x - 2 = 0$$
$$x = -21 \text{ or } \quad x = 2$$
The solutions are $-21, 0, 2$.

131.
$$12x = 6x^3 + 6x^2$$
$$-6x^3 - 6x^2 + 12x = 0$$
$$-6x(x^2 + x - 2) = 0$$
$$-6x(x+2)(x-1) = 0$$
$$-6x = 0 \text{ or } x + 2 = 0 \text{ or } x - 1 = 0$$
$$x = 0 \text{ or } \quad x = -2 \text{ or } \quad x = 1$$
The solutions are $-2, 0, 1$.

132.
$$8x^3 + 10x^2 = 3x$$
$$8x^3 + 10x^2 - 3x = 0$$
$$x(8x^2 + 10x - 3) = 0$$
$$x(4x-1)(2x+3) = 0$$
$$x = 0 \text{ or } 4x - 1 = 0 \text{ or } 2x + 3 = 0$$
$$4x = 1 \text{ or } \quad 2x = -3$$
$$x = \frac{1}{4} \text{ or } \quad x = -\frac{3}{2}$$
The solutions are $-\frac{3}{2}, 0, \frac{1}{4}$.

133. Let $x =$ the number. Then
$$x + 2x^2 = 105$$
$$2x^2 + x - 105 = 0$$
$$(2x+15)(x-7) = 0$$
$$2x + 15 = 0 \text{ or } x - 7 = 0$$
$$2x = -15 \text{ or } \quad x = 7$$
$$x = -\frac{15}{2}$$
The number is $-\frac{15}{2}$ or 7.

134. Let $x =$ width; then $2x - 5 =$ length.

$$x(2x - 5) = 33$$
$$2x^2 - 5x = 33$$
$$2x^2 - 5x - 33 = 0$$
$$(2x - 11)(x + 3) = 0$$
$$2x - 11 = 0 \quad \text{or} \quad x + 3 = 0$$
$$2x = 11 \quad \text{or} \qquad x = -3$$
$$x = \frac{11}{2}$$

Disregard the negative.

Width $= \dfrac{11}{2} = 5\dfrac{1}{2}$ m

Length $= 2\left(\dfrac{11}{2}\right) - 5 = 6$ m

135. $h(t) = -16t^2 + 400$

$$0 = -16t^2 + 400$$
$$0 = -16(t^2 - 25)$$
$$0 = -16(t + 5)(t - 5)$$
$$t + 5 = 0 \quad \text{or} \quad t - 5 = 0$$
$$t = -5 \quad \text{or} \qquad t = 5$$

Disregard the negative. The stunt dummy will reach the ground after 5 seconds.

136. $P(t) = -16t^2 + 1053$

$$P(1) = -16(1)^2 + 1053 = -16 + 1053 = 1037$$

$$P(8) = -16(8)^2 + 1053 = -1024 + 1053 = 29$$

After 1 second, the object is at 1037 feet and after 8 seconds, the object is at 29 feet.

137. $(x + 5)(3x^2 - 2x + 1)$

$$= x(3x^2 - 2x + 1) + 5(3x^2 - 2x + 1)$$
$$= 3x^3 - 2x^2 + x + 15x^2 - 10x + 5$$
$$= 3x^3 + 13x^2 - 9x + 5$$

138. $(3x^2 + 4x - 1.2) - (5x^2 - x + 5.7)$

$$= 3x^2 + 4x - 1.2 - 5x^2 + x - 5.7$$
$$= -2x^2 + 5x - 6.9$$

139. $(3x^2 + 4x - 1.2) + (5x^2 - x + 5.7)$

$$= 3x^2 + 4x - 1.2 + 5x^2 - x + 5.7$$
$$= 8x^2 + 3x + 4.5$$

140. $\left(7ab - \dfrac{1}{2}\right)^2 = (7ab)^2 - 2(7ab)\left(\dfrac{1}{2}\right) + \left(\dfrac{1}{2}\right)^2$

$$= 49a^2b^2 - 7ab + \frac{1}{4}$$

141. $P(x) = -x^2 + x - 4$

$$P(5) = -5^2 + 5 - 4 = -25 + 5 - 4 = -24$$

142. $P(x) = -x^2 + x - 4$

$$P(-2) = -(-2)^2 + (-2) - 4 = -4 - 2 - 4 = -10$$

143. $12y^5 - 6y^4 = 6y^4(2y) + 6y^4(-1) = 6y^4(2y - 1)$

144. $x^2y + 4x^2 - 3y - 12 = x^2(y + 4) - 3(y + 4)$

$$= (y + 4)(x^2 - 3)$$

145. $6x^2 - 34x - 12 = 2(3x^2 - 17x - 6)$

$$= 2(3x + 1)(x - 6)$$

146. $y^2(4x + 3)^2 - 19y(4x + 3)^2 - 20(4x + 3)^2$

$$= (4x + 3)^2(y^2 - 19y - 20)$$
$$= (4x + 3)^2(y - 20)(y + 1)$$

147. $4z^7 - 49z^5 = z^5(4z^2 - 49)$

$$= z^5[(2z)^2 - 7^2]$$
$$= z^5(2z + 7)(2z - 7)$$

148. $5x^4 + 4x^2 - 9 = (x^2 - 1)(5x^2 + 9)$

$$= (x + 1)(x - 1)(5x^2 + 9)$$

149. $\qquad 8x^2 = 24x$

$$8x^2 - 24x = 0$$
$$8x(x - 3) = 0$$
$$8x = 0 \quad \text{or} \quad x - 3 = 0$$
$$x = 0 \quad \text{or} \qquad x = 3$$

150. $\qquad x(x - 11) = 26$

$$x^2 - 11x = 26$$
$$x^2 - 11x - 26 = 0$$
$$(x + 2)(x - 13) = 0$$
$$x + 2 = 0 \quad \text{or} \quad x - 13 = 0$$
$$x = -2 \quad \text{or} \qquad x = 13$$

Chapter 5 Test

1. $(-9x)^{-2} = \dfrac{1}{(-9x)^2} = \dfrac{1}{81x^2}$

2. $-3xy^{-2}(4xy^2)z = -12x^{1+1}y^{-2+2}z = -12x^2z$

3. $\dfrac{6^{-1}a^2b^{-3}}{3^{-2}a^{-5}b^2} = \dfrac{3^2\,a^{2+5}}{6^1\,b^{2+3}} = \dfrac{9a^7}{6b^5} = \dfrac{3a^7}{2b^5}$

4. $\left(\dfrac{-xy^{-5}z}{xy^3}\right)^{-5} = \dfrac{-x^{-5}y^{25}z^{-5}}{x^{-5}y^{-15}}$

$\qquad = \dfrac{x^{-5+5}y^{25-(-15)}}{z^5}$

$\qquad = -\dfrac{y^{40}}{z^5}$

5. $630,000,000 = 6.3\times10^8$

6. $0.01200 = 1.2\times10^{-2}$

7. $5\times10^{-6} = 0.000005$

8. $\dfrac{(0.0024)(0.00012)}{0.00032} = \dfrac{(2.4\times10^{-3})(1.2\times10^{-4})}{3.2\times10^{-4}}$

$\qquad = \dfrac{(2.4)(1.2)}{3.2}\times10^{-3+(-4)-(-4)}$

$\qquad = 0.9\times10^{-3}$

$\qquad = 0.0009$

9. $(4x^3y-3x-4)-(9x^3y+8x+5)$

$\qquad = 4x^3y-3x-4-9x^3y-8x-5$

$\qquad = -5x^3y-11x-9$

10. $-3xy(4x+y) = -3xy(4x)-3xy(y)$

$\qquad = -12x^2y-3xy^2$

11. $(3x+4)(4x-7) = 12x^2-21x+16x-28$

$\qquad = 12x^2-5x-28$

12. $(5a-2b)(5a+2b) = (5a)^2-(2b)^2 = 25a^2-4b^2$

13. $(6m+n)^2 = (6m)^2+2(6m)n+n^2$

$\qquad = 36m^2+12mn+n^2$

14.
$$\begin{array}{r} x^2-6x+4 \\ \times\qquad 2x-1 \\ \hline -x^2+6x-4 \\ 2x^3-12x^2+8x \\ \hline 2x^3-13x^2+14x-4 \end{array}$$

15. $16x^3y-12x^2y^4 = 4x^2y(4x-3y^3)$

16. $x^2-13x-30 = (x-15)(x+2)$

17. $4y^2+20y+25 = (2y+5)(2y+5)$

$\qquad = (2y+5)^2$

18. $6x^2-15x-9 = 3(2x^2-5x-3)$

$\qquad = 3(2x+1)(x-3)$

19. $4x^2-25 = (2x)^2-5^2 = (2x+5)(2x-5)$

20. $x^3+64 = x^3+4^3 = (x+4)(x^2-4x+16)$

21. $3x^2y-27y^3 = 3y(x^2-9y^2)$

$\qquad = 3y(x^2-(3y)^2)$

$\qquad = 3y(x+3y)(x-3y)$

22. $6x^2+24 = 6(x^2+4)$

23. $16y^3-2 = 2(8y^3-1)$

$\qquad = 2((2y)^3-1^3)$

$\qquad = 2(2y-1)(4y^2+2y+1)$

24. $x^2y-9y-3x^2+27 = y(x^2-9)-3(x^2-9)$

$\qquad = (x^2-9)(y-3)$

$\qquad = (x+3)(x-3)(y-3)$

25.
$$3n(7n-20) = 96$$
$$21n^2-60n = 96$$
$$21n^2-60n-96 = 0$$
$$3(7n^2-20n-32) = 0$$
$$3(7n+8)(n-4) = 0$$

$7n + 8 = 0$ or $n - 4 = 0$
$7n = -8$ or $n = 4$
$$n = -\frac{8}{7}$$

The solutions are $-\dfrac{8}{7}$, 4.

26. $(x + 2)(x - 2) = 5(x + 4)$
$$x^2 - 4 = 5x + 20$$
$$x^2 - 5x - 24 = 0$$
$$(x - 8)(x + 3) = 0$$
$x - 8 = 0$ or $x + 3 = 0$
$x = 8$ or $x = -3$
The solutions are 8, –3.

27. $2x^3 + 5x^2 - 8x - 20 = 0$
$$x^2(2x + 5) - 4(2x + 5) = 0$$
$$(2x + 5)(x^2 - 4) = 0$$
$$(2x + 5)(x + 2)(x - 2) = 0$$
$2x + 5 = 0$ or $x + 2 = 0$ or $x - 2 = 0$
$2x = -5$ or $x = -2$ or $x = 2$
$$x = -\frac{5}{2}$$

The solutions are $-\dfrac{5}{2}$, -2, 2.

28. Area $= x^2 - (2y)^2$
         $= (x + 2y)(x - 2y)$ square units

29. $h(t) = -16t^2 + 96t + 880$

a. $-16(1)^2 + 96(1) + 880 = -16 + 96 + 880$
                           $= 960$ feet

b. $-16(5.1)^2 + 96(5.1) + 880$
    $= -416.16 + 489.6 + 880$
    $= 953.44$ feet

c. $0 = -16t^2 + 96t + 880$
$$16t^2 - 96t - 880 = 0$$
$$16(t^2 - 6t - 55) = 0$$
$$(t - 11)(t + 5) = 0$$
$t - 11 = 0$ or $t + 5 = 0$
    $t = 11$ or $t = -5$
Disregard the negative. The pebble will hit the ground in 11 seconds.

Chapter 5 Cumulative Review

1. a. $\sqrt[3]{27} = 3$ since $3^3 = 27$.

    b. $\sqrt[5]{1} = 1$ since $1^5 = 1$.

    c. $\sqrt[4]{16} = 2$ since $2^4 = 16$.

2. a. $\sqrt[3]{64} = 4$ since $4^3 = 64$.

    b. $\sqrt[4]{81} = 3$ since $3^4 = 81$.

    c. $\sqrt[5]{32} = 2$ since $2^5 = 32$.

3. $2(x - 3) = 5x - 9$
     $2x - 6 = 5x - 9$
       $-3x = -3$
          $x = 1$
The solution is 1.

4. $0.3y + 2.4 = 0.1y + 4$
   $10(0.3y + 2.4) = 10(0.1y + 4)$
      $3y + 24 = y + 40$
           $2y = 16$
            $y = 8$
The solution is 8.

5. $A = 10{,}000\left(1 + \dfrac{0.05}{4}\right)^{4(3)}$
    $= 10{,}000(1.0125)^{12}$
    $= 10{,}000(1.160754518)$
    $= 11{,}607.54518$
There will be \$11,607.55 in the account.

6.   The area of the room is
$2(14 \cdot 8) + 2(18 \cdot 8) = 512$ sq ft. Two coats means
$2 \cdot 512 = 1024$ sq ft of wall needs paint.
$$\frac{1}{400} = \frac{x}{1024}$$
$$1024\left(\frac{1}{400}\right) = 1024\left(\frac{x}{512}\right)$$
$$2.56 = x$$
$$x \approx 3$$
3 gallons of paint are needed.

7. a. $\dfrac{1}{4}x \le \dfrac{3}{8}$

$8\left(\dfrac{1}{4}x\right) \le 8\left(\dfrac{3}{8}\right)$

$2x \le 3$

$x \le \dfrac{3}{2}$

$\left\{x \middle| x \le \dfrac{3}{2}\right\}$ or $\left(-\infty, \dfrac{3}{2}\right]$

$\xleftarrow{\qquad\qquad\rule[0.5ex]{2.5cm}{1pt}\rule{0.1pt}{1.5ex}\qquad}$
$\dfrac{3}{2}$

b. $-2.3x < 6.9$

$10(-2.3x) < 10(6.9)$

$-23x < 69$

$\dfrac{-23x}{-23} > \dfrac{69}{-23}$

$x > -3$

$\{x \mid x > -3\}$ or $(-3, \infty)$

$\xleftarrow{\qquad\quad\rule{0.1pt}{1.5ex}\rule[0.5ex]{2.5cm}{1pt}\qquad}$
-3

8. $x + 2 \le \dfrac{1}{4}(x - 7)$

$4(x + 2) \le 4\left[\dfrac{1}{4}(x - 7)\right]$

$4x + 8 \le x - 7$

$3x \le -15$

$x \le -5$

$\{x \mid x \le -5\}$ or $(-\infty, -5]$

$\xleftarrow{\qquad\qquad\rule[0.5ex]{2.5cm}{1pt}\rule{0.1pt}{1.5ex}\qquad}$
-5

9. $-1 \le \dfrac{2x}{3} + 5 \le 2$

$3(-1) \le 3\left(\dfrac{2x}{3} + 5\right) \le 3(2)$

$-3 \le 2x + 15 \le 6$

$-18 \le 2x \le -9$

$-9 \le x \le -\dfrac{9}{2}$

$\left[-9, -\dfrac{9}{2}\right]$

10. $-\dfrac{1}{3} < \dfrac{3x+1}{6} \le \dfrac{1}{3}$

$6\left(-\dfrac{1}{3}\right) < 6\left(\dfrac{3x+1}{6}\right) \le 6\left(\dfrac{1}{3}\right)$

$-2 < 3x + 1 \le 2$

$-3 < 3x \le 1$

$-1 < x \le \dfrac{1}{3}$

$\left(-1, \dfrac{1}{3}\right]$

11. $|y| = 0$

$y = 0$

The solution is 0.

12. $8 + |4c| = 24$

$|4c| = 16$

$4c = 16$ or $4c = -16$

$c = 4$ or $c = -4$

The solutions are –4, 4.

13. $\left|2x - \dfrac{1}{10}\right| < -13$ is impossible; $\varnothing$.

14. $|5x - 1| + 9 > 5$

$|5x - 1| > -4$ is always true.

$(-\infty, \infty)$

15. $y = \dfrac{1}{3}x$

16. $y = 3x$

17. $f(x) = \begin{cases} 2x+3 & \text{if } x \le 0 \\ -x-1 & \text{if } x > 0 \end{cases}$

$f(2) = -2 - 1 = -3 \colon (2, -3)$
$f(-6) = 2(-6) + 3 = -9 \colon (-6, -9)$
$f(0) = 2(0) + 3 = 3 \colon (0, 3)$

18. $f(x) = 3x^2 + 2x + 3$

$\begin{aligned} f(-3) &= 3(-3)^2 + 2(-3) + 3 \\ &= 3(9) - 6 + 3 \\ &= 27 - 6 + 3 \\ &= 24 \end{aligned}$

19. $x = 2$

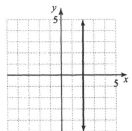

20. $y - 5 = 0$
   $\quad y = 5$

21. $y = 2$
This is a horizontal line.
$m = 0$

22. $f(x) = -2x - 3$
   $m = -2$

23. $y = 3$

24. $x = -3$

25. $x + \dfrac{1}{2}y \ge -4 \qquad$ or $y \le -2$

$\qquad \dfrac{1}{2}y \ge -x - 4 \quad$ or $y \le -2$

$\qquad\quad y \ge -2x - 8 \;$ or $y \le -2$

26. $y - 3 = 0[x - (-2)]$
   $\quad y - 3 = 0$
   $\qquad y = 3$

27. $\begin{cases} 2x + 4y = -6 & (1) \\ \quad x = 2y - 5 & (2) \end{cases}$

Substitute $2y - 5$ for x in E1.
$2(2y - 5) + 4y = -6$
$\quad 4y - 10 + 4y = -6$
$\qquad\qquad\quad 8y = 4$
$\qquad\qquad\quad\; y = \dfrac{1}{2}$

Substitute $\dfrac{1}{2}$ for y in E2.

$x = 2\left(\dfrac{1}{2}\right) - 5 = 1 - 5 = -4$

The solution is $\left(-4, \dfrac{1}{2}\right)$.

28. $\begin{cases} 4x - 2y = 8 & (1) \\ \quad\;\; y = 3x - 6 & (2) \end{cases}$

Substitute $3x - 6$ for y in E1.
$4x - 2(3x - 6) = 8$
$\quad 4x - 6x + 12 = 8$
$\qquad\qquad\; -2x = -4$
$\qquad\qquad\quad\; x = 2$
Substitute 2 for x in E2.
$y = 3(2) - 6 = 6 - 6 = 0$
The solution is $(2, 0)$.

29. $\begin{cases} 2x + 4y \quad\;\; = 1 & (1) \\ 4x \quad\;\; -4z = -1 & (2) \\ \quad\;\; y - 4z = -3 & (3) \end{cases}$

Multiply E2 by -1 and add to E3.

$$-4x \quad +4z = 1$$
$$\underline{\quad y - 4z = -3 \quad}$$
$$-4x + y \quad = -2 \quad (4)$$

Muliply E1 by 2 and add to E4.
$$4x + 8y = 2$$
$$\underline{-4x \; + y = -2 \quad}$$
$$9y = 0$$
$$y = 0$$

Replace y with 0 in E1.
$$2x + 4(0) = 1$$
$$2x = 1$$
$$x = \frac{1}{2}$$

Replace y with 0 in E3.
$$y - 4z = -3$$
$$-4z = -3$$
$$z = \frac{3}{4}$$

The solution is $\left(\dfrac{1}{2}, 0, \dfrac{3}{4}\right)$.

30. $\begin{cases} x + y - \dfrac{3}{2}z = \dfrac{1}{2} \quad (1) \\ \quad -y - 2z = 14 \quad (2) \\ x - \dfrac{2}{3}y \quad = -\dfrac{1}{3} \quad (3) \end{cases}$

Multiply E1 by 2 and E3 by 3 to clear fractions.
$$\begin{cases} 2x + 2y - 3z = 1 \quad (1) \\ \quad -y - 2z = 14 \quad (2) \\ 3x - 2y \quad = -1 \quad (3) \end{cases}$$

Add E1 and E3.
$$5x - 3z = 0 \quad (4)$$

Multiply E2 by 2 and add to E1.
$$-2y - 4z = 28$$
$$\underline{2x + 2y - 3z = 1 \quad}$$
$$2x \quad -7z = 29 \quad (5)$$

Solve the new system $\begin{cases} 5x - 3z = 0 \quad (4) \\ 2x - 7z = 29 \quad (5) \end{cases}$.

Multiply E4 by -2, multiply E5 by 5, and add.
$$-10x + 6z = 0$$
$$\underline{10x - 35z = 145 \quad}$$
$$-29z = 145$$
$$z = -5$$

Replace z with -5 in E4.
$$5x - 3(-5) = 0$$
$$5x + 15 = 0$$
$$5x = -15$$
$$x = -3$$

Replace z with -5 in E2.

$$-y - 2(-5) = 14$$
$$-y + 10 = 14$$
$$-y = 4$$
$$y = -4$$

The solution is $(-3, -4, -5)$.

31. Let $x =$ the first number and $y =$ the second number.
$$\begin{cases} x = y - 4 \quad (1) \\ 4x = 2y + 6 \quad (2) \end{cases}$$

Multiply E1 by -4 and add to E2.
$$-4x = -4y + 16$$
$$\underline{4x = \; 2y + 6 \quad}$$
$$0 = -2y + 22$$
$$2y = 22$$
$$y = 11$$

Replace y with 11 in E1.
$$x = 11 - 4 = 7$$

The numbers are 7 and 11.

32. Let $x =$ ounces of 20% solution and $y =$ ounces of 60% solution.
$$\begin{cases} x \quad + y = 50 \quad\quad (1) \\ 0.20x + 0.60y = 50(0.30) \quad (2) \end{cases}$$

Multiply E2 by 100 to clear decimals.
$$\begin{cases} x \quad + y = 50 \quad (1) \\ 20x + 60y = 1500 \quad (2) \end{cases}$$

Multiply E1 by -20 and add to E2.
$$-20x - 20y = -1000$$
$$\underline{20x + 60y = 1500 \quad}$$
$$40y = 500$$
$$y = \frac{500}{40} = 12.5$$

Replace y with 12.5 in E1.
$$x + 12.5 = 50$$
$$x = 37.5$$

You should mix 37.5 ounces of the 20% solution and 12.5 ounces of the 60% solution.

33. $\begin{cases} 2x - y = 3 \\ 4x - 2y = 5 \end{cases}$

$$\begin{bmatrix} 2 & -1 & | & 3 \\ 4 & -2 & | & 5 \end{bmatrix}$$

Divide R1 by 2.

$$\begin{bmatrix} 1 & -\frac{1}{2} & | & \frac{3}{2} \\ 4 & -2 & | & 5 \end{bmatrix}$$

Multiply R1 by -4 and add to R2.

$$\begin{bmatrix} 1 & -\frac{1}{2} & | & \frac{3}{2} \\ 0 & 0 & | & -1 \end{bmatrix}$$

This corresponds to $\begin{cases} x - \frac{1}{2}y = \frac{3}{2} \\ \quad\quad 0 = -1 \end{cases}$. The last

equation is impossible. The system is inconsistent. The solution set is $\varnothing$.

34. $\begin{cases} 4y = 8 \\ x + y = 7 \end{cases}$

$$\begin{bmatrix} 0 & 4 & | & 8 \\ 1 & 1 & | & 7 \end{bmatrix}$$

Interchange R1 and R2.

$$\begin{bmatrix} 1 & 1 & | & 7 \\ 0 & 4 & | & 8 \end{bmatrix}$$

Divide R2 by 4.

$$\begin{bmatrix} 1 & 1 & | & 7 \\ 0 & 1 & | & 2 \end{bmatrix}$$

This corresponds to $\begin{cases} x + y = 7 \\ \quad\quad y = 2 \end{cases}$.

Replace y with 2 in the equation $x + y = 7$.
$x + 2 = 7$
$\quad x = 5$
The solution is (5, 2).

35. Let x = measure of smallest angle, then
$x + 80$ = measure of largest angle, and
$x + 10$ = measure of remaining angle.
$x + (x + 80) + (x + 10) = 180$
$\qquad\qquad 3x + 90 = 180$
$\qquad\qquad\qquad 3x = 90$
$\qquad\qquad\qquad\quad x = 30$
$x + 80 = 110$
$x + 10 = 40$
The angles measure 30°, 110°, and 40°.

36. $m = \dfrac{1}{2}$, y-intercept (0, 5), $b = 5$
$\quad y = mx + b$
$\quad y = \dfrac{1}{2}x + 5$
$\quad f(x) = \dfrac{1}{2}x + 5$

37. a. $730,000 = 7.3 \times 10^5$

     b. $0.00000104 = 1.04 \times 10^{-6}$

38. a. $8,250,000 = 8.25 \times 10^6$

     b. $0.0000346 = 3.46 \times 10^{-5}$

39. a. $(2x^0 y^{-3})^{-2} = 2^{-2}(1)^{-2}(y^{-3})^{-2} = \dfrac{y^6}{2^2} = \dfrac{y^6}{4}$

     b. $\left(\dfrac{x^{-5}}{x^{-2}}\right)^{-3} = \dfrac{(x^{-5})^{-3}}{(x^{-2})^{-3}} = \dfrac{x^{15}}{x^6} = x^{15-6} = x^9$

     c. $\left(\dfrac{2}{7}\right)^{-2} = \dfrac{2^{-2}}{7^{-2}} = \dfrac{7^2}{2^2} = \dfrac{49}{4}$

     d. $\dfrac{5^{-2}x^{-3}y^{11}}{x^2 y^{-5}} = \dfrac{x^{-3-2}y^{11-(-5)}}{5^2}$
$\qquad\qquad\qquad = \dfrac{x^{-5}y^{16}}{25}$
$\qquad\qquad\qquad = \dfrac{y^{16}}{25x^5}$

40. a. $(4a^{-1}b^0)^{-3} = 4^{-3}(a^{-1})^{-3}(1)^{-3} = \dfrac{a^3}{4^3} = \dfrac{a^3}{64}$

     b. $\left(\dfrac{a^{-6}}{a^{-8}}\right)^{-2} = \dfrac{(a^{-6})^{-2}}{(a^{-8})^{-2}}$
$\qquad\qquad\qquad = \dfrac{a^{12}}{a^{16}}$
$\qquad\qquad\qquad = a^{12-16}$
$\qquad\qquad\qquad = a^{-4}$
$\qquad\qquad\qquad = \dfrac{1}{a^4}$

     c. $\left(\dfrac{2}{3}\right)^{-3} = \dfrac{2^{-3}}{3^{-3}} = \dfrac{3^3}{2^3} = \dfrac{27}{8}$

     d. $\dfrac{3^{-2}a^{-2}b^{12}}{a^4 b^{-5}} = \dfrac{a^{-2-4}b^{12-(-5)}}{3^2}$
$\qquad\qquad\qquad = \dfrac{a^{-6}b^{17}}{9}$
$\qquad\qquad\qquad = \dfrac{b^{17}}{9a^6}$

41. The degree is the degree of the term $x^2 y^2$,
which is $2 + 2 = 4$.

42. $(3x^2 - 2x) - (5x^2 + 3x) = 3x^2 - 2x - 5x^2 - 3x$
$$= -2x^2 - 5x$$

43. a. $(2x^3)(5x^6) = 2(5)x^{3+6} = 10x^9$

   b. $(7y^4z^4)(-xy^{11}z^5) = -7xy^{4+11}z^{4+5}$
   $$= -7xy^{15}z^9$$

44. a. $(3y^6)(4y^2) = 3(4)y^{6+2} = 12y^8$

   b. $(6a^3b^2)(-a^2bc^4) = -6a^{3+2}b^{2+1}c^4$
   $$= -6a^5b^3c^4$$

45. $17x^3y^2 - 34x^4y^2 = 17x^3y^2(1 - 2x)$

46. $12x^3y - 3xy^3 = 3xy(4x^2 - y^2)$
$$= 3xy((2x)^2 - y^2)$$
$$= 3xy(2x + y)(2x - y)$$

47. $x^2 + 10x + 16 = (x + 8)(x + 2)$

48. $5a^2 + 14a - 3 = (5a - 1)(a + 3)$

49. $2x^2 + 9x - 5 = 0$
$(2x - 1)(x + 5) = 0$
$2x - 1 = 0$ or $x + 5 = 0$
$2x = 1$ or $\quad x = -5$
$x = \dfrac{1}{2}$

The solution is $-5, \dfrac{1}{2}$.

50. $3x^2 - 10x - 8 = 0$
$(3x + 2)(x - 4) = 0$
$3x + 2 = 0$ or $x - 4 = 0$
$3x = -2$ or $\quad x = 4$
$x = -\dfrac{2}{3}$

The solution is $-\dfrac{2}{3}, 4$.

Chapter 6

Section 6.1

Practice Exercises

1. a. The denominator of $f(x)$ is never 0.
Domain: $\{x | x$ is a real number$\}$

b. Undefined values when
$x + 3 = 0$, or $x = -3$
Domain: $\{x | x$ is a real number and $x \neq -3\}$

c. Undefined values when
$$x^2 - 5x + 6 = 0$$
$$(x - 3)(x - 2) = 0$$
$$x - 3 = 0 \quad \text{or} \quad x - 2 = 0$$
$$x = 3 \quad \text{or} \qquad x = 2$$
Domain:
$\{x | x$ is a real number and $x \neq 2, x \neq 3\}$

2. a. $\dfrac{5z^4}{10z^5 - 5z^4} = \dfrac{5z^4 \cdot 1}{5z^4(2z - 1)}$

$\qquad = 1 \cdot \dfrac{1}{2z - 1} = \dfrac{1}{2z - 1}$

b. $\dfrac{5x^2 + 13x + 6}{6x^2 + 7x - 10} = \dfrac{(5x + 3)(x + 2)}{(6x - 5)(x + 2)}$

$\qquad = \dfrac{5x + 3}{6x - 5} \cdot 1$

$\qquad = \dfrac{5x + 3}{6x - 5}$

3. a. $\dfrac{x + 3}{3 + x} = \dfrac{x + 3}{x + 3} = 1$

b. $\dfrac{3 - x}{x - 3} = \dfrac{-1(-3 + x)}{x - 3} = \dfrac{-1(x - 3)}{x - 3} = \dfrac{-1}{1} = -1$

4. $\dfrac{20 - 5x^2}{x^2 + x - 6} = \dfrac{5(4 - x^2)}{(x + 3)(x - 2)}$

$\qquad = \dfrac{5(2 + x)(2 - x)}{(x + 3)(x - 2)}$

$\qquad = \dfrac{5(2 + x) \cdot (-1)(x - 2)}{(x + 3)(x - 2)}$

$\qquad = -\dfrac{5(2 + x)}{x + 3}$

5. a. $\dfrac{x^3 + 64}{4 + x} = \dfrac{(x + 4)(x^2 - 4x + 16)}{x + 4}$

$\qquad\qquad = x^2 - 4x + 16$

b. $\dfrac{5z^2 + 10}{z^3 - 3z^2 + 2z - 6} = \dfrac{5(z^2 + 2)}{(z^3 - 3z^2) + (2z - 6)}$

$\qquad\qquad = \dfrac{5(z^2 + 2)}{z^2(z - 3) + 2(z - 3)}$

$\qquad\qquad = \dfrac{5(z^2 + 2)}{(z - 3)(z^2 + 2)}$

$\qquad\qquad = \dfrac{5}{z - 3}$

6. a. $\dfrac{2 + 5n}{3n} \cdot \dfrac{6n + 3}{5n^2 - 3n - 2}$

$\qquad = \dfrac{2 + 5n}{3n} \cdot \dfrac{3(2n + 1)}{(5n + 2)(n - 1)}$

$\qquad = \dfrac{2n + 1}{n(n - 1)}$

b. $\dfrac{x^3 - 8}{-6x + 12} \cdot \dfrac{6x^2}{x^2 + 2x + 4}$

$\qquad = \dfrac{(x - 2)(x^2 + 2x + 4)}{-6(x - 2)} \cdot \dfrac{6x^2}{x^2 + 2x + 4}$

$\qquad = \dfrac{(x - 2)(x^2 + 2x + 4) \cdot 6 \cdot x^2}{-1 \cdot 6(x - 2)(x^2 + 2x + 4)}$

$\qquad = \dfrac{x^2}{-1}$

$\qquad = -x^2$

7. a. $\dfrac{6y^3}{3y^2 - 27} \div \dfrac{42}{3 - y} = \dfrac{6y^3}{3y^2 - 27} \cdot \dfrac{3 - y}{42}$

$\qquad\qquad = \dfrac{6y^3(3 - y)}{3(y + 3)(y - 3) \cdot 42}$

$\qquad\qquad = \dfrac{6y^3 \cdot (-1)(y - 3)}{3(y + 3)(y - 3) \cdot 6 \cdot 7}$

$\qquad\qquad = -\dfrac{y^3}{21(y + 3)}$

b. $\dfrac{10x^2+23x-5}{5x^2-51x+10} \div \dfrac{2x^2+9x+10}{7x^2-68x-20}$

$= \dfrac{10x^2+23x-5}{5x^2-51x+10} \cdot \dfrac{7x^2-68x-20}{2x^2+9x+10}$

$= \dfrac{(5x-1)(2x+5)}{(5x-1)(x-10)} \cdot \dfrac{(7x+2)(x-10)}{(2x+5)(x+2)}$

$= \dfrac{7x+2}{x+2}$

8. $\dfrac{x^2-16}{(x-4)^2} \cdot \dfrac{5x-20}{3x} \div \dfrac{x^2+x-12}{x}$

$= \dfrac{x^2-16}{(x-4)^2} \cdot \dfrac{5x-20}{3x} \cdot \dfrac{x}{x^2+x-12}$

$= \dfrac{(x+4)(x-4)}{(x-4)(x-4)} \cdot \dfrac{5(x-4)}{3x} \cdot \dfrac{x}{(x+4)(x-3)}$

$= \dfrac{5}{3(x-3)}$

9. a. $C(100) = \dfrac{3.2(100)+400}{100} = \dfrac{720}{100} = 7.2$

    $7.20 per tee shirt

b. $C(1000) = \dfrac{3.2(1000)+400}{1000} = \dfrac{3600}{1000} = 3.6$

    $3.60 per tee shirt

Graphing Calculator Explorations

1. $x^2-4=0$

$(x+2)(x-2)=0$

$x+2=0$ or $x-2=0$

$x=-2$ or $x=2$

Domain: $\{x \mid x$ is a real number and $x \neq -2,\, x \neq 2\}$

2. $x^2-9=0$

$(x+3)(x-3)=0$

$x+3=0$ or $x-3=0$

$x=-3$ or $x=3$

Domain: $\{x \mid x$ is a real number and $x \neq -3,\, x \neq 3\}$

3. $2x^2+7x-4=0$

$(2x-1)(x+4)=0$

$2x-1=0$ or $x+4=0$

$2x=1$ or $x=-4$

$x=\dfrac{1}{2}$

Domain:

$\left\{x \mid x \text{ is a real number and } x \neq -4,\, x \neq \dfrac{1}{2}\right\}$

4. $4x^2-19x-5=0$

$(4x+1)(x-5)=0$

$4x+1=0$ or $x-5=0$

$4x=-1$ or $x=5$

$x=-\dfrac{1}{4}$

Domain:

$\left\{x \mid x \text{ is a real number and } x \neq -\dfrac{1}{4},\, x \neq 5\right\}$

Vocabulary and Readiness Check

1. A <u>rational</u> expression is an expression that can be written as the quotient $\dfrac{P}{Q}$ of two polynomials P and Q as long as $Q \neq 0$.

2. A rational expression is undefined if the denominator is <u>0</u>.

3. The <u>domain</u> of the rational function $f(x) = \dfrac{2}{x}$ is

$\{x | x$ is a real number and $x \neq 0\}$.

4. A rational expression is <u>simplified</u> if the numerator and denominator have no common factors other than 1 or −1.

5. The expression $\dfrac{x^2 + 2}{2 + x^2}$ simplifies to <u>1</u>.

6. The expression $\dfrac{y - z}{z - y}$ simplifies to <u>−1</u>.

7. For a rational expression, $-\dfrac{a}{b} = \dfrac{-a}{\underline{b}} = \dfrac{a}{\underline{-b}}$.

8. The statement $\dfrac{a - 6}{a + 2} = \dfrac{-(a - 6)}{-(a + 2)} = \dfrac{-a + 6}{-a - 2}$ is true.

9. $\dfrac{x}{5} \cdot \dfrac{y}{2} = \dfrac{xy}{10}$

10. $\dfrac{y}{6} \cdot \dfrac{z}{5} = \dfrac{yz}{30}$

11. $\dfrac{2}{x} \cdot \dfrac{y}{3} = \dfrac{2y}{3x}$

12. $\dfrac{a}{5} \cdot \dfrac{7}{b} = \dfrac{7a}{5b}$

13. $\dfrac{m}{6} \cdot \dfrac{m}{6} = \dfrac{m^2}{36}$

14. $\dfrac{9}{x} \cdot \dfrac{8}{x} = \dfrac{72}{x^2}$

Exercise Set 6.1

1. 4 is never 0, so the domain of $f(x) = \dfrac{5x - 7}{4}$ is

$\{x | x$ is a real number$\}$.

3. $2t = 0$
$t = 0$

The domain of $s(t) = \dfrac{t^2 + 1}{2t}$ is

$\{t | t$ is a real number and $t \neq 0\}$.

5. $7 - x = 0$
$7 = x$

The domain of $f(x) = \dfrac{3x}{7 - x}$ is

$\{x | x$ is a real number and $x \neq 7\}$.

7. $3x - 1 = 0$
$3x = 1$
$x = \dfrac{1}{3}$

The domain of $f(x) = \dfrac{x}{3x - 1}$ is

$\left\{ x \middle| x \text{ is a real number and } x \neq \dfrac{1}{3} \right\}$.

9. $x^3 + x^2 - 2x = 0$
$x(x^2 + x - 2) = 0$
$x(x + 2)(x - 1) = 0$
$x = 0 \quad$ or $\quad x + 2 = 0 \quad$ or $\quad x - 1 = 0$
$x = 0 \quad$ or $\quad\quad x = -2 \quad$ or $\quad\quad x = 1$

The domain of $R(x) = \dfrac{3 + 2x}{x^3 + x^2 - 2x}$ is

$\{x | x$ is a real number and $x \neq -2,\ x \neq 0,$
$x \neq 1\}$.

11. $x^2 - 4 = 0$
$(x + 2)(x - 2) = 0$
$x + 2 = 0 \quad$ or $\quad x - 2 = 0$
$x = -2 \quad$ or $\quad\quad x = 2$

The domain of $C(x) = \dfrac{x + 3}{x^2 - 4}$ is

$\{x | x$ is a real number and $x \neq 2,\ x \neq -2\}$.

13. $\dfrac{8x - 16x^2}{8x} = \dfrac{8x(1 - 2x)}{8x} = 1 - 2x$

15. $\dfrac{x^2 - 9}{3 + x} = \dfrac{(x + 3)(x - 3)}{3 + x}$
$= \dfrac{(x + 3)(x - 3)}{x + 3}$
$= x - 3$

17. $\dfrac{9y - 18}{7y - 14} = \dfrac{9(y - 2)}{7(y - 2)} = \dfrac{9}{7}$

19. $\dfrac{x^2 + 6x - 40}{x + 10} = \dfrac{(x + 10)(x - 4)}{x + 10} = x - 4$

21. $\dfrac{x-9}{9-x} = \dfrac{-1(9-x)}{9-x} = -1$

23. $\dfrac{x^2-49}{7-x} = \dfrac{(x+7)(x-7)}{7-x}$

$= \dfrac{(x+7)(x-7)}{-1(-7+x)}$

$= \dfrac{(x+7)(x-7)}{-1(x-7)}$

$= -(x+7)$

25. $\dfrac{2x^2-7x-4}{x^2-5x+4} = \dfrac{(2x+1)(x-4)}{(x-1)(x-4)} = \dfrac{2x+1}{x-1}$

27. $\dfrac{x^3-125}{2x-10} = \dfrac{(x-5)(x^2+5x+25)}{2(x-5)}$

$= \dfrac{x^2+5x+25}{2}$

29. $\dfrac{3x^2-5x-2}{6x^3+2x^2+3x+1} = \dfrac{(3x+1)(x-2)}{2x^2(3x+1)+1(3x+1)}$

$= \dfrac{(3x+1)(x-2)}{(3x+1)(2x^2+1)}$

$= \dfrac{x-2}{2x^2+1}$

31. $\dfrac{9x^2-15x+25}{27x^3+125} = \dfrac{9x^2-15x+25}{(3x+5)(9x^2-15x+25)}$

$= \dfrac{1}{3x+5}$

33. $\dfrac{2x-4}{15} \cdot \dfrac{6}{2-x} = \dfrac{2(x-2)}{3 \cdot 5} \cdot \dfrac{2 \cdot 3}{-(x-2)}$

$= \dfrac{2 \cdot 2}{5(-1)}$

$= -\dfrac{4}{5}$

35. $\dfrac{18a-12a^2}{4a^2+4a+1} \cdot \dfrac{4a^2+8a+3}{4a^2-9}$

$= \dfrac{6a(3-2a)}{(2a+1)(2a+1)} \cdot \dfrac{(2a+3)(2a+1)}{(2a+3)(2a-3)}$

$= \dfrac{-6a(2a-3)}{(2a+1)(2a+1)} \cdot \dfrac{(2a+3)(2a+1)}{(2a+3)(2a-3)}$

$= -\dfrac{6a}{2a+1}$

37. $\dfrac{9x+9}{4x+8} \cdot \dfrac{2x+4}{3x^2-3} = \dfrac{9(x+1)}{4(x+2)} \cdot \dfrac{2(x+2)}{3(x^2-1)}$

$= \dfrac{3 \cdot 3(x+1)}{2 \cdot 2(x+2)} \cdot \dfrac{2(x+2)}{3(x+1)(x-1)}$

$= \dfrac{3}{2(x-1)}$

39. $\dfrac{2x^3-16}{6x^2+6x-36} \cdot \dfrac{9x+18}{3x^2+6x+12}$

$= \dfrac{2(x^3-8)}{6(x^2+x-6)} \cdot \dfrac{9(x+2)}{3(x^2+2x+4)}$

$= \dfrac{2(x-2)(x^2+2x+4)}{2 \cdot 3(x-2)(x+3)} \cdot \dfrac{3 \cdot 3(x+2)}{3(x^2+2x+4)}$

$= \dfrac{x+2}{x+3}$

41. $\dfrac{a^3+a^2b+a+b}{5a^3+5a} \cdot \dfrac{6a^2}{2a^2-2b^2}$

$= \dfrac{a^2(a+b)+1(a+b)}{5a(a^2+1)} \cdot \dfrac{6a^2}{2(a^2-b^2)}$

$= \dfrac{(a+b)(a^2+1)}{5a(a^2+1)} \cdot \dfrac{2 \cdot 3 \cdot a \cdot a}{2(a+b)(a-b)}$

$= \dfrac{3a}{5(a-b)}$

43. $\dfrac{x^2-6x-16}{2x^2-128} \cdot \dfrac{x^2+16x+64}{3x^2+30x+48}$

$= \dfrac{(x-8)(x+2)}{2(x^2-64)} \cdot \dfrac{(x+8)(x+8)}{3(x^2+10x+16)}$

$= \dfrac{(x-8)(x+2)}{2(x+8)(x-8)} \cdot \dfrac{(x+8)(x+8)}{3(x+2)(x+8)}$

$= \dfrac{1}{2 \cdot 3}$

$= \dfrac{1}{6}$

45. $\dfrac{2x}{5} \div \dfrac{6x+12}{5x+10} = \dfrac{2x}{5} \cdot \dfrac{5x+10}{6x+12}$

$= \dfrac{2x}{5} \cdot \dfrac{5(x+2)}{6(x+2)}$

$= \dfrac{2x}{5} \cdot \dfrac{5(x+2)}{2 \cdot 3(x+2)}$

$= \dfrac{x}{3}$

47. $\dfrac{a+b}{ab} \div \dfrac{a^2-b^2}{4a^3b} = \dfrac{a+b}{ab} \cdot \dfrac{4a^3b}{a^2-b^2}$

$\qquad = \dfrac{a+b}{ab} \cdot \dfrac{4a^3b}{(a+b)(a-b)}$

$\qquad = \dfrac{4a^2}{a-b}$

49. $\dfrac{x^2-6x+9}{x^2-x-6} \div \dfrac{x^2-9}{4}$

$= \dfrac{x^2-6x+9}{x^2-x-6} \cdot \dfrac{4}{x^2-9}$

$= \dfrac{(x-3)^2}{(x-3)(x+2)} \cdot \dfrac{4}{(x+3)(x-3)}$

$= \dfrac{4}{(x+2)(x+3)}$

51. $\dfrac{x^2-6x-16}{2x^2-128} \div \dfrac{x^2+10x+16}{x^2+16x+64}$

$= \dfrac{x^2-6x-16}{2x^2-128} \cdot \dfrac{x^2+16x+64}{x^2+10x+16}$

$= \dfrac{(x-8)(x+2)}{2(x^2-64)} \cdot \dfrac{(x+8)(x+8)}{(x+2)(x+8)}$

$= \dfrac{(x-8)(x+2)}{2(x-8)(x+8)} \cdot \dfrac{(x+8)(x+8)}{(x+2)(x+8)}$

$= \dfrac{1}{2}$

53. $\dfrac{3x-x^2}{x^3-27} \div \dfrac{x}{x^2+3x+9}$

$= \dfrac{3x-x^2}{x^3-27} \cdot \dfrac{x^2+3x+9}{x}$

$= \dfrac{x(3-x)}{(x-3)(x^2+3x+9)} \cdot \dfrac{x^2+3x+9}{x}$

$= \dfrac{-x(x-3)}{(x-3)(x^2+3x+9)} \cdot \dfrac{x^2+3x+9}{x}$

$= -1$

55. $\dfrac{8b+24}{3a+6} \div \dfrac{ab-2b+3a-6}{a^2-4a+4}$

$= \dfrac{8b+24}{3a+6} \cdot \dfrac{a^2-4a+4}{ab-2b+3a-6}$

$= \dfrac{8(b+3)}{3(a+2)} \cdot \dfrac{(a-2)(a-2)}{b(a-2)+3(a-2)}$

$= \dfrac{8(b+3)}{3(a+2)} \cdot \dfrac{(a-2)(a-2)}{(a-2)(b+3)}$

$= \dfrac{8(a-2)}{3(a+2)}$

57. $\dfrac{x^2-9}{4} \cdot \dfrac{x^2-x-6}{x^2-6x+9}$

$= \dfrac{(x+3)(x-3)}{4} \cdot \dfrac{(x+2)(x-3)}{(x-3)^2}$

$= \dfrac{(x+3)(x+2)}{4}$

59. $\dfrac{2x^2-4x-30}{5x^2-40x-75} \div \dfrac{x^2-8x+15}{x^2-6x+9}$

$= \dfrac{2x^2-4x-30}{5x^2-40x-75} \cdot \dfrac{x^2-6x+9}{x^2-8x+15}$

$= \dfrac{2(x^2-2x-15)}{5(x^2-8x-15)} \cdot \dfrac{(x-3)(x-3)}{(x-3)(x-5)}$

$= \dfrac{2(x-5)(x+3)}{5(x^2-8x-15)} \cdot \dfrac{(x-3)(x-3)}{(x-3)(x-5)}$

$= \dfrac{2(x+3)(x-3)}{5(x^2-8x-15)}$

61. $\dfrac{r^3+s^3}{r+s} = \dfrac{(r+s)(r^2-rs+s^2)}{r+s} = r^2-rs+s^2$

63. $\dfrac{4}{x} \div \dfrac{3xy}{x^2} \cdot \dfrac{6x^2}{x^4} = \dfrac{4}{x} \cdot \dfrac{x^2}{3xy} \cdot \dfrac{6x^2}{x^4} = \dfrac{8}{x^2y}$

65. $\dfrac{3x^2-5x-2}{y^2+y-2} \cdot \dfrac{y^2+4y-5}{12x^2+7x+1} \div \dfrac{5x^2-9x-2}{8x^2-2x-1}$

$= \dfrac{3x^2-5x-2}{y^2+y-2} \cdot \dfrac{y^2+4y-5}{12x^2+7x+1} \cdot \dfrac{8x^2-2x-1}{5x^2-9x-2}$

$= \dfrac{(3x+1)(x-2)(y+5)(y-1)(4x+1)(2x-1)}{(y+2)(y-1)(4x+1)(3x+1)(5x+1)(x-2)}$

$= \dfrac{(y+5)(2x-1)}{(y+2)(5x+1)}$

67. $\dfrac{5a^2-20}{3a^2-12a} \div \dfrac{a^3+2a^2}{2a^2-8a} \cdot \dfrac{9a^3+6a^2}{2a^2-4a}$

$= \dfrac{5a^2-20}{3a^2-12a} \cdot \dfrac{2a^2-8a}{a^3+2a^2} \cdot \dfrac{9a^3+6a^2}{2a^2-4a}$

$= \dfrac{5(a^2-4)}{3a(a-4)} \cdot \dfrac{2a(a-4)}{a^2(a+2)} \cdot \dfrac{3a^2(3a+2)}{2a(a-2)}$

$= \dfrac{5(a+2)(a-2)}{3a(a-4)} \cdot \dfrac{2a(a-4)}{a^2(a+2)} \cdot \dfrac{3a^2(3a+2)}{2a(a-2)}$

$= \dfrac{5(3a+2)}{a}$

69. $\dfrac{5x^4+3x^2-2}{x-1} \cdot \dfrac{x+1}{x^4-1}$

$= \dfrac{(5x^2-2)(x^2+1)}{x-1} \cdot \dfrac{x+1}{(x^2+1)(x^2-1)}$

$= \dfrac{(5x^2-2)(x^2+1)}{x-1} \cdot \dfrac{x+1}{(x^2+1)(x+1)(x-1)}$

$= \dfrac{5x^2-2}{(x-1)^2}$

71. $f(x) = \dfrac{x+8}{2x-1}$

$f(2) = \dfrac{2+8}{2(2)-1} = \dfrac{10}{4-1} = \dfrac{10}{3}$

$f(0) = \dfrac{0+8}{2(0)-1} = \dfrac{8}{0-1} = \dfrac{8}{-1} = -8$

$f(-1) = \dfrac{-1+8}{2(-1)-1} = \dfrac{7}{-2-1} = \dfrac{7}{-3} = -\dfrac{7}{3}$

73. $g(x) = \dfrac{x^2+8}{x^3-25x}$

$g(3) = \dfrac{3^2+8}{3^3-25(3)} = \dfrac{9+8}{27-75} = \dfrac{17}{-48} = -\dfrac{17}{48}$

$g(-2) = \dfrac{(-2)^2+8}{(-2)^3-25(-2)} = \dfrac{4+8}{-8+50} = \dfrac{12}{42} = \dfrac{2}{7}$

$g(1) = \dfrac{1^2+8}{1^3-25(1)} = \dfrac{1+8}{1-25} = \dfrac{9}{-24} = -\dfrac{3}{8}$

75. $R(x) = \dfrac{1000x^2}{x^2+4}$

a. $R(1) = \dfrac{1000 \cdot 1^2}{1^2+4} = \dfrac{1000}{5} = 200$

The revenue at the end of the first year is $200 million.

b. $R(2) = \dfrac{1000 \cdot 2^2}{2^2+4}$

$= \dfrac{1000 \cdot 4}{4+4}$

$= \dfrac{4000}{8}$

$= 500$

The revenue at the end of the second year is $500 million.

c. The revenue during the second year is equal to the revenue at the end of the second year minus the revenue at the end of the first year.

$500 - 200 = 300$

The revenue during the second year is $300 million.

d. $x^2+4 = 0$

$x^2 = -4$

This equation has no solutions. Thus there are no values of x that would make the denominator equal to zero and the function undefined. The domain of $R(x)$ is $\{x | x \text{ is a real number}\}$.

77. $\dfrac{4}{5} + \dfrac{3}{5} = \dfrac{7}{5}$

79. $\dfrac{5}{28} - \dfrac{2}{21} = \dfrac{15}{84} - \dfrac{8}{84} = \dfrac{7}{84} = \dfrac{1}{12}$

81. $\dfrac{3}{8} + \dfrac{1}{2} - \dfrac{3}{16} = \dfrac{6}{16} + \dfrac{8}{16} - \dfrac{3}{16} = \dfrac{11}{16}$

83. a. $\dfrac{-x}{5-x} \ne \dfrac{x}{5-x}$

b. $\dfrac{-x}{-5+x} = \dfrac{x}{-(-5+x)} = \dfrac{x}{5-x}$

c. $\dfrac{x}{x-5} = \dfrac{x}{-5+x} \neq \dfrac{x}{5-x}$

d. $\dfrac{-x}{x-5} = \dfrac{x}{-(x-5)} = \dfrac{x}{-x+5} = \dfrac{x}{5-x}$

85. No; answers may vary

87. $A = l \cdot w$

$$= \left(\dfrac{x+2}{x}\right)\left(\dfrac{5x}{x^2-4}\right)$$

$$= \dfrac{x+2}{x} \cdot \dfrac{5x}{(x+2)(x-2)}$$

$$= \dfrac{5}{x-2}$$

The area is $\dfrac{5}{x-2}$ square meters.

89. Since $A = b \cdot h$, $b = \dfrac{A}{h}$.

$$b = \dfrac{\dfrac{x^2+x-2}{x^3}}{\dfrac{x^2}{x-1}}$$

$$= \dfrac{x^2+x-2}{x^3} \cdot \dfrac{x-1}{x^2}$$

$$= \dfrac{(x+2)(x-1)}{x^3} \cdot \dfrac{x-1}{x^2}$$

$$= \dfrac{(x+2)(x-1)^2}{x^5}$$

The length of the base is $\dfrac{(x+2)(x-1)^2}{x^5}$ feet.

91. answers may vary

93. a. $\dfrac{x+5}{5+x} = \dfrac{x+5}{x+5} = 1$

b. $\dfrac{x-5}{5-x} = \dfrac{x-5}{-(x-5)} = -1$

c. $\dfrac{x+5}{x-5}$ neither

d. $\dfrac{-x-5}{x+5} = \dfrac{-(x+5)}{x+5} = -1$

e. $\dfrac{x-5}{-x+5} = \dfrac{x-5}{-(x-5)} = -1$

f. $\dfrac{-5+x}{x-5} = \dfrac{x-5}{x-5} = 1$

95.

$$\dfrac{x^2-4}{x^2-7x+10} \cdot \dfrac{?}{2x^2+11x+14} = 1$$

$$\dfrac{(x+2)(x-2)}{(x-2)(x-5)} \cdot \dfrac{?}{(2x+7)(x+2)} = 1$$

$$\dfrac{?}{(x-5)(2x+7)} = 1$$

For the fraction to equal 1, the numerator needs to be $(x-5)(2x+7)$.

97. $f(x) = \dfrac{20x}{100-x}$

x	0	10	30	50	70	90	95	99
y	0	$\dfrac{20}{9}$	$\dfrac{60}{7}$	20	$\dfrac{140}{3}$	180	380	1980

99. $\dfrac{x^{2n}-4}{7x} \cdot \dfrac{14x^3}{x^n-2} = \dfrac{(x^n+2)(x^n-2)}{7x} \cdot \dfrac{14x^3}{x^n-2}$

$$= 2x^2(x^n+2)$$

101. $\dfrac{y^{2n}+9}{10y} \cdot \dfrac{y^n-3}{y^{4n}-81}$

$$= \dfrac{y^{2n}+9}{10y} \cdot \dfrac{y^n-3}{(y^{2n}+9)(y^{2n}-9)}$$

$$= \dfrac{y^{2n}+9}{10y} \cdot \dfrac{y^n-3}{(y^{2n}+9)(y^n+3)(y^n-3)}$$

$$= \dfrac{1}{10y(y^n+3)}$$

103. $\dfrac{y^{2n}-y^n-2}{2y^n-4} \div \dfrac{y^{2n}-1}{1+y^n}$

$= \dfrac{y^{2n}-y^n-2}{2y^n-4} \cdot \dfrac{1+y^n}{y^{2n}-1}$

$= \dfrac{(y^n-2)(y^n+1)}{2(y^n-2)} \cdot \dfrac{1+y^n}{(y^n+1)(y^n-1)}$

$= \dfrac{1+y^n}{2(y^n-1)}$

Section 6.2

Practice Exercises

1. a. $\dfrac{9}{11z^2}+\dfrac{x}{11z^2}=\dfrac{9+x}{11z^2}$

b. $\dfrac{x}{8}+\dfrac{5x}{8}=\dfrac{x+5x}{8}=\dfrac{6x}{8}=\dfrac{3x}{4}$

c. $\dfrac{x^2}{x+4}-\dfrac{16}{x+4}=\dfrac{x^2-16}{x+4}$

$\qquad = \dfrac{(x+4)(x-4)}{x+4}$

$\qquad = x-4$

d. $\dfrac{z}{2a^2}-\dfrac{z+3}{2a^2}=\dfrac{z-(z+3)}{2a^2}$

$\qquad = \dfrac{z-z-3}{2a^2}$

$\qquad = \dfrac{-3}{2a^2}$

2. a. $\dfrac{7}{6x^3y^5},\dfrac{2}{9x^2y^4}$

We factor each denominator.

$6x^3y^5 = 2 \cdot 3 \cdot x^3 \cdot y^5$

$9x^2y^4 = 3^2 \cdot x^2 \cdot y^4$

$LCD = 2 \cdot 3^2 \cdot x^3 \cdot y^5 = 18x^3y^5$

b. $\dfrac{11}{x-2},\dfrac{x}{x-3}$

The denominators $x-2$ and $x-3$ do not factor further.

$LCD = (x-2)(x-3)$

c. $\dfrac{b+2}{b^2-16},\dfrac{8}{b^2-8b+16},\dfrac{5b}{2b^2-5b-12}$

We factor each denominator.

$b^2-16=(b-4)(b+4)$

$b^2-8b+16=(b-4)(b-4)$

$2b^2-5b-12=(2b+3)(b-4)$

$LCD=(b-4)^2(b+4)(2b+3)$

d. $\dfrac{y}{y^2-9},\dfrac{3}{12-4y}$

We factor each denominator.

$y^2-9=(y-3)(y+3)$

$12-4y=4(3-y)=4(-1)(y-3)$

$LCD=-4(y-3)(y+3)$

3. a. The LCD is $5p^4q$.

$\dfrac{4}{p^3q}+\dfrac{3}{5p^4q}=\dfrac{4 \cdot 5p}{p^3q \cdot 5p}+\dfrac{3}{5p^4q}$

$\qquad = \dfrac{20p}{5p^4q}+\dfrac{3}{5p^4q}$

$\qquad = \dfrac{20p+3}{5p^4q}$

b. The LCD is the product of the two denominators: $(y+3)(y-3)$.

$\dfrac{4}{y+3}+\dfrac{5y}{y-3}$

$= \dfrac{4 \cdot (y-3)}{(y+3) \cdot (y-3)}+\dfrac{5y \cdot (y+3)}{(y-3) \cdot (y+3)}$

$= \dfrac{4y-12}{(y+3)(y-3)}+\dfrac{5y^2+15y}{(y+3)(y-3)}$

$= \dfrac{4y-12+5y^2+15y}{(y+3)(y-3)}$

$= \dfrac{5y^2+19y-12}{(y+3)(y-3)}$

c. The LCD is either $z - 5$ or $5 - z$.

$$\frac{3z-18}{z-5} - \frac{3}{5-z} = \frac{3z-18}{z-5} - \frac{3}{-1(z-5)}$$
$$= \frac{3z-18}{z-5} - \frac{-1\cdot 3}{z-5}$$
$$= \frac{3z-18-(-3)}{z-5}$$
$$= \frac{3z-18+3}{z-5}$$
$$= \frac{3z-15}{z-5}$$
$$= \frac{3(z-5)}{z-5}$$
$$= 3$$

4. $\dfrac{t}{t^2-25} - \dfrac{3}{t^2-3t-10}$

$$= \frac{t}{(t+5)(t-5)} - \frac{3}{(t-5)(t+2)}$$

The LCD is $(t + 5)(t - 5)(t + 2)$.

$$\frac{t}{(t+5)(t-5)} - \frac{3}{(t-5)(t+2)}$$
$$= \frac{t\cdot(t+2)}{(t+5)(t-5)\cdot(t+2)} - \frac{3\cdot(t+5)}{(t-5)(t+2)\cdot(t+5)}$$
$$= \frac{t^2+2t}{(t+5)(t-5)(t+2)} - \frac{3t+15}{(t+5)(t-5)(t+2)}$$
$$= \frac{t^2+2t-3t-15}{(t+5)(t-5)(t+2)}$$
$$= \frac{t^2-t-15}{(t+5)(t-5)(t+2)}$$

5. $\dfrac{2x+3}{3x^2-5x-2} + \dfrac{x-6}{6x^2-13x-5}$

$$= \frac{2x+3}{(3x+1)(x-2)} + \frac{x-6}{(3x+1)(2x-5)}$$

The LCD is $(3x + 1)(x - 2)(2x - 5)$.

$$= \frac{(2x+3)\cdot(2x-5)}{(3x+1)(x-2)\cdot(2x-5)} + \frac{(x-6)\cdot(x-2)}{(3x+1)(2x-5)\cdot(x-2)}$$
$$= \frac{4x^2-4x-15}{(3x+1)(x-2)(2x-5)} + \frac{x^2-8x+12}{(3x+1)(x-2)(2x-5)}$$
$$= \frac{4x^2-4x-15+x^2-8x+12}{(3x+1)(x-2)(2x-5)}$$
$$= \frac{5x^2-12x-3}{(3x+1)(x-2)(2x-5)}$$

6. $\dfrac{2}{x-2} + \dfrac{3x}{x^2-x-2} - \dfrac{1}{x+1}$

$$= \frac{2}{x-2} + \frac{3x}{(x-2)(x+1)} - \frac{1}{x+1}$$

The LCD is $(x - 2)(x - 1)$.

$$= \frac{2\cdot(x+1)}{(x-2)\cdot(x+1)} + \frac{3x}{(x-2)(x+1)} - \frac{1\cdot(x-2)}{(x+1)\cdot(x-2)}$$
$$= \frac{2x+2}{(x-2)(x+1)} + \frac{3x}{(x-2)(x+1)} - \frac{x-2}{(x-2)(x+1)}$$
$$= \frac{2x+2+3x-x+2}{(x-2)(x+1)}$$
$$= \frac{4x+4}{(x-2)(x+1)}$$
$$= \frac{4(x+1)}{(x-2)(x+1)}$$
$$= \frac{4}{x-2}$$

Vocabulary and Readiness Check

1. The denominators must be the same before performing the operations of addition and subtraction (<u>a, b</u>).

2. To perform the operation of division (<u>d</u>), you multiply the first rational expression by the reciprocal of the second rational expression.

3. Numerator times numerator all over denominator times denominator is multiplication (<u>c</u>).

4. The operations of addition and multiplication (<u>a, c</u>) are commutative (order doesn't matter).

5. Addition: $\dfrac{5}{y} + \dfrac{7}{y} = \dfrac{12}{y}$

6. Subtraction: $\dfrac{5}{y} - \dfrac{7}{y} = -\dfrac{2}{y}$

7. Multiplication: $\dfrac{5}{y} \cdot \dfrac{7}{y} = \dfrac{35}{y^2}$

8. Division: $\dfrac{5}{y} \div \dfrac{7}{y} = \dfrac{5}{y} \cdot \dfrac{y}{7} = \dfrac{5}{7}$

9. $\dfrac{5}{2x} - \dfrac{x+1}{2x} = \dfrac{5-(x+1)}{2x} = \dfrac{-x+4}{2x}$

10. $\dfrac{9}{5x} - \dfrac{6-x}{5x} = \dfrac{9-(6-x)}{5x} = \dfrac{x+3}{5x}$

11. $\dfrac{y+11}{y-2} - \dfrac{y-5}{y-2} = \dfrac{y+11-(y-5)}{y-2} = \dfrac{16}{y-2}$

12. $\dfrac{z-1}{z+6} - \dfrac{z+4}{z+6} = \dfrac{z-1-(z+4)}{z+6} = \dfrac{-5}{z+6}$

Exercise Set 6.2

1. $\dfrac{2}{xz^2} - \dfrac{5}{xz^2} = \dfrac{2-5}{xz^2} = \dfrac{-3}{xz^2} = -\dfrac{3}{xz^2}$

3. $\dfrac{2}{x-2} + \dfrac{x}{x-2} = \dfrac{2+x}{x-2} = \dfrac{x+2}{x-2}$

5. $\dfrac{x^2}{x+2} - \dfrac{4}{x+2} = \dfrac{x^2-4}{x+2}$
$\qquad = \dfrac{(x+2)(x-2)}{x+2}$
$\qquad = x-2$

7. $\dfrac{2x-6}{x^2+x-6} + \dfrac{3-3x}{x^2+x-6} = \dfrac{2x-6+3-3x}{x^2+x-6}$
$\qquad = \dfrac{-x-3}{x^2+x-6}$
$\qquad = \dfrac{-1(x+3)}{(x+3)(x-2)}$
$\qquad = \dfrac{-1}{x-2} \text{ or } \dfrac{1}{-(x-2)}$
$\qquad = \dfrac{-1}{x-2} \text{ or } \dfrac{1}{2-x}$

9. $\dfrac{x-5}{2x} - \dfrac{x+5}{2x} = \dfrac{x-5-x-5}{2x} = \dfrac{-10}{2x} = -\dfrac{5}{x}$

11. $7 = 7$
$5x = 5x$
$\text{LCD} = 7 \cdot 5x = 35x$

13. $x = x$
$x+1 = x+1$
$\text{LCD} = x(x+1)$

15. $x+7 = x+7$
$x-7 = x-7$
$\text{LCD} = (x+7)(x-7)$

17. $3x+6 = 3(x+2)$
$2x-4 = 2(x-2)$
$\text{LCD} = 3 \cdot 2(x+2)(x-2) = 6(x+2)(x-2)$

19. $a^2 - b^2 = (a+b)(a-b)$
$a^2 - 2ab + b^2 = (a-b)^2$
$\text{LCD} = (a+b)(a-b)^2$

21. $x^2 - 9 = (x+3)(x-3)$
$x = x$
$12 - 4x = -4(x-3)$
$\text{LCD} = -4x(x+3)(x-3)$

23. $\dfrac{4}{3x} + \dfrac{3}{2x} = \dfrac{4\cdot2}{3x(2)} + \dfrac{3\cdot3}{2x(3)} = \dfrac{8}{6x} + \dfrac{9}{6x} = \dfrac{17}{6x}$

25. $\dfrac{5}{2y^2} - \dfrac{2}{7y} = \dfrac{5\cdot7}{2y^2 \cdot 7} - \dfrac{2\cdot2y}{7y\cdot2y}$
$\qquad = \dfrac{35}{14y^2} - \dfrac{4y}{14y^2}$
$\qquad = \dfrac{35-4y}{14y^2}$

27. $\dfrac{x-3}{x+4} - \dfrac{x+2}{x-4}$
$\qquad = \dfrac{(x-3)(x-4)}{(x+4)(x-4)} - \dfrac{(x+2)(x+4)}{(x-4)(x+4)}$
$\qquad = \dfrac{x^2-7x+12}{(x+4)(x-4)} - \dfrac{x^2+6x+8}{(x+4)(x-4)}$
$\qquad = \dfrac{x^2-7x+12-x^2-6x-8}{(x+4)(x-4)}$
$\qquad = \dfrac{-13x+4}{(x+4)(x-4)}$

29.
$$\frac{1}{x-5} - \frac{19-2x}{(x-5)(x+4)} = \frac{1 \cdot (x+4)}{(x-5) \cdot (x+4)} - \frac{19-2x}{(x-5)(x+4)}$$
$$= \frac{x+4+19-2x}{(x-5)(x+4)}$$
$$= \frac{3x-15}{(x-5)(x+4)}$$
$$= \frac{3(x-5)}{(x-5)(x+4)}$$
$$= \frac{3}{x+4}$$

31.
$$\frac{1}{a-b} + \frac{1}{b-a} = \frac{1}{a-b} + \frac{1}{-1(-b+a)}$$
$$= \frac{1}{a-b} + \frac{-1}{a-b}$$
$$= \frac{0}{a-b}$$
$$= 0$$

33.
$$\frac{x+1}{1-x} + \frac{1}{x-1} = \frac{x+1}{-(x-1)} + \frac{1}{x-1}$$
$$= \frac{-(x+1)}{x-1} + \frac{1}{x-1}$$
$$= \frac{-x-1+1}{x-1}$$
$$= \frac{-x}{x-1}$$
$$= -\frac{x}{x-1}$$

35.
$$\frac{5}{x-2} + \frac{x+4}{2-x} = \frac{5}{x-2} + \frac{x+4}{-(-2+x)}$$
$$= \frac{5}{x-2} + \frac{-(x+4)}{x-2}$$
$$= \frac{5-x-4}{x-2}$$
$$= \frac{-x+1}{x-2}$$

37. $\dfrac{y+1}{y^2-6y+8}-\dfrac{3}{y^2-16}=\dfrac{y+1}{(y-2)(y-4)}-\dfrac{3}{(y+4)(y-4)}$

$$=\dfrac{(y+1)(y+4)}{(y-2)(y-4)(y+4)}-\dfrac{3(y-2)}{(y-2)(y+4)(y-4)}$$

$$=\dfrac{(y+1)(y+4)-3(y-2)}{(y-2)(y-4)(y+4)}$$

$$=\dfrac{y^2+5y+4-3y+6}{(y-2)(y-4)(y+4)}$$

$$=\dfrac{y^2+2y+10}{(y-2)(y-4)(y+4)}$$

39. $\dfrac{x+4}{3x^2+11x+6}+\dfrac{x}{2x^2+x-15}=\dfrac{x+4}{(3x+2)(x+3)}+\dfrac{x}{(2x-5)(x+3)}$

$$=\dfrac{(x+4)(2x-5)}{(3x+2)(x+3)(2x-5)}+\dfrac{x(3x+2)}{(2x-5)(x+3)(3x+2)}$$

$$=\dfrac{2x^2+3x-20}{(3x+2)(x+3)(2x-5)}+\dfrac{3x^2+2x}{(3x+2)(x+3)(2x-5)}$$

$$=\dfrac{2x^2+3x-20+3x^2+2x}{(3x+2)(x+3)(2x-5)}$$

$$=\dfrac{5x^2+5x-20}{(3x+2)(x+3)(2x-5)}$$

$$=\dfrac{5(x^2+x-4)}{(3x+2)(x+3)(2x-5)}$$

41. $\dfrac{7}{x^2-x-2}-\dfrac{x-1}{x^2+4x+3}=\dfrac{7}{(x-2)(x+1)}-\dfrac{x-1}{(x+3)(x+1)}$

$$=\dfrac{7(x+3)}{(x-2)(x+1)(x+3)}-\dfrac{(x-1)(x-2)}{(x+3)(x+1)(x-2)}$$

$$=\dfrac{7(x+3)-(x-1)(x-2)}{(x-2)(x+1)(x+3)}$$

$$=\dfrac{7x+21-x^2+3x-2}{(x-2)(x+1)(x+3)}$$

$$=\dfrac{-x^2+10x+19}{(x-2)(x+1)(x+3)}$$

43. $\dfrac{x}{x^2-8x+7}-\dfrac{x+2}{2x^2-9x-35}$

$=\dfrac{x}{(x-1)(x-7)}-\dfrac{x+2}{(2x+5)(x-7)}$

$=\dfrac{x(2x+5)}{(x-1)(x-7)(2x+5)}-\dfrac{(x+2)(x-1)}{(2x+5)(x-7)(x-1)}$

$=\dfrac{x(2x+5)-(x+2)(x-1)}{(2x+5)(x-7)(x-1)}$

$=\dfrac{2x^2+5x-(x^2+x-2)}{(2x+5)(x-7)(x-1)}$

$=\dfrac{2x^2+5x-x^2-x+2}{(2x+5)(x-7)(x-1)}$

$=\dfrac{x^2+4x+2}{(2x+5)(x-7)(x-1)}$

45. $\dfrac{2}{a^2+2a+1}+\dfrac{3}{a^2-1}$

$=\dfrac{2}{(a+1)^2}+\dfrac{3}{(a+1)(a-1)}$

$=\dfrac{2(a-1)}{(a+1)^2(a-1)}+\dfrac{3(a+1)}{(a+1)(a-1)(a+1)}$

$=\dfrac{2(a-1)+3(a+1)}{(a+1)^2(a-1)}$

$=\dfrac{2a-2+3a+3}{(a+1)^2(a-1)}$

$=\dfrac{5a+1}{(a+1)^2(a-1)}$

47. $\dfrac{4}{3x^2y^3}+\dfrac{5}{3x^2y^3}=\dfrac{9}{3x^2y^3}=\dfrac{3}{x^2y^3}$

49. $\dfrac{13x-5}{2x}-\dfrac{13x+5}{2x}=\dfrac{13x-5-13x-5}{2x}$

$=\dfrac{-10}{2x}$

$=-\dfrac{5}{x}$

51. $\dfrac{3}{2x+10}+\dfrac{8}{3x+15}=\dfrac{3}{2(x+5)}+\dfrac{8}{3(x+5)}$

$=\dfrac{3\cdot3}{2(x+5)\cdot3}+\dfrac{8\cdot2}{3(x+5)\cdot2}$

$=\dfrac{9}{6(x+5)}+\dfrac{16}{6(x+5)}$

$=\dfrac{25}{6(x+5)}$

53. $\dfrac{-2}{x^2-3x}-\dfrac{1}{x^3-3x^2}=\dfrac{-2}{x(x-3)}-\dfrac{1}{x^2(x-3)}$

$=\dfrac{-2x}{x^2(x-3)}-\dfrac{1}{x^2(x-3)}$

$=\dfrac{-2x-1}{x^2(x-3)}$

55. $\dfrac{ab}{a^2-b^2}+\dfrac{b}{a+b}$

$=\dfrac{ab}{(a+b)(a-b)}+\dfrac{b}{a+b}$

$=\dfrac{ab}{(a+b)(a-b)}+\dfrac{b(a-b)}{(a+b)(a-b)}$

$=\dfrac{ab}{(a+b)(a-b)}+\dfrac{ab-b^2}{(a+b)(a-b)}$

$=\dfrac{ab+ab-b^2}{(a+b)(a-b)}$

$=\dfrac{2ab-b^2}{(a+b)(a-b)}$

$=\dfrac{b(2a-b)}{(a+b)(a-b)}$

57. $\dfrac{5}{x^2-4}-\dfrac{3}{x^2+4x+4}$

$=\dfrac{5}{(x+2)(x-2)}-\dfrac{3}{(x+2)^2}$

$=\dfrac{5(x+2)}{(x+2)(x-2)(x+2)}-\dfrac{3(x-2)}{(x+2)^2(x-2)}$

$=\dfrac{5(x+2)-3(x-2)}{(x+2)^2(x-2)}$

$=\dfrac{5x+10-3x+6}{(x+2)^2(x-2)}$

$=\dfrac{2x+16}{(x+2)^2(x-2)}$

$=\dfrac{2(x+8)}{(x+2)^2(x-2)}$

59.
$$\frac{3x}{2x^2-11x+5}+\frac{7}{x^2-2x-15}=\frac{3x}{(2x-1)(x-5)}+\frac{7}{(x-5)(x+3)}$$
$$=\frac{3x(x+3)}{(2x-1)(x-5)(x+3)}+\frac{7(2x-1)}{(x-5)(x+3)(2x-1)}$$
$$=\frac{3x^2+9x}{(2x-1)(x-5)(x+3)}+\frac{14x-7}{(2x-1)(x-5)(x+3)}$$
$$=\frac{3x^2+9x+14x-7}{(2x-1)(x-5)(x+3)}$$
$$=\frac{3x^2+23x-7}{(2x-1)(x-5)(x+3)}$$

61.
$$\frac{2}{x+1}-\frac{3x}{3x+3}+\frac{1}{2x+2}=\frac{2}{x+1}-\frac{3x}{3(x+1)}+\frac{1}{2(x+1)}$$
$$=\frac{2}{x+1}-\frac{x}{x+1}+\frac{1}{2(x+1)}$$
$$=\frac{2\cdot2}{2(x+1)}-\frac{2\cdot x}{2(x+1)}+\frac{1}{2(x+1)}$$
$$=\frac{4-2x+1}{2(x+1)}$$
$$=\frac{5-2x}{2(x+1)}$$

63.
$$\frac{3}{x+3}+\frac{5}{x^2+6x+9}-\frac{x}{x^2-9}=\frac{3}{x+3}+\frac{5}{(x+3)^2}-\frac{x}{(x+3)(x-3)}$$
$$=\frac{3(x+3)(x-3)}{(x+3)(x+3)(x-3)}+\frac{5(x-3)}{(x+3)^2(x-3)}-\frac{x(x+3)}{(x+3)(x-3)(x+3)}$$
$$=\frac{3x^2-27}{(x+3)^2(x-3)}+\frac{5x-15}{(x+3)^2(x-3)}-\frac{x^2+3x}{(x+3)^2(x-3)}$$
$$=\frac{3x^2-27+5x-15-x^2-3x}{(x+3)^2(x-3)}$$
$$=\frac{2x^2+2x-42}{(x+3)^2(x-3)}$$
$$=\frac{2(x^2+x-21)}{(x+3)^2(x-3)}$$

65. $\dfrac{x}{x^2-9}+\dfrac{3}{x^2-6x+9}-\dfrac{1}{x+3}=\dfrac{x}{(x+3)(x-3)}+\dfrac{3}{(x-3)^2}-\dfrac{1}{x+3}$

$$=\dfrac{x(x-3)}{(x+3)(x-3)^2}+\dfrac{3(x+3)}{(x-3)^2(x+3)}-\dfrac{1(x-3)^2}{(x+3)(x-3)^2}$$

$$=\dfrac{x(x-3)+3(x+3)-(x-3)^2}{(x+3)(x-3)^2}$$

$$=\dfrac{x^2-3x+3x+9-(x^2-6x+9)}{(x+3)(x-3)^2}$$

$$=\dfrac{x^2+9-x^2+6x-9}{(x+3)(x-3)^2}$$

$$=\dfrac{6x}{(x+3)(x-3)^2}$$

67. $\left(\dfrac{1}{x}+\dfrac{2}{3}\right)-\left(\dfrac{1}{x}-\dfrac{2}{3}\right)=\left(\dfrac{3}{3x}+\dfrac{2x}{3x}\right)-\left(\dfrac{3}{3x}-\dfrac{2x}{3x}\right)$

$$=\left(\dfrac{3+2x}{3x}\right)-\left(\dfrac{3-2x}{3x}\right)$$

$$=\dfrac{3+2x-3+2x}{3x}$$

$$=\dfrac{4x}{3x}$$

$$=\dfrac{4}{3}$$

69. $\left(\dfrac{2}{3}-\dfrac{1}{x}\right)\cdot\left(\dfrac{3}{x}+\dfrac{1}{2}\right)=\left(\dfrac{2x}{3x}-\dfrac{3}{3x}\right)\cdot\left(\dfrac{3\cdot2}{2x}+\dfrac{x}{2x}\right)$

$$=\left(\dfrac{2x-3}{3x}\right)\cdot\left(\dfrac{6+x}{2x}\right)$$

$$=\dfrac{(2x-3)(x+6)}{6x^2}\ \text{or}\ \dfrac{2x^2+9x-18}{6x^2}$$

71. $\left(\dfrac{2a}{3}\right)^2\div\left(\dfrac{a^2}{a+1}-\dfrac{1}{a+1}\right)=\dfrac{4a^2}{9}\div\dfrac{a^2-1}{a+1}$

$$=\dfrac{4a^2}{9}\div\dfrac{(a+1)(a-1)}{a+1}$$

$$=\dfrac{4a^2}{9}\div(a-1)$$

$$=\dfrac{4a^2}{9}\cdot\dfrac{1}{a-1}$$

$$=\dfrac{4a^2}{9(a-1)}$$

73. $\left(\dfrac{2x}{3}\right)^2 \div \left(\dfrac{x}{3}\right)^2 = \left(\dfrac{2^2 x^2}{3^2}\right) \div \left(\dfrac{x^2}{3^2}\right)$

$\qquad = \dfrac{2^2 x^2}{3^2} \cdot \dfrac{3^2}{x^2}$

$\qquad = 2^2$

$\qquad = 4$

75. $\left(\dfrac{x}{x+1} - \dfrac{x}{x-1}\right) \div \dfrac{x}{2x+2}$

$\qquad = \left(\dfrac{x \cdot (x-1)}{(x+1)(x-1)} - \dfrac{x \cdot (x+1)}{(x-1)(x+1)}\right) \div \dfrac{x}{2(x+1)}$

$\qquad = \dfrac{x(x-1) - x(x+1)}{(x+1)(x-1)} \div \dfrac{x}{2(x+1)}$

$\qquad = \dfrac{x^2 - x - x^2 - x}{(x+1)(x-1)} \div \dfrac{x}{2(x+1)}$

$\qquad = \dfrac{-2x}{(x+1)(x-1)} \cdot \dfrac{2(x+1)}{x}$

$\qquad = -\dfrac{4}{x-1}$

77. $\dfrac{4}{x} \cdot \left(\dfrac{2}{x+2} - \dfrac{2}{x-2}\right)$

$\qquad = \dfrac{4}{x} \cdot \left(\dfrac{2(x-2)}{(x+2)(x-2)} - \dfrac{2(x+2)}{(x-2)(x+2)}\right)$

$\qquad = \dfrac{4}{x} \cdot \left(\dfrac{2x-4}{(x+2)(x-2)} - \dfrac{2x+4}{(x+2)(x-2)}\right)$

$\qquad = \dfrac{4}{x} \cdot \left(\dfrac{2x-4-2x-4}{(x+2)(x-2)}\right)$

$\qquad = \dfrac{4}{x}\left(\dfrac{-8}{(x+2)(x-2)}\right)$

$\qquad = -\dfrac{32}{x(x+2)(x-2)}$

79. $12\left(\dfrac{2}{3} + \dfrac{1}{6}\right) = 12 \cdot \dfrac{2}{3} + 12 \cdot \dfrac{1}{6} = \dfrac{24}{3} + \dfrac{12}{6} = 8 + 2 = 10$

81. $x^2\left(\dfrac{4}{x^2} + 1\right) = x^2 \cdot \dfrac{4}{x^2} + x^2 \cdot 1 = 4 + x^2$

83. $\sqrt{100} = 10$ because $10^2 = 100$.

85. $\sqrt[3]{8} = 2$ because $2^3 = 8$.

87. $\sqrt[4]{81} = 3$ because $3^4 = 81$.

89. $a^2 + b^2 = c^2$

$\qquad 3^2 + 4^2 = c^2$

$\qquad 9 + 16 = c^2$

$\qquad 25 = c^2$

$\qquad c = 5$ meters

91. $\dfrac{2x-3}{x^2+1} - \dfrac{x-6}{x^2+1} = \dfrac{2x-3-(x-6)}{x^2+1}$

$\qquad = \dfrac{2x-3-x+6}{x^2+1}$

$\qquad = \dfrac{x+3}{x^2+1}$

93. $P = 4s$

$\qquad P = 4 \cdot \left(\dfrac{x}{x+5}\right) = \dfrac{4x}{x+5}$

$\qquad A = s^2$

$\qquad A = \left(\dfrac{x}{x+5}\right)^2$

$\qquad A = \left(\dfrac{x}{x+5}\right)\left(\dfrac{x}{x+5}\right) = \dfrac{x^2}{(x+5)^2}$

The perimeter is $\dfrac{4x}{x+5}$ feet, and the area is

$\dfrac{x^2}{(x+5)^2}$ square feet.

95. Answers may vary

97. Answers may vary

99. Answers may vary

101. $x^{-1} + (2x)^{-1} = \dfrac{1}{x} + \dfrac{1}{2x}$

$\qquad = \dfrac{1 \cdot 2}{x \cdot 2} + \dfrac{1}{2x}$

$\qquad = \dfrac{2+1}{2x}$

$\qquad = \dfrac{3}{2x}$

103. $4x^{-2} - 3x^{-1} = \dfrac{4}{x^2} - \dfrac{3}{x} = \dfrac{4}{x^2} - \dfrac{3x}{x^2} = \dfrac{4-3x}{x^2}$

105.

Section 6.3

Practice Exercises

1. a. $\dfrac{\frac{5k}{36m}}{\frac{15k}{9}} = \dfrac{5k}{36m} \div \dfrac{15k}{9}$

$= \dfrac{5k}{36m} \cdot \dfrac{9}{15k}$

$= \dfrac{5k \cdot 9}{36m \cdot 15k}$

$= \dfrac{1}{12m}$

b. $\dfrac{\frac{8x}{x-4}}{\frac{3}{x+4}} = \dfrac{8x}{x-4} \div \dfrac{3}{x+4}$

$= \dfrac{8x}{x-4} \cdot \dfrac{x+4}{3}$

$= \dfrac{8x(x+4)}{3(x-4)}$

c. $\dfrac{\frac{5}{a}+\frac{b}{a^2}}{\frac{5a}{b^2}+\frac{1}{b}} = \dfrac{\frac{5 \cdot a}{a \cdot a}+\frac{b}{a^2}}{\frac{5a}{b^2}+\frac{1 \cdot b}{b \cdot b}}$

$= \dfrac{\frac{5a+b}{a^2}}{\frac{5a+b}{b^2}}$

$= \dfrac{5a+b}{a^2} \cdot \dfrac{b^2}{5a+b}$

$= \dfrac{b^2(5a+b)}{a^2(5a+b)}$

$= \dfrac{b^2}{a^2}$

2. a. The LCD is $(x-4)(x+4)$.

$\dfrac{\frac{8x}{x-4}}{\frac{3}{x+4}} = \dfrac{\left(\frac{8x}{x-4}\right) \cdot (x-4)(x+4)}{\left(\frac{3}{x+4}\right) \cdot (x-4)(x+4)}$

$= \dfrac{8x(x+4)}{3(x-4)}$

b. The LCD is $a^2 b^2$.

$\dfrac{\frac{b}{a^2}+\frac{1}{a}}{\frac{a}{b^2}+\frac{1}{b}} = \dfrac{\left(\frac{b}{a^2}+\frac{1}{a}\right) \cdot a^2 b^2}{\left(\frac{a}{b^2}+\frac{1}{b}\right) \cdot a^2 b^2}$

$= \dfrac{\frac{b}{a^2} \cdot a^2 b^2 + \frac{1}{a} \cdot a^2 b^2}{\frac{a}{b^2} \cdot a^2 b^2 + \frac{1}{b} \cdot a^2 b^2}$

$= \dfrac{b^3 + ab^2}{a^3 + a^2 b}$

$= \dfrac{b^2(b+a)}{a^2(a+b)}$

$= \dfrac{b^2}{a^2}$

3. $\dfrac{3x^{-1}+x^{-2}y^{-1}}{y^{-2}+xy^{-1}} = \dfrac{\frac{3}{x}+\frac{1}{x^2 y}}{\frac{1}{y^2}+\frac{x}{y}}$

The LCD is $x^2 y^2$.

$= \dfrac{\left(\frac{3}{x}+\frac{1}{x^2 y}\right) \cdot x^2 y^2}{\left(\frac{1}{y^2}+\frac{x}{y}\right) \cdot x^2 y^2}$

$= \dfrac{\frac{3}{x} \cdot x^2 y^2 + \frac{1}{x^2 y} \cdot x^2 y^2}{\frac{1}{y^2} \cdot x^2 y^2 + \frac{x}{y} \cdot x^2 y^2}$

$= \dfrac{3xy^2 + y}{x^2 + x^3 y}$ or $\dfrac{y(3xy+1)}{x^2(1+xy)}$

4. $\dfrac{(3x)^{-1}-2}{5x^{-1}+2} = \dfrac{\frac{1}{3x}-2}{\frac{5}{x}+2}$

$= \dfrac{\left(\frac{1}{3x}-2\right) \cdot 3x}{\left(\frac{5}{x}+2\right) \cdot 3x}$

$= \dfrac{\frac{1}{3x} \cdot 3x - 2 \cdot 3x}{\frac{5}{x} \cdot 3x + 2 \cdot 3x}$

$= \dfrac{1-6x}{15+6x}$

Vocabulary and Readiness Check

1. $\dfrac{\frac{7}{x}}{\frac{1}{x}+\frac{z}{x}} = \dfrac{x\left(\frac{7}{x}\right)}{x\left(\frac{1}{x}\right)+x\left(\frac{z}{x}\right)} = \dfrac{7}{1+z}$

2. $\dfrac{\frac{x}{4}}{\frac{x^2}{2}+\frac{1}{4}}=\dfrac{4\left(\frac{x}{4}\right)}{4\left(\frac{x^2}{2}\right)+4\left(\frac{1}{4}\right)}=\dfrac{x}{2x^2+1}$

3. $x^{-2}=\dfrac{1}{x^2}$

4. $y^{-3}=\dfrac{1}{y^3}$

5. $2x^{-1}=\dfrac{2}{x}$

6. $(2x)^{-1}=\dfrac{1}{2x}$

7. $(9y)^{-1}=\dfrac{1}{9y}$

8. $9y^{-2}=\dfrac{9}{y^2}$

Exercise Set 6.3

1. $\dfrac{\frac{10}{3x}}{\frac{5}{6x}}=\dfrac{10}{3x}\cdot\dfrac{6x}{5}=\dfrac{60x}{15x}=4$

3. $\dfrac{1+\frac{2}{5}}{2+\frac{3}{5}}=\dfrac{5\left(1+\frac{2}{5}\right)}{5\left(2+\frac{3}{5}\right)}=\dfrac{5+2}{10+3}=\dfrac{7}{13}$

5. $\dfrac{\frac{4}{x-1}}{\frac{x}{x-1}}=\dfrac{4}{x-1}\cdot\dfrac{x-1}{x}=\dfrac{4}{x}$

7. $\dfrac{1-\frac{2}{x}}{x+\frac{4}{9x}}=\dfrac{9x\left(1-\frac{2}{x}\right)}{9x\left(x+\frac{4}{9x}\right)}=\dfrac{9x-18}{9x^2+4}=\dfrac{9(x-2)}{9x^2+4}$

9. $\dfrac{\frac{4x^2-y^2}{xy}}{\frac{2}{y}-\frac{1}{x}}=\dfrac{\left(\frac{4x^2-y^2}{xy}\right)\cdot xy}{\left(\frac{2}{y}-\frac{1}{x}\right)\cdot xy}$

$=\dfrac{4x^2-y^2}{2x-y}$

$=\dfrac{(2x-y)(2x+y)}{2x-y}$

$=2x+y$

11. $\dfrac{\frac{x+1}{3}}{\frac{2x-1}{6}}=\dfrac{x+1}{3}\cdot\dfrac{6}{2x-1}=\dfrac{2(x+1)}{2x-1}$

13. $\dfrac{\frac{2}{x}+\frac{3}{x^2}}{\frac{4}{x^2}-\frac{9}{x}}=\dfrac{\left(\frac{2}{x}+\frac{3}{x^2}\right)x^2}{\left(\frac{4}{x^2}-\frac{9}{x}\right)x^2}=\dfrac{2x+3}{4-9x}$

15. $\dfrac{\frac{1}{x}+\frac{2}{x^2}}{x+\frac{8}{x^2}}=\dfrac{x^2\left(\frac{1}{x}+\frac{2}{x^2}\right)}{x^2\left(x+\frac{8}{x^2}\right)}$

$=\dfrac{x+2}{x^3+8}$

$=\dfrac{x+2}{(x+2)(x^2-2x+4)}$

$=\dfrac{1}{x^2-2x+4}$

17. $\dfrac{\frac{4}{5-x}+\frac{5}{x-5}}{\frac{2}{x}+\frac{3}{x-5}}=\dfrac{-\frac{4}{x-5}+\frac{5}{x-5}}{\frac{2(x-5)+3x}{x(x-5)}}$

$=\dfrac{\frac{1}{x-5}}{\frac{2x-10+3x}{x(x-5)}}$

$=\dfrac{1}{x-5}\cdot\dfrac{x(x-5)}{5x-10}$

$=\dfrac{x}{5x-10}$ or $\dfrac{x}{5(x-2)}$

19. $\dfrac{\frac{x+2}{x}-\frac{2}{x-1}}{\frac{x+1}{x}+\frac{x+1}{x-1}}=\dfrac{\frac{(x+2)(x-1)-2x}{x(x-1)}}{\frac{(x+1)(x-1)+(x+1)(x)}{x(x-1)}}$

$\qquad=\dfrac{\frac{x^2+x-2-2x}{x(x-1)}}{\frac{x^2-1+x^2+x}{x(x-1)}}$

$\qquad=\dfrac{x^2-x-2}{x(x-1)}\cdot\dfrac{x(x-1)}{2x^2+x-1}$

$\qquad=\dfrac{(x-2)(x+1)}{x(x-1)}\cdot\dfrac{x(x-1)}{(2x-1)(x+1)}$

$\qquad=\dfrac{x-2}{2x-1}$

21. $\dfrac{\frac{2}{x}+3}{\frac{4}{x^2}-9}=\dfrac{\left(\frac{2}{x}+3\right)\cdot x^2}{\left(\frac{4}{x^2}-9\right)\cdot x^2}$

$\qquad=\dfrac{2x+3x^2}{4-9x^2}$

$\qquad=\dfrac{x(2+3x)}{(2+3x)(2-3x)}$

$\qquad=\dfrac{x}{2-3x}$

23. $\dfrac{1-\frac{x}{y}}{\frac{x^2}{y^2}-1}=\dfrac{\left(1-\frac{x}{y}\right)\cdot y^2}{\left(\frac{x^2}{y^2}-1\right)\cdot y^2}$

$\qquad=\dfrac{y^2-xy}{x^2-y^2}$

$\qquad=\dfrac{y(y-x)}{(x+y)(x-y)}$

$\qquad=\dfrac{-y(x-y)}{(x+y)(x-y)}$

$\qquad=-\dfrac{y}{x+y}$

25. $\dfrac{\frac{-2x}{x-y}}{\frac{y}{x^2}}=\dfrac{-2x}{x-y}\cdot\dfrac{x^2}{y}=-\dfrac{2x^3}{y(x-y)}$

27. $\dfrac{\frac{2}{x}+\frac{1}{x^2}}{\frac{y}{x^2}}=\dfrac{\left(\frac{2}{x}+\frac{1}{x^2}\right)x^2}{\left(\frac{y}{x^2}\right)x^2}=\dfrac{2x+1}{y}$

29. $\dfrac{\frac{x}{9}-\frac{1}{x}}{1+\frac{3}{x}}=\dfrac{\left(\frac{x}{9}-\frac{1}{x}\right)\cdot9x}{\left(1+\frac{3}{x}\right)\cdot9x}$

$\qquad=\dfrac{x^2-9}{9x+27}$

$\qquad=\dfrac{(x+3)(x-3)}{9(x+3)}$

$\qquad=\dfrac{x-3}{9}$

31. $\dfrac{\frac{x-1}{x^2-4}}{1+\frac{1}{x-2}}=\dfrac{\frac{x-1}{x^2-4}}{\frac{x-2+1}{x-2}}=\dfrac{\frac{x-1}{x^2-4}}{\frac{x-1}{x-2}}$

$\qquad=\dfrac{x-1}{x^2-4}\cdot\dfrac{x-2}{x-1}$

$\qquad=\dfrac{x-1}{(x+2)(x-2)}\cdot\dfrac{x-2}{x-1}$

$\qquad=\dfrac{1}{x+2}$

33. $\dfrac{\frac{2}{x+5}+\frac{4}{x+3}}{\frac{3x+13}{x^2+8x+15}}=\dfrac{\frac{2}{x+5}+\frac{4}{x+3}}{\frac{3x+13}{(x+5)(x+3)}}$

$\qquad=\dfrac{\left(\frac{2}{x+5}+\frac{4}{x+3}\right)(x+5)(x+3)}{\frac{3x+13}{(x+5)(x+3)}(x+5)(x+3)}$

$\qquad=\dfrac{2(x+3)+4(x+5)}{3x+13}$

$\qquad=\dfrac{2x+6+4x+20}{3x+13}$

$\qquad=\dfrac{6x+26}{3x+13}$

$\qquad=\dfrac{2(3x+13)}{3x+13}$

$\qquad=2$

35. $\dfrac{x^{-1}}{x^{-2}+y^{-2}}=\dfrac{\frac{1}{x}}{\frac{1}{x^2}+\frac{1}{y^2}}$

$\qquad=\dfrac{x^2y^2\left(\frac{1}{x}\right)}{x^2y^2\left(\frac{1}{x^2}+\frac{1}{y^2}\right)}$

$\qquad=\dfrac{xy^2}{y^2+x^2}$

$\qquad=\dfrac{xy^2}{x^2+y^2}$

37. $\dfrac{2a^{-1}+3b^{-2}}{a^{-1}-b^{-1}}=\dfrac{\frac{2}{a}+\frac{3}{b^2}}{\frac{1}{a}-\frac{1}{b}}$

$\qquad = \dfrac{ab^2\left(\frac{2}{a}+\frac{3}{b^2}\right)}{ab^2\left(\frac{1}{a}-\frac{1}{b}\right)}$

$\qquad = \dfrac{2b^2+3a}{b^2-ab}$

$\qquad = \dfrac{2b^2+3a}{b(b-a)}$

39. $\dfrac{1}{x-x^{-1}}=\dfrac{1}{x-\frac{1}{x}}$

$\qquad = \dfrac{x(1)}{x\left(x-\frac{1}{x}\right)}$

$\qquad = \dfrac{x}{x^2-1}$

$\qquad = \dfrac{x}{(x+1)(x-1)}$

41. $\dfrac{a^{-1}+1}{a^{-1}-1}=\dfrac{\frac{1}{a}+1}{\frac{1}{a}-1}=\dfrac{a\left(\frac{1}{a}+1\right)}{a\left(\frac{1}{a}-1\right)}=\dfrac{1+a}{1-a}$

43. $\dfrac{3x^{-1}+(2y)^{-1}}{x^{-2}}=\dfrac{\frac{3}{x}+\frac{1}{2y}}{\frac{1}{x^2}}$

$\qquad = \dfrac{2x^2y\left(\frac{3}{x}+\frac{1}{2y}\right)}{2x^2y\left(\frac{1}{x^2}\right)}$

$\qquad = \dfrac{6xy+x^2}{2y}$

$\qquad = \dfrac{x(x+6y)}{2y}$

45. $\dfrac{2a^{-1}+(2a)^{-1}}{a^{-1}+2a^{-2}}=\dfrac{\frac{2}{a}+\frac{1}{2a}}{\frac{1}{a}+\frac{2}{a^2}}$

$\qquad = \dfrac{2a^2\left(\frac{2}{a}+\frac{1}{2a}\right)}{2a^2\left(\frac{1}{a}+\frac{2}{a^2}\right)}$

$\qquad = \dfrac{4a+a}{2a+4}$

$\qquad = \dfrac{5a}{2(a+2)}$

47. $\dfrac{5x^{-1}+2y^{-1}}{x^{-2}y^{-2}}=\dfrac{\frac{5}{x}+\frac{2}{y}}{\frac{1}{x^2y^2}}$

$\qquad = \dfrac{x^2y^2\left(\frac{5}{x}+\frac{2}{y}\right)}{x^2y^2\left(\frac{1}{x^2y^2}\right)}$

$\qquad = 5xy^2+2x^2y$

$\qquad = xy(5y+2x)$

49. $\dfrac{5x^{-1}-2y^{-1}}{25x^{-2}-4y^{-2}}=\dfrac{\frac{5}{x}-\frac{2}{y}}{\frac{25}{x^2}-\frac{4}{y^2}}$

$\qquad = \dfrac{x^2y^2\left(\frac{5}{x}-\frac{2}{y}\right)}{x^2y^2\left(\frac{25}{x^2}-\frac{4}{y^2}\right)}$

$\qquad = \dfrac{5xy^2-2x^2y}{25y^2-4x^2}$

$\qquad = \dfrac{xy(5y-2x)}{(5y+2x)(5y-2x)}$

$\qquad = \dfrac{xy}{5y+2x}$ or $\dfrac{xy}{2x+5y}$

51. $\dfrac{3x^3y^2}{12x}=\dfrac{3x\cdot x^2y^2}{3x\cdot 4}=\dfrac{x^2y^2}{4}$

53. $\dfrac{144x^5y^5}{-16x^2y}=\dfrac{16x^2y\cdot 9x^3y^4}{16x^2y\cdot(-1)}=-9x^3y^4$

55. $|x-5|=9$

$\qquad x-5=-9$ or $x-5=9$

$\qquad\qquad x=-4$ or $x=14$

The solution set is $\{-4, 14\}$.

57. $\dfrac{\frac{x+1}{9}}{\frac{y-2}{5}}=\dfrac{x+1}{9}\div\dfrac{y-2}{5}=\dfrac{x+1}{9}\cdot\dfrac{5}{y-2}$

Both a and c are equivalent to the original expression.

59. $\dfrac{a}{1-\frac{s}{770}}=\dfrac{770(a)}{770\left(1-\frac{s}{770}\right)}=\dfrac{770a}{770-s}$

61. $\dfrac{\frac{1}{x}}{\frac{3}{y}} = \dfrac{1}{x} \div \dfrac{3}{y} = \dfrac{1}{x} \cdot \dfrac{y}{3}$

Both a and b are equivalent to the original expression.

63. $\dfrac{1}{1 + (1+x)^{-1}} = \dfrac{1}{1 + \frac{1}{1+x}}$

$= \dfrac{(1+x) \cdot 1}{(1+x)\left(1 + \frac{1}{1+x}\right)}$

$= \dfrac{1+x}{1+x+1}$

$= \dfrac{1+x}{2+x}$

65. $\dfrac{x}{1 - \frac{1}{1+\frac{1}{x}}} = \dfrac{x}{1 - \frac{1}{\frac{x+1}{x}}}$

$= \dfrac{x}{1 - \frac{x}{x+1}}$

$= \dfrac{(x+1)(x)}{(x+1)\left(1 - \frac{x}{x+1}\right)}$

$= \dfrac{x(x+1)}{x+1-x}$

$= \dfrac{x(x+1)}{1}$

$= x(x+1)$

67. $\dfrac{\frac{2}{y^2} - \frac{5}{xy} - \frac{3}{x^2}}{\frac{2}{y^2} + \frac{7}{xy} + \frac{3}{x^2}} = \dfrac{x^2 y^2 \left(\frac{2}{y^2} - \frac{5}{xy} - \frac{3}{x^2}\right)}{x^2 y^2 \left(\frac{2}{y^2} + \frac{7}{xy} + \frac{3}{x^2}\right)}$

$= \dfrac{2x^2 - 5xy - 3y^2}{2x^2 + 7xy + 3y^2}$

$= \dfrac{(2x+y)(x-3y)}{(2x+y)(x+3y)}$

$= \dfrac{x-3y}{x+3y}$

69. $\dfrac{3(a+1)^{-1} + 4a^{-2}}{(a^3 + a^2)^{-1}} = \dfrac{\frac{3}{a+1} + \frac{4}{a^2}}{\frac{1}{a^3 + a^2}}$

$= \dfrac{\frac{3a^2 + 4(a+1)}{a^2(a+1)}}{\frac{1}{a^2(a+1)}}$

$= \dfrac{3a^2 + 4a + 4}{a^2(a+1)} \cdot \dfrac{a^2(a+1)}{1}$

$= 3a^2 + 4a + 4$

71. $f(x) = \dfrac{1}{x}$

  a. $f(a+h) = \dfrac{1}{a+h}$

  b. $f(a) = \dfrac{1}{a}$

  c. $\dfrac{f(a+h) - f(a)}{h} = \dfrac{\frac{1}{a+h} - \frac{1}{a}}{h}$

  d. $\dfrac{\frac{1}{a+h} - \frac{1}{a}}{h} = \dfrac{a(a+h)\left(\frac{1}{a+h} - \frac{1}{a}\right)}{a(a+h) \cdot h}$

      $= \dfrac{a - (a+h)}{ah(a+h)}$

      $= \dfrac{-h}{ah(a+h)}$

      $= \dfrac{-1}{a(a+h)}$

73. $f(x) = \dfrac{3}{x+1}$

  a. $f(a+h) = \dfrac{3}{a+h+1}$

  b. $f(a) = \dfrac{3}{a+1}$

  c. $\dfrac{f(a+h) - f(a)}{h} = \dfrac{\frac{3}{a+h+1} - \frac{3}{a+1}}{h}$

d. $\dfrac{\frac{3}{a+h+1} - \frac{3}{a+1}}{h}$

$= \dfrac{\left(\frac{3}{a+h+1} - \frac{3}{a+1}\right) \cdot (a+h+1)(a+1)}{h \cdot (a+h+1)(a+1)}$

$= \dfrac{3(a+1) - 3(a+h+1)}{h(a+h+1)(a+1)}$

$= \dfrac{3a+3-3a-3h-3}{h(a+h+1)(a+1)}$

$= \dfrac{-3h}{h(a+h+1)(a+1)}$

$= \dfrac{-3}{(a+h+1)(a+1)}$

Section 6.4

Practice Exercises

1. $\dfrac{18a^3 - 12a^2 + 30a}{6a} = \dfrac{18a^3}{6a} - \dfrac{12a^2}{6a} + \dfrac{30a}{6a}$

$\qquad\qquad = 3a^2 - 2a + 5$

2. $\dfrac{5a^3b^4 - 8a^2b^3 + ab^2 - 8b}{ab^2}$

$= \dfrac{5a^3b^4}{ab^2} - \dfrac{8a^2b^3}{ab^2} + \dfrac{ab^2}{ab^2} - \dfrac{8b}{ab^2}$

$= 5a^2b^2 - 8ab + 1 - \dfrac{8}{ab}$

3.
$$
\begin{array}{r}
3x - 2 \\
x+3 \overline{\smash{\big)}\ 3x^2 + 7x - 6} \\
\underline{3x^2 + 9x} \\
-2x - 6 \\
\underline{-2x - 6} \\
0
\end{array}
$$
Answer: $3x - 2$

4.
$$
\begin{array}{r}
3x - 2 \\
2x-1 \overline{\smash{\big)}\ 6x^2 - 7x + 2} \\
\underline{6x^2 - 3x} \\
-4x + 2 \\
\underline{-4x + 2} \\
0
\end{array}
$$
Answer: $3x - 2$

5.
$$
\begin{array}{r}
5x^2 - 6x + 8 \\
x+3 \overline{\smash{\big)}\ 5x^3 + 9x^2 - 10x + 30} \\
\underline{5x^3 + 15x^2} \\
-6x^2 - 10x \\
\underline{-6x^2 - 18x} \\
8x + 30 \\
\underline{8x + 24} \\
6
\end{array}
$$
Answer: $5x^2 - 6x + 8 + \dfrac{6}{x+3}$

6.
$$
\begin{array}{r}
2x^2 + 3x - 2 \\
x^2+0x+1 \overline{\smash{\big)}\ 2x^4 + 3x^3 + 0x^2 - 5x + 2} \\
\underline{2x^4 + 0x^3 + 2x^2} \\
3x^3 - 2x^2 - 5x \\
\underline{3x^3 + 0x^2 + 3x} \\
-2x^2 - 8x + 2 \\
\underline{-2x^2 + 0x - 2} \\
-8x + 4
\end{array}
$$
Answer: $2x^2 + 3x - 2 + \dfrac{-8x+4}{x^2+1}$

7.
$$
\begin{array}{r}
16x^2 + 20x + 25 \\
4x-5 \overline{\smash{\big)}\ 64x^3 + 0x^2 + 0x - 125} \\
\underline{64x^3 - 80x^2} \\
80x^2 + 0x \\
\underline{80x^2 - 100x} \\
100x - 125 \\
\underline{100x - 125} \\
0
\end{array}
$$
Answer: $16x^2 + 20x + 25$

8. Since $x - c = x - 1$, c is 1.
$$
\begin{array}{r|rrrr}
1 & 4 & -3 & 6 & 5 \\
 &   & 4 & 1 & 7 \\
\hline
 & 4 & 1 & 7 & 12
\end{array}
$$
$4x^2 + x + 7 + \dfrac{12}{x-1}$

9. Since $x - c = x + 3 = x - (-3)$, c is -3.

$$
\begin{array}{r|rrrrr}
-3 & 1 & 3 & -5 & 6 & 12 \\
   &   & -3 & 0 & 15 & -63 \\
\hline
   & 1 & 0 & -5 & 21 & -51
\end{array}
$$

$$x^3 - 5x + 21 - \frac{51}{x+3}$$

10. a. $P(x) = x^3 - 5x - 2$

$$P(2) = 2^3 - 5(2) - 2$$
$$= 8 - 10 - 2$$
$$= -4$$

b. Since $x - c = x - 2$, c is 2.

$$
\begin{array}{r|rrrr}
2 & 1 & 0 & -5 & -2 \\
  &   & 2 & 4 & -2 \\
\hline
  & 1 & 2 & -1 & -4
\end{array}
$$

The remainder is -4.

11.

$$
\begin{array}{r|rrrrrr}
3 & 2 & -18 & 0 & 90 & 59 & 0 \\
  &   & 6 & -36 & -108 & -54 & 15 \\
\hline
  & 2 & -12 & -36 & -18 & 5 & 15
\end{array}
$$

$P(3) = 15$

Exercise Set 6.4

1. $\dfrac{4a^2 + 8a}{2a} = \dfrac{4a^2}{2a} + \dfrac{8a}{2a} = 2a + 4$

3. $\dfrac{12a^5 b^2 + 16a^4 b}{4a^4 b} = \dfrac{12a^5 b^2}{4a^4 b} + \dfrac{16a^4 b}{4a^4 b}$
$$= 3ab + 4$$

5. $\dfrac{4x^2 y^2 + 6xy^2 - 4y^2}{2x^2 y}$

$$= \dfrac{4x^2 y^2}{2x^2 y} + \dfrac{6xy^2}{2x^2 y} - \dfrac{4y^2}{2x^2 y}$$

$$= 2y + \dfrac{3y}{x} - \dfrac{2y}{x^2}$$

7.

$$
\begin{array}{r}
x + 1 \\
x+2\overline{\smash{\big)}\,x^2 + 3x + 2} \\
\underline{x^2 + 2x} \\
x + 2 \\
\underline{x + 2} \\
0
\end{array}
$$

$$\frac{x^2 + 3x + 2}{x + 2} = x + 1$$

9.

$$
\begin{array}{r}
2x - 8 \\
x+1\overline{\smash{\big)}\,2x^2 - 6x - 8} \\
\underline{2x^2 + 2x} \\
-8x - 8 \\
\underline{-8x - 8} \\
0
\end{array}
$$

$$\frac{2x^2 - 6x - 8}{x + 1} = 2x - 8$$

11.

$$
\begin{array}{r}
x - \frac{1}{2} \\
2x+4\overline{\smash{\big)}\,2x^2 + 3x - 2} \\
\underline{2x^2 + 4x} \\
-x - 2 \\
\underline{-x - 2} \\
0
\end{array}
$$

$$\frac{2x^2 + 3x - 2}{2x + 4} = x - \frac{1}{2}$$

13.

$$
\begin{array}{r}
2x^2 - \frac{1}{2}x + 5 \\
2x+4\overline{\smash{\big)}\,4x^3 + 7x^2 + 8x + 20} \\
\underline{4x^3 + 8x^2} \\
-x^2 + 8x \\
\underline{-x^2 - 2x} \\
10x + 20 \\
\underline{10x + 20} \\
0
\end{array}
$$

$$\frac{4x^3 + 7x^2 + 8x + 20}{2x + 4} = 2x^2 - \frac{1}{2}x + 5$$

15.

$$
\begin{array}{r}
2x^2 \qquad\quad -6 \\
3x+1\overline{\smash{\big)}\,6x^3 + 2x^2 - 18x - 6} \\
\underline{6x^3 + 2x^2} \\
-18x - 6 \\
\underline{-18x - 6} \\
0
\end{array}
$$

$$\frac{2x^2 + 6x^3 - 18x - 6}{3x + 1} = 2x^2 - 6$$

17.

$$x^2 + 0x - 2 \overline{\smash{\big)}\ 3x^5 + 0x^4 - x^3 + 4x^2 - 12x - 8}$$

$$\begin{array}{r} 3x^3 + 5x + 4 \\ \underline{3x^5 + 0x^4 - 6x^3} \\ 5x^3 + 4x^2 - 12x \\ \underline{5x^3 + 0x^2 - 10x} \\ 4x^2 - 2x - 8 \\ \underline{4x^2 + 0x - 8} \\ -2x \end{array}$$

$$\frac{3x^5 - x^3 + 4x^2 - 12x - 8}{x^2 - 2} = 3x^3 + 5x + 4 - \frac{2x}{x^2 - 2}$$

19.

$$x - 2 \overline{\smash{\big)}\ 2x^4 + \frac{1}{2}x^3 + x^2 + x + 0}$$

$$\begin{array}{r} 2x^3 + \frac{9}{2}x^2 + 10x + 21 \\ \underline{2x^4 - 4x^3} \\ \frac{9}{2}x^3 + x^2 \\ \underline{\frac{9}{2}x^3 - 9x^2} \\ 10x^2 + x \\ \underline{10x^2 - 20x} \\ 21x + 0 \\ \underline{21x - 42} \\ 42 \end{array}$$

$$\frac{2x^4 + \frac{1}{2}x^3 + x^2 + x}{x - 2}$$
$$= 2x^3 + \frac{9}{2}x^2 + 10x + 21 + \frac{42}{x - 2}$$

21. $x - 5 = x - c$ where $c = 5$.

$$\begin{array}{r|rrr} 5 & 1 & 3 & -40 \\ & & 5 & 40 \\ \hline & 1 & 8 & 0 \end{array}$$

$$\frac{x^2 + 3x - 40}{x - 5} = x + 8$$

23. $x + 6 = x - c$ where $c = -6$.

$$\begin{array}{r|rrr} -6 & 1 & 5 & -6 \\ & & -6 & 6 \\ \hline & 1 & -1 & 0 \end{array}$$

$$\frac{x^2 + 5x - 6}{x + 6} = x - 1$$

25. $x - 2 = x - c$ where $c = 2$.

$$\begin{array}{r|rrrr} 2 & 1 & -7 & -13 & 5 \\ & & 2 & -10 & -46 \\ \hline & 1 & -5 & -23 & -41 \end{array}$$

$$\frac{x^3 - 7x^2 - 13x + 5}{x - 2} = x^2 - 5x - 23 - \frac{41}{x - 2}$$

27. $x - 2 = x - c$ where $c = 2$.

$$\begin{array}{r|rrr} 2 & 4 & 0 & -9 \\ & & 8 & 16 \\ \hline & 4 & 8 & 7 \end{array}$$

$$\frac{4x^2 - 9}{x - 2} = 4x + 8 + \frac{7}{x - 2}$$

29. $\dfrac{4x^7y^4 + 8xy^2 + 4xy^3}{4xy^3}$

$$= \frac{4x^7y^4}{4xy^3} + \frac{8xy^2}{4xy^3} + \frac{4xy^3}{4xy^3}$$

$$= x^6y + \frac{2}{y} + 1$$

31.

$$2x - 1 \overline{\smash{\big)}\ 10x^3 - 5x^2 - 12x + 1}$$

$$\begin{array}{r} 5x^2 - 6 \\ \underline{10x^3 - 5x^2} \\ -12x + 1 \\ \underline{-12x + 6} \\ -5 \end{array}$$

$$\frac{10x^3 - 5x^2 - 12x + 1}{2x - 1} = 5x^2 - 6 - \frac{5}{2x - 1}$$

33. $x - 4$ has the form $x - c$, where $c = 4$, so synthetic division can be used.

$2x^3 - 6x^2 - 4 = 2x^3 - 6x^2 + 0x - 4$

$$
\begin{array}{r|rrrr}
4 & 2 & -6 & 0 & -4 \\
  &   & 8 & 8 & 32 \\
\hline
  & 2 & 2 & 8 & 28
\end{array}
$$

$\dfrac{2x^3 - 6x^2 - 4}{x - 4} = 2x^2 + 2x + 8 + \dfrac{28}{x - 4}$

35. $x - 5$ has the form $x - c$, where $c = 5$, so synthetic division can be used.

$$
\begin{array}{r|rrrrr}
5 & 2 & -13 & 16 & -9 & 20 \\
  &   & 10 & -15 & 5 & -20 \\
\hline
  & 2 & -3 & 1 & -4 & 0
\end{array}
$$

$\dfrac{2x^4 - 13x^3 + 16x^2 - 9x + 20}{x - 5}$

$= 2x^3 - 3x^2 + x - 4$

37. $x + 1$ has the form $x - c$, where $c = -1$, so synthetic division can be used.

$7x^2 - 4x + 12 + 3x^3 = 3x^3 + 7x^2 - 4x + 12$

$$
\begin{array}{r|rrrr}
-1 & 3 & 7 & -4 & 12 \\
   &   & -3 & -4 & 8 \\
\hline
   & 3 & 4 & -8 & 20
\end{array}
$$

$\dfrac{7x^2 - 4x + 12 + 3x^3}{x + 1} = 3x^2 + 4x - 8 + \dfrac{20}{x + 1}$

39. $x - \dfrac{1}{3}$ has the form $x - c$, where $c = \dfrac{1}{3}$, so synthetic division can be used.

$$
\begin{array}{r|rrrr}
\frac{1}{3} & 3 & 2 & -4 & 1 \\
            &   & 1 & 1 & -1 \\
\hline
            & 3 & 3 & -3 & 0
\end{array}
$$

$\dfrac{3x^3 + 2x^2 - 4x + 1}{x - \frac{1}{3}} = 3x^2 + 3x - 3$

41. $x - 1$ has the form $x - c$, where $c = 1$, so synthetic division can be used.

$x^3 - 1 = x^3 + 0x^2 + 0x - 1$

$$
\begin{array}{r|rrrr}
1 & 1 & 0 & 0 & -1 \\
  &   & 1 & 1 & 1 \\
\hline
  & 1 & 1 & 1 & 0
\end{array}
$$

$\dfrac{x^3 - 1}{x - 1} = x^2 + x + 1$

43. $\dfrac{25xy^2 + 75xyz + 125x^2yz}{-5x^2y}$

$= \dfrac{25xy^2}{-5x^2y} + \dfrac{75xyz}{-5x^2y} + \dfrac{125x^2yz}{-5x^2y}$

$= -\dfrac{5y}{x} - \dfrac{15z}{x} - 25z$

45. $9x^5 + 6x^4 - 6x^2 - 4x$

$= 9x^5 + 6x^4 + 0x^3 - 6x^2 - 4x + 0$

$$
\require{enclose}
\begin{array}{r}
3x^4 - 2x \\
3x + 2 \enclose{longdiv}{9x^5 + 6x^4 + 0x^3 - 6x^2 - 4x + 0} \\
\underline{9x^5 + 6x^4 } \\
0 + 0x^3 - 6x^2 - 4x \\
\underline{-6x^2 - 4x} \\
0
\end{array}
$$

$(9x^5 + 6x^4 - 6x^2 - 4x) \div (3x + 2) = 3x^4 - 2x$

47.
$$
\begin{array}{r|rrr}
1 & 1 & 3 & -7 & 4 \\
  &   & 1 & 4 & -3 \\
\hline
  & 1 & 4 & -3 & 1
\end{array}
$$
Thus, $P(1) = 1$.

49.
$$
\begin{array}{r|rrrr}
-3 & 3 & -7 & -2 & 5 \\
   &   & -9 & 48 & -138 \\
\hline
   & 3 & -16 & 46 & -133
\end{array}
$$
Thus, $P(-3) = -133$.

51.
$$
\begin{array}{r|rrrrr}
-1 & 4 & 0 & 1 & 0 & -2 \\
   &   & -4 & 4 & -5 & 5 \\
\hline
   & 4 & -4 & 5 & -5 & 3
\end{array}
$$
Thus, $P(-1) = 3$.

53.
$$
\begin{array}{r|rrrrr}
\frac{1}{3} & 2 & 0 & -3 & 0 & -2 \\
            &   & \frac{2}{3} & \frac{2}{9} & -\frac{25}{27} & -\frac{25}{81} \\
\hline
            & 2 & \frac{2}{3} & -\frac{25}{9} & -\frac{25}{27} & -\frac{187}{181}
\end{array}
$$
Thus, $P\left(\dfrac{1}{3}\right) = -\dfrac{187}{81}$.

55.

$$\frac{1}{2} \bigg| \begin{array}{cccccc} 1 & 1 & -1 & 0 & 0 & 3 \\ & \frac{1}{2} & \frac{3}{4} & -\frac{1}{8} & -\frac{1}{16} & -\frac{1}{32} \\ \hline 1 & \frac{3}{2} & -\frac{1}{4} & -\frac{1}{8} & -\frac{1}{16} & \frac{95}{32} \end{array}$$

Thus, $P\left(\dfrac{1}{2}\right) = \dfrac{95}{32}$.

57.
$$7x + 2 = x - 3$$
$$7x - x = -3 - 2$$
$$6x = -5$$
$$x = -\frac{5}{6}$$

The solution is $-\dfrac{5}{6}$.

59.
$$x^2 = 4x - 4$$
$$x^2 - 4x + 4 = 0$$
$$(x - 2)^2 = 0$$
$$x - 2 = 0$$
$$x = 2$$

The solution is 2.

61.
$$\frac{x}{3} - 5 = 13$$
$$3\left(\frac{x}{3} - 5\right) = (13) \cdot 3$$
$$x - 15 = 39$$
$$x = 54$$

The solution is 54.

63. $x^3 - 1 = x^3 - 1^3 = (x-1)(x^2 + x + 1)$

65. $125z^3 + 8 = (5z)^3 + 2^3$
$$= (5z + 2)(25z^2 - 10z + 4)$$

67. $xy + 2x + 3y + 6 = (xy + 2x) + (3y + 6)$
$$= x(y + 2) + 3(y + 2)$$
$$= (y + 2)(x + 3)$$

69. $x^3 - 9x = x(x^2 - 9) = x(x + 3)(x - 3)$

71. $(5x^2 - 3x + 2) \div (x + 2)$ is a candidate for synthetic division since $x + 2$ is in the form $x - c$, where $c = -2$.

73. $(x^7 - 2) \div (x^5 + 1)$ is not a candidate for synthetic division since $x^5 + 1$ does not have the form $x - c$.

75. The degree of the remainder must be less than that of the divisor, or 3 in this case. The choices are a or d.

77.
$$\frac{3x^4 + 6x^2 - 18}{3} = \frac{3x^4}{3} + \frac{6x^2}{3} - \frac{18}{3}$$
$$= x^4 + 2x^2 - 6$$

The length of each piece is $(x^4 + 2x^2 - 6)$ meters.

79.

$$\begin{array}{r} 3x - 7 \\ 5x + 2 \overline{\smash{\big)}\ 15x^2 - 29x - 14} \\ \underline{15x^2 + 6x} \\ -35x - 14 \\ \underline{-35x - 14} \\ 0 \end{array}$$

The width is $(3x - 7)$ inches.

81. $A = bh$ so $h = \dfrac{A}{b} = \dfrac{x^4 - 23x^2 + 9x - 5}{x + 5}$

$$-5 \bigg| \begin{array}{ccccc} 1 & 0 & -23 & 9 & -5 \\ & -5 & 25 & -10 & 5 \\ \hline 1 & -5 & 2 & -1 & 0 \end{array}$$

The height is $(x^3 - 5x^2 + 2x - 1)$ cm.

83.

$$x-1 \overline{\smash{\big)}\, x^4 + \tfrac{2}{3}x^3 + 0x^2 + x + 0}$$

$$x^3 + \tfrac{5}{3}x^2 + \tfrac{5}{3}x + \tfrac{8}{3}$$

$$\underline{x^4 - x^3}$$

$$\tfrac{5}{3}x^3 - 0x^2$$

$$\underline{\tfrac{5}{3}x^3 - \tfrac{5}{3}x^2}$$

$$\tfrac{5}{3}x^2 + x$$

$$\underline{\tfrac{5}{3}x^2 - \tfrac{5}{3}x}$$

$$\tfrac{8}{3}x + 0$$

$$\underline{\tfrac{8}{3}x - \tfrac{8}{3}}$$

$$\tfrac{8}{3}$$

Answer: $x^3 + \dfrac{5}{3}x^2 + \dfrac{5}{3}x + \dfrac{8}{3} + \dfrac{8}{3(x-1)}$

85.

$$2x-1 \overline{\smash{\big)}\, 3x^4 - x^3 + 0x^2 - x + \tfrac{1}{2}}$$

$$\tfrac{3}{2}x^3 + \tfrac{1}{4}x^2 + \tfrac{1}{8}x - \tfrac{7}{16}$$

$$\underline{3x^4 - \tfrac{3}{2}x^3}$$

$$\tfrac{1}{2}x^3 + 0x^2$$

$$\underline{\tfrac{1}{2}x^3 - \tfrac{1}{4}x^2}$$

$$\tfrac{1}{4}x^2 - x$$

$$\underline{\tfrac{1}{4}x^2 - \tfrac{1}{8}x}$$

$$-\tfrac{7}{8}x + \tfrac{1}{2}$$

$$\underline{-\tfrac{7}{8}x + \tfrac{7}{16}}$$

$$\tfrac{1}{16}$$

Answer: $\dfrac{3}{2}x^3 + \dfrac{1}{4}x^2 + \dfrac{1}{8}x - \dfrac{7}{16} + \dfrac{1}{16(2x-1)}$

87.

$$5x+10 \overline{\smash{\big)}\, 5x^4 + 10x^3 - 2x^2 - 4x + 0}$$

$$x^3 - \tfrac{2}{5}x$$

$$\underline{5x^4 + 10x^3}$$

$$-2x^2 - 4x$$

$$\underline{-2x^2 - 4x}$$

$$0$$

Answer: $x^3 - \dfrac{2}{5}x$

89. $\dfrac{f(x)}{g(x)} = \dfrac{25x^2 - 5x + 30}{5x}$

$$= \dfrac{25x^2}{5x} - \dfrac{5x}{5x} + \dfrac{30}{5x}$$

$$= 5x - 1 + \dfrac{6}{x}$$

Setting the denominator equal to 0, we get
$5x = 0$
$x = 0.$

Thus, $x = 0$ is not in the domain of $\dfrac{f(x)}{g(x)}$.

91. $\dfrac{f(x)}{g(x)} = \dfrac{7x^4 - 3x^2 + 2}{x-2}$

$$x-2 \overline{\smash{\big)}\, 7x^4 + 0x^3 - 3x^2 + 0x + 2}$$

$$7x^3 + 14x^2 + 25x + 50$$

$$\underline{7x^4 - 14x^3}$$

$$14x^3 - 3x^2$$

$$\underline{14x^3 - 28x^2}$$

$$25x^2 + 0x$$

$$\underline{25x^2 - 50x}$$

$$50x + 2$$

$$\underline{50x - 100}$$

$$102$$

Therefore, $\dfrac{f(x)}{g(x)} = \dfrac{7x^4 - 3x^2 + 2}{x-2}$

$$= 7x^3 + 14x^2 + 25x + 50 + \dfrac{102}{x-2}$$

Setting the denominator equal to 0, we get
$x - 2 = 0$, or $x = 2$. Thus, $x = 2$ is not in the
domain of $\dfrac{f(x)}{g(x)}$.

93. Answers may vary

95. Answers may vary

97. $\begin{array}{r|rrrr} -3 & 1 & 3 & 4 & 12 \\ & & -3 & 0 & -12 \\ \hline & 1 & 0 & 4 & 0 \end{array}$

Remainder = 0 and

$(x+3)(x^2+4) = x^3 + 3x^2 + 4x + 12$

99. $P(c)$ is equal to the remainder when $P(x)$ is divided by $x - c$. Therefore, $P(c) = 0$.

101. Multiply $(x^2 - x + 10)$ by $(x+3)$ and add the remainder, -2.

$(x^2 - x + 10)(x+3) - 2$

$= (x^3 + 3x^2 - x^2 - 3x + 10x + 30) - 2$

$= x^3 + 2x^2 + 7x + 28$

Section 6.5

Practice Exercises

1. The LCD is 8.

$$\frac{5x}{4} - \frac{3}{2} = \frac{7x}{8}$$

$$8\left(\frac{5x}{4} - \frac{3}{2}\right) = 8\left(\frac{7x}{8}\right)$$

$$8\cdot\frac{5x}{4} - 8\cdot\frac{3}{2} = 8\cdot\frac{7x}{8}$$

$$10x - 12 = 7x$$

$$3x = 12$$

$$x = 4$$

2. The LCD of the denominators x, $5x$, and 5 is $5x$.

$$\frac{6}{x} - \frac{x+9}{5x} = \frac{2}{5}$$

$$5x\left(\frac{6}{x} - \frac{x+9}{5x}\right) = 5x\left(\frac{2}{5}\right)$$

$$5x\cdot\frac{6}{x} - 5x\cdot\frac{x+9}{5x} = 5x\cdot\frac{2}{5}$$

$$30 - (x+9) = 2x$$

$$30 - x - 9 = 2x$$

$$21 = 3x$$

$$7 = x$$

3. The LCD is $x + 3$.

$$\frac{x-5}{x+3} = \frac{2(x-1)}{x+3}$$

$$(x+3)\cdot\frac{x-5}{x+3} = (x+3)\cdot\frac{2(x-1)}{x+3}$$

$$x - 5 = 2(x-1)$$

$$x - 5 = 2x - 2$$

$$-3 = x$$

The number -3 makes the denominator $x + 3$ equal to 0, so it is not a solution. The solution set is { } or $\varnothing$.

4. The LCD is $x(5x - 1)$.

$$\frac{5x}{5x-1} + \frac{1}{x} = \frac{1}{5x-1}$$

$$x(5x-1)\cdot\frac{5x}{5x-1} + x(5x-1)\cdot\frac{1}{x} = x(5x-1)\cdot\frac{1}{5x-1}$$

$$x(5x) + (5x-1) = x$$

$$5x^2 + 5x - 1 - x = 0$$

$$5x^2 + 4x - 1 = 0$$

$$(5x-1)(x+1) = 0$$

$$5x - 1 = 0 \text{ or } x + 1 = 0$$

$$x = \frac{1}{5} \text{ or } \quad x = -1$$

The number $\frac{1}{5}$ makes the denominator $5x - 1$ equal 0, so it is not a solution. The solution is -1.

5. $x^2 - 4 = (x+2)(x-2)$

The LCD is $(x + 2)(x - 2)$.

$$\frac{2}{x-2} - \frac{5+2x}{x^2-4} = \frac{x}{x+2}$$

$$(x+2)(x-2)\cdot\frac{2}{x-2} - (x+2)(x-2)\cdot\frac{5+2x}{(x+2)(x-2)}$$

$$= (x+2)(x-2)\cdot\frac{x}{x+2}$$

$$2(x+2) - (5+2x) = x(x-2)$$

$$2x + 4 - 5 - 2x = x^2 - 2x$$

$$x^2 - 2x + 1 = 0$$

$$(x-1)(x-1) = 0$$

$$x - 1 = 0$$

$$x = 1$$

Since 1 does not make any denominator 0, the solution is 1.

6. $2z^2 - z - 6 = (2z + 3)(z - 2)$

$z^2 - 2z = z(z - 2)$

The LCD is $3z(2z + 3)(z - 2)$.

$$\frac{z}{2z^2 - z - 6} - \frac{1}{3z} = \frac{2}{z^2 - 2z}$$

$$\frac{z}{(2z + 3)(z - 2)} - \frac{1}{3z} = \frac{2}{z(z - 2)}$$

$$3z(2z + 3)(z - 2) \cdot \frac{z}{(2z + 3)(z - 2)} - 3z(2z + 3)(z - 2) \cdot \frac{1}{3z} = 3z(2z + 3)(z - 2) \cdot \frac{2}{z(z - 2)}$$

$$3z(z) - (2z + 3)(z - 2) = 2 \cdot 3(2z + 3)$$

$$3z^2 - (2z^2 - z - 6) = 12z + 18$$

$$3z^2 - 2z^2 + z + 6 = 12z + 18$$

$$z^2 + z + 6 = 12z + 18$$

$$z^2 - 11z - 12 = 0$$

$$(z - 12)(z + 1) = 0$$

$z - 12 = 0$ or $z + 1 = 0$

$z = 12$ or $z = -1$

Neither 12 nor -1 makes any denominator 0, so they are both solutions. The solutions are 12 and -1.

Vocabulary and Readiness Check

1. The LCD of $\dfrac{x}{7}, \dfrac{x}{2},$ and $\dfrac{1}{2}$ is <u>14</u>.

2. The LCD of $\dfrac{9}{x + 1}, \dfrac{5}{(x + 1)^2},$ and $\dfrac{x}{x + 1}$ is <u>$(x + 1)^2$</u>.

3. The LCD of $\dfrac{7}{x - 4}, \dfrac{x}{x^2 - 16} = \dfrac{x}{(x + 4)(x - 4)},$ and $\dfrac{1}{x + 4}$ is <u>$(x + 4)(x - 4)$</u>.

4. The LCD of $3 = \dfrac{3}{1}, \dfrac{1}{x - 5},$ and $\dfrac{2}{x^2 - 5x} = \dfrac{2}{x(x - 5)}$ is <u>$x(x - 5)$</u>.

Exercise Set 6.5

1. $\dfrac{x}{2} - \dfrac{x}{3} = 12$

$$6\left(\frac{x}{2} - \frac{x}{3}\right) = 6(12)$$

$$3x - 2x = 72$$

$$x = 72$$

3. $\dfrac{x}{3} = \dfrac{1}{6} + \dfrac{x}{4}$

$$12\left(\frac{x}{3}\right) = 12\left(\frac{1}{6} + \frac{x}{4}\right)$$

$$4x = 2 + 3x$$

$$x = 2$$

5.
$$\frac{2}{x}+\frac{1}{2}=\frac{5}{x}$$
$$2x\left(\frac{2}{x}+\frac{1}{2}\right)=2x\left(\frac{5}{x}\right)$$
$$4+x=10$$
$$x=6$$

7.
$$\frac{x^2+1}{x}=\frac{5}{x}$$
$$x\left(\frac{x^2+1}{x}\right)=x\left(\frac{5}{x}\right)$$
$$x^2+1=5$$
$$x^2-4=0$$
$$x+2=0 \quad\text{or}\quad x-2=0$$
$$x=-2 \quad\text{or}\quad x=2$$

9.
$$\frac{x+5}{x+3}=\frac{2}{x+3}$$
$$(x+3)\cdot\frac{x+5}{x+3}=(x+3)\cdot\frac{2}{x+3}$$
$$x+5=2$$
$$x=-3$$

which we disregard as extraneous. No solution, or $\varnothing$.

11.
$$\frac{5}{x-2}-\frac{2}{x+4}=-\frac{4}{x^2+2x-8}$$
$$\frac{5}{x-2}-\frac{2}{x+4}=-\frac{4}{(x+4)(x-2)}$$
$$(x-4)(x+2)\left(\frac{5}{x-2}-\frac{2}{x+4}\right)=(x-4)(x+2)\left(-\frac{4}{(x+4)(x-2)}\right)$$
$$5(x+4)-2(x-2)=-4$$
$$5x+20-2x+4=-4$$
$$3x+24=-4$$
$$3x=-28$$
$$x=-\frac{28}{3}$$

13.
$$\frac{1}{x-1}=\frac{2}{x+1}$$
$$(x+1)(x-1)\cdot\frac{1}{x-1}=(x+1)(x-1)\cdot\frac{2}{x+1}$$
$$1(x+1)=2(x-1)$$
$$x+1=2x-2$$
$$-x=-3$$
$$x=3$$

15.
$$\frac{x^2-23}{2x^2-5x-3}+\frac{2}{x-3}=\frac{-1}{2x+1}$$

$$\frac{x^2-23}{(2x+1)(x-3)}+\frac{2}{x-3}=\frac{-1}{2x+1}$$

$$(2x+1)(x-3)\left(\frac{x^2-23}{(2x+1)(x-3)}+\frac{2}{x-3}\right)=(2x+1)(x-3)\left(\frac{-1}{2x+1}\right)$$

$$(x^2-23)+2(2x+1)=-1(x-3)$$

$$x^2-23+4x+2=-x+3$$

$$x^2+5x-24=0$$

$$(x+8)(x-3)=0$$

$x+8=0$ or $x-3=0$

$\quad x=-8$ or $\quad x=3$

We discard 3 as extraneous.

$x=-8$

17.
$$\frac{1}{x-4}-\frac{3x}{x^2-16}=\frac{2}{x+4}$$

$$\frac{1}{x-4}-\frac{3x}{(x+4)(x-4)}=\frac{2}{x+4}$$

$$(x+4)(x-4)\left[\frac{1}{x-4}-\frac{3x}{(x+4)(x-4)}\right]=(x+4)(x-4)\left(\frac{2}{x+4}\right)$$

$$1(x+4)-3x=2(x-4)$$

$$x+4-3x=2x-8$$

$$-2x+4=2x-8$$

$$-4x=-12$$

$$x=3$$

19.
$$\frac{1}{x-4}=\frac{8}{x^2-16}$$

$$\frac{1}{x-4}=\frac{8}{(x+4)(x-4)}$$

$$(x+4)(x-4)\left(\frac{1}{x-4}\right)=(x+4)(x-4)\left(\frac{8}{(x+4)(x-4)}\right)$$

$$1(x+4)=8$$

$$x+4=8$$

$$x=-4$$

which we discard as extraneous. No solution, or $\varnothing$.

21.
$$\frac{1}{x-2}-\frac{2}{x^2-2x}=1$$
$$\frac{1}{x-2}-\frac{2}{x(x-2)}=1$$
$$x(x-2)\left[\frac{1}{x-2}-\frac{2}{x(x-2)}\right]=x(x-2)\cdot 1$$
$$x-2=x(x-2)$$
$$x-2=x^2-2x$$
$$0=x^2-3x+2$$
$$0=(x-2)(x-1)$$
$$x-2=0 \ \text{ or } \ x-1=1$$
$$x=2 \ \text{ or } \quad x=1$$
We discard 2 as extraneous.
$$x=1$$

23.
$$\frac{5}{x}=\frac{20}{12}$$
$$12x\left(\frac{5}{x}\right)=12x\left(\frac{20}{12}\right)$$
$$60=20x$$
$$3=x$$

25.
$$1-\frac{4}{a}=5$$
$$a\left(1-\frac{4}{a}\right)=a(5)$$
$$a-4=5a$$
$$-4=4a$$
$$-1=a$$

27.
$$\frac{x^2+5}{x}-1=\frac{5(x+1)}{x}$$
$$x\left(\frac{x^2+5}{x}-1\right)=x\left[\frac{5(x+1)}{x}\right]$$
$$x^2+5-x=5x+5$$
$$x^2-6x=0$$
$$x(x-6)=0$$
$$x=0 \ \text{ or } \ x-6=0$$
$$x=6$$
We discard 0 as extraneous.
$$x=6$$

29.
$$\frac{1}{2x}-\frac{1}{x+1}=\frac{1}{3x^2+3x}$$
$$\frac{1}{2x}-\frac{1}{x+1}=\frac{1}{3x(x+1)}$$
$$6x(x+1)\left(\frac{1}{2x}-\frac{1}{x+1}\right)=6x(x+1)\left(\frac{1}{3x(x+1)}\right)$$
$$3(x+1)-6x=2$$
$$3x+3-6x=2$$
$$-3x+3=2$$
$$-3x=-1$$
$$x=\frac{1}{3}$$

31.
$$\frac{1}{x}-\frac{x}{25}=0$$
$$25x\left(\frac{1}{x}-\frac{x}{25}\right)=25x(0)$$
$$25-x^2=0$$
$$-(x^2-25)=0$$
$$-(x+5)(x-5)=0$$
$$x+5=0 \quad \text{ or } \ x-5=0$$
$$x=-5 \ \text{ or } \quad x=5$$

33.
$$5-\frac{2}{2y-5}=\frac{3}{2y-5}$$
$$(2y-5)\left(5-\frac{2}{2y-5}\right)=(2y-5)\cdot\frac{3}{2y-5}$$
$$5(2y-5)-2=3$$
$$10y-25-2=3$$
$$10y-27=3$$
$$10y=30$$
$$y=3$$

35.
$$\frac{x-1}{x+2}=\frac{2}{3}$$
$$3(x+2)\left(\frac{x-1}{x+2}\right)=3(x+2)\left(\frac{2}{3}\right)$$
$$3(x-1)=2(x+2)$$
$$3x-3=2x+4$$
$$x=7$$

37.

$$\frac{x+3}{x+2} = \frac{1}{x+2}$$

$$(x+2)\cdot\frac{x+3}{x+2} = (x+2)\cdot\frac{1}{x+2}$$

$$x+3 = 1$$

$$x = -2$$

which we discard as extraneous. No solution, or $\varnothing$.

39.

$$\frac{1}{a-3}+\frac{2}{a+3} = \frac{1}{a^2-9}$$

$$\frac{1}{a-3}+\frac{2}{a+3} = \frac{1}{(a+3)(a-3)}$$

$$(a+3)(a-3)\left(\frac{1}{a-3}+\frac{2}{a+3}\right) = (a+3)(a-3)\cdot\frac{1}{(a+3)(a-3)}$$

$$1(a+3)+2(a-3) = 1$$

$$a+3+2a-6 = 1$$

$$3a-3 = 1$$

$$3a = 4$$

$$a = \frac{4}{3}$$

41.

$$\frac{64}{x^2-16}+1 = \frac{2x}{x-4}$$

$$\frac{64}{(x+4)(x-4)}+1 = \frac{2x}{x-4}$$

$$(x+4)(x-4)\left[\frac{64}{(x+4)(x-4)}+1\right] = (x+4)(x-4)\cdot\frac{2x}{x-4}$$

$$64+1(x+4)(x-4) = 2x(x+4)$$

$$64+(x^2-16) = 2x^2+8x$$

$$x^2+48 = 2x^2+8x$$

$$0 = x^2+8x-48$$

$$0 = (x+12)(x-4)$$

$$x+12 = 0 \quad \text{or } x-4 = 0$$

$$x = -12 \text{ or } \quad x = 4$$

We discard 4 as extraneous.

$$x = -12$$

43.

$$\frac{-15}{4y+1}+4=y$$

$$(4y+1)\left(\frac{-15}{4y+1}+4\right)=(4y+1)y$$

$$-15+4(4y+1)=4y^2+y$$

$$-15+16y+4=4y^2+y$$

$$-11+16y=4y^2+y$$

$$0=4y^2-15y+11$$

$$0=(4y-11)(y-1)$$

$$4y-11=0 \quad \text{or} \quad y-1=0$$

$$4y=11 \quad \text{or} \quad y=1$$

$$y=\frac{11}{4}$$

45.

$$\frac{28}{x^2-9}+\frac{2x}{x-3}+\frac{6}{x+3}=0$$

$$\frac{28}{(x+3)(x-3)}+\frac{2x}{x-3}+\frac{6}{x+3}=0$$

$$(x+3)(x-3)\left[\frac{28}{(x+3)(x-3)}+\frac{2x}{x-3}+\frac{6}{x+3}\right]=(x+3)(x-3)\cdot 0$$

$$28+2x(x+3)+6(x-3)=0$$

$$28+2x^2+6x+6x-18=0$$

$$2x^2+12x+10=0$$

$$2(x^2+6x+5)=0$$

$$2(x+5)(x+1)=0$$

$$x+5=0 \quad \text{or} \quad x+1=0$$

$$x=-5 \quad \text{or} \quad x=-1$$

47.

$$\frac{x+2}{x^2+7x+10}=\frac{1}{3x+6}-\frac{1}{x+5}$$

$$\frac{x+2}{(x+5)(x+2)}=\frac{1}{3(x+2)}-\frac{1}{x+5}$$

$$3(x+5)(x+2)\cdot\frac{x+2}{(x+5)(x+2)}=3(x+5)(x+2)\left[\frac{1}{3(x+2)}-\frac{1}{x+5}\right]$$

$$3(x+2)=1(x+5)-1\cdot 3(x+2)$$

$$3x+6=x+5-3x-6$$

$$3x+6=-2x-1$$

$$5x=-7$$

$$x=-\frac{7}{5}$$

49. Let x = the number.

$$3x+4=19$$

$$3x=15$$

$$x=5$$

The number is 5.

51. Let $w = $ width. Then $w + 5 = $ length.
$$2l + 2w = 50$$
$$2(w+5) + 2w = 50$$
$$2w + 10 + 2w = 50$$
$$4w + 10 = 50$$
$$4w = 40$$
$$w = 10;$$
$$w + 5 = 10 + 5 = 15$$
The length is 15 inches and the width is 10 inches.

53. 36% (reading from the graph)

55. The shortest bar is for the category 12-19 years old.

57. 14% of 284,000
$0.14(284,000) = 39,760$
We would expect approximately 40,000 students to eat breakfast regularly.

59. Answers may vary

61. $f(x) = 20 + \dfrac{4000}{x}$
$$25 = 20 + \dfrac{4000}{x}$$
$$x \cdot 5 = x \cdot \dfrac{4000}{x}$$
$$5 = \dfrac{4000}{x}$$
$$5x = 4000$$
$$x = 800$$
800 pencil sharpeners

63. $x^{-2} - 5x^{-1} - 36 = 0$
$$\dfrac{1}{x^2} - \dfrac{5}{x} - 36 = 0$$
$$x^2\left(\dfrac{1}{x^2} - \dfrac{5}{x} - 36\right) = x^2 \cdot 0$$
$$1 - 5x - 36x^2 = 0$$
$$36x^2 + 5x - 1 = 0$$
$$(9x - 1)(4x + 1) = 0$$
$$9x - 1 = 0 \text{ or } 4x + 1 = 0$$
$$9x = 1 \text{ or } \qquad 4x = -1$$
$$x = \dfrac{1}{9} \text{ or } \qquad x = -\dfrac{1}{4}$$

65. $6p^{-2} - 5p^{-1} + 1 = 0$

$$\frac{6}{p^2} - \frac{5}{p} + 1 = 0$$

$$p^2\left(\frac{6}{p^2} - \frac{5}{p} + 1\right) = p^2 \cdot 0$$

$$6 - 5p + p^2 = 0$$

$$p^2 - 5p + 6 = 0$$

$$(p-2)(p-3) = 0$$

$$p - 2 = 0 \text{ or } p - 3 = 0$$

$$p = 2 \text{ or } \qquad p = 3$$

67.

$$\frac{-8.5}{x+1.9} = \frac{5.7}{x-3.6}$$

$$(x+1.9)(x-3.6) \cdot \frac{-8.5}{x+1.9} = (x+1.9)(x-3.6) \cdot \frac{5.7}{x-3.6}$$

$$-8.5(x-3.6) = 5.7(x+1.9)$$

$$-8.5x + 30.6 = 5.7x + 10.83$$

$$-14.2x = -19.77$$

$$x \approx 1.39$$

69.

$$\frac{12.2}{x} + 17.3 = \frac{9.6}{x} - 14.7$$

$$x\left(\frac{12.2}{x} + 17.3\right) = x\left(\frac{9.6}{x} - 14.7\right)$$

$$12.2 + 17.3x = 9.6 - 14.7x$$

$$32x = -2.6$$

$$x \approx -0.08$$

71. $(4-x)^2 - 5(4-x) + 6 = 0$

Let $u = 4 - x$. Then $u^2 = (4-x)^2$ and

$$u^2 - 5u + 6 = 0$$

$$(u-3)(u-2) = 0$$

$$u = 3 \text{ or } \qquad u = 2$$

$$4 - x = 3 \text{ or } 4 - x = 2$$

$$-x = -1 \text{ or } -x = -2$$

$$x = 1 \text{ or } \qquad x = 2$$

73. $\left(\dfrac{5}{2+x}\right)^2 + \left(\dfrac{5}{2+x}\right) - 20 = 0$

Let $u = \dfrac{5}{2+x}$. Then $u^2 = \left(\dfrac{5}{2+x}\right)^2$ and

$u^2 + u - 20 = 0$
$(u+5)(u-4) = 0$

$u = -5$ or $u = 4$

$\dfrac{5}{2+x} = -5$ or $\dfrac{5}{2+x} = 4$

$5 = -5(2+x)$ or $5 = 4(2+x)$
$5 = -10 - 5x$ or $5 = 8 + 4x$
$5x = -15$ or $-3 = 4x$
$x = -3$ or $-\dfrac{3}{4} = x$

75.

77.

The Bigger Picture

1. $|-7x + 1| < 15$
$-15 < -7x + 1 < 15$
$-16 < -7x < 14$
$\dfrac{16}{7} > x > -2$

The solution set is $\left(-2, \dfrac{16}{7}\right)$.

2. $|-7x + 1| = 15$
$-7x + 1 = 15$ or $-7x + 1 = -15$
$-7x = 14$ $-7x = -16$
$x = -2$ $x = \dfrac{16}{7}$

The solution set is $\left\{-2, \dfrac{16}{7}\right\}$.

3. $x^2 - 121 = 0$

$(x-11)(x+11) = 0$

$x - 11 = 0 \quad$ or $\quad x + 11 = 0$

$\qquad x = 11 \quad$ or $\qquad x = -11$

The solution set is $\{11, -11\}$.

4. $x^2 + x - 2 = (x+2)(x-1)$

The LCD is $(x+2)(x-1)$.

$$\frac{8}{x+2} - \frac{3}{x-1} = \frac{x+6}{x^2+x-2}$$

$$(x+2)(x-1) \cdot \frac{8}{x+2} - (x+2)(x-1) \cdot \frac{3}{x-1} = (x+2)(x-1) \cdot \frac{x+6}{(x+2)(x-1)}$$

$$8(x-1) - 3(x+2) = x+6$$

$$8x - 8 - 3x - 6 = x+6$$

$$5x - 14 = x+6$$

$$4x - 14 = 6$$

$$4x = 20$$

$$x = 5$$

The solution set is $\{5\}$.

5. $9x + 6 = 4x - 2$

$\quad 9x = 4x - 8$

$\quad 5x = -8$

$\quad x = -\dfrac{8}{5}$

The solution set is $\left\{-\dfrac{8}{5}\right\}$.

6. $3x \le 6 \quad$ or $\quad -x \ge 5$

$\quad x \le 2 \quad$ or $\quad x \le -5$

$(-\infty, 2] \cup (-\infty, -5] = (-\infty, 2]$

The solution set is $(-\infty, 2]$.

7. $3x \le 6 \quad$ and $\quad -x \ge 5$

$\quad x \le 2 \quad$ and $\quad x \le -5$

$(-\infty, 2] \cap (-\infty, -5] = (-\infty, -5]$

The solution set is $(-\infty, -5]$.

8. $-9 \le -3x + 21 < 0$

$\quad -30 \le -3x < -21$

$\quad 10 \ge x > 7$

The solution set is $(7, 10]$.

9. $\left|\dfrac{2x-1}{5}\right| > 7$

$\dfrac{2x-1}{5} > 7$ or $\dfrac{2x-1}{5} < -7$

$2x-1 > 35$ or $2x-1 < -35$

$2x > 36$ or $2x < -34$

$x > 18$ or $x < -17$

$(18, \infty) \cup (-\infty, -17)$

The solution set is $(-\infty, -17) \cup (18, \infty)$.

10. $\quad 15x^3 - 16x^2 = 7x$

$15x^3 - 16x^2 - 7x = 0$

$x(15x^2 - 16x - 7) = 0$

$x(3x+1)(5x-7) = 0$

$x = 0$ or $3x+1 = 0$ or $5x - 7 = 0$

$x = 0$ or $3x = -1$ or $5x = 7$

$x = 0$ or $x = -\dfrac{1}{3}$ or $x = \dfrac{7}{5}$

The solution set is $\left\{0, -\dfrac{1}{3}, \dfrac{7}{5}\right\}$.

Integrated Review

1. $\dfrac{x}{2} = \dfrac{1}{8} + \dfrac{x}{4}$

The LCD is 8.

$8 \cdot \dfrac{x}{2} = 8 \cdot \dfrac{1}{8} + 8 \cdot \dfrac{x}{4}$

$4x = 1 + 2x$

$2x = 1$

$x = \dfrac{1}{2}$

The solution set is $\left\{\dfrac{1}{2}\right\}$.

2. $\dfrac{x}{4} = \dfrac{3}{2} + \dfrac{x}{10}$

The LCD is 20.

$20 \cdot \dfrac{x}{4} = 20 \cdot \dfrac{3}{2} + 20 \cdot \dfrac{x}{10}$

$5x = 30 + 2x$

$3x = 30$

$x = 10$

The solution set is $\{10\}$.

3. $\dfrac{1}{8} + \dfrac{x}{4} = \dfrac{1}{8} + \dfrac{x}{4} \cdot \dfrac{2}{2} = \dfrac{1}{8} + \dfrac{2x}{8} = \dfrac{1+2x}{8}$

4. $\dfrac{3}{2} + \dfrac{x}{10} = \dfrac{5}{5} \cdot \dfrac{3}{2} + \dfrac{x}{10} = \dfrac{15}{10} + \dfrac{x}{10} = \dfrac{15+x}{10}$

5. $\dfrac{4}{x+2} - \dfrac{2}{x-1} = \dfrac{4}{x+2} \cdot \dfrac{x-1}{x-1} - \dfrac{2}{x-1} \cdot \dfrac{x+2}{x+2}$

$= \dfrac{4(x-1)}{(x+2)(x-1)} - \dfrac{2(x+2)}{(x+2)(x+1)}$

$= \dfrac{4x-4-2x-4}{(x+2)(x-1)}$

$= \dfrac{2x-8}{(x+2)(x-1)}$

$= \dfrac{2(x-4)}{(x+2)(x-1)}$

6. $\dfrac{5}{x-2} - \dfrac{10}{x+4} = \dfrac{5}{x-2} \cdot \dfrac{x+4}{x+4} - \dfrac{10}{x+4} \cdot \dfrac{x-2}{x-2}$

$= \dfrac{5(x+4)}{(x-2)(x+4)} - \dfrac{10(x-2)}{(x-2)(x+4)}$

$= \dfrac{5x+20-10x+20}{(x-2)(x+4)}$

$= \dfrac{-5x+40}{(x-2)(x+4)}$

$= \dfrac{-5(x-8)}{(x-2)(x+4)}$ or $-\dfrac{5(x-8)}{(x-2)(x+4)}$

7. $\dfrac{4}{x+2} = \dfrac{2}{x-1}$

The LCD is $(x + 2)(x - 1)$.

$(x+2)(x-1) \cdot \dfrac{4}{x+2} = (x+2)(x-1) \cdot \dfrac{2}{x-1}$

$4(x-1) = 2(x+2)$

$4x - 4 = 2x + 4$

$4x = 2x + 8$

$2x = 8$

$x = 4$

The solution set is $\{4\}$.

8. $\dfrac{5}{x-2} = \dfrac{10}{x+4}$

The LCD is $(x - 2)(x + 4)$.

$(x-2)(x+4) \cdot \dfrac{5}{x-2} = (x-2)(x+4) \cdot \dfrac{10}{x+4}$

$5(x+4) = 10(x-2)$

$5x + 20 = 10x - 20$

$5x = 10x - 40$

$-5x = -40$

$x = 8$

The solution set is $\{8\}$.

9. $x^2 - 4 = (x+2)(x-2)$

The LCD is $(x+2)(x-2)$.

$$\frac{2}{x^2-4} = \frac{1}{x+2} - \frac{3}{x-2}$$

$$(x+2)(x-2)\cdot\frac{2}{x^2-4} = (x+2)(x-2)\cdot\frac{1}{x+2} - (x+2)(x-2)\cdot\frac{3}{x-2}$$

$$2 = (x-2) - 3(x+2)$$
$$2 = x - 2 - 3x - 6$$
$$2 = -2x - 8$$
$$2x = -10$$
$$x = -5$$

The solution set is $\{-5\}$.

10. $x^2 - 25 = (x+5)(x-5)$

The LCD is $(x+5)(x-5)$.

$$\frac{3}{x^2-25} = \frac{1}{x+5} + \frac{2}{x-5}$$

$$(x+5)(x-5)\cdot\frac{3}{(x+5)(x-5)} = (x+5)(x-5)\cdot\frac{1}{x+5} + (x+5)(x-5)\cdot\frac{2}{x-5}$$

$$3 = (x-5) + 2(x+5)$$
$$3 = x - 5 + 2x + 10$$
$$3 = 3x + 5$$
$$-2 = 3x$$
$$-\frac{2}{3} = x$$

The solution set is $\left\{-\frac{2}{3}\right\}$.

11.
$$\frac{5}{x^2-3x} + \frac{4}{2x-6} = \frac{5}{x(x-3)} + \frac{4}{2(x-3)}$$
$$= \frac{5}{x(x-3)}\cdot\frac{2}{2} + \frac{4}{2(x-3)}\cdot\frac{x}{x}$$
$$= \frac{10}{2x(x-3)} + \frac{4x}{2x(x-3)}$$
$$= \frac{4x+10}{2x(x-3)}$$
$$= \frac{2(2x+5)}{2x(x-3)}$$
$$= \frac{2x+5}{x(x-3)}$$

12.
$$\frac{5}{x^2-3x} \div \frac{4}{2x-6} = \frac{5}{x^2-3x}\cdot\frac{2x-6}{4}$$
$$= \frac{5}{x(x-3)}\cdot\frac{2(x-3)}{4}$$
$$= \frac{5}{2x}$$

13. $x^2 - 1 = (x-1)(x+1)$

The LCD is $(x-1)(x+1)$.

$$\frac{x-1}{x+1} + \frac{x+7}{x-1} = \frac{4}{x^2-1}$$

$$(x-1)(x+1) \cdot \frac{x-1}{x+1} + (x-1)(x+1) \cdot \frac{x+7}{x-1} = (x-1)(x+1) \cdot \frac{4}{(x-1)(x+1)}$$

$$(x-1)(x-1) + (x+1)(x+7) = 4$$

$$x^2 - 2x + 1 + x^2 + 8x + 7 = 4$$

$$2x^2 + 6x + 8 = 4$$

$$2x^2 + 6x + 4 = 0$$

$$2(x^2 + 3x + 2) = 0$$

$$2(x+1)(x+2) = 0$$

$$x + 1 = 0 \quad \text{or} \quad x + 2 = 0$$
$$x = -1 \quad \text{or} \quad x = -2$$

The number -1 makes the denominator $x + 1$ equal to 0, so it is not a solution. The solution set is $\{-2\}$.

14. $\left(1 - \frac{y}{x}\right) \div \left(1 - \frac{x}{y}\right) = \left(\frac{x}{x} - \frac{y}{x}\right) \div \left(\frac{y}{y} - \frac{x}{y}\right)$

$$= \left(\frac{x-y}{x}\right) \div \left(\frac{y-x}{y}\right)$$

$$= \frac{x-y}{x} \cdot \frac{y}{y-x}$$

$$= \frac{x-y}{x} \cdot \frac{y}{-(x-y)}$$

$$= -\frac{y}{x}$$

15. $\dfrac{a^2-9}{a-6} \cdot \dfrac{a^2-5a-6}{a^2-a-6} = \dfrac{(a+3)(a-3)}{a-6} \cdot \dfrac{(a-6)(a+1)}{(a-3)(a+2)}$

$$= \frac{(a+3)(a+1)}{a+2}$$

16. $\dfrac{2}{a-6} + \dfrac{3a}{a^2-5a-6} - \dfrac{a}{5a+5} = \dfrac{2}{a-6} + \dfrac{3a}{(a-6)(a+1)} - \dfrac{a}{5(a+1)}$

$$= \frac{2}{a-6} \cdot \frac{5(a+1)}{5(a+1)} + \frac{3a}{(a-6)(a+1)} \cdot \frac{5}{5} - \frac{a}{5(a+1)} \cdot \frac{a-6}{a-6}$$

$$= \frac{10a+10}{5(a+1)(a-6)} + \frac{15a}{5(a+1)(a-6)} - \frac{a^2-6a}{5(a+1)(a-6)}$$

$$= \frac{10a+10+15a-a^2+6a}{5(a+1)(a-6)}$$

$$= \frac{-a^2+31a+10}{5(a+1)(a-6)}$$

17. $\dfrac{2x+3}{3x-2} = \dfrac{4x+1}{6x+1}$

The LCD is $(3x-2)(6x+1)$.

$$(3x-2)(6x+1)\cdot\dfrac{2x+3}{3x-2} = (3x-2)(6x+1)\cdot\dfrac{4x+1}{6x+1}$$

$$(6x+1)(2x+3) = (3x-2)(4x+1)$$

$$12x^2+18x+2x+3 = 12x^2+3x-8x-2$$

$$12x^2+20x+3 = 12x^2-5x-2$$

$$20x+3 = -5x-2$$

$$25x+3 = -2$$

$$25x = -5$$

$$x = -\dfrac{5}{25}$$

$$x = -\dfrac{1}{5}$$

The solution set is $\left\{-\dfrac{1}{5}\right\}$.

18. The LCD is $2x(4x+1)$.

$$\dfrac{5x-3}{2x} = \dfrac{10x+3}{4x+1}$$

$$2x(4x+1)\cdot\dfrac{5x-3}{2x} = 2x(4x+1)\cdot\dfrac{10x+3}{4x+1}$$

$$(4x+1)(5x-3) = 2x(10x+3)$$

$$20x^2-12x+5x-3 = 20x^2+6x$$

$$20x^2-7x-3 = 20x^2+6x$$

$$-7x-3 = 6x$$

$$-3 = 13x$$

$$-\dfrac{3}{13} = x$$

The solution set is $\left\{-\dfrac{3}{13}\right\}$.

19. $\dfrac{a}{9a^2-1} + \dfrac{2}{6a-2} = \dfrac{a}{(3a-1)(3a+1)} + \dfrac{2}{2(3a-1)}$

$$= \dfrac{a}{(3a-1)(3a+1)}\cdot\dfrac{2}{2} + \dfrac{2}{2(3a-1)}\cdot\dfrac{(3a+1)}{(3a+1)}$$

$$= \dfrac{2a}{2(3a-1)(3a+1)} + \dfrac{6a+2}{2(3a-1)(3a+1)}$$

$$= \dfrac{8a+2}{2(3a-1)(3a+1)}$$

$$= \dfrac{2(4a+1)}{2(3a-1)(3a+1)}$$

$$= \dfrac{4a+1}{(3a-1)(3a+1)}$$

20.
$$\frac{3}{4a-8}-\frac{a+2}{a^2-2a}=\frac{3}{4(a-2)}-\frac{a+2}{a(a-2)}$$
$$=\frac{3}{4(a-2)}\cdot\frac{a}{a}-\frac{a+2}{a(a-2)}\cdot\frac{4}{4}$$
$$=\frac{3a}{4a(a-2)}-\frac{4(a+2)}{4a(a-2)}$$
$$=\frac{3a}{4a(a-2)}-\frac{4a+8}{4a(a-2)}$$
$$=\frac{3a-4a-8}{4a(a-2)}$$
$$=\frac{-a-8}{4a(a-2)}$$
$$=-\frac{a+8}{4a(a-2)}$$

21. The LCD is x^2.
$$-\frac{3}{x^2}-\frac{1}{x}+2=0$$
$$x^2\cdot-\frac{3}{x^2}-x^2\cdot\frac{1}{x}+x^2\cdot2=0$$
$$-3-x+2x^2=0$$
$$2x^2-x-3=0$$
$$(2x-3)(x+1)=0$$
$$2x-3=0 \quad\text{or}\quad x+1=0$$
$$2x=3 \quad\text{or}\quad x=-1$$
$$x=\frac{3}{2} \quad\text{or}\quad x=-1$$

The solution set is $\left\{-1,\dfrac{3}{2}\right\}$.

22.
$$\frac{x}{2x+6}+\frac{5}{x^2-9}$$
$$=\frac{x}{2(x+3)}+\frac{5}{(x-3)(x+3)}$$
$$=\frac{x}{2(x+3)}\cdot\frac{x-3}{x-3}+\frac{5}{(x-3)(x+3)}\cdot\frac{2}{2}$$
$$=\frac{x(x-3)}{2(x+3)(x-3)}+\frac{10}{2(x+3)(x-3)}$$
$$=\frac{x^2-3x}{2(x+3)(x-3)}+\frac{10}{2(x+3)(x-3)}$$
$$=\frac{x^2-3x+10}{2(x+3)(x-3)}$$

23. $\dfrac{x-8}{x^2-x-2} + \dfrac{2}{x-2} = \dfrac{x-8}{(x-2)(x+1)} + \dfrac{2}{x-2}$

$\qquad = \dfrac{x-8}{(x-2)(x+1)} + \dfrac{2}{x-2} \cdot \dfrac{x+1}{x+1}$

$\qquad = \dfrac{x-8}{(x-2)(x+1)} + \dfrac{2x+2}{(x-2)(x+1)}$

$\qquad = \dfrac{x-8+2x+2}{(x-2)(x+1)}$

$\qquad = \dfrac{3x-6}{(x-2)(x+1)}$

$\qquad = \dfrac{3(x-2)}{(x-2)(x+1)}$

$\qquad = \dfrac{3}{x+1}$

24. $x^2 - x - 2 = (x-2)(x+1)$

The LCD is $(x-2)(x+1)$.

$$\dfrac{x-8}{x^2-x-2} + \dfrac{2}{x-2} = \dfrac{3}{x+1}$$

$$(x-2)(x+1) \cdot \dfrac{x-8}{(x-2)(x+1)} + (x-2)(x+1) \cdot \dfrac{2}{x-2} = (x-2)(x+1) \cdot \dfrac{3}{x+1}$$

$$(x-8) + 2(x+1) = 3(x-2)$$

$$x - 8 + 2x + 2 = 3x - 6$$

$$3x - 6 = 3x - 6$$

$$-6 = -6 \quad \text{True}$$

The solution set is
$\{x | x \text{ is a real number and } x \neq 2, x \neq -1\}$.

25. The LCD is a.

$$\dfrac{3}{a} - 5 = \dfrac{7}{a} - 1$$

$$a \cdot \dfrac{3}{a} - a \cdot 5 = a \cdot \dfrac{7}{a} - a \cdot 1$$

$$3 - 5a = 7 - a$$

$$3 = 7 + 4a$$

$$-4 = 4a$$

$$-1 = a$$

The solution set is $\{-1\}$.

26. $\dfrac{7}{3z-9} + \dfrac{5}{z} = \dfrac{7}{3(z-3)} + \dfrac{5}{z}$

$\qquad = \dfrac{7}{3(z-3)} \cdot \dfrac{z}{z} + \dfrac{5}{z} \cdot \dfrac{3(z-3)}{3(z-3)}$

$\qquad = \dfrac{7z}{3z(z-3)} + \dfrac{15(z-3)}{3z(z-3)}$

$\qquad = \dfrac{7z+15z-45}{3z(z-3)}$

$\qquad = \dfrac{22z-45}{3z(z-3)}$

27. a. $\dfrac{x}{5} - \dfrac{x}{4} + \dfrac{1}{10}$ is an expression.

b. The first step to simplify this expression is to write each rational expression term so that the denominator is the LCD, 20.

c. $\dfrac{x}{5} - \dfrac{x}{4} + \dfrac{1}{10} = \dfrac{x}{5} \cdot \dfrac{4}{4} - \dfrac{x}{4} \cdot \dfrac{5}{5} + \dfrac{1}{10} \cdot \dfrac{2}{2}$

$\qquad = \dfrac{4x}{20} - \dfrac{5x}{20} + \dfrac{2}{20}$

$\qquad = \dfrac{4x-5x+2}{20}$

$\qquad = \dfrac{-x+2}{20}$

28. a. $\dfrac{x}{5} - \dfrac{x}{4} = \dfrac{1}{10}$ is an equation.

b. The first step to solve this equation is to clear the equation of fractions by multiplying each term by the LCD, 20.

c. $\dfrac{x}{5} - \dfrac{x}{4} = \dfrac{1}{10}$

$20 \cdot \dfrac{x}{5} - 20 \cdot \dfrac{x}{4} = 20 \cdot \dfrac{1}{10}$

$4x - 5x = 2$

$-x = 2$

$x = -2$

The solution set is $\{-2\}$.

29. $\dfrac{\triangle + \square}{\triangle} = \dfrac{\triangle}{\triangle} + \dfrac{\square}{\triangle} = 1 + \dfrac{\square}{\triangle}$

b is the correct answer.

30. $\dfrac{\triangle}{\square} + \dfrac{\square}{\triangle} = \dfrac{\triangle}{\square} \cdot \dfrac{\triangle}{\triangle} + \dfrac{\square}{\triangle} \cdot \dfrac{\square}{\square}$

$\qquad = \dfrac{\triangle\triangle}{\square\triangle} + \dfrac{\square\square}{\square\triangle}$

$\qquad = \dfrac{\triangle\triangle + \square\square}{\square\triangle}$

d is the correct answer.

31. $\dfrac{\triangle}{\square} \cdot \dfrac{O}{\square} = \dfrac{\triangle O}{\square\square}$

d is the correct answer.

32. $\dfrac{\triangle}{\square} \div \dfrac{O}{\triangle} = \dfrac{\triangle}{\square} \cdot \dfrac{\triangle}{O} = \dfrac{\triangle\triangle}{\square O}$

a is the correct answer.

33. $\dfrac{\frac{\triangle+\square}{O}}{\frac{\triangle}{O}} = \dfrac{\triangle+\square}{O} \div \dfrac{\triangle}{O} = \dfrac{\triangle+\square}{O} \cdot \dfrac{O}{\triangle} = \dfrac{\triangle+\square}{\triangle}$

d is the correct answer.

Section 6.6

Practice Exercises

1. abc is the LCD.

$\dfrac{1}{a} - \dfrac{1}{b} = \dfrac{1}{c}$

$abc\left(\dfrac{1}{a} - \dfrac{1}{b}\right) = abc\left(\dfrac{1}{c}\right)$

$abc\left(\dfrac{1}{a}\right) - abc\left(\dfrac{1}{b}\right) = abc\left(\dfrac{1}{c}\right)$

$bc - ac = ab$

$bc = ab + ac$

$bc = a(b+c)$

$\dfrac{bc}{b+c} = a$

2. Let n = the number.

$\dfrac{3+n}{11-n} = \dfrac{5}{2}$

$2(11-n) \cdot \dfrac{3+n}{11-n} = 2(11-n) \cdot \dfrac{5}{2}$

$2(3+n) = 5(11-n)$

$6 + 2n = 55 - 5n$

$7n = 49$

$n = 7$

The number is 7.

3. Let x = the number of homes heated by fuel oil.

$$\frac{1}{12} = \frac{x}{36,000}$$
$$12x = 1 \cdot 36,000$$
$$x = \frac{36,000}{12}$$
$$x = 3000$$

3000 homes in the community are heated by fuel oil.

4. Let t = the time it takes them to clean the cages together.

	Time	Part done in one hour
Elissa	3	$\frac{1}{3}$
Bill	2	$\frac{1}{2}$
Together	t	$\frac{1}{t}$

$$\frac{1}{3} + \frac{1}{2} = \frac{1}{t}$$
$$6t\left(\frac{1}{3} + \frac{1}{2}\right) = 6t\left(\frac{1}{t}\right)$$
$$2t + 3t = 6$$
$$5t = 6$$
$$t = \frac{6}{5} \text{ or } 1\frac{1}{5}$$

Elissa and Bill can clean the cages in $1\frac{1}{5}$ hours if they work together.

5. Let x = the speed of the wind.

	Distance $(r \cdot t)$	Rate	Time
Tailwind	$450 + x$	$450 + x$	1
Headwind	$\frac{5}{4}(450 - x)$	$450 - x$	$1\frac{1}{4} = \frac{5}{4}$

$$450 + x = \frac{5}{4}(450 - x)$$
$$4 \cdot (450 + x) = 4 \cdot \frac{5}{4}(450 - x)$$
$$1800 + 4x = 5(450 - x)$$
$$1800 + 4x = 2250 - 5x$$
$$9x = 450$$
$$x = 50$$

The wind speed is 50 mph.

Exercise Set 6.6

1. $$F = \frac{9}{5}C + 32$$
$$F - 32 = \frac{9}{5}C$$
$$C = \frac{5}{9}(F - 32)$$

3. $$Q = \frac{A - I}{L}$$
$$QL = L\left(\frac{A - I}{L}\right)$$
$$QL = A - I$$
$$I = A - QL$$

5. $$\frac{1}{R} = \frac{1}{R_1} + \frac{1}{R_2}$$
$$RR_1R_2 \cdot \frac{1}{R} = RR_1R_2\left(\frac{1}{R_1} + \frac{1}{R_2}\right)$$
$$R_1R_2 = RR_2 + RR_1$$
$$R_1R_2 = R(R_2 + R_1)$$
$$R = \frac{R_1R_2}{R_1 + R_2}$$

7. $$S = \frac{n(a + L)}{2}$$
$$2S = n(a + L)$$
$$n = \frac{2S}{a + L}$$

9. $$A = \frac{h(a + b)}{2}$$
$$2A = h(a + b)$$
$$2A = ah + bh$$
$$2A - ah = bh$$
$$b = \frac{2A - ah}{h}$$

11.
$$\frac{P_1 V_1}{T_1} = \frac{P_2 V_2}{T_2}$$
$$T_1 T_2 \cdot \frac{P_1 V_1}{T_1} = T_1 T_2 \cdot \frac{P_2 V_2}{T_2}$$
$$P_1 V_1 T_2 = P_2 V_2 T_1$$
$$T_2 = \frac{P_2 V_2 T_1}{P_1 V_1}$$

13.
$$f = \frac{f_1 f_2}{f_1 + f_2}$$
$$(f_1 + f_2) f = f_1 f_2$$
$$f_1 f + f_2 f = f_1 f_2$$
$$f_1 f = f_1 f_2 - f_2 f$$
$$f_1 f = f_2 (f_1 - f)$$
$$\frac{f_1 f}{f_1 - f} = f_2$$

15.
$$\lambda = \frac{2L}{n}$$
$$n\lambda = 2L$$
$$\frac{n\lambda}{2} = L$$

17.
$$\frac{\theta}{\omega} = \frac{2L}{c}$$
$$c\omega \cdot \frac{\theta}{\omega} = c\omega \cdot \frac{2L}{c}$$
$$c\theta = 2L\omega$$
$$c = \frac{2L\omega}{\theta}$$

19. Let n = the number. Then
$\dfrac{1}{n}$ = the reciprocal of the number.
$$n + 5\left(\frac{1}{n}\right) = 6$$
$$n + \frac{5}{n} = 6$$
$$n\left(n + \frac{5}{n}\right) = 6n$$
$$n^2 + 5 = 6n$$
$$n^2 - 6n + 5 = 0$$
$$(n-5)(n-1) = 0$$
$$n - 5 = 0 \text{ or } n - 1 = 0$$
$$n = 5 \text{ or } \quad n = 1$$
The numbers are 1 and 5.

21. Let x = the number.
$$\frac{12 + x}{41 + 2x} = \frac{1}{3}$$
$$3(12 + x) = 1(41 + 2x)$$
$$36 + 3x = 41 + 2x$$
$$x = 5$$
The number is 5.

23. Let a = amount of water in 3 minutes.
$$\frac{15}{10} = \frac{a}{3}$$
$$10a = 15(3)$$
$$10a = 45$$
$$a = 4.5$$
The camel can drink 4.5 gallons.

25. Let w = the number of women.
$$\frac{5.5}{50} = \frac{w}{40,639}$$
$$50w = 5.5(40,639)$$
$$50w = 223,514.5$$
$$w = 4470.29$$
There are 4470 women.

27. Let x = number of hours needed working together.
$$\frac{1}{26} + \frac{1}{39} = \frac{1}{x}$$
$$78x\left(\frac{1}{26} + \frac{1}{39}\right) = 78x\left(\frac{1}{x}\right)$$
$$3x + 2x = 78$$
$$5x = 78$$
$$x = \frac{78}{5} = 15.6$$
The roofers together would take 15.6 hours.

29. Let x = time to sort the stack working together.
$$\frac{1}{20} + \frac{1}{30} + \frac{1}{60} = \frac{1}{x}$$
$$60x\left(\frac{1}{20} + \frac{1}{30} + \frac{1}{60}\right) = 60x \cdot \frac{1}{x}$$
$$3x + 2x + x = 60$$
$$6x = 60$$
$$x = 10$$
It takes them 10 minutes to sort the mail when all three work together.

31. Let r = speed of the car. Then
$r + 150$ = speed of the plane.

$$t_{\text{plane}} = t_{\text{car}}$$
$$\frac{600}{r+150} = \frac{150}{r}$$
$$600r = 150(r+150)$$
$$600r = 150r + 22,500$$
$$450r = 22,500$$
$$r = \frac{22,500}{450} = 50$$
$$r + 150 = 50 + 150 = 200$$
The speed of the plane was 200 mph.

33. Let r = speed of the boat in still water.

$$t_{\text{downstream}} = t_{\text{upstream}}$$
$$\frac{20}{r+5} = \frac{10}{r-5}$$
$$20(r-5) = 10(r+5)$$
$$20r - 100 = 10r + 50$$
$$10r = 150$$
$$r = 15$$
The speed of the boat in still water is 15 mph.

35. Let x = the first integer. Then
$x + 1$ = the next integer.

$$\frac{1}{x} + \frac{1}{x+1} = -\frac{15}{56}$$
$$56x(x+1)\left[\frac{1}{x} + \frac{1}{x+1}\right] = 56x(x+1)\left(-\frac{15}{56}\right)$$
$$56(x+1) + 56x = -15x(x+1)$$
$$56x + 56 + 56x = -15x^2 - 15x$$
$$112x + 56 = -15x^2 - 15x$$
$$15x^2 + 127x + 56 = 0$$
$$(15x+7)(x+8) = 0$$
$$15x + 7 = 0 \quad \text{or} \quad x + 8 = 0$$
$$15x = -7 \quad \text{or} \qquad x = -8$$
$$x = -\frac{7}{15} \qquad x + 1 = -8 + 1 = -7$$

$-\dfrac{7}{15}$ is not an integer.

The integers are –8 and –7.

37. Let t = time for 2nd hose to fill the pond.

$$\frac{1}{45} + \frac{1}{t} = \frac{1}{20}$$
$$180t\left(\frac{1}{45} + \frac{1}{t}\right) = 180t \cdot \frac{1}{20}$$
$$4t + 180 = 9t$$
$$180 = 5t$$
$$36 = t$$
The second hose will take 36 minutes to fill the pond alone.

39. Let r = the speed of the first train. Then
$r + 15$ = the speed of the 2nd train.

$$d_{\text{train 1}} + d_{\text{train 2}} = 630$$
$$6r + 6(r+15) = 630$$
$$6r + 6r + 90 = 630$$
$$12r = 540$$
$$r = 45$$
$$r + 15 = 45 + 15 = 60$$
The speed of the trains were 45 mph and 60 mph.

41. Let t = time to travel 1 mile.

$$\frac{0.17}{1} = \frac{1}{t}$$
$$0.17t = 1$$
$$100(0.17t) = 100(1)$$
$$17t = 100$$
$$t = \frac{100}{17} \approx 5.882352941$$

It would take 5.9 hours.

43. Let t = time to fill quota working together.

$$\frac{1}{5} + \frac{1}{6} + \frac{1}{7.5} = \frac{1}{t}$$
$$225t\left(\frac{1}{5} + \frac{1}{6} + \frac{1}{7.5}\right) = 225t \cdot \frac{1}{t}$$
$$45t + 37.5t + 30t = 225$$
$$112.5t = 225$$
$$t = 2$$
It would take 2 hours using all three machines.

45. Let r = the speed of plane in still air.

$$t_{\text{with}} = t_{\text{against}}$$
$$\frac{465}{r+20} = \frac{345}{r-20}$$
$$465(r-20) = 345(r+20)$$
$$465r - 9300 = 345r + 6900$$
$$120r = 16,200$$
$$r = 135$$
The planes speed in still air is 135 mph.

47. Let d = the distance of the run.

$$t_{\text{jogger 2}} = \frac{1}{2} + t_{\text{jogger 1}}$$
$$\frac{d}{6} = \frac{1}{2} + \frac{d}{8}$$
$$24\left(\frac{d}{6}\right) = 24\left(\frac{1}{2} + \frac{d}{8}\right)$$
$$4d = 12 + 3d$$
$$d = 12$$

The run was 12 miles.

49. Let n = numerator. Then
$n + 1$ = the denominator, and

$\dfrac{n}{n+1}$ = the fraction. Now

$$\frac{n-3}{(n+1)-3} = \frac{4}{5}$$
$$\frac{n-3}{n-2} = \frac{4}{5}$$
$$5(n-3) = 4(n-2)$$
$$5n - 15 = 4n - 8$$
$$n = 7$$

Thus, $\dfrac{n}{n+1} = \dfrac{7}{7+1} = \dfrac{7}{8}$ is the fraction.

51. Let t = time to move the cans working together.

$$\frac{1}{2} + \frac{1}{6} = \frac{1}{t}$$
$$6t\left(\frac{1}{2} + \frac{1}{6}\right) = 6t \cdot \frac{1}{t}$$
$$3t + t = 6$$
$$4t = 6$$
$$t = \frac{6}{4} = 1\frac{1}{2}$$

It would take them $1\dfrac{1}{2}$ minutes.

53. Let t = time to complete the job working together.

$$\frac{1}{4} + \frac{1}{5} = \frac{1}{t}$$
$$20t\left(\frac{1}{4} + \frac{1}{5}\right) = 20t \cdot \frac{1}{t}$$
$$5t + 4t = 20$$
$$9t = 20$$
$$t = \frac{20}{9} = 2\frac{2}{9}$$

It would take them $2\dfrac{2}{9}$ hours.

55. Let r = the rate for the 1st portion. Then $r - 2$ = the rate for the cooldown portion.

$$t_{\text{first portion}} = t_{\text{cooldown}}$$
$$\frac{20}{r} = \frac{16}{r-2}$$
$$20(r-2) = 16r$$
$$20r - 40 = 16r$$
$$4r = 40$$
$$r = 10; \ r - 2 = 10 - 2 = 8$$

His rate was 10 mph during the first portion and 8 mph for the cool-down portion.

57. Let t = time if they worked together.

$$\frac{1}{3} + \frac{1}{6} = \frac{1}{t}$$
$$6t\left(\frac{1}{3} + \frac{1}{6}\right) = 6t \cdot \frac{1}{t}$$
$$2t + t = 6$$
$$3t = 6$$
$$t = 2$$

It would take them 2 hours.

59. Let r = the speed of the car. Then $6r$ = speed of the jet.

$$t_{\text{car}} = t_{\text{jet}} + 1$$
$$\frac{240}{r} = \frac{1080}{6r} + 1$$
$$6r \cdot \frac{240}{r} = 6r\left(\frac{1080}{6r} + 1\right)$$
$$1440 = 1080 + 6r$$
$$360 = 6r$$
$$60 = r$$

Thus, $t_{\text{jet}} = \dfrac{1080}{6(60)} = 3; \ t_{\text{car}} = \dfrac{240}{6} = 4$.

She travels 3 hours by jet and 4 hours by car.

61. Let m = the number of movies that cost between $50 and $99 million to make.

$$\frac{5}{7} = \frac{m}{599}$$
$$7m = 5 \cdot 599$$
$$7m = 2995$$
$$m = \frac{2995}{7} \approx 427.86$$

Approximately 428 movies cost between $50 and $99 million to make.

63. $\dfrac{x}{4} = \dfrac{x+3}{6}$

$6x = 4(x+3)$

$6x = 4x + 12$

$2x = 12$

$x = 6$

65. $\dfrac{x-6}{4} = \dfrac{x-2}{5}$

$5(x-6) = 4(x-2)$

$5x - 30 = 4x - 8$

$x = 22$

67. Answers may vary

$\dfrac{705w}{h^2} = 47$

$\dfrac{705(240)}{h^2} = 47$

$169,200 = 47h^2$

$3600 = h^2$

$0 = h^2 - 3600$

$0 = (h+60)(h-60)$

$h + 60 = 0 \quad$ or $\quad h - 60 = 0$

$h = -60 \quad$ or $\qquad h = 60$

Discard the –60. The patient is 60 inches, or 5 feet tall.

69. $\dfrac{1}{R} = \dfrac{1}{R_1} + \dfrac{1}{R_2}$

$\dfrac{1}{2} = \dfrac{1}{3} + \dfrac{1}{R_2}$

$6R_2\left(\dfrac{1}{2}\right) = 6R_2\left(\dfrac{1}{3} + \dfrac{1}{R_2}\right)$

$3R_2 = 2R_2 + 6$

$R_2 = 6$

6 ohms

71. $\dfrac{1}{R} = \dfrac{1}{R_1} + \dfrac{1}{R_2} + \dfrac{1}{R_3}$

$\dfrac{1}{R} = \dfrac{1}{5} + \dfrac{1}{6} + \dfrac{1}{2}$

$30R\left(\dfrac{1}{R}\right) = 30R\left(\dfrac{1}{5} + \dfrac{1}{6} + \dfrac{1}{2}\right)$

$30 = 6R + 5R + 15R$

$30 = 26R$

$R = \dfrac{30}{26} = \dfrac{15}{13}$

$\dfrac{15}{13}$ ohms

Section 6.7

Practice Exercises

1. $y = kx$

$20 = k(15)$

$\dfrac{4}{3} = k$

$k = \dfrac{4}{3}; \; y = \dfrac{4}{3}x$

2. $d = kw$

$9 = k(36)$

$\dfrac{1}{4} = k$

$d = \dfrac{1}{4}w$

$d = \dfrac{1}{4}(75)$

$d = \dfrac{75}{4}$ inches or $18\dfrac{3}{4}$ inches

3. $b = \dfrac{k}{a}$

$5 = \dfrac{k}{9}$

$k = 45; \; b = \dfrac{45}{a}$

4. $P = \dfrac{k}{V}$

$350 = \dfrac{k}{2.8}$

$980 = k$

$P = \dfrac{980}{V}$

$P = \dfrac{980}{1.5}$

$P = 653\dfrac{1}{3}$ kilopascals

5. $A = kap$

6. $y = \dfrac{k}{x^3}$

$\dfrac{1}{2} = \dfrac{k}{2^3}$

$\dfrac{1}{2} = \dfrac{k}{8}$

$4 = k$

$k = 4; \ y = \dfrac{4}{x^3}$

7. $y = \dfrac{kz}{x^3}$

$15 = \dfrac{k \cdot 5}{3^3}$

$81 = k$

$k = 81; \ y = \dfrac{81z}{x^3}$

Vocabulary and Readiness Check

1. $y = 5x$ represents direct variation.

2. $y = \dfrac{700}{x}$ represents inverse variation.

3. $y = 5xz$ represents joint variation.

4. $y = \dfrac{1}{2}abc$ represents joint variation.

5. $y = \dfrac{9.1}{x}$ represents inverse variation.

6. $y = 2.3x$ represents direct variation.

7. $y = \dfrac{2}{3}x$ represents direct variation.

8. $y = 3.1st$ represents joint variation.

Exercise Set 6.7

1. $y = kx$

$4 = k(20)$

$k = \dfrac{1}{5}$

$y = \dfrac{1}{5}x$

3. $y = kx$

$6 = k(4)$

$k = \dfrac{3}{2}$

$y = \dfrac{3}{2}x$

5. $y = kx$

$7 = k\left(\dfrac{1}{2}\right)$

$k = 14$

$y = 14x$

7. $y = kx$

$0.2 = k(0.8)$

$k = 0.25$

$y = 0.25x$

9. $W = kr^3$

$1.2 = k \cdot 2^3$

$k = \dfrac{1.2}{8} = 0.15$

$W = 0.15r^3$

$= 0.15(3)^3$

$= 0.15(27)$

$= 4.05$

The ball weighs 4.05 pounds.

11. $P = kN$

$260,000 = k(442,000)$

$k = \dfrac{10}{17}$

$P = \dfrac{10}{17}N$

$P = \dfrac{10}{17}(348,000) \approx 204,706$

St. Louis produces 204,706 tons.

13. $y = \dfrac{k}{x}$

$6 = \dfrac{k}{5}$

$k = 30$

$y = \dfrac{30}{x}$

15. $y = \dfrac{k}{x}$

$100 = \dfrac{k}{7}$

$k = 700$

$y = \dfrac{700}{x}$

17. $y = \dfrac{k}{x}$

$\dfrac{1}{8} = \dfrac{k}{16}$

$k = 2$

$y = \dfrac{2}{x}$

19. $y = \dfrac{k}{x}$

$0.2 = \dfrac{k}{0.7}$

$k = 0.14$

$y = \dfrac{0.14}{x}$

21. $R = \dfrac{k}{T}$

$45 = \dfrac{k}{6}$

$k = 270$

$R = \dfrac{270}{5} = 54$

The car's speed is 54 mph.

23. $I = \dfrac{k}{R}$

$40 = \dfrac{k}{270}$

$k = 10,800$

$I = \dfrac{10,800}{R} = \dfrac{10,800}{150} = 72$

The current is 72 amps.

25. $I_1 = \dfrac{k}{d^2}$

Replace d by $2d$.

$I_2 = \dfrac{k}{(2d)^2} = \dfrac{k}{4d^2} = \dfrac{1}{4}I_1$

Thus, the intensity is divided by 4.

27. $x = kyz$

29. $r = kst^3$

31. $y = kx^3$

$9 = k(3)^3$

$9 = 27k$

$k = \dfrac{1}{3}$

$y = \dfrac{1}{3}x^3$

33. $y = k\sqrt{x}$

$0.4 = k\sqrt{4}$

$0.4 = 2k$

$\dfrac{0.4}{2} = k$

$0.2 = k$

$y = 0.2\sqrt{x}$

35. $y = \dfrac{k}{x^2}$

$0.052 = \dfrac{k}{5^2}$

$k = 1.3$

$y = \dfrac{1.3}{x^2}$

37. $y = kxz^3$

$120 = k(5)(2^3)$

$120 = k(5)(8)$

$120 = 40k$

$3 = k$

$y = 3xz^3$

39. Weight $= \dfrac{kwh^2}{l}$

$$12 = \dfrac{k\left(\frac{1}{2}\right)\left(\frac{1}{3}\right)^2}{10}$$

$$120 = k \cdot \dfrac{1}{2} \cdot \dfrac{1}{9}$$

$$k = 2160$$

Weight $= \dfrac{2160wh^2}{l} = \dfrac{2160\left(\frac{2}{3}\right)\left(\frac{1}{2}\right)^2}{16} = 22.5$

The beam can support 22.5 tons.

41. $V = kr^2h$

$$32\pi = k(4)^2(6)$$

$$32\pi = k(16)(6)$$

$$32\pi = 96k$$

$$\dfrac{32\pi}{96} = k$$

$$\dfrac{\pi}{3} = k$$

$$V = \dfrac{\pi}{3}r^2h$$

$$V = \dfrac{\pi}{3}(3)^2(5)$$

$$V = 15\pi$$

The volume is 15π cubic inches.

43. $I = \dfrac{k}{x^2}$

$$80 = \dfrac{k}{2^2}$$

$$k = 320$$

$$I = \dfrac{320}{x^2}$$

$$5 = \dfrac{320}{x^2}$$

$$5x^2 = 320$$

$$x^2 = 64$$

$$x = 8$$

The source is 8 feet from the light source.

45. y varies directly as x is written as $y = kx$.

47. a varies inversely as b is written as $a = \dfrac{k}{b}$.

49. y varies jointly as x and z is written as $y = kxz$.

51. y varies inversely as x^3 is written as $y = \dfrac{k}{x^3}$.

53. y varies directly as x and inversely as p^2 is written as $y = \dfrac{kx}{p^2}$.

55. $r = 4$ in.
$C = 2\pi r = 2\pi(4) = 8\pi$ in.
$A = \pi r^2 = \pi(4)^2 = 16\pi$ sq in.

57. $r = 9$ cm
$C = 2\pi r = 2\pi(9) = 18\pi$ cm
$A = \pi r^2 = \pi(9)^2 = 81\pi$ sq cm

59. $\sqrt{81} = 9$

61. $\sqrt{1} = 1$

63. $\sqrt{\dfrac{1}{4}} = \dfrac{1}{2}$

65. $\sqrt{\dfrac{4}{9}} = \dfrac{2}{3}$

67. $y = \dfrac{2}{3}x$ is an example of direct variation; a.

69. $y = 9ab$ is an example of joint variation; c.

71. $H_1 = ks^3$
$H_2 = k(2s)^3 = 8(ks^3) = 8H_1$
It is multiplied by 8.

73. $y_1 = kx$
$y_2 = k(2x) = 2(kx) = 2y_1$
It is multiplied by 2.

75.

x	$\frac{1}{4}$	$\frac{1}{2}$	1	2	4
$y = \frac{3}{x}$	12	6	3	$\frac{3}{2}$	$\frac{3}{4}$

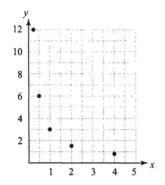

77.

x	$\frac{1}{4}$	$\frac{1}{2}$	1	2	4
$y = \dfrac{1}{2x}$	2	1	$\frac{1}{2}$	$\frac{1}{4}$	$\frac{1}{8}$

Chapter 6 Vocabulary Check

1. A rational expression whose numerator, denominator, or both contain one or more rational expressions is called a <u>complex fraction</u>.

2. To divide a polynomial by a polynomial other than a monomial, we use <u>long division</u>.

3. In the equation $y = kx$, y varies <u>directly</u> as x.

4. In the equation $y = \dfrac{k}{x}$, y varies <u>inversely</u> as x.

5. The <u>least common denominator</u> of a list of rational expressions is a polynomial of least degree whose factors include the denominator factors in the list.

6. When a polynomial is to be divided by a binomial of the form $x - c$, a shortcut process called <u>synthetic division</u> may be used.

7. In the equation $y = kxz$, y varies <u>jointly</u> as x and z.

8. The expressions $(x - 5)$ and $(5 - x)$ are called <u>opposites</u>.

9. A <u>rational expression</u> is an expression that can be written as the quotient $\dfrac{P}{Q}$ of two polynomials P and Q as long as Q is not 0.

10. Which is an expression and which is an equation? An example of an <u>equation</u> is $\dfrac{2}{x} + \dfrac{2}{x^2} = 7$ and an example of an <u>expression</u> is $\dfrac{2}{x} + \dfrac{5}{x^2}$.

Chapter 6 Review

1. 7 is never 0 so the domain of $f(x) = \dfrac{3 - 5x}{7}$ is $\{x | x \text{ is a real number}\}$.

2. 11 is never 0 so the domain of $g(x) = \dfrac{2x + 4}{11}$ is $\{x | x \text{ is a real number}\}$.

3. $x - 5 = 0$
   $x = 5$
   The domain of $F(x) = \dfrac{-3x^2}{x - 5}$ is $\{x | x \text{ is a real number and } x \neq 5\}$.

4. $3x - 12 = 0$
   $3x = 12$
   $x = 4$
   The domain of $h(x) = \dfrac{4x}{3x - 12}$ is $\{x | x \text{ is a real number and } x \neq 4\}$.

5. $x^2 + 8x = 0$
   $x(x + 8) = 0$
   $x = 0 \quad \text{or} \quad x + 8 = 0$
   $x = 0 \quad \text{or} \qquad x = -8$
   The domain of $f(x) = \dfrac{x^3 + 2}{x^2 + 8x}$ is $\{x | x \text{ is a real number and } x \neq 0, x \neq -8\}$.

6. $3x^2 - 48 = 0$

$3(x^2 - 16) = 0$

$3(x+4)(x-4) = 0$

$x+4 = 0$ or $x-4 = 0$

$x = -4$ or $x = 4$

The domain of $G(x) = \dfrac{20}{3x^2 - 48}$ is

$\{x|x$ is a real number and $x \neq -4,\ x \neq 4\}$.

7. $\dfrac{x-12}{12-x} = \dfrac{x-12}{-(x-12)} = -1$

8. $\dfrac{5x-15}{25x-75} = \dfrac{5(x-3)}{25(x-3)} = \dfrac{5}{25} = \dfrac{1}{5}$

9. $\dfrac{2x}{2x^2 - 2x} = \dfrac{2x}{2x(x-1)} = \dfrac{1}{x-1}$

10. $\dfrac{x+7}{x^2 - 49} = \dfrac{x+7}{(x-7)(x+7)} = \dfrac{1}{x-7}$

11. $\dfrac{2x^2 + 4x - 30}{x^2 + x - 20} = \dfrac{2(x^2 + 2x - 15)}{(x+5)(x-4)}$

$= \dfrac{2(x+5)(x-3)}{(x+5)(x-4)}$

$= \dfrac{2(x-3)}{x-4}$

12. $C(x) = \dfrac{35x + 4200}{x}$

a. $C(50) = \dfrac{35(50) + 4200}{50}$

$= \dfrac{1750 + 4200}{50}$

$= \dfrac{5950}{50}$

$= 119$

The average cost is \$119.

b. $C(100) = \dfrac{35(100) + 4200}{100}$

$= \dfrac{3500 + 4200}{100}$

$= \dfrac{7700}{100}$

$= 77$

The average cost is \$77.

c. It will decrease.

13. $\dfrac{4-x}{5} \cdot \dfrac{15}{2x-8} = \dfrac{4-x}{5} \cdot \dfrac{5 \cdot 3}{2(x-4)}$

$= \dfrac{-1(x-4)}{5} \cdot \dfrac{5 \cdot 3}{2(x-4)}$

$= -\dfrac{3}{2}$

14. $\dfrac{x^2 - 6x + 9}{2x^2 - 18} \cdot \dfrac{4x + 12}{5x - 15}$

$= \dfrac{(x-3)(x-3)}{2(x^2 - 9)} \cdot \dfrac{4(x+3)}{5(x-3)}$

$= \dfrac{(x-3)(x-3)}{2(x-3)(x+3)} \cdot \dfrac{4(x+3)}{5(x-3)}$

$= \dfrac{4}{10}$

$= \dfrac{2}{5}$

15. $\dfrac{a-4b}{a^2 + ab} \cdot \dfrac{b^2 - a^2}{8b - 2a}$

$= \dfrac{a-4b}{a(a+b)} \cdot \dfrac{(b-a)(b+a)}{2(4b-a)}$

$= \dfrac{-(4b-a)}{a(a+b)} \cdot \dfrac{(a-b)(a+b)}{2(4b-a)}$

$= \dfrac{a-b}{2a}$

16. $\dfrac{x^2 - x - 12}{2x^2 - 32} \cdot \dfrac{x^2 + 8x + 16}{3x^2 + 21x + 36}$

$= \dfrac{(x-4)(x+3)}{2(x^2 - 16)} \cdot \dfrac{(x+4)(x+4)}{3(x^2 + 7x + 12)}$

$= \dfrac{(x-4)(x+3)}{2(x-4)(x+4)} \cdot \dfrac{(x+4)(x+4)}{3(x+4)(x+3)}$

$= \dfrac{1}{2 \cdot 3}$

$= \dfrac{1}{6}$

17. $\dfrac{4x + 8y}{3} \div \dfrac{5x + 10y}{9} = \dfrac{4x + 8y}{3} \cdot \dfrac{9}{5x + 10y}$

$= \dfrac{4(x + 2y)}{3} \cdot \dfrac{3 \cdot 3}{5(x + 2y)}$

$= \dfrac{12}{5}$

18. $\dfrac{x^2-25}{3}\div\dfrac{x^2-10x+25}{x^2-x-20}$

$=\dfrac{x^2-25}{3}\cdot\dfrac{x^2-x-20}{x^2-10x+25}$

$=\dfrac{(x+5)(x-5)}{3}\cdot\dfrac{(x-5)(x+4)}{(x-5)(x-5)}$

$=\dfrac{(x+5)(x+4)}{3}$

19. $\dfrac{a-4b}{a^2+ab}\div\dfrac{20b-5a}{b^2-a^2}$

$=\dfrac{a-4b}{a^2+ab}\cdot\dfrac{b^2-a^2}{20b-5a}$

$=\dfrac{a-4b}{a(a+b)}\cdot\dfrac{(b+a)(b-a)}{5(4b-a)}$

$=\dfrac{a-4b}{a(a+b)}\cdot\dfrac{-(a+b)(a-b)}{-5(a-4b)}$

$=\dfrac{a-b}{5a}$

20. $\dfrac{3x+3}{x-1}\div\dfrac{x^2-6x-7}{x^2-1}=\dfrac{3x+3}{x-1}\cdot\dfrac{x^2-1}{x^2-6x-7}$

$=\dfrac{3(x+1)}{x-1}\cdot\dfrac{(x+1)(x-1)}{(x-7)(x+1)}$

$=\dfrac{3(x+1)}{x-7}$

21. $\dfrac{2x-x^2}{x^3-8}\div\dfrac{x^2}{x^2+2x+4}$

$=\dfrac{2x-x^2}{x^3-8}\cdot\dfrac{x^2+2x+4}{x^2}$

$=\dfrac{x(2-x)}{(x-2)(x^2+2x+4)}\cdot\dfrac{x^2+2x+4}{x^2}$

$=\dfrac{-x(x-2)}{(x-2)(x^2+2x+4)}\cdot\dfrac{x^2+2x+4}{x^2}$

$=-\dfrac{1}{x}$

22. $\dfrac{5x-15}{3-x}\cdot\dfrac{x+2}{10x+20}\cdot\dfrac{x^2-9}{x^2-x-6}$

$=\dfrac{5(x-3)}{-(x-3)}\cdot\dfrac{x+2}{10(x+2)}\cdot\dfrac{(x+3)(x-3)}{(x-3)(x+2)}$

$=-\dfrac{x+3}{2(x+2)}$

23. $4x^2y^5=2\cdot2x^2y^5$

$10x^2y^4=2\cdot5x^2y^4$

$6y^4=2\cdot3y^4$

The LCD is $2\cdot2\cdot5\cdot3x^2y^5=60x^2y^5$.

24. The LCD is $2x(x-2)$.

25. The LCD is $5x(x-5)$.

26. $5x^3=5\cdot x^3$

$x^2+3x-28=(x+7)(x-4)$

$10x^2-30x=10x(x-3)=2\cdot5\cdot x\cdot(x-3)$

The LCD is

$2\cdot5\cdot x^3\cdot(x-4)(x+7)(x-3)$

$=10x^3(x-4)(x+7)(x-3)$.

27. $\dfrac{4}{x-4}+\dfrac{x}{x-4}=\dfrac{4+x}{x-4}$

28. $\dfrac{4}{3x^2}+\dfrac{2}{3x^2}=\dfrac{4+2}{3x^2}=\dfrac{6}{3x^2}=\dfrac{2}{x^2}$

29. $\dfrac{1}{x-2}-\dfrac{1}{4-2x}=\dfrac{1}{x-2}-\dfrac{1}{2(2-x)}$

$=\dfrac{1}{x-2}-\dfrac{-1}{2(x-2)}$

$=\dfrac{1}{x-2}\cdot\dfrac{2}{2}-\dfrac{-1}{2(x-2)}$

$=\dfrac{2}{2(x-2)}-\dfrac{-1}{2(x-2)}$

$=\dfrac{2+1}{2(x-2)}$

$=\dfrac{3}{2(x-2)}$

30. $\dfrac{1}{10-x}+\dfrac{x-1}{x-10}=\dfrac{-1}{x-10}+\dfrac{x-1}{x-10}$

$=\dfrac{-1+x-1}{x-10}$

$=\dfrac{x-2}{x-10}$

31.

$$\frac{x}{9-x^2} - \frac{2}{5x-15} = \frac{-x}{x^2-9} - \frac{2}{5x-15}$$

$$= \frac{-x}{(x-3)(x+3)} - \frac{2}{5(x-3)}$$

$$= \frac{-x}{(x-3)(x+3)} \cdot \frac{5}{5} - \frac{2}{5(x-3)} \cdot \frac{x+3}{x+3}$$

$$= \frac{-5x}{5(x-3)(x+3)} - \frac{2(x+3)}{5(x-3)(x+3)}$$

$$= \frac{-5x - 2(x+3)}{5(x-3)(x+3)}$$

$$= \frac{-5x - 2x - 6}{5(x-3)(x+3)}$$

$$= \frac{-7x - 6}{5(x-3)(x+3)}$$

32.

$$2x + 1 - \frac{1}{x-3} = 2x \cdot \frac{x-3}{x-3} + 1 \cdot \frac{x-3}{x-3} - \frac{1}{x-3}$$

$$= \frac{2x^2 - 6x}{x-3} + \frac{x-3}{x-3} - \frac{1}{x-3}$$

$$= \frac{2x^2 - 6x + x - 3 - 1}{x-3}$$

$$= \frac{2x^2 - 5x - 4}{x-3}$$

33.

$$\frac{2}{a^2 - 2a + 1} + \frac{3}{a^2 - 1} = \frac{2}{(a-1)(a-1)} + \frac{3}{(a+1)(a-1)}$$

$$= \frac{2}{(a-1)(a-1)} \cdot \frac{a+1}{a+1} + \frac{3}{(a+1)(a-1)} \cdot \frac{(a-1)}{(a-1)}$$

$$= \frac{2(a+1)}{(a-1)^2(a+1)} + \frac{3(a-1)}{(a-1)^2(a+1)}$$

$$= \frac{2a+2}{(a-1)^2(a+1)} + \frac{3a-3}{(a-1)^2(a+1)}$$

$$= \frac{2a+2+3a-3}{(a-1)^2(a+1)}$$

$$= \frac{5a-1}{(a-1)^2(a+1)}$$

34.

$$\frac{x}{9x^2 + 12x + 16} - \frac{3x+4}{27x^3 - 64} = \frac{x}{9x^2 + 12x + 16} - \frac{3x+4}{(3x-4)(9x^2 + 12x + 16)}$$

$$= \frac{x}{9x^2 + 12x + 16} \cdot \frac{3x-4}{3x-4} - \frac{3x+4}{(3x-4)(9x^2 + 12x + 16)}$$

$$= \frac{3x^2 - 4x - 3x - 4}{(3x-4)(9x^2 + 12x + 16)}$$

$$= \frac{3x^2 - 7x - 4}{(3x-4)(9x^2 + 12x + 16)}$$

35.
$$\frac{2}{x-1} - \frac{3x}{3x-3} + \frac{1}{2x-2}$$
$$= \frac{2}{x-1} - \frac{3x}{3(x-1)} + \frac{1}{2(x-1)}$$
$$= \frac{2}{x-1} \cdot \frac{6}{6} - \frac{3x}{3(x-1)} \cdot \frac{2}{2} + \frac{1}{2(x-1)} \cdot \frac{3}{3}$$
$$= \frac{12}{6(x-1)} - \frac{6x}{6(x-1)} + \frac{3}{6(x-1)}$$
$$= \frac{12 - 6x + 3}{6(x-1)}$$
$$= \frac{15 - 6x}{6(x-1)}$$
$$= \frac{3(5 - 2x)}{6(x-1)}$$
$$= \frac{5 - 2x}{2(x-1)}$$

36. Perimeter $= \dfrac{1}{x} + \dfrac{1}{x} + \dfrac{1}{x} + \dfrac{2}{x} + \dfrac{2}{x} + \dfrac{3}{2x} + \dfrac{5}{2x}$
$$= \frac{7}{x} + \frac{8}{2x}$$
$$= \frac{7}{x} \cdot \frac{2}{2} + \frac{8}{2x}$$
$$= \frac{14}{2x} + \frac{8}{2x}$$
$$= \frac{14 + 8}{2x}$$
$$= \frac{22}{2x}$$
$$= \frac{11}{x}$$

37. $\dfrac{1 - \frac{3x}{4}}{2 + \frac{x}{4}} = \dfrac{4\left(1 - \frac{3x}{4}\right)}{4\left(2 + \frac{x}{4}\right)} = \dfrac{4 - 3x}{8 + x}$

38. $\dfrac{\frac{x^2}{15}}{\frac{x+1}{5x}} = \dfrac{x^2}{15} \div \dfrac{x+1}{5x} = \dfrac{x^2}{15} \cdot \dfrac{5x}{x+1} = \dfrac{x^3}{3(x+1)}$

39. $\dfrac{2 - \frac{3}{2x}}{x - \frac{2}{5x}} = \dfrac{10x\left(2 - \frac{3}{2x}\right)}{10x\left(x - \frac{2}{5x}\right)}$
$$= \frac{20x - 15}{10x^2 - 4}$$
$$= \frac{5(4x - 3)}{2(5x^2 - 2)}$$

40. $\dfrac{1 + \frac{x}{y}}{\frac{x^2}{y^2} - 1} = \dfrac{y^2\left(1 + \frac{x}{y}\right)}{y^2\left(\frac{x^2}{y^2} - 1\right)}$
$$= \frac{y^2 + xy}{x^2 - y^2}$$
$$= \frac{y(y + x)}{(x + y)(x - y)}$$
$$= \frac{y}{x - y}$$

41. $\dfrac{\frac{5}{x} + \frac{1}{xy}}{\frac{3}{x^2}} = \dfrac{x^2 y\left(\frac{5}{x} + \frac{1}{xy}\right)}{x^2 y\left(\frac{3}{x^2}\right)} = \dfrac{5xy + x}{3y} = \dfrac{x(5y + 1)}{3y}$

42. $\dfrac{\frac{x}{3} - \frac{3}{x}}{1 + \frac{3}{x}} = \dfrac{3x\left(\frac{x}{3} - \frac{3}{x}\right)}{3x\left(1 + \frac{3}{x}\right)}$
$$= \frac{x^2 - 9}{3x + 9}$$
$$= \frac{(x + 3)(x - 3)}{3(x + 3)}$$
$$= \frac{x - 3}{3}$$

43. $\dfrac{\frac{1}{x-1} + 1}{\frac{1}{x+1} - 1} = \dfrac{(x+1)(x-1)\left(\frac{1}{x-1} + 1\right)}{(x+1)(x-1)\left(\frac{1}{x+1} - 1\right)}$
$$= \frac{x + 1 + (x+1)(x-1)}{x - 1 - (x+1)(x-1)}$$
$$= \frac{x + 1 + x^2 - 1}{x - 1 - x^2 + 1}$$
$$= \frac{x + x^2}{x - x^2}$$
$$= \frac{x(1 + x)}{x(1 - x)}$$
$$= \frac{1 + x}{1 - x}$$

44. $\dfrac{\frac{x-3}{x+3}+\frac{x+3}{x-3}}{\frac{x-3}{x+3}-\frac{x+3}{x-3}} = \dfrac{(x-3)(x+3)\left(\frac{x-3}{x+3}+\frac{x+3}{x-3}\right)}{(x-3)(x+3)\left(\frac{x-3}{x+3}-\frac{x+3}{x-3}\right)}$

$= \dfrac{(x-3)^2+(x+3)^2}{(x-3)^2-(x+3)^2}$

$= \dfrac{x^2-6x+9+x^2+6x+9}{x^2-6x+9-(x^2+6x+9)}$

$= \dfrac{2x^2+18}{x^2-6x+9-x^2-6x-9}$

$= \dfrac{2(x^2+9)}{-12x}$

$= -\dfrac{x^2+9}{6x}$

45. $f(a+h) = \dfrac{3}{a+h}$

46. $f(a) = \dfrac{3}{a}$

47. $\dfrac{f(a+h)-f(a)}{h} = \dfrac{\frac{3}{a+h}-\frac{3}{a}}{h}$

48. $\dfrac{f(a+h)-f(a)}{h} = \dfrac{\frac{3}{a+h}-\frac{3}{a}}{h}$

$= \dfrac{\left(\frac{3}{a+h}-\frac{3}{a}\right)\cdot a(a+h)}{h\cdot a(a+h)}$

$= \dfrac{3a-3(a+h)}{h\cdot a(a+h)}$

$= \dfrac{3a-3a-3h}{h\cdot a(a+h)}$

$= \dfrac{-3h}{h\cdot a(a+h)}$

$= \dfrac{-3}{a(a+h)}$

49. $\dfrac{4xy+2x^2-9}{4xy} = \dfrac{4xy}{4xy}+\dfrac{2x^2}{4xy}-\dfrac{9}{4xy}$

$= 1+\dfrac{x}{2y}-\dfrac{9}{4xy}$

50. $\dfrac{12xb^2+16xb^4}{4xb^3} = \dfrac{12xb^2}{4xb^3}+\dfrac{16xb^4}{4xb^3}$

$= \dfrac{3}{b}+4b$

51.
$$
\begin{array}{r}
3x^3+9x^2+2x+6 \\
x-3\overline{\smash{\big)}\,3x^4+0x^3-25x^2+0x-20} \\
\underline{3x^4-9x^3} \\
9x^3-25x^2 \\
\underline{9x^3-27x^2} \\
2x^2+0x \\
\underline{2x^2-6x} \\
6x-20 \\
\underline{6x-18} \\
-2
\end{array}
$$

Answer: $3x^3+9x^2+2x+6-\dfrac{2}{x-3}$

52.
$$
\begin{array}{r}
2x^3-4x^2+7x-9 \\
x+2\overline{\smash{\big)}\,2x^4+0x^3-x^2+5x-12} \\
\underline{2x^4+4x^3} \\
-4x^3-x^2 \\
\underline{-4x^3-8x^2} \\
7x^2+5x \\
\underline{7x^2+14x} \\
-9x-12 \\
\underline{-9x-18} \\
6
\end{array}
$$

Answer: $2x^3-4x^2+7x-9+\dfrac{6}{x+2}$

53.
$$
\begin{array}{r}
x^2-1 \\
2x+3\overline{\smash{\big)}\,2x^3+3x^2-2x+2} \\
\underline{2x^3+3x^2} \\
-2x+2 \\
\underline{-2x-3} \\
5
\end{array}
$$

Answer: $x^2-1+\dfrac{5}{2x+3}$

54.
$$x^2 + x + 2 \overline{\smash{\big)}\,3x^4 + 5x^3 + 7x^2 + 3x - 2}$$

quotient: $3x^2 + 2x - 1$

$$\underline{3x^4 + 3x^3 + 6x^2}$$
$$2x^3 + x^2 + 3x$$
$$\underline{2x^3 + 2x^2 + 4x}$$
$$-x^2 - x - 2$$
$$\underline{-x^2 - x - 2}$$
$$0$$

Answer: $3x^2 + 2x - 1$

55.
$$\begin{array}{r|rrrr} 2 & 3 & 0 & 12 & -4 \\ & & 6 & 12 & 48 \\ \hline & 3 & 6 & 24 & 44 \end{array}$$

Answer: $3x^2 + 6x + 24 + \dfrac{44}{x-2}$

56.
$$\begin{array}{r|rrrrrr} -1 & 1 & 0 & 0 & 0 & 0 & -1 \\ & & -1 & 1 & -1 & 1 & -1 \\ \hline & 1 & -1 & 1 & -1 & 1 & -2 \end{array}$$

Answer: $x^4 - x^3 + x^2 - x + 1 - \dfrac{2}{x+1}$

57.
$$\begin{array}{r|rrrr} 3 & 1 & 0 & 0 & -81 \\ & & 3 & 9 & 27 \\ \hline & 1 & 3 & 9 & -54 \end{array}$$

Answer: $x^2 + 3x + 9 - \dfrac{54}{x-3}$

58.
$$\begin{array}{r|rrrrr} -2 & 3 & 0 & -2 & 0 & 10 \\ & & -6 & 12 & -20 & 40 \\ \hline & 3 & -6 & 10 & -20 & 50 \end{array}$$

Answer: $3x^3 - 6x^2 + 10x - 20 + \dfrac{50}{x+2}$

59.
$$\begin{array}{r|rrrrrr} 4 & 3 & 0 & 0 & 0 & -9 & 7 \\ & & 12 & 48 & 192 & 768 & 3036 \\ \hline & 3 & 12 & 48 & 192 & 759 & 3043 \end{array}$$

Thus, $P(4) = 3043$.

60.
$$\begin{array}{r|rrrrrr} -5 & 3 & 0 & 0 & 0 & -9 & 7 \\ & & -15 & 75 & -375 & 1875 & -9330 \\ \hline & 3 & -15 & 75 & -375 & 1866 & -9323 \end{array}$$

Thus, $P(-5) = -9323$.

61.
$$\begin{array}{r|rrrrrr} -\frac{1}{2} & 3 & 0 & 0 & 0 & -9 & 7 \\ & & -\frac{3}{2} & \frac{3}{4} & -\frac{3}{8} & \frac{3}{16} & \frac{141}{32} \\ \hline & 3 & -\frac{3}{2} & \frac{3}{4} & -\frac{3}{8} & -\frac{141}{16} & \frac{365}{32} \end{array}$$

Thus, $P\left(-\dfrac{1}{2}\right) = \dfrac{365}{32}$.

62.
$$\begin{array}{r|rrrrr} 3 & 1 & -1 & -6 & -6 & 18 \\ & & 3 & 6 & 0 & -18 \\ \hline & 1 & 2 & 0 & -6 & 0 \end{array}$$

length $= (x^3 + 2x^2 - 6)$ miles

63. The LCD is $3x$.
$$\frac{3}{x} + \frac{1}{3} = \frac{5}{x}$$
$$3x\left(\frac{3}{x} + \frac{1}{3}\right) = 3x\left(\frac{5}{x}\right)$$
$$3x\left(\frac{3}{x}\right) + 3x\left(\frac{1}{3}\right) = 3x\left(\frac{5}{x}\right)$$
$$9 + x = 15$$
$$x = 6$$
The solution set is $\{6\}$.

64. The LCD is $2(5x - 9)$.
$$\frac{2x+3}{5x-9} = \frac{3}{2}$$
$$2(5x-9) \cdot \frac{2x+3}{5x-9} = 2(5x-9) \cdot \frac{3}{2}$$
$$2(2x+3) = (5x-9) \cdot 3$$
$$4x + 6 = 15x - 27$$
$$6 = 11x - 27$$
$$33 = 11x$$
$$3 = x$$
The solution set is $\{3\}$.

65. The LCD is $(x-2)(x+2)$.

$$\frac{1}{x-2} - \frac{3x}{x^2-4} = \frac{2}{x+2}$$

$$(x-2)(x+2)\left(\frac{1}{x-2} - \frac{3x}{x^2-4}\right) = (x-2)(x+2)\left(\frac{2}{x+2}\right)$$

$$(x-2)(x+2)\cdot\frac{1}{x-2} - (x-2)(x+2)\cdot\frac{3x}{(x+2)(x-2)} = (x-2)(x+2)\cdot\frac{2}{x+2}$$

$$(x+2) - 3x = 2(x-2)$$
$$-2x+2 = 2x-4$$
$$-4x+2 = -4$$
$$-4x = -6$$
$$x = \frac{-6}{-4} = \frac{3}{2}$$

The solution set is $\left\{\dfrac{3}{2}\right\}$.

66. The LCD is $7x$.

$$\frac{7}{x} - \frac{x}{7} = 0$$

$$7x\left(\frac{7}{x} - \frac{x}{7}\right) = 7x(0)$$

$$7x\left(\frac{7}{x}\right) - 7x\left(\frac{x}{7}\right) = 0$$

$$49 - x^2 = 0$$

$$(7-x)(7+x) = 0$$

$$7-x = 0 \quad \text{or} \quad 7+x = 0$$
$$7 = x \quad \text{or} \quad x = -7$$

The solution set is $\{-7, 7\}$.

67.
$$\frac{5}{x^2-7x} + \frac{4}{2x-14}$$

$$= \frac{5}{x(x-7)} + \frac{4}{2(x-7)}$$

$$= \frac{5}{x(x-7)} \cdot \frac{2}{2} + \frac{4}{2(x-7)} \cdot \frac{x}{x}$$

$$= \frac{10}{2x(x-7)} + \frac{4x}{2x(x-7)}$$

$$= \frac{10+4x}{2x(x-7)}$$

$$= \frac{2(5+2x)}{2x(x-7)}$$

$$= \frac{5+2x}{x(x-7)}$$

68. The LCD is x^2.

$$3 - \frac{5}{x} - \frac{2}{x^2} = 0$$

$$x^2\left(3 - \frac{5}{x} - \frac{2}{x^2}\right) = x^2(0)$$

$$x^2 \cdot 3 - x^2\left(\frac{5}{x}\right) - x^2\left(\frac{2}{x^2}\right) = 0$$

$$3x^2 - 5x - 2 = 0$$

$$(3x+1)(x-2) = 0$$

$$3x+1 = 0 \quad \text{or} \quad x-2 = 0$$

$$3x = -1 \quad \text{or} \quad x = 2$$

$$x = -\frac{1}{3} \quad \text{or} \quad x = 2$$

The solution set is $\left\{-\frac{1}{3}, 2\right\}$.

69. $\dfrac{4}{3-x} - \dfrac{7}{2x-6} + \dfrac{5}{x}$

$$= \frac{-4}{x-3} - \frac{7}{2(x-3)} + \frac{5}{x}$$

$$= \frac{-4}{x-3} \cdot \frac{2x}{2x} - \frac{7}{2(x-3)} \cdot \frac{x}{x} + \frac{5}{x} \cdot \frac{2(x-3)}{2(x-3)}$$

$$= \frac{-8x}{2x(x-3)} - \frac{7x}{2x(x-3)} + \frac{10x-30}{2x(x-3)}$$

$$= \frac{-8x - 7x + 10x - 30}{2x(x-3)}$$

$$= \frac{-5x - 30}{2x(x-3)}$$

$$= \frac{-5(x+6)}{2x(x-3)}$$

70. $A = \dfrac{h(a+b)}{2}$

$$2A = h(a+b)$$

$$\frac{2A}{h} = a + b$$

$$a = \frac{2A}{h} - b$$

71.

$$\frac{1}{R} = \frac{1}{R_1} + \frac{1}{R_2}$$

$$RR_1R_2\left(\frac{1}{R}\right) = RR_1R_2\left(\frac{1}{R_1}\right) + RR_1R_2\left(\frac{1}{R_2}\right)$$

$$R_1R_2 = RR_2 + RR_1$$

$$R_1R_2 - RR_2 = RR_1$$

$$R_2(R_1 - R) = RR_1$$

$$R_2 = \frac{RR_1}{R_1 - R}$$

72. $I = \dfrac{E}{R+r}$

$$I(R+r) = E$$

$$R + r = \frac{E}{I}$$

$$R = \frac{E}{I} - r$$

73. $A = P + Prt$

$$A - P = Prt$$

$$\frac{A-P}{Pt} = r \text{ or } r = \frac{A-P}{Pt}$$

74. $H = \dfrac{kA(T_1 - T_2)}{L}$

$$HL = kA(T_1 - T_2)$$

$$\frac{HL}{k(T_1 - T_2)} = A \text{ or } A = \frac{HL}{k(T_1 - T_2)}$$

75. Let $x =$ the number.

$$x + 2\left(\frac{1}{x}\right) = 3$$

$$x\left[x + 2\left(\frac{1}{x}\right)\right] = x \cdot 3$$

$$x^2 + 2 = 3x$$

$$x^2 - 3x + 2 = 0$$

$$(x-1)(x-2) = 0$$

$$x - 1 = 0 \quad \text{or} \quad x - 2 = 0$$

$$x = 1 \quad \text{or} \quad x = 2$$

The numbers are 1 and 2.

76. Let x = the number.

$$\frac{3+x}{7+2x} = \frac{10}{21}$$
$$21(3+x) = 10(7+2x)$$
$$63+21x = 70+20x$$
$$63+1x = 70$$
$$x = 7$$

The number is 7.

77. Let x = amount of time required for all three boys to paint the fence together.

$$\frac{1}{4}+\frac{1}{5}+\frac{1}{6} = \frac{1}{x}$$
$$60x\cdot\frac{1}{4}+60x\cdot\frac{1}{5}+60x\cdot\frac{1}{6} = 60x\cdot\frac{1}{x}$$
$$15x+12x+10x = 60$$
$$37x = 60$$
$$x = \frac{60}{37} = 1\frac{23}{37}$$

It will take $1\frac{23}{37}$ hours for all three boys to paint the fence together.

78. Let x = amount of time it takes Tom to type the mailing labels when working alone.

$$\frac{1}{6}+\frac{1}{x} = \frac{1}{4}$$
$$12x\cdot\frac{1}{6}+12x\cdot\frac{1}{x} = 12x\cdot\frac{1}{4}$$
$$2x+12 = 3x$$
$$12 = x$$

It takes Tom 12 hours to complete the task alone.

79. Let x = the speed of the current.

	distance	=	rate	·	time
Upstream	72		$32-x$		$\frac{72}{32-x}$
Downstream	120		$32+x$		$\frac{120}{32+x}$

$$\frac{72}{32-x} = \frac{120}{32+x}$$
$$72(32+x) = 120(32-x)$$
$$2304+72x = 3840-120x$$
$$72x = 1536-120x$$
$$192x = 1536$$
$$x = 8$$

The speed of the current is 8 mph.

80. Let x = the speed of the walker.

	distance	=	rate	·	time
Jogger	14		$x+3$		$\frac{14}{x+3}$
Walker	8		x		$\frac{8}{x}$

$$\frac{14}{x+3} = \frac{8}{x}$$
$$14x = 8(x+3)$$
$$14x = 8x+24$$
$$6x = 24$$
$$x = 4$$

The speed of the walker is 4 mph.

81. $A = kB$

$$6 = k(14)$$
$$k = \frac{6}{14} = \frac{3}{7}$$
$$A = \frac{3}{7}B = \frac{3}{7}(21) = 9$$

82. $$P = \frac{K}{V}$$
$$1250 = \frac{K}{2}$$
$$K = 2500$$
$$P = \frac{2500}{V}$$
$$800 = \frac{2500}{V}$$
$$800V = 2500$$
$$V = 3.125$$

When the pressure is 800 kilopascals, the volume is 3.125 cubic meters.

83. $$\frac{22x+8}{11x+4} = \frac{2(11x+4)}{11x+4} = 2$$

84. $$\frac{xy-3x+2y-6}{x^2+4x+4} = \frac{x(y-3)+2(y-3)}{(x+2)(x+2)}$$
$$= \frac{(x+2)(y-3)}{(x+2)(x+2)}$$
$$= \frac{y-3}{x+2}$$

85. $\dfrac{2}{5x} \div \dfrac{4-18x}{6-27x} = \dfrac{2}{5x} \cdot \dfrac{6-27x}{4-18x}$

$\qquad = \dfrac{2}{5x} \cdot \dfrac{3(2-9x)}{2(2-9x)}$

$\qquad = \dfrac{3}{5x}$

86. $\dfrac{7x+28}{2x+4} \div \dfrac{x^2+2x-8}{x^2-2x-8}$

$\qquad = \dfrac{7x+28}{2x+4} \cdot \dfrac{x^2-2x-8}{x^2+2x-8}$

$\qquad = \dfrac{7(x+4)}{2(x+2)} \cdot \dfrac{(x-4)(x+2)}{(x+4)(x-2)}$

$\qquad = \dfrac{7(x-4)}{2(x-2)}$

87. $\dfrac{5a^2-20}{a^3+2a^2+a+2} \div \dfrac{7a}{a^3+a}$

$\qquad = \dfrac{5a^2-20}{a^3+2a^2+a+2} \cdot \dfrac{a^3+a}{7a}$

$\qquad = \dfrac{5(a^2-4)}{a^2(a+2)+1(a+2)} \cdot \dfrac{a(a^2+1)}{7a}$

$\qquad = \dfrac{5(a+2)(a-2)}{(a+2)(a^2+1)} \cdot \dfrac{a(a^2+1)}{7a}$

$\qquad = \dfrac{5(a-2)}{7}$

88. $\dfrac{4a+8}{5a^2-20} \cdot \dfrac{3a^2-6a}{a+3} \div \dfrac{2a^2}{5a+15}$

$\qquad = \dfrac{4a+8}{5a^2-20} \cdot \dfrac{3a^2-6a}{a+3} \cdot \dfrac{5a+15}{2a^2}$

$\qquad = \dfrac{4(a+2)}{5(a^2-4)} \cdot \dfrac{3a(a-2)}{a+3} \cdot \dfrac{5(a+3)}{2a^2}$

$\qquad = \dfrac{4(a+2)}{5(a-2)(a+2)} \cdot \dfrac{3a(a-2)}{a+3} \cdot \dfrac{5(a+3)}{2a^2}$

$\qquad = \dfrac{6}{a}$

89. $\dfrac{7}{2x} + \dfrac{5}{6x} = \dfrac{7}{2x} \cdot \dfrac{3}{3} + \dfrac{5}{6x}$

$\qquad = \dfrac{21}{6x} + \dfrac{5}{6x}$

$\qquad = \dfrac{21+5}{6x}$

$\qquad = \dfrac{26}{6x}$

$\qquad = \dfrac{13}{3x}$

90. $\dfrac{x-2}{x+1} - \dfrac{x-3}{x-1} = \dfrac{x-2}{x+1} \cdot \dfrac{x-1}{x-1} - \dfrac{x-3}{x-1} \cdot \dfrac{x+1}{x+1}$

$\qquad = \dfrac{(x-2)(x-1)}{(x+1)(x-1)} - \dfrac{(x-3)(x+1)}{(x+1)(x-1)}$

$\qquad = \dfrac{x^2-3x+2}{(x+1)(x-1)} - \dfrac{x^2-2x-3}{(x+1)(x-1)}$

$\qquad = \dfrac{x^2-3x+2-x^2+2x+3}{(x+1)(x-1)}$

$\qquad = \dfrac{-x+5}{(x+1)(x-1)}$

91. $\dfrac{2x+1}{x^2+x-6} + \dfrac{2-x}{x^2+x-6} = \dfrac{2x+1+2-x}{x^2+x-6}$

$\qquad = \dfrac{x+3}{x^2+x-6}$

$\qquad = \dfrac{x+3}{(x+3)(x-2)}$

$\qquad = \dfrac{1}{x-2}$

92.
$$\frac{2}{x^2-16} - \frac{3x}{x^2+8x+16} + \frac{3}{x+4} = \frac{2}{(x+4)(x-4)} - \frac{3x}{(x+4)^2} + \frac{3}{x+4}$$

$$= \frac{2}{(x+4)(x-4)} \cdot \frac{x+4}{x+4} - \frac{3x}{(x+4)^2} \cdot \frac{x-4}{x-4} + \frac{3}{x+4} \cdot \frac{(x+4)(x-4)}{(x+4)(x-4)}$$

$$= \frac{2x+8}{(x+4)^2(x-4)} - \frac{3x^2-12x}{(x+4)^2(x-4)} + \frac{3x^2-48}{(x+4)^2(x-4)}$$

$$= \frac{2x+8-3x^2+12x+3x^2-48}{(x+4)^2(x-4)}$$

$$= \frac{14x-40}{(x+4)^2(x-4)}$$

$$= \frac{2(7x-20)}{(x+4)^2(x-4)}$$

93.
$$\frac{\frac{1}{x}-\frac{2}{3x}}{\frac{5}{2x}-\frac{1}{3}} = \frac{6x\left(\frac{1}{x}-\frac{2}{3x}\right)}{6x\left(\frac{5}{2x}-\frac{1}{3}\right)} = \frac{6-4}{15-2x} = \frac{2}{15-2x}$$

94.
$$\frac{2}{1-\frac{2}{x}} = \frac{x(2)}{x\left(1-\frac{2}{x}\right)} = \frac{2x}{x-2}$$

95.
$$\frac{\frac{x^2+5x-6}{4x+3}}{\frac{(x+6)^2}{8x+6}} = \frac{x^2+5x-6}{4x+3} \div \frac{(x+6)^2}{8x+6}$$

$$= \frac{x^2+5x-6}{4x+3} \cdot \frac{8x+6}{(x+6)^2}$$

$$= \frac{(x+6)(x-1)}{4x+3} \cdot \frac{2(4x+3)}{(x+6)^2}$$

$$= \frac{2(x-1)}{x+6}$$

96.
$$\frac{\frac{3}{x-1}-\frac{2}{1-x}}{\frac{2}{x-1}-\frac{2}{x}} = \frac{\frac{3}{x-1}-\frac{-2}{x-1}}{\frac{2}{x-1}-\frac{2}{x}}$$

$$= \frac{(x)(x-1)\left(\frac{3}{x-1}-\frac{-2}{x-1}\right)}{(x)(x-1)\left(\frac{2}{x-1}-\frac{2}{x}\right)}$$

$$= \frac{3x+2x}{2x-2(x-1)}$$

$$= \frac{5x}{2x-2x+2}$$

$$= \frac{5x}{2}$$

97. $4 + \dfrac{8}{x} = 8$

The LCD is x.

$$x(4) + x\left(\dfrac{8}{x}\right) = x(8)$$
$$4x + 8 = 8x$$
$$8 = 4x$$
$$x = 2$$

The solution set is $\{2\}$.

98. $\dfrac{x-2}{x^2 - 7x + 10} = \dfrac{1}{5x - 10} - \dfrac{1}{x - 5}$

$$\dfrac{x-2}{(x-2)(x-5)} = \dfrac{1}{5(x-2)} - \dfrac{1}{x-5}$$

The LCD is $5(x-2)(x-5)$.

$$5(x-2)(x-5) \cdot \dfrac{x-2}{(x-2)(x-5)} = 5(x-2)(x-5) \cdot \dfrac{1}{5(x-2)} - 5(x-2)(x-5) \cdot \dfrac{1}{x-5}$$
$$5(x-2) = (x-5) - 5(x-2)$$
$$5x - 10 = x - 5 - 5x + 10$$
$$5x - 10 = -4x + 5$$
$$9x - 10 = 5$$
$$9x = 15$$
$$x = \dfrac{15}{9} = \dfrac{5}{3}$$

The solution set is $\left\{\dfrac{5}{3}\right\}$.

99. Let x be the numerator of a fraction. Then $x + 2$ is the denominator.

$$\dfrac{x-3}{x+2+5} = \dfrac{2}{3}$$
$$\dfrac{x-3}{x+7} = \dfrac{2}{3}$$
$$3(x-3) = 2(x+7)$$
$$3x - 9 = 2x + 14$$
$$x - 9 = 14$$
$$x = 23$$
$$x + 2 = 23 + 2 = 25$$

The fraction is $\dfrac{23}{25}$.

100. Let x be the first even integer and $x + 2$ be the next consecutive even integer.

$$\frac{1}{x} + \frac{1}{x+2} = -\frac{9}{40}$$

$$40x(x+2) \cdot \frac{1}{x} + 40x(x+2) \cdot \frac{1}{x+2} = 40x(x+2) \cdot \frac{-9}{40}$$

$$40(x+2) + 40x = -9x(x+2)$$

$$40x + 80 + 40x = -9x^2 - 18x$$

$$80x + 80 = -9x^2 - 18x$$

$$9x^2 + 98x + 80 = 0$$

$$(9x+8)(x+10) = 0$$

$$9x + 8 = 0 \quad \text{or} \quad x + 10 = 0$$

$$9x = -8 \quad \text{or} \quad x = -10$$

$$x = -\frac{8}{9} \quad \text{or} \quad x = -10$$

$-\dfrac{8}{9}$ is not an integer.

$x + 2 = -10 + 2 = -8$

The two integers are -10 and -8.

101. Let $x =$ time it takes to empty a full tank if both pipes are open.

$$-\frac{1}{2.5} + \frac{1}{2} = \frac{1}{x}$$

$$(2.5)(2x) \cdot -\frac{1}{2.5} + (2.5)(2x) \cdot \frac{1}{2} = (2.5)(2x) \cdot \frac{1}{x}$$

$$-2x + 2.5x = 5$$

$$0.5x = 5$$

$$x = 10$$

It takes 10 hours to empty a full tank if both pipes are open.

102. Let $x =$ the speed of the car and
$x + 430 =$ the speed of the jet.

	distance =	rate	· time
Car	210	x	$\frac{210}{x}$
Jet	1715	$x + 430$	$\frac{1715}{x+430}$

$$\frac{210}{x} = \frac{1715}{x+430}$$

$$210(x+430) = 1715x$$

$$210x + 90,300 = 1715x$$

$$90,300 = 1505x$$

$$60 = x$$

$x + 430 = 60 + 430 = 490$

The speed of the jet is 490 mph.

103. One train traveled 382 miles in 6 hours and the second train traveled $382 - 112 = 270$ miles in 6 hours.

Recall $D = rt$ or $r = \dfrac{D}{t}$.

$r = \dfrac{382}{6} = 63\dfrac{2}{3}$ $r = \dfrac{270}{6} = 45$

The speeds of the trains are $63\dfrac{2}{3}$ mph and 45 mph.

104. $C = \dfrac{k}{D}$

$12 = \dfrac{k}{8}$

$96 = k$

$C = \dfrac{96}{D} = \dfrac{96}{24} = 4$

105. $A = kr^2$

$36\pi = k(3)^2$

$36\pi = 9k$

$k = 4\pi$

$A = 4\pi r^2$

$A = 4\pi(4)^2 = 4\pi \cdot 16 = 64\pi$

The surface area is 64π square inches.

106.
$$
\begin{array}{r}
3x^3 + 13x^2 + 51x + 204 \\
x-4\overline{\smash{)}\,3x^4 + x^3 - x^2 + 0x - 2} \\
\underline{3x^4 - 12x^3} \\
13x^3 - x^2 \\
\underline{13x^3 - 52x^2} \\
51x^2 + 0x \\
\underline{51x^2 - 204x} \\
204x - 2 \\
\underline{204x - 816} \\
814
\end{array}
$$

$3x^3 + 13x^2 + 51x + 204 + \dfrac{814}{x-4}$

Chapter 6 Test

1. $1 - x = 0$

$1 = x$

The domain of $f(x) = \dfrac{5x^2}{1-x}$ is

$\{x | x \text{ is a real number and } x \neq 1\}$.

2. $x^2 + 4x + 3 = 0$

$(x+3)(x+1) = 0$

$x + 3 = 0$ or $x + 1 = 0$

$\quad x = -3$ or $\qquad x = -1$

The domain of $g(x) = \dfrac{9x^2 - 9}{x^2 + 4x + 3}$ is

$\{x | x \text{ is a real number and } x \neq -3, x \neq -1\}$.

3. $\dfrac{7x - 21}{24 - 8x} = \dfrac{7(x-3)}{8(3-x)} = \dfrac{7(x-3)}{-8(x-3)} = -\dfrac{7}{8}$

4. $\dfrac{x^2 - 4x}{x^2 + 5x - 36} = \dfrac{x(x-4)}{(x+9)(x-4)} = \dfrac{x}{x+9}$

5. $\dfrac{x^3 - 8}{x-2} = \dfrac{x^3 - 2^3}{x-2}$

$\qquad = \dfrac{(x-2)(x^2 + 2x + 4)}{x-2}$

$\qquad = x^2 + 2x + 4$

6. $\dfrac{2x^3 + 16}{6x^2 + 12x} \cdot \dfrac{5}{x^2 - 2x + 4}$

$= \dfrac{2(x^3 + 8)}{6x(x+2)} \cdot \dfrac{5}{x^2 - 2x + 4}$

$= \dfrac{2(x+2)(x^2 - 2x + 4)}{6x(x+2)} \cdot \dfrac{5}{x^2 - 2x + 4}$

$= \dfrac{5}{3x}$

7. $\dfrac{5}{4x^3} + \dfrac{7}{4x^3} = \dfrac{5+7}{4x^3} = \dfrac{12}{4x^3} = \dfrac{3}{x^3}$

8. $\dfrac{3x^2 - 12}{x^2 + 2x - 8} \div \dfrac{6x + 18}{x+4}$

$= \dfrac{3x^2 - 12}{x^2 + 2x - 8} \cdot \dfrac{x+4}{6x + 18}$

$= \dfrac{3(x^2 - 4)}{(x+4)(x-2)} \cdot \dfrac{x+4}{6(x+3)}$

$= \dfrac{3(x+2)(x-2)}{(x+4)(x-2)} \cdot \dfrac{(x+4)}{6(x+3)}$

$= \dfrac{x+2}{2(x+3)}$

9. $\dfrac{4x-12}{2x-9} \div \dfrac{3-x}{4x^2-81} \cdot \dfrac{x+3}{5x+15} = \dfrac{4x-12}{2x-9} \cdot \dfrac{4x^2-81}{3-x} \cdot \dfrac{x+3}{5x+15}$

$$= \dfrac{4(x-3)}{2x-9} \cdot \dfrac{(2x+9)(2x-9)}{-(x-3)} \cdot \dfrac{x+3}{5(x+3)}$$

$$= \dfrac{4(2x+9)}{-5}$$

$$= -\dfrac{4(2x+9)}{5}$$

10. $\dfrac{3+2x}{10-x} + \dfrac{13+x}{x-10} = \dfrac{-(3+2x)}{x-10} + \dfrac{13+x}{x-10}$

$$= \dfrac{-3-2x+13+x}{x-10}$$

$$= \dfrac{-x+10}{x-10}$$

$$= -\dfrac{x-10}{x-10}$$

$$= -1$$

11. $\dfrac{2x^2+7}{2x^4-18x^2} - \dfrac{6x+7}{2x^4-18x^2} = \dfrac{2x^2+7-6x-7}{2x^4-18x^2}$

$$= \dfrac{2x^2-6x}{2x^4-18x^2}$$

$$= \dfrac{2x(x-3)}{2x^2(x^2-9)}$$

$$= \dfrac{2x(x-3)}{2x^2(x-3)(x+3)}$$

$$= \dfrac{1}{x(x+3)}$$

12. $\dfrac{3}{x^2-x-6} + \dfrac{2}{x^2-5x+6} = \dfrac{3}{(x-3)(x+2)} + \dfrac{2}{(x-3)(x-2)}$

$$= \dfrac{3}{(x-3)(x+2)} \cdot \dfrac{x-2}{x-2} + \dfrac{2}{(x-3)(x-2)} \cdot \dfrac{x+2}{x+2}$$

$$= \dfrac{3(x-2)}{(x-3)(x+2)(x-2)} + \dfrac{2(x+2)}{(x-3)(x+2)(x-2)}$$

$$= \dfrac{3x-6}{(x-3)(x+2)(x-2)} + \dfrac{2x+4}{(x-3)(x+2)(x-2)}$$

$$= \dfrac{3x-6+2x+4}{(x-3)(x+2)(x-2)}$$

$$= \dfrac{5x-2}{(x-3)(x+2)(x-2)}$$

13. $3x - 21 = 3(x - 7)$
$2x - 14 = 2(x - 7)$
The LCD is $3 \cdot 2(x - 7) = 6(x - 7)$.

$$\frac{5}{x-7} - \frac{2x}{3x-21} + \frac{x}{2x-14} = \frac{5}{x-7} \cdot \frac{6}{6} - \frac{2x}{3(x-7)} \cdot \frac{2}{2} + \frac{x}{2(x-7)} \cdot \frac{3}{3}$$

$$= \frac{30}{6(x-7)} - \frac{4x}{6(x-7)} + \frac{3x}{6(x-7)}$$

$$= \frac{30 - 4x + 3x}{6(x-7)}$$

$$= \frac{30 - x}{6(x-7)}$$

14.
$$\frac{3x}{5} \cdot \left(\frac{5}{x} - \frac{5}{2x} \right) = \frac{3x}{5} \cdot \left(\frac{5}{x} \cdot \frac{2}{2} - \frac{5}{2x} \right)$$

$$= \frac{3x}{5} \left(\frac{10}{2x} - \frac{5}{2x} \right)$$

$$= \frac{3x}{5} \left(\frac{10 - 5}{2x} \right)$$

$$= \frac{3x}{5} \left(\frac{5}{2x} \right)$$

$$= \frac{3}{2}$$

15.
$$\frac{\frac{5}{x} - \frac{7}{3x}}{\frac{9}{8x} - \frac{1}{x}} = \frac{24x\left(\frac{5}{x} - \frac{7}{3x} \right)}{24x\left(\frac{9}{8x} - \frac{1}{x} \right)} = \frac{120 - 56}{27 - 24} = \frac{64}{3}$$

16.
$$\frac{\frac{x^2-5x+6}{x+3}}{\frac{x^2-4x+4}{x^2-9}} = \frac{x^2 - 5x + 6}{x + 3} \div \frac{x^2 - 4x + 4}{x^2 - 9}$$

$$= \frac{x^2 - 5x + 6}{x + 3} \cdot \frac{x^2 - 9}{x^2 - 4x + 4}$$

$$= \frac{(x-3)(x-2)}{x+3} \cdot \frac{(x+3)(x-3)}{(x-2)(x-2)}$$

$$= \frac{(x-3)^2}{x-2}$$

17.
$$\frac{4x^2y + 9x + 3xz}{3xz} = \frac{4x^2y}{3xz} + \frac{9x}{3xz} + \frac{3xz}{3xz}$$

$$= \frac{4xy}{3z} + \frac{3}{z} + 1$$

18.

$$2x+1 \overline{)4x^3 + 0x^2 - 5x + 0} \quad \text{with quotient } 2x^2 - x - 2$$

$$\underline{4x^3 + 2x^2}$$
$$-2x^2 - 5x$$
$$\underline{-2x^2 - x}$$
$$-4x + 0$$
$$\underline{-4x - 2}$$
$$2$$

Answer: $2x^2 - x - 2 + \dfrac{2}{2x+1}$

19.

$$\begin{array}{r|rrrrr} -3 & 4 & -3 & 0 & -1 & -1 \\ & & -12 & 45 & -135 & 408 \\ \hline & 4 & -15 & 45 & -136 & 407 \end{array}$$

Answer: $4x^3 - 15x^2 + 45x - 136 + \dfrac{407}{x+3}$

20.

$$\begin{array}{r|rrrrr} -2 & 4 & 0 & 7 & -2 & -5 \\ & & -8 & 16 & -46 & 96 \\ \hline & 4 & -8 & 23 & -48 & 91 \end{array}$$

Thus, $P(-2) = 91$.

21. The LCD is $x - 4$.

$$\frac{x}{x-4} = 3 - \frac{4}{x-4}$$
$$(x-4)\frac{x}{x-4} = (x-4)\cdot 3 - (x-4)\cdot\frac{4}{x-4}$$
$$x = 3(x-4) - 4$$
$$x = 3x - 12 - 4$$
$$x = 3x - 16$$
$$-2x = -16$$
$$x = 8$$

The solution set is $\{8\}$.

22.

$$\frac{3}{x+2} - \frac{1}{5x} = \frac{2}{5x^2 + 10x}$$
$$\frac{3}{x+2} - \frac{1}{5x} = \frac{2}{5x(x+2)}$$
$$5x(x+2)\left(\frac{3}{x+2} - \frac{1}{5x}\right) = 5x(x+2)\cdot\frac{2}{5x(x+2)}$$
$$3(5x) - 1(x+2) = 2$$
$$15x - x - 2 = 2$$
$$14x = 4$$
$$x = \frac{4}{14} = \frac{2}{7}$$

The solution set is $\left\{\dfrac{2}{7}\right\}$.

23.

$$\frac{x^2 + 8}{x} - 1 = \frac{2(x+4)}{x}$$
$$x\left(\frac{x^2+8}{x} - 1\right) = x\left(\frac{2(x+4)}{x}\right)$$
$$(x^2 + 8) - x = 2(x+4)$$
$$x^2 - x + 8 = 2x + 8$$
$$x^2 - 3x = 0$$
$$x(x-3) = 0$$
$$x = 0 \ \text{ or } \ x - 3 = 0$$
$$x = 3$$

Discard the answer 0 as extraneous.
The solution set is $\{3\}$.

24.

$$\frac{x+b}{a} = \frac{4x - 7a}{b}$$
$$ab\left(\frac{x+b}{a}\right) = ab\left(\frac{4x-7a}{b}\right)$$
$$b(x+b) = a(4x - 7a)$$
$$xb + b^2 = 4ax - 7a^2$$
$$b^2 + 7a^2 = 4ax - xb$$
$$b^2 + 7a^2 = x(4a - b)$$
$$x = \frac{b^2 + 7a^2}{4a - b}$$

25. Let $x =$ the number.

$$(x+1)\cdot\frac{2}{x} = \frac{12}{5}$$
$$\frac{2(x+1)}{x} = \frac{12}{5}$$
$$\frac{2x+2}{x} = \frac{12}{5}$$
$$5(2x+2) = 12x$$
$$10x + 10 = 12x$$
$$10 = 2x$$
$$5 = x$$

The number is 5.

26. Let t = time to weed garden together.

Note that 1 hr and 30 min = $\dfrac{3}{2}$ hours.

$$\frac{1}{2}+\frac{1}{3}=\frac{1}{\frac{3}{2}}$$

$$\frac{1}{2}+\frac{2}{3}=\frac{1}{t}$$

$$6t\left(\frac{1}{2}+\frac{2}{3}\right)=6t\left(\frac{1}{t}\right)$$

$$3t+4t=6$$

$$7t=6$$

$$t=\frac{6}{7}$$

It takes them $\dfrac{6}{7}$ hour.

27. $W=\dfrac{k}{V}$

$$20=\frac{k}{12}$$

$$k=20(12)=240$$

$$W=\frac{240}{V}=\frac{240}{15}=16$$

28. $Q=kRS^2$

$$24=k(3)(4)^2$$

$$24=48k$$

$$k=\frac{24}{48}=\frac{1}{2}$$

$$Q=\frac{1}{2}RS^2=\frac{1}{2}(2)(3)^2=9$$

29. $S=k\sqrt{d}$

$$160=k\sqrt{400}$$

$$160=20k$$

$$k=\frac{160}{20}=8$$

$$S=8\sqrt{d}$$

$$128=8\sqrt{d}$$

$$\sqrt{d}=\frac{128}{8}$$

$$\sqrt{d}=16$$

$$d=256$$

The height of the cliff is 256 feet.

Chapter 6 Cumulative Review

1. a. $8x$

  b. $8x+3$

  c. $x\div(-7)$ or $\dfrac{x}{-7}$

  d. $2x-1\dfrac{6}{10}=2x-1.6$

  e. $x-6$

  f. $2(4+x)$

2. a. $x-\dfrac{1}{3}$

  b. $5x-6$

  c. $8x+3$

  d. $\dfrac{7}{2-x}$

3. $\dfrac{y}{3}-\dfrac{y}{4}=\dfrac{1}{6}$

$$12\left(\frac{y}{3}-\frac{y}{4}\right)=12\left(\frac{1}{6}\right)$$

$$4y-3y=2$$

$$y=2$$

4. $\dfrac{x}{7}+\dfrac{x}{5}=\dfrac{12}{5}$

$$35\left(\frac{x}{7}+\frac{x}{5}\right)=35\left(\frac{12}{5}\right)$$

$$5x+7x=84$$

$$12x=84$$

$$x=7$$

5. $$c<200$$
$$-9.2t+527.33<200$$
$$-9.2t<-327.33$$
$$t>35.58\approx 36$$
$$1990+36=2026$$

The consumption of cigarettes will be less than 200 billion per year in 2026 and after.

6. Let x = score on final exam.

$$\frac{78+65+82+79+2x}{6} \geq 78$$

$$\frac{304+2x}{6} \geq 78$$

$$6\left(\frac{304+2x}{6}\right) \geq 6(78)$$

$$304+2x \geq 468$$

$$2x \geq 164$$

$$x \geq 82$$

The minimum score she can make on her final is 82.

7. $\left|\dfrac{3x+1}{2}\right| = -2$ is impossible. The solution set is $\varnothing$.

8. $\left|\dfrac{2x-1}{3}\right| + 6 = 3$

$\left|\dfrac{2x-1}{3}\right| = -3$, which is impossible.

The solution set is $\varnothing$.

9. $\left|\dfrac{2(x+1)}{3}\right| \leq 0$

$$\frac{2(x+1)}{3} = 0$$

$$2(x+1) = 0$$

$$2x+2 = 0$$

$$2x = -2$$

$$x = -1$$

The solution is -1.

10. $\left|\dfrac{3(x-1)}{4}\right| \geq 2$

$$\frac{3(x-1)}{4} \leq -2 \quad \text{or} \quad \frac{3(x-1)}{4} \geq 2$$

$$\frac{3x-3}{4} \leq -2 \quad \text{or} \quad \frac{3x-3}{4} \geq 2$$

$$3x-3 \leq -8 \quad \text{or} \quad 3x-3 \geq 8$$

$$3x \leq -5 \quad \text{or} \quad 3x \geq 11$$

$$x \leq -\frac{5}{3} \quad \text{or} \quad x \geq \frac{11}{3}$$

$$\left(-\infty, -\frac{5}{3}\right] \cup \left[\frac{11}{3}, \infty\right)$$

11. $y = -2x+3$

12. $y = -x+3$

13. a. Function

b. Not a function

c. Function

14. $f(x) = -x^2 + 3x - 2$

a. $f(0) = -(0)^2 + 3(0) - 2 = -2$

b. $f(-3) = -(-3)^2 + 3(-3) - 2$
$$= -9 - 9 - 2$$
$$= -20$$

c. $f\left(\dfrac{1}{3}\right) = -\left(\dfrac{1}{3}\right)^2 + 3\left(\dfrac{1}{3}\right) - 2$

$$= -\frac{1}{9} + 1 - 2$$

$$= -\frac{1}{9} + \frac{9}{9} - \frac{18}{9}$$

$$= \frac{-1+9-18}{9}$$

$$= -\frac{10}{9}$$

15. $x - 3y = 6$
Let $y = 0$.
$x - 3(0) = 6$
$x = 6$
Plot (6, 0).
Let $x = 0$.
$0 - 3y = 6$
$-3y = 6$
$y = -2$
Plot (0, –2).

16. $3x - y = 6$
Let $y = 0$.
$3x - 0 = 6$
$3x = 6$
$x = 2$
Plot (2, 0).
Let $x = 0$.
$3(0) - y = 6$
$-y = 6$
$y = -6$
Plot (0, –6).

17. $y - (-5) = -3(x - 1)$
$y + 5 = -3x + 3$
$y = -3x - 2$

18. $y - 3 = \dfrac{1}{2}\big(x - (-1)\big)$
$y - 3 = \dfrac{1}{2}(x + 1)$
$y - 3 = \dfrac{1}{2}x + \dfrac{1}{2}$
$y = \dfrac{1}{2}x + \dfrac{1}{2} + 3$
$y = \dfrac{1}{2}x + \dfrac{7}{2}$
$f(x) = \dfrac{1}{2}x + \dfrac{7}{2}$

19. $x \geq 1$ and $y \geq 2x - 1$

The solution region is the overlap, which has darker shading, along with its boundary.

20. $2x + y \leq 4$ or $y > 2$

The solution region consists of all shaded regions and the boundary where the boundary line is solid.

21. $\begin{cases} 3x - 2y = 10 & (1) \\ 4x - 3y = 15 & (2) \end{cases}$
Multiply E1 by –4 and E2 by 3, and add.
$-12x + 8y = -40$
$\underline{12x - 9y = 45}$
$-y = 5$
$y = -5$
Replace y with –5 in E1.

$3x - 2(-5) = 10$

$3x + 10 = 10$

$3x = 0$

$x = 0$

The solution is $(0, -5)$.

22. $\begin{cases} -2x + 3y = 6 & (1) \\ 3x - y = 5 & (2) \end{cases}$

Solve E2 for y:

$y = 3x - 5$

Replace y with $3x - 5$ in E1.

$-2x + 3(3x - 5) = 6$

$-2x + 9x - 15 = 6$

$7x = 21$

$x = 3$

Replace x with 3 in the equation $y = 3x - 5$.

$y = 3(3) - 5 = 9 - 5 = 4$

The solution is $(3, 4)$.

23. $\begin{cases} 2x - 4y + 8z = 2 & (1) \\ -x - 3y + z = 11 & (2) \\ x - 2y + 4z = 0 & (3) \end{cases}$

Add E2 and E3.

$-5y + 5z = 11$ (4)

Multiply E2 by 2 and add to E1.

$-2x - 6y + 2z = 22$

$\underline{2x - 4y + 8z = 2}$

$-10y + 10z = 24$ (5)

Solve the new system.

$\begin{cases} -5y + 5z = 11 & (4) \\ -10y + 10z = 24 & (5) \end{cases}$

Multiply E4 by -2 and add to E5.

$10y - 10z = -22$

$\underline{-10y + 10z = 24}$

$0 = 2$, which is impossible.

The solution is $\varnothing$.

24. $\begin{cases} 2x - 2y + 4z = 6 & (1) \\ -4x - y + z = -8 & (2) \\ 3x - y + z = 6 & (3) \end{cases}$

Multiply E2 by -1 and add to E3.

$4x + y - z = 8$

$\underline{3x - y + z = 6}$

$7x = 14$

$x = 2$

Multiply E2 by -2 and add to E1.

$8x + 2y - 2z = 16$

$\underline{2x - 2y + 4z = 6}$

$10x + 2z = 22$ or $5x + z = 11$

Replace x with 2 in the equation $5x + z = 11$.

$5(2) + z = 11$

$10 + z = 11$

$z = 1$

Replace x with 2 and z with 1 in E3.

$3(2) - y + 1 = 6$

$7 - y = 6$

$-y = -1$

$y = 1$

The solution is $(2, 1, 1)$.

25. Let x = measure of the smallest angle,

y = measure of the largest angle and,

z = measure of the remaining angle.

$\begin{cases} x + y + z = 180 & (1) \\ y = x + 80 & (2) \\ z = x + 10 & (3) \end{cases}$

Substitute $x + 80$ for y and $x + 10$ for z in E1.

$x + (x + 80) + (x + 10) = 180$

$3x + 90 = 180$

$3x = 90$

$x = 30$

Replace x with 30 in E2 and E3.

$y = 30 + 80 = 110$

$z = 30 + 10 = 40$

The angles measure $30°$, $110°$, and $40°$.

26. Let x = the price of a ream of paper and

y = the price of a box of manila folders.

$\begin{cases} 3x + 2y = 21.90 & (1) \\ 5x + y = 24.25 & (2) \end{cases}$

Multiply E2 by -2 and add to E1.

$-10x - 2y = -48.50$

$\underline{3x + 2y = 21.90}$

$-7x = -26.60$

$x = 3.80$

Replace x with 3.80 in E2.

$5(3.80) + y = 24.25$

$19 + y = 24.25$

$y = 5.25$

A ream of paper cost \$3.80 and a box of manila folders cost \$5.25.

27. $\begin{cases} x + 2y + z = 2 \\ -2x - y + 2z = 5 \\ x + 3y - 2z = -8 \end{cases}$

$\begin{bmatrix} 1 & 2 & 1 & | & 2 \\ -2 & -1 & 2 & | & 5 \\ 1 & 3 & -2 & | & -8 \end{bmatrix}$

Multiply R1 by 2 and add to R2.

Multiply R1 by -1 and add to R3.

$$\begin{bmatrix} 1 & 2 & 1 & | & 2 \\ 0 & 3 & 4 & | & 9 \\ 0 & 1 & -3 & | & -10 \end{bmatrix}$$

Interchange R2 and R3.

$$\begin{bmatrix} 1 & 2 & 1 & | & 2 \\ 0 & 1 & -3 & | & -10 \\ 0 & 3 & 4 & | & 9 \end{bmatrix}$$

Multiply R2 by -3 and add to R3.

$$\begin{bmatrix} 1 & 2 & 1 & | & 2 \\ 0 & 1 & -3 & | & -10 \\ 0 & 0 & 13 & | & 39 \end{bmatrix}$$

Divide R3 by 13.

$$\begin{bmatrix} 1 & 2 & 1 & | & 2 \\ 0 & 1 & -3 & | & -10 \\ 0 & 0 & 1 & | & 3 \end{bmatrix}$$

This corresponds to $\begin{cases} x+2y+ z = 2 \\ \quad\ y-3z = -10 \\ \qquad\quad z = 3. \end{cases}$

$\begin{aligned} y-3z &= -10 \quad \text{and so} \quad x+2(-1)+(3) = 2 \\ y-3(3) &= -10 \qquad\qquad\quad x-2+3 = 2 \\ y-9 &= -10 \qquad\qquad\qquad\ x+1 = 2 \\ y &= -1 \qquad\qquad\qquad\qquad x = 1 \end{aligned}$

The solution is $(1, -1, 3)$.

28. $\begin{cases} x+ y+ z = 9 \\ 2x-2y+3z = 2 \\ -3x+ y- z = 1 \end{cases}$

$$\begin{bmatrix} 1 & 1 & 1 & | & 9 \\ 2 & -2 & 3 & | & 2 \\ -3 & 1 & -1 & | & 1 \end{bmatrix}$$

Multiply R1 by -2 and add to R2.
Multiply R1 by 3 and add to R3.

$$\begin{bmatrix} 1 & 1 & 1 & | & 9 \\ 0 & -4 & 1 & | & -16 \\ 0 & 4 & 2 & | & 28 \end{bmatrix}$$

Divide R2 by -4.

$$\begin{bmatrix} 1 & 1 & 1 & | & 9 \\ 0 & 1 & -\frac{1}{4} & | & 4 \\ 0 & 4 & 2 & | & 28 \end{bmatrix}$$

Multiply R2 by -4 and add to R3.

$$\begin{bmatrix} 1 & 1 & 1 & | & 9 \\ 0 & 1 & -\frac{1}{4} & | & 4 \\ 0 & 0 & 3 & | & 12 \end{bmatrix}$$

Divide R3 by 3.

$$\begin{bmatrix} 1 & 1 & 1 & | & 9 \\ 0 & 1 & -\frac{1}{4} & | & 4 \\ 0 & 0 & 1 & | & 4 \end{bmatrix}$$

This corresponds to $\begin{cases} x+ y+ z = 9 \\ \quad\ y-\frac{1}{4}z = 4 \\ \qquad\qquad z = 4 \end{cases}$

$\begin{aligned} y-\frac{1}{4}(4) &= 4 & x+5+4 &= 9 \\ y-1 &= 4 \ \text{ and so } & x+9 &= 9 \\ y &= 5 & x &= 0 \end{aligned}$

The solution is $(0, 5, 4)$.

29. a. $7^0 = 1$

b. $-7^0 = -1 \cdot 7^0 = -1 \cdot 1 = -1$

c. $(2x+5)^0 = 1$

d. $2x^0 = 2 \cdot x^0 = 2 \cdot 1 = 2$

30. a. $\begin{aligned} 2^{-2}+3^{-1} &= \frac{1}{2^2}+\frac{1}{3} \\ &= \frac{1}{4}+\frac{1}{3} \\ &= \frac{3}{12}+\frac{4}{12} \\ &= \frac{7}{12} \end{aligned}$

b. $-6a^0 = -6 \cdot a^0 = -6 \cdot 1 = -6$

c. $\dfrac{x^{-5}}{x^{-2}} = x^{-5-(-2)} = x^{-3} = \dfrac{1}{x^3}$

31. a. $\begin{aligned} x^{-b}(2x^b)^2 &= \frac{2^2(x^b)^2}{x^b} \\ &= \frac{4x^{2b}}{x^b} \\ &= 4x^{2b-b} \\ &= 4x^b \end{aligned}$

b. $\dfrac{(y^{3a})^2}{y^{a-6}} = \dfrac{y^{6a}}{y^{a-6}} = y^{6a-(a-6)} = y^{5a+6}$

32. a. $\begin{aligned} 3x^{4a}(4x^{-a})^2 &= 3x^{4a} \cdot 16x^{-2a} \\ &= 48x^{4a+(-2a)} \\ &= 48x^{2a} \end{aligned}$

b. $\dfrac{(y^{4b})^3}{y^{2b-3}} = \dfrac{y^{12b}}{y^{2b-3}}$

$= y^{12b-(2b-3)}$

$= y^{12b-2b+3}$

$= y^{10b+3}$

33. a. $3x^2$ has degree $= 2$.

   b. $-2^3 x^5 = -8x^5$ has degree $= 5$.

   c. y has degree $= 1$.

   d. $12x^2 yz^3$ has degree $= 2 + 1 + 3 = 6$.

   e. 5 has degree $= 0$.

34. $(2x^2 + 8x - 3) - (2x - 7)$

$= 2x^2 + 8x - 3 - 2x + 7$

$= 2x^2 + 6x + 4$

35. $[3 + (2a + b)]^2$

$= 3^2 + 2(3)(2a + b) + (2a + b)^2$

$= 9 + 6(2a + b) + (4a^2 + 2(2a)b + b^2)$

$= 9 + 12a + 6b + 4a^2 + 4ab + b^2$

36. $[4 + (3x - y)]^2$

$= 4^2 + 2(4)(3x - y) + (3x - y)^2$

$= 16 + 8(3x - y) + (9x^2 - 2(3x)y + y^2)$

$= 16 + 24x - 8y + 9x^2 - 6xy + y^2$

37. $ab - 6a + 2b - 12 = a(b - 6) + 2(b - 6)$

$= (b - 6)(a + 2)$

38. $xy + 2x - 5y - 10 = x(y + 2) - 5(y + 2)$

$= (y + 2)(x - 5)$

39. $2n^2 - 38n + 80 = 2(n^2 - 19n + 40)$

40. $6x^2 - x - 35 = (2x - 5)(3x + 7)$

41. $x^2 + 4x + 4 - y^2 = (x^2 + 4x + 4) - y^2$

$= (x + 2)^2 - y^2$

$= [(x + 2) + y][(x + 2) - y]$

$= (x + 2 + y)(x + 2 - y)$

42. $4x^2 - 4x + 1 - 9y^2$

$= (4x^2 - 4x + 1) - 9y^2$

$= (2x - 1)^2 - (3y)^2$

$= [(2x - 1) + 3y][(2x - 1) - 3y]$

$= (2x - 1 + 3y)(2x - 1 - 3y)$

43. $(x + 2)(x - 6) = 0$

$x + 2 = 0 \quad$ or $\quad x - 6 = 0$

$\quad\quad x = -2 \quad$ or $\quad\quad x = 6$

The solutions are -2 and 6.

44. $2x(3x + 1)(x - 3) = 0$

$x = 0 \quad$ or $\quad 3x + 1 = 0 \quad$ or $\quad x - 3 = 0$

$\quad\quad\quad\quad\quad 3x = -1 \quad$ or $\quad\quad x = 3$

$\quad\quad\quad\quad\quad\quad x = -\dfrac{1}{3}$

The solutions are $-\dfrac{1}{3}, 0, 3$.

45. a. $\dfrac{2x^2}{10x^3 - 2x^2} = \dfrac{2x^2}{2x^2(5x - 1)} = \dfrac{1}{5x - 1}$

   b. $\dfrac{9x^2 + 13x + 4}{8x^2 + x - 7} = \dfrac{(9x + 4)(x + 1)}{(8x - 7)(x + 1)} = \dfrac{9x + 4}{8x - 7}$

46. a. Domain: $(-\infty, \infty)$; Range: $[-4, \infty)$

   b. x-intercepts: $(-2, 0), (2, 0)$
      y-intercept: $(0, -4)$

   c. There is no such point.

   d. The point with the least y-value is $(0, -4)$.

   e. $-2, 2$

   f. x-values between $x = -2$ and $x = 2$

   g. The solutions are -2 and 2.

47. $\dfrac{5k}{k^2-4}-\dfrac{2}{k^2+k-2}$

$=\dfrac{5k}{(k+2)(k-2)}-\dfrac{2}{(k+2)(k-1)}$

$=\dfrac{5k(k-1)-2(k-2)}{(k+2)(k-2)(k-1)}$

$=\dfrac{5k^2-5k-2k+4}{(k+2)(k-2)(k-1)}$

$=\dfrac{5k^2-7k+4}{(k+2)(k-2)(k-1)}$

48. $\dfrac{5a}{a^2-4}-\dfrac{3}{2-a}=\dfrac{5a}{(a+2)(a-2)}+\dfrac{3}{a-2}$

$=\dfrac{5a+3(a+2)}{(a+2)(a-2)}$

$=\dfrac{5a+3a+6}{(a+2)(a-2)}$

$=\dfrac{8a+6}{(a+2)(a-2)}$

49. $\dfrac{3}{x}-\dfrac{x+21}{3x}=\dfrac{5}{3}$

$3x\left(\dfrac{3}{x}-\dfrac{x+21}{3x}\right)=3x\left(\dfrac{5}{3}\right)$

$9-(x+21)=5x$

$9-x-21=5x$

$-x-12=5x$

$-12=6x$

$-2=x$

The solution is –2.

50. $\dfrac{3x-4}{2x}=-\dfrac{8}{x}$

$x(3x-4)=-8(2x)$

$3x^2-4x=-16x$

$3x^2+12x=0$

$3x(x+4)=0$

$3x=0$ or $x+4=0$

$x=0$ or $\qquad x=-4$

Discard the answer 0 as extraneous. The solution is –4.

Chapter 7

Section 7.1

Practice Exercises

1. a. $\sqrt{49} = 7$ because $7^2 = 49$ and 7 is not negative.

b. $\sqrt{\dfrac{0}{1}} = \sqrt{0} = 0$ because $0^2 = 0$ and 0 is not negative.

c. $\sqrt{\dfrac{16}{81}} = \dfrac{4}{9}$ because $\left(\dfrac{4}{9}\right)^2 = \dfrac{16}{81}$ and $\dfrac{4}{9}$ is not negative.

d. $\sqrt{0.64} = 0.8$ because $(0.8)^2 = 0.64$.

e. $\sqrt{z^8} = z^4$ because $(z^4)^2 = z^8$.

f. $\sqrt{16b^4} = 4b^2$ because $(4b^2)^2 = 16b^4$.

g. $-\sqrt{36} = -6$. The negative in front of the radical indicates the negative square root of 36.

h. $\sqrt{-36}$ is not a real number.

2. $\sqrt{45} \approx 6.708$

Since $36 < 45 < 49$, then $\sqrt{36} < \sqrt{45} < \sqrt{49}$, or $6 < \sqrt{45} < 7$. The approximation is between 6 and 7 and thus is reasonable.

3. a. $\sqrt[3]{-1} = -1$ because $(-1)^3 = -1$.

b. $\sqrt[3]{27} = 3$ because $3^3 = 27$.

c. $\sqrt[3]{\dfrac{27}{64}} = \dfrac{3}{4}$ because $\left(\dfrac{3}{4}\right)^3 = \dfrac{27}{64}$.

d. $\sqrt[3]{x^{12}} = x^4$ because $(x^4)^3 = x^{12}$.

e. $\sqrt[3]{-8x^3} = -2x$ because $(-2x)^3 = -8x^3$.

4. a. $\sqrt[4]{10,000} = 10$ because $10^4 = 10,000$ and 10 is positive.

b. $\sqrt[5]{-1} = -1$ because $(-1)^5 = -1$.

c. $-\sqrt{81} = -9$ because -9 is the opposite of $\sqrt{81}$.

d. $\sqrt[4]{-625}$ is not a real number. There is no real number that, when raised to the fourth power, is -625.

e. $\sqrt[3]{27x^9} = 3x^3$ because $(3x^3)^3 = 27x^9$.

5. a. $\sqrt{(-4)^2} = |-4| = 4$

b. $\sqrt{x^{14}} = \left|x^7\right|$

c. $\sqrt[4]{(x+7)^4} = |x+7|$

d. $\sqrt[3]{(-7)^3} = -7$

e. $\sqrt[5]{(3x-5)^5} = 3x-5$

f. $\sqrt{49x^2} = 7|x|$

g. $\sqrt{x^2+4x+4} = \sqrt{(x+2)^2} = |x+2|$

6. $f(x) = \sqrt{x+5},\ g(x) = \sqrt[3]{x-3}$

a. $f(11) = \sqrt{11+5} = \sqrt{16} = 4$

b. $f(-1) = \sqrt{-1+5} = \sqrt{4} = 2$

c. $g(11) = \sqrt[3]{11-3} = \sqrt[3]{8} = 2$

d. $g(-5) = \sqrt[3]{-5-3} = \sqrt[3]{-8} = -2$

7. $h(x) = \sqrt{x+2}$
Find the domain.
$x+2 \geq 0$
$\quad x \geq -2$
The domain of $h(x)$ is $\{x \mid x \geq -2\}$.

x	$h(x) = \sqrt{x+2}$
-2	0
-1	1
1	$\sqrt{1+2} = \sqrt{3} \approx 1.7$
2	2
7	3

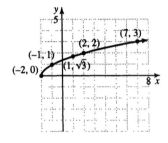

8. $f(x) = \sqrt[3]{x} - 4$

The domain is the set of all real numbers.

x	$f(x) = \sqrt[3]{x} - 4$
0	-4
1	-3
-1	-5
6	$\sqrt[3]{6} - 4 \approx 1.8 - 4 = -2.2$
-6	$\sqrt[3]{-6} - 4 \approx -1.8 - 4 = -5.8$
8	-2
-8	-6

Vocabulary and Readiness Check

1. In the expression $\sqrt[n]{a}$, the n is called the <u>index</u>, the $\sqrt{}$ is called the <u>radical sign</u>, and a is called the <u>radicand</u>.

2. If $\sqrt{a}$ is the positive square root of a, $a \neq 0$, then $-\sqrt{a}$ is the negative square root of a.

3. The square root of a negative number <u>is not</u> a real number.

4. Numbers such as 1, 4, 9, and 25 are called perfect <u>squares</u> where numbers such as 1, 8, 27, and 125 are called perfect <u>cubes</u>.

5. The domain of the function $f(x) = \sqrt{x}$ is $[0, \infty)$.

6. The domain of the function $f(x) = \sqrt[3]{x}$ is $(-\infty, \infty)$.

7. If $f(16) = 4$, the corresponding ordered pair is $(16, 4)$.

8. If $g(-8) = -2$, the corresponding ordered pair is $(-8, -2)$.

9. The radical that is not a real number is $\sqrt{-10}$, choice d.

10. The radicals that simplify to 3 are $\sqrt{9}$ and $\sqrt[3]{27}$, choices a and c.

11. The radical that simplifies to -3 is $\sqrt[3]{-27}$, choice d.

12. The radical that does not simplify to a whole number is $\sqrt{8}$, choice c.

Exercise Set 7.1

1. $\sqrt{100} = 10$ because $10^2 = 100$.

3. $\sqrt{\dfrac{1}{4}} = \dfrac{1}{2}$ because $\left(\dfrac{1}{2}\right)^2 = \dfrac{1}{4}$.

5. $\sqrt{0.0001} = 0.01$ because $(0.01)^2 = 0.0001$.

7. $-\sqrt{36} = -1 \cdot \sqrt{36} = -1 \cdot 6 = -6$

9. $\sqrt{x^{10}} = x^5$ because $(x^5)^2 = x^{10}$.

11. $\sqrt{16y^6} = 4y^3$ because $(4y^3)^2 = 16y^6$.

330

13. $\sqrt{7} \approx 2.646$

Since $4 < 7 < 9$, then $\sqrt{4} < \sqrt{7} < \sqrt{9}$, or $2 < \sqrt{7} < 3$. The approximation is between 2 and 3 and thus is reasonable.

15. $\sqrt{38} \approx 6.164$

Since $36 < 38 < 49$, then $\sqrt{36} < \sqrt{38} < \sqrt{49}$, or $6 < \sqrt{38} < 7$. The approximation is between 6 and 7 and thus is reasonable.

17. $\sqrt{200} \approx 14.142$

Since $196 < 200 < 225$, then $\sqrt{196} < \sqrt{200} < \sqrt{225}$, or $14 < \sqrt{200} < 15$. The approximation is between 14 and 15 and thus is reasonable.

19. $\sqrt[3]{64} = 4$ because $4^3 = 64$.

21. $\sqrt[3]{\dfrac{1}{8}} = \dfrac{1}{2}$ because $\left(\dfrac{1}{2}\right)^3 = \dfrac{1}{8}$.

23. $\sqrt[3]{-1} = -1$ because $(-1)^3 = -1$.

25. $\sqrt[3]{x^{12}} = x^4$ because $(x^4)^3 = x^{12}$.

27. $\sqrt[3]{-27x^9} = -3x^3$ because $(-3x^3)^3 = -27x^9$.

29. $-\sqrt[4]{16} = -2$ because $2^4 = 16$.

31. $\sqrt[4]{-16}$ is not a real number. There is no real number that, when raised to the fourth power, is -16.

33. $\sqrt[5]{-32} = -2$ because $(-2)^5 = -32$.

35. $\sqrt[5]{x^{20}} = x^4$ because $(x^4)^5 = x^{20}$.

37. $\sqrt[6]{64x^{12}} = 2x^2$ because $(2x^2)^6 = 64x^{12}$.

39. $\sqrt{81x^4} = 9x^2$ because $(9x^2)^2 = 81x^4$.

41. $\sqrt[4]{256x^8} = 4x^2$ because $(4x^2)^4 = 256x^8$.

43. $\sqrt{(-8)^2} = |-8| = 8$

45. $\sqrt[3]{(-8)^3} = -8$

47. $\sqrt{4x^2} = 2|x|$

49. $\sqrt[3]{x^3} = x$

51. $\sqrt{(x-5)^2} = |x-5|$

53. $\sqrt{x^2 + 4x + 4} = \sqrt{(x+2)^2} = |x+2|$

55. $-\sqrt{121} = -11$

57. $\sqrt[3]{8x^3} = 2x$

59. $\sqrt{y^{12}} = y^6$

61. $\sqrt{25a^2b^{20}} = 5ab^{10}$

63. $\sqrt[3]{-27x^{12}y^9} = -3x^4y^3$

65. $\sqrt[4]{a^{16}b^4} = a^4b$

67. $\sqrt[5]{-32x^{10}y^5} = -2x^2y$

69. $\sqrt{\dfrac{25}{49}} = \dfrac{5}{7}$

71. $\sqrt{\dfrac{x^2}{4y^2}} = \dfrac{x}{2y}$

73. $-\sqrt[3]{\dfrac{z^{21}}{27x^3}} = -\dfrac{z^7}{3x}$

75. $\sqrt[4]{\dfrac{x^4}{16}} = \dfrac{x}{2}$

77. $f(x) = \sqrt{2x+3}$
$f(0) = \sqrt{2(0)+3} = \sqrt{3}$

79. $g(x) = \sqrt[3]{x-8}$
$g(7) = \sqrt[3]{7-8} = \sqrt[3]{-1} = -1$

81. $g(x) = \sqrt[3]{x-8}$
$g(-19) = \sqrt[3]{-19-8} = \sqrt[3]{-27} = -3$

83. $f(x) = \sqrt{2x+3}$
$f(2) = \sqrt{2(2)+3} = \sqrt{7}$

85. $f(x) = \sqrt{x} + 2$
$x \geq 0$
Domain: $[0, \infty)$

x	$f(x) = \sqrt{x} + 2$
0	$\sqrt{0} + 2 = 2$
1	$\sqrt{1} + 2 = 3$
3	$\sqrt{3} + 2 \approx 3.7$
4	$\sqrt{4} + 2 = 4$

87. $f(x) = \sqrt{x-3}$
$x - 3 \geq 0$
$x \geq 3$
Domain: $[3, \infty)$

x	$f(x) = \sqrt{x-3}$
3	$\sqrt{3-3} = \sqrt{0} = 0$
4	$\sqrt{4-3} = \sqrt{1} = 1$
7	$\sqrt{7-3} = \sqrt{4} = 2$
12	$\sqrt{12-3} = \sqrt{9} = 3$

89. $f(x) = \sqrt[3]{x} + 1$
Domain: $(-\infty, \infty)$

x	$f(x) = \sqrt[3]{x} + 1$
-4	$\sqrt[3]{-4} + 1 \approx -0.6$
-1	$\sqrt[3]{-1} + 1 = 0$
0	$\sqrt[3]{0} + 1 = 1$
1	$\sqrt[3]{1} + 1 = 2$
4	$\sqrt[3]{4} + 1 \approx 2.6$

91. $g(x) = \sqrt[3]{x-1}$
Domain: $(-\infty, \infty)$

x	$g(x) = \sqrt[3]{x-1}$
1	$\sqrt[3]{1-1} = \sqrt[3]{0} = 0$
2	$\sqrt[3]{2-1} = \sqrt[3]{1} = 1$
0	$\sqrt[3]{0-1} = \sqrt[3]{-1} = -1$
9	$\sqrt[3]{9-1} = \sqrt[3]{8} = 2$
-7	$\sqrt[3]{-7-1} = \sqrt[3]{-8} = -2$

93. $(-2x^3y^2)^5 = (-2)^5 x^{3\cdot5} y^{2\cdot5} = -32x^{15}y^{10}$

95. $(-3x^2y^3z^5)(20x^5y^7) = -3(20)x^{2+5}y^{3+7}z^5$
$\qquad\qquad\qquad\qquad\quad = -60x^7y^{10}z^5$

97. $\dfrac{7x^{-1}y}{14(x^5y^2)^{-2}} = \dfrac{7x^{-1}y}{14x^{-10}y^{-4}} = \dfrac{x^9y^5}{2}$

99. $\sqrt{-17}$ is not a real number.

101. $\sqrt[10]{-17}$ is not a real number.

103. Answers may vary

105. $144 < 160 < 169$ so $\sqrt{144} < \sqrt{160} < \sqrt{169}$, or $12 < \sqrt{160} < 13$. Thus $\sqrt{160}$ is between 12 and 13. Therefore, the answer is **b.**

107. $\sqrt{30} \approx 5$, $\sqrt{10} \approx 3$, and $\sqrt{90} \approx 10$ so
$P = \sqrt{30} + \sqrt{10} + \sqrt{90} \approx 5+3+10 = 18$.
Therefore, the answer is **b.**

109. $B = \sqrt{\dfrac{hw}{3131}} = \sqrt{\dfrac{66\cdot135}{3131}}$
$\qquad = \sqrt{\dfrac{8910}{3131}}$
$\qquad \approx 1.69$ sq meters

111. Answers may vary

113. $f(x) = \sqrt{x} + 2$

Domain: $[0, \infty)$

115. $f(x) = \sqrt[3]{x} + 1$

Domain: $(-\infty, \infty)$

Section 7.2

Practice Exercises

1. a. $36^{1/2} = \sqrt{36} = 6$

 b. $1000^{1/3} = \sqrt[3]{1000} = 10$

 c. $x^{1/5} = \sqrt[5]{x}$

 d. $1^{1/4} = \sqrt[4]{1} = 1$

 e. $-64^{1/2} = -\sqrt{64} = -8$

 f. $(125x^9)^{1/3} = \sqrt[3]{125x^9} = 5x^3$

 g. $(3x)^{1/4} = \sqrt[4]{3x}$

2. a. $16^{3/2} = \left(\sqrt{16}\right)^3 = 4^3 = 64$

 b. $-1^{3/5} = -\left(\sqrt[5]{1}\right)^3 = -(1)^3 = -1$

 c. $-(81)^{3/4} = -\left(\sqrt[4]{81}\right)^3 = -(3)^3 = -27$

 d. $\left(\dfrac{1}{25}\right)^{3/2} = \left(\sqrt{\dfrac{1}{25}}\right)^3 = \left(\dfrac{1}{5}\right)^3 = \dfrac{1}{125}$

 e. $(3x+2)^{5/9} = \sqrt[9]{(3x+2)^5}$

3. a. $9^{-3/2} = \dfrac{1}{9^{3/2}} = \dfrac{1}{\left(\sqrt{9}\right)^3} = \dfrac{1}{3^3} = \dfrac{1}{27}$

 b. $(-64)^{-2/3} = \dfrac{1}{(-64)^{2/3}} = \dfrac{1}{\left(\sqrt[3]{-64}\right)^2} = \dfrac{1}{(-4)^2} = \dfrac{1}{16}$

4. a. $y^{2/3} \cdot y^{8/3} = y^{(2/3+8/3)} = y^{10/3}$

b. $x^{3/5} \cdot x^{1/4} = x^{3/5+1/4} = x^{12/20+5/20} = x^{17/20}$

c. $\dfrac{9^{2/7}}{9^{9/7}} = 9^{2/7-9/7} = 9^{-7/7} = 9^{-1} = \dfrac{1}{9}$

d. $b^{4/9} \cdot b^{-2/9} = b^{4/9+(-2/9)} = b^{2/9}$

e. $\dfrac{\left(3x^{1/4}y^{-2/3}\right)^4}{x^4 y} = \dfrac{3^4 (x^{1/4})^4 (y^{-2/3})^4}{x^4 y}$

$= \dfrac{81xy^{-8/3}}{x^4 y}$

$= 81x^{1-4}y^{-8/3-3/3}$

$= 81x^{-3}y^{-11/3}$

$= \dfrac{81}{x^3 y^{11/3}}$

5. a. $x^{3/5}(x^{1/3} - x^2) = x^{3/5}x^{1/3} - x^{3/5}x^2$

$= x^{(3/5+1/3)} - x^{(3/5+2)}$

$= x^{(9/15+5/15)} - x^{(3/5+10/5)}$

$= x^{14/15} - x^{13/5}$

b. $(x^{1/2} + 6)(x^{1/2} - 2)$

$= x^{2/2} - 2x^{1/2} + 6x^{1/2} - 12$

$= x + 4x^{1/2} - 12$

6. $2x^{-1/5} - 7x^{4/5} = (x^{-1/5})(2) - (x^{-1/5})(7x^{5/5})$

$= x^{-1/5}(2 - 7x)$

7. a. $\sqrt[9]{x^3} = x^{3/9} = x^{1/3} = \sqrt[3]{x}$

b. $\sqrt[4]{36} = 36^{1/4} = (6^2)^{1/4} = 6^{2/4} = 6^{1/2} = \sqrt{6}$

c. $\sqrt[8]{a^4 b^2} = (a^4 b^2)^{1/8}$

$= a^{4/8} b^{2/8}$

$= a^{2/4} b^{1/4}$

$= (a^2 b)^{1/4}$

$= \sqrt[4]{a^2 b}$

8. a. $\sqrt[3]{x} \cdot \sqrt[4]{x} = x^{1/3} \cdot x^{1/4}$

$= x^{1/3+1/4}$

$= x^{4/12+3/12}$

$= x^{7/12}$

$= \sqrt[12]{x^7}$

b. $\dfrac{\sqrt[3]{y}}{\sqrt[5]{y}} = \dfrac{y^{1/3}}{y^{1/5}}$

$= y^{1/3-1/5}$

$= y^{5/15-3/15}$

$= y^{2/15}$

$= \sqrt[15]{y^2}$

c. $\sqrt[3]{5} \cdot \sqrt{3} = 5^{1/3} \cdot 3^{1/2}$

$= 5^{2/6} \cdot 3^{3/6}$

$= (5^2 \cdot 3^3)^{1/6}$

$= \sqrt[6]{5^2 \cdot 3^3}$

$= \sqrt[6]{675}$

Vocabulary and Readiness Check

1. It is true that $9^{-1/2}$ is a positive number.

2. It is false that $9^{-1/2}$ is a whole number.

3. It is true that $\dfrac{1}{a^{-m/n}} = a^{m/n}$ (where $a^{m/n}$ is a nonzero real number).

4. To simplify $x^{2/3} \cdot x^{1/5}$, <u>add</u> the exponents.

5. To simplify $(x^{2/3})^{1/5}$, <u>multiply</u> the exponents.

6. To simplify $\dfrac{x^{2/3}}{x^{1/5}}$, <u>subtract</u> the exponents.

7. $4^{1/2} = 2$, A

8. $-4^{1/2} = -2$, B

9. $(-4)^{1/2}$ is not a real number, C

10. $8^{1/3} = 2$, A

11. $-8^{1/3} = -2$, B

12. $(-8)^{1/3} = -2$, B

Exercise Set 7.2

1. $49^{1/2} = \sqrt{49} = 7$

3. $27^{1/3} = \sqrt[3]{27} = 3$

5. $\left(\dfrac{1}{16}\right)^{1/4} = \sqrt[4]{\dfrac{1}{16}} = \dfrac{1}{2}$

7. $169^{1/2} = \sqrt{169} = 13$

9. $2m^{1/3} = 2\sqrt[3]{m}$

11. $(9x^4)^{1/2} = \sqrt{9x^4} = 3x^2$

13. $(-27)^{1/3} = \sqrt[3]{-27} = -3$

15. $-16^{1/4} = -\sqrt[4]{16} = -2$

17. $16^{3/4} = \left(\sqrt[4]{16}\right)^3 = 2^3 = 8$

19. $(-64)^{2/3} = \left(\sqrt[3]{-64}\right)^2 = (-4)^2 = 16$

21. $(-16)^{3/4} = \left(\sqrt[4]{-16}\right)^3$ is not a real number.

23. $(2x)^{3/5} = \sqrt[5]{(2x)^3}$ or $\left(\sqrt[5]{2x}\right)^3$

25. $(7x+2)^{2/3} = \sqrt[3]{(7x+2)^2}$ or $\left(\sqrt[3]{7x+2}\right)^2$

27. $\left(\dfrac{16}{9}\right)^{3/2} = \left(\sqrt{\dfrac{16}{9}}\right)^3 = \left(\dfrac{4}{3}\right)^3 = \dfrac{64}{27}$

29. $8^{-4/3} = \dfrac{1}{8^{4/3}} = \dfrac{1}{\left(\sqrt[3]{8}\right)^4} = \dfrac{1}{2^4} = \dfrac{1}{16}$

31. $(-64)^{-2/3} = \dfrac{1}{(-64)^{2/3}} = \dfrac{1}{\left(\sqrt[3]{-64}\right)^2} = \dfrac{1}{(-4)^2} = \dfrac{1}{16}$

33. $(-4)^{-3/2} = \dfrac{1}{(-4)^{3/2}} = \dfrac{1}{\left(\sqrt{-4}\right)^3}$ is not a real number.

35. $x^{-1/4} = \dfrac{1}{x^{1/4}}$

37. $\dfrac{1}{a^{-2/3}} = a^{2/3}$

39. $\dfrac{5}{7x^{-3/4}} = \dfrac{5x^{3/4}}{7}$

41. $a^{2/3}a^{5/3} = a^{2/3+5/3} = a^{7/3}$

43. $x^{-2/5} \cdot x^{7/5} = x^{-\frac{2}{5}+\frac{7}{5}} = x^{5/5} = x$

45. $3^{1/4} \cdot 3^{3/8} = 3^{\frac{1}{4}+\frac{3}{8}} = 3^{\frac{2}{8}+\frac{3}{8}} = 3^{5/8}$

47. $\dfrac{y^{1/3}}{y^{1/6}} = y^{\frac{1}{3}-\frac{1}{6}} = y^{\frac{2}{6}-\frac{1}{6}} = y^{1/6}$

49. $(4u^2)^{3/2} = 4^{3/2}u^{2(3/2)}$
$= \left(\sqrt{4}\right)^3 u^3$
$= 2^3 u^3$
$= 8u^3$

51. $\dfrac{b^{1/2}b^{3/4}}{-b^{1/4}} = -b^{\frac{1}{2}+\frac{3}{4}-\frac{1}{4}} = -b^{\frac{2}{4}+\frac{3}{4}-\frac{1}{4}} = -b^1 = -b$

53. $\dfrac{(x^3)^{1/2}}{x^{7/2}} = \dfrac{x^{3/2}}{x^{7/2}}$
$= x^{3/2-7/2}$
$= x^{-2}$
$= \dfrac{1}{x^2}$

55. $\dfrac{(3x^{1/4})^3}{x^{1/12}} = \dfrac{3^3 x^{3/4}}{x^{1/12}}$

$= 27x^{\frac{3}{4}-\frac{1}{12}}$

$= 27x^{\frac{9}{12}-\frac{1}{12}}$

$= 27x^{8/12}$

$= 27x^{2/3}$

57. $\dfrac{(y^3 z)^{1/6}}{y^{-1/2} z^{1/3}} = \dfrac{y^{3/6} z^{1/6}}{y^{-1/2} z^{1/3}}$

$= y^{3/6-(-1/2)} z^{1/6-1/3}$

$= y^{1/2+1/2} z^{1/6-2/6}$

$= y^1 z^{-1/6}$

$= \dfrac{y}{z^{1/6}}$

59. $\dfrac{(x^3 y^2)^{1/4}}{(x^{-5} y^{-1})^{-1/2}} = \dfrac{x^{3/4} y^{2/4}}{x^{5/2} y^{1/2}}$

$= x^{\frac{3}{4}-\frac{5}{2}} y^{\frac{2}{4}-\frac{1}{2}}$

$= x^{\frac{3}{4}-\frac{10}{4}} y^{\frac{1}{2}-\frac{1}{2}}$

$= x^{-7/4}$

$= \dfrac{1}{x^{7/4}}$

61. $y^{1/2}(y^{1/2} - y^{2/3}) = y^{1/2} y^{1/2} - y^{1/2} y^{2/3}$

$= y^{1/2+1/2} - y^{1/2+2/3}$

$= y^1 - y^{7/6}$

$= y - y^{7/6}$

63. $x^{2/3}(x - 2) = x \cdot x^{2/3} - 2x^{2/3}$

$= x^{1+2/3} - 2x^{2/3}$

$= x^{5/3} - 2x^{2/3}$

65. $(2x^{1/3} + 3)(2x^{1/3} - 3) = (2x^{1/3})^2 - 3^2$

$= 2^2 (x^{1/3})^2 - 9$

$= 4x^{2/3} - 9$

67. $x^{8/3} + x^{10/3} = x^{8/3}(1) + x^{8/3}(x^{2/3})$

$= x^{8/3}(1 + x^{2/3})$

69. $x^{2/5} - 3x^{1/5} = x^{1/5}(x^{1/5}) - x^{1/5}(3)$

$= x^{1/5}(x^{1/5} - 3)$

71. $5x^{-1/3} + x^{2/3} = x^{-1/3}(5) + x^{-1/3}(x^{3/3})$

$= x^{-1/3}(5 + x)$

73. $\sqrt[6]{x^3} = x^{3/6} = x^{1/2} = \sqrt{x}$

75. $\sqrt[6]{4} = 4^{1/6} = (2^2)^{1/6} = 2^{1/3} = \sqrt[3]{2}$

77. $\sqrt[4]{16x^2} = (16x^2)^{1/4}$

$= 16^{1/4} x^{2/4} = 2x^{1/2} = 2\sqrt{x}$

79. $\sqrt[8]{x^4 y^4} = (x^4 y^4)^{1/8}$

$= x^{4/8} y^{4/8}$

$= x^{1/2} y^{1/2}$

$= (xy)^{1/2}$

$= \sqrt{xy}$

81. $\sqrt[12]{a^8 b^4} = a^{8/12} b^{4/12}$

$= a^{2/3} b^{1/3}$

$= (a^2 b)^{1/3}$

$= \sqrt[3]{a^2 b}$

83. $\sqrt[4]{(x+3)^2} = (x+3)^{2/4} = (x+3)^{1/2} = \sqrt{x+3}$

85. $\sqrt[3]{y} \cdot \sqrt[5]{y^2} = y^{1/3} \cdot y^{2/5}$

$= y^{\frac{1}{3}+\frac{2}{5}}$

$= y^{\frac{5}{15}+\frac{6}{15}}$

$= y^{11/15}$

$= \sqrt[15]{y^{11}}$

87. $\dfrac{\sqrt[3]{b^2}}{\sqrt[4]{b}} = \dfrac{b^{2/3}}{b^{1/4}} = b^{\frac{2}{3}-\frac{1}{4}} = b^{\frac{8}{12}-\frac{3}{12}} = b^{5/12} = \sqrt[12]{b^5}$

89. $\sqrt[3]{x} \cdot \sqrt[4]{x} \cdot \sqrt[8]{x^3} = x^{1/3} \cdot x^{1/4} \cdot x^{3/8}$

$= x^{8/24} \cdot x^{6/24} \cdot x^{9/24}$

$= x^{23/24}$

$= \sqrt[24]{x^{23}}$

91. $\dfrac{\sqrt[3]{a^2}}{\sqrt[6]{a}} = \dfrac{a^{2/3}}{a^{1/6}}$

$= a^{\frac{2}{3}-\frac{1}{6}} = a^{\frac{4}{6}-\frac{1}{6}} = a^{3/6} = a^{1/2} = \sqrt{a}$

93. $\sqrt{3} \cdot \sqrt[3]{4} = 3^{1/2} \cdot 4^{1/3}$
$= 3^{3/6} \cdot 4^{2/6}$
$= (3^3 \cdot 4^2)^{1/6}$
$= (27 \cdot 16)^{1/6}$
$= (432)^{1/6}$
$= \sqrt[6]{432}$

95. $\sqrt[5]{7} \cdot \sqrt[3]{y} = 7^{1/5} \cdot y^{1/3}$
$= 7^{3/15} \cdot y^{5/15}$
$= (7^3 \cdot y^5)^{1/15}$
$= (343y^5)^{1/15}$
$= \sqrt[15]{343y^5}$

97. $\sqrt{5r} \cdot \sqrt[3]{s} = (5r)^{1/2} \cdot s^{1/3}$
$= (5r)^{3/6} \cdot s^{2/6}$
$= [(5r)^3 \cdot s^2]^{1/6}$
$= (125r^3 s^2)^{1/6}$
$= \sqrt[6]{125r^3 s^2}$

99. $75 = 25 \cdot 3$ where 25 is a perfect square.

101. $48 = 4 \cdot 12$ or $16 \cdot 3$ where both 4 and 16 are perfect squares.

103. $16 = 8 \cdot 2$ where 8 is a perfect cube.

105. $54 = 27 \cdot 2$ where 27 is a perfect cube.

107. $B(w) = 70w^{3/4}$
$B(60) = 70(60)^{3/4}$
≈ 1509 calories

109. $f(x) = 33.3x^{4/5}$
$f(10) = 33.3(10)^{4/5}$
≈ 210.1 million subscriptions

111. $\square \cdot a^{2/3} = a^{3/3}$
$\square = \dfrac{a^{3/3}}{a^{2/3}}$
$\square = a^{3/3 - 2/3}$
$\square = a^{1/3}$

113. $\dfrac{\square}{x^{-2/5}} = x^{3/5}$
$x^{-2/5}\left(\dfrac{\square}{x^{-2/5}}\right) = x^{3/5} \cdot x^{-2/5}$
$\square = x^{3/5 - 2/5}$
$\square = x^{1/5}$

115. $8^{1/4} \approx 1.6818$

117. $18^{3/5} \approx 5.6645$

119. $\dfrac{\sqrt{t}}{\sqrt{u}} = \dfrac{t^{1/2}}{u^{1/2}}$

Section 7.3

Practice Exercises

1. a. $\sqrt{5} \cdot \sqrt{7} = \sqrt{5 \cdot 7} = \sqrt{35}$

   b. $\sqrt{13} \cdot \sqrt{z} = \sqrt{13z}$

   c. $\sqrt[4]{125} \cdot \sqrt[4]{5} = \sqrt[4]{125 \cdot 5} = \sqrt[4]{625} = 5$

   d. $\sqrt[3]{5y} \cdot \sqrt[3]{3x^2} = \sqrt[3]{5y \cdot 3x^2} = \sqrt[3]{15x^2 y}$

   e. $\sqrt{\dfrac{5}{m}} \cdot \sqrt{\dfrac{t}{2}} = \sqrt{\dfrac{5}{m} \cdot \dfrac{t}{2}} = \sqrt{\dfrac{5t}{2m}}$

2. a. $\sqrt{\dfrac{36}{49}} = \dfrac{\sqrt{36}}{\sqrt{49}} = \dfrac{6}{7}$

   b. $\sqrt{\dfrac{z}{16}} = \dfrac{\sqrt{z}}{\sqrt{16}} = \dfrac{\sqrt{z}}{4}$

   c. $\sqrt[3]{\dfrac{125}{8}} = \dfrac{\sqrt[3]{125}}{\sqrt[3]{8}} = \dfrac{5}{2}$

   d. $\sqrt[4]{\dfrac{5}{81x^8}} = \dfrac{\sqrt[4]{5}}{\sqrt[4]{81x^8}} = \dfrac{\sqrt[4]{5}}{3x^2}$

3. a. $\sqrt{98} = \sqrt{49 \cdot 2} = \sqrt{49} \cdot \sqrt{2} = 7\sqrt{2}$

   b. $\sqrt[3]{54} = \sqrt[3]{27 \cdot 2} = \sqrt[3]{27} \cdot \sqrt[3]{2} = 3\sqrt[3]{2}$

   c. The largest perfect square factor of 35 is 1, so $\sqrt{35}$ cannot be simplified further.

d. $\sqrt[4]{243} = \sqrt[4]{81 \cdot 3} = \sqrt[4]{81} \cdot \sqrt[4]{3} = 3\sqrt[4]{3}$

4. a. $\sqrt{36z^7} = \sqrt{36z^6 \cdot z} = \sqrt{36z^6} \cdot \sqrt{z} = 6z^3\sqrt{z}$

b. $\sqrt[3]{32p^4q^7} = \sqrt[3]{8 \cdot 4 \cdot p^3 \cdot p \cdot q^6 \cdot q}$
$= \sqrt[3]{8p^3q^6 \cdot 4pq}$
$= \sqrt[3]{8p^3q^6} \cdot \sqrt[3]{4pq}$
$= 2pq^2\sqrt[3]{4pq}$

c. $\sqrt[4]{16x^{15}} = \sqrt[4]{16 \cdot x^{12} \cdot x^3}$
$= \sqrt[4]{16x^{12}} \cdot \sqrt[4]{x^3}$
$= 2x^3\sqrt[4]{x^3}$

5. a. $\dfrac{\sqrt{80}}{\sqrt{5}} = \sqrt{\dfrac{80}{5}} = \sqrt{16} = 4$

b. $\dfrac{\sqrt{98z}}{3\sqrt{2}} = \dfrac{1}{3} \cdot \sqrt{\dfrac{98z}{2}}$
$= \dfrac{1}{3} \cdot \sqrt{49z}$
$= \dfrac{1}{3} \cdot \sqrt{49} \cdot \sqrt{z}$
$= \dfrac{1}{3} \cdot 7 \cdot \sqrt{z}$
$= \dfrac{7}{3}\sqrt{z}$

c. $\dfrac{5\sqrt[3]{40x^5y^7}}{\sqrt[3]{5y}} = 5 \cdot \sqrt[3]{\dfrac{40x^5y^7}{5y}}$
$= 5 \cdot \sqrt[3]{8x^5y^6}$
$= 5 \cdot \sqrt[3]{8x^3y^6 \cdot x^2}$
$= 5 \cdot \sqrt[3]{8x^3y^6} \cdot \sqrt[3]{x^2}$
$= 5 \cdot 2xy^2 \cdot \sqrt[3]{x^2}$
$= 10xy^2\sqrt[3]{x^2}$

d. $\dfrac{3\sqrt[5]{64x^9y^8}}{\sqrt[5]{x^{-1}y^2}} = 3 \cdot \sqrt[5]{\dfrac{64x^9y^8}{x^{-1}y^2}}$
$= 3 \cdot \sqrt[5]{64x^{10}y^6}$
$= 3 \cdot \sqrt[5]{32 \cdot x^{10} \cdot y^5 \cdot 2 \cdot y}$
$= 3 \cdot \sqrt[5]{32x^{10}y^5} \cdot \sqrt[5]{2y}$
$= 3 \cdot 2x^2y \cdot \sqrt[5]{2y}$
$= 6x^2y\sqrt[5]{2y}$

6. Let $(x_1, y_1) = (-3, 7)$ and $(x_2, y_2) = (-2, 3)$.
$d = \sqrt{(x_2 - x_1)^2 + (y_2 - y_1)^2}$
$= \sqrt{[-2 - (-3)]^2 + (3 - 7)^2}$
$= \sqrt{(1)^2 + (-4)^2}$
$= \sqrt{1 + 16}$
$= \sqrt{17} \approx 4.123$
The distance between the two points is exactly $\sqrt{17}$ units, or approximately 4.123 units.

7. Let $(x_1, y_1) = (5, -2)$ and $(x_2, y_2) = (8, -6)$.
$\text{midpoint} = \left(\dfrac{x_1 + x_2}{2}, \dfrac{y_1 + y_2}{2}\right)$
$= \left(\dfrac{5 + 8}{2}, \dfrac{-2 + (-6)}{2}\right)$
$= \left(\dfrac{13}{2}, \dfrac{-8}{2}\right)$
$= \left(\dfrac{13}{2}, -4\right)$
The midpoint of the segment is $\left(\dfrac{13}{2}, -4\right)$.

Vocabulary and Readiness Check

1. The <u>midpoint</u> of a line segment is a <u>point</u> exactly halfway between the two endpoints of the line segment.

2. The <u>distance</u> formula is
$d = \sqrt{(x_2 - x_1)^2 + (y_2 - y_1)^2}$.

3. The <u>midpoint</u> formula is $\left(\dfrac{x_1 + x_2}{2}, \dfrac{y_1 + y_2}{2}\right)$.

4. The statement $\sqrt[n]{a} \cdot \sqrt[n]{b} = \sqrt[n]{ab}$ is <u>true</u>.

5. The statement $\sqrt[3]{7} \cdot \sqrt[3]{11} = \sqrt[3]{18}$ is <u>false</u>.

6. The statement $\sqrt[3]{7} \cdot \sqrt{11} = \sqrt{77}$ is <u>false</u>.

7. The statement $\sqrt{x^7 y^8} = \sqrt{x^7} \cdot \sqrt{y^8}$ is <u>true</u>.

8. The statement $\dfrac{\sqrt[n]{a}}{\sqrt[n]{b}} = \sqrt[n]{\dfrac{a}{b}}$ is <u>true</u>.

9. The statement $\dfrac{\sqrt[3]{12}}{\sqrt[3]{4}} = \sqrt[3]{8}$ is <u>false</u>.

10. The statement $\dfrac{\sqrt[n]{x^7}}{\sqrt[n]{x}} = \sqrt[n]{x^6}$ is <u>true</u>.

Exercise Set 7.3

1. $\sqrt{7} \cdot \sqrt{2} = \sqrt{7 \cdot 2} = \sqrt{14}$

3. $\sqrt[4]{8} \cdot \sqrt[4]{2} = \sqrt[4]{8 \cdot 2} = \sqrt[4]{16} = 2$

5. $\sqrt[3]{4} \cdot \sqrt[3]{9} = \sqrt[3]{4 \cdot 9} = \sqrt[3]{36}$

7. $\sqrt{2} \cdot \sqrt{3x} = \sqrt{2 \cdot 3x} = \sqrt{6x}$

9. $\sqrt{\dfrac{7}{x}} \cdot \sqrt{\dfrac{2}{y}} = \sqrt{\dfrac{7}{x} \cdot \dfrac{2}{y}} = \sqrt{\dfrac{14}{xy}}$

11. $\sqrt[4]{4x^3} \cdot \sqrt[4]{5} = \sqrt[4]{4x^3 \cdot 5} = \sqrt[4]{20x^3}$

13. $\sqrt{\dfrac{6}{49}} = \dfrac{\sqrt{6}}{\sqrt{49}} = \dfrac{\sqrt{6}}{7}$

15. $\sqrt{\dfrac{2}{49}} = \dfrac{\sqrt{2}}{\sqrt{49}} = \dfrac{\sqrt{2}}{7}$

17. $\sqrt[4]{\dfrac{x^3}{16}} = \dfrac{\sqrt[4]{x^3}}{\sqrt[4]{16}} = \dfrac{\sqrt[4]{x^3}}{2}$

19. $\sqrt[3]{\dfrac{4}{27}} = \dfrac{\sqrt[3]{4}}{\sqrt[3]{27}} = \dfrac{\sqrt[3]{4}}{3}$

21. $\sqrt[4]{\dfrac{8}{x^8}} = \dfrac{\sqrt[4]{8}}{\sqrt[4]{x^8}} = \dfrac{\sqrt[4]{8}}{x^2}$

23. $\sqrt[3]{\dfrac{2x}{81y^{12}}} = \dfrac{\sqrt[3]{2x}}{\sqrt[3]{81y^{12}}}$

$$= \dfrac{\sqrt[3]{2x}}{\sqrt[3]{27y^{12}} \cdot \sqrt[3]{3}}$$

$$= \dfrac{\sqrt[3]{2x}}{3y^4 \sqrt[3]{3}}$$

25. $\sqrt{\dfrac{x^2 y}{100}} = \dfrac{\sqrt{x^2 y}}{\sqrt{100}} = \dfrac{\sqrt{x^2}\sqrt{y}}{10} = \dfrac{x\sqrt{y}}{10}$

27. $\sqrt{\dfrac{5x^2}{4y^2}} = \dfrac{\sqrt{5x^2}}{\sqrt{4y^2}} = \dfrac{\sqrt{5}\sqrt{x^2}}{2y} = \dfrac{x\sqrt{5}}{2y}$

29. $-\sqrt[3]{\dfrac{z^7}{27x^3}} = -\dfrac{\sqrt[3]{z^7}}{\sqrt[3]{27x^3}} = -\dfrac{\sqrt[3]{z^6 \cdot z}}{3x} = -\dfrac{z^2\sqrt[3]{z}}{3x}$

31. $\sqrt{32} = \sqrt{16 \cdot 2} = \sqrt{16} \cdot \sqrt{2} = 4\sqrt{2}$

33. $\sqrt[3]{192} = \sqrt[3]{64 \cdot 3} = \sqrt[3]{64} \cdot \sqrt[3]{3} = 4\sqrt[3]{3}$

35. $5\sqrt{75} = 5\sqrt{25 \cdot 3} = 5\sqrt{25} \cdot \sqrt{3} = 5(5)\sqrt{3} = 25\sqrt{3}$

37. $\sqrt{24} = \sqrt{4 \cdot 6} = \sqrt{4} \cdot \sqrt{6} = 2\sqrt{6}$

39. $\sqrt{100x^5} = \sqrt{100x^4 \cdot x} = \sqrt{100x^4} \cdot \sqrt{x} = 10x^2\sqrt{x}$

41. $\sqrt[3]{16y^7} = \sqrt[3]{8y^6 \cdot 2y} = \sqrt[3]{8y^6} \cdot \sqrt[3]{2y} = 2y^2\sqrt[3]{2y}$

43. $\sqrt[4]{a^8 b^7} = \sqrt[4]{a^8 b^4 \cdot b^3} = \sqrt[4]{a^8 b^4} \cdot \sqrt[4]{b^3} = a^2 b\sqrt[4]{b^3}$

45. $\sqrt{y^5} = \sqrt{y^4 \cdot y} = \sqrt{y^4} \cdot \sqrt{y} = y^2\sqrt{y}$

47. $\sqrt{25a^2 b^3} = \sqrt{25a^2 b^2 \cdot b}$

$$= \sqrt{25a^2 b^2} \cdot \sqrt{b}$$

$$= 5ab\sqrt{b}$$

49. $\sqrt[5]{-32x^{10}y} = \sqrt[5]{-32x^{10} \cdot y}$

$$= \sqrt[5]{-32x^{10}} \cdot \sqrt[5]{y}$$

$$= -2x^2\sqrt[5]{y}$$

51. $\sqrt[3]{50x^{14}} = \sqrt[3]{x^{12} \cdot 50x^2}$

$\qquad = \sqrt[3]{x^{12}} \cdot \sqrt[3]{50x^2}$

$\qquad = x^4 \sqrt[3]{50x^2}$

53. $-\sqrt{32a^8 b^7} = -\sqrt{16a^8 b^6 \cdot 2b}$

$\qquad = -\sqrt{16a^8 b^6} \cdot \sqrt{2b}$

$\qquad = -4a^4 b^3 \sqrt{2b}$

55. $\sqrt{9x^7 y^9} = \sqrt{9x^6 y^8 \cdot xy}$

$\qquad = \sqrt{9x^6 y^8} \cdot \sqrt{xy}$

$\qquad = 3x^3 y^4 \sqrt{xy}$

57. $\sqrt[3]{125 r^9 s^{12}} = 5r^3 s^4$

59. $\dfrac{\sqrt{14}}{\sqrt{7}} = \sqrt{\dfrac{14}{7}} = \sqrt{2}$

61. $\dfrac{\sqrt[3]{24}}{\sqrt[3]{3}} = \sqrt[3]{\dfrac{24}{3}} = \sqrt[3]{8} = 2$

63. $\dfrac{5\sqrt[4]{48}}{\sqrt[4]{3}} = 5\sqrt[4]{\dfrac{48}{3}} = 5\sqrt[4]{16} = 5(2) = 10$

65. $\dfrac{\sqrt{x^5 y^3}}{\sqrt{xy}} = \sqrt{\dfrac{x^5 y^3}{xy}} = \sqrt{x^4 y^2} = x^2 y$

67. $\dfrac{8\sqrt[3]{54m^7}}{\sqrt[3]{2m}} = 8\sqrt[3]{\dfrac{54m^7}{2m}}$

$\qquad = 8\sqrt[3]{27m^6}$

$\qquad = 8(3m^2)$

$\qquad = 24m^2$

69. $\dfrac{3\sqrt{100x^2}}{2\sqrt{2x^{-1}}} = \dfrac{3}{2}\sqrt{\dfrac{100x^2}{2x^{-1}}}$

$\qquad = \dfrac{3}{2}\sqrt{50x^3}$

$\qquad = \dfrac{3}{2}\sqrt{25x^2 \cdot 2x}$

$\qquad = \dfrac{3}{2}(5x)\sqrt{2x}$

$\qquad = \dfrac{15x}{2}\sqrt{2x}$

71. $\dfrac{\sqrt[4]{96a^{10}b^3}}{\sqrt[4]{3a^2 b^3}} = \sqrt[4]{\dfrac{96a^{10}b^3}{3a^2 b^3}}$

$\qquad = \sqrt[4]{32a^8}$

$\qquad = \sqrt[4]{16a^8 \cdot 2}$

$\qquad = 2a^2 \sqrt[4]{2}$

73. $(5, 1), (8, 5)$

$d = \sqrt{(8-5)^2 + (5-1)^2}$

$\quad = \sqrt{3^2 + 4^2}$

$\quad = \sqrt{9+16}$

$\quad = \sqrt{25}$

$\quad = 5$ units

75. $(-3, 2), (1, -3)$

$d = \sqrt{[1-(-3)]^2 + (-3-2)^2}$

$\quad = \sqrt{4^2 + (-5)^2}$

$\quad = \sqrt{16+25}$

$\quad = \sqrt{41} \approx 6.403$ units

77. $(-9, 4), (-8, 1)$

$d = \sqrt{[-8-(-9)]^2 + (1-4)^2}$

$\quad = \sqrt{1^2 + (-3)^2}$

$\quad = \sqrt{1+9}$

$\quad = \sqrt{10} \approx 3.162$ units

79. $\left(0, -\sqrt{2}\right), \left(\sqrt{3}, 0\right)$

$d = \sqrt{\left(\sqrt{3}-0\right)^2 + \left[0-\left(-\sqrt{2}\right)\right]^2}$

$\quad = \sqrt{\left(\sqrt{3}\right)^2 + \left(\sqrt{2}\right)^2}$

$\quad = \sqrt{3+2}$

$\quad = \sqrt{5} \approx 2.236$ units

81. $(1.7, -3.6), (-8.6, 5.7)$

$d = \sqrt{(-8.6-1.7)^2 + [5.7-(-3.6)]^2}$

$\quad = \sqrt{(-10.3)^2 + (9.3)^2}$

$\quad = \sqrt{192.58} \approx 13.877$ units

83. $(6, -8), (2, 4)$

$\left(\dfrac{6+2}{2}, \dfrac{-8+4}{2}\right) = \left(\dfrac{8}{2}, \dfrac{-4}{2}\right) = (4, -2)$

The midpoint of the segment is $(4, -2)$.

85. $(-2, -1), (-8, 6)$

$$\left(\frac{-2+(-8)}{2}, \frac{-1+6}{2}\right) = \left(\frac{-10}{2}, \frac{5}{2}\right) = \left(-5, \frac{5}{2}\right)$$

The midpoint of the segment is $\left(-5, \frac{5}{2}\right)$.

87. $(7, 3), (-1, -3)$

$$\left(\frac{7+(-1)}{2}, \frac{3+(-3)}{2}\right) = \left(\frac{6}{2}, \frac{0}{2}\right) = (3, 0)$$

The midpoint of the segment is $(3, 0)$.

89. $\left(\frac{1}{2}, \frac{3}{8}\right), \left(-\frac{3}{2}, \frac{5}{8}\right)$

$$\left(\frac{\frac{1}{2}+\left(-\frac{3}{2}\right)}{2}, \frac{\frac{3}{8}+\frac{5}{8}}{2}\right) = \left(\frac{-1}{2}, \frac{1}{2}\right)$$

The midpoint of the segment is $\left(-\frac{1}{2}, \frac{1}{2}\right)$.

91. $\left(\sqrt{2}, 3\sqrt{5}\right), \left(\sqrt{2}, -2\sqrt{5}\right)$

$$\left(\frac{\sqrt{2}+\sqrt{2}}{2}, \frac{3\sqrt{5}+\left(-2\sqrt{5}\right)}{2}\right) = \left(\frac{2\sqrt{2}}{2}, \frac{\sqrt{5}}{2}\right)$$

$$= \left(\sqrt{2}, \frac{\sqrt{5}}{2}\right)$$

The midpoint of the segment is $\left(\sqrt{2}, \frac{\sqrt{5}}{2}\right)$.

93. $(4.6, -3.5), (7.8, -9.8)$

$$\left(\frac{4.6+7.8}{2}, \frac{-3.5+(-9.8)}{2}\right) = \left(\frac{12.4}{2}, \frac{-13.3}{2}\right)$$

$$= (6.2, -6.65)$$

The midpoint of the segment is $(6.2, -6.65)$.

95. $6x + 8x = (6+8)x = 14x$

97. $(2x+3)(x-5) = 2x^2 - 10x + 3x - 15$
$$= 2x^2 - 7x - 15$$

99. $9y^2 - 8y^2 = (9-8)y^2 = 1y^2 = y^2$

101. $-3(x+5) = -3x - 3(5) = -3x - 15$

103. $(x-4)^2 = x^2 - 2(x)(4) + 4^2$
$$= x^2 - 8x + 16$$

105. $\dfrac{\sqrt[3]{64}}{\sqrt{64}} = \dfrac{4}{8} = \dfrac{1}{2}$

107. $\sqrt[5]{x^{35}} = x^7$

109. $\sqrt[4]{a^{12}b^4c^{20}} = a^3bc^5$

111. $\sqrt[3]{z^{32}} = \sqrt[3]{z^{30} \cdot z^2} = \sqrt[3]{z^{30}} \cdot \sqrt[3]{z^2} = z^{10}\sqrt[3]{z^2}$

113. $\sqrt[7]{q^{17}r^{40}s^7} = \sqrt[7]{q^{14} \cdot q^3 \cdot r^{35} \cdot r^5 \cdot s^7}$
$$= \sqrt[7]{q^{14}r^{35}s^7 \cdot q^3r^5}$$
$$= q^2r^5s\sqrt[7]{q^3r^5}$$

115. $r = \sqrt{\dfrac{A}{4\pi}} = \sqrt{\dfrac{32.17}{4\pi}} \approx \sqrt{2.56} = 1.6$

The radius of a standard zorb is 1.6 meters.

117. $F(x) = 0.6\sqrt{49 - x^2}$

   a. $F(3) = 0.6\sqrt{49 - 3^2}$
$$= 0.6\sqrt{49 - 9}$$
$$= 0.6\sqrt{40} \approx 3.8 \text{ times}$$

   b. $F(5) = 0.6\sqrt{49 - 5^2}$
$$= 0.6\sqrt{49 - 25}$$
$$= 0.6\sqrt{24} \approx 2.9 \text{ times}$$

   c. Answers may vary

Section 7.4

Practice Exercises

1. a. $3\sqrt{17} + 5\sqrt{17} = (3+5)\sqrt{17} = 8\sqrt{17}$

   b. $7\sqrt[3]{5z} - 12\sqrt[3]{5z} = (7-12)\sqrt[3]{5z} = -5\sqrt[3]{5z}$

   c. $3\sqrt{2} + 5\sqrt[3]{2}$
This expression cannot be simplified since $3\sqrt{2}$ and $5\sqrt[3]{2}$ do not contain like radicals.

2. a. $\sqrt{24}+3\sqrt{54}=\sqrt{4\cdot6}+3\sqrt{9\cdot6}$
$=\sqrt{4}\cdot\sqrt{6}+3\cdot\sqrt{9}\cdot\sqrt{6}$
$=2\cdot\sqrt{6}+3\cdot3\cdot\sqrt{6}$
$=2\sqrt{6}+9\sqrt{6}$
$=11\sqrt{6}$

b. $\sqrt[3]{24}-4\sqrt[3]{81}+\sqrt[3]{3}$
$=\sqrt[3]{8}\cdot\sqrt[3]{3}-4\cdot\sqrt[3]{27}\cdot\sqrt[3]{3}+\sqrt[3]{3}$
$=2\cdot\sqrt[3]{3}-4\cdot3\cdot\sqrt[3]{3}+\sqrt[3]{3}$
$=2\sqrt[3]{3}-12\sqrt[3]{3}+\sqrt[3]{3}$
$=-9\sqrt[3]{3}$

c. $\sqrt{75x}-3\sqrt{27x}+\sqrt{12x}$
$=\sqrt{25}\cdot\sqrt{3x}-3\cdot\sqrt{9}\cdot\sqrt{3x}+\sqrt{4}\cdot\sqrt{3x}$
$=5\cdot\sqrt{3x}-3\cdot3\cdot\sqrt{3x}+2\cdot\sqrt{3x}$
$=5\sqrt{3x}-9\sqrt{3x}+2\sqrt{3x}$
$=-2\sqrt{3x}$

d. $\sqrt{40}+\sqrt[3]{40}=\sqrt{4}\cdot\sqrt{10}+\sqrt[3]{8}\cdot\sqrt[3]{5}$
$=2\sqrt{10}+2\sqrt[3]{5}$

e. $\sqrt[3]{81x^4}+\sqrt[3]{3x^4}=\sqrt[3]{27x^3}\cdot\sqrt[3]{3x}+\sqrt[3]{x^3}\cdot\sqrt[3]{3x}$
$=3x\sqrt[3]{3x}+x\sqrt[3]{3x}$
$=4x\sqrt[3]{3x}$

3. a. $\dfrac{\sqrt{28}}{3}-\dfrac{\sqrt{7}}{4}=\dfrac{2\sqrt{7}}{3}-\dfrac{\sqrt{7}}{4}$
$=\dfrac{2\sqrt{7}\cdot4}{3\cdot4}-\dfrac{\sqrt{7}\cdot3}{4\cdot3}$
$=\dfrac{8\sqrt{7}}{12}-\dfrac{3\sqrt{7}}{12}$
$=\dfrac{5\sqrt{7}}{12}$

b. $\sqrt[3]{\dfrac{6y}{64}}+3\sqrt[3]{6y}=\dfrac{\sqrt[3]{6y}}{\sqrt[3]{64}}+3\sqrt[3]{6y}$
$=\dfrac{\sqrt[3]{6y}}{4}+3\sqrt[3]{6y}$
$=\dfrac{\sqrt[3]{6y}}{4}+\dfrac{3\sqrt[3]{6y}\cdot4}{4}$
$=\dfrac{\sqrt[3]{6y}}{4}+\dfrac{12\sqrt[3]{6y}}{4}$
$=\dfrac{13\sqrt[3]{6y}}{4}$

4. a. $\sqrt{5}(2+\sqrt{15})=\sqrt{5}(2)+\sqrt{5}(\sqrt{15})$
$=2\sqrt{5}+\sqrt{5\cdot15}$
$=2\sqrt{5}+\sqrt{5\cdot5\cdot3}$
$=2\sqrt{5}+5\sqrt{3}$

b. $(\sqrt{2}-\sqrt{5})(\sqrt{6}+2)$
$=\sqrt{2}\cdot\sqrt{6}+\sqrt{2}\cdot2-\sqrt{5}\cdot\sqrt{6}-\sqrt{5}\cdot2$
$=\sqrt{2\cdot2\cdot3}+2\sqrt{2}-\sqrt{30}-2\sqrt{5}$
$=2\sqrt{3}+2\sqrt{2}-\sqrt{30}-2\sqrt{5}$

c. $(3\sqrt{z}-4)(2\sqrt{z}+3)$
$=3\sqrt{z}(2\sqrt{z})+3\sqrt{z}(3)-4(2\sqrt{z})-4(3)$
$=6\cdot z+9\sqrt{z}-8\sqrt{z}-12$
$=6z+\sqrt{z}-12$

d. $(\sqrt{6}-3)^2=(\sqrt{6}-3)(\sqrt{6}-3)$
$=\sqrt{6}(\sqrt{6})-\sqrt{6}(3)-3(\sqrt{6})-3(-3)$
$=6-3\sqrt{6}-3\sqrt{6}+9$
$=6-6\sqrt{6}+9$
$=15-6\sqrt{6}$

e. $(\sqrt{5x}+3)(\sqrt{5x}-3)$
$=\sqrt{5x}\cdot\sqrt{5x}-3\sqrt{5x}+3\sqrt{5x}-3\cdot3$
$=5x-9$

f. $(\sqrt{x+2}+3)^2=(\sqrt{x+2})^2+2\cdot\sqrt{x+2}\cdot3+3^2$
$=x+2+6\sqrt{x+2}+9$
$=x+11+6\sqrt{x+2}$

Vocabulary and Readiness Check

1. The terms $\sqrt{7}$ and $\sqrt[3]{7}$ are <u>unlike</u> terms.

2. The terms $\sqrt[3]{x^2y}$ and $\sqrt[3]{yx^2}$ are <u>like</u> terms.

3. The terms $\sqrt[3]{abc}$ and $\sqrt[3]{cba}$ are <u>like</u> terms.

4. The terms $2x\sqrt{5}$ and $2x\sqrt{10}$ are <u>unlike</u> terms.

5. $2\sqrt{3}+4\sqrt{3}=\underline{6\sqrt{3}}$

6. $5\sqrt{7}+3\sqrt{7}=\underline{8\sqrt{7}}$

7. $8\sqrt{x}-\sqrt{x}=\underline{7\sqrt{x}}$

8. $3\sqrt{y}-\sqrt{y}=\underline{2\sqrt{y}}$

9. $7\sqrt[3]{x} + \sqrt[3]{x} = \underline{8\sqrt[3]{x}}$

10. $8\sqrt[3]{z} + \sqrt[3]{z} = \underline{9\sqrt[3]{z}}$

11. $\sqrt{11} + \sqrt[3]{11} = \underline{\sqrt{11} + \sqrt[3]{11}}$

12. $9\sqrt{13} - \sqrt[4]{13} = \underline{9\sqrt{13} - \sqrt[4]{13}}$

13. $8\sqrt[3]{2x} + 3\sqrt[3]{2x} - \sqrt[3]{2x} = \underline{10\sqrt[3]{2x}}$

14. $8\sqrt[3]{2x} + 3\sqrt[3]{2x^2} - \sqrt[3]{2x} = \underline{7\sqrt[3]{2x} + 3\sqrt[3]{2x^2}}$

Exercise Set 7.4

1. $\sqrt{8} - \sqrt{32} = \sqrt{4 \cdot 2} - \sqrt{16 \cdot 2}$
$$= \sqrt{4} \cdot \sqrt{2} - \sqrt{16} \cdot \sqrt{2}$$
$$= 2\sqrt{2} - 4\sqrt{2}$$
$$= -2\sqrt{2}$$

3. $2\sqrt{2x^3} + 4x\sqrt{8x} = 2\sqrt{x^2 \cdot 2x} + 4x\sqrt{4 \cdot 2x}$
$$= 2\sqrt{x^2} \cdot \sqrt{2x} + 4x\sqrt{4} \cdot \sqrt{2x}$$
$$= 2x\sqrt{2x} + 4x(2)\sqrt{2x}$$
$$= 2x\sqrt{2x} + 8x\sqrt{2x}$$
$$= 10x\sqrt{2x}$$

5. $2\sqrt{50} - 3\sqrt{125} + \sqrt{98}$
$$= 2\sqrt{25 \cdot 2} - 3\sqrt{25 \cdot 5} + \sqrt{49 \cdot 2}$$
$$= 2\sqrt{25} \cdot \sqrt{2} - 3\sqrt{25} \cdot \sqrt{5} + \sqrt{49} \cdot \sqrt{2}$$
$$= 2(5)\sqrt{2} - 3(5)\sqrt{5} + 7\sqrt{2}$$
$$= 10\sqrt{2} - 15\sqrt{5} + 7\sqrt{2}$$
$$= 17\sqrt{2} - 15\sqrt{5}$$

7. $\sqrt[3]{16x} - \sqrt[3]{54x} = \sqrt[3]{8 \cdot 2x} - \sqrt[3]{27 \cdot 2x}$
$$= \sqrt[3]{8} \cdot \sqrt[3]{2x} - \sqrt[3]{27} \cdot \sqrt[3]{2x}$$
$$= 2\sqrt[3]{2x} - 3\sqrt[3]{2x}$$
$$= -\sqrt[3]{2x}$$

9. $\sqrt{9b^3} - \sqrt{25b^3} + \sqrt{49b^3}$
$$= \sqrt{9b^2 \cdot b} - \sqrt{25b^2 \cdot b} + \sqrt{49b^2 \cdot b}$$
$$= \sqrt{9b^2} \cdot \sqrt{b} - \sqrt{25b^2} \cdot \sqrt{b} + \sqrt{49b^2} \cdot \sqrt{b}$$
$$= 3b\sqrt{b} - 5b\sqrt{b} + 7b\sqrt{b}$$
$$= 5b\sqrt{b}$$

11. $\dfrac{5\sqrt{2}}{3} + \dfrac{2\sqrt{2}}{5} = \dfrac{5\left(5\sqrt{2}\right) + 3\left(2\sqrt{2}\right)}{3(5)}$
$$= \dfrac{25\sqrt{2} + 6\sqrt{2}}{15}$$
$$= \dfrac{31\sqrt{2}}{15}$$

13. $\sqrt[3]{\dfrac{11}{8}} - \dfrac{\sqrt[3]{11}}{6} = \dfrac{\sqrt[3]{11}}{\sqrt[3]{8}} - \dfrac{\sqrt[3]{11}}{6}$
$$= \dfrac{\sqrt[3]{11}}{2} - \dfrac{\sqrt[3]{11}}{6}$$
$$= \dfrac{3\sqrt[3]{11} - \sqrt[3]{11}}{6}$$
$$= \dfrac{2\sqrt[3]{11}}{6}$$
$$= \dfrac{\sqrt[3]{11}}{3}$$

15. $\dfrac{\sqrt{20x}}{9} + \sqrt{\dfrac{5x}{9}} = \dfrac{\sqrt{4 \cdot 5x}}{9} + \dfrac{\sqrt{5x}}{\sqrt{9}}$
$$= \dfrac{2\sqrt{5x}}{9} + \dfrac{\sqrt{5x}}{3}$$
$$= \dfrac{2\sqrt{5x} + 3\sqrt{5x}}{9}$$
$$= \dfrac{5\sqrt{5x}}{9}$$

17. $7\sqrt{9} - 7 + \sqrt{3} = 7(3) - 7 + \sqrt{3}$
$$= 21 - 7 + \sqrt{3}$$
$$= 14 + \sqrt{3}$$

19. $2 + 3\sqrt{y^2} - 6\sqrt{y^2} + 5 = 2 + 3y - 6y + 5$
$$= 7 - 3y$$

21. $3\sqrt{108} - 2\sqrt{18} - 3\sqrt{48}$
$$= 3\sqrt{36 \cdot 3} - 2\sqrt{9 \cdot 2} - 3\sqrt{16 \cdot 3}$$
$$= 3\sqrt{36} \cdot \sqrt{3} - 2\sqrt{9} \cdot \sqrt{2} - 3\sqrt{16} \cdot \sqrt{3}$$
$$= 3(6)\sqrt{3} - 2(3)\sqrt{2} - 3(4)\sqrt{3}$$
$$= 18\sqrt{3} - 6\sqrt{2} - 12\sqrt{3}$$
$$= 6\sqrt{3} - 6\sqrt{2}$$

23. $-5\sqrt[3]{625} + \sqrt[3]{40} = -5\sqrt[3]{125 \cdot 5} + \sqrt[3]{8 \cdot 5}$
$$= -5(5)\sqrt[3]{5} + 2\sqrt[3]{5}$$
$$= -25\sqrt[3]{5} + 2\sqrt[3]{5}$$
$$= -23\sqrt[3]{5}$$

25. $\sqrt{9b^3} - \sqrt{25b^3} + \sqrt{16b^3}$
$$= \sqrt{9b^2 \cdot b} - \sqrt{25b^2 \cdot b} + \sqrt{16b^2 \cdot b}$$
$$= 3b\sqrt{b} - 5b\sqrt{b} + 4b\sqrt{b}$$
$$= 2b\sqrt{b}$$

27. $5y\sqrt{8y} + 2\sqrt{50y^3} = 5y\sqrt{4 \cdot 2y} + 2\sqrt{25y^2 \cdot 2y}$
$$= 5y(2)\sqrt{2y} + 2(5y)\sqrt{2y}$$
$$= 10y\sqrt{2y} + 10y\sqrt{2y}$$
$$= 20y\sqrt{2y}$$

29. $\sqrt[3]{54xy^3} - 5\sqrt[3]{2xy^3} + y\sqrt[3]{128x}$
$$= \sqrt[3]{27y^3 \cdot 2x} - 5\sqrt[3]{y^3 \cdot 2x} + y\sqrt[3]{64 \cdot 2x}$$
$$= 3y\sqrt[3]{2x} - 5y\sqrt[3]{2x} + 4y\sqrt[3]{2x}$$
$$= 2y\sqrt[3]{2x}$$

31. $6\sqrt[3]{11} + 8\sqrt{11} - 12\sqrt{11} = 6\sqrt[3]{11} - 4\sqrt{11}$

33. $-2\sqrt[4]{x^7} + 3\sqrt[4]{16x^7} = -2\sqrt[4]{x^4 \cdot x^3} + 3\sqrt[4]{16x^4 \cdot x^3}$
$$= -2x\sqrt[4]{x^3} + 3(2x)\sqrt[4]{x^3}$$
$$= -2x\sqrt[4]{x^3} + 6x\sqrt[4]{x^3}$$
$$= 4x\sqrt[4]{x^3}$$

35. $\dfrac{4\sqrt{3}}{3} - \dfrac{\sqrt{12}}{3} = \dfrac{4\sqrt{3}}{3} - \dfrac{\sqrt{4 \cdot 3}}{3}$
$$= \dfrac{4\sqrt{3} - 2\sqrt{3}}{3}$$
$$= \dfrac{2\sqrt{3}}{3}$$

37. $\dfrac{\sqrt[3]{8x^4}}{7} + \dfrac{3x\sqrt[3]{x}}{7} = \dfrac{\sqrt[3]{8x^3 \cdot x}}{7} + \dfrac{3x\sqrt[3]{x}}{7}$
$$= \dfrac{2x\sqrt[3]{x} + 3x\sqrt[3]{x}}{7}$$
$$= \dfrac{5x\sqrt[3]{x}}{7}$$

39. $\sqrt{\dfrac{28}{x^2}} + \sqrt{\dfrac{7}{4x^2}} = \dfrac{\sqrt{28}}{\sqrt{x^2}} + \dfrac{\sqrt{7}}{\sqrt{4x^2}}$
$$= \dfrac{\sqrt{4 \cdot 7}}{x} + \dfrac{\sqrt{7}}{2x}$$
$$= \dfrac{2\sqrt{7}}{x} + \dfrac{\sqrt{7}}{2x}$$
$$= \dfrac{2\left(2\sqrt{7}\right) + \sqrt{7}}{2x}$$
$$= \dfrac{4\sqrt{7} + \sqrt{7}}{2x}$$
$$= \dfrac{5\sqrt{7}}{2x}$$

41. $\sqrt[3]{\dfrac{16}{27}} - \dfrac{\sqrt[3]{54}}{6} = \dfrac{\sqrt[3]{8 \cdot 2}}{\sqrt[3]{27}} - \dfrac{\sqrt[3]{27 \cdot 2}}{6}$
$$= \dfrac{2\sqrt[3]{2}}{3} - \dfrac{3\sqrt[3]{2}}{6}$$
$$= \dfrac{2\left(2\sqrt[3]{2}\right) - 3\sqrt[3]{2}}{6}$$
$$= \dfrac{4\sqrt[3]{2} - 3\sqrt[3]{2}}{6}$$
$$= \dfrac{\sqrt[3]{2}}{6}$$

43. $-\dfrac{\sqrt[3]{2x^4}}{9} + \sqrt[3]{\dfrac{250x^4}{27}} = -\dfrac{\sqrt[3]{x^3 \cdot 2x}}{9} + \dfrac{\sqrt[3]{125x^3 \cdot 2x}}{\sqrt[3]{27}}$
$$= \dfrac{-x\sqrt[3]{2x}}{9} + \dfrac{5x\sqrt[3]{2x}}{3}$$
$$= \dfrac{-x\sqrt[3]{2x} + 3\left(5x\sqrt[3]{2x}\right)}{9}$$
$$= \dfrac{-x\sqrt[3]{2x} + 15x\sqrt[3]{2x}}{9}$$
$$= \dfrac{14x\sqrt[3]{2x}}{9}$$

45. $P = 2\sqrt{12} + \sqrt{12} + 2\sqrt{27} + 3\sqrt{3}$
$$= 2\sqrt{4 \cdot 3} + \sqrt{4 \cdot 3} + 2\sqrt{9 \cdot 3} + 3\sqrt{3}$$
$$= 2(2)\sqrt{3} + 2\sqrt{3} + 2(3)\sqrt{3} + 3\sqrt{3}$$
$$= 4\sqrt{3} + 2\sqrt{3} + 6\sqrt{3} + 3\sqrt{3}$$
$$= 15\sqrt{3} \text{ inches}$$

47. $\sqrt{7}\left(\sqrt{5} + \sqrt{3}\right) = \sqrt{7}\sqrt{5} + \sqrt{7}\sqrt{3}$
$$= \sqrt{35} + \sqrt{21}$$

49. $\left(\sqrt{5}-\sqrt{2}\right)^2 = \left(\sqrt{5}\right)^2 - 2\sqrt{5}\sqrt{2} + \left(\sqrt{2}\right)^2$
$\qquad\qquad = 5 - 2\sqrt{10} + 2$
$\qquad\qquad = 7 - 2\sqrt{10}$

51. $\sqrt{3x}\left(\sqrt{3}-\sqrt{x}\right) = \sqrt{3x}\sqrt{3} - \sqrt{3x}\sqrt{x}$
$\qquad\qquad = \sqrt{9x} - \sqrt{3x^2}$
$\qquad\qquad = 3\sqrt{x} - x\sqrt{3}$

53. $\left(2\sqrt{x}-5\right)\left(3\sqrt{x}+1\right)$
$\qquad = 2\sqrt{x}\left(3\sqrt{x}\right) + 2\sqrt{x}\cdot 1 - 5\left(3\sqrt{x}\right) - 5(1)$
$\qquad = 6x + 2\sqrt{x} - 15\sqrt{x} - 5$
$\qquad = 6x - 13\sqrt{x} - 5$

55. $\left(\sqrt[3]{a}-4\right)\left(\sqrt[3]{a}+5\right)$
$\qquad = \sqrt[3]{a}\left(\sqrt[3]{a}\right) + \sqrt[3]{a}\cdot 5 - 4\sqrt[3]{a} - 4(5)$
$\qquad = \sqrt[3]{a^2} + 5\sqrt[3]{a} - 4\sqrt[3]{a} - 20$
$\qquad = \sqrt[3]{a^2} + \sqrt[3]{a} - 20$

57. $6\left(\sqrt{2}-2\right) = 6\sqrt{2} - 6(2) = 6\sqrt{2} - 12$

59. $\sqrt{2}\left(\sqrt{2}+x\sqrt{6}\right) = \sqrt{2}\sqrt{2} + \sqrt{2}\left(x\sqrt{6}\right)$
$\qquad\qquad = 2 + x\sqrt{12}$
$\qquad\qquad = 2 + x\sqrt{4\cdot 3}$
$\qquad\qquad = 2 + 2x\sqrt{3}$

61. $\left(2\sqrt{7}+3\sqrt{5}\right)\left(\sqrt{7}-2\sqrt{5}\right)$
$\qquad = 2\sqrt{7}\sqrt{7} + 2\sqrt{7}\left(-2\sqrt{5}\right) + 3\sqrt{5}\sqrt{7} + 3\sqrt{5}\left(-2\sqrt{5}\right)$
$\qquad = 2(7) - 4\sqrt{35} + 3\sqrt{35} - 6(5)$
$\qquad = 14 - \sqrt{35} - 30$
$\qquad = -16 - \sqrt{35}$

63. $\left(\sqrt{x}-y\right)\left(\sqrt{x}+y\right) = \left(\sqrt{x}\right)^2 - y^2 = x - y^2$

65. $\left(\sqrt{3}+x\right)^2 = \left(\sqrt{3}\right)^2 + 2\sqrt{3}\cdot x + x^2$
$\qquad\qquad = 3 + 2x\sqrt{3} + x^2$

67. $\left(\sqrt{5x}-2\sqrt{3x}\right)\left(\sqrt{5x}-3\sqrt{3x}\right)$
$\qquad = \left(\sqrt{5x}\right)^2 - \sqrt{5x}\left(3\sqrt{3x}\right) - 2\sqrt{3x}\left(\sqrt{5x}\right)$
$\qquad\qquad\qquad - 2\sqrt{3x}\left(-3\sqrt{3x}\right)$
$\qquad = 5x - 3x\sqrt{15} - 2x\sqrt{15} + 6\cdot 3x$
$\qquad = 23x - 5x\sqrt{15}$

69. $\left(\sqrt[3]{4}+2\right)\left(\sqrt[3]{2}-1\right)$
$\qquad = \sqrt[3]{4}\left(\sqrt[3]{2}\right) + \sqrt[3]{4}\cdot(-1) + 2\sqrt[3]{2} + 2(-1)$
$\qquad = \sqrt[3]{8} - \sqrt[3]{4} + 2\sqrt[3]{2} - 2$
$\qquad = 2 - \sqrt[3]{4} + 2\sqrt[3]{2} - 2$
$\qquad = 2\sqrt[3]{2} - \sqrt[3]{4}$

71. $\left(\sqrt[3]{x}+1\right)\left(\sqrt[3]{x^2} - \sqrt[3]{x} + 1\right)$
$\qquad = \sqrt[3]{x}\left(\sqrt[3]{x^2}\right) - \sqrt[3]{x}\left(\sqrt[3]{x}\right) + \sqrt[3]{x}\left(1\right)$
$\qquad\qquad + 1\left(\sqrt[3]{x^2}\right) - 1\left(\sqrt[3]{x}\right) + 1(1)$
$\qquad = \sqrt[3]{x^3} - \sqrt[3]{x^2} + \sqrt[3]{x} + \sqrt[3]{x^2} - \sqrt[3]{x} + 1$
$\qquad = x + 1$

73. $\left(\sqrt{x-1}+5\right)^2 = \left(\sqrt{x-1}\right)^2 + 2\sqrt{x-1}\cdot 5 + 5^2$
$\qquad\qquad = (x-1) + 10\sqrt{x-1} + 25$
$\qquad\qquad = x + 10\sqrt{x-1} + 24$

75. $\left(\sqrt{2x+5}-1\right)^2 = \left(\sqrt{2x+5}\right)^2 - 2\sqrt{2x+5}\cdot 1 + 1^2$
$\qquad\qquad = (2x+5) - 2\sqrt{2x+5} + 1$
$\qquad\qquad = 2x - 2\sqrt{2x+5} + 6$

77. $\dfrac{2x-14}{2} = \dfrac{2(x-7)}{2} = x - 7$

79. $\dfrac{7x-7y}{x^2-y^2} = \dfrac{7(x-y)}{(x+y)(x-y)} = \dfrac{7}{x+y}$

81. $\dfrac{6a^2b-9ab}{3ab} = \dfrac{3ab(2a-3)}{3ab} = 2a - 3$

83. $\dfrac{-4+2\sqrt{3}}{6} = \dfrac{2\left(-2+\sqrt{3}\right)}{6} = \dfrac{-2+\sqrt{3}}{3}$

85. $P = 2l + 2w$

$\quad = 2\left(3\sqrt{20}\right) + 2\left(\sqrt{125}\right)$

$\quad = 6\sqrt{4\cdot5} + 2\sqrt{25\cdot5}$

$\quad = 6(2)\sqrt{5} + 2(5)\sqrt{5}$

$\quad = 12\sqrt{5} + 10\sqrt{5}$

$\quad = 22\sqrt{5}$ feet

$A = lw$

$\quad = \left(3\sqrt{20}\right)\left(\sqrt{125}\right)$

$\quad = 3\sqrt{4\cdot5}\sqrt{25\cdot5}$

$\quad = 3(2)\sqrt{5}\cdot5\sqrt{5}$

$\quad = 30\cdot5$

$\quad = 150$ square feet

87. a. $\sqrt{3} + \sqrt{3} = 2\sqrt{3}$

b. $\sqrt{3}\cdot\sqrt{3} = \sqrt{9} = 3$

c. Answers may vary

89. Answer may vary

Section 7.5

Practice Exercises

1. a. $\dfrac{5}{\sqrt{3}} = \dfrac{5\cdot\sqrt{3}}{\sqrt{3}\cdot\sqrt{3}} = \dfrac{5\sqrt{3}}{3}$

b. $\dfrac{3\sqrt{25}}{\sqrt{4x}} = \dfrac{3(5)}{2\sqrt{x}} = \dfrac{15}{2\sqrt{x}} = \dfrac{15\cdot\sqrt{x}}{2\sqrt{x}\cdot\sqrt{x}} = \dfrac{15\sqrt{x}}{2x}$

c. $\sqrt[3]{\dfrac{2}{9}} = \dfrac{\sqrt[3]{2}}{\sqrt[3]{9}} = \dfrac{\sqrt[3]{2}\cdot\sqrt[3]{3}}{\sqrt[3]{3^2}\cdot\sqrt[3]{3}} = \dfrac{\sqrt[3]{6}}{3}$

2. $\sqrt{\dfrac{3z}{5y}} = \dfrac{\sqrt{3z}}{\sqrt{5y}} = \dfrac{\sqrt{3z}\cdot\sqrt{5y}}{\sqrt{5y}\cdot\sqrt{5y}} = \dfrac{\sqrt{15yz}}{5y}$

3. $\dfrac{\sqrt[3]{z^2}}{\sqrt[3]{27x^4}} = \dfrac{\sqrt[3]{z^2}}{\sqrt[3]{27x^3}\cdot\sqrt[3]{x}}$

$\quad = \dfrac{\sqrt[3]{z^2}}{3x\sqrt[3]{x}}$

$\quad = \dfrac{\sqrt[3]{z^2}\cdot\sqrt[3]{x^2}}{3x\sqrt[3]{x}\cdot\sqrt[3]{x^2}}$

$\quad = \dfrac{\sqrt[3]{z^2x^2}}{3x\sqrt[3]{x^3}}$

$\quad = \dfrac{\sqrt[3]{x^2z^2}}{3x^2}$

4. a. $\dfrac{5}{3\sqrt{5}+2} = \dfrac{5\left(3\sqrt{5}-2\right)}{\left(3\sqrt{5}+2\right)\left(3\sqrt{5}-2\right)}$

$\quad = \dfrac{5\left(3\sqrt{5}-2\right)}{\left(3\sqrt{5}\right)^2 - 2^2}$

$\quad = \dfrac{5\left(3\sqrt{5}-2\right)}{45-4}$

$\quad = \dfrac{5\left(3\sqrt{5}-2\right)}{41}$

b. $\dfrac{\sqrt{2}+5}{\sqrt{3}-\sqrt{5}} = \dfrac{\left(\sqrt{2}+5\right)\left(\sqrt{3}+\sqrt{5}\right)}{\left(\sqrt{3}-\sqrt{5}\right)\left(\sqrt{3}+\sqrt{5}\right)}$

$\quad = \dfrac{\sqrt{2}\sqrt{3}+\sqrt{2}\sqrt{5}+5\sqrt{3}+5\sqrt{5}}{\left(\sqrt{3}\right)^2 - \left(\sqrt{5}\right)^2}$

$\quad = \dfrac{\sqrt{6}+\sqrt{10}+5\sqrt{3}+5\sqrt{5}}{3-5}$

$\quad = \dfrac{\sqrt{6}+\sqrt{10}+5\sqrt{3}+5\sqrt{5}}{-2}$

c. $\dfrac{3\sqrt{x}}{2\sqrt{x}+\sqrt{y}} = \dfrac{3\sqrt{x}\left(2\sqrt{x}-\sqrt{y}\right)}{\left(2\sqrt{x}+\sqrt{y}\right)\left(2\sqrt{x}-\sqrt{y}\right)}$

$\quad = \dfrac{6\sqrt{x^2}-3\sqrt{xy}}{\left(2\sqrt{x}\right)^2 - \left(\sqrt{y}\right)^2}$

$\quad = \dfrac{6x-3\sqrt{xy}}{4x-y}$

5. $\dfrac{\sqrt{32}}{\sqrt{80}} = \dfrac{\sqrt{16\cdot2}}{\sqrt{16\cdot5}} = \dfrac{4\sqrt{2}}{4\sqrt{5}} = \dfrac{\sqrt{2}}{\sqrt{5}} = \dfrac{\sqrt{2}\cdot\sqrt{2}}{\sqrt{5}\cdot\sqrt{2}} = \dfrac{2}{\sqrt{10}}$

6. $\dfrac{\sqrt[3]{5b}}{\sqrt[3]{2a}} = \dfrac{\sqrt[3]{5b} \cdot \sqrt[3]{25b^2}}{\sqrt[3]{2a} \cdot \sqrt[3]{25b^2}} = \dfrac{\sqrt[3]{125b^3}}{\sqrt[3]{50ab^2}} = \dfrac{5b}{\sqrt[3]{50ab^2}}$

7. $\dfrac{\sqrt{x}-3}{4} = \dfrac{\left(\sqrt{x}-3\right)\left(\sqrt{x}+3\right)}{4\left(\sqrt{x}+3\right)}$

$= \dfrac{\left(\sqrt{x}\right)^2 - (3)^2}{4\left(\sqrt{x}+3\right)}$

$= \dfrac{x-9}{4\left(\sqrt{x}+3\right)}$

Vocabulary and Readiness Check

1. The <u>conjugate</u> of $a + b$ is $a - b$.

2. The process of writing an equivalent expression, but without a radical in the denominator is called <u>rationalizing the denominator</u>.

3. The process of writing an equivalent expression, but without a radical in the numerator is called <u>rationalizing the numerator</u>.

4. To rationalize the denominator of $\dfrac{5}{\sqrt{3}}$, we multiply by $\dfrac{\sqrt{3}}{\sqrt{3}}$.

5. The conjugate of $\sqrt{2} + x$ is $\sqrt{2} - x$.

6. The conjugate of $\sqrt{3} + y$ is $\sqrt{3} - y$.

7. The conjugate of $5 - \sqrt{a}$ is $5 + \sqrt{a}$.

8. The conjugate of $6 - \sqrt{b}$ is $6 + \sqrt{b}$.

9. The conjugate of $-7\sqrt{5} + 8\sqrt{x}$ is $-7\sqrt{5} - 8\sqrt{x}$.

10. The conjugate of $-9\sqrt{2} - 6\sqrt{y}$ is $-9\sqrt{2} + 6\sqrt{y}$.

Exercise Set 7.5

1. $\dfrac{\sqrt{2}}{\sqrt{7}} = \dfrac{\sqrt{2} \cdot \sqrt{7}}{\sqrt{7} \cdot \sqrt{7}} = \dfrac{\sqrt{14}}{\sqrt{49}} = \dfrac{\sqrt{14}}{7}$

3. $\sqrt{\dfrac{1}{5}} = \dfrac{\sqrt{1}}{\sqrt{5}} = \dfrac{1 \cdot \sqrt{5}}{\sqrt{5} \cdot \sqrt{5}} = \dfrac{\sqrt{5}}{5}$

5. $\sqrt{\dfrac{4}{x}} = \dfrac{\sqrt{4}}{\sqrt{x}} = \dfrac{2 \cdot \sqrt{x}}{\sqrt{x} \cdot \sqrt{x}} = \dfrac{2\sqrt{x}}{\sqrt{x^2}} = \dfrac{2\sqrt{x}}{x}$

7. $\dfrac{4}{\sqrt[3]{3}} = \dfrac{4 \cdot \sqrt[3]{9}}{\sqrt[3]{3} \cdot \sqrt[3]{9}} = \dfrac{4\sqrt[3]{9}}{\sqrt[3]{27}} = \dfrac{4\sqrt[3]{9}}{3}$

9. $\dfrac{3}{\sqrt{8x}} = \dfrac{3 \cdot \sqrt{2x}}{\sqrt{8x} \cdot \sqrt{2x}} = \dfrac{3\sqrt{2x}}{\sqrt{16x^2}} = \dfrac{3\sqrt{2x}}{4x}$

11. $\dfrac{3}{\sqrt[3]{4x^2}} = \dfrac{3 \cdot \sqrt[3]{2x}}{\sqrt[3]{4x^2} \cdot \sqrt[3]{2x}} = \dfrac{3\sqrt[3]{2x}}{\sqrt[3]{8x^3}} = \dfrac{3\sqrt[3]{2x}}{2x}$

13. $\dfrac{9}{\sqrt{3a}} = \dfrac{9 \cdot \sqrt{3a}}{\sqrt{3a} \cdot \sqrt{3a}} = \dfrac{9\sqrt{3a}}{3a} = \dfrac{3\sqrt{3a}}{a}$

15. $\dfrac{3}{\sqrt[3]{2}} = \dfrac{3 \cdot \sqrt[3]{4}}{\sqrt[3]{2} \cdot \sqrt[3]{4}} = \dfrac{3\sqrt[3]{4}}{\sqrt[3]{8}} = \dfrac{3\sqrt[3]{4}}{2}$

17. $\dfrac{2\sqrt{3}}{\sqrt{7}} = \dfrac{2\sqrt{3} \cdot \sqrt{7}}{\sqrt{7} \cdot \sqrt{7}} = \dfrac{2\sqrt{21}}{\sqrt{49}} = \dfrac{2\sqrt{21}}{7}$

19. $\sqrt{\dfrac{2x}{5y}} = \dfrac{\sqrt{2x}}{\sqrt{5y}} = \dfrac{\sqrt{2x} \cdot \sqrt{5y}}{\sqrt{5y} \cdot \sqrt{5y}} = \dfrac{\sqrt{10xy}}{5y}$

21. $\sqrt[3]{\dfrac{3}{5}} = \dfrac{\sqrt[3]{3}}{\sqrt[3]{5}} \cdot \dfrac{\sqrt[3]{25}}{\sqrt[3]{25}} = \dfrac{\sqrt[3]{75}}{5}$

23. $\sqrt{\dfrac{3x}{50}} = \dfrac{\sqrt{3x}}{\sqrt{50}}$

$= \dfrac{\sqrt{3x}}{5\sqrt{2}}$

$= \dfrac{\sqrt{3x} \cdot \sqrt{2}}{5\sqrt{2} \cdot \sqrt{2}}$

$= \dfrac{\sqrt{6x}}{5 \cdot 2}$

$= \dfrac{\sqrt{6x}}{10}$

25. $\dfrac{1}{\sqrt{12z}} = \dfrac{1}{\sqrt{4 \cdot 3z}} = \dfrac{1}{2\sqrt{3z}} \cdot \dfrac{\sqrt{3z}}{\sqrt{3z}} = \dfrac{\sqrt{3z}}{6z}$

27. $\dfrac{\sqrt[3]{2y^2}}{\sqrt[3]{9x^2}} = \dfrac{\sqrt[3]{2y^2} \cdot \sqrt[3]{3x}}{\sqrt[3]{9x^2} \cdot \sqrt[3]{3x}} = \dfrac{\sqrt[3]{6xy^2}}{3x}$

29. $\sqrt[4]{\dfrac{81}{8}} = \dfrac{\sqrt[4]{81}}{\sqrt[4]{8}} = \dfrac{3 \cdot \sqrt[4]{2}}{\sqrt[4]{8} \cdot \sqrt[4]{2}} = \dfrac{3\sqrt[4]{2}}{\sqrt[4]{16}} = \dfrac{3\sqrt[4]{2}}{2}$

31. $\sqrt[4]{\dfrac{16}{9x^7}} = \dfrac{\sqrt[4]{16}}{\sqrt[4]{9x^7}} = \dfrac{2 \cdot \sqrt[4]{9x}}{\sqrt[4]{9x^7} \cdot \sqrt[4]{9x}} = \dfrac{2\sqrt[4]{9x}}{\sqrt[4]{81x^8}} = \dfrac{2\sqrt[4]{9x}}{3x^2}$

33. $\dfrac{5a}{\sqrt[5]{8a^9b^{11}}} = \dfrac{5a \cdot \sqrt[5]{4ab^4}}{\sqrt[5]{8a^9b^{11}} \cdot \sqrt[5]{4ab^4}}$

$\qquad = \dfrac{5a\sqrt[5]{4ab^4}}{\sqrt[5]{32a^{10}b^{15}}}$

$\qquad = \dfrac{5a\sqrt[5]{4ab^4}}{2a^2b^3}$

35. $\dfrac{6}{2-\sqrt{7}} = \dfrac{6\left(2+\sqrt{7}\right)}{\left(2-\sqrt{7}\right)\left(2+\sqrt{7}\right)}$

$\qquad = \dfrac{6\left(2+\sqrt{7}\right)}{2^2 - \left(\sqrt{7}\right)^2}$

$\qquad = \dfrac{6\left(2+\sqrt{7}\right)}{4-7}$

$\qquad = \dfrac{6\left(2+\sqrt{7}\right)}{-3}$

$\qquad = -2\left(2+\sqrt{7}\right)$

37. $\dfrac{-7}{\sqrt{x}-3} = \dfrac{-7\left(\sqrt{x}+3\right)}{\left(\sqrt{x}-3\right)\left(\sqrt{x}+3\right)}$

$\qquad = \dfrac{-7\left(\sqrt{x}+3\right)}{\left(\sqrt{x}\right)^2 - (3)^2}$

$\qquad = \dfrac{-7\left(\sqrt{x}+3\right)}{x-9} \text{ or } \dfrac{7\left(\sqrt{x}+3\right)}{9-x}$

39. $\dfrac{\sqrt{2}-\sqrt{3}}{\sqrt{2}+\sqrt{3}} = \dfrac{\left(\sqrt{2}-\sqrt{3}\right)\left(\sqrt{2}-\sqrt{3}\right)}{\left(\sqrt{2}+\sqrt{3}\right)\left(\sqrt{2}-\sqrt{3}\right)}$

$\qquad = \dfrac{\left(\sqrt{2}\right)^2 - 2\sqrt{2}\sqrt{3} + \left(\sqrt{3}\right)^2}{\left(\sqrt{2}\right)^2 - \left(\sqrt{3}\right)^2}$

$\qquad = \dfrac{2 - 2\sqrt{6} + 3}{2-3}$

$\qquad = \dfrac{5 - 2\sqrt{6}}{-1}$

$\qquad = -5 + 2\sqrt{6}$

41. $\dfrac{\sqrt{a}+1}{2\sqrt{a}-\sqrt{b}}$

$\qquad = \dfrac{\left(\sqrt{a}+1\right)\left(2\sqrt{a}+\sqrt{b}\right)}{\left(2\sqrt{a}-\sqrt{b}\right)\left(2\sqrt{a}+\sqrt{b}\right)}$

$\qquad = \dfrac{\sqrt{a} \cdot 2\sqrt{a} + \sqrt{a}\sqrt{b} + 1 \cdot 2\sqrt{a} + 1 \cdot \sqrt{b}}{\left(2\sqrt{a}\right)^2 - \left(\sqrt{b}\right)^2}$

$\qquad = \dfrac{2a + \sqrt{ab} + 2\sqrt{a} + \sqrt{b}}{4a-b}$

43. $\dfrac{8}{1+\sqrt{10}} = \dfrac{8\left(1-\sqrt{10}\right)}{\left(1+\sqrt{10}\right)\left(1-\sqrt{10}\right)}$

$\qquad = \dfrac{8\left(1-\sqrt{10}\right)}{1^2 - \left(\sqrt{10}\right)^2}$

$\qquad = \dfrac{8\left(1-\sqrt{10}\right)}{1-10}$

$\qquad = -\dfrac{8\left(1-\sqrt{10}\right)}{9}$

45.

$$\frac{\sqrt{x}}{\sqrt{x}+\sqrt{y}} = \frac{\sqrt{x}\left(\sqrt{x}-\sqrt{y}\right)}{\left(\sqrt{x}+\sqrt{y}\right)\left(\sqrt{x}-\sqrt{y}\right)}$$

$$= \frac{\sqrt{x}\left(\sqrt{x}-\sqrt{y}\right)}{\left(\sqrt{x}\right)^2 - \left(\sqrt{y}\right)^2}$$

$$= \frac{\sqrt{x}\left(\sqrt{x}-\sqrt{y}\right)}{x-y}$$

$$= \frac{\sqrt{x}\sqrt{x}-\sqrt{x}\sqrt{y}}{x-y}$$

$$= \frac{x-\sqrt{xy}}{x-y}$$

47.

$$\frac{2\sqrt{3}+\sqrt{6}}{4\sqrt{3}-\sqrt{6}} = \frac{\left(2\sqrt{3}+\sqrt{6}\right)\left(4\sqrt{3}+\sqrt{6}\right)}{\left(4\sqrt{3}-\sqrt{6}\right)\left(4\sqrt{3}+\sqrt{6}\right)}$$

$$= \frac{8\cdot 3 + 2\sqrt{18}+4\sqrt{18}+6}{\left(4\sqrt{3}\right)^2-\left(\sqrt{6}\right)^2}$$

$$= \frac{30+6\sqrt{18}}{16\cdot 3 - 6}$$

$$= \frac{30+6(3)\sqrt{2}}{42}$$

$$= \frac{30+18\sqrt{2}}{42}$$

$$= \frac{6\left(5+3\sqrt{2}\right)}{42}$$

$$= \frac{5+3\sqrt{2}}{7}$$

49.

$$\sqrt{\frac{5}{3}} = \frac{\sqrt{5}}{\sqrt{3}} = \frac{\sqrt{5}\cdot\sqrt{5}}{\sqrt{3}\cdot\sqrt{5}} = \frac{\sqrt{25}}{\sqrt{15}} = \frac{5}{\sqrt{15}}$$

51.

$$\sqrt{\frac{18}{5}} = \frac{\sqrt{18}}{\sqrt{5}}$$

$$= \frac{\sqrt{9}\cdot\sqrt{2}}{\sqrt{5}}$$

$$= \frac{3\sqrt{2}}{\sqrt{5}}$$

$$= \frac{3\sqrt{2}\cdot\sqrt{2}}{\sqrt{5}\cdot\sqrt{2}}$$

$$= \frac{3\cdot 2}{\sqrt{10}}$$

$$= \frac{6}{\sqrt{10}}$$

53.

$$\frac{\sqrt{4x}}{7} = \frac{2\sqrt{x}}{7} = \frac{2\sqrt{x}\cdot\sqrt{x}}{7\cdot\sqrt{x}} = \frac{2\sqrt{x^2}}{7\sqrt{x}} = \frac{2x}{7\sqrt{x}}$$

55.

$$\frac{\sqrt[3]{5y^2}}{\sqrt[3]{4x}} = \frac{\sqrt[3]{5y^2}\cdot\sqrt[3]{5^2 y}}{\sqrt[3]{4x}\cdot\sqrt[3]{5^2 y}} = \frac{\sqrt[3]{5^3 y^3}}{\sqrt[3]{100xy}} = \frac{5y}{\sqrt[3]{100xy}}$$

57.

$$\sqrt{\frac{2}{5}} = \frac{\sqrt{2}}{\sqrt{5}} = \frac{\sqrt{2}\cdot\sqrt{2}}{\sqrt{5}\cdot\sqrt{2}} = \frac{\sqrt{4}}{\sqrt{10}} = \frac{2}{\sqrt{10}}$$

59.

$$\frac{\sqrt{2x}}{11} = \frac{\sqrt{2x}\cdot\sqrt{2x}}{11\cdot\sqrt{2x}} = \frac{\sqrt{4x^2}}{11\sqrt{2x}} = \frac{2x}{11\sqrt{2x}}$$

61.

$$\sqrt[3]{\frac{7}{8}} = \frac{\sqrt[3]{7}}{\sqrt[3]{8}}$$

$$= \frac{\sqrt[3]{7}}{2}$$

$$= \frac{\sqrt[3]{7}\cdot\sqrt[3]{7^2}}{2\cdot\sqrt[3]{7^2}}$$

$$= \frac{\sqrt[3]{7^3}}{2\sqrt[3]{49}}$$

$$= \frac{7}{2\sqrt[3]{49}}$$

63.

$$\frac{\sqrt[3]{3x^5}}{10} = \frac{\sqrt[3]{x^3\cdot 3x^2}}{10}$$

$$= \frac{x\sqrt[3]{3x^2}}{10}$$

$$= \frac{x\sqrt[3]{3x^2}\cdot\sqrt[3]{3^2 x}}{10\cdot\sqrt[3]{3^2 x}}$$

$$= \frac{x\sqrt[3]{3^3 x^3}}{10\sqrt[3]{9x}}$$

$$= \frac{x\cdot 3x}{10\sqrt[3]{9x}}$$

$$= \frac{3x^2}{10\sqrt[3]{9x}}$$

65. $\sqrt{\dfrac{18x^4y^6}{3z}} = \dfrac{\sqrt{18x^4y^6}}{\sqrt{3z}}$

$= \dfrac{\sqrt{9x^4y^6 \cdot 2}}{\sqrt{3z}}$

$= \dfrac{3x^2y^3\sqrt{2}}{\sqrt{3z}}$

$= \dfrac{3x^2y^3\sqrt{2} \cdot \sqrt{2}}{\sqrt{3z} \cdot \sqrt{2}}$

$= \dfrac{3x^2y^3 \cdot 2}{\sqrt{6z}}$

$= \dfrac{6x^2y^3}{\sqrt{6z}}$

67. Answers may vary

69. $\dfrac{2-\sqrt{11}}{6} = \dfrac{\left(2-\sqrt{11}\right)\left(2+\sqrt{11}\right)}{6\left(2+\sqrt{11}\right)}$

$= \dfrac{4-11}{12+6\sqrt{11}}$

$= \dfrac{-7}{12+6\sqrt{11}}$

71. $\dfrac{2-\sqrt{7}}{-5} = \dfrac{\left(2-\sqrt{7}\right)\left(2+\sqrt{7}\right)}{-5\left(2+\sqrt{7}\right)}$

$= \dfrac{4-7}{-5\left(2+\sqrt{7}\right)}$

$= \dfrac{-3}{-5\left(2+\sqrt{7}\right)}$

$= \dfrac{3}{5\left(2+\sqrt{7}\right)}$

$= \dfrac{3}{10+5\sqrt{7}}$

73. $\dfrac{\sqrt{x}+3}{\sqrt{x}} = \dfrac{\left(\sqrt{x}+3\right)\left(\sqrt{x}-3\right)}{\sqrt{x}\left(\sqrt{x}-3\right)}$

$= \dfrac{\sqrt{x^2}-9}{\sqrt{x^2}-3\sqrt{x}}$

$= \dfrac{x-9}{x-3\sqrt{x}}$

75. $\dfrac{\sqrt{2}-1}{\sqrt{2}+1} = \dfrac{\left(\sqrt{2}-1\right)\left(\sqrt{2}+1\right)}{\left(\sqrt{2}+1\right)\left(\sqrt{2}+1\right)}$

$= \dfrac{\sqrt{4}-1}{\sqrt{4}+2\sqrt{2}+1}$

$= \dfrac{2-1}{2+2\sqrt{2}+1}$

$= \dfrac{1}{3+2\sqrt{2}}$

77. $\dfrac{\sqrt{x}+1}{\sqrt{x}-1} = \dfrac{\left(\sqrt{x}+1\right)\left(\sqrt{x}-1\right)}{\left(\sqrt{x}-1\right)\left(\sqrt{x}-1\right)}$

$= \dfrac{\sqrt{x^2}-1}{\sqrt{x^2}-2\sqrt{x}+1}$

$= \dfrac{x-1}{x-2\sqrt{x}+1}$

79. $2x-7 = 3(x-4)$

$2x-7 = 3x-12$

$-x-7 = -12$

$-x = -5$

$x = 5$

The solution is 5.

81. $(x-6)(2x+1) = 0$

$x-6 = 0$ or $2x+1 = 0$

$x = 6$ or $\quad 2x = -1$

$\qquad\qquad\qquad x = -\dfrac{1}{2}$

The solutions are $-\dfrac{1}{2}$, 6.

83. $\quad x^2-8x = -12$

$x^2-8x+12 = 0$

$(x-6)(x-2) = 0$

$x-6 = 0$ or $x-2 = 0$

$x = 6$ or $\quad x = 2$

The solutions are 2, 6.

85. $\dfrac{9}{\sqrt[3]{5}} = \dfrac{9}{\sqrt[3]{5}} \cdot \dfrac{\sqrt[3]{25}}{\sqrt[3]{25}} = \dfrac{9\sqrt[3]{25}}{\sqrt[3]{125}} = \dfrac{9\sqrt[3]{25}}{5}$

The smallest number is $\sqrt[3]{25}$.

87. $r = \sqrt{\dfrac{A}{4\pi}}$

$= \dfrac{\sqrt{A}}{\sqrt{4\pi}}$

$= \dfrac{\sqrt{A}}{2\sqrt{\pi}}$

$= \dfrac{\sqrt{A} \cdot \sqrt{\pi}}{2\sqrt{\pi} \cdot \sqrt{\pi}}$

$= \dfrac{\sqrt{A\pi}}{2\pi}$

89. Answers may vary

Integrated Review

1. $\sqrt{81} = 9$ because $9^2 = 81$.

2. $\sqrt[3]{-8} = -2$ because $(-2)^3 = -8$.

3. $\sqrt[4]{\dfrac{1}{16}} = \dfrac{1}{2}$ because $\left(\dfrac{1}{2}\right)^4 = \dfrac{1}{16}$.

4. $\sqrt{x^6} = x^3$ because $(x^3)^2 = x^6$.

5. $\sqrt[3]{y^9} = y^3$ because $(y^3)^3 = y^9$.

6. $\sqrt{4y^{10}} = 2y^5$ because $(2y^5)^2 = 4y^{10}$.

7. $\sqrt[5]{-32y^5} = -2y$ because $(-2y)^5 = -32y^5$.

8. $\sqrt[4]{81b^{12}} = 3b^3$ because $(3b^3)^4 = 81b^{12}$.

9. $36^{1/2} = \sqrt{36} = 6$

10. $(3y)^{1/4} = \sqrt[4]{3y}$

11. $64^{-2/3} = \dfrac{1}{\left(\sqrt[3]{64}\right)^2} = \dfrac{1}{4^2} = \dfrac{1}{16}$

12. $(x+1)^{3/5} = \sqrt[5]{(x+1)^3}$

13. $y^{-1/6} \cdot y^{7/6} = y^{-\frac{1}{6}+\frac{7}{6}} = y^{6/6} = y$

14. $\dfrac{(2x^{1/3})^4}{x^{5/6}} = 16x^{4/3}x^{-5/6}$

$= 16x^{\frac{8}{6}-\frac{5}{6}}$

$= 16x^{3/6}$

$= 16x^{1/2}$

15. $\dfrac{x^{1/4}x^{3/4}}{x^{-1/4}} = x^{\frac{1}{4}+\frac{3}{4}+\frac{1}{4}} = x^{5/4}$

16. $4^{1/3} \cdot 4^{2/5} = 4^{\frac{1}{3}+\frac{2}{5}} = 4^{\frac{5}{15}+\frac{6}{15}} = 4^{11/15}$

17. $\sqrt[3]{8x^6} = (8x^6)^{1/3} = (2^3 x^6)^{1/3} = 2^{3/3} x^{6/3} = 2x^2$

18. $\sqrt[12]{a^9 b^6} = (a^9 b^6)^{1/12}$

$= a^{9/12} b^{6/12}$

$= a^{3/4} b^{1/2}$

$= a^{3/4} b^{2/4}$

$= (a^3 b^2)^{1/4}$

$= \sqrt[4]{a^3 b^2}$

19. $\sqrt[4]{x} \cdot \sqrt{x} = x^{1/4} \cdot x^{1/2} = x^{\frac{1}{4}+\frac{2}{4}} = x^{3/4} = \sqrt[4]{x^3}$

20. $\sqrt{5} \cdot \sqrt[3]{2} = 5^{1/2} \cdot 2^{1/3}$

$= 5^{3/6} \cdot 2^{2/6}$

$= (5^3 \cdot 2^2)^{1/6}$

$= \sqrt[6]{5^3 \cdot 2^2}$

$= \sqrt[6]{500}$

21. $\sqrt{40} = \sqrt{4}\sqrt{10} = 2\sqrt{10}$

22. $\sqrt[4]{16x^7 y^{10}} = \sqrt[4]{16x^4 y^8} \sqrt[4]{x^3 y^2} = 2xy^2 \sqrt[4]{x^3 y^2}$

23. $\sqrt[3]{54x^4} = \sqrt[3]{27x^3} \sqrt[3]{2x} = 3x\sqrt[3]{2x}$

24. $\sqrt[5]{-64b^{10}} = \sqrt[5]{-32b^{10}} \sqrt[5]{2} = -2b^2 \sqrt[5]{2}$

25. $\sqrt{5} \cdot \sqrt{x} = \sqrt{5x}$

26. $\sqrt[3]{8x} \cdot \sqrt[3]{8x^2} = \sqrt[3]{64x^3} = 4x$

27. $\dfrac{\sqrt{98y^6}}{\sqrt{2y}} = \sqrt{\dfrac{98y^6}{2y}}$

$\qquad = \sqrt{49y^5}$

$\qquad = \sqrt{49y^4} \cdot \sqrt{y}$

$\qquad = 7y^2\sqrt{y}$

28. $\dfrac{\sqrt[4]{48a^9b^3}}{\sqrt[4]{ab^3}} = \sqrt[4]{\dfrac{48a^9b^3}{ab^3}}$

$\qquad = \sqrt[4]{48a^8}$

$\qquad = \sqrt[4]{16a^8} \cdot \sqrt[4]{3}$

$\qquad = 2a^2\sqrt[4]{3}$

29. $\sqrt{20} - \sqrt{75} + 5\sqrt{7} = \sqrt{4}\sqrt{5} - \sqrt{25}\sqrt{3} + 5\sqrt{7}$

$\qquad\qquad\qquad\qquad = 2\sqrt{5} - 5\sqrt{3} + 5\sqrt{7}$

30. $\sqrt[3]{54y^4} - y\sqrt[3]{16y} = \sqrt[3]{27y^3}\sqrt[3]{2y} - y\sqrt[3]{8}\sqrt[3]{2y}$

$\qquad\qquad\qquad\qquad = 3y\sqrt[3]{2y} - 2y\sqrt[3]{2y}$

$\qquad\qquad\qquad\qquad = y\sqrt[3]{2y}$

31. $\sqrt{3}\left(\sqrt{5} - \sqrt{2}\right) = \sqrt{3}\sqrt{5} - \sqrt{3}\sqrt{2} = \sqrt{15} - \sqrt{6}$

32. $\left(\sqrt{7} + \sqrt{3}\right)^2 = \left(\sqrt{7}\right)^2 + 2\sqrt{7}\sqrt{3} + \left(\sqrt{3}\right)^2$

$\qquad\qquad\qquad = 7 + 2\sqrt{21} + 3$

$\qquad\qquad\qquad = 10 + 2\sqrt{21}$

33. $\left(2x - \sqrt{5}\right)\left(2x + \sqrt{5}\right) = (2x)^2 - \left(\sqrt{5}\right)^2$

$\qquad\qquad\qquad\qquad\qquad = 4x^2 - 5$

34. $\left(\sqrt{x+1} - 1\right)^2 = \left(\sqrt{x+1}\right)^2 - 2\left(\sqrt{x+1}\right) + 1^2$

$\qquad\qquad\qquad = x + 1 - 2\sqrt{x+1} + 1$

$\qquad\qquad\qquad = x + 2 - 2\sqrt{x+1}$

35. $\sqrt{\dfrac{7}{3}} = \dfrac{\sqrt{7}}{\sqrt{3}} = \dfrac{\sqrt{7}}{\sqrt{3}} \cdot \dfrac{\sqrt{3}}{\sqrt{3}} = \dfrac{\sqrt{21}}{3}$

36. $\dfrac{5}{\sqrt[3]{2x^2}} = \dfrac{5}{\sqrt[3]{2x^2}} \cdot \dfrac{\sqrt[3]{4x}}{\sqrt[3]{4x}} = \dfrac{5\sqrt[3]{4x}}{\sqrt[3]{8x^3}} = \dfrac{5\sqrt[3]{4x}}{2x}$

37. $\dfrac{\sqrt{3} - \sqrt{7}}{2\sqrt{3} + \sqrt{7}}$

$\quad = \dfrac{\sqrt{3} - \sqrt{7}}{2\sqrt{3} + \sqrt{7}} \cdot \dfrac{\left(2\sqrt{3} - \sqrt{7}\right)}{\left(2\sqrt{3} - \sqrt{7}\right)}$

$\quad = \dfrac{\sqrt{3}\left(2\sqrt{3}\right) - \sqrt{3}\sqrt{7} - \sqrt{7}\left(2\sqrt{3}\right) + \sqrt{7}\sqrt{7}}{\left(2\sqrt{3}\right)^2 - \left(\sqrt{7}\right)^2}$

$\quad = \dfrac{6 - \sqrt{21} - 2\sqrt{21} + 7}{12 - 7}$

$\quad = \dfrac{13 - 3\sqrt{21}}{5}$

38. $\sqrt{\dfrac{7}{3}} = \dfrac{\sqrt{7}}{\sqrt{3}} = \dfrac{\sqrt{7}}{\sqrt{3}} \cdot \dfrac{\sqrt{7}}{\sqrt{7}} = \dfrac{7}{\sqrt{21}}$

39. $\sqrt[3]{\dfrac{9y}{11}} = \dfrac{\sqrt[3]{9y}}{\sqrt[3]{11}} = \dfrac{\sqrt[3]{9y}}{\sqrt[3]{11}} \cdot \dfrac{\sqrt[3]{3y^2}}{\sqrt[3]{3y^2}} = \dfrac{\sqrt[3]{27y^3}}{\sqrt[3]{31y^2}} = \dfrac{3y}{\sqrt[3]{33y^2}}$

40. $\dfrac{\sqrt{x} - 2}{\sqrt{x}} = \dfrac{\sqrt{x} - 2}{\sqrt{x}} \cdot \dfrac{\sqrt{x} + 2}{\sqrt{x} + 2}$

$\qquad = \dfrac{\left(\sqrt{x}\right)^2 - 2^2}{\sqrt{x}\sqrt{x} + 2\sqrt{x}}$

$\qquad = \dfrac{x - 4}{x + 2\sqrt{x}}$

Section 7.6

Practice Exercises

1. $\qquad \sqrt{3x - 5} = 7$

$\qquad \left(\sqrt{3x - 5}\right)^2 = 7^2$

$\qquad\qquad 3x - 5 = 49$

$\qquad\qquad\qquad 3x = 54$

$\qquad\qquad\qquad\quad x = 18$

Check:

$\qquad \sqrt{3x - 5} = 7$

$\qquad \sqrt{3(18) - 5} \overset{?}{=} 7$

$\qquad\quad \sqrt{54 - 5} \overset{?}{=} 7$

$\qquad\qquad \sqrt{49} \overset{?}{=} 7$

$\qquad\qquad\quad 7 = 7$

The solution is 18.

2.

$$\sqrt{3-2x} - 4x = 0$$
$$\sqrt{3-2x} - 4x + 4x = 0 + 4x$$
$$\sqrt{3-2x} = 4x$$
$$\left(\sqrt{3-2x}\right)^2 = (4x)^2$$
$$3 - 2x = 16x^2$$
$$16x^2 + 2x - 3 = 0$$
$$(8x-3)(2x+1) = 0$$
$$8x - 3 = 0 \text{ or } 2x + 1 = 0$$
$$x = \frac{3}{8} \text{ or } x = -\frac{1}{2}$$

Check $\dfrac{3}{8}$:

$$\sqrt{3-2x} - 4x = 0$$
$$\sqrt{3-2\left(\frac{3}{8}\right)} - 4\left(\frac{3}{8}\right) \stackrel{?}{=} 0$$
$$\sqrt{\frac{24}{8} - \frac{6}{8}} - \frac{3}{2} \stackrel{?}{=} 0$$
$$\sqrt{\frac{9}{4}} - \frac{3}{2} \stackrel{?}{=} 0$$
$$\frac{3}{2} - \frac{3}{2} = 0$$

Check $-\dfrac{1}{2}$:

$$\sqrt{3-2x} - 4x = 0$$
$$\sqrt{3-2\left(-\frac{1}{2}\right)} - 4\left(-\frac{1}{2}\right) \stackrel{?}{=} 0$$
$$\sqrt{3+1} + 2 \stackrel{?}{=} 0$$
$$2 + 2 \stackrel{?}{=} 0$$
$$4 \neq 0$$

$-\dfrac{1}{2}$ does not check, so the only solution is $\dfrac{3}{8}$.

3.

$$\sqrt[3]{x-2} + 1 = 3$$
$$\sqrt[3]{x-2} = 2$$
$$\left(\sqrt[3]{x-2}\right)^3 = 2^3$$
$$x - 2 = 8$$
$$x = 10$$

Check:

$$\sqrt[3]{x-2} + 1 = 3$$
$$\sqrt[3]{10-2} + 1 \stackrel{?}{=} 3$$
$$\sqrt[3]{8} + 1 \stackrel{?}{=} 3$$
$$2 + 1 = 3$$

The solution is 10.

4.

$$\sqrt{16+x} = x - 4$$
$$\left(\sqrt{16+x}\right)^2 = (x-4)^2$$
$$16 + x = x^2 - 8x + 16$$
$$x^2 - 9x = 0$$
$$x(x-9) = 0$$
$$x = 0 \text{ or } x - 9 = 0$$
$$x = 9$$

Check 0:

$$\sqrt{16+x} = x - 4$$
$$\sqrt{16+0} \stackrel{?}{=} 0 - 4$$
$$\sqrt{16} \stackrel{?}{=} -4$$
$$4 \neq -4$$

Check 9:

$$\sqrt{16+x} = x - 4$$
$$\sqrt{16+9} \stackrel{?}{=} 9 - 4$$
$$\sqrt{25} \stackrel{?}{=} 5$$
$$5 = 5$$

0 does not check, so the only solution is 9.

5.

$$\sqrt{8x+1} + \sqrt{3x} = 2$$
$$\sqrt{8x+1} = 2 - \sqrt{3x}$$
$$\left(\sqrt{8x+1}\right)^2 = \left(2 - \sqrt{3x}\right)^2$$
$$8x + 1 = 4 - 4\sqrt{3x} + 3x$$
$$4\sqrt{3x} = 3 - 5x$$
$$\left(4\sqrt{3x}\right)^2 = (3-5x)^2$$
$$16(3x) = 9 - 30x + 25x^2$$
$$25x^2 - 78x + 9 = 0$$
$$(25x-3)(x-3) = 0$$
$$25x - 3 = 0 \text{ or } x - 3 = 0$$
$$x = \frac{3}{25} \text{ or } x = 3$$

Check $\dfrac{3}{25}$:

$$\sqrt{8x+1} + \sqrt{3x} = 2$$
$$\sqrt{8\left(\frac{3}{25}\right)+1} + \sqrt{3\left(\frac{3}{25}\right)} \stackrel{?}{=} 2$$
$$\sqrt{\frac{24}{25} + \frac{25}{25}} + \sqrt{\frac{9}{25}} \stackrel{?}{=} 2$$
$$\sqrt{\frac{49}{25}} + \sqrt{\frac{9}{25}} \stackrel{?}{=} 2$$
$$\frac{7}{5} + \frac{3}{5} \stackrel{?}{=} 2$$
$$\frac{10}{5} = 2$$

Check 3:
$$\sqrt{8x+1} + \sqrt{3x} = 2$$
$$\sqrt{8(3)+1} + \sqrt{3(3)} \stackrel{?}{=} 2$$
$$\sqrt{25} + \sqrt{9} \stackrel{?}{=} 2$$
$$5 + 3 \neq 2$$

3 does not check, so the only solution is $\dfrac{3}{25}$.

6. $a^2 + b^2 = c^2$
$a^2 + 6^2 = 12^2$
$a^2 + 36 = 144$
$a^2 = 108$
$a = \pm\sqrt{108} = \pm\sqrt{36 \cdot 3} = \pm 6\sqrt{3}$

Since a is a length, we will use the positive value only. The unknown leg is $6\sqrt{3}$ meters long.

7. Consider the base of the tank, and the plastic divider in the diagonal. Use the Pythagorean theorem to find l.

$a^2 + b^2 = c^2$
$12^2 + 7^2 = l^2$
$144 + 49 = l^2$
$l^2 = 193$
$l = \pm\sqrt{193}$

We will use the positive value because l represents length. The divider must be $\sqrt{193} \approx 13.89$ inches long.

Graphing Calculator Explorations

1.

The solution is 3.19.

2.

The solution is 1.55.

3.

There is no solution. The solution set is ∅.

4.

The solution is 0.34.

5.

The solution is 3.23.

6.

The solutions are −5.44 and 7.35.

Vocabulary and Readiness Check

1. A proposed solution that is not a solution of the original equation is called an <u>extraneous solution</u>.

2. The Pythagorean Theorem states that $a^2 + b^2 = c^2$ where a and b are the lengths of the <u>legs</u> of a <u>right</u> triangle and c is the length of the <u>hypotenuse</u>.

3. The square of $x - 5$, or $(x-5)^2 = \underline{x^2 - 10x + 25}$.

4. The square of $4 - \sqrt{7x}$, or
$$\left(4 - \sqrt{7x}\right)^2 = \underline{16 - 8\sqrt{7x} + 7x}.$$

Exercise Set 7.6

1. $\sqrt{2x} = 4$

$\left(\sqrt{2x}\right)^2 = 4^2$

$2x = 16$

$x = 8$

The solution is 8.

3. $\sqrt{x-3} = 2$

$\left(\sqrt{x-3}\right)^2 = 2^2$

$x - 3 = 4$

$x = 7$

The solution is 7.

5. $\sqrt{2x} = -4$

No solution since a principle square root does not yield a negative number.

7. $\sqrt{4x-3} - 5 = 0$

$\sqrt{4x-3} = 5$

$\left(\sqrt{4x-3}\right)^2 = 5^2$

$4x - 3 = 25$

$4x = 28$

$x = 7$

The solution is 7.

9. $\sqrt{2x-3} - 2 = 1$

$\sqrt{2x-3} = 3$

$\left(\sqrt{2x-3}\right)^2 = 3^2$

$2x - 3 = 9$

$2x = 12$

$x = 6$

The solution is 6.

11. $\sqrt[3]{6x} = -3$

$\left(\sqrt[3]{6x}\right)^3 = (-3)^3$

$6x = -27$

$x = -\dfrac{27}{6} = -\dfrac{9}{2}$

The solution is $-\dfrac{9}{2}$.

13. $\sqrt[3]{x-2} - 3 = 0$

$\sqrt[3]{x-2} = 3$

$\left(\sqrt[3]{x-2}\right)^3 = 3^3$

$x - 2 = 27$

$x = 29$

The solution is 29.

15. $\sqrt{13-x} = x-1$

$\left(\sqrt{13-x}\right)^2 = (x-1)^2$

$13 - x = x^2 - 2x + 1$

$0 = x^2 - x - 12$

$0 = (x-4)(x+3)$

$x - 4 = 0 \quad \text{or} \quad x + 3 = 0$

$x = 4 \quad \text{or} \quad\quad x = -3$

We discard –3 as extraneous. The solution is 4.

17. $x - \sqrt{4-3x} = -8$

$x + 8 = \sqrt{4-3x}$

$(x+8)^2 = \left(\sqrt{4-3x}\right)^2$

$x^2 + 16x + 64 = 4 - 3x$

$x^2 + 19x + 60 = 0$

$(x+4)(x+15) = 0$

$x + 4 = 0 \quad \text{or} \quad x + 15 = 0$

$x = -4 \quad \text{or} \quad\quad x = -15$

We discard –15 as extraneous. The solution is –4.

19. $\sqrt{y+5} = 2 - \sqrt{y-4}$

$\left(\sqrt{y+5}\right)^2 = \left(2 - \sqrt{y-4}\right)^2$

$y + 5 = 4 - 4\sqrt{y-4} + (y-4)$

$y + 5 = y - 4\sqrt{y-4}$

$5 = -4\sqrt{y-4}$

$5^2 = \left(-4\sqrt{y-4}\right)^2$

$25 = 16(y-4)$

$25 = 16y - 64$

$89 = 16y$

$\dfrac{89}{16} = y$

We discard $\dfrac{89}{16}$ as extraneous. There is no solution.

21.
$$\sqrt{x-3}+\sqrt{x+2}=5$$
$$\sqrt{x-3}=5-\sqrt{x+2}$$
$$\left(\sqrt{x-3}\right)^2=\left(5-\sqrt{x+2}\right)^2$$
$$x-3=25-10\sqrt{x+2}+(x+2)$$
$$x-3=27-10\sqrt{x+2}+x$$
$$-30=-10\sqrt{x+2}$$
$$3=\sqrt{x+2}$$
$$3^2=\left(\sqrt{x+2}\right)^2$$
$$9=x+2$$
$$7=x$$
The solution is 7.

23.
$$\sqrt{3x-2}=5$$
$$\left(\sqrt{3x-2}\right)^2=5^2$$
$$3x-2=25$$
$$3x=27$$
$$x=9$$
The solution is 9.

25.
$$-\sqrt{2x}+4=-6$$
$$10=\sqrt{2x}$$
$$10^2=\left(\sqrt{2x}\right)^2$$
$$100=2x$$
$$50=x$$
The solution is 50.

27.
$$\sqrt{3x+1}+2=0$$
$$\sqrt{3x+1}=-2$$
No solution since a principle square root does not yield a negative number.

29.
$$\sqrt[4]{4x+1}-2=0$$
$$\sqrt[4]{4x+1}=2$$
$$\left(\sqrt[4]{4x+1}\right)^4=2^4$$
$$4x+1=16$$
$$4x=15$$
$$x=\frac{15}{4}$$
The solution is $\frac{15}{4}$.

31.
$$\sqrt{4x-3}=7$$
$$\left(\sqrt{4x-3}\right)^2=7^2$$
$$4x-3=49$$
$$4x=52$$
$$x=13$$
The solution is 13.

33.
$$\sqrt[3]{6x-3}-3=0$$
$$\sqrt[3]{6x-3}=3$$
$$\left(\sqrt[3]{6x-3}\right)^3=3^3$$
$$6x-3=27$$
$$6x=30$$
$$x=5$$
The solution is 5.

35.
$$\sqrt[3]{2x-3}-2=-5$$
$$\sqrt[3]{2x-3}=-3$$
$$\left(\sqrt[3]{2x-3}\right)^3=(-3)^3$$
$$2x-3=-27$$
$$2x=-24$$
$$x=-12$$
The solution is -12.

37.
$$\sqrt{x+4}=\sqrt{2x-5}$$
$$\left(\sqrt{x+4}\right)^2=\left(\sqrt{2x-5}\right)^2$$
$$x+4=2x-5$$
$$-x=-9$$
$$x=9$$
The solution is 9.

39.
$$x-\sqrt{1-x}=-5$$
$$x+5=\sqrt{1-x}$$
$$(x+5)^2=\left(\sqrt{1-x}\right)^2$$
$$x^2+10x+25=1-x$$
$$x^2+11x+24=0$$
$$(x+8)(x+3)=0$$
$$x+8=0 \quad \text{or} \quad x+3=0$$
$$x=-8 \text{ or} \quad x=-3$$
We discard -8 as extraneous. The solution is -3.

41. $\sqrt[3]{-6x-1} = \sqrt[3]{-2x-5}$

$\left(\sqrt[3]{-6x-1}\right)^3 = \left(\sqrt[3]{-2x-5}\right)^3$

$-6x-1 = -2x-5$

$-4x = -4$

$x = 1$

The solution is 1.

43. $\sqrt{5x-1} - \sqrt{x+2} = 3$

$\sqrt{5x-1} = \sqrt{x} + 1$

$\left(\sqrt{5x-1}\right)^2 = \left(\sqrt{x}+1\right)^2$

$5x-1 = x + 2\sqrt{x} + 1$

$4x-2 = 2\sqrt{x}$

$2x-1 = \sqrt{x}$

$(2x-1)^2 = \left(\sqrt{x}\right)^2$

$4x^2 - 4x + 1 = x$

$4x^2 - 5x + 1 = 0$

$(4x-1)(x-1) = 0$

$4x-1 = 0 \ \text{ or } \ x-1 = 0$

$4x = 1 \ \text{ or } \quad x = 1$

$x = \dfrac{1}{4}$

We discard $\dfrac{1}{4}$ as extraneous. The solution is 1.

45. $\sqrt{2x-1} = \sqrt{1-2x}$

$\left(\sqrt{2x-1}\right)^2 = \left(\sqrt{1-2x}\right)^2$

$2x-1 = 1-2x$

$4x = 2$

$x = \dfrac{2}{4} = \dfrac{1}{2}$

The solution is $\dfrac{1}{2}$.

47. $\sqrt{3x+4} - 1 = \sqrt{2x+1}$

$\sqrt{3x+4} = \sqrt{2x+1} + 1$

$\left(\sqrt{3x+4}\right)^2 = \left(\sqrt{2x+1}+1\right)^2$

$3x+4 = (2x+1) + 2\sqrt{2x+1} + 1$

$3x+4 = 2x+2 + 2\sqrt{2x+1}$

$x+2 = 2\sqrt{2x+1}$

$(x+2)^2 = \left(2\sqrt{2x+1}\right)^2$

$x^2 + 4x + 4 = 4(2x+1)$

$x^2 + 4x + 4 = 8x + 4$

$x^2 - 4x = 0$

$x(x-4) = 0$

$x = 0 \ \text{ or } \ x-4 = 0$

$x = 4$

The solutions are 0 and 4.

49. $\sqrt{y+3} - \sqrt{y-3} = 1$

$\sqrt{y+3} = 1 + \sqrt{y-3}$

$\left(\sqrt{y+3}\right)^2 = \left(1+\sqrt{y-3}\right)^2$

$y+3 = 1 + 2\sqrt{y-3} + (y-3)$

$y+3 = -2 + 2\sqrt{y-3} + y$

$5 = 2\sqrt{y-3}$

$(5)^2 = \left(2\sqrt{y-3}\right)^2$

$25 = 4(y-3)$

$25 = 4y - 12$

$37 = 4y$

$\dfrac{37}{4} = y$

The solution is $\dfrac{37}{4}$.

51. Let $c = $ length of the hypotenuse.

$6^2 + 3^2 = c^2$

$36 + 9 = c^2$

$45 = c^2$

$\sqrt{45} = \sqrt{c^2}$

$\sqrt{9 \cdot 5} = c$

$3\sqrt{5} = c$ so $c = 3\sqrt{5}$ feet

53. Let b = length of the unknown leg.

$$3^2 + b^2 = 7^2$$
$$9 + b^2 = 49$$
$$b^2 = 40$$
$$\sqrt{b^2} = \sqrt{40}$$
$$b = \sqrt{4 \cdot 10}$$
$$b = 2\sqrt{10} \text{ meters}$$

55. Let b = length of the unknown leg.

$$9^2 + b^2 = \left(11\sqrt{5}\right)^2$$
$$81 + b^2 = 121 \cdot 5$$
$$81 + b^2 = 605$$
$$b^2 = 524$$
$$\sqrt{b^2} = \sqrt{524}$$
$$b = \sqrt{4 \cdot 131}$$
$$b = 2\sqrt{131} \approx 22.9 \text{ meters}$$

57. Let c = length of the hypotenuse.

$$7^2 + (7.2)^2 = c^2$$
$$49 + 51.84 = c^2$$
$$100.84 = c^2$$
$$100.84 = \sqrt{c^2}$$
$$c = \sqrt{100.84} \approx 10.0 \text{ mm}$$

59. Let c = amount of cable needed.

$$15^2 + 8^2 = c^2$$
$$225 + 64 = c^2$$
$$289 = c^2$$
$$\sqrt{289} = \sqrt{c^2}$$
$$17 = c$$

Thus, 17 feet of cable is needed.

61. Let c = length of the ladder.

$$12^2 + 5^2 = c^2$$
$$144 + 25 = c^2$$
$$169 = c^2$$
$$\sqrt{169} = \sqrt{c^2}$$
$$13 = c$$

A 13-foot ladder is needed.

63.

$$r = \sqrt{\frac{A}{4\pi}}$$
$$1080 = \sqrt{\frac{A}{4\pi}}$$
$$(1080)^2 = \left(\sqrt{\frac{A}{4\pi}}\right)^2$$
$$1,166,400 = \frac{A}{4\pi}$$
$$14,657,415 \approx A$$

The surface area is approximately 14,657,415 square miles.

65.

$$v = \sqrt{2gh}$$
$$80 = \sqrt{2(32)h}$$
$$(80)^2 = \left(\sqrt{64h}\right)^2$$
$$6400 = 64h$$
$$100 = h$$

The object fell 100 feet.

67.

$$S = 2\sqrt{I} - 9$$
$$11 = 2\sqrt{I} - 9$$
$$20 = 2\sqrt{I}$$
$$10 = \sqrt{I}$$
$$10^2 = \left(\sqrt{I}\right)^2$$
$$100 = I$$

The estimated IQ is 100.

69.

$$P = 2\pi\sqrt{\frac{l}{32}}$$
$$= 2\pi\sqrt{\frac{2}{32}}$$
$$= 2\pi\sqrt{\frac{1}{16}}$$
$$= 2\pi\left(\frac{1}{4}\right)$$
$$= \frac{\pi}{2} \text{ sec} \approx 1.57 \text{ sec}$$

71.
$$P = 2\pi\sqrt{\frac{l}{32}}$$
$$4 = 2\pi\sqrt{\frac{l}{32}}$$
$$\frac{4}{2\pi} = \sqrt{\frac{l}{32}}$$
$$\left(\frac{2}{\pi}\right)^2 = \left(\sqrt{\frac{l}{32}}\right)^2$$
$$\frac{4}{\pi^2} = \frac{l}{32}$$
$$l = 32\left(\frac{4}{\pi^2}\right) \approx 12.97 \text{ feet}$$

73. Answers may vary

75.
$$s = \frac{1}{2}(6+10+14) = \frac{1}{2}(30) = 15$$
$$A = \sqrt{s(s-a)(s-b)(s-c)}$$
$$= \sqrt{15(15-6)(15-10)(15-14)}$$
$$= \sqrt{15(9)(5)(1)}$$
$$= \sqrt{675}$$
$$= \sqrt{225\cdot 3}$$
$$= 15\sqrt{3} \text{ sq mi} \approx 25.98 \text{ sq mi.}$$

77. Answers may vary

79.
$$D(h) = 111.7\sqrt{h}$$
$$80 = 111.7\sqrt{h}$$
$$\frac{80}{111.7} = \sqrt{h}$$
$$\left(\frac{80}{111.7}\right)^2 = \left(\sqrt{h}\right)^2$$
$$0.5129483389 \approx h$$
$$h \approx 0.51 \text{ km}$$

81. Function; no vertical line intersects the graph more than one time.

83. Function; no vertical line intersects the graph more than one time.

85. Not a function; the *y*-axis is an example of a vertical line that intersects the graph more than one time.

87. $\dfrac{\frac{x}{6}}{\frac{2x}{3}+\frac{1}{2}} = \dfrac{\left(\frac{x}{6}\right)6}{\left(\frac{2x}{3}+\frac{1}{2}\right)6} = \dfrac{x}{4x+3}$

89.
$$\frac{\frac{z}{5}+\frac{1}{10}}{\frac{z}{20}-\frac{z}{5}} = \frac{\left(\frac{z}{5}+\frac{1}{10}\right)20}{\left(\frac{z}{20}-\frac{z}{5}\right)20}$$
$$= \frac{4z+2}{z-4z}$$
$$= \frac{4z+2}{-3z}$$
$$= -\frac{4z+2}{3z}$$

91.
$$\sqrt{5x-1}+4 = 7$$
$$\sqrt{5x-1} = 3$$
$$\left(\sqrt{5x-1}\right)^2 = 3^2$$
$$5x-1 = 9$$
$$5x = 10$$
$$x = 2$$

93.
$$\sqrt{\sqrt{x+3}+\sqrt{x}} = \sqrt{3}$$
$$\left(\sqrt{\sqrt{x+3}+\sqrt{x}}\right)^2 = \left(\sqrt{3}\right)^2$$
$$\sqrt{x+3}+\sqrt{x} = 3$$
$$\sqrt{x+3} = 3-\sqrt{x}$$
$$\left(\sqrt{x+3}\right)^2 = \left(3-\sqrt{x}\right)^2$$
$$x+3 = 9-6\sqrt{x}+x$$
$$-6 = -6\sqrt{x}$$
$$(-6)^2 = \left(-6\sqrt{x}\right)^2$$
$$36 = 36x$$
$$1 = x$$

95. a. Answers may vary

b. Answers may vary

97. $\sqrt{(x^2-x)+7} = 2(x^2-x)-1$

Let $t = x^2 - x$. Then
$$\sqrt{t+7} = 2t-1$$
$$\left(\sqrt{t+7}\right)^2 = (2t-1)^2$$
$$t+7 = 4t^2-4t+1$$
$$0 = 4t^2-5t-6$$
$$0 = (4t+3)(t-2)$$
$$t = -\frac{3}{4} \text{ or } t = 2$$

Replace *t* with $x^2 - x$.

$$x^2 - x = -\frac{3}{4} \quad \text{or} \quad x^2 - x = 2$$

$$4x^2 - 4x + 3 = 0 \qquad x^2 - x - 2 = 0$$

which has no real $\qquad (x-2)(x+1) = 0$

solutions $\qquad\qquad x = 2 \text{ or } x = -1$

The solutions are -1 and 2.

99. $x^2 + 6x = 4\sqrt{x^2 + 6x}$

Let $t = x^2 + 6x$. Then

$$t = 4\sqrt{t}$$

$$t^2 = \left(4\sqrt{t}\right)^2$$

$$t^2 = 16t$$

$$t^2 - 16t = 0$$

$$t(t - 16) = 0$$

$$t = 0 \text{ or } t = 16$$

Replace t with $x^2 + 6x$.

$$x^2 + 6x = 0$$

$$x(x + 6) = 0$$

$$x = 0 \text{ or } x = -6$$

or

$$x^2 + 6x = 16$$

$$x^2 + 6x - 16 = 0$$

$$(x + 8)(x - 2) = 0$$

$$x = -8 \text{ or } x = 2$$

The solutions are $-8, -6, 0,$ and 2.

The Bigger Picture

1.
$$\frac{x}{4} + \frac{x+18}{20} = \frac{x-5}{5}$$

$$20\left(\frac{x}{4}\right) + 20\left(\frac{x+18}{20}\right) = 20\left(\frac{x-5}{5}\right)$$

$$5x + (x + 18) = 4(x - 5)$$

$$6x + 18 = 4x - 20$$

$$2x = -38$$

$$x = -19$$

The solution set is $\{-19\}$.

2. $|3x - 5| = 10$

$$3x - 5 = -10 \quad \text{or} \quad 3x - 5 = 10$$

$$3x = -5 \qquad\qquad 3x = 15$$

$$x = -\frac{5}{3} \qquad\qquad x = 5$$

The solution set is $\left\{-\frac{5}{3}, 5\right\}$.

3.
$$2x^2 - x = 45$$

$$2x^2 - x - 45 = 0$$

$$(2x + 9)(x - 5) = 0$$

$$2x + 9 = 0 \quad \text{or} \quad x - 5 = 0$$

$$x = -\frac{9}{2} \qquad\qquad x = 5$$

The solution set is $\left\{-\frac{9}{2}, 5\right\}$.

4. $\quad -6 \le -5x - 1 \le 10$

$$-5 \le -5x \le 11$$

$$1 \ge x \ge -\frac{11}{5}$$

$$-\frac{11}{5} \le x \le 1$$

The solution is $\left[-\frac{11}{5}, 1\right]$.

5. $\quad 4(x - 1) + 3x > 1 + 2(x - 6)$

$$4x - 4 + 3x > 1 + 2x - 12$$

$$7x - 4 > 2x - 11$$

$$5x > -7$$

$$x > -\frac{7}{5}$$

The solution is $\left(-\frac{7}{5}, \infty\right)$.

6. $\sqrt{x} + 14 = x - 6$

$$\sqrt{x} = x - 20$$

$$\left(\sqrt{x}\right)^2 = (x - 20)^2$$

$$x = x^2 - 40x + 400$$

$$0 = x^2 - 41x + 400$$

$$0 = (x - 25)(x - 16)$$

$$x - 25 = 0 \quad \text{or} \quad x - 16 = 0$$

$$x = 25 \qquad\qquad x = 16$$

Discard 16 as an extraneous solution. The solution set is $\{25\}$.

7. $x \ge 10 \quad \text{or} \quad -x < 5$

$$x \ge 10 \quad \text{or} \quad x > -5$$

The solution is $(-5, \infty)$.

8. $\sqrt{3x - 1} + 4 = 1$

$$\sqrt{3x - 1} = -3$$

There is no real number whose square root is negative. The solution set is $\varnothing$.

9. $|x-2| > 15$

$x-2 < -15$ or $x-2 > 15$

$x < -13$ or $x > 17$

The solution is $(-\infty, -13) \cup (17, \infty)$.

10. $5x - 4[x - 2(3x+1)] = 25$

$5x - 4(x - 6x - 2) = 25$

$5x - 4(-5x - 2) = 25$

$5x + 20x + 8 = 25$

$25x = 17$

$x = \dfrac{17}{25}$

The solution set is $\left\{\dfrac{17}{25}\right\}$.

Section 7.7

Practice Exercises

1. a. $\sqrt{-4} = \sqrt{-1 \cdot 4} = \sqrt{-1} \cdot \sqrt{4} = i \cdot 2$, or $2i$

  b. $\sqrt{-7} = \sqrt{-1(7)} = \sqrt{-1} \cdot \sqrt{7} = i\sqrt{7}$

  c. $-\sqrt{-18} = -\sqrt{-1 \cdot 18}$

$= -\sqrt{-1} \cdot \sqrt{9 \cdot 2}$

$= -i \cdot 3\sqrt{2}$

$= -3i\sqrt{2}$

2. a. $\sqrt{-5} \cdot \sqrt{-6} = i\sqrt{5}\left(i\sqrt{6}\right)$

$= i^2\sqrt{30}$

$= -1\sqrt{30}$

$= -\sqrt{30}$

  b. $\sqrt{-9} \cdot \sqrt{-1} = 3i \cdot i = 3i^2 = 3(-1) = -3$

  c. $\sqrt{125} \cdot \sqrt{-5} = 5\sqrt{5}\left(i\sqrt{5}\right)$

$= 5i\left(\sqrt{5}\sqrt{5}\right)$

$= 5i(5)$

$= 25i$

  d. $\dfrac{\sqrt{-27}}{\sqrt{3}} = \dfrac{i\sqrt{27}}{\sqrt{3}} = i\sqrt{9} = 3i$

3. a. $(3 - 5i) + (-4 + i) = (3 - 4) + (-5 + 1)i$

$= -1 - 4i$

  b. $4i - (3 - i) = 4i - 3 + i$

$= -3 + (4 + 1)i$

$= -3 + 5i$

  c. $(-5 - 2i) - (-8) = -5 - 2i + 8$

$= (-5 + 8) - 2i$

$= 3 - 2i$

4. a. $-4i \cdot 5i = -20i^2 = -20(-1) = 20$

  b. $5i(2 + i) = 5i \cdot 2 + 5i \cdot i$

$= 10i + 5i^2$

$= 10i + 5(-1)$

$= 10i - 5$

$= -5 + 10i$

  c. $(2 + 3i)(6 - i) = 2(6) - 2(i) + 3i(6) - 3i(i)$

$= 12 - 2i + 18i - 3i^2$

$= 12 + 16i - 3(-1)$

$= 12 + 16i + 3$

$= 15 + 16i$

  d. $(3 - i)^2 = (3 - i)(3 - i)$

$= 3(3) - 3(i) - 3(i) + i^2$

$= 9 - 6i + (-1)$

$= 8 - 6i$

  e. $(9 + 2i)(9 - 2i) = 9(9) - 9(2i) + 2i(9) - 2i(2i)$

$= 81 - 18i + 18i - 4i^2$

$= 81 - 4(-1)$

$= 81 + 4$

$= 85$

5. a. $\dfrac{4 - i}{3 + i} = \dfrac{(4 - i)(3 - i)}{(3 + i)(3 - i)}$

$= \dfrac{4(3) - 4(i) - 3(i) + i^2}{3^2 - i^2}$

$= \dfrac{12 - 7i - 1}{9 + 1}$

$= \dfrac{11 - 7i}{10}$

$= \dfrac{11}{10} - \dfrac{7i}{10}$ or $\dfrac{11}{10} - \dfrac{7}{10}i$

b. $\dfrac{5}{2i} = \dfrac{5(-2i)}{2i(-2i)}$

$= \dfrac{-10i}{-4i^2}$

$= \dfrac{-10i}{-4(-1)}$

$= \dfrac{-10i}{4}$

$= \dfrac{-5i}{2}$

$= 0 - \dfrac{5i}{2}$ or $0 - \dfrac{5}{2}i$

6. a. $i^9 = i^4 \cdot i^4 \cdot i = 1 \cdot 1 \cdot i = i$

b. $i^{16} = (i^4)^4 = 1^4 = 1$

c. $i^{34} = i^{32} \cdot i^2 = (i^4)^8 \cdot i^2 = 1^8(-1) = -1$

d. $i^{-24} = \dfrac{1}{i^{24}} = \dfrac{1}{(i^4)^6} = \dfrac{1}{(1)^6} = \dfrac{1}{1} = 1$

Vocabulary and Readiness Check

1. A <u>complex</u> number is one that can be written in the form $a + bi$ where a and b are real numbers.

2. In the complex number system, i denotes the <u>imaginary unit</u>.

3. $i^2 = \underline{-1}$

4. $i = \sqrt{-1}$

5. A complex number, $a + bi$, is a <u>real</u> number if $b = 0$.

6. A complex number, $a + bi$, is a <u>pure imaginary</u> number if $a = 0$ and $b \neq 0$.

7. $\sqrt{-81} = 9i$

8. $\sqrt{-49} = 7i$

9. $\sqrt{-7} = i\sqrt{7}$

10. $\sqrt{-3} = i\sqrt{3}$

11. $-\sqrt{16} = -4$

12. $-\sqrt{4} = -2$

13. $\sqrt{-64} = 8i$

14. $\sqrt{-100} = 10i$

Exercise Set 7.7

1. $\sqrt{-24} = \sqrt{-1 \cdot 24} = \sqrt{-1}\sqrt{4 \cdot 6} = i \cdot 2\sqrt{6} = 2i\sqrt{6}$

3. $-\sqrt{-36} = -\sqrt{-1 \cdot 36} = -\sqrt{-1}\sqrt{36} = -i \cdot 6 = -6i$

5. $8\sqrt{-63} = 8\sqrt{-1 \cdot 63}$
$= 8\sqrt{-1}\sqrt{9 \cdot 7}$
$= 8i \cdot 3\sqrt{7}$
$= 24i\sqrt{7}$

7. $-\sqrt{54} = -\sqrt{9 \cdot 6} = -3\sqrt{6}$

9. $\sqrt{-2} \cdot \sqrt{-7} = i\sqrt{2} \cdot i\sqrt{7}$
$= i^2\sqrt{14}$
$= (-1)\sqrt{14}$
$= -\sqrt{14}$

11. $\sqrt{-5} \cdot \sqrt{-10} = i\sqrt{5} \cdot i\sqrt{10}$
$= i^2\sqrt{50}$
$= (-1)\sqrt{25 \cdot 2}$
$= -5\sqrt{2}$

13. $\sqrt{16} \cdot \sqrt{-1} = 4i$

15. $\dfrac{\sqrt{-9}}{\sqrt{3}} = \dfrac{i\sqrt{9}}{\sqrt{3}} = i\sqrt{\dfrac{9}{3}} = i\sqrt{3}$

17. $\dfrac{\sqrt{-80}}{\sqrt{-10}} = \dfrac{i\sqrt{80}}{i\sqrt{10}} = \sqrt{\dfrac{80}{10}} = \sqrt{8} = \sqrt{4 \cdot 2} = 2\sqrt{2}$

19. $(4 - 7i) + (2 + 3i) = (4 + 2) + (-7 + 3)i$
$= 6 + (-4)i$
$= 6 - 4i$

21. $(6 + 5i) - (8 - i) = 6 + 5i - 8 + i$
$= (6 - 8) + (5 + 1)i$
$= -2 + 6i$

23. $6 - (8 + 4i) = 6 - 8 - 4i$
$= (6 - 8) - 4i$
$= -2 - 4i$

25. $-10i \cdot -4i = 40i^2 = 40(-1) = -40$

27. $6i(2-3i) = 12i - 18i^2$
$$= 12i - 18(-1)$$
$$= 18 + 12i$$

29. $\left(\sqrt{3}+2i\right)\left(\sqrt{3}-2i\right)$
$$= \sqrt{3} \cdot \sqrt{3} - \sqrt{3} \cdot 2i + \sqrt{3} \cdot 2i - 4i^2$$
$$= 3 - 4(-1)$$
$$= 3 + 4$$
$$= 7$$

31. $\left(4-2i\right)^2 = (4-2i)(4-2i)$
$$= 16 - 4 \cdot 2i - 4 \cdot 2i + 4i^2$$
$$= 16 - 8i - 8i + 4(-1)$$
$$= 16 - 16i - 4$$
$$= 12 - 16i$$

33. $\dfrac{4}{i} = \dfrac{4(-i)}{i(-i)} = \dfrac{-4i}{-i^2} = \dfrac{-4i}{-(-1)} = -4i$

35. $\dfrac{7}{4+3i} = \dfrac{7(4-3i)}{(4+3i)(4-3i)}$
$$= \dfrac{28-21i}{4^2-9i^2}$$
$$= \dfrac{28-21i}{16+9}$$
$$= \dfrac{28-21i}{25}$$
$$= \dfrac{28}{25} - \dfrac{21}{25}i$$

37. $\dfrac{3+5i}{1+i} = \dfrac{(3+5i)(1-i)}{(1+i)(1-i)}$
$$= \dfrac{3-3i+5i-5i^2}{1^2-i^2}$$
$$= \dfrac{3+2i+5}{1+1}$$
$$= \dfrac{8+2i}{2}$$
$$= \dfrac{8}{2} + \dfrac{2}{2}i$$
$$= 4+i$$

39. $\dfrac{5-i}{3-2i} = \dfrac{(5-i)(3+2i)}{(3-2i)(3+2i)}$
$$= \dfrac{15+10i-3i-2i^2}{3^2-4i^2}$$
$$= \dfrac{15+7i+2}{9+4}$$
$$= \dfrac{17+7i}{13}$$
$$= \dfrac{17}{13} + \dfrac{7}{13}i$$

41. $(7i)(-9i) = -63i^2 = -63(-1) = 63$

43. $(6-3i)-(4-2i) = 6-3i-4+2i = 2-i$

45. $-3i(-1+9i) = 3i - 27i^2$
$$= 3i - 27(-1)$$
$$= 27 + 3i$$

47. $\dfrac{4-5i}{2i} = \dfrac{4-5i}{2i} \cdot \dfrac{-2i}{-2i}$
$$= \dfrac{-8i+10i^2}{-4i^2}$$
$$= \dfrac{-10-8i}{4}$$
$$= \dfrac{-10}{4} - \dfrac{8}{4}i$$
$$= -\dfrac{5}{2} - 2i$$

49. $(4+i)(5+2i) = 20+8i+5i+2i^2$
$$= 20+13i+2(-1)$$
$$= 20+13i-2$$
$$= 18+13i$$

51. $(6-2i)(3+i) = 18+6i-6i-2i^2$
$$= 18+2$$
$$= 20$$

53. $(8-3i)+(2+3i) = 8-3i+2+3i = 10$

55. $(1-i)(1+i) = 1+i-i-i^2 = 1+1 = 2$

57. $\dfrac{16+15i}{-3i} = \dfrac{(16+15i)(3i)}{-3i(3i)}$

$= \dfrac{48i+45i^2}{-9i^2}$

$= \dfrac{-45+48i}{9}$

$= \dfrac{-45}{9} + \dfrac{48}{9}i$

$= -5 + \dfrac{16}{3}i$

59. $(9+8i)^2 = 9^2 + 2(9)(8i) + (8i)^2$

$= 81 + 144i + 64i^2$

$= 81 + 144i - 64$

$= 17 + 144i$

61. $\dfrac{2}{3+i} = \dfrac{2(3-i)}{(3+i)(3-i)}$

$= \dfrac{6-2i}{3^2 - i^2}$

$= \dfrac{6-2i}{9+1}$

$= \dfrac{6-2i}{10}$

$= \dfrac{6}{10} - \dfrac{2}{10}i$

$= \dfrac{3}{5} - \dfrac{1}{5}i$

63. $(5-6i) - 4i = 5 - 6i - 4i = 5 - 10i$

65. $\dfrac{2-3i}{2+i} = \dfrac{(2-3i)(2-i)}{(2+i)(2-i)}$

$= \dfrac{4-2i-6i+3i^2}{2^2 - i^2}$

$= \dfrac{4-8i-3}{4+1}$

$= \dfrac{1-8i}{5}$

$= \dfrac{1}{5} - \dfrac{8}{5}i$

67. $(2+4i) + (6-5i) = 2 + 4i + 6 - 5i = 8 - i$

69. $\left(\sqrt{3}+2i\right)\left(\sqrt{3}-2i\right) = \left(\sqrt{3}\right)^2 - (2i)^2$

$= 3 - 4i^2$

$= 3 - 4(-1)$

$= 7$

71. $(4-2i)^2 = 16 - 2 \cdot 4 \cdot 2i + 4i^2$

$= 16 - 16i + 4(-1)$

$= 16 - 4 - 16i$

$= 12 - 16i$

73. $i^8 = (i^4)^2 = 1^2 = 1$

75. $i^{21} = i^{20} \cdot i = (i^4)^5 \cdot i = 1^5 \cdot i = i$

77. $i^{11} = i^8 \cdot i^3 = (i^4)^2 \cdot i^3 = 1^2 \cdot (-i) = -i$

79. $i^{-6} = \dfrac{1}{i^6} = \dfrac{1}{i^4 \cdot i^2} = \dfrac{1}{1 \cdot (-1)} = -1$

81. $(2i)^6 = 2^6 i^6 = 64i^4 \cdot i^2 = 64(1)(-1) = -64$

83. $(-3i)^5 = (-3)^5 i^5 = -243i^4 \cdot i = -243(1)i = -243i$

85. $x + 50° + 90° = 180°$

$x + 140° = 180°$

$x = 40°$

87. $\underline{1|}\ \ 1\quad -6\quad\ \ 3\quad -4$

$\qquad\qquad 1\quad -5\quad -2$

$\overline{\qquad 1\quad -5\quad -2\quad -6}$

Answer: $x^2 - 5x - 2 - \dfrac{6}{x-1}$

89. 5 people

91. $5 + 9 = 14$ people

93. $\dfrac{5 \text{ people}}{30 \text{ people}} = \dfrac{1}{6} \approx 0.1666$

About 16.7% of the people reported an average checking balance of $201 to $300.

95. $i^3 - i^4 = -i - 1 = -1 - i$

97. $i^6 + i^8 = i^4 \cdot i^2 + (i^4)^2 = 1(-1) + 1^2 = -1 + 1 = 0$

99. $2 + \sqrt{-9} = 2 + i\sqrt{9} = 2 + 3i$

101. $\dfrac{6+\sqrt{-18}}{3} = \dfrac{6+i\sqrt{9\cdot2}}{3}$

$\qquad\qquad = \dfrac{6+3i\sqrt{2}}{3}$

$\qquad\qquad = \dfrac{6}{3}+\dfrac{3\sqrt{2}}{3}i$

$\qquad\qquad = 2+i\sqrt{2}$

103. $\dfrac{5-\sqrt{-75}}{10} = \dfrac{5-i\sqrt{25\cdot3}}{10}$

$\qquad\qquad = \dfrac{5-5i\sqrt{3}}{10}$

$\qquad\qquad = \dfrac{5}{10}-\dfrac{5\sqrt{3}}{10}i$

$\qquad\qquad = \dfrac{1}{2}-\dfrac{\sqrt{3}}{2}i$

105. Answers may vary

107. $\left(8-\sqrt{-4}\right)-\left(2+\sqrt{-16}\right) = (8-2i)-(2+4i)$

$\qquad\qquad\qquad\qquad = 8-2i-2-4i$

$\qquad\qquad\qquad\qquad = 6-6i$

109. $\qquad\qquad x^2+2x = -2$

$\quad (-1+i)^2 + 2(-1+i) = -2$

$\quad (1-2i+i^2)-2+2i = -2$

$\qquad\qquad 1-1-2 = -2$

$\qquad\qquad\qquad -2 = -2$, which is true.

Yes, $-1+i$ is a solution.

Chapter 7 Vocabulary Check

1. The <u>conjugate</u> of $\sqrt{3}+2$ is $\sqrt{3}-2$.

2. The <u>principal square root</u> of a nonnegative number a is written as $\sqrt{a}$.

3. The process of writing a radical expression as an equivalent expression but without a radical in the denominator is called <u>rationalizing</u> the denominator.

4. The <u>imaginary unit</u> written i, is the number whose square is -1.

5. The <u>cube root</u> of a number is written as $\sqrt[3]{a}$.

6. In the notation $\sqrt[n]{a}$, n is called the <u>index</u> and a is called the <u>radicand</u>.

7. Radicals with the same index and the same radicand are called <u>like radicals</u>.

8. A <u>complex number</u> is a number that can be written in the form $a + bi$, where a and b are real numbers.

9. The <u>distance</u> formula is
$$d = \sqrt{(x_2-x_1)^2+(y_2-y_1)^2}.$$

10. The <u>midpoint</u> formula is $\left(\dfrac{x_1+x_2}{2},\dfrac{y_1+y_2}{2}\right)$.

Chapter 7 Review

1. $\sqrt{81}=9$ because $9^2=81$.

2. $\sqrt[4]{81}=3$ because $3^4=81$.

3. $\sqrt[3]{-8}=-2$ because $(-2)^3=-8$.

4. $\sqrt[4]{-16}$ is not a real number.

5. $-\sqrt{\dfrac{1}{49}}=-\dfrac{1}{7}$ because $\left(\dfrac{1}{7}\right)^2=\dfrac{1}{49}$.

6. $\sqrt{x^{64}}=x^{32}$ because $(x^{32})^2=x^{32\cdot2}=x^{64}$.

7. $-\sqrt{36}=-6$ because $6^2=36$.

8. $\sqrt[3]{64}=4$ because $4^3=64$.

9. $\sqrt[3]{-a^6b^9} = \sqrt[3]{-1}\sqrt[3]{a^6}\sqrt[3]{b^9}$
$\qquad\qquad = -1a^2b^3$
$\qquad\qquad = -a^2b^3$

10. $\sqrt{16a^4b^{12}} = \sqrt{16}\sqrt{a^4}\sqrt{b^{12}} = 4a^2b^6$

11. $\sqrt[5]{32a^5b^{10}} = \sqrt[5]{32}\sqrt[5]{a^5}\sqrt[5]{b^{10}} = 2ab^2$

12. $\sqrt[5]{-32x^{15}y^{20}} = \sqrt[5]{-32}\sqrt[5]{x^{15}}\sqrt[5]{y^{20}} = -2x^3y^4$

13. $\sqrt{\dfrac{x^{12}}{36y^2}} = \dfrac{\sqrt{x^{12}}}{\sqrt{36y^2}} = \dfrac{x^6}{6y}$

14. $\sqrt[3]{\dfrac{27y^3}{z^{12}}} = \dfrac{\sqrt[3]{27y^3}}{\sqrt[3]{z^{12}}} = \dfrac{3y}{z^4}$

15. $\sqrt{(-x)^2} = |-x|$

16. $\sqrt[4]{(x^2-4)^4} = |x^2-4|$

17. $\sqrt[3]{(-27)^3} = -27$

18. $\sqrt[5]{(-5)^5} = -5$

19. $-\sqrt[5]{x^5} = -x$

20. $\sqrt[4]{16(2y+z)^{12}} = \sqrt[4]{16}\sqrt[4]{(2y+z)^{12}} = 2\left|(2y+z)^3\right|$

21. $\sqrt{25(x-y)^{10}} = \sqrt{25}\sqrt{(x-y)^{10}}$
$\qquad = 5\left|(x-y)^5\right|$

22. $\sqrt[5]{-y^5} = \sqrt[5]{-1}\sqrt[5]{y^5} = -1y = -y$

23. $\sqrt[9]{-x^9} = \sqrt[9]{-1}\sqrt[9]{x^9} = -1x = -x$

24. $f(x) = \sqrt{x} + 3$
$x \ge 0$
Domain: $[0, \infty)$

x	0	1	4	9
$f(x)$	3	4	5	6

25. $g(x) = \sqrt[3]{x-3}$
Domain: $(-\infty, \infty)$

x	-5	2	3	4	11
$g(x)$	-2	-1	0	1	2

26. $\left(\dfrac{1}{81}\right)^{1/4} = \dfrac{1}{81^{1/4}} = \dfrac{1}{\sqrt[4]{81}} = \dfrac{1}{3}$

27. $\left(-\dfrac{1}{27}\right)^{1/3} = -\dfrac{1}{27^{1/3}} = -\dfrac{1}{\sqrt[3]{27}} = -\dfrac{1}{3}$

28. $(-27)^{-1/3} = \dfrac{1}{(-27)^{1/3}} = \dfrac{1}{\sqrt[3]{-27}} = \dfrac{1}{-3} = -\dfrac{1}{3}$

29. $(-64)^{-1/3} = \dfrac{1}{(-64)^{1/3}} = \dfrac{1}{\sqrt[3]{-64}} = \dfrac{1}{-4} = -\dfrac{1}{4}$

30. $-9^{3/2} = -\left(\sqrt{9}\right)^3 = -3^3 = -27$

31. $64^{-1/3} = \dfrac{1}{64^{1/3}} = \dfrac{1}{\sqrt[3]{64}} = \dfrac{1}{4}$

32. $(-25)^{5/2} = \left(\sqrt{-25}\right)^5$ is not a real number, since there is no real number whose square is -25.

33. $\left(\dfrac{25}{49}\right)^{-3/2} = \dfrac{1}{\left(\dfrac{25}{49}\right)^{3/2}}$

$= \dfrac{1}{\left(\sqrt{\dfrac{25}{49}}\right)^3}$

$= \dfrac{1}{\left(\dfrac{5}{7}\right)^3}$

$= \dfrac{1}{\dfrac{125}{343}}$

$= \dfrac{343}{125}$

34. $\left(\dfrac{8}{27}\right)^{-2/3} = \dfrac{1}{\left(\dfrac{8}{27}\right)^{2/3}} = \dfrac{1}{\left(\sqrt[3]{\dfrac{8}{27}}\right)^2} = \dfrac{1}{\left(\dfrac{2}{3}\right)^2} = \dfrac{1}{\dfrac{4}{9}} = \dfrac{9}{4}$

35. $\left(-\dfrac{1}{36}\right)^{-1/4} = \dfrac{1}{\left(-\dfrac{1}{36}\right)^{1/4}} = \dfrac{1}{\sqrt[4]{-\dfrac{1}{36}}}$ is not a real

number, since there is no real number whose 4th

power is $-\dfrac{1}{36}$.

36. $\sqrt[3]{x^2} = (x^2)^{1/3} = x^{2/3}$

37. $\sqrt[5]{5x^2y^3} = (5x^2y^3)^{1/5}$
$= 5^{1/5}(x^2)^{1/5}(y^3)^{1/5}$
$= 5^{1/5}x^{2/5}y^{3/5}$

38. $y^{4/5} = (y^4)^{1/5} = \sqrt[5]{y^4}$

39. $5(xy^2z^5)^{1/3} = 5\sqrt[3]{xy^2z^5}$

40. $(x+2y)^{-1/2} = \dfrac{1}{(x+2y)^{1/2}} = \dfrac{1}{\sqrt{x+2y}}$

41. $a^{1/3}a^{4/3}a^{1/2} = a^{\frac{1}{3}+\frac{4}{3}+\frac{1}{2}} = a^{\frac{2}{6}+\frac{8}{6}+\frac{3}{6}} = a^{13/6}$

42. $\dfrac{b^{1/3}}{b^{4/3}} = b^{1/3-4/3} = b^{-3/3} = b^{-1} = \dfrac{1}{b}$

43. $(a^{1/2}a^{-2})^3 = (a^{1/2-2})^3$
$= (a^{1/2-4/2})^3$
$= (a^{-3/2})^3$
$= a^{-9/2}$
$= \dfrac{1}{a^{9/2}}$

44. $(x^{-3}y^6)^{1/3} = (x^{-3})^{1/3}(y^6)^{1/3} = x^{-1}y^2 = \dfrac{y^2}{x}$

45. $\left(\dfrac{b^{3/4}}{a^{-1/2}}\right)^8 = (a^{1/2}b^{3/4})^8$
$= (a^{1/2})^8(b^{3/4})^8$
$= a^4b^6$

46. $\dfrac{x^{1/4}x^{-1/2}}{x^{2/3}} = x^{1/4+(-1/2)-2/3}$

$= x^{\frac{3}{12}-\frac{6}{12}-\frac{8}{12}}$

$= x^{-11/12}$

$= \dfrac{1}{x^{11/12}}$

47. $\left(\dfrac{49c^{5/3}}{a^{-1/4}b^{5/6}}\right)^{-1} = \dfrac{49^{-1}c^{-5/3}}{a^{1/4}b^{-5/6}} = \dfrac{b^{5/6}}{49a^{1/4}c^{5/3}}$

48. $a^{-1/4}(a^{5/4} - a^{9/4}) = a^{-1/4}(a^{5/4}) - a^{-1/4}(a^{9/4})$
$= a^{-1/4+5/4} - a^{-1/4+9/4}$
$= a^{4/4} - a^{8/4}$
$= a - a^2$

49. $\sqrt{20} \approx 4.472$

50. $\sqrt[3]{-39} \approx -3.391$

51. $\sqrt[4]{726} \approx 5.191$

52. $56^{1/3} \approx 3.826$

53. $-78^{3/4} \approx -26.246$

54. $105^{-2/3} \approx 0.045$

55. $\sqrt[3]{2} \cdot \sqrt{7} = 2^{1/3} \cdot 7^{1/2}$
$= 2^{2/6} \cdot 7^{3/6}$
$= (2^2 \cdot 7^3)^{1/6}$
$= \sqrt[6]{4 \cdot 343}$
$= \sqrt[6]{1372}$

56. $\sqrt[3]{3} \cdot \sqrt[4]{x} = 3^{1/3} \cdot x^{1/4}$
$= 3^{4/12} \cdot x^{3/12}$
$= (3^4 \cdot x^3)^{1/12}$
$= \sqrt[12]{81x^3}$

57. $\sqrt{3} \cdot \sqrt{8} = \sqrt{24} = \sqrt{4 \cdot 6} = 2\sqrt{6}$

58. $\sqrt[3]{7y} \cdot \sqrt[3]{x^2 z} = \sqrt[3]{7y \cdot x^2 z} = \sqrt[3]{7x^2 yz}$

59. $\dfrac{\sqrt{44x^3}}{\sqrt{11x}} = \sqrt{\dfrac{44x^3}{11x}} = \sqrt{4x^2} = 2x$

60. $\dfrac{\sqrt[4]{a^6 b^{13}}}{\sqrt[4]{a^2 b}} = \sqrt[4]{\dfrac{a^6 b^{13}}{a^2 b}} = \sqrt[4]{a^4 b^{12}} = ab^3$

61. $\sqrt{60} = \sqrt{4 \cdot 15} = 2\sqrt{15}$

62. $-\sqrt{75} = -\sqrt{25 \cdot 3} = -5\sqrt{3}$

63. $\sqrt[3]{162} = \sqrt[3]{27 \cdot 6} = 3\sqrt[3]{6}$

64. $\sqrt[3]{-32} = \sqrt[3]{-8 \cdot 4} = -2\sqrt[3]{4}$

65. $\sqrt{36x^7} = \sqrt{36x^6 \cdot x} = 6x^3 \sqrt{x}$

66. $\sqrt[3]{24a^5 b^7} = \sqrt[3]{8a^3 b^6 \cdot 3a^2 b} = 2ab^2 \sqrt[3]{3a^2 b}$

67. $\sqrt{\dfrac{p^{17}}{121}} = \dfrac{\sqrt{p^{17}}}{\sqrt{121}} = \dfrac{\sqrt{p^{16} \cdot p}}{11} = \dfrac{p^8 \sqrt{p}}{11}$

68. $\sqrt[3]{\dfrac{y^5}{27x^6}} = \dfrac{\sqrt[3]{y^5}}{\sqrt[3]{27x^6}} = \dfrac{\sqrt[3]{y^3 y^2}}{\sqrt[3]{27x^6}} = \dfrac{y\sqrt[3]{y^2}}{3x^2}$

69. $\sqrt[4]{\dfrac{xy^6}{81}} = \dfrac{\sqrt[4]{xy^6}}{\sqrt[4]{81}} = \dfrac{\sqrt[4]{y^4 \cdot xy^2}}{3} = \dfrac{y\sqrt[4]{xy^2}}{3}$

70. $\sqrt{\dfrac{2x^3}{49y^4}} = \dfrac{\sqrt{2x^3}}{\sqrt{49y^4}} = \dfrac{\sqrt{x^2 \cdot 2x}}{7y^2} = \dfrac{x\sqrt{2x}}{7y^2}$

71. $r = \sqrt{\dfrac{A}{\pi}}$

    a. $r = \sqrt{\dfrac{25}{\pi}} = \dfrac{\sqrt{25}}{\sqrt{\pi}} = \dfrac{5}{\sqrt{\pi}}$ meters, or

        $r = \dfrac{5}{\sqrt{\pi}} = \dfrac{5\sqrt{\pi}}{\sqrt{\pi}\sqrt{\pi}} = \dfrac{5\sqrt{\pi}}{\pi}$ meters

    b. $r = \sqrt{\dfrac{104}{\pi}} \approx 5.75$ inches

72. $(x_1, y_1) = (-6, 3),\ (x_2, y_2) = (8, 4)$
$d = \sqrt{(x_2 - x_1)^2 + (y_2 - y_1)^2}$
$= \sqrt{(8+6)^2 + (4-3)^2}$
$= \sqrt{196+1}$
$= \sqrt{197} \approx 14.036$ units

73. $(x_1, y_1) = (-4, -6),\ (x_2, y_2) = (-1, 5)$
$d = \sqrt{(x_2 - x_1)^2 + (y_2 - y_1)^2}$
$= \sqrt{(-1+4)^2 + (5+6)^2}$
$= \sqrt{9+121}$
$= \sqrt{130} \approx 11.402$ units

74. $(x_1, y_1) = (-1, 5),\ (x_2, y_2) = (2, -3)$
$d = \sqrt{(x_2 - x_1)^2 + (y_2 - y_1)^2}$
$= \sqrt{(2+1)^2 + (-3-5)^2}$
$= \sqrt{9+64}$
$= \sqrt{73} \approx 8.544$ units

75. $(x_1, y_1) = \left(-\sqrt{2}, 0\right),\ (x_2, y_2) = \left(0, -4\sqrt{6}\right)$
$d = \sqrt{(x_2 - x_1)^2 + (y_2 - y_1)^2}$
$= \sqrt{\left(0+\sqrt{2}\right)^2 + \left(-4\sqrt{6}-0\right)^2}$
$= \sqrt{2+96}$
$= \sqrt{98}$
$= 7\sqrt{2} \approx 9.899$ units

76. $(x_1, y_1) = \left(-\sqrt{5}, -\sqrt{11}\right)$,

$(x_2, y_2) = \left(-\sqrt{5}, -3\sqrt{11}\right)$

$d = \sqrt{(x_2 - x_1)^2 + (y_2 - y_1)^2}$

$ = \sqrt{\left(-\sqrt{5} + \sqrt{5}\right)^2 + \left(-3\sqrt{11} + \sqrt{11}\right)^2}$

$ = \sqrt{0 + 44}$

$ = \sqrt{44}$

$ = 2\sqrt{11} \approx 6.633 \text{ units}$

77. $(x_1, y_1) = (7.4, -8.6), (x_2, y_2) = (-1.2, 5.6)$

$d = \sqrt{(-1.2 - 7.4)^2 + (5.6 + 8.6)^2}$

$ = \sqrt{(-8.6)^2 + (14.2)^2}$

$ = \sqrt{73.96 + 201.64}$

$ = \sqrt{275.6} \approx 16.601 \text{ units}$

78. $(x_1, y_1) = (2, 6), (x_2, y_2) = (-12, 4)$

$\text{midpoint} = \left(\dfrac{x_1 + x_2}{2}, \dfrac{y_1 + y_2}{2}\right)$

$\phantom{\text{midpoint}} = \left(\dfrac{2 - 12}{2}, \dfrac{6 + 4}{2}\right)$

$\phantom{\text{midpoint}} = \left(\dfrac{-10}{2}, \dfrac{10}{2}\right)$

$\phantom{\text{midpoint}} = (-5, 5)$

79. $(x_1, y_1) = (-6, -5), (x_2, y_2) = (-9, 7)$

$\text{midpoint} = \left(\dfrac{x_1 + x_2}{2}, \dfrac{y_1 + y_2}{2}\right)$

$\phantom{\text{midpoint}} = \left(\dfrac{-6 - 9}{2}, \dfrac{-5 + 7}{2}\right)$

$\phantom{\text{midpoint}} = \left(\dfrac{-15}{2}, \dfrac{2}{2}\right)$

$\phantom{\text{midpoint}} = \left(-\dfrac{15}{2}, 1\right)$

80. $(x_1, y_1) = (4, -6), (x_2, y_2) = (-15, 2)$

$\text{midpoint} = \left(\dfrac{x_1 + x_2}{2}, \dfrac{y_1 + y_2}{2}\right)$

$\phantom{\text{midpoint}} = \left(\dfrac{4 - 15}{2}, \dfrac{-6 + 2}{2}\right)$

$\phantom{\text{midpoint}} = \left(\dfrac{-11}{2}, \dfrac{-4}{2}\right)$

$\phantom{\text{midpoint}} = \left(-\dfrac{11}{2}, -2\right)$

81. $(x_1, y_1) = \left(0, -\dfrac{3}{8}\right), (x_2, y_2) = \left(\dfrac{1}{10}, 0\right)$

$\text{midpoint} = \left(\dfrac{x_1 + x_2}{2}, \dfrac{y_1 + y_2}{2}\right)$

$\phantom{\text{midpoint}} = \left(\dfrac{0 + \frac{1}{10}}{2}, \dfrac{-\frac{3}{8} + 0}{2}\right)$

$\phantom{\text{midpoint}} = \left(\dfrac{1}{20}, -\dfrac{3}{16}\right)$

82. $(x_1, y_1) = \left(\dfrac{3}{4}, -\dfrac{1}{7}\right), (x_2, y_2) = \left(-\dfrac{1}{4}, -\dfrac{3}{7}\right)$

$\text{midpoint} = \left(\dfrac{x_1 + x_2}{2}, \dfrac{y_1 + y_2}{2}\right)$

$\phantom{\text{midpoint}} = \left(\dfrac{\frac{3}{4} - \frac{1}{4}}{2}, \dfrac{-\frac{1}{7} - \frac{3}{7}}{2}\right)$

$\phantom{\text{midpoint}} = \left(\dfrac{\frac{1}{2}}{2}, \dfrac{-\frac{4}{7}}{2}\right)$

$\phantom{\text{midpoint}} = \left(\dfrac{1}{4}, -\dfrac{2}{7}\right)$

83. $(x_1, y_1) = \left(\sqrt{3}, -2\sqrt{6}\right), (x_2, y_2) = \left(\sqrt{3}, -4\sqrt{6}\right)$

$\text{midpoint} = \left(\dfrac{x_1 + x_2}{2}, \dfrac{y_1 + y_2}{2}\right)$

$\phantom{\text{midpoint}} = \left(\dfrac{\sqrt{3} + \sqrt{3}}{2}, \dfrac{-2\sqrt{6} - 4\sqrt{6}}{2}\right)$

$\phantom{\text{midpoint}} = \left(\dfrac{2\sqrt{3}}{2}, \dfrac{-6\sqrt{6}}{2}\right)$

$\phantom{\text{midpoint}} = \left(\sqrt{3}, -3\sqrt{6}\right)$

84. $2\sqrt{50} - 3\sqrt{125} + \sqrt{98}$

$= 2\sqrt{25 \cdot 2} - 3\sqrt{25 \cdot 5} + \sqrt{49 \cdot 2}$

$= 2 \cdot 5\sqrt{2} - 3 \cdot 5\sqrt{5} + 7\sqrt{2}$

$= 10\sqrt{2} - 15\sqrt{5} + 7\sqrt{2}$

$= 17\sqrt{2} - 15\sqrt{5}$

85. $x\sqrt{75xy} - \sqrt{27x^3y} = x\sqrt{25 \cdot 3xy} - \sqrt{9x^2 \cdot 3xy}$

$\phantom{x\sqrt{75xy} - \sqrt{27x^3y}} = x \cdot 5\sqrt{3xy} - 3x\sqrt{3xy}$

$\phantom{x\sqrt{75xy} - \sqrt{27x^3y}} = 2x\sqrt{3xy}$

86. $\sqrt[3]{128} + \sqrt[3]{250} = \sqrt[3]{64 \cdot 2} + \sqrt[3]{125 \cdot 2}$
$$= 4\sqrt[3]{2} + 5\sqrt[3]{2}$$
$$= 9\sqrt[3]{2}$$

87. $3\sqrt[4]{32a^5} - a\sqrt[4]{162a} = 3\sqrt[4]{16a^4 \cdot 2a} - a\sqrt[4]{81 \cdot 2a}$
$$= 3 \cdot 2a\sqrt[4]{2a} - 3a\sqrt[4]{2a}$$
$$= 6a\sqrt[4]{2a} - 3a\sqrt[4]{2a}$$
$$= 3a\sqrt[4]{2a}$$

88. $\dfrac{5}{\sqrt{4}} + \dfrac{\sqrt{3}}{3} = \dfrac{5}{2} + \dfrac{\sqrt{3}}{3} = \dfrac{5 \cdot 3 + 2\sqrt{3}}{6} = \dfrac{15 + 2\sqrt{3}}{6}$

89. $\sqrt{\dfrac{8}{x^2}} - \sqrt{\dfrac{50}{16x^2}} = \dfrac{\sqrt{8}}{\sqrt{x^2}} - \dfrac{\sqrt{50}}{\sqrt{16x^2}}$
$$= \dfrac{\sqrt{4 \cdot 2}}{x} - \dfrac{\sqrt{25 \cdot 2}}{4x}$$
$$= \dfrac{2\sqrt{2} \cdot 4}{x \cdot 4} - \dfrac{5\sqrt{2}}{4x}$$
$$= \dfrac{8\sqrt{2} - 5\sqrt{2}}{4x}$$
$$= \dfrac{3\sqrt{2}}{4x}$$

90. $2\sqrt{32x^2 y^3} - xy\sqrt{98y}$
$$= 2\sqrt{16x^2 y^2 \cdot 2y} - xy\sqrt{49 \cdot 2y}$$
$$= 2 \cdot 4xy\sqrt{2y} - xy \cdot 7\sqrt{2y}$$
$$= 8xy\sqrt{2y} - 7xy\sqrt{2y}$$
$$= xy\sqrt{2y}$$

91. $2a\sqrt[4]{32b^5} - 3b\sqrt[4]{162a^4 b} + \sqrt[4]{2a^4 b^5}$
$$= 2a\sqrt[4]{16b^4 \cdot 2b} - 3b\sqrt[4]{81a^4 \cdot 2b} + \sqrt[4]{a^4 b^4 \cdot 2b}$$
$$= 2a \cdot 2b\sqrt[4]{2b} - 3b \cdot 3a\sqrt[4]{2b} + ab\sqrt[4]{2b}$$
$$= 4ab\sqrt[4]{2b} - 9ab\sqrt[4]{2b} + ab\sqrt[4]{2b}$$
$$= -4ab\sqrt[4]{2b}$$

92. $\sqrt{3}\left(\sqrt{27} - \sqrt{3}\right) = \sqrt{3}\left(\sqrt{9 \cdot 3} - \sqrt{3}\right)$
$$= \sqrt{3}\left(3\sqrt{3} - \sqrt{3}\right)$$
$$= \sqrt{3}\left(2\sqrt{3}\right)$$
$$= 2\sqrt{9}$$
$$= 2(3)$$
$$= 6$$

93. $\left(\sqrt{x} - 3\right)^2 = \left(\sqrt{x}\right)^2 - 2 \cdot \sqrt{x} \cdot 3 + 3^2 = x - 6\sqrt{x} + 9$

94. $\left(\sqrt{5} - 5\right)\left(2\sqrt{5} + 2\right) = 2\sqrt{25} + 2\sqrt{5} - 10\sqrt{5} - 10$
$$= 2(5) - 8\sqrt{5} - 10$$
$$= 10 - 8\sqrt{5} - 10$$
$$= -8\sqrt{5}$$

95. $\left(2\sqrt{x} - 3\sqrt{y}\right)\left(2\sqrt{x} + 3\sqrt{y}\right)$
$$= \left(2\sqrt{x}\right)^2 - \left(3\sqrt{y}\right)^2$$
$$= 2^2\left(\sqrt{x}\right)^2 - 3^2\left(\sqrt{y}\right)^2$$
$$= 4x - 9y$$

96. $\left(\sqrt{a} + 3\right)\left(\sqrt{a} - 3\right) = \left(\sqrt{a}\right)^2 - (3)^2 = a - 9$

97. $\left(\sqrt[3]{a} + 2\right)^2 = \left(\sqrt[3]{a}\right)^2 + 2 \cdot \sqrt[3]{a} \cdot 2 + 2^2$
$$= \sqrt[3]{a^2} + 4\sqrt[3]{a} + 4$$

98. $\left(\sqrt[3]{5x} + 9\right)\left(\sqrt[3]{5x} - 9\right) = \left(\sqrt[3]{5x}\right)^2 - 9^2$
$$= \sqrt[3]{(5x)^2} - 81$$
$$= \sqrt[3]{25x^2} - 81$$

99. $\left(\sqrt[3]{a} + 4\right)\left(\sqrt[3]{a^2} - 4\sqrt[3]{a} + 16\right)$
$$= \left(\sqrt[3]{a}\right)\left(\sqrt[3]{a^2}\right) - 4 \cdot \left(\sqrt[3]{a}\right)^2 + 16\sqrt[3]{a} + 4\sqrt[3]{a^2}$$
$$\quad - 16\sqrt[3]{a} + 64$$
$$= \sqrt[3]{a^3} - 4\sqrt[3]{a^2} + 4\sqrt[3]{a^2} + 64$$
$$= a + 64$$

100. $\dfrac{3}{\sqrt{7}} = \dfrac{3 \cdot \sqrt{7}}{\sqrt{7} \cdot \sqrt{7}} = \dfrac{3\sqrt{7}}{7}$

101. $\sqrt{\dfrac{x}{12}} = \dfrac{\sqrt{x}}{\sqrt{12}}$

$\qquad = \dfrac{\sqrt{x}}{\sqrt{4 \cdot 3}}$

$\qquad = \dfrac{\sqrt{x}}{2\sqrt{3}}$

$\qquad = \dfrac{\sqrt{x} \cdot \sqrt{3}}{2\sqrt{3} \cdot \sqrt{3}}$

$\qquad = \dfrac{\sqrt{3x}}{2 \cdot 3}$

$\qquad = \dfrac{\sqrt{3x}}{6}$

102. $\dfrac{5}{\sqrt[3]{4}} = \dfrac{5 \cdot \sqrt[3]{2}}{\sqrt[3]{4} \cdot \sqrt[3]{2}} = \dfrac{5\sqrt[3]{2}}{\sqrt[3]{8}} = \dfrac{5\sqrt[3]{2}}{2}$

103. $\sqrt{\dfrac{24x^5}{3y^2}} = \sqrt{\dfrac{8x^5}{y^2}}$

$\qquad = \dfrac{\sqrt{8x^5}}{\sqrt{y^2}}$

$\qquad = \dfrac{\sqrt{4x^4 \cdot 2x}}{y}$

$\qquad = \dfrac{2x^2\sqrt{2x}}{y}$

104. $\sqrt[3]{\dfrac{15x^6 y^7}{z^2}} = \dfrac{\sqrt[3]{15x^6 y^7}}{\sqrt[3]{z^2}}$

$\qquad = \dfrac{\sqrt[3]{15x^6 y^7} \cdot \sqrt[3]{z}}{\sqrt[3]{z^2} \cdot \sqrt[3]{z}}$

$\qquad = \dfrac{\sqrt[3]{15x^6 y^7 z}}{\sqrt[3]{z^3}}$

$\qquad = \dfrac{\sqrt[3]{15x^6 y^6 \cdot yz}}{z}$

$\qquad = \dfrac{x^2 y^2 \sqrt[3]{15yz}}{z}$

105. $\dfrac{5}{2 - \sqrt{7}} = \dfrac{5\left(2 + \sqrt{7}\right)}{\left(2 - \sqrt{7}\right)\left(2 + \sqrt{7}\right)}$

$\qquad = \dfrac{5\left(2 + \sqrt{7}\right)}{2^2 - \left(\sqrt{7}\right)^2}$

$\qquad = \dfrac{10 + 5\sqrt{7}}{4 - 7}$

$\qquad = \dfrac{10 + 5\sqrt{7}}{-3}$

$\qquad = -\dfrac{10 + 5\sqrt{7}}{3}$

106. $\dfrac{3}{\sqrt{y} - 2} = \dfrac{3\left(\sqrt{y} + 2\right)}{\left(\sqrt{y} - 2\right)\left(\sqrt{y} + 2\right)}$

$\qquad = \dfrac{3\left(\sqrt{y} + 2\right)}{\left(\sqrt{y}\right)^2 - 2^2}$

$\qquad = \dfrac{3\sqrt{y} + 6}{y - 4}$

107. $\dfrac{\sqrt{2} - \sqrt{3}}{\sqrt{2} + \sqrt{3}} = \dfrac{\left(\sqrt{2} - \sqrt{3}\right)\left(\sqrt{2} - \sqrt{3}\right)}{\left(\sqrt{2} + \sqrt{3}\right)\left(\sqrt{2} - \sqrt{3}\right)}$

$\qquad = \dfrac{2 - \sqrt{2}\sqrt{3} - \sqrt{3}\sqrt{2} + 3}{\left(\sqrt{2}\right)^2 - \left(\sqrt{3}\right)^2}$

$\qquad = \dfrac{5 - \sqrt{6} - \sqrt{6}}{2 - 3}$

$\qquad = \dfrac{5 - 2\sqrt{6}}{-1}$

$\qquad = -5 + 2\sqrt{6}$

108. $\dfrac{\sqrt{11}}{3} = \dfrac{\sqrt{11} \cdot \sqrt{11}}{3 \cdot \sqrt{11}} = \dfrac{11}{3\sqrt{11}}$

109. $\sqrt{\dfrac{18}{y}} = \dfrac{\sqrt{18}}{\sqrt{y}} = \dfrac{3\sqrt{2}}{\sqrt{y}} = \dfrac{3\sqrt{2} \cdot \sqrt{2}}{\sqrt{y} \cdot \sqrt{2}} = \dfrac{3 \cdot 2}{\sqrt{2y}} = \dfrac{6}{\sqrt{2y}}$

110. $\dfrac{\sqrt[3]{9}}{7} = \dfrac{\sqrt[3]{9} \cdot \sqrt[3]{3}}{7 \cdot \sqrt[3]{3}} = \dfrac{\sqrt[3]{27}}{7\sqrt[3]{3}} = \dfrac{3}{7\sqrt[3]{3}}$

111. $\sqrt{\dfrac{24x^5}{3y^2}} = \sqrt{\dfrac{8x^5}{y^2}}$

$= \dfrac{\sqrt{4x^4 \cdot 2x}}{\sqrt{y^2}}$

$= \dfrac{2x^2\sqrt{2x}}{y}$

$= \dfrac{2x^2\sqrt{2x} \cdot \sqrt{2x}}{y \cdot \sqrt{2x}}$

$= \dfrac{2x^2 \cdot 2x}{y\sqrt{2x}} = \dfrac{4x^3}{y\sqrt{2x}}$

112. $\sqrt[3]{\dfrac{xy^2}{10z}} = \dfrac{\sqrt[3]{xy^2}}{\sqrt[3]{10z}}$

$= \dfrac{\sqrt[3]{xy^2} \cdot \sqrt[3]{x^2 y}}{\sqrt[3]{10z} \cdot \sqrt[3]{x^2 y}}$

$= \dfrac{\sqrt[3]{x^3 y^3}}{\sqrt[3]{10x^2 yz}}$

$= \dfrac{xy}{\sqrt[3]{10x^2 yz}}$

113. $\dfrac{\sqrt{x}+5}{-3} = \dfrac{\left(\sqrt{x}+5\right)\left(\sqrt{x}-5\right)}{-3\left(\sqrt{x}-5\right)}$

$= \dfrac{\left(\sqrt{x}\right)^2 - 5^2}{-3\sqrt{x}+15}$

$= \dfrac{x-25}{-3\sqrt{x}+15}$

114. $\sqrt{y-7} = 5$

$\left(\sqrt{y-7}\right)^2 = 5^2$

$y-7 = 25$

$y = 32$

The solution is 32.

115. $\sqrt{2x}+10 = 4$

$\sqrt{2x} = -6$

No solution exists since the principle square root of a number is not negative.

116. $\sqrt[3]{2x-6} = 4$

$\left(\sqrt[3]{2x-6}\right)^3 = 4^3$

$2x-6 = 64$

$2x = 70$

$x = 35$

The solution is 35.

117. $\sqrt{x+6} = \sqrt{x+2}$

$\left(\sqrt{x+6}\right)^2 = \left(\sqrt{x+2}\right)^2$

$x+6 = x+2$

$6 = 2$, which is false.

There is no solution.

118. $2x - 5\sqrt{x} = 3$

$2x-3 = 5\sqrt{x}$

$(2x-3)^2 = \left(5\sqrt{x}\right)^2$

$4x^2 - 12x + 9 = 25x$

$4x^2 - 37x + 9 = 0$

$(4x-1)(x-9) = 0$

$4x-1 = 0 \ $ or $\ x-9 = 0$

$4x = 1 \ $ or $\quad x = 9$

$x = \dfrac{1}{4}$

Discard the solution $\dfrac{1}{4}$ as extraneous. The solution is 9.

119. $\sqrt{x+9} = 2 + \sqrt{x-7}$

$\left(\sqrt{x+9}\right)^2 = \left(2 + \sqrt{x-7}\right)^2$

$x+9 = 4 + 4\sqrt{x-7} + (x-7)$

$x+9 = x-3 + 4\sqrt{x-7}$

$12 = 4\sqrt{x-7}$

$3 = \sqrt{x-7}$

$3^2 = \left(\sqrt{x-7}\right)^2$

$9 = x-7$

$16 = x$

The solution is 16.

120. Let c = length of the hypotenuse.

$$3^2 + 3^2 = c^2$$
$$18 = c^2$$
$$\sqrt{18} = \sqrt{c^2}$$
$$3\sqrt{2} = c$$

The length is $3\sqrt{2}$ centimeters.

121. Let c = length of the hypotenuse.

$$7^2 + \left(8\sqrt{3}\right)^2 = c^2$$
$$49 + 64 \cdot 3 = c^2$$
$$241 = c^2$$
$$\sqrt{241} = \sqrt{c^2}$$
$$\sqrt{241} = c$$

The length is $\sqrt{241}$ feet.

122. Let b = width of the lake.

$$a^2 + b^2 = c^2$$
$$40^2 + b^2 = 65^2$$
$$1600 + b^2 = 4225$$
$$b^2 = 2625$$
$$\sqrt{b^2} = \sqrt{2625}$$
$$b = 51.23475$$

The width is about 51.2 feet.

123. Let c = length of the shortest pipe.

$$a^2 + b^2 = c^2$$
$$3^2 + 3^2 = c^2$$
$$18 = c^2$$
$$\sqrt{18} = \sqrt{c^2}$$
$$4.24264 = c$$

The shortest possible pipe is 4.24 feet.

124. $\sqrt{-8} = i\sqrt{4 \cdot 2} = 2i\sqrt{2}$

125. $-\sqrt{-6} = -i\sqrt{6}$

126. $\sqrt{-4} + \sqrt{-16} = 2i + 4i = 6i$

127. $\sqrt{-2} \cdot \sqrt{-5} = i\sqrt{2} \cdot i\sqrt{5}$
$$= i^2\sqrt{10}$$
$$= -1 \cdot \sqrt{10}$$
$$= -\sqrt{10}$$

128. $(12 - 6i) + (3 + 2i) = (12 + 3) + (-6 + 2)i$
$$= 15 + (-4)i$$
$$= 15 - 4i$$

129. $(-8 - 7i) - (5 - 4i) = -8 - 7i - 5 + 4i$
$$= -13 - 3i$$

130. $(2i)^6 = 2^6 i^6 = 64i^4 \cdot i^2 = 64(1)(-1) = -64$

131. $-3i(6 - 4i) = -18i + 12i^2$
$$= -18i + 12(-1)$$
$$= -12 - 18i$$

132. $(3 + 2i)(1 + i) = 3 + 3i + 2i + 2i^2$
$$= 3 + 5i + 2(-1)$$
$$= 1 + 5i$$

133. $(2 - 3i)^2 = 2^2 + 2 \cdot 2 \cdot (-3i) + (3i)^2$
$$= 4 - 12i + 9i^2$$
$$= 4 - 12i + 9(-1)$$
$$= -5 - 12i$$

134. $\left(\sqrt{6} - 9i\right)\left(\sqrt{6} + 9i\right) = \left(\sqrt{6}\right)^2 - (9i)^2$
$$= 6 - 81i^2$$
$$= 6 + 81$$
$$= 87$$

135. $\dfrac{2 + 3i}{2i} = \dfrac{(2 + 3i) \cdot (-2i)}{2i \cdot (-2i)}$

$$= \dfrac{-4i - 6i^2}{-4i^2}$$
$$= \dfrac{-4i + 6}{4}$$
$$= \dfrac{6}{4} - \dfrac{4}{4}i$$
$$= \dfrac{3}{2} - i$$

136. $\dfrac{1 + i}{-3i} = \dfrac{(1 + i) \cdot (3i)}{-3i \cdot (3i)}$

$$= \dfrac{3i + 3i^2}{-9i^2}$$
$$= \dfrac{3i - 3}{9}$$
$$= \dfrac{-3}{9} - \dfrac{3}{9}i$$
$$= -\dfrac{1}{3} + \dfrac{1}{3}i$$

137. $\sqrt[3]{x^3} = x$

138. $\sqrt{(x+2)^2} = |x+2|$

139. $-\sqrt{100} = -10$

140. $\sqrt[3]{-x^{12}y^3} = -x^4y$

141. $\sqrt[4]{\dfrac{y^{20}}{16x^{12}}} = \dfrac{\sqrt[4]{y^{20}}}{\sqrt[4]{16x^{12}}} = \dfrac{y^5}{2x^3}$

142. $9^{1/2} = \sqrt{9} = 3$

143. $64^{-1/2} = \dfrac{1}{64^{1/2}} = \dfrac{1}{\sqrt{64}} = \dfrac{1}{8}$

144. $\left(\dfrac{27}{64}\right)^{-2/3} = \left(\dfrac{64}{27}\right)^{2/3}$

$\qquad = \left(\sqrt[3]{\dfrac{64}{27}}\right)^2$

$\qquad = \left(\dfrac{4}{3}\right)^2$

$\qquad = \dfrac{16}{9}$

145. $\dfrac{(x^{2/3}x^{-3})^3}{x^{-1/2}} = \dfrac{x^{6/3}x^{-9}}{x^{-1/2}}$

$\qquad = x^{2-9+\frac{1}{2}}$

$\qquad = x^{-13/2}$

$\qquad = \dfrac{1}{x^{13/2}}$

146. $\sqrt{200x^9} = \sqrt{100x^8 \cdot 2x} = 10x^4\sqrt{2x}$

147. $\sqrt{\dfrac{3n^3}{121m^{10}}} = \dfrac{\sqrt{3n^3}}{\sqrt{121m^{10}}} = \dfrac{\sqrt{n^2 \cdot 3n}}{\sqrt{121m^{10}}} = \dfrac{n\sqrt{3n}}{11m^5}$

148. $3\sqrt{20} - 7x\sqrt[3]{40} + 3\sqrt[3]{5x^3}$

$\qquad = 3\sqrt{4}\sqrt{5} - 7x\sqrt[3]{8}\sqrt[3]{5} + 3\sqrt[3]{x^3}\sqrt[3]{5}$

$\qquad = 6\sqrt{5} - 14x\sqrt[3]{5} + 3x\sqrt[3]{5}$

$\qquad = 6\sqrt{5} - 11x\sqrt[3]{5}$

149. $\left(2\sqrt{x} - 5\right)^2 = \left(2\sqrt{x}\right)^2 - 2(5)\left(2\sqrt{x}\right) + 5^2$

$\qquad\qquad\qquad = 4x - 20\sqrt{x} + 25$

150. $(x_1, y_1) = (-3, 5),\ (x_2, y_2) = (-8, 9)$

$d = \sqrt{(x_2 - x_1)^2 + (y_2 - y_1)^2}$

$\quad = \sqrt{(-8+3)^2 + (9-5)^2}$

$\quad = \sqrt{(-5)^2 + (4)^2}$

$\quad = \sqrt{25+16}$

$\quad = \sqrt{41}$

The distance is $\sqrt{41}$ units.

151. $(x_1, y_1) = (-3, 8),\ (x_2, y_2) = (11, 24)$

$\text{midpoint} = \left(\dfrac{x_1 + x_2}{2}, \dfrac{y_1 + y_2}{2}\right)$

$\qquad\quad = \left(\dfrac{-3+11}{2}, \dfrac{8+24}{2}\right)$

$\qquad\quad = \left(\dfrac{8}{2}, \dfrac{32}{2}\right)$

$\qquad\quad = (4, 16)$

152. $\dfrac{7}{\sqrt{13}} = \dfrac{7}{\sqrt{13}} \cdot \dfrac{\sqrt{13}}{\sqrt{13}} = \dfrac{7\sqrt{13}}{13}$

153. $\dfrac{2}{\sqrt{x}+3} = \dfrac{2}{\sqrt{x}+3} \cdot \dfrac{\sqrt{x}-3}{\sqrt{x}-3} = \dfrac{2\sqrt{x}-6}{x-9}$

154. $\sqrt{x} + 2 = x$

$\qquad \sqrt{x} = x - 2$

$\qquad \left(\sqrt{x}\right)^2 = (x-2)^2$

$\qquad\quad x = x^2 - 4x + 4$

$\qquad\quad 0 = x^2 - 5x + 4$

$\qquad\quad 0 = (x-4)(x-1)$

$\quad x - 4 = 0 \quad \text{or} \quad x - 1 = 0$

$\qquad x = 4 \qquad\qquad x = 1$

Discard the extraneous solution 1. The solution set is {4}.

Chapter 7 Test

1. $\sqrt{216} = \sqrt{36 \cdot 6} = 6\sqrt{6}$

2. $-\sqrt[4]{x^{64}} = -x^{16}$

3. $\left(\dfrac{1}{125}\right)^{1/3} = \dfrac{1}{125^{1/3}} = \dfrac{1}{\sqrt[3]{125}} = \dfrac{1}{5}$

4. $\left(\dfrac{1}{125}\right)^{-1/3} = \dfrac{1}{\left(\frac{1}{125}\right)^{1/3}} = \dfrac{1}{\frac{1}{5}} = 5$

5. $\left(\dfrac{8x^3}{27}\right)^{2/3} = \dfrac{(8x^3)^{2/3}}{27^{2/3}}$

$= \dfrac{\left(\sqrt[3]{8x^3}\right)^2}{\left(\sqrt[3]{27}\right)^2}$

$= \dfrac{(2x)^2}{3^2}$

$= \dfrac{4x^2}{9}$

6. $\sqrt[3]{-a^{18}b^9} = \sqrt[3]{-1a^{18}b^9} = (-1)a^6b^3 = -a^6b^3$

7. $\left(\dfrac{64c^{4/3}}{a^{-2/3}b^{5/6}}\right)^{1/2} = \left(\dfrac{64a^{2/3}c^{4/3}}{b^{5/6}}\right)^{1/2}$

$= \dfrac{64^{1/2}(a^{2/3})^{1/2}(c^{4/3})^{1/2}}{(b^{5/6})^{1/2}}$

$= \dfrac{\sqrt{64}a^{1/3}c^{2/3}}{b^{5/12}}$

$= \dfrac{8a^{1/3}c^{2/3}}{b^{5/12}}$

8. $a^{-2/3}(a^{5/4} - a^3) = a^{-2/3}a^{5/4} - a^{-2/3}a^3$

$= a^{-\frac{2}{3}+\frac{5}{4}} - a^{-\frac{2}{3}+3}$

$= a^{-\frac{8}{12}+\frac{15}{12}} - a^{-\frac{2}{3}+\frac{9}{3}}$

$= a^{7/12} - a^{7/3}$

9. $\sqrt[4]{(4xy)^4} = |4xy| = 4|xy|$

10. $\sqrt[3]{(-27)^3} = -27$

11. $\sqrt{\dfrac{9}{y}} = \dfrac{\sqrt{9}}{\sqrt{y}} = \dfrac{3}{\sqrt{y}} = \dfrac{3 \cdot \sqrt{y}}{\sqrt{y} \cdot \sqrt{y}} = \dfrac{3\sqrt{y}}{y}$

12. $\dfrac{4 - \sqrt{x}}{4 + 2\sqrt{x}} = \dfrac{4 - \sqrt{x}}{2(2 + \sqrt{x})}$

$= \dfrac{(4 - \sqrt{x})(2 - \sqrt{x})}{2(2 + \sqrt{x})(2 - \sqrt{x})}$

$= \dfrac{8 - 4\sqrt{x} - 2\sqrt{x} + x}{2\left[2^2 - \left(\sqrt{x}\right)^2\right]}$

$= \dfrac{8 - 6\sqrt{x} + x}{2(4 - x)}$ or $\dfrac{8 - 6\sqrt{x} + x}{8 - 2x}$

13. $\dfrac{\sqrt[3]{ab}}{\sqrt[3]{ab^2}} = \sqrt[3]{\dfrac{ab}{ab^2}}$

$= \sqrt[3]{\dfrac{1}{b}}$

$= \dfrac{1}{\sqrt[3]{b}}$

$= \dfrac{1 \cdot \sqrt[3]{b^2}}{\sqrt[3]{b} \cdot \sqrt[3]{b^2}}$

$= \dfrac{\sqrt[3]{b^2}}{b}$

14. $\dfrac{\sqrt{6} + x}{8} = \dfrac{\left(\sqrt{6} + x\right)\left(\sqrt{6} - x\right)}{8\left(\sqrt{6} - x\right)}$

$= \dfrac{\left(\sqrt{6}\right)^2 - x^2}{8\left(\sqrt{6} - x\right)}$

$= \dfrac{6 - x^2}{8\left(\sqrt{6} - x\right)}$

15. $\sqrt{125x^3} - 3\sqrt{20x^3} = \sqrt{25x^2 \cdot 5x} - 3\sqrt{4x^2 \cdot 5x}$

$= 5x\sqrt{5x} - 3 \cdot 2x\sqrt{5x}$

$= 5x\sqrt{5x} - 6x\sqrt{5x}$

$= -x\sqrt{5x}$

16. $\sqrt{3}\left(\sqrt{16} - \sqrt{2}\right) = \sqrt{3}\left(4 - \sqrt{2}\right)$

$= 4\sqrt{3} - \sqrt{3}\sqrt{2}$

$= 4\sqrt{3} - \sqrt{6}$

17. $\left(\sqrt{x} + 1\right)^2 = \left(\sqrt{x}\right)^2 + 2\sqrt{x} + 1^2$

$= x + 2\sqrt{x} + 1$

18. $\left(\sqrt{2}-4\right)\left(\sqrt{3}+1\right)=\sqrt{2}\sqrt{3}+1\cdot\sqrt{2}-4\sqrt{3}-4$
$$=\sqrt{6}+\sqrt{2}-4\sqrt{3}-4$$

19. $\left(\sqrt{5}+5\right)\left(\sqrt{5}-5\right)=\left(\sqrt{5}\right)^2-5^2$
$$=5-25$$
$$=-20$$

20. $\sqrt{561}\approx23.685$

21. $386^{-2/3}\approx0.019$

22.
$$x=\sqrt{x-2}+2$$
$$x-2=\sqrt{x-2}$$
$$(x-2)^2=\left(\sqrt{x-2}\right)^2$$
$$x^2-4x+4=x-2$$
$$x^2-5x+6=0$$
$$(x-2)(x-3)=0$$
$$x=2 \text{ or } x=3$$
The solutions are 2 and 3.

23. $\sqrt{x^2-7}+3=0$
$$\sqrt{x^2-7}=-3$$
No solution exists since the principle square root of a number is not negative.

24. $\sqrt[3]{x+5}=\sqrt[3]{2x-1}$
$$\left(\sqrt[3]{x+5}\right)^3=\left(\sqrt[3]{2x-1}\right)^3$$
$$x+5=2x-1$$
$$-x=-6$$
$$x=6$$
The solution is 6.

25. $\sqrt{-2}=i\sqrt{2}$

26. $-\sqrt{-8}=-i\sqrt{4\cdot2}=-2i\sqrt{2}$

27. $(12-6i)-(12-3i)=12-6i-12+3i=-3i$

28. $(6-2i)(6+2i)=6^2-(2i)^2$
$$=36-4i^2$$
$$=36+4$$
$$=40$$

29. $(4+3i)^2=4^2+2\cdot4\cdot3i+(3i)^2$
$$=16+24i+9i^2$$
$$=16+24i-9$$
$$=7+24i$$

30. $\dfrac{1+4i}{1-i}=\dfrac{(1+4i)(1+i)}{(1-i)(1+i)}$
$$=\dfrac{1+i+4i+4i^2}{1^2-i^2}$$
$$=\dfrac{1+5i-4}{1-(-1)}$$
$$=\dfrac{-3+5i}{2}$$
$$=-\dfrac{3}{2}+\dfrac{5}{2}i$$

31. $x^2+x^2=5^2$
$$2x^2=25$$
$$x^2=\dfrac{25}{2}$$
$$\sqrt{x^2}=\sqrt{\dfrac{25}{2}}$$
$$x=\dfrac{5}{\sqrt{2}}=\dfrac{5\cdot\sqrt{2}}{\sqrt{2}\cdot\sqrt{2}}=\dfrac{5\sqrt{2}}{2}$$

32. $g(x)=\sqrt{x+2}$
$$x+2\geq0$$
$$x\geq-2$$
Domain: $[-2,\infty)$

x	-2	-1	2	7
$g(x)$	0	1	2	3

33. $(x_1, y_1) = (-6, 3)$, $(x_2, y_2) = (-8, -7)$

$d = \sqrt{(-8-(-6))^2 + (-7-3)^2}$

$\quad = \sqrt{(-2)^2 + (-10)^2}$

$\quad = \sqrt{4+100}$

$\quad = \sqrt{104}$

$\quad = \sqrt{4 \cdot 26}$

$\quad = 2\sqrt{26}$

The distance is $2\sqrt{26}$ units.

34. $(x_1, y_1) = \left(-2\sqrt{5}, \sqrt{10}\right)$,

$(x_2, y_2) = \left(-\sqrt{5}, 4\sqrt{10}\right)$

$d = \sqrt{(x_2 - x_1)^2 + (y_2 - y_1)^2}$

$\quad = \sqrt{\left(-\sqrt{5} + 2\sqrt{5}\right)^2 + \left(4\sqrt{10} - \sqrt{10}\right)^2}$

$\quad = \sqrt{\left(\sqrt{5}\right)^2 + \left(3\sqrt{10}\right)^2}$

$\quad = \sqrt{5 + 90}$

$\quad = \sqrt{95}$

The distance is $\sqrt{95}$ units.

35. $(x_1, y_1) = (-2, -5)$, $(x_2, y_2) = (-6, 12)$

$\text{midpoint} = \left(\dfrac{x_1 + x_2}{2}, \dfrac{y_1 + y_2}{2}\right)$

$\quad = \left(\dfrac{-2-6}{2}, \dfrac{-5+12}{2}\right)$

$\quad = \left(-\dfrac{8}{2}, \dfrac{7}{2}\right)$

$\quad = \left(-4, \dfrac{7}{2}\right)$

36. $(x_1, y_1) = \left(-\dfrac{2}{3}, -\dfrac{1}{5}\right)$, $(x_2, y_2) = \left(-\dfrac{1}{3}, \dfrac{4}{5}\right)$

$\text{midpoint} = \left(\dfrac{x_1 + x_2}{2}, \dfrac{y_1 + y_2}{2}\right)$

$\quad = \left(\dfrac{-\frac{2}{3} - \frac{1}{3}}{2}, \dfrac{-\frac{1}{5} + \frac{4}{5}}{2}\right)$

$\quad = \left(\dfrac{-\frac{3}{3}}{2}, \dfrac{\frac{3}{5}}{2}\right)$

$\quad = \left(-\dfrac{1}{2}, \dfrac{3}{10}\right)$

37. $V(r) = \sqrt{2.5r}$

$\quad V(300) = \sqrt{2.5(300)} = \sqrt{750} \approx 27$ mph

38. $V(r) = \sqrt{2.5r}$

$\quad 30 = \sqrt{2.5r}$

$\quad 30^2 = \left(\sqrt{2.5r}\right)^2$

$\quad 900 = 2.5r$

$\quad r = \dfrac{900}{2.5} = 360$ feet

Chapter 7 Cumulative Review

1. a. $3xy - 2xy + 5 - 7 + xy = 2xy - 2$

b. $7x^2 + 3 - 5(x^2 - 4) = 7x^2 + 3 - 5x^2 + 20$
$\qquad = 2x^2 + 23$

c. $(2.1x - 5.6) - (-x - 5.3) = 2.1x - 5.6 + x + 5.3$
$\qquad = 3.1x - 0.3$

d. $\dfrac{1}{2}(4a - 6b) - \dfrac{1}{3}(9a + 12b - 1) + \dfrac{1}{4}$

$\quad = 2a - 3b - 3a - 4b + \dfrac{1}{3} + \dfrac{1}{4}$

$\quad = -a - 7b + \dfrac{4}{12} + \dfrac{3}{12}$

$\quad = -a - 7b + \dfrac{7}{12}$

2. a. $2(x - 3) + (5x + 3) = 2x - 6 + 5x + 3$
$\qquad = 7x - 3$

b. $4(3x + 2) - 3(5x - 1) = 12x + 8 - 15x + 3$
$\qquad = -3x + 11$

c. $7x + 2(x - 7) - 3x = 7x + 2x - 14 - 3x$
$\qquad = 6x - 14$

3. $\dfrac{x+5}{2} + \dfrac{1}{2} = 2x - \dfrac{x-3}{8}$

$\quad 8\left(\dfrac{x+5}{2} + \dfrac{1}{2}\right) = 8\left(2x - \dfrac{x-3}{8}\right)$

$\quad 4(x + 5) + 4 = 16x - (x - 3)$

$\quad 4x + 20 + 4 = 16x - x + 3$

$\quad 4x + 24 = 15x + 3$

$\quad -11x = -21$

$\quad x = \dfrac{21}{11}$

4. $\dfrac{a-1}{2}+a=2-\dfrac{2a+7}{8}$

$8\left(\dfrac{a-1}{2}+a\right)=8\left(2-\dfrac{2a+7}{8}\right)$

$4(a-1)+8a=16-(2a+7)$

$4a-4+8a=16-2a-7$

$12a-4=9-2a$

$14a=13$

$a=\dfrac{13}{14}$

5. Let x = the sales needed.

$600+0.20x>1500$

$0.20x>900$

$x>\dfrac{900}{0.20}$

$x>4500$

The salesperson needs sales of at least $4500.

6. Let r = their average speed.

$t_{\text{going}}+t_{\text{returning}}=4.5\ \text{hrs}$

$\dfrac{121.5}{r}+\dfrac{121.5}{r}=4.5$

$\dfrac{243}{r}=4.5$

$243=4.5r$

$r=\dfrac{243}{4.5}=54$

Their average speed was 54 mph.

7. $2|x|+25=23$

$2|x|=-2$

$|x|=-1$, which is impossible.

There is no solution, or the solution set is $\varnothing$.

8. $|3x-2|+5=5$

$|3x-2|=0$

$3x-2=0$

$3x=2$

$x=\dfrac{2}{3}$

9. $\left|\dfrac{x}{3}-1\right|-7\ge-5$

$\left|\dfrac{x}{3}-1\right|\ge2$

$\dfrac{x}{3}-1\le-2\ \text{ or }\ \dfrac{x}{3}-1\ge2$

$\dfrac{x}{3}\le-1\ \text{ or }\ \ \dfrac{x}{3}\ge3$

$x\le-3\ \text{ or }\ \ \ x\ge9$

$(-\infty,-3]\cup[9,\infty)$

10. $\left|\dfrac{x}{2}-1\right|\le0$

$\dfrac{x}{2}-1=0$

$\dfrac{x}{2}=1$

$x=2$

11. $y=|x|$

12. $y=|x-2|$

13. a. Domain: $\{2,0,3\}$
Range: $\{3,4,-1\}$

b. Domain: $\{-4,-3,-2,-1,0,1,2,3\}$
Range: $\{1\}$

c. Domain: {Lubbock, Colorado Springs, Omaha, Yonkers, Sacramento}
Range: $\{307,404,445,206,197\}$

14. a. Domain: $(-\infty, 0]$, Range: $(-\infty, \infty)$
       not a function

    b. Domain: $(-\infty, \infty)$, Range: $(-\infty, \infty)$
       function

    c. Domain: $(-\infty, -2] \cup [2, \infty)$
       Range: $(-\infty, \infty)$
       not a function

15. $y = -3$
This is a horizontal line passing through $(0, -3)$.

16. $f(x) = -2$
This is a horizontal line passing through $(0, -2)$.

17. $x = -5$ is a vertical line. The slope is undefined.

18. $y = -3$ is a horizontal line. The slope is 0.

19. $\begin{cases} -\dfrac{x}{6} + \dfrac{y}{2} = \dfrac{1}{2} \\ \dfrac{x}{3} - \dfrac{y}{6} = -\dfrac{3}{4} \end{cases}$ or $\begin{cases} -x + 3y = 3 & (1) \\ 4x - 2y = -9 & (2) \end{cases}$

Solve equation (1) for x.
$-x + 3y = 3$
     $3y - 3 = x$

Replace x with $3y - 3$ in equation (2).
$4(3y - 3) - 2y = -9$
$12y - 12 - 2y = -9$
     $10y - 12 = -9$
        $10y = 3$
          $y = \dfrac{3}{10}$

Substitute $\dfrac{3}{10}$ for y in $x = 3y - 3$.

$x = 3\left(\dfrac{3}{10}\right) - 3 = \dfrac{9}{10} - \dfrac{30}{10} = -\dfrac{21}{10}$

The solution is $\left(-\dfrac{21}{10}, \dfrac{3}{10}\right)$.

20. $\begin{cases} \dfrac{x}{6} - \dfrac{y}{2} = 1 \\ \dfrac{x}{3} - \dfrac{y}{4} = 2 \end{cases}$ or $\begin{cases} x - 3y = 6 & (1) \\ 4x - 3y = 24 & (2) \end{cases}$

Solve equation (1) for x.
$x - 3y = 6$
     $x = 3y + 6$

Replace x with $3y + 6$ in equation (2).
$4(3y + 6) - 3y = 24$
$12y + 24 - 3y = 24$
     $9y + 24 = 24$
        $9y = 0$
         $y = 0$

Substitute 0 for y in $x = 3y + 6$.
$x = 3(0) + 6 = 0 + 6 = 6$
The solution is $(6, 0)$.

21. a. $2^2 \cdot 2^5 = 2^{2+5} = 2^7$

    b. $x^7 x^3 = x^{7+3} = x^{10}$

    c. $y \cdot y^2 \cdot y^4 = y^{1+2+4} = y^7$

22. Let x = number of tee-shirts and
y = number of shorts.
$\begin{cases} x + y = 9 & (1) \\ 3.50x + 4.25y = 33.75 & (2) \end{cases}$
Solve equation (1) for y.
$x + y = 9$
     $y = 9 - x$

Substitute $9 - x$ for y in equation (2).
     $3.50x + 4.25(9 - x) = 33.75$
$3.50x + 38.25 - 4.25x = 33.75$
       $-0.75x + 38.25 = 33.75$
          $-0.75x = -4.5$
             $x = \dfrac{-4.5}{-0.75} = 6$

Replace x with 6 in $y = 9 - x$.
$y = 9 - 6 = 3$
Nana bought 6 shirts and 3 shorts.

23. $\dfrac{2000 \times 0.000021}{700} = \dfrac{(2 \times 10^3) \times (2.1 \times 10^{-5})}{7 \times 10^2}$

$\quad\quad = \dfrac{2(2.1)}{7} \times 10^{3+(-5)-2}$

$\quad\quad = 0.6 \times 10^{-4}$

$\quad\quad = (6 \times 10^{-1}) \times 10^{-4}$

$\quad\quad = 6 \times 10^{-5}$

24. $\dfrac{0.0000035 \times 4000}{0.28} = \dfrac{(3.5 \times 10^{-6}) \times (4 \times 10^3)}{2.8 \times 10^{-1}}$

$\quad\quad = \dfrac{3.5 \times 4}{2.8} \times 10^{-6+3-(-1)}$

$\quad\quad = 5 \times 10^{-2}$

25. $P(x) = 3x^2 - 2x - 5$

a. $P(1) = 3(1)^2 - 2(1) - 5$
$\quad\quad = 3(1) - 2(1) - 5$
$\quad\quad = 3 - 2 - 5$
$\quad\quad = -4$

b. $P(-2) = 3(-2)^2 - 2(-2) - 5$
$\quad\quad = 3(4) - (-4) - 5$
$\quad\quad = 12 + 4 - 5$
$\quad\quad = 11$

26. $(5x^2 - 3x + 6) + (4x^2 + 5x - 3) - (2x - 5)$
$= 5x^2 - 3x + 6 + 4x^2 + 5x - 3 - 2x + 5$
$= 9x^2 + 8$

27. a. $(x + 3)(2x + 5) = 2x^2 + 5x + 6x + 15$
$\quad\quad\quad\quad\quad\quad\quad = 2x^2 + 11x + 15$

b. $(2x - 3)(5x^2 - 6x + 7)$
$= 10x^3 - 12x^2 + 14x - 15x^2 + 18x - 21$
$= 10x^3 - 27x^2 + 32x - 21$

28. a. $(y - 2)(3y + 4) = 3y^2 + 4y - 6y - 8$
$\quad\quad\quad\quad\quad\quad\quad = 3y^2 - 2y - 8$

b. $(3y - 1)(2y^2 + 3y - 1)$
$= 6y^3 + 9y^2 - 3y - 2y^2 - 3y + 1$
$= 6y^3 + 7y^2 - 6y + 1$

29. $20x^3 y = 2^2 \cdot 5x^3 y$
$10x^2 y^2 = 2 \cdot 5x^2 y^2$
$35x^3 = 5 \cdot 7x^3$
$\text{GCF} = 5x^2$

30. $x^3 - x^2 + 4x - 4 = (x^3 - x^2) + (4x - 4)$
$\quad\quad\quad\quad\quad\quad\quad\quad = x^2(x - 1) + 4(x - 1)$
$\quad\quad\quad\quad\quad\quad\quad\quad = (x - 1)(x^2 + 4)$

31. a. $\dfrac{x^3 + 8}{2 + x} = \dfrac{x^3 + 2^3}{x + 2}$

$\quad\quad = \dfrac{(x + 2)(x^2 - 2x + 4)}{x + 2}$

$\quad\quad = x^2 - 2x + 4$

b. $\dfrac{2y^2 + 2}{y^3 - 5y^2 + y - 5} = \dfrac{2(y^2 + 1)}{y^2(y - 5) + 1(y - 5)}$

$\quad\quad = \dfrac{2(y^2 + 1)}{(y - 5)(y^2 + 1)}$

$\quad\quad = \dfrac{2}{y - 5}$

32. a. $\dfrac{a^3 - 8}{2 - a} = \dfrac{a^3 - 2^3}{2 - a}$

$\quad\quad = \dfrac{(a - 2)(a^2 + 2a + 4)}{-1(a - 2)}$

$\quad\quad = -1(a^2 + 2a + 4)$

$\quad\quad = -a^2 - 2a - 4$

b. $\dfrac{3a^2 - 3}{a^3 + 5a^2 - a - 5} = \dfrac{3(a^2 - 1)}{a^2(a + 5) - 1(a + 5)}$

$\quad\quad = \dfrac{3(a^2 - 1)}{(a + 5)(a^2 - 1)}$

$\quad\quad = \dfrac{3}{a + 5}$

33. a. $\dfrac{2}{x^2 y} + \dfrac{5}{3x^3 y} = \dfrac{2 \cdot 3x}{x^2 y \cdot 3x} + \dfrac{5}{3x^3 y}$

$\quad\quad = \dfrac{6x + 5}{3x^3 y}$

b. $\dfrac{3}{x+2}+\dfrac{2x}{x-2}=\dfrac{3(x-2)+2x(x+2)}{(x+2)(x-2)}$

$\qquad\qquad\qquad = \dfrac{3x-6+2x^2+4x}{(x+2)(x-2)}$

$\qquad\qquad\qquad = \dfrac{2x^2+7x-6}{(x+2)(x-2)}$

c. $\dfrac{2x-6}{x-1}-\dfrac{4}{1-x}=\dfrac{2x-6}{x-1}+\dfrac{4}{x-1}$

$\qquad\qquad\qquad = \dfrac{2x-2}{x-1}$

$\qquad\qquad\qquad = \dfrac{2(x-1)}{x-1}$

$\qquad\qquad\qquad = 2$

34. a. $\dfrac{3}{xy^2}-\dfrac{2}{3x^2y}=\dfrac{3\cdot 3x}{xy^2\cdot 3x}-\dfrac{2\cdot y}{3x^2y\cdot y}$

$\qquad\qquad\qquad = \dfrac{9x-2y}{3x^2y^2}$

b. $\dfrac{5x}{x+3}-\dfrac{2x}{x-3}=\dfrac{5x(x-3)-2x(x+3)}{(x+3)(x-3)}$

$\qquad\qquad\qquad = \dfrac{5x^2-15x-2x^2-6x}{(x+3)(x-3)}$

$\qquad\qquad\qquad = \dfrac{3x^2-21x}{(x+3)(x-3)}$

$\qquad\qquad\qquad \text{or } \dfrac{3x(x-7)}{(x+3)(x-3)}$

c. $\dfrac{x}{x-2}-\dfrac{5}{2-x}=\dfrac{x}{x-2}+\dfrac{5}{x-2}=\dfrac{x+5}{x-2}$

35. a. $\dfrac{\frac{5x}{x+2}}{\frac{10}{x-2}}=\dfrac{5x}{x+2}\cdot\dfrac{x-2}{10}=\dfrac{x(x-2)}{2(x+2)}$

b. $\dfrac{\frac{x}{y^2}+\frac{1}{y}}{\frac{y}{x^2}+\frac{1}{x}}=\dfrac{\left(\frac{x}{y^2}+\frac{1}{y}\right)x^2y^2}{\left(\frac{y}{x^2}+\frac{1}{x}\right)x^2y^2}$

$\qquad\qquad = \dfrac{x^3+x^2y}{y^3+xy^2}$

$\qquad\qquad = \dfrac{x^2(x+y)}{y^2(y+x)}$

$\qquad\qquad = \dfrac{x^2}{y^2}$

36. a. $\dfrac{\frac{y-2}{16}}{\frac{2y+3}{12}}=\dfrac{y-2}{16}\cdot\dfrac{12}{2y+3}=\dfrac{3(y-2)}{4(2y+3)}$

b. $\dfrac{\frac{x}{16}-\frac{1}{x}}{1-\frac{4}{x}}=\dfrac{\left(\frac{x}{16}-\frac{1}{x}\right)16x}{\left(1-\frac{4}{x}\right)16x}$

$\qquad\qquad = \dfrac{x^2-16}{16x-64}$

$\qquad\qquad = \dfrac{(x+4)(x-4)}{16(x-4)}$

$\qquad\qquad = \dfrac{x+4}{16}$

37. $\dfrac{10x^3-5x^2+20x}{5x}=\dfrac{10x^3}{5x}-\dfrac{5x^2}{5x}+\dfrac{20x}{5x}$

$\qquad\qquad\qquad\qquad = 2x^2-x+4$

38.
$$\begin{array}{r} x^2+3 \\ x-2\overline{)x^3-2x^2+3x-6} \\ \underline{x^3-2x^2} \\ 3x-6 \\ \underline{3x-6} \\ 0 \end{array}$$

Answer: x^2+3

39.
$$\begin{array}{r|rrrr} 3 & 2 & -1 & -13 & 1 \\ & & 6 & 15 & 6 \\ \hline & 2 & 5 & 2 & 7 \end{array}$$

Answer: $2x^2+5x+2+\dfrac{7}{x-3}$

40.
$$\begin{array}{r|rrrr} 3 & 4 & -12 & -1 & 12 \\ & & 12 & 0 & -3 \\ \hline & 4 & 0 & -1 & 9 \end{array}$$

Answer: $4y^2-1+\dfrac{9}{y-3}$

41. $\dfrac{x+6}{x-2}=\dfrac{2(x+2)}{x-2}$

$(x-2)\left(\dfrac{x+6}{x-2}\right)=(x-2)\left[\dfrac{2(x+2)}{x-2}\right]$

$\qquad\qquad x+6=2(x+2)$

$\qquad\qquad x+6=2x+4$

$\qquad\qquad -x=-2$

$\qquad\qquad x=2$

which we discard as extraneous. There is no solution.

42.

$$\frac{28}{9-a^2} = \frac{2a}{a-3} + \frac{6}{a+3}$$

$$\frac{28}{-(a^2-9)} = \frac{2a}{a-3} + \frac{6}{a+3}$$

$$\frac{-28}{(a+3)(a-3)} = \frac{2a}{a-3} + \frac{6}{a+3}$$

$$(a+3)(a-3)\cdot\frac{-28}{(a+3)(a-3)} = (a+3)(a-3)\cdot\left(\frac{2a}{a-3} + \frac{6}{a+3}\right)$$

$$-28 = 2a(a+3)+6(a-3)$$

$$-28 = 2a^2+6a+6a-18$$

$$0 = 2a^2+12a+10$$

$$0 = 2(a^2+6a+5)$$

$$0 = 2(a+5)(a+1)$$

$a=-5$ or $a=-1$

The solutions are -5 and -1.

43.

$$\frac{1}{x}+\frac{1}{y}=\frac{1}{z}$$

$$xyz\left(\frac{1}{x}+\frac{1}{y}\right) = xyz\left(\frac{1}{z}\right)$$

$$yz+xz = xy$$

$$yz = xy-xz$$

$$yz = x(y-z)$$

$$x = \frac{yz}{y-z}$$

44.

$$A = \frac{h(a+b)}{2}$$

$$2A = h(a+b)$$

$$2A = ah+bh$$

$$2A-bh = ah$$

$$\frac{2A-bh}{h} = a$$

45. $u = \dfrac{k}{w}$

$$3 = \frac{k}{5}$$

$$k = 3(5) = 15$$

$$u = \frac{15}{w}$$

46. $y = kx$

$$0.51 = k(3)$$

$$k = \frac{0.51}{3} = 0.17$$

$$y = 0.17x$$

47. a. $16^{-3/4} = \dfrac{1}{16^{3/4}} = \dfrac{1}{\left(\sqrt[4]{16}\right)^3} = \dfrac{1}{(2)^3} = \dfrac{1}{8}$

    b. $(-27)^{-2/3} = \dfrac{1}{(-27)^{2/3}}$

$= \dfrac{1}{\left(\sqrt[3]{-27}\right)^2}$

$= \dfrac{1}{(-3)^2}$

$= \dfrac{1}{9}$

48. a. $81^{-3/4} = \dfrac{1}{81^{3/4}} = \dfrac{1}{\left(\sqrt[4]{81}\right)^3} = \dfrac{1}{(3)^3} = \dfrac{1}{27}$

    b. $(-125)^{-2/3} = \dfrac{1}{(-125)^{2/3}}$

$= \dfrac{1}{\left(\sqrt[3]{-125}\right)^2}$

$= \dfrac{1}{(-5)^2}$

$= \dfrac{1}{25}$

49. $\dfrac{\sqrt{x}+2}{5} = \dfrac{\left(\sqrt{x}+2\right)\left(\sqrt{x}-2\right)}{5\left(\sqrt{x}-2\right)}$

$= \dfrac{\left(\sqrt{x}\right)^2 - 2^2}{5\left(\sqrt{x}-2\right)}$

$= \dfrac{x-4}{5\left(\sqrt{x}-2\right)}$

50. a. $\sqrt{36a^3} - \sqrt{144a^3} + \sqrt{4a^3}$

$= \sqrt{36a^2 \cdot a} - \sqrt{144a^2 \cdot a} + \sqrt{4a^2 \cdot a}$

$= 6a\sqrt{a} - 12a\sqrt{a} + 2a\sqrt{a}$

$= -4a\sqrt{a}$

    b. $\sqrt[3]{128ab^3} - 3\sqrt[3]{2ab^3} + b\sqrt[3]{16a}$

$= \sqrt[3]{64b^3 \cdot 2a} - 3\sqrt[3]{b^3 \cdot 2a} + b\sqrt[3]{8 \cdot 2a}$

$= 4b\sqrt[3]{2a} - 3b\sqrt[3]{2a} + 2b\sqrt[3]{2a}$

$= 3b\sqrt[3]{2a}$

    c. $\dfrac{\sqrt[3]{81}}{10} + \sqrt[3]{\dfrac{192}{125}} = \dfrac{\sqrt[3]{27 \cdot 3}}{10} + \dfrac{\sqrt[3]{192}}{\sqrt[3]{125}}$

$= \dfrac{3\sqrt[3]{3}}{10} + \dfrac{\sqrt[3]{64 \cdot 3}}{5}$

$= \dfrac{3\sqrt[3]{3}}{10} + \dfrac{4\sqrt[3]{3}}{5}$

$= \dfrac{3\sqrt[3]{3}}{10} + \dfrac{4\sqrt[3]{3} \cdot 2}{5 \cdot 2} = \dfrac{11\sqrt[3]{3}}{10}$

Chapter 8

Practice Exercises

1. $x^2 = 18$

   $x = \pm\sqrt{18}$

   $x = \pm 3\sqrt{2}$

   Check:

   Let $x = 3\sqrt{2}$.　　　Let $x = -3\sqrt{2}$.

   　$x^2 = 18$　　　　　　$x^2 = 18$

   $\left(3\sqrt{2}\right)^2 \overset{?}{=} 18$　　$\left(-3\sqrt{2}\right)^2 \overset{?}{=} 18$

   　$9 \cdot 2 \overset{?}{=} 18$　　　　$9 \cdot 2 \overset{?}{=} 18$

   　$18 = 18$　True　　$18 = 18$　True

   The solutions are $3\sqrt{2}$ and $-3\sqrt{2}$, or the

   solution set is $\left\{-3\sqrt{2}, 3\sqrt{2}\right\}$.

2. First we get the squared variable alone on one side of the equation.

   $3x^2 - 30 = 0$

   $3x^2 = 30$

   $x^2 = 10$

   $x = \pm\sqrt{10}$

   The solutions are $\sqrt{10}$ and $-\sqrt{10}$, or the

   solution set is $\left\{-\sqrt{10}, \sqrt{10}\right\}$.

3. $(x+3)^2 = 20$

   $x + 3 = \pm\sqrt{20}$

   $x + 3 = \pm 2\sqrt{5}$

   $x = -3 \pm 2\sqrt{5}$

   Check:

   $(x+3)^2 = 20$

   $\left(-3 + 2\sqrt{5} + 3\right)^2 \overset{?}{=} 20$

   $\left(2\sqrt{5}\right)^2 \overset{?}{=} 20$

   $4 \cdot 5 \overset{?}{=} 20$

   $20 = 20$　True

   $(x+3)^2 = 20$

   $\left(-3 - 2\sqrt{5} + 3\right)^2 \overset{?}{=} 20$

   $\left(-2\sqrt{5}\right)^2 \overset{?}{=} 20$

   $4 \cdot 5 \overset{?}{=} 20$

   $20 = 20$　True

   The solutions are $-3 + 2\sqrt{5}$ and $-3 - 2\sqrt{5}$.

4. $(5x-2)^2 = -9$

   $5x - 2 = \pm\sqrt{-9}$

   $5x - 2 = \pm 3i$

   $5x = 2 \pm 3i$

   $x = \dfrac{2 \pm 3i}{5}$

   The solutions are $\dfrac{2+3i}{5}$ and $\dfrac{2-3i}{5}$.

5. $b^2 + 4b = 3$

   Add the square of half the coefficient of b to both sides.

   $b^2 + 4b + \left(\dfrac{4}{2}\right)^2 = 3 + \left(\dfrac{4}{2}\right)^2$

   $b^2 + 4b + 4 = 7$

   $(b+2)^2 = 7$

   $b + 2 = \pm\sqrt{7}$

   $b = -2 \pm\sqrt{7}$

   The solutions are $-2 + \sqrt{7}$ and $-2 - \sqrt{7}$.

6. $p^2 - 3p + 1 = 0$

   Subtract 1 from both sides.

   $p^2 - 3p = -1$

   Add the square of half the coefficient of p to both sides.

$$p^2 - 3p + \left(\frac{-3}{2}\right)^2 = -1 + \left(\frac{-3}{2}\right)^2$$

$$p^2 - 3p + \frac{9}{4} = -1 + \frac{9}{4} = \frac{5}{4}$$

$$\left(p - \frac{3}{2}\right)^2 = \frac{5}{4}$$

$$p - \frac{3}{2} = \pm\frac{\sqrt{5}}{2}$$

$$p = \frac{3 \pm \sqrt{5}}{2}$$

The solutions are $\dfrac{3+\sqrt{5}}{2}$ and $\dfrac{3-\sqrt{5}}{2}$.

7. $3x^2 - 12x + 1 = 0$

Divide both sides by 3.

$$3x^2 - 12x + 1 = 0$$

$$x^2 - 4x + \frac{1}{3} = 0$$

$$x^2 - 4x = -\frac{1}{3}$$

Find the square of half of -4.

$$\left(\frac{-4}{2}\right)^2 = (-2)^2 = 4$$

Add 4 to both sides of the equation.

$$x^2 - 4x + 4 = -\frac{1}{3} + 4$$

$$(x-2)^2 = -\frac{1}{3} + \frac{12}{3} = \frac{11}{3}$$

$$x - 2 = \pm\sqrt{\frac{11}{3}} = \pm\frac{\sqrt{33}}{3}$$

$$x = \frac{6}{3} \pm \frac{\sqrt{33}}{3} = \frac{6 \pm \sqrt{33}}{3}$$

The solutions are $\dfrac{6+\sqrt{33}}{3}$ and $\dfrac{6-\sqrt{33}}{3}$.

8. $2x^2 - 5x + 7 = 0$

$$2x^2 - 5x = -7$$

$$x^2 - \frac{5}{2}x = -\frac{7}{2}$$

Since $\dfrac{1}{2}\left(-\dfrac{5}{2}\right) = -\dfrac{5}{4}$ and $\left(-\dfrac{5}{4}\right)^2 = \dfrac{25}{16}$, we add

$\dfrac{25}{16}$ to both sides of the equation.

$$x^2 - \frac{5}{2}x + \frac{25}{16} = -\frac{7}{2} + \frac{25}{16}$$

$$\left(x - \frac{5}{4}\right)^2 = -\frac{56}{16} + \frac{25}{16} = -\frac{31}{16}$$

$$x - \frac{5}{4} = \pm\sqrt{-\frac{31}{16}}$$

$$x = \frac{5}{4} \pm \frac{i\sqrt{31}}{4} = \frac{5 \pm i\sqrt{31}}{4}$$

The solutions are $\dfrac{5+i\sqrt{31}}{4}$ and $\dfrac{5-i\sqrt{31}}{4}$.

9. $A = P(1+r)^t$; $A = 5618$, $P = 5000$, $t = 2$

$$A = P(1+r)^t$$

$$5618 = 5000(1+r)^2$$

$$1.1236 = (1+r)^2$$

$$\pm\sqrt{1.1236} = 1 + r$$

$$-1 \pm 1.06 = r$$

$$0.06 = r \text{ or } -2.06 = r$$

The rate cannot be negative, so we reject -2.06.

Check: $A = 5000(1 + 0.06)^2$

$$= 5000(1.06)^2$$

$$= 5000 \cdot 1.1236$$

$$= 5618$$

The interest rate is 6% compounded annually.

Graphing Calculator Explorations

1. $-1.27, 6.27$

2. $-3.45, 1.45$

3. $-1.10, 0.90$

4. $-1.54, 1.94$

5. No real solutions, or $\varnothing$

6. Answers may vary

Vocabulary and Readiness Check

1. By the square root property, if b is a real number, and $a^2 = b$, then $a = \underline{\pm\sqrt{b}}$.

2. A <u>quadratic</u> equation can be written in the form $ax^2 + bx + c = 0$, $a \neq 0$.

3. The process of writing a quadratic equation so that one side is a perfect square trinomial is called <u>completing the square</u>.

4. A perfect square trinomial is one that can be factored as a <u>binomial</u> squared.

5. To solve $x^2 + 6x = 10$ by completing the square, add $\underline{9}$ to both sides.

6. To solve $x^2 + bx = c$ by completing the square, add $\underline{\left(\dfrac{b}{2}\right)^2}$ to both sides.

7. $m^2 + 2m + \underline{1}$

8. $m^2 - 2m + \underline{1}$

9. $y^2 - 14y + \underline{49}$

10. $z^2 + z + \dfrac{1}{\underline{4}}$

Exercise Set 8.1

1. $x^2 = 16$
$x = \pm\sqrt{16}$
$x = \pm 4$

3. $x^2 - 7 = 0$
$x^2 = 7$
$x = \pm\sqrt{7}$

5. $x^2 = 18$
$x = \pm\sqrt{18}$
$x = \pm\sqrt{9 \cdot 2}$
$x = \pm 3\sqrt{2}$

7. $3z^2 - 30 = 0$
$3z^2 = 30$
$z^2 = 10$
$z = \pm\sqrt{10}$

9. $(x+5)^2 = 9$
$x + 5 = \pm\sqrt{9}$
$x + 5 = \pm 3$
$x = -5 \pm 3$
$x = -8 \ \text{or} \ x = -2$

11. $(z-6)^2 = 18$
$z - 6 = \pm\sqrt{18}$
$z - 6 = \pm 3\sqrt{2}$
$z = 6 \pm 3\sqrt{2}$

13. $(2x-3)^2 = 8$
$2x - 3 = \pm\sqrt{8}$
$2x - 3 = \pm 2\sqrt{2}$
$2x = 3 \pm 2\sqrt{2}$
$x = \dfrac{3 \pm 2\sqrt{2}}{2}$

15. $x^2 + 9 = 0$
$x^2 = -9$
$x = \pm\sqrt{-9}$
$x = \pm 3i$

17. $x^2 - 6 = 0$
$$x^2 = 6$$
$$x = \pm\sqrt{6}$$

19. $2z^2 + 16 = 0$
$$2z^2 = -16$$
$$z^2 = -8$$
$$z = \pm\sqrt{-8}$$
$$z = \pm i\sqrt{8}$$
$$z = \pm 2i\sqrt{2}$$

21. $(x-1)^2 = -16$
$$x - 1 = \pm\sqrt{-16}$$
$$x - 1 = \pm 4i$$
$$x = 1 \pm 4i$$

23. $(z+7)^2 = 5$
$$z + 7 = \pm\sqrt{5}$$
$$z = -7 \pm\sqrt{5}$$

25. $(x+3)^2 = -8$
$$x + 3 = \pm\sqrt{-8}$$
$$x + 3 = \pm i\sqrt{8}$$
$$x + 3 = \pm 2i\sqrt{2}$$
$$x = -3 \pm 2i\sqrt{2}$$

27. $x^2 + 16x + \left(\dfrac{16}{2}\right)^2 = x^2 + 16x + 64$
$$= (x+8)^2$$

29. $z^2 - 12z + \left(\dfrac{-12}{2}\right)^2 = z^2 - 12z + 36$
$$= (z-6)^2$$

31. $p^2 + 9p + \left(\dfrac{9}{2}\right)^2 = p^2 + 9p + \dfrac{81}{4}$
$$= \left(p + \dfrac{9}{2}\right)^2$$

33. $x^2 + x + \left(\dfrac{1}{2}\right)^2 = x^2 + 16x + \dfrac{1}{4}$
$$= \left(x + \dfrac{1}{2}\right)^2$$

35. $x^2 + 8x = -15$
$$x^2 + 8x + \left(\dfrac{8}{2}\right)^2 = -15 + 16$$
$$x^2 + 8x + 16 = 1$$
$$(x+4)^2 = 1$$
$$x + 4 = \pm\sqrt{1}$$
$$x = -4 \pm 1$$
$$x = -5 \text{ or } x = -3$$

37. $x^2 + 6x + 2 = 0$
$$x^2 + 6x = -2$$
$$x^2 + 6x + \left(\dfrac{6}{2}\right)^2 = -2 + 9$$
$$x^2 + 6x + 9 = 7$$
$$(x+3)^2 = 7$$
$$x + 3 = \pm\sqrt{7}$$
$$x = -3 \pm\sqrt{7}$$

39. $x^2 + x - 1 = 0$
$$x^2 + x = 1$$
$$x^2 + x + \left(\dfrac{1}{2}\right)^2 = 1 + \dfrac{1}{4}$$
$$x^2 + x + \dfrac{1}{4} = \dfrac{5}{4}$$
$$\left(x + \dfrac{1}{2}\right)^2 = \dfrac{5}{4}$$
$$x + \dfrac{1}{2} = \pm\sqrt{\dfrac{5}{4}}$$
$$x = -\dfrac{1}{2} \pm \dfrac{\sqrt{5}}{2} = \dfrac{-1 \pm\sqrt{5}}{2}$$

41. $x^2 + 2x - 5 = 0$
$$x^2 + 2x = 5$$
$$x^2 + 2x + \left(\dfrac{2}{2}\right)^2 = 5 + 1$$
$$x^2 + 2x + 1 = 6$$
$$(x+1)^2 = 6$$
$$x + 1 = \pm\sqrt{6}$$
$$x = -1 \pm\sqrt{6}$$

43.
$$3p^2 - 12p + 2 = 0$$
$$3p^2 - 12p = -2$$
$$p^2 - 4p = -\frac{2}{3}$$
$$p^2 - 4p + \left(\frac{-4}{2}\right)^2 = -\frac{2}{3} + 4$$
$$(p - 2)^2 = \frac{10}{3}$$
$$p - 2 = \pm\sqrt{\frac{10}{3}}$$
$$p - 2 = \pm\frac{\sqrt{10} \cdot \sqrt{3}}{\sqrt{3} \cdot \sqrt{3}}$$
$$p - 2 = \pm\frac{\sqrt{30}}{3}$$
$$p = 2 \pm \frac{\sqrt{30}}{3} = \frac{6 \pm \sqrt{30}}{3}$$

45.
$$4y^2 - 12y - 2 = 0$$
$$4y^2 - 12y = 2$$
$$y^2 - 3y = \frac{1}{2}$$
$$y^2 - 3y + \left(\frac{-3}{2}\right)^2 = \frac{1}{2} + \frac{9}{4}$$
$$y^2 - 3y + \frac{9}{4} = \frac{11}{4}$$
$$\left(y - \frac{3}{2}\right)^2 = \frac{11}{4}$$
$$y - \frac{3}{2} = \pm\sqrt{\frac{11}{4}}$$
$$y = \frac{3}{2} \pm \frac{\sqrt{11}}{2} = \frac{3 \pm \sqrt{11}}{2}$$

47.
$$2x^2 + 7x = 4$$
$$x^2 + \frac{7}{2}x = 2$$
$$x^2 + \frac{7}{2}x + \left(\frac{\frac{7}{2}}{2}\right)^2 = 2 + \frac{49}{16}$$
$$x^2 + \frac{7}{2}x + \frac{49}{16} = \frac{81}{16}$$
$$\left(x + \frac{7}{4}\right)^2 = \frac{81}{16}$$
$$x + \frac{7}{4} = \pm\sqrt{\frac{81}{16}}$$
$$x = -\frac{7}{4} \pm \frac{9}{4} = \frac{-7 \pm 9}{4}$$
$$x = -4, \frac{1}{2}$$

49.
$$x^2 - 4x - 5 = 0$$
$$x^2 - 4x = 5$$
$$x^2 - 4x + \left(\frac{-4}{2}\right)^2 = 5 + 4$$
$$x^2 - 4x + 4 = 9$$
$$(x - 2)^2 = 9$$
$$x - 2 = \pm\sqrt{9}$$
$$x = 2 \pm 3$$
$$x = -1, 5$$

51.
$$x^2 + 8x + 1 = 0$$
$$x^2 + 8x = -1$$
$$x^2 + 8x + \left(\frac{8}{2}\right)^2 = -1 + 16$$
$$x^2 + 8x + 16 = 15$$
$$(x + 4)^2 = 15$$
$$x + 4 = \pm\sqrt{15}$$
$$x = -4 \pm \sqrt{15}$$

53.
$$3y^2 + 6y - 4 = 0$$
$$3y^2 + 6y = 4$$
$$y^2 + 2y = \frac{4}{3}$$
$$y^2 + 2y + \left(\frac{2}{2}\right)^2 = \frac{4}{3} + 1$$
$$y^2 + 2y + 1 = \frac{7}{3}$$
$$(y+1)^2 = \frac{7}{3}$$
$$y + 1 = \pm\sqrt{\frac{7}{3}}$$
$$y + 1 = \pm\frac{\sqrt{7} \cdot \sqrt{3}}{\sqrt{3} \cdot \sqrt{3}}$$
$$y + 1 = \pm\frac{\sqrt{21}}{3}$$
$$y = -1 \pm \frac{\sqrt{21}}{3} = \frac{-3 \pm \sqrt{21}}{3}$$

55.
$$2x^2 - 3x - 5 = 0$$
$$2x^2 - 3x = 5$$
$$x^2 - \frac{3}{2}x = \frac{5}{2}$$
$$x^2 - \frac{3}{2}x + \left(\frac{\frac{3}{2}}{2}\right)^2 = \frac{5}{2} + \frac{9}{16}$$
$$x^2 - \frac{3}{2}x + \frac{9}{16} = \frac{49}{16}$$
$$\left(x - \frac{3}{4}\right)^2 = \frac{49}{16}$$
$$x - \frac{3}{4} = \pm\sqrt{\frac{49}{16}}$$
$$x = \frac{3}{4} \pm \frac{7}{4} = \frac{3 \pm 7}{4}$$
$$x = -1, \frac{5}{2}$$

57.
$$y^2 + 2y + 2 = 0$$
$$y^2 + 2y = -2$$
$$y^2 + 2y + \left(\frac{2}{2}\right)^2 = -2 + 1$$
$$y^2 + 2y + 1 = -1$$
$$(y+1)^2 = -1$$
$$y + 1 = \pm\sqrt{-1}$$
$$y = -1 \pm i$$

59.
$$x^2 - 6x + 3 = 0$$
$$x^2 - 6x = -3$$
$$x^2 - 6x + \left(\frac{-6}{2}\right)^2 = -3 + 9$$
$$x^2 - 6x + 9 = 6$$
$$(x-3)^2 = 6$$
$$x - 3 = \pm\sqrt{6}$$
$$x = 3 \pm \sqrt{6}$$

61.
$$2a^2 + 8a = -12$$
$$a^2 + 4a = -6$$
$$a^2 + 4a + \left(\frac{4}{2}\right)^2 = -6 + 4$$
$$a^2 + 4a + 4 = -2$$
$$(a+2)^2 = -2$$
$$a + 2 = \pm\sqrt{-2}$$
$$a + 2 = \pm i\sqrt{2}$$
$$a = -2 \pm i\sqrt{2}$$

63.
$$5x^2 + 15x - 1 = 0$$
$$5x^2 + 15x = 1$$
$$x^2 + 3x = \frac{1}{5}$$
$$x^2 + 3x + \left(\frac{3}{2}\right)^2 = \frac{1}{5} + \frac{9}{4}$$
$$x^2 + 3x + \frac{9}{4} = \frac{49}{20}$$
$$\left(x + \frac{3}{2}\right)^2 = \frac{49}{20}$$
$$x + \frac{3}{2} = \pm\sqrt{\frac{49}{20}}$$
$$x + \frac{3}{2} = \pm\frac{7}{\sqrt{20}}$$
$$x + \frac{3}{2} = \pm\frac{7}{2\sqrt{5}}$$
$$x + \frac{3}{2} = \pm\frac{7 \cdot \sqrt{5}}{2\sqrt{5} \cdot \sqrt{5}}$$
$$x + \frac{3}{2} = \pm\frac{7\sqrt{5}}{10}$$
$$x = -\frac{3}{2} \pm \frac{7\sqrt{5}}{10} = \frac{-15 \pm 7\sqrt{5}}{10}$$

65.
$$2x^2 - x + 6 = 0$$
$$2x^2 - x = -6$$
$$x^2 - \frac{1}{2}x = -3$$
$$x^2 - \frac{1}{2}x + \left(\frac{-\frac{1}{2}}{2}\right)^2 = -3 + \frac{1}{16}$$
$$x^2 - \frac{1}{2}x + \frac{1}{16} = -\frac{47}{16}$$
$$\left(x - \frac{1}{4}\right)^2 = -\frac{47}{16}$$
$$x - \frac{1}{4} = \pm\sqrt{-\frac{47}{16}}$$
$$x - \frac{1}{4} = \pm i\frac{\sqrt{47}}{4}$$
$$x = \frac{1}{4} \pm i\frac{\sqrt{47}}{4} = \frac{1 \pm i\sqrt{47}}{4}$$

67.
$$x^2 + 10x + 28 = 0$$
$$x^2 + 10x = -28$$
$$x^2 + 10x + \left(\frac{10}{2}\right)^2 = -28 + 25$$
$$(x + 5)^2 = -3$$
$$x + 5 = \pm\sqrt{-3}$$
$$x = -5 \pm i\sqrt{3}$$

69.
$$z^2 + 3z - 4 = 0$$
$$z^2 + 3z = 4$$
$$z^2 + 3z + \left(\frac{3}{2}\right)^2 = 4 + \frac{9}{4}$$
$$z^2 + 3z + \frac{9}{4} = \frac{25}{4}$$
$$\left(z + \frac{3}{2}\right)^2 = \frac{25}{4}$$
$$z + \frac{3}{2} = \pm\sqrt{\frac{25}{4}}$$
$$z = -\frac{3}{2} \pm \frac{5}{2} = \frac{-3 \pm 5}{2}$$
$$z = -4, 1$$

71.
$$2x^2 - 4x = -3$$
$$x^2 - 2x = -\frac{3}{2}$$
$$x^2 - 2x + \left(\frac{-2}{2}\right)^2 = -\frac{3}{2} + 1$$
$$x^2 - 2x + 1 = -\frac{1}{2}$$
$$(x - 1)^2 = -\frac{1}{2}$$
$$x - 1 = \pm\sqrt{-\frac{1}{2}}$$
$$x - 1 = \pm i\frac{1}{\sqrt{2}}$$
$$x - 1 = \pm i\frac{1 \cdot \sqrt{2}}{\sqrt{2} \cdot \sqrt{2}}$$
$$x - 1 = \pm i\frac{\sqrt{2}}{2}$$
$$x = 1 \pm i\frac{\sqrt{2}}{2} = \frac{2 \pm i\sqrt{2}}{2}$$

73.
$$3x^2 + 3x = 5$$
$$x^2 + x = \frac{5}{3}$$
$$x^2 + x + \left(\frac{1}{2}\right)^2 = \frac{5}{3} + \frac{1}{4}$$
$$x^2 + x + \frac{1}{4} = \frac{23}{12}$$
$$\left(x + \frac{1}{2}\right)^2 = \frac{23}{12}$$
$$x + \frac{1}{2} = \pm\sqrt{\frac{23}{12}}$$
$$x + \frac{1}{2} = \pm\frac{\sqrt{23}}{2\sqrt{3}}$$
$$x + \frac{1}{2} = \pm\frac{\sqrt{23}\cdot\sqrt{3}}{2\sqrt{3}\cdot\sqrt{3}}$$
$$x + \frac{1}{2} = \pm\frac{\sqrt{69}}{6}$$
$$x = -\frac{1}{2} \pm \frac{\sqrt{69}}{6} = \frac{-3\pm\sqrt{69}}{6}$$

75.
$$A = P(1+r)^t$$
$$4320 = 3000(1+r)^2$$
$$\frac{4320}{3000} = (1+r)^2$$
$$1.44 = (1+r)^2$$
$$\pm\sqrt{1.44} = 1+r$$
$$\pm 1.2 = 1+r$$
$$-1 \pm 1.2 = r$$
$$-2.2 = r \ \text{ or } \ 0.2 = r$$
Rate cannot be negative, so the rate is
$r = 0.2 = 20\%$.

77.
$$A = P(1+r)^t$$
$$16,224 = 15,000(1+r)^2$$
$$\frac{16,224}{15,000} = (1+r)^2$$
$$\pm\sqrt{1.0816} = 1+r$$
$$\pm 1.04 = 1+r$$
$$-1 \pm 1.04 = r$$
$$0.04 = r \ \text{ or } \ -2.04 = r$$
Rate cannot be negative, so the rate is $r = 0.04$, or 4%.

79. Answers may vary

81.
$$s(t) = 16t^2$$
$$1053 = 16t^2$$
$$t^2 = \frac{1053}{16}$$
$$t = \pm\sqrt{\frac{1053}{16}}$$
$$t \approx 8.11 \text{ or } -8.11 \text{ (disregard)}$$
It would take 8.11 seconds.

83.
$$s(t) = 16t^2$$
$$725 = 16t^2$$
$$t^2 = \frac{725}{16}$$
$$t = \pm\sqrt{\frac{725}{16}}$$
$$t \approx 6.73 \text{ or } -6.73 \text{ (disregard)}$$
It would take 6.73 seconds.

85. Simple; answers may vary

87. $\dfrac{3}{5} + \sqrt{\dfrac{16}{25}} = \dfrac{3}{5} + \dfrac{4}{5} = \dfrac{7}{5}$

89. $\dfrac{9}{10} - \sqrt{\dfrac{49}{100}} = \dfrac{9}{10} - \dfrac{7}{10} = \dfrac{2}{10} = \dfrac{1}{5}$

91. $\dfrac{10 - 20\sqrt{3}}{2} = \dfrac{10}{2} - \dfrac{20\sqrt{3}}{2} = 5 - 10\sqrt{3}$

93. $\dfrac{12 - 8\sqrt{7}}{16} = \dfrac{12}{16} - \dfrac{8\sqrt{7}}{16}$
$$= \dfrac{3}{4} - \dfrac{\sqrt{7}}{2}$$
$$= \dfrac{3}{4} - \dfrac{2\sqrt{7}}{4}$$
$$= \dfrac{3 - 2\sqrt{7}}{4}$$

95. $\sqrt{b^2 - 4ac} = \sqrt{(6)^2 - 4(1)(2)}$
$$= \sqrt{36 - 8}$$
$$= \sqrt{28}$$
$$= \sqrt{4 \cdot 7}$$
$$= 2\sqrt{7}$$

97. $\sqrt{b^2 - 4ac} = \sqrt{(-3)^2 - 4(1)(-1)}$
$= \sqrt{9 + 4}$
$= \sqrt{13}$

99. The solutions of $(y - 5)^2 = -9$ are complex, but not real numbers; answers may vary

101. The solutions of $4x^2 = 17$ are real; answers may vary

103. The solutions of $(3m + 2)^2 + 4 = 1$ are complex, but not real numbers; answers may vary

105. $y^2 + \underline{} + 9$
$\left(\dfrac{b}{2}\right)^2 = 9$
$\dfrac{b}{2} = \pm\sqrt{9}$
$\dfrac{b}{2} = \pm 3$
$b = \pm 6$
Answer: $\pm 6y$

107. $x^2 + \underline{} + \dfrac{1}{4}$
$\left(\dfrac{b}{2}\right)^2 = \dfrac{1}{4}$
$\dfrac{b}{2} = \pm\sqrt{\dfrac{1}{4}}$
$\dfrac{b}{2} = \pm\dfrac{1}{2}$
$b = \pm 1$
Answer: $\pm x$

109. $A = \pi r^2$
$36\pi = \pi r^2$
$r^2 = \dfrac{36\pi}{\pi}$
$r^2 = 36$
$r = \pm\sqrt{36}$
$r = 6$ or -6 (disregard)
The radius is 6 inches.

111. $a^2 + b^2 = c^2$
$(4x)^2 + (3x)^2 = 27^2$
$16x^2 + 9x^2 = 729$
$25x^2 = 729$
$x^2 = \dfrac{729}{25}$
$x = \pm\sqrt{\dfrac{729}{25}} = \pm\dfrac{27}{5}$
$x = 5.4$ or -5.4 (disregard)
$3x = 3(5.4) = 16.2$
$4x = 4(5.4) = 21.6$
The sides are 16.2 in. and 21.6 in.

113. $p = -x^2 + 15$
$7 = -x^2 + 15$
$x^2 = 8$
$x = \pm\sqrt{8}$
$x \approx \pm 2.828$
Demand cannot be negative. Therefore, the demand is approximately 2.828 thousand (or 2828) units.

Section 8.2

Practice Exercises

1. $3x^2 - 5x - 2 = 0$
$a = 3, b = -5, c = -2$
$x = \dfrac{-b \pm \sqrt{b^2 - 4ac}}{2a}$
$= \dfrac{-(-5) \pm \sqrt{(-5)^2 - 4(3)(-2)}}{2(3)}$
$= \dfrac{5 \pm \sqrt{25 + 24}}{6}$
$= \dfrac{5 \pm \sqrt{49}}{6}$
$= \dfrac{5 \pm 7}{6}$
$x = \dfrac{5 + 7}{6} = \dfrac{12}{6} = 2$ or $x = \dfrac{5 - 7}{6} = \dfrac{-2}{6} = -\dfrac{1}{3}$

The solutions are $-\dfrac{1}{3}$ and 2, or the solution set is $\left\{-\dfrac{1}{3}, 2\right\}$.

2. $3x^2 - 8x = 2$

Write in standard form.

$3x^2 - 8x - 2 = 0$

$a = 3, b = -8, c = -2$

$x = \dfrac{-b \pm \sqrt{b^2 - 4ac}}{2a}$

$= \dfrac{-(-8) \pm \sqrt{(-8)^2 - 4(3)(-2)}}{2(3)}$

$= \dfrac{8 \pm \sqrt{64 + 24}}{6}$

$= \dfrac{8 \pm \sqrt{88}}{6}$

$= \dfrac{8 \pm 2\sqrt{22}}{6}$

$= \dfrac{4 \pm \sqrt{22}}{3}$

The solutions are $\dfrac{4 + \sqrt{22}}{3}$ and $\dfrac{4 - \sqrt{22}}{3}$, or the

solution set is $\left\{ \dfrac{4 + \sqrt{22}}{3}, \dfrac{4 - \sqrt{22}}{3} \right\}$.

3. $\dfrac{1}{8}x^2 - \dfrac{1}{4}x - 2 = 0$

Multiply both sides of the equation by 8.

$8\left(\dfrac{1}{8}x^2 - \dfrac{1}{4}x - 2 \right) = 8 \cdot 0$

$x^2 - 2x - 16 = 0$

Substitute $a = 1$, $b = -2$, and $c = -16$ into the quadratic formula and simplify.

$x = \dfrac{-(-2) \pm \sqrt{(-2)^2 - 4(1)(-16)}}{2(1)}$

$= \dfrac{2 \pm \sqrt{4 + 64}}{2}$

$= \dfrac{2 \pm \sqrt{68}}{2}$

$= \dfrac{2 \pm 2\sqrt{17}}{2}$

$= 1 \pm \sqrt{17}$

The solutions are $1 + \sqrt{17}$ or $1 - \sqrt{17}$.

4. $x = -2x^2 - 2$

The equation in standard form is

$2x^2 + x + 2 = 0$. Thus, let $a = 2$, $b = 1$, and $c = 2$ in the quadratic formula.

$x = \dfrac{-1 \pm \sqrt{1^2 - 4(2)(2)}}{2(2)}$

$= \dfrac{-1 \pm \sqrt{1 - 16}}{4}$

$= \dfrac{-1 \pm \sqrt{-15}}{4}$

$= \dfrac{-1 \pm i\sqrt{15}}{4}$

The solutions are $\dfrac{-1 + i\sqrt{15}}{4}$ and $\dfrac{-1 - i\sqrt{15}}{4}$.

5. a. $x^2 - 6x + 9 = 0$

In $x^2 - 6x + 9$, $a = 1$, $b = -6$, and $c = 9$.
Thus,

$b^2 - 4ac = (-6)^2 - 4(1)(9) = 36 - 36 = 0$

Since $b^2 - 4ac = 0$, this equation has one real solution.

b. $x^2 - 3x - 1 = 0$

In this equation, $a = 1$, $b = -3$, and $c = -1$.

$b^2 - 4ac = (-3)^2 - 4(1)(-1) = 9 + 4 = 13 > 0$

Since $b^2 - 4ac$ is positive, this equation has two real solutions.

c. $7x^2 + 11 = 0$

In this equation, $a = 7$, $b = 0$, and $c = 11$.

$b^2 - 4ac = 0^2 - 4(7)(11) = -308 < 0$

Since $b^2 - 4ac$ is negative, this equation has two complex but not real solutions.

6. By the Pythagorean theorem, we have

$x^2 + (x + 3)^2 = 15^2$

$x^2 + x^2 + 6x + 9 = 225$

$2x^2 + 6x - 216 = 0$

$x^2 + 3x - 108 = 0$

Here, $a = 1$, $b = 3$, and $c = -108$. By the quadratic formula,

$$x = \frac{-3 \pm \sqrt{3^2 - 4(1)(-108)}}{2(1)}$$

$$= \frac{-3 \pm \sqrt{9 + 432}}{2}$$

$$= \frac{-3 \pm \sqrt{441}}{2}$$

$$= \frac{-3 \pm 21}{2}$$

$$x = \frac{-3 + 21}{2} = \frac{18}{2} = 9 \text{ or}$$

$$x = \frac{-3 - 21}{2} = \frac{-24}{2} = -12$$

The length can't be negative, so reject -12. The distance along the sidewalk is
$x + (x + 3) = 2x + 3 = 2(9) + 3 = 18 + 3 = 21$ feet
A person can save $21 - 15 = 6$ feet by cutting across the lawn.

7. $h = -16t^2 + 20t + 45$
    At the ground, $h = 0$.
    $0 = -16t^2 + 20t + 45$
    Here, $a = -16$, $b = 20$, and $c = 45$. By the quadratic formula,

$$t = \frac{-20 \pm \sqrt{20^2 - 4(-16)(45)}}{2(-16)}$$

$$= \frac{-20 \pm \sqrt{400 + 2880}}{-32}$$

$$= \frac{-20 \pm \sqrt{3280}}{-32}$$

$$= \frac{20 \pm \sqrt{16 \cdot 205}}{32}$$

$$= \frac{20 \pm 4\sqrt{205}}{32}$$

$$= \frac{5 \pm \sqrt{205}}{8}$$

$$t = \frac{5 + \sqrt{205}}{8} \approx 2.4 \text{ or } t = \frac{5 - \sqrt{205}}{8} \approx -1.2$$

Since the time won't be negative, we reject -1.2. The rocket will strike the ground 2.4 seconds after launch.

Vocabulary and Readiness Check

1. The quadratic formula is $x = \dfrac{-b \pm \sqrt{b^2 - 4ac}}{2a}$.

2. For $2x^2 + x + 1 = 0$, if $a = 2$, then $b = \underline{1}$ and $c = \underline{1}$.

3. For $5x^2 - 5x - 7 = 0$, if $a = 5$, then $b = \underline{-5}$ and $c = \underline{-7}$.

4. For $7x^2 - 4 = 0$, if $a = 7$, then $b = \underline{0}$ and $c = \underline{-4}$.

5. For $x^2 + 9 = 0$, if $c = 9$, then $a = \underline{1}$ and $b = \underline{0}$.

6. The correct simplified form of $\dfrac{5 \pm 10\sqrt{2}}{5}$ is $1 \pm 2\sqrt{2}$. The answer is **c**.

Exercise Set 8.2

1. $m^2 + 5m - 6 = 0$
    $a = 1, b = 5, c = -6$

$$m = \frac{-5 \pm \sqrt{(5)^2 - 4(1)(-6)}}{2(1)}$$

$$= \frac{-5 \pm \sqrt{25 + 24}}{2}$$

$$= \frac{-5 \pm \sqrt{49}}{2}$$

$$= \frac{-5 \pm 7}{2}$$

$$= -6 \text{ or } 1$$

The solutions are -6 and 1.

3. $\qquad 2y = 5y^2 - 3$
    $5y^2 - 2y - 3 = 0$
    $a = 5, b = -2, c = -3$

$$y = \frac{2 \pm \sqrt{(-2)^2 - 4(5)(-3)}}{2(5)}$$

$$= \frac{2 \pm \sqrt{4 + 60}}{10}$$

$$= \frac{2 \pm \sqrt{64}}{10}$$

$$= \frac{2 \pm 8}{10}$$

$$= -\frac{3}{5} \text{ or } 1$$

The solutions are $-\dfrac{3}{5}$ and 1.

5. $x^2 - 6x + 9 = 0$

$a = 1, b = -6, c = 9$

$x = \dfrac{6 \pm \sqrt{(-6)^2 - 4(1)(9)}}{2(1)}$

$= \dfrac{6 \pm \sqrt{36 - 36}}{2}$

$= \dfrac{6 \pm \sqrt{0}}{2}$

$= \dfrac{6}{2}$

$= 3$

The solution is 3.

7. $x^2 + 7x + 4 = 0$

$a = 1, b = 7, c = 4$

$x = \dfrac{-7 \pm \sqrt{(7)^2 - 4(1)(4)}}{2(1)}$

$= \dfrac{-7 \pm \sqrt{49 - 16}}{2}$

$= \dfrac{-7 \pm \sqrt{33}}{2}$

The solutions are $\dfrac{-7 + \sqrt{33}}{2}$ and $\dfrac{-7 - \sqrt{33}}{2}$.

9. $8m^2 - 2m = 7$

$8m^2 - 2m - 7 = 0$

$a = 8, b = -2, c = -7$

$m = \dfrac{2 \pm \sqrt{(-2)^2 - 4(8)(-7)}}{2(8)}$

$= \dfrac{2 \pm \sqrt{4 + 224}}{16}$

$= \dfrac{2 \pm \sqrt{228}}{16}$

$= \dfrac{2 \pm \sqrt{4 \cdot 57}}{16}$

$= \dfrac{2 \pm 2\sqrt{57}}{16}$

$= \dfrac{1 \pm \sqrt{57}}{8}$

The solutions are $\dfrac{1 + \sqrt{57}}{8}$ and $\dfrac{1 - \sqrt{57}}{8}$.

11. $3m^2 - 7m = 3$

$3m^2 - 7m - 3 = 0$

$a = 3, b = -7, c = -3$

$m = \dfrac{7 \pm \sqrt{(-7)^2 - 4(3)(-3)}}{2(3)}$

$= \dfrac{7 \pm \sqrt{49 + 36}}{6}$

$= \dfrac{7 \pm \sqrt{85}}{6}$

The solutions are $\dfrac{7 + \sqrt{85}}{6}$ and $\dfrac{7 - \sqrt{85}}{6}$.

13. $\dfrac{1}{2}x^2 - x - 1 = 0$

$x^2 - 2x - 2 = 0$

$a = 1, b = -2, c = -2$

$x = \dfrac{2 \pm \sqrt{(-2)^2 - 4(1)(-2)}}{2(1)}$

$= \dfrac{2 \pm \sqrt{4 + 8}}{2}$

$= \dfrac{2 \pm \sqrt{12}}{2}$

$= \dfrac{2 \pm 2\sqrt{3}}{2}$

$= 1 \pm \sqrt{3}$

The solutions are $1 + \sqrt{3}$ and $1 - \sqrt{3}$.

15. $\dfrac{2}{5}y^2 + \dfrac{1}{5}y = \dfrac{3}{5}$

$2y^2 + y - 3 = 0$

$a = 2, b = 1, c = -3$

$y = \dfrac{-1 \pm \sqrt{(1)^2 - 4(2)(-3)}}{2(2)}$

$= \dfrac{-1 \pm \sqrt{1 + 24}}{4}$

$= \dfrac{-1 \pm \sqrt{25}}{4}$

$= \dfrac{-1 \pm 5}{4}$

$= -\dfrac{3}{2}$ or 1

The solutions are $-\dfrac{3}{2}$ and 1.

17. $\frac{1}{3}y^2 = y + \frac{1}{6}$

$\frac{1}{3}y^2 - y - \frac{1}{6} = 0$

$2y^2 - 6y - 1 = 0$

$a = 2, b = -6, c = -1$

$y = \frac{6 \pm \sqrt{(-6)^2 - 4(2)(-1)}}{2(2)}$

$= \frac{6 \pm \sqrt{36 + 8}}{4}$

$= \frac{6 \pm \sqrt{44}}{4}$

$= \frac{6 \pm 2\sqrt{11}}{4}$

$= \frac{3 \pm \sqrt{11}}{2}$

The solutions are $\frac{3 + \sqrt{11}}{2}$ and $\frac{3 - \sqrt{11}}{2}$.

19. $x^2 + 5x = -2$

$x^2 + 5x + 2 = 0$

$a = 1, b = 5, c = 2$

$x = \frac{-5 \pm \sqrt{(5)^2 - 4(1)(2)}}{2(1)}$

$= \frac{-5 \pm \sqrt{25 - 8}}{2}$

$= \frac{-5 \pm \sqrt{17}}{2}$

The solutions are $\frac{-5 + \sqrt{17}}{2}$ and $\frac{-5 - \sqrt{17}}{2}$.

21. $(m + 2)(2m - 6) = 5(m - 1) - 12$

$2m^2 - 6m + 4m - 12 = 5m - 5 - 12$

$2m^2 - 7m + 5 = 0$

$a = 2, b = -7, c = 5$

$m = \frac{7 \pm \sqrt{(-7)^2 - 4(2)(5)}}{2(2)}$

$= \frac{7 \pm \sqrt{49 - 40}}{4}$

$= \frac{7 \pm \sqrt{9}}{4}$

$= \frac{7 \pm 3}{4}$

$= 1 \text{ or } \frac{5}{2}$

The solutions are 1 and $\frac{5}{2}$.

23. $x^2 + 6x + 13 = 0$

$a = 1, b = 6, c = 13$

$x = \frac{-6 \pm \sqrt{(6)^2 - 4(1)(13)}}{2(1)}$

$= \frac{-6 \pm \sqrt{36 - 52}}{2}$

$= \frac{-6 \pm \sqrt{-16}}{2}$

$= \frac{-6 \pm 4i}{2}$

$= -3 \pm 2i$

The solutions are $-3 + 2i$ and $-3 - 2i$.

25. $(x + 5)(x - 1) = 2$

$x^2 + 4x - 5 = 2$

$x^2 + 4x - 7 = 0$

$a = 1, b = 4, c = -7$

$x = \frac{-4 \pm \sqrt{(4)^2 - 4(1)(-7)}}{2(1)}$

$= \frac{-4 \pm \sqrt{16 + 28}}{2}$

$= \frac{-4 \pm \sqrt{44}}{2}$

$= \frac{-4 \pm 2\sqrt{11}}{2}$

$= -2 \pm \sqrt{11}$

The solutions are $-2 + \sqrt{11}$ and $-2 - \sqrt{11}$.

27.

$$6 = -4x^2 + 3x$$
$$4x^2 - 3x + 6 = 0$$
$$a = 4, b = -3, c = 6$$
$$x = \frac{3 \pm \sqrt{(-3)^2 - 4(4)(6)}}{2(4)}$$
$$= \frac{3 \pm \sqrt{9 - 96}}{8}$$
$$= \frac{3 \pm \sqrt{-87}}{8}$$
$$= \frac{3 \pm i\sqrt{87}}{8}$$

The solutions are $\dfrac{3 + i\sqrt{87}}{8}$ and $\dfrac{3 - i\sqrt{87}}{8}$.

29.

$$\frac{x^2}{3} - x = \frac{5}{3}$$
$$x^2 - 3x = 5$$
$$x^2 - 3x - 5 = 0$$
$$a = 1, b = -3, c = -5$$
$$x = \frac{3 \pm \sqrt{(-3)^2 - 4(1)(-5)}}{2(1)}$$
$$= \frac{3 \pm \sqrt{9 + 20}}{2}$$
$$= \frac{3 \pm \sqrt{29}}{2}$$

The solutions are $\dfrac{3 + \sqrt{29}}{2}$ and $\dfrac{3 - \sqrt{29}}{2}$.

31. $10y^2 + 10y + 3 = 0$
$$a = 10, b = 10, c = 3$$
$$y = \frac{-10 \pm \sqrt{(10)^2 - 4(10)(3)}}{2(10)}$$
$$= \frac{-10 \pm \sqrt{100 - 120}}{20}$$
$$= \frac{-10 \pm \sqrt{-20}}{20}$$
$$= \frac{-10 \pm i\sqrt{4 \cdot 5}}{20}$$
$$= \frac{-10 \pm 2i\sqrt{5}}{20}$$
$$= \frac{-5 \pm i\sqrt{5}}{10}$$

The solutions are $\dfrac{-5 + i\sqrt{5}}{10}$ and $\dfrac{-5 - i\sqrt{5}}{10}$.

33.

$$x(6x + 2) = 3$$
$$x(6x + 2) - 3 = 0$$
$$6x^2 + 2x - 3 = 0$$
$$a = 6, b = 2, c = -3$$
$$x = \frac{-2 \pm \sqrt{(2)^2 - 4(6)(-3)}}{2(6)}$$
$$= \frac{-2 \pm \sqrt{4 + 72}}{12}$$
$$= \frac{-2 \pm \sqrt{76}}{12}$$
$$= \frac{-2 \pm \sqrt{4 \cdot 19}}{12}$$
$$= \frac{-2 \pm 2\sqrt{19}}{12}$$
$$= \frac{-1 \pm \sqrt{19}}{6}$$

The solutions are $\dfrac{-1 + \sqrt{19}}{6}$ and $\dfrac{-1 - \sqrt{19}}{6}$.

35. $\dfrac{2}{5}y^2 + \dfrac{1}{5}y + \dfrac{3}{5} = 0$
$$2y^2 + y + 3 = 0$$
$$a = 2, b = 1, c = 3$$
$$y = \frac{-1 \pm \sqrt{(1)^2 - 4(2)(3)}}{2(2)}$$
$$= \frac{-1 \pm \sqrt{1 - 24}}{4}$$
$$= \frac{-1 \pm \sqrt{-23}}{4}$$
$$= \frac{-1 \pm i\sqrt{23}}{4}$$

The solutions are $\dfrac{-1 + i\sqrt{23}}{4}$ and $\dfrac{-1 - i\sqrt{23}}{4}$.

37.
$$\frac{1}{2}y^2 = y - \frac{1}{2}$$
$$y^2 = 2y - 1$$
$$y^2 - 2y + 1 = 0$$
$$a = 1, b = -2, c = 1$$
$$y = \frac{2 \pm \sqrt{(-2)^2 - 4(1)(1)}}{2(1)}$$
$$= \frac{2 \pm \sqrt{4 - 4}}{2}$$
$$= \frac{2 \pm \sqrt{0}}{2}$$
$$= \frac{2}{2}$$
$$= 1$$
The solution is 1.

39.
$$(n-2)^2 = 2n$$
$$n^2 - 4n + 4 = 2n$$
$$n^2 - 6n + 4 = 0$$
$$a = 1, b = -6, c = 4$$
$$n = \frac{6 \pm \sqrt{(-6)^2 - 4(1)(4)}}{2(1)}$$
$$= \frac{6 \pm \sqrt{36 - 16}}{2}$$
$$= \frac{6 \pm \sqrt{20}}{2}$$
$$= \frac{6 \pm 2\sqrt{5}}{2}$$
$$= 3 \pm \sqrt{5}$$
The solutions are $3 + \sqrt{5}$ and $3 - \sqrt{5}$.

41. $x^2 - 5 = 0$
$$a = 1, b = 0, c = -5$$
$$b^2 - 4ac = 0^2 - 4(1)(-5) = 20 > 0$$
Therefore, there are two real solutions.

43.
$$4x^2 + 12x = -9$$
$$4x^2 - 12x + 9 = 0$$
$$a = 4, b = -12, c = 9$$
$$b^2 - 4ac = (-12)^2 - 4(4)(9)$$
$$= 144 - 144$$
$$= 0$$
Therefore, there is one real solution.

45.
$$3x = -2x^2 + 7$$
$$2x^2 + 3x - 7 = 0$$
$$a = 2, b = 3, c = -7$$
$$b^2 - 4ac = 3^2 - 4(2)(-7)$$
$$= 9 + 56$$
$$= 65 > 0$$
Therefore, there are two real solutions.

47.
$$6 = 4x - 5x^2$$
$$5x^2 - 4x + 6 = 0$$
$$a = 5, b = -4, c = 6$$
$$b^2 - 4ac = (-4)^2 - 4(5)(6)$$
$$= 16 - 120$$
$$= -104 < 0$$
Therefore, there are two complex but not real solutions.

49.
$$9x - 2x^2 + 5 = 0$$
$$-2x^2 + 9x + 5 = 0$$
$$a = -2, b = 9, c = 5$$
$$b^2 - 4ac = 9^2 - 4(-2)(5)$$
$$= 81 + 40$$
$$= 121 > 0$$
Therefore, there are two real solutions.

51.
$$(x+8)^2 + x^2 = 36^2$$
$$(x^2 + 16x + 64) + x^2 = 1296$$
$$2x^2 + 16x - 1232 = 0$$
$$a = 2, b = 16, c = -1232$$
$$x = \frac{-16 \pm \sqrt{(16)^2 - 4(2)(-1232)}}{2(2)}$$
$$= \frac{-16 \pm \sqrt{10,112}}{4}$$
$$x \approx 21 \text{ or } x \approx -29 \text{ (disregard)}$$
$$x + (x+8) = 21 + 21 + 8 = 50$$
$$50 - 36 = 14$$
They save about 14 feet of walking distance.

53. Let x = length of leg. Then
$x + 2$ = length of hypotenuse.
$$x^2 + x^2 = (x+2)^2$$
$$2x^2 = x^2 + 4x + 4$$
$$x^2 - 4x - 4 = 0$$
$$a = 1, b = -4, c = -4$$

$$x = \frac{4 \pm \sqrt{(-4)^2 - 4(1)(-4)}}{2(1)}$$

$$= \frac{4 \pm \sqrt{32}}{2}$$

$$= \frac{4 \pm 4\sqrt{2}}{2}$$

$$= 2 \pm 2\sqrt{2} \text{ (disregard the negative)}$$

$$= 2 + 2\sqrt{2}$$

The sides measure $2 + 2\sqrt{2}$ cm, $2 + 2\sqrt{2}$ cm, and $4 + 2\sqrt{2}$ cm.

55. Let $x =$ width; then $x + 10 =$ length.
Area = length · width
$$400 = (x + 10)x$$
$$0 = x^2 + 10x - 400$$
$$a = 1, b = 10, c = -400$$
$$x = \frac{-10 \pm \sqrt{(10)^2 - 4(1)(-400)}}{2(1)}$$
$$= \frac{-10 \pm \sqrt{1700}}{2}$$
$$= \frac{-10 \pm 10\sqrt{17}}{2}$$
$$= -5 \pm 5\sqrt{17}$$

Disregard the negative length. The width is $-5 + 5\sqrt{17}$ ft and the length is $5 + 5\sqrt{17}$ ft.

57. a. Let $x =$ length.
$$x^2 + x^2 = 100^2$$
$$2x^2 - 10,000 = 0$$
$$a = 2, b = 0, c = -10,000$$
$$x = \frac{0 \pm \sqrt{(0)^2 - 4(2)(-10,000)}}{2(2)}$$
$$= \frac{\pm\sqrt{80,000}}{4}$$
$$= \frac{\pm 200\sqrt{2}}{4}$$
$$= \pm 50\sqrt{2}$$

Disregard the negative length. The side measures $50\sqrt{2}$ meters.

b. Area $= s^2$
$$= \left(50\sqrt{2}\right)^2$$
$$= 2500(2)$$
$$= 5000$$
The area is 5000 square meters.

59. Let $w =$ width; then $w + 1.1 =$ height.
Area = length · width
$$1439.9 = (w + 1.1)w$$
$$0 = w^2 + 1.1w - 1439.9$$
$$a = 1, b = 1.1, c = -1439.9$$
$$w = \frac{-1.1 \pm \sqrt{(1.1)^2 - 4(1)(-1439.9)}}{2(1)}$$
$$= \frac{-1.1 \pm \sqrt{5760.81}}{2}$$
$$= 37.4 \text{ or } -38.5 \text{ (disregard)}$$
Its width is 37.4 ft and its height is 38.5 ft.

61. Let $h =$ height. Then $2h + 4 =$ base.
$$\text{Area} = \frac{1}{2}\text{base} \cdot \text{height}$$
$$42 = \frac{1}{2}(2h + 4)h$$
$$42 = h^2 + 2h$$
$$0 = h^2 + 2h - 42$$
$$a = 1, b = 2, c = -42$$
$$h = \frac{-2 \pm \sqrt{(2)^2 - 4(1)(-42)}}{2(1)}$$
$$= \frac{-2 \pm \sqrt{172}}{2}$$
$$= \frac{-2 \pm 2\sqrt{43}}{2}$$
$$= -1 \pm \sqrt{43} \text{ (disregard the negative)}$$
$$\text{base} = 2\left(-1 + \sqrt{43}\right) + 4 = 2 + 2\sqrt{43}$$

Height: $-1 + \sqrt{43}$ cm
Base: $2 + 2\sqrt{43}$ cm

63. $h = -16t^2 + 20t + 1100$
$$0 = -16t^2 + 20t + 1100$$
$$a = -16, b = 20, c = 1100$$
$$t = \frac{-20 \pm \sqrt{(20)^2 - 4(-16)(1100)}}{2(-16)}$$
$$= \frac{-20 \pm \sqrt{70,800}}{-32}$$
$$\approx 8.9 \text{ or } -7.7 \text{ (disregard)}$$
It will take about 8.9 seconds.

65. $h = -16t^2 - 20t + 180$

$0 = -16t^2 - 20t + 180$

$a = -16, b = -20, c = 180$

$t = \dfrac{20 \pm \sqrt{(-20)^2 - 4(-16)(180)}}{2(-16)}$

$= \dfrac{20 \pm \sqrt{11,920}}{-32}$

≈ 2.8 or -4.0 (disregard)

It will take about 2.8 seconds.

67. $\sqrt{5x-2} = 3$

$\left(\sqrt{5x-2}\right)^2 = 3^2$

$5x - 2 = 9$

$5x = 11$

$x = \dfrac{11}{5}$

69. $\dfrac{1}{x} + \dfrac{2}{5} = \dfrac{7}{x}$

$5x\left(\dfrac{1}{x} + \dfrac{2}{5}\right) = 5x\left(\dfrac{7}{x}\right)$

$5 + 2x = 35$

$2x = 30$

$x = 15$

71. $x^4 + x^2 - 20 = (x^2 + 5)(x^2 - 4)$

$\qquad = (x^2 + 5)(x + 2)(x - 2)$

73. $z^4 - 13z^2 + 36 = (z^2 - 9)(z^2 - 4)$

$\qquad = (z + 3)(z - 3)(z + 2)(z - 2)$

75. $x^2 = -10$

$x^2 + 10 = 0$

$a = 1, b = 0, c = 10$

The correct substitution is **b**.

77. $m^2 + 5m - 6 = 0$

$(m + 6)(m - 1) = 0$

$m + 6 = 0$ or $m - 1 = 0$

$m = -6$ or $m = 1$

The results are the same. Answers may vary.

79. $2x^2 - 6x + 3 = 0$

$a = 2, b = -6, c = 3$

$x = \dfrac{6 \pm \sqrt{(-6)^2 - 4(2)(3)}}{2(2)}$

$= \dfrac{6 \pm \sqrt{12}}{4}$

≈ 0.6 or 2.4

81. From Sunday to Monday

83. Wednesday

85. $f(x) = 3x^2 - 18x + 56$

$f(4) = 3(4)^2 - 18(4) + 56 = 32$

This answers appears to agree with the graph.

87. $f(x) = 115x^2 + 711x + 3946$

    a. $x = 2004 - 2000 = 4$

$f(4) = 115(4)^2 + 711(4) + 3946 = 8630$

There were 8630 stores.

    b. Let $f(x) = 25,000$.

$25,000 = 115x^2 + 711x + 3946$

$0 = 115x^2 + 711x - 21,054$

$a = 115, b = 711, c = -21,054$

$x = \dfrac{-711 \pm \sqrt{711^2 - 4(115)(-21,054)}}{2(115)}$

$= \dfrac{-711 \pm \sqrt{10,190,361}}{230}$

$\approx -3.0913 \pm 13.8793$

$x \approx 10.788 \approx 11$ or $x \approx -16.9706 \approx -17$

We are not concerned with the past, so we reject -17. There will be 25,000 Starbucks in 2011.

89. $\dfrac{-b + \sqrt{b^2 - 4ac}}{2a} + \dfrac{-b - \sqrt{b^2 - 4ac}}{2a}$

$= \dfrac{-b + \sqrt{b^2 - 4ac} - b - \sqrt{b^2 - 4ac}}{2a}$

$= \dfrac{-2b}{2a}$

$= -\dfrac{b}{a}$

91. $3x^2 - \sqrt{12}x + 1 = 0$

$a = 3, b = -\sqrt{12}, c = 1$

$$x = \frac{\sqrt{12} \pm \sqrt{\left(-\sqrt{12}\right)^2 - 4(3)(1)}}{2(3)}$$

$$= \frac{\sqrt{12} \pm \sqrt{12 - 12}}{6}$$

$$= \frac{\sqrt{4 \cdot 3} \pm \sqrt{0}}{6}$$

$$= \frac{2\sqrt{3}}{6}$$

$$= \frac{\sqrt{3}}{3}$$

The solution is $\dfrac{\sqrt{3}}{3}$.

93. $x^2 + \sqrt{2}x + 1 = 0$

$a = 1, b = \sqrt{2}, c = 1$

$$x = \frac{-\sqrt{2} \pm \sqrt{\left(\sqrt{2}\right)^2 - 4(1)(1)}}{2(1)}$$

$$= \frac{-\sqrt{2} \pm \sqrt{2 - 4}}{2}$$

$$= \frac{-\sqrt{2} \pm \sqrt{-2}}{2}$$

$$= \frac{-\sqrt{2} \pm i\sqrt{2}}{2}$$

The solutions are $\dfrac{-\sqrt{2} + i\sqrt{2}}{2}$ and $\dfrac{-\sqrt{2} - i\sqrt{2}}{2}$.

95. $2x^2 - \sqrt{3}x - 1 = 0$

$a = 2, b = -\sqrt{3}, c = -1$

$$x = \frac{\sqrt{3} \pm \sqrt{\left(-\sqrt{3}\right)^2 - 4(2)(-1)}}{2(2)}$$

$$= \frac{\sqrt{3} \pm \sqrt{3 + 8}}{4}$$

$$= \frac{\sqrt{3} \pm \sqrt{11}}{4}$$

The solutions are $\dfrac{\sqrt{3} + \sqrt{11}}{4}$ and $\dfrac{\sqrt{3} - \sqrt{11}}{4}$.

97. Exercise 63:

Exercise 65:

99. $y = 9x - 2x^2 + 5$

There are two *x*-intercepts. There are two real solutions.

Section 8.3

Practice Exercises

1. $x - \sqrt{x+1} - 5 = 0$

Get the radical alone on one side of the equation. Then square both sides.

$$x - \sqrt{x+1} - 5 = 0$$

$$x - 5 = \sqrt{x+1}$$

$$(x-5)^2 = x+1$$

$$x^2 - 10x + 25 = x+1$$

$$x^2 - 11x + 24 = 0$$

$$(x-8)(x-3) = 0$$

$$x - 8 = 0 \quad \text{or} \quad x - 3 = 0$$

$$x = 8 \quad \text{or} \quad x = 3$$

Check:

Let $x = 3$.

$$x - \sqrt{x+1} - 5 = 0$$

$$3 - \sqrt{3+1} - 5 \stackrel{?}{=} 0$$

$$-2 - \sqrt{4} \stackrel{?}{=} 0$$

$$-2 - 2 \stackrel{?}{=} 0$$

$$-4 = 0 \quad \text{False}$$

Let $x = 8$.

$$x - \sqrt{x+1} - 5 = 0$$
$$8 - \sqrt{8+1} - 5 \overset{?}{=} 0$$
$$3 - \sqrt{9} \overset{?}{=} 0$$
$$3 - 3 \overset{?}{=} 0$$
$$0 = 0 \quad \text{True}$$

The solution is 8 or the solution set is $\{8\}$.

2. $\dfrac{5x}{x+1} - \dfrac{x+4}{x} = \dfrac{3}{x(x+1)}$

x cannot be either -1 or 0, because these values cause denominators to equal zero. Multiply both sides of the equation by $x(x+1)$.

$$x(x+1)\left(\frac{5x}{x+1}\right) - x(x+1)\left(\frac{x+4}{x}\right) = x(x+1)\left[\frac{3}{x(x+1)}\right]$$
$$5x^2 - (x+1)(x+4) = 3$$
$$5x^2 - x^2 - 5x - 4 = 3$$
$$4x^2 - 5x - 7 = 0$$

Use the quadratic formula with $a = 4$, $b = -5$, and $c = -7$.

$$x = \frac{-(-5) \pm \sqrt{(-5)^2 - 4(4)(-7)}}{2(4)} = \frac{5 \pm \sqrt{25+112}}{8} = \frac{5 \pm \sqrt{137}}{8}$$

Neither proposed solution will make denominators 0. The solutions are $\dfrac{5+\sqrt{137}}{8}$ and $\dfrac{5-\sqrt{137}}{8}$ or the

solution set is $\left\{ \dfrac{5+\sqrt{137}}{8}, \dfrac{5-\sqrt{137}}{8} \right\}$.

3. $$p^4 - 7p^2 - 144 = 0$$
$$(p^2 + 9)(p^2 - 16) = 0$$
$$(p^2 + 9)(p+4)(p-4) = 0$$
$$p^2 + 9 = 0 \qquad \text{or} \quad p+4 = 0 \quad \text{or} \quad p-4 = 0$$
$$p^2 = -9 \qquad\qquad\quad p = -4 \qquad\qquad p = 4$$
$$p = \pm\sqrt{-9}$$
$$p = \pm 3i$$

The solutions are 4, -4, $3i$, and $-3i$.

4. $(x+2)^2 - 2(x+2) - 3 = 0$

Let $y = x + 2$.
$$y^2 - 2y - 3 = 0$$
$$(y-3)(y+1) = 0$$
$$y - 3 = 0 \quad \text{or} \quad y + 1 = 0$$
$$y = 3 \qquad\qquad y = -1$$

Substitute $x + 2$ for y.
$$x + 2 = 3 \quad \text{or} \quad x + 2 = -1$$
$$x = 1 \qquad\qquad x = -3$$

Both 1 and -3 check. The solutions are 1 and -3.

5. $x^{2/3} - 5x^{1/3} + 4 = 0$

Let $m = x^{1/3}$.

$m^2 - 5m + 4 = 0$

$(m-4)(m-1) = 0$

$m - 4 = 0$ or $m - 1 = 0$

   $m = 4$ $m = 1$

Since $m = x^{1/3}$, we have

$x^{1/3} = 4$ or $x^{1/3} = 1$

   $x = 4^3 = 64$ $x = 1^3 = 1$

Both 64 and 1 check. The solutions are 64 and 1.

6. Let x = the time in hours it takes Steve to groom all the dogs. Then,
$x - 1$ = the time it takes Katy to groom all the dogs.

The part of the job completed in one hour by Steve is $\dfrac{1}{x}$, and the part completed by Katy in one hour is

$\dfrac{1}{x-1}$. In one hour, $\dfrac{1}{4}$ of the job is completed. We have,

$$\frac{1}{x} + \frac{1}{x-1} = \frac{1}{4}$$

$$4x(x-1)\left(\frac{1}{x}\right) + 4x(x-1)\left(\frac{1}{x-1}\right) = 4x(x-1)\left(\frac{1}{4}\right)$$

$$4(x-1) + 4x = x(x-1)$$

$$4x - 4 + 4x = x^2 - x$$

$$0 = x^2 - 9x + 4$$

Use the quadratic formula with $a = 1$, $b = -9$, and $c = 4$.

$$x = \frac{-(-9) \pm \sqrt{(-9)^2 - 4(1)(4)}}{2(1)}$$

$$x = \frac{9 \pm \sqrt{81-16}}{2} = \frac{9 \pm \sqrt{65}}{2}$$

$x \approx 8.53$ or $x \approx 0.47$

Since $x - 1 = 0.47 - 1 = -0.53 < 0$, representing negative time worked, we reject 0.47. It takes Steve
$\dfrac{9+\sqrt{65}}{2} \approx 8.5$ hours and Katy $\dfrac{9+\sqrt{65}}{2} - 1 = \dfrac{7+\sqrt{65}}{2} \approx 7.5$ hours to groom all the dogs when working
alone.

7. Let x = the speed driven to Shanghai. Then
$x + 50$ = the speed driven to Ningbo.

	distance =	rate	· time
To Shanghai	36	x	$\dfrac{36}{x}$
To Ningbo	36	$x + 50$	$\dfrac{36}{x+50}$

The total travel time was 1.3 hours, so

$$\frac{36}{x} + \frac{36}{x+50} = 1.3$$

$$x(x+50)\left(\frac{36}{x}\right) + x(x+50)\left(\frac{36}{x+50}\right) = 1.3x(x+50)$$

$$36(x+50) + 36x = 1.3x^2 + 65x$$

$$36x + 1800 + 36x = 1.3x^2 + 65x$$

$$0 = 1.3x^2 - 7x - 1800$$

Use the quadratic formula with $a = 1.3$, $b = -7$, and $c = -1800$.

$$x = \frac{-(-7) \pm \sqrt{(-7)^2 - 4(1.3)(-1800)}}{2(1.3)} = \frac{7 \pm \sqrt{9409}}{2.6}$$

$$x = \frac{7 + \sqrt{9409}}{2.6} = 40 \quad \text{or} \quad x = \frac{7 - \sqrt{9409}}{2.6} \approx -34.6$$

The speed is not negative, so reject −34.6. The speed to Shanghai was 40 km/hr and to Ningbo it was 40 + 50 = 90 km/hr.

Exercise Set 8.3

1.
$$2x = \sqrt{10 + 3x}$$
$$4x^2 = 10 + 3x$$
$$4x^2 - 3x - 10 = 0$$
$$(4x + 5)(x - 2) = 0$$
$$4x + 5 = 0 \quad \text{or} \quad x - 2 = 0$$
$$x = -\frac{5}{4} \quad \text{or} \quad x = 2$$

Discard $-\frac{5}{4}$. The solution is 2.

3.
$$x - 2\sqrt{x} = 8$$
$$x - 8 = 2\sqrt{x}$$
$$(x - 8)^2 = \left(2\sqrt{x}\right)^2$$
$$x^2 - 16x + 64 = 4x$$
$$x^2 - 20x + 64 = 0$$
$$(x - 16)(x - 4) = 0$$
$$x - 16 = 0 \quad \text{or} \quad x - 4 = 0$$
$$x = 16 \quad \text{or} \quad x = 4 \text{ (discard)}$$

The solution is 16.

5.
$$\sqrt{9x} = x + 2$$
$$\left(\sqrt{9x}\right)^2 = (x+2)^2$$
$$9x = x^2 + 4x + 4$$
$$0 = x^2 - 5x + 4$$
$$0 = (x-4)(x-1)$$
$$x - 4 = 0 \text{ or } x - 1 = 0$$
$$x = 4 \text{ or } \quad x = 1$$
The solutions are 1 and 4.

7. $\dfrac{2}{x} + \dfrac{3}{x-1} = 1$

Multiply each term by $x(x-1)$.
$$2(x-1) + 3x = x(x-1)$$
$$2x - 2 + 3x = x^2 - x$$
$$0 = x^2 - 6x + 2$$
$$x = \frac{6 \pm \sqrt{(-6)^2 - 4(1)(2)}}{2(1)}$$
$$= \frac{6 \pm \sqrt{28}}{2}$$
$$= \frac{6 \pm 2\sqrt{7}}{2} = 3 \pm \sqrt{7}$$
The solutions are $3 + \sqrt{7}$ and $3 - \sqrt{7}$.

9. $\dfrac{3}{x} + \dfrac{4}{x+2} = 2$

Multiply each term by $x(x + 2)$.
$$3(x+2) + 4x = 2x(x+2)$$
$$3x + 6 + 4x = 2x^2 + 4x$$
$$0 = 2x^2 - 3x - 6$$
$$x = \frac{3 \pm \sqrt{(-3)^2 - 4(2)(-6)}}{2(2)}$$
$$= \frac{3 \pm \sqrt{57}}{4}$$
The solutions are $\dfrac{3 + \sqrt{57}}{4}$ and $\dfrac{3 - \sqrt{57}}{4}$.

11. $\dfrac{7}{x^2 - 5x + 6} = \dfrac{2x}{x-3} - \dfrac{x}{x-2}$
$$\frac{7}{(x-3)(x-2)} = \frac{2x}{x-3} - \frac{x}{x-2}$$
Multiply each term by $(x - 3)(x - 2)$.
$$7 = 2x(x-2) - x(x-3)$$
$$7 = 2x^2 - 4x - x^2 + 3x$$
$$0 = x^2 - x - 7$$

$$x = \frac{1 \pm \sqrt{(-1)^2 - 4(1)(-7)}}{2(1)}$$
$$= \frac{1 \pm \sqrt{29}}{2}$$
The solutions are $\dfrac{1 + \sqrt{29}}{2}$ and $\dfrac{2 - \sqrt{29}}{2}$.

13.
$$p^4 - 16 = 0$$
$$(p^2 - 4)(p^2 + 4) = 0$$
$$(p + 2)(p - 2)(p^2 + 4) = 0$$
$$p + 2 = 0 \quad \text{or } p - 2 = 0 \text{ or } p^2 + 4 = 0$$
$$p = -2 \text{ or } \quad p = 2 \text{ or } \quad p^2 = -4$$
$$p = \pm\sqrt{-4}$$
$$p = \pm 2i$$
The solutions are -2, 2, $-2i$, and $2i$.

15.
$$4x^4 + 11x^2 = 3$$
$$4x^4 + 11x^2 - 3 = 0$$
$$(4x^2 - 1)(x^2 + 3) = 0$$
$$(2x + 1)(2x - 1)(x^2 + 3) = 0$$
$$2x + 1 = 0 \quad \text{or } 2x - 1 = 0 \text{ or } x^2 + 3 = 0$$
$$x = -\frac{1}{2} \text{ or } \quad x = \frac{1}{2} \text{ or } \quad x^2 = -3$$
$$x = \pm\sqrt{-3}$$
$$x = \pm i\sqrt{3}$$
The solutions are $-\dfrac{1}{2}, \dfrac{1}{2}, -i\sqrt{3},$ and $i\sqrt{3}$.

17.
$$z^4 - 13z^2 + 36 = 0$$
$$(z^2 - 9)(z^2 - 4) = 0$$
$$(z + 3)(z - 3)(z + 2)(z - 2) = 0$$
$$z = -3, z = 3, z = -2, z = 2$$
The solutions are -3, 3, -2, and 2.

19. $x^{2/3} - 3x^{1/3} - 10 = 0$

Let $y = x^{1/3}$. Then $y^2 = x^{2/3}$ and
$$y^2 - 3y - 10 = 0$$
$$(y - 5)(y + 2) = 0$$
$$y - 5 = 0 \quad \text{or } y + 2 = 0$$
$$y = 5 \quad \text{or } \quad y = -2$$
$$x^{1/3} = 5 \quad \text{or } \quad x^{1/3} = -2$$
$$x = 125 \text{ or } \quad x = -8$$
The solutions are -8 and 125.

21. $(5n+1)^2 + 2(5n+1) - 3 = 0$

Let $y = 5n + 1$. Then $y^2 = (5n+1)^2$ and

$y^2 + 2y - 3 = 0$
$(y+3)(y-1) = 0$
$y+3 = 0$ or $y-1 = 0$
$y = -3$ or $y = 1$
$5n+1 = -3$ or $5n+1 = 1$
$5n = -4$ or $5n = 0$
$n = -\dfrac{4}{5}$ or $n = 0$

The solutions are $-\dfrac{4}{5}$ and 0.

23. $2x^{2/3} - 5x^{1/3} = 3$

Let $y = x^{1/3}$. Then $y^2 = x^{2/3}$ and

$2y^2 - 5y = 3$
$2y^2 - 5y - 3 = 0$
$(2y+1)(y-3) = 0$
$2y+1 = 0$ or $y-3 = 0$
$y = -\dfrac{1}{2}$ or $y = 3$
$x^{1/3} = -\dfrac{1}{2}$ or $x^{1/3} = 3$
$x = -\dfrac{1}{8}$ or $x = 27$

The solutions are $-\dfrac{1}{8}$ and 27.

25. $1 + \dfrac{2}{3t-2} = \dfrac{8}{(3t-2)^2}$

$(3t-2)^2 + 2(3t-2) = 8$
$(3t-2)^2 + 2(3t-2) - 8 = 0$

Let $y = 3t - 2$. Then $y^2 = (3t-2)^2$ and

$y^2 + 2y - 8 = 0$
$(y+4)(y-2) = 0$
$y+4 = 0$ or $y-2 = 0$
$y = -4$ or $y = 2$
$3t-2 = -4$ or $3t-2 = 2$
$3t = -2$ or $3t = 4$
$t = -\dfrac{2}{3}$ or $t = \dfrac{4}{3}$

The solutions are $-\dfrac{2}{3}$ and $\dfrac{4}{3}$.

27. $20x^{2/3} - 6x^{1/3} - 2 = 0$

Let $y = x^{1/3}$. Then $y^2 = x^{2/3}$ and

$20y^2 - 6y - 2 = 0$
$2(10y^2 - 3y - 1) = 0$
$2(5y+1)(2y-1) = 0$
$5y+1 = 0$ or $2y-1 = 0$
$y = -\dfrac{1}{5}$ or $y = \dfrac{1}{2}$
$x^{1/3} = -\dfrac{1}{5}$ or $x^{1/3} = \dfrac{1}{2}$
$x = -\dfrac{1}{125}$ or $x = \dfrac{1}{8}$

The solutions are $\dfrac{1}{8}$ and $-\dfrac{1}{125}$.

29. $a^4 - 5a^2 + 6 = 0$

$(a^2 - 3)(a^2 - 2) = 0$

$a^2 - 3 = 0$ or $a^2 - 2 = 0$
$a^2 = 3$ or $a^2 = 2$
$a = \pm\sqrt{3}$ or $a = \pm\sqrt{2}$

The solutions are $-\sqrt{3}, \sqrt{3}, -\sqrt{2},$ and $\sqrt{2}$.

31. $\dfrac{2x}{x-2} + \dfrac{x}{x+3} = -\dfrac{5}{x+3}$

Multiply each term by $(x+3)(x-2)$.
$2x(x+3) + x(x-2) = -5(x-2)$
$2x^2 + 6x + x^2 - 2x = -5x + 10$
$3x^2 + 9x - 10 = 0$

$x = \dfrac{-9 \pm \sqrt{(9)^2 - 4(3)(-10)}}{2(3)}$

$= \dfrac{-9 \pm \sqrt{201}}{6}$

The solutions are $\dfrac{-9+\sqrt{201}}{6}$ and $\dfrac{-9-\sqrt{201}}{6}$.

33. $(p+2)^2 = 9(p+2) - 20$

$(p+2)^2 - 9(p+2) + 20 = 0$

Let $x = p + 2$. Then $x^2 = (p+2)^2$ and

$x^2 - 9x + 20 = 0$
$(x-5)(x-4) = 0$
$x = 5$ or $x = 4$
$p+2 = 5$ or $p+2 = 4$
$p = 3$ or $p = 2$

The solutions are 2 and 3.

35.
$$2x = \sqrt{11x+3}$$
$$(2x)^2 = \left(\sqrt{11x+3}\right)^2$$
$$4x^2 = 11x+3$$
$$4x^2 - 11x - 3 = 0$$
$$(4x+1)(x-3) = 0$$
$$x = -\frac{1}{4} \text{ (discard) or } x = 3$$
The solution is 3.

37. $x^{2/3} - 8x^{1/3} + 15 = 0$
Let $y = x^{1/3}$. Then $y^2 = x^{2/3}$ and
$$y^2 - 8y + 15 = 0$$
$$(y-5)(y-3) = 0$$
$$y = 5 \quad \text{or} \quad y = 3$$
$$x^{1/3} = 5 \quad \text{or} \quad x^{1/3} = 3$$
$$x = 125 \quad \text{or} \quad x = 27$$
The solutions are 27 and 125.

39.
$$y^3 + 9y - y^2 - 9 = 0$$
$$y(y^2+9) - 1(y^2+9) = 0$$
$$(y^2+9)(y-1) = 0$$
$$y^2 + 9 = 0 \qquad \text{or } y - 1 = 0$$
$$y^2 = -9 \qquad \text{or} \quad y = 1$$
$$y = \pm\sqrt{-9}$$
$$y = \pm 3i$$
The solutions are 1, $-3i$, and $3i$.

41. $2x^{2/3} + 3x^{1/3} - 2 = 0$
Let $y = x^{1/3}$. Then $y^2 = x^{2/3}$ and
$$2y^2 + 3y - 2 = 0$$
$$(2y-1)(y+2) = 0$$
$$y = \frac{1}{2} \quad \text{or} \quad y = -2$$
$$x^{1/3} = \frac{1}{2} \quad \text{or } x^{1/3} = -2$$
$$x = \frac{1}{8} \quad \text{or} \quad x = -8$$

The solutions are -8 and $\frac{1}{8}$.

43. $x^{-2} - x^{-1} - 6 = 0$
Let $y = x^{-1}$. Then $y^2 = x^{-2}$ and
$$y^2 - y - 6 = 0$$
$$(y-3)(y+2) = 0$$
$$y = 3 \quad \text{or} \quad y = -2$$
$$x^{-1} = 3 \quad \text{or} \quad x^{-1} = -2$$
$$\frac{1}{x} = 3 \quad \text{or} \quad \frac{1}{x} = -2$$
$$x = \frac{1}{3} \quad \text{or} \quad x = -\frac{1}{2}$$
The solutions are $-\frac{1}{2}$ and $\frac{1}{3}$.

45.
$$x - \sqrt{x} = 2$$
$$x - 2 = \sqrt{x}$$
$$(x-2)^2 = x$$
$$x^2 - 4x + 4 = x$$
$$x^2 - 5x + 4 = 0$$
$$(x-4)(x-1) = 0$$
$$x = 4 \text{ or } x = 1 \text{ (discard)}$$
The solution is 4.

47.
$$\frac{x}{x-1} + \frac{1}{x+1} = \frac{2}{x^2-1}$$
$$\frac{x}{x-1} + \frac{1}{x+1} = \frac{2}{(x+1)(x-1)}$$
$$x(x+1) + (x-1) = 2$$
$$x^2 + x + x - 1 = 2$$
$$x^2 + 2x - 3 = 0$$
$$(x+3)(x-1) = 0$$
$$x = -3 \text{ or } x = 1 \text{ (discard)}$$
The solution is -3.

49.
$$p^4 - p^2 - 20 = 0$$
$$(p^2-5)(p^2+4) = 0$$
$$p^2 - 5 = 0 \qquad \text{or } p^2 + 4 = 0$$
$$p^2 = 5 \qquad \text{or} \qquad p^2 = -4$$
$$p = \pm\sqrt{5} \quad \text{or} \qquad p = \pm 2i$$
The solutions are $-\sqrt{5}, \sqrt{5}, -2i$, and $2i$.

51. $(x+3)(x^2-3x+9)=0$

$x+3=0$ or $x^2-3x+9=0$

$x=-3$ or

$x=\dfrac{3\pm\sqrt{(-3)^2-4(1)(9)}}{2(1)}$

$=\dfrac{3\pm\sqrt{-27}}{2}$

$=\dfrac{3\pm 3i\sqrt{3}}{2}$

The solutions are -3, $\dfrac{3+3i\sqrt{3}}{2}$, and

$\dfrac{3-3i\sqrt{3}}{2}$.

53.
$$1=\dfrac{4}{x-7}+\dfrac{5}{(x-7)^2}$$

$(x-7)^2-4(x-7)-5=0$

Let $y=x-7$. Then $y^2=(x-7)^2$ and

$y^2-4y-5=0$

$(y-5)(y+1)=0$

$y=5$ or $y=-1$

$x-7=5$ or $x-7=-1$

$x=12$ or $x=6$

The solutions are 6 and 12.

55.
$$27y^4+15y^2=2$$

$27y^4+15y^2-2=0$

$(9y^2-1)(3y^2+2)=0$

$(3y+1)(3y-1)(3y^2+2)=0$

$y=-\dfrac{1}{3}$ or $y=\dfrac{1}{3}$ or $y^2=-\dfrac{2}{3}$

$y=\pm\sqrt{-\dfrac{2}{3}}$

$y=\pm\dfrac{i\sqrt{6}}{3}$

The solutions are $-\dfrac{1}{3},\dfrac{1}{3},-\dfrac{i\sqrt{6}}{3}$, and $\dfrac{i\sqrt{6}}{3}$.

57. Let $x=$ speed on the first part. Then
$x-1=$ speed on the second part.

$d=rt \Rightarrow t=\dfrac{d}{r}$

$t_{\text{on first part}}+t_{\text{on second part}}=1\dfrac{3}{5}$

$\dfrac{3}{x}+\dfrac{4}{x-1}=\dfrac{8}{5}$

$3\cdot 5(x-1)+4\cdot 5x=8x(x-1)$

$15x-15+20x=8x^2-8x$

$0=8x^2-43x+15$

$0=(8x-3)(x-5)$

$8x-3=0$ or $x-5=0$

$x=\dfrac{3}{8}$ or $x=5$

$x-1=4$

Discard $\dfrac{3}{8}$. Her speeds were 5 mph and 4 mph.

59. Let $x=$ time for hose alone. Then
$x-1=$ time for the inlet pipe alone.

$\dfrac{1}{x}+\dfrac{1}{x-1}=\dfrac{1}{8}$

$8(x-1)+8x=x(x-1)$

$8x-8+8x=x^2-x$

$0=x^2-17x+8$

$x=\dfrac{17\pm\sqrt{(-17)^2-4(1)(8)}}{2(1)}$

$=\dfrac{17\pm\sqrt{257}}{2}$

$x\approx 0.5$ (discard) or $x\approx 16.5$

$x-1\approx 15.5$

Hose: 16.5 hrs; Inlet pipe: 15.5 hrs

61. Let $x=$ original speed. Then
$x+11=$ return speed.

$d=rt \Rightarrow t=\dfrac{d}{r}$

$t_{\text{return}}=t_{\text{original}}-1$

$\dfrac{330}{x+11}=\dfrac{330}{x}-1$

$330x=330(x+11)-x(x+11)$

$330x=330x+3630-x^2-11x$

$x^2+11x-3630=0$

$$x = \frac{-11 \pm \sqrt{(11)^2 - 4(1)(-3630)}}{2(1)}$$

$$= \frac{-11 \pm \sqrt{14,641}}{2}$$

$$= \frac{-11 \pm 121}{2} = 55 \text{ or } -66 \text{ (disregard)}$$

$x + 11 = 55 + 11 = 66$

Original speed: 55 mph
Return speed: 66 mph

63. Let x = time for son alone. Then
$x - 1$ = time for dad alone.

$$\frac{1}{x} + \frac{1}{x-1} = \frac{1}{4}$$

$$4(x-1) + 4x = x(x-1)$$

$$4x - 4 + 4x = x^2 - x$$

$$0 = x^2 - 9x + 4$$

$$x = \frac{9 \pm \sqrt{(-9)^2 - 4(1)(4)}}{2(1)}$$

$$= \frac{9 \pm \sqrt{65}}{2}$$

≈ 0.5 (discard) or 8.5

It takes his son about 8.5 hours.

65. Let x = the number.

$$x(x-4) = 96$$

$$x^2 - 4x - 96 = 0$$

$$(x-12)(x+8) = 0$$

$$x = 12 \text{ or } x = -8$$

The number is 12 or –8.

67. a. length $= x - 3 - 3 = x - 6 = (x-6)$ cm

b. $V = lwh$

$$300 = (x-6)(x-6) \cdot 3$$

c. $300 = 3(x-6)^2$

$$100 = x^2 - 12x + 36$$

$$0 = x^2 - 12x - 64$$

$$0 = (x-16)(x+4)$$

$$x = 16 \text{ or } x = -4 \text{ (discard)}$$

The sheet is 16 cm by 16 cm.
Check: $V = 3(x-6)(x-6)$

$$= 3(16-6)(16-6)$$

$$= 3(10)(10)$$

$$= 300 \text{ cubic cm}$$

69. Let x = length of the side of the square.

Area $= x^2$

$$920 = x^2$$

$$\sqrt{920} = x$$

Adding another radial line to a different corner would yield a right triangle with legs r and hypotenuse x.

$$r^2 + r^2 = x^2$$

$$2r^2 = \left(\sqrt{920}\right)^2$$

$$2r^2 = 920$$

$$r^2 = 460$$

$$r = \pm\sqrt{460} = \pm 21.4476$$

Disregard the negative. The smallest radius would be 22 feet.

71. $\dfrac{5x}{3} + 2 \leq 7$

$$\frac{5x}{3} \leq 5$$

$$5x \leq 15$$

$$x \leq 3$$

$(-\infty, 3]$

73.

$$\frac{y-1}{15} > -\frac{2}{5}$$

$$15\left(\frac{y-1}{15}\right) > 15\left(-\frac{2}{5}\right)$$

$$y - 1 > -6$$

$$y > -5$$

$(-5, \infty)$

75. Domain: $\{x \mid x \text{ is a real number}\}$ or $(-\infty, \infty)$
Range: $\{y \mid y \text{ is a real number}\}$ or $(-\infty, \infty)$
It is a function.

77. Domain: $\{x \mid x \text{ is a real number}\}$ or $(-\infty, \infty)$
Range: $\{y \mid y \geq -1\}$ or $[-1, \infty)$
It is a function.

79.
$$y^3 + 9y - y^2 - 9 = 0$$
$$y(y^2 + 9) - (y^2 + 9) = 0$$
$$(y - 1)(y^2 + 9) = 0$$
$$y - 1 = 0 \quad \text{or} \quad y^2 + 9 = 0$$
$$y = 1 \qquad\qquad y^2 = -9$$
$$y = \pm\sqrt{-9} = \pm 3i$$

The solutions are 1, $3i$, and $-3i$.

81.
$$x^{-2} - x^{-1} - 6 = 0$$
$$1 - x - 6x^2 = 0$$
$$(1 - 3x)(1 + 2x) = 0$$
$$1 - 3x = 0 \quad \text{or} \quad 1 + 2x = 0$$
$$1 = 3x \qquad\qquad 2x = -1$$
$$\frac{1}{3} = x \qquad\qquad x = -\frac{1}{2}$$

The solutions are $\dfrac{1}{3}$ and $-\dfrac{1}{2}$.

83.
$$2x^3 = -54$$
$$x^3 = -27$$
$$x^3 + 27 = 0$$
$$(x + 3)(x^2 - 3x + 9) = 0$$
$$x + 3 = 0 \quad \text{or} \quad x^2 - 3x + 9 = 0$$
$$x = -3$$
$$x = \frac{-(-3) \pm \sqrt{(-3)^2 - 4(1)(9)}}{2(1)}$$
$$x = \frac{3 \pm \sqrt{9 - 36}}{2} = \frac{3 \pm \sqrt{-27}}{2}$$
$$x = \frac{3 \pm 3i\sqrt{3}}{2}$$

The solutions are -3, $\dfrac{3 + 3i\sqrt{3}}{2}$, and $\dfrac{3 - 3i\sqrt{3}}{2}$.

85. Answers may vary

87. a. Let x = Bourdais's fastest lap speed and $x + 0.55$ = Pagenaud's fastest lap speed.

Using $t = \dfrac{d}{r}$, we have
$$t_{\text{Bourdais}} = t_{\text{Pagenaud}} + 0.25$$
$$\frac{10{,}391}{x} = \frac{10{,}391}{x + 0.55} + 0.25$$
$$10{,}391(x + 0.55) = 10{,}391x + 0.25x(x + 0.55)$$
$$10{,}391x + 5715.05 = 10{,}391x + 0.25x^2 + 0.1375x$$
$$0 = 0.25x^2 + 0.1375x - 5715.05$$

$$x = \frac{-0.1375 \pm \sqrt{(0.1375)^2 - 4(0.25)(-5715.05)}}{2(0.25)}$$

Using the positive square root, $x \approx 150.92$ feet per second.

b. $\quad x + 0.55 = 150.92 + 0.55$

$\qquad\qquad = 151.47$ feet per second

c. $\quad 5280$ ft = 1 mile, and 3600 sec = 1 hr.

Bourdais: $\dfrac{150.92 \text{ ft}}{\text{sec}} \cdot \dfrac{3600 \text{ sec}}{\text{hr}} \cdot \dfrac{1 \text{ mile}}{5280 \text{ ft}} \approx 102.9$ mph

Fernandez: $\dfrac{151.47 \text{ ft}}{\text{sec}} \cdot \dfrac{3600 \text{ sec}}{\text{hr}} \cdot \dfrac{1 \text{ mile}}{5280 \text{ ft}} \approx 103.3$ mph

Integrated Review

1. $x^2 - 10 = 0$

$\qquad x^2 = 10$

$\qquad x = \pm\sqrt{10}$

2. $x^2 - 14 = 0$

$\qquad x^2 = 14$

$\qquad x = \pm\sqrt{14}$

3. $(x-1)^2 = 8$

$\qquad x - 1 = \pm\sqrt{8}$

$\qquad x - 1 = \pm 2\sqrt{2}$

$\qquad x = 1 \pm 2\sqrt{2}$

4. $(x+5)^2 = 12$

$\qquad x + 5 = \pm\sqrt{12}$

$\qquad x + 5 = \pm 2\sqrt{3}$

$\qquad x = -5 \pm 2\sqrt{3}$

5. $\qquad x^2 + 2x - 12 = 0$

$\qquad x^2 + 2x + \left(\dfrac{2}{2}\right)^2 = 12 + 1$

$\qquad x^2 + 2x + 1 = 13$

$\qquad (x+1)^2 = 13$

$\qquad x + 1 = \pm\sqrt{13}$

$\qquad x = -1 \pm \sqrt{13}$

6. $x^2 - 12x + 11 = 0$

$$x^2 - 12x + \left(\frac{-12}{2}\right)^2 = -11 + 36$$

$$x^2 - 12x + 36 = 25$$

$$(x-6)^2 = \pm\sqrt{25}$$

$$x - 6 = \pm 5$$

$$x = 6 \pm 5$$

$$x = 1 \text{ or } x = 11$$

7.
$$3x^2 + 3x = 5$$

$$x^2 + x = \frac{5}{3}$$

$$x^2 + x + \left(\frac{1}{2}\right)^2 = \frac{5}{3} + \frac{1}{4}$$

$$x^2 + x + \frac{1}{4} = \frac{23}{12}$$

$$\left(x + \frac{1}{2}\right)^2 = \frac{23}{12}$$

$$x + \frac{1}{2} = \pm\sqrt{\frac{23}{12}}$$

$$x + \frac{1}{2} = \pm\frac{\sqrt{23}}{2\sqrt{3}}$$

$$x + \frac{1}{2} = \pm\frac{\sqrt{23}\cdot\sqrt{3}}{2\sqrt{3}\cdot\sqrt{3}}$$

$$x + \frac{1}{2} = \pm\frac{\sqrt{69}}{6}$$

$$x = -\frac{1}{2} \pm \frac{\sqrt{69}}{6} = \frac{-3 \pm \sqrt{69}}{6}$$

8. $16y^2 + 16y = 1$

$$y^2 + y = \frac{1}{16}$$

$$y^2 + y + \left(\frac{1}{2}\right)^2 = \frac{1}{16} + \frac{1}{4}$$

$$y^2 + y + \frac{1}{4} = \frac{5}{16}$$

$$\left(y + \frac{1}{2}\right)^2 = \frac{5}{16}$$

$$y + \frac{1}{2} = \pm\sqrt{\frac{5}{16}}$$

$$y + \frac{1}{2} = \pm\frac{\sqrt{5}}{4}$$

$$y = -\frac{1}{2} \pm \frac{\sqrt{5}}{4} = \frac{-2 \pm \sqrt{5}}{4}$$

9. $2x^2 - 4x + 1 = 0$

$a = 2, b = -4, c = 1$

$$x = \frac{4 \pm \sqrt{(-4)^2 - 4(2)(1)}}{2(2)}$$

$$= \frac{4 \pm \sqrt{8}}{4}$$

$$= \frac{4 \pm 2\sqrt{2}}{4} = \frac{2 \pm \sqrt{2}}{2}$$

10. $\frac{1}{2}x^2 + 3x + 2 = 0$

$$x^2 + 6x + 4 = 0$$

$a = 1, b = 6, c = 4$

$$x = \frac{-6 \pm \sqrt{(6)^2 - 4(1)(4)}}{2(1)}$$

$$= \frac{-6 \pm \sqrt{20}}{2}$$

$$= \frac{-6 \pm 2\sqrt{5}}{2} = -3 \pm \sqrt{5}$$

11. $x^2 + 4x = -7$

$$x^2 + 4x + 7 = 0$$

$a = 1, b = 4, c = 7$

$$x = \frac{-4 \pm \sqrt{(4)^2 - 4(1)(7)}}{2(1)}$$

$$= \frac{-4 \pm \sqrt{-12}}{2}$$

$$= \frac{-4 \pm i\sqrt{4\cdot 3}}{2}$$

$$= \frac{-4 \pm 2i\sqrt{3}}{2} = -2 \pm i\sqrt{3}$$

12. $x^2 + x = -3$

$$x^2 + x + 3 = 0$$

$a = 1, b = 1, c = 3$

$$x = \frac{-1 \pm \sqrt{(1)^2 - 4(1)(3)}}{2(1)}$$

$$= \frac{-1 \pm \sqrt{-11}}{2}$$

$$= \frac{-1 \pm i\sqrt{11}}{2}$$

13. $x^2 + 3x + 6 = 0$
$a = 1, b = 3, c = 6$
$$x = \frac{-3 \pm \sqrt{(3)^2 - 4(1)(6)}}{2(1)}$$
$$= \frac{-3 \pm \sqrt{-15}}{2}$$
$$= \frac{-3 \pm i\sqrt{15}}{2}$$

14. $2x^2 + 18 = 0$
$$2x^2 = -18$$
$$x^2 = -9$$
$$x = \pm\sqrt{-9}$$
$$x = \pm 3i$$

15. $x^2 + 17x = 0$
$x(x + 17) = 0$
$x = 0$ or $x + 17 = 0$
$\phantom{x = 0 \text{ or } x + 17} x = -17$
$x = 0, -17$

16. $4x^2 - 2x - 3 = 0$
$a = 4, b = -2, c = -3$
$$x = \frac{2 \pm \sqrt{(-2)^2 - 4(4)(-3)}}{2(4)}$$
$$= \frac{2 \pm \sqrt{52}}{8}$$
$$= \frac{2 \pm 2\sqrt{13}}{8}$$
$$= \frac{1 \pm \sqrt{13}}{4}$$

17. $(x - 2)^2 = 27$
$$x - 2 = \pm\sqrt{27}$$
$$x - 2 = \pm 3\sqrt{3}$$
$$x = 2 \pm 3\sqrt{3}$$

18. $\frac{1}{2}x^2 - 2x + \frac{1}{2} = 0$
$$x^2 - 4x + 1 = 0$$
$$x^2 - 4x + \left(\frac{-4}{2}\right)^2 = -1 + 4$$
$$x^2 - 4x + 4 = 3$$
$$(x - 2)^2 = 3$$
$$x - 2 = \pm\sqrt{3}$$
$$x = 2 \pm \sqrt{3}$$

19. $3x^2 + 2x = 8$
$3x^2 + 2x - 8 = 0$
$(3x - 4)(x + 2) = 0$
$3x - 4 = 0$ or $x + 2 = 0$
$x = \frac{4}{3}$ or $\quad x = -2$

20. $2x^2 = -5x - 1$
$2x^2 + 5x + 1 = 0$
$a = 2, b = 5, c = 1$
$$x = \frac{-5 \pm \sqrt{(5)^2 - 4(2)(1)}}{2(2)}$$
$$= \frac{-5 \pm \sqrt{17}}{4}$$

21. $x(x - 2) = 5$
$$x^2 - 2x = 5$$
$$x^2 - 2x + \left(\frac{-2}{2}\right)^2 = 5 + 1$$
$$x^2 - 2x + 1 = 6$$
$$(x - 1)^2 = 6$$
$$x - 1 = \pm\sqrt{6}$$
$$x = 1 \pm \sqrt{6}$$

22. $x^2 - 31 = 0$
$$x^2 = 31$$
$$x = \pm\sqrt{31}$$

23. $5x^2 - 55 = 0$
$$5x^2 = 55$$
$$x^2 = 11$$
$$x = \pm\sqrt{11}$$

24. $5x^2 + 55 = 0$

$$5x^2 = -55$$
$$x^2 = -11$$
$$x = \pm\sqrt{-11}$$
$$x = \pm i\sqrt{11}$$

25.
$$x(x+5) = 66$$
$$x^2 + 5x = 66$$
$$x^2 + 5x - 66 = 0$$
$$(x+11)(x-6) = 0$$
$$x+11 = 0 \quad \text{or} \quad x-6 = 0$$
$$x = -11 \quad \text{or} \quad x = 6$$

26. $5x^2 + 6x - 2 = 0$

$a = 5, b = 6, c = -2$

$$x = \frac{-6 \pm \sqrt{(6)^2 - 4(5)(-2)}}{2(5)}$$
$$= \frac{-6 \pm \sqrt{76}}{10}$$
$$= \frac{-6 \pm \sqrt{4 \cdot 19}}{10}$$
$$= \frac{-6 \pm 2\sqrt{19}}{10}$$
$$= \frac{-3 \pm \sqrt{19}}{5}$$

27.
$$2x^2 + 3x = 1$$
$$2x^2 + 3x - 1 = 0$$
$$a = 2, b = 3, c = -1$$
$$x = \frac{-3 \pm \sqrt{(3)^2 - 4(2)(-1)}}{2(2)}$$
$$= \frac{-3 \pm \sqrt{17}}{4}$$

28. $a^2 + b^2 = c^2$

$$x^2 + x^2 = 20^2$$
$$2x^2 = 400$$
$$x^2 = 200$$
$$x = \pm\sqrt{200}$$
$$= \pm 10\sqrt{2} \approx 14.1421$$

Disregard the negative. A side of the room is $10\sqrt{2}$ feet ≈ 14.1 feet.

29. Let x = time for Jack alone. Then
$x - 2$ = time for Lucy alone.

$$\frac{1}{x} + \frac{1}{x-2} = \frac{1}{4}$$
$$4(x-2) + 4x = x(x-2)$$
$$4x - 8 + 4x = x^2 - 2x$$
$$0 = x^2 - 10x + 8$$
$$x = \frac{10 \pm \sqrt{(-10)^2 - 4(1)(8)}}{2(1)}$$
$$= \frac{10 \pm \sqrt{68}}{2}$$
$$\approx 9.1 \text{ or } 0.9 \text{ (disregard)}$$
$$x - 2 = 9.1 - 2 = 7.1$$

It would take Jack 9.1 hours and Lucy 7.1 hours.

30. Let x = initial speed on treadmill. Then
$x + 1$ = speed increased.

$$t_{\text{initial}} + t_{\text{increased}} = \frac{4}{3}$$
$$\frac{5}{x} + \frac{2}{x+1} = \frac{4}{3}$$
$$5 \cdot 3(x+1) + 2 \cdot 3x = 4x(x+1)$$
$$15x + 15 + 6x = 4x^2 + 4x$$
$$0 = 4x^2 - 17x - 15$$
$$0 = (4x+3)(x-5)$$
$$x = -\frac{4}{3} \text{ (disregard) or } x = 5$$
$$x + 1 = 5 + 1 = 6$$

Initial speed: 5 mph
Increased speed: 6 mph

Section 8.4

Practice Exercises

1. $(x-4)(x+3) > 0$

Solve the related equation, $(x-4)(x+3) = 0$.
$$(x-4)(x+3) = 0$$
$$x - 4 = 0 \quad \text{or} \quad x + 3 = 0$$
$$x = 4 \qquad\qquad x = -3$$

Test points in the three regions separated by $x = 4$ and $x = -3$.

Region	Test Point	$(x-4)(x+3)>0$ Result
$A: (-\infty, -3)$	-4	$(-8)(-1)>0$ True
$B: (-3, 4)$	0	$(-4)(3)>0$ False
$C: (4, \infty)$	5	$(1)(8)>0$ True

The points in regions A and C satisfy the inequality. The numbers 4 and -3 are not included in the solution since the inequality symbol is $>$. The solution set is $(-\infty, -3) \cup (4, \infty)$.

2. $x^2 - 8x \leq 0$

Solve the related equation, $x^2 - 8x = 0$.

$x^2 - 8x = 0$
$x(x-8) = 0$
$x = 0 \quad \text{or} \quad x - 8 = 0$
$\qquad\qquad\qquad x = 8$

The numbers 0 and 8 separate the number line into three regions, A, B, and C. Test a point in each region.

Region	Test Point	$x^2 - 8x \leq 0$ Result
$A: (-\infty, 0]$	-1	$1 + 8 \leq 0$ False
$B: [0, 8]$	1	$1 - 8 \leq 0$ True
$C: [8, \infty)$	9	$81 - 72 \leq 0$ False

Values in region B satisfy the inequality. The numbers 0 and 8 are included in the solution since the inequality symbol is $\leq$. The solution set is $[0, 8]$.

3. $(x+3)(x-2)(x+1) \leq 0$

Solve $(x+3)(x-2)(x+1) = 0$ by inspection.
$x = -3 \quad \text{or} \quad x = 2 \quad \text{or} \quad x = -1$
These separate the number line into four regions. Test points in each region.

Region	Test Point	$(x+3)(x-2)(x+1) \leq 0$ Result
$A: (-\infty, -3]$	-4	$(-1)(-6)(-3) \leq 0$ True
$B: [-3, -1]$	-2	$(1)(-4)(-1) \leq 0$ False
$C: [-1, 2]$	0	$(3)(-2)(1) \leq 0$ True
$D: [2, \infty)$	3	$(6)(1)(4) \leq 0$ False

The solution set is $(-\infty, -3] \cup [-1, 2]$. We include the numbers -3, -1, and 2 because the inequality symbol is $\leq$.

4. $\dfrac{x-5}{x+4} \leq 0$

$x + 4 = 0$
$\quad x = -4$

$x = -4$ makes the denominator zero. Solve the related equation $\dfrac{x-5}{x+4} = 0$.

$\dfrac{x-5}{x+4} = 0$
$x - 5 = 0$
$\quad x = 5$

Test points in the three regions separated by $x = -4$ and $x = 5$.

Region	Test Point	$\dfrac{x-5}{x+4} \leq 0$ Result
$A: (-\infty, -4)$	-5	$\dfrac{-10}{-1} \leq 0$ False
$B: (-4, 5]$	0	$\dfrac{-5}{4} \leq 0$ True
$C: [5, \infty)$	6	$\dfrac{1}{10} \leq 0$ False

The solution set is $(-4, 5]$. The interval includes 5 because 5 satisfies the original inequality. This interval does not include -4, because -4 would make the denominator zero.

5. $\dfrac{7}{x+3} < 5$

$x+3 = 0$

$x = -3$

$x = -3$ makes the denominator zero.

Solve $\dfrac{7}{x+3} = 5$.

$(x+3)\left(\dfrac{7}{x+3}\right) = 5(x+3)$

$7 = 5x + 15$

$-8 = 5x$

$-\dfrac{8}{5} = x$

We use these two solutions to divide the number line into three regions and choose test points.

Region	Test Point	$\dfrac{7}{x+3} < 5$ Result
$A: (-\infty, -3)$	-4	$\dfrac{7}{-1} < 5$ True
$B: \left(-3, -\dfrac{8}{5}\right)$	-2	$\dfrac{7}{1} < 5$ False
$C: \left(-\dfrac{8}{5}, \infty\right)$	0	$\dfrac{7}{3} < 5$ True

The solution set is $(-\infty, -3) \cup \left(-\dfrac{8}{5}, \infty\right)$.

Vocabulary and Readiness Check

1. $[-7, 3)$

2. $(-1, 5]$

3. $(-\infty, 0]$

4. $(-\infty, -8]$

5. $(-\infty, -12) \cup [-10, \infty)$

6. $(-\infty, -3] \cup (4, \infty)$

Exercise Set 8.4

1. $(x+1)(x+5) > 0$

$x+1 = 0 \quad$ or $\quad x+5 = 0$

$x = -1 \quad$ or $\quad x = -5$

Region	Test Point	$(x+1)(x+5) > 0$ Result
$A: (-\infty, -5)$	-6	$(-5)(-1) > 0$ True
$B: (-5, -1)$	-2	$(-1)(3) > 0$ False
$C: (-1, \infty)$	0	$(1)(5) > 0$ True

Solution: $(-\infty, -5) \cup (-1, \infty)$

3. $(x-3)(x+4) \le 0$

$x-3 = 0 \quad$ or $\quad x+4 = 0$

$x = 3 \quad$ or $\quad x = -4$

Region	Test Point	$(x-3)(x+4) \le 0$ Result
$A: (-\infty, -4]$	-5	$(-8)(-1) \le 0$ False
$B: [-4, 3]$	0	$(-3)(4) \le 0$ True
$C: [3, \infty)$	4	$(1)(8) \le 0$ False

Solution: $[-4, 3]$

5. $x^2 - 7x + 10 \le 0$

$(x-5)(x-2) \le 0$

$x-5 = 0 \quad$ or $\quad x-2 = 0$

$x = 5 \quad$ or $\quad x = 2$

Region	Test Point	$(x-5)(x-2) \le 0$ Result
$A: (-\infty, 2]$	0	$(-5)(-2) \le 0$ False
$B: [2, 5]$	3	$(-2)(1) \le 0$ True
$C: [5, \infty)$	6	$(1)(4) \le 0$ False

Solution: $[2, 5]$

7. $3x^2 + 16 < -5$

$3x^2 + 16x + 5 < 0$

$(3x + 1)(x + 5) < 0$

$3x + 1 = 0$ or $x + 5 = 0$

$x = -\dfrac{1}{3}$ or $x = -5$

Region	Test Point	$(3x + 1)(x + 5) < 0$ Result
$A: (-\infty, -5)$	-6	$(-17)(-1) < 0$ False
$B: \left(-5, -\dfrac{1}{3}\right)$	-1	$(-2)(4) < 0$ True
$C: \left(-\dfrac{1}{3}, \infty\right)$	0	$(1)(5) < 0$ False

Solution: $\left(-5, -\dfrac{1}{3}\right)$

9. $(x - 6)(x - 4)(x - 2) > 0$

$x - 6 = 0$ or $x - 4 = 0$ or $x - 2 = 0$

$x = 6$ or $x = 4$ or $x = 2$

Region	Test Point	$(x - 6)(x - 4)(x - 2) > 0$ Result
$A: (-\infty, 2)$	0	$(-6)(-4)(-2) > 0$ False
$B: (2, 4)$	3	$(-3)(-1)(1) > 0$ True
$C: (4, 6)$	5	$(-1)(1)(3) > 0$ False
$D: (6, \infty)$	7	$(1)(3)(5) > 0$ True

Solution: $(2, 4) \cup (6, \infty)$

11. $x(x-1)(x+4) \le 0$

$x = 0$ or $x - 1 = 0$ or $x + 4 = 0$

$x = 1$ or $x = -4$

Region	Test Point	$x(x-1)(x+4) \le 0$ Result
$A: (-\infty, -4]$	-5	$-5(-6)(-1) \le 0$ True
$B: [-4, 0]$	-1	$-1(-2)(3) \le 0$ False
$C: [0, 1]$	$\dfrac{1}{2}$	$\dfrac{1}{2}\left(-\dfrac{1}{2}\right)\left(\dfrac{9}{2}\right) \le 0$ True
$D: [1, \infty)$	2	$2(1)(6) \le 0$ False

Solution: $(-\infty, -4] \cup [0, 1]$

13. $(x^2 - 9)(x^2 - 4) > 0$

$(x+3)(x-3)(x+2)(x-2) > 0$

$x + 3 = 0$ or $x - 3 = 0$ or $x + 2 = 0$ or $x - 2 = 0$

$x = -3$ or $x = 3$ or $x = -2$ or $x = 2$

Region	Test Point	$(x+3)(x-3)(x+2)(x-2) > 0$ Result
$A: (-\infty, -3)$	-4	$(-1)(-7)(-2)(-6) > 0$ True
$B: (-3, -2)$	$-\dfrac{5}{2}$	$\left(\dfrac{1}{2}\right)\left(-\dfrac{11}{2}\right)\left(-\dfrac{1}{2}\right)\left(-\dfrac{9}{2}\right) > 0$ False
$C: (-2, 2)$	0	$(3)(-3)(2)(-2) > 0$ True
$D: (2, 3)$	$\dfrac{5}{2}$	$\left(\dfrac{11}{2}\right)\left(-\dfrac{1}{2}\right)\left(\dfrac{9}{2}\right)\left(\dfrac{1}{2}\right) > 0$ False
$E: (3, \infty)$	4	$(7)(1)(6)(2) > 0$ True

Solution: $(-\infty, -3) \cup (-2, 2) \cup (3, \infty)$

15. $\dfrac{x+7}{x-2} < 0$

$x + 7 = 0$ or $x - 2 = 0$

$x = -7$ or $x = 2$

Region	Test Point	$\dfrac{x+7}{x-2} < 0$ False
$A: (-\infty, -7)$	-8	$\dfrac{-1}{-10} < 0$ False
$B: (-7, 2)$	0	$\dfrac{7}{-2} < 0$ True
$C: (2, \infty)$	3	$\dfrac{10}{1} < 0$ False

Solution: $(-7, 2)$

17. $\dfrac{5}{x+1} > 0$

$x + 1 = 0$

$x = -1$

Region	Test Point	$\dfrac{5}{x+1} > 0$ Result
$A: (-\infty, -1)$	-2	$\dfrac{5}{-1} > 0$ False
$B: (-1, \infty)$	0	$\dfrac{5}{1} > 0$ True

Solution: $(-1, \infty)$

19. $\dfrac{x+1}{x-4} \geq 0$

$x + 1 = 0$ or $x - 4 = 0$

$x = -1$ or $x = 4$

Region	Test Point	$\dfrac{x+1}{x-4} \geq 0$ Result
$A: (-\infty, -1]$	-2	$\dfrac{-1}{-6} \geq 0$ True
$B: [-1, 4)$	0	$\dfrac{1}{-4} \geq 0$ False
$C: (4, \infty)$	5	$\dfrac{6}{1} \geq 0$ True

Solution: $(-\infty, -1] \cup (4, \infty)$

21. $\dfrac{3}{x-2} < 4$

The denominator is equal to 0 when $x - 2 = 0$, or $x = 2$.

$\dfrac{3}{x-2} = 4$

$3 = 4x - 8$

$11 = 4x$

$\dfrac{11}{4} = x$

Region	Test Point	$\dfrac{3}{x-2} < 4$ Result
$A: (-\infty, 2)$	0	$\dfrac{3}{-2} < 4$ True
$B: \left(2, \dfrac{11}{4}\right)$	$\dfrac{5}{2}$	$\dfrac{3}{\frac{1}{2}} = 6 < 4$ False
$C: \left(\dfrac{11}{4}, \infty\right)$	4	$\dfrac{3}{2} < 4$ True

Solution: $(-\infty, 2) \cup \left(\dfrac{11}{4}, \infty\right)$

23. $\dfrac{x^2+6}{5x} \geq 1$

The denominator is equal to 0 when $5x = 0$, or $x = 0$.

$$\frac{x^2+6}{5x} = 1$$
$$x^2 + 6 = 5x$$
$$x^2 - 5x + 6 = 0$$
$$(x-2)(x-3) = 0$$
$$x - 2 = 0 \quad \text{or} \quad x - 3 = 0$$
$$x = 2 \quad \text{or} \quad x = 3$$

Region	Test Point	$\dfrac{x^2+6}{5x} \geq 1$ Result
A: $(-\infty, 0)$	-1	$\dfrac{7}{-5} \geq 1$ False
B: $(0, 2]$	1	$\dfrac{7}{5} \geq 1$ True
C: $[2, 3]$	$\dfrac{5}{2}$	$\dfrac{\frac{49}{4}}{\frac{25}{2}} = \dfrac{49}{50} \geq 1$ False
D: $[3, \infty)$	4	$\dfrac{22}{20} \geq 1$ True

Solution: $(0, 2] \cup [3, \infty)$

25. $(x-8)(x+7) > 0$

$$x - 8 = 0 \quad \text{or} \quad x + 7 = 0$$
$$x = 8 \quad \text{or} \quad x = -7$$

Region	Test Point	$(x-8)(x+7) > 0$ Result
A: $(-\infty, -7)$	-8	$(-16)(-1) > 0$ True
B: $(-7, 8)$	0	$(-8)(7) > 0$ False
C: $(8, \infty)$	9	$(1)(16) > 0$ True

Solution: $(-\infty, -7) \cup (8, \infty)$

27. $(2x-3)(4x+5) \leq 0$

$$2x - 3 = 0 \quad \text{or} \quad 4x + 5 = 0$$
$$x = \frac{3}{2} \quad \text{or} \quad x = -\frac{5}{4}$$

Region	Test Point	$(2x-3)(4x+5) \leq 0$ Result
A: $\left(-\infty, -\dfrac{5}{4}\right]$	-2	$(-7)(-3) \leq 0$ False
B: $\left[-\dfrac{5}{4}, \dfrac{3}{2}\right]$	0	$(-3)(5) \leq 0$ True
C: $\left[\dfrac{3}{2}, \infty\right)$	2	$(1)(13) \leq 0$ False

Solution: $\left[-\dfrac{5}{4}, \dfrac{3}{2}\right]$

29. $x^2 > x$

$$x^2 - x > 0$$
$$x(x-1) > 0$$
$$x = 0 \quad \text{or} \quad x - 1 = 0$$
$$x = 1$$

Region	Test Point	$x(x-1) > 0$ Result
A: $(-\infty, 0)$	-1	$-1(-2) > 0$ True
B: $(0, 1)$	$\dfrac{1}{2}$	$\dfrac{1}{2}\left(-\dfrac{1}{2}\right) > 0$ False
C: $(1, \infty)$	2	$2(1) > 0$ True

Solution: $(-\infty, 0) \cup (1, \infty)$

31. $(2x - 8)(x + 4)(x - 6) \le 0$

$2x - 8 = 0$ or $x + 4 = 0$ or $x - 6 = 0$

$x = 4$ or $x = -4$ or $x = 6$

Region	Test Point	$(2x - 8)(x + 4)(x - 6) \le 0$ Result
A: $(-\infty, -4]$	-5	$(-18)(-1)(-11) \le 0$ True
B: $[-4, 4]$	0	$(-8)(4)(-6) \le 0$ False
C: $[4, 6]$	5	$(2)(9)(-1) \le 0$ True
D: $[6, \infty)$	7	$(6)(11)(1) \le 0$ False

Solution: $(-\infty, -4] \cup [4, 6]$

33. $\qquad 6x^2 - 5x \ge 6$

$6x^2 - 5x - 6 \ge 0$

$(3x + 2)(2x - 3) \ge 0$

$3x + 2 = 0$ or $2x - 3 = 0$

$x = -\dfrac{2}{3}$ or $x = \dfrac{3}{2}$

Region	Test Point	$(3x + 2)(2x - 3) \ge 0$ Result
A: $\left(-\infty, -\dfrac{2}{3}\right]$	-1	$(-1)(-5) \ge 0$ True
B: $\left[-\dfrac{2}{3}, \dfrac{3}{2}\right]$	0	$(2)(-3) \ge 0$ False
C: $\left[\dfrac{3}{2}, \infty\right)$	2	$(8)(1) \ge 0$ True

Solution: $\left(-\infty, -\dfrac{2}{3}\right] \cup \left[\dfrac{3}{2}, \infty\right)$

35. $4x^3 + 16x^2 - 9x - 36 > 0$

$4x^2(x + 4) - 9(x + 4) > 0$

$(x + 4)(4x^2 - 9) > 0$

$(x + 4)(2x + 3)(2x - 3) > 0$

$x + 4 = 0$ or $2x + 3 = 0$ or $2x - 3 = 0$

$x = -4$ or $x = -\dfrac{3}{2}$ or $x = \dfrac{3}{2}$

Region	Test Point	$(x+4)(2x+3)(2x-3) > 0$
$A: (-\infty, -4)$	-5	$(-1)(-7)(-13) > 0$ False
$B: \left(-4, -\dfrac{3}{2}\right)$	-3	$(1)(-3)(-9) > 0$ True
$C: \left(-\dfrac{3}{2}, \dfrac{3}{2}\right)$	0	$(4)(3)(-3) > 0$ False
$D: \left(\dfrac{3}{2}, \infty\right)$	4	$(8)(11)(5) > 0$ True

Solution: $\left(-4, -\dfrac{3}{2}\right) \cup \left(\dfrac{3}{2}, \infty\right)$

37.
$$x^4 - 26x^2 + 25 \geq 0$$
$$(x^2 - 25)(x^2 - 1) \geq 0$$
$$(x+5)(x-5)(x+1)(x-1) \geq 0$$
$$x = -5 \quad \text{or} \quad x = 5 \quad \text{or} \quad x = -1 \quad \text{or} \quad x = 1$$

Region	Test Point	$(x+5)(x-5)(x+1)(x-1) \geq 0$ Result
$A: (-\infty, -5]$	-6	$(-1)(-11)(-5)(-7) \geq 0$ True
$B: [-5, -1]$	-2	$(3)(-7)(-1)(-3) \geq 0$ False
$C: [-1, 1]$	0	$(5)(-5)(1)(-1) \geq 0$ True
$D: [1, 5]$	2	$(7)(-3)(3)(1) \geq 0$ False
$E: [5, \infty)$	6	$(11)(1)(7)(5) \geq 0$ True

Solution: $(-\infty, -5] \cup [-1, 1] \cup [5, \infty)$

39. $(2x - 7)(3x + 5) > 0$

$2x - 7 = 0$ or $3x + 5 = 0$

$x = \dfrac{7}{2}$ or $x = -\dfrac{5}{3}$

Region	Test Point	$(2x - 7)(3x + 5) > 0$
A: $\left(-\infty, -\dfrac{5}{3}\right)$	-2	$(-11)(-1) > 0$ True
B: $\left(-\dfrac{5}{3}, \dfrac{7}{2}\right)$	0	$(-7)(5) > 0$ False
C: $\left(\dfrac{7}{2}, \infty\right)$	4	$(1)(17) > 0$ True

Solution: $\left(-\infty, -\dfrac{5}{3}\right) \cup \left(\dfrac{7}{2}, \infty\right)$

41. $\dfrac{x}{x - 10} < 0$

$x = 0$ or $x - 10 = 0$

$x = 10$

Region	Test Point	$\dfrac{x}{x - 10} < 0$ Result
A: $(-\infty, 0)$	-1	$\dfrac{-1}{-11} < 0$ False
B: $(0, 10)$	5	$\dfrac{5}{-5} < 0$ True
C: $(10, \infty)$	11	$\dfrac{11}{1} < 0$ False

Solution: $(0, 10)$

43. $\dfrac{x - 5}{x + 4} \geq 0$

$x - 5 = 0$ or $x + 4 = 0$

$x = 5$ or $x = -4$

Region	Test Point	$\dfrac{x-5}{x+4} \geq 0$ Result
$A: (-\infty, -4)$	-5	$\dfrac{-10}{-1} \geq 0$ True
$B: (-4, 5]$	0	$\dfrac{-5}{4} \geq 0$ False
$C: [5, \infty)$	6	$\dfrac{1}{10} \geq 0$ True

Solution: $(-\infty, -4) \cup [5, \infty)$

45. $\dfrac{x(x+6)}{(x-7)(x+1)} \geq 0$

$x = 0$ or $x + 6 = 0$ or $x - 7 = 0$ or $x + 1 = 0$
$\phantom{x = 0 \text{ or }} x = -6$ or $x = 7$ or $x = -1$

Region	Test Point	$\dfrac{x(x+6)}{(x-7)(x+1)} \geq 0$ Result
$A: (-\infty, -6]$	-7	$\dfrac{-7(-1)}{(-14)(-6)} \geq 0$ True
$B: [-6, -1)$	-3	$\dfrac{-3(3)}{(-10)(-2)} \geq 0$ False
$C: (-1, 0]$	$-\dfrac{1}{2}$	$\dfrac{-\frac{1}{2}\left(\frac{11}{2}\right)}{\left(-\frac{15}{2}\right)\left(\frac{1}{2}\right)} \geq 0$ True
$D: [0, 7)$	2	$\dfrac{2(8)}{(-5)(3)} \geq 0$ False
$E: (7, \infty)$	8	$\dfrac{8(14)}{(1)(9)} \geq 0$ True

Solution: $(-\infty, -6] \cup (-1, 0] \cup (7, \infty)$

47. $\dfrac{-1}{x-1} > -1$

The denominator is equal to 0 when $x - 1 = 0$, or $x = 1$.

$$\dfrac{-1}{x-1} = -1$$
$$-1 = -1(x-1)$$
$$-1 = -x + 1$$
$$x = 2$$

Region	Test Point	$\dfrac{-1}{x-1} > -1$ Result
A: $(-\infty, 1)$	0	$\dfrac{-1}{-1} > -1$ True
B: $(1, 2)$	$\dfrac{3}{2}$	$\dfrac{-1}{\frac{1}{2}} = -2 > -1$ False
C: $(2, \infty)$	3	$\dfrac{-1}{2} > -1$ True

Solution: $(-\infty, 1) \cup (2, \infty)$

49. $\dfrac{x}{x+4} \le 2$

The denominator is equal to 0 when $x + 4 = 0$, or $x = -4$.

$$\dfrac{x}{x+4} = 2$$
$$x = 2x + 8$$
$$-x = 8$$
$$x = -8$$

Region	Test Point	$\dfrac{x}{x+4} \le 2$ Result
A: $(-\infty, -8]$	-9	$\dfrac{-9}{-5} \le 2$ True
B: $[-8, -4)$	-6	$\dfrac{-6}{-2} \le 2$ False
C: $(-4, \infty)$	0	$\dfrac{0}{4} \le 2$ True

Solution: $(-\infty, -8] \cup (-4, \infty)$

51. $\dfrac{z}{z-5} \geq 2z$

The denominator is equal to 0 when $z - 5 = 0$, or $z = 5$.

$$\dfrac{z}{z-5} = 2z$$
$$z = 2z(z-5)$$
$$z = 2z^2 - 10z$$
$$0 = 2z^2 - 11z$$
$$0 = z(2z-11)$$
$$z = 0 \quad \text{or} \quad 2z - 11 = 0$$
$$z = \dfrac{11}{2}$$

Region	Test Point	$\dfrac{z}{z-5} \geq 2z$ Result
A: $(-\infty, 0]$	-1	$\dfrac{-1}{-6} \geq -2$ True
B: $[0, 5)$	1	$\dfrac{1}{-4} \geq 2$ False
C: $\left(5, \dfrac{11}{2}\right]$	$\dfrac{21}{4}$	$\dfrac{\left(\frac{21}{4}\right)}{\left(\frac{1}{4}\right)} \geq \dfrac{21}{2}$ $21 \geq \dfrac{21}{2}$ True
D: $\left[\dfrac{11}{2}, \infty\right)$	6	$\dfrac{6}{1} \geq 12$ False

Solution: $(-\infty, 0] \cup \left(5, \dfrac{11}{2}\right]$

53. $\dfrac{(x+1)^2}{5x} > 0$

The denominator is equal to 0 when $5x = 0$, or $x = 0$.

$$\dfrac{(x+1)^2}{5x} = 0$$
$$(x+1)^2 = 0$$
$$x + 1 = 0$$
$$x = -1$$

Region	Test Point	$\dfrac{(x+1)^2}{5x} > 0$ Result
A: $(-\infty, -1)$	-2	$\dfrac{1}{-10} > 0$ False
B: $(-1, 0)$	$-\dfrac{1}{2}$	$\dfrac{\left(\frac{1}{4}\right)}{\left(-\frac{5}{2}\right)} > 0$ False
C: $(0, \infty)$	1	$\dfrac{4}{5} > 0$ True

Solution: $(0, \infty)$

55. $g(x) = |x| + 2$

57. $F(x) = |x| - 1$

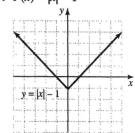

59. $F(x) = x^2 - 3$

61. $H(x) = x^2 + 1$

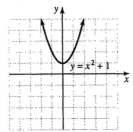

63. Answers may vary

65. Let x = the number. Then

$\dfrac{1}{x}$ = the reciprocal of the number.

$$x - \frac{1}{x} < 0$$

$$\frac{x^2 - 1}{x} < 0$$

$$\frac{(x+1)(x-1)}{x} < 0$$

$$x + 1 = 0 \quad \text{or} \quad x - 1 = 0 \quad \text{or} \quad x = 0$$
$$x = -1 \quad \text{or} \qquad x = 1$$

Region	Test Point	$\dfrac{(x+1)(x-1)}{x} < 0$ Result
$A: (-\infty, -1)$	-2	$\dfrac{(-1)(-3)}{-2} < 0$ True
$B: (-1, 0)$	$-\dfrac{1}{2}$	$\dfrac{\left(\frac{1}{2}\right)\left(-\frac{3}{2}\right)}{\left(-\frac{1}{2}\right)} < 0$ False
$C: (0, 1)$	$\dfrac{1}{2}$	$\dfrac{\left(\frac{3}{2}\right)\left(-\frac{1}{2}\right)}{\left(\frac{1}{2}\right)} < 0$ True
$D: (1, \infty)$	2	$\dfrac{(3)(1)}{2} < 0$ False

Any number less than -1 or between 0 and 1 and its reciprocal satisfy the conditions.

67. $P(x) = -2x^2 + 26x - 44$

$$-2x^2 + 26x - 44 > 0$$
$$-2(x^2 + 13x - 22) > 0$$
$$-2(x - 11)(x - 2) > 0$$
$$x - 11 = 0 \quad \text{or} \quad x - 2 = 0$$
$$x = 11 \quad \text{or} \qquad x = 2$$

Region	Test Point	$-2(x-11)(x-2) > 0$ Result
$A: (0, 2)$	1	$-2(-10)(-3) > 0$ False
$B: (2, 11)$	3	$-2(-8)(1) > 0$ True
$C: (11, \infty)$	12	$-2(1)(10) > 0$ False

The company makes a profit when x is between 2 and 11.

69.

71.

The Bigger Picture

1. $|x - 8| = |2x + 1|$

$x - 8 = 2x + 1 \quad \text{or} \quad x - 8 = -(2x + 1)$
$-9 = x \qquad\qquad x - 8 = -2x - 1$
$\qquad\qquad\qquad\qquad 3x = 7$
$\qquad\qquad\qquad\qquad x = \dfrac{7}{3}$

2. $0 < -x + 7 < 3$
$-7 < -x < -4$
$7 > x > 4$
$4 < x < 7$
Solution: (4, 7)

3. $\sqrt{3x-11}+3=x$

$\sqrt{3x-11}=x-3$

$3x-11=(x-3)^2$

$3x-11=x^2-6x+9$

$0=x^2-9x+20$

$0=(x-4)(x-5)$

$x-4=0$ or $x-5=0$

$x=4$ $x=5$

The solutions are 4 and 5.

4. $x(3x+1)=1$

$3x^2+x-1=0$

$a=3, b=1, c=-1$

$x=\dfrac{-1\pm\sqrt{1^2-4(3)(-1)}}{2(3)}$

$=\dfrac{-1\pm\sqrt{1+12}}{6}$

$=\dfrac{-1\pm\sqrt{13}}{6}$

The solutions are $\dfrac{-1+\sqrt{13}}{6}$ and $\dfrac{-1-\sqrt{13}}{6}$.

5. $\dfrac{x+2}{x-7}\le 0$

$x-7=0$, so $x=7$ makes the denominator 0.

$\dfrac{x+2}{x-7}=0$

$x+2=0$

$x=-2$

Region	Test Point	$\dfrac{x+2}{x-7}\le 0$ Result
A: $(-\infty,-2]$	-3	$\dfrac{-1}{-10}\le 0$ False
B: $[-2,7)$	0	$\dfrac{2}{-7}\le 0$
C: $(7,\infty)$	8	$\dfrac{10}{1}\le 0$ False

Solution: $[-2, 7)$

6. $x(x-6)+4=x^2-2(3-x)$

$x^2-6x+4=x^2-6+2x$

$-6x+4=-6+2x$

$10=8x$

$\dfrac{5}{4}=x$

The solution is $\dfrac{5}{4}$.

7. $x(5x-36)=-7$

$5x^2-36x+7=0$

$a=5, b=-36, c=7$

$x=\dfrac{-(-36)\pm\sqrt{(-36)^2-4(5)(7)}}{2(5)}$

$=\dfrac{36\pm\sqrt{1156}}{10}$

$=\dfrac{36\pm34}{10}$

$x=\dfrac{36+34}{10}=\dfrac{70}{10}=7$ or $x=\dfrac{36-34}{10}=\dfrac{2}{10}=\dfrac{1}{5}$

The solutions are 7 and $\dfrac{1}{5}$.

8. $2x^2-4\ge 7x$

Solve $2x^2-4=7x$.

$2x^2-7x-4=0$

$(2x+1)(x-4)=0$

$2x+1=0$ or $x-4=0$

$2x=-1$ $x=4$

$x=-\dfrac{1}{2}$

Region	Test Point	$2x^2-4\ge 7x$ Result
A: $\left(-\infty,-\dfrac{1}{2}\right]$	-1	$2-4\ge-7$ True
B: $\left[-\dfrac{1}{2},4\right]$	0	$-4\ge 0$ False
C: $[4,\infty)$	5	$50-4\ge 35$ True

Solution: $\left(-\infty,-\dfrac{1}{2}\right]\cup[4,\infty)$

9. $\left|\dfrac{x-7}{3}\right| > 5$

$\dfrac{x-7}{3} > 5 \quad$ or $\quad \dfrac{x-7}{3} < -5$

$x - 7 > 15 \quad$ or $\quad x - 7 < -15$

$x > 22 \quad$ or $\quad x < -8$

Solution: $(-\infty, -8) \cup (22, \infty)$

10. $2(x-5)+4 < 1+7(x-5)-x$

$2x - 10 + 4 < 1 + 7x - 35 - x$

$2x - 6 < 6x - 34$

$28 < 4x$

$7 < x$

Solution: $(7, \infty)$

Section 8.5

Practice Exercises

1. $f(x) = x^2$ and $g(x) = x^2 - 4$

Construct a table of values for $f(x)$ and $g(x)$.

x	$f(x) = x^2$	$g(x) = x^2 - 4$
-2	4	0
-1	1	-3
0	0	-4
1	1	-3
2	4	0

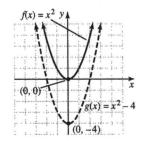

2. a. $f(x) = x^2 - 5$

The graph of $f(x)$ is obtained by shifting the graph of $y = x^2$ downward 5 units.

b. $g(x) = x^2 + 3$

The graph of $g(x)$ is obtained by shifting the graph of $y = x^2$ upward 3 units.

3. $f(x) = x^2$ and $g(x) = (x+6)^2$

Plot points. Notice that the graph of $g(x)$ is the graph of $f(x)$ shifted 6 units to the left.

x	$f(x) = x^2$	x	$g(x) = (x+6)^2$
-2	4	-8	4
-1	1	-7	1
0	0	-6	0
1	1	-5	1
2	4	-4	4

4. a. $G(x) = (x+4)^2$

The graph of $G(x)$ is obtained by shifting the graph of $y = x^2$ to the left 4 units.

b. $H(x) = (x-7)^2$

The graph of $H(x)$ is obtained by shifting the graph of $y = x^2$ to the right 7 units.

5. $f(x) = (x+2)^2 + 2$

The graph of $f(x)$ is the graph of $y = x^2$ shifted 2 units to the left and 2 units upward. The vertex is then $(-2, 2)$, and the axis of symmetry is $x = -2$.

x	$f(x) = (x+2)^2 + 2$
−4	6
−3	3
−1	3
0	6

6. $f(x) = x^2$, $g(x) = 4x^2$, and $h(x) = \dfrac{1}{4}x^2$

Comparing tables of values, we see that for each x-value, the corresponding value of $g(x)$ is four times that of $f(x)$. Similarly, the value of $h(x)$ is one quarter the value of $f(x)$.

x	$f(x) = x^2$	$g(x) = 4x^2$	$h(x) = \frac{1}{4}x^2$
−2	4	16	1
−1	1	4	$\frac{1}{4}$
0	0	0	0
1	1	4	$\frac{1}{4}$
2	4	16	1

7. $f(x) = -\dfrac{1}{2}x^2$

Because $a = -\dfrac{1}{2}$, a negative value, this parabola opens downward. Since $\left| -\dfrac{1}{2} \right| = \dfrac{1}{2} < 1$, the parabola is wider than the graph of $y = x^2$. The vertex is $(0, 0)$, and the axis of symmetry is the y-axis.

x	$f(x) = -\frac{1}{2}x^2$
−2	−2
−1	$-\frac{1}{2}$
0	0
1	$-\frac{1}{2}$
2	−2

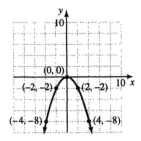

8. $h(x) = \dfrac{1}{3}(x-4)^2 - 3$

This graph is the same as $y = x^2$ shifted 4 units to the right and 3 units downward, and it is wider because a is $\dfrac{1}{3}$. The vertex is $(4, -3)$, and the axis of symmetry is $x = 4$.

x	$h(x) = \frac{1}{3}(x-4)^2 - 3$
2	$-\frac{5}{3}$
3	$-\frac{8}{3}$
4	-3
5	$-\frac{8}{3}$
6	$-\frac{5}{3}$

Graphing Calculator Explorations

1.

2.

3.

4.

5.

6.

Vocabulary and Readiness Check

1. A <u>quadratic</u> function is one that can be written in the form $f(x) = ax^2 + bx + c$, $a \neq 0$.

2. The graph of a quadratic function is a <u>parabola</u> opening <u>upward</u> or <u>downward</u>.

3. If $a > 0$, the graph of the quadratic function opens <u>upward</u>.

4. If $a < 0$, the graph of the quadratic function opens <u>downward</u>.

5. The vertex of a parabola is the <u>lowest</u> point if $a > 0$.

6. The vertex of a parabola is the <u>highest</u> point if $a < 0$.

7. $f(x) = x^2$; vertex: $(0, 0)$

8. $f(x) = -5x^2$; vertex: $(0, 0)$

9. $g(x) = (x-2)^2$; vertex: $(2, 0)$

10. $g(x) = (x+5)^2$; vertex: $(-5, 0)$

11. $f(x) = 2x^2 + 3$; vertex: $(0, 3)$

12. $h(x) = x^2 - 1$; vertex: $(0, -1)$

13. $g(x) = (x+1)^2 + 5$; vertex: $(-1, 5)$

14. $h(x) = (x-10)^2 - 7$; vertex: $(10, -7)$

Exercise Set 8.5

1. $f(x) = x^2 - 1$

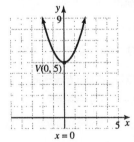

3. $h(x) = x^2 + 5$

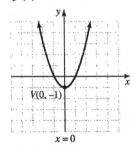

5. $g(x) = x^2 + 7$

7. $f(x) = (x-5)^2$

9. $h(x) = (x+2)^2$

11. $G(x) = (x+3)^2$

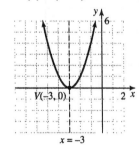

13. $f(x) = (x-2)^2 + 5$

15. $h(x) = (x+1)^2 + 4$

17. $g(x) = (x+2)^2 - 5$

19. $g(x) = -x^2$

21. $h(x) = \frac{1}{3}x^2$

23. $H(x) = 2x^2$

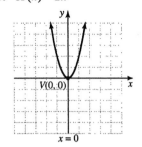

25. $f(x) = 2(x-1)^2 + 3$

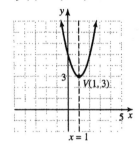

27. $h(x) = -3(x+3)^2 + 1$

29. $H(x) = \frac{1}{2}(x-6)^2 - 3$

31. $f(x) = -(x-2)^2$

33. $F(x) = -x^2 + 4$

35. $F(x) = 2x^2 - 5$

37. $h(x) = (x-6)^2 + 4$

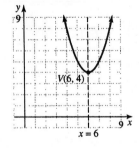

39. $F(x) = \left(x + \dfrac{1}{2}\right)^2 - 2$

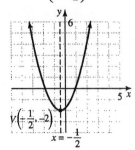

41. $F(x) = \dfrac{3}{2}(x+7)^2 + 1$

43. $f(x) = \dfrac{1}{4}x^2 - 9$

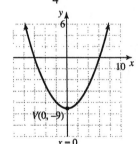

45. $G(x) = 5\left(x + \dfrac{1}{2}\right)^2$

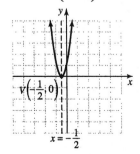

47. $h(x) = -(x-1)^2 - 1$

49. $g(x) = \sqrt{3}(x+5)^2 + \dfrac{3}{4}$

51. $h(x) = 10(x+4)^2 - 6$

53. $f(x) = -2(x-4)^2 + 5$

55. $x^2 + 8x$

$$\left[\frac{1}{2}(8)\right]^2 = (4)^2 = 16$$

$$x^2 + 8x + 16$$

57. $z^2 - 16z$

$$\left[\frac{1}{2}(-16)\right]^2 = (-8)^2 = 64$$

$$z^2 - 16z + 64$$

59. $y^2 + y$

$$\left[\frac{1}{2}(1)\right]^2 = \left(\frac{1}{2}\right)^2 = \frac{1}{4}$$

$$y^2 + y + \frac{1}{4}$$

61.
$$x^2 + 4x = 12$$
$$x^2 + 4x + \left(\frac{4}{2}\right)^2 = 12 + 4$$
$$x^2 + 4x + 4 = 16$$
$$(x+2)^2 = 16$$
$$x + 2 = \pm\sqrt{16}$$
$$x + 2 = \pm 4$$
$$x = -2 \pm 4$$
$$x = -6 \text{ or } 2$$

63.
$$z^2 + 10z - 1 = 0$$
$$z^2 + 10z = 1$$
$$z^2 + 10z + \left(\frac{10}{2}\right)^2 = 1 + 25$$
$$z^2 + 10z + 25 = 26$$
$$(z+5)^2 = 26$$
$$z + 5 = \pm\sqrt{26}$$
$$z = -5 \pm \sqrt{26}$$

65.
$$z^2 - 8z = 2$$
$$z^2 - 8z + \left(\frac{-8}{2}\right)^2 = 2 + 16$$
$$z^2 - 8z + 16 = 18$$
$$(z-4)^2 = 18$$
$$z - 4 = \pm\sqrt{18}$$
$$z - 4 = \pm 3\sqrt{2}$$
$$z = 4 \pm 3\sqrt{2}$$

67. $f(x) = -213(x-0.1)^2 + 3.6$

$a = -213 < 0$, so $f(x)$ opens downward.
The vertex is $(0.1, 3.6)$. The correct answer is **c**.

69. $f(x) = 5(x-2)^2 + 3$

71. $f(x) = 5[x - (-3)]^2 + 6$
$\qquad = 5(x+3)^2 + 6$

73. $y = f(x) + 1$

75. $y = f(x-3)$

77. $y = f(x+2) + 2$

79. $f(x) = 668.7x^2 - 2990.7x + 938$

    a. $x = 2004 - 1985 = 19$
$\qquad f(19) = 668.7(19)^2 - 2990.7(19) + 938$
$\qquad\qquad = 185{,}515.4$
    There were approximately 185,515 thousand subscribers.

    b. $x = 2007 - 1985 = 22$
$\qquad f(22) = 668.7(22)^2 - 2990.7(22) + 938$
$\qquad\qquad = 258{,}793.4$
    There were approximately 258,793 thousand subscribers.

Section 8.6

Practice Exercises

    1. $g(x) = x^2 - 2x - 3$

    Write in the form $y = (x-h)^2 + k$ by completing the square.
$$y = x^2 - 2x - 3$$
$$y + 3 = x^2 - 2x$$
$$y + 3 + \left(\frac{-2}{2}\right)^2 = x^2 - 2x + \left(\frac{-2}{2}\right)^2$$
$$y + 4 = x^2 - 2x + 1$$
$$y = (x-1)^2 - 4$$

    The vertex is at (1, –4).
    Let $g(x) = 0$.
$$0 = x^2 - 2x - 3$$
$$0 = (x-3)(x+1)$$
$$x - 3 = 0 \quad \text{or} \quad x + 1 = 0$$
$$x = 3 \qquad\qquad x = -1$$

    The x-intercepts are (3, 0) and (–1, 0).
    Let $x = 0$.
$$g(0) = 0^2 - 2(0) - 3 = -3$$
    The y-intercept is (0, –3).

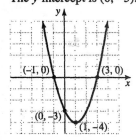

    2. $g(x) = 4x^2 + 4x + 3$
    Replace $g(x)$ with y and complete the square to write the equation in the form $y = a(x-h)^2 + k$.
$$y = 4x^2 + 4x + 3$$
$$y - 3 = 4x^2 + 4x = 4(x^2 + x)$$
$$y - 3 + 4\left(\frac{1}{2}\right)^2 = 4\left[x^2 + x + \left(\frac{1}{2}\right)^2\right]$$
$$y - 3 + 1 = 4\left(x^2 + x + \frac{1}{4}\right)$$
$$y = 4\left(x + \frac{1}{2}\right)^2 + 2$$

    $a = 4$, $h = -\dfrac{1}{2}$, and $k = 2$.

The parabola opens upward with vertex $\left(-\dfrac{1}{2}, 2\right)$, and has an axis of symmetry $x = -\dfrac{1}{2}$.

Let $x = 0$.

$g(0) = 4(0)^2 + 4(0) + 3 = 3$

The y-intercept is (0, 3). There are no x-intercepts.

3. $g(x) = -x^2 + 5x + 6$

   Write $g(x)$ in the form $a(x-h)^2 + k$ by completing the square. Replace $g(x)$ with y.

   $$y = -x^2 + 5x + 6$$

   $$y - 6 = -x^2 + 5x$$

   $$y - 6 = -1(x^2 - 5x)$$

   $$y - 6 - \left(\frac{-5}{2}\right)^2 = -1\left[x^2 - 5x + \left(\frac{-5}{2}\right)^2\right]$$

   $$y - 6 - \frac{25}{4} = -1\left(x^2 - 5x + \frac{25}{4}\right)$$

   $$y - \frac{49}{4} = -\left(x - \frac{5}{2}\right)^2$$

   $$y = -\left(x - \frac{5}{2}\right)^2 + \frac{49}{4}$$

   Since $a = -1$, the parabola opens downward with vertex $\left(\dfrac{5}{2}, \dfrac{49}{4}\right)$ and axis of symmetry $x = \dfrac{5}{2}$.

   Let $x = 0$.

   $y = -0^2 + 5(0) + 6 = 6$

   The y-intercept is (0, 6). Let $y = 0$.

   $0 = -x^2 + 5x + 6$

   $0 = x^2 - 5x - 6$

   $0 = (x - 6)(x + 1)$

   $x - 6 = 0$ or $x + 1 = 0$

        $x = 6$ $x = -1$

   The x-intercepts are (6, 0) and (−1, 0).

4. $g(x) = x^2 - 2x - 3$

   $a = 1$, $b = -2$, and $c = -3$

   $$\frac{-b}{2a} = \frac{-(-2)}{2(1)} = \frac{2}{2} = 1$$

   The x-value of the vertex is 1.

   $g(1) = 1^2 - 2(1) - 3 = 1 - 2 - 3 = -4$

   The vertex is (1, −4).

5. $h(t) = -16t^2 + 24t$

   Find the vertex of $h(t)$ to find its maximum value.

   $a = -16$, $b = 24$, and $c = 0$

   $$\frac{-b}{2a} = \frac{-24}{2(-16)} = \frac{3}{4}$$

   The t-value of the vertex is $\dfrac{3}{4}$.

   $$h\left(\frac{3}{4}\right) = -16\left(\frac{3}{4}\right)^2 + 24\left(\frac{3}{4}\right)$$

   $$= -16\left(\frac{9}{16}\right) + 18$$

   $$= -9 + 18$$

   $$= 9$$

   The vertex is $\left(\dfrac{3}{4}, 9\right)$. Thus, the ball reaches its maximum height of 9 feet in $\dfrac{3}{4}$ second.

Vocabulary and Readiness Check

1. If a quadratic function is in the form $f(x) = a(x-h)^2 + k$, the vertex of its graph is <u>(h, k)</u>.

2. The graph of $f(x) = ax^2 + bx + c$, $a \neq 0$ is a parabola whose vertex has x-value of $\underline{\dfrac{-b}{2a}}$.

	Parabola Opens	*Vertex Location*	*Number of x-intercept(s)*	*Number of y-intercept(s)*
3.	up	Q I	0	1
4.	up	Q III	2	1
5.	down	Q II	2	1
6.	down	Q IV	0	1
7.	up	x-axis	1	1
8.	down	x-axis	1	1
9.	down	Q III	0	
10.	down	Q I	2	
11.	up	Q IV	2	
12.	up	Q II	0	

Exercise Set 8.6

1. $f(x) = x^2 + 8x + 7$

    $-\dfrac{b}{2a} = \dfrac{-8}{2(1)} = -4$ and

    $\begin{aligned} f(-4) &= (-4)^2 + 8(-4) + 7 \\ &= 16 - 32 + 7 \\ &= -9 \end{aligned}$

    Thus, the vertex is (−4, −9).

3. $f(x) = -x^2 + 10x + 5$

    $-\dfrac{b}{2a} = \dfrac{-10}{2(-1)} = 5$ and

    $\begin{aligned} f(5) &= -(5)^2 + 10(5) + 5 \\ &= -25 + 50 + 5 \\ &= 30 \end{aligned}$

    Thus, the vertex is (5, 30).

5. $f(x) = 5x^2 - 10x + 3$

    $-\dfrac{b}{2a} = \dfrac{-(-10)}{2(5)} = 1$ and

    $\begin{aligned} f(1) &= 5(1)^2 - 10(1) + 3 \\ &= 5 - 10 + 3 \\ &= -2 \end{aligned}$

    Thus, the vertex is (1, −2).

7. $f(x) = -x^2 + x + 1$

$-\dfrac{b}{2a} = \dfrac{-1}{2(-1)} = \dfrac{1}{2}$ and

$f\left(\dfrac{1}{2}\right) = -\left(\dfrac{1}{2}\right)^2 + \left(\dfrac{1}{2}\right) + 1$

$\qquad = -\dfrac{1}{4} + \dfrac{1}{2} + 1$

$\qquad = \dfrac{5}{4}$

Thus, the vertex is $\left(\dfrac{1}{2}, \dfrac{5}{4}\right)$.

9. $f(x) = x^2 - 4x + 3$

$-\dfrac{b}{2a} = \dfrac{-(-4)}{2(1)} = 2$ and

$f(2) = (2)^2 - 4(2) + 3 = -1$

The vertex is (2, –1), so the graph is D.

11. $f(x) = x^2 - 2x - 3$

$-\dfrac{b}{2a} = \dfrac{-(-2)}{2(1)} = 1$ and

$f(1) = (1)^2 - 2(1) - 3 = -4$

The vertex is (1, –4), so the graph is B.

13. $f(x) = x^2 + 4x - 5$

$-\dfrac{b}{2a} = \dfrac{-4}{2(1)} = -2$ and

$f(-2) = (-2)^2 + 4(-2) - 5 = -9$

Thus, the vertex is (–2, –9).
The graph opens upward ($a = 1 > 0$).

$x^2 + 4x - 5 = 0$

$(x + 5)(x - 1) = 0$

$x + 5 = 0$ or $x - 1 = 0$

$\qquad x = -5$ or $\qquad x = 1$

x-intercepts: (–5, 0) and (1, 0).

$f(0) = -5$, so the y-intercept is (0, –5).

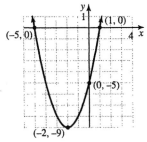

15. $f(x) = -x^2 + 2x - 1$

$-\dfrac{b}{2a} = \dfrac{-2}{2(-1)} = 1$ and

$f(1) = -(1)^2 + 2(1) - 1 = 0$

Thus, the vertex is (1, 0).
The graph opens downward ($a = -1 < 0$).

$-x^2 + 2x - 1 = 0$

$x^2 - 2x + 1 = 0$

$(x - 1)^2 = 0$

$x - 1 = 0$

$x = 1$

x-intercept: (1, 0).

$f(0) = -1$, so the y-intercept is (0, –1).

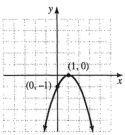

17. $f(x) = x^2 - 4$

$-\dfrac{b}{2a} = \dfrac{-0}{2(1)} = 0$ and

$f(0) = (0)^2 - 4 = -4$

Thus, the vertex is (0, –4).
The graph opens upward ($a = 1 > 0$).

$x^2 - 4 = 0$

$(x + 2)(x - 2) = 0$

$x + 2 = 0$ or $x - 2 = 0$

$\qquad x = -2$ or $\qquad x = 2$

x-intercepts: (–2, 0) and (2, 0).

$f(0) = -4$, so the y-intercept is (0, –4).

19. $f(x) = 4x^2 + 4x - 3$

$-\dfrac{b}{2a} = \dfrac{-4}{2(4)} = -\dfrac{1}{2}$ and

$f\left(-\dfrac{1}{2}\right) = 4\left(-\dfrac{1}{2}\right)^2 + 4\left(-\dfrac{1}{2}\right) - 3 = -4$

Thus, the vertex is $\left(-\dfrac{1}{2}, -4\right)$.

The graph opens upward ($a = 4 > 0$).

$4x^2 + 4x - 3 = 0$

$(2x + 3)(2x - 1) = 0$

$2x + 3 = 0$ or $2x - 1 = 0$

$x = -\dfrac{3}{2}$ or $x = \dfrac{1}{2}$

x-intercepts: $\left(-\dfrac{3}{2}, 0\right)$ and $\left(\dfrac{1}{2}, 0\right)$.

$f(0) = -3$, so the y-intercept is $(0, -3)$.

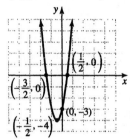

21. $f(x) = x^2 + 8x + 15$

$y = x^2 + 8x + 15$

$y - 15 = x^2 + 8x$

$y - 15 + 16 = x^2 + 8x + 16$

$y + 1 = (x + 4)^2$

$y = (x + 4)^2 - 1$

$f(x) = (x + 4)^2 - 1$

Thus, the vertex is $(-4, -1)$.

The graph opens upward ($a = 1 > 0$).

$x^2 + 8x + 15 = 0$

$(x + 5)(x + 3) = 0$

$x + 5 = 0$ or $x + 3 = 0$

$x = -5$ or $x = -3$

x-intercepts: $(-5, 0)$ and $(-3, 0)$.

$f(0) = 15$, so the y-intercept is $(0, 15)$.

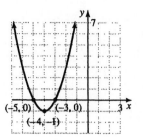

23. $f(x) = x^2 - 6x + 5$

$y = x^2 - 6x + 5$

$y - 5 = x^2 - 6x$

$y - 5 + 9 = x^2 - 6x + 9$

$y + 4 = (x - 3)^2$

$y = (x - 3)^2 - 4$

$f(x) = (x - 3)^2 - 4$

Thus, the vertex is $(3, -4)$.

The graph opens upward ($a = 1 > 0$).

$x^2 - 6x + 5 = 0$

$(x - 5)(x - 1) = 0$

$x = 5$ or $x = 1$

x-intercepts: $(5, 0)$ and $(1, 0)$.

$f(0) = 5$, so the y-intercept is $(0, 5)$.

25. $f(x) = x^2 - 4x + 5$

$y = x^2 - 4x + 5$

$y - 5 = x^2 - 4x$

$y - 5 + 4 = x^2 - 4x + 4$

$y - 1 = (x - 2)^2$

$y = (x - 2)^2 + 1$

$f(x) = (x - 2)^2 + 1$

Thus, the vertex is $(2, 1)$.

The graph opens upward ($a = 1 > 0$).

$x^2 - 4x + 5 = 0$

$x = \dfrac{4 \pm \sqrt{(-4)^2 - 4(1)(5)}}{2(1)} = \dfrac{4 \pm \sqrt{-4}}{2}$

which give non-real solutions.

Hence, there are no x-intercepts.

$f(0) = 5$, so the *y*-intercept is $(0, 5)$.

27.
$$f(x) = 2x^2 + 4x + 5$$
$$y = 2x^2 + 4x + 5$$
$$y - 5 = 2(x^2 + 2x)$$
$$y - 5 + 2(1) = 2(x^2 + 2x + 1)$$
$$y - 3 = 2(x + 1)^2$$
$$y = 2(x + 1)^2 + 3$$
$$f(x) = 2(x + 1)^2 + 3$$

Thus, the vertex is $(-1, 3)$.
The graph opens upward ($a = 2 > 0$).
$$2x^2 + 4x + 5 = 0$$
$$x = \frac{-4 \pm \sqrt{(4)^2 - 4(2)(5)}}{2(2)} = \frac{-4 \pm \sqrt{-24}}{4}$$

which give non-real solutions.
Hence, there are no *x*-intercepts.
$f(0) = 5$, so the *y*-intercept is $(0, 5)$.

29.
$$f(x) = -2x^2 + 12x$$
$$y = -2(x^2 - 6x)$$
$$y + [-2(9)] = -2(x^2 - 6x + 9)$$
$$y - 18 = -2(x - 3)^2$$
$$y = -2(x - 3)^2 + 18$$
$$f(x) = -2(x - 3)^2 + 18$$

Thus, the vertex is $(3, 18)$.
The graph opens downward ($a = -2 < 0$).

$$-2x^2 + 12x = 0$$
$$-2x(x - 6) = 0$$
$$x = 0 \text{ or } x - 6 = 0$$
$$x = 6$$

x-intercepts: $(0, 0)$ and $(6, 0)$
$f(0) = 0$, so the *y*-intercept is $(0, 0)$.

31. $f(x) = x^2 + 1$
$$x = -\frac{b}{2a} = -\frac{0}{2(1)} = 0$$
$$f(0) = (0)^2 + 1 = 1$$

Thus, the vertex is $(0, 1)$.
The graph opens upward ($a = 1 > 0$).
$$x^2 + 1 = 0$$
$$x^2 = -1$$

which give non-real solutions.
Hence, there are no *x*-intercepts.
$f(0) = 1$, so the *y*-intercept is $(0, 1)$.

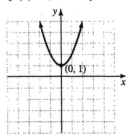

33.
$$f(x) = x^2 - 2x - 15$$
$$y = x^2 - 2x - 15$$
$$y + 15 = x^2 - 2x$$
$$y + 15 + 1 = x^2 - 2x + 1$$
$$y + 16 = (x - 1)^2$$
$$y = (x - 1)^2 - 16$$
$$f(x) = (x - 1)^2 - 16$$

Thus, the vertex is $(1, -16)$.
The graph opens upward ($a = 1 > 0$).

$$x^2 - 2x - 15 = 0$$
$$(x-5)(x+3) = 0$$
$$x = 5 \text{ or } x = -3$$

x-intercepts: $(-3, 0)$ and $(5, 0)$.
$f(0) = -15$ so the y-intercept is $(0, -15)$.

35. $f(x) = -5x^2 + 5x$

$$x = -\frac{b}{2a} = \frac{-5}{2(-5)} = \frac{1}{2} \text{ and}$$

$$f\left(\frac{1}{2}\right) = -5\left(\frac{1}{2}\right)^2 + 5\left(\frac{1}{2}\right) = -\frac{5}{4} + \frac{5}{2} = \frac{5}{4}$$

Thus, the vertex is $\left(\frac{1}{2}, \frac{5}{4}\right)$.

The graph opens downward ($a = -5 < 0$).

$$-5x^2 + 5x = 0$$
$$-5x(x-1) = 0$$
$$x = 0 \text{ or } x - 1 = 0$$
$$x = 1$$

x-intercepts: $(0, 0)$ and $(1, 0)$.
$f(0) = 0$, so the y-intercept is $(0, 0)$.

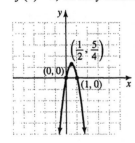

37. $f(x) = -x^2 + 2x - 12$

$$x = -\frac{b}{2a} = \frac{-2}{2(-1)} = 1 \text{ and}$$

$$f(1) = -(1)^2 + 2(1) - 12 = -11$$

Thus, the vertex is $(1, -11)$.
The graph opens downward ($a = -1 < 0$).

$$-x^2 + 2x - 12 = 0$$
$$x^2 - 2x + 12 = 0$$

$$x = \frac{2 \pm \sqrt{(-2)^2 - 4(1)(12)}}{2(1)} = \frac{2 \pm \sqrt{-44}}{2}$$

which yields non-real solutions.
Hence, there are no x-intercepts.
$f(0) = -12$ so the y-intercept is $(0, -12)$.

39. $f(x) = 3x^2 - 12x + 15$

$$x = -\frac{b}{2a} = \frac{-(-12)}{2(3)} = \frac{12}{6} = 2 \text{ and}$$

$$\begin{aligned} f(2) &= 3(2)^2 - 12(2) + 15 \\ &= 12 - 24 + 15 \\ &= 3 \end{aligned}$$

Thus, the vertex is $(2, 3)$.
The graph opens upward ($a = 3 > 0$).

$$3x^2 - 12x + 15 = 0$$
$$x^2 - 4x + 5 = 0$$

$$x = \frac{4 \pm \sqrt{(-4)^2 - 4(1)(5)}}{2(1)} = \frac{4 \pm \sqrt{-4}}{2}$$

which yields non-real solutions.
Hence, there are no x-intercepts.
$f(0) = 15$, so the y-intercept is $(0, 15)$.

41. $f(x) = x^2 + x - 6$

$x = -\dfrac{b}{2a} = \dfrac{-1}{2(1)} = -\dfrac{1}{2}$ and

$f\left(-\dfrac{1}{2}\right) = \left(-\dfrac{1}{2}\right)^2 + \left(-\dfrac{1}{2}\right) - 6$

$\qquad = \dfrac{1}{4} - \dfrac{1}{2} - 6$

$\qquad = -\dfrac{25}{4}$

Thus, the vertex is $\left(-\dfrac{1}{2}, -\dfrac{25}{4}\right)$.

The graph opens upward ($a = 1 > 0$).

$x^2 + x - 6 = 0$

$(x + 3)(x - 2) = 0$

$x = -3$ or $x = 2$

x-intercepts: $(-3, 0)$ and $(2, 0)$.

$f(0) = -6$ so the y-intercept is $(0, -6)$.

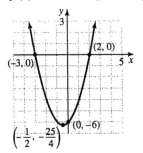

43. $f(x) = -2x^2 - 3x + 35$

$x = -\dfrac{b}{2a} = \dfrac{-(-3)}{2(-2)} = -\dfrac{3}{4}$ and

$f\left(-\dfrac{3}{4}\right) = -2\left(-\dfrac{3}{4}\right)^2 - 3\left(-\dfrac{3}{4}\right) + 35$

$\qquad = -\dfrac{9}{8} + \dfrac{9}{4} + 35$

$\qquad = \dfrac{289}{8}$

Thus, the vertex is $\left(-\dfrac{3}{4}, \dfrac{289}{8}\right)$.

The graph opens downward ($a = -2 < 0$).

$-2x^2 - 3x + 35 = 0$

$2x^2 + 3x - 35 = 0$

$(2x - 7)(x + 5) = 0$

$2x - 7 = 0$ or $x + 5 = 0$

$\qquad x = \dfrac{7}{2}$ or $\qquad x = -5$

x-intercepts: $(-5, 0)$ and $\left(\dfrac{7}{2}, 0\right)$.

$f(0) = 35$ so the y-intercept is $(0, 35)$.

45. $h(t) = -16t^2 + 96t$

$t = -\dfrac{b}{2a} = \dfrac{-96}{2(-16)} = \dfrac{96}{32} = 3$ and

$h(3) = -16(3)^2 + 96(3)$

$\qquad = -144 + 288$

$\qquad = 144$

The maximum height is 144 feet.

47. $C(x) = 2x^2 - 800x + 92,000$

a. $x = -\dfrac{b}{2a} = \dfrac{-(-800)}{2(2)} = 200$

200 bicycles are needed to minimize the cost.

b. $C(200) = 2(200)^2 - 800(200) + 92,000$

$\qquad = 12,000$

The minimum cost is \$12,000.

49. Let x = one number. Then

$60 - x$ = the other number.

$f(x) = x(60 - x)$

$\qquad = 60x - x^2$

$\qquad = -x^2 + 60x$

The maximum will occur at the vertex.

$x = -\dfrac{b}{2a} = \dfrac{-60}{2(-1)} = 30$

$60 - x = 60 - 30 = 30$

The numbers are 30 and 30.

51. Let x = one number. Then

$10 + x$ = the other number.

$f(x) = x(10 + x)$

$\qquad = 10x + x^2$

$\qquad = x^2 + 10x$

The minimum will occur at the vertex.

$$x = -\frac{b}{2a} = \frac{-10}{2(1)} = -5$$
$$10 + x = 10 + (-5) = 5$$
The numbers are –5 and 5.

53. Let x = width. Then $40 - x$ = the length.
Area = length · width
$$A(x) = (40 - x)x$$
$$= 40x - x^2$$
$$= -x^2 + 40x$$
The maximum will occur at the vertex.
$$x = -\frac{b}{2a} = \frac{-40}{2(-1)} = 20$$
$$40 - x = 40 - 20 = 20$$
The maximum area will occur when the length and width are 20 units each.

55. $f(x) = x^2 + 2$

57. $g(x) = x + 2$

59. $f(x) = (x + 5)^2 + 2$

61. $f(x) = 3(x - 4)^2 + 1$

63. $f(x) = -(x - 4)^2 + \frac{3}{2}$

65. $f(x) = 2x^2 - 5$
Since $a = 2 > 0$, the graph opens upward; thus, $f(x)$ has a minimum value.

67. $F(x) = 3 - \frac{1}{2}x^2$

Since $a = -\frac{1}{2} < 0$, the graph opens downward; thus, $F(x)$ has a maximum value.

69. $f(x) = x^2 + 10x + 15$
$$x = -\frac{b}{2a} = \frac{-10}{2(1)} = -5 \text{ and}$$
$$f(-5) = (-5)^2 + 10(-5) + 15 = -10$$
Thus, the vertex is $(-5, -10)$.
The graph opens upward ($a = 1 > 0$).
$f(0) = 15$ so the y-intercept is $(0, 15)$.
$$x^2 + 10x + 15 = 0$$
$$x = \frac{-10 \pm \sqrt{(10)^2 - 4(1)(15)}}{2(1)}$$
$$= \frac{-10 \pm \sqrt{40}}{2}$$
$$\approx -8.2 \text{ or } -1.8$$
The x-intercepts are approximately $(-8.2, 0)$ and $(-1.8, 0)$.

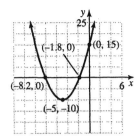

71. $f(x) = 3x^2 - 6x + 7$

$$x = -\frac{b}{2a} = \frac{-(-6)}{2(3)} = 1 \text{ and}$$

$$f(1) = 3(1)^2 - 6(1) + 7 = 4$$

Thus, the vertex is (1, 4).
The graph opens upward ($a = 3 > 0$).
$f(0) = 7$ so the y-intercept is (0, 7).

$$3x^2 - 6x + 7 = 0$$

$$x = \frac{6 \pm \sqrt{(-6)^2 - 4(3)(7)}}{2(3)} = \frac{6 \pm \sqrt{-48}}{6}$$

which yields non-real solutions.
Hence, there are no x-intercepts.

73. $f(x) = 2.3x^2 - 6.1x + 3.2$

$$x = \frac{-(-6.1)}{2(2.3)} \approx 1.33$$

$f(1.33) \approx -0.84$
minimum ≈ -0.84
Alternative solution:

75. $f(x) = -1.9x^2 + 5.6x - 2.7$

$$x = \frac{-5.6}{2(-1.9)} \approx 1.47$$

$f(1.47) \approx 1.43$
maximum ≈ 1.43

Alternate solution:

77. $f(x) = -96x^2 + 1018x + 28,824$

a. It will have a maximum; answer may vary
(e.g., since $a = -96 < 0$).

b. $x = -\frac{b}{2a} = \frac{-1018}{2(-96)} \approx 5.3$

$2000 + 5 = 2005$
In the year 2005.

c. $f(5.3) = -96(5.3)^2 + 1018(5.3) + 28,824$
$= 31,522.76$
The maximum number of McDonald's is
predicted to be about 31,523.

79.

81.

Chapter 8 Vocabulary Check

1. The <u>discriminant</u> helps us find the number and
type of solutions of a quadratic equation.

2. If $a^2 = b$, then $a = \pm\sqrt{b}$.

3. The graph of $f(x) = ax^2 + bx + c$ where a is not
0 is a parabola whose vertex has x-value of $\dfrac{-b}{2a}$.

4. A <u>quadratic inequality</u> is an inequality that can
be written so that one side is a quadratic
expression and the other side is 0.

5. The process of writing a quadratic equation so that one side is a perfect square trinomial is called <u>completing the square</u>.

6. The graph of $f(x) = x^2 + k$ has vertex <u>(0, k)</u>.

7. The graph of $f(x) = (x-h)^2$ has vertex <u>(h, 0)</u>.

8. The graph of $f(x) = (x-h)^2 + k$ has vertex <u>(h, k)</u>.

9. The formula $x = \dfrac{-b \pm \sqrt{b^2 - 4ac}}{2a}$ is called the <u>quadratic formula</u>.

10. A <u>quadratic</u> equation is one that can be written in the form $ax^2 + bx + c = 0$ where a, b, and c are real numbers and a is not 0.

Chapter 8 Review

1. $x^2 - 15x + 14 = 0$
$(x-14)(x-1) = 0$
$x - 14 = 0 \quad \text{or} \quad x - 1 = 0$
$x = 14 \quad \text{or} \qquad x = 1$
The solutions are 1 and 14.

2. $\qquad 7a^2 = 29a + 30$
$7a^2 - 29a - 30 = 0$
$(7a+6)(a-5) = 0$
$7a + 6 = 0 \quad \text{or} \quad a - 5 = 0$
$\quad 7a = -6 \quad \text{or} \qquad a = 5$
$\qquad a = -\dfrac{6}{7}$

The solutions are $-\dfrac{6}{7}$ and 5.

3. $4m^2 = 196$
$\quad m^2 = 49$
$\quad m = \pm\sqrt{49}$
$\quad m = \pm 7$
The solutions are –7 and 7.

4. $(5x-2)^2 = 2$
$5x - 2 = \pm\sqrt{2}$
$\quad 5x = 2 \pm \sqrt{2}$
$\qquad x = \dfrac{2 \pm \sqrt{2}}{5}$

The solutions are $\dfrac{2+\sqrt{2}}{5}$ and $\dfrac{2-\sqrt{2}}{5}$.

5. $\qquad z^2 + 3z + 1 = 0$
$\qquad z^2 + 3z = -1$
$z^2 + 3z + \left(\dfrac{3}{2}\right)^2 = -1 + \dfrac{9}{4}$
$\qquad \left(z + \dfrac{3}{2}\right)^2 = \dfrac{5}{4}$
$\qquad z + \dfrac{3}{2} = \pm\sqrt{\dfrac{5}{4}}$
$\qquad z + \dfrac{3}{2} = \pm\dfrac{\sqrt{5}}{2}$
$\qquad z = -\dfrac{3}{2} \pm \dfrac{\sqrt{5}}{2} = \dfrac{-3 \pm \sqrt{5}}{2}$

The solutions are $\dfrac{-3+\sqrt{5}}{2}$ and $\dfrac{-3-\sqrt{5}}{2}$.

6. $\qquad (2x+1)^2 = x$
$\qquad 4x^2 + 4x + 1 = x$
$\qquad 4x^2 + 3x = -1$
$\qquad x^2 + \dfrac{3}{4}x = -\dfrac{1}{4}$
$x^2 + \dfrac{3}{4}x + \left(\dfrac{\frac{3}{4}}{2}\right)^2 = -\dfrac{1}{4} + \dfrac{9}{64}$
$\qquad \left(x + \dfrac{3}{8}\right)^2 = -\dfrac{7}{64}$
$\qquad x + \dfrac{3}{8} = \pm\sqrt{-\dfrac{7}{64}}$
$\qquad x + \dfrac{3}{8} = \pm\dfrac{i\sqrt{7}}{8}$
$\qquad x = -\dfrac{3}{8} \pm \dfrac{i\sqrt{7}}{8} = \dfrac{-3 \pm i\sqrt{7}}{8}$

The solutions are $\dfrac{-3+i\sqrt{7}}{8}$ and $\dfrac{-3-i\sqrt{7}}{8}$.

7.
$$A = P(1+r)^2$$
$$2717 = 2500(1+r)^2$$
$$\frac{2717}{2500} = (1+r)^2$$
$$(1+r)^2 = 1.0868$$
$$1+r = \pm\sqrt{1.0868}$$
$$1+r = \pm 1.0425$$
$$r = -1 \pm 1.0425$$
$$= 0.0425 \text{ or } -2.0425 \text{ (disregard)}$$
The interest rate is 4.25%.

8. Let x = distance traveled.
$$a^2 + b^2 = c^2$$
$$x^2 + x^2 = (150)^2$$
$$2x^2 = 22,500$$
$$x^2 = 11,250$$
$$x = \pm 75\sqrt{2} \approx \pm 106.1$$
Disregard the negative. The ships each traveled $75\sqrt{2} \approx 106.1$ miles.

9. Two complex but not real solutions exist.

10. Two real solutions exist.

11. Two real solutions exist.

12. One real solution exists.

13. $x^2 - 16x + 64 = 0$
$$a = 1, b = -16, c = 64$$
$$x = \frac{16 \pm \sqrt{(-16)^2 - 4(1)(64)}}{2(1)}$$
$$= \frac{16 \pm \sqrt{256 - 256}}{2}$$
$$= \frac{16 \pm \sqrt{0}}{2}$$
$$= 8$$
The solution is 8.

14. $x^2 + 5x = 0$
$$a = 1, b = 5, c = 0$$
$$x = \frac{-5 \pm \sqrt{(5)^2 - 4(1)(0)}}{2(1)}$$
$$= \frac{-5 \pm \sqrt{25}}{2}$$
$$= \frac{-5 \pm 5}{2}$$
$$= 0 \text{ or } -5$$
The solutions are –5 and 0.

15.
$$2x^2 + 3x = 5$$
$$2x^2 + 3x - 5 = 0$$
$$a = 2, b = 3, c = -5$$
$$x = \frac{-3 \pm \sqrt{(3)^2 - 4(2)(-5)}}{2(2)}$$
$$= \frac{-3 \pm \sqrt{49}}{4}$$
$$= \frac{-3 \pm 7}{4}$$
$$= 1 \text{ or } -\frac{5}{2}$$

The solutions are $-\dfrac{5}{2}$ and 1.

16.
$$9a^2 + 4 = 2a$$
$$9a^2 - 2a + 4 = 0$$
$$a = \frac{2 \pm \sqrt{(-2)^2 - 4(9)(4)}}{2(9)}$$
$$= \frac{2 \pm \sqrt{-140}}{18}$$
$$= \frac{2 \pm i\sqrt{4 \cdot 35}}{18}$$
$$= \frac{2 \pm 2i\sqrt{35}}{18}$$
$$= \frac{1 \pm i\sqrt{35}}{9}$$

The solutions are $\dfrac{1+i\sqrt{35}}{9}$ and $\dfrac{1-i\sqrt{35}}{9}$.

17.
$$6x^2 + 7 = 5x$$
$$6x^2 - 5x + 7 = 0$$
$$a = 6, b = -5, c = 7$$
$$x = \frac{5 \pm \sqrt{(-5)^2 - 4(6)(7)}}{2(6)}$$
$$= \frac{5 \pm \sqrt{25 - 168}}{12}$$
$$= \frac{5 \pm \sqrt{-143}}{12}$$
$$= \frac{5 \pm i\sqrt{143}}{12}$$

The solutions are $\dfrac{5 + i\sqrt{143}}{12}$ and $\dfrac{5 - i\sqrt{143}}{12}$.

18.
$$(2x - 3)^2 = x$$
$$4x^2 - 12x + 9 - x = 0$$
$$4x^2 - 13x + 9 = 0$$
$$a = 4, b = -13, c = 9$$
$$x = \frac{13 \pm \sqrt{(-13)^2 - 4(4)(9)}}{2(4)}$$
$$= \frac{13 \pm \sqrt{169 - 144}}{8}$$
$$= \frac{13 \pm \sqrt{25}}{8}$$
$$= \frac{13 \pm 5}{8}$$
$$= \frac{9}{4} \text{ or } 1$$

The solutions are 1 and $\dfrac{9}{4}$.

19. $d(t) = -16t^2 + 30t + 6$

a.
$$d(1) = -16(1)^2 + 30(1) + 6$$
$$= -16 + 30 + 6$$
$$= 20 \text{ feet}$$

b.
$$-16t^2 + 30t + 6 = 0$$
$$8t^2 - 15t - 3 = 0$$
$$a = 8, b = -15, c = -3$$
$$t = \frac{15 \pm \sqrt{(-15)^2 - 4(8)(-3)}}{2(8)}$$
$$= \frac{15 \pm \sqrt{225 + 96}}{16}$$
$$= \frac{15 \pm \sqrt{321}}{16}$$

Disregarding the negative, we have

$$t = \frac{15 + \sqrt{321}}{16} \text{ seconds}$$
$$\approx 2.1 \text{ seconds.}$$

20. Let x = length of the legs. Then $x + 6$ = length of the hypotenuse.
$$x^2 + x^2 = (x + 6)^2$$
$$2x^2 = x^2 + 12x + 36$$
$$x^2 - 12x - 36 = 0$$
$$a = 1, b = -12, c = -36$$
$$x = \frac{12 \pm \sqrt{(-12)^2 - 4(1)(-36)}}{2(1)}$$
$$= \frac{12 \pm \sqrt{144 + 144}}{2}$$
$$= \frac{12 \pm \sqrt{144 \cdot 2}}{2}$$
$$= \frac{12 \pm 12\sqrt{2}}{2}$$
$$= 6 \pm 6\sqrt{2}$$

Disregard the negative. The length of each leg is $\left(6 + 6\sqrt{2}\right)$ cm.

21.
$$x^3 = 27$$
$$x^3 - 27 = 0$$
$$(x-3)(x^2 + 3x + 9) = 0$$
$$x - 3 = 0 \text{ or } x^2 + 3x + 9 = 0$$
$$x = 3 \qquad a = 1, b = 3, c = 9$$
$$x = \frac{-3 \pm \sqrt{(3)^2 - 4(1)(9)}}{2(1)}$$
$$= \frac{-3 \pm \sqrt{9 - 36}}{2}$$
$$= \frac{-3 \pm \sqrt{-27}}{2}$$
$$= \frac{-3 \pm 3i\sqrt{3}}{2}$$

The solutions are 3, $\dfrac{-3 + 3i\sqrt{3}}{2}$, and $\dfrac{-3 - 3i\sqrt{3}}{2}$.

22.
$$y^3 = -64$$
$$y^3 + 64 = 0$$
$$(y+4)(y^2 - 4y + 16) = 0$$
$$y + 4 = 0 \quad \text{ or } y^2 - 4y + 16 = 0$$
$$y = -4 \qquad a = 1, b = -4, c = 16$$
$$y = \frac{4 \pm \sqrt{(-4)^2 - 4(1)(16)}}{2(1)}$$
$$= \frac{4 \pm \sqrt{16 - 64}}{2}$$
$$= \frac{4 \pm \sqrt{-48}}{2}$$
$$= \frac{4 \pm 4i\sqrt{3}}{2}$$
$$= 2 \pm 2i\sqrt{3}$$

The solutions are -4, $2 + 2i\sqrt{3}$, and $2 - 2i\sqrt{3}$.

23.
$$\frac{5}{x} + \frac{6}{x-2} = 3$$
$$x(x-2)\left(\frac{5}{x} + \frac{6}{x-2}\right) = 3x(x-2)$$
$$5(x-2) + 6x = 3x^2 - 6x$$
$$5x - 10 + 6x = 3x^2 - 6x$$
$$0 = 3x^2 - 17x + 10$$
$$0 = (3x - 2)(x - 5)$$
$$3x - 2 = 0 \text{ or } x - 5 = 0$$
$$x = \frac{2}{3} \text{ or } \quad x = 5$$

The solutions are $\dfrac{2}{3}$ and 5.

24.
$$x^4 - 21x^2 - 100 = 0$$
$$(x^2 - 25)(x^2 + 4) = 0$$
$$(x+5)(x-5)(x^2 + 4) = 0$$
$$x + 5 = 0 \quad \text{ or } x - 5 = 0 \text{ or } x^2 + 4 = 0$$
$$x = -5 \text{ or } \quad x = 5 \text{ or } \quad x^2 = -4$$
$$x = \pm 2i$$

The solutions are -5, 5 $-2i$, and $2i$.

25. $x^{2/3} - 6x^{1/3} + 5 = 0$
Let $y = x^{1/3}$. Then $y^2 = x^{2/3}$ and
$$y^2 - 6y + 5 = 0$$
$$(y-5)(y-1) = 0$$
$$y - 5 = 0 \quad \text{ or } y - 1 = 0$$
$$y = 5 \quad \text{ or } \quad y = 1$$
$$x^{1/3} = 5 \quad \text{ or } x^{1/3} = 1$$
$$x = 125 \text{ or } \quad x = 1$$
The solutions are 1 and 125.

26. $\quad 5(x+3)^2 - 19(x+3) = 4$

$5(x+3)^2 - 19(x+3) - 4 = 0$

Let $y = x + 3$. Then $y^2 = (x+3)^2$ and

$5y^2 - 19y - 4 = 0$

$(5y+1)(y-4) = 0$

$5y+1 = 0 \quad$ or $y - 4 = 0$

$\qquad y = -\dfrac{1}{5} \quad$ or $\quad y = 4$

$x+3 = -\dfrac{1}{5} \quad$ or $\quad x+3 = 4$

$\qquad x = -\dfrac{16}{5} \quad$ or $\qquad x = 1$

The solutions are $-\dfrac{16}{5}$ and 1.

27. $\qquad\qquad\qquad a^6 - a^2 = a^4 - 1$

$a^6 - a^4 - a^2 + 1 = 0$

$a^4(a^2 - 1) - 1(a^2 - 1) = 0$

$(a^2 - 1)(a^4 - 1) = 0$

$(a+1)(a-1)(a^2+1)(a^2-1) = 0$

$(a+1)(a-1)(a^2+1)(a+1)(a-1) = 0$

$(a+1)^2(a-1)^2(a^2+1) = 0$

$(a+1)^2 = 0 \;$ or $(a-1)^2 = 0 \;$ or $a^2 + 1 = 0$

$a+1 = 0 \;$ or $\quad a-1 = 0 \;$ or $\quad a^2 = -1$

$a = -1 \;$ or $\qquad a = 1 \;$ or $\qquad a = \pm i$

The solutions are -1, 1, $-i$, and i.

28. $\quad y^{-2} + y^{-1} = 20$

$\dfrac{1}{y^2} + \dfrac{1}{y} = 20$

$1 + y = 20y^2$

$0 = 20y^2 - y - 1$

$0 = (5y+1)(4y-1)$

$5y+1 = 0 \quad$ or $4y-1 = 0$

$\quad y = -\dfrac{1}{5} \;$ or $\qquad y = \dfrac{1}{4}$

The solutions are $-\dfrac{1}{5}$ and $\dfrac{1}{4}$.

29. Let $x =$ time for Jerome alone. Then $x - 1 =$ time for Tim alone.

$\dfrac{1}{x} + \dfrac{1}{x-1} = \dfrac{1}{5}$

$5(x-1) + 5x = x(x-1)$

$5x - 5 + 5x = x^2 - x$

$0 = x^2 - 11x + 5$

$a = 1, b = -11, c = 5$

$x = \dfrac{11 \pm \sqrt{(-11)^2 - 4(1)(5)}}{2(1)}$

$\quad = \dfrac{11 \pm \sqrt{101}}{2}$

≈ 0.475 (disregard) or 10.525

Jerome: 10.5 hours

Tim: 9.5 hours

30. Let $x =$ the number; then

$\dfrac{1}{x} =$ the reciprocal of the number.

$x - \dfrac{1}{x} = -\dfrac{24}{5}$

$5x\left(x - \dfrac{1}{x}\right) = 5x\left(-\dfrac{24}{5}\right)$

$5x^2 - 5 = -24x$

$5x^2 + 24x - 5 = 0$

$(5x-1)(x+5) = 0$

$5x-1 = 0 \;$ or $\; x+5 = 0$

$\quad x = \dfrac{1}{5} \;$ or $\qquad x = -5$

Disregard the positive value as extraneous. The number is -5.

31. $\qquad\qquad 2x^2 - 50 \le 0$

$2(x^2 - 25) \le 0$

$2(x+5)(x-5) \le 0$

$x+5 = 0 \;$ or $x-5 = 0$

$\quad x = -5 \;$ or $\qquad x = 5$

Region	Test Point	$2(x+5)(x-5) \le 0$ Result
$A: (-\infty, -5]$	-6	$2(-1)(-11) \le 0$ False
$B: [-5, 5]$	0	$2(5)(-5) \le 0$ True
$C: [5, \infty)$	6	$2(11)(1) \le 0$ False

Solution: $[-5, 5]$

32.

$$\frac{1}{4}x^2 < \frac{1}{16}$$

$$x^2 < \frac{1}{4}$$

$$x^2 - \frac{1}{4} < 0$$

$$\left(x + \frac{1}{2}\right)\left(x - \frac{1}{2}\right) < 0$$

$$x + \frac{1}{2} = 0 \quad \text{or} \quad x - \frac{1}{2} = 0$$

$$x = -\frac{1}{2} \quad \text{or} \quad x = \frac{1}{2}$$

Region	Test Point	$\left(x + \frac{1}{2}\right)\left(x - \frac{1}{2}\right) < 0$ Result
A: $\left(-\infty, -\frac{1}{2}\right)$	-1	$\left(-\frac{1}{2}\right)\left(-\frac{3}{2}\right) < 0$ False
B: $\left(-\frac{1}{2}, \frac{1}{2}\right)$	0	$\left(\frac{1}{2}\right)\left(-\frac{1}{2}\right) < 0$ True
C: $\left(\frac{1}{2}, \infty\right)$	1	$\left(\frac{3}{2}\right)\left(\frac{1}{2}\right) < 0$ False

Solution: $\left(-\frac{1}{2}, \frac{1}{2}\right)$

33. $\dfrac{x-5}{x-6} < 0$

$x - 5 = 0$ or $x - 6 = 0$

$x = 5$ or $\quad x = 6$

Region	Test Point	$\dfrac{x-5}{x-6} < 0$ Result
A: $(-\infty, 5)$	0	$\dfrac{-5}{-6} < 0$ False
B: $(5, 6)$	$\dfrac{11}{2}$	$\dfrac{\frac{1}{2}}{-\frac{1}{2}} < 0$ True
C: $(6, \infty)$	7	$\dfrac{2}{1} < 0$ False

Solution: $(5, 6)$

34. $\qquad (x^2 - 16)(x^2 - 1) > 0$

$(x+4)(x-4)(x+1)(x-1) > 0$

$x + 4 = 0 \quad$ or $x - 4 = 0$ or $x + 1 = 0 \quad$ or $x - 1 = 0$

$x = -4$ or $\quad x = 4$ or $\quad x = -1$ or $\quad x = 1$

Region	Test Point	$(x + 4)(x - 4)(x + 1)(x - 1) > 0$ Result
A: $(-\infty, -4)$	-5	$(-1)(-9)(-4)(-6) > 0$ True
B: $(-4, -1)$	-2	$(2)(-6)(-1)(-3) > 0$ False
C: $(-1, 1)$	0	$(4)(-4)(1)(-1) > 0$ True
D: $(1, 4)$	2	$(6)(-2)(3)(1) > 0$ False
E: $(4, \infty)$	5	$(9)(1)(6)(4) > 0$ True

Solution: $(-\infty, -4) \cup (-1, 1) \cup (4, \infty)$

35. $\dfrac{(4x+3)(x-5)}{x(x+6)} > 0$

$4x+3=0,\ x-5=0,\ x=0,\ \text{or}\ x+6=0$

$x=-\dfrac{3}{4},\ x=5,\ x=0,\ \text{or}\ x=-6$

Region	Test Point	$\dfrac{(4x+3)(x-5)}{x(x+6)} > 0$ Result
A: $(-\infty,-6)$	-7	$\dfrac{(-25)(-12)}{-7(-1)} > 0$ True
B: $\left(-6,-\dfrac{3}{4}\right)$	-3	$\dfrac{(-9)(-8)}{-3(3)} > 0$ False
C: $\left(-\dfrac{3}{4},0\right)$	$-\dfrac{1}{2}$	$\dfrac{(1)\left(-\frac{11}{2}\right)}{-\frac{1}{2}\left(\frac{11}{2}\right)} > 0$ True
D: $(0,5)$	1	$\dfrac{(7)(-4)}{1(7)} > 0$ False
E: $(5,\infty)$	6	$\dfrac{(27)(1)}{6(12)} > 0$ True

Solution: $(-\infty,-6)\cup\left(-\dfrac{3}{4},0\right)\cup(5,\infty)$

36. $(x+5)(x-6)(x+2) \le 0$

$x+5=0\ \ \text{or}\ \ x-6=0\ \ \text{or}\ \ x+2=0$

$x=-5\ \ \text{or}\ \ \ x=6\ \ \text{or}\ \ \ \ x=-2$

Region	Test Point	$(x+5)(x-6)(x+2)\le 0$ Result
A: $(-\infty,-5]$	-6	$(-1)(-12)(-4)\le 0$ True
B: $[-5,-2]$	-3	$(2)(-9)(-1)\le 0$ False
C: $[-2,6]$	0	$(5)(-6)(2)\le 0$ True
D: $[6,\infty)$	7	$(12)(1)(9)\le 0$ False

Solution: $(-\infty,-5]\cup[-2,6]$

37. $x^3+3x^2-25x-75 > 0$

$x^2(x+3)-25(x+3) > 0$

$(x+3)(x^2-25) > 0$

$(x+3)(x+5)(x-5) > 0$

$x+3=0\ \ \text{or}\ \ x+5=0\ \ \text{or}\ \ x-5=0$

$x=-3\ \text{or}\ \ \ \ x=-5\ \text{or}\ \ \ \ x=5$

Region	Test Point	$(x+3)(x+5)(x-5) > 0$ Result
A: $(-\infty,-5)$	-6	$(-3)(-1)(-11)>0$ False
B: $(-5,-3)$	-4	$(-1)(1)(-9)>0$ True
C: $(-3,5)$	0	$(3)(5)(-5)>0$ False
D: $(5,\infty)$	6	$(9)(11)(1)>0$ True

Solution: $(-5,-3)\cup(5,\infty)$

38. $\dfrac{x^2+4}{3x} \le 1$

The denominator equals 0 when $3x=0$, or $x=0$.

$\dfrac{x^2+4}{3x}=1$

$x^2+4=3x$

$x^2-3x+4=0$

$x=\dfrac{3\pm\sqrt{(-3)^2-4(1)(4)}}{2(1)}=\dfrac{3\pm\sqrt{-7}}{2}$

which yields non-real solutions.

Region	Test Point	$\dfrac{x^2+4}{3x} \le 1$ Result
A: $(-\infty, 0)$	-1	$\dfrac{5}{-3} \le 1$ True
B: $(0, \infty)$	1	$\dfrac{5}{3} \le 1$ False

Solution: $(\infty, 0)$

39. $\dfrac{(5x+6)(x-3)}{x(6x-5)} < 0$

$x = -\dfrac{6}{5}$ or $x = 3$ or $x = 0$ or $x = \dfrac{5}{6}$

Region	Test Point	$\dfrac{(5x+6)(x-3)}{x(6x-5)} < 0$ Result
A: $\left(-\infty, -\dfrac{6}{5}\right)$	-2	$\dfrac{(-4)(-5)}{-2(-17)} < 0$ False
B: $\left(-\dfrac{6}{5}, 0\right)$	-1	$\dfrac{(1)(-4)}{-1(-11)} < 0$ True
C: $\left(0, \dfrac{5}{6}\right)$	$\dfrac{1}{2}$	$\dfrac{\left(\frac{17}{2}\right)\left(-\frac{5}{2}\right)}{\frac{1}{2}(-2)} < 0$ False
D: $\left(\dfrac{5}{6}, 3\right)$	2	$\dfrac{(16)(-1)}{2(7)} < 0$ True
E: $(3, \infty)$	4	$\dfrac{(26)(1)}{4(19)} < 0$ False

Solution: $\left(-\dfrac{6}{5}, 0\right) \cup \left(\dfrac{5}{6}, 3\right)$

40. $\dfrac{3}{x-2} > 2$

The denominator is equal to 0 when $x - 2 = 0$, or $x = 2$.

$\dfrac{3}{x-2} = 2$

$3 = 2(x-2)$

$3 = 2x - 4$

$7 = 2x$

$\dfrac{7}{2} = x$

Region	Test Point	$\dfrac{3}{x-2} > 2$ Result
A: $(-\infty, 2)$	0	$\dfrac{3}{-2} > 2$ False
B: $\left(2, \dfrac{7}{2}\right)$	3	$\dfrac{3}{1} > 2$ True
C: $\left(\dfrac{7}{2}, \infty\right)$	5	$\dfrac{3}{3} > 2$ False

Solution: $\left(2, \dfrac{7}{2}\right)$

41. $f(x) = x^2 - 4$

Vertex: $(0, -4)$

Axis of symmetry: $x = 0$

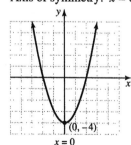

42. $g(x) = x^2 + 7$
Vertex: (0, 7)
Axis of symmetry: $x = 0$

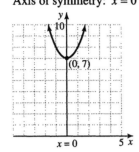

43. $H(x) = 2x^2$
Vertex: (0, 0)
Axis of symmetry: $x = 0$

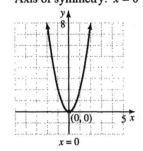

44. $h(x) = -\dfrac{1}{3}x^2$

Vertex: (0, 0)
Axis of symmetry: $x = 0$

45. $F(x) = (x-1)^2$
Vertex: (1, 0)
Axis of symmetry: $x = 1$

46. $G(x) = (x+5)^2$
Vertex: (–5, 0)
Axis of symmetry: $x = -5$

47. $f(x) = (x-4)^2 - 2$
Vertex: (4, –2)
Axis of symmetry: $x = 4$

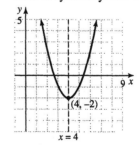

48. $f(x) = -3(x-1)^2 + 1$
Vertex: (1, 1)
Axis of symmetry: $x = 1$

49. $f(x) = x^2 + 10x + 25$

$x = -\dfrac{b}{2a} = \dfrac{-10}{2(1)} = -5$

$f(-5) = (-5)^2 + 10(-5) + 25 = 0$
Vertex: (−5, 0)

$x^2 + 10x + 25 = 0$

$(x+5)^2 = 0$

$x + 5 = 0$

$x = -5$

x-intercept: (−5, 0)

$f(0) = 25$ so the y-intercept is (0, 25).

50. $f(x) = -x^2 + 6x - 9$

$x = -\dfrac{b}{2a} = \dfrac{-6}{2(-1)} = 3$

$f(3) = -(3)^2 + 6(3) - 9 = 0$
Vertex: (3, 0)
x-intercept: (3, 0)
$f(0) = -9$
y-intercept: (0, −9)

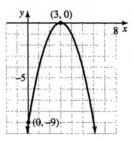

51. $f(x) = 4x^2 - 1$

$x = -\dfrac{b}{2a} = \dfrac{-0}{2(4)} = 0$

$f(0) = 4(0)^2 - 1 = -1$
Vertex: (0, −1)

$4x^2 - 1 = 0$

$(2x+1)(2x-1) = 0$

$x = -\dfrac{1}{2}$ or $x = \dfrac{1}{2}$

x-intercepts: $\left(-\dfrac{1}{2}, 0\right), \left(\dfrac{1}{2}, 0\right)$

$f(0) = -1$
y-intercept: (0, −1)

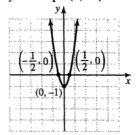

52. $f(x) = -5x^2 + 5$

$x = -\dfrac{b}{2a} = \dfrac{-0}{2(-5)} = 0$

$f(0) = -5(0)^2 + 5 = 5$
Vertex: (0, 5)

$-5x^2 + 5 = 0$

$-5x^2 = -5$

$x^2 = 1$

$x = \pm 1$

x-intercepts: (−1, 0), (1, 0)
$f(0) = 5$
y-intercept: (0, 5)

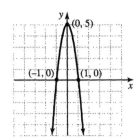

53. $f(x) = -3x^2 - 5x + 4$

$$x = -\frac{b}{2a} = \frac{-(-5)}{2(-3)} = -\frac{5}{6}$$

$$f\left(-\frac{5}{6}\right) = -3\left(-\frac{5}{6}\right)^2 - 5\left(-\frac{5}{6}\right) + 4 = \frac{73}{12}$$

Vertex: $\left(-\frac{5}{6}, \frac{73}{12}\right)$

The graph opens downward ($a = -3 < 0$).

$f(0) = 4 \Rightarrow$ y-intercept: $(0, 4)$

$$-3x^2 - 5x + 4 = 0$$

$$x = \frac{5 \pm \sqrt{(-5)^2 - 4(-3)(4)}}{2(-3)}$$

$$= \frac{5 \pm \sqrt{73}}{-6}$$

$$\approx -2.2573 \text{ or } 0.5907$$

x-intercepts: $(-2.3, 0)$, $(0.6, 0)$

54. $h(t) = -16t^2 + 120t + 300$

a.
$$350 = -16t^2 + 120t + 300$$
$$16t^2 - 120t + 50 = 0$$
$$8t^2 - 60t + 25 = 0$$
$$a = 8, b = -60, c = 25$$
$$t = \frac{60 \pm \sqrt{(-60)^2 - 4(8)(25)}}{2(8)}$$
$$= \frac{60 \pm \sqrt{2800}}{16}$$
$$\approx 0.4 \text{ second and } 7.1 \text{ seconds}$$

b. The object will be at 350 feet on the way up and on the way down.

55. Let $x =$ one number; then
$420 - x =$ the other number.
Let $f(x)$ represent their product.
$$f(x) = x(420 - x)$$
$$= 420x - x^2$$
$$= -x^2 + 420x$$
$$x = -\frac{b}{2a} = \frac{-420}{2(-1)} = 210;$$
$$420 - x = 420 - 210 = 210$$
Therefore, the numbers are both 210.

56. $y = a(x - h)^2 + k$

vertex $(-3, 7)$ gives $y = a(x + 3)^2 + 7$.
Passing through the origin gives
$$0 = a(0 + 3)^2 + 7$$
$$-7 = 9a$$
$$-\frac{7}{9} = a$$

Thus, $y = -\frac{7}{9}(x + 3)^2 + 7$.

57. $x^2 - x - 30 = 0$
$$(x + 5)(x - 6) = 0$$
$$x + 5 = 0 \quad \text{or} \quad x - 6 = 0$$
$$x = -5 \quad \text{or} \quad x = 6$$
The solutions are -5 and 6.

58.
$$10x^2 = 3x + 4$$
$$10x^2 - 3x - 4 = 0$$
$$(5x - 4)(2x + 1) = 0$$
$$5x - 4 = 0 \text{ or } 2x + 1 = 0$$
$$5x = 4 \text{ or } 2x = -1$$
$$x = \frac{4}{5} \text{ or } x = -\frac{1}{2}$$
The solutions are $-\dfrac{1}{2}$ and $\dfrac{4}{5}$.

59.
$$9y^2 = 36$$
$$y^2 = 4$$
$$y = \pm\sqrt{4}$$
$$y = \pm 2$$
The solutions are –2 and 2.

60.
$$(9n + 1)^2 = 9$$
$$9n + 1 = \pm\sqrt{9}$$
$$9n + 1 = \pm 3$$
$$9n = -1 \pm 3$$
$$n = \frac{-1 \pm 3}{9} = \frac{2}{9}, -\frac{4}{9}$$
The solutions are $-\dfrac{4}{9}$ and $\dfrac{2}{9}$.

61.
$$x^2 + x + 7 = 0$$
$$x^2 + x = -7$$
$$x^2 + x + \left(\frac{1}{2}\right)^2 = -7 + \frac{1}{4}$$
$$\left(x + \frac{1}{2}\right)^2 = -\frac{27}{4}$$
$$x + \frac{1}{2} = \pm\sqrt{-\frac{27}{4}}$$
$$x + \frac{1}{2} = \pm\frac{i\sqrt{9 \cdot 3}}{2}$$
$$x + \frac{1}{2} = \pm\frac{3i\sqrt{3}}{2}$$
$$x = -\frac{1}{2} \pm \frac{3i\sqrt{3}}{2} = \frac{-1 \pm 3i\sqrt{3}}{2}$$
The solutions are $\dfrac{-1 + 3i\sqrt{3}}{2}$ and $\dfrac{-1 - 3i\sqrt{3}}{2}$.

62.
$$(3x - 4)^2 = 10x$$
$$9x^2 - 24x + 16 = 10x$$
$$9x^2 - 34x = -16$$
$$x^2 - \frac{34}{9}x = -\frac{16}{9}$$
$$x^2 - \frac{34}{9}x + \left(\frac{-\frac{34}{9}}{2}\right)^2 = -\frac{16}{9} + \frac{289}{81}$$
$$\left(x - \frac{17}{9}\right)^2 = \frac{145}{81}$$
$$x - \frac{17}{9} = \pm\sqrt{\frac{145}{81}}$$
$$x - \frac{17}{9} = \pm\frac{\sqrt{145}}{9}$$
$$x = \frac{17 \pm \sqrt{145}}{9}$$
The solutions are $\dfrac{17 + \sqrt{145}}{9}$ and $\dfrac{17 - \sqrt{145}}{9}$.

63.
$$x^2 + 11 = 0$$
$$a = 1, b = 0, c = 11$$
$$x = \frac{0 \pm \sqrt{(0)^2 - 4(1)(11)}}{2(1)}$$
$$= \frac{\pm\sqrt{-44}}{2}$$
$$= \frac{\pm 2i\sqrt{11}}{2}$$
$$= \pm i\sqrt{11}$$
The solutions are $-i\sqrt{11}$ and $i\sqrt{11}$.

64.
$$(5a - 2)^2 - a = 0$$
$$25a^2 - 20a + 4 - a = 0$$
$$25a^2 - 21a + 4 = 0$$
$$a = \frac{21 \pm \sqrt{(-21)^2 - 4(25)(4)}}{2(25)}$$
$$= \frac{21 \pm \sqrt{441 - 400}}{50}$$
$$= \frac{21 \pm \sqrt{41}}{50}$$
The solutions are $\dfrac{21 + \sqrt{41}}{50}$ and $\dfrac{21 - \sqrt{41}}{50}$.

65. $\dfrac{7}{8} = \dfrac{8}{x^2}$

$7x^2 = 64$

$x^2 = \dfrac{64}{7}$

$x = \pm\sqrt{\dfrac{64}{7}}$

$x = \pm\dfrac{8}{\sqrt{7}} = \pm\dfrac{8\cdot\sqrt{7}}{\sqrt{7}\cdot\sqrt{7}} = \pm\dfrac{8\sqrt{7}}{7}$

The solutions are $-\dfrac{8\sqrt{7}}{7}$ and $\dfrac{8\sqrt{7}}{7}$.

66. $x^{2/3} - 6x^{1/3} = -8$

$x^{2/3} - 6x^{1/3} + 8 = 0$

Let $y = x^{1/3}$. Then $y^2 = x^{2/3}$ and

$y^2 - 6y + 8 = 0$

$(y-4)(y-2) = 0$

$y - 4 = 0$ or $y - 2 = 0$

$y = 4$ or $y = 2$

$x^{1/3} = 4$ or $x^{1/3} = 2$

$x = 64$ or $x = 8$

The solutions are 8 and 64.

67. $(2x-3)(4x+5) \ge 0$

$2x - 3 = 0$ or $4x + 5 = 0$

$x = \dfrac{3}{2}$ or $x = -\dfrac{5}{4}$

Region	Test Point	$(2x-3)(4x+5) \ge 0$ Result
A: $\left(-\infty, -\dfrac{5}{4}\right]$	-2	$(-7)(-3) \ge 0$ True
B: $\left[-\dfrac{5}{4}, \dfrac{3}{2}\right]$	0	$(-3)(5) \ge 0$ False
C: $\left[\dfrac{3}{2}, \infty\right)$	3	$(3)(17) \ge 0$ True

Solution: $\left(-\infty, -\dfrac{5}{4}\right] \cup \left[\dfrac{3}{2}, \infty\right)$

68. $\dfrac{x(x+5)}{4x-3} \ge 0$

$x = 0$ or $x + 5 = 0$ or $4x - 3 = 0$

$x = -5$ or $x = \dfrac{3}{4}$

Region	Test Point	$\dfrac{x(x+5)}{4x-3} \ge 0$ Result
A: $(-\infty, -5]$	-6	$\dfrac{-6(-1)}{-27} \ge 0$ False
B: $[-5, 0]$	-1	$\dfrac{-1(4)}{-7} \ge 0$ True
C: $\left[0, \dfrac{3}{4}\right)$	$\dfrac{1}{2}$	$\dfrac{\frac{1}{2}\left(\frac{11}{2}\right)}{-1} \ge 0$ False
D: $\left(\dfrac{3}{4}, \infty\right)$	1	$\dfrac{1(6)}{1} \ge 0$ True

Solution: $[-5, 0] \cup \left(\dfrac{3}{4}, \infty\right)$

69. $\dfrac{3}{x-2} > 2$

The denominator is equal to 0 when $x - 2 = 0$, or $x = 2$.

$\dfrac{3}{x-2} = 2$

$3 = 2(x-2)$

$3 = 2x - 4$

$7 = 2x$

$\dfrac{7}{2} = x$

Region	Test Point	$\dfrac{3}{x-2} > 2$ Result
$A: (-\infty, 2)$	0	$\dfrac{3}{-2} > 2$ False
$B: \left(2, \dfrac{7}{2}\right)$	3	$\dfrac{3}{1} > 2$ True
$C: \left(\dfrac{7}{2}, \infty\right)$	5	$\dfrac{3}{3} > 2$ False

Solution: $\left(2, \dfrac{7}{2}\right)$

70. $y = 6.46x^2 + 1236.5x + 7289$

a. $x = 2000 - 1980 = 20$

$y = 6.46(20)^2 + 1236.5(20) + 7289$
$= 34,603$ thousand

The passenger traffic was approximately 34,603,000.

b. Let $y = 60,000$.

$60,000 = 6.46x^2 + 1236.5x + 7289$

$0 = 6.46x^2 + 1236.5x - 52,711$

$x = \dfrac{-1236.5 \pm \sqrt{1236.5^2 - 4(6.46)(-52,711)}}{2(6.46)}$

Choosing the positive root, $x \approx 36$, we see that there will be 60,000,000 passengers in $1980 + 36 = 2016$.

Chapter 8 Test

1. $5x^2 - 2x = 7$

$5x^2 - 2x - 7 = 0$

$(5x - 7)(x + 1) = 0$

$5x - 7 = 0 \quad$ or $\quad x + 1 = 0$

$x = \dfrac{7}{5} \quad$ or $\quad x = -1$

The solutions are -1 and $\dfrac{7}{5}$.

2. $(x+1)^2 = 10$

$x + 1 = \pm\sqrt{10}$

$x = -1 \pm \sqrt{10}$

The solutions are $-1 + \sqrt{10}$ and $-1 - \sqrt{10}$.

3. $m^2 - m + 8 = 0$

$a = 1, b = -1, c = 8$

$m = \dfrac{1 \pm \sqrt{(-1)^2 - 4(1)(8)}}{2(1)}$

$= \dfrac{1 \pm \sqrt{1 - 32}}{2}$

$= \dfrac{1 \pm \sqrt{-31}}{2}$

$= \dfrac{1 \pm i\sqrt{31}}{2}$

The solutions are $\dfrac{1 + i\sqrt{31}}{2}$ and $\dfrac{1 - i\sqrt{31}}{2}$.

4. $u^2 - 6u + 2 = 0$

$a = 1, b = -6, c = 2$

$u = \dfrac{-(-6) \pm \sqrt{(-6)^2 - 4(1)(2)}}{2(1)}$

$= \dfrac{6 \pm \sqrt{36 - 8}}{2}$

$= \dfrac{6 \pm \sqrt{28}}{2}$

$= \dfrac{6 \pm 2\sqrt{7}}{2}$

$= 3 \pm \sqrt{7}$

The solutions are $3 + \sqrt{7}$ and $3 - \sqrt{7}$.

5. $7x^2 + 8x + 1 = 0$

$(7x + 1)(x + 1) = 0$

$7x + 1 = 0 \quad$ or $\quad x + 1 = 0$

$7x = -1 \qquad\qquad x = -1$

$x = -\dfrac{1}{7}$

The solutions are $-\dfrac{1}{7}$ and -1.

6.
$$y^2 - 3y = 5$$
$$y^2 - 3y - 5 = 0$$
$$a = 1, b = -3, c = -5$$

$$y = \frac{3 \pm \sqrt{(-3)^2 - 4(1)(-5)}}{2(1)}$$

$$= \frac{3 \pm \sqrt{9 + 20}}{2}$$

$$= \frac{3 \pm \sqrt{29}}{2}$$

The solutions are $\dfrac{3 + \sqrt{29}}{2}$ and $\dfrac{3 - \sqrt{29}}{2}$.

7.
$$\frac{4}{x+2} + \frac{2x}{x-2} = \frac{6}{x^2 - 4}$$

$$\frac{4}{x+2} + \frac{2x}{x-2} = \frac{6}{(x+2)(x-2)}$$

$$4(x-2) + 2x(x+2) = 6$$

$$4x - 8 + 2x^2 + 4x = 6$$

$$2x^2 + 8x - 14 = 0$$

$$x^2 + 4x - 7 = 0$$

$$a = 1, b = 4, c = -7$$

$$x = \frac{-4 \pm \sqrt{(4)^2 - 4(1)(-7)}}{2(1)}$$

$$= \frac{-4 \pm \sqrt{16 + 28}}{2}$$

$$= \frac{-4 \pm \sqrt{44}}{2}$$

$$= \frac{-4 \pm 2\sqrt{11}}{2}$$

$$= -2 \pm \sqrt{11}$$

The solutions are $-2 + \sqrt{11}$ and $-2 - \sqrt{11}$.

8.
$$x^5 + 3x^4 = x + 3$$
$$x^5 + 3x^4 - x - 3 = 0$$
$$x^4(x+3) - 1(x+3) = 0$$
$$(x+3)(x^4 - 1) = 0$$
$$(x+3)(x^2 + 1)(x^2 - 1) = 0$$

$x+3 = 0$ or $x^2 + 1 = 0$ or $x^2 - 1 = 0$
$\quad x = -3$ or $\quad x^2 = -1$ or $\quad x^2 = 1$
$$x = \pm i \text{ or } \quad x = \pm 1$$

The solutions are $-3, -1, 1, -i$, and i.

9.
$$x^6 + 1 = x^4 + x^2$$
$$x^6 - x^4 - x^2 + 1 = 0$$
$$x^4(x^2 - 1) - (x^2 - 1) = 0$$
$$(x^4 - 1)(x^2 - 1) = 0$$
$$(x^2 + 1)(x^2 - 1)(x+1)(x-1) = 0$$
$$(x^2 + 1)(x+1)^2(x-1)^2 = 0$$

$x^2 + 1 = 0$ or $x + 1 = 0$ or $x - 1 = 0$
$\quad x^2 = -1$ $\qquad x = -1$ $\qquad x = 1$
$\quad x = \pm i$

The solutions are $-i, i, -1$, and 1.

10. $(x+1)^2 - 15(x+1) + 56 = 0$

Let $y = x + 1$. Then $y^2 = (x+1)^2$ and

$$y^2 - 15y + 56 = 0$$
$$(y-8)(y-7) = 0$$
$\quad y = 8$ or $\qquad y = 7$
$\quad x + 1 = 8$ or $x + 1 = 7$
$\quad x = 7$ or $\quad x = 6$

The solutions are 6 and 7.

11.
$$x^2 - 6x = -2$$
$$x^2 - 6x + \left(\frac{-6}{2}\right)^2 = -2 + 9$$
$$x^2 - 6x + 9 = 7$$
$$(x-3)^2 = 7$$
$$x - 3 = \pm\sqrt{7}$$
$$x = 3 \pm \sqrt{7}$$

The solutions are $3 + \sqrt{7}$ and $3 - \sqrt{7}$.

12.
$$2a^2 + 5 = 4a$$
$$2a^2 - 4a = -5$$
$$a^2 - 2a = -\frac{5}{2}$$
$$a^2 - 2a + \left(\frac{-2}{2}\right)^2 = -\frac{5}{2} + 1$$
$$a^2 - 2a + 1 = -\frac{3}{2}$$
$$(a-1)^2 = -\frac{3}{2}$$
$$a - 1 = \pm\sqrt{-\frac{3}{2}} = \pm\frac{i\sqrt{3}}{\sqrt{2}}$$
$$a - 1 = \pm\frac{i\sqrt{6}}{2}$$
$$a = 1 \pm \frac{i\sqrt{6}}{2} \quad \text{or} \quad \frac{2 \pm i\sqrt{6}}{2}$$

The solutions are $\dfrac{2+i\sqrt{6}}{2}$ and $\dfrac{2-i\sqrt{6}}{2}$.

13.
$$2x^2 - 7x > 15$$
$$2x^2 - 7x - 15 > 0$$
$$(2x+3)(x-5) > 0$$
$$2x + 3 = 0 \quad \text{or} \quad x - 5 = 0$$
$$x = -\frac{3}{2} \quad \text{or} \quad x = 5$$

Region	Test Point	$(2x+3)(x-5) > 0$ Result
$A: \left(-\infty, -\frac{3}{2}\right)$	-2	$(-1)(-7) > 0$ True
$B: \left(-\frac{3}{2}, 5\right)$	0	$(3)(-5) > 0$ False
$C: (5, \infty)$	6	$(15)(1) > 0$ True

Solution: $\left(-\infty, -\dfrac{3}{2}\right) \cup (5, \infty)$

14. $(x^2 - 16)(x^2 - 25) \geq 0$

$(x + 4)(x - 4)(x + 5)(x - 5) \geq 0$

$x + 4 = 0$ or $x - 4 = 0$ or $x + 5 = 0$ or $x - 5 = 0$

$x = -4$ or $x = 4$ or $x = -5$ or $x = 5$

Region	Test Point	$(x + 4)(x - 4)(x + 5)(x - 5) \geq 0$ Result
A: $(-\infty, -5]$	-6	$(-2)(-10)(-1)(-11) \geq 0$ True
B: $[-5, -4]$	$-\dfrac{9}{2}$	$\left(-\dfrac{1}{2}\right)\left(-\dfrac{17}{2}\right)\left(\dfrac{1}{2}\right)\left(-\dfrac{19}{2}\right) \geq 0$ False
C: $[-4, 4]$	0	$(4)(-4)(5)(-5) \geq 0$ True
D: $[4, 5]$	$\dfrac{9}{2}$	$\left(\dfrac{17}{2}\right)\left(\dfrac{1}{2}\right)\left(\dfrac{19}{2}\right)\left(-\dfrac{1}{2}\right) \geq 0$ False
E: $[5, \infty)$	6	$(10)(2)(11)(1) \geq 0$ True

Solution: $(-\infty, -5] \cup [-4, 4] \cup [5, \infty)$

15. $\dfrac{5}{x + 3} < 1$

The denominator is equal to 0 when $x + 3 = 0$, or $x = -3$.

$\dfrac{5}{x + 3} = 1$

$5 = x + 3$ so $x = 2$

Region	Test Point	$\dfrac{5}{x + 3} < 1$ Result
A: $(-\infty, -3)$	-4	$\dfrac{5}{-1} < 1$ True
B: $(-3, 2)$	0	$\dfrac{5}{3} < 1$ False
C: $(2, \infty)$	3	$\dfrac{5}{6} < 1$ True

Solution: $(-\infty, -3) \cup (2, \infty)$

16. $\dfrac{7x-14}{x^2-9} \le 0$

$\dfrac{7(x-2)}{(x+3)(x-3)} \le 0$

$x-2=0$ or $x+3=0$ or $x-3=0$

$x=2$ or $x=-3$ or $x=3$

Region	Test Point	$\dfrac{7(x-2)}{(x+3)(x-3)} \le 0$ Result
A: $(-\infty, -3)$	-4	$\dfrac{7(-6)}{(-1)(-7)} \le 0$ True
B: $(-3, 2]$	0	$\dfrac{7(-2)}{(3)(-3)} \le 0$ False
C: $[2, 3)$	$\dfrac{5}{2}$	$\dfrac{7\left(\frac{1}{2}\right)}{\left(\frac{11}{2}\right)\left(-\frac{1}{2}\right)} \le 0$ True
D: $(3, \infty)$	4	$\dfrac{7(2)}{(7)(1)} \le 0$ False

Solution: $(-\infty, -3) \cup [2, 3)$

17. $f(x) = 3x^2$
Vertex: (0, 0)

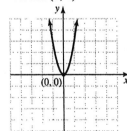

18. $G(x) = -2(x-1)^2 + 5$
Vertex: (1, 5)

19. $h(x) = x^2 - 4x + 4$

$x = -\dfrac{b}{2a} = \dfrac{-(-4)}{2(1)} = 2$

$h(2) = (2)^2 - 4(2) + 4 = 0$
Vertex: (2, 0)
$h(0) = 4 \Rightarrow$ *y*-intercept: (0, 4)
x-intercept: (2, 0)

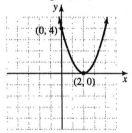

20. $F(x) = 2x^2 - 8x + 9$

$x = -\dfrac{b}{2a} = \dfrac{-(-8)}{2(2)} = 2$

$F(2) = 2(2)^2 - 8(2) + 9 = 1$
Vertex: (2, 1)
$F(0) = 9 \Rightarrow$ *y*-intercept: (0, 9)

$2x^2 - 8x + 9 = 0$
$a = 2, b = -8, c = 9$

$x = \dfrac{8 \pm \sqrt{(-8)^2 - 4(2)(9)}}{2(2)}$

$= \dfrac{8 \pm \sqrt{-8}}{4}$

which yields non-real solutons.
Therefore, there are no *x*-intercepts.

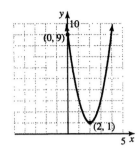

21. Let t = time for Sandy alone. Then $t - 2$ = time for Dave alone.

$$\frac{1}{t} + \frac{1}{t-2} = \frac{1}{4}$$
$$4(t-2) + 4t = t(t-2)$$
$$4t - 8 + 4t = t^2 - 2t$$
$$0 = t^2 - 10t + 8$$
$$a = 1, b = -10, c = 8$$
$$t = \frac{10 \pm \sqrt{(-10)^2 - 4(1)(8)}}{2(1)}$$
$$= \frac{10 \pm \sqrt{68}}{2}$$
$$= \frac{10 \pm 2\sqrt{17}}{2}$$
$$= 5 \pm \sqrt{17}$$
$$\approx 9.12 \text{ or } 0.88 \text{ (discard)}$$

It takes her about 9.12 hours.

22. $s(t) = -16t^2 + 32t + 256$

a. $t = -\dfrac{b}{2a} = \dfrac{-32}{2(-16)} = 1$

$s(1) = -16(1)^2 + 32(1) + 256 = 272$

Vertex: (1, 272)

The maximum height is 272 feet.

b. $\quad -16t^2 + 32t + 256 = 0$
$$t^2 - 2t - 16 = 0$$
$$a = 1, b = -2, c = -16$$
$$t = \frac{2 \pm \sqrt{(-2)^2 - 4(1)(-16)}}{2(1)}$$
$$= \frac{2 \pm \sqrt{68}}{2}$$
$$= \frac{2 \pm 2\sqrt{17}}{2}$$
$$= 1 \pm \sqrt{17}$$
$$\approx -3.12 \text{ and } 5.12$$

Disregard the negative. The stone will hit the water in about 5.12 seconds.

23. $\qquad a^2 + b^2 = c^2$
$$x^2 + (x+8)^2 = (20)^2$$
$$x^2 + (x^2 + 16x + 64) = 400$$
$$2x^2 + 16x - 336 = 0$$
$$x^2 + 8x - 168 = 0$$
$$a = 1, b = 8, c = -168$$
$$x = \frac{-8 \pm \sqrt{(8)^2 - 4(1)(-168)}}{2(1)}$$
$$= \frac{-8 \pm \sqrt{736}}{2}$$
$$\approx -17.565 \text{ or } 9.565$$

Disregard the negative.
$$x \approx 9.6$$
$$x + 8 \approx 9.6 + 8 = 17.6$$
$$17.6 + 9.6 = 27.2$$
$$27.2 - 20 = 7.2$$

They would save about 7 feet.

Chapter 8 Cumulative Review

1. a. $5 + y \geq 7$

b. $11 \neq z$

c. $20 < 5 - 2x$

2. $|3x - 2| = -5$ which is impossible. Thus, there is no solution, or $\emptyset$.

3. $m = \dfrac{5-3}{2-0} = \dfrac{2}{2} = 1$

Plot the given points and draw a line through them.

4. $\begin{cases} -6x + y = 5 & (1) \\ 4x - 2y = 6 & (2) \end{cases}$

Multiply E1 by 2 and add to E2.

$-12x + 2y = 10$

$\underline{4x - 2y = 6}$

$-8x = 16$

$x = -2$

Replace x with -2 in E1.

$-6(-2) + y = 5$

$12 + y = 5$

$y = -7$

The solution is $(-2, -7)$.

5. $\begin{cases} x - 5y = -12 & (1) \\ -x + y = 4 & (2) \end{cases}$

Add E1 and E2.

$-4y = -8$

$y = 2$

Replace y with 2 in E1.

$x - 5(2) = -12$

$x - 10 = -12$

$x = -2$

The solution is $(-2, 2)$.

6. **a.** $(a^{-2}bc^3)^{-3} = (a^{-2})^{-3} b^{-3} (c^3)^{-3}$

$= a^6 b^{-3} c^{-9}$

$= \dfrac{a^6}{b^3 c^9}$

b. $\left(\dfrac{a^{-4}b^2}{c^3} \right)^{-2} = \dfrac{(a^{-4})^{-2}(b^2)^{-2}}{(c^3)^{-2}}$

$= \dfrac{a^8 b^{-4}}{c^{-6}}$

$= \dfrac{a^8 c^6}{b^4}$

c. $\left(\dfrac{3a^8 b^2}{12a^5 b^5} \right)^{-2} = \left(\dfrac{a^3}{4b^3} \right)^{-2}$

$= \dfrac{(a^3)^{-2}}{4^{-2}(b^3)^{-2}}$

$= \dfrac{4^2 a^{-6}}{b^{-6}}$

$= \dfrac{16 b^6}{a^6}$

7. **a.** $(2x - 7)(3x - 4) = 6x^2 - 8x - 21x + 28$

$= 6x^2 - 29x + 28$

b. $(3x^2 + y)(5x^2 - 2y)$

$= 15x^4 - 6x^2 y + 5x^2 y - 2y^2$

$= 15x^4 - x^2 y - 2y^2$

8. **a.** $(4a - 3)(7a - 2) = 28a^2 - 8a - 21a + 6$

$= 28a^2 - 29a + 6$

b. $(2a + b)(3a - 5b)$

$= 6a^2 - 10ab + 3ab - 5b^2$

$= 6a^2 - 7ab - 5b^2$

9. **a.** $8x^2 + 4 = 4(2x^2 + 1)$

b. $5y - 2z^4$ is a prime polynomial.

c. $6x^2 - 3x^3 + 12x^4 = 3x^2(2 - x + 4x^2)$

10. **a.** $9x^3 + 27x^2 - 15x = 3x(3x^2 + 9x - 5)$

b. $2x(3y - 2) - 5(3y - 2)$

$= (3y - 2)(2x - 5)$

c. $2xy + 6x - y - 3 = 2x(y + 3) - 1(y + 3)$

$= (y + 3)(2x - 1)$

11. $x^2 - 12x + 35 = (x - 5)(x - 7)$

12. $x^2 - 2x - 48 = (x + 6)(x - 8)$

13. $3a^2x - 12abx + 12b^2x = 3x(a^2 - 4ab + 4b^2)$
$= 3x(a - 2b)(a - 2b)$
$= 3x(a - 2b)^2$

14. $2ax^2 - 12axy + 18ay^2 = 2a(x^2 - 6xy + 9y^2)$
$= 2a(x - 3y)(x - 3y)$
$= 2a(x - 3y)^2$

15. $3(x^2 + 4) + 5 = -6(x^2 + 2x) + 13$
$3x^2 + 12 + 5 = -6x^2 - 12x + 13$
$9x^2 + 12x + 4 = 0$
$(3x + 2)^2 = 0$
$3x + 2 = 0$
$3x = -2$
$x = -\dfrac{2}{3}$
The solutions is $-\dfrac{2}{3}$.

16. $2(a^2 + 2) - 8 = -2a(a - 2) - 5$
$2a^2 + 4 - 8 = -2a^2 + 4a - 5$
$4a^2 - 4a + 1 = 0$
$(2a - 1)^2 = 0$
$2a - 1 = 0$
$2a = 1$
$a = \dfrac{1}{2}$
The solution is $\dfrac{1}{2}$.

17. $x^3 = 4x$
$x^3 - 4x = 0$
$x(x^2 - 4) = 0$
$x(x + 2)(x - 2) = 0$
$x = 0$ or $x + 2 = 0$ or $x - 2 = 0$
$x = -2$ or $x = 2$
The solutions are –2, 0, and 2.

18. $f(x) = x^2 + x - 12$
$x = -\dfrac{b}{2a} = \dfrac{-1}{2(1)} = -\dfrac{1}{2}$
$f\left(-\dfrac{1}{2}\right) = \left(-\dfrac{1}{2}\right)^2 + \left(-\dfrac{1}{2}\right) - 12$
$= \dfrac{1}{4} - \dfrac{1}{2} - 12$
$= -\dfrac{49}{4}$
Vertex: $\left(-\dfrac{1}{2}, -\dfrac{49}{4}\right)$
$x^2 + x - 12 = 0$
$(x + 4)(x - 3) = 0$
$x + 4 = 0$ or $x - 3 = 0$
$x = -4$ $\qquad$ $x = 3$
x-intercepts: (–4, 0), (3, 0)
$f(0) = 0^2 + 0 - 12 = -12$
y-intercept: (0, –12)

19. $\dfrac{2x^2}{10x^3 - 2x^2} = \dfrac{2x^2}{2x^2(5x - 1)} = \dfrac{1}{5x - 1}$

20. $\dfrac{x^2 - 4x + 4}{2 - x} = \dfrac{(x - 2)^2}{-(x - 2)} = \dfrac{x - 2}{-1} = 2 - x$

21. $\dfrac{2x - 1}{2x^2 - 9x - 5} + \dfrac{x + 3}{6x^2 - x - 2}$
$= \dfrac{2x - 1}{(2x + 1)(x - 5)} + \dfrac{x + 3}{(2x + 1)(3x - 2)}$
$= \dfrac{(2x - 1)(3x - 2) + (x + 3)(x - 5)}{(2x + 1)(x - 5)(3x - 2)}$
$= \dfrac{(6x^2 - 4x - 3x + 2) + (x^2 - 5x + 3x - 15)}{(2x + 1)(x - 5)(3x - 2)}$
$= \dfrac{7x^2 - 9x - 13}{(2x + 1)(x - 5)(3x - 2)}$

22. $\dfrac{a+1}{a^2-6a+8}-\dfrac{3}{16-a^2}$

$=\dfrac{a+1}{(a-4)(a-2)}-\dfrac{3}{(4+a)(4-a)}$

$=\dfrac{a+1}{(a-4)(a-2)}+\dfrac{3}{(4+a)(a-4)}$

$=\dfrac{(a+1)(a+4)+3(a-2)}{(a-4)(a-2)(a+4)}$

$=\dfrac{(a^2+4a+a+4)+3a-6}{(a-4)(a-2)(a+4)}$

$=\dfrac{a^2+8a-2}{(a-4)(a-2)(a+4)}$

23. $\dfrac{x^{-1}+2xy^{-1}}{x^{-2}-x^{-2}y^{-1}}=\dfrac{\dfrac{1}{x}+\dfrac{2x}{y}}{\dfrac{1}{x^2}-\dfrac{1}{x^2y}}$

$=\dfrac{\left(\dfrac{1}{x}+\dfrac{2x}{y}\right)x^2y}{\left(\dfrac{1}{x^2}-\dfrac{1}{x^2y}\right)x^2y}$

$=\dfrac{xy+2x^3}{y-1}$

24. $\dfrac{(2a)^{-1}+b^{-1}}{a^{-1}+(2b)^{-1}}=\dfrac{\dfrac{1}{2a}+\dfrac{1}{b}}{\dfrac{1}{a}+\dfrac{1}{2b}}$

$=\dfrac{\left(\dfrac{1}{2a}+\dfrac{1}{b}\right)2ab}{\left(\dfrac{1}{a}+\dfrac{1}{2b}\right)2ab}$

$=\dfrac{b+2a}{2b+a}$

$=\dfrac{2a+b}{a+2b}$

25. $\dfrac{3x^5y^2-15x^3y-x^2y-6x}{x^2y}$

$=\dfrac{3x^5y^2}{x^2y}-\dfrac{15x^3y}{x^2y}-\dfrac{x^2y}{x^2y}-\dfrac{6x}{x^2y}$

$=3x^3y-15x-1-\dfrac{6}{xy}$

26.
$$\require{enclose}\begin{array}{r}x^2-6x+8\\x+3\enclose{longdiv}{x^3-3x^2-10x+24}\end{array}$$

$\underline{x^3+3x^2}$

$-6x^2-10x$

$\underline{-6x^2-18x}$

$8x+24$

$\underline{8x+24}$

0

Answer: x^2-6x+8

27. $P(x)=2x^3-4x^2+5$

    a. $\quad P(2)=2(2)^3-4(2)^2+5$

$=2(8)-4(4)+5$

$=16-16+5$

$=5$

    b.
$$
\begin{array}{r|rrrr}
2 & 2 & -4 & 0 & 5\\
  &   & 4 & 0 & 0\\
\hline
  & 2 & 0 & 0 & 5
\end{array}
$$
Thus, $P(2)=5$.

28. $P(x)=4x^3-2x^2+3$

    a. $\quad P(-2)=4(-2)^3-2(-2)^2+3$

$=4(-8)-2(4)+3$

$=-32-8+3$

$=-37$

    b.
$$
\begin{array}{r|rrrr}
-2 & 4 & -2 & 0 & 3\\
   &   & -8 & 20 & -40\\
\hline
   & 4 & -10 & 20 & -37
\end{array}
$$
Thus, $P(-2)=-37$.

29. $\dfrac{4x}{5}+\dfrac{3}{2}=\dfrac{3x}{10}$

$10\left(\dfrac{4x}{5}+\dfrac{3}{2}\right)=10\left(\dfrac{3x}{10}\right)$

$2(4x)+5(3)=3x$

$8x+15=3x$

$5x=-15$

$x=-3$

The solution is -3.

30.
$$\frac{x+3}{x^2+5x+6}=\frac{3}{2x+4}-\frac{1}{x+3}$$
$$\frac{x+3}{(x+3)(x+2)}=\frac{3}{2(x+2)}-\frac{1}{x+3}$$
$$2(x+3)=3(x+3)-2(x+2)$$
$$2x+6=3x+9-2x-4$$
$$2x+6=x+5$$
$$x=-1$$

31. Let $x=$ the number.
$$\frac{9-x}{19+x}=\frac{1}{3}$$
$$3(9-x)=1(19+x)$$
$$27-3x=19+x$$
$$-4x=-8$$
$$x=2$$
The number is 2.

32. Let $t=$ time to roof the house together.
$$\frac{1}{24}+\frac{1}{40}=\frac{1}{t}$$
$$120t\left(\frac{1}{24}+\frac{1}{40}\right)=120t\left(\frac{1}{t}\right)$$
$$5t+3t=120$$
$$8t=120$$
$$t=\frac{120}{8}=15$$
It would take them 15 hours to roof the house working together.

33. $y=kx$
$$5=k(30)$$
$$k=\frac{5}{30}=\frac{1}{6} \text{ and } y=\frac{1}{6}x$$

34. $y=\dfrac{k}{x}$
$$8=\frac{k}{14}$$
$$k=8(14)=112 \text{ and } y=\frac{112}{x}$$

35. a. $\sqrt{(-3)^2}=|-3|=3$

b. $\sqrt{x^2}=|x|$

c. $\sqrt[4]{(x-2)^4}=|x-2|$

d. $\sqrt[3]{(-5)^3}=-5$

e. $\sqrt[5]{(2x-7)^5}=2x-7$

f. $\sqrt{25x^2}=\sqrt{25}\cdot\sqrt{x^2}=5|x|$

g. $\sqrt{x^2+2x+1}=\sqrt{(x+1)^2}=|x+1|$

36. a. $\sqrt{(-2)^2}=|-2|=2$

b. $\sqrt{y^2}=|y|$

c. $\sqrt[4]{(a-3)^4}=|a-3|$

d. $\sqrt[3]{(-6)^3}=-6$

e. $\sqrt[5]{(3x-1)^5}=3x-1$

37. a. $\sqrt[8]{x^4}=x^{4/8}=x^{1/2}=\sqrt{x}$

b. $\sqrt[6]{25}=(25)^{1/6}$
$$=(5^2)^{1/6}=5^{2/6}=5^{1/3}=\sqrt[3]{5}$$

c. $\sqrt[4]{r^2s^6}=(r^2s^6)^{1/4}$
$$=r^{2/4}s^{6/4}$$
$$=r^{1/2}s^{3/2}$$
$$=(rs^3)^{1/2}=\sqrt{rs^3}$$

38. a. $\sqrt[4]{5^2}=5^{2/4}=5^{1/2}=\sqrt{5}$

b. $\sqrt[12]{x^3}=x^{3/12}=x^{1/4}=\sqrt[4]{x}$

c. $\sqrt[6]{x^2y^4}=(x^2y^4)^{1/6}$
$$=x^{2/6}y^{4/6}$$
$$=x^{1/3}y^{2/3}$$
$$=(xy^2)^{1/3}=\sqrt[3]{xy^2}$$

39. a. $\sqrt{25x^3}=\sqrt{25x^2\cdot x}=5x\sqrt{x}$

b. $\sqrt[3]{54x^6y^8}=\sqrt[3]{27x^6y^6\cdot 2y^2}$
$$=3x^2y^2\sqrt[3]{2y^2}$$

c. $\sqrt[4]{81z^{11}} = \sqrt[4]{81z^8 \cdot z^3} = 3z^2 \sqrt[4]{z^3}$

40. a. $\sqrt{64a^5} = \sqrt{64a^4 \cdot a} = 8a^2\sqrt{a}$

b. $\sqrt[3]{24a^7b^9} = \sqrt[3]{8a^6b^9 \cdot 3a} = 2a^2b^3\sqrt[3]{3a}$

c. $\sqrt[4]{48x^9} = \sqrt[4]{16x^8 \cdot 3x} = 2x^2\sqrt[4]{3x}$

41. a. $\dfrac{2}{\sqrt{5}} = \dfrac{2 \cdot \sqrt{5}}{\sqrt{5} \cdot \sqrt{5}} = \dfrac{2\sqrt{5}}{5}$

b. $\dfrac{2\sqrt{16}}{\sqrt{9x}} = \dfrac{2 \cdot 4}{3\sqrt{x}} = \dfrac{8 \cdot \sqrt{x}}{3\sqrt{x} \cdot \sqrt{x}} = \dfrac{8\sqrt{x}}{3x}$

c. $\sqrt[3]{\dfrac{1}{2}} = \dfrac{\sqrt[3]{1}}{\sqrt[3]{2}} = \dfrac{1}{\sqrt[3]{2}} = \dfrac{1 \cdot \sqrt[3]{2^2}}{\sqrt[3]{2} \cdot \sqrt[3]{2^2}} = \dfrac{\sqrt[3]{4}}{2}$

42. a. $\left(\sqrt{3}-4\right)\left(2\sqrt{3}+2\right)$
$= \sqrt{3} \cdot 2\sqrt{3} + 2\sqrt{3} - 4 \cdot 2\sqrt{3} - 4 \cdot 2$
$= 2(3) + 2\sqrt{3} - 8\sqrt{3} - 8$
$= 6 - 6\sqrt{3} - 8$
$= -2 - 6\sqrt{3}$

b. $\left(\sqrt{5}-x\right)^2 = \left(\sqrt{5}\right)^2 - 2 \cdot \sqrt{5} \cdot x + x^2$
$= 5 - 2x\sqrt{5} + x^2$

c. $\left(\sqrt{a}+b\right)\left(\sqrt{a}-b\right) = \left(\sqrt{a}\right)^2 - b^2$
$= a - b^2$

43. $\sqrt{2x+5} + \sqrt{2x} = 3$
$\sqrt{2x+5} = 3 - \sqrt{2x}$
$\left(\sqrt{2x+5}\right)^2 = \left(3-\sqrt{2x}\right)^2$
$2x+5 = 9 - 6\sqrt{2x} + 2x$
$-4 = -6\sqrt{2x}$
$(-4)^2 = \left(-6\sqrt{2x}\right)^2$
$16 = 36(2x)$
$16 = 72x$
$x = \dfrac{16}{72} = \dfrac{2}{9}$

The solution is $\dfrac{2}{9}$.

44. $\sqrt{x-2} = \sqrt{4x+1} - 3$
$\left(\sqrt{x-2}\right)^2 = \left(\sqrt{4x+1}-3\right)^2$
$x-2 = (4x+1) - 6\sqrt{4x+1} + 9$
$6\sqrt{4x+1} = 3x+12$
$2\sqrt{4x+1} = x+4$
$\left(2\sqrt{4x+1}\right)^2 = (x+4)^2$
$4(4x+1) = x^2 + 8x + 16$
$16x+4 = x^2 + 8x + 16$
$0 = x^2 - 8x + 12$
$0 = (x-6)(x-2)$
$x-6 = 0 \ \text{ or } \ x-2 = 0$
$x = 6 \ \text{ or } \quad x = 2$
The solutions are 2 and 6.

45. a. $\dfrac{2+i}{1-i} = \dfrac{(2+i) \cdot (1+i)}{(1-i) \cdot (1+i)}$
$= \dfrac{2+2i+1i+i^2}{1^2 - i^2}$
$= \dfrac{2+3i-1}{1+1}$
$= \dfrac{1+3i}{2} \ \text{ or } \ \dfrac{1}{2} + \dfrac{3}{2}i$

b. $\dfrac{7}{3i} = \dfrac{7 \cdot (-3i)}{3i \cdot (-3i)} = \dfrac{-21i}{-9i^2} = \dfrac{-21i}{9} = -\dfrac{7}{3}i$

46. a. $3i(5-2i) = 15i - 6i^2$
$= 15i + 6$
$= 6 + 15i$

b. $(6-5i)^2 = 6^2 - 2(6)(5i) + (5i)^2$
$= 36 - 60i + 25i^2$
$= 36 - 60i - 25$
$= 11 - 60i$

c. $\left(\sqrt{3}+2i\right)\left(\sqrt{3}-2i\right) = \left(\sqrt{3}\right)^2 - (2i)^2$
$= 3 - 4i^2$
$= 3 + 4$
$= 7$

47. $(x+1)^2 = 12$

$x+1 = \pm\sqrt{12}$

$x+1 = \pm 2\sqrt{3}$

$x = -1 \pm 2\sqrt{3}$

The solutions are $-1+2\sqrt{3}$ and $-1-2\sqrt{3}$.

48. $(y-1)^2 = 24$

$y-1 = \pm\sqrt{24}$

$y-1 = \pm 2\sqrt{6}$

$y = 1 \pm 2\sqrt{6}$

The solutions are $1+2\sqrt{6}$ and $1-2\sqrt{6}$.

49. $x - \sqrt{x} - 6 = 0$

Let $y = \sqrt{x}$. Then $y^2 = x$ and

$y^2 - y - 6 = 0$

$(y-3)(y+2) = 0$

$y-3 = 0$ or $y+2 = 0$

$y = 3$ or $\quad y = -2$

$\sqrt{x} = 3$ or $\sqrt{x} = -2$ (can't happen)

$x = 9$

The solution is 9.

50. $\quad\quad m^2 = 4m + 8$

$m^2 - 4m - 8 = 0$

$a = 1, b = -4, c = -8$

$x = \dfrac{4 \pm \sqrt{(-4)^2 - 4(1)(-8)}}{2(1)}$

$= \dfrac{4 \pm \sqrt{16 + 32}}{2}$

$= \dfrac{4 \pm \sqrt{48}}{2}$

$= \dfrac{4 \pm 4\sqrt{3}}{2}$

$= 2 \pm 2\sqrt{3}$

The solutions are $2 + 2\sqrt{3}$ and $2 - 2\sqrt{3}$.

Chapter 9

Practice Exercises

1. $f(x) = x + 2$; $g(x) = 3x + 5$

    a. $(f + g)(x) = f(x) + g(x)$
    $= (x + 2) + (3x + 5)$
    $= 4x + 7$

    b. $(f - g)(x) = f(x) - g(x)$
    $= (x + 2) - (3x + 5)$
    $= x + 2 - 3x - 5$
    $= -2x - 3$

    c. $(f \cdot g)(x) = f(x) \cdot g(x)$
    $= (x + 2)(3x + 5)$
    $= 3x^2 + 6x + 5x + 10$
    $= 3x^2 + 11x + 10$

    d. $\left(\dfrac{f}{g}\right)(x) = \dfrac{f(x)}{g(x)} = \dfrac{x + 2}{3x + 5}$, where $x \neq -\dfrac{5}{3}$.

2. $f(x) = x^2 + 1$; $g(x) = 3x - 5$

    a. $(f \circ g)(4) = f(g(4)) = f(7) = 50$
    $(g \circ f)(4) = g(f(4)) = g(17) = 46$

    b. $(f \circ g)(x) = f(g(x))$
    $= f(3x - 5)$
    $= (3x - 5)^2 + 1$
    $= 9x^2 - 30x + 26$
    $(g \circ f)(x) = g(f(x))$
    $= g(x^2 + 1)$
    $= 3(x^2 + 1) - 5$
    $= 3x^2 - 2$

3. $f(x) = x^2 + 5$; $g(x) = x + 3$

    a. $(f \circ g)(x) = f(g(x))$
    $= f(x + 3)$
    $= (x + 3)^2 + 5$
    $= x^2 + 6x + 14$

    b. $(g \circ f)(x) = g(f(x))$
    $= g(x^2 + 5)$
    $= (x^2 + 5) + 3$
    $= x^2 + 8$

4. $f(x) = 3x$; $g(x) = x - 4$; $h(x) = |x|$

    a. $F(x) = |x - 4|$
    $F(x) = (h \circ g)(x)$
    $= h(g(x))$
    $= h(x - 4)$
    $= |x - 4|$

    b. $G(x) = 3x - 4$
    $G(x) = (g \circ f)(x)$
    $= g(f(x))$
    $= g(3x)$
    $= 3x - 4$

Vocabulary and Readiness Check

1. C

2. E

3. F

4. A

5. D

6. B

Exercise Set 9.1

1. a. $(f + g)(x) = (x - 7) + (2x + 1) = 3x - 6$

    b. $(f - g)(x) = (x - 7) - (2x + 1)$
    $= x - 7 - 2x - 1$
    $= -x - 8$

    c. $(f \cdot g)(x) = (x - 7)(2x + 1) = 2x^2 - 13x - 7$

    d. $\left(\dfrac{f}{g}\right)(x) = \dfrac{x - 7}{2x + 1}$, where $x \neq -\dfrac{1}{2}$.

3. a. $(f + g)(x) = (x^2 + 1) + 5x = x^2 + 5x + 1$

    b. $(f - g)(x) = (x^2 + 1) - 5x = x^2 - 5x + 1$

c. $(f \cdot g)(x) = (x^2 + 1)(5x) = 5x^3 + 5x$

d. $\left(\dfrac{f}{g}\right)(x) = \dfrac{x^2 + 1}{5x}$, where $x \neq 0$

5. a. $(f + g)(x) = \sqrt{x} + x + 5$

b. $(f - g)(x) = \sqrt{x} - (x + 5) = \sqrt{x} - x - 5$

c. $(f \cdot g)(x) = \sqrt{x}(x + 5)$
$$= x\sqrt{x} + 5\sqrt{x}$$

d. $\left(\dfrac{f}{g}\right)(x) = \dfrac{\sqrt{x}}{x + 5}$; where $x \neq -5$.

7. a. $(f + g)(x) = -3x + 5x^2$ or $5x^2 - 3x$

b. $(f - g)(x) = -3x - 5x^2$ or $-5x^2 - 3x$

c. $(f \cdot g)(x) = (-3x)(5x^2) = -15x^3$

d. $\left(\dfrac{f}{g}\right)(x) = \dfrac{-3x}{5x^2}$
$$= -\dfrac{3}{5x}, \text{ where } x \neq 0.$$

9. $(f \circ g)(2) = f(g(2))$
$$= f(-4)$$
$$= (-4)^2 - 6(-4) + 2$$
$$= 16 + 24 + 2$$
$$= 42$$

11. $(g \circ f)(-1) = g(f(-1))$
$$= g(9)$$
$$= -2(9)$$
$$= -18$$

13. $(g \circ h)(0) = g(h(0))$
$$= g(0)$$
$$= -2(0)$$
$$= 0$$

15. $(f \circ g)(x) = f(g(x))$
$$= f(5x)$$
$$= (5x)^2 + 1$$
$$= 25x^2 + 1$$

$(g \circ f)(x) = g(f(x))$
$$= g(x^2 + 1)$$
$$= 5(x^2 + 1)$$
$$= 5x^2 + 5$$

17. $(f \circ g)(x) = f(g(x))$
$$= f(x + 7)$$
$$= 2(x + 7) - 3$$
$$= 2x + 14 - 3$$
$$= 2x + 11$$

$(g \circ f)(x) = g(f(x))$
$$= g(2x - 3)$$
$$= (2x - 3) + 7$$
$$= 2x + 4$$

19. $(f \circ g)(x) = f(g(x))$
$$= f(-2x)$$
$$= (-2x)^3 + (-2x) - 2$$
$$= -8x^3 - 2x - 2$$

$(g \circ f)(x) = g(f(x))$
$$= g(x^3 + x - 2)$$
$$= -2(x^3 + x - 2)$$
$$= -2x^3 - 2x + 4$$

21. $(f \circ g)(x) = f(g(x))$
$$= f(10x - 3)$$
$$= |10x - 3|$$

$(g \circ f)(x) = g(f(x)) = g(|x|) = 10|x| - 3$

23. $(f \circ g)(x) = f(g(x)) = f(-5x + 2) = \sqrt{-5x + 2}$

$(g \circ f)(x) = g(f(x)) = g\left(\sqrt{x}\right) = -5\sqrt{x} + 2$

25. $H(x) = (g \circ h)(x)$
$$= g(h(x))$$
$$= g(x^2 + 2)$$
$$= \sqrt{x^2 + 2}$$

27. $F(x) = (h \circ f)(x)$
$$= h(f(x))$$
$$= h(3x)$$
$$= (3x)^2 + 2$$
$$= 9x^2 + 2$$

29. $G(x) = (f \circ g)(x)$
    $\quad\; = f(g(x))$
    $\quad\; = f\left(\sqrt{x}\right)$
    $\quad\; = 3\sqrt{x}$

31. Answers may vary. For example, $g(x) = x + 2$ and $f(x) = x^2$.

33. Answers may vary. For example, $g(x) = x + 5$ and $f(x) = \sqrt{x} + 2$.

35. Answers may vary. For example, $g(x) = 2x - 3$ and $f(x) = \dfrac{1}{x}$.

37. $x = y + 2$
    $y = x - 2$

39. $x = 3y$
    $y = \dfrac{x}{3}$

41. $\quad x = -2y - 7$
    $\quad 2y = -x - 7$
    $\quad\;\; y = -\dfrac{x + 7}{2}$

43. $(f + g)(2) = f(2) + g(2) = 7 + (-1) = 6$

45. $(f \circ g)(2) = f(g(2)) = f(-1) = 4$

47. $(f \cdot g)(7) = f(7) \cdot g(7) = 1 \cdot 4 = 4$

49. $\left(\dfrac{f}{g}\right)(-1) = \dfrac{f(-1)}{g(-1)} = \dfrac{4}{-4} = -1$

51. Answers may vary.

53. Profit is equal to the revenue minus the cost; $P(x) = R(x) - C(x)$

Section 9.2

Practice Exercises

1. a. $f = \{(4, -3), (3, -4), (2, 7), (5, 0)\}$
        f is one-to-one since each y-value corresponds to only one x-value.

    b. $g = \{(8, 4), (-2, 0), (6, 4), (2, 6)\}$
        g is not one-to-one because the y-value 4 in (8, 4) and (6, 4) corresponds to two different x-values.

    c. $h = \{(2, 4), (1, 3), (4, 6), (-2, 4)\}$
        h is not one-to-one because the y-value 4 in (2, 4) and (-2, 4) corresponds to two different x-values.

d.

Year	1950	1963	1968	1975	1997	2002
Federal Minimum Wage	$0.75	$1.25	$1.60	$2.10	$5.15	$5.15

This function is not one-to-one because the wage $5.15 corresponds to two different years.

e. The function represented by the graph is not one-to-one because the *y*-value 2 in (2, 2) and (3, 2) corresponds to two different *x*-values.

f. The function represented by the diagram is not one-to-one because the score 509 corresponds to two different states.

2. Graphs **a**, **b**, and **c** all pass the vertical line test, so only these graphs are functions. But, of these, only **b** and **c** pass the horizontal line test, so only **b** and **c** are graphs of one-to-one functions.

3. $f(x) = \{(3, 4), (-2, 0), (2, 8), (6, 6)\}$
   Switching the coordinates of each ordered pair gives $f^{-1}(x) = \{(4, 3), (0, -2), (8, 2), (6, 6)\}$

4. $f(x) = 6 - x$
   Replace $f(x)$ with y.
   $y = 6 - x$
   Interchange x and y.
   $x = 6 - y$
   Solve for y.
   $x = 6 - y$
   $y = 6 - x$
   Replace y with $f^{-1}(x)$.
   $f^{-1}(x) = 6 - x$

5. $f(x) = 5x + 2$
   Replace $f(x)$ with y.
   $y = 5x + 2$
   Interchange x and y.
   $x = 5y + 2$
   Solve for y.
   $\quad x = 5y + 2$
   $x - 2 = 5y$
   $\dfrac{x-2}{5} = y$
   Replace y with $f^{-1}(x)$.
   $f^{-1}(x) = \dfrac{x-2}{5}$

6. a. $f(x) = 2x - 3$
$y = 2x - 3$

$x = 2y - 3$
$x + 3 = 2y$
$\dfrac{x+3}{2} = y$

$f^{-1}(x) = \dfrac{x+3}{2}$

b. $f(x) = x^3$
$y = x^3$

$x = y^3$
$\sqrt[3]{x} = y$
$f^{-1}(x) = \sqrt[3]{x}$

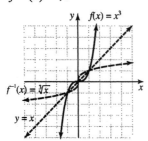

7. $f(x) = 4x - 1;\ f^{-1}(x) = \dfrac{x+1}{4}$

$(f \circ f^{-1})(x) = f(f^{-1}(x))$

$= f\left(\dfrac{x+1}{4}\right)$

$= 4\left(\dfrac{x+1}{4}\right) - 1$

$= x + 1 - 1$

$= x$

$(f^{-1} \circ f)(x) = f^{-1}(f(x))$

$= f^{-1}(4x - 1)$

$= \dfrac{(4x-1)+1}{4}$

$= \dfrac{4x - 1 + 1}{4}$

$= \dfrac{4x}{4}$

$= x$

Since $f \circ f^{-1} = x$ and $f^{-1} \circ f = x$, if

$f(x) = 4x - 1,\ f^{-1}(x) = \dfrac{x+1}{4}.$

Vocabulary and Readiness Check

1. If $f(2) = 11$, the corresponding ordered pair is <u>(2, 11)</u>.

2. The symbol f^{-1} means <u>the inverse of f</u>.

3. If $(7, 3)$ is an ordered pair solution of $f(x)$, and $f(x)$ has an inverse, then an ordered pair solution of $f^{-1}(x)$ is <u>(3, 7)</u>.

4. To tell whether a graph is the graph of a function, use the <u>vertical</u> line test.

5. To tell whether the graph of a function is also a one-to-one function, use the <u>horizontal</u> line test.

6. The graphs of f and f^{-1} are symmetric about the <u>$y = x$</u> line.

7. Two functions are inverse of each other if $(f \circ f^{-1})(x) = \underline{x}$ and $(f^{-1} \circ f)(x) = \underline{x}$.

Exercise Set 9.2

1. $f = \{(-1,-1), (1,1), (0,2), (2,0)\}$
is a one-to-one function.
$f^{-1} = \{(-1,-1), (1,1), (2,0), (0,2)\}$

3. $h = \{(10,10)\}$
is a one-to-one function.
$h^{-1} = \{(10,10)\}$

5. $f = \{(11,12),(4,3),(3,4),(6,6)\}$
    is a one-to-one function.
    $f^{-1} = \{(12,11),(3,4),(4,3),(6,6)\}$

7. This function is not one-to-one because there are two pairs of two months with the same output: (January, 4.6) and (February, 4.6); (March, 4.4) and (April, 4.4).

9. This function is one-to-one.

Rank in Population (input)	1	19	35	4	48
State (output)	California	Maryland	Nevada	Florida	North Dakota

11. $f(x) = x^3 + 2$

    a. $f(1) = 1^3 + 2 = 3$

    b. $f^{-1}(3) = 1$

13. $f(x) = x^3 + 2$

    a. $f(-1) = (-1)^3 + 2 = 1$

    b. $f^{-1}(1) = -1$

15. The graph represents a one-to-one function because it passes the horizontal line test.

17. The graph does not represent a one-to-one function because it does not pass the horizontal line test.

19. The graph represents a one-to-one function because it passes the horizontal line test.

21. The graph does not represent a one-to-one function because it does not pass the horizontal line test.

23. $f(x) = x + 4$
        $y = x + 4$
        $x = y + 4$
        $y = x - 4$
    $f^{-1}(x) = x - 4$

25.
$$f(x) = 2x - 3$$
$$y = 2x - 3$$
$$x = 2y - 3$$
$$2y = x + 3$$
$$y = \frac{x + 3}{2}$$
$$f^{-1}(x) = \frac{x + 3}{2}$$

27.
$$f(x) = \frac{1}{2}x - 1$$
$$y = \frac{1}{2}x - 1$$
$$x = \frac{1}{2}y - 1$$
$$\frac{1}{2}y = x + 1$$
$$y = 2x + 2$$
$$f^{-1}(x) = 2x + 2$$

29.
$$f(x) = x^3$$
$$y = x^3$$
$$x = y^3$$
$$y = \sqrt[3]{x}$$
$$f^{-1}(x) = \sqrt[3]{x}$$

31.
$$f(x) = 5x + 2$$
$$y = 5x + 2$$
$$x = 5y + 2$$
$$5y = x - 2$$
$$y = \frac{x - 2}{5}$$
$$f^{-1}(x) = \frac{x - 2}{5}$$

33.
$$f(x) = \frac{x - 2}{5}$$
$$y = \frac{x - 2}{5}$$
$$x = \frac{y - 2}{5}$$
$$5x = y - 2$$
$$y = 5x + 2$$
$$f^{-1}(x) = 5x + 2$$

35.
$$f(x) = \sqrt[3]{x}$$
$$y = \sqrt[3]{x}$$
$$x = \sqrt[3]{y}$$
$$x^3 = y$$
$$f^{-1}(x) = x^3$$

37. $f(x) = \dfrac{5}{3x+1}$

$y = \dfrac{5}{3x+1}$

$x = \dfrac{5}{3y+1}$

$3y+1 = \dfrac{5}{x}$

$3y = \dfrac{5}{x} - 1$

$3y = \dfrac{5-x}{x}$

$y = \dfrac{5-x}{3x}$

$f^{-1}(x) = \dfrac{5-x}{3x}$

39. $f(x) = (x+2)^3$

$y = (x+2)^3$

$x = (y+2)^3$

$\sqrt[3]{x} = y+2$

$\sqrt[3]{x} - 2 = y$

$f^{-1}(x) = \sqrt[3]{x} - 2$

41.

43.

45.

47. $(f \circ f^{-1})(x) = f(f^{-1}(x))$

$= f\left(\dfrac{x-1}{2}\right)$

$= 2\left(\dfrac{x-1}{2}\right) + 1$

$= x - 1 + 1$

$= x$

$(f^{-1} \circ f)(x) = f^{-1}(f(x))$

$= f^{-1}(2x+1)$

$= \dfrac{(2x+1)-1}{2}$

$= \dfrac{2x}{2}$

$= x$

49. $(f \circ f^{-1})(x) = f(f^{-1}(x))$

$= f\left(\sqrt[3]{x-6}\right)$

$= \left(\sqrt[3]{x-6}\right)^3 + 6$

$= x - 6 + 6$

$= x$

$(f^{-1} \circ f)(x) = f^{-1}(f(x))$

$= f^{-1}(x^3 + 6)$

$= \sqrt[3]{(x^3 + 6) - 6}$

$= \sqrt[3]{x^3}$

$= x$

51. $25^{1/2} = \sqrt{25} = 5$

53. $16^{3/4} = \left(\sqrt[4]{16}\right)^3 = 2^3 = 8$

55. $9^{-3/2} = \dfrac{1}{9^{3/2}} = \dfrac{1}{\left(\sqrt{9}\right)^3} = \dfrac{1}{3^3} = \dfrac{1}{27}$

57. $f(x) = 3^x$

$f(2) = 3^2 = 9$

59. $f(x) = 3^x$

$f\left(\dfrac{1}{2}\right) = 3^{1/2} \approx 1.73$

61. $f(2) = 9$

   a. $(2, 9)$

   b. $(9, 2)$

63. **a.** $\left(-2, \dfrac{1}{4}\right), \left(-1, \dfrac{1}{2}\right), (0,1), (1,2), (2,5)$

   b. $\left(\dfrac{1}{4}, -2\right), \left(\dfrac{1}{2}, -1\right), (1,0), (2,1), (5,2)$

   c, d.

65. Answers may vary.

67. $f(x) = 3x + 1$

      $y = 3x + 1$

      $x = 3y + 1$

      $x - 1 = 3y$

      $y = \dfrac{x-1}{3}$

   $f^{-1}(x) = \dfrac{x-1}{3}$

69. $f(x) = \sqrt[3]{x+1}$

$y = \sqrt[3]{x+1}$

$x = \sqrt[3]{y+1}$

$x^3 = y+1$

$y = x^3 - 1$

$f^{-1}(x) = x^3 - 1$

Section 9.3

Practice Exercises

1.

$f(x) = 2^x$

x	0	1	2	3	−1	−2
$f(x)$	1	2	4	8	$\frac{1}{2}$	$\frac{1}{4}$

$g(x) = 7^x$

x	0	1	2	3	−1	−2
$g(x)$	1	7	49	343	$\frac{1}{7}$	$\frac{1}{49}$

2.

$f(x) = \left(\frac{1}{3}\right)^x$

x	0	1	2	3	−1	−2
$f(x)$	1	$\frac{1}{3}$	$\frac{1}{9}$	$\frac{1}{27}$	3	9

$g(x) = \left(\frac{1}{5}\right)^x$

x	0	1	2	3	−1	−2
$g(x)$	1	$\frac{1}{5}$	$\frac{1}{25}$	$\frac{1}{125}$	5	25

3. $f(x) = 2^{x+3}$

$y = 2^{x+3}$	x	0	-1	-2	-3	-4	-5
	y	8	4	2	1	$\frac{1}{2}$	$\frac{1}{4}$

4. a. $3^x = 9$

Write 9 as a power of 3, $9 = 3^2$.

$3^x = 3^2$, thus, $x = 2$.

b. $8^x = 16$

Write 8 and 16 as powers of 2.

$8 = 2^3$ and $16 = 2^4$.

$$8^x = 16$$
$$(2^3)^x = 2^4$$
$$2^{3x} = 2^4$$
$$3x = 4$$
$$x = \frac{4}{3}$$

c. $125^x = 25^{x-2}$

Write 125 and 25 as powers of 5.

$125 = 5^3$ and $25 = 5^2$.

$125^x = 25^{x-2}$

$(5^3)^x = (5^2)^{x-2}$

$5^{3x} = 5^{2x-4}$

$3x = 2x - 4$

$x = -4$

5. $P = \$3000$, $r = 7\% = 0.07$, $n = 2$, and $t = 4$.

$$A = P\left(1 + \frac{r}{n}\right)^{nt}$$

$$A = 3000\left(1 + \frac{0.07}{2}\right)^{2(4)}$$

$$= 3000(1.035)^8$$

$$\approx 3950.43$$

Thus, the amount A owed is approximately $3950.43.

6. $p(n) = 100(2.7)^{-0.05n}$, $n = 10$ sheets of glass.

$p(10) = 100(2.7)^{-0.05(10)} = 100(2.7)^{-0.5} \approx 60.86$

Thus, approximately 60.86% of the light passes through.

Graphing Calculator Explorations

1.

The expected percent after 2 days is 81.98%.

2.

The expected percent after 10 days is 37.04%.

3.

The expected percent after 15 days is 22.54%.

4.

The expected percent after 25 days is 8.35%.

Vocabulary and Readiness Check

1. A function such as $f(x) = 2^x$ is an <u>exponential</u> function; **C**.

2. If $7^x = 7^y$, then <u>$x = y$</u>; **B**.

3. Yes, the function passes both the vertical- and horizontal-line tests.

4. The function has no x-intercept.

5. The function has a y-intercept of <u>(0, 1)</u>.

6. The domain of this function, in interval notation, is <u>$(-\infty, \infty)$</u>.

7. The range of this function, in interval notation, is <u>$(0, \infty)$</u>.

Exercise Set 9.3

1. $y = 4^x$

3. $y = 2^x + 1$

5. $y = \left(\dfrac{1}{4}\right)^x$

7. $y = \left(\dfrac{1}{2}\right)^x - 2$

9. $y = -2^x$

11. $y = -\left(\dfrac{1}{4}\right)^x$

13. $f(x) = 2^{x+1}$

15. $f(x) = 4^{x-2}$

17. C

19. B

21. $3^x = 27$
$3^x = 3^3$
$x = 3$
The solution is 3.

23. $16^x = 8$
$(2^4)^x = 2^3$
$2^{4x} = 2^3$
$4x = 3$
$x = \dfrac{3}{4}$

The solution is $\dfrac{3}{4}$.

25. $32^{2x-3} = 2$
$(2^5)^{2x-3} = 2^1$
$2^{10x-15} = 2^1$
$10x - 15 = 1$
$10x = 16$
$x = \dfrac{8}{5}$

The solution is $\dfrac{8}{5}$.

27. $\dfrac{1}{4} = 2^{3x}$

$2^{-2} = 2^{3x}$

$3x = -2$

$x = -\dfrac{2}{3}$

The solution is $-\dfrac{2}{3}$.

29. $5^x = 625$

$5^x = 5^4$

$x = 4$

The solution is 4.

31. $4^x = 8$

$(2^2)^x = 2^3$

$2^{2x} = 2^3$

$2x = 3$

$x = \dfrac{3}{2}$

The solution is $\dfrac{3}{2}$.

33. $27^{x+1} = 9$

$(3^3)^{x+1} = 3^2$

$3^{3x+3} = 3^2$

$3x + 3 = 2$

$3x = -1$

$x = -\dfrac{1}{3}$

The solution is $-\dfrac{1}{3}$.

35. $81^{x-1} = 27^{2x}$

$(3^4)^{x-1} = (3^3)^{2x}$

$3^{4x-4} = 3^{6x}$

$4x - 4 = 6x$

$-4 = 2x$

$x = -2$

The solution is -2.

37. $y = 30(2.7)^{-0.004t}$, $t = 50$

$y = 30(2.7)^{-(0.004)(50)}$

$= 30(2.7)^{-0.2}$

≈ 24.6

Approximately 24.6 pounds of uranium will remain after 50 days.

39. $y = 260(2.7)^{0.025t}$, $t = 10$

$y = 260(2.7)^{0.025(10)}$

$= 260(2.7)^{0.25}$

≈ 333

There should be about 333 bison in the park in 10 years.

41. $y = 5(2.7)^{-0.15t}$, $t = 10$

$y = 5(2.7)^{-0.15(10)}$

$= 5(2.7)^{-1.5}$

≈ 1.1

After 10 seconds there will be about 1.1 grams.

43. $p(h) = 760(2.7)^{-0.145h}$

    a. $p(1) = 760(2.7)^{-0.145(1)} \approx 658.1$

       The pressure is 658.1 Pascals at a height of 1 kilometer.

    b. $p(10) = 760(2.7)^{-0.145(10)}$

            $= 760(2.7)^{-1.45}$

            ≈ 180.0

       The pressure is 180.0 Pascals at a height of 10 kilometers.

45. $y = 84{,}949(1.096)^x$

    a. $x = 2000 - 1995 = 5$

       $y = 84{,}949(1.096)^5 \approx 134{,}342$

       134,342 American students studied abroad in 2000.

    b. $x = 2020 - 1995 = 25$

       $y = 84{,}949(1.096)^{25} \approx 840{,}276$

       840,276 American students would be studying abroad in 2020.

47. $A = P\left(1 + \dfrac{r}{n}\right)^{nt}$

$t = 3, P = 6000, r = 0.08,$ and $n = 12$

$A = 6000\left(1 + \dfrac{0.08}{12}\right)^{12(3)}$

$= 6000\left(1 + \dfrac{0.08}{12}\right)^{36}$

≈ 7621.42

Erica would owe $7621.42 after 3 years.

49. $A = P\left(1 + \dfrac{r}{n}\right)^{nt}$

$P = 2000$

$r = 0.06,\ n = 2,$ and $t = 12$

$A = 2000\left(1 + \dfrac{0.06}{2}\right)^{2(12)}$

$= 2000(1.03)^{24}$

≈ 4065.59

Janina has approximately $4065.59 in her savings account.

51. $y = 18(1.24)^x$

$x = 2010 - 1994 = 16$

$y = 18(1.24)^{16} \approx 562$

There will be approximately 562 million cellular phone users in 2010.

53. $5x - 2 = 18$

$5x = 20$

$x = 4$

The solution is 4.

55. $3x - 4 = 3(x + 1)$

$3x - 4 = 3x + 3$

$-4 = 3$

This is a false statement. The solution set is $\varnothing$.

57. $\qquad x^2 + 6 = 5x$

$x^2 - 5x + 6 = 0$

$(x - 2)(x - 3) = 0$

$x = 2$ or $x = 3$

The solutions are 2 and 3.

59. $2^x = 8$

$2^3 = 8$

$x = 3$

61. $5^x = \dfrac{1}{5}$

$5^{-1} = \dfrac{1}{5}$

$x = -1$

63. Answers may vary

65. $y = \left|3^x\right|$

67. $y = 3^{|x|}$

69.

The graphs are the same, since $\left(\dfrac{1}{2}\right)^{-x} = 2^x$.

71.

```
30
Y1=30*2.7^(-0.004X)

40  X=50        Y=24.595095  60
10
```

24.60 pounds remain after 50 days.

73.

18.62 pounds will be available after 120 days.

75.

50.41 grams remain after 10 days.

Section 9.4

Practice Exercises

1. a. $\log_3 81 = 4$ means $3^4 = 81$.

   b. $\log_5 \dfrac{1}{5} = -1$ means $5^{-1} = \dfrac{1}{5}$.

   c. $\log_7 \sqrt{7} = \dfrac{1}{2}$ means $7^{1/2} = \sqrt{7}$.

   d. $\log_{13} y = 4$ means $13^4 = y$.

2. a. $4^3 = 64$ means $\log_4 64 = 3$.

   b. $6^{1/3} = \sqrt[3]{6}$ means $\log_6 \sqrt[3]{6} = \dfrac{1}{3}$.

   c. $5^{-3} = \dfrac{1}{125}$ means $\log_5 \dfrac{1}{125} = -3$.

   d. $\pi^7 = z$ means $\log_\pi z = 7$.

3. a. $\log_3 9 = 2$ because $3^2 = 9$.

   b. $\log_2 \dfrac{1}{8} = -3$ because $2^{-3} = \dfrac{1}{8}$.

   c. $\log_{49} 7 = \dfrac{1}{2}$ because $49^{1/2} = 7$.

4. a. $\log_5 \dfrac{1}{25} = x$

   $\log_5 \dfrac{1}{25} = x$ means $5^x = \dfrac{1}{25}$. Solve

   $5^x = \dfrac{1}{25}$.

   $5^x = \dfrac{1}{25}$

   $5^x = 5^{-2}$

   Since the bases are the same, by the uniqueness of b^x, we have that $x = -2$. The solution is -2 or the solution set is $\{-2\}$.

   b. $\log_x 8 = 3$

     $x^3 = 8$

     $x^3 = 2^3$

     $x = 2$

   c. $\log_6 x = 2$

     $6^2 = x$

     $36 = x$

   d. $\log_{13} 1 = x$

     $13^x = 1$

     $13^x = 13^0$

     $x = 0$

   e. $\log_h 1 = x$

     $h^x = 1$

     $h^x = h^0$

     $x = 0$

5. a. From Property 2, $\log_5 5^4 = 4$.

   b. From Property 2, $\log_9 9^{-2} = -2$.

   c. From Property 3, $6^{\log_6 5} = 5$.

   d. From Property 3, $7^{\log_7 4} = 4$.

6. $y = \log_7 x$ means that $7^y = x$. Find some ordered pair solutions that satisfy $7^y = x$.

$x = 7^y$	y
1	0
7	1
$\frac{1}{7}$	-1
$\frac{1}{49}$	-2

7. $y = \log_{1/4} x$ means that $\left(\dfrac{1}{4}\right)^y = x$. Find some ordered-pair solutions that satisfy $\left(\dfrac{1}{4}\right)^y = x$.

$x = \left(\frac{1}{4}\right)^y$	y
1	0
$\frac{1}{4}$	1
4	-1
16	-2

Vocabulary and Readiness Check

1. A function, such as $y = \log_2 x$ is a <u>logarithmic</u> function; **B.**

2. If $y = \log_2 x$, then <u>$2^y = x$</u>; **C.**

3. Yes, the function passes both the horizontal- and vertical-line tests.

4. The function has an x-intercept of <u>(1, 0)</u>.

5. The function has no y-intercept.

6. The domain of this function, in interval notation, is <u>(0, ∞)</u>.

7. The range of this function, in interval notation, is <u>(−∞, ∞)</u>.

Exercise Set 9.4

1. $\log_6 36 = 2$
   $6^2 = 36$

3. $\log_3 \dfrac{1}{27} = -3$
   $3^{-3} = \dfrac{1}{27}$

5. $\log_{10} 1000 = 3$
   $10^3 = 1000$

7. $\log_9 x = 4$
   $9^4 = x$

9. $\log_\pi \dfrac{1}{\pi^2} = -2$
   $\pi^{-2} = \dfrac{1}{\pi^2}$

11. $\log_7 \sqrt{7} = \dfrac{1}{2}$
    $7^{1/2} = \sqrt{7}$

13. $\log_{0.7} 0.343 = 3$
    $0.7^3 = 0.343$

15. $\log_3 \dfrac{1}{81} = -4$

$\quad\quad 3^{-4} = \dfrac{1}{81}$

17. $\quad 2^4 = 16$

$\quad \log_2 16 = 4$

19. $\quad\quad 10^2 = 100$

$\quad \log_{10} 100 = 2$

21. $\quad\quad \pi^3 = x$

$\quad \log_\pi x = 3$

23. $\quad 10^{-1} = \dfrac{1}{10}$

$\quad \log_{10} \dfrac{1}{10} = -1$

25. $\quad 4^{-2} = \dfrac{1}{16}$

$\quad \log_4 \dfrac{1}{16} = -2$

27. $\quad 5^{1/2} = \sqrt{5}$

$\quad \log_5 \sqrt{5} = \dfrac{1}{2}$

29. $\log_2 8 = 3$ since $2^3 = 8$.

31. $\log_3 \dfrac{1}{9} = -2$ since $3^{-2} = \dfrac{1}{9}$.

33. $\log_{25} 5 = \dfrac{1}{2}$ since $25^{1/2} = 5$.

35. $\log_{1/2} 2 = -1$ since $\left(\dfrac{1}{2}\right)^{-1} = 2$.

37. $\log_6 1 = 0$ since $6^0 = 1$.

39. $\log_{10} 100 = \log_{10} 10^2 = 2$

41. $\log_3 81 = \log_3 3^4 = 4$

43. $\log_4 \dfrac{1}{64} = \log_4 4^{-3} = -3$

45. $\log_3 9 = x$

$\quad\quad 3^x = 9$

$\quad\quad 3^x = 3^2$

$\quad\quad x = 2$

47. $\log_3 x = 4$

$\quad\quad x = 3^4 = 81$

49. $\log_x 49 = 2$

$\quad\quad x^2 = 49$

$\quad\quad x = \pm 7$

We discard the negative base.

$x = 7$

51. $\log_2 \dfrac{1}{8} = x$

$\quad\quad 2^x = \dfrac{1}{8}$

$\quad\quad 2^x = 2^{-3}$

$\quad\quad x = -3$

53. $\log_3 \dfrac{1}{27} = x$

$\quad\quad \dfrac{1}{27} = 3^x$

$\quad\quad 3^{-3} = 3^x$

$\quad\quad -3 = x$

55. $\log_8 x = \dfrac{1}{3}$

$\quad\quad x = 8^{1/3} = 2$

57. $\log_4 16 = x$

$\quad\quad 4^x = 16$

$\quad\quad 4^x = 4^2$

$\quad\quad x = 2$

59. $\log_{3/4} x = 3$

$\quad\quad \left(\dfrac{3}{4}\right)^3 = x$

$\quad\quad \dfrac{27}{64} = x$

61. $\log_x 100 = 2$

$\quad\quad x^2 = 100$

$\quad\quad x = \pm 10$

We discard the negative base.

$x = 10$

63. $\log_2 2^4 = x$

$\qquad 2^x = 2^4$

$\qquad x = 4$

65. $3^{\log_3 5} = x$

$\qquad 5 = x$

67. $\log_x \dfrac{1}{7} = \dfrac{1}{2}$

$\qquad x^{1/2} = \dfrac{1}{7}$

$\qquad x = \dfrac{1}{49}$

69. $\log_5 5^3 = 3$

71. $2^{\log_2 3} = 3$

73. $\log_9 9 = 1$

75. $y = \log_3 x$

$\quad y = 0:$

$\quad \log_3 x = 0$

$\qquad x = 3^0 = 1$

(1, 0) is the only x-intercept. No y-intercept exists.

77. $f(x) = \log_{1/4} x$

$\quad y = 0: \ 0 = \log_{1/4} x$

$\qquad x = \left(\dfrac{1}{4}\right)^0 = 1$

(1, 0) is the x-intercept. No y-intercept exists.

79. $f(x) = \log_5 x$

$\quad y = 0: \ 0 = \log_5 x$

$\qquad x = 5^0 = 1$

(1, 0) is the x-intercept. No y-intercept exists.

81. $f(x) = \log_{1/16} x$

$\quad y = 0:$

$\quad 0 = \log_{1/6} x$

$\qquad x = \left(\dfrac{1}{6}\right)^0 = 1$

(1, 0) is the x-intercept. No y-intercept exists.

83. $\dfrac{x+3}{3+x} = \dfrac{x+3}{x+3} = 1$

85. $\dfrac{x^2 - 8x + 16}{2x - 8} = \dfrac{(x-4)^2}{2(x-4)} = \dfrac{x-4}{2}$

87. $\dfrac{2}{x} + \dfrac{3}{x^2} = \dfrac{2x}{x^2} + \dfrac{3}{x^2} = \dfrac{2x+3}{x^2}$

89. $\dfrac{m^2}{m+1} - \dfrac{1}{m+1} = \dfrac{m^2-1}{m+1}$

$\qquad\qquad = \dfrac{(m+1)(m-1)}{m+1}$

$\qquad\qquad = m-1$

91. $f(x) = \log_5 x; \quad f^{-1}(x) = g(x) = 5^x$

  a. $(2, 25)$ implies $g(2) = 25$.

  b. Since $f^{-1}(x) = g(x)$, $(25, 2)$ is a solution of $f(x)$.

  c. $(25, 2)$ implies $f(25) = 2$.

93. Answers may vary

95. $\log_7(5x - 2) = 1$

$\qquad\quad 5x - 2 = 7^1$

$\qquad\qquad 5x = 9$

$\qquad\qquad\ x = \dfrac{9}{5}$

97. $\log_3\left(\log_5 125\right) = \log_3(3) = 1$

99. $y = 4^x; \ y = \log_4 x$

101. $y = \left(\dfrac{1}{3}\right)^x; \ y = \log_{1/3} x$

103. Answers may vary

105. $\log_{10}(1-k) = \dfrac{-0.3}{H}, \ H = 8$

$\qquad \log_{10}(1-k) = \dfrac{-0.3}{8} = -0.0375$

$\qquad\qquad 1 - k = 10^{-0.0375}$

$\qquad\quad 1 - 10^{-0.0375} = k$

$\qquad\qquad\qquad k \approx 0.0827$

The rate of decay is 0.0827.

Section 9.5

Practice Exercises

1. a. $\log_8 5 + \log_8 3 = \log_8(5 \cdot 3) = \log_8 15$

  b. $\log_2 \dfrac{1}{3} + \log_2 18 = \log_2\left(\dfrac{1}{3} \cdot 18\right) = \log_2 6$

  c. $\log_5(x-1) + \log_5(x+1) = \log_5[(x+1)(x+1)]$
$\qquad\qquad\qquad\qquad\qquad\quad = \log_5(x^2 - 1)$

2. a. $\log_5 18 - \log_5 6 = \log_5 \dfrac{18}{6} = \log_5 3$

  b. $\log_6 x - \log_6 3 = \log_6 \dfrac{x}{3}$

  c. $\log_4(x^2 + 1) - \log_4(x^2 + 3) = \log_4 \dfrac{x^2+1}{x^2+3}$

3. a. $\log_7 x^8 = 8\log_7 x$

  b. $\log_5 \sqrt[4]{7} = \log_5 7^{1/4} = \dfrac{1}{4}\log_5 7$

4. a. $2\log_5 4 + 5\log_5 2 = \log_5 4^2 + \log_5 2^5$
$\qquad\qquad\qquad\qquad = \log_5 16 + \log_5 32$
$\qquad\qquad\qquad\qquad = \log_5(16 \cdot 32)$
$\qquad\qquad\qquad\qquad = \log_5 512$

  b. $2\log_8 x - \log_8(x+3) = \log_8 x^2 - \log_8(x+3)$
$\qquad\qquad\qquad\qquad\quad = \log_8 \dfrac{x^2}{x+3}$

c. $\log_7 12 + \log_7 5 - \log_7 4$
$= \log_7 (12 \cdot 5) - \log_7 4$
$= \log_7 60 - \log_7 4$
$= \log_7 \dfrac{60}{4}$
$= \log_7 15$

5. a. $\log_5 \dfrac{4 \cdot 3}{7} = \log_5 (4 \cdot 3) - \log_5 7$
$= \log_5 4 + \log_5 3 - \log_5 7$

b. $\log_4 \dfrac{a^2}{b^5} = \log_4 a^2 - \log_4 b^5$
$= 2\log_4 a - 5\log_4 b$

6. $\log_b 5 = 0.83$ and $\log_b 3 = 0.56$

a. $\log_b 15 = \log_b (3 \cdot 5)$
$= \log_b 3 + \log_b 5$
$= 0.56 + 0.83$
$= 1.39$

b. $\log_b 25 = \log_b 5^2 = 2\log_b 5 = 2(0.83) = 1.66$

c. $\log_b \sqrt{3} = \log_b 3^{1/2}$
$= \dfrac{1}{2}\log_b 3$
$= \dfrac{1}{2}(0.56)$
$= 0.28$

Vocabulary and Readiness Check

1. $\log_b 12 + \log_b 3 = \log_b (12 \cdot 3) = \log_b \underline{36}$; **a.**

2. $\log_b 12 - \log_b 3 = \log_b \dfrac{12}{3} = \log_b \underline{4}$; **c.**

3. $7\log_b 2 = \underline{\log_b 2^7}$; **b.**

4. $\log_b 1 = \underline{0}$; **c.**

5. $b^{\log_b x} = \underline{x}$; **a.**

6. $\log_5 5^2 = \underline{2}$; **b.**

Exercise Set 9.5

1. $\log_5 2 + \log_5 7 = \log_5 (2 \cdot 7) = \log_5 14$

3. $\log_4 9 + \log_4 x = \log_4 9x$

5. $\log_6 x + \log_6 (x+1) = \log_6 [x(x+1)]$
$= \log_6 (x^2 + x)$

7. $\log_{10} 5 + \log_{10} 2 + \log_{10} (x^2 + 2)$
$= \log_{10} \left[5 \cdot 2\left(x^2 + 2\right) \right]$
$= \log_{10} \left(10x^2 + 20 \right)$

9. $\log_5 12 - \log_5 4 = \log_5 \dfrac{12}{4} = \log_5 3$

11. $\log_3 8 - \log_3 2 = \log_3 \dfrac{8}{2} = \log_3 4$

13. $\log_2 x - \log_2 y = \log_2 \dfrac{x}{y}$

15. $\log_2 (x^2 + 6) - \log(x^2 + 1) = \log_2 \dfrac{x^2 + 6}{x^2 + 1}$

17. $\log_3 x^2 = 2\log_3 x$

19. $\log_4 5^{-1} = -\log_4 5$

21. $\log_5 \sqrt{y} = \log_5 y^{1/2} = \dfrac{1}{2}\log_5 y$

23. $\log_2 5 + \log_2 x^3 = \log_2 5x^3$

25. $3\log_4 2 + \log_4 6 = \log_4 2^3 + \log_4 6$
$= \log_4 8 + \log_4 6$
$= \log_4 (8 \cdot 6)$
$= \log_4 48$

27. $3\log_5 x + 6\log_5 z = \log_5 x^3 + \log_5 z^6$
$= \log_5 x^3 z^6$

29. $\log_4 2 + \log_4 10 - \log_4 5 = \log_4 (2 \cdot 10) - \log_4 5$
$= \log_4 \dfrac{20}{5}$
$= \log_4 4$
$= 1$

31. $\log_7 6 + \log_7 3 - \log_7 4 = \log_7 (6 \cdot 3) - \log_7 4$

$$= \log_7 \frac{18}{4}$$

$$= \log_7 \frac{9}{2}$$

33. $\log_{10} x - \log_{10}(x+1) + \log_{10}(x^2 - 2)$

$$= \log_{10} \frac{x}{x+1} + \log_{10}(x^2 - 2)$$

$$= \log_{10} \frac{x(x^2 - 2)}{x+1}$$

$$= \log_{10} \frac{x^3 - 2x}{x+1}$$

35. $3\log_2 x + \frac{1}{2}\log_2 x - 2\log_2(x+1)$

$$= \log_2 x^3 + \log_2 x^{1/2} - \log_2(x+1)^2$$

$$= \log_2 (x^3 \cdot x^{1/2}) - \log_2(x+1)^2$$

$$= \log_2 x^{7/2} - \log_2(x+1)^2$$

$$= \log_2 \frac{x^{7/2}}{(x+1)^2}$$

37. $2\log_8 x - \frac{2}{3}\log_8 x + 4\log_8 x = \left(2 - \frac{2}{3} + 4\right)\log_8 x$

$$= \frac{16}{3}\log_8 x$$

$$= \log_8 x^{16/3}$$

39. $\log_3 \frac{4y}{5} = \log_3 4y - \log_3 5$

$$= \log_3 4 + \log_3 y - \log_3 5$$

41. $\log_4 \frac{2}{9z} = \log_4 2 - \log_4 9z$

$$= \log_4 2 - (\log_4 9 + \log_4 z)$$

$$= \log_4 2 - \log_4 9 - \log_4 z$$

43. $\log_2 \frac{x^3}{y} = \log_2 x^3 - \log_2 y$

$$= 3\log_2 x - \log_2 y$$

45. $\log_b \sqrt{7x} = \log_b (7x)^{1/2}$

$$= \frac{1}{2}\log_b (7x)$$

$$= \frac{1}{2}\left[\log_b 7 + \log_b x\right]$$

$$= \frac{1}{2}\log_b 7 + \frac{1}{2}\log_b x$$

47. $\log_6 x^4 y^5 = \log_6 x^4 + \log_6 y^5$

$$= 4\log_6 x + 5\log_6 y$$

49. $\log_5 x^3(x+1) = \log_5 x^3 + \log_5(x+1)$

$$= 3\log_5 x + \log_5(x+1)$$

51. $\log_6 \frac{x^2}{x+3} = \log_6 x^2 - \log_6(x+3)$

$$= 2\log_6 x - \log_6(x+3)$$

53. $\log_b 15 = \log_b(5 \cdot 3)$

$$= \log_b 5 + \log_b 3$$

$$= 0.7 + 0.5$$

$$= 1.2$$

55. $\log_b \frac{5}{3} = \log_b 5 - \log_b 3 = 0.7 - 0.5 = 0.2$

57. $\log_b \sqrt{5} = \log_b 5^{1/2} = \frac{1}{2}\log_b 5 = \frac{1}{2}(0.7) = 0.35$

59. $\log_b 8 = \log_b 2^3 = 3\log_b 2 = 3(0.43) = 1.29$

61. $\log_b \frac{3}{9} = \log_b 3 - \log_b 9$

$$= \log_b 3 - \log_b 3^2$$

$$= \log_b 3 - 2\log_b 3$$

$$= -\log_b 3$$

$$= -0.68$$

63. $\log_b \sqrt{\frac{2}{3}} = \log_b \left(\frac{2}{3}\right)^{1/2}$

$$= \frac{1}{2}\log_b \frac{2}{3}$$

$$= \frac{1}{2}\left(\log_b 2 - \log_b 3\right)$$

$$= \frac{1}{2}(0.43 - 0.68)$$

$$= \frac{1}{2}(-0.25)$$

$$= -0.125$$

65. $y = 10^x$ and $y = \log_{10} x$

67. $\log_{10} \dfrac{1}{10} = x$

$\log_{10} 10^{-1} = x$

$-1 = x$

69. $\log_7 \sqrt{7} = x$

$\log_7 7^{1/2} = x$

$\dfrac{1}{2} = x$

71. $\log_9 \dfrac{21}{3} = \log_9 7 = \log_9 21 - \log_9 3$

The correct answers are **a** and **d**.

73. $\log_3 (x + y) = \log_3 x + \log_3 y$ is false.

75. $\log_7 \dfrac{14}{8} = \log_7 14 - \log_7 8$ is true.

77. $(\log_3 6) \cdot (\log_3 4) = \log_3 24$ is false.

Integrated Review

1. $(f + g)(x) = x - 6 + x^2 + 1 = x^2 + x - 5$

2. $(f - g)(x) = x - 6 - (x^2 + 1) = -x^2 + x - 7$

3. $(f \cdot g)(x) = (x - 6)(x^2 + 1) = x^3 - 6x^2 + x - 6$

4. $\left(\dfrac{f}{g}\right)(x) = \dfrac{x - 6}{x^2 + 1}$

5. $(f \circ g)(x) = f(g(x)) = f(3x - 1) = \sqrt{3x - 1}$

6. $(g \circ f)(x) = g(f(x)) = g\left(\sqrt{x}\right) = 3\sqrt{x} - 1$

7. one-to-one; inverse:

$\{(6, -2), (8, 4), (-6, 2), (3, 3)\}$

8. not one-to-one

9. not one-to-one

10. one-to-one

11. not one-to-one

12. $f(x) = 3x$

$y = 3x$

$x = 3y$

$y = \dfrac{x}{3}$

$f^{-1}(x) = \dfrac{x}{3}$

13. $f(x) = x + 4$

$y = x + 4$

$x = y + 4$

$y = x - 4$

$f^{-1}(x) = x - 4$

14. $f(x) = 5x - 1$

$y = 5x - 1$

$x = 5y - 1$

$5y = x + 1$

$y = \dfrac{x + 1}{5}$

$f^{-1}(x) = \dfrac{x + 1}{5}$

15. $f(x) = 3x + 2$

$y = 3x + 2$

$x = 3y + 2$

$3y = x - 2$

$y = \dfrac{x - 2}{3}$

$f^{-1}(x) = \dfrac{x - 2}{3}$

16. $y = \left(\dfrac{1}{2}\right)^x$

17. $y = 2^x + 1$

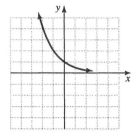

18. $y = \log_3 x$

19. $y = \log_{1/3} x$

20. $2^x = 8$

$2^x = 2^3$

$x = 3$

The solution is 3.

21. $9 = 3^{x-5}$

$3^2 = 3^{x-5}$

$2 = x - 5$

$7 = x$

The solution is 7.

22. $4^{x-1} = 8^{x+2}$

$(2^2)^{x-1} = (2^3)^{x+2}$

$2^{2x-2} = 2^{3x+6}$

$2x - 2 = 3x + 6$

$-8 = x$

The solution is –8.

23. $25^x = 125^{x-1}$

$(5^2)^x = (5^3)^{x-1}$

$5^{2x} = 5^{3x-3}$

$2x = 3x - 3$

$3 = x$

The solution is 3.

24. $\log_4 16 = x$

$4^x = 16$

$4^x = 4^2$

$x = 2$

The solution is 2.

25. $\log_{49} 7 = x$

$49^x = 7$

$(7^2)^x = 7$

$7^{2x} = 7$

$2x = 1$

$x = \dfrac{1}{2}$

The solution is $\dfrac{1}{2}$.

26. $\log_2 x = 5$

$2^5 = x$

$32 = x$

The solution is 32.

27. $\log_x 64 = 3$

$x^3 = 64$

$x^3 = 4^3$

$x = 4$

The solution is 4.

28. $\log_x \dfrac{1}{125} = -3$

$x^{-3} = \dfrac{1}{125}$

$x^{-3} = 5^{-3}$

$x = 5$

The solution is 5.

29. $\log_3 x = -2$

$3^{-2} = x$

$x = \dfrac{1}{3^2} = \dfrac{1}{9}$

The solution is $\dfrac{1}{9}$.

30. $5 \log_2 x = \log_2 x^5$

31. $x \log_2 5 = \log_2 5^x$

32. $3 \log_5 x - 5 \log_5 y = \log_5 x^3 - \log_5 y^5 = \log_5 \dfrac{x^3}{y^5}$

33. $9 \log_5 x + 3 \log_5 y = \log_5 x^9 + \log_5 y^3$

$= \log_5 x^9 y^3$

34. $\log_2 x + \log_2(x-3) - \log_2(x^2+4)$

$= \log_2[x(x-3)] - \log_2(x^2+4)$

$= \log_2(x^2-3x) - \log_2(x^2+4)$

$= \log_2 \dfrac{x^2-3x}{x^2+4}$

35. $\log_3 y - \log_3(y+2) + \log_3(y^3+11)$

$= \log_3 \dfrac{y}{y+2} + \log_3(y^3+11)$

$= \log_3 \dfrac{y(y^3+11)}{y+2}$

$= \log_3 \dfrac{y^4+11y}{y+2}$

36. $\log_7 \dfrac{9x^2}{y} = \log_7 9x^2 - \log_7 y$

$= \log_7 9 + \log_7 x^2 - \log_7 y$

$= \log_7 9 + 2\log_7 x - \log_7 y$

37. $\log_6 \dfrac{5y}{z^2} = \log_6 5y - \log_6 z^2$

$= \log_6 5 + \log_6 y - 2\log_6 z$

Section 9.6

Practice Exercises

1. To four decimal places, $\log 15 \approx 1.1761$.

2. a. $\log \dfrac{1}{100} = \log 10^{-2} = 2$

b. $\log 100,000 = \log 10^5 = 5$

c. $\log \sqrt[5]{10} = \log 10^{1/5} = \dfrac{1}{5}$

d. $\log 0.001 = \log 10^{-3} = -3$

3. $\log x = 3.4$

$x = 10^{3.4}$

$x \approx 2511.8864$

4. $a = 450$ micrometers

$T = 4.2$ seconds

$B = 3.6$

$R = \log\left(\dfrac{a}{T}\right) + B$

$= \log\left(\dfrac{450}{4.2}\right) + 3.6$

$\approx 2.0 + 3.6$

$= 5.6$

The earthquake had a magnitude of 5.6 on the Richter scale.

5. To four decimal places, $\ln 13 \approx 2.5649$.

6. a. $\ln e^4 = 4$

b. $\ln \sqrt[3]{e} = \ln e^{1/3} = \dfrac{1}{3}$

7. $\ln 5x = 8$

$e^8 = 5x$

$\dfrac{e^8}{5} = x$

$x = \dfrac{1}{5} e^8 \approx 596.1916$

8. $P = \$2400$
$r = 6\% = 0.06$
$t = 4$ years
$A = Pe^{rt} = 2400e^{0.06(4)} = 2400e^{0.24} \approx 3051.00$
The total amount of money owed is $3051.00.

9. $\log_8 5 = \dfrac{\log 5}{\log 8} \approx \dfrac{0.6989700043}{0.903089987} \approx 0.773976$

To four decimal places, $\log_8 5 \approx 0.7740$.

Vocabulary and Readiness Check

1. The base of $\log 7$ is <u>10</u>; **c.**

2. The base of $\ln 7$ is <u>e</u>; **a.**

3. $\log_{10} 10^7 = \underline{7}$; **b.**

4. $\log_7 1 = \underline{0}$; **d.**

5. $\log_e e^5 = \underline{5}$; **b.**

6. $\ln e^5 = \underline{5}$; **b.**

7. $\log_2 7 = \dfrac{\log 7}{\log 2} = \dfrac{\ln 7}{\ln 2}$; **a and b.**

Exercise Set 9.6

1. $\log 8 \approx 0.9031$

3. $\log 2.31 \approx 0.3636$

5. $\ln 2 \approx 0.6931$

7. $\ln 0.0716 \approx -2.6367$

9. $\log 12.6 \approx 1.1004$

11. $\ln 5 \approx 1.6094$

13. $\log 41.5 \approx 1.6180$

15. Answers may vary

17. $\log 100 = \log 10^2 = 2$

19. $\log\left(\dfrac{1}{1000}\right) = \log 10^{-3} = -3$

21. $\ln e^2 = 2$

23. $\ln \sqrt[4]{e} = \ln e^{1/4} = \dfrac{1}{4}$

25. $\log 10^3 = 3$

27. $\ln e^{-7} = -7$

29. $\log 0.0001 = \log 10^{-4} = -4$

31. $\ln \sqrt{e} = \ln e^{1/2} = \dfrac{1}{2}$

33. $\ln 2x = 7$
$2x = e^7$
$x = \dfrac{1}{2}e^7 \approx 548.3166$

35. $\log x = 1.3$
$x = 10^{1.3} \approx 19.9526$

37. $\log 2x = 1.1$
$2x = 10^{1.1}$
$x = \dfrac{10^{1.1}}{2} \approx 6.2946$

39. $\ln x = 1.4$
$x = e^{1.4} \approx 4.0552$

41. $\ln(3x - 4) = 2.3$
$3x - 4 = e^{2.3}$
$3x = 4 + e^{2.3}$
$x = \dfrac{4 + e^{2.3}}{3} \approx 4.6581$

43. $\log x = 2.3$
$x = 10^{2.3} \approx 199.5262$

45. $\ln x = -2.3$
$x = e^{-2.3} \approx 0.1003$

47. $\log(2x + 1) = -0.5$
$2x + 1 = 10^{-0.5}$
$2x = 10^{-0.5} - 1$
$x = \dfrac{10^{-0.5} - 1}{2} \approx -0.3419$

49. $\ln 4x = 0.18$

$$4x = e^{0.18}$$

$$x = \frac{e^{0.18}}{4} \approx 0.2993$$

51. $\log_2 3 = \dfrac{\log 3}{\log 2} \approx 1.5850$

53. $\log_{1/2} 5 = \dfrac{\ln 5}{\ln\left(\frac{1}{2}\right)} \approx -2.3219$

55. $\log_4 9 = \dfrac{\ln 9}{\ln 4} \approx 1.5850$

57. $\log_3\left(\dfrac{1}{6}\right) = \dfrac{\log\left(\frac{1}{6}\right)}{\log 3} \approx -1.6309$

59. $\log_8 6 = \dfrac{\log 6}{\log 8} \approx 0.8617$

61. $R = \log\left(\dfrac{a}{T}\right) + B,\ a = 200,\ T = 1.6$

$B = 2.1$

$R = \log\left(\dfrac{200}{1.6}\right) + 2.1 \approx 4.2$

The earthquake measures 4.2 on the Richter scale.

63. $R = \log\left(\dfrac{a}{T}\right) + B,\ a = 400,\ T = 2.6$

$B = 3.1$

$R = \log\left(\dfrac{400}{2.6}\right) + 3.1 \approx 5.3$

The earthquake measures 5.3 on the Richter scale.

65. $A = Pe^{rt},\ t = 12,\ P = 1400, r = 0.08$

$A = 1400e^{(0.08)12} = 1400e^{0.96} \approx 3656.38$

Dana has \$3656.38 after 12 years.

67. $A = Pe^{rt},\ t = 4,\ P = 2000, r = 0.06$

$A = 2000e^{(0.06)4} = 2000e^{0.24} \approx 2542.50$

Barbara owes \$2542.50 at the end of 4 years.

69. $6x - 3(2 - 5x) = 6$

$$6x - 6 + 15x = 6$$

$$21x = 12$$

$$x = \frac{12}{21} = \frac{4}{7}$$

The solution is $\dfrac{4}{7}$.

71. $2x + 3y = 6x$

$$3y = 4x$$

$$x = \frac{3y}{4}$$

73. $\qquad x^2 + 7x = -6$

$$x^2 + 7x + 6 = 0$$

$$(x + 6)(x + 1) = 0$$

$x + 6 = 0 \quad$ or $\quad x + 1 = 0$

$x = -6 \quad$ or $\qquad x = -1$

The solutions are -6 and -1.

75. $\begin{cases} x + 2y = -4 \\ 3x - y = 9 \end{cases}$

Multiply the second equation by 2, then add.

$$x + 2y = -4$$
$$\underline{6x - 2y = 18}$$
$$7x \quad\ = 14$$
$$x = 2$$

Replace x with 2 in the first equation.

$$x + 2y = -4$$
$$2 + 2y = -4$$
$$2y = -6$$
$$y = -3$$

The solution is $(2, -3)$.

77. ln 50 is larger. Answers may vary

79. $f(x) = e^x$

81. $f(x) = e^{-3x}$

83. $f(x) = e^x + 2$

85. $f(x) = e^{x-1}$

87. $f(x) = 3e^x$

89. $f(x) = \ln x$

91. $f(x) = -2\log x$

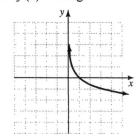

93. $f(x) = \log(x + 2)$

95. $f(x) = \ln x - 3$

97. $f(x) = e^x$

$f(x) = e^x + 2$

$f(x) = e^x - 3$

Answers may vary

Section 9.7

Practice Exercises

1. $5^x = 9$

$\log 5^x = \log 9$

$x \log 5 = \log 9$

$x = \dfrac{\log 9}{\log 5} \approx 1.3652$

The solution is $\dfrac{\log 9}{\log 5}$, or approximately 1.3652.

2. $\log_2(x-1) = 5$

$2^5 = x - 1$

$32 = x - 1$

$33 = x$

Check: $\log_2(x-1) = 5$

$\log_2(33-1) \overset{?}{=} 5$

$\log_2 32 \overset{?}{=} 5$

$2^5 = 32$ True

The solution is 33.

3. $\log_5 x + \log_5(x+4) = 1$

$\log_5 x(x+4) = 1$

$\log_5(x^2 + 4x) = 1$

$5^1 = x^2 + 4x$

$0 = x^2 + 4x - 5$

$0 = (x+5)(x-1)$

$x+5 = 0$ or $x-1 = 0$

$x = -5$ $x = 1$

Since $\log_5(-5)$ is undefined, -5 is rejected. The solution is 1.

4. $\log(x+3) - \log x = 1$

$\log \dfrac{x+3}{x} = 1$

$10^1 = \dfrac{x+3}{x}$

$10x = x + 3$

$9x = 3$

$x = \dfrac{1}{3}$

The solution is $\dfrac{1}{3}$.

5. $y_0 = 60;\ t = 3$

$y = y_0 e^{0.916t}$

$y = 60e^{0.916(3)} = 60e^{2.748} \approx 937$

The population will be approximately 937 rabbits.

6. $P = \$3000;\ r = 7\% = 0.07;\ n = 12;$
$A = 2P = \$6000$

$$A = P\left(1 + \frac{r}{n}\right)^{nt}$$

$$6000 = 3000\left(1 + \frac{0.07}{12}\right)^{12t}$$

$$2 = \left(1 + \frac{0.07}{12}\right)^{12t}$$

$$\log 2 = \log\left(1 + \frac{0.07}{12}\right)^{12t}$$

$$\log 2 = 12t \log\left(1 + \frac{0.07}{12}\right)$$

$$\frac{\log 2}{12\log\left(1 + \frac{0.07}{12}\right)} = t$$

$$9.9 \approx t$$

It takes nearly 10 years to double.

Graphing Calculator Explorations

1. $Y_1 = 5000\left(1 + \dfrac{0.05}{4}\right)^{4x}$, $Y_2 = 6000$

It takes 3.67 years, or 3 years and 8 months.

2. $Y_1 = 1000\left(1 + \dfrac{0.045}{365}\right)^{365x}$, $Y_2 = 2000$

It takes 15.40 years or 15 years and 5 months.

3. $Y_1 = 10,000\left(1 + \dfrac{0.06}{12}\right)^{12x}$, $Y_2 = 40,000$

It takes 23.16 years or 23 years and 2 months.

4. $Y_1 = 500\left(1 + \dfrac{0.04}{2}\right)^{2x}$, $Y_2 = 800$

It takes 11.87 years or 11 years and 10 months.

Exercise Set 9.7

1. $3^x = 6$

$\log 3^x = \log 6$

$x \log 3 = \log 6$

$x = \dfrac{\log 6}{\log 3} \approx 1.6309$

3. $3^{2x} = 3.8$

$\log 3^{2x} = \log 3.8$

$2x \log 3 = \log 3.8$

$x = \dfrac{\log 3.8}{2 \log 3} \approx 0.6076$

5. $2^{x-3} = 5$

$\log 2^{x-3} = \log 5$

$(x - 3) \log 2 = \log 5$

$x - 3 = \dfrac{\log 5}{\log 2}$

$x = 3 + \dfrac{\log 5}{\log 2} \approx 5.3219$

7. $9^x = 5$

$\log 9^x = \log 5$

$x \log 9 = \log 5$

$x = \dfrac{\log 5}{\log 9} \approx 0.7325$

9. $4^{x+7} = 3$

$\log 4^{x+7} = \log 3$

$(x + 7) \log 4 = \log 3$

$x + 7 = \dfrac{\log 3}{\log 4}$

$x = -7 + \dfrac{\log 3}{\log 4} \approx -6.2075$

11. $7^{3x-4} = 11$

$\log 7^{3x-4} = \log 11$

$(3x - 4) \log 7 = \log 11$

$3x - 4 = \dfrac{\log 11}{\log 7}$

$3x = 4 + \dfrac{\log 11}{\log 7}$

$x = \dfrac{1}{3}\left(4 + \dfrac{\log 11}{\log 7}\right) \approx 1.7441$

13. $e^{6x} = 5$

$\ln e^{6x} = \ln 5$

$6x = \ln 5$

$x = \dfrac{\ln 5}{6} \approx 0.2682$

15. $\log_2(x + 5) = 4$

$x + 5 = 2^4$

$x + 5 = 16$

$x = 11$

17. $\log_3 x^2 = 4$

$x^2 = 3^4$

$x^2 = 81$

$x = \pm 9$

19. $\log_4 2 + \log_4 x = 0$

$\log_4 (2x) = 0$

$2x = 4^0$

$2x = 1$

$x = \dfrac{1}{2}$

21. $\log_2 6 - \log_2 x = 3$

$$\log_2\left(\frac{6}{x}\right) = 3$$

$$\frac{6}{x} = 2^3$$

$$\frac{6}{x} = 8$$

$$8x = 6$$

$$x = \frac{3}{4}$$

23. $\log_4 x + \log_4 (x+6) = 2$

$$\log_4 x(x+6) = 2$$

$$x(x+6) = 4^2$$

$$x^2 + 6x = 16$$

$$x^2 + 6x - 16 = 0$$

$$(x+8)(x-2) = 0$$

$x = -8 \quad \text{or} \quad x = 2$

We discard -8 as extraneous, the solution is 2.

25. $\log_5(x+3) - \log_5 x = 2$

$$\log_5\left(\frac{x+3}{x}\right) = 2$$

$$\frac{x+3}{x} = 5^2$$

$$\frac{x+3}{x} = 25$$

$$x+3 = 25x$$

$$3 = 24x$$

$$x = \frac{1}{8}$$

27. $\log_3(x-2) = 2$

$$x - 2 = 3^2$$

$$x - 2 = 9$$

$$x = 11$$

29. $\log_4(x^2 - 3x) = 1$

$$x^2 - 3x = 4$$

$$x^2 - 3x - 4 = 0$$

$$(x-4)(x+1) = 0$$

$x = 4 \quad \text{or} \quad x = -1$

31. $\ln 5 + \ln x = 0$

$$\ln(5x) = 0$$

$$e^0 = 5x$$

$$1 = 5x$$

$$\frac{1}{5} = x$$

33. $3\log x - \log x^2 = 2$

$$3\log x - 2\log x = 2$$

$$\log x = 2$$

$$x = 10^2$$

$$x = 100$$

35. $\log_2 x + \log_2(x+5) = 1$

$$\log_2 x(x+5) = 1$$

$$x(x+5) = 2$$

$$x^2 + 5x - 2 = 0$$

$a = 1, b = 5, c = -2$

$$x = \frac{-5 \pm \sqrt{5^2 - 4(1)(-2)}}{2(1)}$$

$$x = \frac{-5 \pm \sqrt{33}}{2}$$

Discard $\dfrac{-5 - \sqrt{33}}{2}$, the solution is $\dfrac{-5 + \sqrt{33}}{2}$.

37. $\log_4 x - \log_4(2x-3) = 3$

$$\log_4\left(\frac{x}{2x-3}\right) = 3$$

$$\frac{x}{2x-3} = 4^3$$

$$x = 64(2x-3)$$

$$x = 128x - 192$$

$$192 = 127x$$

$$x = \frac{192}{127}$$

39. $\log_2 x + \log_2(3x+1) = 1$

$$\log_2 x(3x+1) = 1$$

$$x(3x+1) = 2$$

$$3x^2 + x - 2 = 0$$

$$(3x-2)(x+1) = 0$$

$3x - 2 = 0 \quad \text{or} \quad x + 1 = 0$

$$x = \frac{2}{3} \quad \text{or} \qquad x = -1$$

We discard -1 as extraneous, the solution is $\dfrac{2}{3}$.

41. $y = y_0 e^{0.043t}$, $y_0 = 83$, $t = 5$

$y = 83e^{0.043(5)} = 83e^{0.215} \approx 103$

There should be 103 wolves in 5 years.

43. $y = y_0 e^{0.023t}$, $y_0 = 294,380$, $t = 8$

$y = 294,380e^{0.023(8)} \approx 354,000$

There will be approximately 354,000 inhabitants in 2015.

45. $y = y_0 e^{-0.00033t}$

$y_0 = 82,400$, $y = 82,000$

$82,000 = 82,400e^{-0.00033t}$

$\dfrac{82,000}{82,400} = e^{-0.005t}$

$t = \dfrac{\ln\left(\frac{82,000}{82,400}\right)}{-0.00033} \approx 14.7$

It will take approximately 14.7 years to reach 82,000.

47. $A = P\left(1 + \dfrac{r}{n}\right)^{nt}$, $P = 600$,

$A = 2(600) = 1200$, $r = 0.07$, $n = 12$

$1200 = 600\left(1 + \dfrac{0.07}{12}\right)^{12t}$

$2 = \left(1 + \dfrac{0.07}{12}\right)^{12t}$

$\log 2 = \log\left(1 + \dfrac{0.07}{12}\right)^{12t}$

$\log 2 = 12t \log\left(1 + \dfrac{0.07}{12}\right)$

$\dfrac{\log 2}{12 \log\left(1 + \frac{0.07}{12}\right)} = t$

$9.9 \approx t$

It takes approximately 9.9 years for the $600 to double.

49. $A = P\left(1 + \dfrac{r}{n}\right)^{nt}$, $P = 1200$,

$A = P + I = 1200 + 200 = 1400$

$r = 0.09$, $n = 4$

$1400 = 1200\left(1 + \dfrac{0.09}{4}\right)^{4t}$

$\dfrac{7}{6} = (1.0225)^{4t}$

$\log\dfrac{7}{6} = \log 1.0225^{4t}$

$\log\dfrac{7}{6} = 4t \log 1.0225$

$t = \dfrac{\log\frac{7}{6}}{4 \log 1.0225}$

$t \approx 1.7$

It would take the investment approximately 1.7 years to earn $200.

51. $A = P\left(1 + \dfrac{r}{n}\right)^{nt}$, $P = 1000$

$A = 2(1000) = 2000$, $r = 0.08$, $n = 2$

$2000 = 1000\left(1 + \dfrac{0.08}{2}\right)^{2t}$

$2 = (1.04)^{2t}$

$\log 2 = \log 1.04^{2t}$

$\log 2 = 2t \log 1.04$

$t = \dfrac{\log 2}{2 \log 1.04}$

$t \approx 8.8$

It takes 8.8 years to double.

53. $w = 0.00185h^{2.67}$, and $h = 35$

$w = 0.00185(35)^{2.67} \approx 24.5$

The expected weight of a boy 35 inches tall is 24.5 pounds.

55. $w = 0.00185h^{2.67}$, and $w = 85$

$85 = 0.00185h^{2.67}$

$\dfrac{85}{0.00185} = h^{2.67}$

$h = \left(\dfrac{85}{0.00185}\right)^{1/2.67} \approx 55.7$

The expected height of the boy is 55.7 inches.

57. $P = 14.7e^{-0.21x}$, $x = 1$

$P = 14.7e^{-0.21(1)}$

$= 14.7e^{-0.21}$

≈ 11.9

The average atmospheric pressure in Denver is approximately 11.9 pounds per square inch.

59. $P = 14.7e^{-0.21x}$, $P = 7.5$

$$7.5 = 14.7e^{-0.21x}$$

$$\frac{7.5}{14.7} = e^{-0.21x}$$

$$-0.21x = \ln\left(\frac{7.5}{14.7}\right)$$

$$x = -\frac{1}{0.21}\ln\left(\frac{7.5}{14.7}\right) \approx 3.2$$

The elevation of the jet is approximately 3.2 miles.

61. $t = \frac{1}{c}\ln\left(\frac{A}{A-N}\right)$

$$t = \frac{1}{0.09}\ln\left(\frac{75}{75-50}\right)$$

$$t = \frac{1}{0.09}\ln(3)$$

$$t \approx 12.21$$

It will take 12 weeks.

63. $t = \frac{1}{c}\ln\left(\frac{A}{A-N}\right)$

$$t = \frac{1}{0.07}\ln\left(\frac{210}{210-150}\right)$$

$$t = \frac{1}{0.07}\ln(3.5)$$

$$t \approx 17.9$$

It will take 18 weeks.

65. $\dfrac{x^2 - y + 2z}{3x} = \dfrac{(-2)^2 - 0 + 2(3)}{3(-2)}$

$$= \frac{4+6}{-6}$$

$$= \frac{10}{-6}$$

$$= -\frac{5}{3}$$

67. $\dfrac{3z - 4x + y}{x + 2z} = \dfrac{3(3) - 4(-2) + 0}{-2 + 2(3)} = \dfrac{9+8}{-2+6} = \dfrac{17}{4}$

69. $f(x) = 5x + 2$

$$y = 5x + 2$$

$$x = 5y + 2$$

$$\frac{x-2}{5} = y$$

$$f^{-1}(x) = \frac{x-2}{5}$$

71. $y = 6{,}123{,}106$; $y_0 = 5{,}130{,}632$; $t = 6$

$$y = y_0 e^{kt}$$

$$6{,}123{,}106 = 5{,}130{,}632e^{k(6)}$$

$$\frac{6{,}123{,}106}{5{,}130{,}632} = e^{6k}$$

$$\ln\frac{6{,}123{,}106}{5{,}130{,}632} = 6k$$

$$k = \frac{1}{6}\ln\frac{6{,}123{,}106}{5{,}130{,}632} \approx 0.029$$

The annual rate of population growth was approximately 2.9%.

73. Answers may vary

75. $Y_1 = e^{0.3x}$, $Y_2 = 8$

$$x \approx 6.93$$

77. $Y_1 = 2\log(-5.6x + 1.3) + x + 1$, $Y_2 = 0$

$$x \approx -3.68,\ 0.19$$

79. $Y_1 = 7^{3x-4} - 11$, $Y_2 = 0$

$x \approx 1.74$

81. $Y_1 = \ln 5 + \ln x$, $Y_2 = 0$

$x = 0.2 = \dfrac{1}{5}$

The Bigger Picture

1. $8^x = 2^{x-3}$

$2^{3x} = 2^{x-3}$

$3x = x - 3$

$2x = -3$

$x = -\dfrac{3}{2}$

2. $11^x = 5$

$\log 11^x = \log 5$

$x \log 11 = \log 5$

$x = \dfrac{\log 5}{\log 11} \approx 0.6712$

3. $-7x + 3 \le -5x + 13$

$-10 \le 2x$

$-5 \le x$

The solution is $[-5, \infty)$.

4. $-7 \le 3x + 6 \le 0$

$-13 \le 3x \le -6$

$-\dfrac{13}{3} \le x \le -2$

The solution is $\left[-\dfrac{13}{3}, -2 \right]$.

5. $|5y + 3| < 3$

$-3 < 5y + 3 < 3$

$-6 < 5y < 0$

$-\dfrac{6}{5} < y < 0$

The solution is $\left(-\dfrac{6}{5}, 0 \right)$.

6. $(x - 6)(5x + 1) = 0$

$x - 6 = 0$ or $5x + 1 = 0$

$x = 6$ $\qquad$ $5x = -1$

$\qquad\qquad x = -\dfrac{1}{5}$

The solutions are 6 and $-\dfrac{1}{5}$.

7. $\log_{13} 8 + \log_{13}(x-1) = 1$

$\log_{13}(8x - 8) = 1$

$13^1 = 8x - 8$

$21 = 8x$

$\dfrac{21}{8} = x$

8. $\left| \dfrac{3x - 1}{4} \right| = 2$

$\dfrac{3x-1}{4} = 2$ or $\dfrac{3x-1}{4} = -2$

$3x - 1 = 8$ $\qquad$ $3x - 1 = -8$

$3x = 9$ $\qquad\qquad$ $3x = -7$

$x = 3$ $\qquad\qquad$ $x = -\dfrac{7}{3}$

The solutions are 3 and $-\dfrac{7}{3}$.

9. $|7x + 1| > -2$ is a true statement for all x, so the solution is $(-\infty, \infty)$.

10. $x^2 = 4$

$x = \pm\sqrt{4} = \pm 2$

The solutions are 2 and -2.

11. $(x + 5)^2 = 3$

$x + 5 = \pm\sqrt{3}$

$x = -5 \pm \sqrt{3}$

The solutions are $-5 + \sqrt{3}$ and $-5 - \sqrt{3}$.

12. $\log_7(4x^2 - 27x) = 1$
$$7^1 = 4x^2 - 27x$$
$$0 = 4x^2 - 27x - 7$$
$$0 = (4x+1)(x-7)$$

$4x + 1 = 0$ or $x - 7 = 0$
$\quad 4x = -1 \qquad\qquad x = 7$
$$x = -\frac{1}{4}$$

The solutions are $-\dfrac{1}{4}$ and 7.

Chapter 9 Vocabulary Check

1. For each one-to-one function, we can find its <u>inverse</u> function by switching the coordinates of the ordered pairs of the function.

2. The <u>composition</u> of functions *f* and *g* is $(f \circ g)(x) = f(g(x))$.

3. A function of the form $f(x) = b^x$ is called an <u>exponential</u> function if $b > 0$, *b* is not 1, and *x* is a real number.

4. The graphs of *f* and f^{-1} are <u>symmetric</u> about the line $y = x$.

5. <u>Natural</u> logarithms are logarithms to base *e*.

6. <u>Common</u> logarithms are logarithms to base 10.

7. To see whether a graph is the graph of a one-to-one function, apply the <u>vertical</u> line test to see if it is a function, and then apply the <u>horizontal</u> line test to see if it is a one-to-one function.

8. A <u>logarithmic</u> function is a function that can be defined by $f(x) = \log_b x$ where *x* is a positive real number, *b* is a constant positive real number, and *b* is not 1.

Chapter 9 Review

1. $(f+g)(x) = f(x) + g(x)$
$$= (x-5) + (2x+1)$$
$$= x - 5 + 2x + 1$$
$$= 3x - 4$$

2. $(f-g)(x) = f(x) - g(x)$
$$= (x-5) - (2x+1)$$
$$= x - 5 - 2x - 1$$
$$= -x - 6$$

3. $(f \cdot g)(x) = f(x) \cdot g(x)$
$$= (x-5)(2x+1)$$
$$= 2x^2 + x - 10x - 5$$
$$= 2x^2 - 9x - 5$$

4. $\left(\dfrac{g}{f}\right)(x) = \dfrac{g(x)}{f(x)} = \dfrac{2x+1}{x-5}, x \neq 5$

5. $(f \circ g)(x) = f(g(x))$
$$= f(x+1)$$
$$= (x+1)^2 - 2$$
$$= x^2 + 2x - 1$$

6. $(g \circ f)(x) = g(f(x))$
$$= g(x^2 - 2)$$
$$= x^2 - 2 + 1$$
$$= x^2 - 1$$

7. $(h \circ g)(2) = h(g(2)) = h(3) = 3^3 - 3^2 = 18$

8. $(f \circ f)(x) = f(f(x))$
$$= f(x^2 - 2)$$
$$= (x^2 - 2)^2 - 2$$
$$= x^4 - 4x^2 + 4 - 2$$
$$= x^4 - 4x^2 + 2$$

9. $(f \circ g)(-1) = f(g(-1)) = f(0) = 0^2 - 2 = -2$

10. $(h \circ h)(2) = h(h(2)) = h(4) = 4^3 - 4^2 = 48$

11. The function is one-to-one.
$$h^{-1} = \{(14, -9), (8, 6), (12, -11), (15, 15)\}$$

12. The function is not one-to-one.

13. The function is one-to-one.

Rank in Auto Thefts (Input)	2	4	1	3
U.S. Region (Output)	West	Midwest	South	Northeast

14. The function is not one-to-one.

15. $f(x) = \sqrt{x+2}$

    a. $f(7) = \sqrt{7+2} = \sqrt{9} = 3$

    b. $f^{-1}(3) = 7$

16. $f(x) = \sqrt{x+2}$

    a. $f(-1) = \sqrt{-1+2} = \sqrt{1} = 1$

    b. $f^{-1}(1) = -1$

17. The graph does not represent a one-to-one function.

18. The graph does not represent a one-to-one function.

19. The graph does not represent a one-to-one function.

20. The graph represents a one-to-one function.

21. $f(x) = x - 9$
$$y = x - 9$$
$$x = y - 9$$
$$y = x + 9$$
$$f^{-1}(x) = x + 9$$

22. $f(x) = x + 8$
$$y = x + 8$$
$$x = y + 8$$
$$y = x - 8$$
$$f^{-1}(x) = x - 8$$

23. $f(x) = 6x + 11$
$$y = 6x + 11$$
$$x = 6y + 11$$
$$6y = x - 11$$
$$y = \frac{x-11}{6}$$
$$f^{-1}(x) = \frac{x-11}{6}$$

24. $f(x) = 12x$
$$y = 12x$$
$$x = 12y$$
$$y = \frac{x}{12}$$
$$f^{-1}(x) = \frac{x}{12}$$

25. $f(x) = x^3 - 5$
$$y = x^3 - 5$$
$$x = y^3 - 5$$
$$y^3 = x + 5$$
$$y = \sqrt[3]{x+5}$$
$$f^{-1}(x) = \sqrt[3]{x+5}$$

26. $f(x) = \sqrt[3]{x+2}$
$$y = \sqrt[3]{x+2}$$
$$x = \sqrt[3]{y+2}$$
$$x^3 = y + 2$$
$$y = x^3 - 2$$
$$f^{-1}(x) = x^3 - 2$$

27. $g(x) = \dfrac{12x-7}{6}$
$$y = \frac{12x-7}{6}$$
$$x = \frac{12y-7}{6}$$
$$6x = 12y - 7$$
$$12y = 6x + 7$$
$$y = \frac{6x+7}{12}$$
$$g^{-1}(x) = \frac{6x+7}{12}$$

28. $r(x) = \dfrac{13}{2}x - 4$
$$y = \frac{13}{2}x - 4$$
$$x = \frac{13}{2}y - 4$$
$$x + 4 = \frac{13}{2}y$$
$$y = \frac{2(x+4)}{13}$$
$$r^{-1}(x) = \frac{2(x+4)}{13}$$

29. $y = g(x) = \sqrt{x}$
$x = \sqrt{y}$
$x^2 = y = g^{-1}(x),\ x \geq 0$

30. $h(x) = 5x - 5$
$y = 5x - 5$
$x = 5y - 5$
$5y = x + 5$
$y = \dfrac{x+5}{5}$
$h^{-1}(x) = \dfrac{x+5}{5}$

31. $f(x) = 2x - 3$
$y = 2x - 3$
$x = 2y - 3$
$y = \dfrac{x+3}{2}$
$f^{-1}(x) = \dfrac{x+3}{2}$

32. $4^x = 64$
$4^x = 4^3$
$x = 3$

33. $3^x = \dfrac{1}{9}$
$3^x = 3^{-2}$
$x = -2$

34. $2^{3x} = \dfrac{1}{16}$
$2^{3x} = 2^{-4}$
$3x = -4$
$x = -\dfrac{4}{3}$

35. $5^{2x} = 125$
$5^{2x} = 5^3$
$2x = 3$
$x = \dfrac{3}{2}$

36. $9^{x+1} = 243$
$(3^2)^{x+1} = 3^5$
$3^{2x+2} = 3^5$
$2x + 2 = 5$
$2x = 3$
$x = \dfrac{3}{2}$

37. $8^{3x-2} = 4$
$(2^3)^{3x-2} = 2^2$
$2^{9x-6} = 2^2$
$9x - 6 = 2$
$9x = 8$
$x = \dfrac{8}{9}$

38. $y = 3^x$

39. $y = \left(\dfrac{1}{3}\right)^x$

40. $y = 4 \cdot 2^x$

41. $y = 2^x + 4$

42. $A = P\left(1 + \dfrac{r}{n}\right)^{nt}$

$A = 1600\left(1 + \dfrac{0.09}{2}\right)^{(2)(7)}$

$A \approx 2963.11$

The amount accrued is \$2963.11.

43. $A = P\left(1 + \dfrac{r}{n}\right)^{nt}$

$A = 800\left(1 + \dfrac{0.07}{4}\right)^{(4)(5)}$

$A \approx 1131.82$

The certificate is worth \$1131.82 at the end of 5 years.

44. $y = 4 \cdot 2^x$

45. $49 = 7^2$

$\log_7 49 = 2$

46. $2^{-4} = \dfrac{1}{16}$

$\log_2 \dfrac{1}{16} = -4$

47. $\log_{1/2} 16 = -4$

$\left(\dfrac{1}{2}\right)^{-4} = 16$

48. $\log_{0.4} 0.064 = 3$

$0.4^3 = 0.064$

49. $\log_4 x = -3$

$x = 4^{-3} = \dfrac{1}{64}$

50. $\log_3 x = 2$

$x = 3^2 = 9$

51. $\log_3 1 = x$

$3^x = 1$

$3^x = 3^0$

$x = 0$

52. $\log_4 64 = x$

$4^x = 64$

$4^x = 4^3$

$x = 3$

53. $\log_x 64 = 2$

$x^2 = 64$

$x = \pm\sqrt{64} = \pm 8$

$x = 8$ since the base must be positive

54. $\log_x 81 = 4$

$x^4 = 81$

$x = \pm 3$

$x = 3$ since the base must be positive

55. $\log_4 4^5 = x$

$\qquad x = 5$

56. $\log_7 7^{-2} = x$

$\qquad x = -2$

57. $5^{\log_5 4} = x$

$\qquad x = 4$

58. $2^{\log_2 9} = x$

$\qquad 9 = x$

59. $\log_2(3x - 1) = 4$

$\qquad 3x - 1 = 2^4$

$\qquad 3x - 1 = 16$

$\qquad 3x = 17$

$\qquad x = \dfrac{17}{3}$

60. $\log_3(2x + 5) = 2$

$\qquad 2x + 5 = 3^2$

$\qquad 2x + 5 = 9$

$\qquad 2x = 4$

$\qquad x = 2$

61. $\log_4(x^2 - 3x) = 1$

$\qquad x^2 - 3x = 4$

$\qquad x^2 - 3x - 4 = 0$

$\qquad (x + 1)(x - 4) = 0$

$\qquad x = -1 \text{ or } x = 4$

62. $\log_8(x^2 + 7x) = 1$

$\qquad x^2 + 7x = 8$

$\qquad x^2 + 7x - 8 = 0$

$\qquad (x + 8)(x - 1) = 0$

$\qquad x = -8 \text{ or } x = 1$

63. $y = 2^x$ and $y = \log_2 x$

64. $y = \left(\dfrac{1}{2}\right)^x$ and $y = \log_{1/2} x$

65. $\log_3 8 + \log_3 4 = \log_3(8 \cdot 4) = \log_3 32$

66. $\log_2 6 + \log_2 3 = \log_2(6 \cdot 3) = \log_2 18$

67. $\log_7 15 - \log_7 20 = \log_7 \dfrac{15}{20} = \log_7 \dfrac{3}{4}$

68. $\log 18 - \log 12 = \log \dfrac{18}{12} = \log \dfrac{3}{2}$

69. $\log_{11} 8 + \log_{11} 3 - \log_{11} 6 = \log_{11} \dfrac{(8)(3)}{6}$

$\qquad\qquad\qquad\qquad\qquad\qquad = \log_{11} 4$

70. $\log_5 14 + \log_5 3 - \log_5 21$

$\qquad = \log_5(14 \cdot 3) - \log_5 21$

$\qquad = \log_5 \dfrac{42}{21}$

$\qquad = \log_5 2$

71. $2\log_5 x - 2\log_5(x + 1) + \log_5 x$

$\qquad = \log_5 x^2 - \log_5(x + 1)^2 + \log_5 x$

$\qquad = \log_5 \dfrac{(x^2)(x)}{(x + 1)^2}$

$\qquad = \log_5 \dfrac{x^3}{(x + 1)^2}$

72. $4\log_3 x - \log_3 x + \log_3(x + 2)$

$\qquad = 3\log_3 x + \log_3(x + 2)$

$\qquad = \log_3 x^3 + \log_3(x + 2)$

$\qquad = \log_3 \left[x^3(x + 2)\right]$

$\qquad = \log_3(x^4 + 2x^3)$

73. $\log_3 \dfrac{x^3}{x + 2} = \log_3 x^3 - \log_3(x + 2)$

$\qquad\qquad\quad = 3\log_3 x - \log_3(x + 2)$

74. $\log_4 \dfrac{x+5}{x^2} = \log_4(x+5) - \log_4 x^2$

$\qquad\qquad = \log_4(x+5) - 2\log_4 x$

75. $\log_2 \dfrac{3x^2 y}{z} = \log_2(3x^2 y) - \log_2 z$

$\qquad\qquad = \log_2 3 + \log_2 x^2 + \log_2 y - \log_2 z$

$\qquad\qquad = \log_2 3 + 2\log_2 x + \log_2 y - \log_2 z$

76. $\log_7 \dfrac{yz^3}{x} = \log_7(yz^3) - \log_7 x$

$\qquad\qquad = \log_7 y + \log_7 z^3 - \log_7 x$

$\qquad\qquad = \log_7 y + 3\log_7 z - \log_7 x$

77. $\log_b 50 = \log_b (5)(5)(2)$

$\qquad\quad = \log_b(5) + \log_b(5) + \log_b(2)$

$\qquad\quad = 0.83 + 0.83 + 0.36$

$\qquad\quad = 2.02$

78. $\log_b \dfrac{4}{5} = \log_b 4 - \log_b 5$

$\qquad\quad = \log_b 2^2 - \log_b 5$

$\qquad\quad = 2\log_b 2 - \log_b 5$

$\qquad\quad = 2(0.36) - 0.83$

$\qquad\quad = 0.72 - 0.83$

$\qquad\quad = -0.11$

79. $\log 3.6 \approx 0.5563$

80. $\log 0.15 \approx -0.8239$

81. $\ln 1.25 \approx 0.2231$

82. $\ln 4.63 \approx 1.5326$

83. $\log 1000 = \log 10^3 = 3$

84. $\log \dfrac{1}{10} = \log 10^{-1} = -1$

85. $\ln \dfrac{1}{e} = \ln e^{-1} = -1$

86. $\ln e^4 = 4$

87. $\ln(2x) = 2$

$\qquad 2x = e^2$

$\qquad x = \dfrac{e^2}{2}$

88. $\ln(3x) = 1.6$

$\qquad 3x = e^{1.6}$

$\qquad x = \dfrac{e^{1.6}}{3}$

89. $\ln(2x-3) = -1$

$\qquad 2x-3 = e^{-1}$

$\qquad x = \dfrac{e^{-1}+3}{2}$

90. $\ln(3x+1) = 2$

$\qquad 3x+1 = e^2$

$\qquad 3x = e^2 - 1$

$\qquad x = \dfrac{e^2-1}{3}$

91. $\qquad \ln \dfrac{I}{I_0} = -kx$

$\qquad \ln \dfrac{0.03 I_0}{I_0} = -2.1x$

$\qquad \ln 0.03 = -2.1x$

$\qquad \dfrac{\ln 0.03}{-2.1} = x$

$\qquad\qquad x \approx 1.67$

The depth is 1.67 millimeters.

92. $\qquad \ln \dfrac{I}{I_0} = -kx$

$\qquad \ln \dfrac{0.02 I_0}{I_0} = -3.2x$

$\qquad \ln 0.02 = -3.2x$

$\qquad \dfrac{\ln 0.02}{-3.2} = x$

$\qquad\qquad x \approx 1.22$

2% of the original radioactivity will penetrate at a depth of approximately 1.22 millimeters.

93. $\log_5 1.6 = \dfrac{\log 1.6}{\log 5} \approx 0.2920$

94. $\log_3 4 = \dfrac{\log 4}{\log 3} \approx 1.2619$

95. $A = Pe^{rt}$

$A = 1450e^{(0.06)(5)}$

$A \approx 1957.30$

The accrued amount is $1957.30.

96. $A = Pe^{rt}$

$A = 940e^{0.11(3)} = 940e^{0.33} \approx 1307.51$

The investment grows to $1307.51.

97. $3^{2x} = 7$

$\log 3^{2x} = \log 7$

$2x \log 3 = \log 7$

$x = \dfrac{\log 7}{2 \log 3} \approx 0.8856$

98. $6^{3x} = 5$

$\log 6^{3x} = \log 5$

$3x \log 6 = \log 5$

$x = \dfrac{\log 5}{3 \log 6} \approx 0.2994$

99. $3^{2x+1} = 6$

$\log 3^{2x+1} = \log 6$

$(2x+1) \log 3 = \log 6$

$2x = \dfrac{\log 6}{\log 3} - 1$

$x = \dfrac{1}{2}\left(\dfrac{\log 6}{\log 3} - 1\right) \approx 0.3155$

100. $4^{3x+2} = 9$

$\log 4^{3x+2} = \log 9$

$(3x+2) \log 4 = \log 9$

$3x = \dfrac{\log 9}{\log 4} - 2$

$x = \dfrac{1}{3}\left(\dfrac{\log 9}{\log 4} - 2\right) \approx -0.1383$

101. $5^{3x-5} = 4$

$\log 5^{3x-5} = \log 4$

$(3x-5) \log 5 = \log 4$

$3x = \dfrac{\log 4}{\log 5} + 5$

$x = \dfrac{1}{3}\left(\dfrac{\log 4}{\log 5} + 5\right) \approx 1.9538$

102. $8^{4x-2} = 3$

$\log 8^{4x-2} = \log 3$

$(4x-2) \log 8 = \log 3$

$4x = \dfrac{\log 3}{\log 8} + 2$

$x = \dfrac{1}{4}\left(\dfrac{\log 3}{\log 8} + 2\right) \approx 0.6321$

103. $2 \cdot 5^{x-1} = 1$

$\log(2 \cdot 5^{x-1}) = \log 1$

$\log 2 + (x-1) \log 5 = 0$

$(x-1) \log 5 = -\log 2$

$x = -\dfrac{\log 2}{\log 5} + 1 \approx 0.5693$

104. $3 \cdot 4^{x+5} = 2$

$4^{x+5} = \dfrac{2}{3}$

$\log 4^{x+5} = \log \dfrac{2}{3}$

$(x+5) \log 4 = \log \dfrac{2}{3}$

$x = \dfrac{\log\left(\frac{2}{3}\right)}{\log 4} - 5 \approx -5.2925$

105. $\log_5 2 + \log_5 x = 2$

$\log_5 2x = 2$

$2x = 5^2$

$2x = 25$

$x = \dfrac{25}{2}$

106. $\log_3 x + \log_3 10 = 2$

$\log_3(10x) = 2$

$10x = 3^2$

$10x = 9$

$x = \dfrac{9}{10}$

74. $\log_4 \dfrac{x+5}{x^2} = \log_4(x+5) - \log_4 x^2$

$\phantom{\log_4 \dfrac{x+5}{x^2}} = \log_4(x+5) - 2\log_4 x$

75. $\log_2 \dfrac{3x^2 y}{z} = \log_2(3x^2 y) - \log_2 z$

$\phantom{\log_2 \dfrac{3x^2 y}{z}} = \log_2 3 + \log_2 x^2 + \log_2 y - \log_2 z$

$\phantom{\log_2 \dfrac{3x^2 y}{z}} = \log_2 3 + 2\log_2 x + \log_2 y - \log_2 z$

76. $\log_7 \dfrac{yz^3}{x} = \log_7(yz^3) - \log_7 x$

$\phantom{\log_7 \dfrac{yz^3}{x}} = \log_7 y + \log_7 z^3 - \log_7 x$

$\phantom{\log_7 \dfrac{yz^3}{x}} = \log_7 y + 3\log_7 z - \log_7 x$

77. $\log_b 50 = \log_b(5)(5)(2)$

$ = \log_b(5) + \log_b(5) + \log_b(2)$

$ = 0.83 + 0.83 + 0.36$

$ = 2.02$

78. $\log_b \dfrac{4}{5} = \log_b 4 - \log_b 5$

$\phantom{\log_b \dfrac{4}{5}} = \log_b 2^2 - \log_b 5$

$\phantom{\log_b \dfrac{4}{5}} = 2\log_b 2 - \log_b 5$

$\phantom{\log_b \dfrac{4}{5}} = 2(0.36) - 0.83$

$\phantom{\log_b \dfrac{4}{5}} = 0.72 - 0.83$

$\phantom{\log_b \dfrac{4}{5}} = -0.11$

79. $\log 3.6 \approx 0.5563$

80. $\log 0.15 \approx -0.8239$

81. $\ln 1.25 \approx 0.2231$

82. $\ln 4.63 \approx 1.5326$

83. $\log 1000 = \log 10^3 = 3$

84. $\log \dfrac{1}{10} = \log 10^{-1} = -1$

85. $\ln \dfrac{1}{e} = \ln e^{-1} = -1$

86. $\ln e^4 = 4$

87. $\ln(2x) = 2$

$2x = e^2$

$x = \dfrac{e^2}{2}$

88. $\ln(3x) = 1.6$

$3x = e^{1.6}$

$x = \dfrac{e^{1.6}}{3}$

89. $\ln(2x-3) = -1$

$2x - 3 = e^{-1}$

$x = \dfrac{e^{-1}+3}{2}$

90. $\ln(3x+1) = 2$

$3x + 1 = e^2$

$3x = e^2 - 1$

$x = \dfrac{e^2 - 1}{3}$

91. $\ln \dfrac{I}{I_0} = -kx$

$\ln \dfrac{0.03 I_0}{I_0} = -2.1x$

$\ln 0.03 = -2.1x$

$\dfrac{\ln 0.03}{-2.1} = x$

$x \approx 1.67$

The depth is 1.67 millimeters.

92. $\ln \dfrac{I}{I_0} = -kx$

$\ln \dfrac{0.02 I_0}{I_0} = -3.2x$

$\ln 0.02 = -3.2x$

$\dfrac{\ln 0.02}{-3.2} = x$

$x \approx 1.22$

2% of the original radioactivity will penetrate at a depth of approximately 1.22 millimeters.

93. $\log_5 1.6 = \dfrac{\log 1.6}{\log 5} \approx 0.2920$

94. $\log_3 4 = \dfrac{\log 4}{\log 3} \approx 1.2619$

95. $A = Pe^{rt}$

$A = 1450e^{(0.06)(5)}$

$A \approx 1957.30$

The accrued amount is \$1957.30.

96. $A = Pe^{rt}$

$A = 940e^{0.11(3)} = 940e^{0.33} \approx 1307.51$

The investment grows to \$1307.51.

97. $3^{2x} = 7$

$\log 3^{2x} = \log 7$

$2x \log 3 = \log 7$

$x = \dfrac{\log 7}{2 \log 3} \approx 0.8856$

98. $6^{3x} = 5$

$\log 6^{3x} = \log 5$

$3x \log 6 = \log 5$

$x = \dfrac{\log 5}{3 \log 6} \approx 0.2994$

99. $3^{2x+1} = 6$

$\log 3^{2x+1} = \log 6$

$(2x+1) \log 3 = \log 6$

$2x = \dfrac{\log 6}{\log 3} - 1$

$x = \dfrac{1}{2}\left(\dfrac{\log 6}{\log 3} - 1 \right) \approx 0.3155$

100. $4^{3x+2} = 9$

$\log 4^{3x+2} = \log 9$

$(3x+2) \log 4 = \log 9$

$3x = \dfrac{\log 9}{\log 4} - 2$

$x = \dfrac{1}{3}\left(\dfrac{\log 9}{\log 4} - 2 \right) \approx -0.1383$

101. $5^{3x-5} = 4$

$\log 5^{3x-5} = \log 4$

$(3x-5) \log 5 = \log 4$

$3x = \dfrac{\log 4}{\log 5} + 5$

$x = \dfrac{1}{3}\left(\dfrac{\log 4}{\log 5} + 5 \right) \approx 1.9538$

102. $8^{4x-2} = 3$

$\log 8^{4x-2} = \log 3$

$(4x-2) \log 8 = \log 3$

$4x = \dfrac{\log 3}{\log 8} + 2$

$x = \dfrac{1}{4}\left(\dfrac{\log 3}{\log 8} + 2 \right) \approx 0.6321$

103. $2 \cdot 5^{x-1} = 1$

$\log(2 \cdot 5^{x-1}) = \log 1$

$\log 2 + (x-1) \log 5 = 0$

$(x-1) \log 5 = -\log 2$

$x = -\dfrac{\log 2}{\log 5} + 1 \approx 0.5693$

104. $3 \cdot 4^{x+5} = 2$

$4^{x+5} = \dfrac{2}{3}$

$\log 4^{x+5} = \log \dfrac{2}{3}$

$(x+5) \log 4 = \log \dfrac{2}{3}$

$x = \dfrac{\log \left(\frac{2}{3} \right)}{\log 4} - 5 \approx -5.2925$

105. $\log_5 2 + \log_5 x = 2$

$\log_5 2x = 2$

$2x = 5^2$

$2x = 25$

$x = \dfrac{25}{2}$

106. $\log_3 x + \log_3 10 = 2$

$\log_3 (10x) = 2$

$10x = 3^2$

$10x = 9$

$x = \dfrac{9}{10}$

107. $\log(5x) - \log(x+1) = 4$

$$\log\frac{5x}{x+1} = 4$$

$$\frac{5x}{x+1} = 10^4$$

$$\frac{5x}{x+1} = 10,000$$

$$5x = 10,000x + 10,000$$

$$x = -1.0005$$

no solution, or $\varnothing$

108. $\ln(3x) - \ln(x-3) = 2$

$$\ln\left(\frac{3x}{x-3}\right) = 2$$

$$\frac{3x}{x-3} = e^2$$

$$3x = e^2 x - 3e^2$$

$$3x - e^2 x = -3e^2$$

$$(3 - e^2)x = -3e^2$$

$$x = \frac{3e^2}{e^2 - 3}$$

109. $\log_2 x + \log_2 2x - 3 = 1$

$$\log_2(x \cdot 2x) = 4$$

$$2x^2 = 2^4$$

$$2x^2 = 16$$

$$x^2 = 8$$

$$x = \pm 2\sqrt{2}$$

$-2\sqrt{2}$ is rejected since $\log_2\left(-2\sqrt{2}\right)$ is undefined. The solution is $2\sqrt{2}$.

110. $-\log_6(4x+7) + \log_6 x = 1$

$$\log_6\frac{x}{4x+7} = 1$$

$$\frac{x}{4x+7} = 6$$

$$x = 6(4x+7)$$

$$x = 24x + 42$$

$$x = -\frac{42}{23}$$

$-\frac{42}{23}$ is rejected since $\log_6\left(-\frac{42}{23}\right)$ is undefined. There is no solution, or $\varnothing$.

111. $y = y_0 e^{kt}$

$$y = 155,000e^{0.06(4)}$$

$$\approx 197,044$$

There will be 197,044 ducks after 4 weeks.

112. $y = y_0 e^{kt}$

$$y = 2,971,650e^{-0.00129(8)}$$

$$= 2,971,650e^{-0.01032}$$

$$\approx 2,941,140$$

The population of Armenia in the year 2015 will be approximately 2,941,140.

113. $y = y_0 e^{kt}$

$$1,500,000,000 = 1,321,851,888e^{0.00606t}$$

$$\frac{1,500,000,000}{1,321,851,888} = e^{0.00606t}$$

$$\ln\frac{1,500,000,000}{1,321,851,888} = \ln e^{0.00606t}$$

$$\ln\frac{1,500,000,000}{1,321,851,888} = 0.00606t$$

$$t = \frac{1}{0.00606}\ln\frac{1,500,000,000}{1,321,851,888}$$

$$t \approx 20.9$$

It will take approximately 20.9 years.

114. $y = y_0 e^{kt}$

$$2(33,390,141) = 33,390,141e^{0.009t}$$

$$2 = e^{0.009t}$$

$$\ln 2 = \ln e^{0.009t}$$

$$\ln 2 = 0.009t$$

$$t = \frac{\ln 2}{0.009}$$

$$t \approx 77.0$$

It will take approximately 77.0 years.

115. $y = y_0 e^{kt}$

$$2(24,821,286) = 24,821,286e^{0.018t}$$

$$2 = e^{0.018t}$$

$$\ln 2 = \ln e^{0.018t}$$

$$\ln 2 = 0.018t$$

$$t = \frac{\ln 2}{0.018}$$

$$t \approx 38.5$$

It will take approximately 38.5 years.

116.
$$A = P\left(1 + \frac{r}{n}\right)^{nt}$$
$$10,000 = 5000\left(1 + \frac{0.08}{4}\right)^{4t}$$
$$2 = (1.02)^{4t}$$
$$\log 2 = \log 1.02^{4t}$$
$$\log 2 = 4t \log 1.02$$
$$t = \frac{\log 2}{4 \log 1.02} \approx 8.8$$

It will take 8.8 years.

117.
$$A = P\left(1 + \frac{r}{n}\right)^{nt}$$
$$10,000 = 6000\left(1 + \frac{0.06}{12}\right)^{12t}$$
$$\frac{5}{3} = (1.005)^{12t}$$
$$\log \frac{5}{3} = \log 1.005^{12t}$$
$$\log \frac{5}{3} = 12t \log 1.005$$
$$t = \frac{1}{12}\left(\frac{\log\left(\frac{5}{3}\right)}{\log(1.005)}\right) \approx 8.5$$

It was invested for approximately 8.5 years.

118. $Y_1 = e^x$, $Y_2 = 2$

$x \approx 0.69$

119. $Y_1 = 10^{0.3x}$, $Y_2 = 7$

$x \approx 2.82$

120.
$$3^x = \frac{1}{81}$$
$$3^x = 3^{-4}$$
$$x = -4$$

121.
$$7^{4x} = 49$$
$$7^{4x} = 7^2$$
$$4x = 2$$
$$x = \frac{1}{2}$$

122.
$$8^{3x-2} = 32$$
$$(2^3)^{(3x-2)} = 2^5$$
$$2^{9x-6} = 2^5$$
$$9x - 6 = 5$$
$$9x = 11$$
$$x = \frac{11}{9}$$

123.
$$\log_4 4 = x$$
$$4^x = 4^1$$
$$x = 1$$

124.
$$\log_3 x = 4$$
$$3^4 = x$$
$$81 = x$$

125.
$$\log_5(x^2 - 4x) = 1$$
$$5^1 = x^2 - 4x$$
$$0 = x^2 - 4x - 5$$
$$0 = (x - 5)(x + 1)$$
$$x - 5 = 0 \quad \text{or} \quad x + 1 = 0$$
$$x = 5 \qquad\qquad x = -1$$

Both check, so the solutions are 5 and −1.

126.
$$\log_4(3x - 1) = 2$$
$$4^2 = 3x - 1$$
$$16 + 1 = 3x$$
$$\frac{17}{3} = x$$

127.
$$\ln x = -3.2$$
$$e^{\ln x} = e^{-3.2}$$
$$x = e^{-3.2}$$

128.
$$\log_5 x + \log_5 10 = 2$$
$$\log_5(10x) = 2$$
$$5^2 = 10x$$
$$\frac{25}{10} = x$$
$$\frac{5}{2} = x$$

129. $\ln x - \ln 2 = 1$

$$\ln \frac{x}{2} = 1$$

$$e^{\ln \frac{x}{2}} = e^1$$

$$\frac{x}{2} = e$$

$$x = 2e$$

130. $\log_6 x - \log_6(4x + 7) = 1$

$$\log_6 \frac{x}{4x + 7} = 1$$

$$6^1 = \frac{x}{4x + 7}$$

$$24x + 42 = x$$

$$23x = -42$$

$$x = -\frac{42}{23}$$

$-\dfrac{42}{23}$ is rejected since $\log_6\left(-\dfrac{42}{23}\right)$ is undefined.

There is no solution, or $\varnothing$.

Chapter 9 Test

1. $f(x) = x$ and $g(x) = 2x - 3$

$(f \cdot g)(x) = f(x) \cdot g(x) = x(2x - 3) = 2x^2 - 3x$

2. $f(x) = x$ and $g(x) = 2x - 3$

$$(f - g)(x) = f(x) - g(x)$$
$$= x - (2x - 3)$$
$$= -x + 3$$
$$= 3 - x$$

3. $(f \circ h)(0) = f(h(0)) = f(5) = 5$

4. $(g \circ f)(x) = g(f(x)) = g(x) = x - 7$

5. $(g \circ h)(x) = g(h(x))$
$$= g(x^2 - 6x + 5)$$
$$= x^2 - 6x + 5 - 7$$
$$= x^2 - 6x - 2$$

6. $f(x) = 7x - 14$, $f^{-1}(x) = \dfrac{x + 14}{7}$

7. The graph represents a one-to-one function.

8. The graph does not represent a one-to-one function.

9. $y = 6 - 2x$ is one-to-one.
$$x = 6 - 2y$$
$$2y = -x + 6$$
$$y = \frac{-x + 6}{2}$$
$$f^{-1}(x) = \frac{-x + 6}{2}$$

10. $f = \{(0,0),(2,3),(-1,5)\}$ is one-to-one.

$$f^{-1} = \{(0,0),(3,2),(5,-1)\}$$

11. The function is not one-to-one.

12. $\log_3 6 + \log_3 4 = \log_3(6 \cdot 4) = \log_3 24$

13. $\log_5 x + 3\log_5 x - \log_5(x+1)$
$$= 4\log_5 x - \log_5(x+1)$$
$$= \log_5 x^4 - \log_5(x+1)$$
$$= \log_5 \frac{x^4}{x+1}$$

14. $\log_6 \dfrac{2x}{y^3} = \log_6 2x - \log_6 y^3$
$$= \log_6 2 + \log_6 x - 3\log_6 y$$

15. $\log_b\left(\dfrac{3}{25}\right) = \log_b 3 - \log_b 25$
$$= \log_b 3 - \log_b 5^2$$
$$= \log_b 3 - 2\log_b 5$$
$$= 0.79 - 2(1.16)$$
$$= -1.53$$

16. $\log_7 8 = \dfrac{\ln 8}{\ln 7} \approx 1.0686$

17. $8^{x-1} = \dfrac{1}{64}$

$8^{x-1} = 8^{-2}$

$x - 1 = -2$

$x = -1$

18. $3^{2x+5} = 4$

$\log 3^{2x+5} = \log 4$

$(2x + 5)\log 3 = \log 4$

$2x = \dfrac{\log 4}{\log 3} - 5$

$x = \dfrac{1}{2}\left(\dfrac{\log 4}{\log 3} - 5\right)$

$x \approx -1.8691$

19. $\log_3 x = -2$

$x = 3^{-2}$

$x = \dfrac{1}{9}$

20. $\ln \sqrt{e} = x$

$\ln e^{1/2} = x$

$\dfrac{1}{2} = x$

21. $\log_8(3x - 2) = 2$

$3x - 2 = 8^2$

$3x - 2 = 64$

$3x = 66$

$x = \dfrac{66}{3} = 22$

22. $\log_5 x + \log_5 3 = 2$

$\log_5(3x) = 2$

$3x = 5^2$

$3x = 25$

$x = \dfrac{25}{3}$

23. $\log_4(x + 1) - \log_4(x - 2) = 3$

$\log_4 \dfrac{x+1}{x-2} = 3$

$\dfrac{x+1}{x-2} = 4^3$

$\dfrac{x+1}{x-2} = 64$

$x + 1 = 64x - 128$

$129 = 63x$

$\dfrac{129}{63} = x$

$\dfrac{43}{21} = x$

24. $\ln(3x + 7) = 1.31$

$3x + 7 = e^{1.31}$

$3x = e^{1.31} - 7$

$x = \dfrac{e^{1.31} - 7}{3} \approx -1.0979$

25. $y = \left(\dfrac{1}{2}\right)^x + 1$

26. $y = 3^x$ and $y = \log_3 x$

Chapter 9 Cumulative Review

27. $A = \left(1 + \dfrac{r}{n}\right)^{nt}$, $P = 4000$, $t = 3$, $r = 0.09$,

and $n = 12$

$A = 4000\left(1 + \dfrac{0.09}{12}\right)^{12(3)}$

$\quad = 4000(1.0075)^{36}$

$\quad \approx 5234.58$

$5234.58 will be in the account.

28. $A = \left(1 + \dfrac{r}{n}\right)^{nt}$, $P = 2000$, $A = 3000$

$r = 0.07$, $n = 2$

$3000 = 2000\left(1 + \dfrac{0.07}{2}\right)^{2t}$

$1.5 = (1.035)^{2t}$

$\log 1.5 = \log 1.035^{2t}$

$\log 1.5 = 2t \log 1.035$

$t = \dfrac{\log 1.5}{2 \log 1.035} \approx 5.9$

It would take 6 years.

29. $y = y_0 e^{kt}$

$y = 57{,}000 e^{0.026(5)}$

$\quad = 57{,}000 e^{0.13}$

$\quad \approx 64{,}913$

There will be approximately 64,913 prairie dogs 5 years from now.

30. $\quad y = y_0 e^{kt}$

$1000 = 400 e^{0.062(t)}$

$2.5 = e^{0.062t}$

$\ln 2.5 = \ln e^{0.062t}$

$0.062t = \ln 2.5$

$t = \dfrac{\ln 2.5}{0.062} \approx 14.8$

It will take the naturalists approximately 15 years to reach their goal.

31. $\log(1 + k) = \dfrac{0.3}{D}$, $D = 56$

$\log(1 + k) = \dfrac{0.3}{56}$

$1 + k = 10^{0.3/56}$

$k = -1 + 10^{0.3/56}$

$k \approx 0.012$

The rate of population increase is approximately 1.2%.

1. **a.** $(-8)(-1) = 8$

    b. $(-2)\dfrac{1}{6} = -\dfrac{1}{3}$

    c. $-1.2(0.3) = -0.36$

    d. $0(-11) = 0$

    e. $\left(\dfrac{1}{5}\right)\left(-\dfrac{10}{11}\right) = -\dfrac{2}{11}$

    f. $(7)(1)(-2)(-3) = 42$

    g. $8(-2)(0) = 0$

2. $\dfrac{1}{3}(x - 2) = \dfrac{1}{4}(x + 1)$

    $4(x - 2) = 3(x + 1)$

    $4x - 8 = 3x + 3$

    $x = 11$

3. $y = x^2$

4. $y = f(x) = -3x + 4$, $m = -3$

    Perpendicular line: $m = \dfrac{1}{3}$, through $(-2, 6)$

    $y - y_1 = m(x - x_1)$

    $y - 6 = \dfrac{1}{3}[x - (-2)]$

    $y - 6 = \dfrac{1}{3}x + \dfrac{2}{3}$

    $y = \dfrac{1}{3}x + \dfrac{20}{3}$

    $f(x) = \dfrac{1}{3}x + \dfrac{20}{3}$

5. Equation 2 is twice the opposite of equation 1 and equation 3 is one-half of equation 1. Therefore, the system is dependent. The solution is $\{(x, y, z) \mid x - 5y - 2z = 6\}$.

6. The angles labeled $y°$ and $(x-40)°$ are alternate interior angles, so $y = x - 40$. The angles labeled $x°$ and $y°$ are supplementary, so $x + y = 180$.

$$\begin{cases} y = x - 40 \\ x + y = 180 \end{cases}$$

Replace y with $x - 40$ in the second equation.

$$x + (x - 40) = 180$$
$$2x = 220$$
$$x = 110$$
$$y = x - 40 = 110 - 40 = 70$$

7. a. $\dfrac{x^7}{x^4} = x^{7-4} = x^3$

b. $\dfrac{5^8}{5^2} = 5^{8-2} = 5^6$

c. $\dfrac{20x^6}{4x^5} = \dfrac{20}{4}x^{6-5} = 5x^1 = 5x$

d. $\dfrac{12y^{10}z^7}{14y^8z^7} = \dfrac{12}{14}y^{10-8}z^{7-7} = \dfrac{6}{7}y^2z^0 = \dfrac{6y^2}{7}$

8. a. $(4a^3)^2 = 4^2(a^3)^2 = 16a^6$

b. $\left(-\dfrac{2}{3}\right)^3 = \dfrac{(-2)^3}{3^3} = \dfrac{-8}{27} = -\dfrac{8}{27}$

c. $\left(\dfrac{4a^5}{b^3}\right)^3 = \dfrac{4^3(a^5)^3}{(b^3)^3} = \dfrac{64a^{15}}{b^9}$

d. $\left(\dfrac{3^{-2}}{x}\right)^{-3} = \dfrac{(3^{-2})^{-3}}{x^{-3}} = \dfrac{3^6}{x^{-3}} = 729x^3$

e. $(a^{-2}b^3c^{-4})^{-2} = (a^{-2})^{-2}(b^3)^{-2}(c^{-4})^{-2}$
$$= a^4b^{-6}c^8$$
$$= \dfrac{a^4c^8}{b^6}$$

9. a. $C(100) = \dfrac{2.6(100) + 10,000}{100}$
$$= 102.60$$
The cost is \$102.60 per disc for 100 discs.

b. $C(1000) = \dfrac{2.6(1000) + 10,000}{1000}$
$$= 12.60$$
The cost is \$12.60 per disc for 1000 discs.

10. a. $(3x-1)^2 = (3x)^2 - 2(3x)(1) + 1^2$
$$= 9x^2 - 6x + 1$$

b. $\left(\dfrac{1}{2}x + 3\right)\left(\dfrac{1}{2}x - 3\right) = \left(\dfrac{1}{2}x\right)^2 - 3^2$
$$= \dfrac{1}{4}x^2 - 9$$

c. $(2x-5)(6x+7) = 12x^2 + 14x - 30x - 35$
$$= 12x^2 - 16x - 35$$

11. a. $\dfrac{x}{4} + \dfrac{5x}{4} = \dfrac{6x}{4} = \dfrac{3x}{2}$

b. $\dfrac{5}{7z^2} + \dfrac{x}{7z^2} = \dfrac{5+x}{7z^2}$

c. $\dfrac{x^2}{x+7} - \dfrac{49}{x+7} = \dfrac{x^2 - 49}{x+7}$
$$= \dfrac{(x+7)(x-7)}{x+7}$$
$$= x - 7$$

d. $\dfrac{x}{3y^2} - \dfrac{x+1}{3y^2} = \dfrac{x-x-1}{3y^2} = -\dfrac{1}{3y^2}$

12. $\dfrac{5}{x-2} + \dfrac{3}{x^2+4x+4} - \dfrac{6}{x+2}$
$$= \dfrac{5}{x-2} + \dfrac{3}{(x+2)^2} - \dfrac{6}{x+2}$$
$$= \dfrac{5(x+2)^2 + 3(x-2) - 6(x-2)(x+2)}{(x-2)(x+2)(x+2)}$$
$$= \dfrac{-x^2 + 23x + 38}{(x-2)(x+2)^2}$$

13.

$$
\begin{array}{r}
3x^2 + 2x + 3 \\
x^2 - 1 \overline{\smash{\big)}\ 3x^4 + 2x^3 \quad\quad -8x + 6} \\
\underline{3x^4 \quad\quad -3x^2} \\
2x^3 + 3x^2 - 8x \\
\underline{2x^3 \quad\quad - 2x} \\
3x^2 - 6x + 6 \\
\underline{3x^2 \quad\quad -3} \\
-6x + 9
\end{array}
$$

Solution: $3x^2 + 2x + 3 + \dfrac{-6x+9}{x^2-1}$

14. a. $\dfrac{\frac{a}{5}}{\frac{a-1}{10}} = \dfrac{a}{5} \cdot \dfrac{10}{a-1} = \dfrac{2a}{a-1}$

b. $\dfrac{\frac{3}{2+a} + \frac{6}{2-a}}{\frac{5}{a+2} - \frac{1}{a-2}} = \dfrac{\frac{3}{a+2} - \frac{6}{a-2}}{\frac{5}{a+2} - \frac{1}{a-2}}$

Multiply the numerator and the denominator by $(a+2)(a-2)$.

$\dfrac{3(a-2) - 6(a+2)}{5(a-2) - 1(a+2)} = \dfrac{3a - 6 - 6a - 12}{5a - 10 - a - 2}$

$\quad\quad = \dfrac{-3a - 18}{4a - 12}$

c. $\dfrac{x^{-1} + y^{-1}}{xy} = \dfrac{\frac{1}{x} + \frac{1}{y}}{xy} = \dfrac{\left(\frac{1}{x} + \frac{1}{y}\right)xy}{(xy)(xy)} = \dfrac{y + x}{x^2 y^2}$

15.

$$\dfrac{2x}{2x-1} + \dfrac{1}{x} = \dfrac{1}{2x-1}$$

$$(2x-1)x\left(\dfrac{2x}{2x-1} + \dfrac{1}{x}\right) = (2x-1)x\left(\dfrac{1}{2x-1}\right)$$

$$2x^2 + 2x - 1 = x$$

$$2x^2 + x - 1 = 0$$

$$(2x-1)(x+1) = 0$$

$$2x - 1 = 0 \quad \text{or} \quad x + 1 = 0$$

$$2x = 1 \quad\quad\quad\quad x = -1$$

$$x = \dfrac{1}{2}$$

$x = \dfrac{1}{2}$ makes the denominator $2x - 1$ zero, so the only solution is $x = -1$.

16. $\dfrac{x^3 - 8}{x - 2} = \dfrac{(x-2)(x^2 + 2x + 4)}{(x-2)}$

$\quad\quad = x^2 + 2x + 4$

17. Use distance = (rate)(time). Let c be the speed of the current.

	d	r	t
Upstream	72	$30 - c$	$1.5t$
Downstream	72	$30 + c$	t

Upstream: $72 = 1.5t(30 - c)$ or $t = \dfrac{72}{1.5(30-c)}$

Downstream: $72 = t(30 + c)$ or $t = \dfrac{72}{30+c}$

$$\dfrac{72}{1.5(30-c)} = \dfrac{72}{30+c}$$

$$72(30+c) = 72(1.5)(30-c)$$

$$2160 + 72c = 3240 - 108c$$

$$180c = 1080$$

$$c = 6$$

The speed of the current is 6 miles per hour.

18.

$$
\begin{array}{r}
2\,\underline{|\ 8 \quad -12 \quad -7} \\
16 \quad\quad 8 \\
\overline{8 \quad\quad 4 \quad\quad 1}
\end{array}
$$

Solution: $8x + 4 + \dfrac{1}{x-2}$

19. a. $\sqrt[4]{81} = \sqrt[4]{3^4} = 3$

b. $\sqrt[5]{-243} = \sqrt[5]{(-3)^5} = -3$

c. $-\sqrt{25} = -\sqrt{5^2} = -5$

d. $\sqrt[4]{-81}$ is not a real number.

e. $\sqrt[3]{64x^3} = \sqrt[3]{4^3 x^3} = 4x$

20.
$$\frac{1}{a+5} = \frac{1}{3a+6} - \frac{a+2}{a^2+7a+10}$$
$$\frac{1}{a+5} = \frac{1}{3(a+2)} - \frac{a+2}{(a+2)(a+5)}$$
$$3(a+2) = a+5-3(a+2)$$
$$3a+6 = a+5-3a-6$$
$$5a = -7$$
$$a = -\frac{7}{5}$$

21. a. $\sqrt{x}\cdot\sqrt[4]{x} = x^{1/2}\cdot x^{1/4} = x^{3/4} = \sqrt[4]{x^3}$

b. $\dfrac{\sqrt{x}}{\sqrt[3]{x}} = \dfrac{x^{1/2}}{x^{1/3}} = x^{\frac{1}{2}-\frac{1}{3}} = x^{1/6} = \sqrt[6]{x}$

c. $\sqrt[3]{3}\cdot\sqrt{2} = 3^{1/3}\cdot 2^{1/2}$
$$= 3^{2/6}\cdot 2^{3/6}$$
$$= 9^{1/6}\cdot 8^{1/6}$$
$$= 72^{1/6}$$
$$= \sqrt[6]{72}$$

22. $y = kx$
$$\frac{1}{2} = 12k$$
$$k = \frac{1}{24},\ y = \frac{1}{24}x$$

23. a. $\sqrt{3}\left(5+\sqrt{30}\right) = 5\sqrt{3}+\sqrt{90} = 5\sqrt{3}+3\sqrt{10}$

b. $\left(\sqrt{5}-\sqrt{6}\right)\left(\sqrt{7}+1\right) = \sqrt{35}+\sqrt{5}-\sqrt{42}-\sqrt{6}$

c. $\left(7\sqrt{x}+5\right)\left(3\sqrt{x}-\sqrt{5}\right)$
$$= 21x-7\sqrt{5x}+15\sqrt{x}-5\sqrt{5}$$

d. $\left(4\sqrt{3}-1\right)^2$
$$= \left(4\sqrt{3}\right)^2 - 2\left(4\sqrt{3}\right)(1)+1^2$$
$$= 16\cdot 3 - 8\sqrt{3}+1$$
$$= 49 - 8\sqrt{3}$$

e. $\left(\sqrt{2x}-5\right)\left(\sqrt{2x}+5\right) = \left(\sqrt{2x}\right)^2 - 5^2$
$$= 2x-25$$

f. $\left(\sqrt{x-3}+5\right)^2 = \left(\sqrt{x-3}\right)^2 + 2\sqrt{x-3}(5)+5^2$
$$= x-3+10\sqrt{x-3}+25$$
$$= x+22+10\sqrt{x-3}$$

24. a. $\sqrt[4]{81} = \sqrt[4]{3^4} = 3$

b. $\sqrt[3]{-27} = \sqrt[3]{(-3)^3} = -3$

c. $\sqrt{\dfrac{9}{64}} = \sqrt{\left(\dfrac{3}{8}\right)^2} = \dfrac{3}{8}$

d. $\sqrt[4]{x^{12}} = x^3$

e. $\sqrt[3]{-125y^6} = -5y^2$

25. $\dfrac{\sqrt[4]{x}}{\sqrt[4]{81y^5}} = \dfrac{\sqrt[4]{x}}{\sqrt[4]{81y^5}}\cdot\dfrac{\sqrt[4]{y^3}}{\sqrt[4]{y^3}} = \dfrac{\sqrt[4]{xy^3}}{3y^2}$

26. a. $a^{1/4}\left(a^{3/4}-a^{7/4}\right) = a^{4/4}-a^{8/4} = a-a^2$

b. $\left(x^{1/2}-3\right)\left(x^{1/2}+5\right)$
$$= x^{2/2}+5x^{1/2}-3x^{1/2}-15$$
$$= x+2x^{1/2}-15$$

27.
$$\sqrt{4-x} = x-2$$
$$\left(\sqrt{4-x}\right)^2 = (x-2)^2$$
$$4-x = x^2-4x+4$$
$$0 = x^2-3x$$
$$0 = x(x-3)$$
$$x = 0 \quad\text{or}\quad x-3 = 0$$
$$x = 3$$
$x = 0$ does not check, so the only solution is $x = 3$.

28. a. $\sqrt{\dfrac{54}{6}} = \sqrt{9} = 3$

b. $\dfrac{\sqrt{108a^2}}{3\sqrt{3}} = \dfrac{1}{3}\sqrt{\dfrac{108a^2}{3}}$

$\qquad\qquad = \dfrac{1}{3}\sqrt{36a^2}$

$\qquad\qquad = \dfrac{1}{3}(6a)$

$\qquad\qquad = 2a$

c. $\dfrac{3\sqrt[3]{81a^5b^{10}}}{\sqrt[3]{3b^4}} = 3\sqrt[3]{\dfrac{81a^5b^{10}}{3b^4}}$

$\qquad\qquad = 3\sqrt[3]{27a^5b^6}$

$\qquad\qquad = 9ab^2\sqrt[3]{a^2}$

29. $3x^2 - 9x + 8 = 0$

$x^2 - 3x + \dfrac{8}{3} = 0$

$x^2 - 3x = -\dfrac{8}{3}$

$x^2 - 3x + \left(\dfrac{-3}{2}\right)^2 = -\dfrac{8}{3} + \left(\dfrac{-3}{2}\right)^2$

$x^2 - 3x + \dfrac{9}{4} = -\dfrac{8}{3} + \dfrac{9}{4}$

$\left(x - \dfrac{3}{2}\right)^2 = -\dfrac{5}{12}$

$x - \dfrac{3}{2} = \pm\sqrt{-\dfrac{5}{12}}$

$x - \dfrac{3}{2} = \pm\dfrac{i\sqrt{5}}{2\sqrt{3}}$

$x - \dfrac{3}{2} = \pm\dfrac{i\sqrt{15}}{6}$

$x = \dfrac{3}{2} \pm \dfrac{i\sqrt{15}}{6}$

$\quad = \dfrac{9}{6} \pm \dfrac{i\sqrt{15}}{6}$

$\quad = \dfrac{9 \pm i\sqrt{15}}{6}$

The solutions are $\dfrac{9 + i\sqrt{15}}{6}$ and $\dfrac{9 - i\sqrt{15}}{6}$.

30. a. $\dfrac{\sqrt{20}}{3} + \dfrac{\sqrt{5}}{4} = \dfrac{2\sqrt{5}}{3} + \dfrac{\sqrt{5}}{4}$

$\qquad\qquad = \dfrac{8\sqrt{5} + 3\sqrt{5}}{12}$

$\qquad\qquad = \dfrac{11\sqrt{5}}{12}$

b. $\sqrt[3]{\dfrac{24x}{27}} - \dfrac{\sqrt[3]{3x}}{2} = \dfrac{2\sqrt[3]{3x}}{3} - \dfrac{\sqrt[3]{3x}}{2}$

$\qquad\qquad = \dfrac{4\sqrt[3]{3x} - 3\sqrt[3]{3x}}{6}$

$\qquad\qquad = \dfrac{\sqrt[3]{3x}}{6}$

31. $\dfrac{3x}{x-2} - \dfrac{x+1}{x} = \dfrac{6}{x(x-2)}$

$3x(x) - (x+1)(x-2) = 6$

$3x^2 - x^2 + x + 2 = 6$

$2x^2 + x - 4 = 0$

$a = 2,\, b = 1,\, c = -4$

$x = \dfrac{-1 \pm \sqrt{1^2 - 4(2)(-4)}}{2(2)} = \dfrac{-1 \pm \sqrt{33}}{4}$

32. $\sqrt[3]{\dfrac{27}{m^4 n^8}} = \dfrac{\sqrt[3]{27}}{\sqrt[3]{m^4 n^8}}$

$\qquad = \dfrac{3}{mn^2\sqrt[3]{mn^2}}$

$\qquad = \dfrac{3 \cdot \sqrt[3]{m^2 n}}{mn^2\sqrt[3]{mn^2} \cdot \sqrt[3]{m^2 n}}$

$\qquad = \dfrac{3\sqrt[3]{m^2 n}}{m^2 n^3}$

33. $x^2 - 4x \le 0$

$x(x - 4) = 0$

$x = 0,\, x = 4$

Region	Test Point	$x(x-4) \le 0$	Result
$x < 0$	$x = -1$	$(-1)(-5) \le 0$	False
$0 < x < 4$	$x = 2$	$2(-2) \le 0$	True
$x > 4$	$x = 5$	$5(1) \le 0$	False

Solution: [0, 4]

34. $c^2 = a^2 + b^2$

$8^2 = 4^2 + b^2$

$64 = 16 + b^2$

$48 = b^2$

$\pm 4\sqrt{3} = b$

$b > 0$ so the length is $4\sqrt{3}$ inches.

35. $F(x) = (x-3)^2 + 1$

36. a. $i^8 = (i^2)^4 = (-1)^4 = 1$

b. $i^{21} = i(i^{20}) = i$

c. $i^{42} = i^2(i^{40}) = i^2 = -1$

d. $i^{-13} = \dfrac{1}{i^{13}} = \dfrac{1}{i(i^{12})} = \dfrac{1}{i} = \dfrac{i}{i^2} = -i$

37. $f(x) = x - 1$ and $g(x) = 2x - 3$

a. $(f+g)(x) = f(x) + g(x)$
$= x - 1 + 2x - 3$
$= 3x - 4$

b. $(f-g)(x) = f(x) - g(x)$
$= x - 1 - (2x - 3)$
$= -x + 2$

c. $(f \cdot g)(x) = f(x) \cdot g(x)$
$= (x-1)(2x-3)$
$= 2x^2 - 5x + 3$

d. $\left(\dfrac{f}{g}\right)(x) = \dfrac{f(x)}{g(x)} = \dfrac{x-1}{2x-3}$, where $x \neq \dfrac{3}{2}$.

38. $4x^2 + 8x - 1 = 0$

$x^2 + 2x - \dfrac{1}{4} = 0$

$x^2 + 2x = \dfrac{1}{4}$

$x^2 + 2x + \left(\dfrac{2}{2}\right)^2 = \dfrac{1}{4} + \left(\dfrac{2}{2}\right)^2$

$x^2 + 2x + 1 = \dfrac{1}{4} + 1$

$(x+1)^2 = \dfrac{5}{4}$

$x + 1 = \pm\sqrt{\dfrac{5}{4}}$

$x + 1 = \pm\dfrac{\sqrt{5}}{2}$

$x = -1 \pm \dfrac{\sqrt{5}}{2}$

$= \dfrac{-2 \pm \sqrt{5}}{2}$

The solutions are $\dfrac{-2+\sqrt{5}}{2}$ and $\dfrac{-2-\sqrt{5}}{2}$.

39. $f(x) = x + 3$
$y = x + 3$
$x = y + 3$
$y = x - 3$
$f^{-1}(x) = x - 3$

40. $\left(x - \dfrac{1}{2}\right)^2 = \dfrac{x}{2}$

$x^2 - x + \dfrac{1}{4} = \dfrac{1}{2}x$

$x^2 - \dfrac{3}{2}x + \dfrac{1}{4} = 0$

$4x^2 - 6x + 1 = 0$

$a = 4,\ b = -6,\ c = 1$

$x = \dfrac{-(-6) \pm \sqrt{(-6)^2 - 4(4)(1)}}{2(4)}$

$= \dfrac{6 \pm \sqrt{20}}{8}$

$= \dfrac{6 \pm 2\sqrt{5}}{8}$

$= \dfrac{3 \pm \sqrt{5}}{4}$

The solutions are $\dfrac{3+\sqrt{5}}{4}$ and $\dfrac{3-\sqrt{5}}{4}$.

41. a. $\log_4 16 = \log_4 4^2 = 2$

b. $\log_{10} \dfrac{1}{10} = \log_{10} 10^{-1} = -1$

c. $\log_9 3 = \log_9 9^{1/2} = \dfrac{1}{2}$

42. $f(x) = -(x+1)^2 + 1$

Vertex: $(-1, 1)$

Axis of symmetry: $x = -1$

Chapter 10

Practice Exercises

1. $x = \dfrac{1}{2}y^2$; $a = \dfrac{1}{2}$, $h = 0$, $k = 0$; vertex: $(0, 0)$

x	y
2	-2
$\dfrac{1}{2}$	-1
0	0
$\dfrac{1}{2}$	1
2	2

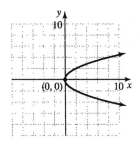

2. $x = -2(y+4)^2 - 1$; $a = -2$, $h = -1$, $k = -4$;
vertex: $(-1, -4)$

x	y
-9	-6
3	-5
-1	-4
-3	-3
-9	-2

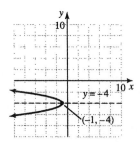

3.
$$y = -x^2 + 4x + 6$$
$$y - 6 = -x^2 + 4x$$
$$y - 6 = -(x^2 - 4x)$$
$$y - 6 - (+4) = -(x^2 - 4x + 4)$$
$$y - 10 = -(x - 2)^2$$
$$y = -(x - 2)^2 + 10$$
$a = -1$, $h = 2$, $k = 10$
vertex: $(2, 10)$

x	y
-1	1
0	6
1	9
2	10
3	9
4	6
5	1

4. $x = 3y^2 + 6y + 4$
Find the vertex.
$$y = \frac{-b}{2a} = \frac{-6}{2(3)} = -1$$

$x = 3(-1)^2 + 6(-1) + 4 = 3 - 6 + 4 = 1$
vertex: $(1, -1)$
The axis of symmetry is the line $y = -1$.
Since $a > 0$, the parabola opens to the right.
$x = 3(0)^2 + 6(0) + 4 = 4$
The x-intercept is $(4, 0)$.

5.
$$x^2 + y^2 = 25$$
$$(x-0)^2 + (y-0)^2 = 5^2$$
center: (0, 0); radius = 5

6. $(x-3)^2 + (y+2)^2 = 4$

$h = 3, k = -2, r = \sqrt{4} = 2$

center: (3, −2)

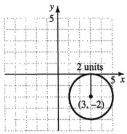

7. Center: (−2, −5); radius = 9

$$(x-h)^2 + (y-k)^2 = r^2$$

$h = -2, k = -5,$ and $r = 9.$

The equation is $(x+2)^2 + (y+5)^2 = 81.$

8.
$$x^2 + y^2 + 6x - 2y = 6$$
$$(x^2 + 6x) + (y^2 - 2y) = 6$$
$$(x^2 + 6x + 9) + (y^2 - 2y + 1) = 6 + 9 + 1$$
$$(x+3)^2 + (y-1)^2 = 16$$

Center: (−3, 1); radius = $\sqrt{16} = 4$

Graphing Calculator Explorations

1. $x^2 + y^2 = 55$
$$y^2 = 55 - x^2$$
$$y = \pm\sqrt{55 - x^2}$$

2. $x^2 + y^2 = 20$
$$y^2 = 20 - x^2$$
$$y = \pm\sqrt{20 - x^2}$$

3. $5x^2 + 5y^2 = 50$
$$5y^2 = 50 - 5x^2$$
$$y^2 = 10 - x^2$$
$$y = \pm\sqrt{10 - x^2}$$

4. $6x^2 + 6y^2 = 105$

$\qquad 6y^2 = 105 - 6x^2$

$\qquad y^2 = 17.5 - x^2$

$\qquad y = \pm\sqrt{17.5 - x^2}$

5. $2x^2 + 2y^2 - 34 = 0$

$\qquad 2y^2 = 34 - 2x^2$

$\qquad y^2 = 17 - x^2$

$\qquad y = \pm\sqrt{17 - x^2}$

6. $4x^2 + 4y^2 - 48 = 0$

$\qquad 4y^2 = 48 - 4x^2$

$\qquad y^2 = 12 - x^2$

$\qquad y = \pm\sqrt{12 - x^2}$

7. $7x^2 + 7y^2 - 89 = 0$

$\qquad 7y^2 = 89 - 7x^2$

$\qquad y^2 = \dfrac{89 - 7x^2}{7}$

$\qquad y = \pm\sqrt{\dfrac{89 - 7x^2}{7}}$

8. $3x^2 + 3y^2 - 35 = 0$

$\qquad 3y^2 = 35 - 3x^2$

$\qquad y^2 = \dfrac{35 - 3x^2}{3}$

$\qquad y = \pm\sqrt{\dfrac{35 - 3x^2}{3}}$

Vocabulary and Readiness Check

1. The circle, parabola, ellipse, and hyperbola are called the <u>conic sections</u>.

2. For a parabola that opens upward the lowest point is the <u>vertex</u>.

3. A <u>circle</u> is the set of all points in a plane that are the same distance from a fixed point. The fixed point is called the <u>center</u>.

4. The midpoint of a diameter of a circle is the <u>center</u>.

5. The distance from the center of a circle to any point of the circle is called the <u>radius</u>.

6. Twice a circle's radius is its <u>diameter</u>.

7. $y = x^2 - 7x + 5$; $a = 1$, upward

8. $y = -x^2 + 16$; $a = -1$, downward

9. $x = -y^2 - y + 2$; $a = -1$, to the left

10. $x = 3y^2 + 2y - 5$; $a = 3$, to the right

11. $y = -x^2 + 2x + 1$; $a = -1$, downward

12. $x = -y^2 + 2y - 6$; $a = -1$, to the left

Exercise Set 10.1

1. $x = 3y^2$

$x = 3(y-0)^2 + 0$

Vertex: $(0, 0)$

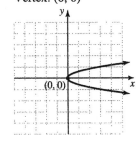

3. $x = (y-2)^2 + 3$

Vertex: $(3, 2)$

5. $y = 3(x-1)^2 + 5$

Vertex: $(1, 5)$

7. $x = y^2 + 6y + 8$

$x - 8 = y^2 + 6y$

$x - 8 + 9 = y^2 + 6y + 9$

$x + 1 = (y+3)^2$

$x = (y+3)^2 - 1$

Vertex: $(-1, -3)$

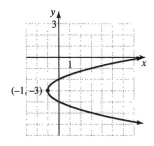

9. $y = x^2 + 10x + 20$

$y - 20 = x^2 + 10x$

$y - 20 + 25 = x^2 + 10x + 25$

$y + 5 = (x+5)^2$

$y = (x+5)^2 - 5$

Vertex: $(-5, -5)$

11. $x = -2y^2 + 4y + 6$

$x - 6 = -2(y^2 - 2y)$

$x - 6 + [-2(1)] = -2(y^2 - 2y + 1)$

$x - 8 = -2(y-1)^2$

$x = -2(y-1)^2 + 8$

Vertex: $(8, 1)$

13. $x^2 + y^2 = 9$

$(x-0)^2 + (y-0)^2 = 3^2$

Center: (0, 0), radius $r = 3$.

15. $x^2 + (y-2)^2 = 1$

$(x-0)^2 + (y-2)^2 = 1^2$

Center: (0, 2), radius $r = 1$.

17. $(x-5)^2 + (y+2)^2 = 1$

$(x-5)^2 + (y+2)^2 = 1^2$

Center: (5, –2), radius $r = 1$.

19. $x^2 + y^2 + 6y = 0$

$x^2 + (y^2 + 6y) = 0$

$x^2 + (y^2 + 6y + 9) = 9$

$(x-0)^2 + (y+3)^2 = 3^2$

Center: (0, –3), radius $r = 3$.

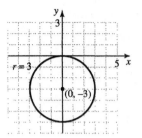

21. $\qquad x^2 + y^2 + 2x - 4y = 4$

$(x^2 + 2x) + (y^2 - 4y) = 4$

$(x^2 + 2x + 1) + (y^2 - 4y + 4) = 4 + 1 + 4$

$(x+1)^2 + (y-2)^2 = 9$

Center: (–1, 2), radius $r = \sqrt{9} = 3$.

23. $\qquad x^2 + y^2 - 4x - 8y - 2 = 0$

$(x^2 - 4x) + (y^2 - 8y) = 2$

$(x^2 - 4x + 4) + (y^2 - 8y + 16) = 2 + 4 + 16$

$(x-2)^2 + (y-4)^2 = 22$

Center: (2, 4), radius $r = \sqrt{22}$.

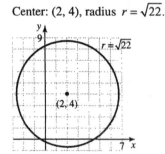

25. Center $(h, k) = (2, 3)$ and radius $r = 6$.

$(x-h)^2 + (y-k)^2 = r^2$

$(x-2)^2 + (y-3)^2 = 6^2$

$(x-2)^2 + (y-3)^2 = 36$

27. Center $(h, k) = (0, 0)$ and radius $r = \sqrt{3}$.

$$(x - h)^2 + (y - k)^2 = r^2$$
$$(x - 0)^2 + (y - 0)^2 = \left(\sqrt{3}\right)^2$$
$$x^2 + y^2 = 3$$

29. Center $(h, k) = (-5, 4)$ and radius $r = 3\sqrt{5}$.

$$(x - h)^2 + (y - k)^2 = r^2$$
$$[x - (-5)]^2 + (y - 4)^2 = \left(3\sqrt{5}\right)^2$$
$$(x + 5)^2 + (y - 4)^2 = 45$$

31. The radius is $\sqrt{10}$.

33. $x = y^2 - 3$

$x = (y - 0)^2 - 3$

Vertex: $(-3, 0)$

35. $y = (x - 2)^2 - 2$

Vertex: $(2, -2)$

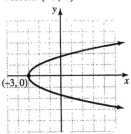

37. $x^2 + y^2 = 1$

Center: $(0, 0)$, radius $r = \sqrt{1} = 1$

39. $x = (y + 3)^2 - 1$

Vertex: $(-1, -3)$

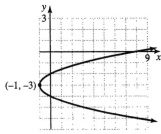

41. $(x - 2)^2 + (y - 2)^2 = 16$

Center: $(2, 2)$, radius $r = \sqrt{16} = 4$

43. $x = -(y - 1)^2$

Vertex: $(0, 1)$

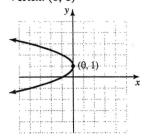

45. $(x - 4)^2 + y^2 = 7$

Center: $(4, 0)$, radius $r = \sqrt{7}$

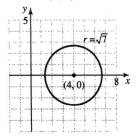

47. $y = 5(x+5)^2 + 3$

Vertex: $(-5, 3)$

49. $\dfrac{x^2}{8} + \dfrac{y^2}{8} = 2$

$8\left(\dfrac{x^2}{8} + \dfrac{y^2}{8}\right) = 8(2)$

$x^2 + y^2 = 16$

Center: $(0, 0)$, radius $r = \sqrt{16} = 4$

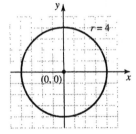

51. $y = x^2 + 7x + 6$

$y - 6 = x^2 + 7x$

$y - 6 + \dfrac{49}{4} = x^2 + 7x + \dfrac{49}{4}$

$y + \dfrac{25}{4} = \left(x + \dfrac{7}{2}\right)^2$

$y = \left(x + \dfrac{7}{2}\right)^2 - \dfrac{25}{4}$

Vertex: $\left(-\dfrac{7}{2}, -\dfrac{25}{4}\right)$

53. $x^2 + y^2 + 2x + 12y - 12 = 0$

$(x^2 + 2x) + (y^2 + 12y) = 12$

$(x^2 + 2x + 1) + (y^2 + 12y + 36) = 12 + 1 + 36$

$(x+1)^2 + (y+6)^2 = 49$

Center: $(-1, -6)$, radius $r = \sqrt{49} = 7$

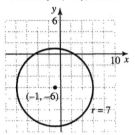

55. $x = y^2 + 8y - 4$

$x + 4 = y^2 + 8y$

$x + 4 + 16 = y^2 + 8y + 16$

$x + 20 = (y+4)^2$

$x = (y+4)^2 - 20$

Vertex: $(-20, -4)$

57. $x^2 - 10y + y^2 + 4 = 0$

$x^2 + (y^2 - 10y) = -4$

$x^2 + (y^2 - 10y + 25) = -4 + 25$

$x^2 + (y-5)^2 = 21$

Center: $(0, 5)$, radius $r = \sqrt{21}$

59.
$$x = -3y^2 + 30y$$
$$x = -3(y^2 - 10y)$$
$$x + [-3(25)] = -3(y^2 - 10y + 25)$$
$$x - 75 = -3(y - 5)^2$$
$$x = -3(y - 5)^2 + 75$$

Vertex: (75, 5)

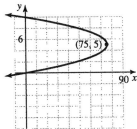

61. $5x^2 + 5y^2 = 25$
$$x^2 + y^2 = 5$$

Center: (0, 0), radius $r = \sqrt{5}$

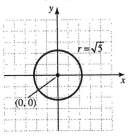

63.
$$y = 5x^2 - 20x + 16$$
$$y - 16 = 5(x^2 - 4x)$$
$$y - 16 + 5(4) = 5(x^2 - 4x + 4)$$
$$y + 4 = (x - 2)^2$$
$$y = (x - 2)^2 - 4$$

Vertex: (2, –4)

65. $y = -3x + 3$

67. $x = -2$

69. $\dfrac{\sqrt{5}}{\sqrt{8}} = \dfrac{\sqrt{5}}{2\sqrt{2}} = \dfrac{\sqrt{5} \cdot \sqrt{2}}{2\sqrt{2} \cdot \sqrt{2}} = \dfrac{\sqrt{10}}{2 \cdot 2} = \dfrac{\sqrt{10}}{4}$

71. $\dfrac{10}{\sqrt{5}} = \dfrac{10 \cdot \sqrt{5}}{\sqrt{5} \cdot \sqrt{5}} = \dfrac{10\sqrt{5}}{5} = 2\sqrt{5}$

73. a. radius $= \dfrac{1}{2}$(diameter) $= \dfrac{1}{2}$(135 meters)
$\qquad\qquad\qquad\qquad = 67.5$ meters

b. The wheel is at ground level or 0 meters.

c. The height of the center is equal to the radius or 67.5 meters.

d. The coordinates of the center are (0, 67.5).

e. $h = 0$, $k = 67.5$, and $r = 67.5$.
$$(x - h)^2 + (y - k)^2 = r^2$$
$$x^2 + (y - 67.5)^2 = 67.5^2$$

75. a. radius $= \dfrac{1}{2}$(diameter) $= \dfrac{1}{2}$(153 meters)
$\qquad\qquad\qquad\qquad = 76.5$ meters

b. height – diameter
$\quad = 160 - 153$
$\quad = 7$ meters from the ground

c. height from ground + radius
= 7 + 76.5
= 83.5 meters from the ground

d. Center: (0, 83.5)

e. $h = 0$, $k = 83.5$, and $r = 76.5$.
$$(x-h)^2 + (y-k)^2 = r^2$$
$$x^2 + (y-83.5)^2 = 76.5^2$$

77. diameter = 20 cm; center: (0, 0)

a.

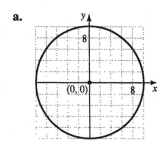

b. $h = 0$, $k = 0$, and $r = \frac{1}{2}(20) = 10$

$$(x-h)^2 + (y-k)^2 = r^2$$
$$x^2 + y^2 = 100$$

c. $h = 0$, $k = 0$, and the radius is the distance from the fountain or 5 feet.
$$x^2 + y^2 = 25$$

79. $5x^2 + 5y^2 = 25$
$$5y^2 = 25 - 5x^2$$
$$y^2 = 5 - x^2$$
$$y = \pm\sqrt{5 - x^2}$$

81. $y = 5x^2 - 20x + 16$

Section 10.2

Practice Exercises

1. $\dfrac{x^2}{25} + \dfrac{y^2}{4} = 1$

The equation is an ellipse with $a = 5$ and $b = 2$. The center is (0, 0). The x-intercepts are (5, 0) and (−5, 0). The y-intercepts are (2, 0) and (−2, 0).

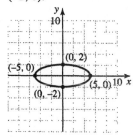

2. $9x^2 + 4y^2 = 36$

$$\frac{9x^2}{36} + \frac{4y^2}{36} = \frac{36}{36}$$

$$\frac{x^2}{4} + \frac{y^2}{9} = 1$$

This is an equation of an ellipse with $a = 2$ and $b = 3$. The ellipse has center (0, 0), x-intercepts (2, 0) and (−2, 0), and y-intercepts (3, 0) and (−3, 0).

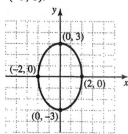

3. $\dfrac{(x-4)^2}{49} + \dfrac{(y+1)^2}{81} = 1$

This ellipse has center (4, −1). $a = 7$ and $b = 9$. Find four points on the ellipse.

$(4 + 7, -1) = (11, -1)$
$(4 - 7, -1) = (-3, -1)$
$(4, -1 + 9) = (4, 8)$
$(4, -1 - 9) = (4, -10)$

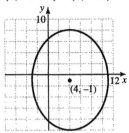

4. $\dfrac{x^2}{9} - \dfrac{y^2}{16} = 1$

This is a hyperbola with $a = 3$ and $b = 4$. It has center $(0, 0)$ and x-intercepts $(3, 0)$ and $(-3, 0)$. The asymptotes pass through $(3, 4)$, $(3, -4)$, $(-3, 4)$, and $(-3, -4)$.

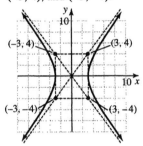

5. $9y^2 - 25x^2 = 225$

$$\dfrac{9y^2}{225} - \dfrac{25x^2}{225} = \dfrac{225}{225}$$

$$\dfrac{y^2}{25} - \dfrac{x^2}{9} = 1$$

This is a hyperbola with $a = 3$ and $b = 5$. The center is at $(0, 0)$ with y-intercepts $(0, 5)$ and $(0, -5)$. The asymptotes pass through $(3, 5)$, $(3, -5)$, $(-3, 5)$, and $(-3, -5)$.

Graphing Calculator Explorations

1. $10x^2 + y^2 = 32$

$$y^2 = 32 - 10x^2$$

$$y = \pm\sqrt{32 - 10x^2}$$

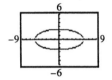

2. $x^2 + 6y^2 = 35$

$$6y^2 = 35 - x^2$$

$$y^2 = \dfrac{35 - x^2}{6}$$

$$y = \pm\sqrt{\dfrac{35 - x^2}{6}}$$

3. $20x^2 + 5y^2 = 100$

$$5y^2 = 100 - 20x^2$$

$$y^2 = 20 - 4x^2$$

$$y = \pm\sqrt{20 - 4x^2}$$

4. $4y^2 + 12x^2 = 48$

$$4y^2 = 48 - 12x^2$$

$$y^2 = 12 - 3x^2$$

$$y = \pm\sqrt{12 - 3x^2}$$

5. $7.3x^2 + 15.5y^2 = 95.2$

$$15.5y^2 = 95.2 - 7.3x^2$$

$$y^2 = \frac{95.2 - 7.3x^2}{15.5}$$

$$y = \pm\sqrt{\frac{95.2 - 7.3x^2}{15.5}}$$

6. $18.8x^2 + 36.1y^2 = 205.8$

$$36.1y^2 = 205.8 - 18.8x^2$$

$$y^2 = \frac{205.8 - 18.8x^2}{36.1}$$

$$y = \pm\sqrt{\frac{205.8 - 18.8x^2}{36.1}}$$

Vocabulary and Readiness Check

1. A <u>hyperbola</u> is the set of points in a plane such that the absolute value of the differences of their distances from two fixed points is constant.

2. An <u>ellipse</u> is the set of points in a plane such that the sum of their distances from two fixed points is constant.

3. The two fixed points are each called a <u>focus</u>.

4. The point midway between the foci is called the <u>center</u>.

5. The graph of $\frac{x^2}{a^2} - \frac{y^2}{b^2} = 1$ is a <u>hyperbola</u> with center <u>(0, 0)</u> and x-intercepts of <u>(a, 0) and (−a, 0)</u>.

6. The graph of $\frac{x^2}{b^2} + \frac{y^2}{a^2} = 1$ is an <u>ellipse</u> with center <u>(0, 0)</u> and x-intercepts of <u>(b, 0) and (−b, 0)</u>.

7. $\frac{x^2}{16} + \frac{y^2}{4} = 1$ is an ellipse.

8. $\frac{x^2}{16} - \frac{y^2}{4} = 1$ is a hyperbola.

9. $x^2 - 5y^2 = 3$ is a hyperbola.

10. $-x^2 + 5y^2 = 3$ or

$\qquad 5y^2 - x^2 = 3$ is a hyperbola.

11. $-\frac{y^2}{25} + \frac{x^2}{36} = 1$ or

$\qquad \frac{x^2}{36} - \frac{y^2}{25} = 1$ is a hyperbola.

12. $\frac{y^2}{25} + \frac{x^2}{36} = 1$ is an ellipse.

Exercise Set 10.2

1. $\frac{x^2}{4} + \frac{y^2}{25} = 1$

$$\frac{x^2}{2^2} + \frac{y^2}{5^2} = 1$$

Center: (0, 0)
x-intercepts: (−2, 0), (2, 0)
y-intercepts: (0, −5), (0, 5)

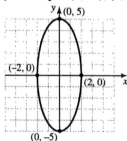

3. $\frac{x^2}{9} + y^2 = 1$

$$\frac{x^2}{3^2} + \frac{y^2}{1^2} = 1$$

Center: (0, 0)
x-intercepts: (−3, 0), (3, 0)
y-intercepts: (0, −1), (0, 1)

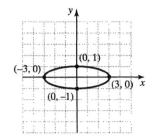

5. $9x^2 + y^2 = 36$

$$\frac{x^2}{4} + \frac{y^2}{36} = 1$$

$$\frac{x^2}{2^2} + \frac{y^2}{6^2} = 1$$

Center: (0, 0)
x-intercepts: (–2, 0), (2, 0)
y-intercepts: (0, –6), (0, 6)

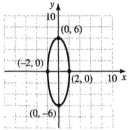

7. $4x^2 + 25y^2 = 100$

$$\frac{x^2}{25} + \frac{y^2}{4} = 1$$

$$\frac{x^2}{5^2} + \frac{y^2}{2^2} = 1$$

Center: (0, 0)
x-intercepts: (–5, 0), (5, 0)
y-intercepts: (0, –2), (0, 2)

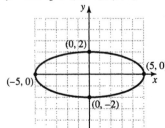

9. $\dfrac{(x+1)^2}{36} + \dfrac{(y-2)^2}{49} = 1$

$$\frac{(x+1)^2}{6^2} + \frac{(y-2)^2}{7^2} = 1$$

Center: (–1, 2)

Other points:
$(-1-6, 2) = (-7, 2)$
$(-1+6, 2) = (5, 2)$
$(-1, 2-7) = (-1, -5)$
$(-1, 2+7) = (-1, 9)$

11. $\dfrac{(x-1)^2}{4} + \dfrac{(y-1)^2}{25} = 1$

$$\frac{(x-1)^2}{2^2} + \frac{(y-1)^2}{5^2} = 1$$

Center: (1, 1)
Other points:
$(1-2, 1) = (-1, 1)$
$(1+2, 1) = (3, 1)$
$(1, 1-5) = (1, -4)$
$(1, 1+5) = (1, 6)$

13. $\dfrac{x^2}{4} - \dfrac{y^2}{9} = 1$

$$\frac{x^2}{2^2} - \frac{y^2}{3^2} = 1$$

$a = 2,\ b = 3$

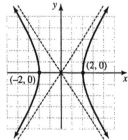

15. $\dfrac{y^2}{25} - \dfrac{x^2}{16} = 1$

$\dfrac{y^2}{5^2} - \dfrac{x^2}{4^2} = 1$

$a = 4, b = 5$

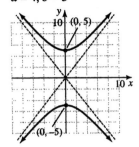

17. $x^2 - 4y^2 = 16$

$\dfrac{x^2}{16} - \dfrac{y^2}{4} = 1$

$\dfrac{x^2}{4^2} - \dfrac{y^2}{2^2} = 1$

$a = 4, b = 2$

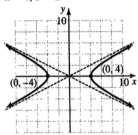

19. $16y^2 - x^2 = 16$

$\dfrac{y^2}{1} - \dfrac{x^2}{16} = 1$

$\dfrac{y^2}{1^2} - \dfrac{x^2}{4^2} = 1$

$a = 4, b = 1$

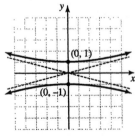

21. Answers may vary

23. $y = x^2 + 4$

Parabola; vertex (0, 4), opens upward

25. $\dfrac{x^2}{4} + \dfrac{y^2}{9} = 1$

$\dfrac{x^2}{2^2} + \dfrac{y^2}{3^2} = 1$

Ellipse; center: (0, 0)

x-intercepts: (–2, 0), (2, 0)

y-intercepts: (0, –3), (0, 3)

27. $\dfrac{x^2}{16} - \dfrac{y^2}{4} = 1$

$\dfrac{x^2}{4^2} - \dfrac{y^2}{2^2} = 1$

Hyperbola; center: (0, 0)

$a = 4, b = 2$

x-intercepts (–4, 0), (4, 0)

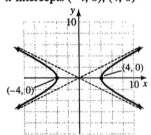

29. $x^2 + y^2 = 16$

Circle; center: (0, 0), radius: $r = \sqrt{16} = 4$

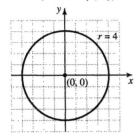

31. $x = -y^2 + 6y$

Parabola: $y = \dfrac{-b}{2a} = \dfrac{-6}{2(-1)} = 3$

$x = -(3)^2 + 6(3) = -9 + 18 = 9$

Vertex: (9, 3), opens to the left

33. $9x^2 + 4y^2 = 36$

$\dfrac{x^2}{4} + \dfrac{y^2}{9} = 1$

$\dfrac{x^2}{2^2} - \dfrac{y^2}{3^2} = 1$

Ellipse; center: (0, 0)

$a = 2, b = 3$

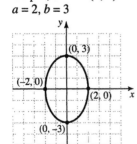

35. $y^2 = x^2 + 16$

$y^2 - x^2 = 16$

$\dfrac{y^2}{16} - \dfrac{x^2}{16} = 1$

$\dfrac{y^2}{4^2} - \dfrac{x^2}{4^2} = 1$

Hyperbola; center: (0, 0)

$a = 4, b = 4$

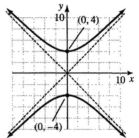

37. $y = -2x^2 + 4x - 3$

Parabola; $x = \dfrac{-b}{2a} = \dfrac{-4}{2(-2)} = 1$

$y = -2(1)^2 + 4(1) - 3 = -1$

Vertex: (1, −1)

39. $x < 5$ or $x < 1$

$x < 5$

$(-\infty, 5)$

41. $2x - 1 \ge 7$ and $-3x \le -6$

$\quad 2x \ge 8$ and $\quad x \ge 2$

$\quad\quad x \ge 4$

$x \ge 4$

$[4, \infty)$

43. $2x^3 - 4x^3 = -2x^3$

45. $(-5x^2)(x^2) = -5x^{2+2} = -5x^4$

47. $\dfrac{x^2}{100} + \dfrac{y^2}{49} = 1$

$\sqrt{100} = 10$, so the distance between the
x-intercepts is $10 + 10 = 20$ units.
$\sqrt{49} = 7$, so the distance between the
y-intercepts is $7 + 7 = 14$ units.
The distance between the x-intercepts is longer
by $20 - 14 = 6$ units.

49. $x^2 + 4y^2 = 36$

$\dfrac{x^2}{36} + \dfrac{y^2}{9} = 1$

$\sqrt{36} = 6$, so the distance between the
x-intercepts is $6 + 6 = 12$ units.
$\sqrt{9} = 3$, so the distance between the
y-intercepts is $3 + 3 = 6$ units.
The distance between the x-intercepts is longer
by $12 - 6 = 6$ units.

51. Circles: B, F
Ellipses: C, E, H
Hyperbolas: A, D, G

53. A: $c^2 = 36 + 13 = 49;\ c = \sqrt{49} = 7$

B: $c^2 = 4 - 4 = 0;\ c = \sqrt{0} = 0$

C: $c^2 = |25 - 16| = 9;\ c = \sqrt{9} = 3$

D: $c^2 = 39 + 25 = 64;\ c = \sqrt{64} = 8$

E: $c^2 = |81 - 17| = 64;\ c = \sqrt{64} = 8$

F: $c^2 = |36 - 36| = 0;\ c = \sqrt{0} = 0$

G: $c^2 = 65 + 16 = 81;\ c = \sqrt{81} = 9$

H: $c^2 = |144 - 140| = 4;\ c = \sqrt{4} = 2$

55. A: $e = \dfrac{7}{6}$

B: $e = \dfrac{0}{2} = 0$

C: $e = \dfrac{3}{5}$

D: $e = \dfrac{8}{5}$

E: $e = \dfrac{8}{9}$

F: $e = \dfrac{0}{6} = 0$

G: $e = \dfrac{9}{4}$

H: $e = \dfrac{2}{12} = \dfrac{1}{6}$

57. They are equal to 0.

59. Answers may vary

61. $a = 130{,}000{,}000 \Rightarrow a^2 = (130{,}000{,}000)^2$
$= 1.69 \times 10^{16}$

$b = 125{,}000{,}000 \Rightarrow b^2 = (125{,}000{,}000)^2$
$= 1.5625 \times 10^{16}$

Thus, the equation is
$\dfrac{x^2}{1.69 \times 10^{16}} + \dfrac{y^2}{1.5625 \times 10^{16}} = 1$.

63. $9x^2 + 4y^2 = 36$

$4y^2 = 36 - 9x^2$

$y^2 = \dfrac{36 - 9x^2}{4}$

$y = \pm\sqrt{\dfrac{36 - 9x^2}{4}} = \pm\dfrac{\sqrt{36 - 9x^2}}{2}$

65. $\dfrac{(x-1)^2}{4} - \dfrac{(y+1)^2}{25} = 1$

Center: $(1, -1)$
$a = 2,\ b = 5$

67. $\dfrac{y^2}{16} - \dfrac{(x+3)^2}{9} = 1$

Center: $(-3, 0)$
$a = 3,\ b = 4$

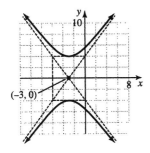

69. $\dfrac{(x+5)^2}{16} - \dfrac{(y+2)^2}{25} = 1$

Center: $(-5, -2)$

$a = 4$, $b = 5$

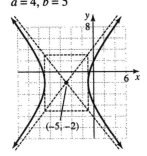

Integrated Review

1. $(x-7)^2 + (y-2)^2 = 4$

Circle; center: $(7, 2)$,

radius: $r = \sqrt{4} = 2$

2. $y = x^2 + 4$

Parabola; vertex: $(0, 4)$

3. $y = x^2 + 12x + 36$

Parabola; $x = \dfrac{-b}{2a} = \dfrac{-12}{2(1)} = -6$

$y = (-6)^2 + 12(-6) + 36 = 0$

Vertex: $(-6, 0)$

4. $\dfrac{x^2}{4} + \dfrac{y^2}{9} = 1$

Ellipse; center: $(0, 0)$

$a = 2$, $b = 3$

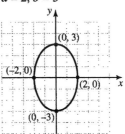

5. $\dfrac{y^2}{9} - \dfrac{x^2}{9} = 1$

Hyperbola; center: $(0, 0)$

$a = 3$, $b = 3$

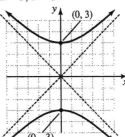

6. $\dfrac{x^2}{16} - \dfrac{y^2}{4} = 1$

Hyperbola; center: $(0, 0)$

$a = 4$, $b = 2$

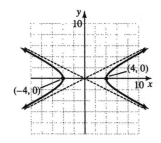

7. $\dfrac{x^2}{16} + \dfrac{y^2}{4} = 1$

Ellipse; center: (0, 0)
$a = 4, b = 2$

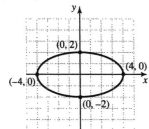

8. $x^2 + y^2 = 16$

Circle; center: (0, 0)
radius: $r = \sqrt{16} = 4$

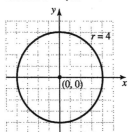

9. $x = y^2 + 4y - 1$

Parabola; $y = \dfrac{-b}{2a} = \dfrac{-4}{2(1)} = -2$

$x = (-2)^2 + 4(-2) - 1 = -5$
Vertex: (-5, -2)

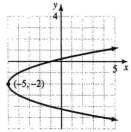

10. $x = -y^2 + 6y$

Parabola; $y = \dfrac{-b}{2a} = \dfrac{-6}{2(-1)} = 3$

$x = -(3)^2 + 6(3) = 9$
Vertex: (9, 3)

11. $9x^2 - 4y^2 = 36$

$\dfrac{x^2}{4} - \dfrac{y^2}{9} = 1$

Hyperbola; center: (0, 0)
$a = 2, b = 3$

12. $9x^2 + 4y^2 = 36$

$\dfrac{x^2}{4} + \dfrac{y^2}{9} = 1$

Ellipse; center: (0, 0)
$a = 2, b = 3$

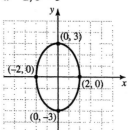

13. $\dfrac{(x-1)^2}{49} + \dfrac{(y+2)^2}{25} = 1$

Ellipse; center: (1, -2),
$a = 7, b = 5$

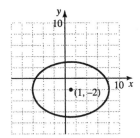

14.
$$y^2 = x^2 + 16$$
$$y^2 - x^2 = 16$$
$$\frac{y^2}{16} - \frac{x^2}{16} = 1$$

Hyperbola; center: $(0, 0)$
$a = 4, b = 4$

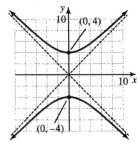

15. $\left(x + \frac{1}{2}\right)^2 + \left(y - \frac{1}{2}\right)^2 = 1$

Circle; center: $\left(-\frac{1}{2}, \frac{1}{2}\right)$, radius: $r = \sqrt{1} = 1$

Section 10.3

Practice Exercises

1. $\begin{cases} x^2 - 4y = 4 \\ x + y = -1 \end{cases}$

Solve $x + y = -1$ for y.
$y = -x - 1$
Replace y with $-x - 1$ in the first equation and solve for x.

$$x^2 - 4(-x - 1) = 4$$
$$x^2 + 4x + 4 = 4$$
$$x^2 + 4x = 0$$
$$x(x + 4) = 0$$
$x = 0$ or $x = -4$
Let $x = 0$,   Let $x = -4$,
$y = -0 - 1 = -1$ $y = -(-4) - 1 = 3$
The solutions are $(0, -1)$ and $(-4, 3)$.

2. $\begin{cases} y = -\sqrt{x} \\ x^2 + y^2 = 20 \end{cases}$

Substitute $-\sqrt{x}$ for y in the second equation.
$$x^2 + \left(-\sqrt{x}\right)^2 = 20$$
$$x^2 + x = 20$$
$$x^2 + x - 20 = 0$$
$$(x + 5)(x - 4) = 0$$
$x = -5$ or $x = 4$
Let $x = -5$.
$y = -\sqrt{-5}$ Not a real number
Let $x = 4$.
$y = -\sqrt{4} = -2$
The solution is $(4, -2)$.

3. $\begin{cases} x^2 + y^2 = 9 \\ x - y = 5 \end{cases}$

Solve the second equation for x.
$x = y + 5$
Let $x = y + 5$ in the first equation.
$$(y + 5)^2 + y^2 = 9$$
$$y^2 + 10y + 25 + y^2 = 9$$
$$2y^2 + 10y + 16 = 0$$
$$y^2 + 5y + 8 = 0$$
By the quadratic formula,
$$y = \frac{-5 \pm \sqrt{5^2 - 4(1)(8)}}{2(1)} = \frac{-5 \pm \sqrt{-7}}{2}$$

$\sqrt{-7}$ is not a real number. There is no real solution, or $\varnothing$.

4. $\begin{cases} x^2 + 4y^2 = 16 \\ x^2 - y^2 = 1 \end{cases}$

Add the opposite of the second equation to the first.

$x^2 + 4y^2 = 16$
$\underline{-x^2 + y^2 = -1}$
$0 + 5y^2 = 15$
$y^2 = 3$
$y = \pm\sqrt{3}$

Let $y = \sqrt{3}$.

$x^2 - \left(\sqrt{3}\right)^2 = 1$
$x^2 - 3 = 1$
$x^2 = 4$
$x = \pm 2$

Let $y = -\sqrt{3}$.

$x^2 - \left(-\sqrt{3}\right)^2 = 1$
$x^2 - 3 = 1$
$x^2 = 4$
$x = \pm 2$

The solutions are $\left(2, \sqrt{3}\right), \left(2, -\sqrt{3}\right)$,

$\left(-2, \sqrt{3}\right),$ and $\left(-2, -\sqrt{3}\right)$.

Exercise Set 10.3

1. $\begin{cases} x^2 + y^2 = 25 \quad (1) \\ 4x + 3y = 0 \quad (2) \end{cases}$

Solve E2 for y.
$3y = -4x$
$y = -\dfrac{4x}{3}$

Substitute into E1.

$x^2 + \left(-\dfrac{4x}{3}\right)^2 = 25$

$x^2 + \dfrac{16x^2}{9} = 25$

$9\left(x^2 + \dfrac{16x^2}{9}\right) = 9(25)$

$9x^2 + 16x^2 = 225$

$25x^2 = 225$

$x^2 = 9$

$x = \pm\sqrt{9} = \pm 3$

$x = 3 : y = -\dfrac{4(3)}{3} = -4$

$x = -3 : y = -\dfrac{4(-3)}{3} = 4$

The solutions are $(3, -4)$ and $(-3, 4)$.

3. $\begin{cases} x^2 + 4y^2 = 10 \quad (1) \\ \quad y = x \quad (2) \end{cases}$

Substitute x for y in E1.

$x^2 + 4x^2 = 10$
$5x^2 = 10$
$x^2 = 2$
$x = \pm\sqrt{2}$

Substitute these values into E2.
$x = \sqrt{2} : y = x = \sqrt{2}$
$x = -\sqrt{2} : y = x = -\sqrt{2}$

The solutions are $\left(\sqrt{2}, \sqrt{2}\right)$ and $\left(-\sqrt{2}, -\sqrt{2}\right)$.

5. $\begin{cases} y^2 = 4 - x \quad (1) \\ x - 2y = 4 \quad (2) \end{cases}$

Solve E2 for x.
$x = 2y + 4$

Substitute into E1.

$y^2 = 4 - (2y + 4)$
$y^2 = -2y$
$y^2 + 2y = 0$
$y(y + 2) = 0$
$y = 0 \text{ or } y + 2 = 0$
$\qquad\qquad y = -2$

Substitute these values into the equation $x = 2y + 4$.
$y = 0 : x = 2(0) + 4 = 4$
$y = -2 : x = 2(-2) + 4 = 0$

The solutions are $(4, 0)$ and $(0, -2)$.

7. $\begin{cases} x^2 + y^2 = 9 \quad (1) \\ 16x^2 - 4y^2 = 64 \quad (2) \end{cases}$

Multiply E1 by 4 and add to E2.

$4x^2 + 4y^2 = 36$
$\underline{16x^2 - 4y^2 = 64}$
$20x^2 \qquad = 100$
$x^2 = 5$
$x = \pm\sqrt{5}$

Substitute 5 for x^2 into E1.

$5 + y^2 = 9$
$y^2 = 4$
$y = \pm 2$

The solutions are $\left(-\sqrt{5}, -2\right), \left(-\sqrt{5}, 2\right)$,

$\left(\sqrt{5}, -2\right),$ and $\left(\sqrt{5}, 2\right)$.

9. $\begin{cases} x^2 + 2y^2 = 2 & (1) \\ x - y = 2 & (2) \end{cases}$

Solve E2 for x: $x = y + 2$

Substitute into E1.

$$(y+2)^2 + 2y^2 = 2$$
$$y^2 + 4y + 4 + 2y^2 = 2$$
$$3y^2 + 4y + 2 = 0$$
$$y = \frac{-4 \pm \sqrt{(4)^2 - 4(3)(2)}}{2(3)} = \frac{-4 \pm \sqrt{-8}}{6}$$

There are no real solutions. The solution is $\varnothing$.

11. $\begin{cases} y = x^2 - 3 & (1) \\ 4x - y = 6 & (2) \end{cases}$

Substitute $x^2 - 3$ for y in E2.

$$4x - (x^2 - 3) = 6$$
$$4x - x^2 + 3 = 6$$
$$0 = x^2 - 4x + 3$$
$$0 = (x - 3)(x - 1)$$
$$x - 3 = 0 \text{ or } x - 1 = 0$$
$$x = 3 \text{ or } \quad x = 1$$

Substitute these values into E1.

$$x = 3: y = (3)^2 - 3 = 6$$
$$x = 1: y = (1)^2 - 3 = -2$$

The solutions are $(3, 6)$ and $(1, -2)$.

13. $\begin{cases} y = x^2 & (1) \\ 3x + y = 10 & (2) \end{cases}$

Substitute x^2 for y in E2.

$$3x + x^2 = 10$$
$$x^2 + 3x - 10 = 0$$
$$(x + 5)(x - 2) = 0$$
$$x + 5 = 0 \quad \text{or } x - 2 = 0$$
$$x = -5 \text{ or } \quad x = 2$$

Substitute these values into E1.

$$x = -5: y = (-5)^2 = 25$$
$$x = 2: y = (2)^2 = 4$$

The solutions are $(-5, 25)$ and $(2, 4)$.

15. $\begin{cases} y = 2x^2 + 1 & (1) \\ x + y = -1 & (2) \end{cases}$

Substitute $2x^2 + 1$ for y in E2.

$$x + 2x^2 + 1 = -1$$
$$2x^2 + x + 2 = 0$$
$$x = \frac{-1 \pm \sqrt{(1)^2 - 4(2)(2)}}{2(2)} = \frac{-1 \pm \sqrt{-15}}{4}$$

There are no real solutions. The solution is $\varnothing$.

17. $\begin{cases} y = x^2 - 4 & (1) \\ y = x^2 - 4x & (2) \end{cases}$

Substitute $x^2 - 4$ for y in E2.

$$x^2 - 4 = x^2 - 4x$$
$$-4 = -4x$$
$$1 = x$$

Substitute this value into E1.

$$y = (1)^2 - 4 = -3$$

The solution is $(1, -3)$.

19. $\begin{cases} 2x^2 + 3y^2 = 14 & (1) \\ -x^2 + y^2 = 3 & (2) \end{cases}$

Multiply E2 by 2 and add to E1.

$$2x^2 + 3y^2 = 14$$
$$\underline{-2x^2 + 2y^2 = 6}$$
$$5y^2 = 20$$
$$y^2 = 4$$
$$y = \pm 2$$

Substitute 4 for y^2 into E2.

$$-x^2 + 4 = 3$$
$$-x^2 = -1$$
$$x^2 = 1$$
$$x = \pm 1$$

The solutions are $(-1, -2)$, $(-1, 2)$, $(1, -2)$, and $(1, 2)$.

21. $\begin{cases} x^2 + y^2 = 1 & (1) \\ x^2 + (y+3)^2 = 4 & (2) \end{cases}$

Multiply E1 by -1 and add to E2.

$$-x^2 - y^2 = -1$$
$$\underline{x^2 + (y+3)^2 = 4}$$
$$(y+3)^3 - y^2 = 3$$
$$y^2 + 6y + 9 - y^2 = 3$$
$$6y = -6$$
$$y = -1$$

Replace y with -1 in E1.

$$x^2 + (-1)^2 = 1$$
$$x^2 = 0$$
$$x = 0$$

The solution is $(0, -1)$.

23. $\begin{cases} y = x^2 + 2 & (1) \\ y = -x^2 + 4 & (2) \end{cases}$

Add E1 and E2.

$$y = x^2 + 2$$
$$\underline{y = -x^2 + 4}$$
$$2y = 6$$
$$y = 3$$

Substitute this value into E1.

$$3 = x^2 + 2$$
$$1 = x^2$$
$$\pm 1 = x$$

The solutions are $(-1, 3)$ and $(1, 3)$.

25. $\begin{cases} 3x^2 + y^2 = 9 & (1) \\ 3x^2 - y^2 = 9 & (2) \end{cases}$

Add E1 and E2.

$$3x^2 + y^2 = 9$$
$$\underline{3x^2 - y^2 = 9}$$
$$6x^2 = 18$$
$$x^2 = 3$$
$$x = \pm\sqrt{3}$$

Substitute 3 for x^2 in E1.

$$3(3) + y^2 = 9$$
$$y^2 = 0$$
$$y = 0$$

The solutions are $\left(-\sqrt{3}, 0\right)$, $\left(\sqrt{3}, 0\right)$.

27. $\begin{cases} x^2 + 3y^2 = 6 & (1) \\ x^2 - 3y^2 = 10 & (2) \end{cases}$

Solve E2 for x^2: $x^2 = 3y^2 + 10$.

Substitute into E1.

$$(3y^2 + 10) + 3y^2 = 6$$
$$6y^2 = -4$$
$$y^2 = -\frac{2}{3}$$

There are no real solutions. The solution is $\varnothing$.

29. $\begin{cases} x^2 + y^2 = 36 & (1) \\ y = \dfrac{1}{6}x^2 - 6 & (2) \end{cases}$

Solve E1 for x^2: $x^2 = 36 - y^2$.

Substitute into E2.

$$y = \frac{1}{6}(36 - y^2) - 6$$
$$y = 6 - \frac{1}{6}y^2 - 6$$
$$6y = -y^2$$
$$y^2 + 6y = 0$$
$$y(y + 6) = 0$$
$$y = 0 \quad \text{or} \quad y = -6$$

Substitute these values into the equation $x^2 = 36 - y^2$.

$$y = 0: x^2 = 36 - (0)^2$$
$$x^2 = 36$$
$$x = \pm 6$$
$$y = -6: x^2 = 36 - (6)^2$$
$$x^2 = 0$$
$$x = 0$$

The solutions are $(-6, 0)$, $(6, 0)$ and $(0, -6)$.

31. $x > -3$

33. $y < 2x - 1$

35. $P = x + (2x - 5) + (5x - 20) = (8x - 25)$ inches

37. $P = 2(x^2 + 3x + 1) + 2(x^2)$
$= 2x^2 + 6x + 2 + 2x^2$
$= (4x^2 + 6x + 2)$ meters

39. Answers may vary

41. There are 0, 1, 2, 3, or 4 possible real solutions.
Answers may vary

43. Let x and y represent the numbers.
$$\begin{cases} x^2 + y^2 = 130 \\ x^2 - y^2 = 32 \end{cases}$$
Add the equations.
$$\begin{array}{r} x^2 + y^2 = 130 \\ \underline{x^2 - y^2 = 32} \\ 2x^2 \quad = 162 \\ x^2 = 81 \\ x = \pm 9 \end{array}$$
Replace x^2 with 81 in the first equation.
$$81 + y^2 = 130$$
$$y^2 = 49$$
$$y = \pm 7$$
The numbers are –9 and –7, –9 and 7, 9 and –7, and 9 and 7.

45. Let x and y be the length and width.
$$\begin{cases} xy = 285 \\ 2x + 2y = 68 \end{cases}$$
Solve the first equation for y: $y = \dfrac{285}{x}$.
Substitute into the second equation.

$$2x + 2\left(\frac{285}{x}\right) = 68$$
$$x + \frac{285}{x} = 34$$
$$x^2 + 285 = 34x$$
$$x^2 - 34x + 285 = 0$$
$$(x - 19)(x - 15) = 0$$
$$x = 19 \text{ or } x = 15$$
Using $x = 19$, $y = \dfrac{285}{x} = \dfrac{285}{19} = 15$.

Using $x = 15$, $y = \dfrac{285}{x} = \dfrac{285}{15} = 19$.

The dimensions are 19 cm by 15 cm.

47. $\begin{cases} p = -0.01x^2 - 0.2x + 9 \\ p = 0.01x^2 - 0.1x + 3 \end{cases}$
Substitute.
$$-0.01x^2 - 0.2x + 9 = 0.01x^2 - 0.1x + 3$$
$$0 = 0.02x^2 + 0.1x - 6$$
$$0 = x^2 + 5x - 300$$
$$0 = (x + 20)(x - 15)$$
$$x + 20 = 0 \quad \text{or} \quad x - 15 = 0$$
$$x = -20 \text{ or} \qquad x = 15$$
Disregard the negative.
$$p = -0.01(15)^2 - 0.2(15) + 9$$
$$p = 3.75$$
The equilibrium quantity is 15,000 compact discs, and the corresponding price is $3.75.

49. $\begin{cases} x^2 + 4y^2 = 10 \\ y = x \end{cases}$

51. $\begin{cases} y = x^2 + 2 \\ y = -x^2 + 4 \end{cases}$

Section 10.4

Practice Exercises

1. $\dfrac{x^2}{36} + \dfrac{y^2}{16} \geq 1$

First graph the ellipse $\dfrac{x^2}{36} + \dfrac{y^2}{16} = 1$ as a solid

curve. Choose (0, 0) as a test point.

$\dfrac{x^2}{36} + \dfrac{y^2}{16} \geq 1$

$\dfrac{0^2}{36} + \dfrac{0^2}{16} \geq 1$

$0 \geq 1$ False

The solution set is the region that does not contain (0, 0).

2. $16y^2 > 9x^2 + 144$

The related equation is $16y^2 = 9x^2 + 144$.

$16y^2 - 9x^2 = 144$

$\dfrac{y^2}{9} - \dfrac{x^2}{16} = 1$

Graph the hyperbola as a dashed curve.

Choose (0, 0), (0, 4), and (0, −4) as test points.

(0, 0): $16(0)^2 > 9(0)^2 + 144$

$\qquad\quad 0 > 144$ False

(0, 4): $16(4)^2 > 9(0)^2 + 144$

$\qquad\quad 256 > 144$ True

(0, −4): $16(-4)^2 > 9(0)^2 + 144$

$\qquad\quad\ 256 > 144$ True

3. $\begin{cases} y \geq x^2 \\ y \leq -3x + 2 \end{cases}$

Solve the related system $\begin{cases} y = x^2 \\ y = -3x + 2 \end{cases}$.

Substitute $-3x + 2$ for y in the first equation.

$x^2 = -3x + 2$

$x^2 + 3x - 2 = 0$

$x = \dfrac{-3 \pm \sqrt{3^2 - 4(1)(-2)}}{2(1)}$

$\quad = \dfrac{-3 \pm \sqrt{17}}{2}$

$\quad \approx 0.56 \text{ or } -3.56$

$y = -3x + 2 \approx -3(0.56) + 2 = 0.32$

$y \approx -3(-3.56) + 2 = 12.68$

The points of intersection are approximately (0.56, 0.32) and (−3.56, 12.68).

Graph $y = x^2$ and $y = -3x + 2$ as solid curves.

The region of the solution set is above the parabola but below the line.

4. $\begin{cases} x^2 + y^2 < 16 \\ \dfrac{x^2}{4} - \dfrac{y^2}{9} < 1 \\ y < x + 3 \end{cases}$

Graph $x^2 + y^2 = 16$, $\dfrac{x^2}{4} - \dfrac{y^2}{9} = 1$, and $y = x + 3$.

The test point (0, 0) gives true statements for all three inequalities; thus, the innermost region is the solution set.

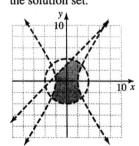

Exercise Set 10.4

1. $y < x^2$

First graph the parabola as a dashed curve.

Test Point	$y < x^2$; Result
(0, 1)	$1 < 0^2$; False

Shade the region which does not contain (0, 1).

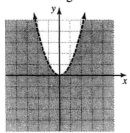

3. $x^2 + y^2 \geq 16$

First graph the circle as a solid curve.

Test Point	$x^2 + y^2 \geq 16$; Result
(0, 0)	$0^2 + 0^2 \geq 16$; False

Shade the region which does not contain (0, 0).

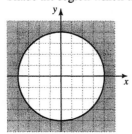

5. $\dfrac{x^2}{4} - y^2 < 1$

First graph the hyperbola as a dashed curve.

Test Point	$\frac{x^2}{4} - y^2 < 1$; Result
(−4, 0)	$\frac{(-4)^2}{4} - 0^2 < 1$; False
(0, 0)	$\frac{(0)^2}{4} - 0^2 < 1$; True
(4, 0)	$\frac{(4)^2}{4} - 0^2 < 1$; False

Shade the region containing (0, 0).

7. $y > (x-1)^2 - 3$

First graph the parabola as a dashed curve.

Test Point	$y > (x-1)^2 - 3$; Result
(0, 0)	$0 > (0-1)^2 - 3$; True

Shade the region containing (0, 0).

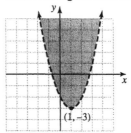

9. $x^2 + y^2 \leq 9$

First graph the circle as a solid curve.

Test Point	$x^2 + y^2 \leq 9$; Result
(0, 0)	$0^2 + 0^2 \leq 9$; True

Shade the region containing (0, 0).

11. $y > -x^2 + 5$

First graph the parabola as a dashed curve.

Test Point	$y > -x^2 + 5$; Result
$(0, 0)$	$0 > -(0)^2 + 5$; False

Shade the region which does not contain $(0, 0)$.

13. $\dfrac{x^2}{4} + \dfrac{y^2}{9} \le 1$

First graph the ellipse as a solid curve.

Test Point	$\dfrac{x^2}{4} + \dfrac{y^2}{9} \le 1$; Result
$(0, 0)$	$\dfrac{(0)^2}{4} + \dfrac{(0)^2}{9} \le 1$; True

Shade the region containing $(0, 0)$.

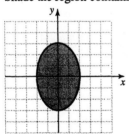

15. $\dfrac{y^2}{4} - x^2 \le 1$

First graph the hyperbola as solid curves.

Test Point	$\dfrac{y^2}{4} - x^2 \le 1$; Result
$(0, -4)$	$\dfrac{(-4)^2}{4} - 0^2 \le 1$; False
$(0, 0)$	$\dfrac{(0)^2}{4} - 0^2 \le 1$; True
$(0, 4)$	$\dfrac{(4)^2}{4} - 0^2 \le 1$; False

Shade the region containing $(0, 0)$.

17. $y < (x - 2)^2 + 1$

First graph the parabola as a dashed curve.

Test Point	$y < (x - 2)^2 + 1$; Result
$(0, 0)$	$0 < (0 - 2)^2 + 1$; True

Shade the region containing $(0, 0)$.

19. $y \le x^2 + x - 2$

First graph the parabola as a solid curve.

Test Point	$y \le x^2 + x - 2$; Result
$(0, 0)$	$0 \le (0)^2 + (0) - 2$; False

Shade the region which does not contain $(0, 0)$.

21. $\begin{cases} 4x + 3y \geq 12 \\ x^2 + y^2 < 16 \end{cases}$

First graph $4x + 3y = 12$ as a solid line.

Test Point	$4x + 3y \geq 12$; Result
(0, 0)	$4(0) + 3(0) \geq 12$; False

Shade the region which does not contain (0, 0). Next, graph the circle $x^2 + y^2 = 16$ as a dashed curve.

Test Point	$x^2 + y^2 < 16$; Result
(0, 0)	$0^2 + 0^2 < 16$; True

Shade the region containing (0, 0). The solution to the system is the intersection.

23. $\begin{cases} x^2 + y^2 \leq 9 \\ x^2 + y^2 \geq 1 \end{cases}$

First graph the circle with radius 3 as a solid curve.

Test Point	$x^2 + y^2 \leq 9$; Result
(0, 0)	$0^2 + 0^2 \leq 9$; True

Shade the region containing (0, 0). Next, graph the circle with 1 as a dashed curve.

Test Point	$x^2 + y^2 \geq 1$; Result
(0, 0)	$0^2 + 0^2 \geq 1$; False

Shade the region which does not contain (0, 0). The solution to the system is the intersection.

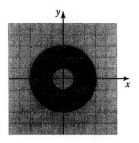

25. $\begin{cases} y > x^2 \\ y \geq 2x + 1 \end{cases}$

First graph the parabola as a dashed curve.

Test Point	$y > x^2$; Result
(0, 1)	$1 > 0^2$; True

Shade the region containing (0, 1). Next, graph $y = 2x + 1$ as a solid line.

Test Point	$y \geq 2x + 1$; Result
(0, 0)	$0 \geq 2(0) + 1$; False

Shade the region which does not contain (0, 0). The solution to the system is the intersection.

27. $\begin{cases} x^2 + y^2 > 9 \\ y > x^2 \end{cases}$

First graph the circle as a dashed curve.

Test Point	$x^2 + y^2 > 9$; Result
(0, 0)	$0^2 + 0^2 > 9$; False

Shade the region which does not contain (0, 0). Next, graph the parabola as a dashed curve.

Test Point	$y > x^2$; Result
(0, 1)	$1 > 0^2$; True

Shade the region containing (0, 1). The solution to the system is the intersection.

29. $\begin{cases} \dfrac{x^2}{4} + \dfrac{y^2}{9} \geq 1 \\ x^2 + y^2 \geq 4 \end{cases}$

First graph the ellipse as a solid curve.

Test Point	$\dfrac{x^2}{4} + \dfrac{y^2}{9} \geq 1$; Result
(0, 0)	$\dfrac{0^2}{4} + \dfrac{0^2}{9} \geq 1$; False

Shade the region which does not contain (0, 0). Next, graph the circle as a solid curve.

Test Point	$x^2 + y^2 \geq 4$; Result
(0, 0)	$0^2 + 0^2 \geq 4$; False

Shade the region which does not contain (0, 0). The solution to the system is the intersection.

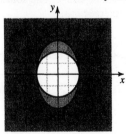

31. $\begin{cases} x^2 - y^2 \geq 1 \\ y \geq 0 \end{cases}$

First graph the hyperbola as solid curves.

Test Point	$x^2 - y^2 \geq 1$; Result
(−2, 0)	$(-2)^2 - 0^2 \geq 1$; True
(0, 0)	$0^2 - 0^2 \geq 1$; False
(2, 0)	$2^2 - 0^2 \geq 1$; True

Shade the region which does not contain (0, 0). Next, graph $y = 0$ as a solid line.

Test Point	$y > 0$; Result
(0, 1)	$1 \geq 0$; True

Shade the region containing (0, 1). The solution to the system is the intersection.

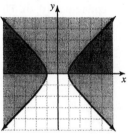

33. $\begin{cases} x + y \geq 1 \\ 2x + 3y < 1 \\ x > -3 \end{cases}$

First graph $x + y = 1$ as a solid line.

Test Point	$x + y \geq 1$; Result
(0, 0)	$0 + 0 \geq 1$; False

Shade the region which does not contain (0, 0). Next, graph $2x + 3y = 1$ as a dashed line.

Test Point	$2x + 3y < 1$; Result
(0, 0)	$2(0) 1 + 3(0) < 1$; True

Shade the region containing (0, 0). Now graph the line $x = -3$ as a dashed line.

Test Point	$x > -3$; Result
(0, 0)	$0 > -3$; True

Shade the region containing (0, 0). The solution to the system is the intersection.

35. $\begin{cases} x^2 - y^2 < 1 \\ \dfrac{x^2}{16} + y^2 \leq 1 \\ x \geq -2 \end{cases}$

First graph the hyperbola as dashed curves.

Test Point	$x^2 - y^2 < 1$; Result
$(-2, 0)$	$(-2)^2 - 0^2 < 1$; False
$(0, 0)$	$0^2 - 0^2 < 1$; True
$(2, 0)$	$2^2 - 0^2 < 1$; False

Shade the region containing $(0, 0)$. Next, graph the ellipse as a solid curve.

Test Point	$\dfrac{x^2}{16} + y^2 \leq 1$; Result
$(0, 0)$	$\dfrac{0^2}{16} + 0^2 \leq 1$; True

Shade the region containing $(0, 0)$. Now graph the line $x = -2$ as a solid line.

Test Point	$x \geq -2$; Result
$(0, 0)$	$0 \geq -2$; True

Shade the region containing $(0, 0)$. The solution to the system is the intersection.

37. This is not a function because a vertical line can cross the graph in more than one place.

39. This is a function because a vertical line can cross the graph in no more than one place.

41. $f(x) = 3x^2 - 2$
$f(-1) = 3(-1)^2 - 2 = 3 - 2 = 1$

43. $f(x) = 3x^2 - 2$
$f(a) = 3(a)^2 - 2 = 3a^2 - 2$

45. Answers may vary

47. $\begin{cases} y \leq x^2 \\ y \geq x + 2 \\ x \geq 0 \\ y \geq 0 \end{cases}$

First graph $y = x^2$ as a solid curve.

Test Point	$y \leq x^2$; Result
$(0, 1)$	$1 \leq 0^2$; False

Shade the region which does not contain $(0, 1)$. Next, graph $y = x + 2$ as a solid line.

Test Point	$y \geq x + 2$; Result
$(0, 0)$	$0 \geq 0 + 2$; False

Shade the region which does not contain $(0, 0)$. Next graph the line $x = 0$ as a solid line, and shade to the right. Now graph the line $y = 0$ as a solid line, and shade above. The solution to the system is the intersection.

Chapter 10 Vocabulary Check

1. A <u>circle</u> is the set of all points in a plane that are the same distance from a fixed point, called the <u>center</u>.

2. A <u>nonlinear system of equations</u> is a system of equations at least one of which is not linear.

3. An <u>ellipse</u> is the set of points on a plane such that the sum of the distances of those points from two fixed points is a constant.

4. In a circle, the distance from the center to a point of the circle is called its <u>radius</u>.

5. A <u>hyperbola</u> is the set of points in a plane such that the absolute value of the difference of the distance from two fixed points is constant.

Chapter 10 Review

1. center $(-4, 4)$, radius 3
$$[x-(-4)]^2 + (y-4)^2 = 3^2$$
$$(x+4)^2 + (y-4)^2 = 9$$

2. center $(5, 0)$, radius 5
$$(x-5)^2 + (y-0)^2 = 5^2$$
$$(x-5)^2 + y^2 = 25$$

3. center $(-7, -9)$, radius $\sqrt{11}$
$$[x-(-7)]^2 + [y-(-9)]^2 = \left(\sqrt{11}\right)^2$$
$$(x+7)^2 + (y+9)^2 = 11$$

4. center $(0, 0)$, radius $\dfrac{7}{2}$
$$(x-0)^2 + (y-0)^2 = \left(\frac{7}{2}\right)^2$$
$$x^2 + y^2 = \frac{49}{4}$$

5. $x^2 + y^2 = 7$

Circle; center $(0, 0)$, radius $r = \sqrt{7}$

6. $x = 2(y-5)^2 + 4$

Parabola; vertex: $(4, 5)$

7. $x = -(y+2)^2 + 3$

Parabola; vertex: $(3, -2)$

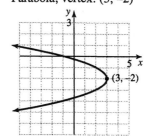

8. $(x-1)^2 + (y-2)^2 = 4$

Circle; center $(1, 2)$, radius $r = \sqrt{4} = 2$

9. $y = -x^2 + 4x + 10$

Parabola; $x = \dfrac{-b}{2a} = \dfrac{-4}{2(-1)} = 2$

$y = -(2)^2 + 4(2) + 10 = 14$

Vertex: (2, 14)

10. $x = -y^2 - 4y + 6$

Parabola; $y = \dfrac{-b}{2a} = \dfrac{-(-4)}{2(-1)} = -2$

$x = -(-2)^2 - 4(-2) + 6 = 10$

Vertex: (10, –2)

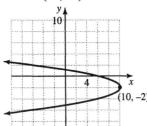

11. $x = \dfrac{1}{2}y^2 + 2y + 1$

Parabola; $y = \dfrac{-b}{2a} = \dfrac{-2}{2\left(\frac{1}{2}\right)} = -2$

$x = \dfrac{1}{2}(-2)^2 + 2(-2) + 1 = -1$

Vertex: (–1, –2)

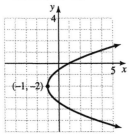

12. $y = -3x^2 + \dfrac{1}{2}x + 4$

Parabola; $x = \dfrac{-b}{2a} = \dfrac{-\frac{1}{2}}{2(-3)} = \dfrac{1}{12}$

$y = -3\left(\dfrac{1}{12}\right)^2 + \dfrac{1}{2}\left(\dfrac{1}{12}\right) + 4 = \dfrac{193}{48}$

Vertex: $\left(\dfrac{1}{12}, \dfrac{193}{48}\right)$

13.
$$x^2 + y^2 + 2x + y = \dfrac{3}{4}$$

$$(x^2 + 2x) + (y^2 + y) = \dfrac{3}{4}$$

$$(x^2 + 2x + 1) + \left(y^2 + y + \dfrac{1}{4}\right) = \dfrac{3}{4} + 1 + \dfrac{1}{4}$$

$$(x+1)^2 + \left(y + \dfrac{1}{2}\right)^2 = 2$$

Circle; center $\left(-1, -\dfrac{1}{2}\right)$, radius $r = \sqrt{2}$

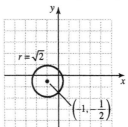

14.
$$x^2 + y^2 - 3y = \dfrac{7}{4}$$

$$x^2 + \left(y^2 - 3y + \dfrac{9}{4}\right) = \dfrac{7}{4} + \dfrac{9}{4}$$

$$x^2 + \left(y - \dfrac{3}{2}\right)^2 = 4$$

Circle; center $\left(0, \dfrac{3}{2}\right)$, radius $r = \sqrt{4} = 2$

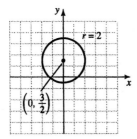

15.
$$4x^2 + 4y^2 + 16x + 8y = 1$$
$$(x^2 + 4x) + (y^2 + 2y) = \frac{1}{4}$$
$$(x^2 + 4x + 4) + (y^2 + 2y + 1) = \frac{1}{4} + 4 + 1$$
$$(x + 2)^2 + (y + 1)^2 = \frac{21}{4}$$

Circle; center $(-2, -1)$, radius $r = \sqrt{\frac{21}{4}} = \frac{\sqrt{21}}{2}$

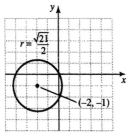

16. $x^2 + \dfrac{y^2}{4} = 1$

Center: $(0, 0)$; $a = 1, b = 2$

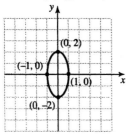

17. $x^2 - \dfrac{y^2}{4} = 1$

Center: $(0, 0)$; $a = 1, b = 2$

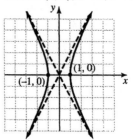

18. $\dfrac{x^2}{5} + \dfrac{y^2}{5} = 1$

$$x^2 + y^2 = 5$$

Center: $(0, 0)$; radius $r = \sqrt{5}$

19. $\dfrac{x^2}{5} - \dfrac{y^2}{5} = 1$

Center: $(0, 0)$; $a = \sqrt{5}, b = \sqrt{5}$

20. $-5x^2 + 25y^2 = 125$

$$\frac{y^2}{5} - \frac{x^2}{25} = 1$$

Center: $(0, 0)$; $a = 5$, $b = \sqrt{5}$

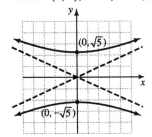

21. $4y^2 + 9x^2 = 36$

$$\frac{y^2}{9} + \frac{x^2}{4} = 1$$

Center: $(0, 0)$; $a = 2$, $b = 3$

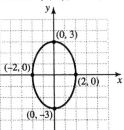

22. $x^2 - y^2 = 1$

Center: $(0, 0)$; $a = 1$, $b = 1$

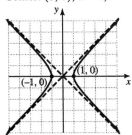

23. $\dfrac{(x+3)^2}{9} + \dfrac{(y-4)^2}{25} = 1$

Center: $(-3, 4)$; $a = 3$, $b = 5$

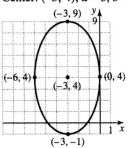

24. $y^2 = x^2 + 9$

$y^2 - x^2 = 9$

$$\frac{y^2}{9} - \frac{x^2}{9} = 1$$

Center: $(0, 0)$; $a = 3$, $b = 3$

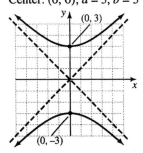

25. $x^2 = 4y^2 - 16$

$16 = 4y^2 - x^2$

$$1 = \frac{y^2}{4} - \frac{x^2}{16}$$

Center: $(0, 0)$; $a = 4$, $b = 2$

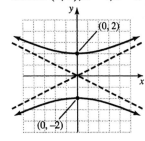

26. $100 - 25x^2 = 4y^2$

$$100 = 25x^2 + 4y^2$$

$$1 = \frac{x^2}{4} + \frac{y^2}{25}$$

Center: $(0, 0)$; $a = 2$, $b = 5$

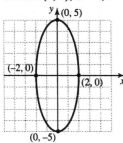

27. $\begin{cases} y = 2x - 4 & (1) \\ y^2 = 4x & (2) \end{cases}$

Substitute $2x - 4$ for y in E2.

$$(2x - 4)^2 = 4x$$

$$4x^2 - 16x + 16 = 4x$$

$$4x^2 - 20x + 16 = 0$$

$$x^2 - 5x + 4 = 0$$

$$(x - 4)(x - 1) = 0$$

$x = 4$ or $x = 1$

Use these values in E1.

$x = 4 : y = 2(4) - 4 = 4$

$x = 1 : y = 2(1) - 4 = -2$

The solutions are $(4, 4)$ and $(1, -2)$.

28. $\begin{cases} x^2 + y^2 = 4 & (1) \\ x - y = 4 & (2) \end{cases}$

Solve E2 for x: $x = y + 4$.
Substitute into E1.

$$(y + 4)^2 + y^2 = 4$$

$$(y^2 + 8y + 16) + y^2 = 4$$

$$2y^2 + 8y + 12 = 0$$

$$y^2 + 4y + 6 = 0$$

$$y = \frac{-4 \pm \sqrt{(4)^2 - 4(1)(6)}}{2(1)} = \frac{-4 \pm \sqrt{-8}}{2}$$

There are no real solutions. The solution is $\varnothing$.

29. $\begin{cases} y = x + 2 & (1) \\ y = x^2 & (2) \end{cases}$

Substitute $x + 2$ for y in E2.

$$x + 2 = x^2$$

$$0 = x^2 - x - 2$$

$$0 = (x - 2)(x + 1)$$

$x = 2$ or $x = -1$

Use these values in E1.

$x = 2 : y = 2 + 2 = 4$

$x = -1 : y = -1 + 2 = 1$

The solutions are $(2, 4)$ and $(-1, 1)$.

30. $\begin{cases} x^2 + 4y^2 = 16 & (1) \\ x^2 + y^2 = 4 & (2) \end{cases}$

Multiply E2 by -1 and add to E1.

$$\begin{array}{r} x^2 + 4y^2 = 16 \\ -x^2 - y^2 = -4 \\ \hline 3y^2 = 12 \\ y^2 = 4 \\ y = \pm 2 \end{array}$$

Replace y^2 with 4 in E2.

$$x^2 + 4 = 4$$

$$x^2 = 0$$

$$x = 0$$

The solutions are $(0, 2)$ and $(0, -2)$.

31. $\begin{cases} 4x - y^2 = 0 & (1) \\ 2x^2 + y^2 = 16 & (2) \end{cases}$

Solve E1 for y^2: $y^2 = 4x$.
Substitute into E2.

$$2x^2 + 4x = 16$$

$$2x^2 + 4x - 16 = 0$$

$$x^2 + 2x - 8 = 0$$

$$(x + 4)(x - 2) = 0$$

$x = -4$ or $x = 2$

Use these values in the equation $y^2 = 4x$.

$x = -4 : y^2 = 4(-4)$

$\qquad y^2 = -16$ (no real solutions)

$x = 2 : y^2 = 4(2)$

$\qquad y^2 = 8$

$\qquad y = \pm\sqrt{8} = \pm 2\sqrt{2}$

The solutions are $\left(2, -2\sqrt{2}\right)$ and $\left(2, 2\sqrt{2}\right)$.

32. $\begin{cases} x^2 + 2y = 9 & (1) \\ 5x - 2y = 5 & (2) \end{cases}$

Add E1 and E2.

$$\begin{aligned} x^2 + 2y &= 9 \\ \underline{5x - 2y} &= \underline{5} \\ x^2 + 5x &= 14 \end{aligned}$$

$$x^2 + 5x - 14 = 0$$
$$(x+7)(x-2) = 0$$
$$x = -7 \text{ or } x = 2$$

Use these values in E1.

$$x = -7 : (-7)^2 + 2y = 9$$
$$49 + 2y = 9$$
$$2y = -40$$
$$y = -20$$

$$x = 2 : (2)^2 + 2y = 9$$
$$4 + 2y = 9$$
$$2y = 5$$
$$y = \frac{5}{2}$$

The solutions are $(-7, -20)$ and $\left(2, \dfrac{5}{2}\right)$.

33. $\begin{cases} y = 3x^2 + 5x - 4 & (1) \\ y = 3x^2 - x + 2 & (2) \end{cases}$

Substitute.

$$3x^2 + 5x - 4 = 3x^2 - x + 2$$
$$6x = 6$$
$$x = 1$$

Use this value in E1.

$$y = 3(1)^2 + 5(1) - 4 = 4$$

The solution is $(1, 4)$.

34. $\begin{cases} x^2 - 3y^2 = 1 & (1) \\ 4x^2 + 5y^2 = 21 & (2) \end{cases}$

Multiply E1 by -4 and add to E2.

$$\begin{aligned} -4x^2 + 12y^2 &= -4 \\ \underline{4x^2 + 5y^2} &= \underline{21} \\ 17y^2 &= 17 \\ y^2 &= 1 \\ y &= \pm 1 \end{aligned}$$

Replace y^2 with 1 in E1.

$$x^2 - 3(1) = 1$$
$$x^2 = 4$$
$$x = \pm 2$$

The solutions are $(-2, -1)$, $(-2, 1)$, $(2, -1)$ and $(2, 1)$.

35. Let x and y be the length and width.

$$\begin{cases} xy = 150 \\ 2x + 2y = 50 \end{cases}$$

Solve the first equation for y: $y = \dfrac{150}{x}$.

Substitute into E2.

$$2x + 2\left(\frac{150}{x}\right) = 50$$
$$x + \frac{150}{x} = 25$$
$$x^2 + 150 = 25x$$

$$x^2 - 25x + 150 = 0$$
$$(x - 15)(x - 10) = 0$$
$$x = 15 \text{ or } x = 10$$

Substitute these values into E1.

$$\begin{array}{ll} 15y = 150 & 10y = 150 \\ y = 10 & y = 15 \end{array}$$

The room is 15 feet by 10 feet.

36. Four real solutions are possible.

37. $y \le -x^2 + 3$

Graph $y = -x^2 + 3$ as a solid curve.

Test Point	$y \le -x^2 + 3$; Result
$(0, 0)$	$0 \le -(0)^2 + 3$; True

Shade the region containing $(0, 0)$.

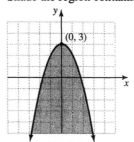

38. $x^2 + y^2 < 9$

First graph the circle as a dashed curve.

Test Point	$x^2 + y^2 < 9$; Result
$(0, 0)$	$0^2 + 0^2 < 9$; True

Shade the region containing $(0, 0)$.

39. $\begin{cases} 2x \le 4 \\ x + y \ge 1 \end{cases}$

First graph $2x = 4$, or $x = 2$, as a solid line, and shade to the left of the line. Next, graph $x + y = 1$ as a solid line.

Test Point	$x + y \ge 1$; Result
$(0, 0)$	$0 + 0 \ge 1$; False

Shade the region which does not contain $(0, 0)$. The solution to the system is the intersection.

40. $\dfrac{x^2}{4} + \dfrac{y^2}{9} \ge 1$

First graph the ellipse as a solid curve.

Test Point	$\dfrac{x^2}{4} + \dfrac{y^2}{9} \ge 1$; Result
$(0, 0)$	$\dfrac{(0)^2}{4} + \dfrac{(0)^2}{9} \ge 1$; False

Shade the region that does not contain $(0, 0)$.

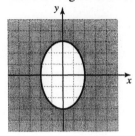

41. $\begin{cases} x^2 + y^2 < 4 \\ x^2 - y^2 \le 1 \end{cases}$

First graph the first circle as a dashed curve.

Test Point	$x^2 + y^2 < 4$; Result
$(0, 0)$	$0^2 + 0^2 < 4$; True

Shade the region containing $(0, 0)$. Next, graph the hyperbola as a solid curve.

Test Point	$x^2 - y^2 \le 1$; Result
$(-2, 0)$	$(-2)^2 - 0^2 \le 1$; False
$(0, 0)$	$0^2 - 0^2 \le 1$; True
$(2, 0)$	$2^2 - 0^2 \le 1$; False

Shade the region containing $(0, 0)$. The solution to the system is the intersection.

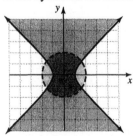

42. $\begin{cases} x^2 + y^2 \le 16 \\ x^2 + y^2 \ge 4 \end{cases}$

First graph the first circle as a solid curve.

Test Point	$x^2 + y^2 \le 16$; Result
$(0, 0)$	$0^2 + 0^2 \le 16$; True

Shade the region containing (0, 0). Next, graph the second circle as a solid curve.

Test Point	$x^2 + y^2 \geq 4$; Result
(0, 0)	$0^2 + 0^2 \geq 4$; False

Shade the region which does not contain (0, 0). The solution to the system is the intersection.

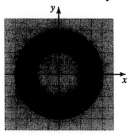

43. center: (−7, 8); radius = 5

$$(x-h)^2 + (y-k)^2 = r^2$$
$$(x+7)^2 + (y-8)^2 = 25$$

44. $3x^2 + 6x + 3y^2 = 9$

$$x^2 + 2x + y^2 = 3$$
$$x^2 + 2x + 1 + y^2 = 3 + 1$$
$$(x+1)^2 + y^2 = 4$$

This is a circle with center (−1, 0) and radius 2.

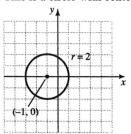

45. $y = x^2 + 6x + 9$

$$y = (x+3)^2$$

This is a parabola that opens upward with vertex (−3, 0).

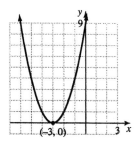

46. $x = y^2 + 6y + 9$

$$x = (y+3)^2$$

This is a parabola that opens to the right with vertex (0, −3).

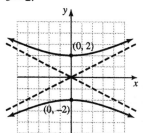

47. $\dfrac{y^2}{4} - \dfrac{x^2}{16} = 1$

This is a hyperbola with center (0, 0), $a = 4$ and $b = 2$.

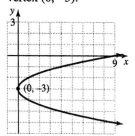

48. $\dfrac{y^2}{4} + \dfrac{x^2}{16} = 1$

This is an ellipse with center (0, 0), $a = 4$ and $b = 2$. The intercepts are (4, 0), (−4, 0), (0, 2), and (0, −2).

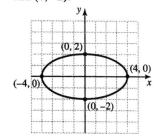

49. $\dfrac{(x-2)^2}{4}+(y-1)^2=1$

This is an ellipse with center (2, 1), $a=2$ and $b=1$.

50. $y^2=x^2+6$

$y^2-x^2=6$

$\dfrac{y^2}{6}-\dfrac{x^2}{6}=1$

This is a hyperbola with center (0, 0), $a=\sqrt{6}$ and $b=\sqrt{6}$.

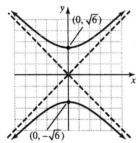

51. $y^2+x^2=4x+6$

$y^2+(x^2-4x)=6$

$y^2+(x^2-4x+4)=6+4$

$y^2+(x-2)^2=10$

This is a circle with center (2, 0) and radius $\sqrt{10}$.

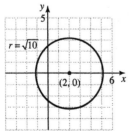

52. $x^2+y^2-8y=0$

$x^2+y^2-8y+16=16$

$x^2+(y-4)^2=16$

This is a circle with center (0, 4) and radius $\sqrt{16}=4$.

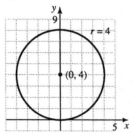

53. $6(x-2)^2+9(y+5)^2=36$

$\dfrac{(x-2)^2}{6}+\dfrac{(y+5)^2}{4}=1$

This is an ellipse with center (2, –5), $a=\sqrt{6}$, and $b=2$.

54. $\dfrac{x^2}{16}-\dfrac{y^2}{25}=1$

This is a hyperbola with center (0, 0), $a=4$, $b=5$, and x-intercepts (4, 0) and (–4, 0).

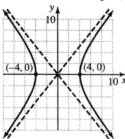

55. $\begin{cases} y=x^2-5x+1 & (1) \\ y=-x+6 & (2) \end{cases}$

Substitute $-x+6$ for y in E2.

$$-x+6 = x^2 -5x+1$$
$$0 = x^2 -4x-5$$
$$0 = (x-5)(x+1)$$
$$x = 5 \text{ or } x = -1$$

Use these values in E2.
$$x = 5: y = -(5)+6 = 1$$
$$x = -1: y = -(-1)+6 = 7$$

The solutions are (5, 1) and (–1, 7).

56. $\begin{cases} x^2 + y^2 = 10 & (1) \\ 9x^2 + y^2 = 18 & (2) \end{cases}$

Multiply E1 by –1 and add to E2.

$$-x^2 - y^2 = -10$$
$$\underline{9x^2 + y^2 = 18}$$
$$8x^2 \qquad = 8$$
$$x^2 = 1$$
$$x = \pm 1$$

Replace x^2 with 1 in E1.
$$1 + y^2 = 10$$
$$y^2 = 9$$
$$y = \pm 3$$

The solutions are (–1, –3), (–1, 3), (1, –3) and (1, 3).

57. $x^2 - y^2 < 1$

First graph the hyperbola as dashed curves.

Test Point	$x^2 - y^2 < 1$; Result
(–2, 0)	$(-2)^2 - 0^2 < 1$; False
(0, 0)	$0^2 - 0^2 < 1$; True
(2, 0)	$2^2 - 0^2 < 1$; False

Shade the region containing (0, 0).

58. $\begin{cases} y > x^2 \\ x + y \geq 3 \end{cases}$

First graph the parabola as a dashed curve.

Test Point	$y > x^2$; Result
(0, 1)	$1 > 0^2$; True

Shade the region containing (0, 1). Next, graph $x + y = 3$ as a solid line.

Test Point	$x + y \geq 3$; Result
(0, 0)	$0 + 0 \geq 3$; False

Shade the region which does not contain (0, 0). The solution to the system is the overlapping region.

Chapter 10 Test

1. $x^2 + y^2 = 36$

Circle; center: (0, 0), radius $r = \sqrt{36} = 6$

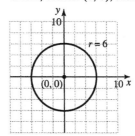

2. $x^2 - y^2 = 36$

$\dfrac{x^2}{36} - \dfrac{y^2}{36} = 1$

Hyperbola; center: $(0, 0)$, $a = 6$, $b = 6$

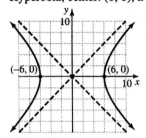

3. $16x^2 + 9y^2 = 144$

$\dfrac{x^2}{9} + \dfrac{y^2}{16} = 1$

Ellipse; center: $(0, 0)$, $a = 3$, $b = 4$

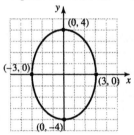

4. $y = x^2 - 8x + 16$

$y = (x-4)^2$

Parabola; vertex: $(4, 0)$

5. $\quad x^2 + y^2 + 6x = 16$

$\quad (x^2 + 6x) + y^2 = 16$

$\quad (x^2 + 6x + 9) + y^2 = 16 + 9$

$\quad (x+3)^2 + y^2 = 25$

6. $\qquad x = y^2 + 8y - 3$

$x + 16 = (y^2 + 8y + 16) - 3$

$\qquad x = (y+4)^2 - 19$

Parabola; vertex: $(-4, -19)$

7. $\dfrac{(x-4)^2}{16} + \dfrac{(y-3)^2}{9} = 1$

Ellipse: center: $(4, 3)$, $a = 4$, $b = 3$

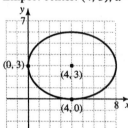

8. $y^2 - x^2 = 1$

Hyperbola: center: $(0, 0)$, $a = 1$, $b = 1$

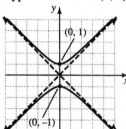

9. $\begin{cases} x^2 + y^2 = 26 & (1) \\ x^2 - 2y^2 = 23 & (2) \end{cases}$

Solve E1 for x^2: $x^2 = 26 - y^2$.

Substitute into E2.

$(26 - y^2) - 2y^2 = 23$

$\qquad -3y^2 = -3$

$\qquad\quad y^2 = 1$

$\qquad\quad y = \pm 1$

Replace y^2 with 1 in E1.

$x^2 + 1 = 26$

$\quad x^2 = 25$

$\quad x = \pm 5$

The solutions are $(-5, -1)$, $(-5, 1)$, $(5, -1)$, and $(5, 1)$.

10. $\begin{cases} y = x^2 - 5x + 6 & (1) \\ y = 2x & (2) \end{cases}$

Substitute $2x$ for y in E1.

$2x = x^2 - 5x + 6$

$0 = x^2 - 7x + 6$

$0 = (x - 6)(x - 1)$

$x = 6 \text{ or } x = 1$

Use these values in E2.

$x = 6: y = 2(6) = 12$

$x = 1: y = 2(1) = 2$

The solutions are $(1, 2)$ and $(6, 12)$.

11. $\begin{cases} 2x + 5y \ge 10 \\ \quad y \ge x^2 + 1 \end{cases}$

First graph $2x + 5y = 10$ as a solid line.

Test Point	$2x + 5y \ge 10$; Result
$(0, 0)$	$2(0) + 5(0) \ge 10$; False

Shade the region which does not contain $(0, 0)$.
Next, graph $y = x^2 + 1$ as a solid curve.

Test Point	$y \ge x^2 + 1$; Result
$(0, 0)$	$0 \ge 0^2 + 1$; False

Shade the region which does not contain $(0, 0)$.
The solution to the system is the intersection.

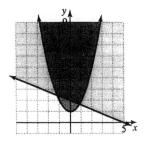

12. $\begin{cases} \dfrac{x^2}{4} + y^2 \le 1 \\ \quad x + y > 1 \end{cases}$

First graph the ellipse as a solid curve.

Test Point	$\dfrac{x^2}{4} + y^2 \le 1$; Result
$(0, 0)$	$\dfrac{0^2}{4} + 0^2 \le 1$; True

Shade the region containing $(0, 0)$. Next, graph $x + y = 1$ as a dashed line.

Test Point	$x + y > 1$; Result
$(0, 0)$	$0 + 0 > 1$; False

Shade the region which does not contain $(0, 0)$.
The solution to the system is the intersection.

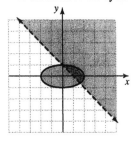

13. $\begin{cases} x^2 + y^2 \ge 4 \\ x^2 + y^2 < 16 \\ \quad y \ge 0 \end{cases}$

First graph the circle $x^2 + y^2 = 4$ as a solid curve.

Test Point	$x^2 + y^2 \ge 4$; Result
$(0, 0)$	$0^2 + 0^2 \ge 4$; False

Shade the region which does not contain $(0, 0)$.

Next graph the circle $x^2 + y^2 = 16$ as a dashed curve.

Test Point	$x^2 + y^2 < 16$; Result
$(0, 0)$	$0^2 + 0^2 < 16$; True

Shade the region containing $(0, 0)$. Now graph the inequality $y \geq 0$ by shading the region above the x-axis. The solution to the system is the intersection.

14. $100x^2 + 225y^2 = 22,500$

$$\frac{x^2}{225} + \frac{y^2}{100} = 1$$

$a = \sqrt{225} = 15$
$b = \sqrt{100} = 10$
Width = 15 + 15 = 30 feet
Height = 10 feet

Chapter 10 Cumulative Review

1. $4 \cdot (9y) = (4 \cdot 9)y = 36y$

2. $3x + 4 > 1$ and $2x - 5 \leq 9$
   $3x > -3$ and $2x \leq 14$
   $x > -1$ and $x \leq 7$
   $-1 < x \leq 7$
   $(-1, 7]$

3. $x = -2y$
   $y = -\dfrac{1}{2}x$

x	$y = -\frac{1}{2}x$
-2	1
0	0
4	-2

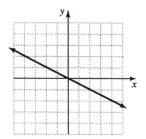

4. $(3, 2), (1, -4)$
   $$m = \frac{-4 - 2}{1 - 3} = \frac{-6}{-2} = 3$$

5. $\begin{cases} 3x + \dfrac{y}{2} = 2 & (1) \\ 6x + y = 5 & (2) \end{cases}$

   Multiply E1 by -2 and add to E2.
   $-6x - y = -4$
   $\underline{6x + y = 5}$
   $ 0 = 1$

   This is a false statement. Therefore, the solution is $\varnothing$.

6. Let $x =$ speed of one plane. Then
   $x + 25 =$ speed of the other plane.
   $d_{\text{plane 1}} + d_{\text{plane 2}} = 650$ miles
   $2x + 2(x + 25) = 650$
   $2x + 2x + 50 = 650$
   $4x = 600$
   $x = 150$
   $x + 25 = 150 + 25 = 175$
   The planes are traveling at 150 mph and 175 mph.

7. **a.** $(5x^2)^3 = 5^3(x^2)^3 = 125x^6$

   b. $\left(\dfrac{2}{3}\right)^3 = \dfrac{2^3}{3^3} = \dfrac{8}{27}$

   c. $\left(\dfrac{3p^4}{q^5}\right)^2 = \dfrac{3^2(p^4)^2}{(q^5)^2} = \dfrac{9p^8}{q^{10}}$

   d. $\left(\dfrac{2^{-3}}{y}\right)^{-2} = \dfrac{(2^{-3})^{-2}}{y^{-2}}$
   $= 2^6 y^2$
   $= 64y^2$

e. $(x^{-5}y^2z^{-1})^7 = (x^{-5})^7(y^2)^7(z^{-1})^7$
$$= x^{-35}y^{14}z^{-7}$$
$$= \frac{y^{14}}{x^{35}z^7}$$

8. a. $\dfrac{4^8}{4^3} = 4^{8-3} = 4^5$

b. $\dfrac{y^{11}}{y^5} = y^{11-5} = y^6$

c. $\dfrac{32x^7}{4x^6} = \dfrac{32}{4}x^{7-6} = 8x$

d. $\dfrac{18a^{12}b^6}{12a^8b^6} = \dfrac{18}{12}a^{12-8}b^{6-6} = \dfrac{3}{2}a^4b^0 = \dfrac{3a^4}{2}$

9. $2x^2 = \dfrac{17}{3}x + 1$
$$3(2x^2) = 3\left(\dfrac{17}{3}x + 1\right)$$
$$6x^2 = 17x + 3$$
$$6x^2 - 17x - 3 = 0$$
$$(6x + 1)(x - 3) = 0$$
$$6x + 1 = 0 \quad \text{or} \quad x - 3 = 0$$
$$6x = -1 \quad \text{or} \quad x = 3$$
$$x = -\dfrac{1}{6}$$

The solutions are $-\dfrac{1}{6}$ and 3.

10. a. $3y^2 + 14y + 15 = (3y + 5)(y + 3)$

b. $20a^5 + 54a^4 + 10a^3$
$$= 2a^3(10a^2 + 27a + 5)$$
$$= 2a^3(2a + 5)(5a + 1)$$

c. $(y - 3)^2 - 2(y - 3) - 8$
Let $u = y - 3$. Then $u^2 = (y - 3)^2$ and
$$u^2 - 2u - 8 = (u - 4)(u + 2)$$
$$= [(y - 3) - 4][(y - 3) + 2]$$
$$= (y - 7)(y - 1)$$

11. $\dfrac{7}{x-1} + \dfrac{10x}{x^2-1} - \dfrac{5}{x+1}$
$$= \dfrac{7}{x-1} + \dfrac{10x}{(x+1)(x-1)} - \dfrac{5}{x+1}$$
$$= \dfrac{7(x+1) + 10x - 5(x-1)}{(x+1)(x-1)}$$
$$= \dfrac{7x + 7 + 10x - 5x + 5}{(x+1)(x-1)}$$
$$= \dfrac{12x + 12}{(x+1)(x-1)}$$
$$= \dfrac{12(x+1)}{(x+1)(x-1)}$$
$$= \dfrac{12}{x-1}$$

12. $\dfrac{2}{3a-15} - \dfrac{a}{25-a^2}$
$$= \dfrac{2}{3(a-5)} + \dfrac{a}{a^2-25}$$
$$= \dfrac{2}{3(a-5)} + \dfrac{a}{(a+5)(a-5)}$$
$$= \dfrac{2(a+5) + 3a}{3(a+5)(a-5)}$$
$$= \dfrac{2a + 10 + 3a}{3(a+5)(a-5)}$$
$$= \dfrac{5a + 10}{3(a+5)(a-5)}$$

13. a. $\dfrac{\frac{2x}{27y^2}}{\frac{6x^2}{9}} = \dfrac{2x}{27y^2} \cdot \dfrac{9}{6x^2} = \dfrac{1}{3y^2} \cdot \dfrac{1}{3x} = \dfrac{1}{9xy^2}$

b. $\dfrac{\frac{5x}{x+2}}{\frac{10}{x-2}} = \dfrac{5x}{x+2} \cdot \dfrac{x-2}{10} = \dfrac{x(x-2)}{2(x+2)}$

c. $\dfrac{\frac{x}{y^2} + \frac{1}{y}}{\frac{y}{x^2} + \frac{1}{x}} = \dfrac{\left(\frac{x}{y^2} + \frac{1}{y}\right)x^2y^2}{\left(\frac{y}{x^2} + \frac{1}{x}\right)x^2y^2}$
$$= \dfrac{x^3 + x^2y}{y^3 + xy^2}$$
$$= \dfrac{x^2(x + y)}{y^2(y + x)}$$
$$= \dfrac{x^2}{y^2}$$

14. a. $(a^{-1} - b^{-1})^{-1} = \left(\dfrac{1}{a} - \dfrac{1}{b}\right)^{-1}$

$= \left(\dfrac{b-a}{ab}\right)^{-1}$

$= \dfrac{ab}{b-a}$

b. $\dfrac{2 - \frac{1}{x}}{4x - \frac{1}{x}} = \dfrac{\left(2 - \frac{1}{x}\right)x}{\left(4x - \frac{1}{x}\right)x}$

$= \dfrac{2x - 1}{4x^2 - 1}$

$= \dfrac{2x - 1}{(2x+1)(2x-1)}$

$= \dfrac{1}{2x+1}$

15.
$$\begin{array}{r} 2x - 5 \\ x+2\overline{\smash{)}2x^2 - x - 10} \\ \underline{2x^2 + 4x} \\ -5x - 10 \\ \underline{-5x - 10} \\ 0 \end{array}$$

Answer: $2x - 5$

16. $\dfrac{2}{x+3} = \dfrac{1}{x^2 - 9} - \dfrac{1}{x-3}$

$\dfrac{2}{x+3} = \dfrac{1}{(x+3)(x-3)} - \dfrac{1}{x-3}$

$2(x-3) = 1 - 1(x+3)$

$2x - 6 = 1 - x - 3$

$2x - 6 = -x - 2$

$3x = 4$

$x = \dfrac{4}{3}$

17.
$$\begin{array}{r|rrrrrrr} 4 & 4 & -25 & 35 & 0 & 17 & 0 & 0 \\ & & 16 & -36 & -4 & -16 & 4 & 16 \\ \hline & 4 & -9 & -1 & -4 & 1 & 4 & 16 \end{array}$$

Thus, $P(4) = 16$.

18. $y = \dfrac{k}{x}$

$3 = \dfrac{k}{\frac{2}{3}}$

$k = 3\left(\dfrac{2}{3}\right) = 2$

Thus, the equation is $y = \dfrac{2}{x}$.

19. $\dfrac{2x}{x-3} + \dfrac{6-2x}{x^2 - 9} = \dfrac{x}{x+3}$

$\dfrac{2x}{x-3} + \dfrac{-2(x-3)}{(x+3)(x-3)} = \dfrac{x}{x+3}$

$\dfrac{2x}{x-3} - \dfrac{2}{x+3} = \dfrac{x}{x+3}$

$\dfrac{2x}{x-3} = \dfrac{x}{x+3} + \dfrac{2}{x+3}$

$\dfrac{2x}{x-3} = \dfrac{x+2}{x+3}$

$2x(x+3) = (x+2)(x-3)$

$2x^2 + 6x = x^2 - x - 6$

$x^2 + 7x + 6 = 0$

$(x+6)(x+1) = 0$

$x + 6 = 0 \quad \text{or} \quad x + 1 = 0$

$x = -6 \quad \text{or} \quad x = -1$

The solutions are -6 and -1.

20. a. $\sqrt[5]{-32} = -2$ because $(-2)^5 = -32$.

b. $\sqrt[4]{625} = 5$ because $5^4 = 625$.

c. $-\sqrt{36} = -6$ because $6^2 = 36$.

d. $-\sqrt[3]{-27x^3} = -(-3x) = 3x$

e. $\sqrt{144y^2} = 12y$

21. Let t = time it will take together.

$$\frac{1}{4}+\frac{1}{5}=\frac{1}{t}$$

$$20t\left(\frac{1}{4}+\frac{1}{5}\right)=20t\left(\frac{1}{t}\right)$$

$$5t+4t=20$$

$$9t=20$$

$$t=\frac{20}{9}=2\frac{2}{9}$$

It will take them $2\frac{2}{9}$ hours. No, they can not finish before the movie starts.

22. a. $\dfrac{\sqrt{32}}{\sqrt{4}}=\sqrt{\dfrac{32}{4}}=\sqrt{8}=\sqrt{4\cdot 2}=2\sqrt{2}$

b. $\dfrac{\sqrt[3]{240y^2}}{5\sqrt[3]{3y^{-4}}}=\dfrac{1}{5}\sqrt[3]{\dfrac{240y^2}{3y^{-4}}}$

$$=\frac{1}{5}\sqrt[3]{80y^6}$$

$$=\frac{1}{5}\sqrt[3]{8y^6\cdot 10}$$

$$=\frac{2y^3\sqrt[3]{10}}{5}$$

c. $\dfrac{\sqrt[5]{64x^9y^2}}{\sqrt[5]{2x^2y^{-8}}}=\sqrt[5]{\dfrac{64x^9y^2}{2x^2y^{-8}}}$

$$=\sqrt[5]{32x^7y^{10}}$$

$$=\sqrt[5]{32x^5y^{10}\cdot x^2}$$

$$=2xy^2\sqrt[5]{x^2}$$

23. a. $\sqrt[3]{1}=1$

b. $\sqrt[3]{-64}=-4$

c. $\sqrt[3]{\dfrac{8}{125}}=\dfrac{\sqrt[3]{8}}{\sqrt[3]{125}}=\dfrac{2}{5}$

d. $\sqrt[3]{x^6}=x^2$

e. $\sqrt[3]{-27x^9}=-3x^3$

24. a. $\sqrt{5}\left(2+\sqrt{15}\right)=2\sqrt{5}+\sqrt{5}\cdot\sqrt{15}$

$$=2\sqrt{5}+\sqrt{75}$$

$$=2\sqrt{5}+5\sqrt{3}$$

b. $\left(\sqrt{3}-\sqrt{5}\right)\left(\sqrt{7}-1\right)$

$$=\sqrt{3}\cdot\sqrt{7}-\sqrt{3}\cdot 1-\sqrt{5}\cdot\sqrt{7}+\sqrt{5}\cdot 1$$

$$=\sqrt{21}-\sqrt{3}-\sqrt{35}+\sqrt{5}$$

c. $\left(2\sqrt{5}-1\right)^2=\left(2\sqrt{5}\right)^2-2\cdot 2\sqrt{5}\cdot 1+1^2$

$$=4(5)-4\sqrt{5}+1$$

$$=21-4\sqrt{5}$$

d. $\left(3\sqrt{2}+5\right)\left(3\sqrt{2}-5\right)=\left(3\sqrt{2}\right)^2-5^2$

$$=9(2)-25$$

$$=18-25$$

$$=-7$$

25. a. $z^{2/3}\left(z^{1/3}-z^5\right)=z^{2/3+1/3}-z^{2/3+5}$

$$=z^{3/3}-z^{2/3+15/3}$$

$$=z-z^{17/3}$$

b. $(x^{1/3}-5)(x^{1/3}+2)$

$$=x^{1/3}\cdot x^{1/3}+2x^{1/3}-5x^{1/3}-5(2)$$

$$=x^{2/3}-3x^{1/3}-10$$

26. $\dfrac{-2}{\sqrt{3}+3}=\dfrac{-2\left(\sqrt{3}-3\right)}{\left(\sqrt{3}+3\right)\left(\sqrt{3}-3\right)}$

$$=\frac{-2\left(\sqrt{3}-3\right)}{\left(\sqrt{3}\right)^2-3^2}$$

$$=\frac{-2\left(\sqrt{3}-3\right)}{3-9}$$

$$=\frac{-2\left(\sqrt{3}-3\right)}{-6}$$

$$=\frac{\sqrt{3}-3}{3}$$

27. a. $\dfrac{\sqrt{20}}{\sqrt{5}}=\sqrt{\dfrac{20}{5}}=\sqrt{4}=2$

b. $\dfrac{\sqrt{50x}}{2\sqrt{2}}=\dfrac{1}{2}\sqrt{\dfrac{50x}{2}}=\dfrac{1}{2}\sqrt{25x}=\dfrac{5\sqrt{x}}{2}$

c.
$$\frac{7\sqrt[3]{48x^4y^8}}{\sqrt[3]{6y^2}} = 7\sqrt[3]{\frac{48x^4y^8}{6y^2}}$$
$$= 7\sqrt[3]{8x^4y^6}$$
$$= 7\sqrt[3]{8x^3y^6 \cdot x}$$
$$= 7 \cdot 2xy^2\sqrt[3]{x}$$
$$= 14xy^2\sqrt[3]{x}$$

d.
$$\frac{2\sqrt[4]{32a^8b^6}}{\sqrt[4]{a^{-1}b^2}} = 2\sqrt[4]{\frac{32a^8b^6}{a^{-1}b^2}}$$
$$= 2\sqrt[4]{32a^9b^4}$$
$$= 2\sqrt[4]{16a^8b^4 \cdot 2a}$$
$$= 2 \cdot 2a^2b\sqrt[4]{2a}$$
$$= 4a^2b\sqrt[4]{2a}$$

28.
$$\sqrt{2x-3} = x-3$$
$$\left(\sqrt{2x-3}\right)^2 = (x-3)^2$$
$$2x-3 = x^2 - 6x + 9$$
$$0 = x^2 - 8x + 12$$
$$0 = (x-6)(x-2)$$
$$x-6 = 0 \text{ or } x-2 = 0$$
$$x = 6 \text{ or } \qquad x = 2$$
Discard 2 as an extraneous solution. The solution is 6.

29. a.
$$\frac{\sqrt{45}}{4} - \frac{\sqrt{5}}{3} = \frac{3\sqrt{5}}{4} - \frac{\sqrt{5}}{3}$$
$$= \frac{9\sqrt{5} - 4\sqrt{5}}{12}$$
$$= \frac{5\sqrt{5}}{12}$$

b.
$$\sqrt[3]{\frac{7x}{8}} + 2\sqrt[3]{7x} = \frac{\sqrt[3]{7x}}{2} + 2\sqrt[3]{7x}$$
$$= \frac{\sqrt[3]{7x}}{2} + \frac{4\sqrt[3]{7x}}{2}$$
$$= \frac{5\sqrt[3]{7x}}{2}$$

30.
$$9x^2 - 6x = -4$$
$$9x^2 - 6x + 4 = 0$$
$$a = 9, b = -6, c = 4$$
$$b^2 - 4ac = (-6)^2 - 4(9)(4)$$
$$= 36 - 144$$
$$= -108$$
Two complex but not real solutions

31.
$$\sqrt{\frac{7x}{3y}} = \frac{\sqrt{7x}}{\sqrt{3y}} = \frac{\sqrt{7x} \cdot \sqrt{3y}}{\sqrt{3y} \cdot \sqrt{3y}} = \frac{\sqrt{21xy}}{3y}$$

32.
$$\frac{4}{x-2} - \frac{x}{x+2} = \frac{16}{x^2-4}$$
$$\frac{4}{x-2} - \frac{x}{x+2} = \frac{16}{(x+2)(x-2)}$$
$$4(x+2) - x(x-2) = 16$$
$$4x+8 - x^2 + 2x = 16$$
$$0 = x^2 - 6x + 8$$
$$0 = (x-4)(x-2)$$
$$x-4 = 0 \text{ or } x-2 = 0$$
$$x = 4 \text{ or } \qquad x = 2$$
Discard the solution 2 as extraneous. The solution is 4.

33.
$$\sqrt{2x-3} = 9$$
$$\left(\sqrt{2x-3}\right)^2 = 9^2$$
$$2x-3 = 81$$
$$2x = 84$$
$$x = 42$$
The solution is 42.

34.
$$x^3 + 2x^2 - 4x \geq 8$$
$$x^3 + 2x^2 - 4x - 8 \geq 0$$
$$x^2(x+2) - 4(x+2) \geq 0$$
$$(x+2)(x^2-4) \geq 0$$
$$(x+2)(x+2)(x-2) \geq 0$$
$$(x+2)^2(x-2) \geq 0$$
$$(x+2)^2 = 0 \text{ or } x-2 = 0$$
$$x+2 = 0 \text{ or } \qquad x = 2$$
$$x = -2$$

Region	Test Point	$(x+2)^2(x-2) \geq 0$ Result
A: $(-\infty, -2)$	-3	$(-1)^2(-5) \geq 0$ False
B: $(-2, 2)$	0	$(2)^2(-2) \geq 0$ False
C: $(2, \infty)$	3	$(5)^2(1) \geq 0$ True

Solution: $[2, \infty)$

35. a. $i^7 = i^4 \cdot i^3 = 1 \cdot (-i) = -i$

b. $i^{20} = (i^4)^5 = 1^5 = 1$

c. $i^{46} = i^{44} \cdot i^2 = (i^4)^{11} \cdot (-1) = 1^{11}(-1) = -1$

d. $i^{-12} = \dfrac{1}{i^{12}} = \dfrac{1}{(i^4)^3} = \dfrac{1}{1^3} = 1$

36. $f(x) = (x+2)^2 - 1$

37.
$$p^2 + 2p = 4$$
$$p^2 + 2p + \left(\frac{2}{2}\right)^2 = 4 + 1$$
$$p^2 + 2p + 1 = 5$$
$$(p+1)^2 = 5$$
$$p + 1 = \pm\sqrt{5}$$
$$p = -1 \pm \sqrt{5}$$

The solutions are $-1 + \sqrt{5}$ and $-1 - \sqrt{5}$.

38. $f(x) = -x^2 - 6x + 4$

The maximum will occur at the vertex.

$$x = \frac{-b}{2a} = \frac{-(-6)}{2(-1)} = -3$$
$$f(-3) = -(-3)^2 - 6(-3) + 4 = 13$$

The maximum value is 13.

39.
$$\frac{1}{4}m^2 - m + \frac{1}{2} = 0$$
$$4\left(\frac{1}{4}m^2 - m + \frac{1}{2}\right) = 4(0)$$
$$m^2 - 4m + 2 = 0$$
$$a = 1, b = -4, c = 2$$
$$m = \frac{-(-4) \pm \sqrt{(-4)^2 - 4(1)(2)}}{2(1)}$$
$$= \frac{4 \pm \sqrt{16 - 8}}{2}$$
$$= \frac{4 \pm \sqrt{8}}{2}$$
$$= \frac{4 \pm 2\sqrt{2}}{2}$$
$$= 2 \pm \sqrt{2}$$

The solutions are $2 + \sqrt{2}$ and $2 - \sqrt{2}$.

40.
$$f(x) = \frac{x+1}{2}$$
$$y = \frac{x+1}{2}$$
$$x = \frac{y+1}{2}$$
$$2x = y + 1$$
$$2x - 1 = y$$
$$f^{-1}(x) = 2x - 1$$

41.
$$p^4 - 3p^2 - 4 = 0$$
$$(p^2 - 4)(p^2 + 1) = 0$$
$$(p+2)(p-2)(p^2 + 1) = 0$$
$$p + 2 = 0 \quad \text{or } p - 2 = 0 \text{ or } p^2 + 1 = 0$$
$$p = -2 \quad \text{or} \quad p = 2 \quad \text{or} \quad p^2 = -1$$
$$p = \pm i$$

The solutions are -2, 2, $-i$, and i.

42. $f(x) = x^2 - 3x + 2$
$g(x) = -3x + 5$

   a. $(f \circ g)(x) = f[g(x)]$
$= f(-3x + 5)$
$= (-3x + 5)^2 - 3(-3x + 5) + 2$
$= 9x^2 - 30x + 25 + 9x - 15 + 2$
$= 9x^2 - 21x + 12$

   b. $(f \circ g)(-2) = f[g(-2)]$
$= f[-3(-2) + 5]$
$= f(11)$
$= (11)^2 - 3(11) + 2$
$= 121 - 33 + 2$
$= 90$

   c. $(g \circ f)(x) = g[f(x)]$
$= g(x^2 - 3x + 2)$
$= -3(x^2 - 3x + 2) + 5$
$= -3x^2 + 9x - 6 + 5$
$= -3x^2 + 9x - 1$

   d. $(g \circ f)(5) = g[f(5)]$
$= g[(5)^2 - 3(5) + 2]$
$= g(12)$
$= -3(12) + 5$
$= -36 + 5$
$= -31$

43. $\dfrac{x + 2}{x - 3} \le 0$
$x + 2 = 0$ or $x - 3 = 0$
   $x = -2$ or $x = 3$

Region	Test Point	$\dfrac{x+2}{x-3} \le 0$ Result
A: $(-\infty, -2)$	-3	$\dfrac{-1}{-6} \le 0$; False
B: $(-2, 3)$	0	$\dfrac{2}{-3} \le 0$; True
C: $(3, \infty)$	4	$\dfrac{6}{1} \le 0$; False

Solution: $[-2, 3)$

44. $4x^2 + 9y^2 = 36$
$\dfrac{x^2}{9} + \dfrac{y^2}{4} = 1$
Ellipse: center $(0, 0)$, $a = 3$, $b = 2$

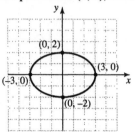

45. $g(x) = \dfrac{1}{2}(x + 2)^2 + 5$
Vertex: $(-2, 5)$, axis: $x = -2$

46. a. $64^x = 4$
$(4^2)^x = 4$
$4^{2x} = 4$
$2x = 1$
$x = \dfrac{1}{2}$

   b. $125^{x-3} = 25$
$(5^3)^{x-3} = 5^2$
$5^{3x-9} = 5^2$
$3x - 9 = 2$
$3x = 11$
$x = \dfrac{11}{3}$

   c. $\dfrac{1}{81} = 3^{2x}$
$3^{-4} = 3^{2x}$
$-4 = 2x$
$-\dfrac{4}{2} = x$
$-2 = x$

47. $f(x) = x^2 - 4x - 12$

$x = \dfrac{-b}{2a} = \dfrac{-(-4)}{2(1)} = 2$

$f(2) = (2)^2 - 4(2) - 12 = -16$

Vertex: $(2, -16)$

48. $\begin{cases} x + 2y < 8 \\ \quad y \geq x^2 \end{cases}$

First, graph $x + 2y = 8$ as a dashed line.

Test Point	$x + 2y < 8$; Result
$(0, 0)$	$0 + 2(0) < 8$; True

Shade the region containing $(0, 0)$. Next, graph the parabola $y = x^2$ as a solid curve.

Test Point	$y \geq x^2$; Result
$(0, 1)$	$1 \geq 0^2$; True

Shade the region containing $(0, 1)$. The solution to the system is the intersection.

49. $(2, -5), (1, -4)$

$d = \sqrt{[-4 - (-5)]^2 + (1 - 2)^2}$

$\quad = \sqrt{1^2 + (-1)^2}$

$\quad = \sqrt{2} \approx 1.414$

50. $\begin{cases} x^2 + y^2 = 36 & (1) \\ \quad\quad y = x + 6 & (2) \end{cases}$

Substitute $x + 6$ for y in E1.

$x^2 + (x + 6)^2 = 36$

$x^2 + (x^2 + 12x + 36) = 36$

$2x^2 + 12x = 0$

$2x(x + 6) = 0$

$2x = 0$ or $x + 6 = 0$

$x = 0$ or $\quad x = -6$

Use these values in E2 to find y.

$x = 0 : y = 0 + 6 = 6$

$x = -6 : y = -6 + 6 = 0$

The solutions are $(0, 6)$ and $(-6, 0)$.

Chapter 11

Practice Problems

1. $a_n = 5 + n^2$

$a_1 = 5 + 1^2 = 5 + 1 = 6$

$a_2 = 5 + 2^2 = 5 + 4 = 9$

$a_3 = 5 + 3^2 = 5 + 9 = 14$

$a_4 = 5 + 4^2 = 5 + 16 = 21$

$a_5 = 5 + 5^2 = 5 + 25 = 30$

Thus, the first five terms of the sequence are 6, 9, 14, 21, and 30.

2. $a_n = \dfrac{(-1)^n}{5n}$

a. $a_1 = \dfrac{(-1)^1}{5(1)} = -\dfrac{1}{5}$

b. $a_4 = \dfrac{(-1)^4}{5(4)} = \dfrac{1}{20}$

c. $a_{30} = \dfrac{(-1)^{30}}{5(30)} = \dfrac{1}{150}$

d. $a_{19} = \dfrac{(-1)^{19}}{5(19)} = -\dfrac{1}{95}$

3. a. $1, 3, 5, 7, \ldots$
These numbers are the first four odd natural numbers, so a general term might be
$a_n = (2n - 1)$.

b. $3, 9, 27, 81, \ldots$
These numbers are all powers of 3 ($3 = 3^1$, $9 = 3^2$, $27 = 3^3$, and $81 = 3^4$), so a general term might be $a_n = 3^n$.

c. $\dfrac{1}{2}, \dfrac{2}{3}, \dfrac{3}{4}, \dfrac{4}{5}, \ldots$
The numerators are the first four natural numbers and each denominator is one greater than the numerator, so a general term might be $a_n = \dfrac{n}{n+1}$.

d. $-\dfrac{1}{2}, -\dfrac{1}{3}, -\dfrac{1}{4}, -\dfrac{1}{5}, \ldots$
The denominators are consecutive natural numbers beginning with 2 and each term is negative, so a general term might be
$a_n = -\dfrac{1}{n+1}$.

4. $v_n = 3950(0.8)^n$

$v_3 = 3950(0.8)^3$
$= 3950(0.512)$
$= 2022.4$

The value of the copier after three years is $2022.40.

Vocabulary and Readiness Check

1. The nth term of the sequence a_n is called the <u>general</u> term.

2. A <u>finite</u> sequence is a function whose domain is $\{1, 2, 3, 4, \ldots, n\}$ where n is some natural number.

3. An <u>infinite</u> sequence is a function whose domain is $\{1, 2, 3, 4, \ldots\}$.

4. $a_n = 7^n$
$a_1 = 7^1 = 7$

5. $a_n = \dfrac{(-1)^n}{n}$
$a_1 = \dfrac{(-1)^1}{1} = -1$

6. $a_n = (-1)^n \cdot n^4$
$a_1 = (-1)^1 \cdot 1^4 = -1$

Exercise Set 11.1

1. $a_n = n + 4$
$a_1 = 1 + 4 = 5$
$a_2 = 2 + 4 = 6$
$a_3 = 3 + 4 = 7$
$a_4 = 4 + 4 = 8$
$a_5 = 5 + 4 = 9$

Thus, the first five terms of the sequence $a_n = n + 4$ are 5, 6, 7, 8, 9.

3. $a_n = (-1)^n$

$a_1 = (-1)^1 = -1$
$a_2 = (-1)^2 = 1$
$a_3 = (-1)^3 = -1$
$a_4 = (-1)^4 = 1$
$a_5 = (-1)^5 = -1$

Thus, the first five terms of the sequence
$a_n = (-1)^n$ are $-1, 1, -1, 1, -1$.

5. $a_n = \dfrac{1}{n+3}$

$a_1 = \dfrac{1}{1+3} = \dfrac{1}{4}$
$a_2 = \dfrac{1}{2+3} = \dfrac{1}{5}$
$a_3 = \dfrac{1}{3+3} = \dfrac{1}{6}$
$a_4 = \dfrac{1}{4+3} = \dfrac{1}{7}$
$a_5 = \dfrac{1}{5+3} = \dfrac{1}{8}$

Thus, the first five terms of the sequence
$a_n = \dfrac{1}{n+3}$ are $\dfrac{1}{4}, \dfrac{1}{5}, \dfrac{1}{6}, \dfrac{1}{7}, \dfrac{1}{8}$.

7. $a_n = 2n$

$a_1 = 2(1) = 2$
$a_2 = 2(2) = 4$
$a_3 = 2(3) = 6$
$a_4 = 2(4) = 8$
$a_5 = 2(5) = 10$

Thus, the first five terms of the sequence
$a_n = 2n$ are $2, 4, 6, 8, 10$.

9. $a_n = -n^2$

$a_1 = -1^2 = -1$
$a_2 = -2^2 = -4$
$a_3 = -3^2 = -9$
$a_4 = -4^2 = -16$
$a_5 = -5^2 = -25$

Thus, the first five terms of the sequence
$a_n = n^2$ are $-1, -4, -8, -16, -25$.

11. $a_n = 2^n$

$a_1 = 2^1 = 2$
$a_2 = 2^2 = 4$
$a_3 = 2^3 = 8$
$a_4 = 2^4 = 16$
$a_5 = 2^5 = 32$

Thus, the first five terms of the sequence
$a_n = 2^n$ are $2, 4, 8, 16, 32$.

13. $a_n = 2n + 5$

$a_1 = 2(1) + 5 = 2 + 5 = 7$
$a_2 = 2(2) + 5 = 4 + 5 = 9$
$a_3 = 2(3) + 5 = 6 + 5 = 11$
$a_4 = 2(4) + 5 = 8 + 5 = 13$
$a_5 = 2(5) + 5 = 10 + 5 = 15$

Thus, the first five terms of the sequence
$a_n = 2n + 5$ are $7, 9, 11, 13, 15$.

15. $a_n = (-1)^n n^2$

$a_1 = (-1)^1 (1)^2 = -1(1) = -1$
$a_2 = (-1)^2 (2)^2 = 1(4) = 4$
$a_3 = (-1)^3 (3)^2 = -1(9) = -9$
$a_4 = (-1)^4 (4)^2 = 1(16) = 16$
$a_5 = (-1)^5 (5)^2 = -1(25) = -25$

Thus, the first five terms of the sequence
$a_n = (-1)^n n^2$ are $-1, 4, -9, 16, -25$.

17. $a_n = 3n^2$

$a_5 = 3(5)^2 = 3(25) = 75$

19. $a_n = 6n - 2$

$a_{20} = 6(20) - 2 = 120 - 2 = 118$

21. $a_n = \dfrac{n+3}{n}$

$a_{15} = \dfrac{15+3}{15} = \dfrac{18}{15} = \dfrac{6}{5}$

23. $a_n = (-3)^n$

$a_6 = (-3)^6 = 729$

25. $a_n = \dfrac{n-2}{n+1}$

$a_6 = \dfrac{6-2}{6+1} = \dfrac{4}{7}$

27. $a_n = \dfrac{(-1)^n}{n}$

$a_8 = \dfrac{(-1)^8}{8} = \dfrac{1}{8}$

29. $a_n = -n^2 + 5$

$a_{10} = -10^2 + 5 = -100 + 5 = -95$

31. $a_n = \dfrac{(-1)^n}{n+6}$

$a_{19} = \dfrac{(-1)^{19}}{19+6} = -\dfrac{1}{25}$

33. 3, 7, 11, 15, or $4(1) - 1$, $4(2) - 1$, $4(3) - 1$, $4(4) - 1$. In general, $a_n = 4n - 1$.

35. $-2, -4, -8, -16$, or $-2, -2^2, -2^3, -2^4$

In general, $a_n = -2^n$.

37. $\dfrac{1}{3}, \dfrac{1}{9}, \dfrac{1}{27}, \dfrac{1}{81}$, or $\dfrac{1}{3}, \dfrac{1}{3^2}, \dfrac{1}{3^3}, \dfrac{1}{3^4}$

In general, $a_n = \dfrac{1}{3^n}$.

39. $a_n = 32n - 16$

$a_2 = 32(2) - 16 = 64 - 16 = 48$ ft
$a_3 = 32(3) - 16 = 96 - 16 = 80$ ft
$a_4 = 32(4) - 16 = 128 - 16 = 112$ ft

41. $0.10, 0.20, 0.40$, or $0.10, 0.10(2), 0.10(2)^2$

In general, $a_n = 0.10(2)^{n-1}$

$a_{14} = 0.10(2)^{13} = \$819.20$

43. $a_n = 75(2)^{n-1}$

$a_6 = 75(2)^5 = 75(32) = 2400$ cases
$a_1 = 75(2)^0 = 75(1) = 75$ cases

45. $a_n = \dfrac{1}{2}a_{n-1}$ for $n > 1, a_1 = 800$

In 2000, $n = 1$ and $a_1 = 800$.

In 2001, $n = 2$ and $a_2 = \dfrac{1}{2}(800) = 400$.

In 2002, $n = 3$ and $a_3 = \dfrac{1}{2}(400) = 200$.

In 2003, $n = 4$ and $a_4 = \dfrac{1}{2}(200) = 100$.

In 2004, $n = 5$ and $a_5 = \dfrac{1}{2}(100) = 50$.

The population estimate for 2004 is 50 sparrows. Continuing the sequence:

In 2005, $n = 6$ and $a_6 = \dfrac{1}{2}(50) = 25$.

In 2006, $n = 7$ and $a_7 = \dfrac{1}{2}(25) \approx 12$.

In 2007, $n = 8$ and $a_8 = \dfrac{1}{2}(12) = 6$.

In 2008, $n = 9$ and $a_9 = \dfrac{1}{2}(6) = 3$.

In 2009, $n = 10$ and $a_{10} = \dfrac{1}{2}(3) \approx 1$.

In 2010, $n = 11$ and $a_{11} = \dfrac{1}{2}(1) \approx 0$.

The population is estimated to become extinct in 2010.

47. $f(x) = (x-1)^2 + 3$

49. $f(x) = 2(x+4)^2 + 2$

51. $(-4, -1)$ and $(-7, -3)$

$$d = \sqrt{[-7-(-4)]^2 + [-3-(-1)]^2}$$
$$= \sqrt{(-7+4)^2 + (-3+1)^2}$$
$$= \sqrt{(-3)^2 + (-2)^2}$$
$$= \sqrt{9+4}$$
$$= \sqrt{13} \text{ units}$$

53. $(2, -7)$ and $(-3, -3)$

$$d = \sqrt{(-3-2)^2 + [-3-(-7)]^2}$$
$$= \sqrt{(-5)^2 + (-3+7)^2}$$
$$= \sqrt{(-5)^2 + (4)^2}$$
$$= \sqrt{25+16}$$
$$= \sqrt{41} \text{ units}$$

55. $a_n = \dfrac{1}{\sqrt{n}}$

$$a_1 = \frac{1}{\sqrt{1}} = \frac{1}{1} = 1$$

$$a_2 = \frac{1}{\sqrt{2}} \approx 0.7071$$

$$a_3 = \frac{1}{\sqrt{3}} \approx 0.5774$$

$$a_4 = \frac{1}{\sqrt{4}} = \frac{1}{2} = 0.5$$

$$a_5 = \frac{1}{\sqrt{5}} \approx 0.4472$$

Thus, the first five terms of the sequence

$a_n = \dfrac{1}{\sqrt{n}}$ are $1, 0.7071, 0.5774, 0.5, 0.4472$.

57. $a_n = \left(1 + \dfrac{1}{n}\right)^n$

$$a_1 = \left(1 + \frac{1}{1}\right)^1 = (2)^1 = 2$$

$$a_2 = \left(1 + \frac{1}{2}\right)^2 = \left(\frac{3}{2}\right)^2 = 2.25$$

$$a_3 = \left(1 + \frac{1}{3}\right)^3 = \left(\frac{4}{3}\right)^3 \approx 2.3704$$

$$a_4 = \left(1 + \frac{1}{4}\right)^4 = \left(\frac{5}{4}\right)^4 \approx 2.4414$$

$$a_5 = \left(1 + \frac{1}{5}\right)^5 = \left(\frac{6}{5}\right)^5 \approx 2.4883$$

Thus, the first five terms of the sequence

$a_n = \left(1 + \dfrac{1}{n}\right)^n$ are $2, 2.25, 2.3704, 2.4414$,

2.4883.

Section 11.2

Practice Problems

1. $a_1 = 4$

$a_2 = 4 + 5 = 9$
$a_3 = 9 + 5 = 14$
$a_4 = 14 + 5 = 19$
$a_5 = 19 + 5 = 24$
The first five terms are $4, 9, 14, 19, 24$.

2. a. $a_n = a_1 + (n-1)d$
   Here, $a_1 = 2$ and $d = -3$.
   $a_n = 2 + (n-1)(-3) = 2 - 3n + 3 = 5 - 3n$

   b. $a_n = 5 - 3n$
   $a_{12} = 5 - 3 \cdot 12 = 5 - 36 = -31$

3. Since the sequence is arithmetic, the ninth term is $a_9 = a_1 + (9-1)d = a_1 + 8d$.
   a_1 is the first term of the sequence, so $a_1 = 3$. d is the constant difference, so
   $d = a_2 - a_1 = 9 - 3 = 6$. Thus,
   $a_9 = a_1 + 8d = 3 + 8 \cdot 6 = 51$.

4. We need to find a_1 and d. The given facts, $a_3 = 23$ and $a_8 = 63$, lead to a system of linear equations.

$$\begin{cases} a_3 = a_1 + (3-1)d \\ a_8 = a_1 + (8-1)d \end{cases} \text{ or } \begin{cases} 23 = a_1 + 2d \\ 63 = a_1 + 7d \end{cases}$$

We solve the system by elimination. Multiply both sides of the second equation by -1.

$$\begin{cases} 23 = a_1 + 2d \\ -1(63) = -1(a_1 + 7d) \end{cases} \text{ or } \begin{cases} 23 = a_1 + 2d \\ -63 = -a_1 - 7d \end{cases}$$
$$\overline{\qquad -40 = \qquad -5d}$$
$$8 = d$$

To find a_1, let $d = 8$ in $23 = a_1 + 2d$.

$23 = a_1 + 2(8)$
$23 = a_1 + 16$
$7 = a_1$

Thus, $a_1 = 7$ and $d = 8$, so

$a_n = 7 + (n-1)(8) = 7 + 8n - 8 = -1 + 8n$ and

$a_6 = -1 + 8 \cdot 6 = 47$.

5. The first term, a_1, is 57,000, and d is 2200.

$$a_n = 57,000 + (n-1)(2200)$$
$$= 54,800 + 2200n$$
$$a_3 = 54,800 + 2200 \cdot 3 = 61,400$$

The salary for the third year is $61,400.

6. $a_1 = 8$

$$a_2 = 8(-3) = -24$$
$$a_3 = -24(-3) = 72$$
$$a_4 = 72(-3) = -216$$

The first four terms are 8, −24, 72, and −216.

7. $a_n = a_1 r^{n-1}$

Here, $a_1 = 64$ and $r = \dfrac{1}{4}$.

Evaluate a_n for $n = 7$.

$$a_7 = 64\left(\frac{1}{4}\right)^{7-1}$$
$$= 64\left(\frac{1}{4}\right)^{6}$$
$$= 64\left(\frac{1}{4096}\right)$$
$$= \frac{1}{64}$$

8. Since the sequence is geometric and $a_1 = -3$, the seventh term must be $a_1 r^{7-1}$, or $-3r^6$. r is the common ratio of terms, so r must be $\dfrac{6}{-3}$, or −2.

$$a_7 = -3r^6$$
$$a_7 = -3(-2)^6 = -192$$

9. Notice that $\dfrac{27}{4} \div \dfrac{9}{2} = \dfrac{3}{2}$, so $r = \dfrac{3}{2}$.

$$a_2 = a_1\left(\frac{3}{2}\right)^{2-1}$$
$$\frac{9}{2} = a_1\left(\frac{3}{2}\right)^{1}, \quad \text{or} \quad a_1 = 3$$

The first term is 3, and the common ration is $\dfrac{3}{2}$.

10. Since the culture is reduced by one-half each day, the population sizes are modeled by a geometric sequence. Here, $a_1 = 4800$ and $r = \dfrac{1}{2}$.

$$a_n = a_1 r^{n-1} = 4800\left(\frac{1}{2}\right)^{n-1}$$
$$a_7 = 4800\left(\frac{1}{2}\right)^{7-1} = 75$$

The bacterial culture should measure 75 units at the beginning of day 7.

Vocabulary and Readiness Check

1. A <u>geometric</u> sequence is one in which each term (after the first) is obtained by multiplying the preceding term by a constant r. The constant r is called the common <u>ratio</u>.

2. An <u>arithmetic</u> sequence is one in which each term (after the first) differs from the preceding term by a constant amount d. The constant d is called the common <u>difference</u>.

3. The general term of an arithmetic sequence is $a_n = a_1 + (n-1)d$ where a_1 is the <u>first</u> term and d is the common <u>difference</u>.

4. The general term of a geometric sequence is $a_n = a_1 r^{n-1}$ where a_1 is the <u>first</u> term and r is the common <u>ratio</u>.

Exercise Set 11.2

1. $a_n = a_1 + (n-1)d$

$a_1 = 4;\ d = 2$

$a_1 = 4$
$a_2 = 4 + (2-1)2 = 6$
$a_3 = 4 + (3-1)2 = 8$
$a_4 = 4 + (4-1)2 = 10$
$a_5 = 4 + (5-1)2 = 12$

The first five terms are 4, 6, 8, 10, 12.

3. $a_n = a_1 + (n-1)d$

$a_1 = 6,\ d = -2$

$a_1 = 6$
$a_2 = 6 + (2-1)(-2) = 4$
$a_3 = 6 + (3-1)(-2) = 2$
$a_4 = 6 + (4-1)(-2) = 0$
$a_5 = 6 + (5-1)(-2) = -2$

The first five terms are 6, 4, 2, 0, −2.

5. $a_n = a_1 r^{n-1}$

$a_1 = 1,\ r = 3$

$a_1 = 1(3)^{1-1} = 1$

$a_2 = 1(3)^{2-1} = 3$

$a_3 = 1(3)^{3-1} = 9$

$a_4 = 1(3)^{4-1} = 27$

$a_5 = 1(3)^{5-1} = 81$

The first five terms are 1, 3, 9, 27, 81.

7. $a_n = a_1 r^{n-1}$

$a_1 = 48,\ r = \dfrac{1}{2}$

$a_1 = 48\left(\dfrac{1}{2}\right)^{1-1} = 48$

$a_2 = 48\left(\dfrac{1}{2}\right)^{2-1} = 24$

$a_3 = 48\left(\dfrac{1}{2}\right)^{3-1} = 12$

$a_4 = 48\left(\dfrac{1}{2}\right)^{4-1} = 6$

$a_5 = 48\left(\dfrac{1}{2}\right)^{5-1} = 3$

The first five terms are 48, 24, 12, 6, 3.

9. $a_n = a_1 + (n-1)d$

$a_1 = 12,\ d = 3$

$a_n = 12 + (n-1)3$

$a_8 = 12 + 7(3) = 12 + 21 = 33$

11. $a_n = a_1 r^{n-1}$

$a_1 = 7,\ d = -5$

$a_n = a_1 r^{n-1}$

$a_4 = 7(-5)^3 = 7(-125) = -875$

13. $a_n = a_1 + (n-1)d$

$a_1 = -4,\ d = -4$

$a_n = -4 + (n-1)(-4)$

$a_{15} = -4 + 14(-4) = -4 - 56 = -60$

15. 0, 12, 24

$a_1 = 0$ and $d = 12$

$a_n = 0 + (n-1)12$

$a_9 = 8(12) = 96$

17. 20, 18, 16

$a_1 = 20$ and $d = -2$

$a_n = 20 + (n-1)(-2)$

$a_{25} = 20 + 24(-2) = 20 - 48 = -28$

19. 2, -10, 50

$a_1 = 2$ and $r = -5$

$a_n = 2(-5)^{n-1}$

$a_5 = 2(-5)^4 = 2(625) = 1250$

21. $a_4 = 19,\ a_{15} = 52$

$\begin{cases} a_4 = a_1 + (4-1)d \\ a_{15} = a_1 + (15-1)d \end{cases}$ or

$\begin{cases} 19 = a_1 + 3d \\ 52 = a_1 + 14d \end{cases}$

$\begin{cases} -19 = -a_1 - 3d \\ \ \ 52 = a_1 + 14d \end{cases}$

Adding yields $33 = 11d$ or $d = 3$. Then $a_1 = 19 - 3(3) = 10$.

$a_n = 10 + (n-1)3$

$\quad = 10 + 3n - 3$

$\quad = 7 + 3n$

and $a_8 = 7 + 3(8)$

$\qquad = 7 + 24$

$\qquad = 31$

23. $a_2 = -1,\ a_4 = 5$

$\begin{cases} a_2 = a_1 + (2-1)d \\ a_4 = a_1 + (4-1)d \end{cases}$ or

$\begin{cases} -1 = a_1 + d \\ 5 = a_1 + 3d \end{cases}$

$\begin{cases} 1 = -a_1 - d \\ 5 = a_1 + 3d \end{cases}$

Adding yields $6 = 2d$ or $d = 3$. Then $a_1 = -1 - 3 = -4$.

$a_n = -4 + (n-1)3$

$\quad = -4 + 3n - 3$

$\quad = -7 + 3n$

and $a_9 = -7 + 3(9)$

$\qquad = -7 + 27$

$\qquad = 20$

25. $a_2 = -\dfrac{4}{3}$ and $a_3 = \dfrac{8}{3}$

Notice that $\dfrac{8}{3} \div \dfrac{-4}{3} = \dfrac{8}{3} \cdot -\dfrac{3}{4} = -2$, so $r = -2$.

Then

$a_2 = a_1(-2)^{2-1}$

$-\dfrac{4}{3} = a_1(-2)$

$\dfrac{2}{3} = a_1$.

The first term is $\dfrac{2}{3}$ and the common ratio is -2.

27. Answers may vary

29. $2, 4, 6$ is an arithmetic sequence.

$a_1 = 2$ and $d = 2$

31. $5, 10, 20$ is a geometric sequence.

$a_1 = 5$ and $r = 2$

33. $\dfrac{1}{2}, \dfrac{1}{10}, \dfrac{1}{50}$ is a geometric sequence.

$a_1 = \dfrac{1}{2}$ and $r = \dfrac{1}{5}$

35. $x, 5x, 25x$ is a geometric sequence.

$a_1 = x$ and $r = 5$

37. $p, p+4, p+8$ is an arithmetic sequence.

$a_1 = p$ and $d = 4$

39. $a_1 = 14$ and $d = \dfrac{1}{4}$

$a_n = 14 + (n-1)\dfrac{1}{4}$

$a_{21} = 14 + 20\left(\dfrac{1}{4}\right) = 14 + 5 = 19$

41. $a_1 = 3$ and $r = -\dfrac{2}{3}$

$a_n = 3\left(-\dfrac{2}{3}\right)^{n-1}$

$a_4 = 3\left(-\dfrac{2}{3}\right)^3 = 3\left(-\dfrac{8}{27}\right) = -\dfrac{8}{9}$

43. $\dfrac{3}{2}, 2, \dfrac{5}{2}, \ldots$

$a_1 = \dfrac{3}{2}$ and $d = \dfrac{1}{2}$

$a_n = \dfrac{3}{2} + (n-1)\dfrac{1}{2}$

$a_{15} = \dfrac{3}{2} + 14\left(\dfrac{1}{2}\right) = \dfrac{17}{2}$

45. $24, 8, \dfrac{8}{3}, \ldots$

$a_1 = 24$ and $r = \dfrac{1}{3}$

$a_n = 24\left(\dfrac{1}{3}\right)^{n-1}$

$a_6 = 24\left(\dfrac{1}{3}\right)^5 = 24\left(\dfrac{1}{243}\right) = \dfrac{8}{81}$

47. $a_3 = 2$, $a_{17} = -40$

$\begin{cases} a_3 = a_1 + (3-1)d \\ a_{17} = a_1 + (17-1)d \end{cases}$ or

$\begin{cases} 2 = a_1 + 2d \\ -40 = a_1 + 16d \end{cases}$

$\begin{cases} -2 = -a_1 - 2d \\ -40 = a_1 + 16d \end{cases}$

Adding yields $-42 = 14d$ or $d = -3$. Then $a_1 = 2 - 2(-3) = 8$.

$a_n = 8 + (n-1)(-3) = 8 - 3n + 3 = 11 - 3n$

and

$a_{10} = 11 - 3(10) = 11 - 30 = -19$

49. $54, 58, 62$

$a_1 = 54$ and $d = 4$

$a_n = 54 + (n-1)4$

$a_{20} = 54 + 19(4) = 54 + 76 = 130$

The general term of the sequence is $a_n = 4n + 50$. There are 130 seats in the twentieth row.

51. $a_1 = 6$ and $r = 3$

$a_n = 6(3)^{n-1} = 2 \cdot 3 \cdot (3)^{n-1} = 2(3)^n$

The general term of the sequence is $a_n = 6(3)^{n-1}$ or $a_n = 2(3)^n$.

53. $a_1 = 486$ and $r = \dfrac{1}{3}$

Initial Height $= a_1 = 486\left(\dfrac{1}{3}\right)^{1-1} = 486$

Rebound 1 $= a_2 = 486\left(\dfrac{1}{3}\right)^{2-1} = 162$

Rebound 2 $= a_3 = 486\left(\dfrac{1}{3}\right)^{3-1} = 54$

Rebound 3 $= a_4 = 486\left(\dfrac{1}{3}\right)^{4-1} = 18$

Rebound 4 $= a_5 = 486\left(\dfrac{1}{3}\right)^{5-1} = 6$

The first five terms of the sequence are 486, 162, 54, 18, 6.

The general term is $a_n = 486\left(\dfrac{1}{3}\right)^{n-1}$ or

$a_n = \dfrac{486}{3^{n-1}}$. Since $a_6 = 2$ and $a_7 = \dfrac{2}{3}$, a_7 is the

first term less than 1. Since a_7 corresponds to the 6th bounce, it takes 6 bounces for the ball to rebound less than 1 foot.

55. $a_1 = 4000$ and $d = 125$

$a_n = 4000 + (n-1)125$ or

$a_n = 3875 + 125n$

$a_{12} = 4000 + 11(125) = 5375$

His salary for his last month of training is \$5375.

57. $a_1 = 400$ and $r = \dfrac{1}{2}$

12 hours = 4(3 hours), so we seek the fourth term after a_1, namely a_5.

$a_n = a_1 r^{n-1}$

$a_5 = 400\left(\dfrac{1}{2}\right)^4 = \dfrac{400}{16} = 25$

25 grams of the radioactive material remain after 12 hours.

59. $\dfrac{1}{3(1)} + \dfrac{1}{3(2)} + \dfrac{1}{3(3)} = \dfrac{1}{3} + \dfrac{1}{6} + \dfrac{1}{9}$

$= \dfrac{6}{18} + \dfrac{3}{18} + \dfrac{2}{18}$

$= \dfrac{11}{18}$

61. $3^0 + 3^1 + 3^2 + 3^3 = 1 + 3 + 9 + 27 = 40$

63. $\dfrac{8-1}{8+1} + \dfrac{8-2}{8+2} + \dfrac{8-3}{8+3} = \dfrac{7}{9} + \dfrac{6}{10} + \dfrac{5}{11}$

$= \dfrac{770}{990} + \dfrac{594}{990} + \dfrac{450}{990}$

$= \dfrac{1814}{990}$

$= \dfrac{907}{495}$

65. $a_1 = \$11,782.40$

$r = 0.5$

$a_2 = (11,782.40)(0.5) = \$5891.20$

$a_3 = (5891.20)(0.5) = \$2945.60$

$a_4 = (2945.60)(0.5) = \$1472.80$

The first four terms of the sequence are \$11,782.40, \$5891.20, \$2945.60, \$1472.80.

67. $a_1 = 19.652$ and $d = -0.034$

$a_2 = 19.652 - 0.034 = 19.618$

$a_3 = 19.618 - 0.034 = 19.584$

$a_4 = 19.584 - 0.034 = 19.550$

69. Answers may vary

Section 11.3

Practice Problems

1. a. $\displaystyle\sum_{i=0}^{4} \dfrac{i-3}{4} = \dfrac{0-3}{4} + \dfrac{1-3}{4} + \dfrac{2-3}{4} + \dfrac{3-3}{4} + \dfrac{4-3}{4}$

$= \left(-\dfrac{3}{4}\right) + \left(-\dfrac{2}{4}\right) + \left(-\dfrac{1}{4}\right) + 0 + \dfrac{1}{4}$

$= -\dfrac{5}{4}$, or $-1\dfrac{1}{4}$

b. $\displaystyle\sum_{i=2}^{5} 3^i = 3^2 + 3^3 + 3^4 + 3^5$

$= 9 + 27 + 81 + 243$

$= 360$

2. a. Since the difference of each term and the preceding term is 5, the terms correspond to the first six terms of the arithmetic sequence $a_n = 5 + (n-1)5 = 5n$. Thus, in summation notation,

$$5 + 10 + 15 + 20 + 25 + 30 = \sum_{i=1}^{6} 5i.$$

b. Since each term is the product of the preceding term and $\frac{1}{5}$, these terms correspond to the first four terms of the geometric sequence $a_n = \frac{1}{5}\left(\frac{1}{5}\right)^{n-1} = \left(\frac{1}{5}\right)^n$.

In summation notation,

$$\frac{1}{5} + \frac{1}{25} + \frac{1}{125} + \frac{1}{625} = \sum_{i=1}^{4}\left(\frac{1}{5}\right)^i.$$

3. $S_4 = \sum_{i=1}^{4} \frac{2+3i}{i^2}$

$\quad = \frac{2+3\cdot1}{1^2} + \frac{2+3\cdot2}{2^2} + \frac{2+3\cdot3}{3^2} + \frac{2+3\cdot4}{4^2}$

$\quad = \frac{5}{1} + \frac{8}{4} + \frac{11}{9} + \frac{14}{16}$

$\quad = 5 + 2 + \frac{11}{9} + \frac{7}{8}$

$\quad = \frac{655}{72}$, or $9\frac{7}{72}$

4. $S_5 = \sum_{i=1}^{5} i(2i-1)$

$\quad = 1(2\cdot1-1) + 2(2\cdot2-1) + 3(2\cdot3-1)$
$\qquad + 4(2\cdot4-1) + 5(2\cdot5-1)$

$\quad = 1 + 6 + 15 + 28 + 45$

$\quad = 95$

There are 95 plants after 5 years.

Vocabulary and Readiness Check

1. A series is an <u>infinite</u> series if it is the sum of all the terms of the sequence.

2. A series is a <u>finite</u> series if it is the sum of a finite number of terms.

3. A shorthand notation for denoting a series when the general term of the sequence is known is called <u>summation</u> notation.

4. In the notation $\sum_{i=1}^{7}(5i-2)$, the Σ is the Greek uppercase letter <u>sigma</u> and the i is called the <u>index of summation</u>.

5. The sum of the first n terms of a sequence is a finite series known as a <u>partial sum</u>.

6. For the notation in Exercise 4 above, the beginning value of i is $\underline{1}$ and the ending value of i is $\underline{7}$.

Exercise Set 11.3

1. $\sum_{i=1}^{4}(i-3) = (1-3) + (2-3) + (3-3) + (4-3)$

$\qquad\qquad = -2 + (-1) + 0 + 1$

$\qquad\qquad = -2$

3. $\sum_{i=4}^{7}(2i+4) = [2(4)+4] + [2(5)+4] + [2(6)+4]$

$\qquad\qquad\qquad\qquad\qquad + [2(7)+4]$

$\qquad\qquad = 12 + 14 + 16 + 18$

$\qquad\qquad = 60$

5. $\sum_{i=2}^{4}(i^2-3) = (2^2-3) + (3^2-3) + (4^2-3)$

$\qquad\qquad = 1 + 6 + 13$

$\qquad\qquad = 20$

7. $\sum_{i=1}^{3}\left(\frac{1}{i+5}\right) = \frac{1}{1+5} + \frac{1}{2+5} + \frac{1}{3+5}$

$\qquad\qquad = \frac{1}{6} + \frac{1}{7} + \frac{1}{8}$

$\qquad\qquad = \frac{28}{168} + \frac{24}{168} + \frac{21}{168}$

$\qquad\qquad = \frac{73}{168}$

9. $\sum_{i=1}^{3}\frac{1}{6i} = \frac{1}{6(1)} + \frac{1}{6(2)} + \frac{1}{6(3)}$

$\qquad\qquad = \frac{1}{6} + \frac{1}{12} + \frac{1}{18}$

$\qquad\qquad = \frac{6+3+2}{36}$

$\qquad\qquad = \frac{11}{36}$

11. $\sum_{i=2}^{6} 3i = 3(2) + 3(3) + 3(4) + 3(5) + 3(6)$

$\qquad\qquad = 6 + 9 + 12 + 15 + 18$

$\qquad\qquad = 60$

13. $\displaystyle\sum_{i=3}^{5} i(i+2) = 3(3+2)+4(4+2)+5(5+2)$

$$= 15+24+35$$
$$= 74$$

15. $\displaystyle\sum_{i=1}^{5} 2^i = 2^1+2^2+2^3+2^4+2^5$

$$= 2+4+8+16+32$$
$$= 62$$

17. $\displaystyle\sum_{i=1}^{4} \frac{4i}{i+3} = \frac{4(1)}{1+3}+\frac{4(2)}{2+3}+\frac{4(3)}{3+3}+\frac{4(4)}{4+3}$

$$= 1+\frac{8}{5}+2+\frac{16}{7}$$
$$= \frac{105}{35}+\frac{56}{35}+\frac{80}{35}$$
$$= \frac{241}{35}$$

19. $1+3+5+7+9$
$a_1 = 1,\ d = 2$
$a_n = 1+(n-1)2 = 2n-1$
$\displaystyle\sum_{i=1}^{5} (2i-1)$

21. $4+12+36+108 = 4+4(3)+4(3)^2+4(3)^3$

$$= \sum_{i=1}^{4} 4(3)^{i-1}$$

23. $12+9+6+3+0+(-3)$
$a_1 = 12,\ d = -3$
$a_n = 12+(n-1)(-3) = -3n+15$
$\displaystyle\sum_{i=1}^{6} (-3i+15)$

25. $12+4+\dfrac{4}{3}+\dfrac{4}{9} = \dfrac{4}{3^{-1}}+\dfrac{4}{3^0}+\dfrac{4}{3}+\dfrac{4}{3^2}$

$$= \sum_{i=1}^{4} \frac{4}{3^{i-2}}$$

27. $1+4+9+16+25+36+49$
$= 1^2+2^2+3^2+4^2+5^2+6^2+7^2$

$$= \sum_{i=1}^{7} i^2$$

29. $a_n = (n+2)(n-5)$

$$S_2 = \sum_{i=1}^{2} (i+2)(i-5)$$
$$= (1+2)(1-5)+(2+2)(2-5)$$
$$= 3(-4)+4(-3)$$
$$= -12-12$$
$$= -24$$

31. $a_n = (-1)^n$

$$S_6 = \sum_{i=1}^{6} (-1)^i$$
$$= (-1)^1+(-1)^2+(-1)^3+(-1)^4+(-1)^5$$
$$\qquad +(-1)^6$$
$$= -1+1+(-1)+1+(-1)+1$$
$$= 0$$

33. $a_n = (n+3)(n+1)$

$$S_4 = \sum_{i=1}^{4} (i+3)(i+1)$$
$$= (1+3)(1+1)+(2+3)(2+1)+(3+3)(3+1)$$
$$\qquad +(4+3)(4+1)$$
$$= 4(2)+5(3)+6(4)+7(5)$$
$$= 8+15+24+35$$
$$= 82$$

35. $a_n = -2n$

$$S_4 = \sum_{i=1}^{4} (-2i)$$
$$= -2(1)+(-2)(2)+(-2)(3)+(-2)(4)$$
$$= -2-4-6-8$$
$$= -20$$

37. $a_n = -\dfrac{n}{3}$

$$S_3 = \sum_{i=1}^{3} -\frac{i}{3} = -\frac{1}{3}-\frac{2}{3}-\frac{3}{3} = -2$$

39. $1, 2, 3, \ldots, 10$

$a_n = n$

$S_{10} = \sum_{i=1}^{10} i = 1 + 2 + 3 + \ldots + 10 = 55$

A total of 55 trees were planted.

41. $a_1 = 6$ and $r = 2$

$a_n = 6 \cdot 2^{n-1}$

$a_5 = 6 \cdot 2^4 = 6 \cdot 16 = 96$

There will be 96 fungus units at the beginning of the 5th day.

43. The general term of the sequence is

$a_n = 50(2)^n$, where n represents the number of 12-hr periods.

$a_4 = 50(2)^4 = 50(16) = 800$

There are 800 bacteria after 48 hours.

45. $a_n = (n+1)(n+2)$

$a_4 = (4+1)(4+2) = 5(6) = 30$

30 opossums were killed in the fourth month.

$S_4 = \sum_{i=1}^{4} (i+1)(i+2)$

$\quad = 2(3) + (3)(4) + (4)(5) + (5)(6)$

$\quad = 6 + 12 + 20 + 30$

$\quad = 68$

68 opossums were killed in the four months.

47. $a_n = 100(0.5)^n$

$a_4 = 100(0.5)^4 = 6.25$

The decay in the fourth year is 6.25 pounds.

$S_4 = \sum_{i=1}^{4} 100(0.5)^i$

$\quad = 100(0.5)^1 + 100(0.5)^2 + 100(0.5)^3$

$\qquad + 100(0.5)^4$

$\quad = 100(0.5) + 100(0.25) + 100(0.125)$

$\qquad + 100(0.0625)$

$\quad = 50 + 25 + 12.5 + 6.25$

$\quad = 93.75$

The decay over the four years is 93.75 pounds.

49. $a_1 = 40$ and $r = \dfrac{4}{5}$

$a_5 = 40\left(\dfrac{4}{5}\right)^4 = 16.384$

The length of the fifth swing is approximately 16.4 inches.

$S_5 = \sum_{i=1}^{5} 40\left(\dfrac{4}{5}\right)^{i-1}$

$\quad = 40\left(\dfrac{4}{5}\right)^0 + 40\left(\dfrac{4}{5}\right)^1 + 40\left(\dfrac{4}{5}\right)^2 + 40\left(\dfrac{4}{5}\right)^3$

$\qquad + 40\left(\dfrac{4}{5}\right)^4$

$\quad = 40 + 32 + 25.6 + 20.48 + 16.384$

$\quad = 134.464$

The pendulum swings about 134.5 inches in five swings.

51. $\dfrac{5}{1-\frac{1}{2}} = \dfrac{5}{\frac{1}{2}} = 5 \cdot \dfrac{2}{1} = 10$

53. $\dfrac{\frac{1}{3}}{1-\frac{1}{10}} = \dfrac{\frac{1}{3}}{\frac{9}{10}} = \dfrac{1}{3} \cdot \dfrac{10}{9} = \dfrac{10}{27}$

55. $\dfrac{3(1-2^4)}{1-2} = \dfrac{3(1-16)}{-1} = \dfrac{3(-15)}{-1} = \dfrac{-45}{-1} = 45$

57. $\dfrac{10}{2}(3+15) = \dfrac{10}{2}(18) = \dfrac{180}{2} = 90$

59. a. $\sum_{i=1}^{7} (i + i^2)$

$\quad = (1+1^2) + (2+2^2) + (3+3^2) + (4+4^2)$

$\qquad + (5+5^2) + (6+6^2) + (7+7^2)$

$\quad = 2 + 6 + 12 + 20 + 30 + 42 + 56$

b. $\sum_{i=1}^{7} i + \sum_{i=1}^{7} i^2$

$\quad = (1+2+3+4+5+6+7)$

$\qquad + (1+4+9+16+25+36+49)$

c. Answers may vary

d. True; answers may vary.

Integrated Review

1. $a_n = n - 3$
   $a_1 = 1 - 3 = -2$
   $a_2 = 2 - 3 = -1$
   $a_3 = 3 - 3 = 0$
   $a_4 = 4 - 3 = 1$
   $a_5 = 5 - 3 = 2$
   Therefore, the first five terms are $-2, -1, 0, 1, 2$.

2. $a_n = \dfrac{7}{1+n}$
   $a_1 = \dfrac{7}{1+1} = \dfrac{7}{2}$
   $a_2 = \dfrac{7}{1+2} = \dfrac{7}{3}$
   $a_3 = \dfrac{7}{1+3} = \dfrac{7}{4}$
   $a_4 = \dfrac{7}{1+4} = \dfrac{7}{5}$
   $a_5 = \dfrac{7}{1+5} = \dfrac{7}{6}$
   The first five terms are $\dfrac{7}{2}, \dfrac{7}{3}, \dfrac{7}{4}, \dfrac{7}{5}$, and $\dfrac{7}{6}$.

3. $a_n = 3^{n-1}$
   $a_1 = 3^{1-1} = 3^0 = 1$
   $a_2 = 3^{2-1} = 3^1 = 3$
   $a_3 = 3^{3-1} = 3^2 = 9$
   $a_4 = 3^{4-1} = 3^3 = 27$
   $a_5 = 3^{5-1} = 3^4 = 81$
   The first five terms are $1, 3, 9, 27$, and 81.

4. $a_n = n^2 - 5$
   $a_1 = 1^2 - 5 = 1 - 5 = -4$
   $a_2 = 2^2 - 5 = 4 - 5 = -1$
   $a_3 = 3^2 - 5 = 9 - 5 = 4$
   $a_4 = 4^2 - 5 = 16 - 5 = 11$
   $a_5 = 5^2 - 5 = 25 - 5 = 20$
   The first five terms are $-4, -1, 4, 11$, and 20.

5. $(-2)^n$; a_6
   $a_6 = (-2)^6 = 64$

6. $-n^2 + 2$; a_4
   $a_4 = -(4)^2 + 2 = -16 + 2 = -14$

7. $\dfrac{(-1)^n}{n}$; a_{40}
   $a_{40} = \dfrac{(-1)^{40}}{40} = \dfrac{1}{40}$

8. $\dfrac{(-1)^n}{2n}$; a_{41}
   $a_{41} = \dfrac{(-1)^{41}}{2(41)} = \dfrac{-1}{82} = -\dfrac{1}{82}$

9. $a_1 = 7$; $d = -3$
   $a_1 = 7$
   $a_2 = 7 - 3 = 4$
   $a_3 = 4 - 3 = 1$
   $a_4 = 1 - 3 = -2$
   $a_5 = -2 - 3 = -5$
   The first five terms are $7, 4, 1, -2, -5$.

10. $a_1 = -3$; $r = 5$
    $a_1 = -3$
    $a_2 = -3(5) = -15$
    $a_3 = -15(5) = -75$
    $a_4 = -75(5) = -375$
    $a_5 = -375(5) = -1875$
    The first five terms are $-3, -15, -75, -375, -1875$.

11. $a_1 = 45$; $r = \dfrac{1}{3}$
    $a_1 = 45$
    $a_2 = 45\left(\dfrac{1}{3}\right) = 15$
    $a_3 = 15\left(\dfrac{1}{3}\right) = 5$
    $a_4 = 5\left(\dfrac{1}{3}\right) = \dfrac{5}{3}$
    $a_5 = \dfrac{5}{3}\left(\dfrac{1}{3}\right) = \dfrac{5}{9}$
    The first five terms are $45, 15, 5, \dfrac{5}{3}, \dfrac{5}{9}$.

12. $a_1 = -12;\ d = 10$

$a_1 = -12$

$a_2 = -12 + 10 = -2$

$a_3 = -2 + 10 = 8$

$a_4 = 8 + 10 = 18$

$a_5 = 18 + 10 = 28$

The first five terms are $-12, -2, 8, 18, 28$.

13. $a_1 = 20;\ d = 9$

$a_n = a_1 + (n-1)d$

$a_{10} = 20 + (10-1)9$

$= 20 + 81$

$= 101$

14. $a_1 = 64;\ r = \dfrac{3}{4}$

$a_n = a_1 r^{n-1}$

$a_6 = 64 \left(\dfrac{3}{4}\right)^{6-1}$

$= 64 \left(\dfrac{3}{4}\right)^5$

$= 64 \left(\dfrac{243}{1024}\right)$

$= \dfrac{243}{16}$

15. $a_1 = 6;\ r = \dfrac{-12}{6} = -2$

$a_n = a_1 r^{n-1}$

$a_7 = 6(-2)^{7-1} = 6(-2)^6 = 6(64) = 384$

16. $a_1 = -100;\ d = -85 - (-100) = 15$

$a_n = a_1 + (n-1)d$

$a_{20} = -100 + (20-1)(15)$

$= -100 + (19)(15)$

$= -100 + 285$

$= 185$

17. $a_4 = -5,\ a_{10} = -35$

$a_n = a_1 + (n-1)d$

$\begin{cases} a_4 = a_1 + (4-1)d \\ a_{10} = a_1 + (10-1)d \end{cases}$

$\begin{cases} -5 = a_1 + 3d \\ -35 = a_1 + 9d \end{cases}$

Multiply eq. 2 by -1, then add the equations.

$\begin{cases} -5 = a_1 + 3d \\ (-1)(-35) = -1(a_1 + 9d) \end{cases}$

$\begin{cases} -5 = a_1 + 3d \\ 35 = -a_1 - 9d \end{cases}$

$30 = -6d$

$-5 = d$

To find a_1, let $d = -5$ in

$-5 = a_1 + 3d$

$-5 = a_1 + 3(-5)$

$10 = a_1$

Thus, $a_1 = 10$ and $d = -5$, so

$a_n = 10 + (n-1)(-5) = -5n + 15$

$a_5 = -5(5) + 15 = -10$

18. $a_4 = 1;\ a_7 = \dfrac{1}{125}$

$a_n = a_1 r^{n-1}$

$a_4 = a_1 r^{4-1}$ so $1 = a_1 r^3$

$a_7 = a_1 r^{71}$ so $\dfrac{1}{125} = a_1 r^6$

Since $a_1 r^6 = (a_1 r^3)r^3,\ \dfrac{1}{125} = 1 \cdot r^3$ and $r = \dfrac{1}{5}$.

$a_5 = a_4 \cdot r$ so $a_5 = 1 \cdot \dfrac{1}{5} = \dfrac{1}{5}$

19. $\displaystyle\sum_{i=1}^{4} 5i = 5(1) + 5(2) + 5(3) + 5(4)$

$= 5 + 10 + 15 + 20$

$= 50$

20. $\displaystyle\sum_{i=1}^{7} (3i + 2)$

$= (3(1) + 2) + (3(2) + 2) + (3(3) + 2)$

$\quad + (3(4) + 2) + (3(5) + 2) + (3(6) + 2)$

$\quad + (3(7) + 2)$

$= 5 + 8 + 11 + 14 + 17 + 20 + 23$

$= 98$

21. $\displaystyle\sum_{i=3}^{7} 2^{i-4}$

$= 2^{3-4} + 2^{4-4} + 2^{5-4} + 2^{6-4} + 2^{7-4}$

$= 2^{-1} + 2^0 + 2^1 + 2^2 + 2^3$

$= \dfrac{1}{2} + 1 + 2 + 4 + 8$

$= 15\dfrac{1}{2}$

$= \dfrac{31}{2}$

22. $\displaystyle\sum_{i=2}^{5} \dfrac{i}{i+1} = \dfrac{2}{2+1} + \dfrac{3}{3+1} + \dfrac{4}{4+1} + \dfrac{5}{5+1}$

$= \dfrac{2}{3} + \dfrac{3}{4} + \dfrac{4}{5} + \dfrac{5}{6}$

$= \dfrac{61}{20}$

23. $S_3 = \displaystyle\sum_{i=1}^{3} i(i-4)$

$= 1(1-4) + 2(2-4) + 3(3-4)$

$= -3 - 4 - 3$

$= -10$

24. $S_{10} = \displaystyle\sum_{i=1}^{10} (-1)^i (i+1)$

$= (-1)^1 (1+1) + (-1)^2 (2+1)$

$\quad + (-1)^3 (3+1) + (-1)^4 (4+1)$

$\quad + (-1)^5 (5+1) + (-1)^6 (6+1)$

$\quad + (-1)^7 (7+1) + (-1)^8 (8+1)$

$\quad + (-1)^9 (9+1) + (-1)^{10} (10+1)$

$= -2 + 3 - 4 + 5 - 6 + 7 - 8 + 9 - 10 + 11$

$= 5$

Section 11.4

Practice Problems

1. 2, 9, 16, 23, 30

Use the formula for S_n of an arithmetic sequence, replacing n with 5, a_1 with 2, and a_n with 30.

$S_n = \dfrac{n}{2}(a_1 + a_n)$

$S_5 = \dfrac{5}{2}(2+30) = \dfrac{5}{2}(32) = 80$

2. Because 1, 2, 3, ..., 50 is an arithmetic sequence, use the formula for S_n with $n = 50$, $a_1 = 1$, and $a_n = 50$.

$S_n = \dfrac{n}{2}(a_1 + a_n)$

$S_5 = \dfrac{50}{2}(1+50) = 25(51) = 1275$

3. The list 6, 7, ..., 15 is the first 10 terms of an arithmetic sequence. Use the formula for S_n with $n = 10$, $a_1 = 6$, and $a_n = 15$.

$S_{10} = \dfrac{10}{2}(6+15) = 5(21) = 105$

There are a total of 105 blocks of ice.

4. $32, \ 8, \ 2, \ \dfrac{1}{2}, \ \dfrac{1}{8}$

Use the formula for the partial sum S_n of the terms of a geometric sequence. Here, $n = 5$, the first term $a_1 = 32$, and the common ratio $r = \dfrac{1}{4}$.

$S_n = \dfrac{a_1(1-r^n)}{1-r}$

$S_5 = \dfrac{32\left[1 - \left(\frac{1}{4}\right)^5\right]}{1 - \frac{1}{4}}$

$= \dfrac{32\left(1 - \frac{1}{1024}\right)}{\frac{3}{4}}$

$= \dfrac{32 - \frac{1}{32}}{\frac{3}{4}}$

$= \dfrac{\frac{1023}{32}}{\frac{3}{4}}$

$= \dfrac{1023}{32} \cdot \dfrac{4}{3}$

$= \dfrac{341}{8}$

$= 42\dfrac{5}{8}$

5. The donations are modeled by the first seven terms of a geometric sequence. Evaluate S_n when $n = 7$, $a_1 = 250{,}000$, and $r = 0.8$.

$S_7 = \dfrac{250{,}000[1 - (0.8)^7]}{1 - 0.8} = 987{,}856$

The total amount donated during the seven years is \$987,856.

6. $7, \dfrac{7}{4}, \dfrac{7}{16}, \dfrac{7}{64}, \ldots$

For this geometric sequence $r = \dfrac{1}{4}$. Since

$|r| < 1$, use the formula for S_∞ of a geometric

sequence with $a_1 = 7$ and $r = \dfrac{1}{4}$.

$$S_\infty = \frac{a_1}{1-r} = \frac{7}{1-\dfrac{1}{4}} = \frac{7}{\dfrac{3}{4}} = \frac{28}{3} = 9\frac{1}{3}$$

7. We must find the sum of the terms of an infinite geometric sequence whose first term, a_1, is 36 and whose common ratio, r, is 0.96. Since $|r| < 1$, we may use the formula for S_∞.

$$S_\infty = \frac{a_1}{1-r} = \frac{36}{1-0.96} = \frac{36}{0.04} = 900$$

The ball travels a total distance of 900 inches before it comes to a rest.

Vocabulary and Readiness Check

1. Each term after the first is 5 more than the preceding term; the sequence is <u>arithmetic</u>.

2. Each term after the first is 2 times the preceding term; the sequence is <u>geometric</u>.

3. Each term after the first is −3 times the preceding term; the sequence is <u>geometric</u>.

4. Each term after the first is 2 more than the preceding term; the sequence is <u>arithmetic</u>.

5. Each term after the first is 7 more than the preceding term; the sequence is <u>arithmetic</u>.

6. Each term after the first is −1 times the preceding term; the sequence is <u>geometric</u>.

Exercise Set 11.4

1. $1, 3, 5, 7, \ldots$

$d = 2;\ a_6 = 1 + (6-1)(2) = 11$

$$S_6 = \frac{6}{2}(1+11) = 3(12) = 36$$

3. $4, 12, 36, \ldots$

$a_1 = 4,\ r = 3,\ n = 5$

$$S_5 = \frac{4(1-3^5)}{1-3} = 484$$

5. $3, 6, 9, \ldots$

$d = 3;\ a_6 = 3 + (6-1)(3) = 18$

$$S_6 = \frac{6}{2}(3+18) = 3(21) = 63$$

7. $2, \dfrac{2}{5}, \dfrac{2}{25}, \ldots$

$a_1 = 2,\ r = \dfrac{1}{5},\ n = 4$

$$S_4 = \frac{2\left[1-\left(\frac{1}{5}\right)^4\right]}{1-\frac{1}{5}} = 2.496$$

9. $1, 2, 3, \ldots, 10$

The first term is 1 and the tenth term is 10.

$$S_{10} = \frac{10}{2}(1+10) = 5(11) = 55$$

11. $1, 2, 3, 7$

The first term is 1 and the fourth term is 7.

$$S_4 = \frac{4}{2}(1+7) = 2(8) = 16$$

13. $12, 6, 3, \ldots$

$a_1 = 12,\ r = \dfrac{1}{2}$

$$S_\infty = \frac{12}{1-\frac{1}{2}} = \frac{12}{\frac{1}{2}} = 12 \cdot \frac{2}{1} = 24$$

15. $\dfrac{1}{10}, \dfrac{1}{100}, \dfrac{1}{1000}, \ldots$

$a_1 = \dfrac{1}{10},\ r = \dfrac{1}{10}$

$$S_\infty = \frac{\frac{1}{10}}{1-\frac{1}{10}} = \frac{\frac{1}{10}}{\frac{9}{10}} = \frac{1}{10} \cdot \frac{10}{9} = \frac{1}{9}$$

17. $-10, -5, -\dfrac{5}{2}, \ldots$

$a_1 = -10,\ r = \dfrac{1}{2}$

$$S_\infty = \frac{-10}{1-\frac{1}{2}} = \frac{-10}{\frac{1}{2}} = -10 \cdot \frac{2}{1} = -20$$

19. $2, -\dfrac{1}{4}, \dfrac{1}{32}, \ldots$

$a_1 = 2, \quad r = -\dfrac{1}{8}$

$S_\infty = \dfrac{2}{1-\left(-\frac{1}{8}\right)} = \dfrac{2}{\frac{9}{8}} = 2 \cdot \dfrac{8}{9} = \dfrac{16}{9}$

21. $\dfrac{2}{3}, -\dfrac{1}{3}, \dfrac{1}{6}, \ldots$

$a_1 = \dfrac{2}{3}, \quad r = -\dfrac{1}{2}$

$S_\infty = \dfrac{\frac{2}{3}}{1-\left(-\frac{1}{2}\right)} = \dfrac{\frac{2}{3}}{\frac{3}{2}} = \dfrac{2}{3} \cdot \dfrac{2}{3} = \dfrac{4}{9}$

23. $-4, 1, 6, \ldots, 41$

The first term is –4 and the tenth term is 41.

$S_{10} = \dfrac{10}{2}(-4+41) = 5(37) = 185$

25. $3, \dfrac{3}{2}, \dfrac{3}{4}, \ldots$

$a_1 = 3, r = \dfrac{1}{2}, n = 7$

$S_7 = \dfrac{3\left[1-\left(\frac{1}{2}\right)^7\right]}{1-\frac{1}{2}} = \dfrac{381}{64}$

27. $-12, 6, -3, \ldots$

$a_1 = -12, r = -\dfrac{1}{2}, n = 5$

$S_5 = \dfrac{-12\left[1-\left(-\frac{1}{2}\right)^5\right]}{1-\left(-\frac{1}{2}\right)} = -\dfrac{33}{4} = -8.25$

29. $\dfrac{1}{2}, \dfrac{1}{4}, 0, \ldots, -\dfrac{17}{4}$

The first term is $\dfrac{1}{2}$ and the twentieth term is

$-\dfrac{17}{4}.$

$S_{20} = \dfrac{20}{2}\left(\dfrac{1}{2} - \dfrac{17}{4}\right) = 10\left(\dfrac{-15}{4}\right) = -\dfrac{75}{2}$

31. $a_1 = 8, r = -\dfrac{2}{3}, n = 3$

$S_3 = \dfrac{8\left[1-\left(-\frac{2}{3}\right)^3\right]}{1-\left(-\frac{2}{3}\right)} = \dfrac{56}{9}$

33. The first five terms are 4000, 3950, 3900, 3850, 3800.

$a_1 = 4000, d = -50, n = 12$

$a_{12} = 4000 + 11(-50) = 3450$

3450 cars will be sold in month 12.

$S_{12} = \dfrac{12}{2}(4000 + 3450) = 44,700$

44,700 cars will be sold in the first year.

35. Firm A:
The first term is 22,000 and the tenth term is 31,000.

$S_{10} = \dfrac{10}{2}(22,000 + 31,000)$

$\qquad = \$265,000$

Firm B:
The first term is 20,000 and the tenth term is 30,800.

$S_{10} = \dfrac{10}{2}(20,000 + 30,800)$

$\qquad = \$254,000$

Thus, Firm A is making the more profitable offer.

37. $a_1 = 30,000, r = 1.10, n = 4$

$a_4 = 30,000(1.10)^{4-1} = 39,930$

She made \$39,930 during her fourth year of business.

$S_4 = \dfrac{30,000(1-1.10^4)}{1-1.10} = 139,230$

She made \$139,230 during the first four years of business.

39. $a_1 = 30, r = 0.9, n = 5$

$a_5 = 30(0.9)^{5-1} = 19.683$

Approximately 20 minutes to assemble the first computer.

$S_5 = \dfrac{30(1-0.9^5)}{1-0.9} = 122.853$

Approximately 123 minutes to assemble the first 5 computers.

41. $a_1 = 20$, $r = \dfrac{4}{5}$

$$S_\infty = \frac{20}{1 - \frac{4}{5}} = 100$$

We double the number (to account for the flight up as well as down) and subtract 20 (since the first bounce was preceded by only a downward flight). Thus, the ball travels $2(100) - 20 = 180$ feet.

43. Player A:
The first term is 1 and the ninth term is 9.

$$S_9 = \frac{9}{2}(1+9) = 45 \text{ points}$$

Player B:
The first term is 10 and the sixth term is 15.

$$S_6 = \frac{6}{2}(10+15) = 75 \text{ points}$$

45. The first term is 200 and the twentieth is
$200 - 19(5) = 105$.

$$S_{20} = \frac{20}{2}(200 + 105) = 3050$$

Thus, $3050 rent is paid for 20 days during the holiday rush.

47. $a_1 = 0.01$, $r = 2$, $n = 30$

$$S_3 = \frac{0.01\left[1 - 2^{30}\right]}{1 - 2} = 10,737,418.23$$

He would pay $10,737,418.23 in room and board for the 30 days.

49. $6 \cdot 5 \cdot 4 \cdot 3 \cdot 2 \cdot 1 = 720$

51. $\dfrac{3 \cdot 2 \cdot 1}{2 \cdot 1} = \dfrac{3 \cdot \cancel{2} \cdot \cancel{1}}{\cancel{2} \cdot \cancel{1}} = 3$

53. $(x+5)^2 = x^2 + 2 \cdot x \cdot 5 + 5^2 = x^2 + 10x + 25$

55. $(2x-1)^3 = (2x-1)^2(2x-1)$
$$= (4x^2 - 4x + 1)(2x - 1)$$
$$= 8x^3 - 4x^2 + 2x - 8x^2 + 4x - 1$$
$$= 8x^3 - 12x^2 + 6x - 1$$

57. $0.\overline{888} = 0.8 + 0.08 + 0.008 + \cdots$
$$= \frac{8}{10} + \frac{8}{100} + \frac{8}{1000} + \cdots$$

This is a geometric series with $a_1 = \dfrac{8}{10}$, $r = \dfrac{1}{10}$.

$$S_\infty = \frac{\frac{8}{10}}{1 - \frac{1}{10}} = \frac{\frac{8}{10}}{\frac{9}{10}} = \frac{8}{10} \cdot \frac{10}{9} = \frac{8}{9}$$

59. Answers may vary.

Section 11.5

Practice Problems

1. $(p+r)^7$

The $n = 7$ row of Pascal's triangle is
1   7   21   35   35   21   7   1

Using the $n = 7$ row of Pascal's triangle as the coefficients, $(p + r)^7$ can be expanded as

$$p^7 + 7p^6 r + 21p^5 r^2 + 35p^4 r^3 + 35p^3 r^4 + 21p^2 r^5 + 7pr^6 + r^7$$

2. a. $\dfrac{6!}{7!} = \dfrac{6 \cdot 5 \cdot 4 \cdot 3 \cdot 2 \cdot 1}{7 \cdot 6 \cdot 5 \cdot 4 \cdot 3 \cdot 2 \cdot 1} = \dfrac{1}{7}$

   b. $\dfrac{8!}{4!2!} = \dfrac{8 \cdot 7 \cdot 6 \cdot 5 \cdot 4!}{4! \cdot 2 \cdot 1}$

$$= \dfrac{8 \cdot 7 \cdot 6 \cdot 5}{2 \cdot 1}$$
$$= 4 \cdot 7 \cdot 6 \cdot 5$$
$$= 840$$

   c. $\dfrac{5!}{4!1!} = \dfrac{5 \cdot 4 \cdot 3 \cdot 2 \cdot 1}{4 \cdot 3 \cdot 2 \cdot 1 \cdot 1} = 5$

   d. $\dfrac{9!}{9!0!} = \dfrac{9!}{9! \cdot 1} = 1$

3. $(a+b)^9$

Let $n = 9$ in the binomial formula.

$$(a+b)^9 = a^9 + \frac{9}{1!}a^8 b + \frac{9 \cdot 8}{2!}a^7 b^2 + \frac{9 \cdot 8 \cdot 7}{3!}a^6 b^3 + \frac{9 \cdot 8 \cdot 7 \cdot 6}{4!}a^5 b^4 + \frac{9 \cdot 8 \cdot 7 \cdot 6 \cdot 5}{5!}a^4 b^5 + \frac{9 \cdot 8 \cdot 7 \cdot 6 \cdot 5 \cdot 4}{6!}a^3 b^6$$
$$+ \frac{9 \cdot 8 \cdot 7 \cdot 6 \cdot 5 \cdot 4 \cdot 3}{7!}a^2 b^7 + \frac{9 \cdot 8 \cdot 7 \cdot 6 \cdot 5 \cdot 4 \cdot 3 \cdot 2}{8!}ab^8 + b^9$$
$$= a^9 + 9a^8 b + 36a^7 b^2 + 84a^6 b^3 + 126a^5 b^4 + 126a^4 b^5 + 84a^3 b^6 + 36a^2 b^7 + 9ab^8 + b^9$$

4. $(a+5b)^3$

Replace b with $5b$ in the binomial formula.

$$(a+5b)^3 = a^3 + \frac{3}{1!}a^2 (5b) + \frac{3 \cdot 2}{2!}a(5b)^2 + (5b)^3$$
$$= a^3 + 3a^2 (5b) + 3a(25b^2) + 125b^3$$
$$= a^3 + 15a^2 b + 75ab^2 + 125b^3$$

5. $(3x-2y)^3$

Let $a = 3x$ and $b = -2y$ in the binomial formula.

$$(3x-2y)^3 = (3x)^3 + \frac{3}{1!}(3x)^2(-2y) + \frac{3\cdot2}{2!}(3x)(-2y)^2 + (-2y)^3$$
$$= 27x^3 + 3(9x^2)(-2y) + 3(3x)(4y^2) - 8y^3$$
$$= 27x^3 - 54x^2y + 36xy^2 - 8y^3$$

6. $(x-4y)^{11}$

Use the formula with $n = 11$, $a = x$, $b = -4y$, and $r + 1 = 7$. Notice that, since $r + 1 = 7$, $r = 6$.

$$\frac{n!}{r!(n-r)!}a^{n-r}b^r = \frac{11!}{6!5!}x^5(-4y)^6$$
$$= 462x^5(4096y^6)$$
$$= 1,892,352x^5y^6$$

Vocabulary and Readiness Check

1. $0! = \underline{1}$

2. $1! = \underline{1}$

3. $4! = 4 \cdot 3 \cdot 2 \cdot 1 = \underline{24}$

4. $2! = 2 \cdot 1 = \underline{2}$

5. $3!0! = 3 \cdot 2 \cdot 1 \cdot 1 = \underline{6}$

6. $0!2! = 1 \cdot 2 \cdot 1 = \underline{2}$

Exercise Set 11.5

1. $(m+n)^3 = m^3 + 3m^2n + 3mn^2 + n^3$

3. $(c+d)^5 = c^5 + 5c^4d + 10c^3d^2 + 10c^2d^3 + 5cd^4 + d^5$

5. $(y-x)^5 = [y+(-x)]^5$
    $$= y^5 - 5y^4x + 10y^3x^2 - 10y^2x^3 + 5yx^4 - x^5$$

7. Answers may vary

9. $\frac{8!}{7!} = \frac{8\cdot7!}{7!} = 8$

11. $\frac{7!}{5!} = \frac{7\cdot6\cdot5!}{5!} = 7\cdot6 = 42$

13. $\frac{10!}{7!2!} = \frac{10\cdot9\cdot8\cdot7!}{7!2!} = \frac{10\cdot9\cdot8}{2\cdot1} = 360$

15. $\dfrac{8!}{6!0!} = \dfrac{8 \cdot 7 \cdot 6!}{6!1} = 8 \cdot 7 = 56$

17. Let $n = 7$ in the binomial theorem.

$$(a+b)^7 = a^7 + \frac{7}{1!}a^6b + \frac{7 \cdot 6}{2!}a^5b^2 + \frac{7 \cdot 6 \cdot 5}{3!}a^4b^3 + \frac{7 \cdot 6 \cdot 5 \cdot 4}{4!}a^3b^4 + \frac{7 \cdot 6 \cdot 5 \cdot 4 \cdot 3}{5!}a^2b^5 + \frac{7 \cdot 6 \cdot 5 \cdot 4 \cdot 3 \cdot 2}{6!}ab^6 + b^7$$
$$= a^7 + 7a^6b + 21a^5b^2 + 35a^4b^3 + 35a^3b^4 + 21a^2b^5 + 7ab^6 + b^7$$

19. Let $b = 2b$ and $n = 5$ in the binomial theorem.

$$(a+2b)^5 = a^5 + \frac{5}{1!}a^4(2b) + \frac{5 \cdot 4}{2!}a^3(2b)^2 + \frac{5 \cdot 4 \cdot 3}{3!}a^2(2b)^3 + \frac{5 \cdot 4 \cdot 3 \cdot 2}{4!}a(2b)^4 + (2b)^5$$
$$= a^5 + 10a^4b + 40a^3b^2 + 80a^2b^3 + 80ab^4 + 32b^5$$

21. Let $a = q$, $b = r$, and $n = 9$ in the binomial theorem.

$$(q+r)^2 = q^9 + \frac{9}{1!}q^8r + \frac{9 \cdot 8}{2!}q^7r^2 + \frac{9 \cdot 8 \cdot 7}{3!}q^6r^3 + \frac{9 \cdot 8 \cdot 7 \cdot 6}{4!}q^5r^4 + \frac{9 \cdot 8 \cdot 7 \cdot 6 \cdot 5}{5!}q^4r^5 + \frac{9 \cdot 8 \cdot 7 \cdot 6 \cdot 5 \cdot 4}{6!}q^3r^6$$
$$+ \frac{9 \cdot 8 \cdot 7 \cdot 6 \cdot 5 \cdot 4 \cdot 3}{7!}q^2r^7 + \frac{9 \cdot 8 \cdot 7 \cdot 6 \cdot 5 \cdot 4 \cdot 3 \cdot 2}{8!}qr^8 + r^9$$
$$= q^9 + 9q^8r + 36q^7r^2 + 84q^6r^3 + 126q^5r^4 + 126q^4r^5 + 84q^3r^6 + 36q^2r^7 + 9qr^8 + r^9$$

23. Let $a = 4a$ and $n = 5$ in the binomial theorem.

$$(4a+b)^5 = (4a)^5 + \frac{5}{1!}(4a)^4b + \frac{5 \cdot 4}{2!}(4a)^3b^2 + \frac{5 \cdot 4 \cdot 3}{3!}(4a)^2b^3 + \frac{5 \cdot 4 \cdot 3 \cdot 2}{4!}(4a)b^4 + b^5$$
$$= 1024a^5 + 1280a^4b + 640a^3b^2 + 160a^2b^3 + 20ab^4 + b^5$$

25. Let $a = 5a$, $b = -2b$, and $n = 4$ in the binomial theorem.

$$(5a-2b)^4 = (5a)^4 + \frac{4}{1!}(5a)^3(-2b) + \frac{4 \cdot 3}{2!}(5a)^2(-2b)^2 + \frac{4 \cdot 3 \cdot 2}{3!}(5a)(-2b)^3 + (-2b)^4$$
$$= 625a^4 - 1000a^3b + 600a^2b^2 - 160ab^3 + 16b^4$$

27. Let $a = 2a$, $b = 3b$, and $n = 3$ in the binomial theorem.

$$(2a+3b)^3 = (2a)^3 + \frac{3}{1!}(2a)^2(3b) + \frac{3 \cdot 2}{2!}(2a)(3b)^2 + (3b)^3$$
$$= 8a^3 + 36a^2b + 54ab^2 + 27b^3$$

29. Let $a = x$, $b = 2$, and $n = 5$ in the binomial theorem.

$$(x+2)^5 = x^5 + \frac{5}{1!}x^4(2) + \frac{5 \cdot 4}{2!}x^3(2)^2 + \frac{5 \cdot 4 \cdot 3}{3!}x^2(2)^3 + \frac{5 \cdot 4 \cdot 3 \cdot 2}{4!}x(2)^4 + (2)^5$$
$$= x^5 + 10x^4 + 40x^3 + 80x^2 + 80x + 32$$

31. 5th term of $(c-d)^5$ corresponds to $r = 4$:

$$\frac{5!}{4!(5-4)!}c^{5-4}(-d)^4 = 5cd^4$$

33. 8th term of $(2c+d)^7$ corresponds to $r = 7$:

$$\frac{7!}{7!(7-7)!}(2c)^{7-7}(d)^7 = d^7$$

35. 4th term of $(2r - s)^5$ corresponds to $r = 3$:

$$\frac{5!}{3!(5-3)!}(2r)^{5-3}(-s)^3 = -40r^2s^3$$

37. 3rd term of $(x + y)^4$ corresponds to $r = 2$: $\frac{4!}{2!(4-2)!}(x)^{4-2}(y)^2 = 6x^2y^2$

39. 2nd term of $(a + 3b)^{10}$ corresponds to $r = 1$: $\frac{10!}{1!(10-1)!}(a)^{10-1}(3b)^1 = 30a^9b$

41. $f(x) = |x|$

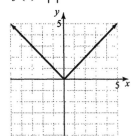

Not one-to-one

43. $H(x) = 2x + 3$

One-to-one

45. $f(x) = x^2 + 3$

Not one-to-one

47. $(\sqrt{x} + \sqrt{3})^5$

Use the binomial theorem with $n = 5$, $a = \sqrt{x}$, , and $b = \sqrt{3}$.

$$(\sqrt{x} + \sqrt{3})^5 = (\sqrt{x})^5 + 5(\sqrt{x})^4(\sqrt{3}) + 10(\sqrt{x})^3(\sqrt{3})^2 + 10(\sqrt{x})^2(\sqrt{3})^3 + 5(\sqrt{x})(\sqrt{3})^4 + (\sqrt{3})^5$$
$$= x^2\sqrt{x} + 5\sqrt{3}x^2 + 30x\sqrt{x} + 30\sqrt{3}x + 45\sqrt{x} + 9\sqrt{3}$$

49. $\dbinom{9}{5} = \dfrac{9!}{5!(9-5)!}$

$= \dfrac{9!}{5!4!}$

$= \dfrac{9\cdot8\cdot7\cdot6\cdot5\cdot4\cdot3\cdot2\cdot1}{(5\cdot4\cdot3\cdot2\cdot1)\cdot(4\cdot3\cdot2\cdot1)}$

$= 126$

51. $\dbinom{8}{2} = \dfrac{8!}{2!(8-2)!}$

$= \dfrac{8!}{2!6!}$

$= \dfrac{8\cdot7\cdot6\cdot5\cdot4\cdot3\cdot2\cdot1}{(2\cdot1)\cdot(6\cdot5\cdot4\cdot3\cdot2\cdot1)}$

$= 28$

53. Answers may vary.

Chapter 11 Vocabulary Check

1. A <u>finite sequence</u> is a function whose domain is the set of natural numbers $\{1, 2, 3, ..., n\}$, where n is some natural number.

2. The <u>factorial of n</u>, written $n!$, is the product of the first n consecutive natural numbers.

3. An <u>infinite sequence</u> is a function whose domain is the set of natural numbers.

4. A <u>geometric sequence</u> is a sequence in which each term (after the first) is obtained by multiplying the preceding term by a constant amount r. The constant r is called the <u>common ratio</u> of the sequence.

5. A sum of the terms of a sequence is called a <u>series</u>.

6. The nth term of the sequence a_n is called the <u>general term</u>.

7. An <u>arithmetic sequence</u> is a sequence in which each term (after the first) differs from the preceding term by a constant amount d. The constant d is called the <u>common difference</u> of the sequence.

8. A triangle array of the coefficients of the terms of the expansions of $(a+b)^n$ is called <u>Pascal's triangle</u>.

Chapter 11 Review

1. $a_n = -3n^2$

$a_1 = -3(1)^2 = -3$
$a_2 = -3(2)^2 = -12$
$a_3 = -3(3)^2 = -27$
$a_4 = -3(4)^2 = -48$
$a_5 = -3(5)^2 = -75$

2. $a_n = n^2 + 2n$

$a_1 = 1^2 + 2(1) = 3$
$a_2 = 2^2 + 2(2) = 8$
$a_3 = 3^2 + 2(3) = 15$
$a_4 = 4^2 + 2(4) = 24$
$a_5 = 5^2 + 2(5) = 35$

3. $a_n = \dfrac{(-1)^n}{100}$

$a_{100} = \dfrac{(-1)^{100}}{100} = \dfrac{1}{100}$

4. $a_n = \dfrac{2n}{(-1)^2}$

$a_{50} = \dfrac{2(50)}{(-1)^2} = 100$

5. $\dfrac{1}{6\cdot1}, \dfrac{1}{6\cdot2}, \dfrac{1}{6\cdot3}, \dots$

In general, $a_n = \dfrac{1}{6n}$.

6. $-1, 4, -9, 16, \dots$

$a_n = (-1)^n n^2$

7. $a_n = 32n - 16$

$a_5 = 32(5) - 16 = 144$ feet
$a_6 = 32(6) - 16 = 176$ feet
$a_7 = 32(7) - 16 = 208$ feet

8. $a_n = 100(2)^{n-1}$

$10,000 = 100(2)^{n-1}$

$100 = 2^{n-1}$

$\log 100 = (n-1)\log 2$

$n = \dfrac{\log 100}{\log 2} + 1 \approx 7.6$

Eighth day culture will be at least 10,000.
Since $n = 1$ corresponds to the end of the first
day, the original amount corresponds to $n = 0$.

$$a_0 = 100(2)^{-1} = 100\left(\frac{1}{2}\right) = 50$$

The original measure of the culture was 50.

9. 2006: $a_1 = 660,000$

2007: $a_2 = 660,000(2) = 1,320,000$

2008: $a_3 = 1,320,000(2) = 2,640,000$

2009: $a_4 = 2,640,000(2) = 5,280,000$

2010: $a_5 = 5,280,000(2) = 10,560,000$

There will be 10,560,000 acres of infested trees
in 2010.

10. $a_n = 50 + (n-1)8$

$a_1 = 50$

$a_2 = 50 + 8 = 58$

$a_3 = 50 + 2(8) = 66$

$a_4 = 50 + 3(8) = 74$

$a_5 = 50 + 4(8) = 82$

$a_6 = 50 + 5(8) = 90$

$a_7 = 50 + 6(8) = 98$

$a_8 = 50 + 7(8) = 106$

$a_9 = 50 + 8(8) = 114$

$a_{10} = 50 + 9(8) = 122$

There are 122 seats in the tenth row.

11. $a_1 = -2, \; r = \dfrac{2}{3}$

$a_1 = -2$

$a_2 = -2\left(\dfrac{2}{3}\right) = -\dfrac{4}{3}$

$a_3 = \left(-\dfrac{4}{3}\right)\left(\dfrac{2}{3}\right) = -\dfrac{8}{9}$

$a_4 = \left(-\dfrac{8}{9}\right)\left(\dfrac{2}{3}\right) = -\dfrac{16}{27}$

$a_5 = \left(-\dfrac{16}{27}\right)\left(\dfrac{2}{3}\right) = -\dfrac{32}{81}$

12. $a_n = 12 + (n-1)(-1.5)$

$a_1 = 12$

$a_2 = 12 + (1)(-1.5) = 10.5$

$a_3 = 12 + 2(-1.5) = 9$

$a_4 = 12 + 3(-1.5) = 7.5$

$a_5 = 12 + 4(-1.5) = 6$

13. $a_n = -5 + (n-1)^4$

$a_{30} = 5 + (30-1)4 = 111$

14. $a_n = 2 + (n-1)\dfrac{3}{4}$

$a_{11} = 2 + 10\left(\dfrac{3}{4}\right) = \dfrac{19}{2}$

15. 12, 7, 2,...

$a_1 = 12, \; d = -5, \; n = 20$

$a_{20} = 12 + (20-1)(-5) = -83$

16. $a_n = a_1 r^{n-1}, \; a_1 = 4, \; r = \dfrac{3}{2}$

$a_6 = 4\left(\dfrac{3}{2}\right)^{6-1} = \dfrac{243}{8}$

17. $a_4 = 18, \; a_{20} = 98$

$\begin{cases} a_4 = a_1 + (4-1)d \\ a_{20} = a_1 + (20-1)d \end{cases}$

$\begin{cases} 18 = a_1 + 3d \\ 98 = a_1 + 19d \end{cases}$

$\begin{cases} -18 = -a_1 - 3d \\ 98 = a_1 + 19d \end{cases}$

Adding yields $80 = 16d$ or $d = 5$.
Then $a_1 = 18 - 3(5) = 3$.

18. $a_3 = -48, \; a_4 = 192$

$r = \dfrac{a_4}{a_3} = \dfrac{192}{-48} = -4$

$a_3 = a_1 r^{3-1}$

$-48 = a_1(-4)^2$

$-48 = 16a_1$

$-3 = a_1$

$r = -4, \; a_1 = -3$

19. $\dfrac{3}{10}, \dfrac{3}{10^2}, \dfrac{3}{10^3}, \ldots$

In general, $a_n = \dfrac{3}{10^n}$

20. 50, 58, 66, ...

$a_n = 50 + (n-1)8$ or $a_n = 42 + 8n$

21. $\frac{8}{3}$, 4, 6, ...

Geometric; $a_1 = \frac{8}{3}$,

$r = \frac{4}{\frac{8}{3}} = 4 \cdot \frac{3}{8} = \frac{12}{8} = \frac{3}{2}$

22. $-10.5, -6.1, -1.7$
Arithmetic; $a_1 = -10.5$,
$d = -6.1 - (-10.5) = 4.4$

23. $7x, -14x, 28x$
Geometric; $a_1 = 7x$, $r = -2$

24. neither

25. $a_1 = 8$, $r = 0.75$
$a_1 = 8$
$a_2 = 8(0.75) = 6$
$a_3 = 8(0.75)^2 = 4.5$
$a_4 = 8(0.75)^3 \approx 3.4$
$a_5 = 8(0.75)^4 \approx 2.5$
$a_6 = 8(0.75)^5 \approx 1.9$
Yes, a ball that rebounds to a height of 2.5 feet after the fifth bounce is good, since $2.5 \geq 1.9$.

26. $a_1 = 25$, $d = -4$
$a_n = a_1 + (n-1)d$
$a_n = 25 + (n-1)(-4) = 29 - 4n$
$a_7 = 25 + 6(-4) = 1$
Continuing the progression as far as possible leaves 1 can in the top row.

27. $a_1 = 1$, $r = 2$
$a_n = 2^{n-1}$
$a_{10} = 2^9 = 512$
$a_{30} = 2^{29} = 536{,}870{,}912$
You save \$512 on the tenth day and \$536,870,912 on the thirtieth day.

28. $a_n = a_1 r^{n-1}$, $a_1 = 30$, $r = 0.7$
$a_5 = 30(0.7)^4 = 7.203$
The length is 7.203 inches on the fifth swing.

29. $a_1 = 900$, $d = 150$
$a_n = 900 + (n-1)150 = 150_n + 750$
$a_6 = 900 + (6-1)150 = 1650$
Her salary is \$1650 per month at the end of training.

30. $\frac{1}{512}, \frac{1}{256}, \frac{1}{128}, ...$

first fold: $a_1 = \frac{1}{256}$, $r = 2$

$a_{15} = \frac{1}{256}(2)^{15-1} = 64$

After 15 folds, the thickness is 64 inches.

31. $\displaystyle\sum_{i=1}^{5}(2i-1) = \left[2(1)-1\right] + \left[2(2)-1\right] + \left[2(3)-1\right]$
$\qquad\qquad + \left[2(4)-1\right] + \left[2(5)-1\right]$
$\qquad = 1 + 3 + 5 + 7 + 9$
$\qquad = 25$

32. $\displaystyle\sum_{i=1}^{5} i(i+2) = 1(1+2) + 2(2+2) + 3(3+2)$
$\qquad\qquad + 4(4+2) + 5(5+2)$
$\qquad = 3 + 8 + 15 + 24 + 35$
$\qquad = 85$

33. $\displaystyle\sum_{i=2}^{4}\frac{(-1)^i}{2i} = \frac{(-1)^2}{2(2)} + \frac{(-1)^3}{2(3)} + \frac{(-1)^4}{2(4)}$
$\qquad = \frac{1}{4} - \frac{1}{6} + \frac{1}{8}$
$\qquad = \frac{5}{24}$

34. $\displaystyle\sum_{i=3}^{5} 5(-1)^{i-1} = 5(-1)^{3-1} + 5(-1)^{4-1} + 5(-1)^{5-1}$
$\qquad = 5(1) + 5(-1) + 5(1)$
$\qquad = 5 - 5 + 5$
$\qquad = 5$

35. $a_n = (n-3)(n+2)$
$S_4 = \displaystyle\sum_{i=1}^{4}(i-3)(i+2)$
$\qquad = (1-3)(1+2) + (2-3)(2+2)$
$\qquad\qquad + (3-3)(3+2) + (4-3)(4+2)$
$\qquad = -6 - 4 + 0 + 6$
$\qquad = -4$

36. $a_n = n^2$

$$S_6 = \sum_{i=1}^{6} i^2$$
$$= (1)^2 + (2)^2 + (3)^2 + (4)^2 + (5)^2 + (6)^2$$
$$= 91$$

37. $a_n = -8 + (n-1)3 = 3n - 11$

$$S_5 = \sum_{i=1}^{5} (3i - 11)$$
$$= [3(1) - 11] + [3(2) - 11] + [3(3) - 11]$$
$$\qquad + [3(4) - 11] + [3(5) - 11]$$
$$= -8 - 5 - 2 + 1 + 4$$
$$= -10$$

38. $a_n = 5(4)^{n-1}$

$$S_3 = \sum_{i=1}^{3} 5(4)^{i-1} = 5(4)^0 + 5(4)^1 + 5(4)^2 = 105$$

39. $1 + 3 + 9 + 27 + 81 + 243$

$$= 3^0 + 3^1 + 3^2 + 3^3 + 3^4 + 3^5$$
$$= \sum_{i=1}^{6} 3^{i-1}$$

40. $6 + 2 + (-2) + (-6) + (-10) + (-14) + (-18)$

$$a_1 = 6, \ d = -4$$
$$a_n = 6 + (n-1)(-4)$$
$$\sum_{i=1}^{7} [6 + (i-1)(-4)]$$

41. $\dfrac{1}{4} + \dfrac{1}{16} + \dfrac{1}{64} + \dfrac{1}{256} = \dfrac{1}{4^1} + \dfrac{1}{4^2} + \dfrac{1}{4^3} + \dfrac{1}{4^4}$

$$= \sum_{i=1}^{4} \frac{1}{4^i}$$

42. $1 + \left(-\dfrac{3}{2}\right) + \dfrac{9}{4} = \left(-\dfrac{3}{2}\right)^0 + \left(-\dfrac{3}{2}\right)^1 + \left(-\dfrac{3}{2}\right)^2$

$$= \sum_{i=1}^{3} \left(-\frac{3}{2}\right)^{i-1}$$

43. $a_1 = 20, \ r = 2$

$a_n = 20(2)^n$ represents the number of yeast, where n represents the number of 8-hour periods. Since $48 = 6(8)$ here, $n = 6$.

$$a_6 = 20(2)^6 = 1280$$

There are 1280 yeast after 48 hours.

44. $a_n = n^2 + 2n - 1$

$$a_4 = (4)^2 + 2(4) - 1 = 23$$
$$S_4 = \sum_{i=1}^{4} (i^2 + 2i - 1)$$
$$= (1 + 2 - 1) + (4 + 4 - 1) + (9 + 6 - 1)$$
$$\qquad + (16 + 8 - 1)$$
$$= 46$$

23 cranes are born in the fourth year and 46 cranes are born in the first four years.

45. For Job A: $a_1 = 39,500, \ d = 2200$;

$$a_5 = 39,500 + (5-1)2200 = \$48,330$$

For Job B: $a_1 = 41,000, \ d = 1400$

$$a_5 = 41,000 + (5-1)1400 = \$46,600$$

For the fifth year, Job A has a higher salary.

46. $a_n = 200(0.5)^n$

$$a_3 = 200(0.5)^3 = 25$$
$$S_3 = \sum_{i=1}^{3} 200(0.5)^i$$
$$= 200(0.5) + 200(0.5)^2 + 200(0.5)^3$$
$$= 175$$

25 kilograms decay in the third year and 175 kilograms decay in the first three years.

47. $15, 19, 23, \ldots$

$$a_1 = 15, \ d = 4, \ a_6 = 15 + (6-1)4 = 35$$
$$S_6 = \frac{6}{2}[15 + 35] = 150$$

48. $5, -10, 20, \ldots$

$$a_1 = 5, \ r = -2$$
$$S_n = \frac{a_1(1 - r^n)}{1 - r}$$
$$S_9 = \frac{5(1 - (-2)^9)}{1 - (-2)} = 855$$

49. $a_1 = 1$, $d = 2$, $n = 30$, $a_{30} = 1 + (30-1)2 = 59$

$$S_{30} = \frac{30}{2}[1+59] = 900$$

50. 7, 14, 21, 28, ...

$a_n = 7 + (n-1)7$

$a_{20} = 7 + (20-1)7 = 140$

$$S_{20} = \frac{20}{2}(7+140) = 1470$$

51. 8, 5, 2, ...

$a_1 = 8$, $d = -3$, $n = 20$

$a_{20} = 8 + (20-1)(-3) = -49$

$$S_{20} = \frac{20}{2}[8 + (-49)]$$
$$= -410$$

52. $\dfrac{3}{4}, \dfrac{9}{4}, \dfrac{27}{4}, ...$

$a_1 = \dfrac{3}{4}$, $r = 3$

$$S_8 = \frac{\frac{3}{4}(1-3^8)}{1-3} = 2460$$

53. $a_1 = 6$, $r = 5$

$$S_4 = \frac{6(1-5^4)}{1-5} = 936$$

54. $a_1 = -3$, $d = -6$

$a_n = -3 + (n-1)(-6)$

$a_{100} = -3 + (100-1)(-6) = -597$

$$S_{100} = \frac{100}{2}(-3 + (-597)) = -30,000$$

55. $5, \dfrac{5}{2}, \dfrac{5}{4}, ...$

$a_1 = 5$, $r = \dfrac{1}{2}$

$$S_\infty = \frac{5}{1-\frac{1}{2}} = 10$$

56. $18, -2, \dfrac{2}{9}, ...$

$a_1 = 18$, $r = -\dfrac{1}{9}$

$$S_\infty = \frac{18}{1+\frac{1}{9}} = \frac{81}{5}$$

57. $-20, -4, -\dfrac{4}{5}, ...$

$a_1 = -20$, $r = \dfrac{1}{5}$

$$S_\infty = \frac{-20}{1-\frac{1}{5}} = -25$$

58. 0.2, 0.02, 0.002, ...

$a_1 = 0.2 = \dfrac{1}{5}$, $r = \dfrac{1}{10}$

$$S_\infty = \frac{\frac{1}{5}}{1-\frac{1}{10}} = \frac{2}{9}$$

59. $a_1 = 20,000$, $r = 1.15$, $n = 4$

$a_4 = 20,000(1.15)^{4-1} = 30,418$

$$S_4 = \frac{20,000(1-1.15^4)}{1-1.15} = 99,868$$

He earned \$30,418 during the fourth year and \$99,868 over the four years.

60. $a_n = 40(0.8)^{n-1}$

$a_4 = 40(0.8)^{4-1} = 20.48$

$$S_4 = \frac{40(1-0.8^4)}{1-0.8} = 118.08$$

He takes 20 minutes to assemble the fourth television and 118 minutes to assemble the first four televisions.

61. $a_1 = 100$, $d = -7$, $n = 7$

$a_7 = 100 + (7-1)(-7) = 58$

$$S_7 = \frac{7}{2}(100+58) = 553$$

The rent for the seventh day is \$58 and the rent for 7 days is \$553.

62. $a_1 = 15$, $r = 0.8$

$S_\infty = \dfrac{15}{1 - 0.8} = 75$ feet downward

$a_1 = 15(0.8) = 12$, $r = 0.8$

$S_\infty = \dfrac{12}{1 - 0.8} = 60$ feet upward

The total distance is 135 feet.

63. 1800, 600, 200,...

$a_1 = 1800$, $r = \dfrac{1}{3}$, $n = 6$

$S_6 = 1800 \dfrac{\left(1 - \left(\frac{1}{3}\right)^6\right)}{1 - \frac{1}{3}} \approx 2696$

Approximately 2696 mosquitoes were killed during the first six days after the spraying.

64. 1800, 600, 200, ...

For which n is $a_n < 1$?

$a_n = 1800 \left(\dfrac{1}{3}\right)^{n-1} < 1$

$\left(\dfrac{1}{3}\right)^{n-1} < \dfrac{1}{1800}$

$(n-1)\log \dfrac{1}{3} < \log \dfrac{1}{1800}$

$(n-1)\log 3^{-1} < \log 1800^{-1}$

$(n-1)(-\log 3) < -\log 1800$

$n - 1 > \dfrac{-\log 1800}{-\log 3}$

$n > 1 + \dfrac{\log 1800}{\log 3}$

$n > 7.8$

No longer effective on the 8th day

$S_8 = \dfrac{1800 \left(1 - \left(\frac{1}{3}\right)^8\right)}{1 - \frac{1}{3}} \approx 2700$

About 2700 mosquitoes were killed.

65. $0.5\overline{55} = 0.5 + 0.05 + 0.005 + \cdots$

$a_1 = 0.5$, $r = 0.1$

$S_\infty = \dfrac{0.5}{1 - 0.1} = \dfrac{0.5}{0.9} = \dfrac{5}{9}$

66. 27, 30, 33, …

$$a_n = 27 + (n-1)(3)$$
$$a_{20} = 27 + (20-1)(3) = 84$$
$$S_{20} = \frac{20}{2}(27 + 84) = 1110$$

There are 1110 seats in the theater.

67. $(x+z)^5 = x^5 + 5x^4z + 10x^3z^2 + 10x^2z^3 + 5xz^4 + z^5$

68. $(y-r)^6 = y^6 + 6y^5(-r) + 15y^4(-r)^2 + 20y^3(-r)^3 + 15y^2(-r)^4 + 6y(-r)^5 + (-r)^6$
$$= y^6 - 6y^5r + 15y^4r^2 - 20y^3r^3 + 15y^2r^4 - 6yr^5 + r^6$$

69. $(2x+y)^4 = (2x)^4 + 4(2x)^3 y + 6(2x)^2 y^2 + 4(2x)y^3 + y^4$
$$= 16x^4 + 32x^3y + 24x^2y^2 + 8xy^3 + y^4$$

70. $(3y-z)^4 = (3y)^4 + 4(3y)^3(-z) + 6(3y)^2(-z)^2 + 4(3y)(-z)^3 + (-z)^4$
$$= 81y^4 - 108y^3z + 54y^2z^2 - 12yz^3 + z^4$$

71. $(b+c)^8 = b^8 + \frac{8}{1!}b^7c + \frac{8\cdot7}{2!}b^6c^2 + \frac{8\cdot7\cdot6}{3!}b^5c^3 + \frac{8\cdot7\cdot6\cdot5}{4!}b^4c^4 + \frac{8\cdot7\cdot6\cdot5\cdot4}{5!}b^3c^5$
$$+ \frac{8\cdot7\cdot6\cdot5\cdot4\cdot3}{6!}b^2c^6 + \frac{8\cdot7\cdot6\cdot5\cdot4\cdot3\cdot2}{7!}bc^7 + c^8$$
$$= b^8 + 8b^7c + 28b^6c^2 + 56b^5c^3 + 70b^4c^4 + 56b^3c^5 + 28b^2c^6 + 8bc^7 + c^8$$

72. $(x-w)^7 = x^7 + \frac{7}{1!}x^6(-w) + \frac{7\cdot6}{2!}x^5(-w)^2 + \frac{7\cdot6\cdot5}{3!}x^4(-w)^3 + \frac{7\cdot6\cdot5\cdot4}{4!}x^3(-w)^4 + \frac{7\cdot6\cdot5\cdot4\cdot3}{5!}x^2(-w)^5$
$$+ \frac{7\cdot6\cdot5\cdot4\cdot3\cdot2}{6!}x(-w)^6 + (-w)^7$$
$$= x^7 - 7x^6w + 21x^5w^2 - 35x^4w^3 + 35x^3w^4 - 21x^2w^5 + 7xw^6 - w^7$$

73. $(4m-n)^4 = (4m)^4 + \frac{4}{1!}(4m)^3(-n) + \frac{4\cdot3}{2!}(4m)^2(-n)^2 + \frac{4\cdot3\cdot2}{3!}(4m)(-n)^3 + (-n)^4$
$$= 256m^4 - 256m^3n + 96m^2n^2 - 16mn^3 + n^4$$

74. $(p-2r)^5 = p^5 + \frac{5}{1!}p^4(-2r) + \frac{5\cdot4}{2!}p^3(-2r)^2 + \frac{5\cdot4\cdot3}{3!}p^2(-2r)^3 + \frac{5\cdot4\cdot3\cdot2}{4!}p(-2r)^4 + (-2r)^5$
$$= p^5 - 10p^4r + 40p^3r^2 - 80p^2r^3 + 80pr^4 - 32r^5$$

75. The 4th term corresponds to $r = 3$.
$$\frac{7!}{3!(7-3)!}a^{7-3}b^3 = 35a^4b^3$$

76. The 11th term corresponds to $r = 10$.
$$\frac{10!}{10!0!}y^{10-10}(2z)^{10} = 1024z^{10}$$

Chapter 11 Test

1. $a_n = \dfrac{(-1)^n}{n+4}$

   $a_1 = \dfrac{(-1)^1}{1+4} = -\dfrac{1}{5}$

   $a_2 = \dfrac{(-1)^2}{2+4} = \dfrac{1}{6}$

   $a_3 = \dfrac{(-1)^3}{3+4} = -\dfrac{1}{7}$

   $a_4 = \dfrac{(-1)^4}{4+4} = \dfrac{1}{8}$

   $a_5 = \dfrac{(-1)^5}{5+4} = -\dfrac{1}{9}$

2. $a_n = 10 + 3(n-1)$

   $a_{80} = 10 + 3(80-1) = 247$

3. $\dfrac{2}{5}, \dfrac{2}{25}, \dfrac{2}{125}, \ldots$

   In general, $a_n = \dfrac{2}{5}\left(\dfrac{1}{5}\right)^{n-1}$ or $a_n = \dfrac{2}{5^n}$.

4. $(-1)^1 9 \cdot 1, \; (-1)^2 9 \cdot 2, \ldots, a_n = (-1)^n 9n$

5. $a_n = 5(2)^{n-1}, S_5 = \dfrac{5(1-2^5)}{1-2} = 155$

6. $a_n = 18 + (n-1)(-2)$

   $a_1 = 18, \; a_{30} = 18 + (30-1)(-2) = -40$

   $S_{30} = \dfrac{30}{2}[18 - 40] = -330$

7. $a_1 = 24, \; r = \dfrac{1}{6}$

   $S_\infty = \dfrac{24}{1-\frac{1}{6}} = \dfrac{144}{5}$

8. $\dfrac{3}{2}, -\dfrac{3}{4}, \dfrac{3}{8}, \ldots$

   $a_1 = \dfrac{3}{2}, \; r = -\dfrac{1}{2}$

   $S_\infty = \dfrac{\frac{3}{2}}{1-\left(-\frac{1}{2}\right)} = 1$

9. $\displaystyle\sum_{i=1}^{4} i(i-2) = 1(1-2) + 2(2-2) + 3(3-2) + 4(4-2)$
$$= -1 + 0 + 3 + 8 - 20 + 40 - 80$$
$$= 10$$

10. $\displaystyle\sum_{i=2}^{4} 5(2)^i (-1)^{i-1} = 5(2)^2 (-1)^{2-1} + 5(2)^3 (-1)^{3-1} + 5(2)^4 (-1)^{4-1} = -20 + 40 - 80 = -60$

11. $(a-b)^6 = a^6 - 6a^5 b + 15a^4 b^2 - 20a^3 b^3 + 15a^2 b^4 - 6ab^5 + b^6$

12. $(2x+y)^5 = (2x)^5 + \dfrac{5}{1!}(2x)^4 y + \dfrac{5\cdot 4}{2!}(2x)^3 y^2 + \dfrac{5\cdot 4\cdot 3}{3!}(2x)^2 y^3 + \dfrac{5\cdot 4\cdot 3\cdot 2}{4!}(2x)y^4 + y^5$
$$= 32x^5 + 80x^4 y + 80x^3 y^2 + 40x^2 y^3 + 10xy^4 + y^5$$

13. $a_n = 250 + 75(n-1)$
$a_{10} = 250 + 75(10-1) = 925$
There were 925 people in the town at the beginning of the tenth year.
$a_1 = 250 + 75(1-1) = 250$
There were 250 people in the town at the beginning of the first year.

14. $1, 3, 5, \ldots$
$a_1 = 1, d = 2, n = 8$
$a_8 = 1 + (8-1)2 = 15$
$1 + 3 + 5 + 7 + 9 + 11 + 13 + 15$
$S_8 = \dfrac{8}{2}[1 + 15] = 64$
There were 64 shrubs planted in the 8 rows.

15. $a_1 = 80, r = \dfrac{3}{4}, n = 4$
$a_4 = 80\left(\dfrac{3}{4}\right)^{4-1} = 33.75$
The arc length is 33.75 cm on the 4th swing.
$S_4 = \dfrac{80\left(1 - \left(\frac{3}{4}\right)^4\right)}{1 - \frac{3}{4}} = 218.75$
The total of the arc lengths is 218.75 cm for the first 4 swings.

16. $a_1 = 80, r = \dfrac{3}{4}$
$S_\infty = \dfrac{80}{1 - \frac{3}{4}} = 320$
The total of the arc lengths is 320 cm before the pendulum comes to rest.

17. 16, 48, 80,...

$a_{10} = 16 + (10-1)32 = 304$

He falls 304 feet during the 10th second.

$S_{10} = \dfrac{10}{2}[16 + 304] = 1600$

He falls 1600 feet during the first 10 seconds.

18. $0.42\overline{42} = 0.42 + 0.0042 + 0.000042$

$a_1 = 0.42 = \dfrac{42}{100}, \ r = 0.01 = \dfrac{1}{100}$

$S_\infty = \dfrac{\frac{42}{100}}{1 - \frac{1}{100}} = \dfrac{42}{100} \cdot \dfrac{100}{99} = \dfrac{14}{33}$

Thus, $0.42\overline{42} = \dfrac{14}{33}$.

Chapter 11 Cumulative Review

1. a. $\dfrac{20}{-4} = -5$

b. $\dfrac{-9}{-3} = 3$

c. $-\dfrac{3}{8} \div 3 = -\dfrac{3}{8} \cdot \dfrac{1}{3} = -\dfrac{1}{8}$

d. $\dfrac{-40}{10} = -4$

e. $\dfrac{-1}{10} \div \dfrac{-2}{5} = \dfrac{1}{10} \cdot \dfrac{5}{2} = \dfrac{1}{4}$

f. $\dfrac{8}{0}$ is undefined.

2. a. $3a - (4a+3) = 3a - 4a - 3 = -a - 3$

b. $(5x-3) + (2x+6) = 7x + 3$

c. $4(2x-5) - 3(5x+1) = 8x - 20 - 15x - 3$
$\qquad = -7x - 23$

3. Let x = the original price, then
$x - 0.08x = 2162$
$0.92x = 2162$
$x = 2350$
The original price is $2350.

4. Let x = the price before taxes, then
$x + 0.06x = 344.50$
$1.06x = 344.50$
$x = 325$
The price before taxes was $325.

5. $3y - 2x = 7$
$3y = 2x + 7$
$y = \dfrac{1}{3}(2x+7)$
$y = \dfrac{2x}{3} + \dfrac{7}{3}$

6. If the line is to be parallel, then the slope has to be the same as the slope of the given line.

Therefore, $m = \dfrac{3}{2}$.

$(y - (-2)) = \dfrac{3}{2}(x-3)$

$y + 2 = \dfrac{3}{2}(x-3)$

$y = \dfrac{3}{2}x - \dfrac{13}{2}$

$f(x) = \dfrac{3}{2}x - \dfrac{13}{2}$

7. a. $(3x^6)(5x) = 3 \cdot 5 x^{6+1} = 15x^7$

b. $(-2.4x^3 p^2)(4xp^{10}) = -2.4 \cdot 4 x^{3+1} p^{2+10}$
$\qquad = -9.6x^4 p^{12}$

8. $\quad y^3 + 5y^2 - y = 5$
$\quad y^3 + 5y^2 - y - 5 = 0$
$\quad (y^3 + 5y^2) + (-y - 5) = 0$
$\quad y^2(y+5) - 1(y+5) = 0$
$\quad (y^2 - 1)(y+5) = 0$
$\quad (y+1)(y-1)(y+5) = 0$
$\qquad\qquad y = -5, -1, 1$

9.

$\begin{array}{r|rrrrr} -2 & 1 & -2 & -11 & 5 & 34 \\ & & -2 & 8 & 6 & -22 \\ \hline & 1 & -4 & -3 & 11 & 12 \end{array}$

Answer: $x^3 - 4x^2 - 3x + 11 + \dfrac{12}{x+2}$

10.
$$\frac{5}{3a-6} - \frac{a}{a-2} + \frac{3+2a}{5a-10}$$
$$= \frac{5}{3(a-2)} - \frac{a}{a-2} + \frac{3+2a}{5(a-2)}$$
$$= \frac{5 \cdot 5 - 3 \cdot 5a + 3(3+2a)}{3 \cdot 5(a-2)}$$
$$= \frac{25 - 15a + 9 + 6a}{15(a-2)}$$
$$= \frac{34 - 9a}{15(a-2)}$$

11. a. $\sqrt{50} = \sqrt{2}\sqrt{25} = 5\sqrt{2}$

b. $\sqrt[3]{24} = \sqrt[3]{8}\sqrt[3]{3} = 2\sqrt[3]{3}$

c. $\sqrt{26} = \sqrt{26}$

d. $\sqrt[4]{32} = \sqrt[4]{16}\sqrt[4]{2} = 2\sqrt[4]{2}$

12. $\sqrt{3x+6} - \sqrt{7x-6} = 0$
$$\sqrt{3x+6} = \sqrt{7x-6}$$
$$\left(\sqrt{3x+6}\right)^2 = \left(\sqrt{7x-6}\right)^2$$
$$3x+6 = 7x-6$$
$$-4x = -12$$
$$x = 3$$

13. $2420 = 2000(1+r)^2$
$$\frac{2420}{2000} = (1+r)^2$$
$$\frac{121}{100} = (1+r)^2$$
$$\pm\sqrt{\frac{121}{100}} = 1+r$$
$$\pm\frac{11}{10} = 1+r$$
$$-1 \pm \frac{11}{10} = r$$
Discard the negative value.
$$r = -1 + \frac{11}{10} = \frac{1}{10} = 0.10$$
The interest rate is 10%.

14. a. $\sqrt[3]{\dfrac{4}{3x}} = \dfrac{\sqrt[3]{4}}{\sqrt[3]{3x}} = \left(\dfrac{\sqrt[3]{9x^2}}{\sqrt[3]{9x^2}}\right) = \dfrac{\sqrt[3]{36x^2}}{3x}$

b. $\dfrac{\sqrt{2}+1}{\sqrt{2}-1} = \dfrac{\sqrt{2}+1}{\sqrt{2}-1} \cdot \left(\dfrac{\sqrt{2}+1}{\sqrt{2}+1}\right)$
$$= \dfrac{2+2\sqrt{2}+1}{2-1}$$
$$= 3+2\sqrt{2}$$

15. $(x-3)^2 - 3(x-3) - 4 = 0$
$$x^2 - 6x + 9 - 3x + 9 - 4 = 0$$
$$x^2 - 9x + 14 = 0$$
$$(x-2)(x-7) = 0$$
$$x = 2, 7$$

16. $\dfrac{10}{(2x+4)^2} - \dfrac{1}{2x+4} = 3$
$$10 - (2x+4) = 3(2x+4)^2$$
$$10 - 2x - 4 = 3(4x^2 + 16x + 16)$$
$$-2x + 6 = 12x^2 + 48x + 48$$
$$12x^2 + 50x + 42 = 0$$
$$6x^2 + 25x + 21 = 0$$
$$(6x+7)(x+3) = 0$$
$$x = -\frac{7}{6}, -3$$

17. $\dfrac{5}{x+1} < -2$
$$x+1 = 0$$
$$x = -1$$
Solve $\dfrac{5}{x+1} = -2$.
$$(x+1)\frac{5}{x+1} = (x+1)(-2)$$
$$5 = -2x - 2$$
$$7 = -2x$$
$$-\frac{7}{2} = x$$

Region	Test Point	$\dfrac{5}{x+1} < -2;$ Result
$\left(-\infty, -\dfrac{7}{2}\right)$	$x = -6$	$\dfrac{5}{-5} < -2;$ False
$\left(-\dfrac{7}{2}, -1\right)$	$x = -2$	$\dfrac{5}{-1} < -2;$ True
$(-1, \infty)$	$x = 4$	$\dfrac{5}{5} < -2;$ False

The solution set is $\left(-\dfrac{7}{2}, -1\right)$.

18. $f(x) = (x+2)^2 - 6$

Axis of symmetry: $x = -2$

vertex: $(-2, -6)$

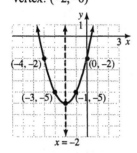

19. $f(t) = -16t^2 + 20t$

The maximum height occurs at the vertex.

$t = \dfrac{-20}{2(-16)} = \dfrac{5}{8}$

$f\left(\dfrac{5}{8}\right) = -16\left(\dfrac{5}{8}\right)^2 + 20\left(\dfrac{5}{8}\right) = \dfrac{25}{4}$

The maximum height of $\dfrac{25}{4}$ feet occurs at

$\dfrac{5}{8}$ second.

20. $f(x) = x^2 + 3x - 18$

$a = 1, b = 3, c = -18$

$x = \dfrac{-3}{2(1)} = -\dfrac{3}{2}$

$f\left(-\dfrac{3}{2}\right) = \left(-\dfrac{3}{2}\right)^2 + 3\left(\dfrac{3}{2}\right) - 18 = -\dfrac{81}{4}$

The vertex is $\left(-\dfrac{3}{2}, -\dfrac{81}{4}\right)$.

21. a. $(f \circ g)(2) = f(g(2)) = f(5) = 5^2 = 25$

$(g \circ f)(2) = g(f(2)) = g(4) = 4 + 3 = 7$

b. $(f \circ g)(x) = f(x+3)$

$= (x+3)^2$

$= x^2 + 6x + 9$

$(g \circ f)(x) = g(x^2) = x^2 + 3$

22. $f(x) = -2x + 3$

$y = -2x + 3$

$x = -2y + 3$

$x - 3 = -2y$

$\dfrac{x-3}{-2} = y$

$f^{-1}(x) = -\dfrac{x-3}{2}$ or $f^{-1}(x) = \dfrac{3-x}{2}$

23. $f^{-1} = \{(1,0), (7,-2), (-6,3), (4,4)\}$

24. a. $(f \circ g)(2) = f(g(2)) = f(3) = 3^2 - 2 = 7$

$(g \circ f)(2) = g(f(2)) = g(2) = 2 + 1 = 3$

b. $(f \circ g)(x) = f(x+1)$

$= (x+1)^2 - 2$

$= x^2 + 2x - 1$

$(g \circ f)(x) = g(x^2 - 2) = x^2 - 2 + 1 = x^2 - 1$

25. a. $2^x = 16$

$2^x = 2^4$

$x = 4$

b. $9^x = 27$

$(3^2)^x = 3^3$

$2x = 3$

$x = \dfrac{3}{2}$

c. $4^{x+3} = 8^x$

$(2^2)^{x+3} = (2^3)^x$

$2^{2x+6} = 2^{3x}$

$2x + 6 = 3x$

$x = 6$

26. a. $\log_2 32 = x$

$$2^x = 32$$
$$2^x = 2^5$$
$$x = 5$$

b. $\log_4 \dfrac{1}{64} = x$

$$4^x = \dfrac{1}{64}$$
$$4^x = 4^{-3}$$
$$x = -3$$

c. $\log_{\frac{1}{2}} x = 5$

$$\left(\dfrac{1}{2}\right)^5 = x$$
$$x = \dfrac{1}{32}$$

27. a. $\log_3 3^2 = 2$

b. $\log_7 7^{-1} = -1$

c. $5^{\log_5 3} = 3$

d. $2^{\log_2 6} = 6$

28. a. $4^x = 64$

$$\left(2^2\right)^x = 2^6$$
$$2x = 6$$
$$x = 3$$

b. $8^x = 32$

$$\left(2^3\right)^x = 2^5$$
$$3x = 5$$
$$x = \dfrac{5}{3}$$

c. $9^{x+4} = 243^x$

$$(3^2)^{x+4} = (3^5)^x$$
$$3^{2x+8} = 3^{5x}$$
$$2x + 8 = 5x$$
$$8 = 3x$$
$$x = \dfrac{8}{3}$$

29. a. $\log_{11} 10 + \log_{11} 3 = \log_{11}(10 \cdot 3) = \log_{11} 30$

b. $\log_3 \dfrac{1}{2} + \log_3 12 = \log_3 \left(\dfrac{1}{2} \cdot 12\right) = \log_3 6$

c. $\log_2(x+2) + \log_2 x = \log_2[(x+2)x]$
$$= \log_2(x^2 + 2x)$$

30. a. $\log 100{,}000 = \log_{10} 10^5 = 5$

b. $\log 10^{-3} = \log_{10} 10^{-3} = -3$

c. $\ln \sqrt[5]{e} = \ln e^{1/5} = \dfrac{1}{5}$

d. $\ln e^4 = 4$

31. $A = Pe^{rt}$
$$A = 1600e^{0.09(5)} \approx 2509.30$$
2509.30 is owed after 5 years.

32. a. $\log_6 5 + \log_6 4 = \log_6(5 \cdot 4) = \log_6 20$

b. $\log_8 12 - \log_8 4 = \log_8 \dfrac{12}{4} = \log_8 3$

c. $2\log_2 x + 3\log_2 x - 2\log_2(x-1)$
$$= 5\log_2 x - \log_2(x-1)^2$$
$$= \log_2 x^5 - \log_2(x-1)^2$$
$$= \log_2 \dfrac{x^5}{(x-1)^2}$$

33. $3^x = 7$

$$\log 3^x = \log 7$$
$$x \log 3 = \log 7$$
$$x = \dfrac{\log 7}{\log 3} \approx 1.7712$$

34. $10{,}000 = 5000\left(1 + \dfrac{0.02}{4}\right)^{4t}$

$$2 = (1.005)^{4t}$$
$$\ln 2 = \ln 1.005^{4t}$$
$$\ln 2 = 4t \ln(1.005)$$
$$t = \dfrac{\ln 2}{4 \ln 1.005} \approx 34.7$$

It takes 34.7 years.

35. $\log_4(x-2)=2$

$$4^2 = x-2$$
$$x-2=16$$
$$x=18$$

36. $\log_4 10 - \log_4 x = 2$

$$\log_4 \frac{10}{x} = 2$$
$$4^2 = \frac{10}{x}$$
$$16 = \frac{10}{x}$$
$$16x = 10$$
$$x = \frac{5}{8}$$

37. $\dfrac{x^2}{16} - \dfrac{y^2}{25} = 1$

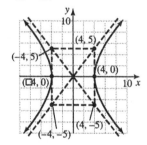

38. $(8, 5), (-2, 4)$

$$d = \sqrt{(-2-8)^2 + (4-5)^2} = \sqrt{101} \text{ units}$$

39. $\begin{cases} y = \sqrt{x} \\ x^2 + y^2 = 6 \end{cases}$

Replace y with $\sqrt{x}$ in the first equation.

$$(x)^2 + \left(\sqrt{x}\right)^2 = 6$$
$$x^2 + x - 6 = 0$$
$$(x+3)(x-2) = 0$$
$$x = -3 \text{(discard) or } x = 2$$
$$x = 2: \ y = \sqrt{x} = \sqrt{2}$$
$$\left(2, \sqrt{2}\right)$$

40. $\begin{cases} x^2 + y^2 = 36 \\ x - y = 6 \Rightarrow x = y+6 \end{cases}$

Replace x with $y + 6$ in the first equation.

$$(y+6)^2 + y^2 = 36$$
$$2y^2 + 12y = 0$$
$$2y(y+6) = 0$$
$$y = 0 \qquad \text{or} \qquad y = -6$$
$$x = 0 + 6 = 6 \qquad\quad x = -6 + 6 = 0$$
$$(0, -6); (6, 0)$$

41. $\dfrac{x^2}{9} + \dfrac{y^2}{16} \le 1$

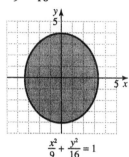

$$\frac{x^2}{9} + \frac{y^2}{16} = 1$$

42.

43. $a_n = n^2 - 1$

$$a_1 = 1^2 - 1 = 0$$
$$a_2 = 2^2 - 1 = 3$$
$$a_3 = 3^2 - 1 = 8$$
$$a_4 = 4^2 - 1 = 15$$
$$a_5 = 5^2 - 1 = 24$$

44. $a_n = \dfrac{n}{n+4}$

$$a_8 = \frac{8}{8+4} = \frac{8}{12} = \frac{2}{3}$$

45. $a_1 = 2, \ d = 9 - 2 = 7$

$$a_{11} = 2 + (11-1)(7) = 72$$

46. $a_1 = 2, \ r = \dfrac{10}{2} = 5$

$$a_6 = 2(5)^{6-1} = 2(5)^5 = 6250$$

47. a. $\displaystyle\sum_{i=0}^{6}\frac{i-2}{2} = \frac{0-2}{2} + \frac{1-2}{2} + \frac{2-2}{2} + \frac{3-2}{2} + \frac{4-2}{2} + \frac{5-2}{2} + \frac{6-2}{2}$

$$= -1 - \frac{1}{2} + 0 + \frac{1}{2} + 1 + \frac{3}{2} + 2$$

$$= \frac{7}{2}$$

b. $\displaystyle\sum_{i=3}^{5} 2^i = 2^3 + 2^4 + 2^5 = 8 + 16 + 32 = 56$

48. a. $\displaystyle\sum_{i=0}^{4} i(i+1) = 0(0+1) + 1(1+1) + 2(2+1) + 3(3+1) + 4(4+1)$

$$= 0 + 2 + 6 + 12 + 20$$

$$= 40$$

b. $\displaystyle\sum_{i=0}^{3} 2^i = 2^0 + 2^1 + 2^2 + 2^3 = 1 + 2 + 4 + 8 = 15$

49. $a_1 = 1$, $a_{30} = 30$

$$S_n = \frac{n}{2}(a_1 + a_n) = \frac{30}{2}(1 + 30) = 465$$

50. $(x-y)^6$ where $a = x$, $b = -y$, $n = 6$, and $r = 2$.

$$\frac{6!}{2!(6-2)!}x^{6-2}y^2 = 15x^4 y^2$$

The third term in the expansion of $(x-y)^6$ is $15x^4 y^2$.

Appendices

1. $\sqrt{216} = \sqrt{36 \cdot 6} = \sqrt{36} \cdot \sqrt{6} = 6\sqrt{6}$

2. $\dfrac{\left(4 - \sqrt{16}\right) - (-7 - 20)}{-2(1 - 4)^2} = \dfrac{(4 - 4) - (-27)}{-2(-3)^2}$

$$= \dfrac{0 + 27}{-2(9)}$$

$$= \dfrac{27}{-18}$$

$$= -\dfrac{3}{2}$$

3. $\left(\dfrac{1}{125}\right)^{-1/3} = 125^{1/3} = \sqrt[3]{125} = \sqrt[3]{5^3} = 5$

4. $(-9x)^{-2} = \dfrac{1}{(-9x)^2} = \dfrac{1}{(-9)^2 x^2} = \dfrac{1}{81x^2}$

5. $\dfrac{\frac{5}{x} - \frac{7}{3x}}{\frac{9}{8x} - \frac{1}{x}} = \dfrac{24x\left(\frac{5}{x} - \frac{7}{3x}\right)}{24x\left(\frac{9}{8x} - \frac{1}{x}\right)}$

$$= \dfrac{24x\left(\frac{5}{x}\right) - 24x\left(\frac{7}{3x}\right)}{24x\left(\frac{9}{8x}\right) - 24x\left(\frac{1}{x}\right)}$$

$$= \dfrac{24 \cdot 5 - 8 \cdot 7}{3 \cdot 9 - 24}$$

$$= \dfrac{120 - 56}{27 - 24}$$

$$= \dfrac{64}{3}$$

6. $\dfrac{6^{-1} a^2 b^{-3}}{3^{-2} a^{-5} b^2} = \dfrac{3^2 a^{2 - (-5)} b^{-3 - 2}}{6^1} = \dfrac{9 a^7 b^{-5}}{6} = \dfrac{3 a^7}{2 b^5}$

7. $\left(\dfrac{64 c^{4/3}}{a^{-2/3} b^{5/6}}\right)^{1/2} = \dfrac{64^{1/2} c^{\frac{4}{3} \cdot \frac{1}{2}}}{a^{-\frac{2}{3} \cdot \frac{1}{2}} b^{\frac{5}{6} \cdot \frac{1}{2}}}$

$$= \dfrac{8 c^{2/3}}{a^{-1/3} b^{5/12}}$$

$$= \dfrac{8 a^{1/3} c^{2/3}}{b^{5/12}}$$

8. $3x^2 y - 27 y^3 = 3y(x^2 - 9y^2)$

$$= 3y[x^2 - (3y)^2]$$

$$= 3y(x + 3y)(x - 3y)$$

9. $16 y^3 - 2 = 2(8 y^3 - 1)$

$$= 2[(2y)^3 - 1^3]$$

$$= 2(2y - 1)[(2y)^2 + 2y \cdot 1 + 1^2]$$

$$= 2(2y - 1)(4y^2 + 2y + 1)$$

10. $x^2 y - 9y - 3x^2 + 27 = y(x^2 - 9) - 3(x^2 - 9)$

$$= (x^2 - 9)(y - 3)$$

$$= (x + 3)(x - 3)(y - 3)$$

11. $(4x^3 y - 3x - 4) - (9x^3 y + 8x + 5)$

$$= 4x^3 y - 3x - 4 - 9x^3 y - 8x - 5$$

$$= 4x^3 y - 9x^3 y - 3x - 8x - 4 - 5$$

$$= -5x^3 y - 11x - 9$$

12. $(6m + n)^2 = (6m)^2 + 2(6m)(n) + n^2$

$$= 36m^2 + 12mn + n^2$$

13. $(2x - 1)(x^2 - 6x + 4)$

$$= 2x(x^2 - 6x + 4) - 1(x^2 - 6x + 4)$$

$$= 2x^3 - 12x^2 + 8x - x^2 + 6x - 4$$

$$= 2x^3 - 13x^2 + 14x - 4$$

14. $\dfrac{3x^2 - 12}{x^2 + 2x - 8} \div \dfrac{6x + 18}{x + 4} = \dfrac{3x^2 - 12}{x^2 + 2x - 8} \cdot \dfrac{x + 4}{6x + 18}$

$$= \dfrac{3(x^2 - 4)}{(x + 4)(x - 2)} \cdot \dfrac{x + 4}{6(x + 3)}$$

$$= \dfrac{3(x + 2)(x - 2)(x + 4)}{(x + 4)(x - 2) \cdot 6(x + 3)}$$

$$= \dfrac{x + 2}{2(x + 3)}$$

15. $\dfrac{2x^2+7}{2x^4-18x^2}-\dfrac{6x+7}{2x^4-18x^2}=\dfrac{(2x^2+7)-(6x+7)}{2x^4-18x^2}$

$\qquad\qquad\qquad = \dfrac{2x^2+7-6x-7}{2x^4-18x^2}$

$\qquad\qquad\qquad = \dfrac{2x^2-6x}{2x^2(x^2-9)}$

$\qquad\qquad\qquad = \dfrac{2x(x-3)}{2x^2(x+3)(x-3)}$

$\qquad\qquad\qquad = \dfrac{1}{x(x+3)}$

16. $\dfrac{3}{x^2-x-6}+\dfrac{2}{x^2-5x+6}$

$\qquad = \dfrac{3}{(x-3)(x+2)}+\dfrac{2}{(x-2)(x-3)}$

$\qquad = \dfrac{3(x-2)}{(x-3)(x+2)(x-2)}+\dfrac{2(x+2)}{(x-2)(x-3)(x+2)}$

$\qquad = \dfrac{3(x-2)+2(x+2)}{(x-3)(x+2)(x-2)}$

$\qquad = \dfrac{3x-6+2x+4}{(x-3)(x+2)(x-2)}$

$\qquad = \dfrac{5x-2}{(x-3)(x+2)(x-2)}$

17. $\sqrt{125x^3}-3\sqrt{20x^3}=\sqrt{25x^2\cdot5x}-3\sqrt{4x^2\cdot5x}$

$\qquad\qquad\qquad = 5x\sqrt{5x}-3\cdot2x\sqrt{5x}$

$\qquad\qquad\qquad = 5x\sqrt{5x}-6x\sqrt{5x}$

$\qquad\qquad\qquad = (5x-6x)\sqrt{5x}$

$\qquad\qquad\qquad = -x\sqrt{5x}$

18. $\left(\sqrt{5}+5\right)\left(\sqrt{5}-5\right)=\left(\sqrt{5}\right)^2-5^2=5-25=-20$

19.

$$
\require{enclose}
\begin{array}{r}
2x^2-x-2 \\
2x+1\enclose{longdiv}{4x^3+0x^2-5x+0} \\
\underline{4x^3+2x^2} \\
-2x^2-5x \\
\underline{-2x^2\ -x} \\
-4x+0 \\
\underline{-4x-2} \\
2
\end{array}
$$

$(4x^3-5x)\div(2x+1)=2x^2-x-2+\dfrac{2}{2x+1}$

20. $\begin{aligned}
9(x+2)&=5[11-2(2-x)+3] \\
9x+18&=5(11-4+2x+3) \\
9x+18&=5(2x+10) \\
9x+18&=10x+50 \\
9x-10x&=50-18 \\
-x&=32 \\
x&=-32
\end{aligned}$

21. $\begin{aligned}
|6x-5|-3&=-2 \\
|6x-5|&=1
\end{aligned}$

$6x-5=-1\quad\text{or}\quad 6x-5=1$

$6x=4\qquad\text{or}\qquad 6x=6$

$x=\dfrac{4}{6}\qquad\text{or}\qquad x=1$

$x=\dfrac{2}{3}$

Both solutions check.

22. $\begin{aligned}
3n(7n-20)&=96 \\
21n^2-60n&=96 \\
21n^2-60n-96&=0 \\
3(7n^2-20n-32)&=0 \\
3(7n+8)(n-4)&=0
\end{aligned}$

$7n+8=0\quad\text{or}\quad n-4=0$

$n=-\dfrac{8}{7}\quad\text{or}\qquad n=4$

Both solutions check.

23. $\begin{aligned}
-3&<2(x-3)\le4 \\
-3&<2x-6\le4 \\
-3+6&<2x-6+6\le4+6 \\
3&<2x\le10 \\
\dfrac{3}{2}&<\dfrac{2x}{2}\le\dfrac{10}{2} \\
\dfrac{3}{2}&<x\le5
\end{aligned}$

$\left(\dfrac{3}{2},5\right]$

24. $|3x+1|>5$

$3x+1<-5\quad\text{or}\quad 3x+1>5$

$3x<-6\qquad\qquad 3x>4$

$x<-2\qquad\qquad x>\dfrac{4}{3}$

$(-\infty,-2)\cup\left(\dfrac{4}{3},\infty\right)$

25.
$$\frac{x^2+8}{x}-1=\frac{2(x+4)}{x}$$

$$x\left(\frac{x^2+8}{x}-1\right)=x\left(\frac{2(x+4)}{x}\right)$$

$$x^2+8-x=2(x+4)$$

$$x^2-x+8=2x+8$$

$$x^2-3x=0$$

$$x(x-3)=0$$

$$x=0 \quad \text{or} \quad x-3=0$$

$$x=3$$

The only solution is 3.

26.
$$y^2-3y=5$$

$$y^2-3y-5=0$$

$$y=\frac{-(-3)\pm\sqrt{(-3)^2-4(1)(-5)}}{2(1)}$$

$$y=\frac{3\pm\sqrt{9+20}}{2}$$

$$y=\frac{3\pm\sqrt{29}}{2}$$

27.
$$x=\sqrt{x-2}+2$$

$$x-2=\sqrt{x-2}$$

$$(x-2)^2=\left(\sqrt{x-2}\right)^2$$

$$x^2-4x+4=x-2$$

$$x^2-5x+6=0$$

$$(x-2)(x-3)=0$$

$$x-2=0 \quad \text{or} \quad x-3=0$$

$$x=2 \quad \text{or} \quad x=3$$

28.
$$2x^2-7x>15$$

$$2x^2-7x-15>0$$

$$(2x+3)(x-5)>0$$

$$2x+3=0 \quad \text{or} \quad x-5=0$$

$$x=-\frac{3}{2} \quad \text{or} \quad x=5$$

Region	Test Point	$2x^2-7x>15$ Result
$\left(-\infty,-\frac{3}{2}\right)$	-3	39 > 15 True
$\left(-\frac{3}{2},5\right)$	0	0 > 15 False
$(5,\infty)$	6	30 > 15 True

$$\left(-\infty,-\frac{3}{2}\right)\cup(5,\infty)$$

29.
$$\begin{cases} \dfrac{x}{2}+\dfrac{y}{4}=-\dfrac{3}{4} \\ x+\dfrac{3}{4}y=-4 \end{cases}$$

$$\begin{cases} -8\left(\dfrac{x}{2}+\dfrac{y}{4}\right)=-8\left(-\dfrac{3}{4}\right) \\ 4\left(x+\dfrac{3}{4}y\right)=4(-4) \end{cases}$$

$$-4x-2y=6$$

$$\underline{4x+3y=-16}$$

$$y=-10$$

Let $y=-10$ in the second equation.

$$x+\frac{3}{4}y=-4$$

$$x+\frac{3}{4}(-10)=-4$$

$$x-\frac{15}{2}=-\frac{8}{2}$$

$$x=\frac{7}{2}$$

The solution is $\left(\dfrac{7}{2},-10\right)$.

30. $4x+6y=7$

$$6y=-4x+7$$

$$y=-\frac{2}{3}x+\frac{7}{6}$$

slope $=-\dfrac{2}{3}$, y-intercept $\left(0,\dfrac{7}{6}\right)$

Plot points: $\left(0,\dfrac{7}{6}\right),\left(\dfrac{7}{4},0\right),\left(-3,\dfrac{19}{6}\right)$

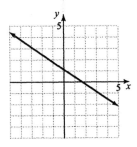

31. $2x - y > 5$

Graph $2x - y = 5$ with a dashed line because the inequality is >.

x	$2x - y = 5$	y
0	$2(0) - y = 5$	-5
1	$2(1) - y = 5$	-3
3	$2(3) - y = 5$	1

Test point $(0, 0)$: $2(0) - 0 \overset{?}{>} 5$

$\qquad\qquad\qquad 0 > 5$ False

Shade the region that does not include $(0, 0)$.

32. $y = -3$

The graph of $y = -3$ is a horizontal line with a y-intercept of $(0, -3)$.

33. $g(x) = -|x + 2| - 1$

x	$g(x) = -|x + 2| - 1$	$g(x)$
-5	$-|-5 + 2| - 1 = -4$	-4
-4	$-|-4 + 2| - 1 = -3$	-3
-3	$-|-3 + 2| - 1 = -2$	-2
-2	$-|-2 + 2| - 1 = -1$	-1
-1	$-|-1 + 2| - 1 = -2$	-2
0	$-|0 + 2| - 1 = -3$	-3
1	$-|1 + 2| - 1 = -4$	-4

Domain: All real numbers, $(-\infty, \infty)$
Range: $(-\infty, -1]$

34. $h(x) = x^2 - 4x + 4$

x-intercept: Let $h(x) = 0$ and solve for x.

$$0 = x^2 - 4x + 4$$
$$0 = (x - 2)^2$$
$$x - 2 = 0$$
$$x = 2$$

x-intercept: $(2, 0)$
y-intercept: Let $x = 0$.

$$h(0) = 0^2 - 4(0) + 4 = 4$$

y-intercept: $(0, 4)$
x-coordinate of vertex:

$$-\frac{b}{2a} = -\frac{-4}{2(1)} = 2$$

vertex: $(2, 0)$

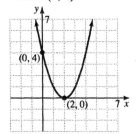

35. $f(x) = \begin{cases} -\dfrac{1}{2}x & \text{if } x \le 0 \\ 2x-3 & \text{if } x > 0 \end{cases}$

If $x \le 0$

x	$-\frac{1}{2}x$	$f(x)$
0	$-\frac{1}{2}(0)$	0
-2	$-\frac{1}{2}(-2)$	1
-4	$-\frac{1}{2}(-4)$	2

If $x > 0$

x	$2x-3$	$f(x)$
1	$2(1)-3$	-1
2	$2(2)-3$	1
3	$2(3)-3$	3

Domain: $(-\infty, \infty)$
Range: $(-3, \infty)$

36. through $(4, -2)$ and $(6, -3)$

$\text{slope} = m = \dfrac{y_2 - y_1}{x_2 - x_1} = \dfrac{-3-(-2)}{6-4} = \dfrac{-1}{2}$

$y - y_1 = m(x - x_1)$

$y - (-2) = -\dfrac{1}{2}(x-4)$

$y + 2 = -\dfrac{1}{2}x + 2$

$y = -\dfrac{1}{2}x$

$f(x) = -\dfrac{1}{2}x$

37. through $(-1, 2)$ and perpendicular to $3x - y = 4$
Find the slope of $3x - y = 4$ by writing the
equation in slope-intercept form.

$3x - y = 4$

$\quad -y = -3x + 4$

$\quad\quad y = 3x - 4$

The slope is 3. The slope of a line perpendicular

to this line is $-\dfrac{1}{3}$.

Substitute $m = -\dfrac{1}{3}$ and $(x_1, y_1) = (-1, 2)$ in the

equation:

$y - y_1 = m(x - x_1)$

$y - 2 = -\dfrac{1}{3}[x - (-1)]$

$y - 2 = -\dfrac{1}{3}(x + 1)$

$y - 2 = -\dfrac{1}{3}x - \dfrac{1}{3}$

$y = -\dfrac{1}{3}x + \dfrac{5}{3}$

$f(x) = -\dfrac{1}{3}x + \dfrac{5}{3}$

38. $(x_1, y_1) = (-6, 3);\ (x_2, y_2) = (-8, -7)$

$d = \sqrt{(x_2 - x_1)^2 + (y_2 - y_1)^2}$

$\quad = \sqrt{[-8-(-6)]^2 + (-7-3)^2}$

$\quad = \sqrt{(-2)^2 + (-10)^2}$

$\quad = \sqrt{4 + 100}$

$\quad = \sqrt{104}$

$\quad = 2\sqrt{26}$ units

39. $(x_1, y_1) = (-2, -5);\ (x_2, y_2) = (-6, 12)$

$\text{midpoint} = \left(\dfrac{x_1 + x_2}{2}, \dfrac{y_1 + y_2}{2} \right)$

$\quad = \left(\dfrac{-2 + (-6)}{2}, \dfrac{-5 + 12}{2} \right)$

$\quad = \left(\dfrac{-8}{2}, \dfrac{7}{2} \right)$

$\quad = \left(-4, \dfrac{7}{2} \right)$

40. $\sqrt{\dfrac{9}{y}} = \dfrac{\sqrt{9}}{\sqrt{y}} = \dfrac{\sqrt{9}}{\sqrt{y}} \cdot \dfrac{\sqrt{y}}{\sqrt{y}} = \dfrac{\sqrt{9} \cdot \sqrt{y}}{\sqrt{y} \cdot \sqrt{y}} = \dfrac{3\sqrt{y}}{y}$

41. $\dfrac{4-\sqrt{x}}{4+2\sqrt{x}} = \dfrac{4-\sqrt{x}}{4+2\sqrt{x}} \cdot \dfrac{4-2\sqrt{x}}{4-2\sqrt{x}}$

$\quad = \dfrac{\left(4-\sqrt{x}\right)\left(4-2\sqrt{x}\right)}{\left(4+2\sqrt{x}\right)\left(4-2\sqrt{x}\right)}$

$\quad = \dfrac{16-12\sqrt{x}+2x}{16-4x}$

$\quad = \dfrac{2\left(8-6\sqrt{x}+x\right)}{2(8-2x)}$

$\quad = \dfrac{8-6\sqrt{x}+x}{8-2x}$

42. Let x = population of New York, then
$x + 1.3$ = Seoul's population, and
$2x - 10.2$ = Tokyo's population.
$x + (x+1.3) + (2x-10.2) = 78.3$
$\qquad\qquad\quad 4x - 8.9 = 78.3$
$\qquad\qquad\qquad\quad 4x = 87.2$
$\qquad\qquad\qquad\quad\ x = 21.8$

$x + 1.3 = 23.1$
$2x - 10.2 = 33.4$
The populations are as follows:
New York: 21.8 million; Seoul: 23.1 million;
Tokyo: 33.4 million

43. Subtract the area of the small square from the
area of the large square.
$x^2 - (2y)^2 = (x+2y)(x-2y)$

44. Let x = the number.
$(x+1)\cdot\left(2\cdot\dfrac{1}{x}\right) = \dfrac{12}{5}$

$\qquad \dfrac{2}{x}(x+1) = \dfrac{12}{5}$

$5x\left[\dfrac{2}{x}(x+1)\right] = 5x\left(\dfrac{12}{5}\right)$

$\qquad 10(x+1) = x \cdot 12$

$\qquad 10x+10 = 12x$

$\qquad\qquad 10 = 2x$

$\qquad\qquad\ 5 = x$

The number is 5.

45. $W = \dfrac{k}{V}$

Find k by substituting $W = 20$ and $V = 12$.

$20 = \dfrac{k}{12}$

$240 = k$

Write the inverse relation equation.

$W = \dfrac{240}{V}$

Let $V = 15$ and find W.

$W = \dfrac{240}{15}$

$W = 16$

46. Use the Pythagorean Theorem.
$c^2 = a^2 + b^2$
$20^2 = x^2 + (x+8)^2$
$400 = x^2 + x^2 + 16x + 64$
$0 = 2x^2 + 16x - 336$
$0 = 2(x^2 + 8x - 168)$

$x = \dfrac{-8 \pm \sqrt{8^2 - 4(1)(-168)}}{2(1)}$

$x = \dfrac{-8 \pm \sqrt{736}}{2}$

$x \approx -17.6$ or $x \approx 9.6$
Discard a negative distance.
$x + 8 + x = 9.6 + 8 + 9.6 = 27.2$
$27.2 - 20 = 7.2$ or about 7
A person saves about 7 feet.

47. a. Find the vertex.
$s(t) = -16t^2 + 32t + 256$

t-value: $\dfrac{-b}{2a} = \dfrac{-32}{2(-16)} = 1$

$s(t)$-value:
$s(1) = -16(1)^2 + 32(1) + 256 = 272$
The maximum height is 272 feet.

b. Let $s(t) = 0$ and solve for t.
$0 = -16t^2 + 32t + 256$
$0 = -16(t^2 - 2t - 16)$

$t = \dfrac{-(-2) \pm \sqrt{(-2)^2 - 4(1)(-16)}}{2(1)}$

$t = \dfrac{2 \pm \sqrt{68}}{2}$

$t = \dfrac{2 \pm 2\sqrt{17}}{2}$

$t = 1 \pm \sqrt{17}$

$t \approx -3.12$ or $t \approx 5.12$
Discard a negative time.
The stone will hit the water in
approximately 5.12 seconds.

48. Let x = amount of 10% solution to add to mixture.

solution	amount of solution	amount of fructose
10%	x	$0.10x$
20%	$20 - x$	$0.20(20 - x)$
17.5%	20	$0.175(20)$

$$0.10x + 0.20(20 - x) = 0.175(20)$$
$$0.10x + 4 - 0.20x = 3.5$$
$$-0.10x = -0.5$$
$$x = 5$$

$20 - x = 15$

Therefore, mix 5 gallons of 10% solution with 15 gallons of 20% solution.

49. $-\sqrt{-8} = -\sqrt{4 \cdot (-1) \cdot 2} = -\sqrt{4} \cdot \sqrt{-1} \cdot \sqrt{2} = -2i\sqrt{2}$

50. $(12 - 6i) - (12 - 3i) = 12 - 6i - 12 + 3i$
$$= 12 - 12 - 6i + 3i$$
$$= 0 - 3i$$
$$= -3i$$

51. $(4 + 3i)^2 = (4 + 3i)(4 + 3i)$
$$= 16 + 12i + 12i + 9i^2$$
$$= 16 + 24i - 9$$
$$= 7 + 24i$$

52. $\dfrac{1 + 4i}{1 - i} = \dfrac{1 + 4i}{1 - i} \cdot \dfrac{1 + i}{1 + i}$
$$= \dfrac{(1 + 4i)(1 + i)}{(1 - i)(1 + i)}$$
$$= \dfrac{1 + 5i + 4i^2}{1 - i^2}$$
$$= \dfrac{1 + 5i - 4}{1 - (-1)}$$
$$= \dfrac{-3 + 5i}{2}$$
$$= -\dfrac{3}{2} + \dfrac{5}{2}i$$

53. $g(x) = x - 7$ and $h(x) = x^2 - 6x + 5$

$(g \circ h)(x) = (x^2 - 6x + 5) - 7 = x^2 - 6x - 2$

54. $f(x) = 6 - 2x$ is a one-to-one function since there is only one $f(x)$ value for each x-value.

Inverse:

$y = 6 - 2x \qquad \Rightarrow \qquad x = 6 - 2y$
$$x + 2y = 6$$
$$2y = -x + 6$$
$$y = \dfrac{-x + 6}{2}$$
$$f^{-1}(x) = \dfrac{-x + 6}{2}$$

55. $\log_5 x + 3\log_5 x - \log_5(x + 1)$
$$= \log_5 x + \log_5 x^3 - \log_5(x + 1)$$
$$= \log_5 x \cdot x^3 - \log_5(x + 1)$$
$$= \log_5 x^4 - \log_5(x + 1)$$
$$= \log_5 \dfrac{x^4}{x + 1}$$

56. $8^{x-1} = \dfrac{1}{64}$
$$(2^3)^{x-1} = \dfrac{1}{2^6}$$
$$2^{3(x-1)} = 2^{-6}$$
$$3(x - 1) = -6$$
$$3x - 3 = -6$$
$$3x = -3$$
$$x = -1$$

57. $3^{2x+5} = 4$
$$\log 3^{2x+5} = \log 4$$
$$(2x + 5)\log 3 = \log 4$$
$$2x + 5 = \dfrac{\log 4}{\log 3}$$
$$2x = \dfrac{\log 4}{\log 3} - 5$$
$$x = \dfrac{1}{2}\left(\dfrac{\log 4}{\log 3} - 5\right)$$
$$x \approx -1.8691$$

58. $\log_8(3x - 2) = 2$
$$8^2 = 3x - 2$$
$$64 = 3x - 2$$
$$66 = 3x$$
$$22 = x$$

59. $\log_4(x+1) - \log_4(x-2) = 3$

$$\log_4 \frac{x+1}{x-2} = 3$$

$$4^3 = \frac{x+1}{x-2}$$

$$64 = \frac{x+1}{x-2}$$

$$64(x-2) = x+1$$

$$64x - 128 = x+1$$

$$63x = 129$$

$$x = \frac{129}{63} = \frac{43}{21}$$

60. $\ln\sqrt{e} = x$

$$\ln e^{1/2} = x$$

$$\frac{1}{2}\ln e = x$$

$$\frac{1}{2} = x$$

61. $y = \left(\frac{1}{2}\right)^x + 1$

x	$\left(\frac{1}{2}\right)^x + 1$	y
-3	$\left(\frac{1}{2}\right)^{-3} + 1 = 9$	9
-2	$\left(\frac{1}{2}\right)^{-2} + 1 = 5$	5
-1	$\left(\frac{1}{2}\right)^{-1} + 1 = 3$	3
0	$\left(\frac{1}{2}\right)^{0} + 1 = 2$	2
1	$\left(\frac{1}{2}\right)^{1} + 1 = 1\frac{1}{2}$	$1\frac{1}{2}$
2	$\left(\frac{1}{2}\right)^{2} + 1 = 1\frac{1}{4}$	$1\frac{1}{4}$
3	$\left(\frac{1}{2}\right)^{3} + 1 = 1\frac{1}{8}$	$1\frac{1}{8}$

62. Let $y_0 = 57{,}000$, $k = 0.026$, $t = 5$.

$$y = y_0 e^{kt}$$

$$y = 57{,}000 e^{0.026(5)}$$

$$y \approx 64{,}913$$

In 5 years, there will be 64,913 prairie dogs.

63. $x^2 - y^2 = 36$

$$x^2 - y^2 = 6^2$$

hyperbola, with x-intercepts $(-6, 0)$, $(6, 0)$

64. $16x^2 + 9y^2 = 144$

$$\frac{16x^2}{144} + \frac{9y^2}{144} = \frac{144}{144}$$

$$\frac{x^2}{9} + \frac{y^2}{16} = 1$$

Ellipse, x-intercepts $(-3, 0)$, $(3, 0)$

y-intercepts $(0, -4)$, $(0, 4)$

65.
$$x^2 + y^2 + 6x = 16$$
$$(x^2 + 6x + 9) + y^2 = 16 + 9$$
$$(x+3)^2 + y^2 = 25$$
$$[x-(-3)]^2 + (y-0)^2 = 5^2$$
circle with center (–3, 0) and radius 5

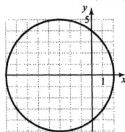

66. $\begin{cases} x^2 + y^2 = 26 \\ x^2 - 2y^2 = 23 \end{cases}$

Multiply equation (2) by –1 and add the equations.
$$x^2 + y^2 = 26$$
$$\underline{-x^2 + 2y^2 = -23}$$
$$3y^2 = 3$$
$$y^2 = 1$$
$$y = \pm 1$$

Substitute $y = -1$ and $y = 1$ into equation (1).
$$x^2 + (-1)^2 = 26$$
$$x^2 = 25$$
$$x = \pm 5$$
$$x^2 + 1^2 = 26$$
$$x^2 = 25$$
$$x = \pm 5$$
The solutions are (–5, –1), (–5, 1), (5, –1), (5, 1).

67. $a_n = \dfrac{(-1)^n}{n+4}$

$$a_1 = \frac{(-1)^1}{1+4} = -\frac{1}{5}$$
$$a_2 = \frac{(-1)^2}{2+4} = \frac{1}{6}$$
$$a_3 = \frac{(-1)^3}{3+4} = -\frac{1}{7}$$
$$a_4 = \frac{(-1)^4}{4+4} = \frac{1}{8}$$
$$a_5 = \frac{(-1)^5}{5+4} = -\frac{1}{9}$$

The first five terms are $-\dfrac{1}{5}, \dfrac{1}{6}, -\dfrac{1}{7}, \dfrac{1}{8}, -\dfrac{1}{9}$.

68. $a_n = 5(2)^{n-1}$
$$a_1 = 5(2)^{1-1} = 5(2)^0 = 5$$
$$r = 2$$
$$n = 5$$
$$S_n = \frac{a_1(1-r^n)}{1-r}$$
$$S_5 = \frac{5(1-2^5)}{1-2} = \frac{5(1-32)}{-1} = 155$$

69. Sequence $\dfrac{3}{2}, -\dfrac{3}{4}, \dfrac{3}{8}, \ldots$

$$a_1 = \frac{3}{2}, r = -\frac{1}{2}$$
$$S_\infty = \frac{a_1}{1-r} = \frac{\frac{3}{2}}{1-\left(-\frac{1}{2}\right)} = \frac{\frac{3}{2}}{\frac{3}{2}} = 1$$

70. $\displaystyle\sum_{i=1}^{4} i(i-2) = 1(1-2) + 2(2-2) + 3(3-2) + 4(4-2)$
$$= 1(-1) + 2(0) + 3(1) + 4(2)$$
$$= -1 + 0 + 3 + 8$$
$$= 10$$

71. $(2x+y)^5 = \binom{5}{0}(2x)^5 + \binom{5}{1}(2x)^4(y) + \binom{5}{2}(2x)^3(y)^2 + \binom{5}{3}(2x)^2(y)^3 + \binom{5}{4}(2x)^1(y)^4 + \binom{5}{5}y^5$

$= 2^5 x^5 + 5 \cdot 2^4 x^4 y + 10 \cdot 2^3 x^3 y^2 + 10 \cdot 2^2 x^2 y^3 + 5 \cdot 2xy^4 + y^5$

$= 32x^5 + 80x^4 y + 80x^3 y^2 + 40x^2 y^3 + 10xy^4 + y^5$

Appendix B.3 Exercise Set

1. $V = lwh$

$= (6 \text{ in.})(4 \text{ in.})(3 \text{ in.})$

$= 72 \text{ cu in.}$

$SA = 2lh + 2wh + 2lw$

$= 2(6 \text{ in.})(3 \text{ in.}) + 2(4 \text{ in.})(3 \text{ in.}) + 2(6 \text{ in.})(4 \text{ in.})$

$= 36 \text{ sq in.} + 24 \text{ sq in.} + 48 \text{ sq in.}$

$= 108 \text{ sq in.}$

3. $V = s^3 = (8 \text{ cm})^3 = 512 \text{ cu cm}$

$SA = 6s^2 = 6(8 \text{ cm})^2 = 384 \text{ sq cm}$

5. $V = \frac{1}{3}\pi r^2 h$

$= \frac{1}{3}\pi(2 \text{ yd})^2(3 \text{ yd})$

$= 4\pi \text{ cu yd}$

$\approx 4\left(\frac{22}{7}\right) \text{ cu yd}$

$\approx 12.57 \text{ cu yd}$

$SA = \pi r\sqrt{r^2 + h^2} + \pi r^2$

$= \pi(2 \text{ yd})\sqrt{(2 \text{ yd})^2 + (3 \text{ yd})^2} + \pi(2 \text{ yd})^2$

$= \pi(2 \text{ yd})\left(\sqrt{13} \text{ yd}\right) + \pi(4 \text{ sq yd})$

$= \left(2\sqrt{13} + 4\right)\pi \text{ sq yd}$

$\approx 3.14\left(2\sqrt{13} + 4\right) \text{ sq yd}$

$\approx 35.20 \text{ sq yd}$

7. $V = \dfrac{4}{3}\pi r^3$

$\quad = \dfrac{4}{3}\pi(5 \text{ in.})^3$

$\quad = \dfrac{500}{3}\pi \text{ cu in.}$

$\quad \approx \dfrac{500}{3}\left(\dfrac{22}{7}\right) \text{ cu in.}$

$\quad = 523\dfrac{17}{21} \text{ cu in.}$

$SA = 4\pi r^2$

$\quad = 4\pi(5 \text{ in.})^2$

$\quad = 100\pi \text{ sq in.}$

$\quad \approx 100\left(\dfrac{22}{7}\right) \text{ sq in.}$

$\quad = 314\dfrac{2}{7} \text{ sq in.}$

9. $V = \dfrac{1}{3}s^2 h = \dfrac{1}{3}(6 \text{ cm})^2(4 \text{ cm}) = 48 \text{ cu cm}$

$SA = B + \dfrac{1}{2}pl$

$\quad = (6 \text{ cm})^2 + \dfrac{1}{2}(24 \text{ cm})(5 \text{ cm})$

$\quad = 36 \text{ sq cm} + 60 \text{ sq cm}$

$\quad = 96 \text{ sq cm}$

11. $V = s^3$

$\quad = \left(1\dfrac{1}{3} \text{ in.}\right)^3$

$\quad = \left(\dfrac{4}{3} \text{ in.}\right)^3$

$\quad = \dfrac{64}{27} \text{ cu in.}$

$\quad = 2\dfrac{10}{27} \text{ cu in.}$

13. $SA = 2lh + 2wh + 2lw$

$\quad = 2(2 \text{ ft})(1.4 \text{ ft}) + 2(2 \text{ ft})(3 \text{ ft}) + 2(1.4 \text{ ft})(3 \text{ ft})$

$\quad = 5.6 \text{ sq ft} + 12 \text{ sq ft} + 8.4 \text{ sq ft}$

$\quad = 26 \text{ sq ft}$

15. $V = \dfrac{1}{3}s^2 h$

$\quad = \dfrac{1}{3}(5 \text{ in.})^2(1.3 \text{ in.})$

$\quad = \dfrac{1}{3}(25 \text{ sq in.})\left(\dfrac{13}{10} \text{ in.}\right)$

$\quad = \dfrac{65}{6} \text{ cu in.}$

$\quad = 10\dfrac{5}{6} \text{ cu in.}$

17. $V = \dfrac{1}{3}s^2 h = \dfrac{1}{3}(12 \text{ cm})^2(20 \text{ cm}) = 960 \text{ cu cm}$

19. $SA = 4\pi r^2 = 4\pi(7 \text{ in.})^2 = 196\pi \text{ sq in.}$

21. $V = (2 \text{ ft})\left(2\dfrac{1}{2} \text{ ft}\right)\left(1\dfrac{1}{2} \text{ ft}\right) = 7\dfrac{1}{2} \text{ cu ft}$

23. $V = \dfrac{1}{3}\pi r^2 h$

$\quad \approx \dfrac{1}{3}\left(\dfrac{22}{7}\right)(2 \text{ cm})^2(3 \text{ cm})$

$\quad = \dfrac{88}{7} \text{ cu cm}$

$\quad = 12\dfrac{4}{7} \text{ cu cm}$

Appendix C Exercise Set

1. $f(x) = 3|x|$

Find and plot ordered-pair solutions.

x	$f(x) = 3|x|$
-1	$3|-1| = 3$
0	$3|0| = 0$
1	$3|1| = 3$

3. $f(x) = \frac{1}{4}|x|$

Find and plot ordered-pair solutions.

x	$f(x) = \frac{1}{4}|x|$
–4	1
0	0
4	1

5. $g(x) = 2|x| + 3$
Write in the form $g(x) = a|x - h| + k$.
$g(x) = 2|x - 0| + 3$

- vertex is $(h, k) = (0, 3)$

- since $a > 0$, V-shape opens up

- since $|a| = |2| = 2 > 1$, the graph is narrower than $y = |x|$

x	$g(x) = 2|x| + 3$
–1	$2|-1| + 3 = 5$
0	$2|0| + 3 = 3$
1	$2|1| + 3 = 5$

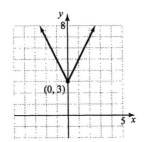

7. $h(x) = -\frac{1}{2}|x|$

- vertex is $(h, k) = (0, 0)$

- since $a < 0$, V-shape opens down

- since $|a| = \left|-\frac{1}{2}\right| = \frac{1}{2} < 1$, the graph is wider than $y = |x|$

x	$h(x) = -\frac{1}{2}|x|$
–2	$-\frac{1}{2}|-2| = -1$
0	$-\frac{1}{2}|0| = 0$
2	$-\frac{1}{2}|2| = -1$

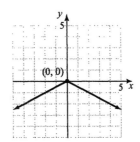

9. $f(x) = 4|x - 1|$
Write in the form $f(x) = a|x - h| + k$.
$f(x) = 4|x - 1| + 0$

- vertex is $(h, k) = (1, 0)$

- since $a > 0$, V-shape opens up

- since $|a| = |4| = 4 > 1$, the graph is narrower than $y = |x|$

x	$f(x) = 4|x - 1|$
–2	$4|-2 - 1| = 12$
0	$4|0 - 1| = 4$
2	$4|2 - 1| = 4$

11. $g(x) = -\frac{1}{3}|x| - 2$

Write in the form $g(x) = a|x - h| + k$.

$g(x) = -\frac{1}{3}|x - 0| + (-2)$

- vertex is $(h, k) = (0, -2)$

- since $a < 0$, V-shape opens down

- since $|a| = \left|-\frac{1}{3}\right| = \frac{1}{3} < 1$, the graph is wider than $y = |x|$

x	$g(x) = -\frac{1}{3}|x| - 2$
-3	$-\frac{1}{3}|-3| - 2 = -3$
0	$-\frac{1}{3}|0| - 2 = -2$
3	$-\frac{1}{3}|3| - 2 = -3$

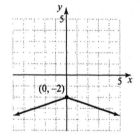

13. $f(x) = -2|x - 3| + 4$
This function is already written in the form $f(x) = a|x - h| + k$.

- vertex is $(h, k) = (3, 4)$

- since $a < 0$, V-shape opens down

- since $|a| = |-2| = 2 > 1$, the graph is narrower than $y = |x|$

x	$f(x) = -2|x - 3| + 4$
-1	$-2|-1 - 3| + 4 = -4$
1	$-2|1 - 3| + 4 = 0$
4	$-2|4 - 3| + 4 = 2$

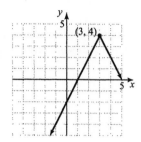

15. $f(x) = \frac{2}{3}|x + 2| - 5$

Write in the form $f(x) = a|x - h| + k$.

$f(x) = \frac{2}{3}|x - (-2)| + (-5)$

- vertex is $(h, k) = (-2, -5)$

- since $a > 0$, V-shape opens up

- since $|a| = \left|\frac{2}{3}\right| = \frac{2}{3} < 1$, the graph is wider than $y = |x|$

x	$f(x) = \frac{2}{3}|x + 2| - 5$
-5	$\frac{2}{3}|-5 + 2| - 5 = -3$
-2	$\frac{2}{3}|-2 + 2| - 5 = -5$
1	$\frac{2}{3}|1 + 2| - 5 = -3$

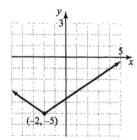

Appendix D

Vocabulary and Readiness Check

1. $\begin{vmatrix} 7 & 2 \\ 0 & 8 \end{vmatrix} = 56$

2. $\begin{vmatrix} 6 & 0 \\ 1 & 2 \end{vmatrix} = 12$

3. $\begin{vmatrix} -4 & 2 \\ 0 & 8 \end{vmatrix} = -32$

4. $\begin{vmatrix} 5 & 0 \\ 3 & -5 \end{vmatrix} = -25$

5. $\begin{vmatrix} -2 & 0 \\ 3 & -10 \end{vmatrix} = 20$

6. $\begin{vmatrix} -1 & 4 \\ 0 & -18 \end{vmatrix} = 18$

Appendix D Exercise Set

1. $\begin{vmatrix} 3 & 5 \\ -1 & 7 \end{vmatrix} = ad - bc = 3(7) - 5(-1) = 21 + 5 = 26$

3. $\begin{vmatrix} 9 & -2 \\ 4 & -3 \end{vmatrix} = ad - bc$
$= 9(-3) - (-2)(4)$
$= -27 + 8$
$= -19$

5. $\begin{vmatrix} -2 & 9 \\ 4 & -18 \end{vmatrix} = ad - bc$
$= -2(-18) - 9(4)$
$= 36 - 36$
$= 0$

7. $\begin{vmatrix} \frac{3}{4} & \frac{5}{2} \\ -\frac{1}{6} & \frac{7}{3} \end{vmatrix} = ad - bc$
$= \left(\frac{3}{4}\right)\left(\frac{7}{3}\right) - \left(\frac{5}{2}\right)\left(-\frac{1}{6}\right)$
$= \frac{7}{4} + \frac{5}{12}$
$= \frac{21}{12} + \frac{5}{12}$
$= \frac{26}{12}$
$= \frac{13}{6}$

9. $\begin{cases} 2y - 4 = 0 \\ x + 2y = 5 \end{cases}$ or $\begin{cases} 0x + 2y = 4 \\ 1x + 2y = 5 \end{cases}$

$D = \begin{vmatrix} 0 & 2 \\ 1 & 2 \end{vmatrix} = 0 - 2 = -2$

$D_x = \begin{vmatrix} 4 & 2 \\ 5 & 2 \end{vmatrix} = 8 - 10 = -2$

$D_y = \begin{vmatrix} 0 & 4 \\ 1 & 5 \end{vmatrix} = 0 - 4 = -4$

$x = \dfrac{D_x}{D} = \dfrac{-2}{-2} = 1$

$y = \dfrac{D_y}{D} = \dfrac{-4}{-2} = 2$

The solution is $(1, 2)$.

11. $\begin{cases} 3x + y = 1 \\ 2y = 2 - 6x \end{cases}$ or $\begin{cases} 3x + 1y = 1 \\ 6x + 2y = 2 \end{cases}$

$D = \begin{vmatrix} 3 & 1 \\ 6 & 2 \end{vmatrix} = 6 - 6 = 0$

Since $D = 0$, Cramer's Rule cannot be used. Notice that equation (2) is equation (1) multiplied by 2.
The solution is $\{(x, y) | 3x + y = 1\}$.

13. $\begin{cases} 5x - 2y = 27 \\ -3x + 5y = 18 \end{cases}$

$D = \begin{vmatrix} 5 & -2 \\ -3 & 5 \end{vmatrix} = 25 - 6 = 19$

$D_x = \begin{vmatrix} 27 & -2 \\ 18 & 5 \end{vmatrix} = 135 + 36 = 171$

$D_y = \begin{vmatrix} 5 & 27 \\ -3 & 18 \end{vmatrix} = 90 + 81 = 171$

$x = \dfrac{D_x}{D} = \dfrac{171}{19} = 9$ and $y = \dfrac{D_y}{D} = \dfrac{171}{19} = 9$

The solution is $(9, 9)$.

15. $\begin{cases} 2x - 5y = 4 \\ x + 2y = -7 \end{cases}$

$D = \begin{vmatrix} 2 & -5 \\ 1 & 2 \end{vmatrix} = 4 + 5 = 9$

$D_x = \begin{vmatrix} 4 & -5 \\ -7 & 2 \end{vmatrix} = 8 - 35 = -27$

$D_y = \begin{vmatrix} 2 & 4 \\ 1 & -7 \end{vmatrix} = -14 - 4 = -18$

$x = \dfrac{D_x}{D} = \dfrac{-27}{9} = -3$ and $y = \dfrac{D_y}{D} = \dfrac{-18}{9} = -2$

The solution is $(-3, -2)$.

17. $\begin{cases} \dfrac{2}{3}x - \dfrac{3}{4}y = -1 \\ -\dfrac{1}{6}x + \dfrac{3}{4}y = \dfrac{5}{2} \end{cases}$

$D = \begin{vmatrix} \dfrac{2}{3} & -\dfrac{3}{4} \\ -\dfrac{1}{6} & \dfrac{3}{4} \end{vmatrix} = \dfrac{1}{2} - \dfrac{1}{8} = \dfrac{3}{8}$

$D_x = \begin{vmatrix} -1 & -\dfrac{3}{4} \\ \dfrac{5}{2} & \dfrac{3}{4} \end{vmatrix} = -\dfrac{3}{4} + \dfrac{15}{8} = \dfrac{9}{8}$

$D_y = \begin{vmatrix} \dfrac{2}{3} & -1 \\ -\dfrac{1}{6} & \dfrac{5}{2} \end{vmatrix} = \dfrac{10}{6} - \dfrac{1}{6} = \dfrac{9}{6}$

$x = \dfrac{D_x}{D} = \dfrac{\frac{9}{8}}{\frac{3}{8}} = 3$ and $y = \dfrac{D_y}{D} = \dfrac{\frac{9}{6}}{\frac{3}{8}} = 4$

The solution is $(3, 4)$.

19. Expand by first row.

$\begin{vmatrix} 2 & 1 & 0 \\ 0 & 5 & -3 \\ 4 & 0 & 2 \end{vmatrix} = 2\begin{vmatrix} 5 & -3 \\ 0 & 2 \end{vmatrix} - 1\begin{vmatrix} 0 & -3 \\ 4 & 2 \end{vmatrix} + 0\begin{vmatrix} 0 & 5 \\ 4 & 0 \end{vmatrix}$

$= 2(10 - 0) - 1(0 + 12) + 0$

$= 20 - 12$

$= 8$

21. Expand by third column.

$\begin{vmatrix} 4 & -6 & 0 \\ -2 & 3 & 0 \\ 4 & -6 & 1 \end{vmatrix} = 0\begin{vmatrix} -2 & 3 \\ 4 & -6 \end{vmatrix} - 0\begin{vmatrix} 4 & -6 \\ 4 & -6 \end{vmatrix} + 1\begin{vmatrix} 4 & -6 \\ -2 & 3 \end{vmatrix}$

$= 0 - 0 + 1(12 - 12)$

$= 0$

23. Expand by first row.

$\begin{vmatrix} 1 & 0 & 4 \\ 1 & -1 & 2 \\ 3 & 2 & 1 \end{vmatrix} = 1\begin{vmatrix} -1 & 2 \\ 2 & 1 \end{vmatrix} - 0\begin{vmatrix} 1 & 2 \\ 3 & 1 \end{vmatrix} + 4\begin{vmatrix} 1 & -1 \\ 3 & 2 \end{vmatrix}$

$= 1(-1 - 4) - 0 + 4(2 + 3)$

$= -5 + 20$

$= 15$

25. Expand by first row.

$\begin{vmatrix} 3 & 6 & -3 \\ -1 & -2 & 3 \\ 4 & -1 & 6 \end{vmatrix} = 3\begin{vmatrix} -2 & 3 \\ -1 & 6 \end{vmatrix} - 6\begin{vmatrix} -1 & 3 \\ 4 & 6 \end{vmatrix} - 3\begin{vmatrix} -1 & -2 \\ 4 & -1 \end{vmatrix}$

$= 3(-12 + 3) - 6(-6 - 12) - 3(1 + 8)$

$= -27 + 108 - 27$

$= 54$

27. $\begin{cases} 3x \quad\;\; + z = -1 \\ -x - 3y + z = 7 \\ 3y + z = 5 \end{cases}$

$D = \begin{vmatrix} 3 & 0 & 1 \\ -1 & -3 & 1 \\ 0 & 3 & 1 \end{vmatrix} = 3\begin{vmatrix} -3 & 1 \\ 3 & 1 \end{vmatrix} - 0\begin{vmatrix} -1 & 1 \\ 0 & 1 \end{vmatrix} + 1\begin{vmatrix} -1 & -3 \\ 0 & 3 \end{vmatrix}$

$= 3(-3 - 3) - 0 + 1(-3 - 0)$

$= -18 - 3$

$= -21$

$D_x = \begin{vmatrix} -1 & 0 & 1 \\ 7 & -3 & 1 \\ 5 & 3 & 1 \end{vmatrix}$

$= -1\begin{vmatrix} -3 & 1 \\ 3 & 1 \end{vmatrix} - 0\begin{vmatrix} 7 & 1 \\ 5 & 1 \end{vmatrix} + 1\begin{vmatrix} 7 & -3 \\ 5 & 3 \end{vmatrix}$

$= -1(-3 - 3) - 0 + 1|21 + 15|$

$= 6 + 36$

$= 42$

$D_y = \begin{vmatrix} 3 & -1 & 1 \\ -1 & 7 & 1 \\ 0 & 5 & 1 \end{vmatrix} = 3\begin{vmatrix} 7 & 1 \\ 5 & 1 \end{vmatrix} + 1\begin{vmatrix} -1 & 1 \\ 5 & 1 \end{vmatrix} + 0\begin{vmatrix} -1 & 1 \\ 7 & 1 \end{vmatrix}$

$= 3(7 - 5) + 1(-1 - 5) + 0$

$= 6 - 6$

$= 0$

$D_z = \begin{vmatrix} 3 & 0 & -1 \\ -1 & -3 & 7 \\ 0 & 3 & 5 \end{vmatrix}$

$= 3\begin{vmatrix} -3 & 7 \\ 3 & 5 \end{vmatrix} - 0\begin{vmatrix} -1 & 7 \\ 0 & 5 \end{vmatrix} - 1\begin{vmatrix} -1 & -3 \\ 0 & 3 \end{vmatrix}$

$= 3(-15 - 21) - 0 - 1(-3 - 0)$

$= -108 + 3$

$= -105$

$x = \dfrac{D_x}{D} = \dfrac{42}{-21} = -2, \quad y = \dfrac{D_y}{D} = \dfrac{0}{-21} = 0,$

$z = \dfrac{D_z}{D} = \dfrac{-105}{-21} = 5$

The solution is $(-2, 0, 5)$.

29. $\begin{cases} x + y + z = 8 \\ 2x - y - z = 10 \\ x - 2y + 3z = 22 \end{cases}$

$D = \begin{vmatrix} 1 & 1 & 1 \\ 2 & -1 & -1 \\ 1 & -2 & 3 \end{vmatrix}$

$\quad = 1\begin{vmatrix} -1 & -1 \\ -2 & 3 \end{vmatrix} - 1\begin{vmatrix} 2 & -1 \\ 1 & 3 \end{vmatrix} + 1\begin{vmatrix} 2 & -1 \\ 1 & -2 \end{vmatrix}$

$\quad = 1(-3-2) - 1(6+1) + 1(-4+1)$

$\quad = -5 - 7 - 3$

$\quad = -15$

$D_x = \begin{vmatrix} 8 & 1 & 1 \\ 10 & -1 & -1 \\ 22 & -2 & 3 \end{vmatrix}$

$\quad = 8\begin{vmatrix} -1 & -1 \\ -2 & 3 \end{vmatrix} - 10\begin{vmatrix} 1 & 1 \\ -2 & 3 \end{vmatrix} + 22\begin{vmatrix} 1 & 1 \\ -1 & -1 \end{vmatrix}$

$\quad = 8(-3-2) - 10(3+2) + 22(-1+1)$

$\quad = -40 - 50 + 0$

$\quad = -90$

$D_y = \begin{vmatrix} 1 & 8 & 1 \\ 2 & 10 & -1 \\ 1 & 22 & 3 \end{vmatrix}$

$\quad = 1\begin{vmatrix} 10 & -1 \\ 22 & 3 \end{vmatrix} - 8\begin{vmatrix} 2 & -1 \\ 1 & 3 \end{vmatrix} + 1\begin{vmatrix} 2 & 10 \\ 1 & 22 \end{vmatrix}$

$\quad = 1(30+22) - 8(6+1) + 1(44-10)$

$\quad = 52 - 56 + 34$

$\quad = 30$

$D_z = \begin{vmatrix} 1 & 1 & 8 \\ 2 & -1 & 10 \\ 1 & -2 & 22 \end{vmatrix}$

$\quad = 1\begin{vmatrix} -1 & 10 \\ -2 & 22 \end{vmatrix} - 1\begin{vmatrix} 2 & 10 \\ 1 & 22 \end{vmatrix} + 8\begin{vmatrix} 2 & -1 \\ 1 & -2 \end{vmatrix}$

$\quad = 1(-22+20) - 1(44-10) + 8(-4+1)$

$\quad = -2 - 34 - 24$

$\quad = -60$

$x = \dfrac{D_x}{D} = \dfrac{-90}{-15} = 6, \quad y = \dfrac{D_y}{D} = \dfrac{30}{-15} = -2,$

$z = \dfrac{D_z}{D} = \dfrac{-60}{-15} = 4$

The solution is $(6, -2, 4)$.

31. $\begin{cases} 2x + 2y + z = 1 \\ -x + y + 2z = 3 \\ x + 2y + 4z = 0 \end{cases}$

$D = \begin{vmatrix} 2 & 2 & 1 \\ -1 & 1 & 2 \\ 1 & 2 & 4 \end{vmatrix} = 2\begin{vmatrix} 1 & 2 \\ 2 & 4 \end{vmatrix} - 2\begin{vmatrix} -1 & 2 \\ 1 & 4 \end{vmatrix} + 1\begin{vmatrix} -1 & 1 \\ 1 & 2 \end{vmatrix}$

$\quad = 2(4-4) - 2(-4-2) + 1(-2-1)$

$\quad = 0 + 12 - 3$

$\quad = 9$

$D_x = \begin{vmatrix} 1 & 2 & 1 \\ 3 & 1 & 2 \\ 0 & 2 & 4 \end{vmatrix} = 1\begin{vmatrix} 1 & 2 \\ 2 & 4 \end{vmatrix} - 3\begin{vmatrix} 2 & 1 \\ 2 & 4 \end{vmatrix} + 0$

$\quad = 1(4-4) - 3(8-2)$

$\quad = -18$

$D_y = \begin{vmatrix} 2 & 1 & 1 \\ -1 & 3 & 2 \\ 1 & 0 & 4 \end{vmatrix} = 2\begin{vmatrix} 3 & 2 \\ 0 & 4 \end{vmatrix} - 1\begin{vmatrix} -1 & 2 \\ 1 & 4 \end{vmatrix} + 1\begin{vmatrix} -1 & 3 \\ 1 & 0 \end{vmatrix}$

$\quad = 2(12-0) - 1(-4-2) + 1(0-3)$

$\quad = 24 + 6 - 3$

$\quad = 27$

$D_z = \begin{vmatrix} 2 & 2 & 1 \\ -1 & 1 & 3 \\ 1 & 2 & 0 \end{vmatrix} = 2\begin{vmatrix} 1 & 3 \\ 2 & 0 \end{vmatrix} - 2\begin{vmatrix} -1 & 3 \\ 1 & 0 \end{vmatrix} + 1\begin{vmatrix} -1 & 1 \\ 1 & 2 \end{vmatrix}$

$\quad = 2(0-6) - 2(0-3) + 1(-2-1)$

$\quad = -12 + 6 - 3$

$\quad = -9$

$x = \dfrac{D_x}{D} = \dfrac{-18}{9} = -2, \quad y = \dfrac{D_y}{D} = \dfrac{27}{9} = 3,$

$z = \dfrac{D_z}{D} = \dfrac{-9}{9} = -1$

The solution is $(-2, 3, -1)$.

33. $\begin{cases} x - 2y + z = -5 \\ 3y + 2z = 4 \\ 3x - y = -2 \end{cases}$

$D = \begin{vmatrix} 1 & -2 & 1 \\ 0 & 3 & 2 \\ 3 & -1 & 0 \end{vmatrix} = 1\begin{vmatrix} 3 & 2 \\ -1 & 0 \end{vmatrix} + 2\begin{vmatrix} 0 & 2 \\ 3 & 0 \end{vmatrix} + 1\begin{vmatrix} 0 & 3 \\ 3 & -1 \end{vmatrix}$

$\quad = 1(0+2) + 2(0-6) + 1(0-9)$

$\quad = 2 - 12 - 9$

$\quad = -19$

$$D_x = \begin{vmatrix} -5 & -2 & 1 \\ 4 & 3 & 2 \\ -2 & -1 & 0 \end{vmatrix}$$

$$= -5 \begin{vmatrix} 3 & 2 \\ -1 & 0 \end{vmatrix} + 2 \begin{vmatrix} 4 & 2 \\ -2 & 0 \end{vmatrix} + 1 \begin{vmatrix} 4 & 3 \\ -2 & -1 \end{vmatrix}$$

$$= -5(0+2) + 2(0+4) + 1(-4+6)$$

$$= -10 + 8 + 2$$

$$= 0$$

$$D_y = \begin{vmatrix} 1 & -5 & 1 \\ 0 & 4 & 2 \\ 3 & -2 & 0 \end{vmatrix} = 1 \begin{vmatrix} 4 & 2 \\ -2 & 0 \end{vmatrix} + 5 \begin{vmatrix} 0 & 2 \\ 3 & 0 \end{vmatrix} + 1 \begin{vmatrix} 0 & 4 \\ 3 & -2 \end{vmatrix}$$

$$= 1(0+4) + 5(0-6) + 1(0-12)$$

$$= 4 - 30 - 12$$

$$= -38$$

$$D_z = \begin{vmatrix} 1 & -2 & -5 \\ 0 & 3 & 4 \\ 3 & -1 & -2 \end{vmatrix}$$

$$= 1 \begin{vmatrix} 3 & 4 \\ -1 & -2 \end{vmatrix} + 2 \begin{vmatrix} 0 & 4 \\ 3 & -2 \end{vmatrix} - 5 \begin{vmatrix} 0 & 3 \\ 3 & -1 \end{vmatrix}$$

$$= 1(-6+4) + 2(0-12) - 5(0-9)$$

$$= -2 - 24 + 45$$

$$= 19$$

$$x = \frac{D_x}{D} = \frac{0}{-19} = 0, \quad y = \frac{D_y}{D} = \frac{-38}{-19} = 2,$$

$$z = \frac{D_z}{D} = \frac{19}{-19} = -1$$

The solution is $(0, 2, -1)$.

35. $\begin{vmatrix} 1 & x \\ 2 & 7 \end{vmatrix} = -3$

$$(1)(7) - x \cdot 2 = -3$$

$$7 - 2x = -3$$

$$-2x = -10$$

$$x = 5$$

37. 0; answers may vary

Appendix E

Viewing Window and Interpreting Window Settings Exercise Set

1. Yes, since every coordinate is between −10 and 10.

3. No, since −11 is less than −10.

5. Answers may vary. Any values such that Xmin < −90, Ymin < −80, Xmax > 55, and Ymax > 80.

7. Answers may vary. Any values such that Xmin < −11, Ymin < −5, Xmax > 7, and Ymax > 2.

9. Answers may vary. Any values such that Xmin < 50, Ymin < −50, Xmax > 200, and Ymax > 200.

11. Xmin = −12   Ymin = −12
       Xmax = 12   Ymax = 12
       Xscl = 3   Yscl = 3

13. Xmin = −9   Ymin = −12
       Xmax = 9   Ymax = 12
       Xscl = 1   Yscl = 2

15. Xmin = −10   Ymin = −25
       Xmax = 10   Ymax = 25
       Xscl = 2   Yscl = 5

17. Xmin = −10   Ymin = −30
       Xmax = 10   Ymax = 30
       Xscl = 1   Yscl = 3

19. Xmin = −20   Ymin = −30
       Xmax = 30   Ymax = 50
       Xscl = 5   Yscl = 10

Graphing Equations and Square Viewing Window Exercise Set

1. Setting A:

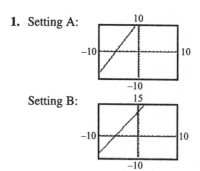

Setting B:

Setting B shows all intercepts.

3. Setting A:

Setting B:

Setting B shows all intercepts.

5. Setting A:

Setting B:

Setting B shows all intercepts.

7. $3x = 5y$

$y = \dfrac{3}{5}x$

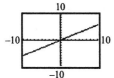

9. $9x - 5y = 30$

$-5y = -9x + 30$

$y = \dfrac{9}{5}x - 6$

11. $y = -7$

13. $x + 10y = -5$

$10y = -x - 5$

$y = -\dfrac{1}{10}x - \dfrac{1}{2}$

15. $y = \sqrt{x}$

17. $y = x^2 + 2x + 1$

19. $y = |x|$

21. $x + 2y = 30$

$2y = -x + 30$

$y = -\dfrac{1}{2}x + 15$

Standard window:

Adjusted window: